"David Allen's *The Extent of the Atonement* is a tremendous accomplishment. He has given us a treasure trove of information on the doctrine of the extent of the atonement, tracing it in detail and providing incisive interaction with the exegetical and theological arguments for and against limited atonement that have been put forth, especially since the Reformation and by Calvinistic authors. As if this were not enough, he also treats us to an extensive and definitive critique of *From Heaven He Came and Sought Her*, which has been touted as the definitive modern work in support of limited atonement. Allen's tome is now the book to own on the extent of the atonement and the place to turn for support of unlimited atonement and refutation of limited atonement."

—Brian Abasciano, adjunct professor of New Testament, Gordon-Conwell Theological Seminary; pastor, Faith Community Church; president, The Society of Evangelical Arminians

"This book is encyclopedic. There is nothing like it in depth and scope. One does not have to hold the author's perspective (though I do) to benefit from his massive research. No one interested in the extent of the atonement can ignore Allen's important contribution."

—Daniel L. Akin, president, Southeastern Baptist Theological Seminary

"This volume represents the fruit of years of careful research and writing, all with a view toward aiding and helping anyone who has wrestled deeply or has had a conversation about the extent of the atonement. David L. Allen has served his readers well by assembling *The Extent of the Atonement: A Historical and Critical Review*. I believe it will soon take its place among the library of volumes one must consult in any discussion related to the work of Christ."

—Jason G. Duesing, provost and associate professor of historical theology, Midwestern Baptist Theological Seminary

"*The Extent of the Atonement* offers a penetrating and perceptive treatment of a thorny, divisive theological issue. David Allen's command of the subject, as well as his ability to lay out clearly and fairly the competing theories and arguments, is masterful. I found his critique of the doctrine of limited atonement fully persuasive. This book is must reading for all who want to understand better the Calvinism debate."

—Craig A. Evans, dean of the School of Christian Thought and John Bisagno Distinguished Professor of Christian Origins, Houston Baptist University

"Baptists have been debating the intent and extent of the atonement since almost the beginning of our movement. The recent popularity of Calvinism among conservative evangelicals—including many Southern Baptists—has helped make this historic debate a current family discussion. To my knowledge, David Allen's *The Extent of the Atonement: A Historical and Critical Review* is the most extensive treatment of this topic that has been written—certainly by a Baptist. I confess I don't agree with everything he argues in this book. However, I strongly agree with Allen that both the Reformed tradition and more Calvinistic Baptist movements have historically included advocates of both limited and universal atonement—a fact too often unrecognized in contemporary discussions about this topic. I'm confident this book will inspire renewed interest in what Baptists and others *have* believed about the atonement. I'm prayerful it will also encourage Southern Baptists to engage in brotherly dialogue, refine our respective views of what we *ought* to believe, and better partner together in proclaiming the gospel to this world that God so loves."

—Nathan A. Finn, dean of the School of Theology and Missions and professor of Christian thought and tradition, Union University

"In this comprehensive historiography, David Allen clarifies the views of Christian thinkers on the extent of the atonement. He argues convincingly from primary sources that unlimited atonement has been the dominant view in the history of the church, even among many Calvinists. Allen challenges readers to discern at which point precisely the atonement was limited—in its intent, extent, or application. Because of the implications for evangelism, he gives special attention to treatments of this doctrine in the Baptist tradition. Allen's study will benefit anyone interested in the question, 'For whom did Christ die?'"

—Adam Harwood, McFarland Chair of Theology, associate professor of theology, and director of the Baptist Center for Theology & Ministry, New Orleans Baptist Theological Seminary

"The extent of the atonement is among the most controversial questions in Reformed theology. It is probably also the most confusing and misunderstood. Is limited atonement the only Reformed position? What did John Calvin himself believe? For whom did Christ die? How do we preach the saving message of the cross to unbelievers? Does God love the world or not? Enter David Allen's monumental book, an absolute *tour de force. The Extent of the Atonement* leaves no stone unturned in tracing the history of the doctrine, critiques every view and proponent with penetrating insight, and is written with a persuasive cogency throughout. The book is an education in how to do theology responsibly and how to read the Bible faithfully. To top it off, Allen writes with the heart of a pastor and the wit and wisdom of a seasoned preacher. A must read for anyone interested in the question of what the cross achieves."

—Brian Rosner, principal, Ridley College, Melbourne, Australia

"The issue of limited atonement has proved a controversial matter for many years and one that is unlikely to disappear at any time in the near future. One of the reasons for this is that the question it seeks to answer is one which developed over time and has a number of subtle and sophisticated facets. Like other doctrines such as the Trinity, an understanding of the history of the doctrine of atonement is thus key to the matter. While David Allen and I disagree on the matter, this work is an irenic and learned contribution to the topic which carries the historical, and thus doctrinal, discussion forward in an extremely helpful way. I am thus happy to recommend this work of a friendly critic. It deserves wide readership and careful engagement."

—Carl R. Trueman, Paul Woolley Chair of Church History and professor of church history, Westminster Theological Seminary

The EXTENT *of the* ATONEMENT

The
EXTENT
of the
ATONEMENT

A Historical and Critical Review

DAVID L. ALLEN

NASHVILLE, TENNESSEE

The Extent of the Atonement: A Historical and Critical Review

Published by B&H Academic
Nashville, Tennessee

ISBN: 978-1-4336-4392-7

Dewey Decimal Classification: 234

SUBHD: ATONEMENT / THEOLOGY / SACRIFICE

Cover design by Darren Welch and art direction by Jade Novak.
Cover images © Shutterstock / Lara Cold and Shutterstock / OlgaSha
Interior design and typesetting by Mandi Cofer / thetinytypesetter.com

Printed in the United States of America
1 2 3 4 5 6 7 8 9 10 VP 21 20 19 18 17 16

Contents

Preface

This work has been a labor of love over the past ten years. The extent of the atonement and its entailments are vital to me as a theologian and preacher. The issue touches very near the heart of the gospel. What one believes about this subject has serious ramifications for both theology and praxis in the church. The necessity of getting the gospel right is basal in my thinking.

The question of the extent of the atonement is controversial and often engenders strong emotion. Some people on either side of the fence tenaciously cling to their view and anathematize opponents. Perhaps one reason for this visceral reaction is the fact that a via media on the extent question is not possible. There are only two options: either Jesus substituted for the sins of all people, or he substituted for the sins of only some people. The subject is delicate but important and must be considered.

Any attempt to cover all the vast literature on this subject can only be judged as ambition on steroids. This work is not a comprehensive treatment. Such is beyond my ability and beside my purpose. I strive for the modest goal of a survey of the lay of the land. I hope to furnish information and sources to enable you to pursue the subject more in depth.

I have attempted to identify and clarify the significant matters in the history of the discussion and to present them in historical context for consideration. Some topics have received less treatment than others. Some of the intricate nuances of the issue I have treated in greater detail, especially where the necessity of linguistic precision requires such. In these latter sections, I trust you will pack a sufficient amount of patience to wade through the issues.

I have written this book as a historian/theologian/preacher rather than as a polemicist. Of course, no author can bring a tabula rasa to the table when writing. Each brings his own paradigm and writes from a particular perspective. I have endeavored to present the issue fairly and with intellectual integrity. Every page is stained with the breath of prayer that I not misrepresent God, his word, or those who have preceded me in theological pursuit. Nevertheless, a final section of this work is a substantive critique of limited atonement. In the final analysis, I believe limited atonement to be a doctrine in search of a text.

I take it for granted that all agree Scripture is the final arbiter on this issue. We must not confuse Scripture with our interpretation of Scripture. The former is infallible. The latter is not. When biblical evidence is presented, such evidence can only be effectively countered if it can be demonstrated that the text is not relevant to the issue at hand or that the text has been misinterpreted exegetically within its context.

There is much misinformation floating around on the question of the extent of the atonement. As a result of loose thought habits, too much reductionist thinking abounds. There is also great need for disambiguation. The relevant information needs to be separated from the irrelevant; the essential from the nonessential.

The problems that obtrude themselves in a study of this nature are legion. In my attempt to thresh the grain, I hope I have not gotten my britches caught on my own pitchfork.

Expressing gratitude to all who have contributed in one way or another to make this work possible is not possible. I stand on the shoulders of so many. But I would be remiss not to thank some who played a key role.

I am deeply grateful for Jim Baird of B&H Publishing for reading the original unedited manuscript and for his decision to publish it. Without the oversight of Chris Thompson and his crack team at B&H, this work could have never seen the light of day. Audrey Greeson brought not only her expertise and efficiency, but also her gracious spirit to the task at hand.

Dr. Jason Duesing, academic provost of Midwestern Baptist Theological Seminary and Baptist historian par excellence, served as the main content editor of this volume. With his keen eye for seeing the big picture as well as historical detail, he has delivered me from many a pitfall. I am deeply grateful to him and thankful for his encouragement in this project.

No one successfully begins or completes a work of this nature without a recognition that he stands indebted to the research of many who got to the top of the mountain first. That is certainly the case with this book. I especially owe a debt of gratitude to David Ponter and Tony Byrne for the generous use I have made of their research websites on Calvinism.

Ponter is a librarian at Reformed Theological Seminary in Jackson, Mississippi, whose encyclopedic knowledge I have ransacked many times. His website Calvin and Calvinism (www.calvinandcalvinism.com) contains the largest collection of quotations and other material on Calvin's view of the extent of the atonement of which I am aware, as well as material from the earliest generation of the Reformed until the present time on the subject. Ponter is an incisive historian of Calvinism, and I am grateful for the opportunity to have interacted with him on a number of issues related to the subject at hand. His suggestions have been invaluable.

Tony Byrne, a former student of mine, hosts the blog Theological Meditations (www.theologicalmeditations.blogspot.com). Byrne's research speciality is in the area of salvation and the love of God, God's universal saving will, the well-meant gospel offer, and other related topics, particularly from the Puritan era. He has ransacked thousands of early English books online (see http://eebo.chadwyck.com/home) and posted material on this subject, much of which has never been published before. His research, writing, and editing assistance has been invaluable. As a Calvinist himself, he has sharpened my thinking about Calvinism and rescued me from many a pitfall of overgeneralization.

As this book passes in review for inspection by readers, I hope it will pass muster in the process. The early church father Cyprian advocated the principle *Salvo jure communionis diversa sentire*, which essentially states, "Provided the law of communion is respected, diversity of opinion is permitted." May differing opinions on the extent of the atonement not lead to any loss of communion among those who follow Christ.

Soli Deo gloria

Introduction

The history concerning the question of the extent of the atonement is fascinating in its own right, variegated in its twists and turns, often either ignored or misunderstood, but essential to a thorough understanding and analysis of the subject. One does not have to read far into the biblical and theological aspects of the extent question before discovering it is knotty and thorny, fraught with potholes and pitfalls.

The question has engendered passionate debate since the Reformation. The extent of the atonement has been a significant controversy not only between the Reformed and the non-Reformed but also within Reformed theology itself. Debates occurred far and wide within Reformed theology, ranging from major events such as Dort and Westminster to individual correspondence and debate (such as occurred between John Owen and Richard Baxter in the seventeenth century and Andrew Fuller and Dan Taylor in the late eighteenth century). Entire Reformed denominations have divided over this issue (at least in part), as, for example, the Secession Church in Scotland in the nineteenth century. The earliest English Baptists (early seventeenth century) designated themselves as "General" and "Particular" Baptists, nomenclature chosen to illustrate their theological differences primarily over the extent of the atonement.

The rise of the neo-Calvinism[1] movement in contemporary American Evangelicalism has once again brought the issue to the fore. Within modern Calvinism, the position of limited atonement is clearly in the catbird seat, while those Calvinists who

1 By "neo-Calvinism," I refer to the growing movement of Calvinism within Evangelicalism over the past twenty years.

affirm unlimited atonement sometimes become clay pigeons. Several recent Calvinist works, mostly of a popular nature, address the question, typically in a tertiary fashion, as part of their explication of Calvinism. Usually only a few pages are devoted to a discussion of this issue and that within the traditional TULIP schema. These treatments are generally descriptive and often superficial. A few scholarly works on the question of the extent of the atonement have appeared in recent years, some written by Calvinists who chronicle the debate within Reformed theology on this topic.[2] Interestingly, these works demonstrate the historical as well as the ongoing debates about this issue.

An important issue in the historical discussion has to do with the recognition that both Reformed and Arminian theologies are not monolithic, nor have they ever been. There is much diversity within these traditions.

In modern times, the question of the extent of the atonement arose in and because of Reformed theology. Though some use the terms interchangeably, "Reformed" and "Calvinism" are not identical in meaning. The former is broader than the later.[3] Reformed theology includes a commitment to Covenant Theology, paedobaptism,[4] and a particular form of church government, along with other theological issues. "Calvinism"[5] usually describes a particular soteriological position that has generally come to be described as belief in the so-called five points of Calvinism: total depravity, unconditional election, limited atonement, irresistible grace, and perseverance of the saints.

However, the TULIP acrostic is imprecise as a descriptor for Calvinism[6] because, as will be shown, many Calvinists historically and today do not affirm limited atonement

---

2 For example, see G. M. Thomas, *The Extent of the Atonement: A Dilemma for Reformed Theology from Calvin to the Consensus (1536–1675)* (Carlisle, UK: Paternoster, 1997); J. Moore, *English Hypothetical Universalism: John Preston and the Softening of Reformed Theology* (Grand Rapids, MI: Eerdmans, 2007); and D. Gibson and J. Gibson, eds., *From Heaven He Came and Sought Her: Definite Atonement in Historical, Biblical, Theological, and Pastoral Perspective* (Wheaton, IL: Crossway, 2013).

3 D. D. Wallace, *Puritans and Predestination: Grace in English Protestant Theology, 1525–1695* (Chapel Hill: University of North Carolina Press, 1982), x–xi, stated:

> The term "Reformed" has been preferred to "Calvinism" as having wider implications, naming a particular kind of theology in the construction of which Calvin was but one figure among many. In English theology the influence of M. Bucer, P. Martyr, H. Bullinger, and others was of great importance, and to refer to this strain as 'Calvinism' can be misleading.

See also the lecture by R. Muller, "Was Calvin a Calvinist? Or, Did Calvin (or Anyone Else in the Early Modern Era) Plant the 'Tulip'?" (Delivered October 15, 2009, at the H. Henry Meeter Center for Calvin Studies at Calvin College, Grand Rapids, MI). Available online at https://www.calvin.edu/meeter/Was%20Calvin%20a%20Calvinist-12-26-09.pdf.

4 Although some Baptists who follow the 1689 confession would argue they are truly Reformed.

5 Actually, the terms "Calvinism" and "Calvinist" arose among the opponents of Calvin, especially from within the Lutheran tradition. By the middle of the sixteenth century, the rift between the early Reformers was evident in the rise of two distinct confessional groups, Lutheran and Reformed. See B. Gerrish, *The Old Protestantism and the New: Essays on the Reformation Heritage* (Chicago: University of Chicago Press, 1982), 27–48.

6 The TULIP schema did not even come into use until the early twentieth century. See, for example, K. Stewart, *Ten Myths about Calvinism* (Downers Grove, IL: InterVarsity, 2011), 78.

but rather affirm a form of unlimited atonement. But even beyond that, as Muller has stated, "there is no historical association between the acrostic TULIP and the Canons of Dort."[7] He went on to state: "Use of the acrostic TULIP has resulted in a narrow, if not erroneous, reading of the Canons of Dort that has led to confused understandings of the Reformed tradition and of Calvin's theology."[8]

Though many, perhaps most, in the Reformed camp argue that it is all or nothing—that is, one must believe in all the tenets of Reformed theology to be considered a "Calvinist"[9]—there are many "Calvinists" who are not "Reformed" in their theology. Calvinistic Baptists are the perfect example. No Baptist is or can be "Reformed" in the confessional sense of that term since Baptists reject aspects of Reformed theology such as paedobaptism, a Presbyterian form of church polity, along with other theological issues.[10] Yet some Baptists are Calvinistic in their soteriology, and some of them are covenantal, while others are not.

The question of the extent of the atonement cannot be studied as an isolated doctrine, divorced from historical considerations, theological method, and the various systems of theology. One's system and methodology invariably impacts one's views on the question of the extent of the atonement. J. I. Packer perceptibly wrote, "Every theological question has behind it a history of study, and narrow eccentricity in handling it is unavoidable unless the history is taken into account."[11]

In considering the historical data on this question, one should be aware of several things. First, there has been and is significant debate over who believed what on the extent of the atonement in the history of Calvinism. Calvin immediately comes to mind. Key theologians such as Calvin must be situated in their immediate theological context, as well as within the broader spectrum of Reformed theological development. That is, we should consider key players along with their stated views synchronically and diachronically.[12]

Second, primary sources must be consulted whenever possible. Some contemporary authors writing from a popular Calvinistic perspective write as if there is only one view historically propounded by Calvinists on this subject. Some may be unaware of the diversity within their own tradition regarding the extent of the atonement.

---

7 Muller, "Was Calvin a Calvinist?," 8.

8 Ibid., 15. Muller also stated, "Calvin did not originate this tradition; he was not the sole voice in its early codification; and he did not serve as the norm for its development" (16). The moral of the story for Muller was "Don't plant TULIP in your Reformed garden" (17).

9 R. Muller, "How Many Points?," *Calvin Theological Journal* 28 (1993): 425–26.

10 For example, see how Kenneth Good maintains that Baptists can indeed be Calvinists in his book *Are Baptists Calvinists?*, rev. ed. (New York: Backus Book, 1988), without being Reformed, as argued in his book *Are Baptists Reformed?* (Lorain, OH: Regular Baptist Heritage Fellowship, 1986).

11 J. I. Packer, "What Did the Cross Achieve? The Logic of Penal Substitution," *Tyndale Bulletin* 25 (1974): 3.

12 As rightly noted by C. Trueman, "Puritan Theology as Historical Event: A Linguistic Approach to the Ecumenical Context," in *Reformation and Scholasticism: An Ecumenical Enterprise*, ed. W. J. van Asselt and E. Dekker (Grand Rapids, MI: Baker, 2001), 253–75.

Jonathan Moore spoke about the failure of some Calvinists to interact carefully with historical theology when addressing the extent of the atonement within Reformed theology:

> Too often Reformed historiography has obsessed at a superficial level about whether or not a particular theologian did or did not state that Christ did or did not "die for all" or "for the world" or some such other ambiguous statement, without actually examining their respective positions on the nature of the atonement itself.[13]

There are essentially three methods of approach to the question of the atonement's extent: deductive, inductive, and abductive.[14] Many who argue for limited atonement approach the subject from a deductive methodology, as we shall see. However, in historical investigation of this kind, the inductive and abductive methods are ultimately the first and best approaches. We must objectively listen to historical theology, and the only way to do this is to read carefully the *primary* sources and those who have engaged the primary sources.[15] Heavy dependence on secondary sources increases the possibility of misinterpreting an author's position. This can be seen in the treatment Arminius and Amyraut have often received at the hands of their detractors.

I will be referencing numerous quotations as evidence of a particular author's view on the extent of the atonement. In each chapter I have arranged these authors chronologically by birth dates. In the chapter on the twenty-first century, I have arranged some of the material chronologically by date of publication. Though space prohibits the citation of quotations in full context, I have attempted to give enough context where possible to minimize mischaracterization and to maximize objectivity. I have also attempted, where possible, to use quotations only from primary sources.[16]

Third, one needs to see the novelty of the limited atonement view as espoused by Theodore Beza and John Owen prior to the late sixteenth century. It has always been

---

13 J. Moore, "The Extent of the Atonement: English Hypothetical Universalism versus Particular Redemption," in *Drawn into Controversie: Reformed Theological Diversity and Debates within Seventeenth-Century British Puritanism,* Reformed Historical Theology 17, ed. M. Haykin and M. Jones (Göttingen: Vandenhoeck & Ruprecht, 2011), 132.

14 The deductive method of reasoning operates on the basis of stated premises, which, if true, render the conclusion true. The inductive method of reasoning operates on the basis of stated premises, which, if true, render the conclusion more or less probable. The abductive method of reasoning moves from an observation to a theory that accounts for the observation, ideally seeking to find the simplest and most likely explanation.

15 R. Muller, R. Godfrey, G. M. Thomas, and J. Moore are four important secondary-source authors who have done significant work in the primary sources. All are Reformed.

16 At times I have retained Old English spelling and grammar; while at other times I have modernized the language. All quotations from the Bible come from the *Holman Christian Standard Bible* (HCSB) unless otherwise specified or appearing in a quotation itself, at which point the quoted version is retained.

the minority view among Christians[17] even after the Reformation. This does not, in and of itself, make it incorrect, but too many Calvinists operate under the assumption that a strictly limited atonement is and has been the only real or orthodox position within Calvinism.[18]

Fourth, not all Calvinists who rejected limited atonement were lockstep in their explication of unlimited atonement. Some were English Hypothetical Universalists, some Amyraldian, some Baxterian, and some eclectic. The one common denominator is their belief in an unlimited atonement understood to mean that Christ died as a substitute for the sins of all people. They differed over supralapsarianism, infralapsarianism, and sublapsarianism. They diverged over the nature and order of God's decrees, the conditionality or unconditionality of the decrees, and other related matters. But they all affirmed universal atonement. This work will not spend much time outlining the many distinctions on these various issues among English Hypothetical Universalism, Amyraldianism, Baxterianism, or other eclectic Reformed theologians.

Loraine Boettner wrote, "The nature of the atonement settles its extent."[19] For many high Calvinists,[20] this belief is true. But for many Calvinists throughout history, it is not. Hunter Bailey spoke of seventeenth-century Scottish Calvinist James Fraser's "universal particularism," by which he meant that Fraser held that Christ died for the sins of all people (universal) and God had decreed to only give saving grace to the elect (particularism). Though the term may seem oxymoronic, it actually expresses the theology of all Calvinists who believe in both a universal atonement and a particular intent to apply it only to the elect. This theology is not only within the boundary of Reformed orthodoxy; it was, in fact, the earliest view of the first generation of the Reformed, as we shall see.

Perhaps a word about my own theological perspective and what this book is and is not attempting to do is in order. I do not write from a Calvinistic perspective. I

---

17 But not necessarily among *Reformed* Christians after the Reformation period.

18 Some, such as R. Muller, G. M. Thomas, and J. Moore, have provided irrefutable evidence concerning the historical diversity within the Reformed camp. For example, consult Muller's lectures at Mid-America Reformed Seminary in November 2008 titled "Revising the Predestination Paradigm: An Alternative to Supralapsarianism, Infralapsarianism and Hypothetical Universalism." He considered the following to be "Hypothetical Universalists" of the non-Amyraldian variety: Musculus, Zanchi, Ursinus, Kimedoncius, Bullinger, Twisse, Ussher, Davenant (and others in the British delegation to Dort), Calamy, Seaman, Vines, Harris, Marshall, Arrowsmith (the latter six were Westminster Divines), Preston, Bunyan, and many other Puritans. Thomas has likewise demonstrated that many early Reformers held to unlimited atonement, and Moore has shown how the Puritan J. Preston, among others, held to unlimited atonement. It is interesting that the authors in *From Heaven He Came and Sought Her* virtually ignore Richard Muller's scholarship. They seem to prefer and uncritically follow Raymond Blacketer's inferior historiography.

19 L. Boettner, *The Reformed Doctrine of Predestination* (Philadelphia: Presbyterian and Reformed, 1965), 152. Homer Hoeksema is an example of an extreme position that fails to understand the history of the issue: "It is simply literally Arminian to teach that Christ died for all men." H. Hoeksema, *Limited Atonement*, ed. H. Hanko, H. Hoeksema, and G. Van Baren (Grandville, MI: Reformed Free, 1976), 49.

20 The term "high Calvinist" refers to one who affirms a strictly limited atonement along with the other four points of the TULIP acrostic.

have great respect for the Calvinistic tradition, and especially the Puritans, but I do not share Reformed soteriology. Neither do I write from an Arminian perspective. I affirm the eternal security of the believer and I do not think election is based on foreseen faith. I recognize this is like entering battle wearing a Confederate blouse and Union pants, but my theological convictions leave me no choice. I write from a Baptist perspective, a rich heritage that has always contained elements of both Calvinistic and Arminian soteriology.

In this volume I make no attempt to analyze the doctrine of the atonement with respect to its nature in terms of the various theories of the atonement. I am not interested in chronicling the historical debate between Arminianism and Calvinism except with specific reference to the extent of the atonement. I have little interest in evaluating other doctrines of Reformed soteriology, such as total depravity, unconditional election, irresistible grace, and perseverance/assurance, except where these impinge directly on the present subject. Of course, these doctrines are certainly related to the extent question.

I am also only slightly interested in following the history of Arminian arguments against limited atonement. I will mostly address arguments against limited atonement from within the Reformed community (though most of these arguments are used by Arminians as well). I will deal with Arminius himself, John Wesley, and a few others within the Arminian tradition, along with a few former Calvinists who converted to Arminianism.

My ultimate goal in this work is simple: to demonstrate historically, and then biblically and theologically, why universal atonement[21] is a more excellent way, and that from the pens of the many Calvinists who have believed such. I will seek to integrate historical theology with exegesis, biblical and systematic theology, and practical theology. In a work of this nature, it is not possible to be exhaustive or fully comprehensive. My goal is more modest: to provide an overview and survey of the question that at least covers all the bases. One of the main purposes of this work is to demonstrate the unity between all moderate Calvinists, Arminians, and non-Calvinists on the specific issue of the extent of the atonement.

As I have read widely in this area in recent years, I have noticed several things that hinder profitable discussion. Perhaps a little clearing of the decks is important at this point.

Confusion often exists in this debate when we fail to note the difference between someone who actually affirms or rejects something and someone who does not mention a specific position. For example, suppose there are two people who affirm Position A (PA). Person 1 (P1) makes no reference to the existence of Position B (PB). Person 2

21 "Universal Atonement" refers to Christ's satisfaction on the cross for the sins of all humanity.

(P2) acknowledges both PA and PB and argues for the truth of PA. The historian would be wise to posit only that P1 *did not affirm or advocate* PB. The historian would still be accurate to suggest that P1 rejected PB *by implication* or *implicitly*, since PA and PB are mutually exclusive. The historian would be on solid ground to say that P2 *explicitly* rejected PB. Furthermore, if it can be established that P1 clearly affirmed PA and never mentions PB, the historian is on solid ground to conclude that P1 *would reject* PB since it is mutually exclusive with PA. These principles will become vital in analysis of historical theology on this subject.

Intent, Extent, and Application of the Atonement

In addition to its nature, it is vital to recognize and distinguish between three major areas comprising the subject of the atonement: (1) intent, (2) extent, and (3) application. One cannot consider the extent question apart from the question of intent and application. The intent of the atonement, since it relates to the differing perspectives on election, answers the questions, What was Christ's saving *purpose* in providing an atonement? Did he equally or unequally desire the salvation of every man? And then, consequently, does his intent necessarily have a bearing upon the extent of his satisfaction?

The classic Arminian and non-Calvinist[22] view of the intent of the atonement is that Christ died for all people *equally* to make salvation possible for all people, as he equally desires all to be saved, as well as secure the salvation of those who do believe (the elect).[23]

Moderate Calvinists[24]—that is, those who reject a strictly limited atonement—believe God's saving *design* or *intent* in the atonement was dualistic: (1) he sent Christ for the salvation of all humanity so that his death paid the penalty for their sins, thus rendering all saveable; and (2) Christ died with the special purpose of ultimately securing the salvation of the elect. High Calvinists[25] believe in a strictly limited *intent* that

22 It is inaccurate to lump all people into the categories of "Arminian" or "Calvinist." There are many who affirm theological positions between these two. I am reminded of R. Muller's comment that historians can be either "lumpers" or "splitters." Like Muller, I wish to engage in splitting, so that the subtle differences between theologians can be seen, not merely their similarities.

23 I am referring here to the classical Arminian position that does not necessarily deny the security of the believer. This would not be the case for most modern Arminians who deny the security of the believer.

24 These are sometimes called four-point Calvinists, but the label is imprecise, as we shall point out. See John Humfrey's comments about "moderate" and "high" sorts of Calvinists in the chapter on the seventeenth century below.

25 Even L. Gatiss, "The Synod of Dort and Definite Atonement," in *From Heaven He Came and Sought Her*, 163, said Hypothetical Universalists are five pointers by Dort standards because Dort's understanding of "particular redemption" does not mandate a strictly limited substitution for sins but does mandate a strictly limited *intent* in that Christ died for the elect with the intent of bringing them to final salvation. Gatiss is getting the five points from Dort and not the modern-day TULIP scheme.

they argue necessarily requires that Christ provided a satisfaction *only* for the elect, and thus he secures salvation only for the elect.[26]

The extent of the atonement answers the question, For whose sins was Christ punished? There are only two possible answers: (1) He died for the sins of all humanity (a) with equal intent (he died for the sins of all as he equally intends their salvation) or (b) with unequal intent (he died for the sins of all but especially intends to save the elect). (2) He died for the sins of the elect only (limited atonement), as he only intends their salvation.[27] All Arminians, non-Calvinists, and moderate Calvinists believe that Jesus died for the sins of all humanity, regardless of the latter's view of a special intent. All high Calvinists and hyper-Calvinists assert Christ died only for the sins of the elect and that it was God's intent that Christ should so die *only* for their sins.

Notice the inclusion of the four words "for the sins of" in the explanation above. Sometimes those who assert limited atonement will also state that Christ died for all people, but in so doing, they are not referring to the *sins* of all people. Usually they are referring to common grace. Virtually all Calvinists and non-Calvinists affirm the notion of common grace, though some distinguish between common and prevenient grace. The essence of the debate over the extent of the atonement has to do with Christ's death in relation to the sins of people. The ultimate question is "For whose sins did Jesus suffer?" and there are only two possible answers to this question, as noted above.

The "application" of the atonement answers the question, When is the atonement applied to the sinner? There are three possible answers to this question. (1) It is applied in the eternal decree of God. This is the view of many hyper-Calvinists. (2) It is applied at the cross to all the elect at the time of Jesus's death. This is called "justification at the cross" and is the position of some hyper-Calvinists and a few high Calvinists. (3) It is applied at the moment the sinner exercises faith in Christ. This is the biblical view and is held by most of the high Calvinists, all moderate Calvinists, all Arminians, and all non-Calvinists. The *ultimate cause* of the application is also in dispute, since Calvinists want to argue that the libertarian free will view grounds the decisive cause of salvation in man's will rather than in God's will.

These three subjects concerning the atonement (intent, extent, and application) should be distinguished but not separated from each other. Our focus here is primarily on the question of the extent of the atonement, but we will also consider the issue in relation to the question of intent and application.

---

26 Not all Calvinists say that Christ's death only provided for the salvation of the elect since they differ among themselves over the meaning of the sufficiency of Christ's death. See the definition of sufficiency below and the discussion of the sufficiency of the atonement in later chapters.

27 Most in this group do admit, however, that Christ's death results in common grace flowing to all. The important point here is sin-bearing. They do *not* admit an unlimited imputation of sin to Christ.

In addition to these distinctions, it is vital to distinguish between Christ's atonement as (1) an actual satisfaction for sins, (2) the extent of this satisfaction, (3) the application of the benefits of the atonement, and (4) the offer of salvation to humanity based on the atonement.

When it comes to the question of the extent of the atonement, one needs to have *all* the options on the table and *all of them rightly represented* before beginning to discriminate between them to see which viewpoint is true biblically.

One of the problems endemic to discussions of Calvinism is the fact that people sometimes make use of the same vocabulary but employ a different dictionary.[28] When individuals or groups do not clearly agree on the definition of terms in the discussion, confusion, misrepresentation, and misunderstanding are likely to result. Consequently, it is necessary to define the terms that will be used in this book. I have attempted to define these terms according to their historical and theological usage. The following are brief definitions of the terms:[29]

- Atonement—in modern usage, this term refers to the expiatory and propitiatory act of Christ on the cross whereby satisfaction for sin was accomplished. One must be careful to distinguish between the *intent*, *extent*, and *application* of the atonement.
- Extent of the Atonement—answers the question, For whom did Christ die? or For whose sins was Christ punished? There are only two options: (1) for the elect *alone* (limited atonement) or (2) for all of humanity. The second option may be further divided into (a) dualists (Christ has an *unequal* will to save all through the death of Christ, which is a universal satisfaction for sins) and (b) Arminians and non-Calvinists (Christ has an *equal* will to save all through the death of Christ, which is a universal satisfaction for sins).
- Limited Atonement—Christ bore the punishment due for the sins of the elect *alone*.[30] This term will be used most often to describe the position of those who affirm Christ died only for the sins of the elect. Other

28 "The use of common terminology does not mean agreement on conceptual content." C. Trueman, "Response by Carl R. Trueman," in *Perspectives on the Extent of the Atonement: 3 Views*, ed. A. D. Naselli and M. A. Snoeberger (Nashville: B&H Academic, 2015), 129.

29 These definitions, with slight modifications, can be found in my chapter "The Atonement: Limited or Universal?," in *Whosoever Will: A Biblical-Theological Critique of Five-Point Calvinism*, ed. D. L. Allen and S. Lemke (Nashville: B&H Academic, 2010), 62–64.

30 While all Calvinists who believe in "definite atonement" believe in a limited imputation of sin to Christ, the majority of them theoretically reject a quantitative "equivalentism"; that is, they do not hold to a *quid pro quo* (tit for tat) theory of expiation, as if there is a quantum of suffering in Christ that corresponds exactly to the number of sins of those he represents. I am not equating "strict particularism" with "equivalentism." In Baptist life, J. L. Dagg and T. Nettles are examples of the quantitative equivalentist view. See T. Nettles, *By His Grace and for His Glory: A Historical, Theological, and Practical Study of the Doctrines of Grace in Baptist Life*, 2nd ed. (Cape Coral, FL: Founders, 2006), 305–16.

synonyms for limited atonement include "definite atonement," "particular redemption,"[31] "strict particularism," and "particularism."

- Unlimited Atonement—Christ bore the punishment due for the sins of *all* humanity, dead and living. (Not to be confused with universal salvation. Throughout this volume, I will regularly use "unlimited atonement" as a synonym for "universal atonement" to avoid confusion.)
- Dualism—the view that Christ bore the punishment due for the sins of all humanity but not for all *equally*—that is, he did not do so with the same *intent, design*, or *purpose*. Most Calvinists who reject (or do not espouse) limited atonement in the Owenic[32] sense are dualists.
- Particularist—someone who holds to particularism—that is, the position of limited atonement. A synonym I will sometimes employ for a particularist is "limitarian."
- Limited Imputation—the sins of the elect *only* were substituted for, atoned for, or imputed to Christ on the cross.
- Unlimited Imputation—the sins of *all* of humanity were substituted for, atoned for, or imputed to Christ on the cross.
- Infinite or Universal Sufficiency—(1) When used by strict particularists, this terminology means, at least by entailment, that the death of Christ *could have been* sufficient or able to atone for all the sins of the world *if God had intended for it to do so*. However, since they think God did not intend for the death of Christ to satisfy the sins of all but only the sins of the elect, it is not *actually* sufficient or able to save any others. (2) When used by moderate Calvinists (dualists) and non-Calvinists, the terminology means that the death of Christ is of such a nature that it is actually able to save all men. It is, *in fact* (not hypothetically), a satisfaction for the sins of all humanity. Therefore, if anyone perishes, it is not for lack of atonement for his sins.[33] The fault lies *totally* within himself.

---

31 There is variety within the group of people who describe themselves by this label. Baptist theologian J. L. Dagg wrote: "Other persons who maintain the doctrine of particular redemption, distinguish between redemption and atonement, and because of the adaptedness referred to, consider the death of Christ an atonement for the sins of all men; or as an atonement for sin in the abstract." See J. L. Dagg, *Manual of Theology* (Harrisonburg, VA: Gano, 1990), 326. Notice that Dagg is affirming there are two particular redemption positions within Calvinism, something that is seldom recognized. Notice also that one of these positions within Calvinism affirms that Christ atoned for the sins of all men.

32 J. Owen, "The Death of Death in the Death of Christ," in *The Works of John Owen*, 16 vols., ed. W. H. Goold (New York: Robert Carter and Brothers, 1852), 10:139–428.

33 C. Hodge (concurring with the Synod of Dort) made this very point in his *Systematic Theology*, 3 vols. (Grand Rapids, MI: Eerdmans, 1993), 2:556–57. The Puritan S. Charnock also argued the point in "The Acceptableness of Christ's Death," in *The Works of Stephen Charnock*, 5 vols. (Edinburgh: Banner of Truth, 1985), 4:563–64.

- Limited Sufficiency—the death of Christ only satisfied for the sins of the elect *alone*, thus it is *limited in its capacity to save* only those for whom he suffered.
- Intrinsic Sufficiency—this speaks to the atonement's internal or infinite, abstract ability to save all humanity (if God so intended), in such a way that it has no direct reference to the actual extent of the atonement.
- Extrinsic Sufficiency—this speaks to the atonement's actual infinite ability to save all and every individual, and this because God indeed wills it to be so, such that Christ *in fact* made a satisfaction for the sins of all men. In other words, the sufficiency enables the unlimited satisfaction to be truly adaptable to all men. Every living person is saveable because there is blood sufficiently shed for him (Heb 9:22).
- Hypothetical Universalism—Christ died for the sins of all people such that if anyone believes, the benefits of the atonement will be applied, resulting in salvation. What is hypothetical is not the actual imputation of all sins of all people to Christ but the conditional fulfillment—in case they do believe.

What exactly is the question we are asking concerning the extent of the atonement? The question is "For whose sins did Christ die?" It is surprising how often those on both sides of the theological fence don't seem to understand the actual state of the question. For example, A. A. Hodge stated: "The question does truly and only relate to the design of the Father and of the Son in respect to the persons for whose benefit the Atonement was made."[34] But stating the question in this fashion fails to reckon with the distinction between the intent and extent of the atonement. The question does not "only" relate to the design of the atonement.

Louis Berkhof saw the question to be "Did the Father in sending Christ, and did Christ coming into the world, to make atonement for sin, do this with the design or for the purpose of saving only the elect or all men? That is the question, and that only is the question."[35] Again, Berkhof fails to distinguish between views on the *intent* of the atonement and the actual issue of its *extent*.

J. Oliver Buswell said: "There is no question . . . as to the fact that the atonement of Christ is universal in three aspects: (1) It is *sufficient* for all. . . . (2) The atonement is *applicable* to all. . . . (3) The atonement is *offered* to all."[36] But again, this does not get to the crux of the issue either. There is debate among Reformed theologians concerning the sufficiency of the atonement for the non-elect, and those within Reformed theology

34 A. A. Hodge, *The Atonement* (Philadelphia: Presbyterian Board of Publication, 1867), 359–60.

35 L. Berkhof, *Systematic Theology* (Grand Rapids, MI: Eerdmans, 1939), 393–94.

36 J. Oliver Buswell, *A Systematic Theology of the Christian Religion* (Grand Rapids, MI: Zondervan, 1962), 2:141–42.

who accept a universal satisfaction for sin don't agree that the atonement is *applicable* to those for whom it was never made.

W. A. Elwell's article in the *Evangelical Dictionary of Theology* informs us that the choices boil down to two: "Either the death of Jesus was intended to secure salvation for a limited number or the death of Jesus was intended to provide salvation for everyone."[37] Yet this is not the question of the *extent* of the atonement. This is the question of the *intent* of the atonement. The two are related but must be distinguished.

Richard Muller, attempting to define the state of the question in his book *Calvin and the Reformed Tradition*, said there are two key questions on this subject from the historical perspective of the sixteenth and seventeenth centuries: "First, the question posed by Arminius and answered at Dort: given the sufficiency of Christ's death to pay the price for all sin, how ought one to understand the limitation of its efficacy to some?"[38] Arminius, and later the Remonstrants, identified the limitation in human choice. The delegates of Dort said the efficacy is limited by God's grace to the elect alone.

Muller continued:

> Second, . . . whether the value of Christ's death was hypothetically universal in efficacy. More simply put, was the value of Christ's death such that, it would be sufficient for all sin if God had so intended—or was the value of Christ's death such that if all would believe all would be saved. On this very specific question Calvin is, arguably, silent. . . . He did frequently state, without further modification, that Christ expiated the sins of the world and that this "favor" is extended "indiscriminately to the whole human race."[39]

Muller's latter statement is a step in the right direction toward the correct statement of the question. When he asked whether the "value" of the atonement was such that if all would believe, all would be saved, we are now dealing with the question of actual substitution: for whose sins did Christ substitute? This is the real question with respect to extent.

On September 12, 2014, Michael Lynch (a PhD student at Calvin Theological Seminary) lectured on "Early Modern Hypothetical Universalism: Reflections on the *Status Quaestionis* and Modern Scholarship" at a Junius Institute Colloquium.[40] Lynch

---

37 W. A. Elwell, "Atonement, Extent of the," *Evangelical Dictionary of Theology*, ed. W. A. Elwell (Grand Rapids, MI: Baker, 1984), 98.

38 R. Muller, *Calvin and the Reformed Tradition: On the Work of Christ and the Order of Salvation* (Grand Rapids, MI: Baker, 2012), 61.

39 R. Muller, "Was Calvin a Calvinist?," 9–10.

40 See J. Ballor, "Colloquium: Early Modern Hypothetical Universalism" (M. Lynch, "Early Modern Hypothetical Universalism: Reflections on the *Status Quaestionis* and Modern Scholarship," delivered at the Junius Institute Colloquium, Junius Institute, Grand Rapids, MI, on September 12, 2014). Available online

sought to correct Louis Berkhof,[41] Wayne Grudem (who sought to improve on Berkhof), Michael Horton, and even, to some extent, Richard Muller himself. Lynch rightly argued that these men are confused (along with most of the contemporary secondary literature) on what does and does not constitute hypothetical universalism because they fail to understand properly how to state the question.

Lynch proposed:

> The key to categorizing the varieties of early modern Reformed theologians on the question of the extent of the satisfaction should lie principally in how they answer this question: for whom, and for whose sins, did God intend for Christ to merit, satisfy, or pay, an objectively sufficient price for sins? In this question, the core issue is *not* whether God intended by the death of Christ *to save* the elect alone (i.e., Berkhof), nor is it merely a question of what actually happened at the atonement (Grudem). Instead it tries to get at the object of satisfaction. What did God intend to be the object of satisfaction? Whether that be the sins of every human being or the sins of the elect alone. In other words, the intention of Christ in his accomplishing of redemption relates directly to the object and sufficiency of the satisfaction, namely whether a sufficient satisfaction was made for non-elect sins.[42]

Notice that Lynch is distinguishing between God's effectual purpose *to save* the elect alone (or that sense of intent) and the object of the satisfaction (or the extent of the atonement) in order to get at a proper understanding of the state of the question.[43]

In this book, I shall attempt to achieve several goals by way of a historical and critical review, which are summarized as follows:

1. Demonstrate that all the early church fathers, including Augustine, held to universal atonement.

---

at *Opuscula Selecta: The Junius Blog*, December 3, 2014, http://www.juniusinstitute.org/blog/colloquium-early-modern-hypothetical-universalism/.

41 Berkhof's definition heavily influenced the authors in *From Heaven He Came and Sought Her.*

42 M. Lynch, "Early Modern Hypothetical Universalism: Reflections on the *Status Quaestionis* and Modern Scholarship," delivered at the Junius Institute Colloquium, Junius Institute, Grand Rapids, MI, on September 12, 2014. (emphasis in original).

43 Lynch argued that André Rivet (1572–1651), a staunch anti-Amyraldian, after reading Davenant and others, agreed with the English variety of so-called hypothetical universalism. Rivet said that, after reading Davenant, he found nothing he disagreed with. Rivet said, "I do not see why I ought to disagree or depart from the two judgments [by Hall and Davenant] of those bishops on the two prior articles [one of which was their articles concerning the death of Christ]." Lynch's translation of Rivet can be read here: M. Lynch, "Translation Tuesday (André Rivet on the Death of Christ, Reprobation, and Private Communion)," *Iconoclastic: Shattering Sloppy History* (blog), August 26, 2014, https://theiconoclastic.wordpress.com/2014/08/26/translation-tuesday-andre-rivet-on-the-death-of-christ-reprobation-and-private-communion/.

2. Demonstrate that the only challenge to universal atonement until the latter sixteenth century came from Lucian in the fifth century at the Council of Arles, and Gottschalk in the ninth century.
3. Demonstrate the subtle shift over the interpretation of the Lombardian formula and the crucial distinction between intrinsic and extrinsic sufficiency with respect to the atonement.
4. Demonstrate that all the first-generation Reformers, including Calvin, held to unlimited atonement.
5. Demonstrate that limited atonement was not an issue of debate within the Reformed community until Beza, after the death of Calvin.
6. Demonstrate that early varieties of Hypothetical Universalism preceded Arminianism, limited atonement, and Amyraldianism in developing Reformed theology.
7. Summarize the debate within Reformed theology on the subject of extent from Beza through the twentieth century.
8. Demonstrate that some at Dort and Westminster differed over the extent question and that the final canons reflect deliberate ambiguity to allow both groups to affirm and sign the canons.
9. Demonstrate that John Owen's *Death of Death*, though viewed as the ultimate defense of limited atonement, was opposed by many within the Reformed tradition, Baxter being chief, and that it contains numerous flaws. It was not well received by the broader English Presbyterian community.
10. Document the many key Calvinists from the seventeenth through twenty-first centuries who held to unlimited atonement and present their arguments from their own words.
11. Demonstrate that Calvinism in Baptist history began to be modified toward hyper-Calvinism by John Gill and others and then was modified away from hyper-Calvinism and high-Calvinism by Fuller, and continued so in the Southern Baptist Convention and the Baptist world at large.
12. Demonstrate that among the many concerns with limited atonement shared by the Reformed and non-Reformed are the issues of God's universal saving will and/or the well-meant gospel offer in preaching and evangelism.

Some may infer at this point that this work is purely within the realm of historical theology and that no chapter treats exegetically the key verses of Scripture on the subject of the extent of the atonement. Quite the contrary, exegetical arguments appear throughout this volume. In the quotations and analyses of various proponents and opponents of limited atonement, time and again their own exegetical discussions of particular passages of Scripture will be listed and evaluated. This will allow us to hear the debate over specific passages of Scripture as it occurs from the Reformation to the present. In addition, the third major section contains my review of *From Heaven He Came and Sought Her*, the latest scholarly work defending limited atonement where multiple authors present the case, biblically and otherwise. Several of these chapters are focused on exegetical issues. In this final section, I will offer a summary evaluation and critique of limited atonement and an argument for the necessity of affirming unlimited atonement when it comes to preaching, missions, and evangelism.

Before proceeding, it will be helpful to ask and answer the question, What is it, precisely, that those who affirm limited atonement as defined above mean by the term? This can, I think, be summed up in three propositions:

1. Christ suffered only for the sins of the elect—that is, he was *punished* for the sins of the elect alone.
2. Only the sins of the elect were *imputed* and/or *laid upon* Christ.
3. Christ only *laid down* a redemptive price and/or ransom for the elect alone.

In addition to these three propositions, those who affirm limited atonement utilize four key major assumptions/arguments in support:

1. The sufficiency of the death of Christ for all the non-elect is only a *hypothetical* sufficiency of value.
2. The double payment argument, that sins cannot be paid for twice (once by Christ on the cross and again by unbelievers in hell), is the key theological argument used to support limited atonement.
3. Christ only died for those for whom he intercedes (a la John 17).
4. The atonement and the application of the atonement are coextensive: those for whom Christ died are those who must be saved due to the effectual nature of the atonement.

The following chart may prove helpful for reference throughout the book.

Four Views on the Extent of the Atonement

	Arminianism	Classic/ Moderate Calvinism	High Calvinism	Hyper-Calvinism
Christ's Death, or the Extent of the Atonement, Expiation, and Redemption*	**Christ suffers for the sins of all mankind** with an *equal* intent to save all people.	**Christ suffers for sins of all mankind**, but with an *unequal* intent/will to save all people.	Christ *only* suffers for the sins of the elect because of his singular intent.	Christ *only* suffers for the sins of the elect because of his singular intent.
	Unlimited Expiation *and* Redemption *and* a Limited Application.	**Some say Unlimited Expiation *and* Redemption** *and* a Designed Limitation in the Effectual Application.**	Expiation *and* Redemption Limited by Design *and* a Designed Limitation in the Effectual Application.	Expiation *and* Redemption Limited by Design *and* a Designed Limitation in the Effectual Application.

*Shading and **Bold** shows agreement.

Others believe in an **Unlimited Expiation with Limited Redemption (i.e., a Designed Limitation in the Effectual Application).

Part One

The Extent of the Atonement in Church History

1

The Early and Medieval Era and the Extent of the Atonement

The Early Church

There is little debate on the issue of the extent of the atonement during the patristic period, with the exception of Augustine. Some Calvinists are prone to argue that he espoused limited atonement. In the patristic era, it is clear from the writings of the Fathers that they understood the Scriptures to affirm that Christ's death satisfied for the sins of all mankind, but only those who believe will receive the benefits of Christ's death.

There are many collections of quotations brought together for the purpose of proving this point in the writings of moderate Calvinists as well as non-Calvinists. Notable examples in the seventeenth century include James Ussher; John Davenant, signatory of Dort; John Goodwin, the Calvinist turned Arminian; and Jean Daillé.[1] Another

1 J. Ussher, *Gotteschalci, et Praedestinatianae Controversiae abe o motae, Historia: Una cum duplice ejusdem Confessione, nunc primum in lucem editâ* (Dublin: Societatis Bibliopolarum, 1631); John Davenant, *An Exposition of the Epistle of St. Paul to the Colossians. With a Dissertation on the Death of Christ*, 2 vols. (London: Hamilton, Adams and Co., 1831). Davenant was a signatory of Dort and probably composed his dissertation on the death of Christ before the synod began in 1618. The dissertation appears at the end of volume two and is more than 150 pages in length, arguing the case for unlimited atonement. J. Goodwin, *Redemption Redeemed: Wherein the Most Glorious Work of the Redemption of the World by Jesus Christ Is Vindicated against the Encroachments of Later*

interesting nineteenth-century source collating many patristic quotes on the subject is Robert Young's *Biblical Notes and Queries*.[2]

Seventeenth-century Calvinists who argued some of the church fathers held to limited atonement include John Owen.[3] John Gill in the eighteenth century cited patristic sources in favor of limited atonement.[4] The references cited by Owen and Gill et al. fail to recognize that sometimes the fathers are speaking of the limited application of the atonement, yet when they speak of the actual extent of the atonement, it is always with universal language.[5] This will be demonstrated below.

The tendency to cherry pick quotations or merely to cite statements without due recognition of the context is a danger for all and must be avoided. For a thorough listing of quotations on the extent of the atonement from the patristics through the post-Reformation era and beyond, consult the research websites of David Ponter[6] and Tony Byrne.[7] Both men are moderate Calvinists with a keen historical eye who have researched this question for many years and have collected the largest databanks on the subject of which I am aware. Other twentieth-century works that provide many quotations from the church fathers to modern times affirming universal atonement include Norman Douty,[8] Robert Lightner,[9] and Curt Daniel.[10]

Consider some examples of how the early church fathers addressed the subject of the extent of the atonement. For the most part, I will only list the quotation and not elaborate.

Irenaeus (AD 130–202)

Christ "gave Himself as a redemption for those who had been led into captivity."[11]

Contextually, Irenaeus understands "those . . . led into captivity" to be all humanity led into the captivity of sin.

Times with a Thorough Discussion of the Great Questions concerning Election, Reprobation, and the Perseverance of the Saints (1561; repr. London: R. Griffin & Co., 1840); J. Daillé, *Apologia Pro duabus Ecclesiarum in Gallia Protestantium Synodis Nationalibus* (Amstelaedami: Ravesteynius, 1655), 2:753–907.

2 R. Young, "The Atonement of Christ," in *Biblical Notes and Queries: A General Medium of Communication Regarding Biblical Criticism and Bible Interpretation, Ecclesiastical History, Antiquities, Biography, and Bibliography, Ancient and Modern Versions, Progress in Theological Science, Reviews of New Religious Books, Etc.* (Edinburgh: George Adam Young & Co., 1869).

3 J. Owen, "The Death of Death in the Death of Christ," 10:139–424.

4 J. Gill, *The Cause of God and Truth* (Grand Rapids, MI: Baker, 1980 [1735–1738]), 241–65.

5 See R. Baxter, *Catholik Theologie: Plain, Pure, Peacable, for Pacification of the Dogmatical Word-Warriours* (London: Robert White, 1645), 2:57–58.

6 D. Ponter, *Calvin and Calvinism: An Elenchus for Classic-Moderate Calvinism* (blog), http://www.calvinandcalvinism.com.

7 T. Byrne, *Theological Meditations* (blog), http://www.theologicalmeditations.blogspot.com.

8 N. Douty, *The Death of Christ* (Irving, TX: Williams & Watrous, 1978).

9 R. Lightner, *The Death Christ Died: A Biblical Case for Unlimited Atonement*, 2nd ed. (Grand Rapids, MI: Kregel, 1998).

10 C. Daniel, "Hyper-Calvinism and John Gill" (PhD diss., University of Edinburgh, 1983).

11 Irenaeus, "Against Heresies," *The Apostolic Fathers, Justin Martyr, Irenaeus*, in *Anti-Nicene Fathers*, 10 vols., ed. A. Roberts and J. Donaldson, rev. by A. C. Coxe (1885; repr. Peabody, MA: Hendrickson, 2004), 1:527.

Mathetes (c. AD 130)

Mathetes's epistle to Diognetus is dated as early as AD 130. Four quotations illustrate his views on the extent of the atonement.

> This [messenger] He sent to them. Was it then, as one might conceive, for the purpose of exercising tyranny, or of inspiring fear and terror? By no means, but under the influence of clemency and meekness. As a king sends his son, who is also a king, so sent He Him; as God He sent Him; as to men He sent Him; as a Saviour He sent Him, and as seeking to persuade, not to compel us; for violence has no place in the character of God. As calling us He sent Him, not as vengefully pursuing us; as loving us He sent Him, not as judging us. (chap. VII)

> For God, the Lord and Fashioner of all things, who made all things, and assigned them their several positions, proved Himself not merely a friend of mankind, but also long-suffering [in His dealings with them]. Yea, He was always of such a character, and still is, and will ever be, kind and good, and free from wrath, and true, and the only one who is [absolutely] good; and He formed in His mind a great and unspeakable conception, which He communicated to His Son alone. (chap. VIII)

> And having made it manifest that in ourselves we were unable to enter into the kingdom of God, we might through the power of God be made able. But when our wickedness had reached its height, and it had been clearly shown that its reward, punishment and death, was impending over us; and when the time had come which God had before appointed for manifesting His own kindness and power, how the one love of God, through exceeding regard for men, did not regard us with hatred, nor thrust us away, nor remember our iniquity against us, but showed great long-suffering, and bore with us, He Himself took on Him the burden of our iniquities, He gave His own Son as a ransom for us, the holy One for transgressors, the blameless One for the wicked, the righteous One for the unrighteous, the incorruptible One for the corruptible, the immortal One for them that are mortal. (chap. IX)

> For God has loved mankind, on whose account He made the world, to whom He rendered subject all the things that are in it, to whom He gave reason and understanding, to whom alone He imparted the privilege of looking upwards to Himself, whom He formed after His own image, to whom He sent His

> only-begotten Son, to whom He has promised a kingdom in heaven, and will give it to those who have loved Him. (chap. X)[12]

The first thing to note in these quotations is that Mathetes does not limit his use of "them" or "men." God sent Christ to the world as a Savior, seeking to persuade "them" out of love. Notice also an implicit teaching of objective reconciliation in Mathetes. God is able to come to mankind in mercy, seeking to persuade people from a heart of love for them. God demonstrates a willingness to be reconciled. In the second quotation, Mathetes thinks of God as a friend to mankind, long-suffering in his dealings with us due to his kindness and goodness.

The third quotation is the most significant. Through the one love of God he bore with us and took on him the burden of our iniquities, and he (the Father) gave his own Son as a ransom for us, who are transgressors, wicked, unrighteous, corruptible, and mortal. These are descriptors of all mankind, not just the elect.

In the fourth quotation, Mathetes makes it explicit that he is talking about mankind and said God loves mankind, whom he formed in his own image and to whom he sent his only Son, promising the kingdom and eternal life to all those who believe in and love him. These statements by Mathetes certainly would indicate an understanding of the atonement as being made for the sins of all people.

Clement of Alexandria (c. AD 150–c. 215)

In his "Exhortation to the Heathen," Clement stated:

> What, then, is the exhortation I give you? I urge you to be saved. This Christ desires. In one word, He freely bestows life on you. And who is He? Briefly learn. The Word of truth, the Word of incorruption, that regenerates man by bringing him back to the truth—the goad that urges to salvation—He who expels destruction and pursues death—He who builds up the temple of God in men, that He may cause God to take up His abode in men.[13]

Clement also stated:

12 Mathetes, "Epistle to Diognetus," *The Apostolic Fathers, Justin Martyr, Irenaeus*, in *ANF*, ed. A. Roberts and J. Donaldson, rev. by A. C. Coxe (1885; repr. Peabody, MA: Hendrickson, 2004), 1:27, 28.

13 Clement, "Exhortation to the Heathen," in *ANF*, 2:204. (From Clement's *Protrepticus*, chapter 11.) Davenant ("Dissertation on the Death of Christ," 2:319) cited a similar passage from Clement's *Pædagogus* chap. 11, as did N. Douty ("Did Christ Die Only for the Elect?," 136). Davenant's quote states, "Christ freely brings and bestows salvation to the whole human race." Douty, relying on Davenant, shortens it to "Christ freely brings . . . salvation to the whole human race." If their citation is correct, and they are not referring to the above passage from the *Protrepticus*, then the original actually says, "He bestows salvation on all humanity abundantly" (Clement, "The Instructor," in *ANF*, 2:234).

> Such is our Instructor, righteously good. "I came not," He said, "to be ministered unto, but to minister." Wherefore He is introduced in the Gospel "wearied," because toiling for us, and promising "to give His life a ransom for many." For him alone who does so He owns to be the good shepherd. Generous, therefore, is He who gives for us the greatest of all gifts, His own life; and beneficent exceedingly, and loving to men, in that, when He might have been Lord, He wished to be a brother man; and so good was He that He died for us.[14]

Origen (AD 184/85–153/54)

Origen clearly affirms unlimited atonement in the following quotations:

> Such great things, then, He is, the Paraclete, the atonement, the propitiation, the sympathizer with our weaknesses, who was tempted in all human things, as we are, without sin; and in consequence He is a great High-Priest, having offered Himself as the sacrifice which is offered once for all, and not for men only but for every rational creature. For without God He tasted death for every one. In some copies of the Epistle to the Hebrews the words are "by the grace of God." Now, whether He tasted death for every one without God, He died not for men only but for all other intellectual beings too, or whether He tasted death for every one by the grace of God, He died for all without God, for by the grace of God He tasted death for every one.[15]

> What and how great things must be said of the Lamb of God, who was sacrificed for this very reason, that He might take away the sin not of a few but of the whole world, for the sake of which also He suffered? If any one sin, we read, "We have an advocate with the Father, Jesus Christ the righteous; and He is the propitiation for our sins, and not for ours only, but for those of the whole world," since He is the Saviour of all men, especially of them that believe, who blotted out the written bond that was against us by His own blood.[16]

> Now, it is not dishonourable to avoid exposing one's self to dangers, but to guard carefully against them, when this is done, not through fear of death, but from a desire to benefit others by remaining in life, until the proper time come for one who has assumed human nature to die a death that will be useful to mankind. And this is plain to him who reflects that Jesus died for the sake of men—a point of which we have spoken to the best of our ability in the preceding pages.[17]

---

14 Clement, "The Instructor," in *ANF*, 2:231.

15 Origen, "Origen's Commentary on the Gospel of John," in *ANF*, 9:318–19.

16 Ibid., 9:378.

17 Origen, "Origen against Celsus," in *ANF*, 4:423 (Book 1, chap. 61).

> Then it is clear also that Jesus, the author of such teaching, is with good reason compared by Celsus to the captain of a band of robbers. But neither was He who died for the common good of mankind, nor they who suffered because of their religion, and alone of all men were persecuted because of what appeared to them the right way of honouring God, put to death in accordance with justice, nor was Jesus persecuted without the charge of impiety being incurred by His persecutors.[18]

> But now is Jesus declared to have come for the sake of sinners in all parts of the world (that they may forsake their sin, and entrust themselves to God), being called also, agreeably to an ancient custom of these Scriptures, the "Christ of God."[19]

Cyprian of Carthage (AD 200–258)

Though there appears to be no direct statement in Cyprian concerning the extent of Christ's death, Owen cited Cyprian as saying of Christ, "'He bare all us, who bare our sins;' that is, he sustained their persons on the cross for whom he died." Yet this quotation is wrongly attributed to Cyprian, according to Goold, Owen's editor.[20]

Eusebius (c. AD 275–339)

Eusebius, the great early church historian, stated with respect to the extent of the atonement: "It was needful that the Lamb of God should be offered for the other lambs whose nature He assumed, even for the whole human race."[21]

Athanasius (AD 298–373)

Athanasius, Bishop of Alexandria, was one of the most important early church fathers. He is best known for his strong stand against the Arians at the Council of Nicea and beyond. His famous works are *Against the Gentiles* and *De Incarnatione*.[22]

> Thus, taking a body like our own, because all our bodies were liable to the corruption of death, He surrendered His body to death in the place of all, and

18 Ibid., 4:448.

19 Ibid., 4:509. This quotation is cited by Davenant, "Dissertation on the Death of Christ," 2:319, but he wrongly attributes it to book 5.

20 J. Owen, "The Death of Death in the Death of Christ," 10:422–23. Goold has an editor's footnote stating that this quote is not actually from Cyprian, but from Ernaldus Bonaevallis's *De cardinalibus operibus Christi usque ad Ascensum*.

21 Eusebius of Caesarea, *Demonstratio Evangelica*. Translations of Christian Literature. Series 1: Greek Texts, ed. W. J. Sparrow-Simpson and W. K. L. Clarke, trans. W. J. Ferrar, 2 vols. (New York: Macmillan, 1920), 2:190–91. This is also quoted in N. Douty, "Did Christ Die Only for the Elect?," 136; and J. Davenant, "Dissertation on the Death of Christ," 2:374.

22 Athanasius, *Against the Heathens (Contra Gentiles)* (New York: Scriptura, 2015); idem, *On the Incarnation* (New York: St. Vladimir's Seminary Press, 1998).

> offered it to the Father. This He did out of sheer love for us, so that in His death all might die, and the law of death thereby be abolished because, when He had fulfilled in His body that for which it was appointed, it was thereafter voided of its power for men.[23]

> The Word perceived that corruption could not be got rid of otherwise than through death; yet He Himself, as the Word, being immortal and the Father's Son, was such as could not die. For this reason, therefore, He assumed a body capable of death, in order that it, though belonging to the Word Who is above all, might become in dying a sufficient exchange for all, and, itself remaining incorruptible through His indwelling, might thereafter put an end to corruption for all others as well, by the grace of the resurrection. It was by surrendering to death the body which He had taken, as an offering and sacrifice free from every stain, that He forthwith abolished death for His human brethren by the offering of the equivalent. For naturally, since the Word of God was above all, when He offered His own temple and bodily instrument as a substitute for the life of all, He fulfilled in death all that was required. Naturally also, through this union of the immortal Son of God with our human nature, all men were clothed with incorruption in the promise of the resurrection. For the solidarity of mankind is such that, by virtue of the Word's indwelling in a single human body, the corruption which goes with death has lost its power over all.[24]

Athanasius spoke of how Jesus the Word died for all humanity, referencing Heb 2:9–15.[25] He also spoke of Christ paying a debt by offering a sacrifice "on behalf of all, surrendering His own temple to death in place of all, . . . so that the due of all might be paid."[26] Athanasius spoke of Christ dying "to ransom all."[27]

Finally, Athanasius stated:

> And this action [giving Himself to death] showed no limitation or weakness in the Word; for He both waited for death in order to make an end of it, and hastened to accomplish it as an offering on behalf of all. Moreover, as it was the death of all mankind that the Saviour came to accomplish, not His own,

---

23 Athanasius, "On the Incarnation of the Word," in *NPNF*, eds. P. Schaff and H. Wace (1892; repr. Peabody, MA: Hendrickson, 2004), 4:40. See also Athanasius, *On the Incarnation*, 34–37, 48–49, 51–52, 69–70, for statements on the universality of the atonement.

24 Ibid., 4:40–41. See also Athanasius, *On the Incarnation*, 35.

25 Ibid., 4:41–42. See also Athanasius, *On the Incarnation*, 36–37.

26 Ibid., 4:47. See also Athanasius, *On the Incarnation*, 49.

27 Ibid., 4:48. See also Athanasius, *On the Incarnation*, 51.

> He did not lay aside His body by an individual act of dying, for to Him, as Life, this simply did not belong; but He accepted death at the hands of men, thereby completely to destroy it in His own body.[28]

Cyril of Jerusalem (AD 315–386)

Cyril stated: "And wonder not that the whole world was ransomed; for it was no mere man, but the only-begotten Son of God, who died on its behalf."[29]

Here is Cyril's statement in its broader context:

> **And wonder not that the whole world was ransomed; for it was no mere man, but the only-begotten Son of God, who died on its behalf.** Moreover one man's sin, even Adam's, had power to bring death to the world; but *if by the trespass of the one death reigned* over the world, how shall not life much rather *reign by the righteousness of the One*? **And if because of the tree of food they were then cast out of paradise, shall not believers now more easily enter into paradise because of the Tree of Jesus?** If the first man formed out of the earth brought in universal death, shall not He who formed him out of the earth bring in eternal life, being Himself the Life? If Phinees, when he waxed zealous and slew the evil-doer, stayed the wrath of God, shall not Jesus, who slew not another, but gave up Himself for a ransom, put away the wrath which is against mankind?

Interestingly, this section in Cyril was quoted by Owen and also Smeaton as evidence of Cyril's belief in limited atonement.[30] Owen quoted Cyril as saying this (which corresponds to the bolded sections above):

> Wonder not if the whole world be redeemed; for he was not a mere man, but the only-begotten Son of God that died. If, then, through the eating of the (forbidden) tree they were cast out of paradise, certainly now by the tree (or cross) of Jesus shall not believers more easily enter into paradise?

Owen then remarked: "So also doth another of them [the church fathers] make it manifest in what sense they use the word *all*."[31] Owen completely failed to note the context and how Cyril used the term "mankind," which corresponds to "the whole

---

28 Ibid. See also Athanasius, *On the Incarnation*, 52.

29 Cyril, "The Catechetical Lectures of S. Cyril, Archbishop of Jerusalem," in *NPNF*, 7:82 (*Catacheses*, 13.2).

30 J. Owen, *The Death of Death in the Death of Christ* (Edinburgh: Banner of Truth, 1989), 311; G. Smeaton, *The Apostles' Doctrine of the Atonement* (Edinburgh: T. & T. Clark, 1870; Grand Rapids, MI: Zondervan, 1957), 498.

31 J. Owen, *The Death of Death*, 311.

world" that was "ransomed" in the first part of the quotation. Owen's mistake is to think that somehow "world" and "mankind" is limited to believers or, as he puts it, "all" in that sense.

Gregory of Nazianzen (AD 324–389)

Gregory stated:

> Take, in the next place, the subjection by which you subject the Son to the Father. What, you say, is He not now subject, or must He, if He is God, be subject to God? You are fashioning your argument as if it concerned some robber, or some hostile deity. But look at it in this manner: that as for my sake He was called a curse, Who destroyed my curse; and sin, who taketh away the sin of the world; and became a new Adam to take the place of the old, just so He makes my disobedience His own as Head of the whole body.[32]

> But that great, and if I may say so, in Its first nature unsacrificeable Victim, was intermingled with the Sacrifices of the Law, and was a purification, not for a part of the world, nor for a short time, but for the whole world and for all time. For this reason a Lamb was chosen for its innocence, and its clothing of the original nakedness. For such is the Victim, that was offered for us, Who is both in Name and fact the Garment of incorruption.[33]

> He is Sanctification, as being Purity, that the Pure may be contained by Purity. And Redemption, because He sets us free, who were held captive under sin, giving Himself a Ransom for us, the Sacrifice to make expiation for the world. And Resurrection, because He raises up from hence, and brings to life again us, who were slain by sin.[34]

Basil (AD 330–379)

> In fact, what can man find great enough that he may give it for the ransom of his soul? But, one thing was found worth as much as all men together. This was given for the price of ransom for our souls, the holy and highly honored blood of our Lord Jesus Christ, which He poured out for all of us; therefore, we were bought with a great price.[35]

---

32 Gregory Nazianzen, "Select Orations," in *NPNF*, 7:311.
33 Ibid., 7:427.
34 Ibid., 7:317.
35 Saint Basil, "Exegetical Homilies," in *The Fathers of the Church*, 46 vols., trans. A. C. Way (Washington, DC: Catholic University of America Press, 1947–1963), 46:318.

Ambrose (AD 338–397)

Although Christ suffered for all, yet He suffered for us particularly, because He suffered for the Church.[36]

Christ suffered for all, rose again for all. But if anyone does not believe in Christ, he deprives himself of that general benefit.[37]

Christ came for the salvation of all, and undertook the redemption of all, inasmuch as He brought a remedy by which all might escape, although there are many who . . . are unwilling to be healed.[38]

So we see how grave a matter it is to deprive another, with whom we ought rather to suffer, of anything, or to act unfairly or injuriously towards one to whom we ought to give a share in our services. . . . If, for instance, the hand tears out the eye, has it not hindered the use of its work? If it were to wound the foot, how many actions would it not prevent? But how much worse is it for the whole man to be drawn aside from his duty than for one of the members only! If the whole body is injured in one member, so also is the whole community of the human race disturbed in one man. The nature of mankind is injured, as also is the society of the holy Church, which rises into one united body, bound together in oneness of faith and love. Christ the Lord, also, Who died for all, will grieve that the price of His blood was paid in vain.[39]

Jerome (AD 347–420)

Matt 20.28. "*Just as the Son of man did not come to be served but to serve*" (NASB). Note what we have frequently said, that he who serves is called the Son of man. "And to give his life as a redemption for many." This took place when he took the form of a slave that he might pour out his blood for the world. And he did not say "to give his life as a redemption" for all, but "for many," that is, for those who wanted to believe.[40]

Michael Haykin concluded from this statement that "Jerome defines the 'many' as 'those who wanted to believe.' While there may be some ambiguity here in Jerome's

---

36 Ambrose, *Exposition of the Holy Gospel According to Saint Luke*, trans. T. Tomkinson (Etna, CA: Center for Traditionalist Orthodox Studies, 1998), 201–2.

37 Ambrose, *In Psalmum David CXVIII Expositio*, Serm. 8. Cited by J. Davenant, "Dissertation on the Death of Christ," 2:411.

38 Ambrose, *De Cain et Abel Libri Duo*, ii. 3. Cited by J. Davenant, "Dissertation on the Death of Christ," 2:425–26.

39 Ambrose, "On the Duties of the Clergy," in *NPNF*, 10:70 (Book 3, chap. 3, sec. 19).

40 Jerome, "Commentary on Matthew," in *The Fathers of the Church*, 117:229.

statement, the words at least hint that Jerome saw Christ's death to be for a particular group of people—believers."[41] In this very same quotation, Jerome clearly affirmed the extent of Christ's death is "for the world." Furthermore, Haykin failed to cite other statements in Jerome that indicate universal atonement. For example, in the same commentary on Matthew, Jerome stated: "Now when Jesus was in Bethany in the house of Simon the leper He was about to suffer for the whole world and to redeem all nations by his blood."[42]

We might also compare Jerome here on Heb 9:28 with what Chrysostom said about the same verse (see below). Notice how Jerome, like Chrysostom, spoke of the universal aspect of the atonement ("that he might pour out his blood for the world") before he spoke of the application to believers only ("but 'for many,' that is, for those who wanted to believe").[43] In both Chrysostom and Jerome, we don't have the language of later Reformed theology where the elect are spoken of in the abstract. Both men primarily spoke of "the elect" *qua* believers, not in the abstract language of "the elect" *qua* elect.

Commenting on Matt 1:3, Jerome stated: "In the Savior's genealogy it is remarkable that there is no mention of holy women, but only those whom Scripture reprehends, so that (we can understand that) he who had come for the sake of sinners, since he was born from sinful women, blots out the sins of everyone."[44] Gill listed Jerome as a particularist on the atonement in *The Cause of God and Truth*, and so Haykin follows suit.[45] Interestingly, Gottschalk, a very staunch ninth-century particularist (see below), on the other hand, associated Jerome with Origen on the subject of universal redemption, and said:

> But Saint Jerome, who rightly execrated this most false revolving, equally believed, as that one [Origen], that Christ suffered for the reprobate, and conjectured that we are called, become, and are holy not according to the purpose of God, but according to that of each of us, and according to our own will.[46]

41 M. Haykin, "'We Trust in the Saving Blood': Definite Atonement in the Ancient Church," in *From Heaven He Came and Sought Her*, 70. See also J. Gill, *The Cause of God and Truth* (London: Waterford, 1855), 260.

42 Jerome, "Commentary on Matthew," 292.

43 See D. Ponter, "Jerome (347–420) on the Death of Christ," *Calvin and Calvinism: An Elenchus for Classic-Moderate Calvinism* (blog), December 6, 2013, http://calvinandcalvinism.com/?p=13256:

> If this reading of Jerome is correct, and I strongly suspect it is, then with regard to the quotation provided by Haykin, there is no reference to the extent of the satisfaction properly speaking. Rather, Jerome speaks to the application of Christ's satisfactory work. His particular interpretation of "the many" would then be perfectly compatible with the doctrine of unlimited satisfaction—as it was with the case of Chrysostom, he could have equally subscribed to the belief that Christ died for (suffered for, etc.) all men.

44 Jerome, "Commentary on Matthew," 59.

45 J. Gill, *The Cause of God and Truth* (Grand Rapids, MI: Baker, 1980), 263–65; M. Haykin, "'We Trust in the Saving Blood': Definite Atonement in the Ancient Church," in *From Heaven He Came and Sought Her*, 70.

46 Gottschalk, "On Predestination," in *Gottschalk & A Medieval Predestination Controversy: Texts Translated from the Latin*, Mediaeval Philosophical Texts in Translation 47, ed. and trans. V. Genke and F. Gumerlock (Milwaukee, WI: Marquette University Press, 2010), 152.

John Chrysostom (c. AD 349–407)

John Chrysostom leaves no doubt as to his views on the universal extent of Christ's death on the cross: "He [Christ] had not died, or would not have died, for all, had not all died or been dead."[47] Here we see that Christ died for all who were "dead." Since all without exception were dead in sins, Christ died for all without exception. Chrysostom also stated: "For it argueth an excess of much love, both to die for so great a world, and to die for it being so affected or disposed as it was."[48]

Chrysostom made clear that Christ died not only for those who believe but for all the world: "Not only for the faithful, but even for the whole world: for He indeed died for all; But what if all have not believed? He hath fulfilled His own [part]. Yet he hath done his part."[49]

Likewise Chrysostom stated: "And yet with it all Christ was not to gain all, yet still He died for all; so fulfilling His own part."[50]

Chrysostom's comment on Heb 9:28 is especially enlightening on the subject.

> Ver. 28. "So Christ was once offered." By whom offered? evidently by Himself. Here he says that He is not Priest only, but Victim also, and what is sacrificed. On this account are [the words] was offered. "Was once offered" (he says) "to bear the sins of many." Why "of many," and not for "all"? Because not all believed. For He died indeed for all, that is His part: for that death was a counterbalance against the destruction of all men. But He did not bear the sins of all men, because they were not willing.
>
> And what is [the meaning of] "He bare the sins"? Just as in the Oblation we bear up our sins and say, "Whether we have sinned voluntarily or involuntarily, do Thou forgive," that is, we make mention of them first, and then ask for their forgiveness. So also was it done here. Where has Christ done this? Hear Himself saying, "And for their sakes I sanctify Myself." (John xvii.19.) Lo! He bore the sins. He took them from men, and bore them to the Father; not that He might determine anything against them [mankind], but that He might forgive them. "Unto them that look for Him shall He appear" (he says) "the second time without sin unto salvation." What is "without sin"? it is as much as to say, He sinneth not. For neither did He die as owing the debt of death, nor yet because of sin. But how "shall He appear"? To punish, you

47 J. Chrysostom, "Homilies on the Second Epistle of St. Paul the Apostle to the Corinthians," in *NPNF*, 12:331.

48 J. Goodwin, *Redemption Redeemed* (1840), 163. See also J. Goodwin, *Redemption Redeemed: A Puritan Defense of Unlimited Atonement*, ed. J. Wagner (Eugene, OR: Wipf & Stock, 2004), 57.

49 J. Chrysostom, "Homilies on the Gospel of St. John and the Epistles to the Hebrews," in *NPNF* (Peabody, MA: Hendrickson, 2004), 14:447–48.

50 J. Chrysostom, "Homilies on the Epistle of St. Paul the Apostle to the Romans," in *NPNF*, 11:529.

> say. He did not however say this, but what was cheering; "shall He appear unto them that look for Him, without sin unto salvation." So that for the time to come they no longer need sacrifices to save themselves, but to do this by deeds.[51]

For Chrysostom in this context, "to bear sin" means "to forgive sin," and it is only the sins of believers that are forgiven. Note carefully Chrysostom affirms that Christ died for the sins of all people, yet not all are forgiven. The statement of the universality of Christ's death precedes the limiting statement concerning all who believe.

Cyril of Alexandria (AD 376–444)

> The death of one flesh is sufficient for the ransom of the whole human race, for it belonged to the Logos, begotten of God the Father.[52]

Theodoret of Cyrus (AD 393–466)

Theodoret, commenting on Heb 9:27–28, said:

> As it is appointed for each human being to die once, and the one who accepts death's decree no longer sins but awaits the examination of what was done in life, so Christ the Lord, after being offered once for us and taking up our sins, will come to us again, with sin no longer in force, that is, with sin no longer occupying a place as far as human beings are concerned. He said himself, remember, when he still had a mortal body, "He committed no sin, nor was guile found in his mouth." It should be noted, of course, that he bore the sins of many, not of all: not all came to faith, so he removed the sins of the believers only.[53]

Theodoret spoke here in the same way as Chrysostom above. Note the use of the concept of "to bear sins." This is not an affirmation of an atonement limited in extent only to the elect. It is an affirmation that the benefits of the atonement are applied only to those who believe. The phrase "he bore the sins of many, not of all" means "since not all come to faith in Christ, the actual removal of sins resulting in salvation is limited only to believers." Theodoret explained what he meant by the phrase in question when he followed it up with the "not all came to faith, so he removed the sins of the believers only."

Theodoret also stated:

---

51 J. Chrysostom, "Homilies on the Gospel of St. John and the Epistles to the Hebrews," in *NPNF*, 14:447–48.

52 Cyril, *Oratorio de Recta Fide*, no. 2, sec. 7. Cited in Smeaton, *The Apostles' Doctrine of the Atonement*, 502.

53 R. C. Hill, *Theodoret of Cyrus: Commentary on the Letters of St. Paul*, 2 vols. (Brookline, MA: Holy Cross Orthodox Press, 2001), 2:175.

> By raising the flesh He has given the promise of resurrection to us all, after giving the resurrection of His own precious body as a worthy pledge of ours. So loved He men even when they hated Him that the mystery of the economy fails to obtain credence with some on account of the very bitterness of His sufferings, and it is enough to show the depths of His loving kindness that He is even yet day by day calling to men who do not believe. And He does so not as though He were in need of the service of men—for of what is the Creator of the universe in want?—but because He thirsts for the salvation of every man. Grasp then, my excellent friend, His gift; sing praises to the Giver, and procure for us a very great and right goodly feast.[54]

Theodoret asserted Christ's love for all and his desire "for the salvation of every man."

Augustine[55] *(AD 354–430)*

Augustine of Hippo was the greatest theologian of the patristic era. His thoughts and writings are hugely influential in Roman Catholicism and in Reformation thought. Both Luther and Calvin were heavily influenced by Augustine. Augustine's late writings on predestination were the fountainhead for Calvin's theological system. Many in the Reformed tradition generally assume that Augustine held to limited atonement. However, an investigation of Augustine's actual statements on the extent of the atonement proves otherwise.[56] Since Augustine is so important not only for the patristic era but for the Reformation as well, we will devote more space to considering his statements on the subject.

Augustine spoke more than once of Jesus as the lamb who "takes away the sins of the world" with no qualification of the meaning of "world."[57] Speaking of Adam and

---

54 Theodoret, "Letter LXXVI to Uranius, Governor of Cyprus," in *NPNF*, 3:272.

55 For an easily accessible collection of in-context quotations of Augustine on the subject of the extent of the atonement, see D. Ponter, "Augustine (354–430) on the Death of Christ," *Calvin and Calvinism: An Elenchus for Classic-Moderate Calvinism* (blog), June 29, 2009, http://calvinandcalvinism.com/?p=13.

56 In an important note appended to the end of volume 2 of the Oxford edition of Augustine's *Homilies on John* (1238–46), translator H. Browne explained the seeming contradictory statements in Augustine with respect to the extent of the atonement. Browne suggested that

> in speaking of redemption, St. Augustine contemplates it not merely as the act of Christ, objectively, consummated once for all on the Cross, but subjectively, as an act taking place in the persons redeemed: in other words, he speaks of it as the actual deliverance of souls from the power of Satan. (1238)

Browne suggested Augustine believed Christ died for all objectively, but God did not purpose the redemption of the reprobate but only the elect, hence Augustine speaks of Christ as not dying for the reprobate in this sense, not in the objective sense of satisfying for the sins of all humanity, which Augustine elsewhere, as Browne showed, also affirmed. Failure to make this distinction in Augustine leads some to mistakenly think that Augustine himself taught limited atonement in the same sense as John Owen taught it. Browne also stated, "The Greek and Latin Fathers before St. Augustine unanimously teach, that God wills the salvation of all men, and that Christ died for all without exception" (1243). Browne also noted that Augustine's disciple, Prosper, in his rebuttal of the semi-Pelagians, also taught unlimited atonement (1245–46).

57 See, for example, Augustine, "On the Trinity," in *NPNF*, 3:223; "Of Holy Virginity," in ibid., 3:430; and "A Treatise on the Merits and Forgiveness of Sins and on the Baptism of Infants," in ibid., 5:25.

Christ, Augustine noted: "As one man brought sin into the world, that is, upon the whole human race, so one man was to take away the sin of the world."[58] He spoke of Jesus's crucifixion as an act that should "abolish in His flesh the sins of the whole world, and not their guilty acts merely, but the evil lusts of their hearts."[59] Augustine spoke of our charity "towards those for whom Christ died, desiring to redeem them by the price of His own blood from the death of the errors of this world."[60] In speaking of the importance of Christians not sinning against the conscience of "weaker brothers," Augustine included among these those who are unsaved and spoke of them as "perishing":

> What account art thou making of their price, if thou disregard the purchase? Consider for how great a price was the purchase made. "Through thy knowledge," saith the Apostle, "shall the weak brother perish;" . . . In this knowledge the weak brother perishes. And lest thou should pay no regard to the weak brother, he added, "for whom Christ died." If thou would disregard him, yet consider his Price, and weigh the whole world in the balance with the Blood of Christ.[61]

Augustine spoke of the fact that if Christ's blood had not been shed, "the world would not have been redeemed."[62] He is not speaking of universalism but of the fact that Christ died for the sins of the world. This same language is used by the early Reformers. In another place, he stated that "the human race was at some time to be redeemed by the precious blood."[63] Augustine spoke of how Christ has "redeemed" the "whole" of the world.[64]

The single most important passage in Augustine that clearly indicates that he believed Christ died for the sins of the world is found in a discussion of Judas's betrayal of Jesus.

> Why so? "For Him whom Thou hast smitten they have themselves persecuted, and upon the pain of my wounds they have added" (ver. 27). How then have they sinned if they have persecuted one by God smitten? What sin is ascribed to their mind? Malice. For the thing was done in Christ which was to be. To suffer indeed He had come, and He punished him through whom He

58 Augustine, "Enchiridion," in *NPNF*, 3:253.

59 Augustine, "On Christian Doctrine," in *NPNF*, 2:591.

60 Augustine, "On the Catechising of the Uninstructed," in *NPNF*, 3:298.

61 Augustine, "Sermons on Selected Lessons of the New Testament: Sermon XII," in *NPNF*, 6:301.

62 Augustine, "Sermons on Selected Lessons of the New Testament: Sermon LXXII," in *NPNF*, 6:472. See also "Homilies on the Gospel of John: Tractate XXXVII," in ibid., 7:217.

63 Ibid., "Tractate VII," 7:50.

64 Augustine, "Exposition on the Book of Psalms," in *NPNF*, 8:179. See also 481 and 592.

> suffered. For Judas the traitor was punished, and Christ was crucified: but us He redeemed by His blood, and He punished him in the matter of his price. For he threw down the price of silver, for which by him the Lord had been sold; and he knew not the price wherewith he had himself by the Lord been redeemed. This thing was done in the case of Judas.[65]

Augustine spoke of Jesus as the "redeemer of all men"[66] and called his death "the ransom for the whole world; He paid the price for the whole world."[67] Augustine often used the language of "world" in a context that precludes the possibility of any meaning other than all people in the world.

> For men were held captive under the devil, and served devils; but they were redeemed from captivity. They could sell, but they could not redeem themselves. The Redeemer came, and gave a price; He poured forth His Blood, and bought the whole world. Ye ask what He bought? Ye see what He hath given; find out then what He bought. The Blood of Christ was the price. What is equal to this? What, but the whole world? What, but all nations? They are very ungrateful for their price, or very proud, who say that the price is so small that it bought the Africans only; or that they are so great, as that it was given for them alone. Let them not then exult, let them not be proud: He gave what He gave for the whole world. He knew what He bought, because He knew at what price He bought it.[68]

Likewise, in another place, Augustine said: "For with righteousness shall He judge the world: not a part of it, for He bought not a part: He will judge the whole, for it was the whole of which He paid the price."[69] Such language cannot be interpreted to mean Christ died only for the elect out of the world.

Speaking of Rom 5:18–19, Augustine again is quite clear in his statement that Christ died for the sins of all people:

> Of this death the Apostle Paul says, "Therefore all are dead, and He died for all, that they which live should not henceforth live unto themselves, but unto Him which died for them and rose again." Thus all, without one exception, were dead in sins, whether original or voluntary sins, sins of ignorance, or sins committed against knowledge; and for all the dead there died the one

---

65 Ibid., 8:309, citing Ps. 69:26–27.

66 Ibid., 8:516.

67 Augustine, "Letters of St. Augustine: Letter LXXVI," in *NPNF*, 1:343.

68 "Exposition on the Book of the Psalms," in *NPNF*, 8:471–72.

69 Ibid., 8:474.

> only person who lived, that is, who had no sin whatever, in order that they who live by the remission of their sins should live, not to themselves, but to Him who died for all, for our sins, and rose again for our justification, that we, believing in Him who justifies the ungodly, and being justified from ungodliness or quickened from death, may be able to attain to the first resurrection which now is.[70]

Speaking of 1 Cor 15:3 and 2 Cor 5:18–20, Augustine affirmed his understanding of Paul's statement to be an indication that Christ died for the sins of all.[71]

Finally, Augustine stated:

> Who is there, moreover, who should not be earnestly disposed to give the return of love to a God of supreme righteousness and also of supreme mercy, who first loved men of the greatest unrighteousness and the loftiest pride, and that, too, so deeply as to have sent in their behalf His only Son, by whom He made all things, and who being made man, not by any change of Himself, but by the assumption of human nature, was designed thus to become capable not only of living with them, but of dying at once for them and by their hands.[72]

From these quotations we may draw several conclusions. First, in numerous places, Augustine spoke of the atonement as being "for the sins of the world" with no restrictive qualification of the meaning of "world." Second, Augustine affirmed universal atonement but also made it clear that the application is only to those who believe. Third, Augustine's view of predestination did not lead him to limit the atonement only to the elect. Fourth, it is clear that Augustine thought that Jesus redeemed Judas. Such a statement could not be made by one who affirmed limited atonement, since Judas was clearly among the reprobate. Fifth, there is no explicit statement in Augustine's writings that the death of Christ is limited only to the elect.

Interestingly, Raymond Blacketer correctly noted that "there is no single statement from the bishop of Hippo that explicitly declares that God's intention in the satisfaction of Christ was to procure redemption for the elect alone." But he then incorrectly concluded that this was "precisely the view that Augustine held."[73] Blacketer confuses

---

70 Augustine, "The City of God," in *NPNF*, 2:425.

71 Augustine, "A Treatise on the Merits and Forgiveness of Sins and on the Baptism of Infants," in *NPNF*, 5:32.

72 Augustine, "On the Catechising of the Uninstructed," in *NPNF*, 3:307.

73 R. Blacketer, "Definite Atonement in Historical Perspective," in *The Glory of the Atonement: Biblical, Historical and Practical Perspectives*, ed. C. Hill and F. James III (Downers Grove, IL: InterVarsity, 2004), 308. Blacketer mentions Augustine's comments on John 10:26, where he explains that Jesus viewed the Pharisees as "predestined to everlasting destruction, not won to eternal life by the price of His own blood." Blacketer then remarks, "It is no stretch to conclude that the implication of this statement is that the price of Christ's blood was paid for those who are predestined to eternal life" (308–9). It is indeed a stretch, since Blacketer's take is quite the opposite of what Augustine is saying.

Augustine's statements about God's predestinarian will for the elect with his view on the actual satisfaction for all sin that Christ accomplished in the atonement. Furthermore, Blacketer's attempt to make Prosper, disciple of Augustine, a proponent of limited satisfaction is likewise a misreading of Prosper. Prosper of Aquitaine is historically viewed as the normative interpreter of Augustine and he *very clearly* held to universal redemption (see below).[74]

Robert Godfrey stated, "While Augustine did not express clearly or discuss at length the doctrine of the definite or limited atonement, he did come very close to this doctrine."[75] He went on to quote Prosper, who "reflected on the sense in which the death of Christ was for all men and the sense in which it was restricted."[76] It appears Godfrey is suggesting that Augustine and Prosper held to an unlimited imputation of sin to Christ (unlimited atonement) but to a limited application only to the elect. Contrary to what many Calvinists have suggested, the evidence supports the position that Augustine did not hold to limited atonement.[77]

Sixth, though Augustine took a limited reading of 1 John 2:2, as many later limitarians would do, he was not repudiating universal atonement. Many Hypothetical Universalists, following Augustine, took a limited reading of this text as well, such as Kimedoncius.[78] Seventh, Augustine often focused on what Christ has done for those who are believers in such a way that there is a certain "ambiguity as to what a theologian may think the work of Christ means for those who are not his own."[79] This critical point made by Godfrey is vital when reading theologians from any era who address the subject of the extent of the atonement, including the biblical authors.

For example, Robert Dabney pointed out that statements in Scripture such as Christ died for "the church" or "his sheep" do not prove a strictly limited atonement because to argue such invokes the negative inference fallacy: "The proof of a proposition does not disprove its converse."[80] One cannot infer a negative (Christ did *not* die for group A) from a bare positive statement (Christ did die for group B) any more than one can infer that Christ died *only* for Paul because Paul said in Gal 2:20,

---

74 See Prosper's *Defense of St. Augustine*, trans. P. De letter (New York: Newman, 1963), 149–51, 159–60, 164.

75 R. Godfrey, "Reformed Thought on the Extent of the Atonement to 1618," *Westminster Theological Journal* 37, no. 2 (Winter 1974): 134.

76 Ibid., 135.

77 As noted, for example, by James Richards (J. Richards, *Mental Philosophy and Theology* [New York: M. W. Dodd, 1846], 302), who, citing J. Milner (*The History of the Church of Christ*, 5 vols. [Boston: Farrand, Mallory, and Co., 1809], 2:445), points out with respect to Augustine that Prosper represented him as maintaining that Christ gave himself a ransom for all, and by C. Daniel ("Hyper-Calvinism and John Gill" [PhD diss., University of Edinburgh, 1983], 497–500) after examining the evidence from the writings of Augustine.

78 J. Kimedoncius, *Of the Redemption of Mankind. Three Books: Wherein the Controversie of the Universalitie of the Redemption and Grace by Christ, and of His Death for All Men, Is Largely Handled. Hereunto Is Annexed a Treatise of Gods Predestination in One Booke*, trans. H. Ince (London: Felix Kingston, 1598), 80–94 [Irregular pagination].

79 Godfrey, "Reformed Thought on the Extent of the Atonement," 134.

80 Dabney, *Systematic Theology*, 521.

"Christ gave himself for me."[81] Additionally, if I frequently repeat that I love my wife, it may be, hypothetically speaking, that I love *only* my wife, but it does not follow with deductive certainty.

This is the same kind of logical mistake that John Owen made numerous times in his *The Death of Death in the Death of Christ*, and it is a logical fallacy constantly made by high Calvinists with regard to the extent of the atonement.[82] Consequently, the fact that many verses speak of Christ dying for his "sheep," his "church," or "his friends" does not prove that he did not die for others not subsumed in these categories. In fact, all of these references in Scripture employing such terminology do not speak of the elect as an abstract class in the sense of all those predestined for eternal life but refer only to the believing elect, those who are in union with Christ by virtue of faith.

The evidence suggests that Augustine, along with all the church fathers, taught an unlimited atonement. In fact, some suggested that it was actually Pelagius, not Augustine, who was the particularist.[83]

Before turning to Augustine's disciple, Prosper, we conclude this section on Augustine with a pertinent quotation from Richard Baxter concerning Augustine's view of the extent of the atonement:

> As for Augustine and some Protestants, they oft deny that Christ redeemeth any but the Faithful, because the word Redemption is ambiguous, and sometimes taken for the price or ransome paid, and often for the very liberation of the captive Sinner. And whenever Austin denieth common Redemption, he taketh Redemption in this last sense, for actual deliverance. But he asserteth it in the first sense, that Christ died for all. Yea, he thought his death is actually applied to the true Justification and Sanctification of some Reprobates that fall away and perish, though the Elect only are so redeemed as to be saved. Read

81 No one should interpret the passage that speaks of hell as prepared "for the devil and his angels" as restrictive in meaning *only* to them.

82 Even R. Reymond, a supralapsarian Calvinist, noted:

> It is true, of course, that logically a statement of particularity in itself does not necessarily preclude universality. This may be shown by the principle of subalternation in Aristotelian logic, which states that if all S is P, then it may be inferred that some S is P, but conversely, it cannot be inferred from the fact that some S is P that the remainder of S is not P. A case in point is the "me" of Gal 2:20: the fact that Christ died for Paul individually does not mean that Christ died only for Paul and for no one else. (R. Reymond, *A New Systematic Theology*, 2nd ed. [Nashville: Thomas Nelson, 1998], 673–74).

83 W. Lorimer spoke of the Pelagians limiting the atonement, at least by necessary consequent or entailment. Since infants don't have original sin, they, or at least some of them who die in the state of infancy without actual sin, don't need a satisfaction for their sin. The Augustinians, far from denying universal redemption, actually used their belief in universal redemption to counter the Pelagians, arguing that if Christ died for all, then he died for infants, and thus infants must in some sense be in need of grace and mercy (W. Lorimer, *An Apology for the Ministers Who Subscribed Only unto the Stating of the Truths and Errors in Mr. William's Book* [London: Printed for John Lawrence, at the Angel in the Poultry, 1694], 184–86). Davenant does not think Pelagius limited the atonement. See his "Dissertation on the Death of Christ," 2:323–30.

> yourself in Augustine, Prosper and Fulgentius, and you will see this with your own eyes.[84]

Notice that Baxter approached Augustine in the same way as H. Browne, translator of some of Augustine's works into English in the nineteenth century, as noted above.

Prosper of Aquitaine (AD 390–455)

Prosper was Augustine's disciple and is viewed by Augustinian scholars as the normative interpreter of Augustine's thought. One can easily discern Prosper's commitment to unlimited atonement in the following two statements:

> Article 9. Objection: The Saviour was not crucified for the redemption of the entire world. . . . Accordingly, though it is right to say that the Saviour was crucified for the redemption of the entire world, because He truly took our human nature and because all men were lost in the first man, yet it may also be said that He was crucified only for those who were to profit by His death.[85]

> Article 1. Objection: Our Lord Jesus Christ did not suffer for the salvation and redemption of all men. . . . Considering, then, on the one hand the greatness and value of the price paid for us, and on the other hand the common lot of the whole human race, one must say that the blood of Christ is the redemption of the entire world. But they who pass through this world without coming to the faith and without having been reborn in baptism, remain untouched by the redemption. Accordingly, since our Lord in very truth took upon Himself the one nature and condition which is common to all men, it is right to say that all have been redeemed and that nevertheless not all are actually liberated from the slavery of sin.[86]

From these two quotations it is clear Prosper held to unlimited atonement. Godfrey concluded that "Prosper was quite concerned to avoid the charge that he was limiting the universality of Christ's death."[87]

In John Owen's list of quotations of the church fathers, he cited Ambrosiaster as

---

84 R. Baxter, *Catholick Theologie* (London: Printed by Robert White, for Nevill Simmons at the Princes Arms in St. Pauls Church-yard, 1675), 2:57–58.

85 Prosper, "Prosper of Aquitaine: Defense of St. Augustine," trans. and annotated P. De Letter, S. J., in *Ancient Christian Writers*, 66 vols. (New York: Newman, 1963), 32:149–50. The work in Latin is *Pro Augustino responsiones ad capitula objectionum allorum calumniantium.*

86 Ibid., 164. Prosper connects the idea of some being "untouched by the redemption" with being "actually liberated from the slavery of sin." This is redemption *applied.*

87 Godfrey, "Reformed Thought on the Extent of the Atonement," 136.

affirming limited atonement.[88] Ambrosiaster is not an actual person. It was once thought that this work, and others, was the work of Ambrose. But when this was proven false, the name "Ambrosiaster" was given to these works. Today this work is believed to be by Prosper. It is now available in English under the title *The Call of the Nations*.[89]

Owen's treatment of this quotation leaves much to be desired. He left out a vital sentence in the quotation that falsifies his limitarian interpretation. Here is Owen's version: "The people of God hath its own fullness. In the elect and foreknown, distinguished from the generality of all, there is accounted a certain special universality; so that the whole world seems to be delivered from the whole world, and all men to be taken out of all men."[90]

Here is the actual quotation from Prosper with the sentence Owen left out italicized:

> God's people, therefore, has a completeness all its own. *It is true that a great part of mankind refuse or neglect the grace of their Saviour*. In the elect, however, and the foreknown who were set apart from the generality of mankind, we have a specified totality. Thus the whole world is spoken of as though the whole of it had been liberated, and all mankind as though all men had been chosen.[91]

The quotation itself, not to mention the rest of the context, indicates that Prosper is engaged in a discussion concerning election, not the extent of the atonement. However, later, Prosper deals with the extent question and it is self-evident he affirms unlimited atonement. For example, "There can, therefore, be no reason to doubt that Jesus Christ our Lord died for the unbelievers and the sinners. If there had been any one who did not belong to these, then Christ would not have died for all. But He did die for all men without exception."[92]

In the entire patristic era there is only one name that can be marshalled in support of limited atonement, and then only in a very tentative and temporary way. In his *History of the Councils of the Church*, Hefele said, as a result of the fifth-century Council of Arles, Lucian, who had leaned toward limited atonement, changed his views to unlimited atonement.[93] It seems that an extreme form of predestinarianism may have raised the possibility of limited atonement in Lucian's mind.[94]

The Council of Arles clearly condemned the view that "Christ has not undergone

---

88 J. Owen, *The Death of Death*, 311. Also in "Death of Death," 10:423.

89 Prosper, *The Call of the Nations*, trans. P. De Letter (London: Longmans, Green & Co., 1952).

90 Owen, *The Death of Death*, 423.

91 Prosper, *The Call of the Nations*, 46.

92 Ibid., 118.

93 C. J. Hefele, *A History of the Councils of the Church*, trans. and ed. W. R. Clark (Edinburgh: T. & T. Clark, 1872), 20–21. According to Hefele, one of the main sources of information on Lucian and the Council of Arles was the letters of Faustus (*Fausti Reiensis Praeter Sermones Pseudo-Eusebianos Opera. Accedunt Ruricii Epistula. Recensuit A. Engelbrecht*, 1891).

94 The Council of Arles primarily dealt with extreme predestination and not the extent of the atonement.

death for the salvation of all men."[95] The council also condemned that view that Christ "does not will that all should be saved."[96] Gould lists two of the anathemas as follows: (1) "and to those who teach that such as are lost did not receive from God means of salvation," and (2) "anathema to those who affirm that Christ sought the salvation of some, not all men."[97]

Conclusion

No statement from the patristics affirms a strictly limited atonement. Many of their statements clearly affirm a universal atonement. What one finds in the patristics is a limitation in the application of redemption, not in its accomplishment.

The Medieval Era

During the medieval period, the only exceptions to the position of unlimited atonement were Gottschalk (ninth century) and Florus of Lyons, a contemporary of Gottschalk. All the leading lights of this period, including the imminent Thomas Aquinas, affirmed an unlimited atonement.

Gottschalk (AD 808–867)

The first person to argue explicitly for limited atonement in church history was Gottschalk of Orbais.[98] Genke correctly summarized Gottschalk's theological views and concluded,

---

95 H. Bettenson, *Documents of the Christian Church*, 2nd ed. (London: Oxford University Press, 1963), 60. See also A. Maria de' Liguori, *The History of Heresies and Their Refutation: Or, the Triumph of the Church* (Dublin: James Duffy, 1857), 116–17. Hilary of Arles (c. 401–449), commenting on 1 John 2:2, said when John says that Christ died for the sins of the "whole world," what he means is that he died for the whole church. (*James, 1–2 Peter, 1–3 John, Jude*, G. Bray, ed., Ancient Christian Commentary on Scripture: XI [Downers Grove, IL: InterVarsity, 2000], 177). This quote doesn't really prove anything. This is a comment on one specific text and following a specific tradition of interpreting a specific passage originating with Augustine. As we saw above, Augustine affirmed an unlimited atonement. What needs to be proved is that Hilary taught that Christ only died for the elect, not that when commenting on a specific passage Hilary believed it only applied to the elect.

96 T. S. Holmes, *The Origin & Development of the Christian Church in Gaul during the First Six Centuries of the Christian Era* (London: Macmillan, 1911), 404–5.

97 S. Baring-Gould, *The Lives of the Saints*, 16 vols. (London: Longmans, Green & Co., 1898), 10:416.

98 G. Michael Thomas, *The Extent of the Atonement: A Dilemma for Reformed Theology from Calvin to the Consensus (1536–1675)* (Carlisle: Paternoster, 1997), 5. For further information on Gottschalk, consult P. Schaff, "Medieval Christianity from Gregory I to Gregory VII A.D. 590–1073, vol. 4," in *History of the Christian Church* (Peabody, MA: Hendrickson, 1996), 523–39; P. N. Archibald, "A Comparative Study of John Calvin and Theodore Beza on the Doctrine of the Extent of the Atonement" (PhD diss., Westminster Theological Seminary, 1998), 20–33; D. E. Nineham, "Gottschalk of Orbais: Reactionary or Precursor of the Reformation?," *Journal of Ecclesiastical History* 40 (1989): 1–18; J. Pelikan, "The Growth of Medieval Theology (600–1300), vol. 3," in *The Christian Tradition: A History of the Development of Doctrine* (Chicago: University of Chicago Press, 1978), 80–95; J. Rainbow, *The Will of God and the Cross* (Allison Park, PA: Pickwick, 1990), 25–32; J. V. Fesko, *Diversity within the Reformed Tradition: Supra- and Infralapsarianism in Calvin, Dort, and Westminster* (Greenville, SC: Reformed Academic Press, 2001), 25–35; V. Genke and F. X. Gumerlock, *Gottschalk & A Medieval Predestination Controversy: Texts Translated from the Latin*, in Mediaeval

among other things, that he taught God does not desire the salvation of all people and Christ died only for the elect.[99]

Gottschalk read Augustine and accepted his predestinarian stance but moved well beyond Augustine into extreme double-predestination. He also moved beyond Augustine when he stated that "Christ was not crucified and put to death for the redemption of the whole world, that is, not for the salvation and redemption of all mankind, but only for those who are saved."[100] As Schaff noted, Gottschalk "measured the extent of the purpose [of the atonement] by the extent of the effect. God is absolutely unchangeable, and his will must be fulfilled. What does not happen, cannot have been intended by him."[101]

Hincmar of Reims (AD 806–882) described Gottschalk's belief:

> God does not wish all men to be saved, but only those who are saved; and that what the Apostle says, "Who desires all men to be saved," is said of all those only who are saved; that Christ did not come that all might be saved,

---

Philosophical Texts in Translation (Milwaukee, WI: Marquette University Press, 2010), 7–63; and L. Gatiss, *For Us and for Our Salvation*, Latimer Studies 78 (London: Latimer Trust, 2012), 61–65.

James Ussher published a book in 1631 about the medieval monk Gottschalk. He agreed with Gottschalk on the subject of unconditional predestination but differed with him on the issue of limited atonement (J. Ussher, *Gotteschalci, et Praedestinatianae Controversiae abe o motae, Historia: Una cum duplice ejusdem Confessione, nunc primum in lucem editâ* [Dublin: Societatis Bibliopolarum, 1631]). See also this work in *The Whole Works of the Most Rev. James Ussher, D.D.*, 17 vols. (Dublin: Hodges and Smith, 1847–1864), 4:207–33. For Ussher's statements on unlimited atonement, see below. Owen Thomas, *The Atonement Controversy in Welsh Theological Literature and Debate, 1707–1841*, trans. J. Aaron (Edinburgh: Banner of Truth, 2002), 116–23, contains a helpful summary of Gottschalk that follows Ussher's treatment.

99 V. Genke and F. X. Gumerlock, *Gottschalk & A Medieval Predestination Controversy*, 58–61.

100 Quoted in J. Davenant, *An Exposition of the Epistle of St. Paul to the Colossians*, 2:334. The 2005 Banner of Truth reprint of Davenant's commentary omits the "Dissertation on the Death of Christ." Davenant contrasts Gottschalk's "novelty of doctrines" with scores of quotes from early church fathers, including Augustine and Prosper. See also Daniel, "Hyper-Calvinism and John Gill," 503. J. Rainbow, *The Will of God and the Cross: An Historical and Theological Study of John Calvin's Doctrine of Limited Redemption* (Allison Park, PA: Pickwick, 1990), 26, mistakenly suggested Gottschalk imbibed his concept of limited atonement from Augustine. Gottschalk interpreted statements in Augustine such as "Christ suffered for all" (*pro cunctis*) to refer to all of the elect and only the elect. While Augustine often spoke of Christ dying for those who were elect unto salvation, he also spoke of Christ dying for the "whole world," and he never limited the actual satisfaction for sins that Christ made exclusively to the elect, as demonstrated above.

101 P. Schaff, *Medieval Christianity*, 528. Schaff is correct as far as this goes. However, later, Schaff stated that Gottschalk "spoke of two redemptions, one common to the elect and the reprobate, another proper and special for the elect only" (531). Schaff follows this comment with the point that this is similar to later Calvinists who spoke of the atonement as efficient only for the elect but sufficient for all people (532). Schaff's statement is misleading for several reasons. First, the "common redemption" that Gottschalk teaches only concerns baptized reprobates, not pagan reprobates. Second, Gottschalk thought that the "redemption" that baptized reprobates have is only one of water baptism that cleanses from past sins, not a redemption in any way related to Christ's death. Third, there is no hint of the sufficiency/efficiency formula in Gottschalk, so comparing him to later Calvinists on that subject has no basis.

Moreover, unlike the vast majority of the Reformed, Gottschalk thought that God does not love the reprobate and in no way wills their salvation. In his thought, Christ's death does not relate to the reprobate, and God has no love or evangelistic saving will for them. One might think of him as a proto-hyper-Calvinist (to use the term anachronistically) on the subject of predestination, not a forerunner to what would later become Reformed orthodoxy.

> nor did he suffer for all, but only for those who are saved by the mystery of his Passion.[102]

In his letter to Egilo (Archbishop of Sens), Hincmar used the presence of Judas at the first Lord's Supper to refute Gottschalk's limited view of Christ's redemption. After quoting Luke 22:19, he stated:

> Judas was also present among those to whom he gave them, having the role of the reprobate, while the other disciples had the role of the elect. For he of course did not say "for all" but "for many" because all were not going to believe. For the shedding of the blood of Christ, of the just for the unjust (1 Pt. 3:18), was of so rich a price that if the universe of those held captive believed in their redeemer, the chains of the devil would have retained no one.[103]

Note Hincmar's sense of Christ's sufficiency when he spoke of "so rich a price." Recall that Augustine likewise said Judas was at the table when Christ spoke of his atoning death.

Fesko said the reason Hincmar opposed Gottschalk's doctrine "was because up until this point in church history, the common opinion was that Christ's atonement was universal, and what negated the efficacy of the atonement for a person's salvation was his refusal to accept the offer of forgiveness."[104]

Both Gottschalk and his extreme views were condemned by three French councils.[105] During the Gottschalk controversy, which was primarily over the issue of predestination, the two views on the extent of the atonement were developed with arguments that would later be used and further developed in the sixteenth and seventeenth centuries.[106]

Important to note here is the fact that the question of the extent of the atonement had not been argued previously, and Gottschalk's views are important "because it is the first extant articulation of a definite atonement in church history."[107] Limited atonement was considered by Gottschalk and the double-predestinarians who supported him to be something of a logical corollary of their doctrine of predestination and not something demonstrated exegetically from the text.[108]

---

102 Hincmar, as quoted by Remigius, "A Reply to Three Letters," in *Gottschalk & A Medieval Predestination Controversy*, 156.

103 Genke and Gumerlock, *Gottschalk & A Medieval Predestination Controversy*, 182. For the dispute on whether Judas was at the table, see G. Gillespie, *Aaron's Rod Blossoming* (London: Printed by E. G. for Richard Whitaker, 1646), 436–60; R. Drake, *A Boundary to the Holy Mount* (London: Abraham Miller, 1653), 7–11; and Daniel, "Hyper-Calvinism and John Gill," 517, 557–78, and 823.

104 Fesko, *Diversity within the Reformed Tradition*, 31.

105 Although he was also exonerated by three other councils: Paris (849), Sens (853), and Valence (855).

106 As noted by Pelikan, *Growth of Medieval Theology*, 90–92, and Archibald, "A Comparative Study," 28–29.

107 Fesko, *Diversity within the Reformed Tradition*, 32.

108 As can be gleaned from P. Schaff's discussion of the events surrounding Gottschalk (*History of the Christian*

Peter Lombard (c. AD 1096–c. 1164)

One of the key influential theologians during the latter part of the Middle Ages was Peter Lombard. He is the author of the now famous sufficiency/efficiency statement. It is vital to say a word about this popular formula first explicitly articulated by Lombard in his *Sentences*:[109] Jesus's death is sufficient for all but efficient only for the elect. Historically this statement indicated that Christ's death paid the price for the sins of the world but that the benefits of the atonement were only applied to the elect (those who believe).

According to Rouwendal, Beza's criticism of the Lombardian formula launched a new stage in the development of the doctrine of limited atonement. Up until his day, the Lombardian formula was accepted by Calvin and all the Reformers.[110] Other Reformers began to accept Beza's critical approach. Gulielmus Bucanus, who was professor at Lausanne from 1591 to 1603, "wrote that Christ's death 'could have been' (instead of 'was') a ransom for the sins of all people." Johannes Piscator (AD 1546–1625) went even further and called the classic formula of the distinction "contradictory."[111] There are many examples of this revision in the writings of high Calvinists at the time.

Nicholas Byfield (AD 1579–1622), for example, said that when Scripture says Christ died for all, one must understand this

> first, in respect of the sufficiency of his death, not in respect of the efficiency of it. Secondly, in respect of the common oblation of the benefits of his death externally in the Gospel unto all. Thirdly, as his death extends to all the Elect: *for all*, that is, for the Elect. Fourthly, *for all*, that is, for all that are saved, so that none that are justified and saved, are so, but by the virtue of his death. Fifthly, *for all*, that is for all indefinitely, for all sorts of men, not for every man of every sort. Lastly, he died *for all*, that is not for the Jews only, but for the Gentiles also.[112]

Church, 4:523–37). Though this is not overtly stated by Gumerlock, it is implied throughout his two-part article on Gottschalk (Francis X. Gumerlock, "Predestination in the Century before Gottschalk [Part 1]," *Evangelical Quarterly* 81.3 [July 2009]: 195–209; and idem, "Predestination in the Century before Gottschalk [Part 2]," *Evangelical Quarterly* 81.4 [October 2009]: 319–37).

109 The formulaic section has been translated as follows:

> He offered himself on the altar of the cross not to the devil, but to the triune God, and he did so for all with regard to the sufficiency of the price, but only for the elect with regard to its efficacy, because he brought about salvation only for the predestined.

P. Lombard, *The Sentences: Book 3; On the Incarnation of the Word*, trans. G. Silano, Mediaeval Sources in Translation 45 (Toronto: Pontifical Institute of Medieval Studies, 2008), 86. The *concept*, however, is *at least* as old as Ambrose (AD 338–397). See his *Exposition of the Holy Gospel according to Saint Luke*, trans. T. Tomkinson (Etna, CA: Center for Traditionalist Orthodox Studies, 1998), 201–2: "Although Christ suffered for all, yet He suffered for us particularly, because He suffered for the Church."

110 P. L. Rouwendal, "Calvin's Forgotten Classical Position on the Extent of the Atonement: About Sufficiency, Efficiency, and Anachronism," *Westminster Theological Journal* 70 (Fall 2008): 320.

111 Ibid.

112 N. Byfield, *An Exposition Vpon the Epistle to the Colossians* (London: E. Griffin for N. Butter, 1617), 99.

Johannes Wollebius (AD 1586–1629) likewise argued in the same manner as Byfield. He stated:

> If we take the plan of God and the intention of Christ into consideration, then it is false to say that Christ died for every person. For this reason others say that his death was sufficient for all, but not effective for all; that is, the merit of Christ, because of his worthiness, is sufficient for all, but it is not effective for all in its application, because Christ did not die with the intention that his death be applied to all.[113]

Leonardus Riissenius (c. AD 1636–1700) expressed the revised version of the formula:

> The satisfaction of Christ might be said to be sufficient for the sins of one and all, if so it had seemed good to God; for since it was of infinite value, it was quite sufficient for the redemption of one and all, if it had seemed good to God to extend it to the whole world. And here belongs a distinction used by the Fathers and retained by various theologians, that Christ died sufficiently for all, but effectually only for the elect; which phrase, understood of the worthiness of Christ's death, is very true, although it is less accurate if referred to the will and counsel of Christ. For the Son gave himself to death, not with the purpose and intention of acting personal substitute in the room of one and all, to give satisfaction for them and secure them salvation; but for the elect only, who were given him by the Father to be redeemed and whose head he was to be, he was willing to give himself up.[114]

William Lyford (AD 1598–1653) was elected to the Westminster Assembly (though he never served). Commenting on the fact that Scripture sometimes speaks of the death of Christ in universal terms and sometimes in limited terms, he informed his readers that they should distinguish between sufficiency and efficiency. Sufficiency denotes the "infinite value and price" of Christ's death, which is "abundantly sufficient to take away the sins of the whole world." With respect to this sufficiency, Lyford spoke of three aspects in which Christ's death should be considered as sufficient. First, with respect

---

113 J. Wollebius, "Compendium Theolgiae Christianae," in *Reformed Dogmatics: Seventeenth-Century Reformed Theology through the Writings of Wollebius, Voetius, and Turrretin*, ed. and trans. J. W. Beardslee (Grand Rapids, MI: Baker, 1965), 105–6. See also J. Wollebius, *The Abridgement of Christian Divinitie*, trans. A. Ross (London: T. Mabb, 1660), 149, and F. Makemie, *An Answer to George Keith's Libel* (Boston: Benjamin Harris, 1694), 48–50.

114 L. Riissenius, *Francisci Turretini Compendium Theologiae didactico-elencticae ex theologorum nostrorum Institutionibus auctum et illustratum* (Amstelodami: Georgium Gallet, 1695), 120 (cited in H. Heppe, *Reformed Dogmatics*, ed. E. Bizer [Grand Rapids, MI: Baker, 1978], 477–78).

to the "price or merit of it." There is sufficient value in Christ's death to atone for all sins that were or shall be committed. Second, the offer of the gospel is "general and universal" based on the sufficiency of the atonement. Third, "redemption is general or universal, in respect of the means, sincerely calling all men unto fellowship with Christ." By this Lyford means that "if there were a thousand worlds more to be saved, they needed no other gospel."[115]

The Leiden Synopsis on the sufficiency/efficiency formula, originally published in 1625 and very popular in Scotland and continental Europe in the seventeenth century, includes the following statement:

> For although with respect to the magnitude, dignity, and sufficiency of the price, considered in itself, it may be extended to all people, yet it is particularly a payment for those whom the Father has chosen and given to the Son, who by the gift of God will believe in God and his Son. Wherefore Scripture everywhere says that he spent himself "for his own," and "for us," "for the sheep," and "the Church." Matthew 20:28, 26:28; 1 John 3:16; Acts 20:28 etc.[116]

The focus is on the value of the sufficiency, not the actual sufficiency for the sins of all. Notice the careful wording "may be extended to all people." The sufficiency for all as understood by Lombard and the early Reformers is here revised to be purely hypothetical.

Herman Witsius (AD 1636–1708) spoke about the issue of sufficiency, and his language is clearly hypothetical as well. The sufferings of Christ "are, on account of the infinite dignity of the person, of that value, as *to have been sufficient* for redeeming not only all and every man in particular, but many myriads besides, *had it so pleased God and Christ, that he should have undertaken and satisfied for them.*"[117]

Hezekiah Holland (c. AD 1617–c. 1661) spoke of Christ paying a sufficient but not efficient price for the world, where he describes sufficiency to mean sufficient in value only but not sufficient in the sense that Christ's death actually satisfied for the sins of all the world.[118]

John Owen knew that he and others were revising Lombard's formula and preferred to put it in hypothetical terms: "The blood of Christ was sufficient *to have been made* a price for all."[119] This reinterpretation was designed to support Owen's argument for

115 W. Lyford, *The Plain Mans Senses Exercised* (London: Printed for Richard Royton at the Angel in Ivie-lane, 1655), 259–62.

116 J. Polyander, A. Walaeus, A. Thysius, and A. Rivet, *Synopsis Purioris Theologiae* (Leiden: Elzevier, 1642 [1625]), 356.

117 H. Witsius, *The Economy of the Covenants between God and Man*, 2 vols., trans. W. Crookshank (Edinburgh: Thomas Turnbull, 1803), 1:260 (emphasis mine).

118 H. Holland, *A Christian Looking-Glasse: Or a Glimps of Christ's Unchangably Everlasting Love* (London: T. R. & E. M., 1649), 13–15.

119 Owen, "The Death of Death in the Death of Christ," 10:296 (emphasis mine). W. Cunningham acknowledged this revision in his *Historical Theology*, 2 vols. (Edinburgh: Banner of Truth, 1994), 2:332.

limited atonement. Richard Baxter called Owen's revision of the Lombardian Formula a "new futile evasion" and he refuted Owen's position thoroughly.[120]

William Cunningham described how the formula was modified by later Calvinists:

> When the subject of the extent of the atonement came to be more fully and exactly discussed, orthodox Calvinists generally objected to adopt this scholastic position, on the ground that it seemed to imply an ascription to Christ of a *purpose* or *intention* of dying in some sense for all men. For this reason they usually declined to adopt it as it stood, or they proposed to alter it into this form,—Christ's death was sufficient for all, efficacious for the elect. By this change in the position, the question was made to turn, not on what Christ did, but on what His death was; and thus the appearance of ascribing to Him personally a purpose or intention of dying, in some sense, for all men, was removed.[121]

The revision of the Lombardian formula occurred historically at the end of the sixteenth century and into the early to mid-seventeenth century. Is it coincidence that the trend of restricting the atonement to the elect began with Beza in the late sixteenth century and corresponds with the revision of the Lombardian formula? Rouwendal noted the importance of acknowledging that the trend toward limited atonement "did not begin until 1588, twenty-four years after Calvin had died."[122]

Many modern Calvinists who assert limited atonement have a distaste for the Lombardian formula for at least two reasons: (1) it can be interpreted to support both limited or unlimited atonement, and (2) historically Lombard intended it to be a consensus statement to indicate the church's belief that Christ did indeed die for the sins of the world, which cuts at the heart of the limited atonement position as argued by Beza, Owen, and others.

Raymond Blacketer thinks the Continental Reformer Zanchi clearly affirmed definite atonement and that his statement "interprets and clarifies" the Lombardian formula.[123] This is a misreading of Zanchi (see below) as well as a failure to recognize the revision of the Lombardian formula that began with Beza. Beza developed the doctrine of definite atonement in detail in several publications. James Arminius,

120 R. Baxter, *Universal Redemption of Mankind by the Lord Jesus Christ* (London: Printed for John Salusbury at the Rising Sun in Cornhill, 1694), 343–45. Clifford said that Owen's

> apparent acceptance of it [the sufficiency-efficiency distinction] is really little more than lip-service; his deliberate redefinition of it means that the atonement is only sufficient for those for whom it is efficient. In other words, if the atonement is strictly limited, then the 'credit facilities' of the gospel are only available to the elect (A. C. Clifford, *Atonement and Justification: English Evangelical Theology, 1640–1790—An Evaluation* [Oxford: Clarendon Press, 1990], 112–13).

121 Cunningham, *Historical Theology*, 2:332.

122 P. L. Rouwendal, "Calvin's Forgotten Classical Position on the Extent of the Atonement," 320.

123 R. Blacketer, "Definite Atonement in Historical Perspective," in *The Glory of the Atonement*, ed. C. E. Hill and F. A. James III (Downers Grove, IL: InterVarsity, 2008), 317.

Beza's student, would later reject Beza's extreme predestinarianism along with limited atonement.

We will see that the debate over the nature of this sufficiency beginning in the early seventeenth century is *the key debate* in the extent question. One often hears statements by Calvinists that "the debate is *not* over the sufficiency of the atonement; all agree the atonement was sufficient to atone for the sins of the whole world." However, the debate is very much about the nature of the sufficiency of Christ's death.

The high Calvinist position on the atonement *entails* that Christ's death is only actually sufficient to save the elect. The non-elect by entailment are not saveable because Jesus did not die for their sins. The sins of the non-elect were not imputed to Jesus on the cross. When one speaks of Jesus's sufficiency in the strictly limited atonement position, one is affirming only an *intrinsic* sufficiency (or a *bare* sufficiency).[124] The idea is that if God had intended for all the world to be saved, then the death of Jesus *could have been* sufficient for all (as it has enough intrinsic merit), but that is not what God intended, according to high Calvinists.

The moderate Calvinist and non-Calvinist position interprets the term "sufficient" to mean Christ actually made satisfaction for the sins of all humanity. Thus, the death of Christ is extrinsically or universally sufficient in capacity to save all people, as it is adapted to the need of every person. This distinction is absolutely crucial to make.

Raymond Blacketer, speaking of Lombard's formula, stated: "Considered abstractly, the death of Christ has more than enough inherent value to cover the sins of every individual; but Lombard limits its efficacy to the elect. This distinction, while a significant move toward the concept of definite atonement and particular redemption, still leaves room for ambiguity."[125] Lombard's formula, rightly understood, is not a move toward definite atonement at all. Nor is there any room for ambiguity when the formula is considered in its original intent. The ambiguity surfaces as a result of the revision of the formula by those advocating limited atonement.

Lombard's formula is fraught with confusion today since it has been used by those on both sides of the post-Reformation extent debate to articulate and defend their position, often without the speaker specifying in what sense he is using the term. Whenever the formula is used, the question must always be asked: What is meant by the term "sufficient"? Is the term being used in a purely hypothetical way such that the sufficiency is limited to worth and value, or is the term understood to refer to an actual sufficiency defined as Christ paid the price for the sins of all people?

124 The "intrinsic" or "bare sufficiency" view is discussed and refuted in the writings of several Calvinists, including J. Davenant, *An Exposition of the Epistle of St. Paul to the Colossians*, 2:401–4; J. Ussher, "An Answer to Some Exceptions," in *The Whole Works of the Most Rev. James Ussher*, 17 vols. (Dublin: Hodges, Smith, and Co., 1864), 12:561–71; E. Polhill, "The Divine Will Considered in Its Eternal Decrees," in *The Works of Edward Polhill* (Morgan, PA: Soli Deo Gloria, 1998), 164; and N. Hardy, *The First General Epistle of St. John the Apostle, Unfolded and Applied* (Edinburgh: James Nichol, 1865), 140–41.

125 R. Blacketer, "Definite Atonement in Historical Perspective," 311.

Thomas Aquinas (c. AD 1225–1274)

Aquinas was undoubtedly the most significant theologian of the medieval period. Called "The Angelic Doctor" and "The Dumb Ox," his writings constituted for the Middle Ages what Augustine's writings did for the patristic era. All the Reformers built on Aquinas in one sense or the other.

David Hogg rightly observed:

> Evidence of the continuity of thought from Peter Lombard's days in the twelfth century through to the middle and late thirteenth century is best exemplified in the works of Thomas Aquinas. Reading through Aquinas's two most famous works, his *Summa Theologiae* and his *Summa Contra Gentiles*, it is evident that while he was clearly influenced by Aristotle, he was no less inspired and affected by Peter's magnum opus.[126]

Aquinas's view on the extent of the atonement is not disputed by most historians.[127] He frequently taught the original sense of the sufficient/efficient formula.[128] According to

---

126 D. S. Hogg, "'Sufficient for All, Efficient for Some,' Definite Atonement in the Medieval Church," in *From Heaven He Came and Sought Her: Definite Atonement in Historical, Biblical, Theological, and Pastoral Perspective*, ed. D. Gibson and J. Gibson (Wheaton, IL: Crossway, 2013), 89–90.

127 D. S. Hogg and R. Blacketer may be the only exceptions. Hogg attempted to argue that Aquinas's pattern of thought "follows a trajectory leading in the direction of the doctrine of definite atonement." See "'Sufficient for All, Efficient for Some,' Definite Atonement in the Medieval Church," 90, 89–95. He says that Aquinas "wrote about predestination, divine foreknowledge, free will, and the atoning death of Christ in a manner that is not only consistent with later Reformation expressions of definite atonement, but preparatory and foundational for this doctrine" (75). Hogg cited R. Blacketer's "Definite Atonement in Historical Perspective," in *The Glory of the Atonement: Biblical, Historical and Practical Perspectives*, 313. Blacketer seems a bit more tentative than Hogg, and maintained that Aquinas's views are "not so clear" (311). Blacketer nevertheless argued that the trajectory of Aquinas's predestinarian thought lends itself to definite atonement.

J. Rainbow dealt with Aquinas's view (*The Will of God and the Cross: An Historical and Theological Study of John Calvin's Doctrine of Limited Redemption* [Allison Park, PA: Pickwick, 1990], 34–38), and thought that Aquinas differed from what Rainbow thinks is Augustine's strict view and sided with Chrysostom instead (34–35). Rainbow maintained that Aquinas harnessed the sufficient-efficient formula "to universalize the saving will of God in the death of Christ" (36). For Thomas, "Christ died sufficiently meant for him that God really wills to save all men through the death of Christ" (ibid.). Rainbow thought that uncertainty about Thomas's position is "virtually eliminated" when we observe how he interpreted such passages as John 12:32 and 1 John 2:2 (37): "Thomas was, in short, a genuine predestinarian who was also a universal redemptionist, and as such he was the precursor of Moyse Amyraut" (38). Later on he stated that "Thomas Aquinas anticipated the thinking of Moyse Amyraut when he combined double predestination and universal redemption in one theological system" (47). Rainbow interpreted R. T. Kendall (*Calvin and English Calvinism to 1649*, rev. ed. [Carlisle, UK: Paternoster, 1997], 16n2) as asserting that Thomas was a limited Redemptionist because he used the "sufficient-efficient" schema (47–48). This is erroneous since, as Rainbow said, "universal redemptionists used the distinction one way, limited redemptionists another" (48). C. Daniel explicates Aquinas's universal view in *Hyper-Calvinism and John Gill* (PhD diss., University of Edinburgh, 1983), 506–10.

128 *The "Summa Theologica" of St. Thomas Aquinas: Part III, Second Number (QQ. XXVII.–LIX.)*, 22 vols., trans. Fathers of the English Dominican Province (New York: R. & T. Washbourne, 1912–36), 16:276 (III, ii, Q. 46, art. 5, ad. 3), 313–14 (III, ii, Q. 48, art. 2, ad. 2), 328 (III, ii, Q. 49, art. 3); *The Summa Contra Gentiles of Saint Thomas Aquinas*, 4 vols., trans. English Dominican Fathers (New York: Benzinger Brothers, 1929), 4:204 (IV. xliv.9), 216 (IV.lv.26 and IV.lv.27), 217 (IV.lv.29); *On Reasons for Our Faith against the Muslims, and a Reply to the Denial of Purgatory by Certain Greeks and Armenians: To the Cantor of Antioch*, trans. P. D. M. Fehlner (New Bedford, MA: Franciscans of the Immaculate, 2002), 52–53; "Exposito Super I Epistolam S. Pauli Apostoli Ad

W. G. T. Shedd, there was in the soteriology of Aquinas "the doctrine of superabundance in the merits of Christ." "The Passion of the Redeemer [in Aquinas's view] was not merely sufficient, it was also a superabundant satisfaction for the sins of the human race."[129]

Thomas dealt with a version of the double payment argument: "If Christ atoned sufficiently for the sins of mankind, it were surely unjust that man should still suffer punishments which Scripture declares to have been inflicted for sin."[130] Thomas answered this objection, and his reply is cited by several Hypothetical Universalists:

> Although Christ, by His death, atoned sufficiently for the sins of mankind, as the twenty-sixth objection argued, each one must seek the means of his own salvation. Christ's death is by way of being a universal cause of salvation, just as the sin of the first man was like a universal cause of damnation. Now a universal cause needs to be applied to each individual, that the latter may have its share in the effect of the universal cause. Accordingly, the effect of the sin of our first parent reaches each individual through carnal origin: and the effect of Christ's death reaches each individual through spiritual regeneration, whereby man is united to and incorporated with Christ. Therefore each one must seek to be regenerated by Christ, and to receive the other things in which the power of Christ's death is effective.[131]

Both Paraeus and Kimedoncius cite Aquinas on Christ's sufficient satisfaction and his teaching on the redemption of all in his comments on Revelation 5:

> The merit of Christ, as to its sufficiency, extends equally to all, but not as to its efficacy, which happens partly on account of free will, and partly on account of the election of God, through which the effects of the merits of Christ are

Timotheum," in *Omnes D. Pauli Apostoli Epistolas Commentaria*, 3 vols. (Leodii: H. Dessain, 1857–1858), 3:68; *Commentary on the Letters of Saint Paul to the Philippians, Colossians, Thessalonians, Timothy, Titus, and Philemon*, trans. F. R. Larcher, ed. J. Mortensen and E. Alarcon (Landor, WY: Aquinas Institute for the Study of Sacred Doctrine, 2012), 265–66; *Commentary on the Epistle to the Hebrews* (South Bend, IN: St. Augustine's Press, 2006), 62.

129 W. G. T. Shedd, *A History of Christian Doctrine*, 2 vols. (1864; repr. Eugene, OR: Wipf & Stock, 1999), 2:310. "Christ's passion was sufficient and superabundant satisfaction for the sins of the whole human race" (*The "Summa Theologica" of St. Thomas Aquinas*, 16:328 [III, ii, Q. 49, art. 3]).

130 *The Summa Contra Gentiles of Saint Thomas Aquinas*, 199 (IV.liii.26).

131 *The Summa Contra Gentiles of Saint Thomas Aquinas*, 4:217 (IV.c.55.29). The following Hypothetical Universalists cite this passage in support of their view: J. Kimedoncius, *Of the Redemption of Mankind* (London: Imprinted for Felix Kingston for Humfrey Lownes, 1598), 235; J. Davenant, "Dissertation on the Death of Christ," in *An Exposition of the Epistle of St. Paul to the Colossians*, 2 vols. (London: Hamilton, Adams, and Co., 1832), 2:342; N. Homes, "Christ's Offering Himself to All Sinners, and Answering All Their Objection," in *The Works of Dr. Nathanael Homes* (London: Printed [by J. Legate] for the Author, 1651), 16. Theophilus Gale (AD 1628–1678) associated Aquinas with Davenant's "ordained sufficiency" view. See *The Court of the Gentiles. Part IV. Of Reformed Philosophie. Wherein Plato's Moral and Metaphysic or Prime Philosophie Is Reduced to an Useful Forme and Method* (London: Printed by J. Macock for Thomas Cockeril at the Sign of the Atlas in Cornhil, near the Royal Exchange, 1677), 357 (II.v.4).

> mercifully bestowed upon some, and withheld from others according to the just judgment of God.[132]

> Of the passion of the Lord we speak after two sorts: either according to the sufficiency, and so his passion redeemed all. For it is sufficient to redeem and save all, although there had been many worlds, as Anselm saith, lib. 2. Cur Deus homo. cap. 14. Or according to efficiency, and so all are not redeemed by his passion, because all cleave not unto the redeemer, and therefore all have not the efficacy of redemption.[133]

It is clear that Aquinas interpreted John 1:29; 1 Tim 2:4–6; and 1 John 2:2 in universal ways.[134]

---

132 Cited in D. Paraeus's contribution (Question 40) to *The Commentary of Dr. Zacharias Ursinus on the Heidelberg Catechism* (1852; repr. Phillipsburg, NJ: P&R, 1985), 224.

133 Cited in J. Kimedoncius, "Of the Redemption of Mankind," 33, 235; D. Paraeus, *Certain Learned and Excellent Discourses: Treating and Discussing Divers Hard and Difficult Points of Christian Religion: Collected, and Published in Latine, by D. David Parreus, out of the Writings of That Late Famous and Worthie Light of God's Church, D. Zachary Ursine. Faithfully Translated* (London: Imprinted by H. Lownes, 1613), 140. Paraeus also cited Ambrose, Cyril, Augustine, Prosper, and Lombard asserting the same (ibid., 135–52).

134 *The Summa Contra Gentiles of Saint Thomas Aquinas*, 4:204 (IV.xliv.9); "Exposito Super I Epistolam S. Pauli Apostoli Ad Timotheum," 3:68; *Commentary on the Letters of Saint Paul to the Philippians, Colossians, Thessalonians, Timothy, Titus, and Philemon*, trans. F. R. Larcher, ed. J. Mortensen and E. Alarcon (Lander, WY: Aquinas Institute for the Study of Sacred Doctrine, 2012), 261–66; *The "Summa Theologica" of St. Thomas Aquinas*, 314 (III, ii, Q. 48, art. 2).

2

The Reformation Era and the Extent of the Atonement

Though there were numerous precursors leading up to the Reformation, most agree it began more or less officially in the first quarter of the sixteenth century. I will address the key theologians and their views on extent chronologically according to the year of their birth.

Early Continental Reformers

Johannes Oecolampadius (AD 1482–1531)

Oecolampadius was a German Reformer, preacher at Basel, and editorial assistant and Hebrew consultant on Erasmus's first edition of the Greek New Testament. His statements make clear he held to unlimited atonement.

> All mankind was damned utterly for their great and many offences, but Christ hath borne upon his Back all our sins satisfying his father for us, and delivering us from everlasting death, so that now we should live to our master Christ.

> Wherefore did Christ dye to deliver us from everlasting death. The exceeding great charity of God did not spare his only begotten son, but for us all did bestow him unto the most cruel death, that who so ever doth believe in him shall not perish, but have everlasting life.
>
> Which at the time appointed of the Father was made man with out any infection of sin, and lived with us in earth, And at last suffered for the sins of all the world.
>
> And your Father in heaven shall forgive your offences. We have remission of sins, where? In the cross, when as Christ suffered for all our sins, that is, the sins of all the world.[1]

Martin Luther (AD 1483–1546)

The Augustinian monk Martin Luther is the undisputed father of the Reformation. The nailing of the Ninety-Five Theses to the chapel door at Wittenberg in 1517 is usually the date given for the launch of the Reformation, though many precursors prepared the way. It is clear that Martin Luther held to unlimited atonement, and all Lutherans subsequently have followed suit.[2]

For example, Luther stated, "Christ has taken away not only the sins of some men but your sins and those of the whole world. The offering was for the sins of the whole world, even though the whole world does not believe."[3] In another place Luther argued poignantly concerning John 1:29:

> You may say: "Who knows whether Christ also bore my sin? I have no doubt that He bore the sin of St. Peter, St. Paul, and other saints; these were pious people." . . . Don't you hear what St. John says in our text: "This is the Lamb of God, who takes away the sin of the world"? And you cannot deny that you are also a part of this world, for you were born of man and woman. You are not a cow or a pig. It follows that your sins must be included, as well as the sins of St. Peter or St. Paul. . . . Don't you hear? There is nothing missing from the Lamb.

---

1 J. Oecolampadius, *A Sarmon, of Ihon Oecolampadius, to Yong Men, and Maydens*, trans. J. Fox (London: Humfrey Powell, 1548), fols. B6r–B7v, B8v, C1v, C5v. In his exposition of Isa 36–37, Oecolampadius also affirmed a universal atonement: "Christ is our 'only mediator, Advocate, and High Priest in the presence of God.' He prayed for transgressors on the cross and continues to do in Heaven. In addition, He offered sacrifice, since voluntarily: He with His innocent blood took away the *sin of the world*" (D. M. Poythress, "Johannes Oecolampadius's Exposition of Isaiah, Chapters 36–37," 2 vols. [PhD diss., Westminster Theological Seminary, 1992], 2:566–67).

2 D. Scaer, "The Nature and Extent of the Atonement in Lutheran Theology," *Journal of the Evangelical Theological Society* 10.4, no. 4 (Winter 1967): 179–87.

3 M. Luther, "Lectures on Galatians (1535): Chapters 1–4," in *Luther's Works*, 55 vols., ed. J. Pelikan, trans. M. H. Bertram (St. Louis, MO: Concordia, 1963), 26:38.

> He bears all the sins of the world from its inception; this implies that He also bears yours, and offers you grace.[4]

In his commentary on Gal 3:13, Luther acknowledged that the sins of the entire world were imputed to Christ on the cross.[5]

The Augsburg Confession (1530), drawn up primarily by Luther's coworker Melanchthon, states in Section 3 that Christ "was crucified, dead, and buried, that he might reconcile the Father unto us, and might be a sacrifice, not only for original guilt, but also for all actual sins of men."[6]

Later in 1551 Melanchthon drew up the Saxon Confession, and it likewise affirms unlimited atonement: "In this sacrifice are to be seen God's justice and wrath against sin, his infinite mercy towards us, and his love, in the Son, toward *the human race*."[7]

A smattering of statements by Luther throughout his works indicates his belief in unlimited atonement.[8]

It is surprising to see a few argue, contrary to all Luther scholars, that Luther most likely held to particular redemption since he was an Augustinian and affirmed double predestination. Shultz cited the fact that Luther took a limited reading of 1 Tim 2:4 where Luther said: "For in an absolute sense Christ did not die for all, because he says: 'This is my blood which is poured out for you' and 'for many'—he does not say: for

---

4 M. Luther, "Sermons on the Gospel of St. John Chapters 1–4," in *Luther's Works*, 22:169. R. Blacketer ("Definite Atonement in Historical Perspective," 313), contrary virtually to all Lutheran historians and theologians, argued that Luther himself held to limited atonement. He cited Luther's comments on one passage, 1 Tim 2:4, as supporting his contention. Blacketer fails to realize that many even in the Reformed tradition who clearly affirm universal atonement take a limited reading of 1 Tim 2:4. T. George (*Theology of the Reformers* [Nashville: Broadman, 1988], 77) and L. Gatiss (*For Us and for Our Salvation* [London: Latimer, 2012], 67) made the same mistake concerning Luther. It is also false to conclude that if one takes an unlimited reading of 1 Tim 2:4, then one affirms unlimited atonement. Both C. Spurgeon ("Salvation by Knowing the Truth," in *Metropolitan Tabernacle Pulpit*, 57 vols. [London: Passmore & Alabaster, 1881], 26:49–50) and J. Piper ("Are There Two Wills in God?," in *Still Sovereign: Contemporary Perspectives on Election, Foreknowledge, and Grace*, ed. T R. Schreiner & B. Ware [Grand Rapids, MI: Baker, 2000], 107–31) take an unlimited reading of 1 Tim 2:4 and yet both affirmed limited atonement.

5 Luther, *Lectures on Galatians*, 26:281.

6 P. Schaff, *The Creeds of Christendom*, 3 vols., 6th ed. (Grand Rapids, MI: Baker, 1993), 3:9.

7 Cited in Young, "The Atonement of Christ," in *Biblical Notes and Queries*, 277. See Schaff, *The Creeds of Christendom*, 1:340–43.

8 M. Luther, *D. Martin Luthers Werke: Kritische Gesamtausgabe, Schriften* [Weimarer Ausgabe], ed. J. K. F. Knaake, G. Kawerau et al., 72 vols. (Weimar: Hermann Böhlaus Nachfolger, 1883–2009), 10.I.2:207; 20:638; 26:277, 280–81, 285, 350; 46:678. See especially his entire sermon on John 1:29 in M. Luther, "Sermons on the Gospel of St. John: Chapters 1–4," in *Luther's Works*, 22:161–70. Luther said,

> He [Christ] helps not against *one* sin only but against *all* my sin; and not against *my* sin only, but against *the whole world's* sin. He comes to take away not sickness only, but death; and not *my* death only, but *the whole world's* death (M. Luther, "Sermon for the First Sunday in Advent, 1533," in *Day by Day We Magnify Thee: Daily Readings for the Entire Year, Selected from the Writings of Martin Luther*, ed. M. D. Johnson (Minneapolis, MN: Augsburg Books, 2008), 10; *D. Martin Luther's Werke* [WA], 37:201); emphasis in original.

See also D. Ponter, "Martin Luther (1483–1546) on the Death of Christ: Unlimited Redemption, Sin-Bearing and Expiation," *Calvin and Calvinism*, January 28, 2008, http://calvinandcalvinism.com/?p=193.

all—'for the forgiveness of sins' (Mark 14:24; Matt 26:28)."[9] Shultz succumbed to faulty logic on this point seeing that many "Augustinians" in the early Reformed tradition affirmed both predestination, even double-predestination, along with unlimited atonement (as, for example, William Twisse). Shultz overlooked the two words "absolute sense" in Luther's statement. Luther meant "absolute" in contrast to "conditional." Luther made clear what he meant: "He does not say for all—'for the forgiveness of sins.'" In other words, if Christ had died for all in an absolute sense, where the sins of all are forgiven, then the result would be universalism.

Early Lutheran Confessions

The Formula of Concord (1577) affirms universal atonement.[10] The Saxon Visitation Articles of 1592 mention "the false and erroneous doctrine of the Calvinists" that "Christ did not die for all men, but only for the elect."[11]

Ulrich Zwingli (AD 1484–1531)

Ulrich Zwingli led the Reformation in Switzerland. Several excerpts from his writings illustrate his belief in an unlimited atonement. For example,

> If then Christ by his death has reconciled all people who are on earth when he poured out his blood on the cross and if we are on earth, then our sins, too, and those of everyone who has ever lived, have been recompensed by the one death and offering.[12]

---

9 Luther, "Lectures on Romans," in *Luther's Works*, 25:375–76; *D. Martin Luther's Werke* (WA), 56:385; G. Shultz, "A Biblical and Theological Defense of a Multi-Intentioned View of the Extent of the Atonement" (PhD diss., Southern Baptist Theological Seminary, 2008), 36–37. Shultz uncritically relies on Blacketer's problematic historiography in some places, such as here. Other than this early pre-Reformation statement (1515–16), there is no other evidence in Luther to support the claim that he held to limited atonement. Some Reformed people use the Romans commentary statement alone (probably because it is the only quote they can find) at the expense of Luther's entire written corpus and thus misrepresent his position. While it is possible that this statement from Luther shows that he held to limited atonement in his pre-Reformation days, as some think, it is likely that he did not even hold it then. First, the comment does not preclude the possibility that Luther held that Christ died *conditionally* for all. We know that this language and theology of Christ dying for all in a conditional sense was being used by Zanchi down to Twisse. Second, it is also not conclusive proof that a given theologian held to limited atonement if he interpreted "the many" as the elect. We know that Zwingli, Musculus, and Oecolampadius understood "the many" as the elect, and yet also affirmed an unlimited redemption and expiation *in principle*. If a Reformational theologian interpreted "the many" in a limited sense, it is not enough to signify an *in principle* affirmation of limited atonement. Similarly, if a Reformed theologian interpreted 1 Tim 2:4 in a limited way, it does not follow that the theologian *in principle* denied that God wishes all men to repent and be saved in his revealed will as taught elsewhere. We also know that Luther later (in 1544) reversed his position on "the many." See *D. Martin Luther's Werke* (WA), 40.3:738–39.

10 G. Bente, ed., *Concordia Triglotta* (St. Louis, MO: Concordia, 1921), 1071–72.

11 "The Saxon Visitation Articles," in *The Creeds of Christendom*, 3:189.

12 U. Zwingli, *Exposition and Basis of the Conclusions or Articles Published by Huldrych Zwingli*, January 29, 1523, 2 vols. (Eugene, OR: Pickwick, 1984), 1:97.

Jacob Kimedoncius said of Zwingli:

> Zwinglius only, the ornament of thy Helvetia, and the brightness of all kind of learning, *Annot. in Evang. & epist. Pauli, per Leonem Juda editis.* There be many such kinds of speakings used afterward in like manner of his successors: "That the son of God took flesh, that he might be made a sacrifice for the sins of the whole world: that his flesh was given for the life and redemption of the whole world: and that he died for all, that he might quicken all by himself, and by his death give life to the universal world: that Christ came to save all, and to give eternal life to all, &c."[13]

Here Kimedoncius asserted Zwingli's affirmation of universal atonement in the use of such phrases as "for the sins of the whole world," "for the life and redemption of the whole world," and "that he died for all." It is also significant that the statement "that Christ came to save all, and to give eternal life to all" speaks of "intent" or "purpose" with respect to the atonement. This would seem to differ with later Reformed orthodoxy, which asserted that the intent of the atonement was to save only the elect, unless Zwingli is using the terms in the sense of God's revealed will.

In commenting on Hebrews 9 and 10, Zwingli declared:

> He obtained eternal salvation for all people for they were all created as well as redeemed through him. And since he is eternal God he is sufficient and worthy enough to take upon himself the sin of all people for eternity and to lead us into eternal salvation, according to Hebrews 9 and 10.[14]

Zwingli asserted that Christ "gave himself up as an expiatory offering for all."[15] Speaking about Heb 9:9, he spoke of Christ, who "made atonement for the sins not only of all who had been, but of all who were yet to come."[16] Concerning John 1:29–31, Zwingli stated that Christ is the lamb that "atones for the universal disease of sin."[17] In another place, Zwingli spoke of Christ making "satisfaction for the sins of all."[18] With respect to John 6:53, Zwingli said:

---

13 J. Kimedoncius, *Of the Redemption of Mankind* (London: Felix Kingston, 1598), 143.

14 H. Zwingli, "A Short Christian Instruction," in *Reformed Confessions of the Sixteenth and Seventeenth Centuries in English Translation*, 4 vols., ed. J. T. Dennison (Grand Rapids, MI: Reformation Heritage, 2010), 1:18. The same language is used again on pages 35–36. For the English translation of Zwingli, see E. J. Furcha and H. W. Pipkin, *Huldrych Zwingli Writings*, vol. 2 of *In Search of True Religion: Reformation, Pastoral and Eucharistic Writings* (Eugene, OR: Pickwick, 1984), 48–75.

15 U. Zwingli, "Early Writings," *Defence Called Archeteles* (Durham, NC: Labyrinth, 1987), 258.

16 U. Zwingli, *Commentary on True and False Religion* (Durham, NC: Labyrinth, 1981), 112.

17 Ibid., 122.

18 Ibid., 123.

> Except ye firmly and heartily believe that Christ was slain for you, to redeem you, and that His blood was shed for you, to wash you thus redeemed (for that is the way we are in the habit of showing bounty and kindness to captives—first freeing them by paying a ransom, then when freed washing away the filth with which they are covered), "ye have no life in you." Since, therefore, Christ alone was sacrificed for the human race, He is the only One through whom we can come to the Father.[19]

Zwingli spoke of Christ's death as a "sufficient ransom for the sins of everyone for all eternity."[20]

Martin Bucer (AD 1491–1551)

Martin Bucer was a Dominican before renouncing his orders and joining the Reformers. He was the leader of the Reformation at Strasbourg. In 1549, Bucer was exiled to England, where he met and worked with Cranmer. He taught at Cambridge and died there in 1551.[21]

Some, like Jonathan Rainbow and W. P. Stevens, have argued that Bucer held to limited atonement.[22] G. Michael Thomas noted that in Bucer's opposition to the Anabaptist Melchior Hoffman, he restricted the atonement to the elect in a statement that he drew up as a basis for Hoffman's examination and expulsion.[23] Shultz relied on Rainbow and claims Bucer for the limitarian camp.[24]

Peterson referenced Rainbow's 1986 dissertation where he argued that Augustine, Gottschalk, and Bucer (Calvin's contemporary) all argued for limited atonement. According to Peterson, Rainbow showed that "Calvin stands in a particularist tradition stretching from Augustine to Bucer."[25] But as we have seen, Augustine did not affirm limited atonement and Gottschalk was judged to be out of the mainstream on the subject. There was no "particularist tradition" on the atonement until Beza.

Jacob Kimedoncius cited Bucer as affirming his own view as well as Zanchi's.[26] Bucer spoke of Christ bearing the sins of the world and being the redeemer of the world.[27] It would seem that Bucer, like Augustine, held to an unlimited expiation of

---

19 Ibid., 128. From this work, see also pp. 129–30; 155–56; 221–22; 234–36. From idem, *On the Providence of God* (Durham, NC: Labyrinth, 1983), 190, 199.

20 Zwingli, *Exposition and Basis*, 103–4.

21 For a concise and helpful summary of Bucer, consult D. F. Wright, "Bucer, Martin (1491–1551)," in *Dictionary of Major Biblical Interpreters*, ed. D. Kim (Downers Grove, IL: InterVarsity, 2007), 247–54.

22 See Rainbow, *The Will of God and the Cross*, 48–63; W. P. Stephens, *The Holy Spirit in the Theology of Martin Bucer* (Cambridge: Cambridge University Press, 1970), 23, 106.

23 G. M. Thomas, *Extent of the Atonement*, 8. Thomas cited Zanchi's *Opera*, 7.1, 342–45 in a footnote.

24 G. Shultz, "A Biblical and Theological Defense of a Multi-Intentioned View of the Extent of the Atonement," 37. See Bucer, *Common Places*, ed. and trans. D. F. Wright (Nashville: Abingdon, 1972), 98–100.

25 R. Peterson, *Calvin and the Atonement* (Fearn, Scotland: Mentor, 1999), 119.

26 J. Kimedoncius, "On the Redemption of Mankind," 239.

27 See D. F. Wright, ed., *Commonplaces of Martin Bucer*, 304. J. C. Ryle included Bucer as taking the same view of

sin with a limited application to the elect. Rainbow and others may be confusing this distinction in Bucer in their treatment of him, just as Rainbow misconstrued Calvin's view on the extent of the atonement, as noted below.

Richard Baxter cited Musculus, Bullinger, Calvin, Amyraut, J. Bergius, C. Bergius, Crocius, Calixtus, Camero, Testard, Daillé, Blondel, Davenant, Preston, Whately, Fenner,[28] Twisse, Paraeus, Zanchi, Ussher, and R. Abbot as supporting universal redemption in his *Catholick Theology*.[29] In the middle of this exchange, Baxter portrayed his Arminian critic as saying, "You may spare your labour of citing *Bullinger* and *Musculus*, or *Melanchthon*, or *Bucer*, or such moderate men: But what are they to the rigid *Calvinists*?"[30] Baxter thought Bucer was a "moderate man." Notice also Baxter's early usage of "moderate" to describe these men with respect to their view of the extent of the atonement.

John Goodwin, in the mid-seventeenth century, stated that Bucer "was as full and thorough for general redemption as any man":

> "Whereas," saith he, "the world was lost or undone by one sin of Adam, the grace of Christ did not only abolish this sin, . . . and that death which it brought" upon the world, "but likewise took away an infinite number of other sins which we the rest of men have added to that first sin." Afterwards, "If we consider that every particular man by his transgressions increaseth the misery of mankind, and that whosoever sinneth doth no less hurt his posterity than Adam did all men, it is a plain case, that the grace of Christ hath removed more evils from men than the sin of Adam brought upon them: for though there be no sin committed in all the world, which hath not its original from that first sin of Adam, yet all particular men who sin, as they sin voluntarily and freely, so do they make an addition to their own proper guilt and misery: all which evils since the alone benefit of Christ hath taken away, it must needs be that it hath taken away the sins of many, and not of one only."[31]

Notice how Bucer spoke of the sin of "all particular men," which the "benefit of Christ hath taken away." Rainbow seems perplexed that Bucer would speak such of "all" here. He completely misunderstands Bucer's assertion that Christ died for the sins of all men in the sense of all particular men, not just "some of all kinds of men." Rainbow concluded about Bucer on Rom 5:17: "So in this case *many* means *all*, but

"love" and "world" as Calvin on John 3:16. See J. C. Ryle, *Expository Thoughts on the Gospels: John 1–6*, 4 vols. (Grand Rapids, MI: Baker, 1979), 3:158. Ryle also included Musculus and Bullinger.

28 See W. Fenner, "Hidden Manna: Or the Mystery of Saving Grace," in *The Works of W. Fenner. B. of Divinity* (Printed by E. Tyler for I. Stafford at the George neer Fleet-Bridge, 1658), 387–90.

29 R. Baxter, *Catholick Theologie*, 2:50–53. W. H. Goold, in his prefatory note to Owen's *Death of Death*, said that Amyraut had the support of Daillé and David Blondel (AD 1591–1655). See J. Owen, *Works*, 10:140.

30 Baxter, *Catholick Theologie*, 2:51.

31 J. Goodwin, *Redemption Redeemed* (1840), 712–13 (from Bucer on Rom 5:16–17).

all does not mean *every*." This is nonsensical. Rainbow is superimposing his own views on Bucer at this point.

Bucer spoke of an "infinite number of other sins" that the human race has added to Adam's sin. According to Bucer, the grace of Christ "took away" this infinite number of sins. This would seem to be a strong statement of unlimited extent.

The bulk of Rainbow's argument that Bucer was a limitarian is based on Bucer's debates with some of the Anabaptists. All the Anabaptists rejected limited atonement, as Bucer correctly noted. Interestingly, Rainbow cannot muster a single quotation from the eight volumes of Bucer's writings that affirms limited atonement. Most of his citations concerning the debates Bucer had with the Anabaptists come from editors Krebs's and Rott's *Quellen zur Geschichte der Täufer*.[32] The issue with specific reference to the atonement between the Anabaptists and Bucer seems to be the same issue that divided the Arminians from the Calvinists—namely, the former argued Christ died for all people, *equally* intending to save all, while the later argued either (1) Christ died for the sins of the elect only, intending their salvation only, or (2) Christ died for the sins of all people, but especially intending the salvation of the elect. Rainbow completely missed this distinction.[33]

Rainbow made another historiographical mistake by assuming Bucer's limited reading of some of the universal texts, such as 1 Tim 2:4, indicated he affirmed limited atonement.[34] But we have already seen how Augustine took a limited reading of some of these texts and yet still affirmed a universal atonement. Calvin will do the same, as we will note below. Rainbow's case for Bucer's limited view of the atonement's extent is circumstantial at best.

Bucer's comment on Rom 5:18 would seem to indicate a belief in unlimited atonement: "As by the fall of one man sin prevailed *in all*, as to render *all* obnoxious to condemnation, so also the righteousness of one man established in *all men* that justification of life may be obtained by *all*."[35]

Curt Daniel asserted Bucer held to an unlimited atonement, and he references both John Goodwin (AD 1594–1670) and Jean Daillé (AD 1594–1670) as also believing Bucer was moderate on the atonement.[36]

32 M. Krebs and H. Georg Rott, "Quellen zur Geschichte der Täufer: Elsaß I, Straßburg 1522–1532, vol. 7," in *Quellen und Forschungen zur Reformationsgeschichte* (Gütersloh: Mohn, 1959); Krebs & H. Georg Rott, "Quellen zur Geschichte der Täufer: Elsaß II, Straßburg 1533–1535, vol. 8.2," in *Quellen und Forschungen zur Reformationsgeschichte* (Gütersloh: Mohn, 1960).

33 J. Rainbow, *The Will of God and the Cross*, 51–60.

34 Ibid., 136–37.

35 Cited by Young, "The Atonement of Christ," in *Biblical Notes and Queries*, 277.

36 Daniel, "Hyper-Calvinism and John Gill," 517. For Daillé's citations of Bucer, see Joannis Dallæi, *Apologia Pro duabus Ecclesiarum in Gallia Protestantium Synodis Nationalibus*, 2 vols. (Amstelaedami: Ravesteynius, 1655), 2:998–1008. He cited Bucer's comments on Matt 23:37, 39; Romans 11; Rom 1:18, 19, 20, 21; 2:4; 1:14; and John 1:4, 5; 3:19, 20, in that order.

Menno Simons (AD 1496–1561)

Simons was an early Reformer in the Netherlands, Anabaptist leader, and founder of the Mennonites, the name later adopted by the Swiss Anabaptists who immigrated to America. His works demonstrate his commitment to unlimited atonement.

> All those, therefore, that seek other remedies for their sins, however great and holy they may appear than the remedy provided by God alone, deny the Lord's death, which He suffered for us, and His innocent blood which He shed for us. (33a; I:52a).
>
> For how could God show and express His love to us more perfectly than that He sent His eternal wisdom and truth, His pure, powerful Word, His blessed Son by whom He created all things, who was like unto Him, and His image, and made Him lower than the angels, a poor, despised, suffering, mortal man and servant who alone had to bear the labor, transgression, curse and death of the whole world. Yea, He so humbled Himself that He became the most despised of men. (I Pet. 2:24; Isa. 53:6).[37]

Wolfgang Musculus (AD 1497–1563)

Musculus was one of the leading early Reformers. He studied under Bucer and later became a professor of theology in Bern from 1549 until his death. He authored several commentaries and a systematic theology.[38] The following quotations illustrate his position on the universal extent of the atonement:

> We know that all be not partakers of this redemption, but yet the loss of them which be not saved, doth hinder nothing at all, why it should not be called an universal redemption, which is appointed not for one nation, but for all the whole world . . . it is not for lack of the grace of God, that the reprobate and desperately wicked men do not receive it: nor is it not right that it should loose his title and glory of universal redemption, because of the children of perdition, seeing that it is ready for all men, and all be called unto it. So he that redeemed the world, what soever do become of the reprobate, is most justly called the Saviour of the world.[39]

> And the only begotten of God himself says: "So God loved the world," (says he), "that he gave his only begotten Son, that everyone which believes in him,

37 J. Horsch, *Menno Simons: His Life, Labors, and Teaching* (Scottsdale, PA: Mennonite, 1916), 239.

38 See, for example, C. S. Farmer, *The Gospel of John in the Sixteenth Century: The Johannine Exegesis of Wolfgang Musculus*, Oxford Studies in Historical Theology (New York: Oxford, 1997).

39 W. Musculus, *Common Places of Christian Religion*, trans. I. Man of Merton (London: Henry Bynneman, 1578), 304–5.

> should not perish, but have life everlasting." So that by the world he means all mankind.[40]

> Redemption is prepared for *all*, and *all* are called to it.[41]

> "But Christ," saith he, "died not only for his friends, but for his enemies also; not for some men only, but for all, without exception. This is the immeasurable or vast extent of the love of God."[42]

Peter Martyr Vermigli (AD 1499–1562)

Vermigli was an early Italian Reformer who fled to Zurich. Upon the invitation of Thomas Cranmer, he came to England to assist with the English Reformation, teaching at Oxford University. Upon the accession of Queen Mary I, he fled England and was teaching theology in Zurich when he died.[43] Vermigli likewise held to universal atonement.

> Even Christ himself, when he had been raised from the dead, carried back with him the scars from his wounds and said to doubting Thomas, "Put your fingers here . . . in my side and in the nail marks, and do not be faithless, but believing" (John 20:27). The wounds had already performed their function, for by them the human race was redeemed, but he still had them after he was raised from the dead, that his body might be displayed as the same one which had suffered earlier.[44]

> The death of the cross, a new kind of sacrifice, is therefore a new altar. He fastened to the cross the handwriting of the decree which was against us and triumphed over his foes. This is the triumphal chariot of Christ. The cross was the balance on which the blood of Christ weighed. The price was paid for the whole world, and if it had not been more precious than the whole world, it would not have redeemed the world.[45]

---

40 Ibid., 963.

41 Young, "The Atonement of Christ," 278.

42 John Goodwin, *Redemption Redeemed* (1840), 711.

43 For Vermigli's life and theology, consult F. A. James III, *Peter Martyr Vermigli and Predestination: The Augustinian Inheritance of an Italian Reformer* (New York: Oxford University Press, 1998); and J. P. Donnelly, *Calvinism and Scholasticism in Vermigli's Doctrine of Man and Grace* (Leiden: Brill, 1976).

44 P. Vermigli, "Resurrection: Commentary on 2 Kings 4," in *Philosophical Works*, trans. J. P. McLelland, Sixteenth Century Essays and Studies 4 (Kirksville, MO: Thomas Jefferson University Press, 1994), 113.

45 P. Vermigli, "On the Death of Christ from Saint Paul's Letter to the Philippians," in *Life, Letters and Sermons*, trans. J. P. Donnelly, Sixteenth Century Essays and Studies 5 (Kirksville, MO: Thomas Jefferson University Press, 1999), 243. For more evidence of Vermigli's affirmation of universal atonement, see D. Ponter, "Peter Martyr Vermigli (1499–1562), Unlimited Redemption and Expiation, Incarnation and Related Issues," *Calvin and Calvinism*, September 2, 2007, http://calvinandcalvinism.com/?p=77.

He affirmed the classical sense of sufficiency, such that Christ actually "redeemed all men sufficiently":

> They [the anti-predestinarians] also grant that "Christ died for us all" and infer from this that his benefits are common to everyone. We gladly grant this, too, if we are considering only the worthiness of the death of Christ, for it might be sufficient for all the world's sinners. Yet even if in itself it is enough, yet it did not have, nor has, nor will have effect in all men. The Scholastics also acknowledge the same thing when they affirm that Christ redeemed all men sufficiently but not effectually.[46]

He also affirmed God's universal saving will: "So that if we respect this will of God, we easilie grant that he will have all men to be saved."[47]

Heinrich Bullinger (AD 1504–1575)

Heinrich Bullinger, the Swiss Reformer and successor to Zwingli, played a major role in the Reformation. Assisted by others, he drew up the First Helvetic Confession in 1536. The confession contained twenty-seven articles and was originally published in Latin. It was formally the first Reformed confession of national authority. Section 11 states: "Christ gave (his whole nature) up unto death for the expiation of *all sin*."

Two years after Calvin's death, Calvin's biblical universalism was reflected in the Second Helvetic Confession (1566).[48] The last of the great Reformation confessions, it was drawn up by Calvin's friend Bullinger.

The confession states in Section 14: "We teach that Christ alone, by his death or passion, is the satisfaction, propitiation, or expiation of *all sins*." Section 15 states: "Christ took upon himself, and bore the sins of the *world*, and satisfied Divine Justice." These combined statements indicate without question the concept of universal satisfaction for the sins of the world.

Richard Muller acknowledged that Bullinger (like Musculus, Zanchi, and Ursinus) taught a form of "non-speculative hypothetical universalism."[49] As noted by G. Michael

---

46 P. Vermigli, *Predestination and Justification: Two Theological Loci*, trans. F. A. James III, Sixteenth Century Essays and Studies 8 (Kirksville, MO: Truman State University Press, 2003), 62.

47 P. Vermigli, "Of Predestination," in *The Common Places*, trans. A. Marten (London: Henrie Denham, 1583), Part 3, 31. The quote appears this way in a modern edition: "Thus if we relate this to the will of God, we will easily grant that he will have all men to be saved" (P. M. Vermigli, *Predestination and Justification*, 8:63).

48 See A. Cochrane, ed., *Reformed Confessions of the Sixteenth Century* (London: SCM, 1966), 220–22; 242, 246.

49 See Muller's review of J. Moore's "English Hypothetical Universalism: John Preston and the Softening of Reformed Theology," *Calvin Theological Journal* 43 (2008): 149–50. Bullinger frequently stressed the universality of the atonement: "Therefore I say, the sins of all men of the world of all ages have been expiated by his death" (H. Bvllingero, "Homilia CLI," in *Isaias Excellentissimus Dei Propheta, Cuius Testimoniis Christus Ipse Dominus Et Eius Apostoli creberrime usi leguntur, expositus Homiliis CXC* [Tiguri: Christophorus Froschouerus, 1567], 266ʳ). Thomas, *Extent*, 74–76, 81, likewise concurred that Bullinger clearly taught universal atonement.

Thomas, central to Bullinger's theology was a universal covenant that necessitated a universal atonement.[50] One can also find a Calvinistic form of universal redemption in the writings of Rudolf Gwalther, Bullinger's student and successor.[51]

A few examples from his sermons will suffice to illustrate Bullinger's belief that Christ died for the sins of all humanity:

> Our Lord therefore became man, by the sacrifice of himself to make satisfaction for us; on whom, as it were upon a goat for the sin-offering, when all the sins of whole world were gathered together and laid, he by his death took away and purged them all: so that now the only sacrifice of God has satisfied for the sins of the whole world.[52]

> And it is not amiss in this place first of all to mark, that Christ is called a propitiation, or satisfaction, not for sinners or people of one or two ages, but for all sinners and all the faithful people throughout the whole world. One Christ therefore is sufficient for all: one intercessor with the Father is set forth unto all.[53]

> Therefore, when Christ was come, and with his death had finished all, then the veil that hung in the temple was rent from the top to the very ground: whereby all men might understand, that the way was opened into the *sanctum sanctorum*, that is, into the very heavens; and that satisfaction was made for all men in respect of the law.[54]

> For the Lord has died for all: but that all are not made partakers of this redemption, it is through their own fault. For the Lord excludes no man, but him only which through his own unbelief, and misbelief excludes himself. &c.[55]

> Wherefore our priest, executing his office before God in heaven, hath need of

---

50 Thomas, *Extent*, 81.

51 R. Gwalther, *A Hundred Threescore and Fifteen Homilies or Sermons upon the Acts of the Apostles*, trans. J. Bridges (Imprinted By Henrie Denham, dwelling in Pater noster rowe, at the signe of the Starre, 1572), 108; 751–52. Gwalther married Regula Zwingli, the daughter of the Swiss Reformer. Ludwig Lavater (1527–1586), Bullinger's son-in-law, also likely held to unlimited atonement. See R. Young, "The Atonement of Christ," in *Biblical Notes & Queries*, 309:

> Some say, I could willingly die, but the magnitude of my sins makes me that I am afraid of death. Such minds are to be raised with this consolation, that we know that God laid our sins on Christ, that for all of us he made satisfaction on the cross.

52 H. Bullinger, *The Decades of Henry Bullinger*, 4 vols., trans. H. I., ed. T. Harding, Parker Society Publications 1 (Cambridge: Cambridge University Press, 1849–52), 1:136.

53 Ibid., 4:218–19.

54 Ibid., 2:147–48.

55 H. Bullinger, *A Hvndred Sermons vpon the Apocalipse of Iesu Christ* (London: Iohn Daye, 1573), 80.

> no altar of incense, no censer, no holy vessels or garments: much less hath he need of the altar of burnt-offerings; for on the cross, which was his altar, he offered up himself but once for all. Neither was there any mortal man worthy to offer to the living God the living Son of God. And that only sacrifice is always effectual to make satisfaction for all the sins of all men in the whole world. . . . Christians know that the sacrifice of Christ once offered is always effectual to make satisfaction for the sins of all men in the whole world, and of all men of all ages: but these men with often outcries say, that it is flat heresy not to confess that Christ is daily offered of sacrificing priests, consecrated to that purpose.[56]

Richard Muller has rightly acknowledged that Bullinger affirmed a universal atonement. He likewise suggested that Calvin and Bullinger agreed on the issue of the sufficiency of the atonement.[57]

Augustine Marlorate (AD 1506–1562)

Though lesser known today than the other first-generation Reformers, Marlorate was an important part of the early Reformed movement. Spurgeon called him "an eminent French reformer, preacher, and martyr," whose commentaries "contain the cream of the older writers."[58]

In his commentary on Matthew, Marlorate spoke of Christ as dying "for salvation of all mankind."[59] By the eternal decree of God, Christ "was ordained a sacrifice to take away the sins of the world."[60] Christ, by his death, "redeemed mankind from death and hell."[61] Speaking of Matt 20:28; Matt 26:28; and 2 Cor 5:18–20, Marlorate said the use of "many" and "world" means "all mankind."[62]

In his commentary on Mark and Luke, Marlorate spoke of Christ's sacrifice "to

56 Bullinger, *The Decades*, 4:287, 296.

57 R. A. Muller, *After Calvin: Studies in the Development of a Theological Tradition*, Oxford Studies in Historical Theology (New York: Oxford University Press, 2003), 14. Venema translated some interesting correspondence between Bullinger and some theologians in Geneva, including Calvin, wherein Bullinger voiced some concerns about their teaching on predestination. He strongly affirmed God's love for all men, as well as his will and desire for the salvation of all men. See C. P. Venema, "Heinrich Bullinger's Correspondence on Calvin's Doctrine of Predestination, 1551–1553," *Sixteenth Century Journal* 17, no. 4 (Winter 1986): 435–50. Venema said that Bullinger "spoke of God's 'counsel' to bless, to justify and to sanctify men in the one Mediator, Jesus Christ. Furthermore, this gracious 'counsel' is 'on account of Jesus Christ, who was made man, suffered and died to expiate the sin of the whole world'" (ibid., 440–41).

58 C. Spurgeon, *Commenting and Commentaries* (Grand Rapids, MI: Kregel, 1988 [1876]), 143.

59 A. Marlorate, *A Catholike and Ecclesiastical Exposition of the Holy Gospel after S. Mathew, Gathered out of All the Singular and Approued Deuines (which the Lorde Hath Geuen to His Churche) by Augustine Marlorate. And Translated out of Latine into Englishe, by Thomas Tymme, Minister, Sene and Allowed according to the Order Appointed* (London: T. Marshe, 1570), 374, 625.

60 Ibid., 631.

61 Ibid., 723.

62 Ibid., 361, 453, 643–44.

make satisfaction for the sins of the world,"[63] Christ is said to be a "redeemer of all men which were, & which should be to the World's end."[64]

In his commentary on John, Marlorate said that by means of the blood of Christ, "salvation belongs to all men."[65] By means of Christ's death, "all the transgressions of the world are wiped away,"[66] and in another place, Christ is said to "make satisfaction for the sins of all men."[67]

John Calvin (AD 1509–1564)

Along with Luther and Zwingli, John Calvin was the third member of the triumvirate of leadership in the early days of the Reformation.[68] Calvin is often (though wrongly) considered *the* father of Reformed theology. A strict Augustinian, Calvin's formulation of his theology is evidenced through successive revisions of his *Institutes* throughout his lifetime. Whether Calvin held to limited atonement has been heavily debated since the early seventeenth century.

Evidence for Calvin as an early example of Hypothetical Universalism is far more abundant than what modern scholarship has for Vermigli, Zanchi, and Musculus, and yet it is recognized that these men clearly affirmed universal atonement. Given the significance of Calvin for Reformed theology, and given the debate that swirls around his statements about the extent of the atonement, we will examine his views on the subject more substantively.

The first place to begin is with the actual statements Calvin made explicitly or implicitly about the extent of the atonement. The following quotations appear from a wide range of Calvin's writings, including his *Institutes*, commentaries, sermons,[69] tracts, and letters.

> *To bear the sins* means to free those who have sinned from their guilt by his satisfaction. He says many meaning all, as in Rom. 5:15. It is of course certain that not all enjoy the fruits of Christ's death, but this happens because their

63 A. Marlorate, *A Catholike and Ecclesiastical Exposition of the Holy Gospel after S. Marke and Lvke*, trans. Thomas Timme (London: T. Marsh, 1583), 323.

64 Ibid., 64.

65 A. Marlorate, *A Catholike and Ecclesiastical Exposition of the Holy Gospel after S. Iohn*, trans. T. Timme (London: T. Marshe, 1575), 542.

66 A. Marlorate, *S. Mathew*, 617.

67 A. Marlorate, *S. Iohn*, 543.

68 This statement needs to be qualified by the fact that there were several men just as important in Reformation theology as Calvin during this time, such as Bullinger, though in modern times many of them are all but forgotten in the wake of Calvin's fame. Technically, Calvin should be viewed as a second-generation Reformer, as Richard Muller classified him. R. Muller, *Calvin and the Reformed Tradition: On the Work of Christ and the Order of Salvation* (Grand Rapids, MI: Baker, 2012), 56.

69 See J. W. Anderson, "The Grace of God and the Non-Elect in Calvin's Commentaries and Sermons" (ThD diss., New Orleans Baptist Theological Seminary, 1976), for numerous examples of statements from Calvin in these writings that indicate his belief in unlimited atonement.

> unbelief hinders them. That question is not dealt with here because the apostle is not discussing how few or how many benefit from the death of Christ, but means simply that He died for others, not for Himself. He therefore contrasts the many to the one.[70]

> Paul makes grace common to all men, not because it in fact extends to all, but because it is offered to all. Although Christ suffered for the sins of the world, and is offered by the goodness of God without distinction to all men, yet not all receive Him.[71]

This statement is on Rom 5:18 and is significant for a number of reasons. Notice Calvin said grace is "common" to "all men" not because it "extends to all" in the sense of application but because it is offered to all. Notice who is doing the "offering": God himself. Christ is said to be offered to all by the "goodness of God." Calvin said Christ suffered for the "sins of the world." It is not possible here to read the elect into the word "world." God's offer of Christ to the world "without distinction" is based on the fact that Christ suffered "for the sins of the world." Though Christ died for all and is offered to all, yet "not all receive him," according to Calvin. This is a clear statement of Calvin's view that Christ died for the sins of all, but only those who believe receive the benefits of Christ's death.

Additional quotations from Calvin include the following:

> Such is also the significance of the term "world" which He had used before. For although there is nothing in the world deserving of God's favour, He nevertheless shows He is favourable to the whole world when He calls all without exception to the faith in Christ, which is indeed an entry into life.[72]

> On the other hand, when Luke speaks of the priests, he is speaking of the responsibility of those who hold public office. Principally, they are ordained to bear God's word. So when some falsehood appears or Satan's wicked disseminations proliferate, it is their duty to be vigilant, confront the situation, and do everything in their power to protect poor people from being poisoned by false teachings and to keep the souls redeemed by the precious blood of our Lord Jesus Christ from perishing, from entering into eternal death.[73]

70 J. Calvin, *The Epistle of Paul the Apostle to the Hebrews and the First and Second Epistles of St. Peter*, ed. D. W. Torrance and T. F. Torrance, trans. W. B. Johnston (Grand Rapids, MI: Eerdmans, 1963), 131.

71 J. Calvin, *The Epistle of Paul the Apostle to the Romans and to the Thessalonians*, ed. D. W. Torrance and T. F. Torrance, trans. R. Mackenzie (Grand Rapids, MI: Eerdmans, 1960), 117–18.

72 J. Calvin, *The Gospel According to St. John 1–10*, ed. D. W. Torrance and T. F. Torrance, trans. T. H. L. Parker (Grand Rapids, MI: Eerdmans, 1961), 74.

73 J. Calvin, *Sermons on Acts 1–7* (Edinburgh: Banner of Truth, 2008), 112.

> We must make every effort to draw everybody to the knowledge of the gospel. For when we see people going to hell who have been created in the image of God and redeemed by the blood of our Lord Jesus Christ, that must indeed stir us to do our duty and instruct them and treat them with all gentleness and kindness as we try to bear fruit this way.[74]

> It is, as I have already said, that, seeing that men are created in the image of God and that their souls have been redeemed by the blood of Jesus Christ, we must try in every way available to us to draw them to the knowledge of the gospel.[75]

> Thus, to head off those who keep on asking about what should be perfectly obvious and familiar to them, as well as those who look for any excuse to dodge God's judgment, I thought it worthwhile to review and revise a sermon which I preached on the topic, the essentials of which had been taken down in writing. The first sermon, therefore, contains a warning against the craven behavior of those who, through God, have come to know the truth of the gospel, but who defile themselves with popish abominations which are completely opposed to the Christian religion, since in doing so they disown, so far as they can, the Son of God who has redeemed them.[76]

Other quotations of Calvin with respect to the extent question include the following:

> But if at this time he spared not the natural branches, (Rom. Xi, 21,) the same punishment will this day be inflicted on us, if we do not answer to his call. The supper which had been prepared for us will not be lost, but God will invite other guests.[77]

> And he has employed the universal term *whosoever*, both to invite all indiscriminately to partake of life, and to cut off every excuse from unbeliev-

---

74 Ibid., 587–88. Notice here that Calvin spoke of those who are "redeemed" and yet they are "going to hell." This could not be said of the elect. Similarly, William Farel (AD 1489–1565) said,

> Let all therefore, whether priests or preachers, have respect to the great shepherd Jesus Christ, who gave his body and his blood for the poor people. Let us prefer to be nothing, if only the poor sheep, gone so far astray, may find the right way, may come to Jesus and give themselves to God. That will be better than if we should gain all the world and lose those for whom Jesus died (J. H. Merle d'Aubigné, *History of the Reformation in Europe in the Time of Calvin*, 8 vols., trans. W. L. B Cates [New York: Robert Carter & Brothers, 1877], 6:238–39).

75 Ibid., 593.

76 J. Calvin, *Faith Unfeigned: Four Sermons Concerning Matters Most Useful for the Present Time, with a Brief Exposition of Psalm 87* (Edinburgh: Banner of Truth, 2010), 1–2.

77 J. Calvin, "Commentary on A Harmony of the Evangelists," in *Calvin's Commentaries*, 22 vols., trans. W. Pringle (Grand Rapids, MI: Baker, 1984), 16:172.

ers. Such is also the import of the term *World*, which he formerly used; for though nothing will be found in *the world* that is worthy of the favour of God, yet he shows himself to be reconciled to the whole world, when he invites all men without exception to the faith of Christ, which is nothing else than everlasting life.[78]

There is, however, still greater force in what follows—that even those that are ignorant or weak have been *redeemed with the blood of Christ*; for nothing were more unseemly than this, that while Christ did not hesitate to die, in order that the weak might not perish, we, on the other hand, reckon as nothing the salvation of those who have *been redeemed with so great a price*. A memorable saying, by which we are taught how precious the salvation of our brethren ought to be in our esteem, and not merely that of all, but of each individual in particular, inasmuch as the *blood of Christ was poured out for each individual*. . . . For if the soul of every one that is weak is the *price of Christ's blood*, that man who, for the sake of a very small portion of meat, hurries back again to death the brother *who has been redeemed by Christ*, shows how contemptible the blood of Christ is in his view.[79]

But the meaning is fuller and more comprehensive—first, that God was in Christ; and, secondly, that he reconciled the world to himself by his intercession.[80]

Since therefore he wishes the benefit of his death to be common to all, an insult is offered to him by those who, by their opinion, shut out any person from the hope of salvation.[81]

Though Christ may be denied in various ways, yet Peter, as I think, refers here to what is expressed by Jude, that is, when the grace of God is turned into lasciviousness; for Christ redeemed us, that he might have a people separated from all the pollutions of the world, and devoted to holiness and innocency. They, then, who throw off the bridle, and give themselves up to all kinds of licentiousness, are not unjustly said to deny Christ by whom they have been redeemed.[82]

---

78 J. Calvin, "Commentary on the Gospel According to John," in *Calvin's Commentaries*, 17.125.

79 J. Calvin, "Commentary on the Epistles of Paul the Apostle to the Corinthians," in *Calvin's Commentaries*, 20.284.

80 Ibid., 20:236.

81 J. Calvin, "Commentaries on the Epistles to Timothy, Titus, and Philemon," in *Calvin's Commentaries*, 21:57.

82 J. Calvin, "Commentaries on the Catholic Epistles," in *Calvin's Commentaries*, 22:393.

So wonderful is his love towards mankind, that he would have them all to be saved, and is of his own self prepared to bestow salvation on the lost. But the order is to be noticed, that God is ready to receive all to repentance, so that none may perish.[83]

By saying that we were reconciled to God by the death of Christ, he means, that it was the sacrifice of expiation, by which God was pacified towards the world, as I have showed in the fourth chapter.[84]

Both points are distinctly stated to us: namely, that faith in Christ brings life to all, and that Christ brought life, because the Heavenly Father loves the human race, and wishes that they should not perish.[85]

The next thing is—that when the weak conscience is wounded, the price of Christ's blood is wasted; for the most abject brother has been redeemed by the blood of Christ: it is then a heinous crime to destroy him by gratifying the stomach.[86]

"Which is shed for many." By the word "many" he means not a part of the world only, but the whole human race; for he contrasts many with one; as if he had said, that he will not be the Redeemer of one man only, but will die in order to deliver many from the condemnation of the curse. It must at the same time be observed, however, that by the words for you, as related by Luke—Christ directly addresses the disciples, and exhorts every believer to apply to his own advantage the shedding of blood. Therefore, when we approach to the holy table, let us not only remember in general that the world has been redeemed by the blood of Christ, but let every one consider for himself that his own sins have been expiated.[87]

And when he says, *the sin* OF THE WORLD, he extends this favor indiscriminately to the whole human race; that the Jews might not think that he had been sent to them alone.[88]

---

83 Ibid., 22:419. Calvin's use of the word "prepared" here implies unlimited atonement.

84 J. Calvin, "Commentaries on the Epistle of St. Paul to the Romans," in *Calvin's Commentaries*, 19:198.

85 J. Calvin, "Commentary on the Gospel According to John," in *Calvin's Commentaries*, 17:123.

86 J. Calvin, "Commentaries on the Epistle of Paul the Apostle to the Romans," in *Calvin's Commentaries*, 19:505.

87 J. Calvin, "Commentary on a Harmony of the Evangelists, Matthew, Mark, and Luke," in *Calvin's Commentaries*, 17:214.

88 J. Calvin, "Commentary on the Gospel According to John," in *Calvin's Commentaries*, 17:64.

He says that this redemption was procured through the *blood of Christ*, for by the sacrifice of his death all the sins of the world were expiated.[89]

"And to give his life a ransom for many." . . . The word "many" (*pollōn*) is not put definitely for a fixed number, but for a large number; for he contrasts himself with all others. And in this sense it is used in Romans 5:15, where Paul does not speak of any part of men, but embraces the whole human race.[90]

For the faithless have no profit at all by the death and passion of our Lord Jesus Christ, but rather are so much the more damnable, because they reject the mean that God had ordained: and their unthankfulness shall be so much the more grievously punished, because they have trodden under foot the blood of our Lord Jesus Christ, which was the ransom for their souls.[91]

God, as we have already said, does not here simply promise salvation but shows that he is indeed ready to save . . . but the obstinacy of men rejects the grace which has been provided and which God willingly and bountifully offers.[92]

Here a question may be raised, how have the sins of the whole world been expiated? I pass by the dotages of the fanatics, who under this pretense extend salvation to all the reprobate, and therefore to Satan himself. Such a monstrous thing deserves no refutation. They who seek to avoid this absurdity, have said that Christ suffered sufficiently for the whole world, but efficiently only for the elect. This solution has commonly prevailed in the schools. Though then I allow that what has been said is true, yet I deny that it is suitable to this passage; for the design of John was no other than to make this benefit common to the whole Church. Then under the word *all* or whole, he does not include the reprobate, but designates those who should believe as well as those who were then scattered through various parts of the world. For then is really made evident, as it is meet, the grace of Christ, when it is declared to be the only true salvation of the world.[93]

The only Lord God, or, God who alone is Lord. Some old copies have, "Christ, who alone is God and Lord." And, indeed, in the Second Epistle of Peter,

---

89 J. Calvin, "Commentaries on the Epistles to the Philippians, Colossians, and Thessalonians," in *Calvin's Commentaries*, 21:148.

90 J. Calvin, "Commentary on a Harmony of the Evangelists," in *Calvin's Commentaries*, 16:427.

91 J. Calvin, *John Calvin's Sermons on Galatians*, trans. Kathy Childress (Audubon, NJ: Old Paths, 1995), 27.

92 J. Calvin, "Commentaries on the Twelve Minor Prophets," in *Calvin's Commentaries*, 13:476–77.

93 J. Calvin, "Commentaries on the Catholic Epistles," in *Calvin's Commentaries*, 22:173.

> Christ alone is mentioned, and there he is called Lord. But He means that Christ is denied, when they who had been redeemed by his blood, become again the vassals of the Devil, and thus render void as far as they can that incomparable price.[94]

> It is incontestable that Christ came for the expiation of the sins of the whole world.[95]

> Our Lord made effective for him [the pardoned thief on the cross] His death and passion which He suffered and endured for all mankind.[96]

In Calvin's last will and testament, he clearly affirmed a form of universal atonement:

> I testify and declare that as a suppliant I humbly implore of him to grant me to be so washed and purified by the blood of that sovereign Redeemer, shed for the sins of the human race, that I may be permitted to stand before his tribunal in the image of the Redeemer himself.[97]

Calvin's discussion in both his commentary and his sermon on the use of "all" in Isa 53:6 ("all we like sheep have gone astray . . . and the Lord hath laid on him the iniquity of us all") clearly made no distinction in usage. "All" like sheep strayed, and on the Servant was laid the sin of us "all." All without exception had sinned and the sin of all without exception had been laid on the suffering Servant. Calvin further stated:

> By adding the term "each one," he [the author of Isaiah] descends from a universal statement, in which he included all, to a particular, that each person may

---

94 Ibid., 433–34.

95 J. Calvin, *Concerning the Eternal Predestination of God*, trans. J. K. S. Reid (London: James Clark, 1961), 148.

96 J. Calvin, *Sermons on the Saving Work of Christ*, trans. L. Nixon (Grand Rapids, MI: Baker, 1980), 151.

97 J. Calvin, *Letters of John Calvin*, 4 vols., ed. and trans. J. Bonnet (New York: Burt and Franklin, 1858), 4:365–69; see also Beza's "Life of Calvin," in Calvin's *Tracts and Treatises*, 3 vols., ed. T. F. Torrance, trans. H. Beveridge (Grand Rapids, MI: Eerdmans, 1958), 1:cxiii–cxxvii. Notice here how Calvin speaks of the blood of Christ being shed not for the "world" but for the "human race." It is impossible to make "human race" refer to the elect. Elijah Waterman (1769–1825) was a graduate of Yale College (1791) and a pastor for many years. In his *Memoirs of the Life and Writings of John Calvin* (Hartford: Hale & Hosner, 1813), he identified Calvin as moderate with respect to the extent of the atonement:

> Some of the professed friends, as well as the avowed enemies of Calvin, have been anxious to establish the point, that Calvin limited the atonement of Christ to the sins of the elect alone. Calvin's opinion however was, that the atonement of Christ was for *Sins*, as he deliberately says in his Will, That the blood of the exalted Redeemer was shed for the sins of the human race.—He is no less explicit in his Commentaries—Rom. v. 18—*Nam etsi passus est Christus pro paccatis totius mundi, atque omnibas indifferente Dei benignitate offertur, non tamen omnes apprehendunt.* "For although Christ SUFFERED FOR THE SINS OF THE WHOLE WORLD, and by the benevolence of God it is indifferently offered to all, yet all do not receive him." *Opera Calvini*, vol. 7. (410–11)

consider in his own mind whether it be so . . . he adds this word "all" to exclude all exceptions . . . even to the last individual . . . all men are included, without any exception.[98]

Calvin stated that "many" means "all" in Isaiah 53:12:

I have followed the ordinary interpretation, that "he bore the sin of many," though we might without impropriety consider the Hebrew word (*răbbīm*) to denote "Great and Noble." And thus the contrast would be more complete, that Christ, while "he was ranked among transgressors," became surety for every one of the most excellent of the earth, and suffered in the room of those who hold the highest rank in the world. I leave this to the judgment of my readers. Yet I approve of the ordinary reading, that he alone bore the punishment of many, because on him was laid the guilt of the whole world. It is evident from other passages, and especially from the fifth chapter of the Epistle to the Romans, that "many" sometimes denotes "all."[99]

In Calvin's commentary and sermon on Gal 2:20, he expressed himself in ways that indicate his commitment to universal atonement: "It will not be enough for any man to contemplate Christ as having died for the salvation of the world, unless he has experienced the consequences of this death, and is enabled to claim it has his own."[100]

In his sermon on this same text, he declared:

And he contenteth not himself to say, that Christ gave himself for the world in common, for that had been but a slender saying; but (sheweth that) every one of us must apply to himself particularly, the virtue of the death and passion of our Lord Jesus Christ. Whereas it is said that the Son of God was crucified, we must not only think that the same was done for the Redemption of the world; but also every one of us must on his own behalf join himself to our Lord Jesus Christ, and conclude, It is for me that he hath suffered . . . but when we once know that the thing was done for the redemption of the whole world, pertaineth to every of us severally: it behooveth every one of us to say also on his own behalf, the son of God has loved me so dearly, that he hath given himself to death for me . . . we be very wretches if we accept not

98 J. Calvin, *Sermons on Isaiah*, 66, 70, 78–79. See K. Kennedy, "Was Calvin a Calvinist? John Calvin on the Extent of the Atonement," in *Whosoever Will*, 191–212, on Calvin's view of the extent of the atonement. Kennedy concluded that Calvin held to universal atonement.

99 J. Calvin, "Commentary on the Book of the Prophet Isaiah," in *Calvin's Commentaries*, 8:131.

100 J. Calvin, "Commentaries on the Epistles of Paul to the Galatians and Ephesians," in *Calvin's Commentaries*, 21:76.

> such a benefit when it is offered to us . . . Lo here a warrant for our salvation, so was we ought to think ourselves thoroughly assured of it.[101]

In his commentary on Gal 2:20, Calvin not only affirmed that one must believe that Christ died for all but added that this alone is not enough. One must also believe that Christ died for him personally. Since it is not possible for one to believe the latter without believing the former, Christ necessarily died for all. This is a different approach than strict particularists who contend one need not believe that Christ died for all people or even for oneself, but that it is sufficient to believe that Christ died for the elect or for "sinners."[102]

In his sermon on Gal 2:20, Calvin affirmed the same notion. Only saving faith appropriates the atonement; the atonement alone does not save. Calvin affirms that Christ was crucified "for the redemption of the world" and this is contrasted with the necessity of believing that "it is for me that he hath suffered." Calvin here indicated that the "warrant for our salvation" is the love of Christ and his atonement for all. Curt Daniel noted: "Particularists limit the warrant to the command to believe; grace and atonement are irrelevant at this point."[103]

In his commentary on Gal 5:12, Calvin grounded the universal offer of the gospel in the unlimited extent of the atonement: "God commends to us the salvation of all men without exception, even as Christ suffered for the sins of the whole world." It is interesting to note here that Helm's treatment of this quotation in his *Calvin and the Calvinists* leaves something to be desired. Helm's treatment is flawed in two ways: (1) he asserted the quotation is from Calvin's sermons on Isaiah, but it actually comes from the commentary on a different passage of Scripture; and (2) Helm elided some of Calvin's words in the quotation in his citation.[104] Calvin taught that one must believe that Christ died for him individually and that the only way he can know this is for the gospel to tell him, and this is exactly what the gospel does.

In Calvin's sermons on Ephesians, he explicitly stated that "Christ is in a general view [or way] the Redeemer of the world."[105] In *The Deity of Christ*, there are several statements affirming the universal nature of the atonement.

> The hour was approaching in which our Lord Jesus would have to suffer for the redemption of mankind.[106]

---

101 J. Calvin, *Sermons of M. John Calvin upon the Epistle of Saint Paul to the Galatians* (London: Henrie Bynneman, 1574), 106.

102 Daniel, "Hyper-Calvinism and John Gill," 824–25. The term "sinners" in the phrase "Christ died for sinners" in many Calvinist writings means "Christ died for *elect* sinners only."

103 Ibid., 825.

104 P. Helm, *Calvin and the Calvinists* (Edinburgh: Banner of Truth, 1982), 45–46. See also the critique in Daniel, "Hyper-Calvinism and John Gill," 788n20.

105 J. Calvin, *Sermons on Ephesians* (Edinburgh: Banner of Truth, 1974), 55.

106 J. Calvin, *The Deity of Christ and Other Sermons* (1950; repr. Audubon, NJ: Old Paths Publications, 1997), 55.

> It was a terrible thing to him to be found before the judgement-seat of God in the name of all poor sinners (for He was there, as it were, having to sustain all our burdens).[107]

> It is that He must be the Redeemer of the world. He must be condemned, indeed, not for having preached the Gospel, but for us He must be oppressed, as it were, to the lowest depths and sustain our curse, since he was there, as it were, in the person of all cursed ones and all transgressors, and of those who had deserved eternal death. Since then, Jesus Christ has this office, and he bears the burdens of all those who had offended God mortally.[108]

> God, to render the wicked all the more inexcusable, willed that Jesus Christ in His death be declared sovereign King of all creatures.[109]

In his commentary on Matt 26:39, Calvin said that Christ was "charged [or burdened] with the sins of the whole world."[110]

In the *Institutes*, Calvin stated: "Christ interceded as his advocate, took upon himself and suffered the punishment that, from God's righteous judgment, threatened all sinners; that he purged with his blood those evils which had rendered sinners hateful to God; that by this expiation he made satisfaction and sacrifice to God the Father."[111]

In one of his sermons Calvin asserted:

> It was to small purpose for us that Jesus Christ had redeemed us from everlasting death, and had shed his blood to reconcile us to God, unless we were certified of this benefit, and it were told us, and God should call us to enter

---

107 Ibid., 155–56.

108 Ibid., 95.

109 Ibid., 153. Note here that Calvin seems to be saying that Christ is Lord and Judge of all people because he died for all people. As C. Daniel noted,

> When a person rejects the gospel, he incurs damnation not just because he rejects it but because he is rejecting that Christ died for him, which the gospel proclaims. The implication is that if Christ did not die for all men, then Christ would not be the sovereign King over all men. Calvin disagrees with the Particularists who contend that Christ is Lord of all merely because of his intrinsic Deity, not because He died for all men.

> Daniel continued and pointed out with respect to the intent of the atonement:

> Why did Christ die for all men if in the secret will of God it was never determined that they will be saved? Answer—Christ died for all so that all would be inexcusable. They incur extra condemnation when they reject the gospel. If Christ did not die for all men, there would be no extra condemnation for failure to believe that Christ died for oneself, as argued by High and Hyper-Calvinists. (Daniel, "Hyper-Calvinism and John Gill," 792)

110 J. Calvin, "Commentary on a Harmony of the Evangelists, Matthew, Mark, and Luke," in *Calvin's Commentaries*, 17:234.

111 J. Calvin, *Institutes of the Christian Religion*, 2 vols., ed. J. T. McNeill, trans. F. L. Battles (Philadelphia: Westminster, 1960), 1:505 (II.xvi.2).

> into possession of this salvation, and to enjoy this price which was thus paid for us. As for example, behold the Turks, which cast away the grace which was purchased for all the world by Jesus Christ.[112]

In another sermon, Calvin distinguished between the nature of the atonement and its application.

> For it is not enough that Jesus Christ suffered in His person and was made a sacrifice for us; but we must be assured of it by the Gospel; we must receive that testimony and doubt not that we have righteousness in Him, knowing that He has made satisfaction for our sins.[113]

One of the key issues in the debate over Calvin's position is his comments on the biblical passages where the words "many" and "all" occur in the context of the atonement. Before entering this discussion, let me point out two important considerations. First, it only takes one clear, unambiguous statement in the biblical text, or in any writer on the subject, that states Jesus died for the sins of all people to affirm unlimited atonement. This is true no matter how many statements are found that indicate Jesus died for the sins of a limited group of people. It would not be at all unusual to find in Scripture and in those writing on the subject of the atonement to sometimes address believers and to speak of what Christ has done for "us," "our sins," "the church," and so on. Such statements do not *ipso facto* indicate a writer is committed to limited atonement. To infer such from these limited statements would be to succumb to the negative inference fallacy.

Second, it only takes one clear, unambiguous statement in the biblical text, or in any writer, that states that Jesus died *only* for the sins of the "elect" or "those who will believe," and so on, to confirm an author's commitment to limited atonement. These two points should be kept in mind at all times in surveying the comments of anyone on the question of the extent of the atonement.

Calvinists who hold to limited atonement are quick to point out that the use of "all" in Scripture does not always mean "all without exception." This is certainly true, but no one I know who holds to unlimited atonement denies this. I cannot but agree with Thomas when he stated:

> It may be granted that citations referring to "all," "the world," "mankind," and "the human race," do not prove that Calvin intended to speak of an unlimited

---

112 J. Calvin, *Sermons of M. John Calvin on the Epistles of Saint Paul to Timothy and Titus*, trans. L.T. (London: G. Bishop and T. Woodcoke, 1579), 177. It is difficult not to see unlimited atonement in this quotation.

113 J. Calvin, *Sermons on Isaiah's Prophecy of the Death and Passion of Christ*, Library of Ecclesiastical History, trans. T. H. L. Parker (Cambridge: James Clarke, 2010), 117.

> universality, since he sometimes could assert that the terms "all" and "world"[114] should be understood of "all sorts" or "all peoples" or the church throughout the world [as in his commentaries on 1 John 2:2 and 1 Tim 2:4–6]. Nevertheless, there are numerous places where an unrestricted universality must be intended.[115]

This is really the issue. Does Calvin use words like "all" and "world" with respect to the atonement when he intends to convey the meaning "all without exception"? It appears clear from his writings that such is indeed the case.

For example, in his commentary on Matt 20:28 and Mark 14:24, Calvin explicitly said that "many" means "all." The same can be said for his commentary on Heb 9:28. In these passages, for particularists, "many" means "some" as opposed to "all"; for Calvin, "many" means "all" as opposed to "some."[116] As demonstrated in the quotation concerning Isa 53:12 above, Calvin explicitly stated that "many" means "all." From what Calvin said in his comments on Rom 5:19, it is clear that "many" means "all" as opposed to "one." He said the same thing in his *Sermons on Deuteronomy*.[117] Here Calvin stated that Christ died for all who have sinned; he is not saying merely that all those for whom Christ died were sinners (as particularists often interpret 2 Cor 5:14–15), as Daniel noted. Furthermore, Calvin grounds their ultimate condemnation in their unbelief, not in lack of atonement.

Daniel's chiding comment concerning Helm's dismissal of this evidence is penetrating:

> Helm mentions this passage but dismisses it, saying it means "all classes" and therefore cannot teach universal atonement (Calvin, p. 44). Later Helm even goes so far in discounting the "many equals all" passages adduced by Kendall that he boldly states: "it is impossible to advance such a far-reaching reconstruction of Calvin's doctrine of the work of Christ on such flimsy foundations" (p. 46). We find it incredible that Helm would class as "flimsy" the many and explicit statements of Calvin himself, especially without producing equally many and explicit examples himself, or at least exegeting the examples given by Kendall by dealing with the crux of the issue.[118]

It seems obvious in many contexts that when Calvin uses "all" and "many," he is not limiting the terms to a definite number of people as a part of humanity, but he is referring to all humanity. Hence on Matt 26:14 he stated that Christ "offered himself as a victim for the salvation of the human race." On John 1:29 Calvin stated that Christ was

114 Calvin probably limits the word "world" only twice: 1 John 2:2 and Jesus's parable of the field. In both cases he is following Augustine.

115 Thomas, *Extent of the Atonement*, 27.

116 Daniel, "Hyper-Calvinism and John Gill," 794.

117 Calvin, *Sermons on Deuteronomy*, 167.

118 Daniel, "Hyper-Calvinism and John Gill," 794.

offered "indiscriminately to the whole human race." Calvin here equates "world" with the "human race." This use of "world" cannot be divorced in its context of meaning from Calvin's phrase "all men without exception who are guilty of unrighteousness." In his commentary on John 3:16, Calvin equated "world" with all "indiscriminately" and spoke of "all without exception." It is clear he is contrasting the few who believe with the rest of the world, not with all who believe. In both his commentary and his sermon on Isa 53:6, Calvin stated the "all" refers to the whole human race and that "none is excepted" because "the prophet includes all, . . . even to the last individual, . . . without any exception."[119]

Consider Calvin's sermon on Isaiah:

> That, then, is how our Lord Jesus bore the sins and iniquities of many. But in fact, the word "many" is often as good as equivalent to "all." And indeed our Lord Jesus was offered to all the world. For it is not speaking of three or four when it says "God so loved the world, that he spared not His only Son." But yet we must notice what the Evangelist adds in this passage: "That whatsoever believes in Him shall not perish but obtain eternal life." Our Lord Jesus suffered for all and there is neither great nor small who is not inexcusable today, for we can obtain salvation in Him. Unbelievers who turn away from Him and who deprive themselves of Him by their malice are today doubly culpable, for how will they excuse their ingratitude in not receiving the blessings in which they could share by faith?[120]

Notice how Calvin asserts that unbelievers are "doubly culpable." Why? Because Christ has shed his blood for them and because they have refused to believe.

Calvin often uses the word "world" when he is speaking of Christ's death as "reconciling" the world to God (Matt 17:5; John 17:1; John 18:32; John 19:2; 2 Cor 5:19).

Two texts that particularists often appeal to in support of Calvin's supposed commitment to limited atonement are 1 Tim 2:4–6 and 1 John 2:2. Calvin said that "all" does not mean "every particular man" in 1 Tim 2:4–6 but rather all sorts of people. Note several things about these verses. Calvin's point, based on what he said about 2:3, is that this passage does not concern God's will for a few individuals but rather his will for the salvation of all classes of people. Notice how Calvin explicitly stated that Christ did not die only for Peter, John, or the Jews but rather for all others, including the Gentiles.[121] This does not indicate Calvin affirmed limited atonement.

119 Calvin, *Sermons on Isaiah*, 66, 70, 79, 81.

120 Ibid., 141.

121 Calvin, *Sermons on Timothy* (Edinburgh: Banner of Truth, 1983), 177. Here Calvin spoke of a group of people ("Turks") "which cast away the grace which was purchased for all the world." See also Ponter, "John Calvin (1509–1564) on Unlimited Expiation, Sin-Bearing, Redemption and Reconciliation," *Calvin and Calvinism*, March 1, 2008, http://calvinandcalvinism.com/?p=230.

Compare how Calvin treats this passage with how Owen, Cunningham, and other high Calvinists treat it. Calvin differs in his exegesis. For Calvin, the "all" of 2:1 has the same referent as the "all" in 2:4 and 2:6. Particularists normally restrict the "all" in 2:6 to the elect. This forces them to interpret the "all" of 2:4 as only "some" according to God's so-called secret will. But Calvin said that 2:4 refers to God's revealed will, not his secret will. If they interpret the "all" of 2:4 as "all" in God's revealed will, then again they are forced to distinguish the "all" of verse 4 with the "all" of verse 6. If they interpret "all" of 2:4 as referring to God's will or call for some to be saved, then they are at odds with Calvin, who said in context that the will of God and the call is universal.[122]

But doesn't Calvin affirm limited atonement in 1 John 2:2? Calvin does take a limited reading of 1 John 2:2, as did Augustine. However, Calvin takes the verse to be about the application of the atonement, not the extent of the atonement.[123] Notice that he considered the "fanatics" to be those who teach a universal application of the atonement, not those who teach a universal atonement with respect to Christ's sin-bearing. Calvin affirmed the original sense of the Lombardian formula but denied its relevance to 1 John 2:2. Calvin said that Christ "suffered sufficiently for the whole world." This statement is a denial of a limited imputation of sin to Christ and thus a denial of limited atonement. Calvin's point seems to be that the atonement is applied to all believers of all nations but to them alone and not to the unbelieving or Satan.

Calvin took "whole world" in 1 John 2:2 as the church, not the abstract class of all the elect. He is following Augustine here. Given Augustine's ecclesiology, where the church is all visible members including some non-elect, this does not implicate either Calvin or Augustine as teaching limited atonement.

Particularists offer other arguments to support their contention that Calvin held to limited atonement. For example, Calvin said Jesus's high priestly prayer of John 17:9 is limited to the elect alone, but his prayer in Luke 23:34, where he prays "Father, forgive them; for they know not what they do" (KJV), is unlimited. But the difference in their contexts is not between Christ's high priestly work on earth and in heaven but between the subjects of his prayers and the content of the prayers. Luke 23:34 is a prayer in the context of atonement and forgiveness; John 17:9 concerns the unity of the believing elect.[124] This is a weak argument for limited atonement. It only argues for a limited intent to apply the atonement.

Particularists appeal to Calvin's engagement with Georgius, Pighius, and Heshusius as evidence of his belief in limited atonement. In Calvin's *On the Eternal Predestination*

---

122 See the discussion of Calvin's interpretation of 1 Tim 2:4–6 in Daniel, "Hyper-Calvinism and John Gill," 796–99.

123 Letham said Calvin cannot be said to have taught universal atonement. "Saving Faith and Assurance in Reformed Theology: Zwingli to the Synod of Dort," 2 vols. (PhD diss., University of Aberdeen, 1979), 2:67. Note the critique by C. Bell, "Calvin and the Extent of the Atonement," *Evangelical Quarterly* 55.2 (April 1983), 115.

124 See Daniel, "Hyper-Calvinism and John Gill," 811.

of God, he refers to one named Georgius who apparently taught universalism based on his interpretation of 1 John 2:2. Georgius's argument was simple: all men will be saved because Christ died for all men. Calvin's refutation of Georgius is to point out that 1 John 2:2 does not refer to the atonement itself but rather to the application of the atonement. Daniel's point is that

> there is not the slightest hint here that Calvin accepts the Particularist *ex opera operato* theory that all for whom Christ died will be saved, though he would agree that all to whom the atonement is applied will necessarily believe. Georgius is the one accepting an *ex opera operato* theory, even though it is Universalist in nature.[125]

Calvin appealed to 1 Tim 2:4 in his refutation of Pighius. Calvin at this point is not dealing with the issue of the extent of the atonement but with the subject of predestination. Calvin argued that this verse deals with the *revealed* will of God and not the *secret* (decretal) will, as Kevin Kennedy pointed out: "When he limits the word 'all' to refer only to classes and not to individuals, he means that this verse tells us nothing about which individuals God, according to his *secret* will, has intended to save."[126]

Kennedy said special note should be taken of Calvin's usage of the word "individuals." Calvin clearly understood the word to refer to a finite and particular group of people and insists,

> 1 Tim. 2:4 is not speaking of those individuals who will actually be saved, but of humanity in general. . . . Thus, his concern was to show that the revealed will of God mentioned here does not preclude that in his secret will God has made certain determinations regarding each individual. Thus this verse is not to be understood as teaching anything about God's actual intention to save certain individuals. Rather, it should be understood only to be dealing with the universal offer of salvation.[127]

Probably the strongest evidence to be marshaled in favor of Calvin as a limitarian has to do with his comments against Heshusius. It is interesting that moderate Calvinists such as Davenant and others in the seventeenth century and beyond have dealt with this passage and concluded that Calvin was not teaching limited atonement. In more recent times, both Daniel and Kennedy have shown why Calvin is not affirm-

---

125 See Calvin, *On the Eternal Predestination of God*, 148–49; Daniel, "Hyper-Calvinism and John Gill," 808; and K. Kennedy, *Union with Christ and the Extent of the Atonement*, Studies in Biblical Literature 48 (New York: Peter Lang, 2002), 49–51.

126 Kennedy, *Union with Christ*, 43.

127 Ibid., 43–44.

ing limited atonement in this passage. My summary discussion is heavily dependent upon their works.[128]

Upon a cursory reading of Calvin's comments on Heshusius, one can see how he might be affirming limited atonement. Upon closer reading, however, it becomes clear this is not the case. As always, context is important to keep in mind.

The point of contention has to do with the bodily presence of Christ in the elements of the Lord's Supper. The context has nothing to do with the extent of the atonement. Calvin rejects the notion of the bodily presence of Christ in the elements. The key quotation is Calvin's query, "I should like to know how the wicked can eat the flesh which was not crucified for them and how they can drink the blood which was not shed to expiate their sins?"[129] When Calvin asks the question "I should like to know," he is using a rhetorical device to express a concept Calvin rejects. This becomes especially clear when one compares other examples of this identical phrase in Calvin's writings. Note also that Calvin uses the term "wicked" here rather than his usual term "reprobate."

Calvin is rejecting the claim apparently made by Heshusius that the "wicked" "eat the flesh that is not crucified for them." As a Lutheran, Heshusius certainly believed in unlimited atonement. How then does one explain Calvin's statement? The answer may lie in Calvin's understanding of true saving faith, which consists in one believing that Christ has died for him. Saving faith is not believing that Christ died for the world but believing that Christ died for me. In the passage in question, genuine partaking of Christ in the elements of the Supper requires that Christ has died for the one partaking. It is Heshusius who wrongly believes that one can truly partake of Christ in the Supper without faith that Christ died for him.

Rouwendal's discussion of this issue hits the nail on the head. He pointed out that this statement by Calvin is a

> single, isolated remark in a tract that deals with quite another subject. Hence, they cannot be viewed as a thoughtful rejection of universal redemption. Second, it is neither fair nor realistic to use this single sentence in order to ignore the many sentences wherein Calvin stated that Christ died for the whole world. Third, it should be noted that even though Calvin states here that Christ did not die for (some) ungodly, no clear doctrine of particular redemption is offered here. Fourth, one should take notice of Calvin's word choice, as well as the context wherein he uses them. The words Calvin chooses do not deny that Christ died for all men, but rather that he died for the ungodly [wicked]. The context does not deal with justification (for

128 Daniel, "Hyper-Calvinism and John Gill," 819–22; Kennedy, *Union with Christ*, 53–56. Kennedy is dependent on Daniel for his treatment.

129 Calvin, *Theological Treatises*, Library of Christian Classics 22, trans. J. K. S. Reid (Philadelphia: Westminster, 1954), 285.

> Calvin surely maintained that it was for the justification of the ungodly that Christ died, and hence, that Christ died for the ungodly), but rather with the Lord's Supper. Calvin's intention was to make clear that Christ is not corporally present. In the immediate context of the quoted sentence, he uses the argument that if Christ were present corporally, the ungodly would eat his flesh and drink his blood, which Calvin deemed impossible. Hence, it is not implausible to interpret the quoted words as follows: "I would like to know how the ungodly can eat from Christ's flesh, and how they can drink the blood of which they have no part through faith." Another (maybe even more plausible) interpretation would be that since the context is about eating and drinking the flesh and blood of Christ by faith, Calvin here had in mind the efficiency of Christ's death, so that the quotation can be read as follows: "I would like to know how the ungodly can eat from Christ's flesh that was not crucified for them effectively, and how they can drink from the blood that was not effectively shed to reconcile their sins."[130]

Given the dozens of clear statements that Calvin affirmed unlimited atonement, one should not give precedence to Calvin's more obscure comments that are not directly addressing the question of the atonement's extent. This is a question of methodology.[131]

With respect to Calvin's view of the extent of the atonement, Rouwendal's conclusion is striking:

> If Calvin taught particular atonement, he would not have used the language [for universal atonement] Clifford has gathered in great number. Thus, the universal propositions in Calvin's works do prove negatively that he did not subscribe to particular atonement, but they do not prove positively that he subscribed to universal atonement. These propositions can be used to falsify the

130 P. L. Rouwendal, "Calvin's Forgotten Classical Position on the Extent of the Atonement: About Sufficiency, Efficiency, and Anachronism," 330–31. See also R. T. Kendall, *Calvin and English Calvinism to 1649*, rev. ed. (Carlisle, UK: Paternoster, 1997), 231–38, where Kendall included Daniel's treatment of this issue. Both Daniel and Kendall follow the same trajectory. Stephen L. Costley has an excellent article on this issue published by D. Ponter, "Understanding Calvin's Argument against Heshusius," *Calvin and Calvinism*, February 12, 2008, http://calvinandcalvinism.com/?p=215.

1. The context of Calvin's theology as a whole does not include limited atonement.
2. The context of Calvin's tract against Heshusius excludes limited atonement.
3. In the famous Heshusius quote, "wicked" does not mean "non-elect."
4. Limited atonement is meaningless and out of place in Calvin's argument against Heshusius.
5. Limited atonement refutes Calvin's own theology of the Lord's Supper as presented and defended by Calvin in the Heshusius tract.
6. In the Heshusius tract, Calvin argued against Christ's local bodily presence in the elements of the Lord's Supper, not against unlimited atonement.

131 Calvin's reference at the beginning of Book 3 of the *Institutes* where he spoke of the "salvation of the human race" has been taken to indicate an underlying assumption of universal atonement for what Calvin wrote in Book 2. So Bell, "Calvin and the Extent of the Atonement," 115.

> conclusion that Calvin was a particularist, but are not sufficient to prove him a universalist.[132]

Rouwendal himself has concluded that the evidence shows Calvin did not subscribe to limited atonement. Note also he *does not* say Calvin *did not* subscribe to universal atonement; rather, he said Calvin's "universal propositions" in his writings "do not prove positively that he subscribed to universal atonement." Frankly, given the clear evidence that Calvin did indeed subscribe to a form of universal atonement, Rouwendal's demurral is unnecessary.

Paul Van Buren's 1957 treatment of Calvin's doctrine of substitution and reconciliation concluded Calvin did not teach limited atonement.[133] John Murray reviewed the book and suggested Van Buren partly misinterpreted and partly ignored the relevant evidence. Part of Van Buren's misunderstanding, according to Murray, was the relation between the universal gospel offer and a universal atonement, since the one does not imply the other.[134]

Amar Djaballah critiqued R. T. Kendall's thesis that Calvin himself held to unlimited atonement. He asserted that nowhere does Calvin advocate clearly a universalist position on extent. Djaballah also claimed that the one text where Calvin "explicitly advocated limited atonement" was Calvin's response to Heshusius.[135]

In 1983, the *Evangelical Quarterly* devoted an issue to the discussion of the "Calvin vs. the Calvinists" debate, including papers given at the 1982 Historical Theology Study Group of the Tyndale Fellowship.[136] Frederick Leahy concluded in his 1992 article that Calvin held to limited atonement.[137] After surveying the debate in the last half of the twentieth century, Andrew McGowan concluded with a quote from William Cunningham that no sufficient evidence had been produced that Calvin believed in a

132 Rouwendal, "Calvin's Forgotten Classical Position on the Extent of the Atonement," 328. Oddly, R. Muller makes no mention of Rouwendal's article in his *Calvin and the Reformed Tradition: On the Work of Christ and the Order of Salvation* (Grand Rapids, MI: Baker, 2012).

133 P. Van Buren, *Christ in Our Place: The Substitutionary Character of Calvin's Doctrine of Reconciliation* (Edinburgh: Oliver & Boyd, 1957), 77–78.

134 J. Murray, "Review of *Christ in Our Place: The Substitutionary Character of Calvin's Doctrine of Reconciliation* by P. van Buren," *Westminster Theological Journal* 22 (1959): 55–60.

135 A. Djaballah, "Calvin and the Calvinists: An Examination of Some Recent Views," *Reformation Canada* 5 (1982), 8–13. Djaballah is professor of biblical studies and dean of the Faculté de Théologie Évangélique in Montreal and contributed a chapter on Amyraldianism in *From Heaven He Came and Sought Her*.

136 P. Helm, "Calvin and the Covenant: Unity and Continuity," *Evangelical Quarterly* 55, no. 2 (April 1983): 65–81; J. B. Torrance, "The Incarnation and 'Limited Atonement,'" *Evangelical Quarterly* 55, no. 2 (April 1983): 83–94; T. Lane, "The Quest for the Historical Calvin," *Evangelical Quarterly* 55.2 (April 1983): 95–113; M. C. Bell, "Calvin and the Extent of the Atonement," *Evangelical Quarterly* 55.2 (April 1983): 115–23.

137 F. S. Leahy, "Calvin and the Extent of the Atonement," *Reformed Theological Journal* 8 (1992): 56. Leahy seriously errs when he writes: "All advocates of universal atonement, of whatever hue, hold that Christ died equally for all with the design of making the salvation of all possible, and nothing more." He overlooks all Hypothetical Universalists and Amyraldians within the Reformed tradition, not to mention the many non-Calvinists who see multiple intentions in the atonement.

universal atonement.[138] McGowan concluded, "This judgment stands."[139] But does it? The evidence suggests otherwise.

Contemporary Analysis of Calvin's Thought on the Extent of the Atonement

Many Calvinists today lean heavily on Roger Nicole in defense of limited atonement.[140] In an unpublished paper, David Ponter refuted Nicole in the most substantive critique of which I am aware entitled "A Brief History of Deviant Calvinism."[141] Ponter is a librarian at Reformed Theological Seminary in Jackson, Mississippi, and hosts the research website www.calvinandcalvinism.com. I have essentially reproduced his critique in summary form below.[142]

One cannot discuss Calvin's view on the extent of the atonement without engaging Roger Nicole's arguments for Calvin's supposed commitment to limited atonement. After summarizing the history of the debate from Amyraut forward, Nicole addressed the arguments for the case that Calvin held to unlimited atonement, followed by arguments to the contrary. Probably the single most important point to note first is that those like Nicole who assert Calvin held to limited atonement admit that Calvin himself has no direct statement in his writings affirming limited atonement. Second, Nicole's approach to the question at hand is often to argue what he himself thinks key verses in the text mean rather than arguing from what Calvin directly said. Third, Nicole assumed a later Reformed Scholastic paradigm and then read Calvin wearing these glasses. For example, he assumed that unlimited atonement *ipso facto* entails an inefficacious atonement and a denial of perseverance, so Calvin could not adhere to a universal atonement. Logically, this begs the question and employs a false dilemma fallacy. The atonement is always efficacious for the elect and the elect always persevere.

Nicole discussed Calvin's interpretation of some Scriptures where he appears to take an unlimited reading. He attempted to explain Calvin's comments on passages such as John 1:29 by appealing to the intrinsic sufficiency of Christ's death. Here Nicole failed to define sufficiency and in fact is using it in its revised version of the later Scholastics and not as it was used by the early Reformers, including Calvin. Nicole argued that

138 W. Cunningham, *The Reformers and the Theology of the Reformation* (London: Banner of Truth: 1967), 395–96.

139 A. McGowan, *The Federal Theology of Thomas Boston (1676–1732)* (Edinburgh: Paternoster, 1997), 48–58.

140 R. Nicole, "John Calvin's View on the Extent of the Atonement," in *Articles on Calvin and Calvinism: An Elaboration of the Theology of John Calvin*, 14 vols., ed. Richard C. Gamble (New York: Garland, 1992), 8:119–47. This essay was also published earlier: R. Nicole, "John Calvin's View of the Extent of the Atonement," *Westminster Theological Journal* 47, no. 2 (Fall 1985): 197–225.

141 Available online at http://calvinandcalvinism.com/wp-content/uploads/2014/05/A-Brief-History-of-Deviant-Calvinism.pdf.

142 D. Ponter, "A Brief Reply to Roger Nicole's Article: 'John Calvin's View on the Extent of the Atonement,'" *Calvin and Calvinism*, July 25, 2008, http://calvinandcalvinism.com/?p=12462.

impetration and application are coextensive, hence the choice is between universalism and definite atonement. Jesus's intercession for those who are among the elect in John 17 cannot logically be construed to indicate that his death was only for the elect. To do so is reductionistic and minimalistic.

Nicole thought Calvin missed "a good opportunity to assert definite atonement" in his remarks on Isa 53:12. He attempted to soften Calvin's statements to be a reference to "all kinds of men" rather than all people without exception. But Nicole has no answer for Calvin's universalizing statements with respect to Isa 53:12. True, Calvin does interpret some of the extent passages in the New Testament to mean "all sorts of men," thus limiting the use of "all" to the elect. However, when Calvin does this in places such as 1 Tim 2:4, the context of his statements is God's election of certain individuals. In other places, such as Isaiah 53 and John 1:29, Calvin does not limit the extent of the atonement to the elect. Nicole ignored this distinction.

Nicole proceeded to offer counterarguments in an effort to establish Calvin's commitment to limited atonement. The first two arguments attempt to pit election against atonement in the unlimited position and then draw the conclusion that Calvin would not "open himself to such self-contradiction."[143] Nicole failed to recognize that Calvin is operating from the traditional understanding of the sufficient/efficient formula. Christ died for all with respect to the sufficiency but only for the elect with respect to the efficiency. This dual intentionality was common among the first generation of Reformers but was obscured by the Scholastics in later generations. All first-generation Reformers affirm elements of universalism and particularism in the design of the atonement.

Nicole argued that Christ has merited repentance and faith for the elect. But even if true, this has no bearing on the extent of the atonement. Nicole's fourth argument attempted to make the accomplishment and application of the atonement coextensive. This is, however, a failure to recognize Calvin's acceptance of the sufficient/efficient formula and an attempt to frame the discussion according to the revision of the formula in later Reformed theology.

Nicole's fifth argument flowed out of the preceding argument. Calvin conjoined Christ's priestly work of substitution with his work of intercession. Since the intercession is limited to the elect, so is the oblation. It is interesting that Calvin himself did not make this argument. Furthermore, Calvin's reference to those who have received the benefits of the atonement as being the recipients of Christ's intercession in no way precludes an unlimited atonement. It assumes the work of atonement and the work of intercession are coextensive, which is an innovation by later Reformed theology. Logically, Nicole's argument proceeds as follows:

143 R. Nicole, "John Calvin's View of the Extent of the Atonement," *Westminster Theological Journal* 47, no. 2 (Fall 1985): 220.

Premise 1: Christ intercedes only for the elect.
Premise 2: Christ's intercession and atonement are coextensive.
Conclusion: Christ only atoned for the elect.

The problem is with premise 2. It remains unproven. This is merely Nicole's assumption, which he imposes on Calvin.

Nicole's sixth argument trades on Calvin's interpretation of texts such as 1 Tim 2:4 and Titus 2:13 where the word "all" is taken to mean "all classes of men." In John 1:29 and 1 John 2:2, the word "world" is understood to indicate John's attempt to transcend a nationalistic Jewish bias. Nicole pressed the point that those who argue for universal atonement never interpret these passages in this fashion. Thus, Calvin did not hold to universal atonement. The problem for Nicole here is that Calvin does take a universal reading of some of the extent passages that he himself cites. Furthermore, so do a number of Calvinists, such as John Davenant, Charles Hodge, Robert Dabney, and W. G. T. Shedd. Nicole's argument can be turned against him. For example, if Calvin held to limited atonement, why did he interpret some of the extent passages in an unlimited way? It is simply not possible to read Calvin's statements on John 1:29 as being limited to the elect. For Calvin, John is not merely contrasting "the world" against "the Jews." Rather, Calvin viewed the Jews as a subset of the world. Jesus bore the sins of the world, which includes the Jews. Nicole has engaged in a category fallacy.

Nicole's seventh argument is that those statements by Calvin that appear to support a universal atonement are actually intended to speak to the indiscriminate gospel call. Nicole failed to apprehend that Calvin's understanding of the atonement is that it is accomplished for all, and this is the ground for it being offered to all. Nicole's eighth argument is especially specious: since Scripture limits the atonement to the elect, Calvin held to limited atonement. Some texts do indeed speak of Christ's atonement for his "sheep" or the "church." But to infer from this that Christ did not die for others is to invoke the negative inference fallacy.

Nicole's ninth argument is Calvin's engagement with Heshusius. Since this is addressed above, we need not rehearse the issue here. Nicole's tenth argument is an appeal to the commercial language of Owen and the later Reformed Scholastics coupled with the biblical language of propitiation, reconciliation, and redemption, which indicates a completed transaction that "transforms the relationship between God and the sinner."[144] But this fails to reflect the fact that the application of the atonement is conditioned on repentance and faith. The work of Christ is accomplished for all and offered to all on the condition of faith. No one is saved by the accomplishment of the atone-

144 Ibid., 223.

ment alone apart from faith, as many Calvinists have rightly pointed out (e.g., Charles Hodge, Dabney, Shedd).

Nicole's eleventh argument is the familiar double-payment argument: if Christ died for the sins of all men as their substitute, then God cannot condemn anyone to hell. Several problems ensue for Nicole. First, notice that Calvin himself does not employ this argument. Second, two theological models of penal substitution can be discerned in Reformed orthodoxy. Third, Nicole assumed a flawed commercial understanding of the atonement. Fourth, he created a false dilemma fallacy: either the atonement is a penal substitution or it is not. If it is, then all men must be saved according to the commercial model or else double payment ensues. But instead of being an either/or situation, it is both/and. Christ substituted himself for all, thus satisfying the law and removing the legal obstacles such that God is objectively reconciled to mankind. However, repentance and faith are necessary for the application of the atonement and for subjective reconciliation to take place (2 Cor 5:19–21).

Nicole's twelfth argument is that unlimited atonement fractures the Trinitarian harmony in the work of redemption, thus Calvin could not have held to limited atonement. Again, this interprets Calvin from a post-Calvin Federalism and fails to take into account Calvin's dualistic understanding of God's will as secret (decretal) and revealed. Nicole also failed to account for the fact that Calvinists such as Davenant, Amyraut, Baxter, and many others like them who affirmed unlimited atonement did so with the understanding that the sufficiency/efficiency formula did not impair the harmonious work of the Trinity in salvation.

Nicole's final argument is that it is not possible for Beza to single-handedly shift the Reformed movement from universal atonement to limited atonement. Of course, no one suggested that Beza single-handedly caused such a shift. Nicole's argument failed to take into account the rise of Federalism, Beza's supralapsarianism, and the general impact of speculative decretalism on Reformed theology. Men such as Amandus Polanus played a significant role in theological development at the time. The rise of Socinianism, Arminianism, and Amyraldianism served to galvanize the majority of Calvinists around limited atonement early in the seventeenth century, but even then there were many Calvinists who rejected this approach and affirmed an unlimited atonement.

In conclusion, Nicole erred by claiming that "all" for Calvin always signified all classes of men and not all men without exception. Nicole failed to take into account Calvin's statements on Isaiah 53 and 2 Pet 3:9, where Calvin explicitly said "all" means elect and non-elect. Thus, Nicole committed two key logical fallacies: (1) he isolated Calvin from his own exegetical and theological tradition and then retrojected a later, more developed, tradition on Calvin; and (2) he isolated Calvin's statements from their context and artificially groups them with other statements of like kind to argue his case. In 1 Tim 2:1–6, Calvin does not follow the trajectory of arguing that "all" becomes "all kinds," which is then transmuted into the meaning "some of all kinds," which is the common approach of later Calvinists.

Ponter also authored a two-part article on Calvin's view of the extent of the atonement that breaks new ground in the debate.[145] Ponter brings to the table new historical data regarding terminology in Calvin and other first-generation Reformers regarding "redeemed souls perishing." Building on G. Michael Thomas, Ponter brings the doctrine of universal vicarious satisfaction directly to bear on Calvin, answering the question whether such satisfaction entails a limited atonement in the minds of the early Reformers.

Ponter showed how Calvin's juxtaposition of individuals with classes explains his real intent: not individuals of nations but nations of individuals. He noted how Calvin conflated John 3:16 with Rom 8:32 in a way that demonstrates his adherence to unlimited atonement. Ponter demonstrates how, for Calvin, the "act" of laying down a price for a person redeemed that person. Ponter compared statements in Latin from Musculus and Zanchi, both of whom held to unlimited atonement, with similar statements in Calvin, demonstrating continuity.

Finally, Ponter's article blows the lid off all attempts to suggest that Amyraut was somehow the deviant, drunk uncle who showed up at the family picnic and compromised the "true" Reformed doctrine of limited atonement.

Ponter's article is initially a response to Tom Nettles's chapter "John Calvin's Understanding of the Death of Christ" in *Whomever He Wills*,[146] a book written in direct response to *Whosoever Will: A Biblical-Theological Critique of Five-Point Calvinism*.[147] Ponter noted that Nettles's approach is to take the universal statements in Calvin and suggest that Calvin merely meant to speak "from the human perspective" and did not intend to state what he actually believed concerning the extent question.[148]

Ponter's purpose is threefold: to show that (1) Nettles has treated Calvin ahistorically and therefore inaccurately, (2) Nettles has misinterpreted critical comments from Calvin, and (3) Nettles has treated Calvin illogically in the conclusions he draws from Calvin's statements.[149]

Ponter followed an inductive or abductive method with the data. He surveyed not only the writings of Calvin but those of his Reformed contemporaries.

---

145 D. Ponter, "Review Essay (Part One): John Calvin on the Death of Christ and the Reformation's Forgotten Doctrine of Universal Vicarious Satisfaction: A Review and Critique of Tom Nettles' Chapter in *Whomever He Wills*," *Southwestern Journal of Theology* 55.1 (Fall 2012): 138–58; "Review Essay (Part Two): John Calvin on the Death of Christ and the Reformation's Forgotten Doctrine of Universal Vicarious Satisfaction: A Review and Critique of Tom Nettles' Chapter in *Whomever He Wills*," *Southwestern Journal of Theology* 55.2 (Spring 2013): 252–70.

146 T. Nettles, "John Calvin's Understanding of the Death of Christ," in *Whomever He Wills: A Surprising Display of Sovereign Mercy*, ed. M. Barrett and T. Nettles (Cape Coral, FL: Founders, 2012), 293–315.

147 D. L. Allen and S. Lemke, eds., *Whosoever Will: A Biblical-Theological Critique of Five-Point Calvinism* (Nashville: B&H Academic, 2010).

148 Ponter, "Review Essay (Part One)," 139.

149 Ibid.

> Rather than fixate on the outdated "Calvin versus the Calvinist" thesis, or rather than treat Calvin in isolation, we should seek to identify and understand the early Reformation doctrine of unlimited vicarious satisfaction. . . . Then the question becomes, "Does the data from Calvin fit this model of satisfaction, rather than the later model as defined by TULIP or strict five-point Calvinist orthodoxy?"[150]

Ponter correctly noted that Nettles's central argument is that salvation is effectually given to all for whom Christ died. Ponter demonstrates that this assertion cannot be proven from Calvin since he never uses this kind of reasoning or argumentation.[151]

Nettles's unstated assumption is there is only one doctrine of substitution as defined by five-point Calvinist orthodoxy. Yet the problem for Nettles is the undeniable fact that Calvin's Reformed contemporaries understood and advocated the position that Christ bore the sins of all men. Ponter demonstrated this beyond any doubt from Zwingli, Bullinger, Musculus, Luther, Gwalther, Juan De Valdes, as well as the English Reformers Hooper and Cranmer.[152]

In Calvin's sermons on Deuteronomy, he rehearsed a hypothetical speech Christ might say to an unbeliever on the final judgment day. Christ suffers the curse of the law for a person who is ultimately unsaved. Calvin spoke of "intentionality" in Christ's death for this unsaved person on the final day of judgment, that he "might be blessed by my grace." Ponter stated: "If we were to assume that Calvin held to the 'substitutionary' satisfaction defined by Nettles and others, such hypothetical language could never have been sensible to Calvin."[153]

Nettles erroneously conflated Calvin's concept of the sufficiency/efficiency of the atonement with that of John Owen's later doctrine of sufficiency. He failed to take notice of the revision of the original Lombardian sufficiency/efficiency formula by Owen and others, as noted above. To read this revision back into Calvin is, as Ponter noted, anachronistic.[154]

Ponter addressed Nettles's proposal that when Calvin spoke of universal satisfaction for sins, he merely meant to describe Christ's death for sins from the human point of view such that no individual is to be *a priori* excluded from redemption. All people are potential candidates for salvation even though Christ only died for the sins of the elect.[155]

Ponter endeavored to show how Calvin's comments on 2 Pet 2:1 and Jude 4 invalidated Nettles's "point-of-view" hermeneutic for Calvin. Ponter asked the pertinent

150 Ibid., 140.
151 Ibid., 141.
152 Ibid., 141–43.
153 Ibid., 144–45.
154 Ibid., 148.
155 Ibid., 151–52.

question: "If we assume for the moment that Calvin really did hold to limited redemption, on what basis would it have been sensible for him to imagine that known apostates . . . had been redeemed by Christ?"[156]

Ponter referenced other statements from Calvin demonstrating that final apostates have been "bought," "ransomed," and "redeemed" by Christ's death. This language of "redeemed souls perishing" is not limited to Calvin but is found in Gwalther, Luther, Tyndale, and others.[157] In addition, Ponter produced several Calvin quotations demonstrating that Calvin spoke of Christ shedding his blood "for the whole world."[158]

Calvin himself identified the "many" of Matt 20:28; Mark 14:24; and Heb 9:28 as equivalent to the "all" in Rom 5:15. Nettles's phenomenological reading of Rom 5:15 "is impossible," according to Ponter.[159]

Ponter concluded that Calvin's language "mirrors the language of his contemporaries," who held to an unlimited satisfaction for sins and thus universal redemption (atonement). How could the same language for Calvin mean something different than his contemporaries? The historical data provides no evidence that such is the case. "It appears that what drives the conclusions of Helm, Rainbow, and now Nettles, is not the actual historical texts understood in terms of their own historical contexts, but their own systematic theological pre-commitments. They approach Calvin assuming that he shares their own *a priori* theological presuppositions."[160]

In part two of his article, Ponter considered the "price of redemption" terminology in Calvin's writings as being "cancelled" or "abolished" such that those for whom the redemptive price was given perish in hell. He cited Calvin's commentary on Gal 2:20 and his sermons on Job and Timothy. This terminology of a "price of redemption for all men" occurs likewise in Musculus, Bullinger, and Zwingli. From this evidence, Ponter concluded: "It was only post-Calvin that the idea of Christ properly or actually laying down a redemptive price for all men was denied."[161]

What was Calvin's concept of "all," "classes" of men, and "world" from 1 Tim 2:4–6? For Nettles, Calvin's use of "all" would have no real quantitative extension in the sense that Christ literally died for the sins of all. Ponter challenged this and submitted direct statements from Calvin on 1 Tim 2:4–6 and elsewhere to show otherwise.

> When we read Calvin's language of classes and orders, we must ask ourselves "Did Calvin effectively mean *some men of all kinds*, or did he mean *all men of*

156 Ibid., 152.
157 Ibid., 153–54.
158 Ibid., 156.
159 Ibid.
160 Ibid., 158.
161 Ibid. (Part Two), 251–55.

> *every kind*?" The idea that Paul, and by extension Calvin, meant some of all kinds of men dates back to Augustine.[162]

Ponter showed that Augustine was speaking about God's hidden or decretive will in 1 Tim 2:4–6, while Calvin was speaking of God's revealed will. For Calvin, the phrase "all people" or "all nations" is distributed to mean all men of all people and all nations. Note in context Calvin's reference to all men being God's "image bearers."

Ponter provided other examples from Calvin's writings where the will of God is not to be limited to any single individual to the exclusion of others but rather to be extended to all people in a given class.

> In each case, when Calvin refers to "all," he means all people of every kind or class or order. "All" for Calvin functions in this inclusive quantitative and qualitative sense. Furthermore, there are other examples in Calvin where he states that God desires the salvation of the whole human race, and where "world" means "all mankind."

The restrictive reading of Calvin by Nettles and others actually reverses what Calvin is saying.[163]

Ponter considered Nettles's assertion (assumption) that for Calvin Christ's expiation and intercession refer to the same group of people—namely, the elect, and hence supported limited atonement. Ponter noted that no quotation of Calvin proffered by Nettles indicated such. Ponter wondered whether Nettles was engaging in the logical fallacy known as "affirming the consequent: If A then B, B therefore A." There is no necessary reason to believe that Calvin taught Christ's intercession limits the extent of the expiation on the cross. Ponter cited Augustine Marlorate, a French Reformer, who cited Musculus affirming Christ died for all men but limited the intercession to those who believe.[164]

Nettles argued that salvation is infallibly applied to all for whom it was purchased. Ponter countered that there is no evidence of this line of reasoning in Calvin. In Rom 8:32 Nettles has confused what Paul has said to and about believers and broadened statements into an abstraction concerning all the "elect." Nettles's *modus tollens* argument simply does not follow and merely begs the question at hand. Paul's *a fortiori* argument is limited in its conclusions and application to believers. There is no argument for limited atonement here.[165]

---

162 Ibid., 257–58.
163 Ibid., 259–60.
164 Ibid., 260–61.
165 Ibid., 262.

Ponter quoted Calvin's comments in his *Sermons on Timothy* to demonstrate that Calvin did not believe that the "purchased blessings of salvation are infallibly applied to any and all for whom they were obtained."[166]

Ponter concluded his two-part review essay with a summary of each of Nettles's arguments and how counter-factual evidence negates those arguments. "I would argue that there is no evidence in Calvin's writings which prove or entail the doctrine of a limited satisfaction for the sins of the elect alone."[167]

In one of the important, recent books on the subject of the extent of the atonement in Reformed thought, G. Michael Thomas pointed out that "Calvin's freedom in presenting redemption in universal terms is undeniable, and is grounded in the person of Christ, in that, through his incarnation, Christ bears a relation to the whole human race."[168] Although Calvin can speak of the atonement as limited in certain respects, he can also speak of it in ways where "an unrestricted universality must be intended."[169]

> In addition to such clear statements, it is significant that in his "Antidote to the Acts of the Council of Trent" Calvin wrote that he "would not touch" the assertion of the Council's Sixth Session that "Though He died for all, all do not receive the benefit of His death." Furthermore, he showed no hesitation in repeating, without modification, the biblical statements about the possibility of some for whom Christ died perishing.[170]

Thomas disputed Muller's claim "that on this basis Calvin spoke of a universal expiation and propitiation, but of a particular redemption and reconciliation" as a claim that "cannot be substantiated, for the terminology of redemption and reconciliation is often applied in a universal context, for example on Mark 10:45."[171] Here Calvin stated:

> He declares that His life was the price of our redemption. From this it follows that our reconciliation with God is free. . . . "Many" is used, not for a definite number, but for a large number. . . . And this is its meaning also in Rom 5:15, where Paul is not talking of a part of mankind but of the whole human race.[172]

166 Ibid., 263–64.
167 Ibid., 268–70.
168 Thomas, *Extent*, 27.
169 Ibid.
170 Ibid., 28. See Calvin, "Acts of the Council of Trent, with the Antidote," in *Tracts and Treatise*, 3 vols., trans. E. Beveridge (Grand Rapids, MI: Eerdmans, 1958), 3:93, 109. See also *Sermons on Isaiah*, 126, "For how many unbelievers do we see perishing, for whom the death and passion of our Lord Jesus Christ serves only for more severe condemnation, because they trample underfoot His sacred blood and reject His grace offered to them?"
171 Ibid., 29–30.
172 J. Calvin, "Commentary on A Harmony of the Evangelists," in *Calvin's Commentaries*, 16:427.

Thomas agreed that Muller rightly detected both universal and particular aspects in Calvin's teaching on the atonement, yet he concluded "it is not possible to categorize Calvin's use of words in this respect, and he over-simplifies when he concludes that 'this distinction well fits what is loosely called "limited atonement" not only in Calvin's thought but in later Reformed theology.'"[173]

Calvin appeared

> willing to place the work of Christ in conjunction with the electing purpose of God, and so present the atonement as having a particular as well as universal aspect. . . . This double aspect is illustrated in the reference to "reconciliation . . . offered to all through him" and "the benefit . . . peculiar to the elect" in the above citation. Calvin's exposition of several crucial passages of Scripture brings these two facts to light repeatedly.[174]

Thomas made the crucial point:

> How is it that Calvin could teach limited and universal redemption in the same place? Only by appreciating that he viewed the atonement from two vantage points can this apparent confusion be understood. From the perspective of election, Christ died for "all sorts" but not all individuals. From the perspective of the promise of the gospel, he died for all the world, even for those who do not participate in the purchased benefit.[175]

Thomas's statement is not without its problems and needs careful unpacking. When he said "from the perspective of election, Christ died for 'all sorts' but not all individuals," he apparently means Christ's death is not *efficacious* (applied) to any but the elect. However, when Thomas said Calvin believed Christ "died for all the world," he (Thomas, and Calvin, too) must mean more than Christ died merely to bring common grace to the whole world. Thomas's point is that Calvin had a dualistic approach to the atonement, which was in line with the Lombardian formula—namely, that Christ died sufficiently for the whole world in the sense that he satisfied for the sins of the world but that Christ died efficaciously only for the elect (those who believe). This reading of Calvin's various statements on the atonement and its extent harmonizes all the data.

Those who advocate the position that Calvin taught limited atonement tend to deal deductively with the data. Based on Calvin's theology of election, they presume

173 Thomas, *Extent,* 30.
174 Ibid., 31.
175 Ibid., 33.

he must have held to limited atonement since universal atonement is purportedly inconsistent with election. Passages in Calvin that appear to teach universal atonement must be interpreted to mean something else than what they appear to mean on the surface. On the other hand, advocates for the position that Calvin taught an unlimited atonement tend to view the data inductively, as was the case with Davenant, Daillé, Ussher, Morison, and in more recent times Curt Daniel, David Ponter, and Paul Hartog.

One of the most significant but often overlooked treatments of Calvin's view of the extent of the atonement is found in Curt Daniel's dissertation "Hyper-Calvinism and John Gill."[176] Daniel cited dozens of quotations from Calvin's *Institutes*, commentaries, sermons, and letters demonstrating Calvin's adherence to unlimited atonement. He interacted with William Cunningham, Roger Nicole, Robert Letham, Paul Helm, and Jonathan Rainbow on the topic, all of whom argued that Calvin held to limited atonement. Daniel demonstrated quite well the occasional faulty logic and even historical errors made with respect to Calvin by these men.

William Cunningham, Robert Letham, and Paul Helm contended that Calvin did not speak to the subject of the extent of the atonement. William Cunningham's methodology is problematic. He first suggested Calvin does not address the subject, but then he said Calvin did not teach universalism. Finally, he concluded Calvin held to particularism.[177] Cunningham barely mentioned the many quotations of Calvin adduced by others. He dismissed the forty pages of quotations from Calvin adduced by Jean Daillé as "irrelevant and inconclusive."[178] When Cunningham contended that proof of Calvin's universalism cannot be derived from Calvin's writings, he merely demonstrated his own bias. Strangely, after all this, Cunningham cautioned against affirming conclusively that Calvin taught particularism.[179]

Cunningham noted one does not find in Calvin's writings "explicit statements as

---

176 Daniel, "Hyper-Calvinism and John Gill." See especially Appendix A, "Did John Calvin Teach Limited Atonement?," 777–828. For Daniel's listing of quotations of Calvin on the extent question, see pages 787–89. Roger Nicole said of Daniel's collection of Calvin quotations,

> This is by far the most extensive treatment of this topic I have ever seen. It provides more quotations of Calvin related to this precise issue than any previous writer; it discusses adequately and fairly the arguments advanced by those who have published materials in this area; it has extensive bibliographies of previous studies; it takes cognizance of three Aberdeen doctoral dissertations that were not available to me by Robert Letham, Robert Doyle, and M. Charles Bell.

See R. Nicole, "John Calvin's View of the Extent of the Atonement," *Westminster Theological Journal* 47, no. 2 (Fall 1985): 197–225.

177 See his *The Reformers and the Theology of the Reformation* (London: Banner of Truth, 1967), 395–402. A. A. Hodge, in his *The Atonement* (Philadelphia: Presbyterian Board of Publication, 1867), 347–429, argued much the same way as Cunningham.

178 Ibid., 395. Cunningham wrote of Daillé's *Apologia pro duabus Synodis*: "This work of nearly five hundred pages contains a listing of quotations from writers from the patristics through the mid-seventeenth century affirming universal atonement." Cunningham references Amyraut's *Eschantillon de la Doctrine de Calvin touchant la Praedestination* "as written to show Calvin supported his views about the extent of the atonement."

179 Ibid., 400–401.

to any limitation in the object of the atonement, or in the number of those for whom Christ died."[180] "But we think it is likewise true, that no sufficient evidence has been produced that Calvin believed in a universal or unlimited atonement."[181] Cunningham admitted the Lombardian formula was considered "sound and orthodox" for Calvin but argued Calvin never explained in what sense he affirmed it. Cunningham also acknowledged the modification of the formula by the later orthodox.[182]

Cunningham's support for Calvin's limitarian position is twofold. First, he argued Calvin "consistently, unhesitatingly, and explicitly" denied God's universal grace and love to all men in the sense that God desired or intended to save all. Cunningham smugly stated that this is "too evident to any one who has read his writings, to admit of doubt or to require proof."[183] This is a truly amazing statement in light of the clear evidence in Calvin's writings to the contrary. Cunningham is quite mistaken on this point. He compounded his error by asserting, "The doctrine of a universal atonement necessitates, in logical consistency, a denial of the Calvinistic doctrine of election."[184] This is also surprising given that Cunningham immediately admitted that Amyraut, Daillé, Davenant, and Baxter all affirmed both universal atonement and election. Nevertheless, Cunningham concluded on the supposed grounds of Calvin's denial of God's universal saving grace and love that we are warranted to infer that Calvin did not hold to universal atonement.[185]

Cunningham's second reason for concluding Calvin held to limited atonement is the limited interpretation he gave to certain key texts concerning the extent of the atonement. He specifically referenced 1 Tim 2:4 and 1 John 2:2 and the fact that many after Calvin who clearly affirmed limited atonement interpreted these texts in the same way. Cunningham failed to note that many Calvinists who interpret these passages in the same way as Calvin nevertheless reject limited atonement and affirm unlimited atonement.[186]

Unlike some limitarians who see nothing in it to support Calvin's unlimited view, Cunningham mentioned Calvin's *Antidote* to the earlier sessions of the Council of Trent, where he made no comment or argument against the fourth chapter of the sixth session, which contains an explicit statement that Christ died for all men. Cunningham rightly noted that Calvin overlooks this "not tacitly . . . but with the explicit statement—'*tertium et quartum caput non attingo*,' as if he found nothing there to

180 Ibid., 396.

181 Ibid.

182 Ibid., 397.

183 Ibid., 398. Cunningham's use of "or" is ambiguous. He confuses the issue by using "desired" and "intended" together. Most Calvinists today use "desire" for God's *revealed* will and reserve the stronger volitional term "intends" for God's *secret* or *efficacious* will, so that none of them would say God "intends" (in the sense of efficaciously *purposes*) the salvation of the non-elect, though they say God desires their salvation in his revealed will. The issue here is that, with respect to Calvin's view of God's *revealed* will, along with his view of God's general benevolence and general grace, Cunningham is misrepresenting him. What he says is not accurate because it is not qualified.

184 Ibid., 399.

185 Ibid.

186 See D. L. Allen, "The Atonement: Limited or Universal?," 82–83.

object to."[187] It seems unlikely that Calvin would have remained silent on this point if he did indeed affirm limited atonement.

Robert Letham concluded that Calvin was uncommitted on the question of the extent of the atonement. Letham's brief comments on Calvin in his two-volume PhD dissertation are not surprising given the theme of his work is the subject of assurance. Letham affirmed that universal atonement was the position of Luther and Zwingli but that particularism was introduced by Calvin and Bullinger—whom he suggested wavered on the issue—and then was taught explicitly by Beza, Peter Martyr, Bucer, and Zanchi. As we have demonstrated previously with Martyr and Bucer, and shall demonstrate in the case of Zanchi, all held to unlimited atonement. However, Letham's chronology is not entirely unfounded. If, as we will attempt to demonstrate below, Beza was the first to inject the concept of strict particularism into Reformed theology, then Letham's basic assessment is correct: the earliest Reformers held to unlimited atonement, and then the next generation began to move more toward limited atonement.[188]

However, the evidence suggests that Calvin himself was not uncommitted on the issue of the extent of the atonement. Bell noted, for example,

> Calvin's use of the term "all" becomes consistent when we bear in mind the relation between atonement and faith in his writings. In several places he maintains that while Christ's atonement is universal, the gift of saving faith is limited to the elect. This is precisely the situation in 1 John 2:2.[189]

Daniel pointed out that Letham argued Calvin made "ambiguous and contradictory statements" on the subject. Nevertheless, Letham assumed Calvin taught limited atonement.[190]

Paul Helm's argument and logic that Calvin held to limited atonement is especially problematic. He concluded: (1) Calvin did not teach universal atonement; (2) therefore, he can be said to teach limited atonement, even though Calvin does not explicitly say that he taught limited atonement. This is, of course, question begging and special pleading. Helm's methodology is faulty.[191] Helm furthermore concluded that John Owen explicitly taught what Calvin implicitly held: limited atonement.

Some have argued that Calvin actually changed his position from limited atonement to universal atonement.[192] As James Richards noted,

---

187 Cunningham, *The Reformers*, 401.

188 Letham, "Saving Faith and Assurance in Reformed Theology," 1:125–26; 2:62, 66–67. See also Daniel, "Hyper-Calvinism and John Gill," 514–16.

189 See Bell, "Calvin and the Extent of the Atonement," 118. Bell cited Calvin's commentary on Matt 15:13; the *Institutes* 3.3.21; and his commentary on Rom 10:16.

190 Daniel, "Hyper-Calvinism and John Gill," 780.

191 So noted by Daniel, Ibid., 779.

192 So A. H. Strong, *Systematic Theology* (Valley Forge, PA: Judson, 1907), 778. But as Daniel pointed out, this tends

> But whatever might have been his opinions in early life, his commentaries, which were the labors of his riper years, demonstrate in the most unequivocal manner that he received and taught the doctrine of a *general* or *universal* atonement. This is distinctly asserted by Dr. Watts, and several striking examples of his interpretation given.[193]

Lee Gatiss set his sights on R. T. Kendall's thesis concerning Calvin and concluded that Helm's response to Kendall is an adequate refutation. Though Kendall's thesis is overstated at points, his arguments concerning Calvin's adherence to universal atonement have been confirmed and strengthened by more recent treatments. Gatiss is correct to note there is no explicit statement in Calvin supporting limited atonement, though he himself considered Calvin's statements to be best interpreted along this line.[194]

Robert Peterson's latest edition of his *Calvin and the Atonement* is much more judicious on the subject in confessing uncertainty concerning Calvin's position.[195] He stated that some passages in Calvin's commentaries might be considered to favor limited atonement, "but the data is insubstantial." Peterson likewise is not persuaded by attempts to appeal to systematic themes in Calvin that would lend themselves toward limited atonement.[196]

Peterson is swayed by Nicole, Helm, and Rainbow to the extent that he thinks limited atonement harmonizes well with Calvin's soteriology. He nonetheless stated: "I am not persuaded that it is proper to claim Calvin as an advocate of particular redemption."[197] For Peterson, antinomy is unavoidable.

This represents a change in viewpoint by Peterson since his 1983 work. The key factor in this shift was Rainbow's 1986 dissertation on the subject (later published in 1990 as *The Will of God and the Cross*). Rainbow argued that Calvin agreed with his historical antecedents Augustine, Gottschalk, and Bucer (his contemporary) in advocating limited atonement, and thus stood within this "particularist tradition" from Augustine to Bucer.[198]

But as we have seen, there is no such tradition. Augustine did not hold to limited atonement and it seems unlikely Bucer did either. Peterson now considers limited

---

to ignore the fact that Calvin was frequently revising his *Institutes* and that evidence for universal atonement can be found not only in the *Institutes* but also in the commentaries and sermons (Daniel, "Hyper-Calvinism and John Gill," 783).

193 J. Richards, "On the Extent of the Atonement," in *Lectures on Mental Philosophy and Theology* (New York: M. W. Dodd, 1846), 308. Richards's "Dr. Watts" is a reference to Isaac Watts. See I. Watts, "The Ruin and Recovery of Mankind," in *The Works of the Reverend and Learned Isaac Watts, D.D.*, 6 vols. (New York: AMS, 1971), 6:151–54.

194 L. Gatiss, *For Us and for Our Salvation* (London: Latimer, 2012), 67–75.

195 Peterson, *Calvin and the Atonement*, 118.

196 Ibid., 117–18.

197 Ibid., 118–19.

198 Ibid., 119.

atonement was not a debated issue within Reformed circles until Beza. "The debate over the matter waiting until Moses Amyrald and John Cameron began promoting unlimited atonement and thereby precipitated responses from the defenders of reformed orthodoxy."[199] But Peterson runs into a problem with this line of thinking: G. Michael Thomas, among others, demonstrated that many, even most, of Calvin's early Reformed contemporaries clearly affirmed predestination, election, reprobation, and the like, and yet also did not affirm limited atonement.[200] The debate actually began around the time of Beza with the introduction of limited atonement, not the other way around. Peterson's appeal to antinomy in Calvin is problematic since Calvin himself does not speak in this fashion or even hint at such an idea.

Finally, Ponter critiqued Peterson's conclusion that limited satisfaction best fits Calvin's theology:

> Notwithstanding his own denial of reading paradigm(s) back into Calvin, Peterson is, in fact, doing exactly that. He reads back into Calvin a version of vicarious satisfaction which contains key theological contours which arose post-Calvin. Further, Calvin's particularistic language well fits the then contemporary theological paradigm of election and reprobation, existing alongside unlimited satisfaction.[201]

Paul Archibald's 1998 dissertation on Calvin's view on the extent of the atonement attempted to show there are only minor variations between Calvin and Beza on the subject, and whereas Beza was explicit in his advocacy of the limitarian view, Calvin can best be described as also affirming limited atonement.[202]

Archibald found antecedents to limited atonement and even limited atonement itself in Augustine, Gottschalk, some of the medieval scholastics, possibly in Luther, Bucer, Calvin, and Beza.[203] There are several historical missteps in this section. Augustine clearly taught an unlimited atonement, as we have demonstrated, though he interpreted some of the key passages in a limited fashion, such as 1 Tim 2:4–6. The Lombardian formula originally signified a universal atonement with respect to extent and a limited application only to the elect. As we have seen, the formula was revised in the late sixteenth and seventeenth centuries to fit the paradigm of limited atonement. Luther clearly taught an unlimited atonement, though he, as an Augustinian, interpreted some of the passages to

---

199 Ibid., 119–20.

200 G. Michael Thomas, *The Extent of the Atonement: A Dilemma for Reformed Theology from Calvin to the Consensus (1536–1675)* (Carlisle, UK: Paternoster, 1997).

201 D. Ponter, "Robert Peterson on Calvin and the Extent of the Atonement; Contra Jonathan Rainbow," *Calvin and Calvinism*, November 7, 2014, http://calvinandcalvinism.com/?p=15569.

202 P. Archibald, "A Comparative Study of John Calvin and Theodore Beza on the Doctrine of the Extent of the Atonement" (PhD diss., Westminster Theological Seminary, 1998).

203 Ibid., 9–46.

be referencing "all" in the sense of "all kinds of people." Bucer, as we have seen, most likely held to unlimited atonement, as did Calvin.

Much has happened in the field since Archibald's dissertation was written. Archibald's claim that Zwingli, Bullinger, Vermigli, and Zanchi did or may have held to limited atonement has been demonstrated by Richard Muller and others to be incorrect.

Archibald also misinterpreted Curt Daniel when he stated: "Daniel assumes that acceptance of the infinite worth of Christ's sacrifice implies redemptive universalism. On that basis, every Reformer would be a redemptive universalist, including Beza. Practically speaking, Daniel regards as particularists only those who completely rejected the common solution."[204]

It is significant that Archibald dealt first with the systematic theology of Calvin and Beza before dealing with the actual biblical texts as addressed by them. This is especially important with Calvin, since Archibald is forced to admit that Calvin did not address the subject directly. Here is an example of systematic theology preceding exegesis. This is a deductive approach to a subject that should be treated inductively first.[205]

Archibald first considered the evidence favoring Calvin as subscribing to an unlimited atonement.[206] He resorted to the usual arguments in an attempt to show that though Calvin made much use of universal language in atonement contexts, nevertheless, these can be explained by assuming Calvin is using such language to refer to the offer of salvation and not the atonement itself; sometimes "all" does not mean "all without exception," and so on. The tendentious nature of Archibald's arguments can be seen in numerous places, such as when he asserted that Calvin's comments on Gal 5:12 that appear to indicate his belief in unlimited atonement actually demonstrate that "Calvin is only saying what the Apostle *would* say about the imposters, the 'wolves,' if he were to take a man-centered point of view."[207]

Archibald considered evidence in Calvin that would seem to favor limited atonement.[208] Yet there is not a single, clear, unambiguous statement of limited atonement in Calvin that Archibald can point to. Furthermore, most of the references Archibald mentioned can best be explained as having to do with the application of the atonement to the limited group of the elect, not the actual extent of the atonement. Here Archibald falls prey to the negative inference fallacy by assuming that statements like "Christ died for his sheep" indicate that Christ died for only his sheep. Archibald does correctly note that, unlike Calvin, Beza's statements on the limited extent of the atonement are clear and precise.

Archibald's historical conclusion that the Reformers more or less contemporaneous

204 Ibid., 66. Citing Daniel, "Hyper-Calvinism and John Gill," 519.
205 Ibid., 118–272.
206 Ibid., 273–323.
207 Ibid., 315.
208 Ibid., 323–53.

with Calvin and Beza held to limited atonement is simply incorrect, especially with respect to Calvin, and would be correct only for those contemporaries of Beza toward the end of the sixteenth century. Also incorrect is that Beza's writings indicate he held to limited atonement prior to Calvin's death.[209]

Kevin Kennedy's *Union with Christ and the Extent of the Atonement in Calvin* is another significant work advocating Calvin taught universal atonement. Kennedy demonstrated that the concept of union with Christ is central though not necessarily programmatic to Calvin's soteriology.[210] The question is often raised by particularists: How can the atonement be substitutionary for those who don't actually receive the benefits of Christ's death? Calvin's concept of union with Christ is the key to answering this question, according to Kennedy. For Calvin, union with Christ is "the effectual event in the actual application of our salvation."[211]

The elect and the reprobate are separated not at the point of the cross but at the point of union with Christ. Trevor Hart took a similar tack earlier:

> When grace is interpreted from a Christological perspective, being seen not as some *tertium quid* of external divine decree or an infused substance, but rather as the self-giving of God himself for us and to us in the person of Christ, the dilemma which has so long plagued Western Christianity is disposed of. For the question of whether "grace" is objective or subjective to the believer presupposes a framework in which the mediatory capacity of the Saviour is short-circuited. When it is realized that Jesus mediates not as some third party to the dispute, but as the one *in whose very persons* the two estranged parties are brought together and reconciled, then the focus of questioning must alter. For then we realize that the privilege which we are given is not restricted to the possession of "benefits" earned for us by some external transaction in which Christ is the main agent; but rather that we have been adopted into the relationship which the incarnate Son has with the Father in the Spirit, namely into the very Trinitarian life of God himself. This is ours by virtue of our union with Christ; apart from him we have and we are nothing.[212]

---

209 Ibid., 356–58.

210 T. L. Wenger, "The New Perspective on Calvin: Responding to Recent Calvin Interpretations," *Journal of the Evangelical Theological Society* 50, no. 2 (June 2007): 311–28, critiqued those who want to redefine the relationship of justification and sanctification in Calvin's thought and argue that Calvin subsumed all his soteriology under the rubric of union with Christ (311). He accused those who take this approach of questionable historiography, erratic collections of Calvin's own words, and "out-prooftext[ing]" the other, leading to futile stalemates (321). Kennedy escapes Wenger's critique because he does not attempt to subsume Calvin's soteriology under the single rubric of union with Christ.

211 K. Kennedy, *Union with Christ and the Extent of the Atonement in Calvin*, Studies in Biblical Literature 48 (New York: Peter Lang, 2002), 149.

212 T. Hart, "Humankind in Christ and Christ in Humankind: Salvation as Participation in Our Substitute in the Theology of John Calvin," *Scottish Journal of Theology* 42, no. 1 (April 1989): 84. Emphasis original.

Muller is rather tendentious in his critique of Kennedy when he chided him for failing to properly handle the terminology "limited atonement," given the fact that Kennedy is actually clear on what he means by the term "limited atonement"—namely, a limited substitution of sin on the cross such that only the sins of the elect were imputed to Christ when he died on the cross.[213]

Kennedy's "Hermeneutical Discontinuity between Calvin and Later Calvinism" demonstrated that Calvin's interpretation of biblical passages related to the extent question differed significantly from later Reformed tradition.[214] Calvin operated from a different hermeneutic from what would come to be entrenched in later Reformed theology. Kennedy showed how Calvin's discussion of the passages that state Christ died for the "many" indicate Calvin interpreted "many" to mean "all."

Calvin does not always interpret some extent passages that employ "all" to mean "all without distinction" rather than "all without exception," as is the case with later Reformed theology. Since many post-Calvin and modern interpreters of Calvin find some similarity in his treatment of some of the "all" passages with those arguing for limited atonement in the later tradition, this is viewed as evidence Calvin held to limited atonement. Kennedy showed the fallacy of such reasoning. Kennedy's work provides additional theological support for the position that Calvin affirmed universal atonement.

Paul Hartog is a professor at Faith Baptist Bible College and Theological Seminary in Ankeny, Iowa. His *A Word for the World: Calvin on the Extent of the Atonement* is a stout argument that Calvin affirmed unlimited atonement.[215]

Hartog listed and summarized the four general approaches that are usually taken with respect to Calvin's view of extent.

1. Calvin believed in limited atonement, though he did not emphasize it specifically. John Murray, Jonathan Rainbow, Roger Nicole, Frederick Leahy, Paul Helm, William Cunningham, Henri Blocher, and W. Robert Godfrey are examples of scholars who fall into this category.
2. Calvin held a form of unlimited atonement along with particular election. In this group would be a number of post-Reformation scholars such as John Davenant, Amyraut, Jean Daillé, Bishop Ussher, and Richard Baxter, along with modern scholars such as R. T. Kendall, Alan Clifford, Charles Bell, Curt Daniel, Kevin Kennedy, and David Ponter.

213 Muller, *Calvin and the Reformed Tradition*, 73, 75. Muller is unclear on the nature of the sufficiency of Christ's atonement since he does not acknowledge the distinction between intrinsic and extrinsic sufficiency nor clarify the ambiguity in his own use of the term.

214 K. Kennedy, "Hermeneutical Discontinuity between Calvin and Later Calvinism," *Scottish Journal of Theology* 64, no. 3 (August 2011): 299–312.

215 P. Hartog, *A Word for the World: Calvin on the Extent of the Atonement* (Schaumburg, IL: Regular Baptist, 2009). See also his forthcoming revision, *Calvin on Christ's Death: A Word for the World.*

3. Calvin's view cannot be determined due to the ambiguity of the evidence. G. Michael Thomas, Robert Peterson, and Hans Boersma fit into this category.
4. Calvin espoused neither limited nor unlimited atonement but adhered to the Lombardian formula, which, according to Hartog, following Rouwendal, left the question open-ended.[216]

This categorization is helpful, though it does appear that the fourth general approach is not much different from the third.

Hartog discussed the complex structure of Calvin's theology around twelve issues in chapter 3.[217]

1. All people will not ultimately be saved.
2. Christ offers salvation to all indiscriminately.
3. Not everyone believes the gospel because not everyone is efficaciously drawn by the Holy Spirit.
4. Unconditional election distinguishes those efficaciously called from those not so called.
5. People do not experience salvation prior to their belief.
6. Calvin coordinated a universal provision in the death of Christ with the general call of the gospel. Here Hartog cited statements from Calvin's *Institutes*, commentaries, sermons, and other writings in support. For example, Calvin stated it is "incontestable that Christ came for the expiation of the sins of the whole world."[218] Calvin said in his commentary on Col 1:14: "This redemption was procured by the blood of Christ, for by the sacrifice of His death all the sins of the world have been expiated."[219] According to Calvin, Christ suffered "for the redemption of the whole world."[220] Calvin stated Jesus was "sent to be the Redeemer of the human race" and was "burdened with the sins of the world."[221] Hartog appeals to several other Calvin quotations as proof of this point.
7. Hartog argued that, for Calvin, the universal provision of Christ in the universal offer of the gospel is important to the elect themselves. The Holy Spirit applies the work of Christ through the preaching of the universal gospel promises, which are grounded in a universal provision.[222]

---

216 Ibid., 9–18.

217 Ibid., 19–35.

218 Ibid., 23. Citing Calvin's *Concerning the Eternal Predestination*, 148.

219 Ibid. Citing Calvin, *Epistle of Paul the Apostle to the Galatians, Ephesians, Philippians and Colossians*, 308.

220 Ibid. Citing Calvin, *Deity of Christ and Other Sermons*, 55.

221 Ibid. Citing Calvin, *Harmony of the Gospels*, 3:150–52.

222 Ibid., 24. See Calvin, *Sermons on Isaiah's Prophecy*, 117; and *A Harmony of the Gospels Matthew, Mark and Luke*, 1:56; and many other Calvin references in Hartog, *A Word for the Worlds*, 25–26 nn. 49–57.

8. Hartog argued that Calvin sees ramifications of Christ's universal satisfaction for sins in the ministry of evangelism. Calvin appeals to evangelistic urgency "when we see people going to hell who have been created in the image of God and redeemed by the blood of our Lord Jesus Christ."[223]
9. Calvin affirmed that unbelievers despise the grace that is offered them.[224]
10. Calvin distinguished between God's revealed will in Scripture's universal promises and his secret will in his eternal decrees.[225]
11. Calvin believed Christ died "as a sufficient expiation and redemption for the sins of all humanity, and He died intentionally for the efficacious salvation of the elect."[226]
12. Calvin affirmed Trinitarian unity in the work of redemption.[227]

Hartog's twelve points are well supported primarily from Calvin's own writings but also from other secondary sources who affirm Calvin's commitment to a universal atonement.

Hartog's fourth chapter addressed evidences for limited atonement in Calvin's writings. Those who assert Calvin held to limited atonement put forth three key passages from his writings: Calvin's "Reply to Heshusius" in 1561, his commentary on 1 John 2:2, and his commentary on 1 Tim 2:4.[228]

Hartog replied to each of these, demonstrating that none of the three implicate Calvin as clearly asserting limited atonement. Hartog carefully looked at the context of each, along with secondary literature that has answered the arguments.

Hartog concluded that Calvin affirmed a form of universal atonement in tandem with personal, unconditional election. He rightly noted that Calvin should not be anachronistically labeled "Amyraldian," as he did not examine how Christ's universal satisfaction for sins worked within the framework of God's decretal will. Though Calvin spoke of the decretal will of God, he focused on God's revealed will in his commentaries and sermons.[229]

Richard Muller is considered by all as the doyen of sixteenth- and seventeenth-century Reformed historiography. His labor in this area of Reformed studies is the high-water mark of scholarship. Regarding the question of Calvin's view on the extent of the atonement, Muller is discreet. He comes ever so close to affirming that Calvin held to

223 Ibid., 26. Citing Calvin, *Sermons on the Acts of the Apostles, Chapters 1–7*, 87, along with other Calvin quotations.

224 Ibid., 29. Citing Calvin, *Sermons of M. John Calvin, on the Epistles of S. Paule to Timothie and Titus*, 177, and other Calvin quotations.

225 Ibid., 30–31. Citing Calvin, *Concerning the Eternal Predestination*, 106, and other Calvin quotations.

226 Ibid., 32. Citing Calvin, *Sermons on Isaiah's Prophecy*, 16, and other Calvin quotations.

227 Ibid., 33–34.

228 Ibid., 37–48.

229 Ibid., 49–61.

unlimited atonement with respect to the actual expiation of sin, but he never quite tips his hand, so far as I can tell, either way.

It is common among Reformed writers to suggest that there is little if any difference between Calvin's view of the extent of the atonement and later Reformed writers in the post-Reformation scholastic era. For example, Richard Muller has stated:

> Reformed theology also presented, both in the Reformation and in the era of orthodoxy, a doctrine of the mediatorial work of Christ that paralleled the Reformed emphases on salvation by grace alone and on divine election. Whereas Calvin, Bullinger, and others of their generation did not themselves make a major issue of the limitation of Christ's atoning work to the elect alone, later Reformed thinkers elaborated the point, particularly because of the controversies in which they became involved. There has been some scholarly disagreement on this point and sometimes a doctrinal wedge is driven between "Calvin" and the "Calvinists," as if Calvin taught a "universal atonement" and later Reformed writers taught a "limited atonement." Yet, when the terms and definitions are rightly sorted out, there is significant continuity in the Reformed tradition on this point.[230]

Muller's statement calls for clarification on several points. First, while he and others have shown that the "Calvin against the Calvinists" argument was flawed at a number of points,[231] this did not solve the question of Calvin's view of the extent of the atonement, nor does Muller claim it does. An inductive investigation of Calvin's writings on this subject compared with later Reformed authors, particularly those in the seventeenth century, reveals a development in Reformed thought on the question of the extent of the atonement, a fact that Muller himself conceded.[232]

Second, many have argued that Calvin and Bullinger did not "make a major issue of the limitation of Christ's atoning work to the elect alone" because they did not believe Christ's satisfaction for sins was limited only to the elect.

---

230 R. Muller, "John Calvin and Later Calvinism: The Identity of the Reformed Tradition," in *The Cambridge Companion to Reformation Theology*, ed. D. Bagchi and D. C. Steinmetz (New York: Cambridge University Press, 2005), 147.

231 R. Muller, "Calvin and the 'Calvinists': Assessing Continuities and Discontinuities between the Reformation and Orthodoxy," *Calvin Theological Journal* 30, no. 2 (November 1995): 345–75; idem, "Calvin and the 'Calvinists': Assessing Continuities and Discontinuities between the Reformation and Orthodoxy, Part II," *Calvin Theological Journal* 31, no. 1 (April 1996): 125–60. Muller delimits the period of Post-Reformation Reformed orthodoxy as 1565–1699 ("Calvin and the 'Calvinists,' Part II," 375).

232 Muller, "Calvin and the 'Calvinists,'" Part II, 137:

> And it ought also to be quite evident, after broad reading in Calvin's sermons and Old Testament commentaries, that presumed differences between his teaching, and that of Bullinger or that of the later Reformed federal tradition is not nearly as great as has sometimes been asserted. By way of further example, recent examination and reappraisal of the Synod of Dort has demonstrated an enormous variety of opinion and definition within the confessionally identifiable bounds of Reformed orthodoxy on the issues of "limited atonement."

Third, there is continuity, which Muller mentioned, but there is also significant discontinuity among Calvin, Bullinger, and other first-generation Reformers when compared to many within the orthodox period following the death of Calvin.

Fourth, Calvin and the first generation of Reformers believed the application of the atonement was designed and intended only for the elect, as did those in the subsequent Reformed tradition. In this sense, it was clearly limited. This is a part of the continuity in the tradition. However, when the terms and definitions are sorted out, there is a significant difference on the extent of the atonement between Calvin and Bullinger on the one hand and the later Reformed tradition as expressed by some at the Synod of Dort and later by John Owen.

Muller followed the previous long quotation with this paragraph:

> The terms "universal" and "limited atonement" do not represent the sixteenth- and seventeenth-century Reformed view or, for that matter, the view of its opponents. The issue was not over "atonement," but over the "satisfaction" made by Christ for sin and the debate was never over whether or not Christ's satisfaction was limited: all held it to be utterly sufficient to pay the price for all sin, and all held it to be effective or efficient only for those who were saved. The question concerned the identity of those saved and, therefore, the ground of the limitation—God's will or human choice. Thus, both Calvin and Bullinger taught the sufficiency of Christ's work of satisfaction for all sin as well as the universal preaching of the gospel and, at the same time, recognized the efficacy of Christ's work for the faithful alone and both taught that faith is the gift of God, made available to the elect only. The Reformed orthodox did teach the doctrine more clearly. In response to Arminius, they brought the traditional formula of sufficiency for all sin and efficiency for the elect alone to the forefront of their definition, where Calvin and Bullinger hardly mentioned it at all. The orthodox also more clearly connected the doctrine of election to the language of the limitation of the efficacy of Christ's death. This solution is presented in the Canons of Dort in concise formulas.[233]

Again, several comments are in order. First, Muller is correct that the specific terms "limited" and "universal" don't represent the usage of the Reformed in the sixteenth and seventeenth century. However, the concepts that those terms represent were very much debated, and not only by the Reformed against their opponents but by the Reformed among themselves, as is evidenced by what happened at Dort and beyond.

---

233 Muller, "John Calvin and Later Calvinism," 147. Also in Richard Muller, *After Calvin: Studies in the Development of a Theological Tradition*, Oxford Studies in Historical Theology (New York: Oxford University Press, 2003), 14.

Second, Muller is correct that the issue concerned the nature and extent of the satisfaction made by Christ for sin. He is incorrect, however, to suggest that the debate was "never over whether or not Christ's satisfaction was limited." From at least as early as the late sixteenth century, the debate was indeed over whether Christ satisfied for the sins of all people or only for the elect. Again, this debate was carried on not only between the Reformed and their opponents but among the Reformed themselves.

Third, when Muller stated that all held the death of Christ to be "utterly sufficient to pay the price for all sin," he is trading on the ambiguity of the word "sufficient." In the sense of an intrinsic sufficiency—namely, that the death of Christ could have been a satisfaction for the sins of all people had God intended it to be so—all in the Reformed tradition affirmed this. However, if by "sufficient" one means "extrinsic sufficiency"—namely, that the death of Christ was actually a sufficient price for all sin because it did, in fact, pay the price for the sins of all people—then again, from Dort (if not earlier) and well beyond Dort, the debate raged over this point *in the Reformed camp.*

Fourth, Muller stated that Calvin and Bullinger both "taught the sufficiency of Christ's work of satisfaction for all sin."[234] The question here is what Muller means by "sufficiency." Given that he followed this statement with a statement about the limited efficacy of the atonement, one would naturally assume he is speaking of an extrinsic sufficiency.

Perhaps Muller's most recent and significant work, *Calvin and the Reformed Tradition: On the Work of Christ and the Order of Salvation*, will clarify these issues. In chapter 3, he addressed the issue of Calvin's view on Christ's satisfaction for sins and limited atonement. Muller correctly pointed out the problem of anachronism in that the term "limited atonement" was not in use in Calvin's day. "In short, fixation on the anachronistic term 'limited atonement' and on the ancient but inherently vague language that 'Christ died for all people' or, by contrast, 'for the elect,' has led to fallacious argumentation on all sides of the issue."[235]

Muller continued:

> The problem for the doctrine of "limited atonement," therefore, lies in the fact that the sixteenth- and early seventeenth-century debate concerned neither the objective sacrificial death of Christ considered as the atonement or *expiatio* offered to God for the price of sin, upon which all parties in the debate were agreed, or the unlimited value, worth, merit, power, or "sufficiency" of the *satisfactio*, upon which all parties were also agreed, nor precisely, indeed,

234 Muller, "After Calvin," 14.

235 R. Muller, *Calvin and the Reformed Tradition: On the Work of Christ and the Order of Salvation* (Grand Rapids, MI: Baker, 2012), 73.

> the limited *efficacia* or *applicatio*, inasmuch as all parties to the debate denied universal salvation.[236]

Again, the question is what meaning Muller attaches to "sufficiency": intrinsic or extrinsic. As has been shown, the nature of the sufficiency of the atonement had been modified from the original meaning of the Lombardian formula early on in Reformed theology. Some among the Reformed redefined the issue of sufficiency to be intrinsic in nature rather than extrinsic. Davenant himself made much of this problem in his *Dissertation on the Death of Christ*. As far as I can tell, Muller nowhere acknowledges this revision of the Lombardian formula.

Muller is closer to the truth of the situation in this statement:

> The actual issues relevant to the debate were (1) the divine intention concerning the sufficiency of Christ's satisfaction, specifically, the relationship between the hypothetical, "if all would believe," and the infinite value or merit of Christ's death, namely, its "sufficiency" for all sin; (2) the divine intention concerning the effective application of salvation to individuals, specifically, the grounds of limitation of the efficiency or efficacy of Christ's work; and (3) the relationship between the value or sufficiency and efficiency of Christ's satisfaction and the universal or, more precisely, indiscriminate proclamation and call of the gospel.[237]

Though Muller did not mention it, David Pareaus (1548–1622) was advocating the position that God willed Christ to die for all as to the actual sufficiency and that he also willed that Christ die for the elect alone as to the efficiency (efficacy) of the atonement.[238] There is no difference in Pareaus's statement of double intentionality in the death of Christ and that found some forty years later in the teachings of John Cameron, Moise Amyraut, or John Davenant, or in Calvin approximately twenty-five years earlier.

Muller seems to come very near affirming that Calvin held to a universal satisfaction for sin in the following statement:

> Thus, given that Calvin did understand Christ's satisfaction as fully paying the price for sin, that is, as having an infinite or universal value or power, how did he frame the grounds of its limited application to or efficacy for believers? In addition, did Calvin offer an explanation of the divine intention underlying

236 Ibid., 76.

237 Ibid., 77. Muller has a helpful footnote outlining the seven distinct patterns of formulation of these issues among the early Reformed.

238 D. Pareus, *Commentary on the Heidelberg Catechism*, trans. G. W. Willard (1852; repr. Phillipsburg, NJ: P&R, 1985), 223.

> the sufficient satisfaction of Christ, specifically with regard to the question of whether God in some sense intended Christ's objective reconciliation for all sin to be such that if all believed all would be saved?[239]

Does Muller mean by "Calvin did understand Christ's satisfaction as fully paying the price for sin" that Calvin taught an unlimited substitution? Muller remains unclear here. Muller's statement is true, but it is true because of Calvin's underlying doctrine of universal imputation of sin to Christ. Calvin specifically stated that Christ suffered for the sins of all men. This is not limited atonement (a satisfaction only for the sins of the elect) as the concept was understood and taught by Beza, most of the delegates at Dort, John Owen, and many of the Puritans.

Muller's statement with reference to Calvin's view that "the universal offer here extends to all, elect and reprobate alike, and it is a valid offer given the full expiation (in itself sufficient) made for all sin—but the particularity of the application is limited by divine election"[240] certainly appears to affirm the point that Calvin held to an unlimited satisfaction for the sin of all people. It is difficult to invest his "full expiation (in itself sufficient) made for all sin" with any other meaning.

Muller's statement also confirms Calvin's view that the gospel is indeed an offer, and an offer to all, whether elect or reprobate. This understanding of Calvin on the offer of the gospel is confirmed by Beach, who one year before Muller's *Calvin and the Reformed Tradition*, surveyed the history of scholarship on Calvin's view of the free offer of the gospel and concluded from Calvin's writings "that Calvin freely employed the language of 'offer' and 'invitation,' terms that apply to all sinners. . . . Calvin linked the language of gospel-offer unto all sinners to the notion of God's love, favor, kindness, or goodness. . . . Calvin does not feel obliged to distinguish elect and reprobate sinners from one another."[241] However, Beach wrote his entire article without once referencing Calvin's view on the extent of the atonement, and it appears he presumed Calvin held to limited atonement.

Muller spoke of Calvin's use of the word "world" in his understanding of the divine intention in salvation as intent to actually save only the elect.

> In none of the contexts where he interprets "world" as indicating the universal human race, uniformly locked in sin and indiscriminately made aware of the promise of salvation, does Calvin indicate a divine intention to save all people or to send Christ to save all people—in fact, he consistently points toward the limit of salvation to the elect. Yet, as we have seen, Calvin also consistently

239 Muller, *Calvin and the Reformed Tradition*, 78.

240 Ibid., 93.

241 J. M. Beach, "Calvin's Treatment of the Offer of the Gospel and Divine Grace," *Mid-America Journal of Theology* 22 (2011): 67.

> points to Christ's death as full payment for the sins of the world, undergirding, as it were, the indiscriminate proclamation of the gospel.[242]

The operative word here is "intention." Of course Calvin, as did all the Reformed, taught a limited intention by divine decree to save only the elect. That is not in question. But this does not preclude that Calvin held that Christ was ordained to be the Savior of the world and that he was ordained to make a "full payment for the sins of the world," as Muller put it. This is the meaning of Calvin's universal language.

If Muller is denying Calvin believed God has a universal saving will, then he is incorrect on this point.[243] Muller seems unclear concerning Calvin's dualism with respect to intentionality. Calvin's understanding of intentionality does not appear to differ one bit from Davenant's understanding some fifty years later. Both held that God intended for the death of Christ to expiate the sins of all people but that he also intended to save only the elect.

Muller continued:

> Calvin taught that the value, virtue, or merit of Christ's work served as sufficient payment for the sins of all human beings, and provided the basis for the divine promise that all who believe will be saved, assuming that believers are recipients of God's grace and that unbelievers are "left without excuse"—as also did, granting different nuancings of the relation of divine intentionality to the value or suf-

---

242 Muller, *Calvin and the Reformed Tradition*, 82.

243 Although Muller has had many opportunities in his writings to affirm Calvin's belief that God desires the salvation of all men in the revealed will, the most he does is *imply* it. Noting Calvin's comments on Nah 1:3, Muller said that "frequently, God defers punishment and 'suspends' his anger against the ungodly in order to demonstrate his willingness to pardon sin—but neither does he tolerate the abuse of his patience" (R. Muller, *Post-Reformation Reformed Dogmatics: The Rise and Development of Reformed Orthodoxy, ca. 1520 to ca. 1725*, 4 vols. [Grand Rapids, MI: Baker, 2003], 3:583). Again, observing Calvin's comments on Jonah 4:2, Muller said,

> Indeed, God works toward the salvation of the human race at the very same time that he is angry at sin: the ground of our hope of mercy and pardon is, therefore, the "infinite and inexhaustible" goodness of God, who does not respond in anger to the constant provocation of sinful humanity. (ibid., 3:583–84)

On this text, Calvin himself clearly said, "This slowness to wrath proves that God provides for the salvation of mankind, even when he is provoked by their sins. Though miserable men provoke God daily against themselves, he yet continues to have a regard for their salvation" (John Calvin, *Commentaries on the Twelve Minor Prophets*, 14 vols., trans. John Owen [Grand Rapids, MI: Baker, 1984], 3:125). Calvin is abundantly clear in his exposition of 2 Pet 3:9: "So wonderful is his love towards mankind, that he would have them all to be saved, and is of his own self prepared to bestow salvation on the lost."

In another work Muller considered Calvin's exegesis of various texts related to mission and evangelism. Regarding 1 Tim 2:4, Muller noted that Calvin's sermon "offers an even more direct promotion of the universal task of preaching the gospel: 'that God would have all the world to be saved: to the end that as much as lies in us, we should also seek their salvation'" (R. Muller, "'To Grant this Grace to All People and Nations:' Calvin on Apostolicity and Mission," in *For God So Loved the World: Missiological Reflections in Honor of Roger S. Greenway*, ed. A. C. Leder [Belleville, Ontario: Essence, 2006], 225). J. H. Merle d'Aubigné correctly expounded Calvin's view of God's revealed will in 1 Tim 2:4 and *explicitly* says, "Calvin declares that it is the will of God that all men should be saved" (J. H. Merle d'Aubigné, *History of the Reformation in Europe in the Time of Calvin*, 8 vols., trans. W. L. B Cates [New York: Robert Carter & Brothers, 1877], 7:90–94).

> ficiency of Christ's death, Theodore Beza, the Canons of Dort, John Davenant, Pierre Du Moulin, Moise Amyraut, Francis Turretin, and a host of other often forgotten and sometimes maligned Reformed writers of the next two centuries, among them both particularists and hypothetical universalists.[244]

Again the key question here is, What does Muller mean by "sufficient"? It appears he has in mind an intrinsic sufficiency. That would be the only kind of sufficiency that Calvin, Beza, Davenant, Du Moulin, Amyraut, and Turretin could agree on. Here it is crucial to distinguish between intrinsic and extrinsic sufficiency. Beza, Du Moulin, and Turretin clearly did not hold to an extrinsic sufficiency in the death of Christ—there was no satisfaction made for the sins of the non-elect, hence Christ's death was only intrinsically sufficient to save all but not extrinsically sufficient to do so.

Muller again appeared to suggest that Calvin affirmed Christ satisfied for the sins of all people in the following statement:

> In the case of the doctrine of Christ's satisfaction for sin, since Christ paid the price of all sin and accomplished a redemption capable of saving the whole world, his benefits are clearly placed before, proffered, or offered to all who hear: what Calvin does not indicate is any sort of universalizing intentionality flowing from the sufficiency into the actual efficacy of this offering. Calvin's approach to the value, merit, or sufficiency of Christ's work assumed that it was unlimited and could therefore undergird the universality of the promise and the indiscriminate preaching of the gospel, but, equally so, his approach to the eternal divine will and intention to save in Christ, to the efficacy or application of Christ's work, and to Christ's own high-priestly intercession assumed its limitation to the elect. The conditional or hypothetical dimension of Calvin's doctrine, therefore, belongs to the revealed will of God in the promise of salvation to all who believe and not, clearly not, to an ultimate willing of God to save all on condition of belief.[245]

What Muller said is correct as far as it goes: Christ did pay the price for sin. However, Calvin said more than this. As the quotations from Calvin above demonstrate, Christ paid the price for sin *for the world*, not merely for sin that was sufficient for the world. Unless Muller meant to indicate an extrinsic sufficiency in Calvin, he has failed to represent him correctly.

Muller's statement that, for Calvin, Christ's high-priestly intercession "assumed its [Christ's work on the cross] limitation to the elect" is problematic. It is true that for

244 R. Muller, *Calvin and the Reformed Tradition*, 105.
245 Ibid., 105–6.

Calvin the expiation and intercession are inseparable, but in the sense that the expiation grounds the intercession, making the latter possible. But from this it cannot be assumed that Calvin reversed the logic and believed that limited intercession entailed or proved limited expiation. If this is Muller's approach, then it is logically fallacious.

Muller compared Davenant to Du Moulin:

> Du Moulin raises the issue of the extent of Christ's death and does so using the sufficiency-efficiency distinction of the Synod of Dort. The dispute is over the issue of whether Christ died for all human beings, specifically whether he died equally for the reprobate and for the elect. It is utterly true, Du Moulin argues, "that the death of Jesus Christ was a price sufficient to save all human beings if all human beings would believe in him."[246]

Notice several things about this statement. Muller said the dispute at Dort was over whether Christ died "equally" for the reprobate and the elect. This was the position of the Remonstrants, which Dort rejected. However, as will be demonstrated below in the discussion of Dort, though all the Reformed (before and after Dort, the Remonstrants excepted) denied Christ died "equally" for all; some of them, like Davenant, argued that Christ did in fact die for the sins of all in the sense of universal expiation but not with an "equal" will or intent to save all.

Second, Muller quoted Du Moulin as saying the death of Christ is "sufficient" to save all if all would believe. However, clearly here Du Moulin did *not* mean an extrinsic sufficiency since he clearly argued elsewhere that Christ died *only* for the elect. Hence, there was no price paid for the non-elect and the only sufficiency in the atonement that could be used in regard to the non-elect is an intrinsic sufficiency. Du Moulin, like all high Calvinists, collapsed the sufficiency into the efficiency and revised or reinterpreted the Lombardian formula.

In his *Anatomy of Arminianism*, Du Moulin clearly denied Hypothetical Universalism and employed all the standard arguments for a limited satisfaction such as double payment, expiation-intercession, and so on. Muller is simply mistaken when he asserted: "Davenant and Du Moulin were both proponents of the assumption that Christ's death paid for the sins of the whole world and was therefore sufficient to save all if all would believe—and therefore can be identified as hypothetical universalists."[247]

---

246 Ibid., 155.

247 Ibid., 156. Muller repeated the same erroneous claim about Du Moulin in "Beyond Hypothetical Universalism: Moïse Amyraut (1596–1664) on Faith, Reason, and Ethics," in *The Theology of the French Reformed Churches: From Henri IV to the Revocations of the Edict of Nantes*, ed. M. I. Klauber (Grand Rapids, MI: Reformation Heritage Books, 2014), 206. The label "Hypothetical Universalism" surfaced in the available documents for the first time in a letter written by Guillaume Rivet in July 1645 and was intended pejoratively. Rivet was likely the first to employ the term as a label for the theologians of Saumur, as noted by F. P. Van Stam, *The Controversy over the Theology of Saumur, 1635–1650* (Amsterdam: APA-Holland University Press, 1988), 277–78.

For all its benefits, Muller's work with respect to Calvin's views on the extent of the atonement is problematic on three fronts. First, he makes no attempt to define and distinguish the concept of sufficiency as intrinsic or extrinsic. Though it appears in most of his uses of the term, he means an extrinsic sufficiency. Second, he makes no mention of how Beza and others changed the Lombardian formula by the beginning of the seventeenth century. This appears to be a historical oversight on his part. Third, he sidesteps some of Calvin's clear statements about the universality of the satisfaction of Christ for sin, such as Calvin's sermon on 2 Tim 2:19 and his statement "it is not a little thing, that souls perish that have been purchased by the blood of Jesus Christ." Muller spoke of "vagueness" and "difficulty" in using such phrases as "for whom Christ died."[248] But there is no vagueness here. It is quite clear. For example, with respect to Calvin's comments on 1 Tim 2:4, it seems clear that Calvin was not interpreting the word "all" to mean "some of all kinds" but rather "every one of all kinds."

Muller's actual understanding of Calvin's view of the extent of the atonement remains unclear to me. It is difficult to discern whether he is in essential agreement with Cunningham, Nicole, Helm, Letham, and Rainbow who argue Calvin held to a limited satisfaction for sins (the elect only) or whether he has conceded Calvin held to a form of universal satisfaction for all sins (elect and non-elect). What does not seem unclear is Calvin's own position given all the data. It is growing ever more difficult to deny the notion that Calvin understood the atonement to be a universal satisfaction for sins.

One final interesting piece of evidence that may support the view that Calvin did not affirm limited atonement comes from the Bolsec controversy over predestination that occurred in Geneva from 1551 to 1555.[249] Jerome Bolsec, a Carmelite monk and doctor of theology in Paris, had come to Geneva in early 1551 to work as a physician. He immediately became a critic of Calvin's doctrine of predestination. At a regular Friday preaching event, one of the Genevan ministers preached on predestination. Apparently thinking Calvin was out of town, Bolsec rose to speak and criticized Calvin's doctrine of predestination with sharp invective. Calvin, who had apparently come in late to the meeting and was sitting in the back, was incensed, and stalwartly defended his views of predestination.

The city magistrates arrested Bolsec and placed him on trial. Letters were sent to Reformed leaders in Basel, Zurich, and Bern requesting advice on how to deal with the issue. The responses made it clear that these other Reformed leaders, including Bullinger,[250] did not share what they considered to be Calvin's extreme view of predes-

248 R. Muller, *Calvin and the Reformed Tradition*, 97.

249 For sources on this controversy, consult P. E. Hughes, ed. and trans., *The Register of the Company of Pastors in Geneva* (Grand Rapids, MI: Eerdmans, 1966), which includes full documentary evidence of the trial. The most detailed discussion of the controversy is P. C. Holtrop, *The Bolsec Controversy on Predestination from 1551–1555: The Statements of Jerome Bolsec, and the Responses of John Calvin, Theodore Beza, and Other Reformed Theologians*, 2 vols. (Lewiston, NY: Edwin Mellen, 1993).

250 C. P. Venema, "Heinrich Bullinger's Correspondence on Calvin's Doctrine of Predestination, 1551–1553," *The*

tination, and they thought that some of Bolsec's views were not entirely in error and counseled leniency with Bolsec. Calvin was deeply disappointed. Nevertheless, the trial proceeded and Bolsec was banished permanently from Geneva.

Of interest here is that nowhere during the controversy and trial is Bolsec ever challenged by Calvin for holding the view that the atonement was unlimited. If Calvin himself believed in limited atonement, and if he believed that unconditional election mandated limited atonement, he did not utilize the opportunity during the controversy and trial to say so.

Conclusion

In spite of the evidence supporting Calvin's understanding of the atonement as unlimited, debate within the Reformed community will no doubt continue. Some will agree with the trajectory articulated by Stephen Holmes: "There is no fundamental divergence between Calvin and the later tradition on the question of limited atonement; the later teaching is no more than a making explicit of what was implicit in Calvin's theology."[251] Gatiss likewise continues to press for Calvin's view of the atonement as limited.[252]

Others, such as Strehle, will continue to contend that Calvin's theological system as a whole actually demands an unlimited understanding of the atonement:

> The extent of the atonement is discovered, not in the intention of an event, but in the extent of the Savior's power. The atonement is unlimited because Christ is the Savior only by virtue of the fact that he has gained the lordship over all hostile forces within the divine economy.[253]

Strehle also contended that although Arminianism is "a ground for advocating unlimited atonement, it is not true that Calvinism's understanding of predestination is a ground for advocating limited atonement."[254]

Sometimes interpreters of Calvin appear more prone to evaluate his statements theologically than historically. The result is Calvin sometimes is interpreted more on the grounds of what he *could*, *would*, or *should* have said based on the interpreter's presuppositions rather than what he did in fact say. Calvin must be read within his own historical framework, not that of later Reformed orthodoxy.

Alister McGrath stated: "It may be stressed that at no point does Calvin himself

---

Sixteenth Century Journal 17 (Winter 1986): 435–50.

251 S. Holmes, *Listening to the Past: The Place of Tradition in Theology* (Carlisle, UK: Paternoster, 2002), 80.

252 Gatiss, *For Us and for Our Salvation*, 75.

253 S. Strehle, "The Extent of the Atonement within the Theological Systems of the Sixteenth and Seventeenth Centuries" (ThD diss., Dallas Theological Seminary, 1980), 92–93.

254 Ibid., 94–95. Calvin never engaged in speculation concerning God's decrees and rebuked those who did (*Institutes*, 3.23.5).

suggest that Christ died only for the elect."[255] Likewise Robert Godfrey rightly concluded that Calvin's writings did not explicitly speak of or affirm limited atonement.[256]

However, in light of the quotations assessed above by Calvin on the subject, one is hard pressed to agree with Godfrey that Nicole's conclusion on the question still seems accurate: "Definite atonement fits better than universal grace into the pattern of Calvin's teaching."[257] In fact, the more research done on Calvin's writings on the extent of the atonement, the more difficult it is to affirm the position that Calvin himself held to limited atonement.

Many Calvinists since the earliest days of the Reformation have argued that Calvin held to unlimited atonement. Among them are Davenant, Ussher, and Baxter in the seventeenth century, including many others since that time. When all the evidence is considered from Calvin's own writings, I do not see how one can assert that (1) Calvin held to limited atonement, (2) Calvin was unclear on his views on the extent of the atonement, or (3) Calvin stated no particular position on the extent of the atonement.

Calvin's own writings indicate he believed Christ died for the sins of all people but only those who believe in Christ actually receive the benefit of the atonement applied to them. For those Calvinists wishing to locate Calvin in the particularist camp who yet acknowledge that there are both universal and particular statements in his writings, it seems they are operating under the baseball rule "tie goes to the runner," and they are the runners.

High Calvinists have a vested interest in claiming Calvin for their view on the question of extent. Given Muller and others now argue that most, if not all, of the early Reformers held to a form of universal atonement, it is difficult to relinquish Calvin. If he falls into the universal category, then the thesis that Beza was essentially the first (excepting Gottschalk) to argue for limited atonement becomes even more probable, and there is a significant discontinuity between the first generation of Reformers and later generations on the specific issue of the extent of the atonement.

Curt Daniel's pointed statement may rankle some of his Calvinist cohorts, but it is difficult to deny: "If Calvin did not teach limited atonement, then those who do are not Calvinists on the subject of the extent of the atonement,"[258] though they are certainly within the bounds of Reformed confessional orthodoxy.

Benedictus Aretius (AD 1505–1574)

Aretius was a scientist, theologian, and professor of theology at Strasbourg from 1564 to 1574. The following quotation indicates his belief in unlimited atonement: "Christ

255 A. McGrath, *A Life of John Calvin: A Study in the Shaping of Western Culture* (Oxford: Blackwell, 1990), 216.

256 So noted by Godfrey, "Reformed Thought on the Extent of the Atonement," 137.

257 Ibid., 138.

258 Daniel, "Hyper-Calvinism and John Gill," 827.

died for all, yet, notwithstanding, all do not embrace the benefit of His death . . . they despise the offered grace."[259]

Girolamo Zanchi (AD 1516–1590)

Zanchi was an Italian Reformer, pastor, and professor. After teaching at Strasbourg, he departed to become the pastor of the Italian Protestant congregation in the Graubünden in Chiavenna. In 1568 he received a call to the University of Heidelberg, where he took over the chair of dogmatics formerly occupied by Ursinus. After the Electorate of the Palatinate returned to Lutheranism during the reign of Elector Ludwig VI, Zanchi moved with many other Reformed professors to the Reformed academy in Neustadt. He died during a return visit to Heidelberg.

Zanchi was a voluminous writer whose works include *Confession of the Christian Religion* and *Observation on the Divine Attributes*. He is perhaps best known for his *The Doctrine of Absolute Predestination*, which is still in publication today.[260]

A careful reading of Zanchi on the extent of the atonement reveals his essential dualism: Christ died for all according to the revealed will of God, but with respect to the purpose and intent of God, he died especially, and in that sense only, for the elect.

> 6. For *Christ*, according to the purpose of his Father, for the Elect only, that is, for those who according to the eternal Election should believe in him, was born, suffered and died, and rose again, and makes intercession at the right hand of his Father.[261]
>
> 25. Christ according to the purpose, of both his Father's and his own will, neither prayed nor suffered but for the Elect only: which is proved fully by many places of Scripture.[262]

With respect to Christ's advocacy for the elect, Zanchi stated:

> Christ is the Advocate of the elect only, & (that) of all which have been from the beginning of the world, and shall be to the end.

259 B. Aretius, *Commentarii in Epistolas D. Pauli ad Timoth. Ad Titus, & ad Philemonem* (Bern: Le Preux, 1580), 48–49. Also cited in Davenant, "Dissertation on the Death of Christ," 2:338.

260 Zanchi's *De Praedestinatione Sanctorum* has been used to assert Zanchi held to limited atonement. However, scholars on Zanchi's theology, such as Patrick J. O'Banion, have pointed out in various places that, although *Absolute Predestination* is Zanchi's most well-known work, it was not technically written by him. It is a translation and abridgement of a section of Zanchi's work completed by Augustus Toplady in the eighteenth century, and it is difficult to determine exactly how much of it is a translation of Zanchi and how much was added by Toplady. For those investigating Zanchi's own thought, this hybrid translation is problematic at best.

261 G. Zanchius, *Speculum Christianum or A Christian Survey for the Conscience* (London: George Eld, 1614), 336.

262 Ibid., 344.

> *Christ* also is the propitiation only for the sins of the elect of the whole word; therefore is he their advocate only. So the Church of *Smyrna* to all the parishes of Paul "saith, *Christ* did suffer for the salvation of all the World which are to be saved: but the Elect only are saved." So *Ambrose. To. 2. de fide ad Gratianum. lib. 4.c.1.* If thou does not believe, he descended not for thee, he suffered not for thee. Therefore he suffered only for the believers.
>
> The (world) is sometimes taken for the whole World, and all men, as well as Elect as Reprobate; sometime for the more special part, to wit the Elect; sometime for the worse part of the World, that is, the Reprobate. The Author also of the book *de vocatione Gentium. lib. 1.c.3.* does declare by examples of many Scriptures often-times for a part of the Earth, the whole Earth, for a part of the World the whole World for a part of men all men to be nominated; and this as well touching the wicked as the godly. Therefore when he says, that "Christ is the propitiation for the sins of the whole world," we are not enforced by the name of (the whole World) to understand universally all men.
>
> There is a difference between the work of our redemption, and the force (or fruit) of our redemption: for the first is once done; the other is eternal, extending itself as well to them which were from the beginning of the World, even before the work of our redemption was accomplished, as to them who after the work of redemption effected shall be to the end of the World. *Hilasmos* is properly the efficacy of redemption & propitiation; nothing therefore does let, but that Christ has been and is perpetually the Atonement for the sins even of them which were elected, even from the beginning of the world.[263]

From these statements, one might easily presume Zanchi is committed to limited atonement in the sense of a limited imputation of the sins of the elect to Christ. It is important to note, however, that he is speaking of Christ's priestly advocacy for the elect only. Limitarians are all too prone to read these kinds of statements in the writings of early Calvinists and presume from them that limited atonement is being advocated. This is a mistake. Though Zanchi affirmed Christ's limited intercessory advocacy for the elect alone, in some of his other statements it is clear he believed in an unlimited imputation of sin to Christ. In these statements, Zanchi spoke of mankind itself being "redeemed":

> I. The gospell, what it is.
>
> Concerning the gospell therefore, according to the signification received

263 Ibid., 345–47.

and used in the church, we beleeve that it is nothing else but the heavenly doctrine concerning Christ, preached by Christ himselfe and the apostles, and contained in the bookes of the Newe testament, bringing the best and most gladsome tidings to the world, namely, that mankinde is redeemed by the death of Iesus Christ, the onely, begotten Sonne of God. So that there is prepared for all men, if they repent and beleeve in Iesus Christ, a free remission of al their sinns, salvation, and eternall life. Wherefore it is fitlie called of the Apostle: "The gospel of our salvation."[264]

Furthermore, both John Davenant (of Dort fame) and William Twisse (of Westminster fame) interpreted Zanchi's writings to indicate Christ died for all (Hypothetical Universalism). John Davenant cited Zanchi's statement that each man is bound to believe he is elect. Speaking of his (Davenant's) opponent, he said:

His second reason why absolute Reprobation is against God's Justice, is, "Because it makes God to require faith in Christ of those to whom he has precisely in his absolute purpose denied both a power to believe, and a Christ to believe in." And Zanchi says, "That every man is bound to believe that he is chosen in Christ to salvation," &c. I hold it improper to say that God commands or binds any man to believe his own Predestination or Election, though some learned Divines spake in that manner.[265]

William Twisse, proculator of the Westminster Assembly and himself a Hypothetical Universalist, wrote the following:

Look in what sense *Arminius* says Christ died for us, in the same sense we may be held to say (without prejudice to our Tenet) of absolute reprobation, that all who hear the Gospel are bound to believe that Christ died for them. For the meaning Arminius makes of Christ's dying for us, is this, Christ died, for this end, that satisfaction being made for sin, the Lord now may pardon sin, upon what condition he will; which indeed is to die for obtaining a possibility of the redemption of all, but for the actual redemption of none at all.

Secondly, But I lift not to content myself and this; therefore, I farther answer, by distinction of the phrase dying for us, that we may not cheat ourselves by the confounding of things that differ. To die for us, or for all, is to die for our bene-

264 G. Zanchi, *De religione christiana Fides* [*Confession of Christian Religion*], ed. L. Baschera and C. Moser (London: Brill, 2007), 253.

265 J. Davenant, *Animadversions Written by the Right Reverend Father in God, John, Lord Bishop of Salisbury, upon a Treatise Entitled "God's Love to Mankind"* (London: Printed for John Partridge, 1641), 254–55.

> fit, or for the benefit of all: Now these benefits are of a different nature, whereof some are bestowed upon man only conditionally (though for Christ's sake) and they are the pardon of sin and Salvation of the Soul, and these God does confer only upon the condition of faith and repentance. Now I am ready to profess, and that, I suppose, as out of the mouth of all our Divines, that every one who hears the Gospel (without distinction between Elect and Reprobate) is bound to believe that Christ died for him, so far as to procure both the pardon of his sins, and the salvation of his soul, in case he believe and repent.
>
> And here first I observe, *Zanchi* is not charged to maintain, that every hearer of the Gospel, is bound to believe, that he is elect in Christ unto faith and repentance, but only to salvation: that puts me in good heart, that *Zanchi* & I shall shake hands of fellowship in the end, and part good friends.
>
> Now to accommodate that opinion of *Zanchi*, I say it may have a good sense, to say that every hearer is bound to believe, both that Christ died to procure salvation for him, in the case he do believe, and that God ordained that he should be saved, in case he do believe; where belief is made the condition only of salvation, not of the Divine ordination.[266]
>
> Notice several points made by Twisse.
>
> 1. He asserted his agreement with Arminius that Christ died for the sins of all people.
> 2. He disagreed with Arminius that Christ died to make salvation only possible but actual for none.
> 3. He distinguished between Christ dying absolutely for all and conditionally for those who believe.
> 4. He asserted that everyone who hears the gospel is bound to believe that Christ died for him.
> 5. He asserted his agreement with Zanchi concerning the death of Christ for all people such that if they do believe, they will be saved.

Finally, notice how Thomas seemed to confirm Zanchi's dualism by his quotations, revealing how in one sense, Zanchi held that Christ died for all and in another sense (God's intention of effectual application), Christ died only for the elect.

266 W. Twisse, *The Riches of God's Love unto the Vessels of Mercy, Consistent with His Absolute Hatred or Reprobation of the Vessels of Wrath* (Oxford: Printed by L. L. and H. H. Printers to the University, for Tho. Robinson, 1653), I:153–55.

Here are three quotes from Zanchi cited by Thomas illustrating how Zanchi affirmed Christ died for the sins of all people:

> It is not false that Christ died for all men, regarding the conditional will: namely, if they want to be partakers of his death by faith. For the passion of Christ is offered to all in the Gospel. No-one is excluded from it unless he excludes himself.[267]

> We are ordered to believe the gospel, and the gospel both assumes that we have been redeemed through Christ and proclaims that we have been predestined in Christ, so we are commanded to believe simply that we have been predestined in Christ from eternity to obtain redemption.[268]

> Those who, looking at the revealed will of God, teach that God both wills that all be saved, and that Christ died for the salvation of all, cannot be condemned.[269]

Though Zanchi affirmed an unlimited atonement, he also affirmed the limited effectual application of the atonement only for the elect, as these quotes cited by Thomas illustrate:

> The elect alone are saved . . . therefore God wills simply to save only them, and for them alone Christ died and for them alone he intercedes.[270]

> Regarding the plan and counsel of the Lord, and the eternal will of God, he died for the elect alone.[271]

> It cannot be said that it was properly and simply the will of God that Christ should die for the salvation of all . . . and . . . that Christ, according to the Father's plan died for all . . . sufficiently.[272]

Thomas concluded from Zanchi's treatment of 1 John 2:1 that the latter limited the propitiation to the elect alone. Zanchi was "openly contending" for limited atonement as early as 1565 and was thus the "first public champion" of limited atonement from

---

267 Thomas, *Extent of the Atonement*, 96. (Also cited in Davenant, "Dissertation on the Death of Christ," 2:339.)
268 Ibid., 98.
269 Ibid., 102.
270 Ibid.
271 Ibid.
272 Ibid.

the Reformed camp.[273] Thomas has misread Zanchi, failing to see the latter's dualism on the issue and failing to notice that many who held to Hypothetical Universalism, such as Calvin, still took a limited reading of some of the key texts on the extent of the atonement. Likewise, Robert Godfrey has misread Vermigli and Zanchi, as the quotations he cites do not indicate these men held to limited atonement as Godfrey suggests.[274]

Thomas's statement concerning Zanchi being the "first public champion" of limited atonement in 1565 is significant. Notice it is not Calvin in Thomas's mind who first championed limited atonement, since Calvin died in 1564.

Theodore Beza (AD 1519–1605)

Beza was professor of Greek at Lausanne until 1558. In 1559 he became a professor in Calvin's newly founded academy in Geneva. He traveled to France to consult on the Huguenot problem and remained there from 1561 to 1563. Returning to Geneva in May of 1564, he arrived just three weeks before Calvin's death. When Calvin died, the reins of leadership in Geneva were taken up by Beza. Twenty-two years later Beza would become the first one among the key leaders of the Reformed movement to articulate limited atonement.[275]

In 1582 Beza published *De Praedestinationis doctrina*, in which his scholastic tendencies are evident. According to Hall, "Beza re-opened the door to speculative determinism which Calvin had attempted to close."[276] Beza debated the Lutheran Jacob Andreae at the Colloquy of Montbéliard in 1586. Michael Jinkins suggested Beza's own willingness to engage in speculation concerning an *ordo salutis* inadvertently opened the door for the speculative theological musings of seventeenth-century Federal theologians and their notion of the intra-Trinitarian "Covenant of Redemption." Andreae attacked limited atonement. Beza countered, responding that "Christ did not die for the damned."

Jinkins joined Bray, Maruyama, and Raitt in understanding Beza "as a key transitional figure between Calvin and Calvinist Scholasticism."[277] Beza clearly framed his dogmatics around a supralapsarian Calvinism. His influence on Perkins and Ames is evident.

Jinkins pointed out how Beza, in his attempt to ground the assurance of election

273 Ibid., 99.

274 Godfrey, "Reformed Thought on the Extent of the Atonement," 146.

275 See his *Tabula Praedestinationis*. For Beza's doctrine of predestination and soteriology based on his *Tabula*, consult J. S. Bray, *Theodore Beza's Doctrine of Predestination* (Nieuwkoop: B. De Graaf, 1975); S. Manetsch, *Theodore Beza and the Quest for Peace in France, 1572–1598* (Leiden: Brill, 2000); J. Mallinson, *Faith, Reason, and Revelation in Theodore Beza: 1519–1605*, Oxford Theological Monographs (Oxford: Oxford University Press, 2003); P. Geisendorf, *Théodore de Bèze* (Geneva: Julien, 1967); R. Letham, "Theodore Beza: A Reassessment," *Scottish Journal of Theology* 40, no. 1 (February 1987): 25–40. See also M. Jinkins, "Theodore Beza: Continuity and Regression in the Reformed Tradition," *Evangelical Quarterly* 64, no. 2 (April–June 1992): 131–54; and Thomas, *Extent of the Atonement*, 47–48.

276 B. Hall, "Calvin against the Calvinists," in *John Calvin: A Collection of Distinguished Essays*, ed. G. Duffield (Grand Rapids, MI: Eerdmans, 1966), 27.

277 Jinkins, "Theodore Beza," 145.

in the free grace of God and not conditioned by human actions, tended to sever Christ as the second person of the Trinity from Christ in his temporal activity as revelation of the fullness of God and as Redeemer. Only the loving fatherhood of God is revealed to the elect. For the rest of the non-elect, God remains a judge. This drives a wedge between God and Christ, where God controls the eternal decree of election and Christ executes the decree in the economical scheme of salvation. "Beza, in this, is at odds with Calvin."[278] For Beza, predestination drives everything. For Calvin, predestination is important but it does not drive his theology, as is evidenced its appearance in the 1559 edition of Calvin's *Institutes* at the end of Book III in the context of the discussion of the Christian life, as Jinkins pointed out.[279] Unlike Calvin, one does not sense, however, that at bottom, atonement is an essentially filial matter for Beza.[280]

It was not until 1586 at the Colloquy of Montbéliard and 1587 with the publication of Beza's *Ad Acta Colloquia Montisbelgardensis Tubingae Edita, Theodori Bezae Responsionis*[281] that his clear position on the extent of the atonement can be discerned. Beza considered it "blasphemous" for one "to say that those whose sins have been expiated through the death of Christ, or for whom Christ has satisfied, can be condemned."[282]

In his dispute with Andreae, Beza understood Andreae's position on the universality of the atonement to imply that people cannot be condemned for their sins but are condemned solely for failure to believe in Christ. Since unbelief is a sin, Beza thought Andreae should maintain that it too has been expiated by the death of Christ and thus the unbelieving are saved. Beza, like John Owen would later argue, held that if sins are expiated, salvation must follow. Thus the atonement is limited only to the elect and guarantees their salvation.

Thomas rightly noted that this argument represents a departure from Calvin. For Calvin, the atonement did indeed accomplish the salvation of the elect but not without the necessary faith for the benefit to be applied. Unlike Calvin, Beza said that application is certain for all those for whom Christ died—namely, the elect. For Beza, Christ's death, by necessity, must be effective for all for whom it was performed.[283] Salvation was not made possible in Christ; it was made actual only for the elect. Beza stated that the atonement was limited because Jesus did not die for the damned.[284]

Unlike Calvin, who believed that the sufficiency of the death of Christ meant that it actually atoned for the sins of all people, Beza understood sufficiency to mean the

278 Ibid., 148.
279 Ibid., 149.
280 Ibid., 151.
281 T. Beza, *Ad Acta Colloquia Montisbelgardensis Tubingae Edita, Theodori Bezae Responsionis, Pars Altera*, Edito Prima (Genevae: Joannes le Preux, 1588), 215.
282 Ibid.
283 Thomas, *Extent of the Atonement*, 57–58.
284 Godfrey, "Reformed Thought on the Extent of the Atonement," 142.

death of Christ was of infinite value but was not for all people individually "either with respect to the intention of the Father in sending His Son to die or with respect to the actual effect of the death."[285] Godfrey's next statement is vital to note: "Beza's contention at this point was his unique contribution to this discussion."[286] Whereas Calvin had affirmed the validity of the Lombardian formula, Beza clearly rejected it.[287]

In addition, Beza's understanding of God's universal love differs from that of Calvin. Referring to correspondent J. Andreae's enquiry about John 3:16, G. Michael Thomas stated,

> Beza replied that the world God loves is not to be understood universally, but indefinitely, with reference to those who believe in Christ, just as Christ said that he did not pray for the world but for those given him by his Father. "The world" in John 3:16 means the elect throughout the world. A will of God to save all individuals cannot be meant, because what God decrees, he also performs, since he cannot be impeded or changed.[288]

David Steinmetz stated how Beza "allowed the doctrine of election to qualify the doctrine of the atonement. According to Beza, Christ died only for the elect. While Calvin may have entertained this idea, only Beza flatly stated it."[289] Strehle, following Kickel, pointed out how Beza's supralapsarianism was harsher than Calvin's (supposed) infralapsarianism. For Beza, the work of Christ has no autonomous value but finds its identity within the supralapsarian purposes of God. "Christ is taken from the centrality he held in Calvin's theology and is demoted to the position of a secondary cause; [Kickel, *Vernunft und Offenbarung*, 167–68] in particular, a formal and material cause [Beza, *Tract.* III, 437]."[290] Kickel argued that Beza groups both Christ and his atonement, along with the elect, in God's decree.[291] Thus, Beza limited the extent of the atonement to the elect alone.[292] Strehle concluded this was the logical result of listing Christ with the elect, as a minister to and for them alone.[293] Christ must

285 Ibid. Beza maintains, "The one and only sacrifice of Christ once made, is sufficient for the abolishing of all the sins of all the faithful." T. Beza, *Cours sur les épîtres aux Romains et aux Hebrieux 1564–66; d'après les notes de Marcus Widler*, ed., P. Fraenkel and L. Perrotet (Genève: Droz, 1988), 406.

286 Godfrey, "Reformed Thought on the Extent of the Atonement," 142.

287 Beza, *Ad Acta Colloquia Montisbelgardensis*, 217.

288 Thomas, *Extent of the Atonement*, 56. William Strong (d. 1654), a Westminster delegate, links Beza with Calvin in teaching that, in distinction from God's peculiar and fatherly love for his people, "there is also a common love, whereby he loves whatever is of his own in any of the Creatures. So Beza and Calvin." See William Strong, *A Discourse of the Two Covenants* (London: J. M. for Francis Tyton, 1678), 101.

289 D. C. Steinmetz, *Reformers in the Wings* (Oxford: Oxford University Press, 2001), 118.

290 Strehle, "The Extent of the Atonement," 132.

291 Kickel, "Vernunft und Offenbarung bei Theodore Beza: Zum Problem des Verhältnisses," in *Philosophie und Staat* (Neukirchen-Vluyn: Neukirchener Verlag, 1967), 105.

292 Beza, *Ad Acta Col. Mont.*, 215, 221.

293 Strehle, "The Extent of the Atonement," 133; see Beza, *Correspondance de Théodore de Bèze Tome I, 1539–1555*

be considered as active within both decrees of God; showing his mercy in salvation, displaying his wrath in judgment. It is only within the soteriological scheme of Luther and Calvin that this dual activity of Christ has a true ontological foundation in his work on the cross.[294]

With Beza, something of a corner is turned in Reformed theology. His rejection of the Lombardian formula[295] and affirmation of strict particularism is something new in Reformed theology. It would appear Beza is allowing his doctrine of predestination to drive his doctrine of the extent of the atonement. Beza can and should be distinguished from the theology of Calvin and the first generation of Reformers.

At this juncture it is important to differentiate between Beza as the father of Reformed Scholasticism (as some would argue) and Beza as the fountainhead of limited atonement. Post-Reformation theological method underwent a change. As McGrath noted,

> It became increasingly important to demonstrate the internal consistency and coherence of Calvinism. As a result, many Calvinist writers turned to Aristotle, . . . Theology was understood to be grounded upon Aristotelian philosophy, and particularly Aristotelian insights into the nature of method; later Reformed writers are better described as philosophical, rather than biblical, theologians.[296]

Beza used Aristotle's "four causes" (material, formal, efficient, and final) as a theological method to support supralapsarianism and double predestination.

Though the so-called Calvin against the Calvinists debate has abated significantly, one should not assume there was no shift in theological method or development of Reformed theology beyond the first generation of Reformers.[297] Polmen noted that Beza's theological system became so detached from Scripture that the theological chair at Geneva was eventually split in two, teaching theology and the Scriptures as separate subjects.[298] Likewise, Jinkins admitted that while the case for discontinuity between Calvin and the later Calvinists has been at times overstated, "it is conversely

---

(Genève: Droz, 1960), 171 (40).

294 Strehle, "The Extent of the Atonement," 134.

295 Godfrey noted that this rejection of the traditional distinction between sufficiency and efficiency "was not accepted by the majority of the Reformed theologians." Ibid., 144.

296 A. McGrath, *Christian Theology: An Introduction*, 2nd ed. (Oxford: Blackwell, 1994), 74. See also P. Benedict, *Christ's Churches Purely Reformed: A Social History of Calvinism* (New Haven, CT: Yale University Press, 2002), 298–99.

297 For both sides of the debate, consult W. F. Graham, ed., *Later Calvinism: International Perspectives* (Kirksville, MO: Sixteenth Century Journal, 1994); C. Trueman and R. S. Clark, eds., *Protestant Scholasticism: Essays in Reassessment* (Carlisle, UK: Paternoster, 1999); and W. J. van Asselt and E. Dekker, eds., *Reformation and Scholasticism: An Ecumenical Enterprise* (Grand Rapids, MI: Baker, 2001).

298 Strehle, "The Extent of the Atonement," 128, citing Pontien Polmen, *L'Elément Historique dans la controverse religeùse du XVIe Siècle* (Gembloux: J. Duculot, 1932), 127.

true that there is a danger for those who appreciate Beza to minimize the creeping ratiocination that finds a place in his theology. Beza's theology *does* represent structurally a more consistent, but also a more scholastic, more rigid and deterministic distillation of Calvinist doctrine."[299]

This neither solves the question of Calvin's view of the extent of the atonement nor sets aside the evidence that Beza, not Calvin or any of the other first-generation Reformers, is the first purveyor of limited atonement in the Reformation era.

Rudolf Gwalther (AD 1519–1586)

Gwalther is a lesser-known early Reformer in Zurich. He became Zwingli's son-in-law and worked alongside Bullinger with the church in Zurich, following him as pastor in 1575. Gwalther, like Zwingli and Bullinger, held to unlimited atonement. In a number of places, Gwalther spoke of Christ being the Savior and redeemer of mankind and the world.[300] "For as every man is created after the image of God: so are they redeemed and purchased with the blood of the Son of God."[301] "Every man created after the image of God" cannot mean the elect alone. Christ reconciles mankind,[302] his death is sufficient for the sins of the world,[303] and he purged the sins of all the world.[304] Christ "made oblation unto God the heavenly Father, with a perfect and sufficient sacrifice for the sins of all the world,"[305] and "he has made a full satisfaction by the sacrifice of his body, once offered upon the cross, for the sins of all the world."[306] Gwalther said "the redemption made by Christ Jesus, is offered of God to all men, and appertains to all men."[307] Like Calvin, he spoke of redeemed souls perishing.[308]

Gwalther wrote:

> Again, when he commends the preaching of the Gospel to his Apostles, he will first have repentance to be taught, next after which, he will have remissions of sins to be joined. Therefore Peter does not without a cause proceed

299 M. Jinkins, "Theodore Beza," 147. See also T. Lane, "The Quest for the Historical Calvin," *Evangelical Quarterly* 55.2 (April 1983): 98, who claims there is no absolute contrast between Calvin and later Calvinism, "but there is a significant shift in emphasis." For Lane, the most serious change came about with the "increasing role given to logical deduction and the increased willingness to speculate" (99).

300 R. Gwalther, *An Hundred, Threescore and Fifteen Sermons, uppon the Actes of the Apostles*, trans. J. Bridges (London: Henrie Denham, 1572), 59, 71, 74, 86, 93, 106, 112, 127, 320, 375, 407, 450, 451, 454, 532, 650, 667, 727, 859, 900; R. Gwalther, *Antichrist* (Sothwarke: Christopher Trutheall, 1556), 22ʳ, 41ᵛ, 96ʳ, 122ʳ [irregular pagination], 148ʳ, 179ᵛ, 180ʳ, 188ʳ. R. Gwalther, *Certain Godly Homilies or Sermons upon the Prophets Abdias and Ionas: Conteyning a Most Fruitefull Exposition of the Same* (London: Henrie Bynneman, 1573), 236.

301 Gwalther, *Actes of the Apostles*, 752.

302 Ibid., 482, 450.

303 Gwalther, *Antichrist*, 31ʳ, 175ᵛ, 195ᵛ⁻ʳ [irregular pagination].

304 Gwalther, *Actes of the Apostles*, 23, 53, 65, 452, 662, 795.

305 Gwalther, *Antichrist*, 31ʳ.

306 Gwalther, *Actes of the Apostles*, 127.

307 Ibid., 75.

308 Ibid., 632.

in this order, that speaking of the death of Christ, he first proves his hearers to be guilty, and to be the authors thereof. And so it is necessary to have Christ's death preached in these days, that all men might understand the Son of God died for their sins, and that they were the authors thereof. For thus it shall come to pass, that men shall learn to be sorry in their heart for their sins, and shall embrace the salvation offered them in Christ with the more fervency of faith.[309]

Zacharias Ursinus (AD 1534–1583)

Ursinus became professor of dogmatics at Heidelberg in 1562 and was the prime mover behind the production of the famous Heidelberg Catechism (1563). In Ursinus's answer to Question 20 of the Catechism, he spoke to the extent of the atonement:

> Q 20. Are all men, then, as they perished in Adam, saved by Christ? Ans: No; only those engrafted into him, and receive all his benefits by truth faith.
>
> The answer to this question consists of two parts:—Salvation through Christ is not bestowed upon all who perished in Adam; but only upon those who, by a true faith, are engrafted into Christ, and receive all his benefits.
>
> The first part of this answer is clearly proven by experience, and the word of God. "He that believes not the Son, shall not see life, but the wrath of God abides on him." "Not every one that says unto me, Lord, Lord, shall enter into the kingdom of heaven." "Except a man be born again, he cannot see the kingdom of God." (John 3:36; 3:3; Matt. 7:21.) The reason why all are not saved through Christ, is not because of any insufficiency of merit and grace in him—for the atonement of Christ is for the sins of the whole world, as it respects the dignity and sufficiency of the satisfaction which he made—but it arises from unbelief; because men reject the benefits of Christ offered in the gospel, and so perish by their own fault, and not because of any insufficiency in the merits of Christ. The other part of the answer is also evident from the Scriptures. "As many as received him to them, gave he power to become the sons of God." "By his knowledge shall my righteous servant justify many." (John 1:12. Is. 53:11.) The reason why only those who believe are saved, is, because they alone lay hold of, and embrace the benefits of Christ; and because in them alone God secures the end for which he graciously delivered his Son to death; for only those that believe know the mercy and grace of God, and return suitable thanks to him.

309 Ibid., 108.

The sum of this whole matter is therefore this: that although the satisfaction of Christ, the mediator for our sins, is perfect, yet all do not obtain deliverance through it, but only those who believe the gospel, and apply to themselves the merits of Christ by a true faith.[310]

The Heidelberg Catechism on Question 37 states:

What dost thou understand by the word *Suffered*?

Answer. That all the time he lived on earth, but especially at the end of his life, he bore, in body and soul, the wrath of God against the sin of the whole human race, in order that by his passion, as the only atoning sacrifice, he might redeem our body and soul from everlasting damnation, and obtain for us the grace of God, righteousness, and eternal life.[311]

Ursinus, in his commentary on the Heidelberg Catechism, said:

Question: If Christ made a satisfaction for all, then all ought to be saved. But all are not saved. Therefore he did not make a perfect satisfaction.

Answer: Christ satisfied for all, as it respects the sufficiency of the satisfaction which he hath made, but not as it respects the application thereof.[312]

Roger Nicole went to great lengths to explain away this language of the Heidelberg Catechism:

G. Voetius, in his crystal clear *catechisatie*, advances two possible explanations of the phrase under scrutiny. The second one—in the author's judgment the less plausible—is that "the whole human race" here means "people of all sorts, conditions and nations out of the whole human race." (ed. Kuyper. Rotterdam: Hague, 1891, I, 440) His first suggestion is that the words "against the sin of the whole human race" refer to the range of the wrath of God, not to the range of the substitutionary sin bearing of Christ.[313]

---

310 Z. Ursinus, *The Commentary of Dr. Zacharias Ursinus on the Heidelberg Catechism*, trans. G. W. Willard (Phillipsburg, NJ: P&R, 1994), 106. Ursinus also stated: "Grace exceeds sin as regards the satisfaction, but not as regards the application" (ibid., 107). Concerning John 3:16, Ursinus stated, "Christ has made a sufficient satisfaction for the offences of all men" (ibid.). These would seem to be strong statements of universal atonement.

311 Schaff, *Creeds of Christendom*, 3:319.

312 Z. Ursinus, *Commentary*, 215.

313 R. Nicole, "The Doctrine of the Definite Atonement in the Heidelberg Catechism," *The Gordon Review* 3 (1964): 142.

This kind of attempt to massage the words of the Catechism to fit one's own theological view is tendentious at best.

Ursinus clearly affirmed a universal satisfaction in the following statements:

> Christ was ordained by God the Father . . . to offer himself a sacrifice propitiation for the sins of all mankinde . . . and lastly to apply effectually his sacrifice unto us . . . by enlightening and moving the Elect.[314]

> Therefore, as he has died for *all* in the sufficiency of his ransom, only for those believing in its efficiency, so also he willed to die for *all in common* as to the sufficiency of his merit, that is, he wished, by his death, to merit grace, righteousness, life sufficiently for all, because he wished nothing to be wanting in him and his merit, that all the impious who perish might be without apology.[315]

> The reason why all are not saved through Christ, is not because of any insufficiency of merit and grace in him—for the atonement [expiation] of Christ is for the sins of the whole world, as it respects the dignity and sufficiency of the satisfaction which he made—but it arises from unbelief; because men reject the benefits of Christ offered in the gospel, and so perish by their own fault, and not because of any insufficiency in the merits of Christ.[316]

> The dignity of the person who suffered appears in this, that it was God . . . who died for the sins of the world; which is infinitely more than the destruction of all creatures, and avails more than the holiness of all the angels and men.[317]

Richard Muller concluded rightly that Bullinger, Musculus, and Ursinus held to a form of universal atonement. Nicole erred historically when he argued Ursinus was committed to limited atonement.[318]

---

314 Ursinus, *The Summe of Christian Religion*, 116–17, as cited in Thomas, *Extent of the Atonement*, 111 (cf. 118, 122, 132).

315 Ursinus, *Catech. par. ii. quest.* 11; cited in Young, "The Atonement of Christ," *Biblical Notes & Queries*, 309 (also partially cited in Thomas, *Extent of the Atonement*, 111; emphasis in original).

316 Ursinus, *Commentary*, 106.

317 Ibid., 88.

318 R. Muller, "Review of Jonathan Moore's *English Hypothetical Universalism*," *Calvin Theological Journal* 43, no. 1 (2008): 150. Nicole said that "Those who, to the author's knowledge, have taken a cue from this statement [Question 37 in the Heidelberg Catechism] to justify a universal extent and intent of redemption are representatives of rather seriously deviant tendencies within the Reformed family" (Nicole, "Doctrine of the Definite Atonement," 142). This kind of statement would entail that John Davenant, the English delegate to Dort, was of "seriously deviant tendencies within the Reformed family," contrary to the judgment of modern Reformed scholarship.

Caspar Olevianus (AD 1536–1587)

Olevianus was co-laborer with Ursinus and one of the compilers of the Heidelberg Catechism. His major work, *De Substantia Foederis Gratuiti inter Deum et Electos*, was published in 1585.

Thomas interpreted the following statement as evidence of Olevianus's commitment to limited atonement:

> If he had made intercession and sacrifice for reprobates too, then clearly, their sins having been paid for by the sacrifice of the Son of God, the justice of God would not allow him to require a debt already paid by the Son, nor would the justice of God be able to punish them with eternal death for their sins inasmuch as satisfaction has been made by him.[319]

David Paraeus (AD 1548–1622)

Paraeus was a student of Ursinus, a pastor, and then a professor who attracted students far and wide. His writings indicate that he, like his mentor, held to unlimited atonement.

> "Thou wast slain" that is, by dying for the sins of the world, that declares thyself to be the Messiah, whom Isaiah forward should be led "as a sheep to the slaughter," to take away the sins of the world.
>
> Hence we observe two things: "First" that the death of Christ is truly a ransom satisfactory for our sins: and that our redemption by it, is not metaphorical (as the new "Samosatenians" blasphemously affirm) but proper: for the redemption which is made by a price is proper. But such is ours by Christ, because by the shedding of his blood, he has paid a full ransom, and satisfied the justice of God, as the Scripture witnesses Matt. 20:28. and 1 Tim. 2:6. being the same with what is here said, "that has redeemed us by thy blood:" and Chap. 1:5. "who has washed us in his blood," and Heb. 1:3. "purged our sins by himself:" unless that by the word "redemption" is properly signified the whole work of our salvation: by "washing" and "purging" a part thereof, viz. our justification or sanctification. This place therefore and so many others, proving Christ's satisfactory ransom, are to be opposed against "Socinian blasphemies."
>
> *Secondly*, that the redemption by Christ's blood, is truly universal, as sufficient, and propounded not only to one nation, or a few, but to all nations, tongues and peoples: yet not so, as if all promiscuously should be saved: but

319 C. Olevianus, *De Substantia Foederis Gratuiti inter Deum et Electos* (Genève: Eustache Vignon, 1585), 68; cited in Thomas, *Extent of the Atonement*, 114.

> those of every tribe, people and language, who believe in Christ. And this much the Elders teach us: "Thou have redeemed us of every tribe."[320]
>
> But are not all redeemed by Christ, died he not for all? Says not the Apostle Peter that he bought these "false prophets," by whom he is denied? To this Augustine well answers, that all are said to be redeemed, according to the dignity of the price: which would suffice for the redemption of all men, if all by faith did receive the benefit offered. But as many as pass the time of their being in this life in infidelity, they remain unredeemed through their own fault. The sealed therefore are only redeemed, because they alone by faith receive the grace of redemption, through the grace of election, which God vouchsafed them (not to the others) from all eternity.[321]

The following section is a truncated portion of Paraeus's more lengthy statement in Ursinus's commentary on the Heidelberg Catechism that indicates Paraeus's view on the extent of the atonement:

> III. Did Christ Die For All? . . . we must make a distinction, so as to harmonise those passages of Scriptures which seem to teach contradictory doctrines. . . . There are some who interpret these general declarations of the whole number of the faithful. . . . Others reconcile these seemingly contradictory passages of Scripture by making a distinction between the sufficiency, and efficacy of the death of Christ. For there are certain contentious persons, who deny that these declarations which speak in a general way, are to be restricted to the faithful alone. [As he died sufficiently for all and efficaciously for the faithful alone,] . . . he willed to die for all in general, as touching the sufficiency of his merit, that is, he willed to merit by his death, grace, righteousness, and life in the most abundant manner for all; because he would not that any thing would be wanting as far as he and his merits are concerned, so that all the wicked who perish may be without excuse. But he willed to die for the elect alone as touching the efficacy of his death, that is, he would not only sufficiently merit grace and life for them alone, but also effectually confers these upon them, grants faith, and the Holy Spirit, and brings it to pass that they apply to themselves, by faith, the benefits of his death, and so obtain for themselves the efficacy of his merits.[322]

---

320 D. Paraeus, *A Commentary upon the Divine Revelation of the Apostle and Evangelist John* (London: Printed for John Allen, at the rising-Sun in S. Paul's Church-yard, 1659), 103–4.

321 Ibid., 333–34.

322 Ursinus, *Commentary*, 221–23. See also Godfrey, "Reformed Thought on the Extent of the Atonement to 1618," *Westminster Theological Journal* 37 (1975): 149.

> Obj. 2., Christ died for all. Therefore his death does not merely extend to such as believe. Ans. *Christ died for all as it regards the merit and sufficiency* of the ransom which he paid; but only for those that believe as it respects the application and efficacy of his death; for seeing that the death of Christ is applied to such alone, and is profitable to them, it is correctly said to belong properly to them alone, as has been already shown.[323]

Paraeus has a fascinating discussion of the extent question where he affirmed unlimited atonement and cited quotations from Ambrose, Cyril, Augustine, Prosper, Aquinas, and Lombard as asserting the same.[324]

One of the clearest statements found in Paraeus with respect to the extent of the atonement occurs in his comment on Heb 2:9: "That which is here said, '*for every man,*' pertains to the amplification of the death of Christ. *Not for some few did he die*, but its efficacy pertains to *all men*. Therefore to *all* afflicted consciences life is prepared in the death of Christ."[325] Paraeus included a section under "The Death of Christ" entitled "Whether Christ Died for All." His marginal note stated that Ursinus never addressed this question directly and that the section, put together on the basis of scattered comments, has been included because the subject had come into contention.

Paraeus considered the argument that Christ satisfied only for the sins of the elect to be false:

> Article 5. That Christ satisfied only for the elect. This is an argument about words or a false accusation. Christ carried, paid, and expiated the sins of all people: if we consider the magnitude of the price or the sufficiency of the ransom: Not the sins of all people, but only of those who have faith: if we consider the efficacy, fruit, and application of the ransom. For so the Scripture: Behold, the Lamb of God, who takes away the sins of the world (John 1:29). And also: If you do not believe, you will die in your sins (John 8:24). So Ambrose: If you do not believe, Christ did not suffer for you. So Pope Innocent: The blood of Christ was poured out for only the predestined as far as concerns the efficacy, but was poured out for all men as far as concerns the sufficiency. So Lyra: He is the propitiation for the sins of the whole world, as far as concerns the sufficiency, but for the elect so much as regards the efficacy. There is no disagree-

323 Ursinus, *Commentary*, 221–25.

324 D. Paraeus, *Certain Learned and Excellent Discourses: Treating and Discussing Divers Hard and Difficult Points of Christian Religion: Collected, and Published in Latin, by D. David Parreus, out of the Writings of That Late Famous and Worthy Light of God's Church, D. Zachary Ursine. Faithfully Translated* (London: H. L., 1613), 135–52. For an accessible copy of this section of Paraeus, see Ponter, "David Paraeus (1548–1622) on the Death of Christ: Unlimited Expiation and Redemption," *Calvin and Calvinism*, August 29, 2007, http://calvinandcalvinism.com/?p=30.

325 D. Parei, *In divinam Ad Hebraeos S. Pauli Apostoli epistolam Commentarivs* (Heidelbergae: J. Rosae, 1613), 116; cited in Young, "The Atonement of Christ," *Biblical Notes & Queries*, 279.

> ment adjoining this understanding. If a Papist or Lutheran thinks otherwise, they consent in error against Scripture and all antiquity.[326]

John Davenant, signatory of Dort, understood Paraeus to be teaching unlimited atonement:

> The cause and matter of the passion of Christ was the sense and sustaining of the anger of God excited against the sin, not of some men, but of the whole human race; whence it arises, that the whole of reconciliation was not obtained or restored to all [*Act. Synod. Dortrect.* 217].[327]

Richard Baxter understood Paraeus to be teaching universal atonement when he quoted Paraeus in his *Irenicum*: "That the sins of all men lay on Christ; and so he died for all, that is, for all mens sins as the cause of his death: And you may tell any wicked man, Thy sins killed Christ (what-ever the deniers say to excuse them)."[328]

Likewise, G. Michael Thomas confirmed Paraeus's commitment to universal atonement when he quoted Paraeus: "Christ carried, dissolved, expiated the sins of all, if we consider the magnitude of the price or sufficiency of the ransom, but only the faithful and not of all, if we consider the efficacy, fruit and application of the ransom."[329] In Paraeus's *Aphorismes of the Orthodoxall Doctrine of the Reformed Churches* (1593), he stated, "We believe also that this death of Christ alone, is a perfect and sufficient ransome, to expiate and abolish all the sins of the whole world."[330]

Jacob Kimedoncius (AD 1550–1596)

Kimedoncius was a Dutch Heidelberg Reformed pastor, professor, and student of Ursinus. His work *Of the Redemption of Mankind* contains numerous references to the extent of the atonement being universal.[331]

326 D. Pareus, *Irenicum sive de Unione et Synodo Evangelicorum concilianda Liber Votivus, Paci Ecclesiae et desiderijs pacificorum dicatus* (Heidelberg: Johannes Lancellot, 1615), 142. Translation by Michael Lynch, "Translation Tuesday (Pareus on the Extent of the Satisfaction)," *Iconoclastic: Shattering Sloppy History*, July 22, 2014, https://theiconoclastic.wordpress.com/2014/07/22/translation-tuesday-pareus-on-the-extent-of-the-satisfaction/.

327 D. Parie, "Epitome of Arminianism: Or, the Examination of the Five Articles of the Remonstrants, in the Netherlands," in *Theological Miscellanies of Doctor David Pareus*, trans. A. R. (London: Printed by James Young, 1645), 830; cited by Davenant, "Dissertation on the Death of Christ," 2:356.

328 Baxter, *Catholick Theologie*, I.ii.53.

329 Thomas, *Extent of the Atonement*, 116.

330 Z. Ursinus, *The Summe of Christian Religion. First Englished by D. Henry Parry. To this Work of Ursinus Are Now at Last Annexed the Theological Miscellanies of D. David Pareus* (London: Printed by J. Young, 1645), 694. R. Nicole said, "It is very likely indeed that Paraeus understood rightly the teaching of Ursinus," but Nicole mistakenly did not think either Ursinus or Paraeus taught an unlimited expiation (Nicole, "Doctrine of the Definite Atonement in the Heidelberg Catechism," 144).

331 J. Kimedoncius, *The Redemption of Mankind: Three Books: Wherein the Controversy of the Universality of the Redemption and Grace by Christ, and His Death for All Men, Is Largely Handled*, trans. Hugh Ince (London: Felix Kingston, 1598).

> For there is one God, and one Mediator also of God and men, the man Christ Jesus, who gave himself a price of redemption for all, as the Apostle says.[332]

> For whereas it was not lawful to offer sacrifice but unto God alone, how much more ought this peculiar sacrifice to be offered to none, but to God alone, which the eternal high priest offered upon the Altar of the cross, by the sacrifice of his flesh and effusion of his blood, and which only by the propitiation for the sins of the world.[333]

> Therefore all men must hope in him alone, who only is the Mediator of God and man, the redemption, propitiation, and salvation of all men.[334]

> But to proceed to my purpose, the Lord from the time of his coming and appearing in the flesh, sustained all his whole life both in body and soul, the wrath of God against the sin of all mankind: but especially in his end, when he bare our sins in his body upon the tree, and took out of way the hand-writing of death that was against us, nailing it to the cross.[335]

Quoting from one of Bernard of Clairvaux's Psalm sermons, Kimedoncius stated: "He that dwells *&c* very well says: 'Christ according to the time died for the wicked: but in respect of predestination he died for his brethren and friends.'"[336] Speaking about the question of whether Christ suffered for the redemption of all and against those who falsely accuse the Reformed of denying that Christ died for the sins of all men, Kimedoncius said:

> But in the very entrance (as it is said) they run on ground, fastening as a false opinion, against which afterwards they perpetually fight. For we willingly acknowledge these manner of speeches: "That Christ is made the propitiation for the sins of the whole world, and has given himself the price of redemption for all men." For who can deny that, which the Scripture would have to be expressed in so many words?[337]

Kimedoncius appealed approvingly to the sufficiency/efficiency formula as used by Aquinas and others during the medieval period. He quoted Aquinas on Revelation 5:

332 Ibid., 4.
333 Ibid., 7.
334 Ibid., 13.
335 Ibid., 14.
336 Ibid., 26.
337 Ibid., 32.

> "Of the passion of the Lord" (says he) "we speak after two sorts: either according to sufficiency, and so his passion redeemed all. For it is sufficient to redeem and save all, although there had been many worlds, as Anselm says *lib.2 cur Deus homo. cap. 14.* Or according to the efficiency, and so all are not redeemed by his passion, because all cleave not unto the redeemer, and therefore all have not the efficacy of redemption."[338]

Speaking in reference to Augustine, Kimedoncius stated:

> Moreover, Augustine the chief of the ancient sound writers, does not only acknowledge that distinction, but also does expound it largely, *Tom.7* answering unto Articles that were false fathered upon him, whereof the first was, that he was reported to maintain, that "our Lord Jesus Christ suffered not for the redemption of all men." But he distinguishes after this manner: "As touching the greatness and might of the price, (says he) and as touching the only cause of mankind, the blood of Christ is the redemption of the whole world, and so all are well said to be redeemed."[339]

Kimedoncius spoke of "our adversaries" as believing "that Christ without any difference died for the sins of all men," and that all the sins of all men are satisfied and cleansed by sacrifice, not only sufficiently, but also effectually:

> Unto this opinion as new and unheard of, and many ways erroneous (as it shall appear) we cannot subscribe: but following the old distinction we affirm, that Christ suredly exhibited that which was sufficient to have taken away all sins, and so they are taken away, and that all are redeemed, as touching the sufficiency or greatness and power of the price, as Augustine expounded. But as touching the efficiency, we say that by the death of Christ, the sins only of the elect are blotted out, who believe in him, and stick unto him as members to the head: but such as are not incorporated into Christ, cannot receive the effect of his passion. For as the Lord says: "God so loved the world, that he gave his son that every one that believes in him should not perish, but have eternal life. He that believes is not condemned: but he that believes not, is condemned already," Joh. 3. Which in that place John Baptist confirming testified: "He that believes in the Son, has eternal life: but he that believes not in the Son shall not see life, but the wrath of God abides on him."[340]

338 Ibid., 33.
339 Ibid., 34–35.
340 Ibid., 38.

First of all, as touching the testimonies of the death of Christ for all, we grant also after a sort, that Christ suffered and died for all men, as many as have been, are, and shall be.[341]

This answer use Theophilact upon Heb 2. whom Anselm there seems to follow. His words are these: *He tasted death not for the faithful only, but for the whole world. For albeit all are not saved in very deed, yet he wrought that which was his part to do.* See how it does not follow, that if Christ died for all, all are straightway saved, which is the divinity of Huberus, *thes.* 270. Upon the 9. Chapter to the Hebr. The same interpreter has left it written thus: *He has taken away the sins of many. Why said he of many, and of all? Because all mortal men have not believed. The death of Christ surely was equivalent to the perdition of all, that is, was of value sufficient that all, and as much as lay in him he died for all: yet he took not away the sins of all: because they that refuse him make the death of Christ altogether unprofitable unto themselves.*[342]

But what shall we say to that which follows, "Who gave himself a ransom for all?" The answer is plain by the things that have been spoken before. For he truly gave himself a price of redemption sufficient for all, none excepted at all of the whole universality of men: but because the unbelievers do not apply redemption to themselves, the wrath of God abides on them. Also, he gave himself the price of reconciliation for all that belongs to the universality of the elect, and to his own body. Again, for all indefinitely, that is, for whomsoever Jews and Gentiles, high and low, masters and servants, as it has been often already said.[343]

Secondly, though we grant that the iniquities of all men were laid upon Christ; we deny the consequence that therefore by the sacrifice of Christ the sins of all be in very deed cleansed, and that all are justified, and received into grace.[344]

The seventh place is the tenth of John, where that good shepherd says: "I lay down my life for the sheep: my sheep hear my voice, and I know them and they follow me, and I give unto them eternal life, neither shall they perish for ever, neither shall any man take them out of mine hand." Here it appears, that howsoever Christ after a sort died for all, yet specially he died for such as shall be saved, because he died for his sheep.[345]

341 Ibid., 49.
342 Ibid., 50 (emphasis in original).
343 Ibid., 56.
344 Ibid., 104.
345 Ibid., 185.

Kimedoncius cited Musculus and provided three reasons why the atonement should be considered universal:

> Nevertheless, according to the reasons assigned of Musculus, this redemption is rightly termed universal. 1. Because it comes not to pass by the defect of grace, that many do perish, but by the defect of faith, seeing grace is prepared for all, to wit that do not refuse it, as all things were ready for the marriage. 2. Because all are called unto it. 3. Because so it is appointed for all, that no man without it can be redeemed. Where now he does understand this appointing otherwise than before: yet rightly, because albeit many are not redeemed nor justified, yet all by Christ are redeemed and justified, because no man is redeemed but by him. Of all which things plainly appear, that Musculus, as well as others, is against the adversary, and nothing at all on his side.[346]

Finally, in his dedication to Fredrick the Fourth concerning the work *Of the Redemption of Mankind*, Kimedoncius wrote:

> At this day we are slandered of malicious men with a new crime that is feigned against us, as though we should deny that Christ died for all men, an impudent reproach. For according to the Scriptures we also confess the same, but we deny, that thereupon it followeth that all mankind without exception of any one, are by the death of Christ indeed justified, saved, and restored into the bosom of grace, having received the pardon of their sins, whether they believe or no.[347]

One should not miss the irony here. The Heidelberg Reformer Kimedoncius, writing one of the first books on the atonement from a Calvinistic perspective, affirmed Christ died for the sins of all people and is concerned that he not be slandered by a view that has come to be thought of as orthodox among the Reformed today: Christ died *only* for the sins of the elect. Further irony is the fact that Kimedoncius, unlike many high Calvinists in Reformed history, did not believe that universal atonement entails universalism.

Conclusion

We are now in a position to summarize the views of the earliest key Continental Reformers.

---

346 Ibid., 145.

347 Ibid., A6^{v-r}.

1. Oecolampadius,[348] Luther, Zwingli, Bucer, Musculus, Vermigli, Bullinger, and Calvin all held to a form of universal atonement. There is no statement in any of their writings that explicitly affirms the notion that Christ died only for the sins of the elect as one finds in later Reformed orthodoxy.
2. Calvin's statements on the subject are often similar if not identical to his fellow Reformers. We have seen that Richard Muller lists Musculus, Vermigli, and Bullinger as affirming Hypothetical Universalism.
3. We have observed that some of these men took a limited reading of some of the key passages on the extent question even though it is clear they affirmed unlimited atonement in the sense that the sins of all men were imputed to Christ on the cross.
4. All these men affirmed the Lombardian formula of sufficiency/efficiency, where sufficiency is understood as an objective satisfaction for all sins and efficiency is understood as the application of the atonement only to those who believe (the elect).
5. While Bucer, Calvin, Musculus, Vermigli, and Bullinger affirmed Christ died for the sins of all, in good Reformed fashion they did not affirm that he died for all equally. There was a sense in which Christ died especially for the sins of the elect with the direct intent of bringing them to salvation via election.
6. Among the second-generation key Reformers, Zanchi, Gwalther, and Ursinus all affirmed universal atonement, though they often spoke with strong language to the effect that Christ died only for the sins of the elect with respect to God's intention and purpose for the atonement.
7. We have seen that several interpreters have failed to discern the dualism in these men with respect to the atonement and have wrongly concluded that some of them were limitarians with respect to the objective nature of the atonement.
8. Of all the key first- and second-generation Reformers, the only one who clearly affirmed limited atonement was Beza.

James Richards harbored no doubts that most of the earliest Reformers held to universal atonement.

> But, that *Luther, Melancthon, Osiander, Brentius, Ecolampadius, Zwinglius, and Bucer*, held the doctrine of a general atonement, there is no reason to doubt.

348 Letham's attempt to have Oecolampadius teach limited expiation on the basis that the Reformed held that "the many" of Isaiah 53 refers to the elect is another example of faulty logic. Musculus took an identical reading of Isaiah 53 and still held to unlimited expiation as has been demonstrated above. We have seen that Calvin held that the "many" in Isaiah 53 referred to all mankind. Again, the point needs to be made that some of the Reformers took a limited reading of passages like Isaiah 53; 1 Tim 2:4, and 1 John 2:2 while still affirming unlimited atonement.

> We might infer it from their Confession at *Marpurge*, signed A.D. 1529, as the expressions they employ on this subject are of a comprehensive character, and best agree with this sentiment. From their subsequent writings, however, it is manifest that these men, and the German Reformers generally, embraced the doctrine of a *universal propitiation*. Thus, also, it was with their immediate successors, as the language of the Psalgrave Confession testifies. This Confession is entitled, "A Full Declaration of the Faith and Ceremonies professed in the dominions of the most illustrious and noble Prince Frederick V., Prince Elector Palatine." It was translated by John Rolte, and published in London, A.D. 1614.[349]

It is difficult to assess just how pervasive limited atonement was in Reformed thought at the end of the sixteenth century. Beza's influence was significant, even in England. Perhaps Shultz is correct when he asserted, "Particular redemption, however, was widely accepted, and by the end of the sixteenth century it was the majority view concerning the extent of the atonement in Reformed theology."[350]

Early English Reformers

Like their Continental counterparts, all the early English Reformers, with the possible exception of John Bradford, held to universal atonement.

John Wycliffe (AD 1320–1384)

John Wycliffe, known as the "Morning Star of the Reformation," was an Oxford theologian, preacher, and early Reformer. He is most known for his translation of the Bible from the Latin Vulgate into English.

In his sermon "The Sondai Withnne Octave of Twelthe Dai," he stated:

> This gospel tellith a witnesse, how Baptist witnesside of Crist, both of his godhede and eke of his manhede. The storye seith thus, that Joon say Jesus comynge to him and saide thus of oure Lord, Lo the loomb of God; lo him that takith awey the synnes of this world, for he is bothe God and man. Crist

349 Richards, *Mental Philosophy and Theology*, 304. Compare Richards's statement with G. Shultz who said Bucer, Oecolampadius, and Vermigli held to particular redemption ("A Biblical and Theological Defense of a Multi-Intentioned View of the Extent of the Atonement" [PhD diss., Southern Baptist Theological Seminary, 2008], 45). Shultz is dependent on Robert Letham for this viewpoint (R. Letham, "Theodore Beza: A Reassessment," *Scottish Journal of Theology* 40 [1987]: 30). For the Psalgrave Confession, see *A Full Declaration of the Faith and Ceremonies Professed in the dominions of the most Illustrious and noble Prince Fredericke, 5. Prince, Elector Palatine. Published for the Belefit and Satisfaction of all God's people. According to the Original printed in the High Dutch tongue*, trans. J. Rolte (London, imprinted for William Welby, 1614) 12–14.

350 G. Shultz, "A Biblical and Theological Defense of a Multi-Intentioned View of the Extent of the Atonement," 49.

> is clepid Goddis lombe, for many resouns of the lawe. In the olde lawe weren thei wont to offre a lombe withouten wem, the whiche shulde be of o gere, for the synne of the puple. Thus Crist, that was with outen wem, and of o geer in mannis elde was offrid in the cros for the synne of al this worlde, and where siche lambren that weren offrid felden sum tyme to the preestis, this lombe that made ende of other felde fulli to Goddis hond. And other lambren in a maner fordide the synne of o cuntre, but this lombe proprely fordide the synne of alle this worlde. . . . And so, al if preestis have power to relese synne as Cristis vikeris, netheles thei have this power in as myche as thei acorden with Crist; so tha yif ther keies and Cristis wille be discording atwynne, thei feynen hem falsely to assoile, and than thei neither loosen ne bynden; so that in ech siche worchynge the godhede of Crist mut first wirche.[351]

Here Wycliffe spoke twice of Christ being offered for the sins of the world.[352]

Hugh Latimer (AD 1487–1555)

Hugh Latimer, along with Cranmer, was one of the crucial leaders of the English Reformation. Having served as Bishop of Worcester prior to the Reformation, he became chaplain to Edward VI and was instrumental in many ways in fostering the English Reformation. He was martyred along with Ridley under Queen Mary in 1555.

Latimer's commitment to unlimited atonement is unquestioned. His sermons furnish a plethora of statements clearly affirming a universal atonement.[353] Here is one example:

> For Christ only, and no man else, merited remission, justification, and eternal felicity, for as many as will believe the same; they that will not believe it, shall not have it, for it is no more but believe and have. For Christ shed as much

351 J. Wyclif, *Select English Works*, 3 vols., ed. T. Arnold (Oxford: Clarendon, 1869–1871), 1:77.

352 Shultz, following Rainbow, asserted Wycliffe held to limited atonement (Shultz, "A Biblical and Theological Defense of a Multi-Intentioned View of the Extent of the Atonement," 30). Shultz argued that Wycliffe followed Aquinas in using the sufficient/efficient formula but used it instead to defend particular redemption: "Wycliffe employed the formula to affirm that Christ's atonement considered in and of itself was theoretically sufficient for an infinite number of people, although in reality it only bought salvation for the elect (and was therefore efficient only for them)" (ibid., 35. Shultz footnotes *Wycliffe's Latin Works*, 25 vols. [London: The Wycliffe Society, 1883–1914], 10:439–40). However, as Wycliffe's comments on John 1:29 demonstrate above, Shultz is mistaken about Wycliffe.

353 See, among others, H. Latimer, *Sermons by Hugh Latimer, Sometime Bishop of Worcester*, 2 vols. (Cambridge: Cambridge University Press, 1844–1845), 1:7; 1:234–35; 1:330–31; 1:520–22, for explicit statements concerning the universal extent of the atonement. William Lorimer also claims Latimer taught the "middle-way," in addition to the first Reformers, Luther, Calvin, Hooper, and the Church of England. See W. Lorimer, *An Apology for the Ministers Who Subscribed Only unto the Stating of the Truths and Errours in Mr. William's Book* (London: Printed for John Lawrence, at the Angel in the Poultry, 1694), 192. Henry Hickman (d. AD 1692) also said that both Hooper and Latimer "asserted universal redemption." See his *Historia Quinq-Articularis Exarticulata; or, Animadversions on Doctor Heylin's Quinquarticular History* (London: Printed for R. Boulter, 1674), 180.

> blood for Judas as He did for Peter; Peter believed it, and therefore he was saved; Judas would not believe and therefore he was condemned—the fault being in him only, and in nobody else.[354]

Gatiss mentioned Augustus Toplady's *Historic Proof for the Doctrinal Calvinism of the Church of England* (1774) as presenting "copious amounts of evidence" to prove that some bishops and clergy in England, including Latimer, held to limited atonement.[355] In addition to Latimer, he lists Ridley, Bucer, and the British delegation to Dort.

Gatiss's comment here is problematic since it can be shown beyond any doubt that Ridley and Latimer held to unlimited atonement, and even Gatiss himself just a few pages previously mentions Davenant and the British delegation as affirming Hypothetical Universalism and not limited atonement. Toplady is in error concerning these men.

Toplady attempted to argue that "world" for Latimer always meant the world of believers. This can be easily falsified by even a cursory reading of Latimer. Toplady asserted that Latimer held to limited atonement because the latter said Christ did not die for the impenitent.[356] But the context reveals that Latimer means that Christ did not die to save anyone as long as they remain in unbelief. No unbeliever can appropriate the saving benefit of Christ's death as long as he remains in unbelief. This is no indication of limited atonement.

Toplady argued, with no evidence whatsoever, that when Latimer spoke of Christ shedding his blood as much for Judas as for Peter, he meant only the intrinsic sufficiency of Christ's death. Finally, Toplady appealed to Latimer's statements concerning a Christian's participation in the Lord's Table.[357] Latimer said to the communicant that he should not consider the death of Christ for the world generally but think of his death for you specifically. Toplady found in this evidence for limited atonement. But it is obvious that Latimer is saying the Christian at the Lord's Table is to think and apply what Christ has done for him personally. Interestingly, this kind of language is common to both Calvin and Bullinger, both of whom held to unlimited atonement.

Miles Coverdale (AD 1488–1568)

Miles Coverdale was best known for his publication of the first complete English Bible in print (1535). He served as king's chaplain in the court of Edward VI and became Bishop of Exeter in 1551 but was deposed in 1553 by the new Queen Mary. His belief in unlimited atonement can be discerned in several places in his writings.[358]

354 Latimer, *Sermons,* 1:521.

355 L. Gatiss, *For Us and for Our Salvation,* 109–10.

356 A. Toplady, *Historic Proof of the Doctrinal Calvinism of the Church of England,* 2 vols. (London: Printed for George Keith, in Gracechurch-street, 1774), 1:312–25.

357 Ibid., 1:315.

358 D. Wallace, *Puritans and Predestination: Grace in English Protestant Theology, 1525–1695* (Eugene, OR: Wipf & Stock, 2004), 16.

Thomas Cranmer (AD 1489–1556)

Thomas Cranmer was the leading theologian and preacher of the English Reformation.

Cranmer was primarily responsible for *The Forty-Two Articles* in 1553. These articles reflected the influence of the Swiss Reformers. The articles contain clear affirmations of justification by faith, humanity's fallen state, the idea that repentance and faith are only the result of God's gift, unconditional election, and the perseverance of the elect.[359] There is no mention in *The Forty-Two Articles* of any notion that the atonement is limited in its extent only to the elect. John Ponet's catechism, published with *The Forty-Two Articles*, likewise made no mention of limited atonement.

During the reign of Edward VI, the *Book of Homilies* was published, with most of the sermons written by Cranmer. It was banned during the reign of Mary, but reinstated by the Elizabethan Injunctions of 1559. A second book of homilies was authorized in 1563.[360] These homilies covered the lay of the land of Protestant theology, but one searches in vain for any statement that the extent of the atonement was limited only to the elect.

Cranmer clearly affirms universal atonement in the following:

> This is the honour and glory of this our high priest, wherein he admitteth neither partner nor successor. For by his own oblation he satisfied his Father for all men's sins, and reconciled mankind unto his grace and favour. And whosoever deprive him of his honour, and go about to take it to themselves, they be very antichrists, and most arrogant blasphemers against God and against his Son Jesus Christ, whom he hath sent.[361]

Notice in this statement how Cranmer spoke of Christ's death as being for the sins of "all men" and "mankind." Here is unlimited atonement. But then, just a few paragraphs beyond, Cranmer spoke of the benefits of Christ's atonement to those who believe.

> But now to speak somewhat more largely of the priesthood and sacrifices of Christ, he was of such an high bishop, that he, once offering himself, was sufficient, by once effusion of his blood, to abolish sin unto the world's end. He was so perfect a priest, that by one oblation he purged an infinite heap of sins, leaving an easy and a ready remedy for all sinners, that his one sacrifice should suffice for many years unto all men that would not shew themselves unworthy. And he took unto himself not only their sins that many years before were dead,

359 Ibid., 32.

360 T. Cranmer, *Writings and Disputations of Thomas Cranmer*, 2 vols. (Cambridge: Cambridge University Press, 1844–46), 1:346.

361 Ibid., 1:346–47.

> and put their trust in him, but also the sins of those that, until his coming again, should truly believe in his gospel.[362]

If one were to fail to read Cranmer's latter statements in context, one might wrongly conclude that Cranmer is affirming limited atonement. Cranmer has already established the death of Christ for the sins of "all men" and "mankind." Here his focus is on Christ's death as benefiting all who believe. This is the kind of dualism that we find in virtually all of the early Reformers. Failure to recognize this dualism leads to a false assessment that Cranmer and others affirmed limited atonement.

William Tyndale (AD 1494–1536)

Tyndale was perhaps best known for his Bible translation, but he was an important part of the early English Reformation. He authored numerous works and was martyred in 1536. The following quotation illustrates Tyndale's belief in unlimited atonement: "And I wonder that M. More can laugh at it, and not rather weep for compassion, to see the souls for which Christ shed his blood to perish."[363]

Additional examples from his writings supporting his belief in unlimited atonement can be found in his *Doctrinal Treatises* and his *Exposition of the First Epistle of St. John*.[364]

John Hooper (c. AD [1495–1500]–1555)

John Hooper was Bishop of Gloucester and Worcester. He spent the better part of two years (1547–1849) on the continent in Strassburg and Zurich. While in Zurich he met on many occasions with Bullinger, whose commentaries on Paul's Epistles played a significant role in Hooper's conversion sometime before 1546. Hooper was martyred in 1555. His commitment to universal atonement can be found in several places in his writings. For example, Article 25 of his "Brief and Clear Confession of the Christian Faith, Contained in an Hundred Articles According to the Order of the Apostles Creed" states:

> I believe, that all this (the sufferings of Christ) was done, not for himself, who never committed sin, in whose mouth was never found deceit nor lie; but for the love of us poor and miserable sinners, whose place he occupied upon the

362 See, for example, Miles Coverdale, "The Passion of Christ," in *The Writings and Translations of Miles Coverdale*, ed. G. Pearson (Cambridge: Cambridge University Press, 1844), 211; idem, "The Old Faith," in *The Writings and Translations of Miles Coverdale*, 75–76; and "The Sending of the Holy Ghost," in *The Writings and Translations of Miles Coverdale*, 403–4.

363 W. Tyndale, "Answer to Sir Thomas More's Dialogue," in *The Works of the English Reformers William Tyndale and John Frith*, 3 vols., ed. T. Russell (London: Printed for Ebenezer Palmer, 1831), 2:131.

364 W. Tyndale, "Prologue to the Prophet Jonas," *Doctrinal Treatises and Introductions to Different Portions of the Holy Scriptures*, ed. H. Walter (Cambridge: Cambridge University Press, 1848), 464, where he stated: "Because we be *all equally created* and *formed of one God our Father*, and *indifferently bought and redeemed with one blood of our Saviour Jesus Christ*." See also his "Exposition of First Epistle of St. John," in *Works*, 2:406; 2:425; 2:453–54; 2:467.

cross, as a pledge, or as one that represented the person of all the sinners that ever were, now are, or shall be, unto the world's end.[365]

John Bradford (AD 1510–1555)

Bradford was an early English Reformer and martyr who died at the hands of Mary in 1555. He was a prebendary at St. Paul's. Bradford is the one who saw a criminal on his way to execution and allegedly said, "There, but for the grace of God, go I."

In the late seventeenth century, John Humfrey listed Bradford, along with Cranmer, Ridley, and Latimer, as affirming unlimited atonement from the Church of England Catechism: "Where the child is made to answer there, *Who hath redeemed me and all mankind*."[366]

Trueman alleged that Bradford's doctrine of election also included a doctrine of limited atonement. Bradford "places a limitation upon the extent of the atonement, and allows that Christ is a general saviour only in a qualified sense."[367] In Hart's controversy with Bradford, he charges that Bradford's doctrine of election "denies that the virtue of Christ's blood extends to all men."[368] Bradford said in reference to John 17, "For whom he [Christ] 'prayed not,' for them he died not."

Each of these reasons listed by Trueman and Hart do not in and of themselves indicate a strictly limited atonement. The final statement by Bradford may indicate a commitment to limited atonement, but Bradford may be using the term "died" to mean "died effectually for," in the sense of "died with the intent to apply the atonement to the elect." If the latter is his intended meaning, this is no proof of limited atonement.

John Jewel (AD 1522–1571)

Jewel was Bishop of Salisbury and was influenced by the writings of Peter Martyr Vermigli. He wrote that on the cross, Christ declared, "It is finished" to signify "that the price and ransom was now full paid for the sin of all mankind."[369] In a sermon, Jewel stated: "The death of Christ is available for the redemption of all the world."[370]

---

365 J. Hooper, "Extracts from a Brief and Clear Confession of the Christian Faith," in *Writings of Dr. John Hooper* (London: Religious Tract Society, 1831), 417–20. See idem, "A Declaration of Christ and His Office," in *Writings of Dr. John Hooper*, 41–42; idem, "Homily to Be Read in Times of Pestilence," in *Writings of Dr. John Hooper*, 233; idem, *Early Writings of Bishop Hooper* (Cambridge: Cambridge University Press, 1843), 115–16; and idem, "Copy of Bishop Hooper's Visitation Book," in *Later Writings of Bishop Hooper* (Cambridge: Cambridge University Press, 1852), 122.

366 J. Humfrey, *Peace at Pinners-Hall* (London: Randal Taylor, 1692), 2–4.

367 C. Trueman, *Luther's Legacy: Salvation and English Reformers, 1525–1556* (Oxford: Clarendon, 1994), 257; citing Bradford, *Writings*, 1:320.

368 Trueman, *Luther's Legacy*, 261.

369 J. Jewel, "An Apology or Answer in Defense of the Church of England," in *The Works of John Jewel, Bishop of Salisbury*, 8 vols., ed. J. Ayre (Cambridge: Cambridge University Press, 1848), 3:66.

370 J. Jewel, "An Homily of the Worthy Receiving and Reverent Esteeming of the Sacrament of the Body and Blood of Christ," in *The Two Books of Homilies Appointed to be Read in Churches*, ed. J. Griffiths (Oxford: Oxford University Press, 1859), 444.

The early years of the English Reformation were led by men who believed in unlimited atonement. With the influence of Beza on the continent, attitudes toward the extent of the atonement began to change in England toward the last third of the sixteenth century.

The account leading up to this may be summarized, beginning with the reign of Edward VI. When he acceded to the throne, Continental Reformed theologians such as Bucer and Vermigli were invited to England. Bucer's influence on England was already significant when he received the Regius Professor of Divinity at Cambridge. Vermigli was made professor of divinity at Oxford. These men provided theological leadership and often served in an advising capacity to the English bishops.[371] No doubt their commitment to unlimited atonement was disseminated within their sphere of influence.

John Bridges's 1571 sermon at Paul's Cross on John 3:16 is important to note. He interpreted the word "world" as a reference to the elect. Bridges continued to assert that God only desires the salvation of the elect. But nowhere did Bridges explicitly affirm limited atonement or address the subject of the extent of the atonement. Some have reasoned that his interpretation of "world" as the elect pointed to his belief in limited atonement. One thing is clear: Bridges was making the point that the death of Christ was *designed* for the elect, even though this would not necessarily commit him to particular redemption. Bridges also supported the necessity of the universal gospel call through preaching.[372]

When Samuel Harsnett, later to become Archbishop of York, preached his sermon on Ezek 33:11 at Paul's Cross in October of 1594,[373] he may very well have been opposing the teaching of William Perkins (Perkins's first publication appeared in 1590). Harsnett stated in his sermon that God desires and wills the salvation of all and that Christ died for the sins of all according to passages such as John 1:29; 1 John 2:2; Matt 23:27; and 1 Tim 2:4.

In February of 1597, John Dove also preached a sermon on Ezek 33:11 at Paul's Cross. It is possible this sermon was a response to Harsnett's sermon three years earlier.[374] Dove's main point was, "It is not the will of God that all men should be saved."[375] By this point in time, the views of Beza and Perkins[376] were well established in England, though clearly not accepted by all, and the debate over the extent of the atonement was just getting under way in England as well as on the continent.

Peter Baro, Lady Margaret Professor of Divinity at Cambridge from 1574, had been ordained at Geneva by Calvin in 1560. Baro declared firmly in a sermon that Christ

---

371 D. Wallace, *Puritans and Predestination*, 5, 10.

372 See the discussion in J. Moore, *English Hypothetical Universalism: John Preston and the Softening of Reformed Theology* (Grand Rapids, MI: Eerdmans, 2007), 55–57.

373 Wallace, *Puritans and Predestination*, 66.

374 N. Tyacke, *Anti-Calvinists: The Rise of English Arminianism c. 1590–1640*, 2nd ed. (Oxford: Clarendon, 1990), 164.

375 Moore, *English Hypothetical Universalism*, 64.

376 Moore's statement that Perkins, "with his popular, supralapsarianism, particular redemptionism, may perhaps be seen, at least in this respect, as more the end of an era than, as is more usually stated, the beginning of a new one" (ibid., 226) is wide of the mark.

died for the sins of all, not just the elect. He also differed with the Reformed orthodox on the subject of predestination in his opposition to the Lambeth Articles of 1595 (articles that strongly asserted predestination but not limited atonement). This garnered the attention of Cambridge and he was not reelected to his professorship in 1596. Others at Cambridge agreed with Baro, including John Overall and Lancelot Andrewes.[377] John Overall found members of his parish at Epping distressed because "they could not be persuaded that Christ died for them." In response, Overall preached a sermon teaching that Christ died for all.[378] Richard Thompson affirmed that Christ died not for the elect only and was answered by the Bishop of Salisbury, Robert Abbot.[379]

A posthumous work by Abbot published in 1618 argued the Arminian view of the atonement made salvation only possible but not actual. Abbot made the high Calvinist distinction between the infinite value of Christ's death and the intention of Christ to provide satisfaction for the elect only. God loved the world in an indefinite sense, but such love was not saving love.[380]

By the last decade of the sixteenth century, the wrangling over the extent of the atonement, aided by William Perkins, was in full swing. In addition to Perkins's publications, Robert Some (AD 1542–1609), of Cambridge, published in 1596 a tract listing eight reasons for limited atonement.[381]

William Perkins (AD 1558–1602)

Perkins was the most eminent English Reformed theologian of the late sixteenth century and the first English Calvinist to earn a major European reputation. His homiletical and theological output was nothing short of astounding in his lifetime. Between 1590 and 1618, of the approximately two-hundred ten books printed by the primary publishing house in Cambridge, Perkins authored no fewer than fifty.[382] The most influential of these was his systematic theology, *A Golden Chaine*, which reached eight editions in English by 1600.[383] Perkins's *A Christian and Plaine Treatise of the Manner and Order of Predestination*, combined with *A Golden Chaine*, constructed a strong statement of predestination and an elaborate and speculative *ordo salutis*.

---

377 For Andrewes on universal atonement, see L. Andrewes, "Ninety Six Sermons: Sermons of the Nativity and of Repentance and Fasting, vol. 1," in *The Works of Lancelot Andrewes*, ed. J. Bliss and J. P. Wilson (Oxford: John Henry Parker, 1841), 268; and *Works*, 3:310.

378 Wallace, *Puritans and Predestination*, 75.

379 Ibid., 67–68.

380 R. Abbot, in his *De Gratia et perseverantia sanctorum, exercitationes aliquot habitæ in Academia Oxoniensi* (Londini: Ioannem Billium, 1618), 166.

381 R. Some, *Three Questions, Godly, and Plainly, and Briefly Handled . . . III. Christ Died Effectually for the Elect Alone: Therfore Not for Every Severall Man* (Cambridge: John Legat, 1596), 20–30. His texts were Matt 1:21; John 10:15, 26; 17:9; Heb 7:25; Rom 8:33–34; 1 John 2:1–2; Matt 26:28; Rev 5:9; Rom 5:19; Heb 9:28; Col 1:14; and John 11:49–52. See also Gatiss, *For Us and for Our Salvation*, 76.

382 R. Some, *Three Questions*, 27–28.

383 See W. Perkins, "A Golden Chaine," in *The Work of William Perkins*, ed. I. Breward (Appleford, England: Sutton Courtenay, 1970), 204–8, for his argument for limited atonement.

Perkins taught that God had decreed Adam's fall but denied that God was the author of sin. He also taught double predestination and was a supralapsarian. Moore noted how Perkins's doctrine of particular redemption "was intimately linked with three main areas of his thought: predestinarianism, federalism, and the doctrine of the unity of Christ's priestly work."[384] Jacob Arminius, already chaffing under what he considered to be the extreme predestinarian theology of Beza, responded to Perkins in his *Examen Modestum Libelli*.

Perkins opposed Arminianism and its understanding of universal atonement. Perkins, according to Moore, was not opposing English Hypothetical Universalism or the later development of Amyraldianism.[385] In fact, Perkins made statements that could possibly be interpreted in support of Hypothetical Universalism, such as Christ "hath perfectly alone by himself accomplished all things that are needful for the salvation of mankind" on the grounds that he made "satisfaction to his Father for the sinne of man."[386] Perkins likewise wrote, "I doe willingly acknowledge and teach universall redemption and grace, so farre as it is possible by the word," and "universall redemption of all men, we grant: the Scripture saith so."[387]

However, as Moore noted, Perkins is simultaneously maintaining that Christ died "only for those which are elected and predestinated." "Perkins sees that 'there is an universalitie among the Elect and beleevers.' Similarly, Perkins can concede that 'Christ died for all men in the sense of Scripture,' but simultaneously denies that 'Christ died for every man without exception.'"[388] Though Perkins retained the universal language of Scripture concerning Christ's satisfaction for sin, it appears he interpreted such language only in the sense of an infinite intrinsic sufficiency[389] and not in an objective extrinsic sufficiency such that Christ's death actually paid the price for the sins of the world. Perkins stated that the

384 Moore, *English Hypothetical Universalism*, 39.

385 Ibid., 43.

386 W. Perkins, "The Foundation of Christian Religion," in *The Works of that Most Famous and Worthy Minister of Christ in the University of Cambridge, Mr. William Perkins*, 2 vols. (London: John Legatt, 1616), 1:4; cited by Moore, *English Hypothetical Universalism*, 38.

387 Perkins, *Workes*, 2:605; cited by Moore, *English Hypothetical Universalism*, 39.

388 Perkins, *Workes*, 2:609; cited by Moore, *English Hypothetical Universalism*, 39.

389 Moore, *English Hypothetical Universalism*, 37–39. On Perkins's treatment of specific texts related to the extent of the atonement, see Moore, *English Hypothetical Universalism*, 38–55. Moore noted the "great length to which Perkins goes to defend his interpretation of 1 Timothy 2:4 is indicative of how dangerous to his system Perkins considered the notion of a universal saving will in God to be" (51). Perkins attempts to defend his interpretation of key extent passages, such as 1 Tim 2:4, while arguing simultaneously that the gospel call is universal and should be preached to all. Moore's portrayal of Perkins on the will of God is not without its problems. In Perkins's lectures on Revelation, he spoke of Christ standing at the door of every man's heart with "a desire of their conversion, which he heartily seeks and longs for." He "pursues them with mercy, and offers mercy to them that refused it." Christ "comes by the ministry of the Gospel to work our conversion," and "it is an earnest knocking of one that would fain enter . . . to save men's souls." He "knocks in good earnest" which is "the first token of Christ's love, his desire of their conversion, which he shows by two signs; first his waiting, secondly his knocking, and that joined with crying." See W. Perkins, *Lectures upon the Three First Chapters of the Revelation* (London: Richard, 1604), 331–34. In this same work (326) Perkins affirmed God's love for all mankind. See also his treatment of Matt 23:27 in *A Treatise of God's Free Grace, and Man's Free Will* (Cambridge: John Legat, 1601), 23, 44–47.

> virtue and efficacy of this price being paid, in respect of merit and operation is infinite; but yet it must be distinguished for it is either potentiall or actuall. The potentiall efficacy is, whereby the price is in itself sufficient to redeeme every one without exception from his sins, albeit there were a thousand worlds of me. But if we consider the actual efficacy, the price is payd in the counsel of God, and as touching the event, onely for those which are elected and predestinated. For the Sonne doth not sacrifice, for those, for whom he doth not pray: because to make intercession and to sacrifice are conjoined: but he prayeth onely for the elect and for believers.[390]

Moore's quotations from Perkins leave no doubt that he taught a limited atonement: "Wee utterly denie, that [Christ] died for all and every one alike in respect of God, or as well for the damned as elect, and that effectually on God's part."[391] Likewise, Perkins can state unequivocally that God "giveth them no Saviour. For Christ is onely the Redeemer of the Elect, and of no more."[392] Perkins leaves no doubt when he asserted "the price is appointed and limited to the elect alone by the Fathers decree, and the Sonnes intercession and oblation."[393] Prior to but in the same vein as John Owen, Perkins interpreted the "world" of John 3:16 as the elect among the Jews and Gentiles.[394]

Moore continued, demonstrating that Perkins's polemical statements against universal redemption are further evidence of his commitment to limited atonement. Perkins styles universal redemption as "a mere devise," "very absurd," and "flat against Gods word." Perkins saw it as a "forgerie of mans brain," and "the conceit of popish writers." Moore referenced Baxter's belief that no one had written more confidently against universal redemption than had Perkins.[395]

William Ames (AD 1566–1633)

Ames was a leading English Puritan who had been a student of Perkins at Cambridge from 1594 to 1610. For whatever reason, authorities of the Church of England thought him too radical, and he was stripped of his ecclesiastical and academic positions in 1610. He left England for the Netherlands where he served from 1613 to 1618. Ames was an observer at Dort and was professor of theology at Franeker in Friesland from 1622 to 1633. He published four polemical books against Arminianism. His best-known work is *The Marrow of Theology* (1623).

Ames used the following syllogism to express his views on limited atonement:

---

390 W. Perkins, "The Order of Predestination," in *The Works of that Famous and Worthy Minister of Christ in the University of Cambridge, M. William Perkins*, 3 vols. (London: John Haviland, 1631), 2:609.

391 Perkins, *Workes*, 2:609; cited by Moore, *English Hypothetical Universalism*, 40.

392 Perkins, *Workes*, 1:415; cited by Moore, *English Hypothetical Universalism*, 40.

393 Perkins, *Workes*, 2:609; cited by Moore, *English Hypothetical Universalism*, 40.

394 Perkins, *Workes*, 1:296; cited by Moore, *English Hypothetical Universalism*, 45.

395 Moore, *English Hypothetical Universalism*, 43.

> For whom it is intended, to them it is applied.
> But not to all is it applied.
> Therefore not to all is it intended.[396]

The most this argument can prove is a limited intent to apply, not a limited satisfaction for sin. And as others have argued, if Christ's death is in fact sufficient for all, then it must have been intended to be sufficient for all. If it was intended to be sufficient for all, then God must intend the salvation of all through faith in that all-sufficient satisfaction.

For Ames, the issue was how intent, extent, and application were related to each other. He viewed all three as co-extensive.[397]

On the sufficiency of the atonement, Ames stated:

> As for the intention of application, it is rightly said that Christ made satisfaction only for those whom he saved, though in regard to the sufficiency in the mediation of Christ it may also rightly be said that Christ made satisfaction for each and all. Because these counsels of God are hidden to us, it is the part of charity to judge well of every one, although we may not say of all collectively that Christ equally pleads the cause of each before God.[398]

This statement is quite interesting. Ames asserted that Christ, with respect to the intention of application, made satisfaction *only* for those who are saved. Yet he also stated that with regard to the sufficiency of the atonement that Christ "made satisfaction for each and all." These statements seem contradictory. If Ames is speaking about a hypothetical sufficiency of merit and value, which is how all limitarians describe sufficiency, he cannot follow that by saying it can be said that Christ "made satisfaction for each and all." He would have to say that Christ *could have made satisfaction for all if that was God's intention in the actual extent of the atonement.* But this is not what Ames seems to be saying. He said Christ made satisfaction "for each and all."

William Perkins made similar inconsistent statements.

---

396 Translation from Latin by S. Lewis Johnson. The Latin states: "Quibus intenditur, iis applicatur. Sed non omnibus intendatur. Ergo non omnibus intendatur" ("De Arminii sententia," in *Opera*, 5 vols. [Amsterdam, 1658], 5:A2v), quoted in H. A. Krop, "Philosophy and the Synod of Dort. Aristotelianism, Humanism, and the Case against Armininism," in *Revisiting the Synod of Dordt (1618–1619)*, ed. A. Goudriaan and F. van Lieburg; Brill's Series in Church History 19 (Leiden: Brill, 2011), 72n74.

397 Godfrey, "Reformed Thought on the Extent of the Atonement," 163–64. See Ames's *Rescriptio Scholastica et brevis ad Nic. Grevinchovii Respondum illud prolixum, quod opposuit Dissertationi De Redemptione generali, et Electione ex fide praevisa*, Editio altera (Amsteledami: Henricum Laurentium, 1615), 1, where the first five chapters discuss the work of Christ where Ames argued that the central errors of the Arminians were in separating the oblation and intercession of Christ and in separating the extent and application of Christ's death. See also K. L. Sprunger, *The Learned Doctor William Ames: Dutch Backgrounds of English and American Puritanism* (Urbana: University of Illinois Press, 1972).

398 W. Ames, *The Marrow of Theology*, trans. J. D. Eusden (Durham, NC: Labyrinth, 1983), 150.

> I do now exhibit unto thee a view and picture of this Doctrine, composed of these principles, and do publish the same, that I might, to my power, help out those that stick in the difficulties of this doctrine of Predestination: and that I might clear the truth, that is (as they call it) the Calvinists doctrine, of those reproaches which are cast upon it: and that I might mitigate and appease the minds of some of our Brethren, which have been more offended at it then was fit. For I do willingly acknowledge and teach universal redemption and grace, so far as it is possible by the word.[399]

Both Ames and Perkins, although high Calvinists, still have something of the earlier Reformed tradition of Hypothetical Universalism in their thinking. Notice that Perkins and Ames say things in ways that Calvin never did before them (Calvin never limited the extent of the atonement) and that Owen and Turretin never did after them (who never made any statements like Perkins and Ames such as "Christ made satisfaction for the sins of each and all.")

Ames and Perkins appear to be transitional figures between the first generation of Reformers who never advocated limited atonement and the Owen and Turretin generation, which staunchly advocated a strictly limited atonement. The lingering remnants of an earlier Hypothetical Universalism model continue to emerge, but they are negated by statements arguing for a strictly limited position.

At the accession of Queen Elizabeth to the throne of England (1558), the year of Perkins's birth, one is hard pressed to find evidence for particular redemption in the Anglican Church, with the possible exception of John Bradford. Article 31 of the Thirty-Nine Articles (1563) clearly affirmed universal atonement, as did other articles. But toward the latter half of Elizabeth's reign, as a result of the growing influence of Beza and Perkins, a strict redemption view was espoused by a growing number, but if it ever had been the dominant viewpoint during this time, which is debatable, there were many who affirmed and argued for universal atonement. Before the turn of the seventeenth century, there was growing unrest over the strict predestinarian theology advocated by Beza and Perkins, including the notion of limited atonement.

In reference to Some's 1596 tract in support of limited atonement, Lee Gatiss stated: "The question of whether Christ died effectually for the elect alone or for everyone was certainly discussed in the sixteenth century."[400] But it was not discussed until the late sixteenth century. Gatiss's use of the term "effectually" is problematic and lacks proper nuance. No one doubts that Christ died *effectually* only for the elect—that is,

---

399 W. Perkins, "Master Perkinses Epistle to the Reader," in *A Christian and Plaine Treatise of the Manner and Order of Predestination* (London: Printed for William Welby and Martin Clarke, 1606), iv.

400 Gatiss, *For Us and for Our Salvation*, 75. In fact, all of the propositions drawn up by the Remonstrants in Holland leading up to the Synod of Dort were discussed in England in the 1590s. (H. C. Porter, *Reformation and Reaction in Tudor Cambridge* [Cambridge: Cambridge University Press, 1958], 277–87).

for all who believe. The issue concerning the extent of the atonement is whether Christ actually substituted himself for the sins of all people and not just for the elect.

In the early seventeenth century, debate over the meaning of the extent of the atonement and the nuances and entailments of such ambiguous phrases as "Christ died for the sins of the world," Christ's death was "sufficient" for the sins of the world, and so on would reach fever pitch. Important to note at this point is the fact that such debates occurred not only between the Reformed and the Arminians but among the Reformed themselves. Peter White stated: "At perhaps no point were the tensions within international Calvinism [in England] more acute than on the extent of the Atonement."[401] We shall see that the same would be true for Reformed theology on the continent as well.

Early Reformed Confessions

One of the earliest Protestant confessions was the Anglican Catechism of 1553. It was published just a few months prior to the untimely death of King Edward VI and illustrates the emerging Reformed Anglicanism during Edward's reign under the auspices of Cranmer and Latimer. It stated concerning Christ's death: "Then He truly died and was truly buried, that by His most sweet sacrifice He might pacify His Father's wrath against mankind."[402]

Another early confession is the English Confession of Faith, also called the Genevan Confession (1556), written by the English exiles in Geneva, signed by John Knox, and approved by the Church of Scotland at that time. It states that Christ "offered up himself as the only sacrifice to purge the sins of all the world."[403] Clearly, at face value, the confession affirms an unlimited atonement.

This was soon followed by the Second Helvetic Confession of 1562, written by Bullinger. This confession was influential in the Swiss churches and was adopted by the Reformed Church abroad. It states that Christ is the "Savior of the human race, and thus of the whole world" and that Christ is the "Redeemer and Savior of the world."[404] The confession speaks of Christ as the "satisfaction, propitiation or expiation of all sins (Isa., ch. 53; I Cor. 1:30)," and further stated that "Christ took upon himself and bore the sins of the world, and satisfied divine justice." Under the section on the Lord's Supper, the confession refers to Christ's "redemption and that of all mankind" whose body was "given and his blood shed, not only for men in general, but particularly for every faithful communicant." It is clear that the Second Helvetic Confession affirms an unlimited atonement.

---

401 P. White, *Predestination, Policy and Polemic: Conflict and Consensus in the English Church from the Reformation to the Civil War* (Cambridge: Cambridge University Press, 1992), 187.

402 "Anglican Catechism (1553)," in *Reformed Confessions of the Sixteenth and Seventeenth Centuries in English Translation*, 4 vols., ed. J. T. Dennison (Louisville, KY: Westminster John Knox, 2003), 2:23.

403 A. C. Cochrane, ed., *Reformed Confessions of the Sixteenth Century* (Philadelphia: Westminster, 1966), 132. See also *Dunlop's Harmony of Confessions*, 2:55.

404 Ibid., 246.

The Hungarian *Confessio Catholica* of 1562 likewise affirms unlimited atonement,[405] basing the universal gospel call upon Christ's death for all.

One of the most important confessions in church history is the Thirty-Nine Articles. Article 31, "Of the One Oblation of Christ Finished upon the Cross," addresses the issue of the extent of the atonement:

> The offering of Christ once made is *the* perfect redemption, propitiation, and satisfaction for all the sins of the whole world, both original and actual; and there is none other satisfaction for sin, but that alone. Wherefore the sacrifices of Masses, in the which it was commonly said that the Priests did offer Christ for the quick and the dead, to have remission of pain or guilt, were blasphemous fables, and dangerous deceits.[406]

Article 31 was regularly interpreted as affirming an unlimited atonement from its inception.

Lee Gatiss made an abortive attempt to argue that Article 31 does not teach universal atonement.[407] He stated, "Thus it is abundantly plain that this Article, when read in its immediate context, is an assertion of the *sufficiency* of the atonement designed to undercut the doctrine and practice of Mass sacrifice." Gatiss considers it "irresponsible" to interpret the first half of Article 31 "as if it thoughtfully reflected a doctrine of universal atonement."[408] But Gatiss has failed to read Article 31 in light of Article 2, which states Christ "truly suffered, was crucified, dead and buried, to reconcile his father to us, and to be a sacrifice not only for original guilt, but also for all actual sins of men."

Gatiss also fails to discern that the statement in Article 31 is not *only* about the universal sufficiency of the atonement (interpreted by Gatiss to be an intrinsic, hypothetical sufficiency). The statement actually says Christ died "for all the sins of the whole world." This is a direct statement concerning the atonement's extent and cannot be explained away by merely positing that the statement is only about the hypothetical sufficiency of the atonement.

Davenant himself appealed to Article 31 as affirming the universal extent of the atonement.[409] Fesko rightly noted that "a qualified universalism, that is, that Christ's satisfaction in some sense extended to all, was part of the confessional air that the Westminster

---

405 "The Hungarian *Confessio Catholica* (1562)," in *Reformed Confessions of the Sixteenth and Seventeenth Centuries in English Translation*, 4 vols., ed. J. T. Dennison (Grand Rapids, MI: Reformation Heritage, 2010), 2:487.

406 I have updated the old English spellings to modern English. P. Schaff, "The Evangelical Protestant Creeds, with Translations, vol. 3," in *Creeds of Christendom* (Grand Rapids, MI: Baker, 1966), 507.

407 Gatiss, *For Us and for Our Salvation*, 102–6.

408 Ibid., 104. Article 31 of the *Thirty-Nine Articles* (1563) states: "The offering of Christ once made is the perfect redemption, propitiation and satisfaction for all the sins of the whole world, both original and actual; and there is no other satisfaction for sin, but that alone" (P. Schaff, *The Evangelical Protestant Creeds, with Translations*, 507. I have updated the old English spellings to modern English.)

409 Davenant, "Dissertation on the Death of Christ," 2:355.

divines breathed, found both in the Thirty-Nine Articles and in the Canons of Dort with its use of the sufficient-efficient distinction."[410]

Conclusion

A survey of the English Reformed scene during the sixteenth century indicates a firm belief in universal atonement. With the possible exception of John Bradford, no sixteenth-century early English Reformer advocated limited atonement. Any hint of a limited atonement does not appear until late in the sixteenth century.

410 J. V. Fesko, *The Theology of the Westminster Standards: Historical Context & Theological Insights* (Wheaton, IL: Crossway, 2014), 194–95.

3

The Post-Reformation Era and the Extent of the Atonement

Jacob Arminius and the Synod of Dort

In the late sixteenth and early seventeenth century leading up to Dort, the theological scene was anything but monolithic.[1] The Lutherans and the Reformed had long been engaged in debates. The newer theology of Faustus Socinus (AD 1539–1604)[2] and the Socinians also began to be engaged by the Reformed, and that with a vengeance. Finally, the rise of the Arminians brought another group to the fray. From the perspective of the Reformed, they found themselves doing battle on three fronts: Lutherans, Socinians, and Arminians.

Unfortunately for the Arminians, they were often wrongly shackled with the epithet

---

1 A good overview is J. Rohls, "Calvinism, Arminianism, and Socinianism in the Netherlands until the Synod of Dort," in *Socinianism and Arminianism: Antitrinitarians, Calvinists, and Cultural Exchange in Seventeenth-Century Europe*, ed. M. Mulsow and J. Rohls (Leiden: Brill, 2005), 3–48.

2 On Socinianism, the primary sources are the writings of Faustus and Laelius Socinus, collected in the *Bibliotheca Fratrum Polonarum*, 8 vols. (Amsterdam: Sumptibus Irenici, 1656–1698). See also *The Racovian Catechism, with Notes and Illustrations*, trans. T. Rees (1605; repr. London: Printed for Longman, Hurst, Rees, Orme, and Brown, 1818), for the official doctrine of Socinianism. For a helpful summary of the Socinian view of the atonement, see S. Strehle, "The Extent of the Atonement within the Theological Systems of the Sixteenth and Seventeenth Centuries" (PhD diss., Dallas Theological Seminary, 1980), 179–87.

of Socinianism by their Calvinist opponents. Whereas Socinianism had a flawed anthropology, Christology, and soteriology (denying predestination and substitutionary atonement), Arminius and the Arminians affirmed all of these, though they differed with the orthodox Reformed on predestination and were noncommittal on eternal security.[3]

But even that does not tell the whole story, because when it came to the extent of the atonement, the influence of Beza and Perkins and those who identified with their theology created a division within the Reformed camp.[4] For example, in 1595 Piscator wrote against the views of Andreae Schaafmann, who had argued for unlimited atonement,[5] and Piscator wrote again on the subject in 1614. Like Beza, he found the Lombardian formula confusing and unhelpful. He affirmed the infinite value (intrinsic sufficiency) of the death of Christ but maintained that the crucial question was Christ's intention in his death. This intention, according to Piscator, was strictly limited to the elect.

Jacob Arminius (AD 1560–1609)[6]

Arminius had himself studied under Beza at Geneva from 1582 to 1586. He found Beza's and Perkins's predestinarian theology to be on the extreme side of things. His two-hundred-page critique of Perkins's 1598 publication *On the Order and Mode of Predestination* was completed in 1600 but not published until 1612.

We are specifically interested in Arminius's approach to the question of the extent of the atonement. He clearly rejected Beza's and Perkins's understanding and supported universal atonement.[7]

---

3 For a helpful historical summary analysis of Arminianism from a Reformed perspective, see J. I. Packer, "Arminianisms," in *Through Christ's Word: A Festschrift for Dr. Philip E. Hughes*, ed. W. R. Godfrey and J. Boyd III (Phillipsburg, NJ: P&R, 1985), 121–48. Packer dealt with Arminius and his immediate successors through John Wesley and John Fletcher in the eighteenth century.

4 In Godfrey's survey of the period before the Arminian controversies, he pointed out that "there was a general Reformed consensus on the death of Christ. There were differences and ambiguities of expression to be sure, but the issue was not a matter of controversy within the Reformed community. Most theologians wrote sparingly on the subject and few followed Beza in rejecting the traditional distinction between sufficiency and efficiency" (Godfrey, "Reformed Thought on the Extent of the Atonement," 150).

5 J. Piscator, *Disputatio theological de praedestinatione opposite disfiutationi Andreae Schaafmanni* (Herbornae Nassoviorum: Christophori Corvini, 1598), 38–77. See note 97 in Godfrey, "Reformed Thought on the Extent of the Atonement," 162, for reference to F. L. Bos, *Johann Piscator: ein Beitrag zur Geschichte der reformierten Theologie* (Kampen: J. H. Kok, 1932), 206–7.

6 In the latest, scholarly, and more than seven-hundred-page defense of limited atonement, *From Heaven He Came and Sought Her*, Arminius garnered only ten references in the index, three of which are footnotes. Yet, as a member of the Reformed community, Arminius's arguments against limited atonement are significant and should be addressed.

7 The best place to begin a study of Arminius on the question of the extent of the atonement is his own writings. See *The Works of James Arminius*, 3 vols., trans. J. Nichols and W. Nichols (Grand Rapids, MI: Baker, 1986). Three outstanding secondary sources on Arminius are G. Brandt, *The Life of James Ariminius*, trans. J. Guthrie (Nashville: E. Stevenson & F. A. Owen, 1857); C. Bangs, *Arminius: A Study in the Dutch Reformation*, 2nd ed. (Grand Rapids, MI: Zondervan, 1985); and K. Stanglin and T. McCall, *Jacob Arminius: Theologian of Grace* (Oxford: Oxford University Press, 2012), 141–88. See also J. M. Pinson, "The Nature of the Atonement in the Theology of Jacobus Arminius," *Journal of the Evangelical Theological Society* 53 (2010): 773–85. For a Reformed perspective on Arminius and Arminianism, consult the survey of Arminius scholarship in R. A. Muller, *God, Creation, and Providence in the Thought of Jacob Arminius: Sources and Directions of Scholastic Protestantism in the*

Arminius was unhappy with the traditional Reformed order of the decrees to elect and to redeem. He reversed the order of the decrees in Reformed theology, placing the decree to send Christ as redeemer prior to the decree of election.[8] His reasoning was twofold: (1) he viewed Christ as the actual foundation of the decree of election, not just the executor of it, and (2) he distinguished between the oblation (death) of Christ and the intercession of Christ for believers, as did many classical Calvinists.

Arminius offered a lengthy and substantive critique of William Perkins's views on predestination and limited atonement. Concerning the sufficiency of the atonement, Arminius correctly understood Perkins's position to be that the sufficiency was limited only to the worth and value of the cross, and hence, for Arminius, this was no sufficiency at all.

> But, if I rightly understand you, you seem to me not to acknowledge the sufficiency of that price simply, but with the condition added,—"provided that God had willed it to be offered for the sins of the whole world:" and so what the Schoolmen enunciated categorically,—that Christ died for all and each sufficiently,—must, according to your idea, be pro-pounded under supposition; in this sense, forsooth, that "Christ's death would be a sufficient price for the sins of the whole world and of more worlds, provided that God had willed it to be offered for all men." In which sense, truly, the sufficiency is simply taken away. . . . Therefore, the death of Christ might be said to be sufficient for redeeming the sins of all men, if God had willed Him to die for all: but the λυτρον cannot be called sufficient, unless it has actually been paid for all.[9]

Arminius continued:

> But truly, my dear Perkins, Scripture in many places most plainly teaches that Christ died "for all," and "for the life of the world," and that by the command and grace of God but the decree of predestination sets no bounds to the universality of the price paid for all by the death of Christ. For it is posterior to the death of Christ and its proper efficacy. For it relates to the application of the benefits obtained for us by the death of Christ: but death is the price by which those benefits were acquired. Wrongly, therefore and in inverse order is it expressed, when Christ is said to have "died only for the elect and predestinated." For predestination rests not merely on the death, but also on the merit of the death of Christ: and therefore Christ has not died for the predestinated,

Era of Early Orthodoxy (Grand Rapids, MI: Baker, 1991), 3–14.

8 Arminius, *Works*, 1:653–57; Stanglin and McCall, *Jacob Arminius*, 134–40.

9 Arminius, *Works*, 3:324–25.

> but those are predestinated for whom Christ has died, though not all. For the universality of the death of Christ extends more widely than the object of predestination. Whence also it is concluded that the death of Christ and its merit are antecedent by nature and order to predestination.[10]

In response to Perkins's argument for limited atonement from Christ's intercessory prayer in John 17:9 that the sacrifice and intercession of Christ are conjoined and thus Christ did not die for those for whom he did not pray, Arminius made three arguments. First, he pointed out that the sacrifice is prior to the intercession. Christ could not enter heaven to intercede except through his shed blood. For Arminius, "the sacrificing belongs to the merit, the intercession to the application of the merit."[11] The two are in that sense conjoined, yet ought to be distinguished, according to Arminius.

Second, Arminius noted that Christ not only prayed for his own, but he also prayed for his enemies—those who crucified him—among whom were some who were non-elect. The context of John 17 indicates the purpose of the prayer was for believers and those who would believe that they should attain the benefits of the atonement and that they may be one in unity with the Father and the Son.

Third, "world" in John 17

> properly signifies those who rejected Christ, when proclaimed to them in the word of the Gospel, and who should thereafter reject Him. Which is apparent from the opposition: "I pray not for the world, but for those whom Thou hast given Me," whom He defined as those who believed and those who were about to believe. . . . Therefore the amplitude of the sacrifice is not to be circumscribed by the narrow terms of the intercession.[12]

Arminius noted that Perkins had stated that Christ was destined to be the ransom paid for sin "by the intercession and offering of the Son." But intercession is posterior to the atonement, therefore the latter was not destined by the former.[13]

Perkins had argued Christ intercedes only for those whom he represented as a substitute on the cross—namely, the elect. But Scripture indicates Christ died for more than the elect, as, for example, in John 1:29. For Arminius, Christ's incarnation necessitated that he substituted for the sins of all humanity on the cross.[14]

Arminius stated that the *philanthropia* of God toward humanity "is not in every

10 Ibid., 325.
11 Ibid., 326.
12 Ibid., 326–27.
13 Ibid., 327.
14 Ibid., 328–29.

respect equal towards all men and each; but I also deny that there is such a difference of that Divine love towards men, that He has determined not to deal with the fallen angels; according to this grace with all men fallen in Adam."[15] Arminius argued that God

> has determined to display every good—in which also mercy and long-suffering are comprehended (Exod. xxxiii.19, and xxxiv.6, 7)—in the welfare or salvation of men:—unless we are willing to do away with, in great part, that difference which most theologians set forth as existing between the fall of angels and that of men. For they say that the angels fell beyond hope of restoration, but that man can be restored entirely: and they assign as the reason, that the angels sinned of their own motion and instinct, but man at the instigation and persuasion of a bad angel.[16]

Because of the death of Christ for the sins of humanity, God may now impart the benefits of the cross to those who meet his conditions for salvation.

Arminius stated that if God were unwilling to be satisfied for some people's sins by the death of Christ, "then by no right can faith in Christ be required for them, by no right can they be condemned on account of unbelief, nor can Christ by any right be appointed their Judge."[17]

Perkins had argued that the death of Christ and the application of the atonement were both accomplished only for the elect. Arminius countered that Perkins had labored under a "notorious falsity"—namely, the confusion and conflation of redemption accomplished with redemption applied.[18] Arminius quoted Heb 9:12, where Christ is said to have "entered into the holy place, having obtained eternal redemption," which Christ "communicates to believers by the Holy Ghost."[19] "There is a perpetual error in the confusion of dissimilar things, or the mixing together of things which should be divided. For obtaining, and the act itself which obtains, are confounded with the application, and the former are substituted in the place of the latter."[20]

Arminius continued to press Perkins on his failure to distinguish properly redemption accomplished and redemption applied:

> You add moreover that "Christ is the perfect Saviour of those whom He saves, not by meriting their salvation only, but by effectually working it out." Who denies this? But these two functions and operations of Christ—to wit, the recovering,

15 Ibid., 330.
16 Ibid.
17 Ibid., 332.
18 Ibid., 333.
19 Ibid., 334–35.
20 Ibid., 335.

> through the blood of Christ, of the salvation lost by sin; and the actual communication or application, by the Holy Spirit, of the salvation obtained by that blood—are distinct from each other. The former is antecedent to faith; the latter requires faith preceding, according to the decree of God. Wherefore, although Christ be not said perfectly to save those who are not actually saved, yet He is called the Saviour even of others than believers, in 1 Tim.iv.10. As to which place, I do not see how it can fittingly be explained, except by the distinction either of salvation sufficient and efficacious, or of salvation recovered and applied. The passages which you cite from the Fathers, in part have nothing to do with the present business; and in part do refer to it, but teach nothing else than that the death and passion of Christ, which are a price sufficient for redeeming the sins of all men, actually profit to salvation only the elect and believers.[21]

On the nature of God's love for the elect and the non-elect, Arminius explained that "as saving gifts are conferred on any one by that act which is called election, it is properly 'love:' as that bestowal is restricted to some, to the exclusion of others, it is called 'election.'"[22] Arminius then made a crucial point that would come to be a major point of contention at Dort: "Whence it appears, first, that loving which is according to election would not be less towards the elect than it now is, even though it should not be according to election, that is, even though God should declare the same favour and love of His to all men universally."[23] Here Arminius asserts that God's love, *qua* love, is *equal* for all people.

Arminius's second contention with respect to God's love was

> that they who make the loving in Christ the cause of man's salvation, and the only cause, do no injury to grace, even though they deny that loving to be according to election, that is, restricted to a few by any decree of God. They deny, indeed, what is true, but without injury to grace and mercy: for I presuppose that they lay down the same love as the cause of salvation, which they lay down who urge election.[24]

In what sense, then, can there be said to be any distinction in the love of God with respect to the elect and the non-elect? Arminius explained:

> But some one will say, that by the reprobation of some,—that is, by election joined with love (dilection,)—the elect are more convinced of the unmerited

21 Ibid., 336.
22 Ibid., 337.
23 Ibid.
24 Ibid.

> love of God towards themselves, than if that same love were bestowed by God on all without distinction. I grant it, truly, and Scripture often uses that argument; but even without that argument the free and unmerited love towards us can be perfectly proved and impressed upon our hearts. Whence also it is evident that there is no absolute necessity for bringing forward that argument.[25]

Returning to the sufficiency question, Arminius stated that Perkins's comments needed more careful consideration. Due to the crucial nature of this issue in the discussion of the atonement's extent, and to gain the full effect of Arminius's argument, a rather lengthy quotation from Arminius is in order.

> You say, that "the efficacy of that price, as far as merit is concerned, is infinite"; but you make a distinction between "actual and potential efficacy," You also define "potential efficacy" as synonymous with a sufficiency of price for the whole world. This, however, is a phrase, hitherto unknown among Theologians, who have merely made a distinction between the efficacy and the sufficiency of the merit of Christ. I am not sure, also, but that there is an absurdity in styling efficacy "potential," since there is a contradiction in terms. For all efficacy is actual, as that word has been, hitherto, used by Theologians. But, laying aside phrases, let us consider the thing itself. The ransom or price of the death of Christ, is said to be universal in its sufficiency, but particular in its efficacy, i. e. sufficient for the redemption of the whole world, and for the expiation of all sins, but its efficacy pertains not to all universally, which efficacy consists in actual application by faith and the sacrament of regeneration, as Augustine and Prosper, the Aquitanian, say. If you think so, it is well, and I shall not very much oppose it. But if I rightly understand you, it seems to me that you do not acknowledge the absolute sufficiency of that price but with the added condition, if God had willed that it should be offered for the sins of the whole world. So then, that, which the Schoolmen declare categorically, namely, that Christ's death was sufficient for all and for each, is, according to your view, to be expressed hypothetically, that is, in this sense—the death of Christ would be a sufficient price for the sins of the whole world, if God had willed that it should be offered for all men. In this sense, indeed, its sufficiency is absolutely taken away. For if it is not a ransom offered and paid for all, it is, indeed, not a ransom sufficient for all. For the ransom is that, which is offered and paid. Therefore the death of Christ can be said to be sufficient for the redemption of the sins of all men, if God had wished that he should die for all; but it cannot be said to be a sufficient ransom, unless it has, in fact, been paid for all. Hence, also, Beza noted an incorrect phraseology, in

25 Ibid., 338.

> that distinction, because the sin-offering is said to be absolutely sufficient, which is not such, except on the supposition already set forth. But, indeed, my friend Perkins, the Scripture says, most clearly, in many places, that Christ died for all, for the life of the world, and that by the command and grace of God.
>
> The decree of Predestination prescribes nothing to the universality of the price paid for all by the death of Christ. It is posterior, in the order of nature, to the death of Christ and to its peculiar efficacy. For that decree pertains to the application of the benefits obtained for us by the death of Christ: but his death is the price by which those benefits were prepared. Therefore the assertion is incorrect, and the order is inverted, when it is said that "Christ died only for the elect, and the predestinate." For predestination depends, not only on the death of Christ, but also on the merit of Christ's death; and hence Christ did not die for those who were predestinated, but they for whom Christ died, were predestinated, though not all of them. For the universality of the death of Christ extends itself more widely than the object of Predestination. From which it is also concluded that the death of Christ and its merit is antecedent, in nature and order, to Predestination. What else indeed, is predestination than the preparation of the grace obtained and provided for us by the death of Christ, and a preparation pertaining to the application, not to the acquisition or provision of grace, not yet existing? For the decree of God, by which He determined to give Christ as a Redeemer to the world, and to appoint him the head only of believers, is prior to the decree, by which He determined to really apply to some, by faith, the grace obtained by the death of Christ.[26]

Here Arminius correctly analyzed the hypothetical sufficiency doctrine that had been first espoused by Beza. A ransom not paid for a person cannot be said to be sufficient for that person. This would become the very argument used by virtually all moderate Calvinists against their limitarian counterparts within Reformed theology.

Later in his response, Arminius reminded Perkins what belief in election and reprobation meant and entailed. God accomplishes everything necessary for the redemption of the elect, and those whom God has reprobated are excluded from all these things so that there is no hope of salvation. Perkins had argued that God could have withheld grace from all people, condemned all people to hell, and done so without any injustice. To which Arminius replied: "Who denies it?" Arminius agreed with Perkins on this point.

The point for Arminius was this:

> Whether it can be said with truth, that when God willed His Son to become man and die for sins, he willed it with this distinction, that He should assume

26 Ibid., 345–47.

the human nature, which He has in common with all men, only for a certain few; that he should suffer death for some few only, which might have been the price for all the sins of all men, and for the first sin which all equally had committed in Adam: that is, Whether God determined within Himself to deal with the greatest part of men according to the rigour of His justice, according to the rule of the law, and the condition required in the law; but with a few according to His mercy and grace, according to the Gospel and the righteousness of faith, and the condition set forth in the Gospel: whether He determined to impute to a certain few the sin which they had perpetrated in Adam, in their own person, without any hope of remission. This, I say, is what is asked. To this question you reply in the affirmative, and therefore confess that that crimination is justly objected to your doctrine.[27]

Here is the crux of Arminius's dispute with Perkins:

You adduce, Secondly, another reply; namely, that "Christ may be said to have died for all:" but you adjoin an explanation of such a sort as corrupts the interpretation, and simply takes away what you seemed in word to concede. For you add, that "He has not died for all and each equally with respect to God, not for the damned the same as for the elect, not efficiently on the part of God." Let us stop here a little, and weigh what you say . . . "Not equally," you say, "as regards God." But what does this mean, "as regards God?" does it mean the same as "by the decree of God?" Truly Christ "by the grace of God tasted death for every man," as says the Scripture. (Heb. ii. 9.)[28]

You therefore add, "has not died equally for the reprobate" (for so you ought to have called them, and not "the damned") "and for the elect." You consider these things in a perverted order. For the death of Christ in the order of causes precedes the decree of election and reprobation, whence arises the difference between men elect and reprobate . . . But that phrase, "Christ died for the elect," does not signify this, that some were elect before Christ received from God the command to offer His own life as the redemption-price for the life of the world . . . But that the death of Christ goes to the benefit of the elect only, which comes to pass by the application of Christ and of His benefits.[29]

Wherefore also the phrase used by the Schoolmen is to be so understood, that "Christ has died for all sufficiently, but efficaciously only for the elect and believers." But truly that form of expression is in my judgment

27 Ibid., 420–21.
28 Ibid., 421.
29 Ibid., 421–22.

> absurd,—"efficiently on God's part." For what is meant by, "Christ died, efficiently on God's part, for the elect, not for the reprobate?" Those expressions cannot be conjoined in any proper sense. I know you meant to signify that the efficacy of Christ's death is applied to them, and not to others. But if you intend this, you should also have spoken so as to be understood to mean this. For if you will please examine rigidly both that phrase of yours and that of the Schoolmen, you will find it cannot be employed without injury to the death of Christ and its merit. For sufficiency is attributed to the death of Christ, efficacy is taken away, since the death of Christ is on that account a sufficient price for the life of the world, because it was efficacious for abolishing sin and making satisfaction to God. We are not talking, you will say, of the efficacy, but of the application, of His death. Nay, the very contrary is plainly evident: for you take away the efficacy from that thing to which you attribute the sufficiency: but you attribute the sufficiency to the death of Christ. For how shall a price be sufficient which is not a price? That is not a price which is not offered, not paid, not reckoned up. "But Christ did not offer Himself as a price except for some few, namely, the elect." Certainly, these are mere words and subterfuges, of which you avail yourself in order to escape the stroke of truth.[30]

Arminius's critique of Perkins's less-than-careful use of language and logic and the resulting lack of clarity is actually quite penetrating.

Arminius next showed a fallacy in Perkins's logic regarding his use of certain Scriptures, such as Matt 7:23. Since Christ denied he ever knew some people, Perkins reasoned, he did not die for them. Arminius responded: "The argumentation is inconsequent . . . Whence it appears that there is here the fallacy of *ignoratio elenchi*, and of 'the cause for the non-cause.'"[31]

Arminius cited another argument by Perkins for limited atonement:

> The Second argument which you advance is of no greater force. "If all and each be effectually redeemed, all and each also are reconciled to God: But all are not reconciled, nor do all receive the remission of sins: therefore all and each have not been effectually redeemed." . . . For you confound the effect accomplished with the action and passion from which it arises. . . . You also confound the reconciliation achieved with God by the death and sacrifice of Christ with the application of the same; which are plainly distinguished in 2 Cor.v.19 . . . . For satisfaction precedes, as consisting in the death and obedience of Christ: but

30 Ibid., 422–23.
31 Ibid., 423.

> remission of sins consists in the application of satisfaction by faith in Christ, which cannot actually follow satisfaction accomplished. . . . The passage from Prosper entirely agrees with what I have here said.[32]

Notice here that Arminius appealed to Prosper's comments on 2 Cor 5:19 to support his point.

Perkins argued that those who are not partakers of sanctification are not those for whom Christ paid the redemption price. Arminius countered that this is in error "because the action of Christ is confounded with its result, and the application of the benefits with the obtaining of the same."[33]

Perkins claimed that faith was obtained by Christ on the cross for the elect only. Arminius responded:

> Unless it has been obtained for all, faith in Christ can by no right be required from all: and unless it has been obtained for all, by no right can any one be blamed on account of refusing the offer of redemption. . . . If Christ has not obtained redemption for all, He cannot be the Judge of all.[34]

First Timothy 2:4 has always played a significant role in debates over the extent of the atonement. Perkins attempted to argue that Paul's use of "all" in this passage does not indicate "all without exception" but rather something along the lines of "all people without distinction"—namely, all kinds of people. Arminius responded with several counterarguments.

> For the scope of the Apostle is to exhort that "prayers be made for all men," and for magistrates. . . . Whence it appears that the word "all" is taken in the same sense in the reasoning, in which it was taken in the exhortation. Otherwise the connexion would be dissolved, and there would be four terms in the syllogism . . . "I beseech that prayers and supplications be instituted for all who are to be saved: for God wills all who are to be saved to be saved."[35]

For Perkins, God willed some of each kind of people to be saved. Arminius does not dispute this but countered that Perkins had

> explained the distributive acceptation of that word for the collective, and the contrary. For all animals *distributively* were in Noah's ark, but all men

32 Ibid., 423–24.
33 Ibid., 424.
34 Ibid., 425–26.
35 Ibid., 427.

> *collectively* . . . . But it is not used for the kinds of each, but for each of all kinds; because the will of God tends to each one of classes, or to each separate man. For He wishes every man to come to the knowledge of the truth and be saved; that is, all and each, rich, poor, noble, ignoble, men, women, &c. And as the knowledge of the truth, and salvation, belongs to every man, and is really prepared for each that is to be saved by predestination, not for the classes of each; and is denied by reprobation to each that is to be condemned, not to the classes of each: so also, as the more general providence precedes the decree of predestination and reprobation in the order of nature, the will of God is employed about each one of the classes, and not about the classes of each. For the providence which is employed about the classes of each relates to the conservation of species; but that which is concerned about each one of kinds relates to the conservation of individuals.[36]

Arminius pointed out that the efficacy of redemption belongs to the application, which is made in response to faith. Believing is prior to efficacious application of the atonement and the object of faith is prior to the faith itself. Arminius stated: "But everyone is bound to believe on Christ the Saviour, that He has died for his sake, and has obtained for him reconciliation with God and redemption." People cannot be condemned on account of unbelief unless they were bound to believe such.

Arminius accused Perkins of making use of a distinction that is unnecessary when Perkins asserted that the elect individual "is bound to believe, in order that by believing he may become partaker of election; the *reprobate*, in order that by not believing he may be rendered 'inexcusable,' even according to God's intention."[37] Arminius thinks this is beside the point. According to him, Perkins's statement, "In order that he may become partaker of election," is "absurd." Arminius continued:

> In order that he may become partaker of the benefits prepared for him by election: nay, if we wish to confine ourselves within the terms, "In order that he may become actually partaker of the redemption obtained for him by Christ." But the reprobate also is bound to believe from that same cause. Say that he absolutely cannot become partaker, and I will say that for that very reason the reprobate is not bound to believe. For the end of faith bestowed is the application of redemption, and of all the benefits obtained for us by the merit of Christ: the end of faith commanded and required is that that

36 Ibid., 427–28. Arminius's point here serves as a critique of the kind of exegesis of passages like 1 Tim 2:4–6 one finds in most high Calvinists who attempt to differentiate between "all without distinction" and "all without exception" in an effort to support limited atonement.

37 Ibid., 436.

> application may be made. But how absurdly is it affirmed, that "the reprobate is therefore bound to believe, that by not believing he may become inexcusable!"[38]

At this point, Arminius brings to light Perkins's denial of God's universal saving will and Perkins's understanding of human inability to respond to the gospel:

> I will say in a word,—No one can allow himself to be guilty of a fault on account of repudiating a promise made by word, if the mind of the speaker determines not to fulfil that promise to him; or rather if he who promises by word has appointed by a sure decree that the promise shall not and cannot belong to him. You make an objection to yourself, as your own adversary, and say, "But you will allege that he could not." Not that only but this also:—How do you confute that saying, in order that it may thence not follow that he is without blame who could not receive the offered salvation? You say that "that inability is voluntary and born with us, and therefore does not deserve excuse." You are mistaken, O Perkins, and confound the inability to perform the law propagated down to us by Adam, with the inability to believe in Christ, and receive the grace of the Gospel offered to us by the word. For by what deed have we acquired for ourselves that inability? Not by a deed preceding that promise: therefore by one following, that is, by a rejection of the evangelic promise; which rejection also cannot be imputed to us as a fault, if we were then already unable when the promise was first set forth to us. Nothing therefore is answered, on account of the confusion between the two inabilities, which constitutes a fallacy of *ignoratio elenchi*, and of equivocation.[39]

Arminius continued:

> Secondly, you reply, that "that is true which every one is bound to believe,—is bound, unless he has placed an obstacle before himself by not believing." Is it so in truth? Can any one place an obstacle before himself by his unbelief, so that that should not be true which he is bound to believe? Absurd.[40]

In conclusion, Arminius pressed Perkins on the issue of conflating the atonement with its application. Whereas Perkins's language tended to equate atonement with efficacy, Arminius argued that the two should be distinguished. In fact, Arminius reminded

---

38 Ibid.
39 Ibid., 437.
40 Ibid.

Perkins of the necessity of properly distinguishing the atonement's "extent," "sufficiency," "efficacy," and "universality of its offering."

> For the question is, not "whether all men and every man are actually regenerated and renovated;" but whether God has reprobated any man without respect of sin as the meritorious cause; whether He has determined absolutely to deny to any man the grace of remission and of the renewing of the Holy Spirit, without consideration of the unworthiness by which he has rendered himself unworthy of that grace.[41]

Following his death, Arminius's followers came to be called "Remonstrants" or "Arminians." Forty-three (some say forty-five) Arminian ministers met in 1610 and framed a statement of their convictions known as the "Remonstrance." This document was submitted to the States-General of the Netherlands.[42] The second article dealt with the atonement and stated that Christ died with a saving intention for all:

> That, accordingly, Jesus Christ the Savior of the world, died for all men and for every man, so that he has obtained for them all, by his death on the cross, redemption and the forgiveness of sins; yet that no one actually enjoys this forgiveness of sins except the believer, according to the word of the Gospel of John 3:16, "For God so loved the world, that he gave his only begotten Son, that whosoever believes in him should not perish, but have everlasting life." And in the First Epistle of John 2:2: "And he is the propitiation for our sins: and not for ours only, but also for *the sins of* the whole world."[43]

Note the following:

1. The statement affirms Christ "died for all men and for every man." Understood in this statement is that Christ died *for the sins* of all. The phrase "for every man" clearly indicates the death of Christ is understood to encompass all people without exception.
2. Christ's death obtained "redemption" for all people and "the forgiveness of sins." In light of the immediately following clause, it is clear that the benefits of the atonement are only applied to those who believe.

---

41 Ibid., 438–39.

42 The five Remonstrant articles, in Dutch, Latin, and English, can be found in Schaff, *Creeds of Christendom,* 3:546–49.

43 Ibid., 545–46.

3. Two verses of Scripture are cited to support Article 2: John 3:16 and 1 John 2:2.
4. Though not overtly stated, the implication of the statement is that Christ died equally for all people—that is, with equal intent to save all.

Most of the states of Holland were unwilling to convene a national synod, but they did call for a conference to be held in the hopes of determining the nature and seriousness of the differences and finding means of mutual toleration. In preparation for this conference, those who opposed the Arminians drew up a Contra-Remonstrance that answered the points made in the Remonstrance. The fourth point of this document addressed the extent of the atonement.[44] This conference made little headway and tensions continued to grow.

The Synod of Dort (AD 1618–1619)

The popular perception today, especially among the so-called new Calvinists, is that limited atonement was enshrined at Dort. Such is not the case.[45]

The Remonstrants created such a stir that Dutch authorities finally determined to call a national synod held at Dort to address the issues. The Synod of Dort and the Westminster Assembly in England were the two most significant religious events of the seventeenth century for the Reformed movement.

At first, the Remonstrants were allowed to attend the early meetings of the synod, but then they were systematically excluded from participation and their doctrines were considered without the benefit of their presence for dialogue or cross-examination. Additional evidence that the deck was stacked against the Arminians at Dort was that Ames, a strict high Calvinist who employed the revised Lombardian formula, actually served as the private secretary to the president of the synod. The concluding report of the synod condemned the Remonstrants and their doctrines.[46]

Godfrey pointed out that the Remonstrants viewed the love of God in a two-fold manner: God's love that was antecedent to salvation and his love for believers subsequent to salvation. This reflected the Arminian understanding of the order of

---

44 Godfrey, "Reformed Thought on the Extent of the Atonement," 155–56.

45 Moore, "The Extent of the Atonement," 144, 147. Notice how Rainbow failed to discern this situation in Dort and Westminster (*The Will of God and the Cross*, 183). Likewise, Tom Ascol's historiography with respect to Dort is in error: "The Synod of Dort represents a watershed in the development of the orthodox Reformed view of the atonement. The second chapter, or canon, from that assembly's published confession clearly rejects *any understanding* which views Christ's death as indefinite, universal, or general in nature." See T. Ascol, "The Doctrine of Grace: A Critical Analysis of Federalism in the Theologies of John Gill and Andrew Fuller" (PhD diss., Southwestern Baptist Theological Seminary, 1989), 215 (emphasis mine).

46 As a result, some two hundred Arminian pastors were deprived of their right to serve the churches, many were forced into exile, and van Oldenbarnevelt was decapitated (W. Rex, *Essays on Pierre Bayle and Religious Controversy*, International Archives of the History of Ideas 8 [The Hague: Martinus Nijhoff, 1965], 81).

God's decrees.[47] Without denying election, but defining it differently than orthodox Calvinism and placing the decree of election after the decree to send Christ as redeemer, the logical result was universal atonement.[48]

Furthermore, the Remonstrants argued that unlimited atonement was nothing new in Reformed theology, and they appealed to Calvin, Zanchi, Bullinger, Musculus, and Gwalther, all of whom, as we have seen, affirmed a form of unlimited atonement.

The Contra-Remonstrants denied that Christ died for all, except in the sense that his death was sufficient for all. As we have seen, some within the Reformed camp agreed with the Arminians that Christ's death satisfied for the sins of all people and thus was extrinsically sufficient. But most understood this sufficiency only in an intrinsic sense. For example, William Ames made use of the Lombardian formula but defined sufficiency to mean only an infinite intrinsic sufficiency.[49]

The single, most disputed issue among the Reformed delegates at the Synod of Dort concerned the extent of the atonement. Some of the delegates agreed with the Remonstrants that the death of Christ satisfied for the sins of all people and thus rejected the concept that Christ died for the sins of the elect only.

The history of this debate within the synod is fascinating in itself.[50] It should be noted that the synod did not include all of the Reformed churches (the Reformed Church of Anhalt was not invited), nor were the Lutheran churches invited. The synod was not a council of the Protestant churches of Europe or even of the Reformed Church of Europe but a national Dutch synod to which various Reformed theologians from various parts of Europe were invited.[51]

Final agreement on the Canons of Dort only occurred as a result of the final committee's deliberate ambiguity in the modification of the language of the Second Canon on the subject of the extent of the atonement. This was done to accommodate those

---

47 Godfrey, "Reformed Thought on the Extent of the Atonement," 157.

48 Ibid., 158.

49 Ibid., 164.

50 In addition to the primary sources such as J. Quick, *Synodicon in Gallia Reformata, or, the Acts, Decisions, Decrees, and Canons of those Famous National Councils of the Reformed Churches in France*, 2 vols. (London: Printed for T. Parkhurst and J. Robinson, 1692), and the "Letters from the Synod of Dort, from an Authentik Hand," in *The Golden Remains of the Ever Memorable John Hales* (London: Printed by T. Newcomb, for R. Pawlet, 1673), the following modern treatments of the Synod of Dort on the specific question of the extent of the atonement are important: G. M. Thomas, *The Extent of the Atonement: A Dilemma for Reformed Theology from Calvin to the Consensus* (Carlisle, UK: Paternoster, 1997). This is an important summary work on the subject. More treatments include W. R. Godfrey, "Tensions within International Calvinism: The Debate on the Atonement at the Synod of Dort" (PhD diss., Stanford University, 1974); S. Strehle, "The Extent of the Atonement within the Theological Systems of the Sixteenth and Seventeenth Centuries," 216–35; idem, "The Extent of the Atonement in the Synod of Dort," *Westminster Theological Journal* 51 (1989): 1–23; W. A. McComish, *The Epigones: A Study of the Theology of the Genevan Academy at the Time of the Synod of Dort, with Special Reference to Giovanni Diodati* (Allison Park, PA: Pickwick, 1989), 85–105; N. R. N. Tyacke, *Anti-Calvinists: The Rise of English Arminianism 1590–1640* (Oxford: Clarendon, 1990), 87–105; and P. White, *Predestination, Policy, and Polemic: Conflict and Consensus in the English Church from the Reformation to the Civil War* (New York: Cambridge University Press, 1992), 187–92.

51 "Dort, Synod of," in *Cyclopedia of Biblical, Theological, and Ecclesiastical Literature*, 12 vols., ed. J. McClintock and J. Strong (Grand Rapids, MI: Baker, 1968), 2:870.

delegates who affirmed strict particularism and those like John Davenant and members of the British and Bremen delegations who rejected strict particularism and who believed Jesus's death paid the penalty for the sins of all humanity.[52] As Thomas stated the issue: "Agreement to the final articles was possible by including within them statements that were both disharmonious and unexplained."[53] Blacketer noted: "The issue of the extent of the atonement was certainly the most difficult and contentious matter the Synod faced. Formulating the final statement on this issue took a great deal of debate and compromise."[54] James Richards likewise noted:

> Yet, in the Synod of Dort, there were many able advocates for the doctrine that *Christ died for all*, in the only sense in which it is contended for now, by that part of the Calvinistic school who plead for a *general propitiation*. The delegates from England, *Hesse* and *Bremen*, were explicit in their declaration to this effect. But all were not of the same mind; and, therefore, though they agreed upon a *form of words*, under which every man might take shelter, still it wears the appearance of a compromise, and is not sufficiently definite to satisfy the rigid inquirer.[55]

Dort's "Second Head of Doctrine—the Death of Christ, and the Redemption of Men Thereby"[56] stated the following in Articles 3, 5, 6, and 8, and these are the key points relative to our discussion:

> Article 3. *The* death of the Son of God is the only and most perfect sacrifice and satisfaction for sin; and is of infinite worth and value, abundantly sufficient to expiate the sins of the whole world.
>
> Article 5. Moreover, the promise of the gospel is, that whosoever believeth in Christ crucified, shall not perish, but have everlasting life. This promise, together with the command to repent and believe, ought to be declared and published to all nations, and to all persons promiscuously and without distinction, to whom God out of his good pleasure sends the gospel.
>
> Article 6. And, whereas many who are called by the gospel, do not repent, nor believe in Christ, but perish in unbelief; this is not owing to any defect or

52 See Godfrey, "Tensions within International Calvinism," 252–69; and R. Muller, *Post-Reformation Reformed Dogmatics*, 4 vols. (Grand Rapids, MI: Baker, 2003), 1:76–77. See also Rex, *Essays on Pierre Bayle*, 87. Richard Muller even said that the same confessional compromises on the language of the extent of the atonement occurred at Westminster so as to allow both views.

53 Thomas, *Extent of the Atonement*, 132.

54 Blacketer, "Definite Atonement in Historical Perspective," 319.

55 J. Richards, *Lectures on Mental Philosophy and Theology* (New York: M. W. Dodd, 1846), 306.

56 Schaff, *Creeds of Christendom*, 3:586–87. The canons were published in English under the title *The Judgement of the Synode Holden at Dort, concerning the Five Articles* (London: John Bill, 1619).

insufficiency in the sacrifice offered by Christ upon the cross, but is wholly to be imputed to themselves.

Article 8. For this was the sovereign counsel, and most gracious will and purpose of God the Father, that the quickening and saving efficacy of the most precious death of his Son should extend to all the elect, for bestowing upon them alone the gift of justifying faith, thereby to bring them infallibly to salvation: that is, it was the will of God, that Christ by the blood of the cross, whereby he confirmed the new covenant, should effectually redeem out of every people, tribe, nation, and language, all those, and those only, who were from eternity chosen to salvation, and given to him by the Father; that he should confess upon them faith, which together with all the other saving gifts of the Holy Spirit, he purchased for them by his death; should purge them from all sin, both original and actual, whether committed before or after believing; and having faithfully preserved them even to the end, should at last bring them free from every spot and blemish to the enjoyment of glory in his own presence forever.[57]

These articles were further explained by an immediately following "statement of errors," which the synod rejected. The vital denials are found in statements 1, 3, and 6:[58]

The true doctrine having been explained, the Synod rejects the errors of those:

1. Who teach: That God the Father has ordained his Son to the death of the cross without a certain and definite decree to save any, so that the necessity, profitableness and worth of what Christ merited by his death might have existed, and might remain in all its parts complete, perfect and intact, even if the merited redemption had never in fact been applied to any person. For this doctrine tends to the despising of the wisdom of the Father and of the merits of Jesus Christ, and is contrary to Scripture. For thus says our Saviour:

   "I lay down my life for the sheep, and I know them," John 10:15, 27. And the prophet Isaiah says concerning the Saviour: "When thou shalt make his soul an offering for sin, he shall see his seed, he shall prolong

57 With respect to this article, Thomas noted, "There is no attempt to resolve the apparent contradiction between the assertion of universal sufficiency, preaching and inexcusability, on the one hand, and limited saving will and efficacy on the other" (*Extent of the Atonement*, 133).

58 Schaff, *Creeds of Christendom*, 3:563–64. For valuable appendices containing biographical information of delegates at Dort, the opinions of the Remonstrants, the Canons of Dort, and so on, consult P. Y. De Jong, ed. *Crisis in the Reformed Churches: Essays in Commemoration of the Great Synod of Dort, 1618–1619* (Grand Rapids, MI: Reformed Fellowship, 1968), 197–262.

his days, and the pleasure of Jehovah shall prosper in his hand," Isa. 53:10. Finally, this contradicts the article of faith according to which we believe the Catholic Christian Church.

3. Who teach: That Christ by his satisfaction merited neither salvation itself for anyone, nor faith, whereby this satisfaction of Christ unto salvation is effectually appropriated; but that he merited for the Father only the authority or the perfect will to deal again with man, and to prescribe new conditions as he might desire, obedience to which, however, depended on the free will of man, so that it therefore might have come to pass that either none or all should fulfill these conditions. For these adjudge too contemptuously of the death of Christ, do in no wise acknowledge the most important fruit or benefit thereby gained, and bring again out of hell the Pelagian error.
6. Who use the difference between meriting and appropriating, to the end that they may instill into the minds of the imprudent and inexperienced this teaching that God, as far as he is concerned, has been minded of applying to all equally the benefits gained by the death of Christ; but that, while some obtain the pardon of sin and eternal life, and others do not, this difference depends on their own free will, which joins itself to the grace that is offered without exception, and that it is not dependent on the special gift of mercy, which powerfully works in them, that they rather than others should appropriate unto themselves this grace. For these, while they feign that they present this distinction, in a sound sense, seek to instill into the people the destructive poison of the Pelagian errors.

Note carefully what is stated in Article 8 under the Second Head of Doctrine, on the Death of Christ: "That the quickening and saving efficacy of the most precious death of his Son should extend to all the elect," and "it was the will of God, that Christ by the blood of the cross, whereby he confirmed the new covenant, should effectually redeem out of every people, tribe, nation, and language, all those, and those only, who were from eternity chosen to salvation."[59] Here the canon is saying that Christ's *effectual* redemption is designed to be accomplished for the elect only. The canon is not saying that Christ's redemptive work was accomplished *only* for the elect. Furthermore, there is nothing in the denials that would undercut this reading.

This is how Davenant and the other delegates who affirmed universal atonement could sign the documents in good faith. What is formally affirmed is that the death of Christ is actually effective only for the elect. What is formally denied is the Arminian

59 P. Schaff, *The Creeds of Christendom*, 6th ed., P. Schaff, rev. D. S. Schaff (Grand Rapids, MI: Baker, 1993), 3:587.

understanding of the *intent* of the atonement—that is, that Christ died *equally* for all (note the use of the word "equally" in denial 6 above). What is *not* formally denied is that Christ died for the sins of all with respect to *extent*.[60] Again, one must recognize that the early Reformed made a clear distinction between the intent to apply the atonement and its extent. Later particularists conflated the *intent to apply* with the *extent* and viewed them as co-extensive. Hypothetical Universalists did not view the *intent to apply* and *extent* co-extensively.[61]

Although today the denials are rarely listed with the Second Head of Doctrine, on the Death of Christ, in the Canons of Dort, according to Sinnema, the drafting committee of the final documents used the term "Canons" to refer only to the denials. The positive articles, what have come to be known as the "Canons of Dort," were folded into the final document in order to support the denials. Thus, it is vital to interpret the Canons of Dort in the light of the denials.[62] When this is done, it becomes even clearer that though the majority of delegates personally were committed to limited atonement, the final canons were written with sufficient ambiguity so as not to enshrine limited atonement as the "official" position of Dort.

The English delegation,[63] led by John Davenant, were among those who argued that the death of Christ was unlimited in its extent in that it satisfied for the sins of all men.[64] At this point, Davenant and others were in agreement with the Remonstrants but in disagreement with their fellow strict particularists, who conflated the intent to apply and the extent of the atonement. Thomas made a crucial point when he noted:

> The twofold approach of the British submission is powerfully reminiscent of Ursinus' approach to the question of the extent of the atonement. It is more

60 J. Moore, "The Extent of the Atonement," 145–46.

61 Notice Wallace's ambiguous statement: "The English delegates at Dort agreed that predestination was unconditional, that atonement was limited to the elect." If Wallace intends to say that the atonement was efficaciously limited to the elect, that is, in its application, then his statement is true. If he means to suggest that the synod concluded that the atonement was limited in its extent to the elect only, then he is mistaken (*Puritans and Predestination,* 81). Wallace likewise stated: "Meanwhile, Ussher took time in his letters to explicate such matters as limited atonement" (ibid., 97). As we shall see below, Ussher wrote clearly *against* limited atonement and in favor of Hypothetical Universalism.

62 D. Sinnema, "The Canons of Dordt: From Judgment on Arminianism to Confessional Standard," in *Revisiting the Synod of Dordt (1618–1619),* ed. A. Goudriaan and F. van Lieburg; Brill's Series in Church History 49 (Leiden: Brill, 2011), 313–33; and Moore, "The Extent of the Atonement," 146.

63 For a detailed study, see A. Milton, *The British Delegation and the Synod of Dort (1618–1619)* (Suffolk: Boydell, 2005).

64 The English delegation declared:

> God, pitying the fall of the *human race*, sent his Son, who gave himself, the price of redemption, for the sins of the *whole world*... Since that price, which was paid for *all men,* which will certainly benefit *all who believe* to eternal life, yet doth not profit *all* men.... So then Christ died for *all* men, that all and each, by the mediation of faith, through the virtue of this corresponding ransom, might obtain remission of sins and eternal life. (*Acta Synodi Nationalis, in Nomine Domini Nostri Iesv Christi, Autoritate Illvstr. Et Praepotentvm D.D. Ordinvm Generalivm Foederati Belgij Prouinciarum, Dordrechti Habitæ anno M.DC.XVIII & M.DC.XIX* [Hanoviæ: Impensis Egenolphi Emmelii, 1620], II:78)

> than likely that the British were influenced by it, since his exposition of the Heidelberg Catechism had been widely circulated in England during the previous 30 years. Indeed, it was almost word for word quotation when the British said, "We consider two things in this offering of Christ—the manner of calling people to actual participation, and the fruit."[65]

We have seen how both Ursinus and the Heidelberg Catechism championed universal atonement.

Likewise, the Breman delegation argued for unlimited atonement and included as one of their reasons the necessity to ground the well-meant gospel offer to all in the fact that Christ had satisfied for the sins of all. For example, Martinius stated:

> If this redemption be not supposed a common blessing bestowed on all men, the indiscriminate and promiscuous preaching of the gospel committed to the apostles to be exercised among all nations, will have *no true* foundation in truth . . . for how from a benefit, sufficient indeed, but not designed for me by a sincere intention, can the necessity of believing that it belongs to me be deduced? . . . This redemption is the payment of a price due for us captives, not that we should go forth from captivity at all events, but that we should be able and be bound to go forth; and in fact we should go forth if we would believe in the Redeemer.[66]

Martinius held that a universal atonement was actually necessary, "For how can a necessity of believing that a benefit pertains to me be deduced from a benefit that is indeed sufficient, but not destined to be such by a true intention?"[67] Thus, there were some at Dort, like Davenant and Martinius, who held a dualistic approach to the question of the design of the atonement: Christ died for all in that he satisfied for the sins of all, but he died especially with the intent of saving the elect, and election is what determines who can and will believe. "Redemption accomplished did not have to be co-extensive with redemption applied"[68] in the minds of those who fostered universal atonement at Dort.

No one was more influential at Dort in arguing for unlimited atonement than John Davenant (1572–1641), Lady Margaret Professor of Divinity at Cambridge, who was

65 Thomas, *Extent of the Atonement,* 134. See also Robert Godfrey's remarks on the similarity between Martinius's statements in Thesis XXV and those of Ursinus in in his commentary ("Tensions within International Calvinism," 196–98).

66 E. Griffin, "A Humble Attempt to Reconcile the Differences of Christians Respecting the Extent of the Atonement," in *The Atonement: Discourses and Treatises* (Boston: Congregational Board of Publication, 1859), 371; quoting and translating Martinius.

67 Cited in Thomas, *Extent of the Atonement,* 137.

68 Ibid., 137, 147.

appointed Bishop of Salisbury shortly after his return to England from Dort. Davenant wrote a very important work on the extent of the atonement called "A Dissertation on the Death of Christ."[69] Often ignored or neglected, it is one of the most significant works in the history of Reformed theology that argues for unlimited atonement.

Consider the following from his "Dissertation," which exhibits his thinking on this subject, especially with respect to the views of the church fathers, Augustine, and Prosper:

> I think that it may be truly affirmed, that before the dispute between Augustine and Pelagius, there was no question concerning the death of Christ, whether it was to be extended to all mankind, or to be confined only to the elect. For the Fathers, when speaking of the death of Christ, describe it to us as undertaken and endured for the redemption of the human race; and not a word (that I know of) occurs among them of the exclusion of any persons by the decree of God. They agree that it is actually beneficial to those only who believe, yet they everywhere confess that Christ died in behalf of all mankind. . . .
>
> Their adversaries were nevertheless accustomed to object to Augustine, that they taught that Christ was crucified for the predestinate alone; and from this objection of the Pelagians, some in succeeding ages seized a handle for kindling the afore-mentioned controversy. This is manifest from the objections of the Vincentians, in which this takes the lead, that *our Lord Jesus Christ did not suffer for the salvation and redemption of all men.* It is manifest from the Answers of Prosper to the *Capitula* of the Gallican Divines, where their ninth objection is given after this manner: *That the Savior was not crucified for the redemption of the whole world.* The Semipelagians objected to this as new, invidious, and erroneous. But Prosper meets these objections, not by maintaining that Christ suffered only for the elect, but by shewing whence it arises, that the passion of Christ is profitable and saving to the elect alone. . . .
>
> We assert, therefore, that Augustine never attempted to impugn that proposition of the Semipelagians, that *Christ died for the whole human race,* but with all his might refuted the addition they had made to it; and shewed that the property or benefit of redemption, that is, eternal life, belongs to the predestinate alone, because they only do not pass through life in unbelief, they never die in their impiety . . . For neither did Augustine ever oppose as erroneous the proposition *that Christ died not for all men, but for the predestinate alone.*[70]

69 J. Davenant, "A Dissertation on the Death of Christ," in *An Exposition of the Epistle of St. Paul to the Colossians,* 2 vols., trans. J. Allport (London: Hamilton, Adams, and Co., 1832), 2:309–569.

70 Ibid., 318–20, 328, 330 (emphasis in original).

Since Davenant was the leader of the English delegation at Dort, it proves helpful to consider what the English delegation submitted as their understanding of the extent of the atonement as reflected in "The Collegiate Suffrage of the Divines of Great Britain, concerning the Five Articles Controverted at the Synod of Dort" concerning the second article. In "The First Position," the delegation clearly affirmed that Christ died for the elect based on a special love by God and Christ for them. In "The Second Position," the delegates stated that all the gifts of grace proceed to the elect upon the fulfillment of the conditions of the covenant. "The Third Position" is vital to an understanding of the British delegation's view of the extent of Christ's death. They state in unequivocal terms that God sent Christ to give himself a ransom "for the sins of the whole world."

Furthermore, it is on the grounds of this universal atonement for the sins of all that all men are saveable and the gospel may be therefore preached to all. That the price for sins was paid for all in no way interdicts the doctrine of election. "The Fourth Position" stated:

> Christ therefore so dyed for all, that all and every one by the meanes of faith might obtaine remission of sins, and eternall life by virtue of that ransome paid once for all mankind. But Christ so dyed for the elect, that by the merit of his death in speciall manner destinated unto them according to the eternall good pleasure of God, they might infallibly obtaine both faith and eternall life.

The foundation for the universal gospel offer is the death of Christ for the sins of all people. If anyone believes, he may obtain forgiveness of sins and eternal life.[71]

Davenant and the English delegation signed the final canons of the Synod of Dort. We will consider Davenant in more detail below.

Ludwig Crocius (AD 1586/7–1653/5)

Ludwig Crocius was a German Calvinist and delegate to the Synod of Dort who also held to universal atonement. He stated that Christ died for all and this furnishes the ground for a genuine offer of salvation to all who hear the gospel. On these grounds, all people are required to repent and believe the gospel, though not all will do so. Crocius cited the following texts as evidence: John 1:29; 3:16; 1 Tim 4:10; Heb 2:9; 1 Cor 5:15; 2 Pet 2:1; 1 Cor 8:11; and Heb 10:29.[72]

---

71 Milton, *The British Delegation*, 243–51. Milton is working from the original source, George Carleton, et al., *The Collegiat Suffrage of the Divines of Great Britaine, concerning the Five Articles Controverted in the Low Countries. Which Suffrage Was by Them Delivered in the Synod of God, March 6, Anno 1619. Being Their Vote or Voice Forgoing the Joint and Publique Judgment of that Synod* (London: Robert Milbourne, 1629), 43–64.

72 Ludovici Crocie, *Syntagma sacrae theologiae quatuor libris adornatum, Quo exhibetur idea Dogmatum Ecclesiasticorum, Pro conditione ecclesiae Sardensis* (Bremae: Typis Bertholdi Villeriani, 1636), 1013–14.

Letham acknowledged Crocius believed God's love included the whole human race but seemed to suggest that Crocius himself held to limited atonement:

> For Crocius, God's revealed will as it finds expression in the gospel promise has predominance over the doctrine of election. The mercy of God, which is the source of our salvation, is that by which God embraces the whole human race and so wishes all men to be saved. His grace is, consequently, not restricted to the elect alone but to the entire race. Yet this universal love of God does not oppose election. Nor does it follow that all men are elect. Therefore, while he holds to limited atonement he can stress with considerable emphasis the universal sufficiency of the atonement. Christ's sacrifice is of infinite value because of who he is and because of what his offering actually was. His atoning work is offered to all men and is effective for them upon repentance and faith. But its intention and efficacy is for the elect only.[73]

Tony Byrne rightly noted Letham's potentially confusing language in this quote.

> One should be careful with Letham's confused way of describing things. The modern interpreter may read Letham's statement that Crocius held to "limited atonement" (his modern label) and think Crocius did *not* believe Christ satisfied for all men. That is not the case. Even the Latin that Letham cites in footnote #290 reveals Crocius to be using the language of the *moderate* Calvinists at the Synod of Dort, such as Davenant and Martinius. Crocius' view of sufficiency does not read as a "bare sufficiency," but as an "ordained sufficiency" for all that properly grounds the serious, *bona fide* offer to all in the Gospel. Like all Calvinists, however, Crocius sees an effectual limitation *in the application* of Christ's death to the elect alone, which stems from Christ's effectual *intent.* When Crocius cites Calvin [*ad. Johann.* 3.17] in support of his point concerning the effectual *application* to the elect alone, it is not as though he thinks Calvin did not teach that Christ satisfied for all men, as Letham seems to infer in footnote #291. To cite Calvin in support of an *application* that is effectual to the elect alone does not tell us anything about Crocius' opinion of Calvin's view of the satisfaction itself (i.e. whether it was for all men or not), contrary to Letham's inference.[74]

---

73 R. W. Letham, "Saving Faith and Assurance in Reformed Theology: Zwingli to the Synod of Dort," 2 vols. (PhD diss., University of Aberdeen, 1979), 2:124. See Heinrich Heppe, *Reformed Dogmatics* (Grand Rapids, MI: Baker, 1978), 372, where Heppe quotes Crocius on John 3:16, indicating Crocius's interpretation of "world" as all people and not the elect only.

74 T. Byrne, "Robert Letham on the Primacy of the Gospel over Election in Ludwig Crocius," *Theological Meditations* (blog), July 14, 2012, http://www.theologicalmeditations.blogspot.com/2012/07/letham-on-primacy-of-gospel-over.html.

Conclusion

In summary, several conclusions can be drawn. First, at the beginning of the seventeenth century, the Reformed community was divided over the question of the extent of the atonement. The proceedings at Dort made this clear. On the continent and in England, some in the Reformed tradition were making strong arguments for a universal atonement, arguing that this was the original position of the earliest theologians in the Reformed tradition.

Notable examples were James Ussher (AD 1581–1656); Archbishop of Armagh, one of Britain's most influential Reformed leaders in the seventeenth century;[75] and the prolific Puritan author and preacher John Preston (AD 1587–1628),[76] about whom we will have more to say.

Second, the synod, and indeed all in the Reformed tradition, rejected the Arminian position on the question of the *intent* of the atonement—namely, that it was designed and intended *equally* for the salvation of all but not designed for any particular person. Particularists and universalists were united in their conviction that Christ died efficaciously for the elect only and not efficaciously for all equally.[77]

Third, there were some delegates who agreed with the Arminians on the question of the *extent* of the atonement—namely, that Christ satisfied for the sins of all humanity.

Fourth, that men such as Davenant, Ussher, and so on, should be accused by some of their Reformed brethren, past and present, as being Arminian because of their position on the extent of the atonement is nothing short of gross misunderstanding or historical revisionism.[78]

Fifth, the final language of the canon on the atonement was constructed with deliberate ambiguity to permit both sides of the debate to sign in good conscience. Thus,

---

75 J. Ussher, "The True Intent and Extent of Christ's Death and Satisfaction upon the Cross," in *The Whole Works of the Most Rev. James Ussher, D. D.*, 17 vols., ed. C. Elrington (Dublin: Hodges, Smith, and Co., 1864), 12:553–71.

76 See Moore, *English Hypothetical Universalism*, 94–140, for a thorough interaction with Preston's writings and his conclusion that Preston was a hypothetical universalist.

77 J. Moore, "Extent of the Atonement," 147.

78 For example, Wallace (*Puritans and Predestination*, 103) records a remarkable scene involving Davenant and Samuel Harsnett:

> One of these Episcopalian Calvinists, Bishop Davenant, preaching before the king in 1630, in a counterattack on the Arminians took the liberty of touching on the forbidden points, maintaining that election precluded human merit and free will in salvation. As punishment, Davenant was forced to appear before the Privy Council on his knees and was berated by Samuel Harsnett, by then advanced to the archbishopric of York. In defense, Davenant insisted that he had preached no more than what all ministers of the English church were obliged to subscribe in the Thirty-Nine Articles. In correspondence, Bishop Hall agreed with Davenant's views, declaring he would "live and die" in agreement with the Synod of Dort, and Ussher marveled that the established doctrine of the church could be so questioned. No longer required to be silent after the convening of the Long Parliament, Davenant then wrote against the Arminian Samuel Hoard, defending "the absolute decree of predestination" and "the absolute decree of negative Reprobation" as the official teaching of the Church of England and warning against any setting forth of God's general love to mankind that obscured "the special love and mercy of God prepared from all eternitie and bestowed in due time upon elect men."

the Canons of Dort did not exclude the strict particular view, but neither did it exclude Hypothetical Universalism. The work of Robert Godfrey, Richard Muller, Robert Letham, Carl Trueman, G. Michael Thomas, among many others, demonstrate this beyond doubt.

Sixth, Dort surfaced a mind-set among some of the more extreme delegates who affirmed strict particularism that would portend difficulty down the road for the Reformed. Those delegates from Gelderland and Friesland, in response to the question "Why is the gospel to be preached to all?" answered that there is no obligation to preach the gospel to all. Thus, even at Dort, there was exhibited an early form of hyper-Calvinism.

I have argued elsewhere that the jump to hyper-Calvinism cannot be made without the platform of limited atonement.[79] The important point here is that one does not have to wait until the eighteenth century to encounter hyper-Calvinism; the connection between limited atonement and hyper-Calvinism can already be seen in some Reformed theologians as early as Dort.[80]

Seventh, this question of the well-meant gospel offer became a major issue of discussion at Dort and continued so over the next centuries. The reason why this became such a controversial issue was due in no small part to the doctrine of limited atonement. The debate at Dort illustrated the problem faced by those who want to affirm a strictly limited atonement: How is it that the gospel can be genuinely offered to all if Christ did not die for the sins of all? This problem looms large in John Owen's defense of limited atonement.[81] We will explore the question of the well-meant gospel offer from the platform of limited atonement in greater detail below.

Richard Muller's comments on Dort are especially important:

> Clear statements of nonspeculative hypothetical universalism can be found (as Davenant recognized) in Heinrich Bullinger's *Decades* and commentary on the Apocalypse, in Wolfgang Musculus' *Loci communes*, in Ursinus' catechetical lectures, and in Zanchi's *Tractatus de praedestinatione sanctorum*, among other places. In addition, the Canons of Dort, in affirming the standard distinction of a sufficiency of Christ's death for all and its efficiency for the elect, actually refrain from canonizing either the early form of hypothetical universalism or the assumption that Christ's sufficiency serves only to leave the nonelect with-

79 Allen, "The Atonement: Limited or Universal?," in *Whosoever Will*, 96.

80 Thomas, *Extent of the Atonement*, 149, noted concerning these strict particularists, "So, in striving for theological consistency, some of the more particularistic theologians were eroding a major part of the Reformed heritage, by qualifying and restricting that preaching of the word."

81 Martin Foord concluded from John Owen's *Death of Death in the Death of Christ* that Owen grounded the free offer of the gospel in God's particular love for the elect only. Owen's views thus tend "toward the so-called 'hyper-Calvinism' that developed in the eighteenth century" (M. Foord, "John Owen's Gospel Offer: Well-Meant or Not?," in *The Ashgate Research Companion to John Owen's Theology*, ed. K. M. Kapic and M. Jones [Farnham, UK: Ashgate, 2012], 283).

> out excuse. Although Moore can cite statements from the York conference that Dort "either overtly or covertly denied the universality of man's redemption" (156), it remains that various of the signatories of the Canons were hypothetical universalists—not only the English delegation (Carleton, Davenant, Ward, Goad, and Hall) but also the [*sic*] some of the delegates from Bremen and Nassau (Martinius, Crocius, and Alsted)—that Carleton and the other delegates continued to affirm the doctrinal points of Dort while distancing themselves from the church discipline of the Belgic Confession, and that in the course of seventeenth-century debate even the Amyraldians were able to argue that their teaching did not run contrary to the Canons. In other words, the nonspeculative, non-Amyraldian form of hypothetical universalism was new in neither the decades after Dort nor a "softening" of the tradition: The views of Davenant, Ussher, and Preston followed out a resident trajectory long recognized as orthodox among the Reformed.[82]

Robert Godfrey concluded: "Out of the Synod's debate, however, emerged a balanced compromise statement of the Reformed doctrine of the extent of the atonement which accommodated the considerable varieties of thought on that subject within the international Reformed community."[83] Thomas's conclusion on the question of the extent of the atonement in early Reformed theology is vital to a proper understanding of the situation through the Synod of Dort. The Canons of Dort exhibited a

> mixture of the conditional-universal, and the absolute-restricted interpretations of the atonement. . . . "Nor can it be claimed, on the basis of a survey of the Reformation and classical period that there was ever such a thing as a coherent and agreed 'Reformed position' on the extent of the atonement. This is the most obvious conclusion to emerge from all the detail of the present survey, and one which challenges on this point existing, if not from Calvin, at least from Beza onwards."[84]

Oliver Crisp has drawn several significant conclusions that support our understanding of what occurred at the Synod of Dort and beyond with respect to Hypothetical Universalism. First, it was never repudiated by any Reformed synod or council. The so-called Three Forms of Unity—the Belgic Confession, the Heidelberg Catechism, and the Canons of the Synod of Dort—as well as the Anglican Articles of Religion

82 R. Muller, "Review of Jonathan Moore's *English Hypothetical Universalism*," *Calvin Theological Journal* 43 (2008): 150.

83 Godfrey, "Reformed Thought on the Extent of the Atonement," 171.

84 Thomas, *Extent of the Atonement*, 249–50.

(Thirty-Nine Articles), "are consistent with hypothetical universalism."[85] Second, the same is true for the Westminster Confession.[86] Third, "contrary to some popular presentations on the matter, there is no good reason to think that Dort affirmed a doctrine of atonement that excludes hypothetical universalism."[87] Fourth, Article 2.8 of the Synod of Dort clearly affirms that the atonement will be applied only to the elect, but it makes no statement limiting the actual extent of the atonement.[88]

We have seen that all the key Reformers following Calvin, with the exception of Beza and possibly Olevianus, held to a form of unlimited atonement. Muller himself concluded that most of these men held to Hypothetical Universalism. Additionally, Ussher, Davenant, and Martinius likewise held to unlimited atonement. The important point here is all of this was before Dort and before the Amyraldian controversy.

These facts are important for several reasons. First, it is often believed that it was the Arminians and the Amyraldians who first promulgated the notion of universal atonement among the Reformed. Second, many within the Reformed camp have made historical errors in their statements that these men held to limited atonement.[89] Third, there was no such thing as a Reformed consensus on the extent question unbroken until Amyraut and the Amyraldians.

Historically, sometimes people on either side of the aisle try to claim Dort as advocating their view. This is especially the case with limitarians. Strictly speaking, neither moderates nor high Calvinists can make such a claim since the final canons leave a certain deliberate ambiguity on the issue.[90] The details are left sufficiently broad enough to allow both groups to interpret the canons as they will, yet the details clearly disavow the Arminian notion that Christ died *equally* for the salvation of all people. It appears not only possible but likely that Turretin and the Geneva School in the mid-seventeenth century attempted to use Dort to drive a wedge between their strictly limitarian view and that of the more moderate group in an effort to portray the moderates as beyond the boundaries of Dortian orthodoxy.

---

85 O. Crisp, *Deviant Calvinism: Broadening Reformed Theology* (Minneapolis, MN: Fortress, 2014), 178.

86 Ibid., 181.

87 Ibid., 179.

88 Ibid., 181.

89 For example, Roger Nicole argued Ursinus was committed to limited atonement ("The Doctrine of the Definite Atonement in the Heidelberg Catechism," *The Gordon Review* 3 [1964]: 143–44), and Shultz stated, "The majority of the Reformers following Calvin, such as Beza, Musculus, Casper Olevianus, Zacharius Ursinus, David Pareus, Peter Vermigli, Jerome Zanchi and William Perkins all held to particular redemption" (Shultz, "A Biblical and Theological Defense," 49). As we have seen, among this listing of names only Beza and Perkins can be said to hold to particular redemption understood as a limited substitution for the sins of the elect only.

90 During the Christian Reformed Synod of 1967, H. Boer reported that Dr. Henry Zwaanstra told them about the broad opinions present at the Synod of Dort. Boer wrote: "In conclusion, it may be observed that if, as Professor Zwaanstra declared at synod, views that were as far apart as those of Herman Hoeksema [a hyper-Calvinist] and Harold Dekker [who affirmed unlimited atonement] were accepted at the Synod of Dort as valid expressions of the Reformed faith, then we have in our Confession a far wider and larger spectrum through which to reflect the light of the Word of God than many of us assumed" (H. Boer, "Decision on a Controversy," *The Reformed Journal* 17 [1967]: 9).

Amyraut, Amyraldianism, and the Saumur School[91]

John Cameron (AD 1579–1625) was professor of theology at the French Reformed Academy at Saumur in 1618–1621. Cameron had studied under Paraeus at Heidelberg for one year. We have already seen Paraeus's belief in universal atonement. Cameron left an indelible impression on Amyraut. As a preacher as well as theologian, his concern for preaching the gospel informed his approach to the extent of the atonement. Cameron proceeded on the assumption that people cannot be called upon to believe that Christ died for them, unless it is known to be true that he did.[92]

Moïse Amyraut (AD 1596–1664) was a student of John Cameron. He became a pastor in Saumur from 1626 to 1633, at the end of which time he began teaching at the academy, becoming its principal in 1640 until his death.

Amyraut opposed Arminianism as an extreme theological system but also taught that it was the extreme Calvinism of Beza that was largely responsible for the new Arminian errors. The publication of his treatise on predestination in 1634 created a firestorm.[93] He faced charges of heterodoxy at three national councils over a twenty-two-year period but was exonerated at all three. He tirelessly maintained his acceptance of the Canons of Dort.[94]

Whereas Beza limited the atonement by design, extent, and application only to the elect, Amyraut argued he was teaching nothing more than what Calvin had taught with

91 On the Amyraldian controversy, key works include L. Proctor, "The Theology of Moise Amyraut Considered as a Reaction against Seventeenth-Century Calvinism" (PhD diss., University of Leeds, 1952); B. Armstrong, *Calvinism and the Amyraut Heresy: Protestant Scholasticism and Humanism in Seventeenth-Century France* (1969; repr. Eugene, OR: Wipf & Stock, 2004), 158–262; and F. P. van Stam, *The Controversy over the Theology of Saumur 1635–1650: Disrupting Debates among the Huguenots in Complicated Circumstances* (Amsterdam: APA-Holland University Press, 1988).

92 Thomas, *Extent of the Atonement*, 175. Cameron also stated that "Christ dyed sufficiently for the wicked, and efficaciously for the believers; which is, indeed, my opinion. But then, I extend the term *sufficiently*, in this subject, further, it may be, than some others." See Cameron's letter to J. Capell (May 16, 1612) in R. Wodrow, *Collections Upon the Lives of the Reformers and Most Eminent Ministers of the Church of Scotland*, ed. W. J. Duncan, 2 vols. (Glasgow: Edward Khull [Maitland Club], 1834–1845), 2:102; emphasis in original. Gootjes wrongly inferred from this statement that "Cameron wants to go beyond the traditional sufficiency-efficiency distinction, for he argues that the word 'sufficiency' means more than most assume it does." See A. Gootjes, "John Cameron (ca. 1579–1625) and the French Universalist Tradition," in *The Theology of the French Reformed Churches: From Henri IV to the Revocations of the Edict of Nantes*, ed. M. I. Klauber (Grand Rapids, MI: Reformation Heritage Books, 2014), 185. Cameron was simply asserting that he had a more extended sense of the "sufficiency" term than others did, since he believed Christ satisfied for the sins of all men. It is the others, not Cameron, who went beyond the traditional or classical sense of Lombard's formula.

93 M. Amyraut, *Brief traitté de la prédestination et des ses principales dépendances* (Saumur: Jean Lesnier & Isaac Desbordes, 1634). For an accessible English translation, see R. Lum, "Brief Treatise on Predestination and Its Dependent Principles: A Translation and Introduction" (PhD diss., Dallas Theological Seminary, 1985); and M. Harding, "A Critical Analysis of Moise Amyraut's Atonement Theory Based on a New and Critical Translation of *A Brief Treatise on Predestination*" (PhD diss., Southwestern Baptist Theological Seminary, 2014), 183–314.

94 For an accessible survey of Amyraut biographically and theologically, see A. Clifford, "The Case for Amyraldianism," in *Christ for the World: Affirming Amyraldianism*, ed. A. Clifford (Norwich, UK: Charenton Reformed, 2007), 7–20; A. Clifford, "A Quick Look at Amyraut," in *Christ for the World*, 21–43; A. Djaballah, "Controversy on Universal Grace: A Historical Survey of Moïse Amyraut's *Brief Triaitté de la Predestination*," in *From Heaven He Came and Sought Her*, 165–200.

respect to Christ's objective satisfaction for the sins of all people as the grounds for the universal gospel offer.[95]

Amyraut, like his teacher Cameron, was concerned for preaching the gospel. How could people believe the gospel unless they were persuaded the atonement was for them? If the object of faith was not suitable to all, faith could not be commanded of all. Universal atonement was necessary to Amyraut's universal, conditional covenant and expression of the universal saving will of God. All were ultimately founded on the nature of God himself.[96]

Prior to Amyraut, most of the Reformed operated within a two-covenant system: covenant of works and covenant of grace. Amyraut and the Saumur School postulated a threefold covenant, viewed as three successive steps in God's saving program unfolded in history. The covenant of nature established by God with Adam involved obedience to the divine law as disclosed in the natural order. The covenant of law established by God with Israel involved obedience to the law of Moses. The covenant of grace established by God with all humanity requires faith in Christ.[97]

In Amyraldianism the covenant of grace was divided into a universal, conditional covenant (for all humanity on the condition of faith in Christ) and an unconditional covenant of particular grace (whereby God gives saving grace to the elect thus creating faith).

Amyraut understood God's will to have two aspects, a universal/conditional aspect and a particular/unconditional aspect.[98] God wills the salvation of all humanity but on the condition that one must believe the gospel. Since humanity, as a result of total depravity, has no moral ability to believe the gospel unless renewed by the Holy Spirit, no unrenewed sinner can or will ever come to faith. Here God's particular, unconditional will comes into play. God wills to create faith in the elect. This latter aspect of the will of God is "hidden," in distinction to the "revealed" will of God one finds in Scripture. Like Calvin, Amyraut believed that all speculation of God's secret

---

95 See Amyraut, *Defensio doctrinae J. Calvini de absolute reprobationis decreto* (Saumur: Isaac Desbordes, 1641), published three years later in French as *Defense de la doctrine de Calvin: sur le sujet de l'election et de la reprobation* (Saumur: Isaac Desbordes, 1644). Richard Muller's admission concerning the effectiveness of Amyraut's evidence against his opponents that Calvin held to unlimited atonement is significant (R. Muller, *The Unaccommodated Calvin* [Oxford: Oxford University Press, 2000], 62).

96 Thomas, *Extent of the Atonement*, 201–2.

97 B. Demarest, "Amyraldianism," in *Evangelical Dictionary of Theology*, ed. W. Elwell (Grand Rapids, MI: Baker, 1984), 41–42.

98 Amyraut has often been caricatured as believing there are two wills in God rather than distinctions within the one will of God. Carson is an example of this. In his lecture at the 2015 EFCA (Evangelical Free Church America) theology pre-conference, Carson spoke as if Amyraut believed there is a separation in the wills of God or "two different wills" rather than distinctions within the one will (faculty) of God. Notice how Carson compared what he thinks is the correct conception of God's will to "distinctions" within the love of God. There are not separations or multiple kinds of love, as Carson noted, but different senses of God's love. Contra Carson, for Amyraut, the same is true of the will of God. Carson's comments occur at the 57:25–61:52 minute marks in the recorded lecture. See D. A. Carson, "Calvinism/Reformed" (lecture, 2015 EFCA Pre-Conference, Trinity International University, January 28, 2015, available online, http://go.efca.org/resources/media/calvinismreformed).

purposes in his hidden, decretal will of election and reprobation was pointless and counterproductive.

For Amyraut, God's intent as to the actual extent of the atonement was that Christ should substitute for the sins of all humanity. God's intent in the atonement with respect to salvation applied was limited to the elect only. The atonement is itself an objective satisfaction, which is sufficient for the sins of all people because it actually atoned for the sins of all people. The limitation is not in the atonement itself but rather in the application of the atonement to the elect, per God's design and purpose in his particular/unconditional will.

Amyraut claimed that his theology differed in no wise from Calvin himself with respect to the two aspects of God's one unified will and the universal extent of the atonement. Amyraut continued to reject Arminianism and agreed with it only on the specific question of the actual extent of the atonement.

Our discussion of Amyraut and Amyraldianism is limited in focus to the question of the extent of the atonement. Thomas noted in his assessment of Amyraut's theology, "Christ dies for all conditionally, but only the elect fulfill the condition; so Christ died for the elect with respect to result rather than intention."[99] Amyraut, according to Thomas, placed predestination logically after the external call, thus preventing it from dominating the extent of the atonement. "The doctrine which produced limited atonement in Reformed theology was unquestionably that of the absolute predestination of certain individuals."[100]

Amyraut's position was criticized as inconsistent, even absurd, since double predestination, which Amyraut affirmed, negated the possibility of God's universal saving will according to Amyraut's critics. If Christ died for the sins of all the non-elect, then the result would be an empty atonement.[101] If the atonement is universal, then how was predestination not undercut? How could Jesus die to save those whom God had already predestined, or passed over, to destruction?[102]

The Reformed ultra-orthodox considered the Saumur doctrine of the extent of the atonement a serious threat. Some falsely identified Amyraut and the Saumur School as Arminians.

However, as Thomas rightly concluded:

> It would be just as incorrect, though, to represent the Saumur doctrine of the extent of the atonement as a new and odd departure from a monolithic Reformed

99 Thomas, *Extent of the Atonement*, 203. Amyraut employed descriptions of the atonement in metaphors such as a medicine and captives being set free, reminiscent of some of the first-generation Reformers, as well as Davenant, who used the same analogies.

100 Ibid.

101 Ibid., 232.

102 J. Moore, "The Extent of the Atonement," 124–25.

> tradition as it would to view it as simply a rediscovery of Calvin's Calvinism after years of neglect. It was rather an ambitious attempt to restate in an emphatic way, in the face of an orthodoxy in the process of excluding positions that were too close to those of the Arminian enemy, a doctrine that could be discovered in Calvin and seen clearly in Musculus and Bullinger, and that had been maintained in the German tradition.[103]

Likewise, John Menzeis, a seventeenth-century high Calvinist, said: "The [Popish] Pamphleter might have known that Protestants do not exclude from the Reformed Churches, the learned Camero, Amyrald, Capellus, Dallaeus [Daillé] who with many others especially in the French Church assert universal redemption."[104]

Francis Turretin played a significant role in the Amyraldian controversy. He rejected Amyraldianism but never argued that it was outside the boundaries of Reformed orthodoxy. He considered Amyraldianism's approach to the divine decrees to be near that of the Remonstrants, yet acknowledged they differed from the Arminians. Turretin studied in Saumur and Paris and maintained a lengthy correspondence with Jean Daillé, a leading Amyraldian.[105] Turretin also played an important role in the adoption of the Helvetic Consensus, which rejected Amyraldianism.[106]

One of the most important sources for Reformed theology in the seventeenth century is John Quick's *Synodicon*.[107] Quick analyzed Amyraut and the Amyraldians as affirming an unlimited atonement with respect to extent but affirming also God's intent to save only the elect. Amyraut was not an unqualified universalist. Roger Nicole quoted Quick on the Amyraldians and their beliefs and rightly noted Amyraut held a "twofold reference" view on the atonement and not an unqualified universalism.[108] This admission by Nicole, a strict particularist, is significant since it is not uncommon to find Amyraut viewed as something of an Arminian universalist by some Reformed writers, past and present.

The Genevan reactions to the Salmurian doctrine of Hypothetical Universalism were harsh. Alexandre Morus was a candidate for ministry in Geneva in 1641. However, the Genevan pastors did not readily accept his application because, among other reasons, he was suspected of being an Amyraldian. The pastors drew up a list of theses,

---

103 Thomas, *Extent of the Atonement*, 220.

104 J. Menzeis, *Roma Mendax* (London: Printed for Abel Roper, at the sign of the Sun over against St. Dunstanes Church in Fleet-street, 1675), 190.

105 B. T. Inman, "God's Covenant in Christ: The Unifying Role of Theology Proper in the Systematic Theology of Francis Turretin" (PhD diss., Westminster Theological Seminary, 2004), 390–93.

106 See P. Schaff, "The Helvetic Consensus Formula," in *The Creeds of Christendom*, 1:477–89.

107 J. Quick, *Synodicon in Gallia Reformata: Or, The Acts, Decisions, Decrees and Canons of the Seven Last National Councils of the Reformed Churches in France*, 2 vols. (London: J. Richardson, 1692).

108 Quoted in R. Nicole, *Moyse Amyraut (1596–1664) and the Controversy on Universal Grace: First Phase (1634–1637)* (PhD diss., Harvard University, 1966), 81, 110. See Quick's *Synodicon*, 2:354. However, Nicole, in some of his criticisms of Amyraldian theology, seems to presuppose Amyraut was an unqualified universalist.

which they demanded Morus assent to and sign. The theses were organized under five headings: Original Sin, Predestination, Redemption, Disposition of Man to Grace, and Promises Made to the Faithful. The third head dealt directly with the extent of the atonement and was presented in four affirmations and one denial:

1. Since the end is destined only to those to whom the means are destined, the coming of Christ into the world, his death, his satisfaction, and his salvation are destined only to those to whom God decreed from all eternity by his pure good pleasure to give faith and repentance, and to whom he confers them effectively in time; the universality of saving grace is contrary to Scripture and the experience of all the centuries.
2. Christ, from the pure good pleasure (*eudokia*) of the Father, was destined and given as mediator to a certain number of men who constitute his mystical body according to God's election.
3. It was precisely for them that Christ, perfectly conscious of his calling, wanted and decided to die and to add to the infinite worth of his death the most efficacious and particular intention of his will.
4. The universal propositions that are found in Scripture do not indicate that Christ died, made satisfaction, and so on, for each and every man according to the counsel of the Father and his will, but either they are to be restricted to the universality of the body of Christ or they must be referred to the economy (*oikonomian*) of the new covenant, by which the external distinction of all people having been taken away, the Son took all nations to himself as an inheritance. That is, he opens and accords the grace of proclamation to nations and peoples together by his will, and he gathers the Church from there, which is the foundation of the general proclamation of the Gospel.

Rejection of the errors of those

who teach that Christ died for each and every one sufficiently not only with regard to the worth, but even by reason of the intention, or for all conditionally if they believe; or who assert that Scripture teaches that Christ died for all men in general, and particularly that the Scripture passages Ezek. 18:21, etc., and 33:11; John 3:16; I Tim. 2:4; II Pet. 3:9 ought to extend to each and every man, and that the universality of love and grace is proved by them.[109]

109 D. Grohman, "The Genevan Reactions to the Saumur Doctrines of Hypothetical Universalism: 1635–1685" (ThD diss., Knox College in cooperation with Toronto School of Theology, 1971), 233–35.

These original theses finally resulted in 1649 in the doctrinal statement known as the Genevan Article. Theodore Tronchin, one of the two men responsible for drafting the theses, had been a representative of Geneva at Dort. Part of the presentation at Dort by the Genevan delegates is included word for word in the 1649 theses, especially in the section on redemption. Grohman stated:

> It is interesting to notice that the Company attached more importance to what their representatives said at Dort than to what the Synod itself said. This is true undoubtedly because the Synod actually adopted a position which was a compromise between the conservative Genevan delegates and the liberal delegates from Bremen and England on the subject of the extent of grace. As Rex points out, "the Calvinism at Dordrecht allowed for both conservatism and for a certain liberalism: the Canons decidedly did not rule out the liberal theology of the delegates from England and Bremen." Thus, the Canons of the Synod of Dort were not as precise on the subject of grace as the Genevan representatives had wished. It is also interesting that the 1649 theses clearly reject Beza's supralapsarian position, accepting instead the infralapsarian position held by both Tronchin and Morus.[110]

It has been previously pointed out with respect to Dort that there was an incipient hyper-Calvinism present among some of the delegates. These Genevan theses exhibit this as well.

However, as we have also seen with respect to Dort, the final canons provided room for Hypothetical Universalism within Reformed orthodoxy. The Genevan Article leaves no such room.

The Genevan Article is at variance with Dort here and also stands in contradiction to the exegesis and teaching of many of the early Reformers. Even Calvin and Bullinger would have never been ordained to the ministry under these theses. Mainstream high and moderate Calvinism have rejected some of the content of the Genevan Article.[111]

After surveying the Reformed debates on the extent of the atonement during the sixteenth and seventeenth centuries, Thomas's conclusion appears undeniable: neither Cameron nor Amyraut can be blamed for introducing universal atonement into Reformed theology,[112] since, as we have seen, the majority of first-generation Reformed theologians held it. Thomas continued:

"It seems fair to conclude that the question of the extent of the atonement, already

110 Ibid., 154–56. Grohman's "conservative" and "liberal" descriptions are problematic and potentially misleading.

111 Ponter, "Donald Grohman on Dort and the 1649 Genevan Articles," *Calvin and Calvinism*, November 11, 2010, http://calvinandcalvinism.com/?p=9719.

112 Thomas, *Extent of the Atonement*, 164.

handled ambiguously by the Synod of Dort, was never satisfactorily answered by the Reformed Churches throughout their early and classical period."[113]

Miscellaneous Seventeenth-Century Theologians

Jean Daillé (AD 1594–1670)

Daillé was a French Huguenot, pastor, theologian, and commentator of Scripture. He defended the Hypothetical Universalism of Amyraut in his *Apologie des Synodes d'Alençon et de Charenton* (1655). He wrote commentaries on Philippians and Colossians and in both affirmed his commitment to universal atonement, speaking of Christ's "expiation" and "propitiation" "for the sins of the world" in contexts where it is clear he means all humanity. He also used terminology such as Christ died for the "salvation" and "redemption" of the world.[114] Daillé wrote: "A Christian looks not upon any man on earth as his enemy; he knows that they are all the creation of the Lord his God, and that his Master died for them, and shed his blood to save them."[115]

Daillé compiled a lengthy list of quotations (more than 150 pages) from the patristic era throughout the sixteenth century demonstrating the priority of universal atonement in the church and the rarity of any affirmation of limited atonement.[116]

Hermann Hildebrand (AD 1590–1649)

Herman Hildebrand was a German Reformed theologian and Bremen pastor who published his views on the extent of the atonement in 1641.[117] Hildebrand sent his theses to various leading Reformed theologians asking for their opinion. Among those who received Hildebrand's theses were Joseph Hall, John Davenant, André Rivet, and Ludwig Crocius. In support of his own views of universal atonement and to demonstrate that his views were not out of step with church history, he published more than two hundred pages of quotations from the patristic, medieval, and early Reformed eras.

One needs to read no further than the first three pages of his theses to discern Hildebrand's clear affirmation of universal atonement. First, he stated that one should accept the biblical data that affirms: (1) Christ died for the sins of all, (2) yet also he died for the church, and (3) Christ intercedes for believers and not the "world"

---

113 Ibid., 241.

114 J. Daillé, *The Epistle of Saint Paul to the Philippians* (London: Henry G. Bohn, 1843), 57, 60, 62, 95, 139; idem, *An Exposition of the Epistle of Saint Paul to the Colossians* (London: Henry G. Bohn, 1843), 30.

115 Daillé, *Colossians*, 244. See also 27, 30, 53, 55–57, 60, 62, 79, 141, 242–44.

116 J. Daillé, *Apologia pro duabus Ecclesiarum in Gallia Protestantium Synodis Nationalibus*, 2 vols. (Amstelaedami: Ravesteynius, 1655), 2:753–907.

117 H. Hildebrand, *Orthodoxa Declaratio Articulorum Trium, De Mortis Christi Sufficientia et Efficacia, Reprobationis Causa Meritoria, Privata Denique Communione* (Bremen: Bertholdus Villierianus, 1642).

in John 17. The real question to ask is in what sense did and did not Christ die for all. Second, Hildebrand clearly affirmed that Christ bore the sins of all, paid for the sins of all, and expiated the sins of all. Third, he spoke of the sufficiency of Christ's death for the sins of all, not in a hypothetical way as Beza, Turretin, and Owen were prone to do, but in actuality, as we find in Davenant's "ordained sufficiency." Fourth, Hildebrand cited the following Scriptures as supporting an unlimited atonement for the whole world: John 1:29; 3:16; 1 John 2:2; Heb 2:16; 2 Cor 5:14–15; 1 Tim 2:6; Heb 2:9; Rom 14:15; 1 Cor 8:11; Heb 10:29; and 2 Pet 1:9; 2:1.[118]

Francis Turretin (AD 1623–1687)

Turretin served as the pastor of the Italian church in Geneva and professor of theology. He was one of the authors of the Helvetic Consensus and a zealous opponent of Amyraldianism. His systematic theology served as a standard text for the Reformed until the late nineteenth century.[119]

Turretin's theology of the extent of the atonement is accessible today in the republication of his three-volume *Institutes of Elenctic Theology*. Turretin is a strong advocate of limited atonement. He is also a clear example of one who has revised the Lombardian formula in an effort to make it conform to limited atonement.

> Hence the state of the question is easily elicited. (1) It is not asked with respect to the value of the sufficiency of the death of Christ—whether it has in itself sufficient for the salvation of all men. For it is confessed by all that since its value is infinite, it would have been entirely sufficient for the redemption of each and every one, if God had seen fit *to extend it to the whole world*. And here belongs the distinction used by the fathers and retained by many divines—that Christ "died sufficiently for all, but efficiently for the elect only." For this being understood of the *dignity* of Christ's death is perfectly true (although the phrase would be less accurate if referred to the will and purpose of Christ).[120]

Notice carefully Turretin's injection of a hypothetical meaning in the Lombardian formula: "If God had seen fit to extend it to the whole world." This is a revisionist read-

118 Ibid., 1–3.

119 On Turretin and his soteriology, see J. Mark Beach, *Christ and the Covenant: Francis Turretin's Federal Theology as a Defense of the Doctrine of Grace*, Reformed Historical Theology 1 (Göttingen: Vandenhoeck & Ruprecht, 2007). Beach offers an excellent treatment of Turretin's Federal theology. His discussion on the redemptive scope of the covenant of grace (224–43) summarizes well Turretin's arguments for limited atonement and against the Arminians, and particularly Amyraldianism and the Saumur school.

120 F. Turretin, *Institutes of Elenctic Theology*, 3 vols., ed. J. T. Dennison, trans. G. M. Giger (Phillipsburg, NJ: P&R, 1994), 2:458–59 (14.14.9). If Turretin is correct in his advocacy of limited atonement, the Lombardian formula is not "less accurate" with respect to the will and purpose of Christ, but it is actually inaccurate.

ing of the formula in the same vein as John Owen, for which Richard Baxter chided Owen by calling this revision a "new, futile evasion."[121]

Beach explained Turretin's forceful defense of limited atonement:

> Turretin's vigorous denial of the universality of the covenant of grace and rigorous polemic to defend its particular scope, is born of a desire to safeguard the efficacious nature of the covenant of grace. God does not fail in his salvific purpose, that he does not intend or try to save certain persons whom he fails to save—as if they are unsavable, somehow beyond his reach. If that were true, believer's confidence in his or her own salvation would be undermined, for the inescapable implication would be that any person who is an object of God's mercy and saving intention might prove to be unsaveable, or, in being saved, subsequently fall away; and in that way and to that degree sin would prove to be greater than God's grace.
>
> Moreover, in that way and to that degree the covenant of grace would be thwarted in its purpose and so would fail, at least partially, in its intention. Such a notion cuts against the grain of the covenant as a divine testament, even as it emasculates Christ's suretyship. In fact, federal theologians of the seventeenth century, like their Reformed predecessors of the sixteenth century, were resolute (believing the gospel itself to be at stake in this matter) in affirming that no class of persons and no individual person is beyond the reach of God's ability to save them, but certain persons may well be outside the scope of God's purpose to save them, something altogether inscrutable to us.[122]

Contrast Turretin here with Amyraut, who believed that Christ "died to fulfill the decree of the Father, which proceeded from an equal love to all."[123] Turretin said: "A love of God towards the human race" such that "Christ was sent into the world by the Father through that love . . . to procure salvation for each and every one under the condition of faith" is an Arminian tenet.[124] Turretin spent four pages in a vain attempt to make the case that John 3:16 speaks only about the elect.[125]

Cornelius Otto Jansen (AD 1585–1638)

Jansen, Catholic Bishop of Ypres, wrote a work on Augustine that was published posthumously in 1640. Jansen allegedly argued for limited atonement, but that may not be

121 R. Baxter, *Universal Redemption of Mankind by the Lord Jesus Christ*, 345.
122 Beach, *Christ and the Covenant*, 241–42.
123 Quoted by F. Turretin, *The Atonement of Christ*, trans. J. R. Wilson (Grand Rapids, MI: Baker, 1978), 155.
124 Turretin, *Institutes of Elenctic Theology*, 2:457.
125 Ibid., 1:405–8.

the case. Jansenists were said to believe that "it is semi-Pelagian to say that Christ died and shed his blood for all men."[126]

Conclusion

"Hypothetical Universalism," in the bare sense of an unlimited substitution of Christ for the sins of all the world, was the default position of the first generation of the Reformed tradition. Many advocates of limited atonement fail to make this point and write so as to give the impression that Hypothetical Universalism came on the scene in the early seventeenth century as a challenge to limited atonement.[127]

The term itself did indeed originate in the seventeenth century as an epithet for the Salmurian School's teaching on the extent of the atonement. Van Stam identified the source of the label "Hypothetical Universalism":

> Another sign of the hardening of the conflict is the rise, a half year after the national synod of Charenton, of a designation for the adherents of Saumur that was intended to be unfavorable. The expression in question is "les hypothetiques," the "hypotheticals." In the later history of dogma the theology of Saumur would be known as "hypothetical universalism," a phrase in which the pejorative element occurs as adjective. The Reformed in France adopted the concept "les hypothetiques" as a fixed designation for the theologians of Saumur while the Swiss Reformed before 1650 described them as "universalists." The term "les hypothetiques" was a reference to the problem in Amyraut's theology that on the one hand it declared that God willed to save all and on the other hand it acknowledged that this is not realized in all. Amyraut's intent was to make plain that whoever believes may rest assured that God will save him or her and has in fact elected that person. But his opponents objected

126 "Jansenism: The 'Five Propositions,' 1653," in *Documents of the Christian Church*, 4th ed., ed. H. Bettenson and C. Maunder (Oxford: Oxford University Press, 2011), 273. "The five propositions were admitted [by the Jansenists] to be heretical [*de jure*], but in 'fact' [*de facto*] they were declared unrepresentative of Jansen's doctrine, which the Jansenists held to be a fair representation of the teaching of St Augustine" ("Jansenism," in *The Oxford Dictionary of the Christian Church*, 3rd ed, ed. F. L. Cross and E. A. Livingstone [New York: Oxford University Press, 1997], 862). Arnauld, a Jansenist, said, "Let the five propositions be heretical, yet, with the exception of the first, they are to be found neither in letter nor in spirit in the writings of Jansen" ("Jansen or Jansenius, Cornelius," in *Cyclopedia of Biblical, Theological, and Ecclesiastical Literature*, 12 vols., ed. J. McClintock and J. Strong [1867–1887; repr. Grand Rapids, MI: Baker, 1981], 4:772). For Jansen's original work, see C. Iansenii, *Augustinus seu doctrina Sancti Augustini de humanae naturae sanitate, aegritudine, medicina adversus Pelagianos & Massilienses*, 3 vols. (Lovanii: Jacobi Zegeri, 1640), especially "Caput XX. Quomodo Christus sit redemptor omnium, pro omnibus crucifixus & mortuus," in *Augustinus*, 3:380–92, where he cited Prosper and the use of the sufficiency-efficiency solution. Abercrombie cited this section in *Augustinus* (3:382, 384–86) and represented Jansen as teaching a strict view of Christ's redemption, and concluded that "the fifth proposition, therefore, does him little injustice; but it is not, perhaps, perfectly representative of his exact expression." See N. Abercrombie, *The Origins of Jansenism* (Oxford: Clarendon Press, 1936), 148, 158. See also T. Gale, *The True Idea of Jansenism, Both Historick and Dogmatick* (London: Printed for Th. Gilbert in Oxen, 1669). John Owen wrote a preface to Gale's book.

127 For example, L. Gatiss, *For Us and for Our Salvation*, 90–99, along with many contributors in *From Heaven He Came and Sought Her.*

> that he made God's will to save all people "frustratoire." It was a reduction to absurdity of a small part of Amyraut's total point of view and the expression "hypothetical universalism" is therefore ill-suited to serve as a summary of the core of Amyraut's theology.
>
> The term "les hypothetiques" surfaced in the available documents for the first time in a letter written by Guillaume Rivet in July 1645. . . . Thus the term proves to have become popular among the opponents of Saumur, enabling them to show their aversion for certain fellow believers without having to argue their case any more.[128]

Given this history of usage, and given the fact that there is nothing "hypothetical" in the satisfaction for all sin according to all Calvinists who affirm such, "Hypothetical Universalism" is an unhelpful term. Some in the Reformed tradition have even inaccurately associated "Hypothetical Universalism" (at least the Saumur variety) with Pelagianism and Arminianism.[129]

Anglicans, Puritans, and Westminster (AD 1550–1700)

The English Puritan era can be roughly defined as spanning 130 years from c. 1560 to 1689. Some would extend it even further; others would restrict it. It is often falsely

128 Van Stam, *The Controversy over the Theology of Saumur*, 277–78. This work is one of the most important secondary sources concerning the history and theology of Amyraut and the controversy over the Samaur school's teaching of universal expiation of sin.

129 Van Stam noted the following: 1. Guillaume Rivet accused Amyraut of Arminianism; 2. Philippe Vincent thought Amyraut's teaching was venomous and that he was speaking the language of Socinus and Arminius; 3. Jean Daillé noted that Amyraut's opponents put the worst possible construction on his teaching, saying that "Socinius and Arminius are [deemed] angels by comparison with him"; 4. J. Bogerman, M. Schotanus, and J. Maccovius regarded the theology of Saumur as a new Arminianism, Pelagianism, and Socinianism; 5. Du Moulin asserted that the teaching of Amyraut and Testard was like that of the Arminians as two peas in a pod, yet Amyraut pointed out contradictions between Du Moulin's criticism and Andre Rivet's, noting that while Du Moulin had accused him of Arminianism, Rivet had not; 6. In Spanheim's work against Amyraut, Amyraut's views were mentioned in one breath with those of Arminius and semi-Pelagians; 7. Spanheim repeatedly made the mere assertion that Amyraut's teaching was also advocated by Pelagius and other heretics; 8. The theology of Saumur was equated with Arminianism, Socinianism, Papism, and even atheism. Ibid., 30, 33, 70, 98, 125–27, 217, 244, 291, 300, 325, 366, 415, 420, 428–30, 435. R. Nicole concluded that Pierre Du Moulin "was not free of exaggeration" when he expressed that "Amyraut and Testard were inclined to Arminianism, or at least to semi-Arminianism." He noted that a cursory count shows that Du Moulin's *Examen de la doctrine de MM. Amyraut & Testard* (Amsterdam: n.p., 1638) "discloses that he used the terms 'Arminius, Arminian and Arminianism' no less than 67 times in 114 pages, to say nothing of the mention of Pighius, Vortius, Corvinus, and semi-Pelagianism." In Franeker and Groningen, some letters were used "as an occasion to denounce very roundly the Salmurian views as infected with Arminianism, Pelagianism, Socinianism, and Jesuitical speculation." See R. Nicole, *Moyse Amyraut (1596–1664) and the Controversy on Universal Grace: First Phase (1634–1637)* (PhD diss., Harvard University, 1966), 104, 130.

Other modern examples would be the Hoeksemians (followers of the Dutch American Calvinist Herman Hoeksema, long-tenured pastor of the First Protestant Reformed Church in Grand Rapids and who, along with others, established the Protestant Reformed Churches when he broke with the Christian Reformed Church. He died in 1965). Likewise, R. C. Sproul Sr., in light of his comment that he would call a four-point Calvinist an Arminian. (See under R. C. Sproul below.)

assumed that all English Puritans (including those who came to America and their subsequent generations) held to limited atonement.[130]

An understanding of this period necessitates recognition of the fact that the debate between Calvinism and Arminianism was not the only game in town, though it was the biggest. Several competing theologies were in play at the dawn of the seventeenth century in England that impacted this debate, including Socinianism[131] and Grotius's governmental theory of the atonement.[132]

Andrew Kingsmill (AD 1538–1569)

Kingsmill was an early Puritan who stated that Christ sought Judas's salvation and laid down his life for him. Speaking about Christ's question to Judas in the Garden of Gethsemane,

> Even as that lamentable question [imposeth?], Judas, betrayest thou the sonne of man with a kiss? Which was to say, thou whom I have chose of many a thousand, one of my twelve familiars, . . . art thou become the betrayer of my soul? whose salvation I have sought by so many means, doest thou thirst my blood? for whom I am content to lay down my life, art thou become my hangman?[133]

Here we have an early Puritan affirming unlimited atonement in a publication dated 1574, long before Arminius or Amyraut. But notice that Kingsmill died in 1569, thus his view antedates 1569 (remember, Calvin died in 1564).

Ezekiel Culverwell (AD 1554–1631)

Culverwell was an Anglican clergyman and a Puritan leader. In his *Treatise of Faith* (1623), he sought to modify the doctrine that Christ died only for the elect. When Alexander Leighton accused him of Arminianism, Culverwell issued a spirited defense in 1626 affirming his adherence to the Synod of Dort.[134]

---

130 This is the misleading impression that is left by Joel Beeke and Randall Pederson's book *Meet the Puritans* (Grand Rapids, MI: Reformation Heritage, 2006).

131 Named for Faustus Socinus, an Italian theologian who denied the preexistence of Christ, rejected predestination, and denied that the death of Christ made satisfaction for sin. His *De Jesu Christo Servatore* was written in 1578 and published in Poland in 1594. This school of thought came to be known as Socinianism and was vigorously opposed by the Calvinists.

132 Grotius had come to England in 1613 and published his major work advocating the governmental theory of the atonement in 1617.

133 A. Kingsmill, *A View of Man's Estate, Wherein the Great Mercie of God in Man's Free Justification by Christ, Is Very Comfortably Declared* (London: H. Bynneman, 1574), 62 (no pagination, pages numbered manually from the beginning of the treatise).

134 B. Usher, "Culverwell, Ezekiel," in *Puritans and Puritanism in Europe and America: A Comprehensive Encyclopedia*, 2 vols., ed. F. J. Bremer and T. Webster (Santa Barbara, CA: ABC-CLIO, 2006), 1:69–70.

He agreed with Ussher that the extent of the atonement is universal[135] and acknowledged that John 3:16 asserts an unlimited atonement.[136]

Robert Rollock (AD 1555–1599)

Lesser known than many of the Puritans like Baxter and Bunyan, Robert Rollock was the first principal at the University of Edinburgh and author of several commentaries and other works. His commentaries and sermons were influential in Scotland. His theology of covenant closely resembled that of Ussher, and he was influential on the Westminster Assembly. His collected works are available today in a two-volume reprint.[137]

Rollock affirmed unlimited atonement:

> So long, therefore, as thy conscience is not purged, when thou goest to present thyself before his majesty, if thy conscience be wakened, thou wilt find God marking thy sins,—laying them to thy charge,—and wilt find him as a terrible judge, compassed about with burning wrath, ready to destroy thee: and if he mark thee, thou hast no standing, and if thou appear not clothed with the righteousness and perfect satisfaction that Jesus, through his blood, hath purchased for thee, thou darest not presume to approach, for then his fierce wrath shall be poured out upon thee.[138]

In another sermon, after describing the mistreatment of Jesus at the cross by unbelievers, Rollock addressed unbelievers:

> All this lets us see how dearly the Lord hath bought our life and salvation; and we are more than miserable if we see not this. And also, it lets us see what should have become of us if he had not satisfied for us, and what should become of thee, if thou be not in Christ in that great day. And it tells thee, seeing all this is for thy sin, that thou shouldst have a sad heart to have such a Redeemer made such a spectacle, and thou shouldst groan under the burden of sin; and when thou readest of the cross, thine heart should be sorrowful that ever thou shouldst have moved the God of glory to such vengeance of

---

135 E. Culverwell, *A Treatise of Faith* (London: John Dawson, 1633), 14–17. Moore concurred that Culverwell affirmed unlimited atonement (*English Hypothetical Universalism*, 175–76).

136 E. Culverwell, *A Briefe Answer to Certain Objections against the Treatise of Faith Made by Ez. Culverwell. Clearing Him from the Errors of Arminius, Unjustly Layd to His Charge* (London: John Dawson, 1646), A7^{v-r}. He said,

> I professe, I cannot find any one clear place where the WORLD must of necessity be taken for the ELECT *onely*. For the *wicked* in the world it is oft used; and more generally, for all *Mankind*, as Mr. *Calvin*, with sundry other great *Divines* understand it, even in the place where he mis aleageth [*sic*] him to the contrary. (A7^{v})

Baxter cited this in *Universal Redemption of Mankind* (London: John Salusbury, 1694), 295.

137 R. Rollock, *Select Works of Robert Rollock*, 2 vols., ed. W. Gunn (Grand Rapids, MI: Reformation Heritage, 2008).

138 R. Rollock, "Sermon XII. Psalm cxxx. 1–4," in *Select Works of Robert Rollock*, 1:464.

> his dear Son for thee. Think not that every man shall be relieved of his sin by him; no, only those who learn to groan under the burden of their own sins, by the which they have pierced him, and turn to the Lord unfeignedly, and get favour. So, if thou learnest not at one time or other to groan under the burden of thy sin, thou shalt never be relieved by him.[139]

Notice how Rollock spoke of Jesus as "purchasing" through his blood "perfect satisfaction" for the unsaved. Rollock also spoke of Jesus as having "bought" our salvation and having "satisfied" for us. In context where Rollock is speaking to the unsaved, it is clear he is affirming an unlimited atonement.

Commenting on John 3:16, Rollock utilized a syllogism for the gospel:

> Major Premise: Jesus came to save sinners.
> Minor Premise: I am a sinner.
> Conclusion: Jesus came to save me.

For Rollock, the syllogism is only valid if the major premise means Christ died for all people. As he stated: "Out of which it followeth, that in the publishing of the Gospel, God hath respect not only of all men in common, but also distinctly of every several person."[140]

Andrew Willet (AD 1562–1621)

Willet was Anglican through and through. A voracious and broad reader in theology and church history, he digested the church fathers, councils, ecclesiastical histories, the civil and canon law, and numerous other writers. His understanding and retention was renowned such that he was dubbed "a living library."[141]

His pen was no less prolific. One of his voluminous and important publications appeared in the late sixteenth century, entitled *Synopsis Papismi*. It was published in 1594, dedicated to Queen Elizabeth, exceeded thirteen hundred pages, and passed through five editions. Some considered it the best refutation of Catholicism available. In this work, Willet affirmed that Calvin held to unlimited atonement.

> *Calvin* himself excepted the manner: *Excepto, quod deloribus mortis, &c.* It must be excepted that Christ could not be held in the sorrows of death, as the reprobate are: *ibid.* The punishment then, which Christ did bear, and the reprobate

139 R. Rollock, "Sermon XVI. The Crucifixion, Continued," in *Select Works of Robert Rollock*, 2:188–89. See also Wallace, *Puritans and Predestination*, 141.

140 Rollock, *Select Works*, 1:215.

141 See J. F. Wilkinson, "Willet, Andrew," in *Dictionary of National Biography*, 63 vols., ed. L. Stephen and S. Lee (London: Smith, Elder & Co., 1885–1900), 61:288–92.

> suffer, differ in the perpetuity: wherefore the Frier impudently does object to the two first punishments produced, which do include a continuance and perpetuity forever.[142]

In the broader context of this quotation, Willet affirmed Augustine, like Calvin, also held to unlimited atonement.

John Davenant (AD 1572–1641)

John Davenant, Bishop of Salisbury and signatory of Dort, wrote what is probably the most important work in seventeenth-century England arguing against limited atonement and in favor of universal atonement. His "A Dissertation on the Death of Christ" was not published until 1650, the same year as Owen's refutation of Baxter. It was translated from the Latin by Josiah Allport and appeared at the end of Davenant's *An Exposition of the Epistle of St. Paul to the Colossians*.[143]

Owen's rejoinder to Baxter was already at the printer when Davenant's work was published, but Owen was able to provide a brief assessment of it in the preface of his work, using some of the harsh language reminiscent of places in his *Death of Death in the Death of Christ*. For example, Owen used phrases like "repugnant unto truth," not "founded on the word," "several parts thereof are mutually conflicting and destructive of each other, to the great prejudice of the truth therein contained," "unscriptural distinctions," and "inextricable entanglements."[144]

One of Davenant's key criticisms of the advocates of limited atonement was virtually identical to that of Baxter—namely, that they do not handle the Lombardian formula correctly.

Contrary to Owen and other strict particularists, Davenant argued that the sufficiency of Christ's death was not a "bare sufficiency" but an "ordained sufficiency."[145] Davenant's meaning here is that Christ, both as to intent (the will of God and Christ) and to extent, by his death satisfied for the sins of all people.

Davenant's understanding of sufficiency is much more than the "mere sufficiency" of the particularists, which goes beyond the intrinsic value of the sacrifice

142 A. Willet, *Synopsis Papismi* (London: Felix Kyngson, 1614), 1081. This work was originally published in 1594.

143 J. Davenant, "A Dissertation on the Death of Christ," in *Colossians*, 2:309–569.

144 Owen, *Works*, 10:432–33.

145 Davenant, "Dissertation," 2:378, 401–3, 409, 412. Some recent works on Owen's *Death of Death in the Death of Christ* have offered salient critiques of his arguments. Neil Chambers has subjected Owen's limitarian theology to trenchant scrutiny and found flaws in his exegesis, logic, and theology on the extent of the atonement ("A Critical Examination of John Owen's Argument for Limited Atonement in 'The Death of Death in the Death of Christ,'" [ThM thesis, Reformed Theological Seminary, 1998]). M. Foord ("John Owen's Gospel Offer" 283–95) has shown how Owen essentially denied the well-meant gospel offer, which is generally considered within orthodox Calvinism to be biblical. As Mark Jones puts it, "Foord claims that Owen holds essentially to a hyper-Calvinist position on the gospel offer, as opposed to Thomas Manton" (*Antinomianism: Reformed Theology's Unwelcome Guest?* [Phillipsburg, NJ: P&R, 2013], 15).

alone. It was God's will that atonement be made for the sins of all in an objective sense whereby all legal obstacles from God's side, which would preclude any one from salvation are removed. As Davenant stated, "God would not be actually pacified and reconciled to any man, as soon as he should believe, that is, on the performance of the condition of faith, unless he were placable and reconcilable to any man before he should believe."[146] Davenant believed that all people without exception are save-able. Davenant's theology here could not be clearer when he stated that the death of Christ was even "capable of application to Judas, if Judas had repented and believed in Christ."[147]

Unlike strict particularists, Davenant understood passages like 2 Cor 5:18–21 to express an objective and subjective side to reconciliation. God is objectively reconciled to all by virtue of the death of Christ such that all legal barriers to any person's salvation have been removed. But God has determined that no one can actually be reconciled to God who does not repent and believe the gospel (subjective reconciliation). Davenant considered the specter of eternal justification constantly looming in the theology of all those who affirm limited atonement. The atonement itself does not bring reconciliation to any one of the elect until they believe. Nor does it bring about the faith of the elect, as Perkins had argued. The atonement does not *ipso facto* come with its own application. A separate decree of predestination is what in the final analysis separates the non-elect from the elect.[148]

For Davenant, such a universal atonement guarantees the genuineness of the offer of salvation made to all people through the preaching of the gospel. The atonement "is as far applicable as it is announceable," to use Davenant's alliterative phrase.[149]

Davenant tackled the particularist double payment argument later made popular by Owen. God himself stipulated a condition on the reception of this proffered reconciliation—namely, that faith in Christ is a necessary condition for the application of the atonement to any person. This being the case, there is no injustice with God who eternally punishes those who do not meet this condition.[150]

> Since God himself of his own accord provided that his price should be paid to himself, it was in his own power to annex conditions, which being performed, this death should be advantageous to any man, nor being performed it should not profit any man. Therefore no injustice is done to those persons who are punished by God after the ransom was accepted for the sins of the human

146 Davenant, "Dissertation on the Death of Christ," 2:427.
147 Ibid., 342.
148 Moore, *English Hypothetical Universalism*, 194–96.
149 Davenant, "Dissertation," 2:418.
150 Ibid., 2:376. See also Moore, *English Hypothetical Universalism*, 206.

race, because they offered nothing to God as a satisfaction for their sins, nor performed that condition, without the performance of which God willed not that this satisfactory price should benefit any individual.[151]

Davenant's "Dissertation" is outlined with propositions that he then explained and defended. Here is his summary of the first three propositions:

> We have exhibited the universal virtue and efficacy of the death of Christ, explained in three propositions. In the *first* it was demonstrated, that this death of Christ was appointed by God and proposed to the human race, as an universal remedy applicable to all men individually. In the *second*, we have shewn in what sense Christ is said to have died for all, or in what sense the death of Christ may be acknowledged to have been established as an universal cause of salvation, for the good of the whole human race; namely, not as some assert, by reason of its mere sufficiency, or intrinsic value, in which respect the death of Christ, or the blood of the Son of God, is a price more than sufficient to redeem each and all men and angels; but by reason of the Evangelical covenant established and confirmed by this death and blood of Christ, according to the tenor of which covenant a right accrued to all men individually, on condition of faith, of claiming for themselves remission of sins and eternal life. To these two propositions we have subjoined a *third*, in which it was shewn, that universal virtue of the death of Christ having been stated, and the universal covenant of the Gospel having regard to every man, yet that every individual person has indeed, by the sole benefit of this death, God under obligation to enter into peace with him and give him life, if he should believe; but has not actual justification or reconciliation, or an actual state of grace and salvation, before he believes.[152]

Davenant concluded his "Dissertation" in such a way that leaves no doubt he adhered to universal atonement:

> Therefore, let this be the sum and conclusion of this whole controversy on the death of Christ; That Jesus Christ, the Mediator between God and man, in confirming the evangelical covenant, according to the tenor of which eternal life is due to everyone that believeth, made no division or separation of men, so that we can say that anyone is not excluded from the benefit of his

151 Ibid., 2:376.
152 Ibid., 2:473.

> death, if he should believe. And in this sense we contend, in agreement with the Scriptures, the fathers, and solid arguments, that Christ suffered on the cross and died for all men, or for the whole human race. We add, moreover, that this Mediator, when he had determined to lay down his life for sin, had also this special intention, that, by virtue of his merits, he would effectually and infallibly quicken and bring to eternal life, some persons who were specially given to him by the Father. And in this sense we contend that Christ laid down his life for the elect alone, or in order to purchase his Church; that is, that he died for them alone, with the special and certain purpose of effectually regenerating and saving them by the merit of his death. Therefore, although the merit of Christ equally regards all men as to its sufficiency, yet it does not as to its efficacy: which is to be understood, not only on account of the effect produced in one and not in another, but also on account of the will, with which Christ himself merited, and offered his merits, in a different way for different persons. Now, the first cause and source of this diversity, was the election and will of God, to which the human will of Christ conformed itself.[153]

Davenant quoted Robert Abbot (AD 1560–1617), Bishop of Salisbury:

> Although we do not deny that Christ died for all men, yet we believe that he died specially and peculiarly for the Church, nor does the benefit of redemption pertain in any equal degree to all. And from the peculiarity of this benefit, and from the human will, in some degree depends the efficacy of all means, that they are for those only, and for their use, whom Christ redeemed with some peculiar regard to their being elected in him. Nor do they obtain the effect because of being willing, but because God, according to the purpose of his own grace, works in the elect and redeemed to will that to which he chooses them.[154]

Davenant made a vital point that must be addressed by defenders of limited atonement. With respect to John 3:16, God's love does not result in the salvation of all, but it does result in God giving Jesus to die for the sins of all without exception. Salvation is always promised upon condition of faith. Yet nowhere in Scripture do we read that Christ's death was given conditionally to the human race. His death was for the sins of all.[155]

---

153 Ibid., 2:556–57.

154 Cited in M. Fuller, *The Life, Letters, and Writings of John Davenant, D.D. 1572–1641* (London: Methuen & Co., 1897), 238–39.

155 Davenant, "Dissertation," 2:384.

Joseph Hall (AD 1574–1656)

Joseph Hall was one of the original English delegates to Dort but was forced to return to England due to illness. He affirmed a universal atonement, speaking of God who

> sent his own Son, that he should give himself as a ransom for the sins of the whole world: so as there is no living soul that may not be truly and seriously invited, by his faith to take hold of the forgiveness of his sins and everlasting life, by the virtue of this death of Christ, with certain assurance of obtaining both.

Hall said that it is the "universal merit" of Christ's death that grounds the universal offer of the gospel "to all men through the whole world." Hall appealed to Calvin's understanding of the extent of the atonement as universal and stated, "Neither is there any man living to whom it may be singularly said, Christ died not for thee." He also stated that since mankind is composed of individual men, "why should we fear to say unto all, that Christ died for them?"[156]

Robert Boyd (AD 1578–1627)

In 1614 King James appointed Robert Boyd to be principal and professor of divinity in the University of Glasgow, a position he occupied until 1621. He was principal of the University of Edinburgh from 1622 to 1623. Boyd had been a student of Rollock. Though reserved in temperament, he was a brilliant scholar. He held to unlimited atonement. Boyd's major work was a *Commentary on the Epistle to the Ephesians*, published after his death.[157]

James Ussher (AD 1581–1656)

The Irish Anglican Archbishop James Ussher wrote against limited atonement.[158] Ussher drafted the Irish Articles of 1615, a significant portion of which would be later utilized by the Westminster Assembly where Ussher was invited, but declined, to serve as a delegate. The Irish Articles did not affirm limited atonement. Ussher was likely the prime influencer on Davenant on the extent of the atonement. According

---

156 J. Hall, "Via Media: The Way of Peace," in *The Works of the Right Reverend Joseph Hall*, 9 vols., ed. P. Wynter (Oxford: University Press, 1863), 9:492, 510–11.

157 R. Bodii [Robert Boyd], *In epistolam Pauli Apostoli ad Ephesios praelectiones supra CC lectione varia, multifaria eruditione, & pietate singulari refertae* (Londini: Soc. Stationariorum, 1652).

158 J. Ussher, "The True Intent and Extent of Christ's Death and Satisfaction upon the Cross," in *The Whole Works of the Most Rev. James Ussher*, 17 vols., ed. C. R. Elrington (Dublin: Hodges, Smith, and Co., 1864), 12:553–59. See also idem, "An Answer of the Archbishop of Armagh to Some Exceptions Taken against His Aforesaid Letter," in *Whole Works*, 12:561–71; and idem, *The Judgment of the Late Archbishop of Armagh and Primate of Ireland, 1. Of the Extent of Christ's Death, and Satisfaction, &c.*, ed. N. Bernard (London: For John Crook, 1657). Below the title of this work appears this statement: "Written in answer to the request of a friend, March 3, 1617."

to Richard Baxter, Ussher was responsible for bringing both John Davenant and John Preston to the position of universal redemption.[159]

Ussher employed the medicine imagery for the death of Christ, which was common among earlier Reformers.

> We may safely conclude, out of all these premises, that "the Lamb of God, offering himself a sacrifice for the sins of the whole world," intended . . . to prepare a medicine for the sins of the whole world, which should be denied to none that intended to take the benefit of it.

Christ provided and offers a medicine for the sins of the world, but only those who receive the medicine are actually saved from their sins.[160]

Just before the Synod of Dort convened, Ussher was asked by a friend to express his views on the extent of the atonement. Ussher responded with several points. First, he suggested there were "two extremes," the first of which he considered to be unlimited atonement according to Arminianism, whereby Christ died *equally* for all people, and the second limited atonement. With respect to this second extreme, Ussher asserted it would entail "that a man should be bound in conscience to believe that which is untrue, and charged to take that wherewith he hath nothing to do."[161] Second, he said one must "carefully put a distinction betwixt the satisfaction of Christ absolutely considered, and the application thereof to every one in particular."[162] Third, Ussher employed several biblical texts to support his position. Fourth, after quoting Rev 22:17 and John 6:44, he stated:

> For the universality of the satisfaction derogates nothing from the necessity of the special grace in the application; neither doth the speciality of the one any-

159 J. Moore, "James Ussher's Influence on the Synod of Dordt," in *Revisiting the Synod of Dordt*, 163–79. See also Moore, *English Hypothetical Universalism*, 174. Moore (178–79), citing Alan Ford for the point, also corrected C. Trueman concerning Ussher's views:

> Carl Trueman concludes from the book *Body of Divinitie* that Ussher was a rigorous particularist (James Ussher, *A Body of Divinitie, or the Summe and Substance of Christian Religion, Catechistically Propounded, and Explained, by Way of Question and Answer* [London: M. F. for Thomas Downes and George Badger, 1645], p. 173; Carl R. Trueman, *The Claims of Truth: John Owen's Trinitarian Theology* [Carlisle, UK: Paternoster Press, 1998], p. 200). However, even if the evidence in this book had been compelling, it is not relevant, for Ussher was not in fact its author and was displeased at its publication under his name, even expressing disagreement with some of its content. (Ussher, The Judgement, II:23–25; Nicholas Bernard, *The Life & Death of the Most Reverend and Learned Father of Our Church Dr. James Ussher* [London: E. Tyler for John Crook, 1656], 41–42; Samuel Clarke, *A General Martyrologie, Containing a Collection of All the Greatest Persecutions Which Have Befallen the Church of Christ, from the Creation, to Our Present Times* [London: For William Birch, 1677], II: 283; Parr, *The Life of the Most Reverend Father in God, James Usher*, I:62; Ussher, *Works*, I:248–50).

160 Ussher, "True Intent," 12:559.

161 Ibid., 554.

162 Ibid.

> ways abridge the generality of the other. Indeed, Christ our Saviour saith, John xvii. 6, I pray not for the world, but for them that thou hast given me: but the consequence hereby referred may well be excepted against,—namely he prayed not for the world, therefore he paid not for the world; because the latter is an act of his satisfaction, the former of his intercession, which being divers parts of his priesthood, are distinguishable one from another by sundry differences. This his satisfaction doth properly give contentment to God's justice, in such sort as formerly hath been declared: his intercession doth solicit God's mercy. The first contains the preparation of the remedy necessary for man's salvation; the second brings with it an application of the same; and, consequently, the one may well appertain to the common nature, which the Son assumed, when the other is a special privilege vouchsafed to such particular persons only as the Father hath given him; and therefore we may safely conclude, out of all these premises, that the Lamb of God offering himself a sacrifice for the sins of the whole world, intended, by giving sufficient satisfaction to God's justice, to make the nature of man, which he assumed, a fit subject for mercy, and to prepare a medicine for the sins of the whole world, which should be denied to none that intended to take the benefit of it: Howsoever he intended not by applying this all-sufficient remedy unto every person in particular, to make it effectual unto the salvation of all, or to procure thereby actual pardon for the sins of the whole world. So in one respect he may be said to have died for all, and, in another respect, not to have died for all, yet, so as in respect of his mercy he may be counted a kind of universal cause of the restoring of our nature, as Adam was of the depraving of it; for, as far as I can discern, he rightly hits the nail on the head that determineth the point in this manner.[163]

Ussher also made an important point for those within the Reformed tradition who reject limited atonement: the inadequacy of understanding sufficiency merely as an intrinsic sufficiency where Christ's death is viewed as being of infinite value but not actually satisfying for the sins of all people. Ussher stated: "For he is much deceived that thinks a preaching of a bare sufficiency is able to yield sufficient ground of comfort to a distressed soul, without giving a further way to it, and opening a further passage."[164]

Ussher affirmed that only the elect would have Christ's death for their sins applied via effectual calling. But he went on to add,

> It may be well concluded, that Christ, in a special manner, died for these [the elect]; but to infer from hence, that in no manner of respect he died for any

163 Ibid., 558–59.

164 Ussher, "An Answer," 12:568.

> others, is but a very weak conclusion, specially the respect by me expressed being so reasonable, that no sober mind advisedly considering thereof can justly make question of it,—namely, that the Lamb of God offering himself a sacrifice for the sins of the world, intended by giving satisfaction to God's justice to make the nature of man which he assumed, a fit subject for mercy, and to prepare a sovereign medicine that should not only be a sufficient cure for the sins of the whole world, but also should be laid open to all, and denied to none, that indeed do take the benefit thereof: for he is much deceived that thinks a preaching of a bare sufficiency is able to yield sufficient ground of comfort to a distressed soul, without giving a further way to it, and opening a further passage.[165]

After this letter was published, and in spite of his clear statements to the contrary, some Calvinists falsely accused Ussher of leaning toward Arminianism.[166]

Hugo Grotius (AD 1583–1645)

The Dutch jurist and Calvinist-turned-Arminian Hugo Grotius is known for championing the "governmental" theory of the atonement,[167] which would become influential among Arminians and some moderate Calvinists, especially among the New Divinity men. Grotius arrived in England in 1613 and published his views on the governmental theory of the atonement in 1617, arguing against the Socinian view of the atonement. Socinus had written against the doctrine of satisfaction and the deity of Christ in 1578, and his work was published in 1594 in Poland.[168]

Grotius supported the Remonstrants and was given a life prison sentence after the Synod of Dort's victory over the Arminians. After two years' imprisonment, through the resourcefulness of his wife, he was smuggled out of prison in a chest of books. Grotius clearly held to unlimited atonement.[169]

---

165 Ibid., 567–68.

166 A. Robertson, *History of the Atonement Controversy in Connection with the Secession Church from Its Origin to the Present Time* (Edinburgh: William Oliphant and Sons, 1846), 318.

167 H. Grotius, "Defensia fidei catholicae de satisfaction Christi Adversus Faustum Socinum Senensem," in *Hugo Grotius Opera Theologica*, ed. E. Rabbie, trans. H. Mulder (Assen/Maastricht: Van Gorcum, 1990). This work was translated into English as *A Defense of the Catholic Faith concerning the Satisfaction of Christ, against Faustus Socinus*, trans. F. H. Foster (Andover, MA: Warren F. Draper, 1889).

168 For a helpful summary of Grotius and the governmental theory of the atonement, see Strehle, "The Extent of the Atonement," 187–93. G. Williams has sought to correct misunderstanding in some of the secondary sources concerning Grotius's view of divine justice and the governmental emphasis among Reformed writers. His doctoral dissertation is very helpful on this point. See G. Williams, "A Critical Exposition of Hugo Grotius's Doctrine of the Atonement in *De satisfaction Christi*" (PhD diss., University of Oxford, 1999). See also idem, "Punishment God Cannot Inflict: The Double Payment Argument *Redivivus*," in *From Heaven He Came and Sought Her*, 490–93.

169 See Williams, "A Critical Exposition," for an excellent treatment of Grotius and the governmental theory.

Thomas Adams (AD 1583–1652)

Adams was a Cambridge graduate, pastor, and occasional preacher at St. Paul's. He was called by Robert Southey "the prose Shakespeare of puritan theologians."[170] Adams authored a commentary on 2 Peter in which at numerous points he affirmed unlimited atonement.

> Some understand it thus; that this purging is meant by the shedding of Christ's blood, whereby, the whole world is purged, John i. 29. But that all men are purged by Christ's blood, is neither a true position in itself, nor a true exposition of this place. The blood of Christ only purgeth his church, Eph. v. 26. And there are none admitted to stand before the throne, but such as have "washed their robes, and made them white in the blood of the Lamb," Rev. vii. 14. If any soul be thus washed, he shall never be confounded. If this man were thus purged, how could he forget it? "God was in Christ, reconciling the world unto himself," 2 Cor. v. 19. Yet no man thinks that the whole world shall go to heaven, for then were hell made to no purpose. So God loved the world, that he gave his Son; yet "the whole world lieth in wickedness," 1 John v. 19. Thus it is clear, expiation was offered for the world, and offered to the world; but those that are blessed by it, are separated from the world: "I have chosen you out of the world," John xv. 19. Salvation may be said to belong to many, that belong not to salvation. Now the reprobate forgets that a purgation was made for him by the shedding of the Messiah's blood, which is a wretched thing, to forget so great a ransom.[171]

Notice how Adams affirmed the atonement as "all-sufficient"—a special intent on God's part to save the elect, Christ died for all—and his reference to Chrysostom, whom he is quoting: "In regard of the all-sufficient price paid for them. So Christ is said to be that Lamb which taketh away the sins of the world. Though he meant not to save all, yet he died for all, performing his part. (Chrysost.)"[172]

Commenting on 2 Pet 2:1, Adams repeatedly affirmed the verse teaches an unlimited atonement.[173]

Robert Jenison (AD 1584–1682)

Jenison was a seventeenth-century Puritan and friend of Richard Sibbes. His moderate views on the extent of the atonement can be found in his 1642 work, *Two Treatises*:

---

170 A. B. Grosart, "Adams, Thomas," in *Dictionary of National Biography*, 63 vols., ed. L. Stephen (New York: MacMillan and Co., 1885), 1:102.

171 T. Adams, *An Exposition upon the Second Epistle General of St. Peter, by Rev. Thomas Adams, Rector of St. Gregory's* (1633; repr. Morgan, PA: Soli Deo Gloria, 1990), 108.

172 Ibid., 222. See also 216, 219, 671, and 812, where Adams asserted unlimited atonement.

173 Ibid., 222–25.

> Our Church then doth not deny universal redemption: for we truly say with it and with Scripture, *Christ died for all.* Yet it denies that equall and universall Application of this redemption, whose event is suspended, & hangs either on the libertie of mans will, or on any condition in man (which God will not work.) We deny not, but say that Christ paid a price for all, but such as is to bee applied to each by the meanes of faith, which is not of all, and not by the very act or fact of his oblation, so that, faith being presupposed, & comming betweene, all and each are capable of salvation, and they are such as, beleeving, shall be saved.[174]
>
> Here is then the *mystery*: Though God invite all, and promise life to all upon the condition of faith, and that promise be grounded, as is granted, upon the merits of Christs death, yet the fruit of Christs death doth actually belong only to such as beleeve. The price paid for all, and which shall certainely bee to the salvation of beleevers, yet profits not all, because *faith is not given to all* (as not the meanes of faith) but to the Elect onely.
>
> We therefore preach and teach that *Christ dyed for all,* so as that all and each, *may* by the vertue of Christs death, through faith (the Gospell once comming to them) *may* I say obtaine remission of sin and life; and so Christs death hath purchased a possibility of salvation for all men, if all men can beleeve.
>
> But wee say againe that Christ so dyed for the Elect that, by vertue of the merit of his death (which was specially intended for them according to Gods eternall decree) they not onely *might*, but *should* infallibly attaine faith here, and obtaine life eternall hereafter, and that without any co[m]pulsion of their wills.[175]

John Preston (AD 1587–1628)

One of the most prolific Puritan authors was John Preston. Contrary to many modern examinations of Preston's theology, Jonathan Moore has demonstrated that Preston actually affirmed Hypothetical Universalism.[176] Several strands of evidence support

---

174 R. Jenison, *Two Treatises: The First concerning Gods Certaine Performance of His Conditional Promises, as Touching the Elect, or, A Treatise of Gods Most Free and Powerfull Grace. Lately Published without the Authours Privitie, and Printed Corruptly, by the Name and Title of Solid Comfort for Sound Christians. The Second, concerning the Extent of Christ's Death and Love, Now Added to the Former. With an Additionall Thereunto* (London: E. G., 1642), 216–17.

175 Ibid., 232–33.

176 Moore, *English Hypothetical Universalism*, 96. Prior to Moore, P. Toon, *The Emergence of Hyper-Calvinism in English Non-Conformity* (Eugene, OR: Wipf & Stock, 2011), 23; N. Douty, *Did Christ Die for the Elect? A Treatise on the Extent of the Atonement* (Eugene, OR: Wipf & Stock, 2007), 101–2; and C. Daniel, "Hyper-Calvinism and John Gill," 735, all cited Preston as a universal Redemptionist. J. R. Beeke and R. J. Pederson also observed that "Preston espoused a modified and moderate form of Calvinism. Especially his later sermons reveal that he embraced the system of English hypothetical universalism, teaching that Christ died for all without exception and placing great stress on human responsibility in the covenant relationship" (*Meet the Puritans*, 491–92).

his claim. Richard Baxter, who was influenced by Preston's writings, frequently cited Preston as in agreement with himself on the question of the extent of the atonement.[177]

In Preston's collection of sermons, *Riches of Mercy*, his belief in unlimited atonement is clear. Preston's approach to some of the key texts on extent, such as John 3:16; 1 Tim 2:6; and Heb 9:28, differs from particularists. For example, Preston interpreted the "all" of 1 Tim 2:6 to mean "all without exception." Of interest is the fact that Preston limited Christ's intercessory ministry to the elect, as is common to most Calvinists, but clearly repudiated the notion that Christ's death was only for those for whom he made effectual intercession.[178]

Moore concluded that, for Preston, "Christ as High Priest makes satisfaction for all without exception, but Christ as High Priest makes intercession only for the elect. It would appear that the decree of election can be removed almost altogether for propitiation and lodged solely in the limited and discriminating intercession of Christ."[179]

In his *Opera*, Preston never stated that Christ died only for the elect.[180] Preston affirmed God's love for all people and grounded the sincerity of the Gospel call in Christ's death for all people.[181] Notice Preston's use of the phrase "Christ is dead for him" in the following statement: "Goe and tell every man without exception, that there is good newes for him, Christ is dead for him, and if he will take him, and accept of his rightousnesse, he shall have it; restaine it not, but goe and tell every man under Heaven."[182]

Moore made note of the fact:

> A reading of the Geneva Bible in comparison with the Authorised Version gives evidence that the phrase "is dead for" was used in translation to mean "died for." . . . Furthermore, the interchangeability of the two phrases is also evident in other theological literature of the period. Even in the context of the extent of Christ's satisfaction, Hugh Ince translated "Christus mortuus est pro omnibus" as both Christ "died for all" and also "is dead for all," evidently without seeking to convey any distinction by the variation in the English rendering.[183]

---

177 R. Baxter, *Universal Redemption*, 480. In a work on the life and times of Baxter, published only five years after his death, one again finds evidence that Preston held to universal redemption. See R. Baxter, *Reliquiae Baxterianae: Or, Mr. Richard Baxter's Narrative of the Most Memorable Passages of his Life and Times*, ed. M. Sylvester (London: For T. Parkhurst, J. Robinson, J. Lawrence, and J. Dunton, 1696), 206. See also Moore, *English Hypothetical Universalism*, 174.

178 J. Preston, *Riches of Mercy to Men in Their Misery* (London: J. T., 1658), 425–26, as cited in Moore, *English Hypothetical Universalism*, 101. See also Thomas Ball's record of John Preston's discussions with Francis White in Thomas Ball, *The Life of the Renowned Doctor Preston*, ed. E. W. Harcourt (London: Parker and Co., 1885), 130–36.

179 Moore, *English Hypothetical Universalism*, 101.

180 Ibid., 101–2.

181 Ibid., 109.

182 J. Preston, *The Breastplate of Faith and Love*, 6th ed. (London: G. Purstow, 1651), I:8.

183 Moore, *English Hypothetical Universalism*, 121.

Preston implied that one cannot be expected to believe the gospel unless he can believe that Christ died for him in particular.[184] Like the first generation of Reformers, Preston affirmed a universal atonement with a designed application only for the elect.

The York House Conference (AD 1626)

During the first quarter of the seventeenth century, a growing number of Arminians within the Anglican Church created concern for the Calvinists, especially the high Calvinists. For some Calvinists, the Thirty-Nine Articles was insufficient to clinch a strong Calvinism, and many desired revisions to the confession to strengthen the hand of high Calvinism. Some desired to see the Canons of Dort become the official interpretive grid for the Thirty-Nine Articles. Particularly clear was the Thirty-Nine Articles' lack of affirmation of a limited atonement. In fact, the confession clearly affirmed an unlimited atonement.

The York House Conference was the effort of Calvinists to persuade George Villiers, the Duke of Buckingham, to declare Calvinism (as defined by Dort) the theological position of the Church of England. The conference failed to produce the effect the high Calvinists had desired.

Moore summarized the proceedings of the York House Conference well.[185] The Puritan Calvinist John Preston was a key player in this conference. He squared off against Francis White, an Arminian leader. White pointed out that the Church of England

> in the Catechism [1549][186] and many other places, hath taught us to believe that Christ died for all, "and hath redeemed me and all mankind," that is, paid the ransom and the price for all without exception; and that if any man be damned, it is not because man's own fault, is not applied unto him. Adding hereunto, that a great and manifest mischief it was, to have our people taught that Christ died not for them all.[187]

In answer to White's pressing question to Preston concerning the extent of the atonement, Preston acknowledged his own Hypothetical Universalism by clearly responding that Christ died for the sins of all people. Where Preston differed with White concerned not the actual extent of the atonement but the intent. White, like all Arminians, argued that Christ died *with equal intent to apply* the atonement to all people. Preston, like all Calvinists, argued that Christ died *with the intent to apply the atonement only to the elect.*

184 Ibid., 123. See Preston, *The Breastplate*, 1:32–33.

185 Moore, *English Hypothetical Universalism*, 141–69.

186 Where the catechumen is to state his belief "in God the Son who hath redeemed me and all mankind." See Schaff, *Creeds of Christendom*, 3:518.

187 J. Cosin, "The Sum and Substance of the Conferences Lately Had at York House Concerning Mr. Mountague's Books," in *The Works of the Right Reverend Father in God John Cosin, Lord Bishop of Durham*, 5 vols. (Oxford: John Henry Parker, 1844), 2:63, as cited by Moore, *English Hypothetical Universalism*, 157.

Where Preston differed with his high Calvinist cohorts was in the actual extent of the atonement. Here Preston agreed with White and the Arminians.

Preston also interpreted the passages that employ "all" in the context of the atonement's extent as meaning "all without exception" rather than "all without distinction," as was the standard interpretation of the high Calvinists. Preston felt this was the plain meaning of these texts. For example, he stated: "Christ was indeed a ransome for all, 1 Tim. 2:6 yet the Saviour only of his body, . . . he redeemed all, but called, justified, & glorified, whom he knew before, and had predestined to be formable to the image of his Son."[188] Preston took "ransom" and "redemption" to refer to all without exception.

John Goodwin (AD 1594–1665)

John Goodwin was one of the most prolific authors during the English Revolution, publishing sixty books and pamphlets from 1640 to 1663. Educated at Queens' College, Cambridge, he was pastor of St. Stephen's, Coleman Street, a flagship Puritan parish in London, from 1633 to 1645 and again from 1649 to 1660.[189] A contemporary of John Owen, Goodwin was a Calvinist turned Arminian. He defended the minority view at Dort on the extent of the atonement in his *Theomachia* (1644).

Goodwin published a major work on the extent of the atonement in 1651 entitled *Redemption Redeemed.*[190] Wallace probably is correct in his suggestion that Goodwin had more in common with moderate Calvinists than with some within Anglican Arminianism.[191] Goodwin was the chief advocate of what came to be called the "New Arminianism," which took root during the Cromwellian era. His influence over the General Baptists is not as great as sometimes assumed, according to J. Matthew Pinson.[192]

Goodwin's lengthy tome critiqued Calvinism, especially with respect to predestination and limited atonement. Our focus on Goodwin concerns what he said about the extent of the atonement. His critique is formidable, arguing the case by appealing to Scripture, theology, logic, the patristics, and early Reformed leaders.

188 T. Ball, *The Life of the Renowned Doctor Preston*, ed. by E. W. Harcourt (London: Parker and Co., 1885), 132; cited by Moore, *English Hypothetical Universalism*, 162.

189 For an excellent study of Goodwin's life and thought, consult J. Coffey, *John Goodwin and the Puritan Revolution: Religion and Intellectual Change in Seventeenth-Century England* (Woodbridge: Boydell, 2006). On Goodwin's conversion from Calvinism to Arminianism, see especially pages 207–9.

190 J. Goodwin, *Apolytrosis Apolytroseos, or, Redemption Redeemed: Wherein the Most Glorious Work of the Redemption of the World by Jesus Christ Is Vindicated against the Encroachments of Later Times with a Thorough Discussion of the Great Questions concerning Election, Reprobation, and the Perseverance of the Saints* (London: John Macock, 1651). Goodwin's *Redemption Redeemed* was reprinted from the 1651 edition and published in London in 1840 by R. Griffin & Co. A revised edition has recently been republished under the title *Redemption Redeemed: A Puritan Defense of Unlimited Atonement*, ed. J. Wagner (Eugene, OR: Wipf & Stock, 2004). Like Davenant, Goodwin cited a number of the patristics demonstrating their adherence to universal atonement.

191 Wallace, *Puritans and Predestination*, 130–31.

192 J. Matthew Pinson, "The Diversity of Arminian Soteriology: Thomas Grantham, John Goodwin, and Jacob Arminius" (paper presented at the national meeting of the American Society of Church History, Florida State University, Tallahassee, FL: Spring 1998), 3.

In introducing his discussion of the extent of the atonement, Goodwin said:

> I shall . . . evince both from the main and clear current of the Scriptures themselves, as likewise by many impregnable and undeniable demonstrations and grounds of reason, to be a most ancient and divine truth; yea, to be none other but the heart and soul, the spirit and life, the strength and substance, and brief sum of the glorious gospel itself: yea, I shall make it appear from ancient records of best credit, and from the confessions of modern divines themselves, of best account adversaries in the point, that universal atonement by Christ was a doctrine generally taught and held in the churches of Christ for three hundred years together next after the apostles.
>
> Neither doth anything nor all things that I could ever yet meet with either from the tongues or pens of the greatest patrons of particular redemption, deliver me from under much admiration, that conscientious and learned men, professing subjection of judgment to the Scriptures, should either deny universal or assert particular redemption; considering that the Scriptures, in particularity, plainness, and expressness of words and phrase, do more than ten times over deliver the former; whereas the latter is nowhere asserted by them, but only stands upon certain venturous consequences and deductions, which the weak judgments of men, so much accustomed to error and mistake, presume to levy from them; together with such arguments and grounds, which, upon examination, will be found either to have no consistency with the sound principles either of reason or religion, or else no legitimate coherence with the cause which they pretend unto.[193]

Goodwin began by considering no less than twenty-six passages in the New Testament affirming universal redemption. He often referenced aspects of Greek lexicography, syntax, and grammar, and interspersed in his analysis of these passages are occasional quotations from the church fathers and early Reformers indicating their agreement with Goodwin's understanding of said passages.

On the question of the meaning of "all men" in passages like 1 Tim 2:1–6, Goodwin has a lengthy and penetrating discussion showing why it is not possible to interpret this phrase to mean "some of all sorts of men" to support a limited atonement reading,[194] an approach common today among Calvinists defending limited atonement.[195]

Goodwin's lengthy treatment of John 3:16–17 is exegetically solid and supports

193 J. Goodwin, *Redemption Redeemed (1840)*, 129–30.

194 Ibid., 158–77.

195 See, for example, T. Schreiner, "Problematic Texts for Definite Atonement in the Pastoral and General Epistles," in *From Heaven He Came and Sought Her*, 375–97.

unlimited atonement. Goodwin demonstrated from Calvin's writings, as well as others on this passage, that Calvin himself taught unlimited atonement.[196]

Goodwin asserted that apart from an unlimited atonement, gospel preaching to all people "will have no true foundation."[197] Responding to the assertion that limited atonement and the well-meant gospel offer are compatible, on such a supposition, Goodwin stated that God

> cannot, either with honour or otherwise, or with truth, make any such offer or promise. . . . Suppose the devil had certainly known, as very possibly he might, that the Lord Christ would not have fallen down and worshipped him, upon any terms or conditions whatsoever, would this have excused him from vanity, in promising him all the kingdoms of the world upon such a condition, when, as all the world knew, that not one of these kingdoms were at his disposal.[198]

Goodwin concluded that no one, including God, can say with truth to every person "if you believe you shall be saved" unless undergirding this offer is a salvation purchased for all people. The truth of this assertion "cannot be salved by this, that all men or every particular man will not believe."[199]

On the sufficiency question, Goodwin asserted:

> So that to affirm and grant, that Christ died sufficiently for all men, and yet deny that he died intentionally for all men, is to speak contradictions. . . . But in this sense the actual salvation of particular men, under any other consideration than as believers, is none of his intentions. . . . Besides, If Christ died sufficiently for all men, either God intended this sufficiency of his death for or unto all men or not. . . . If then, God did intend the sufficiency of his death for or unto all men, why may it not be said that he intended his death itself accordingly? and so, that Christ died intentionally, on God's part, for all men? . . . Therefore the argument follows roundly; if God intended the sufficiency of Christ's death for all men, then he intended his death itself for all men; and consequently, Christ died not sufficiently only, but intentionally also for all men. And so the distinction vanisheth.[200]

Notice here that Goodwin is articulating in essence the same argument of Davenant's "ordained sufficiency."

196 Goodwin, *Redemption Redeemed (1840)*, 132–45.
197 Ibid., 144.
198 Ibid., 179.
199 Ibid.
200 Ibid., 155.

Goodwin continued to press his argument by making several points. "How can he, who payeth nothing at all for a man, nor intends to pay any thing, be notwithstanding said to pay that which is sufficient for him?"[201] Goodwin personalizes with an illustration. He asks how a sum of money can be considered sufficient to ransom him, which was only paid for the ransom of another.[202] If there is a sufficiency in Christ's death for all people, and yet God did not intend Christ's death to be for the sins of all people, but only for some, "then will the death of Christ be found rather matter of dishonour or disparagement unto him, than of honour?"[203]

Goodwin likewise asserted that if Christ died sufficiently for all people, yet not intentionally for all, "then he died as much for the devils themselves as he did for the greatest part of men."[204]

Finally, Goodwin chided those who distinguish between Christ's dying for all people sufficiently and intentionally, affirming the former but denying the latter, as speaking

> things most unworthy of God, and which render him a far greater deluder or derider of his poor creature, man, than a benefactor or well-willer to him, in all his declarations and professions of love unto him, in the gift of his Son Jesus Christ to make his atonement, and procure redemption for him.[205]

Later, Goodwin asserted "the distinction of Christ dying sufficiently for all men, but not intentionally, is ridiculous, and unworthy from first to last of any intelligent or considering man."[206]

What is of interest at this point in Goodwin's argument is his quotation of Beza and Piscator, both of whom deny in strong terms that the atonement can be said to be "sufficient" for anyone other than the elect. Piscator is particularly terse in his statement to his antagonist on the subject:

> The proposition laid down is false, viz. that Christ died sufficiently for every particular or single man; this is thy assertion. For Christ died most sufficiently for the elect, paying the price of their redemption, I mean his precious blood, that blood of the Son of God. But for reprobates Christ died neither in one kind nor other, *neither sufficiently* nor efficaciously.[207]

201 Ibid., 156.
202 Ibid.
203 Ibid.
204 Ibid., 157.
205 Ibid.
206 Ibid., 180.
207 Ibid., 158. (See Piscator, *Piscator contra Schaffman*, 123.)

Concerning 1 Tim 2:4 and 2 Pet 3:9, Goodwin stated:

> If it be the will of God to have all men without exception, saved, &c., most certain it is that Christ died, and intentionally on God's part, for ALL men, without exception; because it is not imaginable that God should be willing to have those saved for whom he was unwilling that salvation should be procured.[208]

Goodwin made a strong point concerning unlimited atonement from Rom 5:20–21. Sin reigned over "all men" without exception; therefore, grace must have proportionately reigned unto life by putting all people into a capacity of life and salvation. "If so, it undeniably follows that Christ died for all men, without exception for any, because otherwise all men could not be put into an estate of grace or salvation by Him."[209] Goodwin enlisted Martin Bucer for support: "That our reparation is made by Christ, and that it is more efficacious than the sin of Adam, and that it is of *larger extent*, is that which the apostle argueth in this and the following section."[210] Here is further evidence that Bucer affirmed an unlimited atonement.

Goodwin expostulated on Bucer's comment:

> Doubtless, if all men, without exception, were brought into a condition of misery by the sin of Adam, and but a handful only, in comparison, made happy by the grace of Christ; the grace of Christ cannot be said to have profited mankind more than the sin of Adam damnified it.[211]

Goodwin proceeded to examine Bucer's additional comments on this passage, concluding with these statements by Bucer:

> For though there be no sin committed in all the world which hath not its original from that first sin of Adam, yet all particular men who sin, as they sin voluntarily and freely, so do they make an addition of their own proper guilt and misery. *All which evils*, since the alone *benefit of Christ hath taken away*, it must needs be that it hath taken away the sins of many, and not of one only. Manifest, therefore, it is, that more evils have been removed by Christ, than were brought in by Adam.[212]

208 Ibid., 166–67.
209 Ibid., 174.
210 Ibid.
211 Ibid., 175.
212 Ibid.

Goodwin concluded with this quotation of Bucer: "As by the fall of one, sin prevailed over all, so as to make all liable unto condemnation: so likewise the righteousness of one so far took place on the behalf of all men, that all men may obtain the justification of life thereby."[213] Bucer appears to be asserting unlimited atonement.

Goodwin cited the following names, with quotations, as advocating that Christ died for the sins of all people:

> Augustine, Ambrose, Jerome, Chrysostom, Athanasius, Hilarius, Cyril of Jerusalem, Eusebius, Arnobius, Didymus, Basil, Gregory Nyssen, Gregory Nazianzen, Epiphanius, Tertullian, Origen, Cyprian, Clement of Alexandria, Justin Martyr, Ireneus, Prosper, Cyril of Alexandria, Theodoret, Leo, Fulgentius, Primasius, Gregorius, Bede, Theophylact, Anselm, Oecumenius, Bernard, the Synod at Mentzin opposition to Gottschalk, some of the statements made by those at the Synod of Dort, Luther, Melancthon, Chemnitius, Calvin, Vermigli, Bucer, Pareus, Gwalther, Hemmingius, Ursinus, Aretius, J. Fox, Lavater, Chamier, Perkins,[214] Zanchius, Bullinger, Grynaeus, Davenant, Kimedoncius.[215]

One year after Goodwin's publication, Richard Resbury dismissed several of Goodwin's quotes merely by calling it "wresting of Quotations."[216] However, Resbury is engaging in special pleading here, as it is clear that Goodwin is thoroughly familiar with the patristic literature (Goodwin's analysis of this aspect of church history is just shy of seventy pages) and is not cherry picking quotations.

In his preface to the 1959 Banner of Truth edition of Owen's *Death of Death*, J. I. Packer stated that this work must be reckoned with in any attempt to answer the

---

213 Ibid., 176.

214 It is likely Goodwin errs in his assessment of Perkins. See above under Perkins.

215 See Goodwin, *Redemption Redeemed (1840)*, 524–61; 672–719. Goodwin's treatment here is formidable. Notice that Goodwin cited Pope Leo the Great (c. AD 400–461). Leo clearly taught that Christ "died for all men" ("Sermons of Leo the Great: Sermon LXXXV," in *NPNF*, Second Series, eds. P. Schaff and H. Wace [1895; repr. Peabody, MA: Hendrickson, 2004], 12:197), and that Christ "propitiated for the human race," "took up the cause of all," and was "the propitiation of the world" ("Letters of Leo the Great: Letter CXXIV," in *NPNF*, Second Series, 12:92). Leo is important because both Kimedoncius and Jeremias Bastingius (AD 1551–1595), a Dutch Reformed theologian, sought to establish a case for continuity between their view of the extent of Christ's satisfaction with that of Leo's. See J. Kimedoncius, *The Redemption of Mankind*, 12; and J. Bastingius, *An Exposition or Commentary Vpon the Catechisme of Christian Religion, which is taught in the Schooles and Churches both of the Low Countries, and of the Dominions of the Countie Palatine* (Printed at London by Iohn Legatt, Printer to the University of Cambridge, 1614), 159. Bastingius also said that "it was necessary that Christ should come between to make intercession, that he should take upon himself and abide the punishment, which by the just judgement of God did hang over the head of all sinners" (ibid., 4). Christ "suffered in his soul the wrath of God against the sin of all mankind," and he "is the only sacrifice of reconciliation for the sins of the whole world" (ibid., 154, 159). For an overview of Bastingius's life, see J. Beeke, "Bastingius, Jeremias," in *The Oxford Encyclopedia of the Reformation*, ed. H. J. Hillerbrand, 4 vols. (New York: Oxford University Press, 1996), 1:127–28.

216 R. Resbury, *The Lightless-Starre: or, Mr. John Goodwin Discovered a Pelagio-Socinian: And This by the Examination of His Preface to His Book Entitled Redemption Redeemed* (London: Printed for John Wright at the Kings-Head in the Old-Bayly, 1652), 21–24.

arguments for limited atonement.[217] Actually, in Owen's own generation, both Richard Baxter and John Goodwin provided significant biblical and theological refutations of Owen. Goodwin's treatment has been virtually ignored by high Calvinists, even though his *Redemption Redeemed* is almost 750 pages in length. It garners not a single citation in the index of *From Heaven He Came and Sought Her*, reputed to be the definitive modern defense of limited atonement, which I will review in part 3 below.

Henry Hammond (AD 1605–1660)

Hammond was an Anglican Royalist. He was a well-read scholar, knowledgeable in patristics, and was the first English scholar to compare manuscripts of the New Testament. He authored numerous published works along with many sermons and letters.[218]

Hammond spoke of the purpose of Christ's death as "to satisfie for the sin of Adam, and for all the sins of all mankind."[219] In his 1648 *A Brief Vindication of Three Passages in the Practical Catechisme*, he asserted, "Christ redeemed all men." He spoke of the benefits of Christ's death as being "general" and designed in such a way that all conditionally[220] (John 3:16) may be saved if they perform the condition. Hammond appealed to Prosper as affirming the same thing and noted that the Catechism at this point appeals to Heb 2:9, where Hammond asserted "every man" "signifies all mankind" and that "tasting death for them" means "satisfying for their sins."

Hammond appealed to other passages in support of universal atonement: 2 Pet 2:1; 1 Cor 8:11; and 2 Cor 5:14. Concerning the latter, he stated,

> Where speaking of the constraining obliging love of Christ, he saith, we thus judge, that if one died for all, then were all dead, that is, surely, All in the full latitude, not only the elect but All others; and this conclusion the Apostle infers by this medium, because one, i.e. Christ died for all, which being a proof of the other, must certainly be as true, and as acknowledged (if not more) as that which 'tis brought to prove; and particularly the [all] for whom he died, be as unlimited as the [all] that were prov'd from thence to be dead, or else the Apostle could not judge (as he saith he doth) or conclude the death of all in Adam by that medium. From this arguing of the Apostle I shall make no question to infer, that in S. Pauls divinity, Christ died for all who are dead in

217 J. I. Packer, "Introduction," in *The Death of Death in the Death of Christ* (Edinburgh: Banner of Truth, 1959), 1–25. The entire introduction can be read here at http://www.johnowen.org/media/packer_quest_for_godliness_ch_8.pdf.

218 For Hammond's role in the Church of England between 1643 and 1660, see J. W. Packer, *The Transformation of the Church of Anglicanism: 1643–1660, with Special Reference to Henry Hammond* (Manchester: University of Manchester, 1969).

219 H. Hammond, *Practical Catechism*, 2nd ed. (London: Printed for R. Royston, at the Angel in Ivy-Lane, 1646), 3.

220 It is standard fare for moderate Calvinists to distinguish between Christ dying for all absolutely and dying for all conditionally. Notice how Hammond uses the term "conditional." Many Puritans make use of this distinction as well.

> Adam; and on that occasion I shall adde, by the way, that the contrary doctrine [of Christs not dying for all] was by the Ancients affixt on Pelagius upon that ground, of his affirming that all (i.e. that Infants) were not faln in Adam, and so needed not to be redeem'd by Christ. Thus it appears by S. August: cont. 2. Epist. Pelag: l. 2. c. 2. Pelagiani *dicunt Deum non esse omnium aetatum in hominibus mundatorem, salvatorem, liberatorem*, &c. and when the Massilians, to vindicate themselves from that charge of S. Augustines, confesse that Christ died for all mankind, (as it appears by Prospers Epistle) Prosper expresses no manner of dislike of that confession, but forms other charges against them. And the truth is, there is scarce any ancient writer before Pelagius, but hath directly asserted Christs dying for all.

Several things should be observed. First, Hammond suggested 2 Cor 5:14 can be interpreted in no other logical way than as an assertion of unlimited atonement. Second, he stated that it was actually Pelagius who argued that Christ did not die for all people, and he quoted Augustine as making the point. Third, he appealed to Prosper in support of Augustine's belief that Christ died for all.

Hammond professed to have learned this notion of unlimited atonement not only from Scripture but also from the Church of England's Thirty-Nine Articles and the Practical Catechism in the *Book of Liturgy*, both of which affirm Christ died for all. From the Practical Catechism, "I was taught," Hammond said, "to believe . . . in God the Son, who redeemed me and all mankind."[221]

William Jenkyn (AD 1613–1685)

Jenkyn was a popular preacher and one of those ejected by the Act of Uniformity in 1662. He was arrested and placed in Newgate Prison, where he died in 1685. He authored an excellent commentary on Jude.[222]

In his controversy with the Arminian John Goodwin, he indicated his adherence to unlimited atonement: "*Chrysostome* would have informed you [John Goodwin], that those of whom Christ is Redeemer in respect of the sufficiency of the price, may perish, though not those to whom the price is applied."[223] This is a refutation of Goodwin's notion of the possibility of loss of salvation. Jenkyn agreed with Goodwin on the extent question.

---

221 H. Hammond, *A Brief Vindication of Three Passages in the Practical Catechisme, from the Censures Affixt on Them by the Ministers of London, in a Book Entitled, A Testimony to the Truth of Jesus Christ, &c.* (London: Printed for Richard Royston in Ivy-lane, 1648), 3–7.

222 W. Jenkyn, *An Exposition upon the Epistle of Jude Delivered in Christ's Church, London* (Edinburgh: J. Nichols, 1865).

223 W. Jenkyn, ΟΔΗΓΟΣ ΤΥΦΟΣ, *The Blinde Guide, or the Doting Doctor* (London: M. B., 1648), 107. Goodwin affirmed universal atonement and the possibility of loss of salvation.

John Owen (AD 1616–1683)

John Owen is rightly considered one of the foremost English Puritan theologians.[224] His collected works today fill sixteen volumes. At the age of thirty-one, he published in 1648 his now famous *Death of Death in the Death of Christ*,[225] considered by many to be the classic work defending limited atonement.[226] Three leading concerns undergird Owen's defense of limited atonement: Trinitarian, covenantal, and exegetical.[227]

Owen could not conceive of any such thing as "potential" reconciliation. Either the cross reconciled sinners or it did not. Owen refused to see in passages such as 2 Cor 5:14–21 an objective and subjective aspect to reconciliation. He relied heavily on the so-called covenant of redemption and logic in his arguments for limited atonement: the "double payment" and "triple choice" arguments. Owen also argued the sufficiency of Christ's death for all but interpreted that sufficiency as a mere hypothetical sufficiency, accepting the revision of the Lombardian formula promulgated by Beza and Piscator earlier.

Owen's theology of limited atonement is heavily dependent upon several notions. One is his notion of the eternal Trinitarian covenant (covenant of redemption), whereby the Father and the Son agreed together to redeem the elect. For Owen, the eternal priesthood of Christ and his mediatorial office is ultimately defined by the covenant of redemption.[228] This in turn functions as the causal ground for the decree of election.[229] Trueman noted the progression in Owen here: Christ's death is part of his priesthood, Christ's priesthood is part of his mediatorial office, and his mediatorial office is created and defined by the terms of the covenant of redemption.[230]

Another key concept for Owen is commercialism, where notions of sin and guilt are viewed somewhat quantitatively and where faith is said to be purchased for all the elect. Owen's understanding of Christ's satisfaction on the cross is rooted in his adherence to Anselm's commercial theory of the atonement. Owen defines "satisfaction" as "a full compensation of the creditor from the debtor."[231] Owen is dependent upon

224 D. Wallace, "The Life and Thought of John Owen to 1660" (PhD diss., Princeton University, 1962).

225 J. Owen, *Salus Electorum, Sanguis Jesu*; or the English short title "The Death of Death in the Death of Christ," in *Works of John Owen*, 10:139–428.

226 Two key arguments Owen develops are the now famous "double payment" argument and the "triple choice" argument.

227 Moore, "Extent of the Atonement," 128–31. On Owen's exegetical methodology, Moore cited Henry Knapp and Barry Howson, but omitted an important modern critique of Owen's hermeneutics and exegesis by N. Chambers, "A Critical Examination of John Owen's Argument for Limited Atonement in 'The Death of Death in the Death of Christ'" (ThM thesis, Reformed Theological Seminary, 1998).

228 C. Trueman, *The Claims of Truth: John Owen's Trinitarian Theology* (Carlisle, UK: Paternoster, 1998), 205. For the role of Christ's priesthood in Owen's atonement theology, consult E. M. Tay, *Priesthood of Christ: Atonement in the Theology of John Owen (1616–1683)*, Studies in Christian History and Thought (Milton Keynes, UK: Paternoster, 2014).

229 Ibid., 218.

230 Ibid., 205.

231 Owen, "The Death of Death in the Death of Christ," 10:265. Even Carl Trueman, Owen's defender, conceded that Owen's double-payment argument relied "on a crudely commercial theory of the atonement" (*Claims of Truth*, 140).

Grotius's distinction between *solutio ejusdem* (the same as) and *solutio tantidem* (as good as) with respect to the atonement.

A third is his conception of the will and purpose of God, which cannot be thwarted or fail.[232] A fourth is Owen's concept of the mediatorial office of Christ. The most recent significant study of this aspect of Owen's soteriology is Tay's *The Priesthood of Christ*.[233]

Tay believes that Owen's later works must be considered in evaluating his views on the atonement's nature and extent. I certainly agree. But it should be noted that Owen's views never departed from those expressed in his *Death of Death*. Tay draws primarily on Owen's massive commentary on Hebrews as the major exegetical source behind his atonement theology.[234]

Owen viewed the incarnation of Christ as primarily a means to an end. The goal is to achieve the work of atonement (oblation) and intercession for the salvation of the elect.[235]

> Owen's use of oblation and intercession as unifying heads reveals what he was intending to establish theologically against universal redemption. It allowed him to develop a particularistic and actualistic view of the atonement against the threat of a general ransom that merely secured the universal potentiality of salvation. The crux of the matter lies in the inseparability of oblation and intercession. Both acts are united by the nature of their relations since oblation is the foundation for intercession and intercession is the continuation of oblation so that what was procured by the oblation is bestowed by virtue of the intercession.[236]

In addition, Tay correctly noted that the relation between divine intentionality and application of the atonement is absolutely fundamental for Owen.

Owen's view of Christ's satisfaction for sin is expressed in commercialistic language. The debtor is man, the debt is sin, that which is required to make satisfaction is death, the obligation that binds the debtor is the law, the creditor that requires the payment is God, and Christ pays the ransom to God.[237] Tay attempted to demonstrate, in spite of this language, which is shot through Owen's *Death of Death*, that we should not mistake this as Owen's acceptance of commercialism. Other metaphors of the atonement are clearly in play for Owen, but there is no mistaking the fact that the commercial concept is dominant. Nothing in Owen's later writings obviates the fact

---

232 Owen ("The Death of Death in the Death of Christ," 10:200) wrote that the entire controversy over the extent of the atonement pivots on the issue of God's intended purpose for the atonement, which for Owen was the salvation of the elect alone.

233 E. M. Tay, *The Priesthood of Christ: Atonement in the Theology of John Owen (1616–1683)* (Milton Keynes, UK: Paternoster, 2015).

234 Ibid., 9.

235 Ibid., 16.

236 Ibid., 18. See Owen, "The Death of Death in the Death of Christ," 10:181.

237 Tay, *The Priesthood of Christ*, 21. See Owen, "The Death of Death in the Death of Christ," 10:265–66.

that commercialism is his dominant category for understanding the atonement. It is not so much Owen's commercial *language* per se that is the problem (except his notion of God as creditor) but Owen's view of Christ's death as a *literal* payment.

Tay argued that Owen's atonement theology is built around three theological loci: (1) the triune God, (2) the mediatorial office of Christ, and (3) the satisfaction for sin.[238]

With respect to the nature of the sufficiency of the atonement, Owen argued for the infinite sufficiency of Christ's death, but limited this sufficiency only to an intrinsic sufficiency such that Christ did not actually pay for the sins of the non-elect.[239] For Owen, the sufficiency of the atonement is necessarily understood in tandem with God's intended purpose, and that purpose is to redeem only the elect, hence the doctrine of limited atonement. The atonement, given the covenant of redemption, must have one, and only one, end: the salvation of the elect.[240]

For Owen, the sufficiency of the atonement is determined by the value of the sacrifice, which in Christ's case is infinite, coupled with the relation of Christ's sacrifice to God's intended purpose, which is the salvation of the elect.[241]

Trueman noted Owen concurrently argued for the infinite sufficiency of the atonement in terms of worth and value while denying any unconditional relationship between sufficiency and the saving purposes of God, which is limited only to the elect.[242] Jonathan Lindell pointed out that it is Owen's Christology, specifically his view of the intercessory ministry of Jesus,[243] which undergirded and provided the continuity

---

238 Tay, *The Priesthood of Christ*, 22.

239 Owen, "The Death of Death in the Death of Christ," 10:295–96:

> It was, then, the purpose and intention of God that his Son should offer a sacrifice of infinite worth, value, and dignity, sufficient in itself for the redeeming of all and every man, if it had pleased the Lord to employ it to that purpose . . . It was in itself of infinite value and sufficiency to have been made a price to have bought and purchased all and every man in the world. That it did formally become a price for any is solely to be ascribed to the purpose of God, intending their purchase and redemption by it.

He also stated:

> It is denied that the blood of Christ was a sufficient price and ransom for all and every one, not because it was not sufficient, but because it was not a ransom.

H. Boersma correctly observed that "Owen only acknowledges an internal sufficiency: a sufficiency located in the infinite value of Christ's sacrifice itself. It would only be sufficient for the whole world *if* indeed it were meant for all (*A Hot Pepper Corn: Richard Baxter's Doctrine of Justification in Its Seventeenth-Century Context of Controversy* [Vancouver: Regent College, 2004], 254).

240 Owen, "The Death of Death in the Death of Christ," 10:200.

241 Ibid., 10:295–96.

242 Trueman, *Claims of Truth*, 202.

243 Owen's take on Christ's prayer from the cross, "Father forgive them," reveals the tortuous exegesis he is constrained to engage in. He makes an effort to limit this prayer to a particular people present on that day alone who crucified him, but only those among them who did so in ignorance, as if they are a subclass within the group of those who crucified him. He then argued that Christ did not pray that they believe, but only that they be forgiven for that one particular sin they did in ignorance. Then Owen goes on to say that the prayer was effectual, in a sense, for those people who came to *believe* in the book of Acts. But how can this be when Owen has informed us that the prayer *was not* about their believing? But when Owen is done with it, it turns out to be about the belief *of the elect among them*, since some in Acts came to believe in accordance with Christ's prayer. See Owen, "The Death of Death in the Death of Christ," 10:195–96.

Owen argued for in the infinite intrinsic sufficiency of the atonement and its extrinsic efficiency for the elect alone.[244]

Owen's primary argument is that the purpose of God would fail if the atonement is universal because that which Christ intended to accomplish by his death—namely, the salvation of those for whom he died—is in fact not accomplished for the reprobate. This is the single thread that runs through the warp and woof of Owen's theological tapestry.[245]

Since Richard Baxter carried on a debate with Owen over several years on the subject of the nature and extent of the atonement, we shall consider Baxter's views briefly, especially noting his critique of Owen on the extent question. Following this, we will turn our attention to a critique of Owen's views on extent.

Richard Baxter (AD 1615–1691)

Not all Anglicans and Puritans were persuaded by Owen's arguments. Richard Baxter's prolific pen (his literary output was twice that of Owen) was put into action against Owen's arguments. Baxter's most extensive defense of universal atonement, *Universal Redemption of Mankind*, was not published until three years after his death.[246]

Baxter and Owen carried on a significant debate over the extent of the atonement and the issue of justification.[247] Baxter took issue with Owen over the nature of the satisfaction of Christ's death. Owen had maintained that the death of Christ met the exact legal requirement and discharged the exact sin debt in a commercial fashion.

Baxter maintained that the satisfaction made by Christ was an equivalent value for all sins, thus meeting the law's requirements.[248] Baxter understood the concept of "debt" not in literal but rather in analogical terms.[249] Thus, for Baxter, Christ's death is extrinsically sufficient for all (contra Owen) but effectual only for the elect.[250]

---

244 J. Lindell, "John Owen and Richard Baxter: A Conflict Concerning the Nature of Divine Satisfaction" (ThM thesis, Dallas Theological Seminary, 2010), 15.

245 See, for example, Owen, "The Death of Death in the Death of Christ," 10:149, 176, 182, 193, 209, 224, 238, 241, 258, 288, 296, 312, 329, 335, 345, 359, 381, and 417. A. Clifford said Owen's argument reveals the strong influence of Aristotle's teleology along with the commercial implications of Anselm's theory of the atonement (*Atonement and Justification* [Oxford: Clarendon Press, 1990], 111).

246 R. Baxter, *Universal Redemption of Mankind, by the Lord Jesus Christ: Stated and Cleared by the Late Learned Mr. Richard Baxter. Whereunto Is Added a Short Account of Special Redemption, by the Same Author* (London: For John Salusbury, 1694).

247 For a good summary of the 1649–58 debate, see Boersma, *A Hot Pepper Corn*, 41–44. Boersma spoke of the verbosity of both in dragging out the debate. Boersma addressed the extent of the atonement on pages 209–20; 254–56.

248 Baxter, *Universal Redemption*, 78. Boersma summarized Baxter well: "Christ's payment is equivalent in value, though not equivalent in what it *ipso facto* procures. The benefits of Christ's death are applied by means of a condition" (*Hot Pepper Corn*, 247).

249 Baxter, *Universal Redemption*, 79. Baxter said that sin conceived as "debt" in Scripture is a metaphor. Baxter argued against Owen's view that Christ's death made an equivalent payment (*solutio tantidem*).

250 Ibid., 135–36. Trueman summarized Baxter's views, noting that Baxter "argues using the Thomist terminology that Christ dies to gain salvation antecedently for all and consequently for those who will believe" (*Claims of Truth*, 205).

Owen sees the death of Christ as determined by the covenant of redemption, which is the causal ground of election. Baxter places the death of Christ and the decree of God that makes it salvific logically prior to any consideration of the election of individuals.[251]

Among his arguments against Owen and limited atonement, Baxter discussed Matt 22:1–13, the parable of the Marriage Feast. In order to see the full thrust of Baxter's point, I have provided a rather lengthy quotation.

> Here it is agreed on that God is the King: The Wedding feast, is Christ and the benefits of his Death offered by the Gospel. The killing of the Fatling most say, doth intimate the killing of Christ that he may be to us the Bread of Life, and his Flesh Meat indeed, and his Blood Drink indeed. The Messengers are Preachers: The message is the Gospel Invitation or Offer. Hence therefore I thus argue; If all the things are ready before hand which upon coming in to Christ are to be received, yea and ready for those that refused to come, and only their not coming, or not coming preparedly do hinder their participation, then Christ was a Sacrifice made ready even for all that refused to come. But, *&c. Ergo, &c.*
>
> I mean not that Christ was appointed to save final refusers considered as such: But he was a Sacrifice for all the Sins of the same Men, except their final refusal, and thereby made ready for them all those saving benefits, which upon coming in they were to receive. This message any Minister of the Gospel may now deliver to unbelievers: Come in to Christ; accept him as a Redeemer, Lord and Saviour, and with him pardon and Salvation; for all this is ready: All that is prerequisit to believing or coming in, is done by Christ, as far as concerned him as a Sacrifice and a Donor of his Testamentory benefits; and as far as unsatisfied Justice did require: All things that are requisite objectively to your believing are ready. Now this could not be a truth; if Christ had not been a sacrifice for these Mens Sins: For how is all ready when the very first and most needful thing is unready, that is, an expiatory Sacrifice for sin? When satisfaction to justice is unready? Can they make this? Or are they called to make it? Or would their coming in make it, which was not before made? Or would coming in serve turn without satisfaction? Rather it should be said to them (as to the Devils) come not, for nothing is ready. For where Christ is not ready, and satisfaction for sin not ready, there nothing is ready which a sinner is called to by the Gospel. The Cause being wanting, all the Effects must needs be wanting.
>
> Obj. *All may be said to be ready, in that Christ's Death is sufficient for All.*

251 C. Trueman, *The Claims of Truth: John Owen's Trinitarian Theology* (Carlisle, UK: Paternoster, 1998), 218.

> Ans. That's true; and I desire no more; if you understand it as Divines have hitherto done, and as this Text proves it; that is, that it is a sufficient Ransom, Sacrifice, *&c.* for All. But according to the new futile evasion, it is false, *viz.* that Christ's Death was only sufficient to have been a Sacrifice or Ransom for All, if God or Christ had so been willing: but indeed was no Ransom for them at all. For is this making all ready? Is Christ any readier for those he died not for, than for the Devils? or than if he had never died at all? Will you send to a Prisoner and say, I have paid 1000 *l.* for thy fellow Prisoner that owed by 500 *l.* the sum is sufficient to have discharged thy debt too, if I had ever intended it, therefore come and receive a discharge, for all is ready? Or will you bid your Servant go to all the Town and say, I have killed and dressed meat enough for you all, resolving that some of you shall never taste of it on any conditions, therefore come now and partake of it all, for all things are ready? The Readiness that Christ speaks of here is such, as supposeth all things to be ready except receiving by Faith: nothing but coming is wanting.[252]

In addition to the argument based on Matt 22:1–13, notice Baxter's reference to Owen's hypothetical understanding of the sufficiency of Christ's death as a "new futile evasion." If Christ has not satisfied for all, then Christ's death is not sufficient for all.[253] For Baxter, those who say Christ did not suffer for all are in effect denying the sufficiency of his death even for those who believe.[254] Furthermore, Baxter asserted if Christ has not satisfied for the sins of all, then no one has a sufficient ground for coming to faith in Christ. Baxter called this an "uncomfortable uncertainty."[255]

Baxter listed thirty "absurd consequences" for denying universal atonement. If Christ did not die for all, then it is no sin to reject the gospel, which was not intended for their recovery.[256] Interestingly, Baxter shows how William Perkins's preaching is different from his theology.[257] Baxter believed if there is no universal satisfaction for sins in the atonement, the preacher has nothing to declare that can encourage any sinner to believe with confidence.[258]

Baxter addressed the question of just what the phrase "Christ died for" means:

> 99. The particle [*For*] when we question whether Christ died [*For*] All is ambiguous: 1. It may mean [*In the strict representation of the persons of all as*

252 Baxter, *Universal Redemption*, 343–45.
253 Ibid., 133.
254 Ibid., 138.
255 Ibid., 168.
256 Ibid., 173.
257 Ibid., 124.
258 Ibid., 122.

> *several, so that they may be said to have died or satisfied in and by him, as civilly in their own persons, though not naturally*]. And thus Christ died not *for all*, or for *any man*: which yet is in some mens conceits, who thence say that Christ died not *for all*, because he did not so *personate* all. 2. It may signify [*to die by the procurement of all mens sins, as the assumed promeritorious cause.*] And thus *Pareus* himself in his *Irenicon* saith, that *the sins of all men lay on Christ*; and so he *died for all*, that is, *for all mens sins as the cause of his death*: And you may tell any wicked man, *Thy sins killed Christ* (what-ever the deniers say to excuse them). 3. Or it meaneth, that Christ died *finally for the good of all men*. And that is true, as afore explained. He died for the *good of all*; but not *equally*; that is, not with the same absolute Will, Decree or Intention of attaining their Salvation.[259]

Speaking about the sufficiency of the atonement, Baxter stated:

> The old Solution which Schoolmen and Protestants have acquiesced in, is, that Christ died for All, as to the sufficiency of his death, but not as to the efficiency of their salvation: Which is true, but must be thus explained: Christ's Death and Obedience were not only sufficient but effectual as to their first effects; that is, They effected that which is commonly called, Satisfaction and Merit; and hence and from the Covenant of God they were also effectual to procure the Covenant of Grace as of universal tenor, and therein a free pardon of Sin and gift of Right to life-eternal to all, on condition of due acceptance: This conditional Gift of Christ and Life is effected: And this efficacy of the antecedent Mercies, must either be called part of the sufficiency of Redemption, as to the consequent Mercies (viz. Actual Pardon and Salvation) or else an efficiency beyond the sufficiency, antecedent to the said special efficiency. That Christ's Death hath effectually procured the Act of Oblivion or conditional Gift of Life to all Mankind; but it doth not effect the actual salvation of all: To the universal Grace it is both sufficient and efficient; but to the special Grace and actual Salvation it is sufficient to All (as after shall be opened) but not efficient, (which is by the Refuser's fault and forfeiture.)
>
> When we say, that either Christ's Death or Grace is sufficient to more than it effecteth, the meaning is, that it hath all things on its part which is absolutely necessary to the effect, but that somewhat else is supposed necessary to it, which is wanting.[260]

---

259 Baxter, *Catholick Theologie*, I.ii.53 (emphasis in original). Baxter is citing David Paraeus here.

260 R. Baxter, *An End of Doctrinal Controversies, which Have Lately Troubled the Churches, by Reconciling Explication without Much Disputing* (London: Printed for John Salusbury, 1691), 161–62.

At the time of the Westminster Assembly, Baxter said that half of the divines in England were Amyraldians.[261] This is probably not strictly accurate in that Baxter is probably referring to most Hypothetical Universalists as Amyraldian, which is an oversimplification. However, if Baxter can be trusted on this point, the statement does illustrate the large number within the Reformed ranks who rejected limited atonement.

Richard Baxter's position on the extent of the atonement can be summed up, according to Curt Daniel, in the following sentence: "Christ therefore died for all, but not for all equally, or with the same intent, design or purpose."[262]

Owen did not take Baxter's criticism lying down and responded with his own *Of the Death of Christ*.[263]

Critique of Owen

It is not uncommon to see Calvinists appealing to Owen's *Death of Death in the Death of Christ* as the definitive statement on limited atonement. This is sometimes followed with a bold statement along the lines of "Owen has never been refuted." As we have seen, that is not entirely accurate, given the work of Baxter and Goodwin in Owen's generation as well as the various twentieth-century critiques of Owen, including Alan Clifford.

One of the little-known and seldom-recognized critiques of Owen was done by Neal Chambers in a four-hundred-page 1998 master's thesis at Reformed Theological Seminary.[264] I will summarize chapter by chapter Chambers's critique of Owen.

- Chapter 1: "Limited Atonement and John Owen" (3–22)
- Chapter 2: "The Death of Death" (23–110)
- Chapter 3: "A Consideration of the 'World'" (111–189)
- Chapter 4: "Faith" (190–234)
- Chapter 5: "Owen's Commercial Language" (235–285)
- Chapter 6: "The Covenant of Redemption" (286–339)
- Chapter 7: "Conclusion" (340–384)
- Appendix A: "Appendix A" (385–391)

261 R. Baxter, *Certain Disputations of Right to Sacraments, and the True Nature of Visible Christianity* (London: Printed by R. W. for Nevil Simmons,1658), B2v.

262 Daniel, "Hyper-Calvinism and John Gill," 192.

263 J. Owen, *Of the Death of Christ, the Price He Paid, and the Purchase He Made. or, the Satisfaction and Merit of the Death of Christ Cleared, the Universality of Redemption Thereby Oppuned: And the Doctrine Concerning These Things Formerly Delivered in a Treatise against Universal Redemption Vindicated from the Exceptions, and Objections of Mr Baxter* (London: Peter Cole, 1650). See also Owen, *Works*, 10:429–79.

264 N. Chambers, "A Critical Examination of John Owen's Argument for Limited Atonement in 'The Death of Death in the Death of Christ'" (ThM thesis, Reformed Theological Seminary, 1998). This is a substantive critique of Owen, and yet it is usually ignored by limitarians. It is not referenced in *From Heaven He Came and Sought Her.*

In chapter 1 Chambers mapped the lay of the land for the discussion and oriented the reader to Owen's theological methodology. For Owen, the Bible is infallible, thus all true interpretation of the Bible is infallible. Thus, consequences rightly deduced from these interpretations are infallibly true.[265] This raises the question whether Owen has left his argument hostage to an alien form of reasoning, as Clifford had alleged.[266]

In chapter 2 Chambers summarized Owen's book. Owen was at Oxford from 1628 to 1635 when Arminianism was growing in popularity. In 1628 a royal declaration banned all university disputing on points at issue between Arminians and Calvinists. The election of Bishop Laud as chancellor of Oxford led to a change in Oxford theology. After 1631 Calvinist doctrine disappeared from the Oxford Act. Owen was also distressed about the Hypothetical Universalism of Amyraut. Thomas More's *The Universality of God's Free Grace* was published in 1646. Owen is directly refuting More in his *Death of Death.*

Owen's argument is "long, complex and repetitious."[267] *Death of Death* is structured in four books. Books one and two establish the theological superstructure, which supports Owen's particular sixteen arguments against universal redemption in book three. Book four contains his exegesis of key universalist texts and refutation of More's eighteen proofs. Chambers rightly pointed out that the argument is won or lost in books one and two, for one's acceptance of Owen's presuppositions here makes his conclusions and exegesis inevitable, as Owen himself suggested at the conclusion of book two.[268]

Owen's major argument in book one is simple: Restriction of the benefit of the atonement to the elect argues for a restriction in the purpose of Christ's death to benefit them alone. Owen considered that if all are not saved, Christ has failed in his intention. For Owen, the only way to avoid this is to embrace universalism.

Owen considered faith to have been purchased for the elect. Denial of this places the determinative role of human faith in one's salvation, a point that Owen rejected. For Owen, Christ's death must be directly causally responsible for the faith of those who are saved.[269]

Owen believed all action can be considered in terms of agent, end, and means. This becomes the structure of the remainder of book one and all of book two:

- Agent = Trinity (chaps. 3–5, book one)
- Means = Christ's death, Oblation, and Intercession (chaps. 6–8, book one)
- End = Salvation of the Elect (book two)

265 Ibid., 16.
266 Clifford, *Atonement and Justification*, 96–98.
267 Chambers, "A Critical Examination," 30.
268 Ibid., 31.
269 Ibid., 35.

Owen detailed the relationship of means to ends. Means can be either the meritorious or the instrumental efficient cause of the end, which is the first principle or moving cause of the whole. With God, outcome and intention are coextensive. This crucial observation is vital to understanding Owen's argument. Owen arrived at God's intention directly from its outcome. Thus, every statement in Scripture concerning the result of Christ's work becomes a statement of the intention of that work. This is the argument Owen employed repeatedly in book three, where he argues that the death of Christ was only intended for those who are actually reconciled.[270]

Owen discussed the role of each person of the Trinity and posited a covenant of redemption where God the Father entered into covenant with the Son concerning the work of redemption. The Father promised the Son the attainment of the end of the covenant—namely, the redemption of the elect. This end is the purpose and goal of Christ's work on the cross. The content of this promise by the Father to the Son is explicated principally from Isaiah 49, 53; and John 17. According to Owen's understanding of the covenant of redemption, the Father lays on the Son the punishment for the sins of the elect.

Owen proceeded to lay out his now famous triple choice dilemma: Christ died for either (1) all the sins of all men, (2) all the sins of some men, or (3) some sins of all men.[271] Unbelief cannot be the cause of all people not being saved, as unbelief is a sin. If it is a sin, it is atoned for on the universal atonement theory, and thus, how can one suffer for a sin already atoned for?

But this raises a number of questions that Owen did not answer:

1. Is substitution conceived quantitatively in Scripture?
2. If unbelief is atoned for, why are the elect not saved at the cross?
3. What is the relationship of unbelief to the unforgivable sin?

In considering the work of Christ, Owen adamantly refused any attempt to separate impetration from application. Thus, Christ intercedes only for those for whom he died. Since Christ's intercession is always effective, Owen considered it impossible that Christ could be interceding for any who ultimately perish. Thus, Christ cannot be conceived as having died for those for whom he does not intercede. Owen drew this conclusion from Rom 8:33–34 and considered this argument to be the death knell of universal atonement.[272] Owen then proceeded to give six arguments why intercession and oblation are equal.[273]

Owen criticized his opponents for drawing universal conclusions from indefinite

270 Ibid., 36.

271 See Owen, "The Death of Death in the Death of Christ," 10:173.

272 Chambers, "A Critical Examination," 42–43. See Owen, "The Death of Death in the Death of Christ," 10:181.

273 Chambers, "A Critical Examination," 45.

propositions. But, as Chambers rightly pointed out, if it is wrong to draw universal conclusions from indefinite propositions, does not Owen's own position seek to have these indefinite propositions read in a definite sense, as referring ultimately to the elect, converting in the process qualitative indefinite terms into quantitative references?[274] Owen's conclusion in book one that Christ never intends to save more than for whom he dies precedes any exegesis of the disputed passages.

In his summary of book two, Chambers noted that, for Owen, the final goal of Christ's work on the cross can be conceived either as the ultimate end (glory of God) or as the intermediate end (our salvation). The elect actually have a right to salvation based on Christ's purchase of their faith on the cross. The covenant of redemption makes salvation for the elect not just a possibility but a certainty by right.[275] Here Owen imported both covenantal and commercial notions into his argument.

Chambers quoted Owen's statement of the purpose of Christ's death:

> Jesus Christ, according to the counsel and will of his Father, did offer himself upon the cross, to the procurement of those things before recounted; and maketh continual intercession with this intent and purpose, that all the good things so procured by his death might be actually and infallibly bestowed on and applied to all and every one for whom he died, according to the will and counsel of God.[276]

Owen denied Thomas More's suggestion that a work can have more than one end.[277] For Owen, the purpose of Christ's death was not to make all men saveable but to actually save the elect.

Owen's opponents respond that redemption is not obtained absolutely but upon a condition, and what is obtained upon condition only becomes actually applied on fulfillment of that condition. Owen replied that if this were so, and the intention of the cross was universal, the condition ought to be universally made known, which it isn't.[278] Owen stated: "Christ did not die for any upon condition, if they do believe; but he died for all God's elect, that they should believe. . . . faith itself is among the principal effects and fruits of the death of Christ."[279]

Chambers summarized Owen's argument in book two, including his dependence on the notions of the so-called purchase of faith and commercial language to describe the atonement:

---

274 Ibid., 46.
275 See Owen, "The Death of Death in the Death of Christ," 10:207.
276 Ibid., 10:208.
277 Chambers, "A Critical Examination," 57.
278 Ibid., 63.
279 Owen, "The Death of Death in the Death of Christ," 10:235.

> But it is also apparent that if Owen's position is granted then Christ's work could never have any intention for good for any more than those who are actually saved [the elect], and no more than the elect ever had a stake in that work, just as none but they are objects of God's love in this work. Further, this legitimates Owen's use of those scriptures which speak of the outcome of Christ's death for believers as scriptures which also prove the restriction of the atonement to the elect and thus overthrow the general ransom theory, for it, for example, believers and only believers are sanctified by Christ's blood, and faith is purchased by that blood for all for whom He died, then as not all are sanctified it is plain that Christ's death could not be for all. This is at the heart of the sixteen arguments against the universality of redemption that make up Book Three.[280]

In book three, Owen marshalled sixteen arguments for limited atonement:

1. As the new covenant is restricted to the elect, so there is a restriction in the intent of that which inaugurates the new covenant, Christ's death.
2. Faith comes through hearing. But the gospel is not preached to all, and thus the condition is not possible to all. According to universal atonement, something has been obtained that can never be applied. As God is sovereign, if the gospel is not made known to some, Owen concluded it was not intended for them. If it is not intended for them, then it was not obtained for them. For Owen, Christ's death cannot be universally intended because it is not universally made known. The corollary to this is if they don't hear, they were never intended to be saved. Chambers noted, while not requiring it, that one can see how Owen's view can conduce complacency in evangelism.[281]
3. There are implications for affirming and denying the purchase of faith. If Christ died for all, then he did so either absolutely or upon some condition to be fulfilled by all. If he procured these benefits absolutely, then all ought to be saved, which they are not. If he procured them conditionally, they must answer whether the condition is procured absolutely or conditionally. If the condition is procured absolutely, then it is the same as "dying for" absolutely, and all will be saved for whom Christ died. Intention and effect are coextensive.

   Furthermore, if the condition is not purchased, how can any be saved? Chambers said this "rhetorical flourish" indicated Owen's larger argument

280 Chambers, "A Critical Examination," 65.
281 Ibid., 67.

that there can be no condition of salvation that was not purchased for those for whom Christ died if there is to be real salvation for any.[282] But if faith is viewed as purchased, some will object that this makes a mockery of preaching and the command to repent and believe, for God is now requiring something of humanity that it cannot do. Owen responded that the commands indicate what our duty is, not what God intends should be done, and our duty is the same regardless of our ability to perform it. Owen also argued that the promises associated with a command to believe do not indicate that it is God's purpose that Christ's death should benefit us if we do believe but rather indicate that faith is God's appointed means to salvation, and thus faith and salvation are inseparably joined. (Owen will return to the implications of his position for preaching in book four, chap. 7.)[283]

4. There is an argument from the reality of election and reprobation. Owen acknowledged that there is no direct statement in Scripture that says Christ died for the elect only. Yet Owen believed the sense of a limited atonement can be clearly derived from the context. But Chambers noted that this defense works only if the terms are mutually exclusive and comprehensive, neither of which is the case.[284]
5. Scripture nowhere makes an explicit universal affirmation of the death of Christ. (In book 4, chap. 4, Owen will offer an exegesis of the many passages that appear to support an unlimited atonement.)
6. The doctrine of substitution undercuts universal atonement. If unbelief is a sin Christ died for, then substitution entails universalism.
7. Based on Owen's understanding of Christ's priesthood and his limited intercession, Owen deduces a limited atonement, the restriction of Christ's mediatorial work to the elect. Those for whom Christ does not pray, he does not pay.
8. There is the notion of the purchase of faith. (Owen will go into more detail later.)
9. Faith is procured only for the elect, and faith is not common to all. Therefore Christ died only for the elect. Owen asserted both premises are true, therefore the conclusion is true. Chambers makes the interesting observation that the scriptural evidence for this is introduced by Owen only as the last of his five proofs.
10. There is an argument from type to antitype. Since Old Testament redemption was confined only to Israel, so New Testament redemption is confined only to spiritual Israel, which Owen understood to be the elect.

---

282 Ibid., 69.

283 Ibid., 71.

284 Ibid., 72.

11. To show the nature of redemption itself, Owen asserted the terms in Scripture that are used to describe the action of the cross necessarily include the outcome.
12. If reconciliation is the immediate effect of the death of Christ, and if all are not reconciled, then it is plain Christ did not die for all.
13. The nature of Christ's death as a satisfaction for sins is a lengthy treatment, three chapters, due to the controversy on this issue in Owen's day, as Chambers noted.
14. There is the compatibility of universal redemption with the merit of Christ. Since Christ has obtained the merit of redemption for the elect via the covenant of redemption, this merit must be bestowed on the elect, otherwise injustice ensues.
15. The biblical phrases with the Greek prepositions *hyper* and *anti* indicate that the nature of substitution denies universal atonement.
16. Owen examines several texts that he maintains teach limited atonement: Gen 3:15; Matt 7:32; 11:25–26; and John 10.

With respect to the John 10, Owen's syllogistic thinking is clear:

> Christ died for his sheep
> Not all are his sheep
> Therefore, Christ did not die for all.

Owen, however, committed two major logical fallacies at this point: (1) the negative inference fallacy and (2) the fact that his conclusion is only valid if the word "only" can be included in the major premise, which is to assume what he is trying to prove, thus begging the question.

Owen also appealed to Rom 8:32–34; Eph 1:7; 5:25; 2 Cor 5:21; and John 17:9 to support limited atonement.

Chambers summarized book three:

> To think of Christ's death as effectual is to think of the death of Christ as necessitating the salvation of those for whom he dies. Central to the force of Owen's arguments has been the demonstrated unity of impetration and application, the insistence that whatever is obtained must be applied to all those for whom it is obtained. The foundation of this assertion is the conceptualization of the Atonement as being the temporal outworking of the agreement between the Father and the Son in eternity, the Covenant of Redemption, which guarantees that the objects of Christ's oblation and his intercession are one and the same, and that the intercession is always to be effective. The crucial test of the

truthfulness of this position is the notion of the purchase of faith, which is at the heart of the necessary salvation of the elect.[285]

In book four, Owen addressed arguments made in favor of universal atonement. He listed ten principles he considered as fundamental to the correct interpretation of the three classes of texts that are alleged against limited atonement: (1) general and indefinite expressions, (2) some for whom Christ died do not obtain salvation, and (3) general offers are made to all indiscriminately.

1. The infinite sufficiency of Christ's death is the foundation of universal preaching and the universal call to all to believe the gospel. Here Owen dealt with the Lombardian formula, to which he adds qualifications. Owen here depends on the covenant of redemption. For him, sufficiency is an abstraction considered in itself and not in relation to human need. Owen argued the objection of a lack of atonement for the non-elect fails to take notice of the use of means by which God uses to bring the elect to himself. Also the nature of the gospel is not to "believe that Jesus died for you particularly" but to "believe that only in Jesus can salvation be found."[286]
2. The extent of the new covenant is for all kinds of people and nations. General passages in Scripture that speak of "all" are interpreted by Owen to mean "all distributively" not "all universally." Thus, "all" means "some of all kinds."
3. One must acknowledge the distinction between man's duty and God's purpose.
4. General terms such as "all" or "world" must be seen as opposing Jewish nationalism and not as a reference to all without exception.
5. "All" and "world" do not always mean "all" but "some of all kinds."
6. Scripture uses phenomenological language to speak of people as they appear to be, not necessarily as they actually are.
7. We must employ the "judgment of charity" according to 1 Thess 1:4. Paul did not assume that all within the church were saved.
8. Believers will be saved, but the language of Scripture does not necessarily indicate a conditional will for all to be saved.
9. The general offer of the gospel to all people is necessary only because the elect are mixed in with the non-elect.
10. Owen explains what people are being asked to believe when they encounter the gospel. This is Owen's effort to address the objection that if Christ did not die for all, then people have no proper object for their faith presented in

285 Ibid., 82–83.
286 Owen, "The Death of Death in the Death of Christ," 10:407.

> the gospel. Owen claims there is an orderly progression in what the gospel commands people to believe. (1) Salvation is not to be found in themselves. (2) Salvation is only to be found in the "promised seed." (3) Jesus crucified is the promised Savior and salvation is in no one else. (4) One must rest upon Christ as an all-sufficient Savior.

Owen observed that when these four are "firmly seated in the soul," then

> we are every one called in particular to believe the efficacy of the redemption that is in the blood of Jesus towards our own souls in particular; which every one may assuredly do in whom the free grace of God hath wrought the former acts of faith, and doth work also.[287]

Chambers queried exactly where it is in Scripture that the gospel is presented in this fashion? Where is the exhortation for the believer to move from one step to the next? Apart from step one, Owen offered no biblical reference in support. Noticeably absent here and in the entire work is 1 Cor 15:3–4. For Paul, Christ dying for sins is an important element of the gospel and is foremost among those elements of the gospel that we must believe. McLeod Campbell critiqued Owen on this very point.[288]

Owen laid out the general foundations of the answers he will give to the particular objections to his doctrine that follow and then proceeded to respond to those particular objections. As Chambers noted, in this approach, book four duplicates the pattern of the whole treatise: Owen laid down general principles that will determine the outcome of his presentation of the biblical material before he comes to examine the texts themselves. Owen's approach is deductive rather than inductive.

Owen proceeded to consider the texts that appear to affirm Christ died for the "world," for "all," or "every," along with the texts that speak of the perishing of some of those for whom Christ died. Owen concluded that "world" refers to either the elect, the Gentile elect, or the habitable world, but never a universality of individuals and never all people at all times in all places. He concluded that "all" in atonement contexts means "all sorts of men." He also concluded that Christ is never spoken of as "dying for" any that ultimately perish where "dying for" is understood to mean "by the command of his Father, and with the intention to make satisfaction for sins."[289]

Owen proceeded to cite and reject Thomas More's six arguments for universal atonement. Owen stated that consolation cannot be found in statements like "Christ died for sinners." But as Chambers noted, in Scripture, it is not believers *qua* believers

287 Ibid., 10:315.

288 J. M. Campbell, *The Nature of the Atonement and Its Relation to Remission of Sins and Eternal Life* (Cambridge: MacMillan and Co., 1856), 58–61; cited in Chambers, "A Critical Examination," 94.

289 Owen, "The Death of Death in the Death of Christ," 10:302–10, 317–19, 325–60.

or elect *qua* elect that need someone to die for them but believers and elect as sinners, which is the relevant inclusive category.

Chambers drew an interesting contrast between Owen and Spurgeon on the issue of comfort a sinner can have when it comes to the gospel and the death of Christ. For Owen, there is no comfort to be had. However, Spurgeon concluded his sermon, "Particular Redemption," with these surprising words:

> Your only question is "Did Christ die for me?" And the only answer we can give is "this is a faithful saying, and worthy of all acceptation, that Christ came into the world to save sinners." Can you write your name down among the sinners . . . ? Are you a sinner? That felt, that known, that professed, you are now invited to believe that Christ died for you, because you are a sinner.[290]

Owen never spoke like this. He never suggested that a sinner should "believe that Christ died for you." Owen's approach rules out any place for the sufficiency of Christ's death in providing assurance to sinners *qua* sinners.[291] Spurgeon's statement here is, in fact, inconsistent with his own commitment to limited atonement. We shall see other examples of this kind of inconsistency in Spurgeon below.

Chambers concluded his summary of book four by noting that systematic considerations form the parameters within which Owen conducts his interpretation of the atonement passages. Owen reasoned that it is beyond dispute that limited intention is the reason for limited provision.

In his next three chapters, Chambers critiqued Owen's notion of faith as purchased, his commercial language in explaining the atonement and its extent, and his reliance on the covenant of redemption. These three issues are the linchpins of Owen's argument, and Chambers finds fault with all three.

Owen argued that faith itself is purchased by Christ on the cross and bestowed on the elect unconditionally. In a startling statement, Owen asserted that if this not true, then universal atonement and free will is "established."

Owen considered the intermediate end of Christ's work to be the "bringing of many sons to glory."[292] This end can be considered in two parts: (1) the end itself and (2) the means for obtaining the end, which is faith. Faith is bestowed by God on the elect "absolutely upon no condition at all."[293] Thus, the elect have a right to the means of salvation purchased for them by Christ. This notion is central to Owen's case for limited atonement. Chambers pointed out that this language of purchase allows Owen

290 C. H. Spurgeon, "Particular Redemption," in *New Park Street Pulpit*, 6 vols. (Pasadena, TX: Pilgrim, 1981), 4:136.

291 Chambers, "A Critical Examination," 106–7.

292 Owen, "The Death of Death in the Death of Christ," 10:202.

293 Ibid., 203.

to present the elect's coming to faith as directly, causally, and thus intentionally brought about by Christ's death.

Owen began with two premises. First, all one receives in Christ is procured by Christ's death because of the foundational role of the covenant of redemption. If this axiom is accepted, limited atonement is inevitable according to Owen. Second, since faith is the absolute necessity for salvation, the cause of faith will be the prime, principal cause of salvation.

Owen offered four deductive proofs for faith as a purchase before he made any attempt to support this notion from Scripture itself. Owen's foundation for his notion of faith as a purchase is limited to only three proof texts: Phil 1:29; Eph 1:3; and Heb 12:2. Chambers demonstrated that none of these texts support Owen's claim.[294] There is simply no statement in the New Testament asserting Christ purchased faith for the elect. Chambers rightly noted the distinction between faith as a gift and faith as a purchase.[295] The two are not equivalent. There is no causal link between the death of Christ and the subjective faith of one who believes the gospel. Owen has engaged in category confusion: faith becomes something of an object instead of a relational response.

Chambers correctly noted that gift is the language of grace; purchase moves into the language of rights.[296] Owen's notion of the "purchase of faith" is not a self-evident biblical construct but a theoretical, causal construct dependent on the covenant of redemption, as Chambers noted. Such a concept has the potential to obscure the nature of faith and the relation of the cross to faith in time. Dependence on the covenant of redemption and faith as purchased for the elect blurs the distinction between the cross viewed from eternity and the cross viewed as a temporal work. This further underlies the subjugation of the sufficiency of the atonement to its efficiency as far as Owen is concerned. The result is a distortion of his exegesis of texts.[297]

At this point, Chambers considered Owen's dependence upon commercial language in defining the atonement and its extent. One need only make a cursory reading of *Death of Death* to observe how pervasive the language of "purchase" is in Owen. What exactly is it that is being purchased and from whom is it being purchased? Owen's answer is that salvation and means of salvation have been purchased by Christ for the elect with payment made to God the Father based on the contractual obligation between the Father and Son in the covenant of redemption. The result is the elect have a right to receive the benefits of the atonement. For Owen, such a notion established and required the limitation of the death of Christ for the elect only.

294 Ibid., 205–17.
295 Ibid., 224–29.
296 Ibid., 229.
297 Ibid., 204.

Chambers deftly dismantled Owen's approach to sin as debt in Scripture, demonstrating Owen's failure to recognize the figurative use of this concept. Terms from the realm of commerce are infrequent in the New Testament and are mainly employed in the context of a need for forgiveness. Owen misconstrued Col 2:14, a passage that stresses the nature of our debt, which is a failure to keep the law. This "certificate of debt" is "cancelled" with no statement in the text of payment to anyone.

Owen appealed to the *lutron* word group in the New Testament, with translations like "ransom," "redemption," and "bought." But nowhere in Scripture are we ever said to be redeemed from God nor is Christ's death said to be a ransom paid to God or anyone else. Revelation 5:9 speaks of those who have been bought *for* God, not *from* God, as Chambers noted. In Scripture, it is only persons who are said to be purchased, never "faith" or "salvation."[298]

Owen turned to the double payment argument in support of limited atonement. If the ransom is paid, justice demands those for whom it is paid must go free. It cannot be said to be paid for any who are not free. Hence, Owen deduced limited atonement. But, as Chambers noted, there is a difference between Christ's death as a sacrifice and as a ransom. This is a referential fallacy on the part of Owen. For him, all that can be said of one is assumed to be true of the other. One of Owen's major mistakes is his linguistic assumption about metaphor. Somehow metaphor is less truthful than literal language. Owen insisted on a literal ransom based on the covenant of redemption and God's prior agreement to accept Christ's death as a ransom for the elect. Thus, as Chambers noted, Owen winds up distorting Scripture.

Like many who affirm limited atonement, Owen is mixing legal debt and commercial debt categories. For him, to die for someone is equivalent to saving them. In this approach, quantitative connotations are introduced into the equation. For Owen, if more were paid than the debt of those actually released, the blood of Christ is wasted.

Chambers pointed out that when it comes to preaching, the cross of Christ is always viewed in relation to human need. For Owen, the death of Christ is infinitely sufficient only in abstraction. The atonement *could have been* sufficient for the entire world had God *intended* it to be so. But for Owen, God only intended the atonement to be actually sufficient for the elect. Owen failed to see that something that is non-existent cannot be sufficient.

Chambers concluded that Owen's double payment argument does not work because Jesus paid the equivalent penalty for sin, but the unsaved in eternity will pay the exact price. Chambers also appealed to Charles Hodge's critique of Owen's double payment argument: "There is no grace in accepting a pecuniary satisfaction. It cannot be refused. It *ipso facto* liberates. The moment the debt is paid the debtor

298 Ibid., 291.

is free; and that without any condition. Nothing of this is true in the case of judicial satisfaction."[299]

Chambers found four major problems with the double payment argument:

1. It undermines grace. The elect are "owed" salvation.
2. The question must be asked, Why the elect are not justified at the cross?
3. It undermines the role of faith by denying the need for any condition in salvation.
4. It undermines the urgency of preaching. Ultimately preaching is merely revealing to the elect their saved status rather than an urgent call to all to repent and believe.[300]

Chambers next dealt with Owen's concept of the covenant of redemption as the foundation for limited atonement. The covenant of redemption is a seventeenth-century construct of federal theology that attempts to ground an *ordo salutis* in the Trinity to undergird certainty of the covenant's fulfillment. In a nutshell, the covenant of redemption can be summarized as follows:

1. God promises to Christ success in gaining the salvation of the elect.
2. What is promised is the goal and that alone is what the Son achieves and intends to achieve. The atonement is thus limited to the elect.
3. The Son agrees to be the constituted representative of the elect.
4. This new relation between the Father and the Son is the basis of the Son's subordination to the Father in the work of redemption.
5. The incarnation is only undertaken with reference to the elect.

Owen sought evidence for this covenant of redemption in Jesus's obedience to the Father and his perfect fulfillment of the Father's will as expressed in John's Gospel. Owen appealed also to Luke 22:29 as proof of the existence of this covenant, but here Christ operates as the fulfillment of new covenant, not the covenant of redemption. The same is true for Heb 7:22; 10:5–7; and 12:24—all refer to the new covenant.

Chambers noted that Owen's *a priori* presupposition behind the covenant of redemption is that all covenant relationships involving promise and obedience in Scripture are covenant relationships from eternity.

Several theological problems accompany Owen's notion of a covenant of redemption:[301]

---

299 C. Hodge, *Systematic Theology*, 3 vols. (Grand Rapids, MI: Eerdmans, 1993), 2:557. See the entire context of Hodge's critique in 2:554–57.

300 Chambers, "A Critical Examination," 286–93.

301 See the critique by K. Barth, *Church Dogmatics: The Doctrine of Reconciliation*, 13 vols., ed. G. W. Bromiley and T.

1. No such covenant within the Godhead is revealed in Scripture. No such covenant is needed.
2. A covenant implies a prior state of non-agreement, which is problematic for the doctrine of the Trinity.
3. Such a covenant becomes a threat to eternal love. Scripture reveals Christ dies for mankind out of love, not out of legal agreement.
4. One might query where the Holy Spirit is in the covenant of redemption.
5. In Scripture, Christ comes in the incarnation in the stead of all humanity, not just the elect.
6. Owen subordinates all temporal covenants in the Bible to the covenant of redemption. This shifts the focus from God's revealed will in Scripture to a focus on God's secret will in eternity.
7. This notion of covenant has the tendency to work from eternity into time. What is most speculative becomes the controlling element undergirding all else. There is a tenuous connection with Scripture in this approach.

Chambers exposed Owen's methodological fallacy in his treatment of the covenant of redemption. Such a covenant structure is introduced prior to any examination of Scripture. For Owen, his theology precedes exegesis. Owen also commits a hermeneutical fallacy—the promises made to the Messiah in the Old Testament are made to reflect promises made to the Son in eternity.

Chambers offered a sevenfold critique of Owen's covenant of redemption.

1. It has negative implications for theology proper. God can be righteous as he is in himself, but cannot be merciful as he is in himself.
2. It has negative implications for the Trinity. How is it possible to have legal dealings among the Godhead? In Owen's construct, the Father demands payment for sins and the Son agrees to make the payment.
3. It has negative implications for the biblical concept of covenant. In Scripture, man is God's covenant partner, never a member of the Godhead.
4. It has negative implications hermeneutically. Given Owen's notion of the eternal intention of the covenant of redemption, he is forced to interpret all potentially universalistic statements concerning the extent of the atonement in a restricted sense in the light of the covenant of redemption. Since all are not

F. Torrance (Edinburgh: T. & T. Clark, 1956), IV:1:54–66. Barth called the notion of a "Covenant of Redemption" a contract that is "mythology," which has no place in a correct understanding of the doctrine of the Trinity. For Barth, the covenant of redemption introduces an unbiblical dualism into the Godhead. How can there be an antecedent logical moment where God is somehow not capable of being both righteous and merciful? (65). Barth also argued that the construct of the first two divine persons in the Godhead as two legal subjects is problematic because it jeopardizes the unity of the Godhead and suggests disunity of will within the Godhead.

saved, all were never intended by God to be redeemed. Thus, Christ died only for the elect, and all extent passages, even those with universalistic language, must be interpreted in a limited fashion.

5. It has negative implications for the doctrine of grace. The elect have a right to salvation both as to means and ends. The grace principle is destroyed.
6. It has negative implications for the doctrine of faith. Contrary to Scripture, faith becomes something like a commodity that is "purchased."
7. It has negative implications for the doctrine of the atonement's sufficiency. The death of Christ, considered in itself, could have been sufficient to save all had God intended such to be the case. The sufficiency of the atonement is limited to an intrinsic sufficiency of worth.

In addition to the critiques leveled by Barth and Chambers, Keith Loftin found another serious flaw with the covenant of redemption. If Barth is correct, the wedge between God's righteousness and mercy is disastrous for an orthodox conception of the divine nature. On such a view, God must be "righteous *in abstracto*." Loftin considered it logically sound to assert that if one affirms the covenant of redemption, one thereby surrenders an orthodox doctrine of the divine nature. Proponents of a covenant of redemption have made logical space for at least three divine wills: that of the Father, that of the Son, and that of the covenanted Father and Son.[302] Once the covenant of redemption is eliminated, the theological basis for limited atonement is undercut. Having no scriptural basis, limited atonement collapses.

Chambers summarized Owen's theology of atonement in a concluding chapter. The covenant of redemption is central to Owen's thesis. From it, Owen developed the unity of the atonement's impetration and application with its essential element, the purchase of faith for the elect. Christ's death obtained not only the end of salvation (redemption from sin) but the means (faith) as well. This faith must be applied to the elect by right. The biblical terms for salvation (ransom, reconciliation, satisfaction, redemption) are understood to mean "to die for = to save." For Owen, Christ cannot be said to have died for anyone who will not be saved.[303]

Demonstrating exclusive intent in the atonement is dependent upon demonstrating compatibility with all that is taught in Scripture concerning the intention of Christ's death. But it is precisely here that Chambers demonstrates how Owen fails at each juncture to achieve scriptural support. "World" in John's Gospel entails a loss of and distortion of meaning when the concept of the elect is substituted.

Chambers queried if Christ had any real love for the world beyond the elect. Did

302 R. Keith Loftin, "A Barthian Critique of the Covenant of Redemption" (unpublished paper, Southwestern Baptist Theological Seminary, 2014), 20–21.

303 Chambers, "A Critical Examination," 294–348.

Christ die in some sense other than common grace for the elect? John 3:16–17, among other places, appears to indicate that such is the case. First John 2:2 indicates Christ's death must be understood as making a real provision for the sins of the world.

For Owen, the notion of the purchase of faith is indispensable to limited atonement. Chambers asserted Owen makes a category confusion and distorts the nature of faith and the reception of grace by taking a relational term predominantly seen as a human activity and responsibility and transferring it into a different field of relations—namely, commerce and rights. This places it in an entirely different frame of reference where it could be seen as the responsibility of Christ and not the believer. Passivity on the part of the believer is thus encouraged. The chief support for the notion of purchase, upon which Owen built all his arguments, is the covenant of redemption.

In contrast to Owen, Scripture relates faith to the presentation of the atonement's objective sufficiency as the object of faith in the preaching of the gospel. Owen's stress on the efficiency of the cross, expressed in the triple choice argument in which Owen considers the unbelief of the elect and its relation to Christ's work, further distorted the picture by proving too much, according to Chambers. The elect were in effect saved at the cross, a notion contrary to Scripture.

Chambers pointed out how Owen's discussion of commercial language for atonement is at the heart of his argument for the necessity of the application to the elect. The language of sin as "debt" in Scripture is restricted and never associated as such with Christ's death. A survey of commercial terms in Scripture does not support Owen's view of faith as purchase. It is always believers who are "bought," never "faith." Also, the ransom is never spoken of as being paid to the Father. Owen's view of language here and his failure to respect metaphor left him wide open for criticism, according to Chambers.

Nineteenth-century theologians like Charles Hodge and Robert Dabney began to point out the difficulties of a commercial portrayal of satisfaction.[304] Scripture supports neither the prominence Owen gave to commercial language in his system nor the specific content he associated with its use.

Chambers noted that the suggestion that the elect were saved at the cross logically undermines both the nature and urgency of gospel preaching.

For all its impressiveness, Chambers opined that the central pillars of Owen's argument are unsound. They give rise to unhelpful and unbiblical notions, such as payment to the Father, dominance of commercial language, subjugation of sufficiency,

304 Hodge, *Systematic Theology*, 2:554: "Where it is taught that the satisfaction of Christ was in all respects analogous to the payment of a debt, it is clear that the work of Christ can justify the offer of salvation to those only whose debts He has actually cancelled." See also R. L. Dabney, *Systematic Theology* (1878; repr. Edinburgh: Banner of Truth, 2002), 523, 526. Daniel makes the point that the introduction of particularism coupled with the rejection of assurance as the essence of faith "slowly opened the door for hyper-Calvinism" ("Hyper-Calvinism and John Gill," 515). Joel Beeke's chapter, "The Assurance Debate: Six Key Questions," in *Drawn into Controversie*, 263–83, on Owen's concept of assurance fails to examine what Owen said about assurance in his *Death of Death*, nor does Beeke probe the relationship of those views to limited atonement.

intrusion of rights, dissonance within the Trinity, understanding of the gospel, and assurance of salvation.[305]

Chambers's suggestion that Owen's *Death of Death* should no longer be viewed as an argument for limited atonement will no doubt chafe many Calvinists. But his point is well taken that there has been a change since Owen's day in the understanding of language, exegesis, and the systematic assumptions that Owen took for granted, such as federal theology. "Those who think Owen's position is necessary for a fully fledged Calvinism and the rejection of modern Arminianism and its offshoots . . . will need to advance new arguments that carry conviction within this changed context."[306] High Calvinists like Wayne Grudem continue to employ many of Owen's arguments.[307] The same occurs in many of the chapters in the more recent tome defending limited atonement, *From Heaven He Came and Sought Her*.

However, Chambers assumed his own Dortian understanding of unconditional election as biblical when he said, "In the end Arminian universal redemption founders on the modification of the scriptural teaching on election that it entails."[308] Chambers chided both high Calvinists and Arminians:

> Both make indefinite statements definite . . . distorting their function as inclusive invitations . . . and both reason to assert either the absolute freedom of the human will or the limitation of God's love to the elect . . . both seek to prescribe what is consistent with almighty love. For Owen, to love equals to save. For the universal redemptionist, to love equals giving all opportunity of being saved. In both cases God's being loving is made to be dependent on His treatment of His creatures and the positions adopted in relationship to the atonement are deduced from the premise of God's love.[309]

Chambers referenced other critiques of various aspects of Owen's soteriology, including McLeod Campbell, James Torrance, A. C. Clifford, and Trevor Hart. Campbell and Torrance faulted Owen's doctrine of God for making God's justice absolute and his love relative. Hart critiqued both those who espouse universal atonement and those who support limited atonement. What lies behind both is a notion of omnipotent love, "which must succeed in bringing about its desired goal or else it ceases by definition to be omnipotent love."[310] Since we don't know what is and is not consistent with divine

---

305 Chambers, "A Critical Examination," 356–58.
306 Ibid., 358.
307 W. Grudem, *Systematic Theology* (Grand Rapids, MI: Zondervan, 1994), 594–603.
308 Chambers, "A Critical Examination," 362.
309 Ibid., 365–66.
310 T. Hart, "Universalism: Two Distinct Types," in *Universalism and the Doctrine of Hell*, ed. N. M. de S. Cameron (Grand Rapids, MI: Baker, 1992), 28–31.

love, we best not make deductions based on its assumed content, especially when there is no warrant in Scripture to do so.

Chambers pointed out how difficult it is to derive a single intent in the atonement from Scripture since both indefinite and definite statements are used by the biblical authors. Scripture relates Christ's death sometimes to sinners as sinners and sometimes to the church. Most statements on the extent of Christ's death appear in a global context, not a restricted context. Chambers is correct that there are no specifically exclusive statements on the extent of the atonement.

Owen sought to bolster his inferred exclusiveness of the definite statements by arguing from outcome to intent, from the salvation of the elect alone to an exclusive intent in the death of Christ to save the elect alone. Chambers discerned the problem here: To make exclusive statements of God's intention in Christ's death, one must have exhaustive knowledge of the outcome, which deals comprehensively with every aspect of the relation of the atonement to the end. But no one has such knowledge.

Chambers also questioned Owen's assumption that the substitutionary nature of Christ's death entails limited atonement. Throughout Reformed history, many have disagreed. One need only read Charles Hodge and Robert Dabney as examples.[311]

Chambers critiqued J. I. Packer's adherence to Owen's logic in arguing that if the atonement is a penal substitution, one is left with either universalism or limited atonement.[312] Robert Letham made the same argument.[313] Biblically, there is nothing in a sacrifice per se, whether Passover or the Day of Atonement, that makes the sacrifice as constituting an exclusive one-to-one relationship with any of the participants. What includes Israelites in the effectiveness of those sacrifices is faith. Faith constitutes the one-to-one substitution. According to Chambers, Packer wants substitution to be constitutive of faith.

Chambers understood Packer's logic as follows: (1) substitution saves me, (2) substitution secures my faith; therefore, (3) there must be a substitutionary relationship prior to faith. Several things follow from this:

1. We must abandon the biblical model of sacrifice in our understanding of substitution. Many for whom the Passover and Day of Atonement sacrifice were made were not saved. Faith is the context for acceptable sacrifice (Ps 51:15–19).
2. This model is dependent on the covenant of redemption and thus stands or falls with it. Payment of a legal debt in itself does not entitle one to any other benefit than being spared punishment. Here Owen's triple choice argument comes into play.

311 Hodge, *Systematic Theology*, 2:544; Dabney, *Systematic Theology*, 521.

312 Chambers, "A Critical Examination," 372–76.

313 R. Letham, *The Work of Christ*, Contours of Christian Theology, ed. Gerald Bray (Downers Grove, IL: InterVarsity, 1993), 231–32.

3. This notion that substitution entails salvation proves too much. Chambers quoted William Sailer:

> If it be argued that God cannot but acquit those for whom Christ died then the question arises whether God can ever manifest wrath toward them—even for a time. But Scripture plainly asserts that prior to conversion the elect are the objects of God's wrath [Eph 2:3; Col 2:13]. Now if Christ took their place and they died with him does it not follow that these can never be under the wrath of God? This is the conclusion reached by Karl Barth, who maintains that there is no transition from wrath to grace in history and that men need only be told that they are already in Christ.[314]

4. Packer has abandoned his own stated aim. Penal substitution should be evaluated as a model of the atonement rather than its mechanics. Yet in his reasoning from substitution to limited atonement, he is using substitution as a causative mechanism rather than an explanatory model, thus trying to solve the "how" problem of why some believe and others do not.
5. The Scriptures cited by Packer that faith is secured at the cross do not say such.

Chambers concluded his four-hundred-page thesis with a consideration of limited atonement's effect on preaching. Preaching to all the nations is an activity central and necessary to Christology. Salvation is mediated by the Word and experienced by believing the Word (Rom 10:5–17). The gospel contains the message of Christ's death for all sins according to 1 Cor 15:1–3.

Chambers noted that it is not only Owen's limited atonement that threatens the role of preaching; Barth's understanding of election, Vernon White's attempt at universalism, and Pinnock's and Sanders's inclusivism all undermine, potentially or actually, the role that Scripture gives to preaching. According to Chambers, minimizing salvation through preaching is to seek a theology of glory rather than a theology of the cross. Anything that operates to undermine the universality, centrality, and necessity of the gospel in salvation works against the specific testimony of Scripture and the whole pattern of God's dealings with people.[315]

Chambers boldly proclaimed that any view that encourages preachers to be complacent about seeking out hearers or hesitant about driving the gospel home to all is wrong. Such would be the logical consequence if it were denied that, from the preacher's viewpoint, God saves by making all saveable by Christ's work. Saveability must

314 W. S. Sailer, "The Nature and Extent of the Atonement: A Wesleyan View," *Bulletin of the Evangelical Theological Society* 10 (1967): 198.

315 Chambers, "A Critical Examination," 383–90.

be seen as the outcome of the atonement for the elect. But preachers are not asked to operate on a hypothesis that, after reflection, would show to be untrue. Rather, the real provision is the death of Christ for all, because it is the death required for all and every person. Chambers appealed again to Charles Hodge: "God in effecting the salvation of his own people, did whatever was necessary for the salvation of all men, and therefore to all the offer may be, and in fact is made in the gospel."[316] Hodge can affirm what Owen must deny because he rejected both limited atonement and the purchase of faith.

Chambers concluded his critique of Owen by noting Christ's death is sufficient for all not just as a statement of its infinite intrinsic worth but as a real provision for the sins of the whole world. This atonement is effective for those who have the work of atonement applied to them by the Spirit through the preaching of the Word coupled with their faith.

Chambers saw "no reality" in the objection that if there is a general provision of atonement, somehow God may have failed in his purpose. Such an objection only arises out of the framework of the Covenant of Redemption, the dominance of commercial analogies and the idea that provision includes the purchase of faith. God's purpose may well include the magnifying of his mercy in that provision and the demonstration of human culpability and the sinfulness of sin in its rejection. There was provision made for many in the exodus, but only two of those who began the journey as adults attained the land. Did God's purpose fail?

Chambers offered this pointed critique regarding the failure of Owen's exegesis: "Owen has an enduring appeal because it gives logical consistency to the theological system of which it is a part, not because of the transparent appropriateness or adequacy of its exegesis."[317]

In addition to Chambers, another significant critique of the logic of Owen's *Death of Death* is a series of posts by Arminian Dan Chapa on his website.[318] Chapa's strategy is to distill Owen's arguments in syllogistic form and examine them.

Chapa began with Owen's attempt to prove that the death of Christ and his intercession for the elect are coextensive. This is vital to Owen's entire argument. For Owen, Christ's death effects five things: (1) reconciliation, (2) justification, (3) sanctification, (4) adoption, and (5) eternal inheritance. Owen argues from these five effects that if one supports unlimited atonement, he is forced to assert either that God failed in his intended plan or that universalism results.

Whereas Arminianism treats Christ's actual death on the cross and his intercession as high priest as a two-step process, Owen must make these coextensive to support his

316 C. Hodge, *Systematic Theology*, 2:556.

317 Chambers, "A Critical Examination," 390.

318 D. Chapa, "Index to Review of John Owen's the Death of Death in the Death of Christ," *Traditional Baptist Chronicles* (blog), July 4, 2010, http://www.traditionalbaptistchronicles.com/2010/07/index-to-review-of-john-owens-death-of.html.

view of limited atonement. But as Chapa correctly pointed out, if Christ's death immediately accomplishes the five things Owen mentions, where is room left for justification by faith?

Chapa stated Owen's argument in syllogistic form:

> P1: Intercession is inseparably connected with oblation.
> P2: Christ's intercession is made for the elect alone.
> C1: Therefore, Christ's oblation was made for the elect alone.

Owen sought biblical support for P1 in Isa 53:11–12 and Rom 8:32–34.

Even if P1 and P2 are valid, the conclusion does not follow. Just because Christ died for everyone whom he intercedes for does not mean he did not die for anyone else. The passages cited do support the fact that Christ's death is the basis for justification, but Owen's conclusion does not follow.

Owen's second argument:

> P3: Christ died with the intent of justifying those he died for.
> P4: Not all are justified.
> C2: Therefore, either Christ's aim failed, or he did not die for all.
> P5: Christ's aim cannot fail.
> C3: Therefore, Christ did not die for all.

P3 requires clarification. If Owen meant Christ died with the intent of immediately justifying those for whom he died, or justifying them without also interceding for them, then P3 is false. But if Owen meant that Christ died with the intention of everyone coming to faith and being justified, then P3 is true. Chapa concluded if this is the case, then P5 is false. Christ did come to save the world (John 3:17), but not all the world is saved.

Owen's third argument:

> P6: Christ's oblation was for an equivalent number of people as his intercession.
> P2: Christ's intercession is made for the elect alone.
> C1: Therefore, Christ's oblation was made for the elect alone.

Again Owen appeals to Rom 8:32–34.

P6 is Owen's interpretation, but it is false. The scope of Rom 8:32–34 is limited to people who have been justified. Owen is attempting to apply the passage to all the elect as an abstract class. Paul is referring only to the believing elect. There is no ground to work backward from what is stated in this text and exclude some from Christ's death. No one doubts that Christ died for those who are believers and that his blood has been applied to them through Christ's intercession. Romans 8:32–34 does not address those who have not been justified. Therefore, while the text does prove that Christ died for everyone he intercedes for, it does not prove that he died for no one else. This is Owen's logical mistake.

Owen's fourth argument:

> P1: A high priest wouldn't be fulfilling his duties if he offers a sacrifice on someone's behalf, but didn't intercede for them
> P2: Christ is a faithful high priest, fulfilling his duties
> C1: Therefore, Christ does not make an offering for someone without also interceding for them.

Owen found biblical support for P1 in 1 John 2:1–2. He continues the argument by positing:

> P3: Christ offered his blood to God at the entrance of the holy place.
> P4: Christ entered the holy place by his blood to intercede for the elect.
> C2: Therefore, offering and intercession are two parts of the same tabernacle function.

Owen adduced biblical support for P1 from 1 John 2:1–2 and for P3 and P4 from Heb 9:7–14.

Chapa asserted P1, P3, and P4 are incorrect. With respect to P1, Owen neglects to quote the second half of 1 John 2:2: "And not for ours only, but also for the sins of the whole world." Even then, the text does not state that advocacy and propitiation are two parts of one ceremonial function performed by a high priest. Propitiation is certainly the basis of advocacy, but that does not entail that the two are inseparable duties of a high priest.

With respect to P3 and P4, the Hebrews text does not state that offering and intercession are part of the same ceremonial function. It is plain from Hebrews 9 that P3 is false since the text states that Christ enters the Holy of Holies to offer his blood to God. At this point, he has not already offered it. P4 is false on three counts: (1) Owen confused offering with intercession, (2) Christ's intercession is done at the right hand of God *after* he has made his offering, and (3) the offering is once for all, but the intercession is continuous. Christ's duty as mediator begins after his cross work and is in fact based on it.

Owen's fifth argument:

P1: Christ's intercession is not vocal or supplication but rather a presentation of Christ himself.
P2: The presentation of Christ to God is joined with the offering of Christ to God.
C1: Therefore, intercession is joined with the offering of Christ to God.

Owen adduced Heb 9:12–14, 24 in support of P1.

Chapa asserted P1 is false on the grounds that Owen is confusing the once-for-all offering of Christ on the cross with the continuous heavenly intercession. In John 17 Christ prays to the Father to sanctify believers. Owen's claim that this intercession is not vocal is a mystery. Again, he is conflating and thus confusing oblation with intercession.

Another argument Owen posited in this vein:

P1: In John 17 Christ both offered and interceded.
P2: Christ intercedes for the elect alone.
C1: Therefore, Christ offered for the elect alone.

Owen's support for P1 is John 17:4; 1 Cor 15:17; and Heb 9:12.

Chapa noted P1 and P2 are true, but the conclusion does not follow. Just because Christ offered for everyone he intercedes for does not mean he intercedes for everyone he offers for. Christ's offering is the basis for his intercession. The two are linked but not identical.

Chapa addressed one final Owen argument:

P1: The strict connection between Christ's offering and his intercession gives assurance to those who believe Christ offered for them.
P2: Arminians think Christ may offer for those whom he does not intercede.
C1: For Arminianism, those who believe Christ offered himself to the Father for them lack assurance.

Biblical support for P1 is Rom 8:34.

But the conclusion does not logically follow, according to Chapa. The connection between Christ's offering and intercession is not the only way to explain the assurance that believers in Christ possess. They have assurance because of the intercession of Christ for them as believers. It is true that everyone who believes in Christ has assurance; it's just not true because of P1.

C1 should actually read: According to Arminianism, those who believe Christ offered himself to the Father for them have no assurance due to a strict connection between Christ's offering and his intercession. To which Chapa replies, "So what?" Arminians have assurance for other reasons. As Romans 8 continues, Christ "is even at the right hand of God, who also makes intercession for us."

Chapa has found some chinks in Owen's logical armor. One might find any number of Reformed theologians to consult who take issue with Owen on the notion that Christ's death and intercession must be treated as one, beginning with Owen's interlocutor, Richard Baxter.[319]

John Corbet (AD 1620–1680)

Corbet affirmed unlimited atonement as being an expression of God's goodwill toward all people "and doth convict the negligent of being inexcusable despisers of his Grace towards them."[320]

Corbet also stated: "We differ not from the Established Doctrine of the Church of England, and we approve her moderation used in those articles, which we take in the same sense with the English Episcopal Divines in general, that lived in Queen Elizabeth's and King James' time."[321]

Thomas Watson (AD 1620–1686)

Watson was a Nonconformist, Puritan preacher, and author of many books, including some of the best devotional literature of the Puritan era. He served as pastor of St. Stephen's in Walbrook, London, for sixteen years.

Watson's belief in unlimited atonement may be seen in his discussion of the issue of mistakes concerning sin's forgiveness. The first mistake is to assume our sins are forgiven when they are not. This mistake flows from two grounds. First, God's mercy. Second,

> Because Christ died for their sins, therefore they are forgiven. *Ans.* That Christ died for remission of sin is true; but, that, therefore, all have remission is false; then Judas should be forgiven. Remission is limited to believers, Acts xiii. 39. "By him all that believe are justified;" but all do not believe: some slight and trample Christ's blood under foot, Heb. x. 29. So that, notwithstanding

319 D. Ponter, "Sources on John 17:9," *Calvin and Calvinism*, July 14, 2011, http://calvinandcalvinism.com/?page_id=8409.

320 J. Corbet, *A Humble Endeavour of Some Plain and Brief Explication of the Decrees and Operations of God about the Free Actions of Men: More Especially of the Operations of Divine Grace* (London: Printed for Tho. Parkhurst, at the Bible and Three Crowns in Cheapside, near Mercers-Chappel, 1683), A2r, referenced in D. P. Field's *Rigide Calvinisme in a Softer Dresse: The Moderate Presbyterianism of John Howe, 1630–1705* (Edinburgh: Rutherford, 2004), 144.

321 J. Corbet, *An Account of the Principles and Practices of Several Nonconformists* (London: Printed for T. Parkhurst, at the Bible and 3 Crowns near Mercers Chappel, at the lower end of Cheap-side, 1682), 21–22.

> Christ's death, all are not pardoned. Take heed of this dangerous mistake. Who will seek after pardon, that thinks he has it already?[322]

Watson's comment about Judas is revealing. Judas's possible forgiveness can only be true (hypothetically) because Christ died for his sins. As David Ponter noted, there is a functional equivalency in Watson's statement between Christ dying for sins and the implication of Christ dying for Judas. Ponter gleaned a second theological inference from Watson's statement:

> Watson's comments entail a denial of the double payment dilemma. The very connection Watson seeks to refute, is, in fact, the core of Owen's trilemma, namely, if Christ dies for a man, that man cannot fail to be saved (*i.e.*, pardoned). Watson is arguing that Christ's death, even for Judas, is conditional. That is, the benefits of Christ's death are only conditionally applied. The condition being faith.[323]

John Humfrey (AD 1621–1719)

Humfrey spoke of the distinction between two sorts of Calvinists who opposed Arminianism: "high" Calvinists who affirmed limited atonement and "moderate" Calvinists who held to a form of universal atonement.[324] Referencing John 3:16 and Heb 2:9, he stated that Scripture clearly taught Christ died for the sins of the world, and that the "world" must be more than the elect.

Humfrey made the salient point concerning Rom 8:29–30 so often missed by Calvinists who affirm limited atonement—namely, that Paul omits redemption from the chain of salvation. "And why is *Redemption* here left out of the Apostolical Chain, but because *those he hath redeemed*, are all the world? If the Doctrine that this Gentleman hath received were right [limited atonement], the Apostle would have said, *Whom he did predestinate, them he Redeemed*."[325]

This is an important point Humfrey is making. Moderate Calvinists affirm eternal

---

322 Thomas Watson, *Body of Divinity*, 2 vols. (Berwick: W. George, 1806), 2:294.

323 D. Ponter, "Thomas Watson (1620–1686) on Conditional Satisfaction (Contra Owen's Double Payment Trilemma)," *Calvin and Calvinism*, August 8, 2014, http://calvinandcalvinism.com/?p=14517.

324 Humfrey stated,

> Sir, you know there are two sorts of such as oppose Arminianism. One that is the high sort, and the other the moderate sort that are for the middle way in these Controversies, and I confess myself one who have wrote several pieces, so called. We that are of this sort, do hold Election to be of particular persons (not the choosing Believers to be saved with the Arminian and Lutherans, but the choosing Persons to believe): But Redemption we hold to be Universal (J. Humfrey, *Peace at Pinners-Hall Wish'd and Attempted in a Pacifick Paper Touching the Universality of Redemption, the Conditionality of the Covenant of Grace, and Our Freedom from the Law of Works* [London: Randal Taylor, 1692], 2–3).

325 Ibid. See also J. Humfrey, *The Middle-Way, in One Paper of Election & Redemption, with Indifferency between the Arminian & Calvinist* (London: Printed for T. Parkhurst, at the Three Bibles in Cheap-Side, 1673).

election and the effectual call but also affirm an unlimited atonement. Joseph Truman also called himself a "moderate" several times in opposing certain free will advocates.[326]

Edward Polhill (AD 1622–1694)

Edward Polhill was a significant Puritan writer in the seventeenth century. He spent sixty-five pages refuting particular redemption and defending Hypothetical Universalism in his 1673 work, *The Divine Will.*[327]

> But if Christ no way died for all men, how came the minister's commission to be so large. They command men to repent that their sins may be blotted out for whom Christ was not made sin? They beseech men to be reconciled to God, but how shall they be reconciled for whom Christ paid no price at all? They call and cry out to men to come to Christ that they may have life, but how can they have life, for whom Christ was no surety in his death? If then Christ died for all men, the ministry is a true ministry as to all; but if Christ died only for the elect, what is the ministry as to the rest? Those exhortations, which as to the elect are real undissembled offers of grace, as to the rest seem to be but golden dreams and shadows. Those calls, which as to the elect are right ministerial acts, as to the rest appear as extra-ministerial blots and erratas. Those invitations to the gospel feast, which as the elect are the cordial wooings and beseechings of God himself, as to the rest look like the words of mere men speaking at random, and without commission; for alas! why should they come to that feast for whom nothing is prepared? How should they eat and drink for whom the Lamb was never slain? Wherefore, I conclude that Christ died for all men, so far as to found the truth of the ministry towards them.[328]

John Flavel (AD 1627–1691)

Flavel was one of the Puritan ministers of 1662 ejected for his nonconformity. He was a prolific author. In a sermon Flavel preached in 1689, just two years before his death, his phraseology suggests that he might have been a moderate Calvinist. In presenting motives for why his unregenerate hearers should come to Christ, he stated that Christ has a right to the sinner's soul "by redemption; Christ hath bought thy soul, and that

---

326 J. Truman, *A Discourse of Natural and Moral Impotency* (London: Printed for R. Clavel; and are to be sold at the Sign of the Peacock in St. Paul's yard, 1675), 115, 124.

327 E. Polhill, *The Divine Will Considered in Its Eternal Decrees and Holy Execution of Them* (London: For Henry Eversden, 1673), 281–346. See idem, *Essay on the Extent of the Death of Christ from the Treatise on the Divine Will* (Berwick: Thomas Melrose, 1842), 1–33.

328 E. Polhill, "The Divine Will Considered in Its Eternal Decrees," in *The Works of Edward Polhill* (Morgan, PA: Soli Deo Gloria, 1998), 165.

at the invaluable price of his own blood. Who then can dispute the right of Christ to enter into his own house?"[329]

While some high Calvinists have spoken similarly, this strong language by Flavel may indicate his moderation on the atonement.[330]

George Swinnock (AD 1627–1673)

Swinnock was also one of the ejected preachers in 1662. He returned to the pastorate in Maidstone in 1672 and served until his death.

Swinnock told all his unbelieving readers that "he [Christ] redeemed them" and "paid the price" of their ransom. Notice his usage of Acts 3:36. Baxter used the same passage to teach the same doctrine.[331] Observe also the connection he made between the willingness of Christ to save sinners, the gospel offer, and Christ paying the ransom price for his hearers:

> Consider friend, did Christ esteem Regeneration worth his blood, to merit it; and is it not worth thy prayers, and tears, and utmost endeavours to obtain it? Did Christ come to destroy the works of the Devil which is sin, 1 Joh. 3.8. and wilt thou build them up? did the Lord Jesus Come to build up the temple of holiness, and wilt thou pull it down? did Christ think it worth the while to be reproached, condemned, crucified, and all to make thee holy; and wilt thou be such an enemy to the cross of Christ, as by continuing in sin, to deprive him of that which he earned so dearly? Why wilt thou bind thy self to be a slave to Satan, when he redeemed thee with such a vast sum?

---

329 J. Flavel, *Christ Knocking at the Door of Sinners' Hearts; or, A Solemn Entreaty to Receive the Saviour and His Gospel in This the Day of Mercy* (New York: American Tract Society, 1850), 135–36. This statement by Flavel suggests an unlimited imputation of sin to Christ:

> The death of Christ, doubtless, contained the greatest and acutest pains imaginable: because these pains of Christ alone, were intended to equalize all that misery which the sin of men deserved, all that pain which the damned shall, and the elect deserve to feel. Now, to have pains meeting at once upon one person, equivalent to all the pains of the damned; judge you what a plight Christ was in (J. Flavel, "The Fountain of Life Opened Up," in *The Whole Works of the Rev. Mr. John Flavel*, 6 vols. (London: Printed for W. Baynes and Son, 1820), 1:322–23).

330 In the case of some Puritans, they spoke more broadly about the extent of Christ's death in their sermons and gospel appeals than they did in their formal doctrinal or theoretical statements. Obadiah Sedgwick (c. AD 1600–1658), a high Calvinist and Westminster divine, is a classic example. See Sedgwick's strong gospel offer language with reference to the death of Christ in *The Humbled Sinner Resolved What He Should Do to be Saved: or, Faith in the Lord Jesus Christ* (London: T. R. & E. M. for A. Byfield, 1656), 88–89, 161–63, 166, 167, 181; along with similar statements his *The Riches of Grace Displayed in the Offer and Tender of Salvation to Poor Sinners* (London: Printed by T. R. & E. M. for A. Byfield, 1657); and *The Fountain Opened: And the Water of Life Flowing Forth, for the Refreshing of Thirsty Sinners* (London: Printed by T. R. and E. M. for A. Byfield, 1657). For Sedgwick's strict views and arguments against universal redemption, see *The Bowels of Tender Mercy Sealed in the Everlasting Covenant* (London: E. Mottershed, for A. Byfield, 1661), 280–312. If Flavel was not moderate on the *extent* question, then he was like Sedgwick in this respect. Like all Calvinists, however, there is no doubt that Flavel limited the Son's *intention* or saving *design* in dying. See his "The Method of Grace in the Gospel-Redemption," in *The Whole Works of the Rev. Mr. John Flavel*, 6 vols. (London: Printed for W. Baynes and Son, 1820), 2:21–22.

331 R. Baxter, *Universal Redemption of Mankind by the Lord Jesus Christ*, 236.

> Did the merciful God send his Son into the world to bless thee, in turning thee from thine iniquity, and canst thou look upon that great blessing as they bondage? Act. 3.26. Believe it, God had servants enough (even Angels, that are ever ready to do his will) to send ordinary gifts by, surely them twas some extraordinary Present that he thought none worthy to carry, and would trust none with but his only Son. God sent him to bless you, in turning every one of you from your iniquities. I hope, Reader, thou wilt have higher thoughts of holiness, and worse thoughts of sin all thy days: Surely the Son of God was not so prodigal of his most precious blood, as to pour it out for anything that was not superlatively excellent.[332]

Swinnock also stated: "Jesus Christ is willing that sinners should live, or he would not so willingly have died such a death; he hath paid the price of thy ransom, and offereth thee an happier estate than that of which Adam deprived thee."[333] Again, Swinnock connected Christ's universal willingness that sinners should live with his death and the gospel call: "If he had not been willing that poor sinners should live, he would not have died; if he had been unwilling that I should come, why doth he call me?"[334]

Speaking of the love of God for the unsaved, Swinnock said:

> When God sent his Son into the world, he did, as it were, say to him, My dear Son, thou Son of my chiefest love and choicest delight, go to the wicked, unworthy world, commend me to them, and tell them, that in thee I have sent them such a love-token, such an unquestionable testimony of my favor and good-will towards them, that hereafter they shall never have the least color of reason to suspect my love, or to say, "Wherein hast thou loved us?" Mal. i. 2.[335]

Swinnock here affirmed God's universal saving will as well as his love for all humanity.

Stephen Charnock (AD 1628–1680)

Another important Puritan who is often mistaken as holding limited atonement is Stephen Charnock. Charnock connected the love of God for all people with the death of Christ for all.[336] He referenced Amyraut's writings for a proper understanding of

332 George Swinnock, "The Door of Salvation Opened by the Key of Regeneration," in *The Works of George Swinnock*, 5 vols. (Edinburgh: James Nichol, 1868), 5:181–82.

333 Ibid., 5:245. Note the similarity of this to what Bucer said earlier as referenced by Goodwin.

334 Ibid., 216.

335 G. Swinnock, "Heaven and Hell Epitomised," in *The Works of George Swinnock*, 3:342–46.

336 S. Charnock, "A Discourse of the Subjects of the Lord's Supper," in *The Complete Works of Stephen Charnock*, 5 vols. (Edinburgh: James Nichol, 1865), 4:464.

the phrase "takes away the sin of the World" in John 1:29.[337] Siekawitch's study of Charnock concluded that the Saumur School had an immense influence on Charnock:

> If number of citations are any indication it would appear the School of Saumur in France made the largest impression on Charnock next to puritanism. In his *Works* he cited Moise Amyraut 130 times and Jean Daillé 79 times. The next largest number of citations of anyone not affiliated with the School of Saumur was the Roman Catholic Francisco Suarez with 44 and Johannes Cocceius 33 times. From the School of Saumur and those affiliated with it he referred to Amyraut, Daillé, Louis Cappel, Jean Mestrezat, John Cameron, Paul Testard, Michel Le Faucheur, Josue de Place (Placeus) and the *Theses Salmuriensis* a total of 254 times . . . After the ejection Charnock visited France for an extended period and brought back the French reformers' books as well as their ideas.[338]

Charnock also stated:

> There is no want on Christ's part. There hath been by him satisfaction enough for the payment of our debts, and merit enough for our restoration to our happiness. He hath done all things necessary for the salvation of the world: he hath expiated sin, which plunged it into misery; he hath presented his death to God as a sacrifice of infinite value, sufficient for all the world, and by opening the throne of grace, hath given liberty to approach to God, and solicit him for the application of the benefit he hath purchased; . . .
>
> The title of our Lord Jesus in his first coming was Saviour, not Judge; he presented men with that which might warrant them from condemnation; but if they will not rejoice in their happiness, they exclude themselves from the benefit; and by not embracing the ransom God hath provided, they expose themselves to pay that satisfaction in their persons which the law exacts. The satisfaction of Christ they cannot plead, because the conditions of it are not embraced; they must therefore pay what the law demands, which would else be insignificant, and the honour of God's justice would suffer in their safety.

337 S. Charnock, "A Discourse of Christ Our Passover," in *The Works of Stephen Charnock*, 5 vols. (1865; repr. Edinburgh: Banner of Truth, 1985), 4:507.

338 L. D. Siekawitch, "Stephen Charnock's Doctrine of the Knowledge of God: A Case Study of the Balance of Head and Heart in Restoration Puritanism" (PhD diss., University of Wales, 2007), 70. See also L. D. Siekawitch, *Balancing Head and Heart in Seventeenth Century Puritanism: Stephen Charnock's Doctrine of the Knowledge of God*, Studies in Christian History and Thought (Milton Keynes, UK: Paternoster, 2012), 51. This argues against the broad brushing of Beeke and Jones who said without qualification that the "Puritans also opposed the views of the Amyraldians and their hypothetical universalism" (*A Puritan Theology: Doctrine for Life* [Grand Rapids, MI: Reformation Heritage, 2012], 360). Clearly Beeke is not aware of Charnock's moderate Calvinism or his fondness for Amyraldian theology, even on the extent of Christ's satisfaction.

> When, therefore, every offer of mercy shall accompany men to the tribunal of the judge, and this charge be heard from his mouth: I have redeemed you by my blood, and you have trod it under foot; I have invited you to faith and repentance, but you would rather wallow in the excrement of sin; I have called you by the motions of my Spirit, and you have proved rebellious; I have encouraged you by promises of great reward, but you made no account of them; wherein have I been wanting? With what face can any man now lay the fault upon God? And when a king proclaims pardon to a rebellious city, upon the condition that they yield up themselves to his son; as it is equity that those that surrender themselves should have the promised benefit, so it is just that those that willfully resist so easy and reasonable a condition, should fall under the threatened penalty; they have no reason to large their ruin upon any want of clemency in the king, since the proffer was made to all, but upon their own obstinacy, because they perish by their own folly.[339]

Note Charnock's language of "expiated sin," "ransom," "satisfaction," and "redeemed" in the context of those who are as yet unbelievers. This indicates clearly Charnock's belief in unlimited atonement.

John Howe (AD 1630–1705)

John Howe, theologian and chaplain to Oliver Cromwell, was as well-known and as influential in his own lifetime as John Owen but is seldom read or recognized today as one of the great Puritan thinkers of the seventeenth century.[340] Howe is often pegged as a limitarian with respect to the extent of the atonement, but as the quotations below illustrate—out of many that could be provided—he clearly affirmed universal atonement.

> Again, is it righteous to deny the Lord that bought thee, to neglect that great salvation which he is the author of? And whereas he came to bless thee in turning thee from thine iniquities, wilfully to remain still in an accursed servitude to sin? when he was made manifest to destroy the works of the devil, still to yield thyself a captive at his will? Whereas he died that thou mightest not any longer live to thyself, but to him that died for thee, and rose again; and that he might redeem thee from thy vain conversation; and that thou art so expressly told, that such as still lead sensual lives, mind earthly things,

---

339 Stephen Charnock, "The Misery of Unbelievers," in *The Complete Works*, 4:342–43.

340 One of the most important modern sources on Howe is David Field's, *"Rigide Calvinisme in a Softer Dresse": The Moderate Presbyterianism of John Howe 1630–1705*, Rutherford Studies of Historical Theology (Edinburgh: Rutherford, 2004), which confirms Howe's moderate Calvinism. Howe's writings are available today in *The Works of the Reverend John Howe (1630–1705)*, 3 vols. (1848; repr. Ligonier, PA: Soli Deo Gloria, 1990).

> have not their conversation in heaven, are enemies to the cross of Christ. Is it no unrighteousness, that in these respects thy whole life should be nothing else but a constant contradiction to the very design of his dying? a perpetual hostility, a very tilting at his cross? Is there no unrighteousness in thy obstinate infidelity, that wickedly denies belief to his glorious truths, acceptance of his gracious offers, subjection to his holy laws? No unrighteousness in thy obstinate, remorseless impenitency? thy heart that cannot repent? that melts not, while a crucified Jesus, amidst his agonies and dying pangs, cries to thee from the cross, O sinner, enough, thy hard heart breaks mine! yield at last, and turn to God.[341]

> If thou wilt not be reconciled, Christ did, as to thee, die in vain; thou canst be nothing the better. Think what it must come to, that so precious blood, (infinitely exceeding the value of all corruptible things; silver and gold, &c. 1 Pet. i. 18, 19,) should be shed, to redeem and save such as thou, and yet do thee no good?[342]

> When he actually makes his demand and lays his claim, what amazing guilt, how swift destruction must they incur, that dare adventure to deny the Lord that bought them![343]

> We speak to them in the name of the eternal God that made them, of the great Jesus who bought them with his blood, and they regard it not.[344]

James Fraser of Brea (AD 1639–1698)

Fraser was a Scottish Covenanter who was imprisoned on the Bass Rock for two years, where he studied Hebrew and Greek and wrote *Justifying Faith*. He was freed in 1679 but was again arrested in 1681 and confined in Blackness Castle. He was exiled from Scotland on his release six weeks later but then again imprisoned in London. He returned to Scotland in 1687 and became parish minister in Culross, Fife, until his death.[345]

James Walker outlined Fraser's commitment to universal atonement, stating that Fraser "wrought out a theory of universal redemption from the extremest positions of

341 J. Howe, "The Blessedness of the Righteous," in *The Works of the Rev. John Howe*, 3 vols. (1848; repr. Ligonier, PA: Soli Deo Gloria, 1990), 2:151–52. Howe (like Swinnock and Baxter) referenced Acts 3:26 in this quotation to support his view of the atonement.

342 J. Howe, "Of Reconciliation between God and Man," in *Works*, 1:460.

343 J. Howe, "The Redeemer's Tears, etc.," in *Works*, 2:321.

344 Ibid., 2:323.

345 See J. Fraser, *Memoirs of the Rev. James Fraser of Brea, 1639–1698* (Inverness: Melven Brothers, 1891).

his ultra-Calvinistic masters."[346] Christ died for all, but God's intention in the atonement is to save only the elect. Fraser believed a universal atonement laid the foundation for a genuine gospel offer to all and also provided the grounds of judgment for the reprobate. Walker was especially disturbed by this latter purpose of universal redemption: "That whole notion of gospel vengeance was altogether out of keeping with the spirit of the Bible. How monstrous the idea of the Father satisfied, and the Saviour made the wrath-inflicter!"[347] Yet this was essentially Calvin's position as well, along with many in the Reformed tradition.

Fraser argued from 2 Pet 2:1 that Christ paid for the sins of the reprobates. He also queried why it is in Scripture

> that God has elected the whole world, sanctified every man; for in that sense it is as true that God elected, sanctified, justified and glorified them all, as that he died for them all; for he elected, justified and sanctified all sorts and ranks of persons? Why are comprehensive universalities used in the matter of redemption, when such restrictions are used in the matter of election and justification?

Referencing Edward Polhill's identical argument, Fraser stated, "Redemption has a larger sphere then election has, and therefore the Scripture contracts election in words of specialty only, while they open and dilate redemption in emphatic generalities."[348]

Fraser rejected the double payment argument so often used to bolster limited atonement. It is no injustice if salvation bought by Christ comes with conditions that must be fulfilled on the part of the one who may receive that salvation, and yet the conditions are not met by the recipient. Salvation was not purchased to be given to anyone absolutely whether they believed or not, but only upon the exercise of faith.

> In case the satisfaction made and ransom paid by consent of both the payer, and he to whom it was paid, was not to liberate the man absolutely but conditionally, then and in that case by the mutual consent of both parties, especially the payer if the condition be not performed, then either the principal or the cautioner who has paid once may take and seek satisfaction of him that performs not the condition.[349]

---

346 J. Walker, *The Theology and Theologians of Scotland 1560–1750* (1872; repr. Edinburgh: Knox, 1982), 81. It is interesting that Walker does not even acknowledge the large number of Scottish Calvinists who rejected limited atonement during the time period 1560–1750.

347 Ibid., 83.

348 James Fraser, *A Treatise on Justifying Faith, Wherein Is Opened the Grounds of Believing, or the Sinner's Sufficient Warrant to Take Hold of what is Offered in the Everlasting Gospel: Together with an Appendix Concerning the Extent of Christ's Death, Unfolding the Dangerous and Various Pernicious Errors that Hath Been Vented about It* (Edinburgh: William Gray, 1749), 195.

349 Ibid., 228.

Fraser added an interesting twist when he argued that injustice does not occur when double payment is

> not made to one and the same person . . . for it is the person of the Father to whom Christ made satisfaction, and it is the person of the Son to whom satisfaction in hell is made by reprobates (*for the Father judges no man*) now these are two distinct persons, tho' essentially they be the same.[350]

According to Fraser, if Christ satisfied for the sins of the elect, which he certainly did,

> how does the law and justice of God punish the elect before conversion for sins committed by them, . . . and seeing *Adam's* first sin is satisfied for, how comes that sin by law to be imputed to them, to defile the elect with original corruption? . . . Yet while the law lives until we be married to Christ by faith, while we are under it and not under grace, how comes it to punish and exact satisfaction in the elect for these sins for which Christ without doubt has satisfied? Shall they suffer and Christ, too, and that without violation of justice? And may not reprobates suffer law punishments in a higher measure in hell eternally, tho' Christ satisfied justice for the same sins for which they suffer? Why, just in the one case, and not in the other: More or less punishments either as to measure of sufferings or duration of longer or shorter time do not vary the kind, it may make it more or less just, but it cannot make a thing simply or absolutely equal or unequal, and the infinitely holy God cannot be charged with the least injustice, Zeph. iii 5. Hab. i. 13.[351]

Matthew Henry (AD 1662–1714)[352]

Matthew Henry's name is well known today for his devotional commentary on the Bible, which remains in print. He was one of the leading Puritans of England.

In Henry's catechism, he stated that Jesus is a "universal redeemer" who "gave himself a ransom for all, 1 Tim 2:5."[353] He also noted that Christ is the redeemer "in a spe-

---

350 Ibid., 229 (emphasis in original).

351 Ibid., 231. See Hunter M. Bailey, "*Via Media Alia*: Reconsidering the Controversial Doctrine of Universal Redemption in the Theology of James Fraser of Brea" (PhD diss., University of Edinburgh, 2008), for the best scholarly analysis of Fraser's theology of the atonement.

352 One should note that Henry's commentary on the Bible was completed after his death. Romans through Revelation was written by thirteen Nonconformist ministers, partly based upon notes taken by Henry's hearers, and edited by George Burder and John Hughes in 1811. The names of the thirteen are given by John Evans (1767–1827) in the *Protestant Dissenters* magazine, 1797, on page 472, from a memorandum by Isaac Watts. The complete edition of 1811 was edited by G. Burder and J. Hughes. See A. Gordon, "Henry, Matthew," in *Dictionary of National Biography*, 26:124.

353 M. Henry, "Scripture Catechism in the Method of the Assembly's," in *The Miscellaneous Works of the Rev. Matthew Henry, V.D.M.* (London: Joseph Ogle Robinson, 1830), 878.

cial manner" of the elect. He asks, "Is all mankind redeemed from among devils? Yes: for none must say as they did, What have we to do with thee, Jesus, thou Son of God, Matt. 8:29. But are the elect redeemed from among men? Yes: these were redeemed from among men, Rev. 14:4."[354]

In an American edition of Henry's catechism, the question "Is he a universal Redeemer? Yes: he gave himself a ransom for all" was deleted by the editor, Colin McIver, with the explanation given in the preface:

> In this edition, the typographical errors, found in the London Edition, are carefully corrected. The Shorter Catechism, which Mr. Henry, in this work, has beautifully illustrated in the language of scripture, is here presented, in the very words of the Westminster Divines. This is here mentioned, inasmuch as, in the London Edition of this work, there are to be found some few deviations from the language employed by the Westminster Divines, though none of them are such as to affect the sentiment. Of the illustrative questions and answers contained in the London Edition, one only is, in this edition, omitted. This is done, under an impression which is believed to be well founded, that the question and answer here alluded to, was never written by Mr. Henry; but was, in some unaccountable way, interpolated into the London Edition of this work. If inquiry be made into the ground of this supposition, the reply to such inquiry must be, that the question and answer here referred to, considered in connexion, exhibit a palpable misapplication of a text of scripture, and convey an erroneous sentiment, which is flatly contradicted, in other parts of Mr. Henry's published works.[355]

This is quite astounding for two reasons. First, there is no textual evidence of any later addition of this statement. Second, McIver offered no reference to any statements in Henry's works to prove this alleged contradiction. As David Ponter rightly concluded concerning McIver's interpolation, "It is nothing more than the paradigm adjusting the facts, rather than the facts being allowed to adjust the paradigm."[356] The paradigm, of course, being that of limited atonement.

As surprising as it may seem to some, many of the Puritans, along with many Anglicans, opposed the doctrine of limited atonement and affirmed a form of universal atonement. The list of names includes such stellar men as Ussher, Davenant, Baxter, Bunyan, Charnock, Preston, Howe, and Henry. All these men held some form

354 Ibid.

355 C. McIver, ed., *The Westminster Assembly's Shorter Catechism, with Which Is Incorporated "A Scripture Catechism in the Method of the Assembly's; by the Rev. Matthew Henry, V.D.M"* (Princeton, NJ: Franklin Merrill, 1846), ii.

356 D. Ponter, "Matthew Henry (1662–1714) on the Universal Redemption of Mankind," *Calvin and Calvinism*, August 2, 2011, http://calvinandcalvinism.com/?p=10733.

of Hypothetical Universalism in the sense that they all believed Christ satisfied for the sins of all people in his death.[357]

Second, one also discovers that by the middle of the seventeenth century, some high Calvinists began to express their theology of predestination and limited atonement in more extreme ways than some of their predecessors.[358]

Third, Jonathan Moore's research on Preston undermines Jonathan Rainbow's treatment of some similar statements made by Calvin concerning the universality of the atonement.[359] As David Ponter pointed out, Rainbow's thesis is also rebutted when Calvin's statement on Acts 20:28 is placed side by side with Gwalther on the same verse. The statements are virtually identical and Gwalther clearly held to universal atonement.[360]

Westminster Assembly (AD 1643–1649)

The Westminster Assembly[361] was appointed by the Long Parliament to restructure the Church of England. It also included representatives of religious leaders from Scotland. Composed of approximately 150 people, the assembly met from 1643 to 1649 in more than 1,150 sessions and in the process produced the Westminster Standards, which are the major confessional standards of the Presbyterian Church, including the Westminster Confession of Faith and the Westminster Larger and Shorter Catechisms. The completed work of the Westminster Assembly was eventually adopted with revisions in England. It was later revoked during the Restoration in 1660. However, these documents were fully accepted by the Church of Scotland and formed the theological foundation of the Presbyterian Church in Europe and America.

It is often assumed that all those who were members of the Westminster Assembly held to limited atonement (strict particularism).[362] They did not. For example, consider Henry Scudder (AD 1585–1652):

---

357 In Beeke and Pederson's *Meet the Puritans*, the authors fail to mention the moderation of many of the Puritans. In his most recent book on the Puritans, Beeke engages in the same misleading generalizations and broadbrushing (or historical lumping) when he said the "Puritans also opposed the views of the Amyraldians and their hypothetical universalism" (*A Puritan Theology*, 360).

358 This is documented by Wallace, *Puritans and Predestination*, 110–11; 144.

359 See Rainbow, *The Will of God*, 159–74. Remarkably, Rainbow states that it "was not theologically true" for Calvin that "God loves all sinners and wills all sinners to be saved" (ibid., 171). A similar statement is made by W. Cunningham in *The Reformers and the Theology of the Reformation* (London: Banner of Truth, 1967), 398. Calvin's comments on 2 Pet 3:9 concerning God's love toward mankind and his revealed will in the gospel such that he would have them all to be saved refutes both of these claims.

360 See Ponter, "Review Essay (Part One): John Calvin on the Death of Christ and the Reformation's Forgotten Doctrine of Universal Vicarious Satisfaction: A Review and Critique of Tom Nettles' Chapter in Whomever He Wills," *Southwestern Journal of Theology* 55.1 (Fall 2012): 138–58. Or see D. Ponter, "Rudolph Gualther (1519–1586) on the Death of Christ," *Calvin and Calvinism*, June 23, 2008, http://calvinandcalvinism.com/?p=309.

361 For helpful secondary material on the Westminster Assembly, consult R. Letham, *The Westminster Assembly* (Phillipsburg, NJ: P&R, 2009); J. V. Fesko, *The Theology of the Westminster Standards* (Wheaton, IL: Crossway, 2014); L. Gatiss, "'Shades of Opinion within a Generic Calvinism.' The Particular Redemption Debate at the Westminster Assembly," *Reformed Theological Review* 69 (2010): 101–18; and L. Gatiss, "A Deceptive Clarity? Particular Redemption in the Westminster Standards," *Reformed Theological Review* 69 (2010): 180–96.

362 Some of the material in this section appeared in my "The Atonement: Limited or Universal?," 67–78.

> It must be granted, that Christ gave himself a ransom for all. This ransom may be called general, and for all, in some sense: but how? namely, in respect of the common nature of man, which he took, and of the common cause of mankind, which he undertook; and in itself it was of sufficient price to redeem all men; and because applicable to all, without exception, by the preaching and ministry of the gospel. And it was so intended by Christ, that the plaster should be as large as the sore, and that there should be no defect in the remedy, that is, in the price, or sacrifice of himself offered upon the cross, by which man should be saved, but that all men, and each particular man, might in that respect become salvable by Christ.[363]

In the broader context of this quotation, Scudder discussed the fact that the death of Christ was for all people. He denied the argument that all people will be saved because Christ ransomed all mankind. Scudder did not deny this by rejecting the premise that Christ ransomed all mankind;[364] rather, he argued that the new covenant of grace is conditional: only those who believe will obtain salvation.[365]

Further, in granting that Christ died for the sins of every individual person, he based that truth on Christ's common humanity. This is classical Christology in accord with Heb 2:5–14. The sufficiency of which Scudder spoke is an *extrinsic* sufficiency, whereby Christ bore the sin of all humanity. Scudder grounded God's universal offer upon the fact of that extrinsic sufficiency. He further associated God's "general and common love to mankind" with Christ's death for all mankind.[366] All men are "salvable" (an archaic word meaning "saveable") by virtue of what Christ did on the cross. None are left without a remedy for their sin. Therefore, those who hear the gospel and perish have only themselves to blame.[367] One will also notice that Scudder did not use "world" to connote the elect in his scriptural references and allusions.

---

363 H. Scudder, *The Christian's Daily Walk in Security and Peace* (Glasgow: William Collins, 1826), 279–82. J. Moore made an important point when he noted:

> John Owen himself who wrote a recommendatory preface in 1674 to Westminster Divine Henry Scudder's *The Christians Daily Walk*, in which a recommendatory preface by Baxter also appeared. In this book Scudder spends a section of five pages defending a hypothetical universalist position, and in his recommendation Owen covers himself accordingly by distancing himself from some unspecified expressions in the book. But his willingness to commend it warmly on the basis of the plain and practical godliness it promotes is indicative of the relative importance given to this in-house Reformed debate, at least in Post-Restoration England, even by one of the staunchest defenders of particularism. ("The Extent of the Atonement: English Hypothetical Universalism versus Particular Redemption," in *Drawne into Controversie*, 155).

364 Like those who accept the double payment argument.

365 This was also how Ursinus handled the issue. See *The Commentary of Dr. Zacharias Ursinus on the Heidelberg Catechism*, 215.

366 This is also true of Charnock. See S. Charnock, "A Discourse of the Subjects of the Lord's Supper," in *Works*, 4:464. Amyraut also frequently made this connection. See L. Proctor, "The Theology of Moise Amyraut Considered as a Reaction against Seventeenth-Century Calvinism" (PhD diss., University of Leeds, 1952), 200–259.

367 C. Hodge, *Systematic Theology*, 2:556–57, made all of these points.

William Jenkyn confirmed Scudder's moderate views on the atonement. In Jenkyn's ΟΔΗΓΟΣ ΤΥΦΟΣ, *The Blinde Guide, or the Doting Doctor*, he quoted from one of Scudder's letters:

> Master John Goodwin hath alledged some passages in my book, as if I did concur with him, or favor his opinion. I have hereupon considered and weighed well what I have there written, and find nothing tending to the maintaenance of his error; but something expressly against free will to good. I declaring, that notwithstanding Christ may be said to give himself a ransome for all, &c. yet this doth not argue universal Redemption, nor that all men may be saved if they will. I appeal to any judicious and impartial Reader, whether in any thing I have there written, I have justified his opinion; which I am utterly against.[368]

This statement is important in that it revealed Scudder was not rejecting that Christ gave himself a ransom for all (in fact he positively asserts it), but he rejected John Goodwin's sense of universal redemption that Christ died for the sins of all people since he *equally* intends their salvation. When Scudder said "nor that all men may be saved if they will," he means "if they will" in the sense of *free will.* He was not rejecting the idea that all men are saveable by virtue of what Christ has done. He was rejecting the free will sense of that as maintained by Goodwin. Otherwise, Scudder would be contradicting himself in what he said elsewhere on the death of Christ in *The Christian's Daily Walk.*

George Walker (AD 1581–1651) served on the Westminster Assembly and appears to be an advocate for Hypothetical Universalism:

> Quest. Doth not Christ as well make Intercession for all, as hee dyed for all mankind?
>
> Answ. Though Christ dyed and fulfilled the law for a common benefit to all man-kind and his ransome is sufficient to save all; yet he never purposed to redeeme all men by his death. For he knew that many were already damned, and past all hope of redemption before he dyed, and that Judas was a son of perdition, and therefore hee did not purpose to give himselfe a ransome for them. Besides he himself testifieth that hee did not pray for the world, but only for his Elect given to him by his father out of the world, Joh. 17.9. Therefore he did much lesse dye with an intent, purpose and desire to redeeme and save them.[369]

---

368 W. Jenkyn, ΟΔΗΓΟΣ ΤΥΦΟΣ, *The Blinde Guide, or the Doting Doctor* (London: M. B., 1648), 112–13.

369 G. Walker, *The Key of Saving Knowledge* (London: T. Badger, 1641), 49–50.

Walker continued:

> Quest. You have well shewed that Christ both in respect of his Person and Offices, is an all sufficient Redeemer and Saviour, and is able by the infinite worth of his Mediation to save all men: Now then tell me why all men are not saved?
>
> Answ. Though Christ [in] his ransome and satisfaction is able to save and redeeme all that are partakers thereof, even all mankind, if they had grace to receive and apply him and all his merits by Faith, Yet because none have spiritual communion with him, but only they whom God hath chosen to eternall life in him, and predestined to be effectually called, according to his purpose, to the state of grace, and to be made conformable to his image: Therefore many who are not elect, follow their own evil ways, and have no will nor care to repent of their sins, and beleeve in Christ, but run wilfully into destruction and perish.[370]

Notice how Walker distinguished between the "ransome" or "satisfaction" and the application of the atonement. The former is universal, but the latter is limited to those "whom God hath chosen."

> Quest. Doth the benefit of Christ the Mediator, and Redeemer reach only to the Elect?
>
> Answ. Though the saving vertue of Christ belongeth only to the elect; yet there is a common benefit of Christ, whereof reprobates are partakers, which reacheth also to all the world. For hee is said to preserve man and beasts, that is, to keep them in life and being, Psal. 36.6 and to be the Saviour of all, especially of them that beleeve, 1 Tim. 4.10 and to give himself a ransome for all, 1 Tim. 2.6. and by him all things are said to consist, Coloss. 1.17.[371]

Walker spoke of the "common benefit" of the atonement but does not limit these non-salvific benefits to common grace only.[372] Christ is also the Savior of all people and has given himself as a ransom for all.

---

370 Ibid., 52–53.

371 Ibid., 55.

372 Walker certainly did connect Christ's "ransom" with "common benefits" that reach "all in some measure, manner, and degree, even to infidels" (*The Doctrine of the Sabbath* [Amsterdam: Richt Right Press, 1638], 108), and he limited the "world" of John 3:16, 2 Cor 5:19, and 1 John 2:2 to the elect (*The History of the Creation as It Is Written by Moses in the First and Second Chapters of Genesis* [London: Printed for John Barlet, 1641], 22). However, he still called Christ "the common Saviour, and Redeemer of all mankind" (*The Doctrine of the Sabbath*, 104) and granted as true a premise in a question that "the sufferings of one man [Christ] satisfy for all men" (*The Key of Saving Knowledge*, 47).

Another important Westminster delegate was Edmund Calamy (AD 1600–1666). He said:

> I am far from universal redemption in the Arminian sense; but that that I hold is in the sense of our divines in the Synod of Dort, that Christ did pay a price for all,—absolute intention for the elect, conditional intention for the reprobate in case they do believe,—that all men should be *salvabiles, non obstante lapsu Adami* . . . that Jesus Christ did not only die sufficiently for all, but God did intend, in giving of Christ, and Christ in giving Himself, did intend to put all men in a state of salvation in case they do believe.[373]

> I argue from John 3:16, in which words a ground of God's intention of giving Christ, God's love to the world, a philanthropy the world of elect and reprobate, and not of elect only; it cannot be meant of the elect, because of that "whosoever believeth" . . . If the covenant of grace is to be preached to all, then Christ redeemed, in some sense, all—both elect and reprobate.[374]

One should observe several salient points in these quotations. First, Calamy said he holds to a form of universal redemption distinct from the Arminian view. Second, he saw his view expressed by some at the Synod of Dort. Third, he spoke of an intentional sufficiency (conditional for the non-elect; absolute for the elect) such that Christ did actually pay a price for all. This objective price paid for all renders all men saveable, but they must believe to obtain the benefit. Notice that Calamy used John 3:16 as a proof of his view, and he argued that "world" cannot mean the "elect only" in that passage. He also argued that a universal proclamation presupposes a form of universal atonement.

In his *Chain of Principles*, John Arrowsmith (AD 1602–1659), like Calamy, interpreted John 3:16 to refer to "the undeserving world of mankind," not to the "elect world."[375] Thomas Ford (AD 1598–1674), also a member of the Westminster Assembly, held to universal atonement and argued such from John 3:16. Ford argued that the unsaved who die in their sins perish not for lack of a remedy in the death of Christ for their sins but because of their failure to apply that remedy. He stated:

373 A. F. Mitchell & J. P. Struthers, eds., *Minutes of the Sessions of the Westminster Assembly of Divines* (Edinburgh: W. Blackwood and Sons, 1874), 152.

374 Ibid., 154.

375 J. Arrowsmith, *Armilla Catechetica. A Chain of Principles; or an Orderly Concatenation of Theological Aphorism and Exercitations; Wherein, the Chief Heads of Christian Religion Are Asserted and Improved* (Cambridge: John Field, 1659), 182. Mitchell and Struthers (*Minutes*, lvii) said that Thomas Gataker (AD 1574–1654), Joseph Caryl (AD 1602–1673), Jeremiah Burroughs (c. AD 1600–1646), and William Strong (d. AD 1654) concurred with this interpretation of John 3:16.

> For proof hereof, I appeal to John 3:16, "God so loved the world, that he gave his only begotten Son, that whosoever believes on him, should not perish." Here's enough said, to show, that God is not wanting to me, but that they are wanting to themselves. There's provision made such, and so much, as none can perish, but they who refuse to make use of it. . . .
>
> Let it also be considered, that the word [world] cannot rationally be taken in any other sense. For in the next verse, [John 3:17] it is meant of the world, whereof some are saved, and some perish, (as Reverend Davenant observes) and that they who perish, perish only because they believe not on the Son of God.

Ford also questioned the reasonableness of preaching to all and attempting to persuade all to believe in Christ if the preacher himself is not persuaded that there is a sufficient provision (unlimited atonement) in the death of Christ if any should exercise faith in Christ:

> As I take it, we should not persuade men to believe on Christ, by telling them: "If they believe, then Christ died for them." Rather, as I suppose, we may safely tell them, "That Christ died for them, and thereupon persuade them, to believe on him." We are bound to believe, that the thing is true, before we can believe our share in it. The object is in order of nature, before the action. My believing makes not a thing true; but it is true in itself and therefore I believe it. And this is the method of Scripture, as far as I know. The Feast was first prepared, and the Guests were invited: All things are ready, come unto the marriage, Mat. 22:4. The Jews, who are the guests there invited, refused to come: But were they not cast utterly off, and put into that condition, wherein they abide unto this day, upon this account "That the Son of God came to his own, and his own received him not"? [John 1:11.]. How could they refuse, if there were no provision made for them? Or justly perish only for refusing? I am very willing to believe: "That Christ was offered for me, before he was offered to me, and that if I die in my sins, it is only for my not receiving Christ offered to me." Sure I am, that Scripture never lays the death of Sinners, upon the want of a λυτρον, or price of redemption; but always upon unbelief, disobedience, neglect of, and setting light by Christ, and the things of Christ. And this is enough to serve my turn: "That Scripture never hints any impediment to men's salvation, more than an evil heart of unbelief. . . ."
>
> And to these I say, if they die in their sins, it is not upon the account of Christ's not dying for them, but only for their not-believing on him. And for this I appeal to the whole tenor of Scripture, and in particular to John 3.16. where the gift of Christ is common, but the efficacy of it limited to believing.
>
> Let others dispute, for whom Christ died, (I cannot hinder them). I am sure Christ never suffered or satisfied for any, so as they shall have the saving

> benefits of his death, without laying hold on him by a lively Faith. And I shall be as sure, on the other side: "That whosoever shall believe on the Lord Jesus, with all his heart, he shall be saved by him." And this I take to be sound doctrine, that may be safely preached to all, and every one, without exception, *viz.*: "You, O man, whoever you are, Christ died for you; and if you believe on him, with all your heart, as God hath commanded you, you shall be saved." In this we preach the tenor of the Gospel.[376]

William Twisse (AD 1578–1646) served as the Prolocutor of the Westminster Assembly and preached the opening sermon. He was an interesting fellow: a supralapsarian Calvinist, a premillennialist, and a Hypothetical Universalist. Twisse's belief in universal atonement can be illustrated in numerous quotations from his writings.

> I am ready to profess, and that I suppose, as out of the mouth of all divines, that everyone who hears the gospel (without distinction between elect and reprobate) is bound to believe that Christ died for him (1 John 5.10,11), so far as to secure both the pardon of his sins, and the salvation of his soul, in case he repents and believes.[377]

Notice that this statement by Twisse contains the usual terminology found in the writings of the Hypothetical Universalists: "Everyone who hears the gospel . . . is bound to believe that Christ died for him . . . in case he repents and believes." With respect to 1 John 2:2, Twisse preferred to take "world" as the elect, but notice he also said "we willingly confesse, that Christ dyed to obtaine salvation for all and every one that beleeve in him." Twisse (and Baxter) both assert that there is a universal satisfaction for the sins of all people coupled with the conditionality of salvation: repentance and faith.[378]

Joseph Hall quoted Twisse as saying,

> When we say Christ died for mankind, we mean that Christ died for the benefit of mankind. Now, let this benefit be distinguished, and contentions hereabouts will cease: for, if this benefit be considered as the remission of sins, and the salvation of our souls; these are benefits obtainable only, upon the condition of faith and repentance: on the one side, no man will say that Christ died to this end to procure forgiveness and salvation to every one, whether they believe and repent,

376 Thomas Ford, *Autokatakritos; or, The Sinner Condemned of Himself* (London: Printed for Edward Brewster, and are to be sold by Giles Widowes, at the Maiden-head, over against the Half-Moon, in Aldersgate-street, near Jewen-street, 1668), 22–23, 39–40, 46–56.

377 W. Twisse, *The Riches of God's Love unto the Vessels of Mercy, Consistent with his Absolute Hatred or Reprobation of the Vessels of Wrath* (Oxford: L. L. and H. H., 1653), I:154.

378 So noted by Boersma, *Hot Pepper Corn*, 197.

> or no; so, on the other, none will deny but that he died to this end, that salvation and remission should redound to all and every one, in case they should repent and believe: for this depends upon the sufficiency of that price, which our Saviour paid for the redemption of the world, &c. And to pay a price sufficient for the redemption of all and every one, is, in a fair sense, to redeem all and every one.[379]

When Twisse spoke of Christ dying "for mankind," he intended a reference to the provision of salvation (extent) and not about God's will behind that provision (intent), hence Christ died "for the benefit of mankind." Notice he said one should "distinguish" the "benefit" and "contentions will cease." He then explained the distinction. No one receives the benefit of Christ's death for sins apart from "the condition of faith and repentance." The death of Christ does not *ipso facto* bring forgiveness of sins apart from conditions. On the other hand, "none will deny" that Christ died for the sins of all people conditionally: "In case they should repent and believe." Twisse affirmed a universal sufficiency in Christ's death: "To pay a price sufficient for the redemption of all and every one." Notice the specificity of this language. Twisse was drawing a distinction between redemption accomplished (which is for all people) and redemption applied (which is only for those who believe).

J. I. Packer commented:

> Baxter now remembered that Twisse, his oracle, had himself asserted that Christ had died for all in such a sense that salvation could be offered to all without exception, on condition of faith (though, plainly, he had failed to integrate this idea with the rest of his soteriology), and, reviewing the case, was converted to a belief in universal redemption.[380]

---

379 Hall's reference reads: "D. Twisse in his *Animadversions upon D. Jackson.* And, to the same effect, D Rivetius Disp. 6. [5. de statu humil. Christi.] *de Redemptione.*" Cited in J. Hall, "The Peacemaker, Laying Forth the Right Way of Peace, in Matters of Religion," in *The Works of the Right Reverend Joseph Hall, D.D.*, 9 vols., ed. P. Wynter (Oxford: Oxford University Press, 1863), 7:636. Notice that Hall linked Rivet's position with Twisse's mediating or moderate view of the atonement. See A. Rivet, "Disputationes Theologicae Undecim, In Synopsi purioris Theologiae Professorum Leydensium: Disputatio V. Thesis XXIII," in *Operum theologicorum quae Latine edidit*, 3 vols. (Rotterdam: Arnoldi Leers, 1651–1660), 3:760; or "XXVII. De Statu Humiliationis Christi," in *Synopsis Purioris Theologiae* (Lugduni Batavorum: Apud Didericum Donner, 1881), 268. In Denlinger's excellent chapter on Scottish Hypothetical Universalism, he noted that Robert Baron (c.1596–1639) appealed to André Rivet to support his moderate position on the atonement, along with Gregory of Nazianzus, Ambrose, Chrysostom, Augustine, Prosper of Aquitaine, the British delegates to the Synod of Dort (especially Martinius), Bullinger, Bucer, Calvin, Marlorat, Musculus, Gwalther, Pareus, and Cameron, among others. See A. C. Denlinger, "Scottish Hypothetical Universalism: Robert Baron (c.1596–1639) on God's Love and Christ's Death for All," in *Reformed Orthodoxy in Scotland: Essays on Scottish Theology 1560–1775*, ed. A. C. Denlinger (London: Bloomsbury Academic, 2015), 88, 90–91, 95, 97–98.

380 J. I. Packer, *The Redemption & Restoration of Man in the Thought of Richard Baxter* (Vancouver: Regent College, 2003), 204. The section to which Packer refers in Baxter's work on *Universal Redemption* states:

> And for the first some say by the World, is meant the Elect part of the World; some say (as Dr. Twisse and others) it is meant of Mankind as distinct from Angels, excluding none, and not of the Elect only; and withal that it speaks only of the sufficiency of Christ's Satisfaction; which if it were

Additional evidence for Twisse's commitment to unlimited atonement can be found in several of his works[381] and in Hans Boersma's *A Hot Pepper Corn: Richard Baxter's Doctrine of Justification in Its Seventeenth-Century Context of Controversy.*[382]

Robert Letham, in his significant work *The Westminster Assembly*, correctly identified Calamy as a Hypothetical Universalist and cited from the *Minutes of the Sessions* how Calamy distinguished his position from Arminianism.

> They [Arminians] say Christ did not purchase any impetration. Calamy insisted his views "doth neither intrude upon either [the] doctrine of speciall election or speciall grace." His point was that Arminianism asserted that Christ simply suffered; all people are in a potentially salvable situation, so that any who believe will be saved. In contrast, he himself believed that Christ's death saves his elect and grants a conditional possibility of salvation to the rest. Seaman, supporting Calamy, argued that the views of the Remonstrants were irrelevant; what mattered was the truth or falsity of the case. Calamy, he insisted, was talking not of a salvability in relation to man, but to God; he has so far reconciled himself to the world that he would have mercy on whom he would have mercy.[383]

Letham continued:

> In each case, the hypothetical universalists failed to gain the approval of the Assembly, which remained steadfast. This was despite roughly one-third of the recorded speeches favoring Calamy's position. They could claim backing from the Thirty-nine Articles and legitimately disavow any connection with Arminianism. It is also inaccurate to describe them as Amyraldian as hypothetical universalism in England antedated Amyraut and did not go as far as he did in decretal dualism. . . . The Assembly was not a partisan body within the boundaries of its generic Calvinism, but allowed differing views to coexist.[384]

> not sufficient for All, there were no place for the General Promise, *Whoever believeth shall be Saved.* There is more truth and soundness in this exposition, than will stand with some other contradictory passages in the same Authors. For my part I stand to this exposition of Dr. Twisse (as you may find him industriously explaining this text, *Vindic. Grat. lib. 1. part 2. § 7. pag. [mihi]* 203).

(R. Baxter, *Universal Redemption of Mankind by the Lord Jesus Christ* [London: Printed for John Salusbury at the Rising Sun in Cornhill, 1694], 287).

381 See Twisse, *The Doctrine of the Synod of Dort and Arles Preface*, 15–17, 143–44, 152, 165; idem, *The Riches of God's Love unto the Vessels of Mercy, Consistent with His Absolute Hatred or Reprobation of the Vessels of Wrath* (Oxford: L. L. and H. H., 1653), I:5–6, 153–55; and *A Discovery of D. Iacksons Vanitie* (Amsterdam: Giles Thorp/London: W. Jones, 1631), 526–27.

382 Boersma, *Hot Pepper Corn*, 80–88.

383 R. Letham, *The Westminster Assembly: Reading Its Theology in Historical Context* (Phillipsburg, NJ: P&R, 2009), 176–77.

384 Ibid., 181–82.

David Ponter has questioned the accuracy of some of Letham's statements and conclusions. Noting that Letham's comments are helpful in showing the diversity of the question of the extent of the atonement at Westminster, he nonetheless erred on several points. For example, Amyraut "explicitly grounded foreknowledge in the unconditioned decree of God." But Letham may be relying on Warfield's and/or Smeaton's "faulty definition of Amyraut's theology," who themselves relied on Amyraut's opponents to formulate their definitions, when he described Amyraut's belief about God's decree "as based on the foreknowledge of God, simply considered." Ponter continued:

> The allegation that Amyraut posited a dualistic *decree* is misleading as it implies a twofold *univocal* decree (as Smeaton and Warfield exactly do imply). However, for Amyraut, the universal decree was an expression of the *revealed will*, and so does not contradict the absolute secret decree of God respecting the salvation of the elect. And, thus, when Amyraut did speak of distinct and seemingly sequential decrees, he did not attribute a univocal meaning to each decree, as is found in standard infra- and supralapsarian orderings. It is simply unhelpful to speak of Amyraut's distinctions as if they had the same logical relationship and nature one finds in the infra-and supralapsarian schemas.[385]

Letham also erred in his characterization of English Hypothetical Universalists "as not subscribing to the tenet that God in some way *intends* the salvation of all men." Theophilus Gale spoke of Davenant's statements on this issue demonstrating that Letham is in error.[386] Some Calvinists, such as Davenant, will use the strong volitional term "intent" for God's revealed will.[387]

Letham, following Moore, also erred in drawing a sharp dichotomy between the English and Salmurian Hypothetical Universalists with the original Reformers. As Ponter noted, "Richard Muller has rebutted this claim. Furthermore, no hard dichotomy exists between the Salmurian school and the English Hypothetical Universalists. Such attempted dichotomies, more often than not, rest on the mischaracterizations of Amyraut's doctrine of the decrees (Turretin, Smeaton, Warfield, *et. al.*)."[388]

---

385 D. Ponter, "Robert Letham on the English Hypothetical Universalists at the Westminster Assembly," *Calvin and Calvinism*, http://calvinandcalvinism.com/?p=5229.

386 As noted by Theophilus Gale, *The Court of the Gentiles. Part IV. Of Reformed Philosophie. Wherein Plato's Moral and Metaphysic or Prime Philosophie Is Reduced to a Useful Forme and Method* (London: J. Macock, 1677), 357 (II.v.4). For more on Gale, consult D. D. Wallace, *Shapers of English Calvinism, 1660–1714: Variety, Persistence, and Transformation* (Oxford: Oxford University Press, 2011), 87–119. Wallace stated that Calvinist Peter Sterry (b. AD 1613), parliament preacher in the 1640s and advisor to Oliver Cromwell in the 1650s, held to unlimited atonement (76).

387 Other Calvinists, whether high or moderate on the atonement, also used the strong volitional term "intent" for God's legislative will or for his desire for the salvation of all people expressed in the revealed will. Included in this list are J. Calvin, M. Martinius, J. Burroughs, A. Burgess, T. Gale, H. Scudder, J. Edwards, J. Flavel, J. Howe, E. Polhill, G. Swinnock, and G. Whitefield, to name a few.

388 Ponter, "Robert Letham on the English Hypothetical Universalists."

Ponter argued, contra Warfield, and as Muller has demonstrated,

> the WCF documents were not written to exclude the theology of the English Hypothetical Universalists. The suggestion that about one third of the assembly delegates would sign a document that repudiated a core element of their theology is nonsensical. This, along with the fact that many English Hypothetical Universalists continued to subscribe to the WCF documents in the proceeding decades makes Warfield's claims highly implausible.[389]

Letham did, however, make the important point that it is historically inaccurate to ascribe the designation "Amyraldians" to the moderate Calvinists at the Westminster Assembly:

> Amyraut held that God, foreseeing the fall, sent his Son to atone for the sins of all people. God also foreseeing that not all would accept the gospel, elected some to salvation. Calamy and the English hypothetical universalists held to an atonement effective for the elect and conditional for the non-elect, to a decree of election with the rest passed by. For these theological reasons, it is a mistake to describe these Assembly men as Amyraldians, as Fesko does; it is also historically erroneous, since this strand of thought was present in England long before Amyraut wrote on the subject.[390]

A. Craig Troxel demonstrated confusion about Hypothetical Universalism at the Westminster Assembly when he suggested that "forms of Pelagianism and Arminianism . . . fall, in general, under the heading of 'Hypothetical Universalism.'"[391] Troxel did not cite Amyraut from any primary sources. He also wrongly identified Millard Erickson as an Amyraldian Hypothetical Universalist.[392]

At the time of the Westminster Assembly, Fesko noted Gisbert Voetius offered a basic taxonomy of four views on the extent of the atonement:

1. Universal satisfaction for every person (the Remonstrants).
2. Those who affirm the universal sufficiency of Christ's satisfaction and argue that it is applied in some sense to all but only effectively for the elect. (This is

389 Ibid.

390 Letham, *The Westminster Assembly*, 178. See also J. Fesko, "The Westminster Confession and Lapsarianism: Calvin and the Divines," in *The Westminster Confession into the 21st Century: Essays in Remembrance of the 350th Anniversary of the Westminster Assembly*, 3 vols., ed. J. L. Duncan III (Fearn, Scotland: Mentor, 2004), 2:477–525.

391 A. Troxel, "Amyraut 'At' the Assembly: The *Westminster Confession of Faith* and the Extent of the Atonement," *Presbyterion* 22 (1996): 46.

392 Ibid., 54–55.

misleading because it fails to distinguish which kind of sufficiency, intrinsic or extrinsic, is meant.)

3. Those who admit the universal sufficiency of Christ's satisfaction but deny its application to all (the scholastics, e.g., Lombard, Aquinas, as well as Calvin, and others; same ambiguity as #2 above).
4. Those who hold that Christ died solely for the elect.[393]

Fesko classified these respectively as universalism, Hypothetical Universalism, the classical sufficient/efficient position, and strict particularism.[394]

But there are problems with Voetius's taxonomy. With respect to the actual extent of the atonement, considered in distinction from God's intent to apply, the first three positions were in agreement: Christ satisfied for the sins of all people. The Hypothetical Universalists asserted their agreement with the Remonstrants on the simple question of the extent of the atonement. As we have seen, the Lombardian sufficient/efficient formula originally asserted that Christ died for the sins of all people but only effectually applied to the elect. All Hypothetical Universalists agreed with this. In fact, as we have demonstrated, it was the advocates of limited atonement who self-consciously qualified and modified the original sufficient/efficient formula into a mere hypothetical sufficiency.

Any taxonomy on the question of the extent of the atonement must carefully distinguish between the intent to apply and extent. It was on the question of intent where the Remonstrants differed with both Hypothetical Universalists and strict particularists. But when it came to the actual extent of the atonement considered in and of itself, Arminians, English Hypothetical Universalists, and Amyraldians were in agreement: Christ satisfied for the sins of all people. This is the key distinction within Reformed theology: only Fesko's fourth category of strict particularism denies Christ suffered for the sins of all men.

We may summarize the Westminster Assembly with respect to the extent of the atonement as follows:

1. Many at the assembly affirmed universal atonement and rejected limited atonement.[395] "About two-thirds of the delegates were for limited atonement; one-third were for either universal atonement or a 'dual' approach."[396]

---

393 J. V. Fesko, *The Theology of the Westminster Standards: Historical Context & Theological Insights* (Wheaton, IL: Crossway, 2014), 191; citing and translating G. Voetius, "Problematum de Merito Christi, Pars Secunda," in *Select arum Disputationum Theologicarum, Pars Secunda* (Utrecht: Johannem a Waesberge, 1654), 251–53.

394 Fesko, *The Theology of the Westminster Standards*, 189.

395 Moore, *English Hypothetical Universalism*, 148–52. "The Reformed Orthodox had to wait until 1675 before a Reformed Confession unequivocally and without any possible means of escape explicitly condemned and excluded Hypothetical Universalism in all its forms: *Formula Consensus Helvetica.* But it never obtained widespread use" (152). See also Wallace, *Puritans and Predestination*, 133–34.

396 C. Daniel, *The History and Theology of Calvinism* (Springfield, IL: Good Books, 2003), 51.

2. The Westminster standards were not written in such a way as to exclude English Hypothetical Universalism or Amyraldianism, as Baxter, Muller, Fesko, Gatiss, and others correctly noted.[397]
3. Upon examination of the early and classical period of Reformed theology, including the Westminster Assembly, the extent question was never satisfactorily answered.[398]

Richard Baxter said of Chapter VIII of the Westminster Confession, "I have spoken with an eminent Divine, yet living, that was of the Assembly, who assured mee that they purposely avoided determining that Controversie, and som of them profest themselves for the middle way of Universal Redemption."[399]

For the evidence that many at Westminster did not affirm limited atonement (strict particularism), consult Mitchell and Struthers's *Minutes of the Sessions of the Westminster Assembly of Divines.*[400]

Conclusion

John Spurr has argued convincingly for the fluidity of Calvinism within Puritan theology during the seventeenth century. It was a theology "constantly being defined in religious controversy, in intellectual speculation, and in pastoral practice."[401] The debates over the extent of the atonement within Calvinism during this period serve as exhibit A for Spurr's claim.

A significant number of Anglicans and Puritans in England during this period subscribed to a form of universal atonement. In fact, Baxter went so far as to estimate that "half the divines of England" held to universal atonement.[402] Furthermore,

---

397 R. Baxter, *Certain Disputations of Right to Sacraments and the True Nature of Visible Christianity* (London: William Du Gard, 1657), B4r; R. Muller, "John Cameron and Covenant Theology," *Mid-America Journal of Theology* 17 (2006): 36–38; J. V. Fesko, *The Theology of the Westminster Standards* (Wheaton, IL: Crossway, 2014), 202–3; Gatiss, "A Deceptive Clarity?," 194; and L. Gatiss, "'Shades of Opinion within a Generic Calvinism.' The Particular Redemption Debate at the Westminster Assembly," *Reformed Theological Review* 69 (2010): 101–18. Muller wrote: "The Westminster Confession was in fact written with this diversity in view, encompassing confessionally the variant Reformed views on the nature of the limitation of Christ's satisfaction to the elect, just as it is written to be inclusive of the infra- and the supralapsarian views on predestination" (R. Muller, *Post-Reformation Reformed Dogmatics: The Rise and Development of Reformed Orthodoxy, ca. 1520–ca. 1725,* 4 vols., 2nd ed. [Grand Rapids, MI: Baker, 2003], 1:76–77).

398 Thomas, *Extent of the Atonement,* 250. For more on the Westminster Assembly and its theology, especially the influence of Ussher on the Hypothetical Universalists and those like Calamy, Twisse, and others who espoused Hypothetical Universalism, consult J. V. Fesko, *The Theology of the Westminster Standards,* esp. 169–206.

399 Baxter, *Certain Disputations of Right,* B4r.

400 Mitchell and Struthers, *Minutes,* liv–lxi. Schaff (*Creeds of Christendom,* 1:770) also mentioned the name of Thomas Gataker in his analysis of the Westminster Confession. C. Daniel noted the diverse theological makeup of the delegates at Westminster: "About 3/4 of the divines were Infralapsarian, 1/4 Supralapsarian. About 2/3 were for limited atonement, 1/3 for either universal atonement or a 'dual' approach" (*The History and Theology of Calvinism,* 51).

401 J. Spurr, *English Puritanism: 1603–1689* (New York: St. Martin's, 1998), 166–70.

402 R. Baxter, *Certain Disputations of Right,* B2v.

Hypothetical Universalism antedated Particular Redemption, Arminianism, and Amyraldianism. It is historically inaccurate to label those like Ussher, Davenant, and Preston as Amyraldians since they rejected what would later be known as the Amyraldian view of the divine decree.[403]

Further, it is a gross historical inaccuracy to use "Hypothetical Universalism" as something of a catch-all term to include Pelagianism and Arminianism as some in the Reformed tradition have been prone to do.[404] It is also unhelpful to attempt to merge Hypothetical Universalism and Amyraldianism in an effort to forge one unified "middle way" between Arminianism and high Calvinism as Baxter did.[405] The evidence demonstrates clearly that far more was happening than an open-range feud between the Reformed and the Arminians.[406]

Joseph Truman (AD 1631–1671) illustrated the viewpoint of those in the Reformed tradition toward the end of the seventeenth century who rejected limited atonement and yet affirmed, contrary to Arminianism, God's intention to save only the elect. Regarding the two sets of passages in the New Testament that speak of Christ dying for all people and those that speak of his dying for a select group like the church, Truman stated:

> Though God and Christ did, as one saith, *æque* intend this satisfaction, a propitiation conditionally applicable to every one; yet he did not *ex æquo*, as fully intend it for to be actually applied to every man. . . . You cannot say, the Devils continue to be condemned, because they reject Christ; because, if they should accept him, they would still perish; for there was no satisfaction made for them: And may not the same be said of them that perish, if no satisfaction be made for them? . . .
>
> If Election and Redemption were of the same latitude and strictness, you might as well say to sinners, Repent, for you are elected, for you are foreknown in the Scripture-sense, for you are given to Christ by the Father, in that special sense; as, Repent, for you are redeemed, Christ dyed for you; *you are bought with a price: therefore glorifie God with your bodies and spirits, which are his*: But the Apostle would not venture to speak thus, You are elected; therefore repent, glorifie God: for he should have spoken what he knew not to be true.
>
> I will say no more but this here: Whether is it a more likely way to lay a foundation for Religion in this World, to encourage and draw mens hearts to repent, return, to tell them Christ hath dyed for you, and hath obtained this

403 Moore, *English Hypothetical Universalism*, 217.

404 These inaccuracies have been pointed out by Moore, *English Hypothetical Universalism*, 217.

405 Ibid., 219.

406 For the situation with the Anglican Reformed tradition during the late seventeenth and early eighteenth centuries, consult S. Hampton, *Anti-Arminians: The Anglican Reformed Tradition from Charles II to George I* (Oxford: Oxford University Press, 2008).

> of the Father for you, that if you return, you shall live, notwithstanding all your former sins; or, to say, Repent, return: for, any thing you know, Christ hath dyed for you; for any thing you know, he hath obtained this from God, that if you turn, you shall live; though it is ten to one he hath not: or however, we cannot tell whether he hath or no. And if he hath not, then as this is true, that if the Devils should repent and return, they should yet perish, because no Satisfaction was made for them; so if you should repent and believe, you should yet perish, because no Satisfaction was made for you.[407]

Toward the end of the seventeenth century, William Lorimer (AD 1640–1722) assessed the controversy over the extent of the atonement and the so-called middle-way approach, with which he himself identified. He noted that the controversy began with Beza and Piscator and their writing on limited atonement. He correctly identified the Arminian position on extent as Christ died "equally" for all people. He identified the Arminian position and the strict particularist position as "extremes" and uses the term "middle way" to describe the position that historically antedates Arminianism and limited atonement and was correctly expressed in the Lombardian formula.

Lorimer affirmed that all the Reformed agreed that Christ died efficaciously for the elect alone. Important for our purposes is his affirmation that the "middle way" was not only tolerated but approved by the Synod of Dort, and that long before Dort, the view was held by the earliest Reformers in England and on the continent, including Calvin.[408]

It is now recognized by Reformed scholarship that the Westminster Confession did not ensconce limited atonement to the exclusion of unlimited atonement. The standards clearly leave room for Hypothetical Universalism. Fesko argued:

> Confirmation that the Standards leave hypothetical universalism as an option appears when we compare the Confession with Turretin's *Formula Consensus* (1675), which was written specifically to refute Amyraut, though not necessarily the view of Davenant, Ussher, or Twisse. Turretin likely considered those three within the pale of orthodoxy, since Davenant and other hypothetical universalists were signatories to Dort, whereas Amyraut's views arose some fifteen years later. The Formula Consensus states:
>
> We cannot approve the contrary doctrine of those who affirm that of His own intention, by His Own counsel and that of the Father who sent Him, Christ died for all and each upon the impossible condition, provided they believe; that He obtained for all a salvation which, nevertheless, is not applied

407 J. Truman, *The Great Propitiation; or, Christ's Satisfaction; and Man's Justification by it upon His Faith; that Is, Belief of, and Obedience to the Gospel* (London: A. Maxwell, 1672), 216–20.

408 W. Lorimer, *An Apology for the Ministers Who Subscribed Only unto the Stating of the Truths and Errours in Mr. William's Book* (London: Printed for John Lawrence, at the Angel in the Poultry, 1694), 191–92.

> to all, and by His death merited salvation and faith for no one individually and certainly (*proprie et actu*), but only removed the obstacle of Divine justice, and acquired for the Father the liberty of entering into a new covenant of grace with all men.
>
> Nothing of this nature appears in the Westminster Standards. And even the Formula characterizes Amyraut's view as "contrary to the plain scriptures and the glory of Christ" (§ 16), but not as heresy.[409]

The earliest Reformed confession to affirm a *strictly* limited atonement is probably Turretin's *Formula Consensus* (AD 1675). As noted above, it clearly and without equivocation advocates limited atonement to the exclusion of unlimited atonement.

Herman Bavinck assessed the situation in England with respect to the debate over the extent of the atonement in the seventeenth century:

> In England, over against the rigorously Reformed school of Twisse, Rutherford, Gillespie, [Thomas] Goodwin, and others, there was a moderate group represented by Davenant, Calamy, Arrowsmith, Seaman, and others and especially by Richard Baxter. Their view completely agreed in substance with that of the French theologians Cameron, Testard, Amyraut, and others. There was an antecedent decree by which Christ had conditionally satisfied for all, on condition of faith, and another subsequent particular decree by which he had so made satisfaction for the elect that he would in time also grant them faith and infallibly lead them to salvation.[410]

After the return of the Monarchy under Charles II (AD 1660), many new bishops were appointed in the Church of England, and very few of these were Calvinists. In 1662, as a result of the Act of Uniformity, two thousand ministers, mostly Calvinists, resigned rather than conform to the new laws of the Church of England. From that time forward, Calvinism never held the position it had once enjoyed in the Anglican Church. Though some Calvinists retained a commitment to limited atonement, others were certainly more moderate on the extent of the atonement, affirming a limited *intent* to apply the atonement only to the elect, but simultaneously affirming an unlimited *extent* of the atonement.

---

409 Fesko, *The Theology of the Westminster Standards*, 201.

410 H. Bavinck, *Sin and Salvation in Christ*, vol. 3 of *Reformed Dogmatics* (Grand Rapids, MI: Baker, 2006), 461.

4

The Modern Era and the Extent of the Atonement

The Eighteenth Century

The eighteenth century witnessed the birth of the modern missionary movement with William Carey; great revivals in England and America with the preaching of Wesley, Whitefield, and Edwards; and religious cross-pollination between England and America. During this century, the debates over the extent of the atonement continued between the Reformed and non-Reformed as well as among the Reformed themselves.

The Marrow Controversy[1]

One major controversy in the eighteenth century that related to the extent of the atonement, although not limited to that subject, was the Marrow controversy in Scotland and England. Fisher's *The Marrow of Modern Divinity* became very popular after its

1 E. Fisher, *The Marrow of Modern Divinity*, ed. C. G. M'Crie (Glasgow: David Bryce & Son, 1902). An accessible edition is E. Fisher, *The Marrow of Modern Divinity with Notes by Thomas Boston* (Fearn, Scotland: Christian Focus, 2009). See also Robertson, *History of the Atonement Controversy*; D. C. Lachman, *The Marrow Controversy: An Historical and Theological Analysis* (Edinburgh: Rutherford, 1988); D. Wright and N. M. De S. Cameron, *Dictionary of Scottish Church History and Theology* (Edinburgh: InterVarsity, 1993). The most recent and probably best analysis of the history and theology of the controversy is W. Van Doodewaard, *The Marrow Controversy and Seceder Tradition* (Grand Rapids, MI: Reformation Heritage, 2011).

publication in 1646, passing through numerous editions. Thomas Boston discovered it and republished it in 1718.[2] *The Marrow* stated:

> Wherefore, as Paul and Silas said to the jailor, so say I unto you, believe on the Lord Jesus Christ, and thou shalt be saved: that is, be verily persuaded in your heart, that Jesus Christ is yours, and that you shall have life and salvation by him: that whatsoever Christ did for the redemption of mankind, he did it for you.[3]

> Go preach the gospel to every creature, that is, Go and tell every man without exception, that *here is good news for* him; *Christ is dead* for him; *and if he will take him and accept of his righteousness, he shall have him.*[4]

The Marrow's appearance in Scotland raised controversy, and a growing opposition ensued, led by Principal Hadow of St. Andrews. The General Assembly of the Church appointed a committee for "Purity of Doctrine," divided into two sections; one meeting at Edinburgh and the other at St. Andrews. At Edinburgh, four men were examined, including Hog, who had written the preface to the republished *The Marrow* in 1718, and Hamilton of Airth. Hamilton affirmed two kinds of sufficiency with respect to the death of Christ: an "absolute and intrinsic sufficiency" based on the deity of Christ, and a "federal and legal sufficiency" based on the fullness of Christ's satisfaction of the law in his death and seen in Scripture passages affirming that Christ gave himself a ransom for all, he tasted death for every man, and he became a propitiation for the sins of the whole world.[5]

The publication of pamphlets and frequent presbyterial and synodical debates prolonged the affair. At the 1720 General Assembly, *The Marrow* was condemned and preachers were prohibited from recommending the book in their preaching, writing, or printing. But this act of condemning *The Marrow* did not sit well with many. Hog, Ebenezer and Ralph Erskine, Bathgate, and Wardlaw drew up a draft to be presented to the General Assembly. Some were not satisfied with it, and Thomas Boston drew up another version, which, after further editing, was submitted to the committee of the General Assembly.[6] This was ultimately to no avail, and another committee was appointed by the General Assembly to draw up a vindication for the assembly's act of censure. The result was the Assembly of 1722 issued a second act that explained and

2 For Boston's agreement with the theology of the Marrow Men, see below under Thomas Boston.
3 E. Fisher, *Marrow of Modern Divinity*, 112.
4 Ibid.
5 Robertson, *History of the Atonement Controversy*, 16.
6 Ibid., 20–21.

confirmed the act of 1720 with a refusal to repeal it.[7] The so-called Marrow Men began to experience "grievous persecution."[8]

Over the next ten years, the situation continued to broil. A petition containing almost two thousand signatures to rescind the Act of 1720 was presented to the General Assembly in 1732, only one year before the famous Secession in the Scottish Church took place. It was dismissed by the assembly without any hearing.[9]

The Marrow controversy served as a major cause of the secession from the Church of Scotland in 1733. In 1742 the secessionists issued the "Act Concerning the Doctrine of Grace" wherein "the said doctrine . . . is asserted and vindicated from the errors vented and published in some Acts of the Assemblies of this Church."[10] In this document the authors speak, as did *The Marrow of Modern Divinity*, of the "Deed of Gift, or Grant" that God had made with all mankind and guarantees the universal offer of the gospel.

> Now this Deed of Gift, or Grant, made to all mankind, in the Word, is the very foundation of our faith, and the ground and warrant of the ministerial offer, without which no minister could have authority to preach the gospel to every creature, or to make a full, free, and unhampered offer of Christ, his grace, righteousness, and salvation to all mankind, to whom they have access in providence. . . . This Deed of Gift, or Grant, of Christ in the Word unto mankind-sinners, as such, is expressly set forth in several texts of Scripture.[11]

At the same time, the document affirmed, in good Reformed style, that Christ died efficaciously only for the elect and that the Arminian doctrine of an atonement made with an equal intent to apply to all people is erroneous.[12]

> Holding such sentiments, the Fathers of the Secession, were accustomed, along with other orthodox divines, to restrict the terms,—substitute,—representative,—and surety,—to Christ as undertaking for the elect; and hence, they scrupled not to affirm, that he represented and suffered for them only. But while thus refusing to admit, that Christ died for all, destinated for all alike, they notwithstanding strenuously contended for the doctrine, that Christ "was dead for all," and dead for all alike,—that is, as they explained it, dead for all to come to, Christ with his grace and righteousness, and salvation being accessible to all, and not only so, but actually made over to the

7 Ibid., 38. It should be noted that issues other than the extent of the atonement, such as the nature of faith, etc., were a part of this dispute.
8 Ibid., 41.
9 Ibid., 42.
10 Ibid., 46–47.
11 Ibid., 52.
12 Ibid., 48–49.

> acceptance of all, by a Deed of Gift, which Deed of Gift afforded to all, a full, legal, and equal right to appropriate Christ and all his benefits.[13]

Robertson commented on the significance of the "Deed of Gift":

> From these extracts, it appears, that the Marrowmen did not resolve the Deed of Gift into the simple offer of the gospel, but considered it rather as the ground upon which the offer is made, the latter presupposing the former. Hence the minister of the gospel is to offer salvation to all, not merely because he is commanded by God to do so, but because he can point to the Father's Deed of Gift, which constitutes the ground upon which the offer is based.[14]

In a sermon on Heb 11:7, Ebenezer Erskine spoke of Christ's human nature and how all mankind is related to him: "It is impossible to conceive how all mankind, especially gospel hearers, should not have an interest in his death—I mean such as warrants them to say in faith—'He loved me, and gave himself for me.'"[15]

What is important to note here is that these Calvinists affirmed both a particular redemption with respect to the elect and perhaps an unlimited atonement for all people, or at least an atonement that removed "all legal bars that stood in the sinner's way."[16] This "unlimited" scope of the atonement is an expression of God's love to all humanity. The Marrow Men referred to this love as God's "giving love" and they appealed to verses like John 3:16 to establish it.

In 1828 William Pringle preached two sermons on the text "It Is Finished" (John 19:30), in which he asserted Christ died for all men and this was the foundation for the universal gospel offer. Forrester, who was assisting Pringle with the Lord's Supper at the time of the sermon, complained to the Presbytery of Perth. Robertson noted:

> From the evidence adduced, it appeared Mr Pringle did not deny that, in connexion with the decree of election Christ died for the elect only, but that in addition to this, he maintained that Christ died for all in the sense of his atonement being sufficient for all, this universal sufficiency constituting the basis upon which the invitations of the gospel proceeded.[17]

The synod took up the matter in 1830 and found that the accusation was groundless in that Pringle did not teach anything inconsistent with doctrinal standards of the

13 Ibid., 57.
14 Ibid., 61.
15 Ibid., 65–66.
16 Ibid., 49.
17 Ibid., 154.

church. What happened next is most interesting. The synod appointed a committee to address how the subject of the extent of the atonement should be treated by ministers. Preachers were enjoined

> to be on their guard against introducing discussions in their ministrations, or employing language which may seem to oppose the doctrine of particular redemption, or that Christ in making atonement for sin was substituted in the room of the elect only, and which may unsettle the minds of the people on this point, or give occasion to members of other churches to suspect the purity of our faith. . . . and it recommends likewise the avoidance of such language as may seem to oppose the doctrine, "that Christ in making atonement for sin was substituted in the room of the elect only."[18]

The charge continued to state:

> The Gospel Call, as addressed by God, to sinners of mankind as such is founded on the all sufficient virtue of the death of Christ for the salvation of guilty men, without exception,—on God's Gift of his Son, that whosoever believeth on him might not perish, but have everlasting life, and on his command to all to whom it comes to believe in the name of his Son whom he hath sent.[19]

The Marrow controversy demonstrated that some Calvinists in Scotland affirmed a form of unlimited atonement along with their commitment to particular redemption in terms of God's intent to save only the elect.

Thomas Boston (AD 1676–1732)

Thomas Boston republished Fisher's *The Marrow of Modern Divinity* in 1718 in Scotland, leading to the Marrow controversy. He was himself likely committed to unlimited atonement:

> But that God hath given eternal life to a certain select set of men, can never, in reason be deemed to be a warrant for *all* men to believe. Moreover, the great sin of unbelief lies in *not believing* this *record*; but it doth not lie in not believing that God hath given eternal life to *actual believers*, or to the *elect*; for the most desperate unbelievers believe *that*, insomuch that their belief of it adds to their torment; but it lies in their not believing, that to mankind-sinners, and to *themselves* in particular, God hath given eternal life. This is what flies in

18 Ibid., 156–57.
19 Ibid., 157.

the face of the gospel of God, which is to the proclaimed deed of the *gift* and *grant* of Christ and all his benefits to sinners of mankind, declaring the grant thereof to be *made* to them, and calling them to *take* possession of the same as their *own*.[20]

In one of his sermons, Boston stated the following:

Christ is given to mankind-sinners indefinitely. It is not to the elect only, but to sinners indefinitely, elect or not elect; sinners of the race of Adam without exception, whatever they have been, whatever they are, whatever qualifications they have, whatever they want.

1. This gift and grant is conceived in the same ample terms, without any restriction to any particular set of men.
2. Christ is given to mankind-sinners as the manna was given to the Israelites. Now the manna was given to the Israelites indefinitely; to those who loathed it as well as to them that loved it.
3. There is made to mankind-sinners indefinitely a gift of the benefits of his purchase, which yet are never given but in and through himself.
4. Lastly, if Christ were not given to mankind-sinners indefinitely, but there were some of the world who have no part in the gift of Christ, then the ministers of the gospel might not offer him to all, nor might all receive him.

Behold here, admire, and believe that the great love of God to a lost world, in providing a Saviour, and such a Saviour for them, even his own Son! The Scripture speaks of this in a very high strain. John 3.16, "God so loved the world, that he gave his only begotten Son," &c. There was a man-love in God, Titus 3:4, "But the kindness and love of God our Saviour towards man appeared,"—a love of the kind, mankind. It has appeared in two eminent instances: first, in securing by an irreversible decree the salvation of some of them; second, in providing a Saviour for the whole of the kind, constituting his own Son Saviour to the lost family of Adam indefinitely. Believe it with application to yourselves. If upon this a secret murmur begins to go through your heart—*But it was not for me*; crush it in the bud, for it is a bud of hell. If you are not one of the devil kind, but of sinful mankind, it *was* for you. The Father gave Christ a Saviour for you, that if you would believe on him, you

20 T. Boston, *A View of the Covenant of Grace from the Sacred Records* (Edinburgh: J. Gray, 1775), 261–62 (emphasis in original).

should not perish; he sent his Son from heaven with full instructions and ample powers to save you, if you will believe.[21]

These statements appear to indicate Boston was likely moderate on the atonement, though in other places Boston sounded stricter in his view of extent.

Daniel Whitby (AD 1638–1726)

Whitby was an Arminian Priest in the Church of England. In 1710 he wrote his *Discourse on the Five Points*[22] against Calvinism, which eventually drew responses from the English Particular Baptist John Gill (*The Cause of God and Truth* [1735]) and the American Congregationalist Jonathan Edwards (*Freedom of the Will* [1754]). Whitby's treatment of the extent of the atonement is in Discourse II and covers eighty pages.[23]

Whitby rejected as "absurd" the notion that Christ died sufficiently for all but intentionally only for the elect, leaving all the non-elect "under an impossibility of pardon and salvation."[24] This being the case, it cannot be the duty of any besides the elect to believe in Christ. Whitby likewise rejected the moderate Calvinist understanding of the intent of the atonement (though he agreed with them on the actual extent of the atonement), as well as universalism such that all for whom Christ died will be saved.

Whitby affirmed Christ died *equally* for all with the intent to save all who meet the condition of faith.[25] The new covenant is equally established "to all who perform the conditions of it." He noted there is "not one word" in Scripture declaring Christ died only for the elect.[26]

Whitby answered a number of objections raised by limitarians, including the usage of the word "many" in extent-related contexts. Christ cannot be said to die for "many" exclusive of "all" any more than Daniel can be said to affirm a limited resurrection when he said "many shall rise from the dead" (Dan 12:2). Daniel's statement does not contradict the New Testament statement that "all" people shall rise from the dead.[27]

---

21 T. Boston, "Christ, the Son of God, Gifted to Sinners," in *The Whole Works of the Late Reverend Thomas Boston of Ettrick*, 12 vols., ed. S. McMillan (Aberdeen: George and Robert King, 1851), 10:196–97. Also cited in J. Morison, *The Extent of the Atonement; or, the Question, for Whom Did Christ Die? Answered* (Kilmarnock: J. Davie; London: Thomas Ward & Co., 1842), 83–85.

22 D. Whitby, *A Discourse concerning I. the True Import of the Words and the Things Signified by Them in the Holy Scripture. II. The Extent of Christ's Redemption. III. The Grace of God; where It Is Enquired, Whether It Be Vouchsafed Sufficiently to Those Who Improve It Not, and Irresistibly to Those Who Do Improve It; and Whether Men Be Wholly Passive in the Work of Their Regeneration. IV. The Liberty of the Will in a State of Trial and Probation. V. The Perseverance and Defectibility of the Saints, with Some Reflections on the State of Heathens, the Providence and Prescience of God*, 3rd ed. (1710; repr. London: F. C. & J. Rivington, 1816). For biographical information, consult D. Wallace, "Whitby, Daniel," in *Dictionary of Major Biblical Interpreters*, 2nd ed., ed. D. K. McKim (Downers Grove, IL: InterVarsity, 2007), 1048–52; and A. Gordon, "Whitby, Daniel," in *Dictionary of National Biography*, 61:28–30.

23 Whitby, *A Discourse*, 106–86.

24 Ibid., 106–7.

25 Ibid., 108.

26 Ibid., 113.

27 Ibid., 115.

Whitby addressed key passages such as 1 Tim 2:4–6; Titus 2:11–12; Heb 2:9; and 2 Pet 3:9 as statements affirming unlimited atonement.[28] He also covered all the "world" passages in extent-related contexts, concluding that "world" cannot be restricted to mean "the elect."[29] He then turned to passages that indicate Christ died for the sins of those who ultimately perish eternally.[30]

The necessity of all people to believe in Christ furnished Whitby with another argument for unlimited atonement.[31] Whitby answered objections from Scripture raised by limitarians to unlimited atonement,[32] followed by his presentation of arguments from reason for and against unlimited atonement.[33]

Experience Mayhew (AD 1673–1758)

Experience Mayhew was a Calvinist missionary to the Wampanoag Indians in Martha's Vineyard, Massachusetts.[34] He received an honorary degree from Harvard at age twenty-five. His work *Indian Converts* (1727) is an important historical account that traces four generations of Wampanoag Indians on Martha's Vineyard in colonial America.

In Mayhew's final published sermon entitled *Grace Defended* (1744), he wrote:

> Now that which I here intend is this, that Mankind have, since their Fall into a State of Sin and Death, had so much done for them, in order to their Recovery out of that miserable Estate, as thereby to be put into a State of Salvability: For otherwise there would be no Room for an Offer of Salvation to be made to them. Now Mankind, since their Apostacy, may be conceived to be in a salvable Condition in two Respects, or on a two-fold Account. (1) In Respect of the Sufficiency of God to find out and provide a Way for their Salvation, whatever seeming Difficulties, in Respect of the Threatening denounced against Sinners, and of his own Truth and Justice, seemed to lie against it; yet this notwithstanding, I say, the Wisdom, Goodness, and Power of God was such, that it was, in that Respect, possible for him to find out and provide a Way, in which such Sinners as Mankind were, might be eternally saved. But this is not what I principally here intend. Wherefore, (2) Mankind may be said to be in a salvable State, in Respect of a Price already paid, . . .
>
> It is in Respect of this Price of Redemption, that I here affirm Mankind to be in a salvable Estate. They are so now, in Respect of a Price already paid for

28 Ibid., 118–23.
29 Ibid., 124–32.
30 Ibid., 132–36.
31 Ibid., 136–42.
32 Ibid., 142–47.
33 Ibid., 148–86.
34 For information about Mayhew and his Calvinism, consult L. A. Leibman, ed., *Experience Mayhew's Indian Converts: A Cultural Edition* (Amherst, MA: University of Massachusetts Press, 2008), 10–16.

> them, in order to their eternal Happiness. And this I suppose to be a Truth, with Respect to all Mankind without Exception: So that though there are many who never will be saved, yet the Reason of this is not, because there is not a sufficient Price paid for their Redemption, nor because this is not a Remedy applicable to them, according to the Tenor of the new Covenant, but for other Reasons hereafter to be mentioned.[35]

Mayhew then averred that this truth is

> clearly revealed in the Word of God; and that the reason why it is not so generally believed so to be, is not because it is not sufficiently asserted in Scripture, but because many have, without sufficient Grounds, supposed that a Belief of this cannot be reconciled to some other Articles of Faith, which they think clearly and fully revealed.[36]

At this point, Mayhew appealed to Rom 5:12–19; John 3:16; 1 John 2:2; Heb 2:9; 1 Tim 2:6; 2 Cor 5:14–15; and 1 Tim 4:10 as scriptural support that the atonement is universal.

Mayhew continued:

> The most obvious Sense of these Texts of Scripture, is, that Jesus Christ died for all Men without Exception, I think very evident. Nor is it at our Liberty to recede from this, without some urgent Necessity compelling us to it, which I suppose can never be shown; but instead thereof, I will show a Necessity of taking of them in the full Latitude in which they are expressed. I do not therefore wonder, that there have been a great many eminent Divines, in the *English* Nation, who have been far from being *Arminians*, that have plainly and fully asserted Christ's dying for all, as I could easily manifest, did I rely on human Authorities, as I do not.[37]

Mayhew appealed to Twisse (*The Riches of God's Love to the Vessels of Mercy*) to explain the debate over extent. Twisse asked whether one should use the phrase "Christ died for me," and Mayhew concluded in the affirmative:

---

35 E. Mayhew, *Grace Defended: In a Modest Plea for an Important Truth: Namely, That the Offer of Salvation Made to Sinners in the Gospel, Comprises in It an Offer of the Grace Given in Regeneration; and Shewing the Consistency of This Truth with the Free and Sovereign Grace of God, in the Whole Work of Man's Salvation; in Which the Doctrine of Original Sin and Humane Impotence, the Object and Extent of Redemption, the Nature of Regeneration, the Difference between Common and Special Grace, the Nature of Justifying Faith, and Other Important Points, Are Considered and Cleared* (Boston: B. Green and Company, 1744), 40–41.

36 Ibid., 42.

37 Ibid., 41.

> I am bound to believe that Christ died for the procuring of these Benefits unto me, in such Manner as God hath ordained; to wit, not absolutely but conditionally, to wit, in Case I do believe and repent. For God hath not otherwise ordained, that I should reap the Benefits of Pardon and Salvation, by virtue of Christ's Death and Passion, unless I believe in him and repent.[38]

Mayhew continued to quote Twisse as saying that everyone who hears the gospel is bound to believe that Christ died for him. Twisse even stated that Judas could have been saved had he repented and believed.[39]

Mayhew made a vital point: "It is not supposed in what is here maintained, that Jesus died equally, or in the same Sense, for all Mankind, Elect and Non-elect."[40] He grounded this claim in the covenant of redemption, whereby the members of the Trinity designed to effectually bring the benefits of the atonement to the elect, and the covenant of grace, which is a covenant with all mankind. Mayhew explained that all men, elect and non-elect, are on level ground. In this covenant, the benefits of salvation are offered on condition of faith in Christ. And since there is atonement made for all men, all men are saveable if they believe. Of course, from a Reformed perspective, the non-elect will not believe because they cannot believe (they possess natural ability to believe but no moral ability to believe) unless they are effectually called, which God has not willed to occur. As Mayhew pointed out, if one does not believe, "it is not because there is not a sufficient Remedy provided, but for such other Reasons as are given in God's Word."[41]

Mayhew proceeded to inquire how it is possible that the gospel can be preached to any sinner for whom Christ has not died. He responded in the negative since there is no price paid for that sinner by Christ. "I may very seriously say, I know of no Kindness that can be shown in such an offer, i.e., an Offer of Salvation made to Sinners that are not in a salvable State."[42]

Quoting Rom 3:24–26, Mayhew noted:

> In which Words we are assured, that it would not have stood with the Justice of God to have justified a Sinner, though a Believer, had not Christ been set forth, as in the Words expressed. And it will no more consist with the Justice of God to offer Salvation to a Sinner for whom Christ died not, than actually to save him without Christ's dying for him. And Salvation might have been

38 Ibid., 42.
39 Ibid., 43.
40 Ibid.
41 Ibid., 45.
42 Ibid., 46.

> as well offered to the whole World, if Christ had not died at all, as to any one Sinner for whom he died not.[43]

Thus, for Mayhew, the universal extent of the atonement was the necessary ground for the free offer of the gospel to all.

Isaac Watts (AD 1674–1748)

Though remembered more for his hymnology than his theology, Watts was important in eighteenth-century English Calvinism. His writings leave no doubt he held to unlimited atonement.

Speaking of the many universal passages in Scripture with respect to the atonement, Watts stated that such passages can only be explained by supposing that the death of Christ provided "a sufficient conditional pardon, and conditional salvation, for the non-elect, while it also provides absolute, effectual, and certain pardon and salvation for those whom God has elected."[44] Watts asserted:

> Here let it be observed, that when the Remonstrants assert, that Christ died for all mankind, merely to purchase conditional salvation for them, and when those who profess to be the strictest Calvinists assert Christ died only and merely to procure absolute and effectual pardon and salvation for the elect; it is not because the whole Scripture every where expressly or plainly reveals, or asserts, the particular sentiments of either of these sects, with an exclusion of the other; but the reason of these different assertions of men is this, that the holy writers, in different texts, pursuing different subjects, and speaking to different persons, sometimes seem to favour each of these two opinions, and men being at a loss to reconcile them by any medium, run into different extremes, and entirely follow one of these tracks of thought, and neglect the other. . . .
>
> Nor indeed can I conceive why the remonstrant should be uneasy to have pardon and salvation absolutely provided for the elect, since all the rest of mankind, especially such as hear the gospel, have the same conditional salvation which they contend for, sincerely proposed to their acceptance; nor can I see any reason, why the strictest Calvinist should be angry, that the all sufficient merit of Christ should overflow so far in its influence, as to provide conditional salvation for all mankind, since the elect of God have that certain and absolute salvation, which they contend for, secured to them by the same merit; and especially since that great and admirable reformer, John Calvin,

43 Ibid., 47.

44 I. Watts, "The Ruin and Recovery of Mankind," in *The Works of the Reverend and Learned Isaac Watts, D.D.*, 6 vols. (London: Printed by and for John Barfield, 1810), 6:151.

> whose name they affect to wear, and to whose authority they pay so great a regard, has so plainly declared in his writings, that there is a sense in which Christ died for the sins of the whole world, or all mankind; and he sometimes goes so far as to call this the redemption of all. See his comments on the following Scriptures.[45]

Watts then proceeded to list Matt 24:28; Rom 5:18; 1 Cor 8:11–12; 1 John 2:2; 2 Pet 2:1; and Jude 4, along with Calvin's comments on each, demonstrating his contention and concluding with this statement: "Thus it appears that Calvin himself thought that Christ and his salvation are offered to all, and that in some sense he died for all."[46]

One gets a feel for Watts's dualistic understanding of the atonement, illustrated in his description of Christ dying "absolutely" for the sins of the elect but "conditionally" for the sins of all humanity:

> Yet further, one Christian may delight more to fix his Eye and Hope on Christ, as a Surety or Representative of his Elect, or of those whom he certainly and finally saves, and on that account he suffered Death particularly in their room and stead, and secured to them certain Deliverance and Salvation; yet he cannot therefore affirm, that Christ did not, in any Sense, die for all Men, as a general Friend of Man, or suffer Death for their Good; nor can he say, that the Benefits of his Death do not any way reach to all Mankind. Another perhaps will say, since all are dead, he died for all as a common Mediator betwixt God and Man, or as a general Benefactor to procure conditional Salvation for all Men, and offer it to them if they are willing to come to him and receive it; but he cannot say, that he was not a proper Surety, or Representative of his Elect, whereby he has secured certain Salvation to them only: For as I have shown in former Papers, that he by his Righteousness and Death has directly and absolutely procured this Salvation for his Elect, as their Head and Representative, but yet he has also procured Salvation, with all the Glories of it, conditionally, for the rest of Mankind, upon which Foundation these Blessings are offer'd to all Men in the Gospel.[47]

The final clause of this indicates Watts believed that a universal atonement is foundational for the well-meant offer of the gospel to all people.

---

45 Ibid., 6:151–54. This quotation is also cited by Edward Griffin, "An Humble Attempt to Reconcile the Differences of Christians Respecting the Extent of the Atonement," in *The Atonement: Discourses and Treatises* (Boston: Congregational Board of Publication, 1859), 251–52.

46 Ibid., 6:154.

47 I. Watts, *Orthodoxy and Charity United: In Several Reconciling Essays on the Law and Gospel, Faith and Works* (London: T. Longman & T. Shewel, 1745), 254–55. Also in Isaac Watts, "A View of the Manifold Salvation of Man by Jesus Christ, Represented in Order to Reconcile Christians of Different Sentiments," in *Works*, 3:674.

Herman Venema (AD 1697–1787)[48]

Venema succeeded Vitringa in 1723 as professor of theology at Franecker, a post he held for more than fifty years. His *Institutes of Theology* was published posthumously in English in 1850. Venema appears to be a Hypothetical Universalist, believing that Christ substituted for the sins of all people and that if all would repent and believe the gospel, all would be saved.

> Scripture assures us that the love of God towards men as such is universal—that he has "no pleasure in the death of him that dies" that he "will have all men to be saved and to come unto the knowledge of the truth"—that he is "not willing that any should perish, but that all should come to repentance," Ezek. xviii. 32; 1 Tim. ii. 4; 2 Pet. iii. 9. From these passages we infer that there is a general will or purpose of God held forth in the gospel by which he has linked together faith and salvation without excluding any man, and declares that it is agreeable to him that all should believe and live. If this be denied then it follows that he absolutely willed that some should perish and that, according to his good pleasure, the proposition "he that believes shall be saved" should not apply to them. What becomes, in this case, of his universal love? What are we to make of the passages in which he declares that he wills not the death of the sinner, that he will have all men to be saved?[49]

This quote from Venema demonstrates his belief in God's universal saving will. Venema may have been moderate on the atonement, but this statement alone does not overtly indicate such.

Philip Doddridge (AD 1702–1751)

Doddridge was a pastor, teacher, author, and prolific hymn writer, authoring more than four hundred hymns.[50] His most famous work, *The Rise and Progress of Religion in the Soul,* was dedicated to his friend Isaac Watts and was widely circulated. It was credited with bringing about the conversion of the famous abolitionist William Wilberforce.

His hymn "Grace: 'Tis a Charming Sound" expresses his commitment to unlimited

48 See Muller, *Post-Reformation Reformed Dogmatics,* 1:51, 308–9; Johannes Cornelis de Bruïne, *Herman Venema: Een Nederland[d]se theoloog in de tijd der Verlichting* (Franeker: Wever, 1973), which contains a bibliography of Venema's works on pp. 174–78; and H. J. M. Nellen and E. Rabbie, eds., *Hugo Grotius, Theologian: Essays in Honor of G. H. M. Posthumus Meyjes,* Studies in the History of Christian Thought 55 (Leiden: Brill, 1994), 215.

49 Muller, *Post-Reformation Reformed Dogmatics,* 1:306. See also H. Venema, *Institutes of Theology,* trans. A. W. Brown (Andover, MA: W. F. Draper Brothers, 1853), 163–64, 252.

50 J. Stoughton, *Philip Doddridge: His Life and Labors* (London: Jackson and Walford, 1851).

atonement in the refrain: "Saved by grace alone, this is all my plea. Jesus died for all mankind, and Jesus died for me."[51]

Jonathan Edwards (AD 1703–1758)

Considered by many to be the greatest theologian America ever produced, Jonathan Edwards was America's most well-known Calvinist. His writings today continue to be influential, especially among the new Calvinist movement in Evangelicalism. It comes as something of a surprise to Calvinists and non-Calvinists alike to learn that Edwards affirmed unlimited atonement.

In his voluminous writings, seldom did Edwards address directly the subject of the extent of the atonement. However, a careful reading of his writings provides sufficient evidence to confirm Edwards's commitment to universal atonement.

For example, Edwards wrote in the *Miscellanies* under the heading "Universal Redemption":

> 424. UNIVERSAL REDEMPTION. Christ did die for all in this sense, that all by his death have an opportunity of being [saved]; and he had that design in dying, that they should have that opportunity by it. For it was certainly a thing that God designed, that all men should have such an opportunity, or else they would not have it; and they have it by the death of Christ.[52]

Likewise, Edwards wrote:

> From these things it will inevitably follow, that however Christ in some sense may be said to *die for all*, and to redeem[53] all visible Christians, yea, the whole world, by his death; yet there must be something *particular* in the design of his death, with respect to such as he intended should actually be saved thereby.[54]

One can see that Edwards is advocating a form of dualism on the extent of the atonement. Christ may be said to die for all in that he *redeemed* all, but there is still

51 See also A. Clifford, "The Christian Mind of Philip Doddridge (1702–1751)," *Evangelical Quarterly* 56.4 (Oct.–Dec. 1984): 227–42, for additional evidence from Doddridge's writings that he held to universal atonement.

52 J. Edwards, "Miscellanies," in *Works of Jonathan Edwards Online*, 73 vols., ed. H. S. Stout (Jonathan Edwards Center, Yale University, 2008), 13:478.

53 It is crucial to note Edwards's universal use of the term "redeemed" here, which is like Calamy's above. While some high Calvinists do say that "Christ died for all" in the sense of purchasing common grace for even the non-elect, they are careful *not* to say that Christ "redeemed" any of the non-elect, since this involves paying their ransom price.

54 J. Edwards, "On the Freedom of the Will," in *The Works of Jonathan Edwards*, 2 vols., ed. E. Hickman (1834; repr. Edinburgh: Banner of Truth, 1979), 1:88. This is not to claim that Edwards saw no sense of particularity in the design or intent of Christ's death, but only that he did not see any limitation in the *extent* of Christ's suffering on behalf of the whole world.

something particular in his work in the case of the elect such that he purposes that they alone should obtain the benefit through faith. Redemption *applied* is limited, but redemption *accomplished* is unlimited.

Stephen Holmes referred to this same quotation in Edwards and stated that though Edwards wants to hold to the theological point of limited atonement, he is unhappy with the expression of it. Holmes spoke of Edwards as "suggesting that there is genuinely a universal component to the atonement" such that all people would have the opportunity to be saved.[55] Clearly Edwards means by this universal expiation of sin, but it is unclear if Holmes is asserting that this is Edwards's meaning or not.[56]

Under the heading "Universal Redemption," Edwards wrote,

> In some sense, redemption is universal of all mankind: all mankind now have an opportunity to be saved otherwise than they would have had if Christ had not died. A door of mercy is in some sort opened for them. This is one benefit actually consequent on Christ's death; but the benefits that are actually consequent on Christ's death and are obtained by Christ's death, doubtless Christ intended to obtain by his death. It was one thing he aimed at by his death; or which is the same thing, he died to obtain it, as it was one end of his death.[57]

Likewise Edwards wrote,

> Christ's incarnation, his labors and sufferings, his resurrection, etc., were for the salvation of such as are not elected, in Scripture language, in the same sense as the means of grace are for their salvation; in the same sense as the instruction, counsels, warnings and invitations that are given them, are for their salvation.[58]

In Edwards's "Life of David Brainerd," he stated:

> II. How and in what sense He "takes away the sin of the world:" not because all the world shall actually be redeemed from sin by Him, but because (1) He has done and suffered sufficient to answer for the sins of the world, and so to redeem all mankind; (2) He actually does take away the sins of the elect world.[59]

---

55 S. Holmes, *God of Grace and God of Glory: An Account of the Theology of Jonathan Edwards* (Grand Rapids, MI: Eerdmans, 2001), 159.

56 Ibid., 157–59.

57 J. Edwards, "Book of Minutes on the Arminian Controversy," Gazeteer Notebook, in *Works of Jonathan Edwards Online*, 37:10–11.

58 J. Edwards, "'Controversies,' Notebook," in *Works of Jonathan Edwards Online*, 27:Part III.

59 J. Edwards, "The Life of David Brainerd," in *The Works of Jonathan Edwards*, 2:374.

> He was enabled to do and to suffer the whole will of God; and he obtained the whole of the end of his sufferings—a full atonement for the sins of the whole world, and the full salvation of every one of those who were given him in the covenant of redemption, and all that glory to the name of God, which his mediation was designed to accomplish, not one jot or tittle has failed.[60]

Consider these additional statements by Edwards:

> Jesus Christ, the Redeemer, will have no pity on you. Though he had so much love to sinners, as to be willing to lay down his life for them, and offers you the benefits of his blood, while you are in this world, and often calls upon you to accept them; yet then he will have no pity upon you. You never will hear any more instructions from him; he will utterly refuse to be your instructor: on the contrary, he will be your judge, to pronounce sentence against you.[61]

Contextually, Edwards is speaking to and about those who will eventually be lost, hence the non-elect. Edwards said that after they perish, Jesus Christ will no longer take pity on them. However, to this same group of "sinners," Edwards also said Jesus "loved" them so as "to be willing to lay down his life for them."

Edwards stated:

> When Christ hung dying upon the cross, he was doing that that was the most wonderful act of love that ever was; and the posture that he died in was very suitable to signify his free and great [love]: he died with his arms spread open as being ready to embrace all that would come to him. He was lift up [upon the] cross above the earth with arms thus open, and there he made an offer of his love to the world; he was presented in open [view to] the world as their Saviour.[62]

Edwards stated:

> II. Let all be exhorted to accept the grace of the gospel. One would think, that there should be no need of such exhortations as this, but alas, such is the dreadful wickedness and the horrible ingratitude of man's heart, that he needs abundance of persuading and entreating to accept of God's kindness, when offered them. We should count it horrible ingratitude in a poor, necessitous

60 J. Edwards, "Christ's 'Agony,'" in *The Works of Jonathan Edwards*, 2:874.

61 J. Edwards, "The End of the Wicked Contemplated by the Righteous," in *The Works of Jonathan Edwards*, 2:211.

62 J. Edwards, "'Miscellanies,' no. 304," in *Works of Jonathan Edwards Online*, 13:390.

creature, to refuse our help and kindness when we, out of mere pity to him, offer to relieve and help him. If you should see a man in extremity of distress, and in a perishing necessity of help and relief, and you should lay out yourself, with much labor and cost, out of compassion to him, that he might be relieved, how would you take it of him, if he should proudly and spitefully refuse it and snuff at it, instead of thanking you for it? Would you not look upon it as a very ungrateful, unreasonable, base thing? And why has not God a thousand times the cause, to look upon you as base and ungrateful, if you refuse his glorious grace in the gospel, that he offers you? When God saw mankind in a most necessitous condition, in the greatest and extremist distress, being exposed to hellfire and eternal death, from which it was impossible he should ever deliver himself, or that ever he should be delivered by any other means, He took pity on them, and brought them from the jaws of destruction by His own blood. Now what great ingratitude is it for them to refuse such grace as this?

But so it is: multitudes will not accept a free gift at the hands of the King of the World. They have the daring, horrible presumption as [to] refuse a kindness offered by God himself, and not to accept a gift at the hands of Jehovah, nor not his own Son, his own Son equal with himself. Yea, they'll not accept of him, though he dies for them; yea, though he dies a most tormenting death, though he dies that they may be delivered from hell, and that they may have heaven, they'll not accept of this gift, though they are in such necessity of it, that they must be miserable forever without it. Yea, although God the Father invites and importunes them, they'll not accept of it, though the Son of God himself knocks and calls at their door till his head is wet with the dew, and his locks with the drops of the night, arguing and pleading with them to accept of him for their own sakes, though he makes so many glorious promises, though he holds forth so many precious benefits to tempt them to happiness, perhaps for many years together, yet they obstinately refuse all. Was ever such ingratitude heard of, or can greater be conceived of?

What would you have God do for you, that you may accept of it? Is the gift that he offers too small, that you think it too little, for you to accept of? Don't God offer you his Son, and what could God offer more? Yea, we may say God himself has not a greater gift to offer. Did not the Son of God do enough for you, that you won't accept of him; did he [not] die, and what could he do more? Yea, we may say that the Son of God could not do a greater thing for man. Do you refuse because you want to be invited and wooed? You may hear him, from day to day, inviting of you, if you will but hearken. Or is it because you don't stand in need of God's grace? Don't you need it so much as that you must either receive it or be damned to all eternity, and what greater need can there possibly be?

Alas, miserable creatures that we are, instead of the gift of God offered in the gospel's not being great enough for us, we are not worthy of anything at all: we are less than the least of all God's mercies. Instead of deserving the dying Son of God, we are not worthy of the least crumb of bread, the least drop of water, or the least ray of light; instead of Christ's not having done enough for us by dying, in such pain and ignominy, we are not worthy that he should so much as look on us, instead of shedding his blood. We are not worthy that Christ should once make an offer of the least benefit, instead of his so long urging of us to be eternally happy.

Whoever continues to refuse Christ, will find hereafter, that instead of his having no need of him, that the least drop of his blood would have been more worth to them, than all the world; wherefore, let none be so ungrateful to God and so unwise for themselves, as to refuse the glorious grace of the gospel.[63]

Speaking of God's love for the unsaved, Edwards stated:

As great as this wrath is, it is not greater than that love of God which you have slighted and rejected. God, in infinite mercy to lost sinners, has provided a way for them to escape future misery, and to obtain eternal life. For that end he has given his only-begotten Son, a person infinitely glorious and honorable in himself—being equal with God, and infinitely near and dear to God. It was ten thousand times more than if God had given all the angels in heaven, or the whole world, for sinners. Him he gave to be incarnate, to suffer death, to be made a curse for us, and to undergo the dreadful wrath of God in our room, and thus to purchase for us eternal glory. This glorious person has been offered to you times without number, and he has stood and knocked at your door, until his hairs were with the dews of the night. But all that he has done has not won upon you. You see no form nor loveliness in him, no beauty that you should desire him. When he has thus offered himself to you as your Savior, you never freely and heartily accept of him. This love which you have thus abused, is as great as that wrath of which you are in danger. If you would have accepted of it, you might have had the enjoyment of this love instead of enduring this terrible wrath. So that the misery you have heard of is not greater than the love you have despised, and the happiness and glory which you have rejected. How just then would it be in God to execute upon you this dreadful wrath, which is not greater than that love which you have despised! Heb. 2:3, "How shall we escape if we neglect so great salvation?"[64]

---

63 J. Edwards, "Sermons and Discourses 1720–1723," in *Works of Jonathan Edwards Online*, 10:397–98.

64 J. Edwards, "The Portion of the Wicked," in *The Works of Jonathan Edwards*, 2:887.

In the following statement, Edwards spoke of all mankind as being "capable subjects of saving mercy":

> God deals with the generality of mankind, in their present state, far differently, on occasion of the redemption by Jesus Christ, from what he otherwise would do; for, being capable subjects of saving mercy, they have a day of patience and grace, and innumerable temporal blessings bestowed on them; which, as the apostle signifies, (Acts xiv. 17.) are testimonies of God's reconcilableness to sinful men, to put them upon seeking after God.[65]

Notice Edwards's language here. He spoke of "God's reconcilableness to sinful men." This is more than common grace given the context where Edwards is speaking about the "generality of mankind."

Edwards also stated:

> Christ is become a most importunate suitor to sinners, that he may become their sovereign. He is often setting before them the need they have of him, the miserable condition in which they are, and the great provision that is made for the good of their souls and he invites them to accept of this provision, and promises it shall be theirs upon their mere acceptance.
>
> All the persons of the Trinity are now seeking your salvation. God the Father hath sent his Son, who hath made way for your salvation, and removed all difficulties, except those which are with your own heart.[66]

One of the clearest examples of Edwards's belief in an unlimited atonement is found in this statement:

> His blood which he spilled, his life which he laid down, was an infinite price because it was the blood of God, as it was expressly called. Acts 20:28. Now upon this account, the price offered was equivalent to the demerit of the sins of all mankind, [and] his sufferings equivalent to the eternal sufferings of the whole world, [of] all mankind.[67]

Following this quotation, McMullen noted that Edwards considered vitally important the question of the price paid by Christ for the sins of the world since he made

65 J. Edwards, "The Great Christian Doctrine of Original Sin Defended," in *The Works of Jonathan Edwards*, 1:227.

66 J. Edwards, "The End of the Wicked Contemplated by the Righteous," in *The Works of Jonathan Edwards*, 2:212.

67 J. Edwards, "The Sacrifice of Christ Acceptable," in *Works of Jonathan Edwards Online*, 14:452; cited in M. McMullen, "'The Wisdom of God in the Work of Redemption': Soteriological Aspects of the Theology of Jonathan Edwards 1703–1758" (PhD diss., University of Aberdeen, 1992), 132.

several entries on this subject in his *Miscellanies.* For Edwards, God's threats were without foundation unless Christ had actually paid the price of all sins. Edwards considered Christ's death as belonging to every human being. As Adam's sin is the sin of all humanity, so there is a sense in which all humanity die in Christ's death, as Edwards noted in Miscellany 281.[68]

Edwards's view of the sufficiency of the atonement is that Christ's death is a provision for the sins of all people. Furthermore, Edwards affirmed the possibility of salvation for all people, as he indicated here:

> The possibility of obtaining. Though it be attended with so much difficulty, yet it is not a thing impossible . . . However sinful a person is, and whatever his circumstances are, there is, notwithstanding, a possibility of his salvation. He himself is capable of it, and God is able to accomplish it, and has mercy sufficient for it; and there is sufficient provision made through Christ, that God may do it consistent with the honour of his majesty, justice and truth. So that there is no want either of sufficiency in God, or capacity in the sinner, in order to this.[69]

Other examples could be given, but these are sufficient to indicate Edwards believed in unlimited atonement.

In the comment thread on a blog post where I argued against limited atonement, one commenter used the following Edwards quote in an attempt to show that I was mistaken about Edwards's view of the extent of the atonement:

> Universal redemption must be denied in the very sense of Calvinists themselves, whether predestination is acknowledged or no, if we acknowledge that Christ knows all things. For if Christ certainly knows all things to come, he certainly knew, when he died, that there were such and such men that would never be the better for his death. And therefore, it was impossible that he should die with an intent to make them (particular persons) happy. For it is a right-down contradiction [to say that] he died with an intent to make them happy, when at the same time he knew they would not be happy—Predestination or no predestination, it is all one for that. This is all that Calvinists mean when they say that Christ did not die for all, that he did not die intending and designing that such and such particular persons should be the better for it; and that is evident to a demonstration. Now Arminians, when [they] say that Christ died for all,

68 McMullen, "'The Wisdom of God in the Work of Redemption,'" 132–33.

69 J. Edwards, "Pressing into the Kingdom of God," in *The Works of Jonathan Edwards,* 1:656, cited in McMullen, "'The Wisdom of God in the Work of Redemption,'" 198.

> cannot mean, with any sense, that he died for all any otherwise than to give all an opportunity to be saved; and that, Calvinists themselves never denied. He did die for all in this sense; 'tis past all contradiction.[70]

In response, I pointed out that Edwards was affirming unlimited atonement with respect to *extent*! What Edwards was denying is that Jesus died with intent to actually save all people. Notice Edwards acknowledged that many will never be saved—that is, they will never partake of the benefits of the atonement. Edwards said, "It is impossible that he [Christ] should die with an *intent* to make them happy." Furthermore, Edwards stated it is a "contradiction [to say that] he died with an *intent* to make them happy," when Jesus in fact knew they would never be saved. Edwards then said, "This is all that Calvinists mean when they say that Christ did not die for all, that he did not die *intending* and *designing* that such and such particular persons should be the better for it."

Notice then Edwards stated what the Arminians mean by the extent of Christ's death: "They cannot mean, with any sense, that he died for all any otherwise than to give all an opportunity to be saved." In other words, Edwards correctly affirmed what Arminians believe: Christ died to make salvation *possible for all.* No Arminian believes Christ died with the *design or intent* to save any particular person, which of course is exactly what Edwards and all Calvinists do in fact believe—that Christ did indeed die with the *intent or design* to save the elect. Then comes the money quote from Edwards: the statement that Arminians believe Christ did die for all to give all an opportunity to be saved, "that, Calvinists themselves never denied. He did die for all in this sense; 'tis past all contradiction." This is a clear statement that Edwards believed Calvinists and Arminians agreed that Christ died for all people *with respect to the extent of the atonement, but that Calvinists and Arminians differed with respect to the intent of the atonement.*

Should the limitarian interpret Edwards to mean that the design of the atonement was limited to the elect, therefore Edwards believed the extent of the atonement was limited as well, the logical mistakes would be obvious. First, there is the conflation of intent with extent. The assumption is that by "design" Edwards means "design to send Christ to die for any man," when Edwards means design in the sense "to apply the atonement to any man." Second, this assumes a limited extent, which limitarians are attempting to prove, based on a limited intent to apply only to the elect.

Third, Edwards did in fact agree with the Arminians that Christ did die to give all people an opportunity to be saved. Therefore, one should draw the conclusion that Edwards believed that the *extent* of the atonement was universal, so that all people would have the opportunity to be saved; but he also believed, as a good Calvinist, that the *intent* of the atonement was limited only to the elect such that it would be applied only to them according to unconditional election.

---

70 J. Edwards, "The Miscellanies," in *The Works of Jonathan Edwards Online*, 13:174.

Fourth, Edwards asserted it is possible for the non-elect to be redeemed should they believe the gospel because he believed Christ died for the sins of all. Logic dictates that even though Calvinists affirm by virtue of a penal relationship with the elect alone, thereby only making their salvation possible, it is still possible for the non-elect to be saved, *if they were to believe*. The death of Christ for sins is a necessary precondition for anyone's salvation, *whether they believe or not*. Without this precondition, even if they were to believe, they could not be saved because no atonement exists for their sins according to limited atonement. This is why, among other reasons, I have argued that limited atonement is not only theologically flawed but logically flawed.[71]

High Calvinists presume that the intent to apply and the extent are and must be coextensive, though we have demonstrated that numerous Calvinists from the beginning of the Reformation distinguished the two from their exegesis of the biblical texts and held to a form of universal atonement, as did Edwards.

Oliver Crisp drew a number of compelling conclusions from his comparison of Edwards with Joseph Bellamy, a New Divinity Calvinist who held to unlimited atonement. He first noted how the Reformed understanding of the atonement's extent has never been monolithic, even before Dort.[72] Second, he correctly pointed out the nineteenth-century skirmish between the Princetonian Calvinists and the New Divinity theology, where Charles Hodge and Warfield "sought to outmaneuver their opponents by claiming the high Calvinistic ground."[73]

Third, Crisp appears to have missed the fact that Edwards, like many before him, held that the atonement with respect to its extent (scope) actually atoned for the sins of all people, but that God's intent was only to apply its benefits to the elect.[74] The quotations from Edwards above indicate that there was a very real sense in which Christ's death included the sins of the reprobate. Fourth, Crisp is correct that Edwards himself affirmed a penal substitutionary atonement.[75]

Crisp concluded his chapter by addressing the question of why Edwards endorsed Bellamy's doctrine. Crisp thinks that Edwards's difference with Bellamy was that of a "different mechanism" for the atonement in Edwards's view, yet "it yielded equivalent outcomes."[76] "It would appear that Edwards thought there was a sufficient similarity or family resemblance between his doctrine and Bellamy's that he was willing to endorse

---

71 D. Allen, "The Atonement: Limited or Universal?," *Whosoever Will*, 93–94.

72 O. Crisp, "The Moral Government of God: Jonathan Edwards and Joseph Bellamy on the Atonement," in *After Jonathan Edwards: The Courses of the New England Theology*, ed. O. Crisp and D. Sweeney (Oxford: Oxford University Press, 2012), 79–80.

73 Ibid., 81.

74 Ibid., 85.

75 Ibid.

76 Ibid., 88.

Bellamy's work."[77] Perhaps the better explanation is that Edwards and Bellamy agreed on the scope of the atonement's extent.

Edwards's preface to Joseph Bellamy's *True Religion Delineated* has caused no small consternation among Edwardsian scholars. Edwards praises Bellamy's work. Did Edwards affirm Bellamy's view of the atonement? In that Bellamy clearly affirmed an unlimited atonement, both the preface and the foregoing evidence would seem to indicate that Edwards agreed with Bellamy on the question of the atonement's extent. The scholarly debate need not detain us here, but an accessible and helpful survey can be found in McMullen's dissertation on Edwards's view of the atonement, where McMullen cautiously, and I think correctly, concluded that Edwards likely held to unlimited atonement but did not fully endorse all of the governmental aspects of the New Divinity with respect to the atonement.[78]

Through Jonathan Edwards and his successors, the governmental approach to the atonement passed over into New England Calvinism and was widely held by New England Congregationalists and New School Presbyterians.[79] Some of these Calvinists affirmed a combination of penal substitutionary atonement with the governmental theory.

George Whitefield (AD 1714–1770)

The fiery evangelist of the Great Awakening was George Whitefield. Whitefield was a Calvinist, but whether he held to limited atonement is at least debatable given that some of his statements would be inconsistent with a limited substitution for sin by Christ on the cross:

> Now, my dear sisters, I shall speak a few words to those of you who have not yet espoused yourselves to the Lord Jesus. It is a great sin, and surely you highly affront the Lord that bought you. It is likewise your folly to refuse and neglect the gracious proffers of being the spouse of Christ.[80]

> Christ's invitations to be his spouse are earnest. He doth call upon you, and not only call, but earnestly too; yea he uses many arguments with you: he will press you to come unto him; he is loath to take any denial from you: he knocks, and knocks hard at the door of your hearts for entertainment; and surely you will not deny the Lord of life and glory who died for you, and gave

77 Ibid., 89.

78 See McMullen, "'The Wisdom of God in the Work of Redemption,'" 147–64.

79 W. A. Brown, "Expiation and Atonement (Christian)," in *Encyclopædia of Religion and Ethics*, 13 vols., ed. J. Hastings (New York: Charles Scribner's Sons, 1908), 5:647.

80 G. Whitefield, "Christ the Best Husband," in *The Works of the Reverend George Whitefield*, 6 vols. (London: Edward and Charles Dilly, 1771–1772), 5:71.

himself for you: O my dear sisters, let this be the evening of your espousals to the Lord Jesus Christ.[81]

Now you enjoy the means of grace, as the preaching of his word, prayer, and sacraments; and God has sent his ministers out into the fields and highways, to invite, to woo you to come in; but they are tiresome to thee, thou hadst rather be at thy pleasures: ere long, my brethren, they will be over, and you will be no more troubled with them; but then thou wouldst give ten thousand worlds for one moment of that merciful time of grace which thou had abused; then you will cry for a drop of that precious blood which now you trample under your feet; then you will wish for one more offer of mercy, for Christ and his free grace to be offered to you again; but your crying will be in vain: for as you would not repent here, God will not give you an opportunity to repent hereafter: if you would not in Christ's time, you shall not in your own. In what a dreadful condition will you then be? . . .

O that this would awaken and cause you to humble yourselves for your sins, and to beg pardon for them, that you might find mercy in the Lord. . . .

Do not go away, let not the devil hurry you away before the sermon is over; but stay, and you shall have a Jesus offered to you, who has made satisfaction for all your sins.[82]

Would we now and then draw off our thoughts from sensible objects, and by faith meditate a while on the miseries of the damned, I doubt not but we should, as it were, hear many an unhappy soul venting his fruitless sorrows, in some such piteous moans as these. . . .

But, alas! these reflections come now too late: these wishes now are vain and fruitless. I have not suffered, and therefore must not reign with them. I have in effect denied the Lord that bought me, and therefore justly am I now denied by him. But must I live for ever tormented in these flames? Must this body of mine, which not long since lay in state, was cloathed in purple and fine linen, and fared sumptuously every day, must it be here eternally confined, and made the mockery of insulting devils? O eternity! that thought fills me with despair: I must be miserable forever.[83]

Hence then we may trace infidelity to its fountain head: for it is nothing else, but a pride of the understanding, an unwillingness to submit to the truths of God,

81 Ibid., 5:75.

82 G. Whitefield, "A Penitent Heart, the Best New Year's Gift," in *Works*, 6:12–13.

83 G. Whitefield, "The Eternity of Hell-Torments," in *Works*, 5:401–2.

> that makes so many, professing themselves wise, to become such fools as to deny the Lord, who has so dearly bought them; and dispute the divinity of that eternal Word, "in whom they live, and move, and have their being:" Whereby it is justly to be feared, they will bring upon themselves sure, if not swift destruction.[84]

Even though Whitefield was staunchly against Wesley's Arminian view of universal redemption (Christ died *with equal intent to save* all people), he still told unbelievers that Christ died for them, bought them, was given for them, and satisfied for their sins. While Whitefield does not go into detail on his view of the atonement, it is quite remarkable that he would proclaim the gospel that way to those he plainly thinks are unbelievers. If he did indeed affirm limited atonement, then these statements above, and many more like them, are clearly at variance with that belief.

David Brainerd (AD 1718–1747)

Brainerd was a missionary to the North American Indians. Coughing up blood from his tubercular lungs, he preached the gospel indefatigably to them. It is clear he held to universal atonement.

> II. Considered how and in what sense he "takes away the sin of the world:" and observed, that the means and manner, in and by which he takes away the sins of men, was his "giving himself for them," doing and suffering in their room and stead, &c. And he is said to take away the sin of *the world*, not because *all* the world shall *actually* be redeemed from sin by him; but because, (1.) He has done and suffered *sufficient* to answer for the sins of the world, and so to redeem all mankind. (2.) He *actually* does take away the sins of the *elect* world.[85]

> And, *secondly*, I frequently endeavoured to open to them the *fulness*, *all-sufficiency*, and *freeness* of that *redemption*, which the Son of God has wrought out by his obedience and sufferings, for perishing sinners: how this provision he had made, was suited to all their wants; and how he called and invited them to accept of everlasting life freely, notwithstanding all their sinfulness, inability, unworthiness, &c.[86]

When Brainerd spoke of Jesus taking way "the sin of the world," he defined that as Christ suffering "in the stead of" the world. Brainerd did not interpret "world" to mean the elect when he said Christ "suffered in their room and stead," and "redeemed

---

84 G. Whitefield, "The Extent and Reasonableness of Self-Denial," in *Works*, 5:429–30.

85 "Life and Diary of the Rev. David Brainerd," in *The Works of Jonathan Edwards*, 2:374.

86 Ibid., 2:432.

all mankind," as many particularists did and do. When Brainerd spoke of "the elect world's" sin being taken away, he has in view the forgiveness of sins or the application of Christ's death. Clearly he did not teach universal salvation.

Christ's death on the cross paid the price for the sins of the world. Brainerd stated that the benefits of the atonement will only be applied to the elect and then only when they believe on Christ. He also affirmed that the universal offer of the gospel is based on the universal sufficient atonement of Christ. Brainerd's missionary zeal is not based merely on a hypothetical sufficiency of the atonement but on an actual sufficiency where Christ has suffered for the sins of all people. This is something he "frequently endeavored to open" to all the lost so they could see the "provision he had made, was suited to all their wants."

Joseph Bellamy (AD 1719–1790)

Joseph Bellamy was an American Congregationalist pastor and a leading theologian in New England in the second half of the eighteenth century. The following extract from Bellamy illustrates his belief in unlimited atonement and his belief that a limited provision for sin precludes an unlimited free offer of the gospel.

> What Christ has done, is, in fact, sufficient to open a door for God, through him, to become reconcilable to the whole world. . . . God may now, therefore, through Jesus Christ, stand ready to pardon the whole world. . . . So that there is nothing in the way, but that mankind may, through Christ, be received into full favor, and entitled to eternal life.
>
> And God has expressly declared that it was the design of Christ's death to open this door of mercy to all. "God so loved the world, that he gave his only begotten Son, that whosoever believes in him should not perish, but have everlasting life." . . .
>
> And now, all things being thus ready on God's side, and the offers, invitations, and calls of the gospel being to every one, without exception; . . .
>
> And now, because the door of mercy is thus opened to the whole world by the blood of Christ, therefore, in Scripture, he is called the Savior of the world. "The Lamb of God, which takes away the sin of the world." "A propitiation for the sins of the whole world." "That he gave himself a ransom for all." "And tasted death for every man." The plain sense of all which expressions may, I think, without any danger of mistake, be learned from John iii. 16, "God so loved the world, that he gave his only begotten Son, that whosoever believes in him should not perish, but have everlasting life."
>
> Besides, if Christ died merely for the elect, that is, to the intent that they, only upon believing, might, consistently with the divine honor, be received

> to favor, then God could not, consistently with his justice, save any besides, if they should believe, "For without shedding of blood, there can be no remission." If Christ did not design, by his death, to open a door for all to be saved conditionally, that is, upon the condition of faith, then there is no such door opened: the door is not opened wider than Christ designed it should be; there is nothing more purchased by his death than he intended: if this benefit was not intended, then it is not procured; if it be not procured, then the non-elect cannot any of them be saved, consistently with divine justice. And, by consequence, if this be the case, then, first, the non-elect have no right at all to take any, the least encouragement, from the death of Christ, or the invitations of the gospel, to return to God through Christ, in hopes of acceptance; for there are no grounds of encouragement given. Christ did not die for them in any sense. It is impossible their sins should be pardoned consistently with justice; as much impossible as if there had never been a Savior: as if Christ had never died; and so there is no encouragement at all for them; and therefore it would be presumption in them to take any; all which is apparently contrary to the whole tenor of the gospel, which every where invites all, and gives equal encouragement to all. "Come, for all things are ready," said Christ to the reprobate Jews. . . .
>
> And now, if Christ's atonement and merits be thus sufficient for all, . . .
>
> And hence we may see upon what grounds it is that the poor, convinced, humbled sinner is encouraged and emboldened to venture his all upon Christ, and return to God through him.[87]

Notice two important points in Bellamy's statements. First, he believed that all legal barriers between God and man have been removed by the atonement of Christ. Second, Bellamy clearly made the point that if this is not the case, there is no possible way for salvation to be offered to one for whom no provision exists in the atonement.

John Newton (AD 1725–1807)

The great pastor and hymn writer John Newton is best known for his famous hymn "Amazing Grace." In his sermon on John 1:29, he seems to affirm universal atonement. The sermon is structured around three points, the third of which is "The Extent of it, 'The sin of the world.'"

At the beginning of his third point, Newton opined: "Many of my hearers need not be told, what fierce and voluminous disputes have been maintained concerning the extent of the death of Christ. I am afraid the advantage of such controversies has not

87 J. Bellamy, "True Religion Delineated," in *The Works of Joseph Bellamy*, 2 vols. (Boston: Doctrinal Tract and Book Society, 1853), 1:292–95, 297 (some spelling modernized).

been answerable to the zeal of the disputants."[88] After denying universalism, affirming the designed intent of the atonement is to save the elect, and denying quantitative equivalentism, Newton appeared to ground the universal offer of the gospel to all people in the sufficient death of Christ for all people. For Newton, this sufficiency seems to be an objective sufficiency in that Christ died for the sins of all people.

> III. The designed extent of this gratuitous removal of sin, by the oblation of the Lamb of God, is expressed in a large and indefinite manner: He taketh away the sin of the world. Many of my hearers need not to be told, what fierce and voluminous disputes have been maintained concerning the extent of the death of Christ. I am afraid the advantages of such controversies have not been answerable to the zeal of the disputants. For myself, I wish to be known by no name but that of a Christian, and implicitly to adopt no system but the Bible. I usually endeavour to preach to the heart and the conscience, and to wave, as much as I can, all controversial points. But as the subject now lies directly before me, I shall embrace the occasion, and simply and honestly open to you the sentiments of my heart concerning it.[89]

> But, on the other hand, I cannot think the sense of the expression is sufficiently explained, by saying, that the world, and the whole world is spoken of, to teach us that the sacrifice of the Lamb of God was not confined, like the Levitical offerings, to the nation of Israel only; but that it is available for the sins of a determinate number of persons, called the Elect, who are scattered among many nations, and found under a great variety of states and circumstances in human life. This is undoubtedly the truth, so far as it goes; but not, I apprehend, fully agreeable to the scriptural manner of representation. That there is an election of grace, we are plainly taught; yet it is not said, that Jesus Christ came into the world to save the elect, but that he came to save sinners, to seek and to save them that are lost, 1 Tim. i. 15; Luke xix. 10. Upon this ground, I conceive that ministers have a warrant to preaching the gospel to every human creature, and to address the conscience of every man in the sight of God; and that every person who hears this gospel has thereby a warrant, an encouragement, yea, a command, to apply to Jesus Christ for salvation. And that they who refuse, thereby exclude themselves, and perish, not because they never had, nor possibly could have any interest in his atonement, but simply because they will not come unto him that they may have life.[90]

---

88 J. Newton, "Sermon XVI: The Lamb of God, The Great Atonement," in *The Works of the Rev. John Newton*, 2 vols. (Philadelphia: Uriah Hunt, 1839), 2:270.

89 Ibid.

90 Ibid., 2:271.

Newton also repudiated the notion of a quantitative equivalency in the atonement in this sermon: "But this nicety of computation does not seem analogous to that unbounded magnificence and grandeur which overwhelm the attentive mind in the contemplation of the divine conduct in the natural world."[91]

Jonathan Edwards Jr. (AD 1745–1801)

Jonathan Edwards Jr. served as a pastor for many years and then for a brief stint as president of Union College in New York before his death in 1801. His most important sermons are the three on the atonement that he delivered at New Haven in 1785. In these sermons he affirmed his belief in universal atonement.[92]

Edward Williams (AD 1750–1813)

Williams was a native of Wales who pastored Carr's Lane in Birmingham, served as principal of Independent Academy at Rotherham, and was one of the founders of the London Missionary Society. His main work, *An Essay on the Equity of Divine Government and the Sovereignty of Divine Grace*, addressed the subject of God's sovereignty and human responsibility in salvation. Williams's theology was influential in Wales and contributed to the debates there over the extent of the atonement in the eighteenth and nineteenth centuries.

Williams's comments about Calvin's view of the extent of the atonement coupled with his comments about his own views are instructive:

> Having endeavored to explain and illustrate what I presumed to call "the harmonizing principle," in reference to the great topic of redemption, I will now advert to his Lordship's declarations on the subject. It is asserted, in the first place, that the doctrine of universal redemption—was directly opposed by CALVIN. His Lordship I hope will excuse me for asserting, in return, that this eminent reformer did not "directly" oppose the doctrine of universal redemption, in the sense now explained, as far as I have been able to collect by a frequent search into his voluminous writings. He admitted a universal price of redemption; but he had reasons innumerable against the notion of an actual redemption of all men from sin and misery. He maintained that the remedy was universal, and that it was universally proposed to mankind, according to God's rectoral design; by it not that it was the sovereign design of God by it to make mankind universally and indiscriminately submissive, and compliant with the terms on which the

91 Ibid., 2:270.

92 J. Edwards, "Sermons 1, 2, 3," in *The Works of Jonathan Edwards, with a Memoir of His Life and Character*, 2 vols., ed. T. Edwards (Andover, MA: Allen, Morrill & Wardwell, 1842), 2:11–52. These sermons can also be found in J. Smalley et al., *Sermons, Essays and Extracts by Various Authors Selected with Special Respect to the Great Doctrine of Atonement* (New York: George Forman, 1811), 325–85.

blessings resulting from it were to be enjoyed. Had this been his design, not one of the human race could perish; for "who hath resisted his will?" If God were to design this, and to exert his power on the heart accordingly, who could prevent him? What CALVIN'S ill digested reprobating decree implied indirectly, is another consideration.

CALVIN, however, certainly did "oppose" his Lordship's notion of universal redemption,—which we now proceed to examine. The explanatory clauses, indicating what was intended by the phrase "universal redemption," are these: "namely, that *the benefits* of Christ's passion extend to the *whole human race*;" or, "that every man *is enabled* to attain salvation through the merits of Christ." If by "*the* benefits" be meant *some* benefits, what Calvinist, ancient or modern, ever denied it? But if by "*the* benefits" be meant *all* the benefits of Christ's passion, surely his Lordship will not deliberately maintain it, as it is "directly opposed," by obvious innumerable *facts*. For instance, a clean heart, a right spirit, justification, adoption, divine love shed abroad in the heart, being kept by divine power through faith unto salvation, an introduction to the heavenly Jerusalem, a glorious resurrection, and eternal life—all these are benefits of Christ's passion; but are they extended to "the whole human race?" If it be said that they are extended conditionally, proposed objectively, or in such a manner that all *may* obtain them, were it for their own fault; this I have already admitted.[93]

Williams indicated his belief that Calvin himself never asserted limited atonement. In another work Williams stated:

The *mediatorship*, atonement and merits of Christ, are the foundation of all gospel offers; and the rectoral designation of them extends to all human characters on earth: but the *suretyship* of Christ, the exertion of his power, and the application of his grace, is the foundation of justification, regeneration, sanctification, and perseverance; and the *decretive* designation of them extends only to persons who eventually love GOD and enjoy heaven; the *chosen*, the *called*, the *faithful*. Every new-covenant blessing, flows through the mediation and merits of Christ; when therefore overtures of pardon and reconciliation, righteousness and peace, are made to *sinners* as such, and not merely to elect sinners, can the consequence be avoided, that the blessings, purchased by the death of Christ, are rectorally designed for them? Must not the *provision* be equally extensive with the *overture*? Is the proposal made, *delusive* or *real*? If the latter, must not the advantages proposed be the purchase of the mediator? Or

93 E. Williams, *A Defence of Modern Calvinism: Containing an Examination of the Bishop of Lincoln's Work, Entitled a "Refutation of Calvinism"* (London: Printed for and sold by James Black, 1812), 192–93 (some spelling modernized; emphasis in original).

> is the overture made founded on the foreseen *aversion* of the sinner to the thing proposed, and the *certainty* of a refusal if left in the hand of his own counsel? And then the proposal would be hypothetical; thus: If you perform, what it is *certain* you will not, you shall be saved. That is, if you believe a falsehood, that there is provision made for sinners, *as such*, when, on the supposition, there is provision only for *elect* sinners, which election cannot be known as a qualification for believing, GOD is willing to bestow pardon! But is such a proposal worthy of the great Supreme, or better than *delusive*?—We conclude, therefore, that the *rectoral* design of the death of Christ (whatever higher speciality there is in it) extends to all the *human race*; not merely to those who have been, or actually shall be but also such as may be evangelized or discipled—that is, *all the nations*, past, present, and future.[94]

These statements by Williams indicate his belief in an unlimited atonement as a necessary ground for the free offer of the gospel to all.

John Wesley (AD 1703–1791)

Wesley's life and ministry are well known, as is his commitment to universal atonement, demonstrated from his sermons and writings and the immense secondary literature on his life.[95] Though his life dates are earlier, we here mention him before turning to the next century

Allan Coppedge explored the Wesleyan hymns, which John Wesley edited for publication, as a source of his theology. Coppedge noted: "An examination of Wesley's preaching . . . along with his hymns and early publications on predestination, has already demonstrated his strong commitment to the doctrine of universal redemption."[96]

---

94 E. Williams, *An Essay on the Equity of Divine Government and the Sovereignty of Divine Grace* (London: J. Burditt, 1899), 107–9. In a footnote by Williams in this section, he stated: "That illustrious reformer and admirable writer, CALVIN, has treated much of predestination and the doctrines of special grace; but though his works consist of nine volumes folio, I do not think that there is one sentence in them all that militates against the above representation; and in many places he expresses himself in a manner that abundantly justifies it, particularly his comments on several passages of the New Testament." Williams then quoted Calvin's comments in the Latin text on Matt 26:8 and Rom 5:18.

95 See, for example, John Wesley, "Predestination Calmly Considered," in *The Works of John Wesley*, 14 vols. (Peabody, MA: Hendrickson, 1991), 10:225, where Wesley appeals to 2 Cor 5:14–15 and 1 John 2:2 in support of unlimited atonement; and his sermon "Free Grace," in *Doctrinal and Controversial Treatises I*, in *Works of John Wesley*, 14 vols., ed. R. Maddox (New York: Abingdon, 2012), 3:73–86. Here Wesley strongly asserted and defended unlimited atonement. For secondary literature, consult K. J. Collins, *The Theology of John Wesley* (Nashville: Abingdon, 2007), 99–103; W. R. Cannon, *The Theology of John Wesley* (New York: Abingdon Cokesbury, 1946), 250; J. E. Vickers, "Wesley's Theological Emphases," *The Cambridge Companion to John Wesley*, ed. R. L. Maddox and J. E. Vickers (Cambridge: Cambridge University Press, 2010), 190–97. Calvinist Baptist Isaac Backus surveyed Wesley's critique of limited atonement and responded in his *Isaac Backus on Church, State, and Calvinism: Pamphlets 1754–1789*, ed. W. McLoughlin (Cambridge, MA: Harvard University Press, 2013), 453–55. See Backus, *The Atonement of Christ, Explained and Vindicated against Late Attempts to Exclude It out of the World* (Boston: Printed by Samuel Hall, in State-Street, and sold by Philip Freeman, in Union-Street, 1787).

96 A. Coppedge, *John Wesley in Theological Debate* (Wilmore, KY: Wesley Heritage, 1987), 134.

Concerning whether or not Wesley held to penal substitution, Collins remarked, "A broad agreement exists in the secondary literature that Wesley's satisfaction view of the atonement is best comprehended in terms of penal substitution."[97]

Conclusion

As the eighteenth century came to a close, many Calvinists of all denominations in Great Britain and in America were affirming unlimited atonement, including such a stellar figure as Jonathan Edwards. These Calvinists all affirmed a special *intent* of the atonement such that God's design was to save only the elect. But with respect to *extent*, they affirmed a universal atonement such that Christ's death paid the penalty for the sin of all people. They asserted the *application* of the atonement was limited by God's intent to the elect only.

The Nineteenth Century

The nineteenth century witnessed a spate of books and articles on the question of the extent of the atonement. Leading Calvinist theologians such as Thomas Chalmers in Scotland and Charles Hodge, Robert Dabney, and W. G. T. Shedd in the United States all argued against limited atonement and critiqued many of the arguments of Owen and other strict particularists.

In the first half of the century, the debate over the extent of the atonement among the Reformed was in full swing in Great Britain. The debate in Wales is best chronicled by Owen Thomas (1812–1891) in his 1874 biography of the stellar Welsh preacher John Jones.[98] This is the most important source on the debates over the extent of the atonement during the period of the eighteenth and early nineteenth centuries in Wales.

The book is divided into three main parts: (1) controversies between Calvinists and Arminians (1707–1831), (2) controversies among Calvinists (1811–1841), and (3) controversies among the Calvinistic Methodists (1814–1841). A lengthy section of this biography (338 pages) contains a historical survey of the debates among the Reformed between the years 1811 and 1841. This section of the biography was translated into English by John Aaron and published in 2002.[99]

Following a summary of the issue from the early church through about the end of the eighteenth century, Thomas covered the crucial thirty years from 1811 to 1841 in

97 Collins, *The Theology of John Wesley*, 102.

98 O. Thomas, *The Life of John Jones, Talsarn* (Wrexham: Hughes and Son, 1874).

99 O. Thomas, *The Atonement Controversy in Welsh Theological Literature and Debate, 1707–1841*, trans. J. Aaron (Edinburgh: Banner of Truth, 2002). One can also see something of this controversy in Owen Jones, *Some of the Great Preachers of Wales* (London: Passmore and Alabaster, 1886). See especially the chapter on Christmas Evans (159–222), as well as the chapters on Henry Rees (357–462) and John Jones (463–538).

Wales.[100] The book illustrates quite well one of the main theses of this volume—namely, that there has never been a consensus on the extent of the atonement among Calvinists from the Reformation era through modern times. As in England and Scotland during the eighteenth and early to mid-nineteenth centuries, many Welsh Calvinists affirmed universal atonement along with particular redemption in terms of application to the elect.

Thomas noted that the views of several in England, such as Andrew Fuller, who argued for a universal aspect to the atonement, were well known in Wales early in the nineteenth century, and some Welsh Calvinist pastors were preaching "similar views" in 1809.[101] Ironically, what launched the debate into the open was a publication by the colorful Welsh Baptist Christmas Evans, who argued for limited atonement by positing the commercial nature of the atonement in strong quantitative equivalentist terms such that the nature of Christ's substitution is defined as the exact amount of sins of each of the elect was borne by Christ on the cross. "The price, or the suffering, had to be equivalent to the measure of the sins, as far as number, weight and extent."[102] As a consequence, Evans argued there is no actual sufficiency in the atonement for the non-elect.

Thomas suggested that the many Calvinists who affirmed a universal aspect to the atonement were reluctant to say much publicly "since there was great prejudice amongst all the Calvinistic parties against anything that might appear to have any connection with Arminianism."[103] In 1814, John Roberts published a short, twenty-four-page book containing two letters to a friend concerning the nature and extent of the atonement.[104] The gist of Roberts's argument was that Christ had both general (universal) and particular intentions in the atonement. It is clear that Roberts believed Christ suffered for the sins of all people, not just the elect.

Two years later Thomas Jones published a fifty-eight-page book, which was expanded and republished in 1819, making the case for a strictly limited atonement.[105] Jones argued the case for the sufficiency of the atonement based on its merit or worth and this, to his mind, grounded the universal call of the gospel. Here Jones differed significantly from Christmas Evans, who argued there is no sufficiency in the atonement for the non-elect.

---

100 O. Thomas, *The Atonement Controversy*, 151–283.

101 Ibid., 152.

102 C. Evans, *The Particular Nature of Redemption Sought out, Taking Notice of All that It Entails. Together with Select Remarks from the Works of Andrew Fuller, Kettering* (Aberystwyth: James and Williams, 1811), iv.

103 Thomas, *The Atonement Controversy*, 158.

104 J. Roberts, *A Humble Attempt at Explaining What We Are Taught in the Scriptures of Truth concerning the General and Particular Purposes of the Suffering of Jesus Christ, in Two Letters to a Friend* (Llanbryn-mair, Carmarthen: J. Evans, 1814).

105 T. Jones, *Conversations upon Redemption between Two Friends, Enquirer and Oldman* (Denbigh: Thomas Gee, 1816), reprinted as *Conversations upon Redemption between Enquirer and Oldman; One Tending towards a Degree of Generality in the Redemption; and the Other Tending to the Opposite, Which Is Much Worse, and Setting a Limit to the Merit of Christ's Sacrifice! and a Cywydd, Etc., on the Same Matters* (Denbigh: Thomas Gee, 1819).

Owen Thomas quoted the main statements in each of these three works in an effort to let the authors speak for themselves and then engaged them as to the strengths and weaknesses of their arguments. Thomas perceptively pointed out with respect to Jones's critique of Roberts's use of "all," "every man," and "the whole world," that Jones does not attempt to demonstrate

> why, or on what grounds, he believes that the same phrases are sufficient to prove a general offer of the gospel which is still consistent with a particular and effective call, whilst arguing that they are completely insufficient to prove an universal atonement which might, as is argued, be consistent with an effective, particular redemption.[106]

This is an absolutely crucial point to make and highlights a major problem in the argument for limited atonement conjoined with the argument for a universal gospel offer.

Thomas summarized what he considered to be the main difficulty in each author. The difficulty with Christmas Evans he considered to be

> how to reconcile the sincere, honest universal call of the gospel upon all without distinction, with a sufficiency for the elect alone? And if the sufficiency of the sacrifice only corresponds to the number and iniquity of the sins of those for whom Christ suffered, and if he suffered more for some of his people than for others, and if there could not be a sufficiency in him for others without his having suffered more, how can we account for such words as "He is the propitiation," "but now once in the end of world hath he appeared to put away sin by the sacrifice of Himself," and similar phrases? And, especially, how can such a view be reconciled with the justice of punishing those who ultimately refuse Christ?[107]

The difficulty with John Roberts was

> how could Jesus Christ be an atonement for the sins of all without having been appointed for all; for sins are associated only with persons? Or, if he is appointed for all persons, where is the particular relationship (for which Roberts argues) between him in his death and the elect for whom he is Mediator?[108]

---

106 Thomas, *The Atonement Controversy*, 173.

107 Ibid., 178.

108 Ibid., 177.

The difficulty with Thomas Jones was "how to reconcile the general sufficiency for all, with a specific appointment for only some? And if there can be in him a sufficiency for those for whom he was not appointed, what need was there for an appointment for any?"[109]

Christmas Evans wasted no time in replying to Thomas Jones.[110] Evans claimed to have modified his views on the commercial and quantitative equivalentist nature of the atonement, though it is difficult to see just how he had softened on this point. However, he continued his stringent arguments to prove the limited sufficiency of the atonement. Evans had been uncharitable in his response and even at times "completely misrepresents" the views of both Jones and Roberts.[111]

Within a few weeks of Evans's book, Thomas Jones responded in a short, eight-page letter,[112] narrating two amicable conversations the two men had in 1819. However, Jones ended his letter "with a very unfraternal reference, expressed in a rather reproachful spirit."[113]

Shortly after this letter was published, some Baptists replied to Thomas Jones in a letter asking a series of questions intimating Jones's error.[114] This was followed by yet another anonymous letter, likely written by Christmas Evans, in a vituperative style, consisting "mainly of attacks on Jones for *accusing, slandering, reviling, libelling, abusing, blaspheming and mocking* Christmas Evans."[115]

At this point John Roberts replied to Thomas Jones in an effort to further the argument that Christ died for the sins of the non-elect as well as the elect.[116] Thomas called this work a remarkable book in the history of Welsh theological controversy because it served as something of an index to the views of Welsh Independents who held to some form of unlimited atonement.[117] Thomas summarized the book chapter by chapter and offered his evaluative comments.[118]

The controversy over the extent of the atonement in Wales continued and increased during the period 1820–1827 with a series of published sermons and articles on the

109 Ibid.

110 C. Evans, *Redempton within the Compass of Election . . . Together with a Refutation of the Misinterpretations of Mr. Thomas Jones of Denbigh of a Booklet of Similar Title to This* (Caernarvon: L. E. Jones, 1819).

111 O. Thomas, *The Atonement Controversy*, 185.

112 T. Jones, *A Letter for T. Jones to All Who Read It and Especially to Those Ministers and Members of That Body of People Known as Baptists, concerning a Booklet Written by Mr Christmas Evans* (Denbigh: T. Gee, 1820).

113 O. Thomas, *The Atonement Controversy*, 189.

114 *A Letter from a Few Members in Denbighshire of That Body of People Known as Baptists . . . in Answer to a Letter Written to Us by Him and Relating to a Book by Mr Christmas Evans on the Particular Nature of Redemption* (Trefriw: John Jones, 1820). For the specific questions of this letter, see Owen Thomas, *The Atonement Controversy*, 190–93.

115 O. Thomas, *The Atonement Controversy*, 193 (emphasis in original).

116 J. Roberts, *A Serious Call for Inquirers after the Truth to Consider the Testimony of the Scriptures Relating to the Extent of Christ's Atonement, and Containing Comments on a Book by the Rev. Thomas Jones of Denbigh on Redemption* (Llanbryn-mair, Dolgelley: Richard Jones, 1820).

117 O. Thomas, *The Atonement Controversy*, 197–98.

118 Ibid., 198–217.

issue. John Hurrion's four sermons defending particular redemption appeared in 1820 with a short introduction by John Elias, which opposed Arminianism and those within Calvinism who affirmed a universal atonement.[119] This was followed by a reply to Elias by C. Jones[120] in 1820 and John Griffiths in 1821.[121] John Davies, influenced by Andrew Fuller's view of the atonement and its universal extent, published two sermons. This engendered a supportive response from Richard Foulkes, a Baptist, in the April 1822 edition of *Gomer's Star*. Other articles appeared over a period of several months continuing the debate.[122]

The period of 1826–1841 likewise continued to produce sermons, books, and articles on the subject.[123] By 1841, it had become evident that both sides had presented their case, neither party was moving any closer to the other, and little remained to be said. Both groups agreed that the most important work at hand was the preaching of the gospel.

The final section of Thomas's *The Atonement Controversy* dealt with the discussions and debates over the subject among the Calvinistic Methodists in Wales. One result of the arrival of the Wesleyan Methodists in Wales was the pendulum swing of some already strict Calvinists into positions and beliefs opposing Arminianism that bordered on the extreme. This fact was acknowledged by some Welsh Calvinists who themselves held firmly to limited atonement.

Thomas's book illustrates well that the question of the extent, nature, and sufficiency of the atonement were hot topics during the early to mid-eighteenth century in Wales, with many Calvinists affirming that Christ died for the sins of all.

Likewise in Scotland, from the early to mid-nineteenth century, a torrent of books, pamphlets, and articles debating the extent question appeared with no abatement until early into the twentieth century.[124] The key controversy was the extent of the atonement. By the mid- to late nineteenth century, the controversy shifted more to the nature of the atonement. Many of the key players and their views will be considered below.

In America, the late eighteenth and early nineteenth centuries witnessed the rise of the New Divinity in New England. Works on the atonement, including its extent, were published by Stephen West, Jonathan Edwards Jr., and John Smalley within a

119 J. Hurrion, *A Defense of the Scriptural Doctrine of Particular Redemption*, trans. Evan Evans (Trefriw: J. Jones, 1820).

120 C. Jones, *A Defense of the Nonconformists* (Dolgelley: R. Richards, 1820).

121 J. Griffiths, *A Letter to the Rev. John Elias* (Dolgelley: R. Jones, n.d. [1821]).

122 For citations, details, and other works on the controversy published through 1827, see Thomas, *The Atonement Controversy*, 221–27.

123 Ibid., 239–83.

124 Malcolm Kinnear noted that in the second and third decades of the 1800s, fewer than twenty books, pamphlets, and articles on the atonement appeared in Scotland in each decade. Yet between 1840 and 1850, more than 120 books, pamphlets, and articles appeared ("Scottish New Testament Scholarship and the Atonement c. 1845–1920" [PhD dissertation, University of Edinburgh, 1995], 402). Kinnear's bibliography is very helpful on the primary source material produced in this period (404–13).

period of twelve months from 1785 to 1786. During this same period of time New England experienced a strong push toward universalism, whose advocates derived some of their arguments from notions of commercialism inherent in the limited atonement scheme.

Maxcy followed Edwards as president of Union College and wrote on the atonement in 1796. Edwards Park noted how there were several Baptists who were persuaded toward the Edwardsian theory following the publication of Maxcy's work on the atonement. From 1800 to 1826, Nathanael Emmons would advocate the Edwardsian approach as well. Griffin published his *Humble Attempt to Reconcile the Differences of Christians* in 1819, a significant work advocating universal atonement. Three years later, Caleb Burge published a work defending unlimited atonement.[125]

All of these men were Calvinists who described the nature of the atonement in governmental categories and, like their earlier counterparts, affirmed an unlimited atonement. It is often assumed by limitarians that all who affirmed a governmental understanding of the atonement had come to reject penal substitution. This is false.

R. Larry Shelton surveyed Arminian and Wesleyan theologians with respect to Grotius's governmental theory, demonstrating that many held both to a form of substitution and to rectoral justice.[126] For example, "Curcellaeus emphasized the idea of sacrifice rather than satisfaction of wrath through punishment, thus describing the priestly work of Christ as propitiatory, but not penal."[127] "Wesley's followers generally developed some form of the governmental theory of atonement. Richard Watson developed a modified governmental theory which emphasized the atonement as substitutionary and penal."[128] "William Pope was drawn to the governmental theory but tended to relate Christ's vicarious work to the concept of penalty."[129] The nineteenth-century American Methodist theologian John Miley held that the atonement is a satisfaction for sins but is not penally retributive. "For Miley, atonement is made, not in its satisfaction, but in fulfillment of the rectoral office of justice."[130] Shelton noted that H. Orton Wiley affirmed a penal understanding of the cross but rejected the penal satisfaction theory. Wiley mistakenly believed that the penal substitutionary theory led to either universalism or unconditional election/limited atonement. Here Wiley is giving too much ground to a commercialistic understanding

125 C. Burge, "Essay on the Scripture Doctrine of Atonement: Showing its Nature, Its Necessity, and its Extent," in *The Atonement: Discourses and Treatises*, ed. E. Park (Boston: Congregational, 1859), 429–546. This work by Burge originally appeared in 1822.

126 R. Larry Shelton, "A Covenant Concept of Atonement," *Wesleyan Theological Journal* 19 (1984): 91–108.

127 Ibid., 101; citing Curcellaeus, *Institutes*, V19.15.

128 Ibid., 102; citing R. Watson, *Theological Institutes*, 2 vols. (New York: Carlton & Phillips, 1856), 2:139; 87–102.

129 Ibid., 103; citing W. B. Pope, *A Compendium of Christian Theology*, 3 vols. (London: Wesleyan Conference Office, 1880), 2:265, 313–14.

130 Ibid.; citing J. Miley, *Systematic Theology*, 2 vols. (New York: Easton and Mains, 1984), 2:186. Shelton noted that Miley quoted Miner Raymond for support of his position (M. Raymond, *Systematic Theology*, 3 vols. [New York: Phillips and Hunt, 1880], 2:257–58).

of penal substitution, causing him to draw the same false dilemma conclusions that many Calvinists draw.[131]

In a work published in 1859, Edwards Park charted the waters of the rise of the Edwardsian theory of the atonement, a common synonym for New Divinity theology reflecting the influence of Jonathan Edwards.[132] Park noted that according to Emmons, a leading proponent of the New Divinity, the atonement was designed to make the salvation of all men possible by removing all the obstacles that the law and distributive justice presented against the salvation of the non-elect as well as the elect. God grants regenerating grace only to the elect, yet without particular respect to the atonement. Even though only the elect are regenerated on the grounds of the atonement, Emmons denied that the regeneration of one person rather than another is a consequence of the atonement itself.[133]

Joseph Bellamy was also a leading light espousing the Edwardsian theory of the atonement. Park discussed Joseph Bellamy's understanding of the extent of the atonement.

> What Christ has done, is, in fact, sufficient to open a door for God, through him, to become reconcilable to the whole world. The sufferings of Christ, all things considered, have as much displayed God's hatred to sin, and as much secured the honor of his law, as if the whole world had been damned; as none will deny, who believe the infinite dignity of his divine nature. God may now, therefore, through Jesus Christ, stand ready to pardon the whole world. There is nothing in the way. And the obedience of Christ has brought as much honor to God, and to his law, as the perfect obedience of Adam, and of all his race, would have done; the rights of the God head are as much asserted and maintained. So that there is nothing in the way, but that mankind may, through Christ, be received into full favor, and entitled to eternal life. God may stand ready to do it, consistently with his honor. What Christ has done is every way sufficient. "All things are now ready."[134]

Bellamy frequently spoke of Christ's death removing the obstacles to salvation of all people. If Christ died only for the elect, then the non-elect have no door of salvation opened to them since there is no atonement for their sins. They have no grounds to take encouragement in the gospel. Furthermore, no one can rationally take any encourage-

131 Ibid.; citing Wiley, *Christian Theology* (Kansas City: Beacon Hill, 1952), 2:221–26; 245–49.

132 E. Park, "The Rise of the Edwardean Theory of the Atonement," in *The Atonement: Discourses and Treatises*, vii–lxxx.

133 Ibid., xiii. See N. Emmons, *The Works of Nathanael Emmons*, 6 vols., ed. J. Ide (Boston: Crocker & Brewster, 1842), 5:66.

134 J. Bellamy, "True Religion Delineated," in *The Works of Joseph Bellamy*, 2 vols. (Boston: Doctrinal Tract and Book Society, 1853), 1:292; cited in Park, *The Rise of the Edwardean Theory*, xlv–xlvi. Jonathan Edwards wrote the preface to Bellamy's work, commending it warmly.

ment from the gospel on this scheme until he knows he is elected because, until then, he cannot know that there is any ground for such encouragement.[135]

Park took note of the fact that Bellamy and Hopkins were close friends with Jonathan Edwards, and that the views of these three on the atonement are in essential agreement with that doctrine adopted by the school of the younger Jonathan Edwards.[136]

From the perspective of the New Divinity approach to the atonement and its extent, the illogic of positing God as a Sovereign who does that which he is obligated in distributive justice to do (the limited atonement scheme) is alleviated by ascribing the application of the atonement to both God's sovereign right as well as his sovereign grace.[137] Park's treatment is helpful in tracking the rise of the New Divinity in New England and its influence on the founding and early faculty of Andover Theological Seminary.

Space will not permit a full examination of everything written on the extent question during this century, but we will attempt coverage of the major works.

Ezra Styles Ely's *A Contrast between Calvinism and Hopkinsianism* was published in 1811.[138] Ely's goal was to compare and contrast what he considered to be historic Calvinism with the revision of Calvinism promulgated by Samuel Hopkins in late eighteenth-century New England and dubbed "Hopkinsianism," also known as the New Divinity. The roots of the New Divinity trace back to Jonathan Edwards. Of course, Hopkins was a Calvinist, but he was moderate on the extent of the atonement. One of the key tenets of Hopkins and those who agreed with his teachings was the belief that Christ died for the sins of all people.

One of the older books on the subject of the extent of the atonement in my personal library is *Sermons, Essays and Extracts by Various Authors Selected with Special Respect to the Great Doctrine of Atonement*, published in 1811. This work is a collection of various sermons and writings by Calvinist authors on the subject, mostly written or preached in the eighteenth century, and arguing for unlimited atonement. The first two chapters are sermons on John 6:44 by John Smalley (1734–1820), a pastor in Farmington, Michigan. Both were preached in the latter half of the eighteenth century. Sermon 2 is of special interest and is entitled "The Natural Ability of Men to Understand and Embrace the Gospel Considered; and the Subject Applied."[139]

> Sin stands in our way of obtaining salvation. Not in our power to erase. Until sin is dealt with, it is not consistent with the honor of God's character and the

---

135 Ibid., 1:294–96; cited in Park, *The Rise of the Edwardean Theory*, xlvi–xlvii.

136 Park, *The Rise of the Edwardean Theory*, lxii.

137 Ibid., lxxvii.

138 E. S. Ely, *A Contrast between Calvinism and Hopkinsianism* (New York: S. Whiting & Co., 1811).

139 J. Smalley, *Sermons, Essays and Extracts by Various Authors Selected with Special Respect to the Great Doctrine of Atonement* (New York: George Forman, 1811), 35–78.

> rights of his government to show favor to the sinner. But Christ has removed every difficulty of this kind. By his all-sufficient sacrifice he has made full atonement for sin, and opened a way for the exercise of Grace. God stands ready to justify every sinner who is willing to submit to Christ's righteousness and consents to forsake his sins and be saved in this way. And now he can say, and has actually said: "all things are now ready." . . . There is nothing on earth; there is nothing in all the decrees of heaven; there is nothing in all the power of hell that can hinder your salvation if you do not hinder it yourself.[140]

Smalley affirmed that Christ has satisfied for the sins of all people. Smalley elsewhere appealed to Jonathan Edwards's distinction between natural and moral ability in fallen humanity. People have the natural ability to believe in Christ, but they lack the moral ability.[141] When sinners don't come to Christ through their moral inability, they have no one to blame but themselves. The fact that God sovereignly chose to give the moral ability only to the elect to repent and believe the gospel does not impugn God's character according to Edwards and Smalley.

Smalley continued:

> The things which have been said may help us to see that there is a universal door of mercy opened to sinners, and a glorious hope set before all without exception, for which they have infinite reason to glorify God and to be thankful; the limitation in the text notwithstanding. Had no sufficient provision been made for the salvation of but only a remnant of mankind; or, were the terms of obtaining an interest in the covenant of grace *naturally impossible* to men, without that special divine influence which is given only to an elect number, it would indeed seem, as some have objected, that the offers of mercy could not, with any sincerity, be made to the non-elect; and that it could not be their fault that they are not saved. But neither of these is truly the case.[142]

Smalley quoted Heb 2:9 and 1 John 2:2 with respect to his claim for universal atonement. However, it is interesting to note he offered no scriptural support for the concept of moral inability. Such statements as these above simply could not consistently be said by one who held to limited atonement.

---

140 Ibid., 71–72.

141 For more on this subject from Smalley, see J. Smalley, *Consistency of the Sinner's Inability to Comply with the Gospel. The Consistency of the Sinner's Inability to Comply with the Gospel; with His Inexcusable Guilt in Not Complying with It, Illustrated and Confirmed in Two Discourses, on John VIth, 44th* (Hartford, CT: Green & Watson, 1769).

142 J. Smalley, "The Law in All Respects Satisfied by Our Saviour, in Regard to Those Only Who Belong to Him; or, None but Believers Saved through the All-Sufficient Satisfaction of Christ," in *Sermons, Essays and Extracts*, 162.

Also tucked away in this 1811 volume is an excerpt from John Newton's *Messiah*, entitled "The Lamb of God, the Great Atonement," demonstrating that Newton rejected a quantitative view of the atonement and likely held to a form of universal atonement.[143]

Following Newton is a two-part sermon on Heb 2:10 delivered on November 11 and 25, 1796, in the chapel of Rhode Island College by president Jonathan Maxcy, entitled "A Discourse, Designed to Explain the Doctrine of Atonement: In Two Parts."[144] The most important section dealt with how the atonement made full satisfaction for justice without obligating justice for the deliverance of sinners but leaving their deliverance an act of pure grace. "How can those be subjects of forgiveness who owe nothing since Christ has paid the price?" Here Maxcy is addressing and critiquing the so-called double payment or double jeopardy argument popularized by John Owen. Crucial to us is what he said about limited atonement. It "represents Christ suffering on the ground of distributive justice." "To represent Christ's sufferings to be the same as those of his people, is to destroy all grace in salvation. For if in Him they have endured all to which they were exposed, from what are they delivered? In what respect are they forgiven?"[145] Maxcy is making the argument that if Christ only suffered for the sins of the elect in the sense of distributive justice, then the atonement is owed the elect and the principle of grace in the application goes out the window.

There is much more in this book, including material from Andrew Fuller and Jonathan Edwards Jr., which the editors included as evidence that these men affirmed universal atonement. We will consider Fuller below.

James Willson's *A Historical Sketch of Opinions on the Atonement* was published in 1817.[146] Willson was a high Calvinist. This is a lengthy work that rather hops, skips, and jumps through church history. Most of this work deals with the atonement more generally and only occasionally touches on the question of extent.

The tone of the book is at times condescending, especially in criticism of Arminius and Arminianism. There are some historical errors in his assessment, coupled with other statements in need of nuance. For example, he cited Luther as limiting the extent of the atonement to the elect only.[147] His assessment of Arminius's beliefs is also not entirely accurate.[148] He indicated that the Arminians at Dort were called "Remonstrants" because of their written opposition to the Canons of Dort, but the

143 J. Newton, "The Lamb of God, the Great Atonement," 177–78.

144 J. Maxcy, "A Discourse Designed to Explain the Doctrine of Atonement: In Two parts—Delivered in the Chapel of Rhode-Island College, on the 11th and 25th of November, 1796," 179–212.

145 Ibid., 210–11.

146 J. R. Willson, *A Historical Sketch of Opinions on the Atonement, Interspersed with Biographical Notices of the Leading Doctors, and Outlines of the Sections of the Church, from the Incarnation of Christ to the Present Time; with Translations from Francis Turretin, on the Atonement* (Philadelphia: Edward Earle, 1817).

147 Ibid., 22.

148 Ibid., 32.

Arminians were called "Remonstrants" prior to Dort.[149] He spoke of the Baptists as differing with other denominations only in the question of baptism and church polity. This is much too simplistic. Interestingly, and correctly I think, he perceived a closer link of Baptists to the Anabaptists than many Baptists themselves, especially Calvinistic Baptists, are willing to admit.[150] He also rightly affirmed Andrew Fuller's commitment to unlimited atonement.[151]

Of the Thirty-Nine Articles of the Church of England, along with the Book of Homilies, Willson conceded that there is no explicit affirmation of definite atonement,[152] but Willson cannot fathom how these articles could be given any Arminian reading with respect to the extent of the atonement. He also appeared to misunderstand the diversity at Dort and Westminster with respect to the question of the extent of the atonement.

In America, as early as 1732, tenets of Arminianism were finding their way into Yale and spreading among New England pastors. Willson charged that the doctrine of general atonement began to prevail among the pastors of New England. He appears to fail to distinguish between Arminians who affirmed a general atonement and moderate Calvinists who likewise affirmed a universal satisfaction for sins with respect to extent.

He referenced the French Amyraldians who came to England as a result of the revocation of the Edict of Nantes and spoke of the large number of London pastors who "embraced" these errors[153] and how the close connection with their New England counterparts influenced them as well. This indicates the large number of Calvinistic pastors who embraced unlimited atonement in France, England, and New England in the late seventeenth and early eighteenth centuries.

Willson concluded that the doctrine of indefinite atonement was responsible for many churches succumbing to Socinianism.[154]

Concerning the faculty and early student body of Andover Seminary, founded in 1808, Willson stated: "The number of pupils is upwards of sixty; among all of whom, professors and pupils, there is probably not one who does not maintain the doctrine of general atonement."[155] If this statement is accurate, it would likely confirm both Adoniram Judson and Luther Rice (Andover graduates and early Congregationalist missionaries turned Baptist) as Calvinists who affirmed universal atonement. In fact, Willson called Andover "an American Saumur."[156] Willson's book was published only nine years after the founding of Andover Seminary.

---

149 Ibid., 37.
150 Ibid., 114.
151 Ibid., 116.
152 Ibid., 78, 80, 83.
153 Ibid., 132.
154 Ibid., 155.
155 Ibid., 163.
156 Ibid.

Willson also discussed Ely's *A Contrast between Calvinism and Hopkinsianism.*[157]

His conclusion concerning the situation with respect to views on the extent of the atonement in early nineteenth-century New England is that "a very large majority of the professors of religion in the United States, are either Hopkinsians, or entire Arminians, and as such opposed to the doctrine of a definite atonement."[158]

These works, published prior to 1820, illustrate the diversity within Calvinism on the question of the extent of the atonement from the eighteenth century in New England. This also impinges on the situation surrounding the founding of the Southern Baptist Convention in 1845, as we shall see below.

Hypothetical Dialogues on the Atonement's Extent

During the late eighteenth and nineteenth centuries, some authors, such as Andrew Fuller, presented their views on the extent of the atonement via a hypothetical dialogue between two or three interlocutors.[159] Generally, one speaker would represent unlimited atonement and the other limited atonement.

One of the best of these types of strategies can be found in the 1823 edition of the *Utica Christian Repository*, entitled "Dialogue on the Atonement."[160] The dialogue partners are Paulinus (P.) and Aspasio (A.), where P. affirms a version of unlimited atonement and A. represents a Calvinist who affirms limited atonement. I will present the gist of the dialogue with only rare comment or footnote so the reader can more easily follow the flow of discussion and understand the arguments that Calvinists who affirm universal atonement make against limited atonement.

P. inquires of A. why God chooses to save a part rather than the whole of mankind. A. responds he supposes that God loved a part of humanity more than he did the rest, and so gave his Son to die for them and not for the rest. P. then queries why God

> should love the elect before regeneration more than the non-elect? No reason appears. They are no better by nature, nor is their happiness in itself any more valuable. That he does love them any more is a mere assumption of your own, and has no countenance from the word of God.[161]

---

157 Ibid., 172–75.

158 Ibid., 215.

159 See, for example, A. Fuller, "Three Conversations between Andrew, James, and John on Imputation, Substitution, and Particular Redemption," in *Dialogues and Essays on Various Subjects*, in *The Works of Andrew Fuller*, 8 vols. (New Haven: S. Converse, 1824), 4:79–111. See also Anon., *A Dialogue on the Extent of the Atonement Between Clericus and Honestus* (Edinburgh: J. Leslie et al., 1842), 1–38. The editor and publisher, John Leslie, touts this work as the substance of a "friendly debate" in dialogue form that actually took place, between a minister and layman (labeled so as to identify the speakers as "Minister," who argued for limited atonement, and "Passenger," who argues for unlimited atonement) who were traveling to Edinburgh by steamboat. See also L. Edwards, *The Doctrine of the Atonement* (London: Hodder & Stoughton, 1888).

160 W. R. Weeks, "Dialogue on the Atonement," *Utica Christian Repository* (Utica, NY: Merrell & Hastings, 1823); and later published in *The Atonement: Discourses and Treatises*, 549–83.

161 *A Dialogue on the Extent*, 551.

P. contends that God has no greater love for the elect than the non-elect. God exercised his love for all in giving Christ to die for all.

A. argues that the reason Christ died was ultimately only the salvation of those for whom he died, the elect. God did not intend to save any but the elect, hence Christ could not have died for any but the elect. P. agrees with A. that only a part of mankind was given to the Son in the Covenant of Redemption but suggests that this does not logically entail a limited atonement exclusively. God had other purposes for the atonement.

A. queries P. as to the purpose or motive God had in Christ dying for those whom he had no intention of saving. P. responds that the great purpose of God is to promote his own glory. A. counters by questioning just how it is that the glory of God is promoted by Christ's death for the non-elect.

P. responds:

> His mercy is glorified in the offer of forgiveness, which is made to them for Christ's sake; his truth and sincerity are glorified in his inviting them to turn and live; his patience and long-suffering are glorified in his bearing so long with all their ingratitude, and contempt of offered mercy; and finally, his justice is glorified in their aggravated condemnation for having rejected the Saviour that was provided for them.[162]

A. counters this response by asking why God could not have his mercy be glorified in the offer of forgiveness to the non-elect, even if Christ had not died for them. P. responds: "Could mercy have been glorified in the pardon of sinners, if no atonement had been made?" P. continues:

> If, then, where no atonement is made, no forgiveness can be granted, it follows that where no atonement is made, no forgiveness can be offered; at least, there is no manifestation of mercy in such an offer. For if the offer should be accepted, the forgiveness could not be granted. What will the non-elect think in the great day, if they find that forgiveness was offered them on the part of God, with the greatest appearance of compassion for them, and at the same time discover that if they had accepted the offer forgiveness would have been refused?[163]

A. responds that this is a situation that never can happen. P. counters:

> The non-elect are either able or unable to accept the offer. If they are able, then the case can happen; and the appearance of mercy, expressed in the offer,

162 Ibid., 554.
163 Ibid.

> should be judged accordingly. If they are unable, then the difficulty is greatly increased; for they are not only tantalized with the offer of forgiveness which cannot be granted, but they are mocked with proposals which they cannot comply with. It is like calling upon a drowning man to take hold of a rope and save himself, when there is not only no rope within his reach, but he has no hands to take hold of one if there were. But if Christ has died for all men, they can all be forgiven if they will repent and believe.[164]

According to P., if Christ has died for all, then the truth and sincerity of God are glorified in his inviting all to salvation. P. illustrates this point by a man who makes a feast and invites twenty persons to come and partake of it. Does the invitation say to all invited, "Come, for there is provision made" or "Come for there is no provision made"?[165] The obvious answer is the former.

A. responds that preachers of the gospel do not know who the elect are. P. answers that the invitation to come to the feast is not that of the preachers, who are servants, but the invitation is from the Master. He knows for how many he has made provision. P. asks how God can sincerely invite all to come when provision has only been made for some.

A. deflects this question by arguing that the gospel invitation is not made to the entire human race since a great part of the world has never heard the gospel. P. counters by asking A. if he thinks that all are elected who hear the gospel preached. A. answers he does not think that. P. responds: "Then the fact that the gospel has not been actually preached to every creature will avail you nothing."[166]

A. suggests that the gospel invitation may be given to all people as sincerely upon his limited atonement scheme as upon P.'s unlimited atonement scheme. He proceeds with an illustration:

> Suppose a thousand captives are confined in prison—suppose a person wishes to redeem one hundred of them, and, for that purpose, pays to the authority which holds them in prison a pearl of great value, sufficient to redeem all the captives in prison; but the person paying it has in view only to redeem his own friends; this intention in the redeemer, and the acceptance of the price by the authority which holds them in bondage, constitutes the pearl a ransom, and confines it to the number for whom it was designed. But the pearl itself is sufficient to ransom all the rest of the captives if it had been applied to their advantage. To carry on the allusion, suppose that the person undertaking to redeem

164 Ibid.

165 Ibid., 555.

166 Ibid., 556.

> his friends should say, "I will have proclamation made in the prison that everyone who will acknowledge me as his deliverer, and will submit himself to my authority, may immediately come forth on the footing of the ransom which I have paid; for none but my friends will accept these terms, the remainder will prefer their prison to liberty, which can only be had by submission to me, whom they inveterately hate." Now the person commissioned to carry these tidings to the prison would feel himself authorized to proclaim deliverance to everyone who was willing to accept the terms, and to use arguments and motives to induce them to submit; but the event would be, that none would accept the offer but the real friends of the redeemer. This he knew from the beginning, and therefore he paid the ransom for no others. Is there anything insincere in this whole transaction?[167]

P. responds with the question: "Was the pearl paid for the whole, or only for a part?" A. responded that it was paid for the hundred who were intended from the beginning to be redeemed, but it was not paid for the rest. P. responds, "Then its value makes no difference."[168]

A. says that it was foreseen that none of them for whom there was no price paid would accept the offer. P. says this does not alleviate the problem. There is a wide difference between being hindered from receiving something because of voluntary refusal and being hindered because of the lack of a price being paid for one's release.

P. asks if the demons are bound to receive Christ as Savior. A. responds in the negative, stating it is not a reasonable duty for them because their condition and circumstances are different than humanity's. P. responds that for the same reason, according to limited atonement, the non-elect are not bound to believe in Christ because there is no atonement for them since Christ did not die for them. For the same reason as with demons, it cannot be the duty of the non-elect, on the limited atonement scheme, to believe in Christ. It is not possible they should have Christ to be their savior since he did not die for them.

For this reason, P. asserts that the non-elect, according to limited atonement, by entailment, cannot be charged with unbelief. Thus, the patience of God in sparing them from immediate destruction is, according to the unlimited atonement scheme, more gloriously displayed than on the limited scheme.

When A. asks P. to agree that God's justice is glorified in the condemnation of the non-elect, even though Christ did not die for them, P. responds that such is the case, "but in a degree far less."[169] Since Christ did not die for the non-elect, the justice of

167 Ibid.
168 Ibid., 557.
169 Ibid., 559.

God cannot be glorified in condemning them for rejecting Christ, since there is no Savior for them to reject. P. continues to press the case, pointing out that since Christ has died for the sins of the non-elect, "they are placed in a situation very different from that in which they would have been if he had not died for them."[170]

At this point, A. proffers another argument for limited atonement. The death of Christ, as a full expiation, propitiation, and satisfaction to God's law and justice, therefore must be efficacious in behalf of those for whom he died. Consequently, if Christ died for all people, then all must be saved. All are not saved, so Christ did not die for all. A. employs the double payment argument when he queries how God can punish the same crimes twice and remain just?

P. responds by clarifying the purpose of the atonement in order to understand its nature. He asks

> whether an atonement was necessary to restore to man his moral agency. . . . 2. I ask whether an atonement was necessary to be made in order to excite the compassion of God. . . . If you mean that a propitiation is that which renders it consistent for the person to whom it is offered to show favor, I have no objection to the idea. But if you mean that a propitiation is that which renders the person to whom it is offered disposed to show favor; if you mean it is intended to move him to show favor, when without it he would have no such inclination, it cannot be correct as applied to God. . . . 3. I ask whether an atonement was necessary to pay God for favors to be bestowed upon us. . . .
>
> I ask, fourthly, whether an atonement was necessary to satisfy commutative justice. . . . There are three kinds of justice, differing from each other as they have relation to different things. These are, commutative justice, which relates to commercial transactions, distributive justice, which relates to moral character, and public justice, which relates to the public good. . . . It is evident, then, that an atonement was not necessary to satisfy commutative justice. I acknowledge that some of "the words by which the death of Christ is frequently expressed, signify the price paid for the redemption of captives, and that the life of Christ is called a ransom." But this language is evidently figurative. The blood of Christ was not gold nor silver, nor any other commercial medium. To take figurative language, and draw conclusions from it, as if it was literal, will certainly lead us into mistakes. If this language were to be understood literally, it would indeed follow, as you say, that "When a sufficient price is paid for the redemption of a captive, he cannot with propriety be detained in slavery." It would indeed follow that those for whom the ransom price was paid will surely be actually redeemed. . . . But all such literal conclusions, drawn from

170 Ibid., 561.

> figurative language as if it were literal, are drawn without any foundation, and are a most unwarrantable perversion of the word of God. The atonement, therefore, was not a commercial transaction, and it was not necessary that an atonement should be made to satisfy commutative justice. . . . 5. I ask whether an atonement was necessary to take away our ill desert. . . . 6. I ask whether an atonement was necessary to satisfy distributive justice?[171]

A. responds and asks how the atonement could accomplish salvation for sinners without satisfying distributive justice. P. responds that the atonement satisfies public justice. A. counters by asking if distributive justice is not satisfied for sinners, then when they are exempted from punishment, why is it that no injustice is done?

P. responds by pointing out that distributive justice demands that the soul that sins should die. No injustice is done since injustice consists in treating persons worse than they deserve. When persons are treated better than they deserve, that is not injustice, but grace. Jesus did not undergo distributive justice when he died because he was not himself a sinner.

A. asks how, then, it follows from this view of the atonement that it is universal. P. responds that the atonement was a satisfaction to public justice by which the ends of punishment are answered. The atonement is, from its very nature, as sufficient for one man as for another, and for all men as for one man.[172]

P. then turns the discussion in another direction and asks A. if he believes that the elect are under the judgment of God until the moment they believe in Christ. A. responds in the affirmative. P. then states there is a difference between "a cover for" and "a cover of." The atonement is "a cover for sin, because it is adapted to be a cover of sin; but it does not become a cover of sin to any individual till he puts it on, that is, till he actually believes in Christ and receives his pardon."[173]

P. asks how it is, on the limited atonement scheme, the unbelieving elect are still under the judgment of God. He asserts that Scripture differentiates between atonement and reconciliation.

A. offers a fourth argument for limited atonement: Christ only intercedes for those for whom he died. P. responds that to draw this conclusion is to take it for granted that he could not possibly die for any but the elect, and hence to beg the question. Furthermore, P. does not grant that Christ intercedes only for the elect. A. counters that the Scripture says Christ prays not for the world "but for them which Thou hast given

171 Ibid., 563–67.

172 This, incidentally, is the same argument for universal atonement made by Andrew Fuller and Charles Hodge, among many other Calvinists who could be listed. However, they would disagree with some of the categories and arguments that P. uses in the dialogue.

173 *A Dialogue on the Extent*, 571.

me."[174] P. responds that contextually, in that particular prayer, Christ is praying specifically for his disciples and not others. To assert from this statement that Christ does not pray at all for the world is to beg the question. The mediatorial work of Christ includes atonement and intercession. A. does agree that in some respects Jesus does intercede for the non-elect.

A. presents his fifth argument for limited atonement. Limited atonement, per the covenant of redemption, procures the gift of faith for the elect. Only the elect receive the gift of faith, therefore Christ only died for the sins of the elect.

P. responds that the syllogistic argument is logically fallacious, and provides two examples of this kind of faulty logic.

> God is the giver of all good things.
> God is the giver of faith.
> Faith comes only to the elect,
> Therefore God gives no good things to any but the elect.
>
> The rain and sun produces vegetation.
> But there is no vegetation on a barren rock.
> Therefore, the rain never falls and the sun never shines upon the barren rock.[175]

Both conclusions are false. P. says that for A. to make his argument correct, he would have to say:

> The death of Christ secures the enjoyment of all spiritual blessings to those for whom he died.
> It therefore secures the gift of faith.
> Faith is given to none but the elect.
> Therefore, Christ died for none but the elect.[176]

P. states:

> This would be a correct syllogism, and the conclusion would follow, if it were true, that the death of Christ does actually secure the enjoyment of all spiritual blessings to all those for whom he died. To assume that it does is to assume the very point in dispute. It is begging the question again. This argument, however, is good on the other side, and proves that Christ died for all men.[177]

---

174 Ibid., 573.
175 Ibid.
176 Ibid.
177 Ibid.

A. makes another argument for limited atonement. If Christ died for all men, then he died for those already in hell whose salvation is impossible and who can never receive the offer of salvation. P. turns the tables and asks how it is that Christ can die for the salvation of those of the elect who are already in heaven, whose salvation is complete and who can never receive the offer of salvation.

A. responds that those already in heaven are there by faith in Christ who was to come in the future. P. counters that those already in hell had gone there in spite of lack of faith in the Savior who was to come. A.'s problem according to P. is that A. is assuming Christ could not have any purpose or intention in dying for anyone unless he intended to save them. This is begging the question again.

A. reasons that if Christ died for all, then God's justice was exacting punishment from both the sinner and Jesus. How can the same crimes be punished twice over without injustice? P. responds that they cannot be punished twice. Christ, according to P., was not punished at all. The satisfaction he made was not a satisfaction to the law or to distributive justice. Only on the principles of limited atonement is the law satisfied twice.

A. then argued the point that if Christ died for all people, then he atoned for sins that are never pardoned such as blasphemy against the Holy Spirit and final unbelief. This is absurd. P. responded by saying that on the same principle, while the elect are without repentance, their sin cannot be pardoned. Therefore, to suppose the sin of the elect atoned for while they are still unbelieving is absurd.

A. offers another argument in favor of limited atonement. The death of Christ is of no benefit to those who never hear the gospel. If Christ died for all people, how is it that God allows so many millions of them to remain in ignorance of the gospel?

P. responds that such a situation assumes Christ could not die for any unless he intended their salvation, hence A. is begging the question. P. returns the favor with a few questions of his own for A., such as "Why does he [God] not actually save all men? Why does he not, at least, save all who enjoy the light of the gospel? . . . Why does he convert one [of the elect] in the morning of life and another not till the close of it?"[178] These, and the like questions, are ultimately unanswerable because Scripture does not answer them. So, concludes P., is the question about those who have never heard the gospel. Scripture provides no answer.

A. puts forth another argument for limited atonement: it dishonors Christ that so many of those for whom he died should ultimately perish in their unbelief. P. responds that argument again begs the question by supposing that Christ did not die for any but the elect.

A. then argues that Scripture says in some places that the death of Christ is restricted to a group of people like the church, the sheep, and so on. But P. responds that lim-

178 Ibid., 575.

itarians should not infer from these statements that Christ could not or did not die for others, since to do so, once again, begs the question.[179]

A. continues by insisting that unlimited atonement is inconsistent with the doctrine of particular election. Here P. and A. engage in the lapsarian discussion so common in intramural debates among the Reformed. This part of the dialogue is less helpful on the issue of the extent of the atonement since throughout Reformed history, one can find supralapsarians who held to a form of Hypothetical Universalism (like William Twisse), as well as infralapsarians (like Charles Hodge and W. G. T. Shedd) and non-lapsarians (like R. L. Dabney) who held to unlimited atonement. Herman Bavinck, like Dabney, argued against lapsarian speculation, and yet, as we shall see, he held to a strict view of the atonement.[180] Contrary to popular opinion, then, one's view on lapsarianism or decretal ordering is not decisive for where one falls on the extent question.

A. offers one final argument in favor of limited atonement: atonement and redemption signify the same thing, thus all who are atoned for are redeemed. Only the elect are redeemed, therefore the atonement was made only for the elect. P. counters that atonement and redemption are not the same thing. "Atonement is satisfaction *for* sin; redemption is deliverance *from* sin. If atonement and redemption were the same thing, it would be as improper to pray for redemption as for atonement."[181]

At this point A. invites P. to state his arguments for unlimited atonement. Since most of P.'s arguments have been presented in his rebuttal of A.'s arguments, P. briefly repeats them in summary fashion.

1. A sincere offer of the gospel that invites all people to partake of its blessings necessitates an unlimited atonement. The gospel invitation declares that there is salvation provided and available for all, not just some. Without an unlimited atonement, such a universal offer is untrue, and such an invitation is a mere mockery.
2. All who hear the gospel have a duty to respond to it. But if Christ has not died for all, it cannot be the duty of all to obey the gospel. It cannot be the duty of demons to believe the gospel, for Christ did not die for demons.
3. All who finally reject Christ are condemned and punished for their unbelief. How can they be justly punished for rejecting a salvation never provided for them?
4. The nature of public justice, which the atonement satisfied, requires a universal atonement.

179 It also employs the negative inference fallacy, which says that the proof of a proposition does not disprove its converse.

180 Herman Bavinck, *Reformed Dogmatics: God and Creation*, 4 vols., ed. J. Bolt, trans. J. Vriend (Grand Rapids, MI: Baker, 2004), 2:388–92; *Reformed Dogmatics: Sin and Salvation in Christ*, 3:455–75.

181 *A Dialogue on the Extent*, 579 (emphasis in original).

5. Since all people receive blessings from God as a consequence of the death of Christ, there must be a sense in which Christ died for all.
6. The death of Christ places all people in a state of probation where they have an opportunity to receive the benefit of the atonement if they meet God's condition of salvation. But the non-elect have no such opportunity since Christ did not die for their sins. No matter what they do, they could never receive salvation.
7. Scripture clearly asserts an unlimited atonement in numerous places.[182]

To this last argument, A. responds that P. must admit that "world" and "all" are sometimes used in a limited sense, thus they may so be used in all passages that speak of the atonement's extent. P. admits that these words are on occasion used in a limited sense. However, when such is the case, context is clear in mandating the limitation. It is not possible that all the atonement passages that speak of intent using these words can be limited.

The dialogue between A. and P. is designed to support the unlimited atonement position within the Reformed tradition. This kind of hypothetical dialogue is valuable in that it takes lofty and sometimes obtuse theological vocabulary and concepts and places them on the level where virtually all can easily access the meaning. This strategy is still occasionally employed in theological discourse.

For example, compare the dialogue above with this hypothetical dialogue posted on John Piper's website between an evangelist who believes in limited atonement and an unbeliever. My comments will appear in brackets.

Unbeliever: So what are you offering me?

Evangelist: Salvation from God's wrath and from your sin. Everlasting life.

U: How?

E: Because when Jesus, the Son of God, died, he absorbed God's wrath, removed it, and he bore the guilt of sin for all who trust him. [Here is limited atonement—Christ only bore the sin for all who trust him.]

U: Did he do that for me?

E: If you will have him—receive him—you will have all that he is for you and all that he did for you. If you will trust him, yes, he did it for you. [Notice how difficult and awkward such an answer is to an unbeliever. If you believe, yes he did it for you; if you don't believe, either he didn't do it for you, or, if you are one of the elect, this call you are currently receiving is the general call, not the special call to salvation, which you will receive at some point in the future and you will respond to the special call.]

182 Ibid., 579–80.

U: So you don't know if he did it for me? [Exactly. The evangelist does not know whether Christ died for this unbeliever or not, given his belief in limited atonement.]

E: He is offering himself to you right now freely. He is offering you a wonderful, finished work of redemption—all that he accomplished in absorbing God's wrath and cancelling sins. All of that is yours for the having, right now. If you won't have it, it's not yours. If you will, it is. There's only one way to know if your sins were cancelled and your death sentence was commuted in the death of Jesus. Believe on him. His promise is absolute: If you believe, you will be saved. If you won't believe, you remain in your sin, and under God's wrath. [Notice the problems here if this person is actually one of the non-elect. First, the evangelist is mistakenly telling this non-elect unbeliever that God is offering him something when in fact what is being offered does not exist. There is no atonement for his sins; he could not be saved even if he wanted to. Second, and more problematic, God himself is offering salvation to this non-elect unbeliever. Yet how can this be when God himself has not provided atonement for this non-elect unbeliever's sins? This brings into question God's sincerity in the offer, and in fact his very character.]

U: So what are you asking me to receive?

E: Jesus. Receive Jesus! Because Jesus really did these things. He really secured the freedom of his people from the wrath of God. He really bore their sins in his body on the tree. If you receive him, you are one of them. You are included. All that is true for you. He offers to you freely right now. [Notice Jesus secured the freedom "of his people"—limited atonement. But would not there be a lingering question in the back of the mind of this unbeliever if he did in fact believe?—"What if my faith was not real? Perhaps I'm one of the non-elect and am deceived?"]

U: I thought I could know Jesus died for me before I believed? That's what I've always been told: Believe on him, because he died for everybody.

E: I can't say for sure, but the people who taught you that probably meant this: Jesus died so that the gospel could be offered to all, and all who believe would be saved. That's true. But if I assured you before you believe that your sins were cancelled and your freedom from God's wrath was obtained, I would mislead you. Imagine if I said to you, Jesus certainly obtained your deliverance from God's wrath and certainly covered all your sins. Now believe that. What would you say? [Here things really go awry. No one I know who believes in unlimited atonement says to any unbeliever that their sins are cancelled and their freedom from God's wrath is already obtained merely because Christ died for their sins. Here the evangelist is trading on two errors: a commercial theory of the atonement that conflates the extent of the atonement with its application and failure to recognize the conditional nature of the atonement's application: it only is applied when the unbeliever believes.]

U: I'd say, great. Now what if I don't believe? Then I'm still saved, right? Since my sins were certainly covered. It's done. [Now the unbeliever is confused as well.]

E: Yes, that's probably what you would say, and you'd be wrong. Because I would have misled you. The good news that Jesus has for you before you believe on him is not that your sins are certainly cancelled. The good news is that Jesus really propitiated the wrath of God, and really covered the sins of his people. It is finished. And that is what I offer you. It's free. It's full. It's complete. It's glorious. And his absolute promise to you is this: It's yours if you will receive him. Believe on the Lord Jesus Christ, and you will be saved. [Again notice the illogic of this response by the evangelist. The unbeliever is being offered something which neither he nor the evangelist can be sure exists for him. Once again, on the limited atonement scheme, the offer from the evangelist, and God himself, cannot be a genuine, sincere offer if this unbeliever is among the non-elect.][183]

We now consider some of the key names who played a role in the debate over extent in the nineteenth century.

James Richards (AD 1747–1843)

Richards was professor of theology in the Theological Seminary at Auburn, New York, from 1823 to 1843. Lecture XIII in his *Lectures on Mental Philosophy and Theology* (1846) dealt with the extent of the atonement. We have already seen that Richards affirms a universal atonement. His lecture is important for many reasons.

First, he listed numerous patristic authors who affirmed unlimited atonement. Second, he listed the earliest Reformers, including Calvin, and Lutherans as affirming unlimited atonement. With respect to Calvin, Richards made an important point concerning Calvin's exegesis of the word "all" in some atonement passages.

> It is but candid, however, to allow that in some passages where the word all is brought into question, this writer supposes that it signifies all of every kind, or all sorts, rather than all, every one. But this he might easily do and consistently maintain as the doctrine of the New Testament, that the death of Christ was

183 See John Piper, "A Five-Pointer Shares the Gospel," *Desiring God* (blog), March 9, 2011, http://www.desiringgod.org/articles/a-five-pointer-shares-the-gospel.

> a full and perfect sacrifice for the sins of all men absolutely. This doctrine he most certainly did maintain, as several of the extracts from his writings now presented clearly evince. We need not be afraid therefore, that our *Calvinism* will be essentially marred by holding the doctrine of a *general propitiation*, unless we wish to be more Calvinistic than John Calvin himself.[184]

Third, he correctly noted the posture of the Church of England's Thirty-Nine Articles reflected unlimited atonement. Fourth, he correctly noted that Dort's final canon on the subject was written in such a way that both parties, the limitarians and those who affirmed unlimited imputation of sins to Christ, could sign. Fifth, he addressed and answered the theological arguments often made against an unlimited atonement. Finally, he addressed certain biblical passages that indicate a universal atonement.[185]

For Richards, the atonement "was a true and proper sacrifice for sin," and "this sacrifice bore such a relation to the sins of men, that a way was thereby opened for the restoration of the whole human family to the favor of God."[186]

George Hill (AD 1750–1819)

Hill was a moderate leader in the Scottish church, professor of divinity, and subsequently principal of St. Mary's College, St. Andrews. He published his *Lectures in Divinity* early in the nineteenth century. These were used for many years after his death as a standard textbook in university faculties of divinity until the 1870s when Charles Hodge's *Systematic Theology* became popular.

Hill's work was less Calvinistic in spirit than that of the later Free Church leaders; he was little interested in federal theology. He spoke of Christ's death not as the very punishment due to sinners but as an alternative means to fulfill man's sinful obligation.[187] Hill was more comfortable with the developing New Divinity of American Calvinists in the early nineteenth century. Hill appears to lean toward an unlimited atonement. For example, on John 6, he stated, "Here are the doctrines of particular and of universal redemption seemingly taught in the same discourse."[188]

Hill stated:

> If the efficacy of the remedy is inseparably connected with its being accepted, it cannot be, in the intention of the Almighty, an universal remedy, since he has withheld the means of accepting it from many of those for whom it was said to have been provided. The words of the apostle, then, "God will have all men

184 J. Richards, *Lectures on Mental Philosophy and Theology* (New York: M. W. Dodd, 1846), 311 (emphasis in original).

185 Ibid., 302–27.

186 Ibid. See also R. B. Welch, "Rev. Dr. James Richards and His Theology," *The Presbyterian Review* 5.18 (April 1884): 401–42.

187 G. Hill, *Lectures in Divinity*, ed. Alexander Hill (Philadelphia: Herman Hooker, 1844), 505–12.

188 G. Hill, *Extracts from Lectures in Divinity* (Edinburgh: William Blackwood & Sons, 1861), 88.

> to be saved, and to come to the knowledge of the truth," must receive from the event an interpretation different from that which is the most obvious; and all the other texts urged in favour of universal redemption are in like manner limited by the imperfect publication of the Gospel.[189]

Alexander Ranken (AD 1755–1827) was a theologian and a moderator of the Church of Scotland. He published his *Institutes of Theology* in 1822,[190] which was something of an attempt to provide a shorter version of Hill's work. He had hoped that moderate Calvinism and moderate Arminianism might find grounds for rapprochement. He leaned toward the governmental theory of the atonement and affirmed a universal atonement.

Timothy Dwight (AD 1752–1817)

Dwight was a leading American Congregationalist preacher, theologian, author, and president of Yale College from 1795 until 1817. He was an influential Calvinist. Many of his sermons were published posthumously in 1818–1819 in four volumes under the title *Theology Explained and Defended.*[191]

In volume two, sermon 56, under heading V, Dwight addressed the extent of the atonement. He stated: "*The atonement of Christ was sufficient in its extent to open the door for the pardon of all human sinners.*"[192] This doctrine "is so often and so plainly declared in the Scriptures, that I am surprised to find a doubt concerning it, entertained by any man."[193] He continued to list six arguments in favor of universal atonement:

1. If the atonement was such that God can consistently forgive one sinner, he might with equal consistency forgive any number of sinners. The atonement necessary to save the world was equally necessary, and in the same manner and degree, to save an individual sinner.
2. The atonement is, by the infinite dignity of Christ, rendered infinitely meritorious. An infinitely meritorious is sufficient for all the world.
3. Christ suffered in the place of those whom he came to redeem.
4. If Christ had not made a sufficient atonement for others beside the elect, then his salvation cannot be offered to them at all, and they are not guilty for not receiving it. But this is contrary to Scripture.
5. The gospel is good news for all people, not just the elect. If the atonement is limited, the gospel is not addressed to the non-elect at all.

---

189 Hill, *Lectures in Divinity*, 510.

190 A. Ranken, *Institutes of Theology, or, A Concise System of Divinity* (Glasgow, University Press, 1822).

191 T. Dwight, *Theology Explained and Defended in a Series of Sermons*, 4 vols., 4th ed. (New Haven, CT: S. Converse, 1825).

192 Ibid., 2:217 (emphasis in original).

193 T. Dwight, "Sermon 56," in *Theology Explained and Defended*, 2:217.

6. Preachers are required to preach repentance and faith to all sinners as their duty. But if no atonement exists for their sins, they cannot believe, for Christ is not a possible object of their faith.[194]

To the question why all people are not saved, Dwight responded that all do not believe in Christ. "No man is pardoned merely because of the Atonement made by Christ; but because of his own acceptance, also, of that atonement, by faith."[195]

John Chavis (AD 1763–1838)

Chavis studied at Princeton for three years then completed his studies at Washington College in 1802. He was the first ordained African American Presbyterian preacher and he held to unlimited atonement.[196]

Chavis fell victim to the 1832 law in North Carolina prohibiting blacks from teaching or preaching, effectively depriving him of his livelihood. Shortly thereafter, Chavis decided to write a sermon on the atonement since the topic was being debated within his own denomination. He sided with the New School Presbyterians, most of whom adhered to unlimited atonement. His intention was to have the sermon published, but the Orange Presbytery refused to publish it. Finally, it was published in 1837 in Raleigh, North Carolina.

Chavis's main argument for an unlimited atonement is the command of God to preach the gospel to all people. "The character of the Saviour, the plan of Redemption, reason and common sense forbid such a belief [in a limited atonement]."[197]

Edward Dorr Griffin (AD 1770–1837)

A graduate of Yale, Griffin was licensed to preach in 1792. In 1815 he became pastor of the Second Presbyterian Church in Newark, New Jersey, and later in 1821 he became president of Williams College in Massachusetts until 1836. Griffin was a significant preacher during the Second Great Awakening.

He wrote on the extent of the atonement under an unusual title: *A Humble Attempt to Reconcile the Differences of Christians Respecting the Extent of the Atonement, by Showing That the Controversy Which Exists on the Subject Is Chiefly Verbal.*[198] In this volume

194 Ibid., 217–18.

195 Ibid., 218.

196 See H. C. Othow, *John Chavis, African American Patriot, Preacher, Teacher and Mentor (1763–1838)* (Jefferson, NC: McFarland and Company, 2001).

197 John Chavis, "Letter upon the Doctrine of the Extent of the Atonement of Christ," in *Preaching with Sacred Fire: An Anthology of African American Sermons, 1750 to the Present*, ed. M. Simmons and F. Thomas (New York: W. W. Norton and Co., 2010), 35. The entire sermon can be found on pp. 32–44, and also in Othow, *John Chavis*, 13–32.

198 E. Griffin, *A Humble Attempt to Reconcile the Differences of Christians Respecting the Extent of the Atonement, by Showing That the Controversy Which Exists on the Subject is Chiefly Verbal. To Which Is Added an Appendix Exhibiting the Influence of Christ's Obedience* (New York: Stephen Dodge, 1819).

Griffin argued for universal atonement. He refuted the double payment argument.[199]

Griffin's concept of atonement is general: Christ died for the sins of all people. His concept of redemption is twofold: what he called "lower redemption" essentially corresponds to atonement and speaks of the atonement as satisfying the law for the sins of all people. "Higher redemption" for Griffin meant deliverance effected. Thus, Christ died for the sins of all (atonement and lower redemption) but only efficaciously for the sins of the elect (higher redemption).[200]

Throughout his *Humble Attempt*, Griffin appealed to Calvin, Isaac Watts, and other Calvinists who affirmed unlimited atonement. Griffin considered the evidence from Calvin's sermons and commentaries to be "decisive" in implicating Calvin's belief in an unlimited atonement, "the same as that of the schoolmen and fathers before him."[201]

In Griffin's sermons there is further evidence of his belief in general atonement. In his sermon "The Brazen Serpent" on John 3:14–15, he affirmed Christ's death as an expiation for the sins of the world.[202]

Griffin was comfortable with the governmental approach to the atonement, but as with many who affirmed this approach, he likewise held to a form of penal satisfaction for sins. "Atonement removed the penal bar which sin had raised."[203]

Griffin viewed the atonement as complete provision for the sins of all people as moral agents. Griffin's concern with some of his fellow Calvinists was their failure to distinguish between persons as moral agents and persons as passive receivers. "The mistake lies in not perceiving that an atonement intended merely for agents, is completely for them without reference to the question whether the same creatures are to be regenerated."[204] For Griffin, as for all Calvinists, this lay in the purview of God's sovereign election.

For example, he stated that the death of Christ is the cause of all spiritual blessings and thus it is the cause of "the gift of faith." But Griffin stated that "this has nothing to do with the extent of the atonement."[205] Christ died for the non-elect and if they perish it is due to their own hardness of heart and refusal to believe. Griffin explained his point by asking the two questions: For whom did Christ *atone*? and For whom did Christ *die*? The former should be answered universally. The latter answers the question, Whom did Christ *intend* to save by the work of effectual calling and the gift of faith on them as passive recipients? Christ only *intends* to save the elect.[206]

This is commensurate with Griffin's acceptance of the covenant of redemption as

---

199 Ibid., 113–14.
200 Ibid., 95–101.
201 Ibid., 379–80.
202 E. Griffin, *The Life and Sermons of Edward D. Griffin*, 2 vols. (Edinburgh: Banner of Truth, 1987), 2:15–27.
203 Ibid., 175.
204 Ibid., 179.
205 Ibid., 180.
206 Ibid., 181–82.

a valid construct in understanding soteriology.[207] Yet the Covenant of Redemption, election, the purchased gift of faith by Christ for the elect, and the like have no bearing on the extent of the atonement, according to Griffin.[208]

Just as man must be viewed as both moral agent and passive recipient, so Griffin said God must be viewed as both Moral Governor and as Sovereign Efficient Cause. These are the two "great departments of the divine administration. And they are so distinct that when a man opens his eyes in one, he cannot, so to speak, see the other."[209]

This work by Griffin provides insight into how supporters of a governmental approach to the atonement think about the issues.

Ralph Wardlaw (AD 1779–1853)

Wardlaw was a Scottish Congregationalist and key figure in the later Marrow controversy. As a preacher, Wardlaw held a prominent place in Scotland, but it was by his theological writings that he was most widely known both in Great Britain and in America.

Wardlaw purposed to consider the Calvinistic views on extent under three categories: hyper-Calvinism, orthodox Calvinism, and moderate Calvinism. Of this latter category, Wardlaw stated it is "ably elucidated by the late Andrew Fuller," along with others, and it is "now embraced by a growing proportion of Calvinistic ministers and professing Christians."[210]

Concerning the hyper-Calvinist position on the extent of the atonement, Wardlaw considered the view to be quantitative equivalentism.[211] He did not mince words about his disdain for the view: "I have before expressed my unqualified reprobation of this doctrine, as having in it a littleness, a meanness, and an utter incongruity with the divine dignity of the Mediator, utterly revolting to both my judgment and feelings."[212] He listed and discussed several objections to this view. For example,

> If it be granted, as it generally is, by the advocates of atonement, that it was from the divinity of Jesus that His sacrifice derived its value; I might, I apprehend, go a step further, and affirm the idea of an exact equivalent for the deserts of the

207 Ibid., 175.

208 Ibid., 192.

209 Ibid., 209.

210 R. Wardlaw, *Systematic Theology*, 3 vols., ed. J. R. Campbell (Edinburgh: Adam and Charles Black, 1856–1857), 2:439. Wardlaw's full discussion on the subject can be found at 2:438–84.

211 Wardlaw (ibid., 2:439) described equivalentists as

> those who hold a limited atonement in the sense of its being sufficient only, in the way of legal compensation, for the salvation of the elect; so that, if more in number had been to be saved, more suffering must have been endured; that Christ, standing in the room of the elect, and appearing as their substitute and representative, bore their sins exclusively, making an atonement adequate for their remission and for no more; paying precisely (to use the ordinary but much abused phraseology) their amount of debt. This view of the atonement has been held by not a few, and has been advanced anew, and maintained as the only just and scriptural view, by some modern writers.

212 Ibid.

> elect alone an impossibility in the very nature of things. The infinite dignity of His mediatorial person put it necessarily and for ever out of the question that the value of His propitiatory sufferings should be measured and bounded by the amount of penalty due to finite creatures. His substitution and obedience unto death must, of necessity, have infinitely exceeded an equivalent for the penal sufferings of any conceivable number of the race of men.[213]

Another objection is that equivalentism renders it impossible for those other than the elect who might desire salvation to be saved since the impossibility would arise not from themselves "but in the very nature and constitution of the plan of redemption." There is no atonement for them.[214] Wardlaw argued there cannot be a genuine universal offer of the gospel with such a theology.[215] Finally, Wardlaw argued that the commercialism of this position negates the principle of grace in that the benefit of the atonement is owed to the elect.[216]

Wardlaw's treatment of the second view, orthodox Calvinism, is the standard view of limited or definite atonement, whereby Christ substituted only for the sins of the elect. Wardlaw considered this view to rightly uphold the full intrinsic sufficiency of the atonement. However, he thought the view undercuts the ground for the universal offer of the gospel. This position essentially invites sinners to that which has no existence.[217]

The moderate Calvinist view "holds the atonement to have been a general remedy, with a particular application."[218] In his critique of the second view above, Wardlaw rightly queried how it can be consistent to claim at one and the same time that the atonement is limited only to the elect while its value "is admitted to have been contained, infinitely beyond the actual amount of salvation that shall arise from it."[219]

Wardlaw further stated that there would be no ground for the universal gospel offer in this approach and the same objections made against the position of quantitative equivalentism can be leveled against the so-called orthodox Calvinist position as well.

Wardlaw is not impressed with the double payment argument. As with the quantitative equivalentist position, Wardlaw considered definite atonement to negate the principle of grace: "It is surely very clear, then, that there can be no grace in bestowing what it would be an act of injustice to withhold."[220] He continued:

213 Ibid., 440–41.
214 Ibid., 442.
215 Ibid., 442–43.
216 Ibid., 443–44.
217 Ibid., 443.
218 Ibid., 445.
219 Ibid., 446.
220 Ibid., 451.

> But, according to the present hypothesis, the grace must have lain exclusively in the sovereign determination of God that the redemption price or ransom should be paid. When it had been paid, God could not, consistently with this hypothesis, be said to "justify freely by His grace" those for whom it had been paid, but was laid, by the payment of it, under an obligation of justice to pardon and save them. There might be grace in admitting the proposal of a surety to pay the debt; but there was no grace, when the debt had been paid, in absolving the debtor. There might be grace in allowing a voluntary substitute to bear the merited penalty; but there could be none, when the substitute had borne the penalty, in remitting it to the transgressor.[221]

For Wardlaw, quoting Payne approvingly, "Strictly speaking, the atonement was not made for one man, or for all men; it was made to God for sin, i.e., on account of sin."[222] Wardlaw found no inconsistency in this position on the extent of the atonement combined with the special intention of God to apply it only to the elect.[223]

At this point Wardlaw turned to a consideration of the key passages in the New Testament that affirm an unlimited atonement. He pointed out that those who argue for definite atonement attempt to reconcile the universal passages by restricting the meaning of "world" and "all" to the elect. Wardlaw considered the ploy one that to "no candid mind, can ever be satisfactory." He objected to this approach on two grounds: it is "forced and unnatural," and "it introduces into some statements of the sacred penmen inconsistency and absurdity."[224] For Wardlaw, this approach subverted the principles of sound biblical hermeneutics.

Wardlaw concluded his discussion of the extent of the atonement with a summary of the position for which he has argued in this section in his *Systematic Theology*.

> The atonement is a grand general remedy, glorifying all the divine perfections in the forgiveness and salvation of the guilty on account of it; possessing sufficiency of value for the salvation of all, and, on this ground, proclaiming and offering salvation alike to all; but limited as to its actually saving efficacy by the sovereign purpose of God in the election of grace: in the former view,

221 Ibid., 451–52.

222 Ibid., 454.

223 Ibid., 456:

> The view which I have thus given does appear to my mind much more self-consistent and free from embarrassing difficulties than either the exact equivalent scheme or the special destination scheme. Its great advantage is, that it leaves all open; and thus, by introducing no previous restrictions having reference to the atonement itself, it preserves, free of all encroachment, a basis for the universal obligation of sinners of mankind to accept the offered mercy, and for the sincerity of the universal offer of it, in order to such acceptance. On neither of the other schemes do we feel our way clear; the restriction, whether in the way of limited sufficiency or of limited destination in the propitiation itself.

224 Ibid., 460–61.

> answering the rectoral design of God, as moral governor of the world; and in the latter, the sovereign purpose of God in the free and unfettered exercise of His everlasting mercy.[225]

Wardlaw expressed his thoughts on the subject in another work entitled *Discourse on the Nature and Extent of the Atonement*:

> By pleading for the universality of the atonement, we are neither, on the one hand, obliged to grant the universality of pardon and salvation, nor, on the other hand, to deny sovereign electing grace. We can, with perfect consistency, disown the one, and embrace the other.—If the *atonement* and the *remission of sins* were necessarily coincident in their extent,—so that atoned or expiated sin must necessarily be pardoned and cancelled sin;—it surely is a remarkable fact, that the same terms of universality are not used alike with regard to both. The force of the following questions ought, I think, to be acknowledged. It will be by every candid mind.—"If, after all, it be true, that by such expressions as these,—'the world,' 'the whole world,' 'all men,' 'every man,'—God means only the elect, how comes it to pass that equally extensive terms" (that is, with those used respecting atonement) "are not employed in speaking of election and justification? If these two and the atonement be really co-extensive, how do we never read that God *elected* 'the world,' and 'the whole world,' and 'all men,' and 'every man,'—and *justified* 'the world,' and 'the whole world,' and 'all men,' and 'every man?' Limitarians allow that the one might be said as well as the other:—and how comes it to pass, then, that it is never said?—Not only must this be accounted for, but on the face of the case there appears so plain and palpable a difference between the extent of atonement and the extent of election and justification, and the sudden identification of these is so preposterous, that, unless a solid and decisive demonstration be given of their co-extensiveness, the system of limitation falls to the ground, and the universal atonement comes to be received as a matter of course. There is so vast a difference between the language that describes atonement, and that which describes election and justification, in point of extent; and the general easy unstrained meaning of Scripture teaches so plainly the unlimited propitiation by Christ's blood, that it can never be displaced except by solid and irrefragable proof of direct limitation."*—I confess myself unable to see any possibility of satisfactorily answering such questions as are thus put, on the ground of atonement and justification being necessarily co-extensive.—But by admitting the universality of the atonement, and the sovereign restriction of

225 Ibid., 483.

justification to them who believe, and who are the objects of God's gracious choice,—the difference in the language on the one subject and on the other is at once accounted for. It is precisely what we perceive it must have been, supposing it to have been constructed on this principle. Is not this, then, the truth?—The more restricted terms which are used in regard to actual forgiveness, or justification, are in correspondence with the restrictive character of God's electing love, and of his published determination to justify sinners only through faith. There is a limited *purpose to save*. The atonement is the ground on which this purpose to save rests. But the purpose to save on the ground of the atonement does not, and cannot, enter into the essence of the atonement itself. The purpose, and that on which the purpose rests, can, in no respect, be the same thing. But still, there existed in the divine mind, both in providing and in making the atonement, this sovereign purpose to save,—this sovereign purpose that, while made for mankind,—made for the indefinite design of glorifying God in the forgiveness of sin and the acceptance and salvation of sinners,—it should take actual effect in the salvation of some, while others remained inexcusably guilty in their rejection of it. And surely the existence of such a purpose gives quite a sufficiency of peculiarity to those texts which use the terms of limitation,—without supposing limitation in the atonement itself; a supposition which gives rise to superlative difficulty, and to every kind of unnaturalness and straining, in the interpretation of those other passages in which the terms are universal, and in which they cannot be understood otherwise than in their universal sense, without rendering them, especially in some of their occurrences, self-contradictory.[226]

Wardlaw also stated:

The *purpose* or *intention to save*, which is represented as the peculiarity of the atonement in its relation to the elect, is not, as I think must be obvious to you, any part of the atonement itself,—does not at all enter into its nature:—it is a purpose, or intention, relative to *the effects or results of the atonement*:—it is a purpose respecting the persons to whom the atonement, in itself indefinite and the same to all, shall, by the grace of God, be rendered savingly efficacious. It is not, then, the atonement itself, but this sovereign purpose, connected with it though not essentially belonging to it, that secures their salvation. There can be nothing in the *nature* or *essence* of the atonement for one more than for another;

226 R. Wardlaw, *Discourse on the Nature and Extent of the Atonement of Christ* (1843; repr. London: Forgotten Books, 2013), 222–24. The asterisk refers to Wardlaw's quotation of Robert Morison's "Difficulties connected with the doctrine of a limited atonement."

> so that if, on the one hand, the atonement was for all, and a "purpose to save" belonged to its nature, all must have been saved:—and if, on the other hand, a purpose effectually to save did not properly belong to its nature, but was connected with it, determining and limiting its effects; then what have we here but the very thing we contend for,—a universal atonement, as the ground of universal invitation,—and a special purpose, the result of a special but unmerited and sovereign favour, with regard to its actual application, or saving efficiency?[227]

As a Calvinist himself, Wardlaw's warning about forcing an interpretation on Scripture to make it fit one's preconceived theology is all the more significant:

> I have ever thought that Calvinists in general, in supporting the doctrine of particular redemption, have laid themselves greatly open to animadversion for the unnatural interpretations which they have put upon some parts of Scripture phraseology, to some of which we have had occasion to make pointed reference. That principle of interpretation should certainly be adopted as the right one, which, with the least appearance or reality of forced and unnatural explanation of words and phrases, harmonizes the various and, at first view, seemingly conflicting passages of the divine word.[228]

Thomas Chalmers (AD 1780–1847)

Many consider Thomas Chalmers the greatest preacher in Scotland in the nineteenth century. Prior to the Disruption in 1843, he was a successful pastor, preacher, and professor. He was in essence the founder and key leader of the evangelical Free Church of Scotland, serving as the moderator of the first assembly. He also affirmed universal atonement and considered it crucial for the foundation of the free offer of the gospel to all people. "If Christ died only for the elect, and not for all," preachers "are puzzled to understand how they should proceed with the calls and invitations of the gospel."[229] "We tell you of God's beseeching voice. We assure you, in His name, that he wants you not to die. We bid you venture for pardon on the atonement made by Him who died for all."[230]

In the same sermon on Romans, Chalmers explicitly stated Christ died for all men and the fervor with which he exhorts his hearers to follow Christ is evident:

> We tell you of God's beseeching voice. We assure you, in His name, that he wants you not to die. We bid you venture for pardon on the atonement made

227 See R. Wardlaw's explanation in ibid., 207–8.

228 Wardlaw, *Systematic Theology*, 483.

229 T. Chalmers, *Institutes of Theology*, 2 vols. (Edinburgh: Sutherland and Knox, 1849), 2:418.

230 T. Chalmers, *Lectures on the Epistle of Paul the Apostle to the Romans* (New York: Robert Carter & Brothers, 1863), 398.

by Him who died for all men. We bid you apply forthwith to the spirit of all grace and holiness, that you may be qualified to enter into that beatific heaven from whose battlements there wave the signals of welcome, and whose gates are widely opened to receive you. We would bring this plain word of salvation nigh unto every conscience, and knock with it at the door of every heart; and commissioned as we are to preach the gospel not to a chosen few, while we keep it back from the hosts of the reprobate, but to preach it to every creature under heaven, we again entreat that none here present shall forbid themselves—for most assuredly God has not forbidden them. But come unto Christ all of you who labour and are heavy-laden, and ye shall have rest. Look unto Him, all ye ends of the earth; and though now placed at the farthest outskirts of a moral distance and alienation, even look unto Him and ye shall be saved.[231]

His biographer, citing one of Chalmers's hearers, wrote of his passion in this area:

He would bend over the pulpit and press us to take the gift, as if he held it that moment in his hand, and would not be satisfied till every one of us had got possession of it. And often when the sermon was over and the psalm was sung, and he rose to pronounce the blessing, he would break out afresh with some new entreaty, unwilling to let us go until he had made one more effort to persuade us to accept it.[232]

In a sermon on Romans, Chalmers affirmed his belief that Christ died for the sins of all people:

It is nowhere said in the Bible that Christ so died for me in particular, as that by His simple dying the benefits of His atonement are mine in possession. But it is everywhere said in the Bible, that He so died for me in particular, as that by His simple dying the benefits of His atonement are mine in offer. They are mine if I will.[233]

Chalmers addressed his students and affirmed both universal atonement and the importance of boldly proclaiming the gospel:

This you are fully warranted to do by the terms in which the message of the gospel is conceived—by words, for example, of such universal and at the same

231 Ibid.

232 W. Hanna, *Memoirs of the Life and Writings of Thomas Chalmers*, 4 vols. (Edinburgh: Edmonston and Douglass Hamilton, Adams, and Co., London, 1867), 1:318.

233 Chalmers, *Romans*, 167.

time of such pointed and specific application, as "whosoever", and "all", and "any", and "every" being associated with the calls and invitations of the New Testament.[234]

The following statement is crystal clear on the issue:

> Christ did not so die for all as that all do actually receive the gift of salvation; but He so died for all, as that all to whom He is preached have the real and honest offer of Salvation. He is not yours in possession till you have laid hold of Him by faith. But he is yours in offer. He is as much yours as anything of which you can say—I have it for the taking. You, one and all of you, my brethren, have salvation for the taking; and it is because you do not choose to take it if it do not indeed belong to you.[235]

Chalmers made the point clear that the offer is universal because the atonement is universal:

> The remedy [for human sin], in fact, is much more extensive in proposition than it is in effect. It may be held out, in proposition, to all, while at the same time, and effectively, it is limited to those who repent and believe, while most assuredly all those who do so repent and believe shall be saved. And it is also quite true, that though the offer of redemption were rejected by all, there is a sense in which that redemption might still be called universal. The offer could not be made without it; and now that Christ hath died, the offer might be made to one and all of the species.[236]

This statement is important because of the distinction Chalmers made between the offer and the atonement ("redemption"). Chalmers said that "redemption" may be called "universal." His views are further confirmed by his explicit statement that he agreed with Arminian William Paley that "Christ died for the whole world, because now and in consequence of His death, the offer of the remission of sins may be made to the whole world."[237]

---

234 T. Chalmers, "Prelections on Butler's Analogy," in *Posthumous Works of the Rev. Thomas Chalmers*, 9 vols., ed. W. Hanna (Edinburgh: T. Constable and Co., 1852), 9:167. Chalmers said much the same thing in the *Institutes* (168): "I do not object, you will observe, to the object of their faith being in this particular form, that He died for my sins—as I hold the precious terms of all, and any and whosoever, wherein the overtures of the gospel are couched, abundantly warrant this blessed application."

235 Chalmers, *Romans*, 319. For more on the free offer of the Gospel, see Chalmers, *Institutes*, 2:409–12.

236 Chalmers, "Prelections on Butler's Analogy," 9:326.

237 Ibid., 9:107–8.

In a sermon on Luke 2:14 entitled "On the Universality of the Gospel Offer," Chalmers addresses the unsaved: "As the remission of sins without the shedding of blood is impossible, he cleared the way between Him and a guilty world of this mighty barrier. Rather than lose you for ever, he sent His Son to pour out His soul unto death for you."[238] Chalmers passionately pleaded to his unsaved hearers:

> He no longer grieves for the hardness of your hearts, when thy give up their resistance to the impressive consideration of His good-will to you; and to the affecting proofs of His good-will, in His Son suffering for you, His Son dying for you, His Son bearing for your sakes a load of mysterious agony, and pouring out the blood of atonement to wash you from the guilt and the pollution of all your iniquities.[239]

Chalmers considered "as unfortunate the assertion that Christ did not die for all men, but only for those of every nation who are in the end to be saved."[240]

Finally, Chalmers links the necessity of a universal atonement as the grounds for the free offer of the gospel:

> If Christ died not for all, how I can make a tender of His salvation to all? If He died only for the elect, in what terms can I declare the readiness of God to take into acceptance the multitude before me? How can I represent Him as waiting to be gracious, if, in the exercise of a discriminating grace, He has purposes of mercy only for certain some who are unknown to me, while He has no such purpose for certain others, who are alike unknown to me? . . .
>
> We read that Christ died for the world; but did He die for me in particular? Is the foundation laid in Zion by His atoning death, a foundation broad enough for me to rest upon? Are the overtures of reconciliation that have come from heaven such as I can entertain in the form of overtures addressed to myself? How can I so take them up, after being told that Christ died only for some; and it is nowhere said that I am included in the happy number? The perplexity felt by a minister in the pulpit as to the terms in which he should propose the message of reconciliation, is the very perplexity felt by the individual hearer as to the terms in which he should receive it. . . .
>
> If Christ did not so far die for me, as that He is yet mine in possession, He at least so far died for me, as that He is mine in offer. . . .

238 T. Chalmers, "On the Universality of the Gospel Offer," in *The Select Works of Thomas Chalmers*, 4 vols. (New York: Robert Carter & Brothers, 1850), 3:237.

239 Ibid., 240.

240 "Prelections on Butler's Analogy," 9:356.

> I should hold it a most grievous effect of that doctrine on your conduct of the business of the pulpit, if you did not address all men, as the subjects of the proposed pardon and justification—if you did not assure them of a reconciliation on their turning to God, and having faith in the Lord Jesus Christ—if you did not, for this purpose, urge them so to turn, and expound to them, affectionately as well as fully, the truth as it is in Jesus—if you did not tell them, just as these universal redemptionists do, that their salvation depends on their faith. The remedy, in fact, is much more extensive in proposition than it is in effect. It may be held out, and honestly held out, in proposition, to all, while at the same time, and effectively, it is limited to those who repent and believe, while most assuredly all who do so repent and believe shall be saved. And it is also quite true, that though the offer of redemption were rejected by all, there is a sense in which that redemption might still be called universal.[241]

George Payne (AD 1781–1848)

Payne was an English Congregationalist. His 1836 work, *Lectures on Divine Sovereignty, Election, the Atonement, Justification, and Regeneration*,[242] was answered by J. A. Haldane, among others, to whom Payne replied in the final edition of 1846.

Payne advanced the governmental approach to the atonement. He stated as his third proposition,

> While, on the one hand, the Saviour cannot have intended to secure the salvation of all men by the act of offering up himself a sacrifice for sin,—yet that sacrifice must, on the other hand, have been in itself adequate to the salvation of all men, so as to become a suitable foundation for the general and unlimited calls of the gospel.[243]

Payne acknowledged the ambiguity in the question of whether Christ died with a *design* to save some men or all men.

> To save, it might be said, may mean to lay for men a foundation of salvation, i.e., to supply them with the means of salvation;—or again, to render those means effectual to their salvation: and, accordingly, the answer to the question must vary, as one or other of these senses is attached to the words. If the question be, "Did Christ die with the design of laying a foundation of salvation for *all* men, or for *some* men?" I answer, that, in this sense, he died for all men. If

241 Ibid., 317–18, 321, 326.

242 G. Payne, *Lectures on Divine Sovereignty, Election, the Atonement, Justification, and Regeneration* (London: Hamilton, Adams, and Co., 1836). Lecture 13 is on "The Extent of the Atonement."

243 Ibid., 208–9.

> the question be, "Did he die with the design of rendering these means effectual to the salvation of *all* men, or of *some* men?" I answer, that, in this sense, he died for *some* men only.
>
> I believe in the unlimited, universal, infinite sufficiency of the atonement of Christ—I believe it was the intention of God, *as the moral Governor*, in giving his Son as a sacrifice for sin, . . . to provide a remedy commensurate with the disease. I believe, on the other hand, in the limited application of the atonement. I believe it was the intention of God, *as a Sovereign*, to render that remedy effectual, by special and sovereign influence, in the case of certain individuals *only* who are affected with the general disease, so that the intention of God, as a *Sovereign*, and as a *Ruler*, in reference to the atonement, is different, the one being general, the other particular.[244]

Payne described the atonement as a satisfaction for sin rendered to God as the moral governor of the world, which removed every obstacle on God's part such that he could respond in grace and salvation to sinners. Payne reasoned that if this truly described the nature of the atonement, then the death of Christ must have been sufficient for the salvation of the entire world. Payne stated:

> Now, if this be the nature of the atonement, the sacrifice of our Lord must have been in itself sufficient for the salvation of the whole world. To conceive any limitation in reference to its own intrinsic worth or adequacy, is utterly impossible. To suppose that the death of Christ has removed the obstacles which must otherwise have prevented the salvation of some men, and not those which would have obstructed the salvation of others, is to suppose not only what is unscriptural, but what is absurd.[245]

"If Christ's death was of the nature of a moral and not a pecuniary satisfaction, then that satisfaction which was sufficient for one must be sufficient for all," reasoned Payne.[246] Unless the atonement is universal, the consistency of the biblical exhortations and threats is impossible to vindicate.[247]

Concerning the sufficiency of the atonement, Payne registered his astonishment that some could give credence to the "monstrous proposition" that no atoning provision exists for multitudes who are nevertheless invited by God to partake of them and

244 Ibid., 210.

245 Ibid., 211.

246 Ibid., 212. Payne cited sermon 35 by Timothy Dwight: "The atonement, in other words, which was necessary for a world, was equally necessary, and in just the same manner and degree, for an individual sinner" (213).

247 Ibid., 214.

yet damned for rejecting them.[248] For Payne, "It is absurd to rest the *sufficiency* of the atonement upon the divine purpose in reference to its application."[249] If the atonement were not sufficient independent of God's will as to whom it should be applied, Payne argued it could not have been efficient for even one person. Furthermore, if the atonement is sufficient in itself in terms of worth and value, as all Calvinists would agree, then according to Payne, it may be rendered efficient in the case of all, should God have willed it so.

Payne made the point that if one supposes the sufficiency of the atonement rests only upon God's purpose for application to the elect, the result must be a limited sufficiency since it has no power to secure salvation except those to whom God has determined beforehand should receive it. Yet God invites all to receive it. Payne might have made explicit what is implicit in his reasoning—namely, that on the limited atonement scheme, the atonement cannot be sufficient for those for whom it does not exist, the non-elect.

For Payne, God's moral government of his creatures simply cannot support the notion of limited atonement. A door of mercy is opened to all people. It is thus necessary that the ground for reception of salvation, the atonement, "should be in itself sufficient for the salvation of all."[250]

Robert Morison (c. AD 1781–1855; Father of James Morison)

In 1841 he published *Difficulties Connected with the Doctrine of a Limited Atonement*,[251] in which, like his son James, he clearly advocated unlimited atonement. He suffered the same fate at the hands of the synod as his son.[252]

Morison did not find the typical passages used by limitarians to support limited atonement "at all conclusive of limitation."[253] He concluded, "If limitation be not clearly, and complete, and the *onus probandi*, or burthen of proof, lies incontestably on the side of the limitarians."[254]

Morison incisively critiqued the limitarian notion of sufficiency when he asked what they mean by it:

> Is it merely meant that there is so much abstract worth in the work of Christ that it would suffice for all men, had it been so designed? If this be all that is

248 Ibid.

249 Ibid., 214–15.

250 Ibid., 217.

251 R. Morison, *Difficulties Connected with the Doctrine of a Limited Atonement; or, The Question for Whom Did Christ Die?* (Kilmarnock: J. Davie, 1841), 3–37.

252 See A. Robertson, *History of the Atonement Controversy: In Connexion with the Session Church, from Its Origin to the Present Time* (Edinburgh: William Oliphant and Sons, 1846), 170–75.

253 R. Morison, *Difficulties Connected*, 4.

254 Ibid., 10.

meant, the next question is, Was it no way designed for all men? And if it was designed in some way for all men, then what is that way? If it was designed for all men, but was designed to be less than a propitiation for their sins, what was it designed to be to them?

If on the other hand it is affirmed, it was not designed for all men, but is in its nature a thing sufficient for all men, then I ask can it, in any available sense, be sufficient for that for which it was never designed? Either it was designed for all men, as an expiation of their sins, or it can no more become available to those for whom it was not designed, that it can be available to fallen angels.

If the atonement of Christ was only a work that might have sufficed, had it been so intended, that does not imply that it actually does suffice, or is sufficient, but merely that on certain supposable conditions it would have been so. Its intrinsic value is not the thing here. The intention is everything. This sufficiency must, in fact, be determined by its efficiency.

In one view, the efficiency of the atonement (that is, its actual fruits) is measured by its application, or the purpose of application, and in this vague sense of efficiency it is of a restricted nature. But another and still more important view of its efficiency, is its propitiatory character, as legally "putting away sin." This character it does possess antecedent to application, and it is in this that its proper efficiency consists.

It is just sufficient accordingly for the removal of all the sins, and all the sins of all the sinners, for which it was efficient as a propitiation. It is sufficient for all this, but for no more. As a *bona fide* transaction in behalf of sinners, its sufficiency is bounded by its efficiency, and springs out of it; or, in other words, it does not actually suffice for any except those for whose sins it was a propitiation.

If it was an efficient propitiation for the sins of the whole world, then it suffices or is sufficient for the salvation of the whole world; but if it was not an efficient propitiation for the sins of the whole world, then it suffices not or is not sufficient, for the salvation of the whole world—and is not sufficient, just because it was not efficient.

It is therefore a serious difficulty connected with the doctrine of a limited atonement, that by denying the unlimited efficiency of Christ's blood as a propitiation, it nullifies its universal sufficiency for the salvation of mankind sinners without exception.[255]

Morison questioned how the sinner can know the love of God to him, the gift of Christ to him, and the propitiation that Christ accomplished on the cross was actually for his sins, "except on the principle of the universal atonement. This is the only

255 Ibid., 14–16.

means the Bible supplies, by which he may know that the propitiation was for his sins." Morison did not think it possible for anyone to believe the gospel unless he "proceed practically on the principle of the unlimited atonement. Without this, there is no available testimony he can see coming directly to him that he can believe."[256]

Morison continued his critique by arguing that limited atonement "represents God in a most unfavourable light in the preaching of the gospel."[257] "A man never really preaches the gospel, in Paul's sense of the word, unless all that he brings forward is so arranged as to throw the souls of his hearers upon the grand fact, 'Christ died for your sins according to the scriptures.'"[258] The universal call of the gospel and the universal command to believe the gospel indicates a provision of the gospel for all people.[259]

Concerning propitiation, Morison believed there can be propitiation where there is not salvation, but there cannot be salvation where there is no propitiation. In unlimited atonement, propitiation extends beyond salvation. But on the limitarian scheme, propitiation only exists for a select few, and consequently salvation only exists for a select few. Such a scheme "represents God as sending an insincere and deceptive message."[260]

In conclusion, Morison saw no conflict with his own views and those of Westminster. He quoted Twisse, the moderator at Westminster, as saying, "Every man who hears the gospel (without distinction between elect and reprobate,) is bound to believe that Christ died for him." Morison continued to quote Twisse on John 3:16: "This gives a fair light of exposition to those places where Christ is said to have died for the sins of the world, yea, of the whole world," and concluded by stating, "Surely Dr. Twisse knew what was agreeable to the Westminster standards!"[261]

John Brown (AD 1784–1858)

John Brown was a Scottish pastor and professor of theology in the Secession Church. He was the grandson of the famed John Brown of Haddington. Brown was involved in the atonement controversy between 1840 and 1845, leading to the formation of the Secession Church. He was tried before the Presbyterian synod for affirming the extent of the atonement was universal. He was honorably acquitted.[262]

Illustrating his moderate Calvinistic dualism with respect to the atonement, Brown stated,

256 Ibid., 17.

257 Ibid., 19–20.

258 Ibid., 20.

259 Ibid.

260 Ibid., 21.

261 Ibid., 34.

262 See J. Brown, J. Hay, and A. Marshall, *Report of Proceedings in Trial by Libel of John Brown, D.D.* (Edinburgh: W. Oliphant, David Robertson, 1845).

> Nothing almost in the New Testament seems plainer to me, than that in one sense Christ gave Himself a ransom for all, and in another and higher sense gave Himself for the Church. The declaration, that He died with a special reference to those who are actually saved, does in no degree interfere with the declaration, that He died with a general reference, "the just for the unjust."[263]

Speaking of Heb 9:28, Brown said, "The sins of the whole world, were laid on Him."[264] Speaking of Heb 9:14, Brown spoke of the blood of Christ, "which He came to offer for the sins of mankind."[265] In Brown's *Discourses and Sayings of Our Lord*, he likewise spoke twice of Christ's death in universal terms as "for the sins of mankind."[266] In his commentary on Romans, Brown interpreted 1 John 2:2 to mean that Christ died for the sins of all people, not just the elect.[267]

With respect to John 3:16, Brown discussed the meaning of the word "world" as applying to all humanity. In good Calvinist fashion, he affirmed God's special love for the elect but maintained that Christ satisfied for the sins of the world in such a way that

> not merely was the atonement offered by Christ Jesus sufficient for the salvation of the whole world, but it was intended and fitted to remove out of the way of the salvation of sinners generally, every bar which the perfections of the Divine moral character, and the principles of the Divine moral government, presented. Without that atonement, no sinner could have been pardoned in consistency with justice. In consequence of that atonement, every sinner may be, and if he believe in Jesus certainly shall be, pardoned and saved.[268]

Particularists often appeal to Jesus's intercessory prayer in John 17 as evidence for limited atonement. Brown argued against this interpretation through careful exegesis of the passage.[269]

Robertson recorded Brown's comments to the synod with respect to his views concerning the extent of the atonement:

---

263 J. Brown, *An Exposition of the Epistle of the Apostle Paul to the Hebrews*, 2 vols., ed. D. Smith (Edinburgh: W. Oliphant and Co., 1862), 1:429.

264 Ibid., 1:430–31.

265 Ibid., 2:341.

266 J. Brown, *Discourses and Sayings of Our Lord Jesus Christ*, 2 vols. (New York: Robert Carter and Brothers, 1857), 1:38–39; 42. See also his comments on p. 526 that "there is no doubt" that Jesus is the propitiation for the sins of the whole world.

267 J. Brown, *Analytical Exposition of the Epistle of Paul to the Romans* (New York: Robert Carter and Brothers, 1857), 556. Brown likewise affirmed his commitment to an unlimited atonement in his *Expository Discourses of the First Epistle of the Apostle Peter*, 3 vols. (Edinburgh: William Oliphant and Co., 1866), 2:87–90.

268 J. Brown, *Discourses and Sayings*, 49–50.

269 J. Brown, *An Exposition of Our Lord's Intercessory Prayer* (Edinburgh: William Oliphant and Co., 1866), 101–4.

> That he was equally persuaded, that, by divine appointment, the death of Jesus Christ removes the legal bars in the way of the salvation, and opens the door of mercy to all mankind, making it consistent with the perfections of the divine character, and the principles of the divine government, to make a free offer of salvation to every human being, through the faith of the truth, and that, by the divine appointment, the death of Jesus Christ secures the actual salvation of those whom God, in sovereign mercy, from all eternity, elected to everlasting life.[270]

Robertson continued to reference Brown as affirming that Christ satisfied for the sins of the human race, not just the elect.

William Cogswell (AD 1787–1850)

Cogswell was a pastor in Dedham, Massachusetts, for fourteen years. He later served as professor of history in Dartmouth College, and then as president of Gilmanton Theological Seminary and professor of Christian theology, and authored many books, including *The Theological Class Book; Containing A System of Divinity in the Form of Question and Answer*.[271]

In the section on the atonement, question 10 asks, "How extensive is the atonement?" The answer given stated: "It is general, and extends in its sufficiency to all the human family."[272] Notice the way Cogswell answers this question by stating the atonement is "general"—that is, "for the sins of all people"—and that it "extends in its sufficiency" to all humanity. Here Cogswell understands "sufficiency" to be more than the value or dignity of Christ's death, so that the sufficiency is only hypothetical. Rather, the sufficiency consists in the fact that Christ actually substituted for the sins of all people.

Question 11 asks "How does this appear to be the case?" The answer explains:

> 1. From the character of Christ. The Saviour is a being of infinite dignity and worth. Hence His sufferings and death are of infinite value and efficacy; and hence the atonement is sufficient for all mankind. To conclude otherwise, would be derogatory to the glorious character of the Redeemer. 2. The atonement from its nature appears to be as sufficient for all, as for a part of the human race. It is that, on account of which God can consistently dispense grace to the guilty—can be just and still the justifier of all, who believe, how-

---

270 Robertson, *History of the Atonement Controversy*, 179–81.

271 William Cogswell, *The Theological Class Book; Containing a System of Divinity in the Form of Question and Answer, Accompanied with Scripture Proofs, Designed for the Benefit of Theological Classes, and the Higher Classes in Sabbath Schools* (Boston: Crocker & Brewster, 1831).

272 Ibid., 79.

ever large the number. 3. This doctrine may be proved from the commands, invitations, and exhortations of Scripture. God is sincere in all his dealings with men. Consequently, he would not command, invite, and exhort all to accept of salvation, if it were not provided for them. The inference, then, is, that the atonement is sufficient for all. 4. Another argument to prove the sufficiency of the atonement, is the command, given in the Scriptures, to pray for all men. God would not command us to pray for all men, unless salvation were provided for all. 5. The Scriptures teach this doctrine by express declarations.[273]

First, Cogswell deduced from the character and nature of Christ and his sufferings that it is not possible that Christ should suffer for some sins and not for others. Such would be "derogatory" to the character of the Savior. Second, based on Christ's death for all, God can dispense grace to the guilty in a just manner, no matter how large the number. Hence, it is possible that all could be saved if all would repent and believe the gospel because there is a sufficient atonement made for the sins of all people. Third, God's sincerity in commanding and inviting all people to believe the gospel hinges on an atonement made for all who hear these commands and invitations. Otherwise, God is insincere in these offers. Fourth, the command to pray for all implies a salvation provided for all. Fifth, these truths are taught by "express declaration" in Scripture. They are not merely logically deduced but actually taught.

Cogswell also pointed out that if we properly distinguish between atonement and redemption, where "atonement" has to do with the penalty paid for sin and "redemption" is reserved to speak of actual deliverance from sin's penalty by means of the application of the atonement, then "none would ever infer the doctrine of universal salvation from the general extent of the atonement." The atonement's "sufficiency depends upon its nature; but its efficiency depends upon its application, by the Spirit of God."[274]

Daniel Dewar (AD 1788–1867)

Dewar was principal of Marischal College, Aberdeen, and a minister of the Church of Scotland. His *Nature, Reality, and Efficacy of the Atonement* was published in 1831.[275] He affirmed a strictly limited atonement.

Dewar's approach to the extent question can be summarized as follows:

1. Scripture affirms Christ died for his people, his sheep.
2. Christ's death is restricted to those who have been given him by the Father.

273 Ibid., 80–81.

274 Ibid., 83.

275 D. Dewar, *The Nature, Reality, and Efficacy of the Atonement* (Edinburgh: Waugh and Inns, 1831).

3. Atonement and intercession are linked.
4. There is an inseparable connection between the gift of the Son and the gift of the Spirit.
5. Since Christ's death expresses his greatest or infinite love, it can only be for his elect.
6. The nature of Christ's suretyship guarantees the salvation of all those for whom he died.
7. Christ merited faith, holiness, and eternal life for those for whom he died.[276]

Dewar grounded the universal gospel offer on the intrinsic sufficiency of Christ's atonement.[277]

Charles Hodge (AD 1797–1878)

It would be difficult to name someone more illustrious than Charles Hodge as a Reformed theologian in the nineteenth century. Hodge's credentials are impeccable. He served as professor of theology at Princeton and was influential on some Southern Baptist founders, especially J. P. Boyce.

Hodge made a pertinent point about the necessity of biblical theology serving as the foundation for systematic theology in the following two quotations:

> This is what is meant when it is said, or implied in Scripture, that Christ gave Himself as a propitiation, not for our sins only, but for the sins of the whole world. He was a propitiation effectually for the sins of his people, and sufficiently for the sins of the whole world. Augustinians have no need to wrest the Scriptures. They are under no necessity of departing from their fundamental principle that it is the duty of the theologian to subordinate his theories to the Bible, and teach not what seems to him to be true or reasonable, but simply what the Bible teaches.[278]

> It is the duty of the theologian to subordinate his theories to the Bible, and teach not what seems to him to be true or reasonable, but simply what the Bible teaches.[279]

In several places in his *Systematic Theology* and his sermons, Hodge made clear his affirmation of universal atonement. For example, in a sermon he stated:

276 Ibid., 385–89.
277 Ibid., 391.
278 C. Hodge, *Systematic Theology*, 2:558–59.
279 Ibid., 2:559.

> It is here [in John 3:16], as well as elsewhere taught, that it was the design of God to render the salvation of all men possible, by the gift of his Son. There was nothing in the nature, or the value, or the design of his work to render it available for any one class of men only. Whosoever believeth, etc. This is not inconsistent with other representations that it entered into God's design to render the salvation of his people certain by the death of his Son.[280]

Hodge's *The Orthodox Doctrine Regarding the Extent of the Atonement Vindicated*[281] is an often overlooked work that sheds light on the subject and indicates Hodge's commitment to a form of unlimited atonement. Hodge is responding to Nathan Beman's *Christ, the Only Sacrifice: Or the Atonement in Its Relations to God and Man.* Key to Hodge's comments is his distinction between the intent of the atonement and the extent of the atonement.

Hodge critiqued commercialism.[282] He stated that the work of Christ "would have been the same, had God purposed to save one soul or the souls of all mankind."[283] For Hodge, the distinction is in the *design* or *purpose* of the atonement, not its nature. With respect to the atonement, Hodge stated, "As to its nature [it is] as much adapted to one man as to another, to all as to one."[284] That Hodge is here affirming a universal sin-bearing on the part of Christ is made clear by his statement "that the Reformed and Lutherans do not differ at all as to the nature of Christ's satisfaction, though they do differ as to its design." When Hodge spoke of "nature," he is including the notion of "extent."

Hodge critiqued Beman's notion that the single purpose of the atonement is to lay a foundation for the offer of salvation to all people. Hodge does not totally disagree with Beman here, but he argued that the atonement "not merely removes obstacles out of the way, but actually secures the salvation of his people." He followed this up by saying this removal of obstacles "lays the foundation for a free, full, and unrestrained offer of salvation to all men."[285] Notice the connection here. It is the removal of all legal barriers via an unlimited atonement that lays the foundation for the universal offer of the gospel to all. This is a crucial distinction missed by most Calvinists who affirm a limited extent in Christ's sin-bearing.

Hodge also affirmed an unlimited satisfaction for sin in Christ's death when he noted that Christ's death, to secure the salvation of the elect, fulfilled the conditions of the law "under which they and all mankind were placed." Those conditions were

280 C. Hodge, *Princeton Sermons* (London: Thomas Nelson and Sons, 1879), 17.

281 C. Hodge, *The Orthodox Doctrine regarding the Extent of the Atonement Vindicated* (Edinburgh: John Johnstone, 1846).

282 Ibid., 47–48.

283 Ibid., 54.

284 Ibid.

285 Ibid., 60.

perfect obedience and satisfaction to divine justice "by bearing the penalty threatened against sin."[286] Notice Hodge does not say "against the sin of the elect." He continued: "That righteousness is precisely what the law demands of every sinner, in order to his justification before God. It is, therefore, in its nature, adapted to all sinners who are under the law." This is unlimited sin-bearing by Christ on the cross, according to Hodge. Notice carefully his next statement: "Its nature is not altered by the fact that it was wrought out for a portion only of such sinners, or that it is secured to them by the covenant between the Father and the Son."[287] Here again is Hodge making the distinction between the *intent* of the atonement and its *extent*. "What is necessary for the salvation of one man, is necessary for the salvation of another, and of all."[288]

Hodge spoke of the atonement as being "adapted to all men" and of infinite value so as to be "sufficient for all." He continued: "On these two grounds, its adaptation to all and its sufficiency for all, rests the offer made in the gospel to all."[289] Hodge's next sentence is important: "With this its design has nothing to do." Hodge is again distinguishing between the atonement's *extent* and *intent*. He then makes this startling statement: "If one of the non-elect should believe . . . to him that righteousness would be imputed to his salvation." How could the non-elect be saved if they were to believe on the limited atonement scheme? They could not, for no atonement exists for their sins. But Hodge indicated they could be saved if they believe. Why? Because an atonement exists for their sins. The atonement "opens the door for mercy, as far as legal obstructions are concerned."[290]

Where does one read those who hold to limited atonement speaking like this? Which Reformed theologian who asserts limited atonement speaks of the death of Christ removing all legal obstructions blocking humanity from salvation?[291] No one I know. This is not the language of limited atonement but unlimited atonement with respect to the actual extent of Christ's death.

Hodge also made the point that the application of the atonement is delayed and does not *ipso facto* liberate those for whom it was made at the point of Christ's death on the cross. The elect are still children of wrath (Eph 2:1–3). Hodge is rejecting the double payment argument.[292]

Albert Barnes (AD 1798–1870)

Albert Barnes, an American Presbyterian preacher and author of an extensive and widely used set of commentaries on the whole Bible, was brought to trial in 1835 by the Second

286 Ibid., 68.
287 Ibid.
288 Ibid.
289 Ibid.
290 Ibid., 69.
291 One possible exception would be A. A. Hodge, son of Charles Hodge. A. A. Hodge spoke of the barriers being removed by the death of Christ but, unlike his father, seemed to affirm inconsistently a limited atonement.
292 See Hodge, *Systematic Theology*, 2:471–72, 555, 557–58.

Presbytery of Philadelphia for his belief in unlimited atonement. Barnes's trial served as one of the issues that led to the division in the Presbyterian Church in the United States in 1837.[293] In his own defense at his trial, he reminded his hearers that the sermon he had preached that caused consternation among the high Calvinists in no way violated the confession of faith. Barnes pointed out that the word "atonement" is not used in the confession but the term "redemption" is used. He further pointed out how the confession "in no instance denies" his use of the term "atonement" to refer to Christ's satisfaction for the sins of all men, concluding, "How this can be a grave offense against our standards does not appear."[294] He was acquitted of the charges.

Barnes wrote an extensive treatise arguing for unlimited atonement entitled *The Atonement in Its Relation to Law and Moral Government*.[295] His views on the extent of the atonement may also be found in his commentaries and sermons.

In his sermon on *The Way of Salvation*, Barnes expressed clearly his affirmation of unlimited atonement. God's plan of salvation is to provide a healing balm designed by God to extend as far as the sickness of sin. Jesus died for the human race so that a way of salvation might be opened for all people.[296]

Quoting John Owen, Barnes asserted the atonement, in and of itself, secured the salvation of no one. Only on the condition of repentance and faith would anyone receive God's salvation. In rhetoric expressive of his passion, Barnes stated:

> I hold no doctrines—and by the grace of God never can hold any—which will be in *my* views inconsistent with the free and full offer of the Gospel to all men; or which will bind my hands, or palsy my tongue, or freeze my heart, when I stand before sinners to tell them of a dying Saviour.[297]

In his work, *The Atonement*, in distinguishing between "atonement" and "redemption," Barnes stated that the exact number of the elect was not fixed by the nature and extent of the atonement. Barnes distinguished the purpose and intent of the atonement from the actual nature of the atonement. For the latter, Barnes, like many of his contemporaries, chose to use the term "atonement." For the actual application of the atonement Barnes chose to use the word "redemption." In this sense, for Barnes, the death of Christ is unlimited as to its nature (atonement) but limited as to its application

293 E. Moyer, "Barnes, Albert," in *Wycliffe Biographical Dictionary of the Church*, rev. and enlarged by E. E. Cairns (Chicago: Moody Press, 1982), 29.

294 A. Barnes, *The Way of Salvation: A Sermon, Delivered at Morristown New Jersey, together with Mr Barnes Defence of the Sermon, Read before the Synod of Philadelphia, at Lancaster, October 29, 1830, and His "Defence" before the Second Presbytery of Philadelphia, in Reply to the Chargers of the Rev. Dr. George Junkin*, 7th ed. (New York: Leavitt, Lord & Co, 1836), 67–69.

295 A. Barnes, *The Atonement in Its Relation to Law and Moral Government* (Philadelphia: Lindsay & Blakiston, 1860). The work was republished under the title *The Atonement* (Minneapolis, MN: Bethany, 1980).

296 A. Barnes, *The Way of Salvation*, 18.

297 Ibid., 22 (emphasis in original).

(redemption). This distinction appears in the later Andrew Fuller as well as in such nineteenth-century Calvinist theologians as Dabney and Shedd.

Among the many arguments Barnes adduced for universal atonement is the analogy of the remedial arrangements God has placed in creation, which are of universal applicability. The laws of healing are the same in all men, and the remedial system is adapted alike to all. There is no limit to the provisions made for healing disease. Barnes stated: "If this may be allowed to be an indication of what a plan of redemption would be, it would, therefore, indicate that the plan would be of universal applicability."[298] Barnes did not make too much of this argument from analogy, as he admitted God could limit the extent of the atonement if he so designed. But Barnes saw in nature "an obvious inference that the impressions which God has designed to make in regard to his character in his works will be found to be sustained and confirmed in the provisions for salvation."[299]

Barnes noted one common objection against universal atonement is the supposition that Christ died for many who will not be redeemed; hence that portion of the atonement is a waste.[300] One sees the argument regularly made throughout Reformed history: Christ's blood is wasted on the general atonement view.

Barnes rightly countered that such an objection is rooted in a commercial view of the atonement and/or a quantitative equivalentism view, where the same amount of suffering must be endured by Christ that would have been endured by those for whom he died. These problems aside, and they are difficult to overcome, Barnes stated that the "wasted blood" argument assumes more than we have a right to assume about God and his intentions in the atonement. How often does the rain descend on barren rocks or sterile fields where neither humanity nor animals benefit?[301] Nowhere in Scripture is the "wasted blood" argument ever made.

Barnes deduced from the nature of the atonement certain entailments.

> If, as I endeavored to show, the atonement is (a) something *substituted* in the place of the penalty of the law, which will answer the same ends as the punishment of the offender himself would have done; (b) that it secures reconciliation between God and man; and (c) that it is a manifestation of the character of God to the inhabitants of other worlds, in showing to them how justice and mercy may be blended in the pardon of offenders, then it would seem clearly to follow that it may be *general* in its nature, and may be applicable to any number of offenders. It has no peculiar adaptedness to one more than to another. It is in this respect like the light of the sun, or like running fountains

298 Barnes, *The Atonement*, 317–18.
299 Ibid., 321–22.
300 Ibid., 323.
301 Ibid., 329–30.

> or streams—adapted to all; like medicine—applicable to no one class of the human race exclusively, but having an original applicability to *disease* wherever it may be found.[302]

Barnes asked his readers to contemplate the incarnation of Christ and ask what would be the proper interpretation of the extent of the atonement from such contemplation. The fact would suggest itself that the design of the atonement would be for all humanity. The idea of it being limited to a few would appear wholly incongruous with the incarnation.[303] If there is a limitation, it should be placed in the purpose of God and not in the nature of the atonement.

Barnes queried, "If we take our views of the atonement from his character, and allow those views to interpret the atonement, we could not fail to come to the conclusion that it was designed to be unlimited."[304]

Barnes considered the biblical texts themselves that support unlimited atonement, beginning with John 3:16–17. He opined against the limitarian interpretation of John 3:16, arguing that if limitation were intended, "the declaration should have been such as to embrace that fact, and not such that its obvious interpretation would be contradictory to it and irreconcilable with it."[305] Other texts Barnes considered include Heb 2:9; 1 John 2:2; 2 Cor 5:14; and 2 Pet 2:1.

Barnes considered the gospel offer in light of the atonement's nature. His first point is that the gospel offer is first made by God, not man. Second, the offer is sincere because there is an atonement made for the sins of all people.

> On the ground of the gospel of Christ, he assures men that he is ready to save them, nothing can be more certain than that the Redeemer died for them. It will not meet the case to say that the atonement is "sufficient" in its own nature for all men if God had chosen that it should have been made with reference to all.[306]

The sufficiency question was crucial for Barnes:

> It is this—that the offer of salvation is made not on the ground of an original *sufficiency in the atonement itself*, but on the ground that it *had such a reference to sinners* as to justify an offer of pardon. It is *not* offered to the one class on the ground that it was made for them, and to the other on the ground that it

302 Ibid., 337 (emphasis in original).
303 Ibid., 341.
304 Ibid., 342.
305 Ibid., 345.
306 Ibid., 348.

> was sufficient for them though not intended for them. Of any such distinction there is no trace whatever in the Scriptures. If there had been such a distinction in the mind of God, every consideration of sincerity and truthfulness required that all the facts should be made known; or, at least, that the communication made to men should not be so made as to leave a false impression.[307]

Howard Malcolm (AD 1799–1879)

Malcolm was an American Baptist pastor and educator in New England. He served as president at Georgetown College in Kentucky until 1850. His *Extent and Efficacy of the Atonement* was published in 1833. He argued the case for limited atonement based on the argument that extent and efficacy are coextensive.[308] In an appendix to this work, Malcom argued that Andrew Fuller did not assert universal atonement, as many were claiming.

In the quotations on the nature and extent of the atonement from Fuller that Malcolm adduced, he apparently failed to take note of the fact that the Fuller used the word "design" or "intent" as distinguished from "extent" in virtually every case. Fuller's statements that God limits the intent or design of the atonement to the elect in no way supports limited atonement in light of his statements that, with respect to sinners as sinners, the atonement is adapted to all.

Notice how Malcom himself said, "The consistency of particular redemption or of a limited design in the death of Christ."[309] He equated "particular redemption" (extent) with "limited design" (intent). This is what the later Fuller did not do.

John McLeod Campbell (AD 1800–1872)

Campbell was an influential nineteenth-century Scottish Calvinist preacher and theologian. He articulated his views on the extent of the atonement in his famous work *The Nature of the Atonement*, published in 1856.[310] Campbell was well acquainted with the writings of the early church fathers as well as the Reformers. He argued for an unlimited atonement but denied the substitutionary nature of the atonement. He also taught universal pardon, that all people were actually, rather than potentially, forgiven, and that their failure to enjoy the benefit of this forgiveness was the result of their not believing it. He was accused of heresy, brought to trial by the General Assembly, and found guilty of teaching contrary to the Westminster Standards. Robertson proffered

---

307 Ibid., 349.

308 H. Malcolm, *The Extent and Efficacy of the Atonement*, 2nd ed. (New York: Robert Carter, 1840), 117–21.

309 Ibid., 119.

310 J. M. Campbell, *The Nature of the Atonement* (1856; repr. Grand Rapids, MI: Eerdmans, 1996). Campbell's work was very influential in Scotland and beyond and went through six editions by 1866. Reprints continued until 1915. For a helpful discussion of Campbell's view of the atonement, his influencers, and those he influenced, see Kinnear, "Scottish New Testament Scholarship and the Atonement," 68–123.

the suggestion that it was the exclusivity of the limited atonement position that drove Campbell to the opposite extreme.[311]

Wright attempted to co-opt Campbell to support the notion that if atonement is substitutionary, limited extent is a necessary corollary, as Owen had said. In answering Owen, Campbell denied the atonement was substitutionary, thinking this would protect unlimited atonement. He bought into the same erroneous either/or fallacy of a commercial understanding of the atonement just as Owen had done. Campbell assumed Owen's triple choice argument was unassailable, and hence Campbell denied that the death of Christ satisfied God's justice; rather, Christ died to offer a substitute repentance.[312]

Nevertheless, Campbell's *Nature of the Atonement* provides many excellent arguments in favor of universal atonement.

Erskine Mason (AD 1805–1851)

A graduate of Princeton Theological Seminary, Mason was a pastor of the prestigious Bleeker Street Presbyterian church in New York City from 1830 until his death. He also served as professor of church history at Union Theological Seminary.

In his sermon on 1 John 2:2 entitled "Extent of the Atonement," Mason presented a strong appeal for understanding this passage as teaching an unlimited atonement. In careful logic coupled with descriptive prose, Mason passionately pressed his hearers at the end of this sermon to come to a Savior who has died for their sins.

Mason began by noting that the question of the extent of the atonement is no matter of speculative theology but of serious practicality. Like many Calvinists in the nineteenth century, he draws a distinction between atonement and redemption, which he stated should be carefully maintained in the discussion. The one does not necessarily imply the other. For Mason, atonement speaks of the actual work of Christ on the cross with respect to sin. Redemption includes atonement as well as the actual results of the atonement as applied—namely, actual salvation. Redemption is not general; atonement is.[313]

Mason distinguished the nature of the atonement, which he asserted was general, from the purpose of the atonement, which, as a Calvinist, he asserted was for the elect alone. With respect the atonement's extent, Mason is clear: "Every legal bar and obstruction in the way of the salvation of all men is removed."[314]

---

311 Robertson, *History of the Atonement Controversy*, 159. See also A. Drummond and J. Bulloch, *The Scottish Church 1688–1843: The Age of the Moderates* (Edinburgh: Saint Andrew Press, 1973), 201–10. Drummond and Bulloch state that Edward Irving discussed with John McLeod Campbell that Christ died for all (201–2). See also J. Goroncy, "'*Tha mi a' toirt fainear dur gearan*': J. McLeod Campbell and P. T. Forsyth on the Extent of Christ's Vicarious Ministry," in *Evangelical Calvinism: Essays Resourcing the Continuing Reformation of the Church*, ed. M. Habets and B. Grow (Eugene, OR: Wipf & Stock, 2012), 253–87.

312 See R. K. McGregor Wright, *No Place for Sovereignty* (Downers Grove, IL: InterVarsity, 1996), 149–54.

313 E. Mason, *A Pastor's Legacy: Being Sermons on Practical Subjects* (New York: Charles Scribner, 1853).

314 Ibid., 276.

Mason made the same analogical arguments for general atonement as Barnes did in his appeal to nature and how God provides sun and rain for all. Likewise, there is an unlimited provision in the atonement for the sins of all, though not all benefit from this provision. This can be demonstrated from the universal terms used by Scripture to speak of the atonement.

Mason's language is strong concerning the absolute necessity of a universal atonement to ground the well-meant offer of the gospel to all people:

> If the entire population of the globe were before me, and there should be one in the mighty assembly for whom there was no provision, I could not preach the gospel; for how could I say in sincerity and honesty to all and to each, come and take of the waters of life freely?[315]

Mason continued:

> With these views of the gospel offer, I cannot advocate a limited atonement; I cannot put a restriction of the provision which I do not find in the offer; I cannot believe that God would make to a sinner in his wants and his woes the tender of a relief which did not exist, or which he did not wish him to embrace; I cannot believe that God would command his creatures to embrace a provision which had never been made for them, or sanction by the peril of one's everlasting interests a commandment which he never meant should be obeyed, and which itself precluded the possibility of obedience.[316]
>
> It does not at all meet the difficulty of the case to say, at this point, that we are required thus indiscriminately to offer the gospel and thus to enforce its acceptance upon all, because we do not know the persons for whom the provision is made, and whom God designs shall accept it. The offer is not ours; we are but the channel through which it comes. God himself makes the offer; we but take up God's words, and announce them as he has given them to us. We are ambassadors of Christ, not speaking in our own name, but according to our instructions, which bind us to say to each and every one of our hearers, "Come, for all things are now ready." In this matter we have no responsibility beyond the simple utterance of the message, "This is the will of God, that ye believe on him whom he hath sent;" and the question returns upon us, how can we reconcile a universal offer with a limited provision? How can we acquit God of the charge of insincerity in making to men a tender, and enforcing upon them by the high

315 Ibid., 282.
316 Ibid., 283.

> sanctions of eternity the acceptance of that which not only was never designed for them in any sense, but which, in fact, has never been provided?[317]

Mason proceeded to counter another criticism made by limitarians against universal atonement—namely, how can one reconcile an unrestricted provision with a limited result? Why should God make a provision he knew would be unnecessary for many? Mason's response is penetrating.

> I do not know, my brethren, a better example than the foregoing questions furnish, of that rule of logic which forbids us to allow a weak argument to stand isolated and unprotected, and requires us to combine such arguments and present them in one view, so that they may help each other, and have the appearance, at least, of overwhelming force. When you take all the questions together, they seem to have no little weight; but when taken singly they are wholly pointless and irrelevant.
>
> For we may ask in return, what has any secret purpose to do with our role of judgment and action? "Secret things," we are told, "belong unto the Lord our God; but things which are revealed, unto us and to our children." The question taken from the hidden purposes of the divine mind can have no force whatever, because it is an appeal to our ignorance. We know, and can know nothing about them. One thing, however, we do know. God must be always and everywhere consistent with himself; and whether we can understand it or not, it is certain that there can be no inconsistency between revealed and unrevealed truths; and if God has made an offer of eternal life through the atonement unto all men, and commanded all men to embrace it, there cannot be in any purpose of God concerning its nature, anything which will clash with, and so contradict this universal offer.
>
> This argument, however, from God's purpose, which is so often brought forward to limit the nature and availableness of Christ's atonement, like many other arguments, destroys itself by proving too much.[318]

Mason further countered this argument by quoting an uncited source:

> Its necessity does not arise from the number of sinners, but from the nature of sin. The very nature of sin requires an infinite atonement in order to its honorable remission. Such an atonement as Christ offered, was indispensably necessary to the pardon of one act of sin—and as the sun must be what it is,

317 Ibid., 284.
318 Ibid., 285–86.

> whether it lightens one man, or every man who cometh into the world, so it makes no difference as to the nature or availableness of the sufferings of Christ, whether one sinner, or a race of sinners, is to be saved by them. There is no more waste or unnecessary expenditure in the one case than in the other.[319]

Mason's final portion of the sermon is a passionate appeal to his unsaved hearers to respond to the all-sufficient atonement made for the sins of all people. I am struck by one of his final sentences concerning the importance of preaching and the extent of the atonement: "There is no more waste in preaching, than there has been in making an atonement which is not received."[320]

Henry Carpenter (AD 1806–1864)

Carpenter was a pastor in Liverpool at St. Michael's Church. He published in 1857 *Did Christ Die for All Men, Or for the Elect Only?*[321] The work is a published letter to a friend on the subject of the extent of the atonement.

Carpenter was unpersuaded by the common arguments used in favor of limited atonement. He boldly asserted: "But there is not, I am persuaded, a single passage in the Bible where it can be proved that the word 'world' is used to signify the elect only—no place where, by any just canon of interpretation, this restricted and exclusive meaning ought to be given to it."[322]

Concerning the Thirty-Nine Articles of the Anglican Church, Carpenter noted how Article 2 speaks of Christ as one

> "who truly suffered, was crucified, dead and buried, to reconcile his father to us, and to be a sacrifice not only for original guilt, but also for all actual sins of men." From this we see that the minister of the Church of England is, by her teaching, authorized to say to each individual—to every human being, "The death of Christ was a sacrifice for all the sins you ever committed."[323]

Carpenter appealed to the authors of the Thirty-Nine Articles, which explicitly taught universal atonement by stating that the sins of the "world" means to convey the sins of all humanity: "For what is expressed concerning his death, in reference to 'the world,' in the 15th and 31st Articles, the same is said of it, in reference to 'men' and 'mankind', in the 2d and 7th Articles."[324]

---

319 Ibid., 288.
320 Ibid., 292.
321 H. Carpenter, *Did Christ Die for All Men, or for the Elect Only?* (London: T. Hatchard, 1857).
322 Ibid., 7.
323 Ibid., 5.
324 Ibid., 7–8.

Carpenter adduced further evidence for universal atonement from the Prayer of Consecration, the Anglican Catechism, and the Book of Homilies. The Prayer of Consecration speaks of Christ "who made there (by his one oblation of himself once offered) a full, perfect, and sufficient sacrifice, oblation, and satisfaction for the sins of the whole world."[325] The catechism employs this statement: "I believe in God the Son, who has redeemed me and all mankind." The homilies likewise employ similar language. In the first part of the Sermon Concerning the Sacrament, the author spoke of our having "sure and constant faith . . . that the death of Christ is available for the redemption of all the world." Likewise, the Second Homily on the Death and Passion of Christ employs these words: "Was not this a singular token of great love? But to whom did he give him? He gave him to the whole world—that is to say, to Adam and all that should come after him."[326]

Carpenter enlisted a strong argument against limited atonement when he noted that the universal language that is used to describe the Son's death for sins is nowhere used concerning the work of the Holy Spirit.

> We never read that the Spirit is the Sanctifier of the world, as we read that Christ is the Saviour of the world. We never read of the Spirit's purifying every man, as we read of Christ's tasting death for every man. The world is redeemed by the Son, but the elect only are sanctified by the Spirit. But it is a distinction we look for in vain, in their writings, who deny the doctrine of General Redemption.[327]

To the argument that God's intentions cannot be frustrated, therefore limited atonement must be true, Carpenter suggested caution that we

> be certain what his purpose is before we can pronounce with any measure of confidence that it is frustrated. . . . Study the history of the fall of Adam and of the angels; study the history of the flood, and of Nineveh repenting; weigh these facts, and consider what is written on these and similar subjects, and you will see that God speaks at times in his word as though his expectations were disappointed and his intentions frustrated.[328]

Carpenter packed quite a punch against limited atonement in these short twenty-four pages.

---

325 Ibid., 8.
326 Ibid., 9.
327 Ibid., 10.
328 Ibid., 20.

Robert Candlish (AD 1806–1873)

Robert Candlish, along with Thomas Chalmers, was a key leader in the formation of the Free Church of Scotland in 1843. Pastor of St. George's in Edinburgh, he was well known for his preaching skills. He succeeded William Cunningham as principal of New College while retaining his pastorate. Along with excellent commentaries on Genesis and 1 John, Candlish authored *The Atonement; Its Reality, Completeness and Extent* in 1861, which was based upon a smaller work on the subject in 1845.[329] He was firmly committed to limited atonement, as can be seen in his discussion of John 3:16.

He explained that the gospel has a "gracious aspect" to the world—that is, mankind as such—without reference to elect or non-elect. But Candlish argued that here there is nothing said about God giving his Son for all. Rather, the terms themselves "imply a limitation of it to them that believe."

> It is the gift of his Son, with this limited design, which is represented as being an index and measure of his love to the world at large, or to mankind as such; and it is so, through the manifestation which the cross gives to all alike and indiscriminately, of what it is in the mind and heart of God to do for a race of guilty sinners.[330]

How Candlish can reason that such a limitation in the extent of the atonement to only some of the human race is in any way a demonstration of God's love to mankind at large is difficult to comprehend.

Furthermore, other statements by Candlish would appear to be inconsistent with his avowed commitment to limited atonement:

> He is the propitiation for all sinners and for all sins. No-sin, no sinner, is at any time beyond the reach of that great atonement. It meets the case of all mankind, or all the world, and therefore it meet thy case, by thy backsliding ever so grievous, thy guilt ever so aggravated. Thou couldst not venture to appropriate Christ as the propitiation for thy sins otherwise than as he is the propitiation for the sins of the whole world. It is only because thou believest and art sure that no sin no sinner, in all the world is debarred from that wondrous fountain filled with blood, that thou canst summon courage to plunge in it thyself afresh.[331]

---

329 R. Candlish, *An Inquiry into the Completeness of the Atonement with Especial Reference to the Universal Offer of the Gospel, and the Universal Obligation to Be Believed* (Edinburgh: John Johnstone, 1845). See also R. Candlish, *The Atonement; Its Reality, Completeness and Extent* (London: T. Nelson & Sons, 1861).

330 R. Candlish, *An Inquiry*, xxv–xxvii.

331 R. Candlish, *First Epistle of John* (Grand Rapids, MI: Kregel, 1979), 75. Candlish appears to be inconsistent here as a high Calvinist.

Notice the inconsistency here. Candlish spoke of Christ being the propitiation for "all sinners and all sins." He further stated that one cannot venture to appropriate the benefits of this propitiation for his own sins if he is not convinced that it was also a propitiation for the world. One is forced to query Candlish as to exactly how this squares with limited atonement as a limited substitution for the sins of the elect alone.

Candlish quoted Moses Stuart on Heb 2:9 in an effort to support his own limited atonement interpretation, but in the process he has misunderstood Stuart. Stuart said "all" means all men, Jew and Gentile. This does not help Candlish. All without distinction here still means all without exception for Stuart. Furthermore, Stuart's point was to inveigh against universal salvation, not universal atonement.[332] Candlish missed this contextual point. Stuart questions whether limitarian language with respect to the extent of the atonement can ground the sincere offer of the gospel to all people in a consistent way.

> The question, in all these phrases, evidently respects the offer of salvation, the opportunity to acquire it through a Redeemer; not the actual application of promises, the fulfillment of which is connected only with repentance and faith. But whether such an offer can be made with sincerity to those who are reprobates . . . consistently with the grounds which the advocates for particular redemption maintain, is a question for the theologian, rather than the commentator, to discuss.[333]

Stuart raised the problem of the well-meant gospel offer for those who affirm limited atonement. Taking the "all" passages in Scripture separately, Candlish said one must ask what is the precise point under discussion. For example, in Rom 5:18 and 2 Cor 5:14, Candlish tried to deflect what these passages say about the extent of the atonement by suggesting Paul focuses on imputation, not the extent of the atonement. In Rom 5:18 he attempted to explain away the possibility of universal extent by saying if taken in this fashion, the result is universalism. In 2 Cor 5:14, Candlish stated Paul's theme is union with Christ and the question of the extent of the atonement is not in Paul's mind.

But the passages under consideration address more than just imputation and union with Christ. They make statements concerning the extent of the atonement that cannot be set aside.

332 R. Candlish, *An Inquiry*, xi–xii.
333 Ibid., xii.

Alexander C. Rutherford (AD 1810–1878)

The Scottish Rutherford authored *Universal Atonement Proved from the Nature of the Gospel Offer in Four Letters to the Rev. William Fraser.*[334] He made this interesting statement: "But, while the forefathers of the Secession would not admit a universal atonement, in the Arminian sense of the expression, they contended for the thing expressed by it, as it is used and understood by every enlightened Calvinist."[335]

Referencing the Act of the Associate Presbytery, passed on October 21, 1742, Rutherford stated:

> The persons to whom this grant and offer are made, are NOT THE ELECT ONLY, but mankind, considered as lost. For the record of God, being such a thing as warrants all to believe on the Son of God, it is evident that it can be no such warrant to tell men that God hath given eternal life to the elect: As the offering of a gift to a certain select company, can never be a warrant for all men to receive or take possession of it.[336]

In a letter to William Fraser, Rutherford said that Fraser, in affirming limited atonement, had

> receded from the grand doctrine for which our forefathers so strenuously contended. The manna was actually rained down for all. Even so the atonement, in the sense explained, was actually made for all. This you deny; and, in denying this you occupy the precise ground occupied by the General Assembly of 1720 and 1722. We, then, contend for the same truth for which the Erskines struggled. But it is painful to think, that the honoured descendant of an Erskine should be our assailant. You have discharged against us the precise weapons, too, which the Assembly flung so recklessly and unjustly against the supporters of the Marrow. You call us Arminians, &c. I forget not that you are a father; and I will not throw back the words. I do hope, however, that the position occupied by you, will never be taken up by the Synod of the Succession.[337]

Thomas Crawford (AD 1812–1875)

Crawford was a Scottish theologian who entered the ministry in 1834 and was appointed professor of divinity at Edinburgh in 1859. He served as moderator of the

334 A. Rutherford, *A Universal Atonement Proved from the Nature of the Gospel Offer: In Four Letters to the Rev. William Fraser* (Edinburgh: W. Oliphat and Son, 1841).

335 Ibid., 27.

336 Ibid.

337 Ibid., 28.

General Assembly in 1867. Crawford was a contributor to the theological debate surrounding the atonement in the 1860s and 1870s. He affirmed limited atonement.

One of his three major works, published in 1883, dealt specifically with the atonement.[338] Crawford's work is refreshing in that he attempted painstakingly to follow the inductive method to understand the biblical teaching on the atonement. From the data, he educed a series of twelve inferences on the subject.

Crawford asserted:

> From MAN'S standpoint (the only point of view from which we can regard it), it [the atonement] cannot be otherwise looked at or dealt with than as "a propitiation for the sins of the whole world"—*sufficient for all, suitable for all,* and beyond all controversy, *pressed on the acceptance of all.*[339]

Notice he said "from man's standpoint."

Crawford treated the issue of universal gospel offers from the platform of limited atonement and admitted the "great difficulty" in harmonizing the two. First, he asserted that our inability to reconcile these two need not be proof of any real inconsistency. On the other hand, that might just be the case. When he averred that universal invitations of the gospel are "fully consistent with the truth of the case,"[340] he was begging the question as to extent. When he stated that "certain benefits purchased by the atonement shall certainly be obtained by any sinner provided he meets conditions for obtaining them (repentance and faith),"[341] he is confusing the categories of an atonement procured and an atonement applied. No one denies that Scripture teaches all those who repent and believe the gospel will have the benefit of the atonement applied to them.

Second, Crawford reminded us that the same Bible speaks of universal gospel offers but limited references "to those who are given to Christ by the Father." But this has nothing to do with the extent of the atonement. Again, this is begging the question. Crawford assumed no insincerity on God's part in this because he thinks both are taught in Scripture.[342]

Third, Crawford assumed a deterministic understanding of sovereignty and rejected libertarian free will when he finds a difference between God's universal gospel invitations and the purposes of his secret will.

> But while the commandments are thus expressive of what He *desires, approves of,* and *delights in,* as congenial to the goodness and holiness of His moral

338 T. Crawford, *The Doctrine of Holy Scripture Respecting the Atonement,* 4th ed. (Edinburgh: Blackwood, 1883).

339 Ibid., 201–2 (emphasis in original).

340 Ibid., 510.

341 Ibid.

342 Ibid., 511.

> nature, they are not declarative of what he has *purposed*, or *determined*, in His government of the universe to carry into effect. For if they were so, it is certain that they would be unfailingly and universally obeyed by all His creatures; whereas they are frequently violated, without any interference on His part to vindicate their authority and secure their observance.[343]

Fourth, Crawford asserted there is no difference between all parties on the sufficiency of the atonement. He quoted John Owen and Charles Hodge.[344] But Crawford failed to note the difference between Owen and Hodge. Owen spoke only of a hypothetical sufficiency. Hodge spoke of an actual sufficiency in that the atonement is "adapted to all" and that Christ substituted for the sins of all people. Hodge held to universal atonement, as we have seen.

Crawford misunderstood Hypothetical Universalism when he said that they (Hypothetical Universalists) "deny the special destination of the atonement for the benefit of those who are eventually saved."[345] This is a caricature of the position. No Hypothetical Universalist denies the special destination of the atonement for the elect only. They merely, in addition to God's special destination, affirm a universal satisfaction for all sins.

Crawford attempted to show that Calvinist advocates of universal atonement with limited intent do not improve their position over the limitarians:

> The fact is that, as regards the *actual attainment* of salvation through the sacrifice of Christ, there is a limitation on the principles of either party, while as regards *the removal of such obstacles as stood in the way of salvation being attainable by all sinners in the event of their faithful compliance with the terms of the Gospel*, there is, on the principles of either party, the same perfectly suitable and adequate provision made in the all-sufficient merits and sufferings of the Son of God. And thus does it appear that the advocates of what is called "universal atonement," combined with a limited purpose in the divine mind as to its application, are really in no better position than those who differ from them, when they come to explain the unrestricted language in which the Scriptures speak of the Lord Jesus Christ as "the Saviour of the world," and invite all sinners to receive His offered grace.[346]

---

343 Ibid., 512 (emphasis in original).

344 Ibid., 513.

345 Ibid., 514. Crawford calls them "semi-Arminians." This pejorative is not new. Morris Fuller mentions a letter by Samuel Ward (AD 1572–1643) written to Archbishop James Ussher in which Ward says, "Some of us [English moderates at Dort] were held by some [as] half Remonstrants, for extending the oblation [of Christ] made to the Father to all, and for holding sundry effects thereof offered *serio*, and some really communicated to the reprobate" (M. Fuller, *The Life, Letters & Writings of John Davenant D.D. 1572–1641, Lord Bishop of Salisbury* [London: Methuen & Co., 1897], 90; emphasis in original).

346 Ibid., 515–16 (emphasis in original).

For Crawford, widening the extent of the atonement compromises its efficacy.[347]

Crawford's explanation fails to recognize the different limitations in play for both parties. For the high Calvinist, the limitation is at the point of the actual atonement itself; it is limited in the sense that Christ only substituted himself for the elect. For Calvinists who affirm unlimited atonement, the limitation is at the point of the effectual application alone. Crawford fails to reckon with the fact that on his scheme, he has no gospel to offer the non-elect. They are effectively unsaveable.

C. John Kennedy (AD 1813–1900)

Kennedy was a Scottish Congregational minister, author, and educator. He studied at Aberdeen, Edinburgh, and Glasgow universities. He was pastor of a Congregational church in Aberdeen from 1836 to 1846, then the Stepney Congregational Meeting House in London until his retirement in 1882. From 1872 to 1876 he was professor of apologetics at New College, London.

Kennedy wrote *The Doctrine of Universal Atonement Vindicated*[348] in response to John Smyth's *Treatise on the Forgiveness of Sins, as the Privilege of the Redeemed; In Opposition to the Doctrine of Universal Pardon.*[349] Smyth was the minister at St. George's in Glasgow and championed limited atonement.

Smyth was reacting to Thomas Erskine's notion of unlimited atonement and universal pardon.[350] Smyth took as his foundational text Eph 1:7, and deduced from it the following syllogism:

> Christ's redemption is not of universal extent.
> Forgiveness is a primary blessing of redemption.
> Therefore, forgiveness is not universal.

Of course, Smyth's first proposition assumed the point to be proven and thus the syllogism is false. Furthermore, there is nothing in Eph 1:7 about the extent of the atonement.

Smyth attempted to argue the point that unless the atonement is limited only to those for whom it actually saves, then the blood of Christ is wasted and Christ died in vain. He stated that "wherever the blood of Christ is mentioned in relation to the scheme of our salvation, it is uniformly described as effectual for saving purposes."[351]

He proceeded to discuss the key passages that appear to support unlimited

---

347 Ibid., 516.

348 C. J. Kennedy, *The Doctrine of Universal Atonement Vindicated; in Seven Letters to the Rev. John Smyth* (Glasgow: David Robertson, 1841).

349 J. Smyth, *Treatise on the Forgiveness of Sins, as the Privilege of the Redeemed; in Opposition to the Doctrine of Universal Pardon* (Glasgow: Thomas Ogilvie, 1830).

350 See T. Erskine, *The Unconditional Freeness of the Gospel*, new rev. ed. (Edinburgh: Edmonton and Douglas, 1870).

351 Smyth, *Treatise on the Forgiveness of Sins*, 118.

atonement. Here he takes the well-worn path of attempting to demonstrate that "world" and "all" do not always mean "all people without exception" in a universal sense.[352] Smyth moved to consider passages that speak of those for whom Christ died who will not be saved and explains each from a limited atonement interpretation.[353]

He considered several practical issues surrounding three questions concerning unlimited atonement: Does it bring glory to God? Does it humble the sinner? Does it exalt the Savior? In response to the first question, Smyth considered universal atonement to dishonor the electing grace of God, the redeeming grace of the Son, and the renovating grace of the Holy Spirit.[354]

Finally, he concluded with a series of assertions followed by his defense from a limited atonement framework. (1) Universal atonement opposes the moral supremacy of God as the law-giver and judge of his creatures. (2) Universal atonement unavoidably leads to universal salvation. (3) Universal atonement removes many powerful motives to a life of faith and holiness and retards missionary zeal. (4) Universal atonement rests on principles of interpretation that are alike untenable and dangerous.[355]

Kennedy responded to Smyth's treatment of "world," "all," and "all men" by showing that in their proper application and ordinary meaning they are unrestricted and signify absolute universality. Though there are cases where these terms do not signify "all without exception," nevertheless, limitation is the exception, not the rule. Kennedy charged Smyth with putting the exception for the rule. "You proceed to apply these terms as if you were at liberty to *assume* that their signification is restricted, whenever it suits you to do so." In fact, Smyth restricted these terms in every single passage where they are used with reference to the extent of the atonement. Kennedy reminded Smyth: rules guide, exceptions cannot.[356]

Kennedy sagaciously turned the tables on Smyth's logic.

> If you are entitled to employ the help of such instances to neutralize those passages of holy writ which teach that Christ died strictly for all, an Arian is equally well entitled to employ their help to neutralize the passages which teach that Christ is truly and properly *God over all*. . . . The Universalists can easily furnish you with instances in which the words, translated "forever," "eternal," and "everlasting" do not refer to duration strictly endless but to limited duration. You can produce no one word denoting or referring to duration which they cannot prove to be sometimes used in the Bible in a limited sense.[357]

---

352 Ibid., 50–70.

353 Ibid., 71–95.

354 Ibid., 97–118.

355 Ibid., 119–45.

356 Kennedy, *The Doctrine of Universal Atonement Vindicated*, 3–5 (emphasis in original).

357 Ibid., 6 (emphasis in original).

Kennedy offered a careful linguistic analysis of *kosmos*, noting that his method is one of patient inductive examination. From the biblical data, especially 1 John 2:2 and 5:19, Kennedy concluded that "whole world" means the whole unregenerate world.[358] All humanity without exception are subsumed under the two classes of people: believers (1 John 2:2) and the rest of the unbelieving world (1 John 5:19).

Kennedy adduced seven classes of meaning for "the world" in the New Testament:

1. Passages in which "the world" means all mankind.
2. Passages in which "the world" means all the ungodly.
3. Passages in which "the world" means all the finally lost.
4. Passages in which "the world" means all the ungodly living at one time.
5. Passages in which "the world" means the public, or all that part of mankind with which one has to do.
6. Passages in which "the world" means all the ungodly part of the public.
7. Passages in which "the world" means the Gentiles as opposed to the Jews.[359]

Kennedy turned to a consideration of the Greek word *pas*—"all." When used in the singular, it means "every"; when plural, it means "all." He concluded:

> The words translated "the world," "every man," "all men," in their natural and proper sense express universality. Whenever these terms are not restricted in their meaning, either by the texts in which they occur, by their contexts, or by other plain passages of the word of God, they are to be taken as denoting universality.[360]

At this point Kennedy began to unravel and expose the flaws in Smyth's interpretive methodology. "According to your principle and your mode of applying it, restriction when *proved* to exist in *one* case, may be *assumed* to exist in *any* case. Yours is a principle which sanctions *arbitrary* limitations; mine; a principle which admits only of *regulated, ascertainable*, and *proveable* limitations."[361] Kennedy continued:

> Both principles are based on a different purpose. On the one principle, the context is to be consulted to discover whether it may not *forbid* restriction: on the other, to discover whether it does not *require* restriction. On the one principle, proof of the unlimited meaning is required, and, if that proof is not

358 Ibid., 12.
359 Ibid., 14–15.
360 Ibid., 17.
361 Ibid., 21 (emphasis in original).

forthcoming, the passage is interpreted as one in which these terms may have a limited meaning. On the other principle, proof of the *limitation* is required; and, if that proof is not produced, the terms in question are taken in the full latitude of meaning which is natural to them.[362]

In relentless fashion, Kennedy pressed Smyth further:

> With regard to passages appealed to as proof of universal atonement, you observe, "It is necessary to premise, that every one of them is expressed in *general terms*, the precise extent of which is to be ascertained by the context, or by a comparison with others of a more definite character."

Kennedy pointed out how Smyth assumed that the meaning of the universal terms such as "world" and "all" "needs *to be ascertained*; and that such passages are not of any very *definite* character. In accordance with these views of the passages in question, you proceed to impose upon them the meaning that suits best with your system."[363] Kennedy disputed Smyth's claim that these passages employ "general terms" that are "of an indefinite character" and noted they more accurately can be said to employ universal terms that are quite definite.

Throughout Smyth's treatment of the passages he thinks support limited atonement, he consistently falls prey to the negative inference fallacy. Smyth assumed that passages that speak of the blood of Christ in the atonement is shed only for elect sinners, but Kennedy countered that these passages speak of the blood as having been *actually applied*.[364]

One of the most important statements in Kennedy's critique of Smyth, which applies to all Calvinists who assert limited atonement, is this sentence: "When you prove the efficacy of the atonement you do not disprove the universality of the atonement."[365]

Smyth attempted to blunt the direct statement for universal atonement in 2 Pet 2:1 by arguing that the phrase "the Lord that bought them" is not the object of Peter's belief but those of the false teacher's denial—that is, Peter is speaking of what the false teachers actually disavowed. Smyth averred that it is common in the Epistles to address people "agreeably" to their own confession of faith. Kennedy responded that there is something even more common in the Epistles—namely, the biblical writers address people "agreeably to the truth."[366] The clear meaning of 2 Pet 2:1 is that the phrase "the Lord that bought them" was the object of Peter's belief as well as the false teachers'

362 Ibid., 24 (emphasis in original).
363 Ibid., 25 (emphasis in original).
364 Ibid., 33.
365 Ibid., 34.
366 Ibid., 36.

denial. "As Redeemer, and *only* as Redeemer, can it be said that the Lord *bought* any human being," Kennedy asserted.[367]

Smyth attempted to make Jude 4 support limited atonement by taking the Greek term *despotēs* to refer to someone other than Christ. Kennedy demonstrated why this is not exegetically feasible or even possible. Adding insult to injury, Kennedy stated:

> Zealous to overthrow the doctrine of universal atonement, you seem reckless as to the safety of other doctrines. You cannot destroy the corroborative evidence which this passage affords of the unlimitedness of the atonement, without first destroying the direct evidence which it affords of our Saviour's proper Divinity. You have sacrificed the one to screen your system from the other.[368]

Text by text, Kennedy countered Smyth's exegesis and logic. For example, Matt 1:21 is a key text used by limitarians. Yet Kennedy rightly noted that this text does not tell us for how many Christ died, but simply whom he will ultimately save. With respect to John 1:9, Smyth said, "The obvious import of the passage, is, that every man who received the true light for his guidance heavenward, receives it from the Lord Jesus Christ." Kennedy reveals the lacuna in Smyth's reading of the text:

> No, Rev. Sir, the obvious import of the passage is, that *every man that cometh into the world* receives the true light for his guidance heavenward from the Lord Jesus Christ. . . . The text asserts one thing. Instead of it, you assert another.—another which is only a part of what the text says.[369]

Regarding John 1:7, Kennedy corrected Smyth's reading (God determined that all who are capable of believing should actually believe) to "God intended that all men through Christ might believe."[370]

Smyth interpreted John 3:16 as teaching a limited atonement. He asserted that "not one word" is affirmed by John 3:16 respecting the extent of God's love, except as it eventually saves those who believe (the elect). Kennedy responded with a query of Smyth as to whether the text teaches that God loves the world or that God loves those who believe.

Building on the analysis of the sevenfold usage of "world," Kennedy visually substituted each meaning for "world" in John 3:16 to determine which are valid interpretive possibilities.

367 Ibid., 40 (emphasis in original).
368 Ibid., 45.
369 Ibid., 87–88 (emphasis in original).
370 Ibid., 93.

God so loved:	1. all mankind
	2. all unbelievers
	3. all the finally lost
	4. all unbelieving living at one time—that whosoever believes in him shall not perish
	5. all the public
	6. all unbelieving of the public
	7. the Gentiles as opposed to the Jews

According to Kennedy, the only meaning that makes sense in the context is the first. If "the world" in John 3:16 should be interpreted as all mankind, it must receive the same interpretation in verse 17 as well.[371]

Kennedy noted how John 6:51, 57 are expressing different things: the former is about the unlimited extent of Christ's goodwill for all people; the latter focuses on the efficacy of Christ's death in saving those who believe.[372]

Kennedy devoted eight pages to an analysis of 2 Cor 5:18–19 and a refutation of Smyth's take on it. He noted the following points:

1. The act of reconciling is past; it has been performed by Christ.
2. The reconciling here cannot be equivalent to the pardoning of believers because that, with regard to all believers, is not an act already past.
3. Scripture speaks of no actual reconciliation between God and man except that which takes place at conversion.
4. The passage, therefore, cannot refer to the actual and completed reconciliation of the world to God.
5. If so, there would be no need for Paul to exhort people to be reconciled to God.

371 Ibid., 99–100. The entire discussion is on pp. 93–101.

372 Ibid., 103.

6. What then was this reconciliation? It is the providing of means whereby people can be reconciled via Christ's death.[373]

God is not in a state of actual reconciliation (subjective reconciliation) with all people. He is in a state of intentional reconciliation (objective reconciliation) with all people. There are no barriers on God's part hindering the salvation of any person.

Kennedy noted that John 3:36 affirms that the wrath of God is abiding on those who sins are actually expiated, both elect and non-elect. Kennedy continued to illustrate the faulty logic of Smyth.

If Jesus is the propitiation for the sins of every individual,
Then all are at peace with God.
All are not at peace with God,
Therefore Jesus is not the propitiation for the sins of every individual.

If one grants the premises, it is impossible to deny the conclusion.

If Jesus is the propitiation for the sins of each one of the elect,
Then all the elect are reconciled to him.
But all the elect are not reconciled, because the unbelieving elect are still under God's wrath.
Therefore Jesus is not the propitiation for the sins of every individual of the elect.

Kennedy concluded that whatever absurdity attaches itself to the doctrine of universalism does not attach to the doctrine of universal atonement.

Kennedy devoted twelve pages to a treatment of 2 Cor 5:14–15. The "all" in Paul's conclusion in verse 15 must have the same extent as the "all" in the minor proposition in verse 14:

> "Christ died for all:" otherwise, it follows, not indeed that the doctrine of universal depravity is false; for that doctrine may be capable of being proved by other arguments,—but it does follow, that, if the "all" in the conclusion exceeds in extent the "all" in the minor premise, then the Apostle argued inconclusively. For then he argued thus: Those for whom Christ died were dead; (in trespasses and sins); Since Christ died for all the elect; Then all, whether elect or non-elect, were dead in trespasses and sins.[374]

373 Ibid., 106–14.
374 Ibid., 130.

Kennedy noted how this argument is inconclusive. Rather, the conclusion ought to be "then all the elect were dead in trespasses and sins."

> If then, the conclusion is to be extended to all men whatever, the minor proposition must be altered, so as to include all men whatever; and the Apostle's enthymeme expanded to a syllogism, will be to the following effect: Those for whom Christ died were dead in trespasses and sins. Since Christ died for all men whatever, whether elect or non-elect; then all men whatever, whether elect or non-elect were dead in trespasses and sins.[375]

Kennedy's argument is clear:

> If, as is evident from the tenor of the passage and its context, and as is commonly admitted even by Calvinists, the Apostle does here conclude that all men whatever are dead in trespasses and sins; then he must be taking it for certain that Christ died for all men whatever: otherwise his argument would be an inconclusive argument—a mere sophism.[376]

Limit the "all" in the passage and the "verses become incapable of proving that all men are dead in trespasses and sins."[377]

If, in defiance of consistency, Smyth limited the "all men" in the latter clause of the verse, may not others be justified in limiting the "all men" in the first clause to make the declaration harmonize with his system as well? Sauce for the goose.

Kennedy quoted Smyth's translation of the verses:

> For the love of Christ constraineth us, having thus judged, that if one died on account of all (believers), then these all died, and he died on account of all (of them), in order that they, living should no longer live for themselves, but for him who died on their account and who rose (was raised) from the dead.[378]

Kennedy rejected Smyth's interpretive translation:

> Here you alter the common version without reason. "For" is quite as exact an English equivalent for *huper* as "on account of" is: nay, the former is the better rendering of the two. "To themselves" and "to him who died," are as correct

375 Ibid.

376 Ibid., 130–31.

377 Ibid., 135.

378 Smyth, *Treatise on the Forgiveness of Sins*, 96; cited by Kennedy, *The Doctrine of Universal Atonement Vindicated*, 138.

> translations of *heautois* and *tō huper apothananti* as "for themselves" and "for him who died." You insert, "from the dead," without any authority in the text, even as quoted by yourself, for the insertion. You have likewise ventured to insert, as supplements, the words "believers" and "of them," though they are utterly unauthorized and unnecessary. This last is rather a daring act. As these supplements rest on no better authority than yours, I shall dismiss them.
>
> You insert likewise the word *these* before "all," whereas there is no corresponding word in the original, *hoi pantes* (literally "the all" meaning simply "all.") In v. 10, we have an instance of the article occurring before the word rendered "all" without altering its extent of meaning.[379]

Kennedy analyzed 1 Tim 2:6, a key passage that would seem to assert clearly unlimited atonement, and a passage that limitarians like Smyth spend lots of ink in explaining why the passage refers to "all kinds or classes of people" and not all people without exception. Reverting to his earlier comments concerning "all," Kennedy stated that

> the universality of meaning in particular instances does not need to be proved; it is enough that it cannot be disproved. As every man is to be considered innocent by his fellow men, until he is proved to be guilty,—so every "all" is to be regarded as denoting universality until it is proved to be limited in its meaning.[380]

Kennedy informed Smyth that he has no need whatever to prove that "all" must in the text

> be taken *absolutely*; it is for you to *prove that it must be taken restrictedly*. Unless you can prove *your* position to be true, I have a sufficient warrant to abide by mine as true. I am entitled to say to you, Prove "all" to be limited in its meaning, or admit it to be universal. But you are not to think it enough to prove a *possible* restriction. I require you to prove a *necessary* or an *actual* restriction. You are not to make out a *may be* but a *must be*.[381]

The text indicates that Paul exhorts his readers to pray for all men on the grounds that Christ gave himself a ransom for all. But if Jesus did not give himself a ransom for all without exception, then surely Paul has not produced a sufficient reason why

---

379 Kennedy, *The Doctrine of Universal Atonement Vindicated*, 139.

380 Ibid., 150.

381 Ibid., 150–51 (emphasis in original).

Christians should pray for all men without exception. Furthermore, Kennedy queried why Christians should pray for those for whom Christ did not pray. "Why should we pray for those for whom Jesus refused to die? . . . Are we, miserable sinners, to be more gracious than God?—more pitiful and benevolent than the incarnate Word who was full of grace."[382]

Kennedy landed another blow when he asked Smyth:

> Do you insinuate that the "all men" for whom we are to pray are only all kings and all others that are in authority? If you do, then since the "all men" in v. 1 and the "all" in v. 6 are evidently the same persons,—I ask do you maintain that Christ Jesus gave himself a ransom for all kinds and rulers. . . . If you do not maintain that it was for all those men who are kings and rulers that Christ Jesus gave himself a ransom; what is there in the preceding quotation from your Treatise that has any tendency to prove, that Christ did not give himself a ransom for all men without exception? I can see nothing.[383]

Kennedy's final letter to Smyth listed seven advantages of unlimited atonement over limited atonement, followed by a response to three common objections to limited atonement.

1. The doctrine of universal atonement magnifies the divine philanthropy.
2. The doctrine of unlimited atonement illustrates the grace of Immanuel.
3. The doctrine of universal atonement vindicates the righteousness of God in consigning to endless destruction all such as reject the offer of mercy made to them through Christ.
4. The doctrine of universal atonement affords rich and satisfying encouragement to penitent sinners.
5. The doctrine of universal atonement forms the only available ground for satisfying personal assurance of salvation.
6. The doctrine of unlimited atonement is peculiarly favorable to the exercise of simple, unmixed dependence on the free grace of God, expressed in the promises of the Gospel.
7. The doctrine of unlimited atonement is eminently and evidently favorable to the spirit of zealous exertion for the salvation of men.[384]

Commenting on this seventh point, Kennedy pointed out how whenever limitarians

382 Ibid., 152–53.
383 Ibid., 154.
384 Ibid., 173–95.

> yield themselves to the influence of uncommon earnestness for the salvation of their fellow men, they are led irresistibly to address him in language which would induce any plain man to believe that they hold the doctrine of Unlimited atonement; in language precisely similar to what is employed by those who do believe in that doctrine.[385]

Kennedy listed and answered three objections regularly made against universal atonement. First, if Christ died for all men, all must be saved. Second, if Christ died for all, and if the actual salvation of people depends on their accepting it when offered to them through Christ, then it would be uncertain whether any would be saved at all. Third, if Christ died for all and if the actual salvation of people depends on their accepting it when offered, then a person must be entitled to the glory of his own salvation.

With respect to the latter, Kennedy asserted no one is entitled to his own glory. Though faith is a condition, it is not a meritorious condition of salvation. "The opportunity to believe, the inclination to believe, and the ability to believe, are freely bestowed on us, by God."[386]

Kennedy's *The Doctrine of Universal Atonement Vindicated* concluded with an appendix that critiqued Ralph Wardlaw, a fellow moderate Calvinist, on his interpretation of 1 Tim 2:4–6 where Wardlaw takes the "all" as meaning "all kinds of men." We have already seen this interpretation of the passage from Augustine to the present, noting that many Calvinists who clearly affirm a universal atonement take the Timothy text to be referring to classes of people. This is especially important to note since many Calvinists are prone to measure an individual's view of the extent question based on how he interprets 1 Tim 2:4–6.

Edward A. Litton (AD 1813–1897)

Litton was an Anglican theologian, educator, and preacher. He affirmed an unlimited atonement in his *Introduction to Dogmatic Theology*, originally published in 1882. For Litton, the term "particular redemption" correctly expressed redemption in its actual completion in the salvation of the elect.

> If one substitutes the word "redemption" with "atonement," or "expiation," then there is truth to the statement that Christ died for the sins of the non-elect. If redemption is particular, it does not follow that atonement or expiation for sin should not be a universal benefit. And this distinction, in truth, seems the only method or reconciling the various statements of Scripture on the subject. The

385 Ibid., 189.
386 Ibid., 191.

> death of Christ placed mankind as a whole in a new and favourable position as regards God, though by many this position may never be realized or made their own; it was a propitiation not for our sins only, but also for the sins of the whole world (1 john ii.2).[387]

For Litton, the full sufficiency of the atonement for all people grounds the universal gospel offer: "This proclamation could not be made if there had not been effected by the death of Christ a general expiation for our fallen race."[388]

George Smeaton (AD 1814–1889)

Another key nineteenth-century Calvinist writing on the extent of the atonement was Scottish theologian and professor George Smeaton. Smeaton studied under Thomas Chalmers and taught exegetical theology at New College, Edinburgh, for more than thirty years.

His two works, *The Doctrine of the Atonement According to Christ* and *The Doctrine of the Atonement According to the Apostles*, published in 1868 and 1870 respectively, present the case for limited atonement employing the standard limitarian arguments.[389] An appendix to the second volume contains a good survey of the history of the doctrine of the atonement.[390] The overriding issue for Smeaton when it comes to the extent of the atonement is divine intention.

Smeaton followed in the trajectory of covenant theology as articulated in nineteenth-century Scotland by John Dick (1764–1833),[391] professor of theology in the United Secession Church, and William Symington (1795–1862) of the Reformed Presbyterian Church.[392] Other Scottish advocates of limited atonement during this time were A. Marshall,[393] William Cunningham (1805–1861), professor of church history in New College,[394] and Hugh Martin.[395]

Smeaton opposed Amyraldianism or any form of Hypothetical Universalism, which

---

387 E. A. Litton, *Introduction to Dogmatic Theology: On the Basis of the XXXIX Articles of the Church of England*, new ed., ed. P. E. Hughes (1882; repr. London: James Clarke & Co., 1960), 235.

388 Ibid., 236.

389 G. Smeaton, *The Doctrine of the Atonement according to Christ* (Grand Rapids, MI: Sovereign Grace, n.d. [1868]); idem, *The Doctrine of the Atonement according to the Apostles* (1870; repr. Peabody, MA: Hendrickson, 1988). Both volumes have been reprinted by Banner of Truth and by Hendrickson.

390 Smeaton, *Doctrine of the Atonement according to the Apostles*, 479–544. For discussion of George Smeaton's doctrine of the atonement, see Kinnear, "Scottish New Testament Scholarship and the Atonement," 124–80.

391 J. Dick, *Lectures on Theology*, 2nd ed. (Edinburgh: Oliver & Boyd, 1838).

392 W. Symington, *The Atonement and Intercession of Jesus Christ* (Edinburgh: White, 1834).

393 A. Marshall, *The Atonement, or the Death of Christ the Redemption of His People* (Glasgow: Murray, 1868).

394 W. Cunningham, *Historical Theology: A Review of the Principal Doctrinal Discussions in the Christian Church since the Apostolic Age*, 3rd ed. (Edinburgh: T. & T. Clark, 1870). For further information on Smeaton, Dick, Symington, Marshall, and Cunningham, consult J. Walker, *The Theology and Theologians of Scotland 1560–1750* (Glasgow: MacLehose, 1872).

395 H. Martin, *The Atonement* (Edinburgh: Knox, 1870).

had found supporters in the United Presbyterian Church in Scotland.[396] Smeaton did seem to accept, albeit cautiously, the concept of God's character as holy love and sought to integrate God's love into the penal understanding of the atonement.[397]

Kinnear faulted Smeaton's imbalance between justice and love and his distorted view of the Trinity when Smeaton stated, "Only when sin is expiated can proper Fatherhood begin."

Such an approach creates Trinitarian disharmony in the act of atonement. Smeaton's excess at this point would be rejected by most within the Reformed tradition.[398]

Kinnear was probably correct when he noted that Smeaton's two volumes on the atonement "were the first comprehensive, scholarly exegetical analysis of the New Testament teaching on the atonement from a British author in this period, and in thoroughness and detail his work has not been paralleled since in the English language."[399]

S. G. Burney (AD 1814–1893)

Burney served in several pastorates in the Cumberland Presbyterian Church from 1841 through 1872. He founded the College for Women in Oxford, Mississippi, and served as president of Union Female College from 1852 to 1861. He was elected to the chair of English literature at the University of Mississippi from 1866 to 1872 and also served as professor of philosophy. In 1881 he became professor of systematic theology and later served as professor of biblical literature in the Theological School of Cumberland University in Lebanon, Tennessee.

He devoted twenty pages to the extent of the atonement in his *Atonement: Soteriology*.[400] Burney affirmed and argued for an unlimited atonement. Christ's human nature as well as the law mandated he offer a sacrifice for the sins of all people.

> If any one of the race is excluded the law is not fulfilled. The law requires me to love all men, even my enemies, and if the sacrifice of my natural life will save their souls, and nothing else could save them, then the law requires the sacrifice. Should I refuse to make the sacrifice, then I would not fulfill the law, because I would not love my neighbor as myself. Or, if I should love half, and make provision for them, and leave all others unprovided for, I would not obey the law, but be guilty before the law. . . . But if there ever was or ever will be a human being, or one of the great brotherhood for whom he did not give himself as a sacrifice unto God, it is plain that he has not kept the law or honored

396 J. MacGregor, *The Question of Principle as Raised in the Free Church Specially Regarding the Atonement* (Edinburgh: MacLaren, 1870).

397 See Kinnear, "Scottish New Testament Scholarship and the Atonement," 170–72.

398 Ibid., 176–79.

399 Ibid., 179.

400 S. G. Burney, *Atonement, Soteriology: The Sacrificial, in Contrast with the Penal, Substitutionary, and Merely Moral or Exemplary Theories of Propitiation* (Nashville: Cumberland Presbyterian, 1888), 380–400.

> it. In light of these facts, what becomes of the dogma of a limited atonement? . . . It is simply swept to the winds, and utterly demolished.[401]

Burney continued to support unlimited atonement by considering the universal Fatherhood of God and his love toward all people, the divinity of Christ and its implications for the extent of the atonement, and natural revelation. Concerning the latter, Burney pointed out that hunger and thirst are endemic to humanity and indicate that there is a provision available for both. This kind of reasoning could be replicated dozens of times on the physical plane. Mentally, the same is the case according to Burney. The human mind longs for a happy future, even immortality. "The irresistible conclusion, therefore, is that God created all men for such a state, and that its attainment in some stage of every person's live is possible."[402]

Such a condition would lead one to conclude that in the spiritual realm, as in the natural realm, God has provided by his grace a means for humanity to experience salvation from sins through an all-sufficient, universal atonement. But Burney was careful to point out that possibility and actuality are separated by conditions, and it is only when the conditions of repentance and faith are met that salvation becomes a reality for any individual.[403]

Henry B. Smith (AD 1815–1877)

Henry Smith emerged as the leading spokesman of the New School theology in the decades following 1840. Smith was professor of systematic theology at Union Theological Seminary from 1854 to 1874. He played a role in the reunion of the Presbyterian Church in the 1860s.[404]

Like many American Presbyterians during the nineteenth century, Smith distinguished between atonement and redemption, where the former refers to the actual sacrifice on the cross, including its extent, and the latter refers to the application of the atonement.[405] For Smith, the former is unlimited while the latter is limited.

Smith spoke positively of the covenant of redemption but with this additional point: "Only in this Covenant there should be included all that Christ's work accomplished: Propitiation for the sins of the whole world and the General Offer of Salvation as well as the Provision for the Elect."[406]

---

401 Ibid., 385–86.

402 Ibid., 399.

403 Ibid., 400.

404 E. Smith, ed., *Henry Boynton Smith, His Life and Work* (New York: A. C. Armstrong, 1881); L. F. Stearns, *Henry Boynton Smith* (Boston: Houghton Mifflin & Co., 1892); D. H. Holcomb, "The Theology of Henry B. Smith (1815–1877): With Special Reference to Contemporary Influences" (ThM thesis, Southern Baptist Theological Seminary, 1963).

405 H. B. Smith, *System of Christian Theology*, 2nd ed. (New York: A. C. Armstrong and Son, 1884), 437.

406 Ibid., 377–78.

Smith quoted Soame Jenyns, who asserted

> Christ suffered and died as an atonement for the sins of the world is a doctrine so constantly infused through the New Testament that whoever will seriously peruse these writings and deny that it is there, may with as much reason and truth, after reading the works of Thucydides and Livy, assert that in them no mention is made of any facts in relation to the history of Greece and Rome.[407]

Smith devoted a chapter in his *System of Christian Theology* to the extent of the atonement. After explaining the differences between the Lutheran, Arminian, and Reformed understandings of the question, including the necessary differences within these groups, he asserted that the intent of the atonement is to save the elect, but that the actual atonement in and of itself saves no one until it is applied.[408]

Under the heading "Proof of General Atonement," Smith adduced six points:

1. The key passage is 1 Tim 4:10.
2. God's offer of salvation to all indicates provision for all. Smith here rejects the interpretation of "all" in key biblical texts as meaning "some among all classes," and so on, for three reasons. First, this is "an unscriptural distinction." Second, "we do not know that the offer, in the sense of 'effectual calling,' is made to 'some in all' these cases." Third, the sincerity of God is at stake. "He offers to all a salvation which He has not provided for all."
3. Special guilt is ascribed to those who reject the atonement (Matt 23:37; Luke 14:17; John 3:19; Acts 7:51).
4. Scripture declares the atonement to be universal (John 1:29; 3:17; 12:47; 1 Tim 2:6; 2 Cor 5:14–15; Heb 2:9; 1 John 2:2).
5. All people receive some benefits from the atonement: (1) the offer of eternal life, (2) knowledge of the divine plan and ways, and (3) the continuance of probation and many temporal blessings.
6. The argument for general atonement *ex concessis*—if it is conceded to be "sufficient" for all, then it was designed to be for all. Therefore, it is consistent for God to offer salvation to all, and if to offer to all, then to grant on conditions salvation to all who meet those conditions.

Smith proceeded to list four other arguments in favor of general atonement:

---

407 Ibid., 450.
408 Ibid., 478.

1. The parallel between Adam and Christ (Rom 5:18).
2. Christ died for some who are not saved (Rom 14:15; 1 Cor 8:11; Heb 10:29; 2 Pet 2:1).
3. From the connection of truths: (1) from the view it gives of the glorious character of the divine government—God is the God of grace, (2) from the moral influence of the doctrine on people, and (3) from the view it gives of the final condemnation of the lost.
4. The relationship of Christ to the universe is consistent only with general atonement.

Finally, Smith listed and answered six objections to general atonement:

1. It supposes different and inconsistent purposes in God. But Smith queries how it is inconsistent if God has a purpose to make salvation possible for all, but a second purpose to save only some.
2. God makes provision for an end, which he determines never to effect. Smith responds that such is not the case. God makes provision in order to make the salvation of all men possible.
3. It is inconsistent with the doctrine of election. Smith counters that the condemnation of the non-elect is, in part, on the ground of their refusal, not on the ground of their non-election.
4. The divine holiness demands the salvation of all for whom provision is made. Smith rejects this argument by noting such is not the case if other good reasons forbid the salvation of some.
5. The Scripture says Christ died to save his people. Smith affirms this is correct, but adds that the Scripture also teaches Christ died for the sins of the whole world.

> Christ's special design does not exclude a more general design. To say, Christ came to save, redeem, deliver, sanctify his people, is most certainly true, but is, in this argument, a *petitio principii*; it assumes that Christ in his work had only one design. The doctrine of General Atonement does not assert that the purpose of God in Christ's death had equal respect to the elect and the non-elect, in the sense that God intended to apply it equally.[409]

6. Scripture affirms the union of Christ and his people, thus all that Christ did he did for those who are united to him by faith. Again Smith agreed with this

409 Ibid., 480.

statement but said it is irrelevant to the question at hand. "The doctrine of General Atonement does not assert that all that Christ did and does, He does for all mankind."[410]

J. C. Ryle (AD 1816–1900)

J. C. Ryle became the first Anglican Bishop of Liverpool in England in 1880 after thirty-eight years in the pastorate. He was an Evangelical Calvinist author and preacher. Speaking on the subject of election and the extent of the atonement, Ryle remarked, "We know not who are God's Elect, and whom he means to call and convert. Our duty is to invite all. To every unconverted soul without exception we ought to say, 'God loves you, and Christ has died for you.'"[411]

Of John 3:16, Ryle stated concerning Calvin's view of the extent of God's love for the "world,"

> Calvin observes on this text, "Christ brought life, because the heavenly Father loves the human race, and wishes that they should not perish." Again he says, "Christ employed the universal term whosoever, both to invite indiscriminately all to partake of life, and to cut off every excuse from unbelievers. Such also is the import of the term world. Though there is nothing in the world that is worthy of God's favor, yet He shows Himself to be reconciled to the whole world, when he invites all men without exception to the faith of Christ." The same view of God's "love" and the "world," in this text, is taken by Brentius, Bucer, Calvinius, Glassius, Chemnitius, Musculus, Bullinger, Bengal, Nifanius, Dyke, Scott, Henry, and Manton.[412]

Ryle clearly affirmed an unlimited atonement. Notice also his reference to Bucer among the names of those who take a similar interpretation of "world" in John 3:16.

Commenting on John 1:29, Ryle wrote,

> Christ is . . . a Saviour for all mankind. . . . He did not suffer for a few persons only, but for all mankind. . . . What Christ took away, and bore on the cross, was not the sin of certain people only, but the whole accumulated mass of all the sins of all the children of Adam. . . . I hold as strongly as anyone, that Christ's death is profitable to none but the elect who believe in His Name. But I dare not limit and pare down such expressions as the one before us. I dare not say that no atonement has been made, in any sense, except for the elect. I believe

410 Ibid., 478–81.

411 J. C. Ryle, *Expository Thoughts on the Gospels: John 1–6*, 3:157.

412 Ibid, 3:158.

> it is possible to be more systematic than the Bible in our statements. . . . I dare not confine the intention of redemption to the saints alone. Christ is for every man. . . . I repudiate the idea of universal salvation as a dangerous heresy and utterly contrary to Scripture. But the lost will not prove to be lost because Christ did nothing for them. He bore their sins, He carried their transgressions, He provided payment; but they would not put in their claim to any interest in it. . . . The atonement was made for all the world, though it is applied and enjoyed by none but believers.[413]

James Morison (AD 1816–1893)

Morison was a Scottish pastor who in the spring of 1839, on his way to preach to a struggling church, read Charles Finney's *Revivals of Religion*. The next Sunday he laid aside his manuscript and preached from his heart. He regarded this event as his actual conversion.

Morison abandoned his high Calvinist view on limited atonement. On March 2, 1841, the Presbytery began a trial of Morison in light of his views on unlimited atonement.[414] The synod appointed a committee to deal with Morison's views and report back.

> The Committee being appointed, Mr Morison met with them, but on perceiving that nothing would satisfy them short of a distinct acknowledgment of the special reference of the atonement, he declined meeting with them again; and having disregarded the sentence of suspension imposed by the Presbytery, and continued by the Synod, he was declared to be no longer in connexion with the Secession Church.[415]

Morison wrote a book on the extent of the atonement in which he stated, "I do most firmly believe, O anxious sinner, whomsoever you be, and whatsoever may have been your character, that all that Jesus did on Calvary He did for *you*."[416] "Jesus came into the world to save sinners. . . . The word *sinners* in this blessed passage is no crust that conceals beneath it the word the 'elect'. It is an honest word. . . . It is as great as the world. What word is more universal than 'sinner'?"[417]

Morison enlisted the church fathers, along with Davenant, to come to his aid on the issue:

413 Ibid., 3:61–62.

414 And other issues, but the extent question was the primary issue.

415 Robertson, *History of the Atonement Controversy*, 164.

416 J. Morison, *The Extent of the Propitiation; or, The Question for Whom Did Christ Die? Answered* (Kilmarnock: J. Davie, 1842), 6 (emphasis in original).

417 Ibid., 26 (emphasis in original).

> For the Fathers, when speaking of the death of Christ, describe it to us as undertaken and endured for the redemption of the human race; and not a word (that I know of) occurs among them of the exclusion of any person by the decree of God. They agree that it is actually beneficial to those only who believe, yet they everywhere confess that Christ died in behalf of all mankind. . . .
>
> Bishop Davenant goes on to give some further details respecting the opinions of Augustine . . . "We assert, therefore, . . . that Augustine never attempted to impugn that proposition of the Semipelagians [*sic*], that Christ died for the whole human race, . . . For neither did Augustine ever oppose as erroneous the proposition 'that Christ died for the redemption of the whole human race;' nor did he ever acknowledge or defend as his own, 'that Christ died, not for all men, but for the pre-destinate alone.'"[418]

Morison clearly believed in an unlimited atonement coupled with the doctrine of election. "I am not an Arminian; call me a low-Calvinist, or a no-Calvinist, if you like, but I am not an Arminian."[419]

Robertson noted Morison's view on the atonement was

> that Christ in making atonement sustained no special relationship to any portion of mankind, but stood in the same common relationship to every sinner of our race, his atonement doing for all, whatever it did for any,—it being intended to do nothing more than to open the door of mercy, and to render it consistent with the righteous character of God to extend forgiveness to the guilty.[420]

Interestingly, at the same synod, Robert Walker, who had been charged by the Presbytery of Perth with holding views similar to Morison, was questioned. Unlike Morison, he did not deny the atonement's special reference to the elect but did maintain the atonement had a general reference to all people, opening a door of mercy to all. The examining committee found in favor of Walker.[421] It would appear the synod feared that Morison's view tended too much toward Arminianism.

Morison made an interesting comment in his defense of unlimited atonement and its impact on preaching and missions.

> If it were not true that Christ died for the heathen, pray, what gospel is the missionary to preach when he lands on a foreign shore? Is he to tell them that

418 Ibid., 66–67.

419 O. Smeaton, *Principle James Morison: The Man and His Work* (Edinburgh: Oliver & Boyd, 1902), 114. See also Robertson, *History of the Atonement Controversy*, 161–74, 323–25, for the specifics on Morison.

420 Robertson, *History of the Atonement Controversy*, 163.

421 Ibid., 166.

> God loved a few men scattered somewhere or other throughout the world, and that therefore, for aught that he could know, there may happen to be some of these favoured ones among them, and for these Christ died. . . . Men need not go to heathen lands with the doctrine of a limited atonement in their creeds; or, if they go with it, they must hide it, and preach in a manner practically contradictory to it. One of the greatest missionaries of modern times . . . when asked by me what he preached to his poor Africans, replied, that it was a maxim with him and his true yoke-fellow to tell all and sundry that Christ died for them. [Morison identifies this missionary as the famous Robert Moffat.][422]

In his work on the nature of the atonement, Morison devoted a chapter explaining why the atonement is not a payment of a debt in a commercial sense.[423] According to Morison, the atonement is never represented in Scripture as a debt payment in a commercial sense for the following reasons:

> 1. Debts when paid cease to be debts; but sin, though atoned for, is a debt still.
> 2. Debts that are paid cannot be forgiven; but though sin is atoned for, it must also be forgiven.
> 3. Debts may be forgiven without any payment; but sin could not be forgiven without an atonement.
> 4. Debts are transferable; sins are not.
> 5. The satisfactory payment of a debt does not depend on the dignity of the person who pays it; but the whole value of the propitiation depends upon the high and glorious rank and character of the sufferer.
> 6. Sin was atoned for as a crime, not as a debt.
> 7. The propitiation of Christ, then, is a something, in consideration of which God is ready, instead of exacting payment, to forgive us our debts.

In answering the question "What is the propitiation?" Morison responded in several points.

> 1. The propitiation is a reality, independent of the sinner's faith.

> The sinner is not called upon to believe that he is pardoned, justified, redeemed, or at one with God. Were he to believe this, he would be believing what is not

422 J. Morison, *The Extent of the Propitiation*, 64–65.

423 J. Morison, *The Nature of the Atonement* (London: Simpkin, Marshall, Hamilton, Kent & Co., 1890), 61–73. This work is a reprint with only slight revision from an edition published earlier in Morison's ministry.

true till he become a believer. The sinner is, however, called upon to believe that his sins have been atoned for; and consequently this must be something that is true whether he believe it or not. When we assert that Jesus atoned for sins, . . . we mean this, that He removed every *legal* obstacle standing between them and pardon, justification, redemption, and reconciliation; so that if they be not pardoned, justified, redeemed, reconciled, it is their own fault, and they remain for ever "without excuse."[424]

2. Jesus has removed every legal obstacle, but not every obstacle of every kind. Unbelief remains an obstacle.
3. If one is an unbeliever, his sins remain unpardoned.

Morison concluded this book like a sermon addressing an unbeliever—with strong, urgent appeals on the basis of the atonement of Christ out of love for the sinner to repent and believe the gospel.[425] In a note at the end on Rom 3:24 and Heb 9:15, Morison argued that the word "redemption" "does not mean *the price of deliverance*, but the *actual deliverance procured by the price*."[426] He appeals to the leading lexicographers and quotes numerous Calvinists, including many who affirm limited atonement, as making this very point.[427]

Robert L. Dabney (AD 1820–1898)

Few Calvinist theologians were as loved and respected as Robert Dabney, the premier southern Presbyterian theologian of the nineteenth century. Dabney served as Confederate Army chaplain and as chief of staff and biographer to Stonewall Jackson. His most important work is his *Lectures on Systematic Theology*.

At the 1863 General Assembly of the Old School Southern Church, a committee including Dabney was formed to discuss the prospect of reunion with the New School Southern Church. The greatest barrier to reunion was accusation by the Old School that the New School did not adhere to the standards of confessional orthodoxy with respect to the extent of the atonement. Benjamin Palmer and A. A. Porter charged Dabney with teaching indefinite atonement. At one point, Dabney responded to Porter, "He demands that we shall say Christ was only the elect's substitute, and bore the guilt only of the elect's sins. We reply, show us the place where either the Bible or Confession of Faith says so."[428] Dabney's writings on the nature and

---

424 Ibid., 75–76.
425 Ibid., 85–101.
426 Ibid., 93 (emphasis in original).
427 Ibid., 93–95.
428 B. M. Palmer, "The Proposed Plan of Union between the General Assembly and the United Synod of the South," *Southern Presbyterian Review* 16 (1864): 304.

extent of the satisfaction demonstrate substantial disagreement with traditional Old School opinion.[429]

In his *Lectures on Systematic Theology*, Dabney identified what he believed the atonement of Christ on the cross secured. These include (1) the purchase of redemption for the elect (all believers); (2) a temporary "reprieve of doom" and a "postponement of death" for all the non-elect, including temporal benefits (common grace); (3) God's mercy to all the non-elect who "live under the Gospel" along with "sincere offers of salvation on terms of faith"; (4) a "justly enhanced condemnation" for all who reject the gospel, including a display of God's "righteousness and reasonableness" in condemning those who refuse to believe; and (5) a disclosure of God's "infinite tenderness" and compassion to all.[430]

Speaking of these blessings that Christ secured for the non-elect via the atonement, Dabney strongly criticized William Cunningham for his rejection of the notion that Christ satisfied for the sins of all people:

> In view of this fact, the scorn which Dr. William Cunningham heaps on the distinction of a special, and general design in Christ's satisfaction, is thoroughly shortsighted. All wise beings (unless God be the exception), at times frame their plans so as to secure a combination of results from the same means. This is the very way they display their ability and wisdom. Why should God be supposed incapable of this wise and fruitful acting? I repeat, the design of Christ's sacrifice must have been to effectuate just what it does effectuate. And we see, that, along with the actual redemption of the elect, it works out several other subordinate ends. There is then a sense, in which Christ "died for" all those ends, and for the persons affected by them.[431]

When Dabney spoke of what God "designed" or "purposed," he is speaking of God's decretal will and not God's revealed will. But it must be noted that Dabney spoke of common grace as flowing from the cross as well. Notice that the rejection of the gospel offered by God to all results in an "enhanced condemnation." Dabney's strong words concerning Cunningham ("scorn," which Cunningham "heaps on the distinction of a general and special design in the atonement") are surprising and should be noted carefully. Cunningham is a high Calvinist who denied Christ died in any way for the non-elect. Notice Dabney referred to Cunningham as "shortsighted" in this.[432]

429 See M. J. Lynch, "'*In Mediis Ibis*': An Examination of Robert Lewis Dabney's View of the Extent of Christ's Satisfaction" (paper presented at the annual meeting of the Evangelical Theological Society, San Diego, November 2014). The audio is available at http://www.Wordmp3.com/speakers/profile/.aspx?id=1732.

430 R. L. Dabney, *Systematic Theology* (Edinburgh: Banner of Truth, 2002), 528–29.

431 Ibid., 529.

432 For Cunningham's approach to the atonement's extent, including his separation of the well-meant gospel offer from the sufficiency of the atonement, see his *Historical Theology*, 2 vols. (Edinburgh: Banner of Truth, 1994), 2:343–70.

Speaking of the Westminster Confession, Dabney made a salient point with respect to the extent of the atonement when he noted,

> It carefully avoids confusing the two concepts of legal satisfaction for guilt with the consequent at-one-ment, or reconciliation, for the believing sinner. And it gives no countenance to the quid-pro-quo theory of expiation, which affects, with a mischievous over-refinement, to affix a commercial ratio between the sins of the elect and the one indivisible and infinite merit of the divine sacrifice.[433]

Speaking of the extrinsic sufficiency of Christ's sacrifice, Dabney said,

> But sacrifice, expiation, is one—the single, glorious, indivisible act of the divine Redeemer, infinite and inexhaustible in merit. Had there been but one sinner, Seth, elected of God, this whole divine sacrifice would have been needed to expiate his guilt. Had every sinner of Adam's race been elected, the same one sacrifice would be sufficient for all. We must absolutely get rid of the mistake that expiation is an aggregate of gifts to be divided and distributed out, one piece to each receiver, like pieces of money out of a bag to a multitude of paupers. Were the crowd of paupers greater, the bottom of the bag would be reached before every pauper got his alms, and more money would have to be provided. I repeat, this notion is utterly false as applied to Christ's expiation, because it is a divine act. It is indivisible, inexhaustible, sufficient in itself to cover the guilt of all the sins that will ever be committed on earth. This is the blessed sense in which the Apostle John says (1 Jn. 2:2): "Christ is the propitiation (the same word as expiation) for the sins of the whole world."[434]

Just two pages following this quotation, Dabney stated, "We are bound to assert that, while the expiation is infinite, redemption is particular."[435] What Dabney meant by this statement is the expiation for sin by Christ on the cross is unlimited, but the application of the atonement, governed by God's intent and purpose as understood by Reformed theology, is for the elect alone. Further confirmation of this is the fact that Dabney went on to ground his statement in the electing work of God and not on any of the key scriptural passages on the extent of the atonement that are usually argued by Calvinists to support limited atonement.

---

433 R. L. Dabney, "The Doctrinal Contents of the Westminster Confession of Faith," in *Discussions: Miscellaneous Writings*, 5 vols., ed. J. H. Vamer (Harrisonburg, VA: Sprinkle, 1999), 5:130. For Dabney's rejection of quantitative equivalentism and his affirmation of a universal atonement, see also B. M. Palmer, "The Proposed Plan of Union," 278, 297, 304.

434 R. L. Dabney and Jonathan Dickinson, *The Five Points of Calvinism* (Harrisonburg, VA: Sprinkle, 1992), 61.

435 Ibid., 63.

Perhaps Dabney is clearest on his affirmation of a universal atonement when speaking of John 3:16. He rejected the attempt to connect "world" with the elect and clearly affirms that Christ's death on the cross resulted in unlimited expiation of sins, not just a limited expiation.[436]

Rejecting the interpretation of Owen and others that "world" here means "the elect," Dabney demonstrated how exegetically the connection between John 3:17 and 18 shows that the "world" of verse 17 is inclusive of those who believe and those who do not believe in verse 18.

> It is hard to see how, if the tender of Christ's sacrifice is in no sense a true manifestation of divine benevolence to that part of "the world" which "believeth not," their choosing to slight it is the just ground of a deeper condemnation, as is expressly stated in verse 19.[437]

Finally, Dabney declared Christ paid the "penal debt of the world."[438] Dabney argued against John Owen's double payment argument, the linchpin argument used by supporters of limited atonement.[439]

W. G. T. Shedd (AD 1820–1894)

William G. T. Shedd completes the American triumvirate of nineteenth-century Reformed theologians (Charles Hodge and Robert Dabney being the other two) who rejected limited atonement. A graduate of Andover Theological Seminary, where he was influenced by Leonard Woods, about whom we will have more to say below, he taught for a brief time at Auburn Theological Seminary, then became professor of church history at Andover from 1853 to 1862. Following this, he served for two years as the pastor of the Brick Presbyterian Church in New York City. Later, Shedd taught at Union Theological Seminary from 1874 to 1892, where he completed his systematic theology.

Like Robert Dabney and Charles Hodge, Shedd believed there was no contradiction between an unlimited satisfaction for sin by Christ on the cross, predestination, and the universal offer of the gospel to all.[440] Shedd clearly affirmed that the death of Christ is not merely hypothetically sufficient as high Calvinists affirmed, but it is actually sufficient because it expiated all sins.

Shedd appealed to 1 John 2:2 to argue for an unlimited satisfaction for sins on the

---

436 R. L. Dabney, "God's Indiscriminate Proposals of Mercy as Related to His Power, Wisdom, and Sincerity," *The Princeton Review* 54 (July 1878): 64–65. See also in Dabney's *Discussions: Evangelical and Theological*, 5 vols., ed. C. R. Vaughn (Harrisonburg, VA: Sprinkle, 1982), 1:282–313. See also his *Systematic Theology*, 535, where he stated, "There is, perhaps, no Scripture which gives so thorough and comprehensive an explanation of the design and results of Christ's sacrifice, as John 3:16–19."

437 Ibid.

438 R. L. Dabney, *Christ Our Penal Substitute* (Richmond, VA: Presbyterian Committee of Publication, 1898), 24.

439 R. L. Dabney, *Systematic Theology*, 521.

440 W. G. T. Shedd, *Dogmatic Theology* (Phillipsburg, NJ: P&R, 2003), 349.

cross. He spoke of God's justice being "completely satisfied for the sin of man by the death of Christ," is an "ample oblation for the sin of the world," and that the death of Christ on the cross has "completely expiated human guilt."[441] Shedd argued that the death of Christ was "related to the claims of the law upon all mankind" and "cancels those claims wholly." In fact, Shedd stated,

> The death of the God-man naturally and necessarily cancelled all legal claims. When a particular person trusts in this infinite atonement, and it is imputed to him by God, it then becomes his atonement for judicial purposes as really as if he had made it himself, and then it naturally and necessarily cancels his personal guilt.[442]

He went on to point out that

> For as the case now stands, there is no necessity, so far as the action of *God* is concerned, that a single human being should ever be the subject of future punishment . . . all the legal obstacles to the exercise of this great attribute [mercy] have been removed by the death of the Son of God for the sins of the whole world (1 John 2:2).[443]

Shedd answered the question, If Christ's death removes all legal obstacles and expiates all sin, how it is that universalism does not result? Shedd's simple answer is the same all moderate Calvinists have pointed out since the earliest debates on this subject: no one is saved unless they exercise faith in Christ. The atonement in and of itself saves no one.[444] For Shedd, as for all moderate Calvinists and non-Calvinists, the application of the atonement is limited; the expiation is unlimited. He believed that this understanding took into consideration all biblical texts—those asserting Christ died for all as well as those asserting he died for the church.[445] Furthermore, Shedd clearly drew a distinction between the intent and extent of the atonement. The former is limited by God's design and purpose; the latter is unlimited.[446]

Shedd understood the sufficiency of the atonement to be such that it expiates "the sin of all men indiscriminately; . . . There is no sin of man for which an infinite atonement has not been provided." Shedd then grounds the universal offer of the gospel on this universal atonement.[447]

441 Ibid., 709.
442 Ibid., 724–25.
443 Ibid., 930.
444 Ibid., 726.
445 Ibid., 743.
446 Ibid., 739–42.
447 Ibid., 743.

Not only did Shedd articulate his understanding of the atonement as universal in his theology, but he also did so in his preaching. Consider the sermon "The Guilt of the Pagan." Here Shedd clearly stated that Christ's blood was shed for those who ultimately would reject him.[448]

Like Dabney, Shedd argued against the double payment argument commonly used in support of limited atonement.[449]

Hugh Martin (AD 1821–1885)

Hugh Martin was a Scottish theologian and pastor. His work, *The Atonement: In Its Relations to the Covenant, the Priesthood, the Intercession of our Lord*, appeared in 1877.[450] As the title indicates, it is a defense of limited atonement arguing primarily from the priestly office and ministry of Christ. Martin attempted to demonstrate that Christ only prayed for the elect (John 17), hence he only suffered for the sins of the elect.

A. A. Hodge (AD 1823–1886)

Hodge was the son of the famed Charles Hodge of Princeton Seminary. An American Presbyterian leader and theologian, A. A. Hodge served as the principal of Princeton Seminary between 1878 and 1886.

He published a significant work on the atonement in 1867.[451] Hodge addressed the intent of the atonement first from the Arminian perspective then from the Hypothetical Universalism perspective.[452] He divided the latter category into two groups: (1) those like Amyraut, Wardlaw, Balmer, John Brown, and James Richards of Auburn Theological Seminary; and (2) Jenkyn, Taylor, and Fiske, whom Hodge charged with departing from the "true faith" on the nature of the atonement, "whose views as to its indefinite universality is a necessary corollary of their views as to its nature."[453]

Hodge is particularly condescending to those in the first group of Hypothetical Universalists: they possess "a hardly conscious dissatisfaction with the peculiarities of Calvinism, giving rise to an unconscious Arminianism; or their divergence is to be referred solely to an absence of clearness of thought, and consequent inaccuracy in the use of terms."[454] The latter group "lacks either candour or competent knowledge as to the true state of the controversy."[455] Hodge is referring here to the fact that the latter group denies penal substitution.

---

448 W. G. T. Shedd, *The Guilt of the Pagan: A Sermon* (Boston: American Board of Commissioners for Foreign Missions, 1864), 23–24.

449 Shedd, *Dogmatic Theology*, 727.

450 H. Martin, *The Atonement: In Its Relations to the Covenant, the Priesthood, the Intercession of Our Lord* (1877; repr. Edinburgh: Banner of Truth, 2013). See especially chapters three and four.

451 A. A. Hodge, *The Atonement* (Philadelphia: Presbyterian Board of Publication, 1867).

452 Ibid., 348–54.

453 Ibid., 351.

454 Ibid., 351–52.

455 Ibid., 353.

Hodge outlined his treatment on the extent question as follows:

1. Statement of the question in the debate
2. Relationship of the nature of the atonement with its design
3. Outline of history on the subject
4. Calvin on the question
5. Biblical evidence
6. Response to arguments by advocates of general atonement

For Hodge, the question at hand did not relate to the sufficiency of the satisfaction. Here he is speaking only of intrinsic value.[456] This is an inaccurate assessment as the question is very much about the nature of the sufficiency of the atonement. Neither does the question relate to the applicability of the satisfaction rendered by Christ to the demands of the law. For Hodge,

> Christ died and suffered precisely what the law demanded of each man personally and of every man indiscriminately, and it may be at any time applied to the redemption of one man as well as to another, as far as the satisfaction itself is concerned. Putting these two things together, therefore, the sufficiency for all and the exact adaptation to each, it is plain as the sun in the heavens that the death of Christ did remove all legal obstacles out of the way of God's saving any man he pleases. In this sense, if you please, Christ did make the salvation of all men indifferently possible, *a parte Dei*. He can apply it to any whomsoever he will.[457]

Hodge sounds very much like his own father when he stated,

> It necessarily follows that whosoever believes on him, non-elect (if that were subjectively possible) just as truly as the elect, would find a perfect atonement and cordial welcome ready for him when he comes. . . . but the Atonement of Christ is itself *objectively* most certainly and freely *available* to each and every sinner to whom it is offered, upon condition *that he believes*.[458]

Yet there is a subtle difference between A. A. Hodge at this point and his father, Charles Hodge. As we have seen, Charles Hodge affirmed that there was an objective atonement made for the sins of all people, even though the intent of God in the

456 Ibid., 355.
457 Ibid., 356–57.
458 Ibid., 538.

atonement is to save only the elect. A. A. Hodge would appear to affirm the same when he spoke of the law of God as "satisfied" by Christ's death. Yet, Hodge argued for a limited atonement. This is a serious inconsistency.

Notice in the second quote above that Hodge seemed to think that he can speak about an atonement that is "objectively" available to "each and every sinner" and yet affirm a limited substitution by Christ on the cross. But Hodge did not explain how this atonement can be available to the non-elect when such an atonement for their sins does not exist. The question of the extent does not relate to the actual application of the saving benefits of Christ's work to each and every person, according to Hodge. For Hodge, God's intention in the atonement is the salvation of the elect only.

Hodge said the question "does not relate to the universal offer in perfect good faith of a saving interest in Christ's work on the condition of faith. This is admitted by all."[459] Actually, this is not admitted by all. All non-Calvinists and moderate Calvinists do not believe the offer of the gospel can be in "good faith" for those for whom there is no atonement.

Finally, the question does not relate "to the *design* of Christ in dying *as it stands related to all the benefits* secured to mankind by his death."[460]

Having determined what the question is not, Hodge turned to identify the correct understanding of the question. He stated that the question

> does truly and only relate to the design of the Father and of the Son in respect to the persons for whose benefit the Atonement was made; that is, to whom in the making of it they intended it should be applied. . . . (a.) Its essential nature, involving its exact adaption to the legal relations and necessities of each and every man indifferently; (b) its intrinsic sufficiency for all; (c) its honest and authoritative offer to all; (d) its *actual* application; (e) its *intended* application. . . . The fifth all Calvinists must believe to be limited to the elect.[461]

Hodge found the Lombardian formula to be "inaccurate and inadequate rather than false."[462]

He queried whether God's motive in giving Christ to die was "personal love of certain definite individuals foreknown from eternity" or "a general and impersonal philanthropy, yet allowing the majority of those so loved to perish."[463] This is, of course, a false dichotomy on Hodge's part. How can God's love for "humanity" be impersonal? I know of no Arminian or non-Calvinist who asserts such a thing.

---

459 Ibid., 357.
460 Ibid., 359 (emphasis in original).
461 Ibid., 360.
462 Ibid., 361.
463 Ibid., 363.

Hodge asked:

> Did Christ die with the design and effect of making the salvation of all men indifferently possible, and the salvation of none certain, or did he die in pursuance of an eternal covenant between the Father and himself for the purpose as well as with the result of effecting the salvation of his own people?

Again, this is a false dichotomy. Where in Scripture is this either/or false dilemma stated?

Hodge set the issue in some additional questions that cannot detain us here. Suffice it to say that he continued to create false dilemmas by unwarranted either/or fallacies.

Like his father, Hodge correctly rejected the commercialistic understanding of the atonement and characterized it as a "vicarious penal satisfaction."[464] Like all limitarians, Hodge affirmed that redemption "must be in order to accomplish the purpose of the sovereign election of some, then it is certain that Christ died in order to secure the salvation of the elect, and not in order to make the salvation of all men possible."[465] But this is a false dichotomy for non-Calvinists and Calvinists who affirm an unlimited redemption. Why cannot God accomplish both purposes, and even others beyond?

Hodge returned again to the notion that the atonement removes all legal obstacles from God's way of saving any person. "That in a strictly objective sense the Atonement is as freely available, on the condition of faith, to the gospel-hearing non-elect as it is to the elect."[466] How this can be the case given Hodge's commitment to limited atonement he does not say.

Concerning the phrase "Christ died for the whole world," Hodge said it may be taken in three senses:

> (a.) That he died for Jews as well as Gentiles, for a people elect out of all nations and generations. (b.) That he died to secure many advantages for all men from Adam to the last generation, especially for all citizens in Christian lands, (c.) That he died to secure the salvation of each and every man that ever lived; that is, that he died in the same sense for the non-elect as for the elect. The first two we affirm; the latter we deny.[467]

But here Hodge failed to include a fourth usage that comports better with Scripture: Christ died objectively for the sins of all people, thus making salvation possible for all, yet also with a view to saving only those who believe (the elect in Reformed theology).

---

464 Ibid., 368.
465 Ibid., 370.
466 Ibid., 371–72.
467 Ibid.

Hodge thought that the unlimited extent view within Reformed theology developed only in the seventeenth century with Amyraut and the Samaur School and the eighteenth century with the Marrow controversy.[468] Like so many, Hodge wishes to label the unlimited atonement view within Reformed orthodoxy as a "novelty." He condescendingly spoke of this "novelty" as "not heresy, but an evidence of absurdly confused thought and disordered language upon the subject."[469] In fact, Hodge has the temerity to say, "If men will be consistent in their adherence to these 'Novelties,' they must become Arminians."[470]

> It has always been a marked characteristic of the Arminians, in their controversies with Calvinists, that they insist upon the importance of the distinction between the Impetration and the Application of Redemption. I challenge anyone to show (1) how the *intended* application of the Atonement could have been any more general than its *actual* application? And (2) if the *intended* application is admitted to have been limited to the elect, what remains to the general reference of the Atonement except (a) the intrinsic sufficiency; (b) the exact adaptation; and (c) the *bona fide* offer—all which, it is agreed on all hands, is without any limit at all?[471]

The answer to Hodge's challenge can be seen in the many statements of moderate Calvinists already cited in this work.

Hodge addressed the problem of the well-meant gospel offer from a limitarian platform. He admitted difficulty on this issue, identifying three areas where there would appear to be inconsistency. First, the warrant for all gospel offers "must be found alone in the great commission. . . . Even if the Atonement can be demonstrated to be universal, our right to offer it to all men cannot rest upon that demonstration, but, as said before, upon the plain terms of that commission which we already have." Second, the same goes for the warrant of personal faith. Third, the warrant for God acting as he does lies in his sovereignty.[472]

> Viewing the matter from the *stand-point of the Calvinistic Universalists*, we challenge our opponents to show us wherein there is any more inconsistency with the good faith of the indiscriminate offer of an interest in the redemption of Christ upon our view that it was designed only for the elect, than there is upon their view that God foreknew and intended that the conditions

468 Ibid., 375.
469 Ibid., 377.
470 Ibid., 384.
471 Ibid., 385.
472 Ibid., 418–20.

> upon which it is offered to all men should be impossible. Remember that the question between them and us respects the single point as to the *design* of the Atonement.[473]

The problem with Hodge's point above is his misrepresentation of the "Calvinistic Universalists." They too believe that the atonement was *designed* only for the elect with respect to application but that it was also designed to be a universal satisfaction for sins. The accuracy of Hodge's last sentence depends upon what he means by "design."

Finally, with reference to the use of "all" and "world" in atonement contexts, Hodge attempted to argue, following Candlish, "that particular and definite expressions must limit the interpretation of the general ones, rather than the reverse." Hodge cannot find a plausible reason why Christ, "if he died to make the salvation of all possible, he should nevertheless be said in any connection to have died for the purpose of certainly saving his elect."[474]

But surely it is evident that the few passages that speak of Christ dying for a specific group such as his "church," especially in contexts addressed to the church, cannot be interpreted to mean that he died for them only without invoking the negative inference fallacy, and this especially so in light of the many universal passages.

One final point of interest with Hodge: he did not like the phrase "limited atonement," yet he believed that Christ in some sense satisfied the justice of God by bearing the penalty of the law. Hodge stated: "When thoroughly analyzed and accurately defined, the true doctrine that Christ satisfied the retributive justice of God by bearing the very penalty of the law, *does not* logically lead to any consequences which can be accurately expressed by the phrase *limited* atonement."[475] But Hodge did indeed believe the atonement is limited in terms of its satisfaction for sins since it is restricted to the sins of the elect only. Hodge never explained how it is that Christ can satisfy the law and justice of God without satisfying for the sins of all people who are condemned by that law.

Herman Bavinck (AD 1854–1921)

Bavinck was a Dutch Reformed theologian whose magnum opus is his four-volume *Reformed Dogmatics*, published between 1895 and 1901.[476]

Bavinck addressed the issue of extent historically and then biblically/theologically. He rightly noted that the church fathers prior to Augustine affirm an unlimited atonement. He mistakenly concluded that Augustine himself taught a limited atonement

473 Ibid., 421 (emphasis in original).

474 Ibid., 424–25.

475 Ibid., 343.

476 H. Bavinck, *Reformed Dogmatics*, 4 vols., ed. J. Bolt, trans. J. Vriend (1895–1901; repr. Grand Rapids, MI: Baker, 2003–8). The second revised and expanded edition appeared between 1906 and 1911, followed by a third, unaltered edition in 1918, and a fourth, unaltered edition in 1928 with different pagination. The section on limited atonement appears in volume three, "Sin and Salvation in Christ," 445–75.

based on three grounds: (1) election, (2) Augustine's explanation of 1 Tim 2:4–6, and (3) Augustine's repeated linking the work of Christ "only with the elect."[477]

With respect to the earliest Reformers, Bavinck stated: "The Reformed theologians accordingly, with their doctrine of particular satisfaction, stood virtually alone. Add to this that they were not at all unanimous among themselves and gradually diverged even further from one another as well."[478] This is also a misreading of early Reformed history, as most, if not all, of the early Reformed theologians did not affirm limited atonement. Bavinck correctly noted there were those Calvinists who rejected limited atonement, but he incorrectly indicated they all diverged from the original position of limited atonement. By the late nineteenth century, Bavinck stated the doctrine of limited atonement "has been almost universally abandoned."[479]

Considering the biblical data, Bavinck listed several Scriptures that he interpreted as linking Christ's sacrifice "only to the church." Here Bavinck committed the negative inference fallacy. None of the Scriptures he cited limit the atonement only to the restricted groups mentioned. He argued that "Scripture implies that the sacrifice and intercession of Christ, hence also the acquisition and application of salvation, are inseparably connected."[480] Bavinck and other limitarians interpret John 17 in this fashion.

Bavinck engaged in a false dichotomy when he stated: "We have to make a choice: either God loved all people and Christ made satisfaction for all—and then they will all, without fail, be saved—or Scripture and experience testify that this is not the case."[481] This is of course based on a commercialistic understanding of the atonement whereby the atonement *ipso facto* secures its own application.

When Bavinck suggested that "God, therefore, had ordained his Son to the death of the cross without a definite plan to save anyone without fail," he caricatured and misrepresented Arminians and moderate Calvinists alike.[482] Bavinck's final argument against universal atonement is the so-called disunity it creates between members of the Trinity. We have already seen this issue addressed by many moderate Calvinists, and I will address it in more detail later.

Richard Webster (AD 1811–1856)

Among the many articles that appeared during this century is a three-part article in *The Presbyterian* by the author "R. W." that made the case for limited atonement using the standard arguments:

1. Penal substitution entails limited atonement.

477 H. Bavinck, "Sin and Salvation in Christ," in *Reformed Dogmatics*, 3:456–57.
478 Ibid., 460.
479 Ibid., 463.
480 Ibid., 466.
481 Ibid., 467.
482 Ibid., 468.

2. The extent of the atonement is not to be decided on the basis of sufficiency (value) or on the basis of love. If infinite love is the measure of the provision, why should it also not be the measure of the application? (Free will.)
3. The main question is, What was the intention of God for the atonement? Like Owen, purpose must be argued from result. God did not purpose to save all since all are not saved.
4. The covenant of redemption is the basis of limited atonement.
5. Limited intercession entails limited atonement the efficacy and limitation of intercession are inseparable.
6. The gift of the Spirit is restricted, so also the gift of the Son in making atonement is limited.[483]

Arminian Theologians of the Nineteenth Century

Charles Finney (AD 1792–1875)

When it comes to the Second Great Awakening and revival in American history, few names are as prominent as the Presbyterian preacher Charles Finney. Some call him the father of modern revivalism. Finney taught at Oberlin College and served as its second president from 1851 to 1866. Finney rejected some of his Calvinist background, which brought down the ire of Presbyterian leader Charles Hodge.

Finney's views on the extent of the atonement are best expressed in his *Lectures on Systematic Theology*, first published in 1846.[484] In the first sentence of his lecture on the extent question, Finney stated that God's own glory is the supreme reason for all his conduct, including the atonement, which was made to "satisfy Himself."

Reasoning from the nature of the atonement itself, Finney concluded it was designed and adapted to benefit "all the inhabitants of this world."[485] Finney reasoned that the atonement was made for all humanity because: (1) it is offered to all indiscriminately; (2) sinners are universally condemned for not receiving it; (3) God is insincere in making an offer of salvation to all people through the atonement; (4) if the atonement were made only for a part of humanity, no one could know whether he had a

483 R. W. [Richard Webster], "The Extent of the Atonement, No. 1," *The Presbyterian Magazine* 4, ed. C. V. Bensselaer (November 1854): 496–502; "The Extent of the Atonement, No. 2," *The Presbyterian Magazine* 4 (December 1854): 533–40; "The Extent of the Atonement, No. 3," *The Presbyterian Magazine* 5 (February 1855): 49–57.

484 C. G. Finney, *Lectures in Systematic Theology* (Oberlin, OH: James Fitch, 1846). This was actually volume two of Finney's *Systematic Theology*, with volume three appearing in 1847. In 1851, volumes two and three were combined and published as *Finney's Systematic Theology*. Volume one did not appear until c. 1860 and was composed of previously unpublished manuscripts. In 1878, all three volumes of *Finney's Systematic Theology* were abridged from the 1851 version. All subsequent versions have been taken from the 1878 version. *Finney's Systematic Theology* was republished in 1976 and again in 1994, the latter being an expanded edition containing two lectures on truth from the 1847 and 1851 editions and combined into one section. See C. Finney, *Finney's Systematic Theology*, ed. D. Carroll, B. Nicely, and L. G. Parkhurst (Minneapolis, MN: Bethany House, 1994).

485 Finney, *Finney's Systematic Theology*, 223.

right to embrace it unless God revealed such to him; and (5) if preachers do not believe the atonement was made for all, how can they "heartily and honestly" press the gospel upon every individual or congregation?[486]

Finney linked the sufficiency of the atonement with its general nature, indicating the impossibility of its being sufficient for those for whom it was not made. Citing texts such as Prov 1:20–23; Isa 1:18; and Isa 48:17, 18, he inferred the universality of the atonement based on the fact that "God expostulates with them for not accepting His invitations." Likewise, God "complains" when sinners reject his overtures of mercy, as per Prov 1:24; Zech 7:11–13; and Matt 22:2–6.[487]

Finney made the point that those who object to a general atonement

> take exactly substantially the same course to evade this doctrine, that Unitarians do to set aside the doctrine of the Trinity and the Divinity of Christ. They quote those passages that prove the unity of God and the humanity of Christ, and then take it for granted that they have disproved the doctrine of the Trinity and Christ's Divinity.[488]

Concerning the wasted blood argument (if Christ shed his blood for a single soul that is not effectually redeemed, then his blood is "wasted") of high Calvinists, Finney rejoined that the objection presumes a commercialistic understanding of the atonement. Furthermore, even if sinners don't respond to the preaching of the gospel, the atonement still provides benefits to humanity as well as the universe. Even if all people rejected the atonement, it would still "be of infinite value to the universe, as the most glorious revelation of God."[489] Finally, for Finney, the atonement does not entail universalism because it is not a literal debt payment in a pecuniary fashion.[490]

Thomas Summers (AD 1812–1882)

Summers was an American Methodist theologian writing in the last quarter of the nineteenth century. He served as professor of systematic theology and later dean at Vanderbilt University, later to be known as Vanderbilt Divinity School.

His chapter on the extent of the atonement contains an excellent analysis of 2 Cor 5:14–15 as supporting unlimited atonement. He interacted with many translators of the passage and studied how church fathers such as Chrysostom and Augustine treated

---

486 Ibid., 224–25.
487 Ibid., 225–26.
488 Ibid., 228.
489 Ibid.
490 Finney is not without his theological problems. For a critique of Finney from a high-Calvinist perspective, consult Michael Horton's essay, "The Legacy of Charles Finney," in *Modern Reformation* 4 (1995): 5–9. Also available online at http://www.modernreformation.org/default.php?page=articledisplay&var2=625.

the passage, deriving an unlimited atonement interpretation from it. He concluded this chapter with a list of sixteen proofs of universal atonement.[491]

John Miley (AD 1813–1895)

One of the most important Arminian theologians of the nineteenth century was John Miley.[492] Calvinism "holds the divine destination of the atonement to be determinative of its extent. We fully accept this position. Calvinism is right, not in the limitation of the atonement, but in the determining law of its extent."[493] Citing Turretin, Miley considered the pivot on which the controversy turns, "what was the purpose of the Father in sending his Son to die, and the object which Christ had in view in dying; not what is the value and efficacy of his death." This assessment is only partially correct. It is true the issue is not the value of the death of Christ. But the issue is larger than the question of purpose as well, unless we interpret purpose to refer to God's purpose to expiate the sins of all people (which Miley clearly believed) and not to God's purpose to save only the elect (which Miley disavowed). Miley was correct when he asserted that the question of God's sovereignty is indifferent to either limited or unlimited atonement.[494]

Miley addressed the question of God's relation to humanity as Creator and Father of all and discerns no difference in his relationship, which could be a reason for the limitation of the atonement.[495] There is no difference in humanity's state of evil either. Atonement originated in God's compassion for a lost and sinful humanity. Miley found it difficult to conceive "how God's love could impose upon itself an arbitrary limitation when the very reason of it existed alike in all? Could it be the pleasure of the Father to limit the atonement to a part when his compassion, in which it originated, equally embraced all?"[496] Furthermore, God's justice, holiness, wisdom, and goodness provide no reason for limitation in the atonement. How could God, in the presence of an infinitely greater good, have preferred a limited atonement?[497]

Given that Calvinists believe in the sufficiency of the atonement as the grounds for the sincerity of the universal gospel offer, what reason or motive from the amount of suffering necessary could there be for God to have preference for a limited atonement?[498]

Miley raised the important point, sometimes raised by Calvinists who reject limited

491 T. Summers, *Systematic Theology: Complete Body of Wesleyan Arminian Divinity, Consisting of Lectures on Twenty-five Articles of Religion*, 2 vols., ed. J. J. Tigert (Nashville: Methodist Episcopal Church, South, 1888), 1:234–37.

492 J. Miley, *Systematic Theology*, 2 vols. (New York: Hunt and Eaton, 1889), 2:217–40 is the section where the extent of the atonement is addressed. See also Miley, *Systematic Theology*, 2 vols. (Peabody, MA: Hendrickson, 1989), 2:217–40.

493 Ibid., 2:221. As has been demonstrated, Calvinism is not so monolithic, as Miley represents it to be.

494 Ibid., 222.

495 Ibid., 223.

496 Ibid.

497 Ibid., 224.

498 Ibid., 225.

atonement, that all passages that speak of Christ dying for a limited group, such as "the church," "his friends," or "his body," "are a distinct and limited class as actually saved, not as redeemed [objectively atoned for], and especially not before their redemption." In other words, it is a mistake to think of all the elect as an abstract class and apply texts such as these in such a fashion. These verses are always speaking of the believing elect.[499]

Referencing 1 Tim 4:10, Miley said if God "is not in some similarity of meaning the Saviour of all men, as he is especially the Saviour of believers, there is here a comparison without any basis in analogy."[500] More than once in Scripture do we find a coextension of sin and atonement set forth. "The overture of saving grace to all; the opportunity of salvation for all; the duty of all to believe; and the guilt of unbelief imperatively require a universal atonement, and, so requiring, affirm its truth."[501]

Miley presented nine fallacies in the defense of a limited atonement.

1. Certain facts about the great commission must be admitted: the gospel is for all, salvation is the privilege of all under the gospel, and saving faith in Christ is the duty of all.
2. All admit the divine sincerity in the gospel offer, but limited atonement is inconsistent with God's sincerity. On the limited view, the gospel cannot consistently or sincerely be preached to those for whom Christ's death was not divinely destined as an atonement.
3. Limitarians attempt a vindication of divine sincerity on an alleged sufficiency of the atonement for all, but the sufficiency is only intrinsic, not "a real and available sufficiency for all."[502]
4. A true sense of sufficiency is not merely intrinsic but an actual sufficiency. "An intrinsic sufficiency is from what a thing is in its own capability. An actual sufficiency is from its appropriation." An intrinsic sufficiency is not able to be appropriated by all but is only fit to rescue or liberate those for whom it is actually available. This view cannot vindicate God in his universal overture or uphold the duty of all to have faith in Christ. "Only an actual and available sufficiency will so answer."[503]
5. The extent of the atonement is determined by its divine destination. "The sufferings of Christ have no atoning value except as they were vicariously endured for sinners with the purpose of an atonement. . . . The divine destination absolutely fixes the limit of its extent. There is no atonement

499 Ibid., 226–27.
500 Ibid., 227.
501 Ibid., 232.
502 Ibid., 233.
503 Ibid.

beyond." A "plea for a sufficient atonement for all, while maintaining its limited destination is firmly maintained, is the sheerest fallacy. It is as utterly insufficient for all for whom it was not divinely destined as though no atonement had been made for any."[504]

6. Limited atonement is as utterly insufficient for any and all for whose sins penal satisfaction is not rendered to justice as though no atonement were made, or there were no Christ to make one. According to limited atonement, from its own principles the atonement of satisfaction is necessarily efficient just as broadly as it is sufficient. A contingent sufficiency that might have been but is not is not a real sufficiency. Thus, divine sincerity in offering the gospel to all is impossible to reconcile.
7. Our inability to reconcile the contradiction is said by Calvinists to be of no import. But such a conjectural solution will not answer for a real difficulty. "We may accept in faith what is above our reason, but we cannot by any mere conjecture solve, nor even relieve, a difficulty which is contradictory to our reason."[505]
8. Limitarians attempt to vindicate their view on the assumption of a necessity arising out of the mixed state of the elect and non-elect.

Let the atonement be preached, with the announcement of its partialism, and that the non-elect have no interest in it and no duty respecting it, and the result, as determined by an absolute sovereignty working monergistically, will be the very same. And a limited atonement still contradicts facts divinely given. It must, therefore, be an error.[506]

9. Distinguishing between the secret and preceptive will of God will not solve the problem. "Can the precepts and purposes of God run counter to each other? Can he openly offer a grace, and with the forms of gracious invitation and promise, which he secretly intends not to give, and by an eternal purpose withholds?"[507]

Miley concluded: "The atonement, as a provision of infinite love for a common race in a common ruin of sin, with its unrestricted overture of grace and requirement of saving faith in Christ, is, and must be, an atonement for all."[508]

Miley's critique of the penal substitutionary theory that it "leads of necessity either to

504 Ibid., 233–34.
505 Ibid., 238.
506 Ibid., 239.
507 Ibid.
508 Ibid.

universalism on the one hand, or unconditional election on the other" is the same false dilemma based on a commercialistic view of the atonement that high Calvinist employ. Nevertheless, in his *Systematic Theology*, he confirmed that many nineteenth-century Congregationalists and New School Presbyterians affirmed unlimited atonement.

Conclusion

The nineteenth century witnessed a broad spectrum of debate over the extent of the atonement within the ranks of the Reformed themselves. In Great Britain as well as America, the Reformed were continuing to move away from a strictly limited atonement. In America, the triumvirate of Charles Hodge, Robert Dabney, and W. G. T. Shedd were strongly influential in continuing to move Presbyterian Calvinism away from limited atonement.

The Auburn Declaration (1837) originated during the conflict that preceded the division of the American Presbyterian Church in 1837. Those who later became known as New School Presbyterians had been charged with rejecting aspects of "true Calvinism" and the Westminster Standards,[509] which supposedly included limited atonement. The New School party responded with a statement of their beliefs and presented them to the general assembly that met in 1837.[510] These doctrinal statements were subsequently adopted by a representative convention at Auburn, New York, in 1837. The New School group organized into a separate church in 1838, but the two dissenting groups were reunited in 1870.[511] The confession affirms unlimited atonement.

A perusal of many of the books of sermons published by Calvinists in America during this century reveals that a number of them in their preaching affirmed an unlimited atonement. For example, Thomas Williams's *Sermons on Important Subjects* appeared in 1810 and is a series of ten sermons on key atonement texts: 1 Tim 2:4; Luke 14:17; Rev 22:17; John 5:40; and six sermons on John 6:37. Williams was a strict Calvinist in every way but held to an unlimited atonement.[512]

The Twentieth Century

The nineteenth-century torrent of works on the extent of the atonement dissipated significantly in the twentieth century. Discussion and debate over the extent of the

509 These charges are listed in E. D. Morris, "The Auburn Declaration," *Presbyterian Quarterly and Princeton Review* 17 (January 1876): 7–8.

510 Both the charges, called the "Errors," and the response, called "True Doctrines," may be found in W. Moore, *A New Digest of the Acts and Deliverances of the General Assembly of the Presbyterian Church in the United States of America* (Philadelphia: Presbyterian Publication Committee, 1861), 315–18. See also E. D. Morris "The Auburn Declaration," 5–40.

511 See B. Dickinson, "The Auburn Declaration," in *The Creeds of Christendom*, 3:777–80.

512 T. Williams, *Sermons on Important Subjects* (Hartford: Peter B. Gleason, 1810), 17, 27.

atonement was ameliorated by several other pressing theological issues that came to the forefront.

Within Reformed theology, for roughly the first two-thirds of the century, limited atonement was championed by four theologians dominating the scene: B. B. Warfield, Louis Berkhof, R. B. Kuiper, and John Murray.

B. B. Warfield (AD 1851–1921)

Like Charles Hodge, Warfield was a giant of Princetonian Reformed theology. Warfield is an avowed high Calvinist whose defense of limited atonement is sometimes fraught with straw-man arguments. For example, he took the Amyraldians to task for their position of conditional substitution but missed the point that the Amyraldian view was not conditional substitution but conditional application of the atonement; conditioned upon repentance and faith. Warfield misread Amyraldianism.

Second, Warfield erred when he concluded that either Christ's death removed all legal obstacles from God's perspective or Christ died to save only a limited number of people. This is the false dilemma fallacy. No Reformed theologian believed one at the expense of the other, as we have seen above. Furthermore, no moderate Calvinist believes *all* obstacles have been removed by the cross of Christ. That is a caricature of the moderate Calvinist and non-Calvinist position. Unbelief has certainly not been removed.

Broughton Knox criticized Warfield for failing to apprehend the significance of the point that the elect are not saved at the moment of Christ's death on the cross but only at the point of application of the atonement when their sin is removed at regeneration. Until that point, as Knox correctly noted, the elect remain under the wrath of God (Eph 2:1–3).[513]

Third, Warfield attempted to shackle those Calvinists and non-Calvinists who affirmed an unlimited substitution with the governmental theory of the atonement, though many, even most, affirmed a penal substitutionary theory of the atonement.

Fourth, he erroneously concluded that if the atonement only made salvation possible for all men, then it did nothing for any man.[514] Clearly the atonement made salvation possible, even if only for the elect according to Reformed theology, since they remain under the wrath of God until the point of belief.

In an article appearing in 1921, Warfield interpreted the phrase "for the whole world" in 1 John 2:2 to refer not to each and every individual but to all the sins of all

---

513 B. Knox, "Some Aspects of the Atonement," in *The Doctrine of God, D. Broughton Knox Selected Works*, 3 vols., ed. T. Payne (Kingsford, NSW: Matthias Media, 2000), 1:260–66. Knox went on to note Edwin Palmer's erroneous use of the doctrine of substitution to establish, "conclusively" in Palmer's words, limited atonement. Palmer succumbed to a combination of commercialism and the either/or fallacy. See E. Palmer, *The Five Points of Calvinism* (Grand Rapids, MI: Baker, 1972), 48.

514 B. B. Warfield, *The Plan of Salvation* (Philadelphia: Presbyterian Board of Publications, 1915), 121–22.

believers throughout the world.[515] Warfield considered John to be "a universalist; he teaches the salvation of the whole world. But he is not an 'each and every' universalist: he is an 'eschatological' universalist . . . and at the end, therefore, we will see nothing less than a world saved by him."[516]

In a sermon on Heb 2:9, Warfield interpreted the phrase "tasted death for everyone" to mean the human race at large, not every single person in humanity.[517] But he offered no exegesis or explanation about how or why this phrase should mean what he said it means. Furthermore, would not the human race at large include all individuals?

In the same volume, Warfield has a sermon on John 3:16. He attempted to wrangle from the word "world" the meaning of God's elect in the world, as Owen had done before him. The "love" here celebrated by John is God's saving love, which is reserved only for the elect. Warfield said this is what the text means and what it "must" mean.[518] For Warfield, "God's love of the world is shown by His saving so great a multitude as He does save out of the world."[519] The eisegesis reflected in Warfield's treatment of John 3:16 is actually quite surprising.

Louis Berkhof (AD 1873–1957)

Berkhof was an American Dutch Reformed theologian best known for his *Systematic Theology* published in 1932. He served as president of Calvin Theological Seminary (1931–1944), where he taught for almost four decades. Berkhof was committed to limited atonement.[520]

Berkhof's chief error is in identifying limited atonement as "the Reformed position." Though he is aware of Calvinists who reject limited atonement, he writes as if the unlimited atonement position within Calvinism is somehow a deviation: "The Calvinistic Universalists sought to mediate between the Reformed position and that of the Arminians."[521] Berkhof seems unaware of the fact that the Calvinistic universalists were on the scene prior to those who held to limited atonement. He refers to the Amyraldians as holding this "dubious and very unsatisfactory view."[522] He mentions this view was held by some English scholars, the New Divinity men, and by some of the Marrow Men, though he does not carefully distinguish between Amyraldianism and Hypothetical Universalism.[523]

---

515 B. B. Warfield, *Selected Shorter Writings*, 2 vols., ed. J. Meeter (Phillipsburg, NJ: P&R, 2001), 1:170. See also idem, "Jesus Christ the Propitiation for the Whole World," *The Expositor* 21 (1921): 241–53.

516 Ibid., 176–77.

517 B. B. Warfield, *The Saviour of the World: Sermons Preached in the Chapel of Princeton* (New York: Hodder and Stoughton, 1913), 181–82.

518 Ibid., 111.

519 Ibid., 114.

520 L. Berkhof, *Systematic Theology* (Grand Rapids, MI: Eerdmans, 1939), 393–98.

521 Ibid., 394.

522 Ibid.

523 Ibid.

R. B. Kuiper (AD 1886–1966)

Kuiper (not to be confused with Abraham Kuyper) was one of the founding members of Westminster Theological Seminary and professor of systematic theology there. He wrote an important work on the subject of the extent of the atonement, *For Whom Did Christ Die?*,[524] where he makes the case for limited atonement. He also argued that common grace is one of the fruits of the atonement and that it is the ground for the offer of the gospel to all people, though Christ only died for the elect. Kuiper suggested we simply must live with this paradox.

John Murray (AD 1898–1975)

Murray was one of the founders and professor of theology at Westminster Seminary. He wrote an important work, *Redemption Accomplished and Applied*,[525] where he advocated limited atonement clearly and concisely. Murray divided the book into two sections. The first is the attempted biblical and theological rationale for limited atonement: redemption accomplished.

Following chapters on the "Necessity," "Nature," and "Perfection" of the atonement, Murray discussed the "Extent" of the atonement.[526] Murray first tried to blunt the force of the universal language in Scripture with respect to the extent question by attempting to show that "all," "world," and the like do not always mean "all without exception." He argued that Christ came not to make salvation possible but actually to save. This is a false dilemma fallacy, as Christ came to do both. For Murray, the limitation in the atonement "insures its efficacy and conserves its essential character as efficient and effective redemption."[527]

Murray set forth two biblical arguments in favor of limited atonement based on Rom 8:31–39; 2 Cor 5:14–21; and similar passages. He then addressed two passages used to affirm unlimited atonement: 2 Cor 5:14–15 and 1 John 2:2.

The second section covers Murray's understanding of and justification for the Reformed *ordo salutis*. Among Murray's other writings related to the subject at hand is "The Atonement and the Free Offer of the Gospel," where he attempted to justify the well-meant gospel offer to all people even though Christ only died for the sins of the elect.[528]

Resurgent Calvinism in the Late Twentieth Century

Four significant Calvinists have had a strong influence on the resurgence of Calvinism within Evangelicalism in the last third of the twentieth century and into the twenty-first

524 R. B. Kuiper, *For Whom Did Christ Die?: A Study of the Divine Design of the Atonement* (Eugene, OR: Wipf & Stock, 2003).

525 J. Murray, *Redemption Accomplished and Applied* (Grand Rapids, MI: Eerdmans, 1955).

526 Ibid., 69–85.

527 Ibid., 74.

528 J. Murray, "The Atonement and the Free Offer of the Gospel," in *The Claims of Truth*, in *Collected Works of John Murray*, 4 vols. (Edinburgh: Banner of Truth, 1976), 1:59–85.

century: Roger Nicole, R. C. Sproul, and John MacArthur in America, and J. I. Packer in Britain. We will consider Nicole in the chapter below on North American Baptists.

J. I. Packer (b. AD 1926)

A leading Evangelical Calvinist who has strongly defended limited atonement is the British Anglican J. I. Packer. Packer's contribution to the debate comes in three phases. Phase one centers around his introduction to the 1959 Banner of Truth edition of John Owen's *Death of Death*.[529] Phase two centers around Packer's 1974 article on the logic of penal substitution.[530] Phase three centers around his contributions to this subject in the twenty-first century.

Packer's 1973 article is a key resource in the debate about extent. In it, Packer pointed out that Scholastic Reformed theology rightly fought back against Socinianism but erred in "conceding the Socinian assumption that every aspect of God's work of reconciliation will be exhaustively explicable in terms of a natural theology of divine government, drawn from the world of contemporary legal and political thought. Thus, in their zeal to show themselves rational, they became rationalistic."[531]

Packer suggested we should think of Christ's substitution on the cross "as a definite, one-to-one relationship" between Christ and each individual sinner. If so, then the cross guarantees salvation for those for whom Christ substituted. Christ's death secured reconciliation with God as gifts to be received. Likewise, faith is a gift given to those for whom Christ substituted. Packer argues that if this is the case, then we have only two options: universalism or limited atonement.

If one rejects these, Packer thinks we are left with only one option: to suppose that God purposed to save every person through the atonement, yet some thwart his purpose by unbelief. This can only be the case, Packer said, if one maintains that God makes faith possible and leaves it to the individual to make faith actual. This forces one to redefine substitution in imprecise terms or drop the term altogether, "for they are committing themselves to deny that Christ's vicarious sacrifice ensures anyone's salvation."[532] Furthermore, the double payment argument comes into effect.

> So it seems that if we are going to affirm penal substitution for all without exception we must either infer universal salvation or else, to evade this inference, deny the saving efficacy of the substitution for anyone; and if we are going to affirm penal substitution as an effective saving act of God we must either infer universal

529 See below for an analysis of this introduction.

530 J. I. Packer, "What Did the Cross Achieve? The Logic of Penal Substitution," *Tyndale Bulletin* 75 (1974): 3–45. This is the publication of Packer's Tyndale Biblical Theology Lecture in 1973.

531 Ibid., 5.

532 Ibid., 37.

salvation or else, to evade this inference, restrict the scope of the substitution, making it a substitution for some, not all.[533]

This is the same argument put forth by John Murray,[534] as we saw above.

Does substitution entail salvation? That is the key question. Packer said the New Testament writers constantly take for granted that the atonement is the act of God that has made certain the salvation of those who are saved.[535] Yet one should notice the ambiguity here. Arminians could affirm this statement as well with reference to salvation, though most affirm the possibility of loss of salvation.

For Packer, the cross is decisive as the procuring cause of salvation, and this leads to limited atonement.[536]

R. C. Sproul Sr. (b. AD 1939)

Sproul is an American Presbyterian theologian, philosopher, author, and pastor. He is the founder and chairman of Ligonier Ministries and hosts the radio program *Renewing Your Mind.* He is a strong proponent of limited atonement who has made injudicious statements on the subject. At one of his conferences, when asked what he would call someone who self-identified as a four-point Calvinist, he responded with "Arminian."[537]

John MacArthur (b. AD 1939)

John MacArthur is a well-known and influential evangelical pastor who has served Grace Community Church in Sun Valley, California, since 1969. He is also known for his nationally syndicated radio program *Grace to You.* He is a prolific and influential author. In his early ministry, MacArthur seemed to affirm a universal atonement, as exampled in a sermon on 1 Tim 2:5–8 delivered in 1986.[538]

However, in the late 1980s or early 1990s, he seems to have moved to limited atonement. Since that time he has advocated limited atonement in his sermons, writings,[539]

533 Ibid.

534 John Murray, *The Atonement* (Philadelphia: P&R, 1962), 27.

535 Packer, "What Did the Cross Achieve?," 37–38.

536 Ibid., 39. In a 2007 volume co-authored with Mark Dever, *In My Place Condemned He Stood* (Wheaton, IL: Crossway, 2007), three of Packer's key works on the atonement are brought together in one place. These include his famous introduction to the 1959 Banner of Truth edition of Owen's *Death of Death in the Death of Christ*, "The Heart of the Gospel" from Packer's famous *Knowing God*, and "The Logic of Penal Substitution," a lecture given at the Tyndale House in 1973 and published in 1974.

537 R. C. Sproul, *The Truth of the Cross* (Lake Mary, FL: Reformation Trust, 2007), 141–43.

538 J. MacArthur, "Evangelistic Praying: Part 3" (delivered at Grace Community Church, Sun Valley, California, on January 26, 1986), available at http://www.gty.org/resources/sermons/54–13. MacArthur said: "He was a ransom for all. Would you just circle that? That's the point here. Did Christ die for a few? He died for all. That's what it says. And that's Paul's key idea. He is not here, by the way, intending to give a complex treatment on the theology of the atonement. He is not here trying to emphasize all that could be said about the substitutionary ransom of Jesus Christ. His point here is the 'all.' What he wants you to understand is that Christ who is the one mediator came to do a work on the cross in behalf of man and God that would provide a ransom for all men."

539 See J. MacArthur, *The Freedom and Power of Forgiveness* (Wheaton, IL: Crossway, 1998), 20, 21, 26.

commentaries, and study Bible.[540] MacArthur has sometimes spoken of Christ dying for all mankind, as in a sermon on Titus 2:11, "Saving Grace," but he clarified what he meant by this.[541] He believed the atonement brings temporal blessings to the non-elect, but in terms of actual sin-bearing, Christ died only for the sins of the elect.

MacArthur employs the double payment argument of Owen in his sermon on 2 Cor 5:18–21.

> Did Christ actually pay the penalty for everybody's sins? And if he did pay the penalty for everyone's sins, then the suffering for sin was already accomplished. How in the world could someone then have to suffer eternally for their sin? . . . If sinners are sent to hell to pay forever for their sins, their sins could not have been paid for by Christ on the cross.
>
> The actual atonement was made only for those who would believe. Only their sins were expiated, otherwise nobody could go to hell if God had in Christ borne the punishment for their sins. There would be no sins for them to be punished for.[542]

In MacArthur's commentary on John 1–11, published in 2003, he affirmed a limited atonement.

> Redemption is the work of God. Christ died to accomplish it, not merely to make it possible and then finally accomplished when the sinner believes. The Bible does not teach that Jesus died for everyone potentially, but no one actually. On the contrary, Christ procured salvation for all whom God would call and justify; He actually paid the penalty in full for all who would ever believe. Sinners do not limit the atonement by their lack of faith; God does by His sovereign design.[543]

In his commentary on 2 Corinthians, MacArthur asserted that "Christ did not die for all men without exception but for all men without distinction."[544] Many other places in his commentaries could be cited.

540 See *MacArthur Study Bible*, notes on key atonement passages such as 2 Cor 5:14–21; Heb 2:9; and 1 John 2:2. The note on 1 John 2:2 reads: "Christ actually paid the penalty only for those who would repent and believe. . . . Most of the world will be eternally condemned to hell to pay for their own sins, so they could not have been paid for by Christ. . . . His sacrifice was sufficient to pay the penalty for all the sins of all whom God brings to faith . . . the actual satisfaction and atonement was made only for those who believe."

541 J. MacArthur, "Saving Grace: Part 1" (delivered at Grace Community Church on May 2, 1993), at http://www.gty.org/resources/sermons/56–18.

542 Transcribed from J. MacArthur, "The Ministry of Reconciliation" (delivered at Grace Community Church on March 26, 1995), available at http://www.gty.org/resources/sermons/47–38. See also J. MacArthur, *Truth Endures: Landmark Sermons from Forty Years of Unleashing God's Truth One Verse at a Time* (Wheaton, IL: Crossway, 2011), 163–67. In this sermon on 2 Cor 5:21, MacArthur clearly affirmed limited atonement.

543 J. MacArthur, *John 1–11* (Chicago: Moody, 2006), 259. See also his *1–3 John* (Chicago: Moody, 2007), 49–50, where he clearly affirmed limited atonement.

544 J. MacArthur, *2 Corinthians* (Chicago: Moody, 2003), 202.

MacArthur has been prone in recent years to make statements equating Calvinism with the gospel and to speak of Jesus and Paul as Calvinists.[545]

Though we will consider a few other limitarians in this chapter, most of the names to be discussed from this point forward will be Calvinists who championed unlimited atonement in the twentieth century, along with a few Arminians.

Henry C. Sheldon (AD 1845–1928)

A two-time graduate of Yale, Sheldon was a pastor of two churches from 1871 to 1875 and professor and chair of systematic theology at the Boston University School of Theology from 1875 until his retirement in 1921.

In his *System of Christian Doctrine*, published in 1903, Sheldon discussed the extent of the atonement. He incorrectly assumed the penal satisfaction view of the atonement was commercialistic in nature and hence entailed limited atonement. He was correct to note the logical connection between a commercialist understanding of the atonement and a limited extent of the satisfaction for sins.[546] Sheldon was incorrect to assume that this must necessarily be the case. He quoted Charles Hodge's description of how penal satisfaction functions but did not seem to realize that Hodge himself rejected commercialism and affirmed that Christ died equally for the sins of all people with respect to the actual satisfaction for sins but with a special intent, based on the covenant of redemption, to save only the elect.[547]

Sheldon was on theological *terra firma* when he challenged advocates of limited atonement to point to a single verse of Scripture that necessarily implies "anything more than that the sufferings of Christ afforded a general ground for a gracious economy, and in that sense contemplated all sins in need of pardon."[548] He was on less firm ground when he stated that penal satisfaction is "exposed to all the serious objections, scriptural and rational, which hold against the doctrines of limited atonement and unconditional election."[549] This would only be the case if penal satisfaction were inextricably linked to limited atonement.

Sheldon made a good case for the necessity of the interrelation of all the divine attributes playing a role in the atonement. The love of God is the inseparable companion of the righteousness of God. However one understands the atonement and its extent, the

545 Allen, "The Atonement: Limited or Universal?," 102. An interesting wrinkle concerning MacArthur is some have questioned how he could sign the IFCA doctrinal statement which states: "We believe that the Lord Jesus Christ died on the cross for all mankind as a representative, vicarious, substitutionary sacrifice" (Section 3b). The use of the phrase "for all mankind" would seem to clearly prohibit limited atonement.

546 H. C. Sheldon, *System of Christian Doctrine* (Cincinnati: Jennings and Graham, 1903), 401. His critique of commercialism entailing limited atonement is similar to that of moderate Calvinists who have raised the same objections. For example, forgiveness becomes a matter of justice more than grace; faith becomes less a condition of salvation and is reduced to mere instrumentality; and it is difficult to reconcile with God's universal saving will as expressed in Scripture.

547 Ibid., 397–98.

548 Ibid., 400.

549 Ibid.

love of God should never be made to play second fiddle to the justice of God.[550] In terms of atonement theory, he opted for a modification of the governmental view but warned that the analogy can be and has been pushed too far from the days of Grotius until the present time.[551] He argued for both the objective and subjective aspects of the atonement. "The economy of grace, as brought to manifestation in Christ, provides a basis for the salvation of all men on equal conditions, rather than strictly purchases or absolutely guarantees the salvation of any."[552]

Referencing Rom 5:18–19, Sheldon stated:

> Indeed he [Paul] asserts that the justification offered through the one was meant to be as universal as the condemnation occasioned by the other, if not in truth to overmatch it. The tone of the passage indicates that Paul would have considered it a slander against the largeness of God's grace, if one had interrupted him with the suggestion that the area of possible salvation through Christ was fenced in and contracted, as compared with that of condemnation through Adam.[553]

For Sheldon, limitarians

> are obliged to admit that God authorizes a universal offer and imposes a universal obligation of acceptance, while yet He has made only a limited provision, and has no wish or intention that all men should avail themselves of the gracious overtures.[554] How do they explain and justify this incongruity? They cannot explain it, except by a denial of their own premises. No human subtlety is adequate to justify a picture of God which represent Him as holding a universal offer in an outstretched hand, and keeping all the time in the hand behind His back a sentence of nullification against its universality.[555]

If limited atonement is true, "it follows inevitably that if all men are solicited to appropriate the benefits of Christ's death some must be solicited to take what has no existence for them."[556]

Sheldon critiqued the moderate Calvinist approach to the atonement as well:

---

550 Ibid., 403–4.
551 Ibid., 407.
552 Ibid., 411.
553 Ibid., 427.
554 Orthodox Calvinism actually posits God's universal saving will, though high Calvinists struggle to justify it on the limited atonement scheme.
555 Ibid., 428.
556 Ibid., 429.

> An artificial verbal advantage in scriptural interpretation may be secured by those predestinarians who say that Christ died for all, though God has no intention of applying the benefits of His death to others than the subjects of His unconditional choice. But, as has been noticed already, such a representation is self-cancelling. A purpose that Christ should die for all, followed by such total indifference to some that they are consigned to eternal perdition, although they could be saved without any violence to their moral nature, as the advocates of the theory are compelled by their own premises to admit, is palpable contradiction.[557]

Sheldon's discussion is a substantive contribution to the issue.

Olin Alford Curtis (AD 1850–1918)

After serving in three pastorates, Curtis taught at Boston University from 1889 to 1895 and then served as professor of systematic theology at Drew Theological Seminary from 1896 to 1914. His major theological work is *The Christian Faith: A System of Doctrine*, first published in 1905.

Curtis affirmed a universal atonement, viewing Christ's death from more of a governmental perspective, but including the element of penal substitution. The suffering of Christ on the cross was representative suffering "as the Race-Man, for the whole race."[558]

Lewis Sperry Chafer (AD 1851–1952) and Dallas Theological Seminary

Lewis Sperry Chafer, founder and first president of Dallas Theological Seminary, affirmed unlimited atonement.[559] The doctrinal statement of Dallas Theological Seminary clearly affirms unlimited atonement in a portion of Article 6:

> We believe that, in infinite love for the lost, He voluntarily accepted His Father's will and became the divinely provided sacrificial Lamb and took away the sin of the world, bearing the holy judgments against sin which the righteousness of God must impose. His death was therefore substitutionary in the most absolute sense—the just for the unjust—and by His death He became the Savior of the lost (John 1:29; Rom. 3:25–26; 2 Cor. 5:14; Heb. 10:5–14; 1 Pet. 3:18).[560]

---

557 Ibid.

558 O. A. Curtis, *The Christian Faith: A System of Doctrine* (1905; repr. Grand Rapids, MI: Kregel, 1971), 321.

559 L. S. Chafer, *Systematic Theology*, 8 vols. (Dallas: Dallas Seminary Press, 1976), 2:183–205. See also Chafer, "For Whom Did Christ Die?," *Bibliotheca Sacra* 137.4 (October 1980): 310–26. This article was originally printed in *Bibliotheca Sacra* 105.1 (January 1948): 7–35. The 1976 reprint has undergone minor editing.

560 Dallas Theological Seminary, "Doctrinal Statement," accessed February 9, 2016, http://www.dts.edu/about/doctrinalstatement/. For details on the dispute between J. F. Walvoord and S. L. Johnson over the extent of the atonement in the early days at DTS that led to Johnson's departure, see J. D. Hannah, *An Uncommon Union: Dallas Theological Seminary and American Evangelicalism* (Grand Rapids, MI: Zondervan, 2009), 174–76.

Chafer's discussion on this subject is lucid and penetrating. He suggested four positions on this issue: (1) extreme limited Redemptionists (ultra-Calvinists who would equate with hyper-Calvinism), (2) Calvinists who are limited Redemptionists, (3) Calvinists who are unlimited Redemptionists, and (4) Arminians.[561] Regarding some in categories one and two who affirm equivalentism, Chafer is clear this approach is erroneous. Regarding the third category, where Chafer falls, he noted that the death of Christ "does render all men *saveable*."

Chafer pointed out that the issue of Christ's sin-bearing on the cross is one thing, while to assert that the bearing of sin is equivalent to the salvation of the one for whom Christ died is something quite different. He considered it "unscriptural and misleading" to imply there is no distinction between the atonement and its application.[562]

Like many Calvinists before him, Chafer made the point:

> Men cannot reject what does not even exist, and if Christ did not die for the non-elect, they cannot be condemned for unbelief (cf. John 3:18). Both salvation and condemnation are conditioned on the individual's reaction to one and the same thing, namely, the saving grace of God made possible through the death of Christ.[563]

Chafer argued that people cannot be condemned for unbelief if Christ did not die for their sins. All agree that divine judgment is delayed on the ground of the atonement, an atonement with universal value. Therefore, it is an "insignificant" step from the position of limited atonement to that of universal atonement.[564]

Chafer deftly noted the distinction between the group of words that includes "redemption," "reconciliation," and "propitiation" and the group of words that includes "forgiveness," "regeneration," "justification," and "sanctification." The latter group refers to aspects of truth that *belong only to those who are saved.* The former group refers to what Christ has accomplished by his death on the cross for the unsaved. "Redemption" speaks of the relationship between the sinner and his sins. "Reconciliation" speaks of the relationship between God and the sinner with respect to barriers removed such that God can now be reconciled with those who meet his condition for reconciliation. "Propitiation" speaks of the relationship between God and the sinner with respect to the satisfaction of God's justice so that he can be just when he justifies the sinner.[565]

Chafer continued:

561 Chafer, *Systematic Theology*, 3:184–85 (emphasis in original).
562 Ibid., 186.
563 Ibid., 187.
564 Ibid.
565 Ibid., 189–90.

> According to 2 Corinthians 5:19 there is a reconciliation declared to be world-wide and wrought wholly of God; yet, in the verse which follows in the context, it is indicated that the individual sinner has the responsibility, in addition to the universal reconciliation wrought of God, to be reconciled himself to God. Thus there is a reconciliation which of itself saves no one, but which is a basis for the reconciliation of any and all who will believe.[566]

Limitarians claim that redemption necessitates the salvation of all those for whom Christ died. But Christ's death of itself forgives no sinner, nor does it render unnecessary the regenerating work of the Holy Spirit. People are not saved by the act of Christ in dying but rather by the divine *application* of the atonement when they believe. In the Old Testament, the blood of the Passover lamb became efficacious only when applied to the doorpost.[567]

Chafer rightly noted that while people are in their unregenerate state, no vital distinction between the elect and the non-elect is recognized in the Scripture. He also pointed out the problem of the well-meant gospel offer in the limited atonement scheme.

> How, it may be urged, can a universal gospel be preached if there is no universal provision? To say, at one time, that Christ did not die for the non-elect and, at another time, that His death is the ground on which salvation is offered to all men, is perilously near contradiction.[568]

Chafer is concerned that this state of affairs hinders preaching the gospel to every person. "To believe that some are elect and some non-elect creates no problem for the soul-winner provided he is free in his convictions to declare that Christ died for everyone to whom he speaks . . . it becomes rather a question of *truthfulness* in the declaration of the message."[569] The gospel is *actual* in its availability because Christ died for all. The gospel is *potential* in its application because no one is saved apart from faith in Christ. People are condemned for their unbelief according to John 3:18 and, by implication, John 16:7–11.[570]

According to limitarians, the non-elect die because (1) they were non-elect and (2) their sins were not borne by Christ. But Scripture says the condition on which one may avoid dying in their sins is not based on Christ not dying for them but rather based on their *believing* on Christ.[571]

---

566 Ibid., 192.
567 Ibid., 193.
568 Ibid., 194.
569 Ibid., 195.
570 Ibid., 196.
571 Ibid., 197.

Chafer raised the challenge of Owen's triple choice argument against unlimited atonement. Did Christ bear all the sins of all the non-elect? If so, he bore the sin of unbelief as well. Therefore, how can anyone be condemned? But as we have already seen, Owen's argument proves too much. If Christ bore the sin of unbelief along with the other sins of the elect, then how can an elect sinner in his unregenerate state be subject to God's condemnation and judgment?[572]

Chafer demonstrated the illogic of some limitarians when they appeal to such passages as Christ died for his church as furnishing sufficient grounds to contend that Christ did not die for anyone else. It could then be argued

> with inexorable logic that Christ died only for Israel (cf. John 11:51; Isa 53:8); and that He died only for the Apostle Paul, for Paul declares "who loved me and gave himself for me" (Gal. 2:20). As well might one contend that Christ restricted His prayers to Peter because of the fact that he said to Peter: "But I have prayed for thee" (Luke 22:32).[573]

At this point, Chafer considered various passages in the New Testament that affirm an unlimited atonement.[574]

Chafer concluded by noting three important points. First, if God did intend for Christ to die for the sins of all people in order to provide a legitimate gospel offer to all, could he have used any more explicit language in Scripture than that which is used? Second, it is "wholly impossible" for the limitarian, when preaching the gospel, "to hide with any completeness his conviction that the death of Christ is only for the elect." Third, if the preacher believes that some to whom he is preaching could not be saved under any circumstances, "those addressed have a right to know what the preacher believes and in time will know."

For Chafer, "No greater wrong could be imposed than that, by a philosophical contemplation of truths that are throbbing with glory, light, and blessing, the evangelistic fervor of even one who is called to preach salvation through Christ to lost men should be dampened."[575]

Henry Thiessen (AD 1883–1947)

Thiessen was a moderate Calvinist who served as professor of theology at Dallas Theological Seminary and also as chairman of the faculty of the graduate school at Wheaton College, Illinois. His major work, *Lectures in Systematic Theology* (1949), was influential and regularly used in many Bible colleges and seminaries.

572 Ibid., 198.
573 Ibid., 202.
574 Ibid., 203–4.
575 Ibid., 205.

For Thiessen, the answer to the extent question is related to one's conception of decretal order. Supralapsarians believe Christ died for the elect; sublapsarians hold, in some sense, that Christ died for the world.[576] This is an over-generalization, as we have seen that William Twisse, a supralapsarian, also held to universal atonement. Thiessen listed the two extent positions along with Scripture passages supporting each one. Quoting Augustus Strong, Thiessen indicated his support for unlimited atonement.[577]

T. F. Torrance (AD 1913–2007)

Torrance's lifetime work on the atonement has been published under the title *Atonement: The Person and Work of Christ.*[578] Torrance asked the question, Whom did Christ represent in his incarnation and in his death? This in turn raises two more questions. (1) What is the relation of the incarnation to the atonement? (2) What is the relation between the redemptive work of Christ and election?

If the incarnation and atonement cannot be separated, then Christ represents in his death all whom he represents in his incarnation. If they can be separated, does Christ represent only the elect, and if so, how so? Torrance argued for the inseparability of atonement and incarnation and for their range of representation. In the incarnation, Christ takes on the nature of all humanity and thus represents them all. Torrance repudiated the notion that the humanity of Christ was merely instrumental in the hands of God to procure the salvation of the elect.[579] "God's election cannot be separated from Christ and is essentially corporate in him. We cannot speak of an election or a predestination behind the back of Jesus Christ, and so divide God's saving action in two, into election and into the work of Christ on the cross."[580] For Torrance, election is essentially corporate in the covenant, which is wholly fulfilled in the death of Christ who, as the representative of all, loves all.[581]

Torrance queried, What is the relation between the death of Christ and the Father in heaven? "It is impossible to divide the deity and the humanity of Christ, or Christ from the Father."[582] He thought limited atonement divided Christ's divinity from his humanity and thus rests upon a basic Nestorian heresy (two persons, divine and human, in Christ).[583]

Torrance continued his critique:

---

576 H. Thiessen, *Lectures in Systematic Theology* (Grand Rapids, MI: Eerdmans, 1949), 329.

577 Ibid., 330.

578 T. F. Torrance, *The Person and Work of Christ,* ed. R. T. Walker (Downers Grove, IL: InterVarsity, 2009). See pages 181–92 for his specific treatment of the extent question.

579 Ibid., 182.

580 Ibid., 183.

581 Ibid., 183–84.

582 Ibid., 184.

583 Ibid., 185.

> How can we think of the cross as only a partial judgment against sin? That's what it is if limited atonement is the case. It would mean a partial substitution. It would mean a divorce of the cross from final judgment. It would mean that outside of Christ there is still a God of wrath who will judge humanity apart from the cross. But that is to divide God from Christ, and to eliminate the biblical teaching of the wrath of the lamb (Rev. 6:26), that God has committed all judgment to the Son. (John 5:22).[584]

Torrance moved to the question of the nature of the efficacy of the atonement and found a distinction between "sufficiency" and "efficacy." He asked the question whether the atonement flows from the will of God or the nature of God. Noting that "predestination is used to supply a notion of causal efficacy—it saves only the elect," Torrance asked how, then, one preserves the freedom and transcendence of God. If one thinks the atonement rests upon the arbitrary will (freedom) of God, as Samuel Rutherford, then predestination becomes the controlling category and the divine nature of love becomes something of a secondary issue.

According to Torrance, if one thinks the atonement flows out of the nature of God but that God only loves some (the elect) and not others, such as John Owen's approach, then the nature of God (his omnibenevolence) is impugned. If, as Owen suggested, the nature of God is absolute causality and the atonement flows out of the divine nature, then logically one cannot escape the conclusion that unlimited atonement entails universalism, as Owen in fact argued.[585]

Torrance concluded that both universalism and limited atonement are bound up in rationalism: "Both refuse to bow their reason before the cross." For Torrance, unlimited atonement is the only inescapable reality based on the incarnation and the nature of God and his love.

Leon Morris (AD 1914–2006)

Morris was an Anglican evangelical New Testament scholar, theologian, and writer. He authored many New Testament commentaries, including volumes on Luke, John, Romans, and 1 Corinthians. Examining Morris's comments on key extent texts in John, Romans, and 1 Corinthians evidences his support of universal atonement.[586]

Broughton Knox (AD 1916–1994)

Broughton Knox was an Anglican theologian and principal of Moore Theological

---

584 Ibid.

585 Ibid., 186–87.

586 See, for example, L. Morris, *The Gospel According to John*, NICNT, rev. ed. (Grand Rapids, MI: Eerdmans, 1995), 130–31, on John 1:29. See also idem, *The Atonement: Its Meaning and Significance* (Leicester: InterVarsity, 1983); *The Cross in the New Testament* (Grand Rapids: Eerdmans, 1999).

College in Sydney, Australia, until his retirement in 1985. He held to unlimited atonement. His discussion of the subject is succinct but both lucid and penetrating.

Knox began by noting that certain truths, viewed in and of themselves, indicate the universal nature of the atonement. These include Christ's incarnation, where he took on the nature of humanity, not the elect alone; his life of perfect obedience to the law, which fulfilled all humanity's obligation, not the elect alone; his victory over Satan, which was for all humanity, not the elect alone; and Christ's bearing of the curse, which was for all humanity, not merely the elect alone.[587]

With respect to preaching, Knox noted that from the point of view of the preacher, "Christ has died for all his audience." Were this not so, he continued, it would not be possible to extend a universal offer of the gospel, since the offer must rest on adequate grounds. The only way a genuine offer can be made to any individual is if Christ has died for all, such that the preacher can press the gospel to each individual by saying, "Christ died for you."[588]

Knox correctly noted that the extent of the atonement is limited only in the "intentions and purposes of God." He further noted that the Calvinist notion of unconditional election does not make limited atonement necessary, calling such a *non sequitur*. As a Calvinist, Knox stated, "It is not what limited atonement states positively, but what it states negatively, that is objectionable (that is, the use of the word 'only' for the more appropriate 'specifically,' or 'especially')."[589] Knox spoke of limited atonement as a "textless doctrine," since nowhere in Scripture are we told that Christ died *only* for the elect or that he did not die for all men.

He rejected the commercialism that undergirds limited atonement. "If Christ's substitution is conceived of in this pecuniary way, it would follow that all the saints are free from the wrath the moment the substitution is made and accepted. Otherwise God would be unjust."[590]

Knox concluded: "Limited atonement as commonly propounded, introduces unscriptural concepts into the doctrine of God's relation to the world, and may prove an Achilles' heel for the revival of Reformed theology."[591]

John Stott (AD 1921–2011)

Stott was a leading Anglican evangelical until his death in 2011. He authored more than fifty books, one of the most important of which is *The Cross of Christ*.[592] Though he wrote next to nothing specifically about the extent of the atonement, it appears from

587 B. Knox, "Some Aspects of the Atonement," 260.

588 Ibid., 261.

589 Ibid., 262.

590 Ibid., 265.

591 Ibid., 266. For a critique of Knox from a limitarian perspective, see G. Williams, "The Definite Intent of Penal Substitutionary Atonement," in *From Heaven He Came and Sought Her*, 468–72.

592 J. Stott, *The Cross of Christ* (Downers Grove, IL: InterVarsity, 2006).

a brief section discussing Isa 53:12 in his *The Cross of Christ* that he was a moderate Calvinist who rejected limited atonement.[593]

Homer Hoeksema (AD 1923–1989)

Hoeksema is the son of Reformed theologian Herman Hoeksema and was pastor of two Protestant Reformed congregations from 1949 to 1959. From 1959 until his death he served as a professor in the Protestant Reformed Seminary. He served for many years as the editor of *The Standard Bearer*. His main work was *The Voice of the Fathers*, a study of the Canons of Dort.

Hoeksema contributed a chapter on limited atonement in *The Five Points of Calvinism*.[594] He argued that the Canons of Dort assert limited atonement. His discussion of sin as "debt" indicates his commitment to a commercial understanding of the atonement as the foundation for limited atonement. If the atonement is a substitutionary satisfaction for sins, then limited atonement naturally follows.

James B. Torrance (AD 1923–2003)

The Scottish theologian James Torrance, along with his brother T. F. Torrance, have lodged significant arguments against limited atonement. J. B. Torrance's 1983 article on the incarnation and limited atonement interconnects the atonement in Trinitarian fashion by speaking of a "moment of eternity," the eternal love of the Father; "a moment of history," Christ's death on the cross; and a "moment of experience," when the Holy Spirit applies the atonement.[595]

Torrance considered it a mistake to interpret Christ's headship over all as mediator and the effectual calling of the Spirit in terms of an Aristotelian dichotomy between "actuality" and "possibility."[596]

Torrance critiqued John Owen's notion of God's love, or lack thereof, for the non-elect. For Owen, if God loves all, and all are not saved, then God loves them in vain. Therefore, he does not love all. Owen argued love is not God's nature, but rather an act of his will. Referencing 1 John 4:7–11, Torrance flagged this as logic flying in the face of Scripture.[597]

Torrance viewed the mistake of Calvin's successors as twofold: (1) the Scholastic Calvinists made election prior to grace, and (2) they gave priority of natural law over grace. The double decree of predestination and reprobation grounds the doctrines of grace, incarnation, and atonement as God's method of fulfilling the decree. Logically,

---

593 Ibid., 147.

594 H. Hoeksema, "Limited Atonement," in *The Five Points of Calvinism*, ed. H. Hanko, H. Hoeksema, and G. Van Baren (Grandville, MI: Reformed Free, 1976), 45–66.

595 J. B. Torrance, "The Incarnation and 'Limited Atonement,'" *Evangelical Quarterly* 55, no. 2 (April 1983): 83.

596 Ibid., 84.

597 Ibid., 84–85.

Christ died only for the elect. This fails, according to Torrance, to see the significance of the Trinity.[598] If one makes this double decree the logical starting place, the result is federal Calvinism and covenant theology.[599]

Torrance saw federal Calvinists as having a "deep seated confusion" between "covenant" and "contract." Owen took federalism to the logical conclusion that justice is the essential attribute of God, while love becomes arbitrary.[600]

Torrance claimed that our salvation is made certain, not merely possible, by the combined work of the Trinity and not by the cross alone, taken in isolation.

Torrance's point in this article was also argued previously by James Orr.[601] Orr stated that Calvin never taught limited atonement. Orr and Torrance argue that Calvin erred when he subordinated God's love to God's sovereignty.[602]

Donald Bloesch (AD 1928–2010)

Bloesch was an influential evangelical theologian whose *Essentials of Evangelical Theology* was widely read. He affirmed an unlimited atonement: "In our opinion those who emphasize the universal atonement of Christ are more faithful to the witness of Scripture."[603] Bloesch wrestled with the issue of whether Scripture explicitly teaches that all humanity is in actuality in a state of redemption by virtue of the atonement, a motif that he said is implicit, if not explicit, in Barth's theology. Bloesch correctly rejected this Barthian concept, noting that Christ died as a substitute for the sins of all people, but his death is efficacious only for believers.[604]

Michael Green (b. AD 1930)

Green is an Anglican evangelical pastor, theologian, and since 1997, is senior research fellow and head of evangelism and apologetics at Wycliffe Hall, Oxford. Green affirms unlimited atonement and considers limited atonement a very serious error that

> verges on the blasphemous, and it totally contradicts 1 John 2:2 where the writer assures us that "he is the expiation for our sins, and not for ours only, but for the sins of the whole world." There is a glorious prodigality of grace in God. There is no parsimonious and precise equating of the work of Christ with those who will respond.[605]

---

598 Ibid., 87.
599 Ibid., 88.
600 Ibid., 92.
601 J. Orr, *Progress of Dogma* (London: Hodder & Stoughton, 1901), 297.
602 Torrance, "The Incarnation and Limited Atonement," 93–94.
603 D. Bloesch, "God, Authority, and Salvation," in *Essentials of Evangelical Theology*, 2 vols. (New York: Harper & Row, 1978), 1:165.
604 Ibid., 166–67.
605 M. Green, *The Empty Cross of Jesus* (Downers Grove, IL: InterVarsity, 1984), 84.

Robert Lightner (b. AD 1931)

Lightner is professor of systematic theology emeritus at Dallas Theological Seminary, where he has taught courses in biblical studies and theology since 1968. He wrote a significant work on the subject in 1967, *The Death Christ Died: A Biblical Case for Unlimited Atonement.*[606] This work presents historical, biblical, and theological evidence for universal atonement.

Lightner used three terms to help distinguish between the three views: "obtained," "secured," and "provided." The general atonement position sees the death of Christ as *obtaining* redemption for all but securing it for none. The limited atonement view understands Christ's death to *secure* salvation for the elect—but only for the elect. The singular redemption position understands Christ's death to *provide* salvation for all humanity, but the benefits of the atonement are secured only for those who believe, and those benefits are applied at the time of their conversion.

Therefore, in the words of Robert Lightner, the singular redemption view can be summed up thusly: "Christ died to make possible the salvation of all men and to make certain the salvation of those who believe."[607]

Lightner summarized his own view:

> We, therefore, reject the idea that Christ died to secure the salvation of all men or that He provided every man with sufficient grace to cooperate with God. If that be true, God is defeated because all men will not be saved. We also reject the idea that Christ died to secure the salvation of the elect only. If that be true the cross can no longer be the basis of condemnation for those who do not believe (John 3:18). We believe rather that the twofold testimony of Scripture can be harmonized only in the view that believes Christ died to make possible the salvation of all men and to make certain the salvation of those who believe.[608]

Lightner considered 1 John 2:2 to be the most important text in the New Testament supporting universal atonement. Lightner's discussion can be summarized as follows.

First, some adherents to limited atonement believe that propitiation is not related to Christ's death as a sacrifice for sin but is associated with the mercy seat (Lev 16:14) in the holy of holies where the high priest on the Day of Atonement sprinkled the blood. Christ's death typologically fulfilled this action, and his death is understood to be "for his people only," just as the blood sprinkled on the mercy seat was for Israel only.[609]

---

606 R. Lightner, *The Death Christ Died: A Biblical Case for Unlimited Atonement* (1967; repr. Grand Rapids, MI: Kregel, 1998).

607 Ibid., 47.

608 Ibid., 46.

609 Ibid., 82.

However, Lightner correctly noted that propitiation is inextricably linked to Christ's substitutionary work on the cross, as evidenced by 1 John 4:10; Rom 3:24–25; and other places where the *hilasmos* word group is used. Christ was not only the place of propitiation (the mercy seat) but the sacrifice itself.

Second, the Old Testament makes clear that the blood sprinkled on the mercy seat was for all the people of Israel. To attempt to restrict the event to only the "elect" within Israel has no textual support and is theologically anachronistic.

Third, Lightner noted that if one construes both the first phrase "for our sins" and the last phrase "for the whole world" as referring to the elect, then John's statement is reduced to redundancy.[610]

Fourth, Lightner said the attempt to construe "our sins" with the sins of elect Jews and "sins of the whole world" with elect Gentiles is likewise untenable.[611] Lightner appealed to Westcott's comment on this passage: "But for all alike Christ's propitiation is valid. The propitiation extends as far as the need of it (l.c.) through all places and all time. Comp. iv. 14 (John iv. 42; xii. 32; xvii. 22–24)." Lightner also enlisted A. T. Robertson in support of this interpretation of 1 John 2:2.[612]

Fifth, Lightner said some who support a limited reading of the passage take it to mean that the propitiation is not for John or his readers alone but for all the redeemed of all time and not a distinction between Jew and Gentile. The problem here is enforcing the meaning of "redeemed" on the word "world," an invalid lexical move.[613]

Sixth, Lightner listed and critiqued John Murray's three arguments to explain the apparent universal meaning of 1 John 2:2. Murray admitted there is no text in Scripture that presents more plausible support for universal atonement. His reasoning as to why this text does not teach unlimited atonement is that other texts teach a limited atonement, therefore this text must be interpreted to teach it as well. According to Murray, John sets forth the scope of the propitiation as not limited to the immediate disciples. Second, John emphasizes the "exclusiveness" of the propitiation: only Jesus is the propitiation. Third, John speaks of the "perpetuity" of the propitiation; it endures forever.[614]

Lightner pointed out that John is not dealing so much with the nature of the atonement as with its extent. Murray fails to deal with the problem that limited atonement faces in this text.[615]

Seventh, Lightner cited John Owen's take on this verse:

> That as by the world in other places, men living in the world are denoted, so by the whole world in this can nothing be understood, but men living throughout

610 Ibid.
611 Ibid.
612 Ibid., 83.
613 Ibid., 83–84.
614 Ibid.
615 Ibid.

> the whole world, in all the parts and regions thereof (in opposition to the inhabitants of any one nation, place, or country as such).[616]

But Owen is assigning a meaning to the word "world" that is inadmissible lexically. There is no textual evidence to support Owen's interpretation.

Since its appearance fifty years ago, Lightner's *The Death Christ Died* has often been cited by proponents of unlimited atonement. It remains one of the best overall arguments in favor of unlimited atonement and against limited atonement.

Norman Geisler (b. AD 1932)

Geisler is a Christian apologist, theologian, author, and co-founder of Southern Evangelical Seminary in North Carolina. He has written on the subject of the extent of the atonement, making the case for unlimited atonement, in his multi-volume *Systematic Theology* and in his popular *Chosen but Free*.[617]

Geisler methodically treats the biblical basis for unlimited atonement, beginning with Isaiah 53 and then moving to the New Testament. Concerning Matt 22:14 and contra John Owen, who had argued that God's commands reveal our duty, not God's purpose, Geisler stated: "It would be both deceptive and absurd for God to command everyone to be saved if He had not provided salvation for all."[618] Geisler asserted Owen failed to consider another alternative: "God commands *not only* what He would have us to do *but also* what He desires (wills) to be done."[619]

Addressing John Gill's take on Matt 23:37, where Gill said Jesus's weeping over Jerusalem means not a gathering to salvation but only a gathering to hear Christ preach and thus to be brought to the kind of faith that could preserve them from temporal ruin, Geisler calls this a "desperate interpretation." Such a conclusion would have one believe that Christ's concern for our temporal condition supersedes his concern for our eternal souls.[620]

With respect to Rom 5:18–19, Geisler made a good case for why "the many" means "all," including support from Calvin himself, who affirmed such.[621] The same is the case with Geisler's treatment of 2 Cor 5:14–15 and Paul's nomenclature of "world" and "he died for all."[622]

Geisler proceeded to address 1 Tim 2:3–6; 4:10; Heb 2:9; 2 Pet 2:1; 3:9; and 1 John

---

616 Ibid., 85.

617 N. Geisler, "Sin, Salvation," in *Systematic Theology*, vol. 3 (Minneapolis, MN: Bethany House, 2004), 347–87; *Chosen but Free: A Balanced View of God's Sovereignty and Free Will*, 3rd ed. (Minneapolis, MN: Bethany House, 2010).

618 Geisler, *Sin, Salvation*, 348.

619 Ibid.

620 Ibid., 348–49.

621 Ibid., 351–53.

622 Ibid., 353–54.

2:2, all key texts supporting unlimited atonement. With reference to the latter, and in conjunction with 1 John 5:19, Geisler concluded: "It goes far beyond the strain of one's credulity to somehow conclude that *kosmos* in 1 John 2 refers only to the elect; if that interpretation is correct, only those whom God has chosen are under the power of the devil!"[623]

Geisler then proceeded to respond to objections against limited atonement based on the following passages: Eph 1:4; 1 Cor 15:3; John 5:21; 6:37; 17:9; Eph 5:25; Rom 5:15; Mark 10:45; Rom 9:11–13; 1 Cor 15:22; 1 Pet 3:18; and 1 Pet 2:24.[624]

Geisler next turned to the theological basis for unlimited atonement. He deals with God's omnibenevolence and addresses five objections raised against it.[625] He also considers a number of philosophical problems for limited atonement, such as the relationship between God's nature and God's will (essentialism and voluntarism).[626]

Finally, Geisler briefly surveyed the historical basis for unlimited atonement in the early church and medieval fathers, Reformation leaders including Calvin, and later theologians and historians including Philip Schaff, Earl Radmacher, and Millard Erickson.[627]

R. T. Kendall (b. AD 1935)

Kendall was pastor of the famed Westminster Chapel following Martyn Lloyd-Jones and in later years has carried on an itinerant preaching, teaching, and writing ministry. He is the author of more than fifty books, the most significant for the subject at hand being *Calvin and English Calvinism*.[628]

Kendall is usually held responsible for initiating the so-called Calvin against the Calvinists debate[629] with the publication of this book, although the debate antedated Kendall by many years. He argued that Calvin himself did not hold to limited atonement.

623 Ibid., 359.

624 Ibid., 359–69.

625 Ibid., 369–73.

626 Ibid., 373–79.

627 Ibid., 379–87.

628 R. T. Kendall, *Calvin and English Calvinism to 1689* (New York: Oxford University Press, 1979).

629 C. Trueman, in his foreword to Moore's *English Hypothetical Universalism*, asserted that Moore's work "dispatches to the ash can of history two of the central theses of the 'Calvin against the Calvinists' argument, as found in the influential work of R. T. Kendall. By demonstrating that Preston's hypothetical universalism could happily co-exist with his commitment to experimental predestinarianism, he cuts the tight connection between limited atonement and the latter upon which Kendall and his followers place so much weight. Further, by careful study of the decretal order in Reformed Orthodoxy, he also puts to death the simplistic connection drawn by Kendall, Clifford, and others between hypothetical universalism and Amyraldianism. The two are not different sides of the same coin, and are not connected in any significant organic or structural way; rather, hypothetical universalism was developed within an orthodox ordering of the decrees and, as one option within a heterogeneous English Calvinism" ("Foreword," in *English Hypothetical Universalism*, x). Trueman's statement needs slight nuance since it implies that hypothetical universalism developed *after* limited atonement, which is inaccurate historically. The various attempts to order the decrees in hypothetical universalism did develop in the time of Amyraut and hypothetical universalists in the sixteenth century, but the universal nature of the atonement expressed in both Amyraldianism and other forms of hypothetical universalism antedates limited atonement in Reformed theology.

Though Kendall went too far in shackling later Calvinists with distorting early Reformed theology via Scholasticism, his point about Calvin's position on the issue cannot be so easily dismissed, as we have seen.

Brian Armstrong (AD 1936–2011)

Armstrong was a professor at Georgia State University, historian, and author who served tenures as president of the Calvin Studies Society, the Sixteenth Century Studies Society, and the International Congress for Calvin Research.

He authored an important work on Amyraut and the Reformed debates over the extent of the atonement in seventeenth-century France.[630] Armstrong argued that Amyraut held essentially the same views of Calvin, especially on the universal extent of the atonement. Armstrong is thoroughly familiar with Amyraut's writings. One great concern for Amyraut was what he considered to be the dishonest exegesis of Scripture the Reformed orthodox employed in formulating their understanding of limited atonement by beginning with decretal theology rather than Scripture.[631] "In a word, Amyraut and his friends seem to be saying that a faulty a priori methodology had produced in orthodoxy a barrier to honest historico-exegetical research."[632] Amyraut also made a strong case from Calvin's own writings that Calvin himself held to unlimited atonement.

Armstrong noted that Amyraut further contended "that the orthodox methodology and doctrine had destroyed the effectiveness of Reformed preaching."[633] For Amyraut, when it comes to preaching, the universality of the atonement is crucial.[634] Theology impacts methodology. Armstrong demonstrated Amyraut's clear commitment to God's universal saving will. For Amyraut, "God wills the salvation of all men on the condition that they believe."[635]

Key to Amyraut's theology is God's provision of atonement is for all, but it is only applied to those who meet God's condition of salvation: belief. What is hypothetical in Amyraut's understanding of the extent of the atonement is that salvation is only made effectual when God's condition is fulfilled.

Armstrong's book remains a major contribution to the subject of the extent of the atonement historically and theologically considered.

Gary Long (b. AD 1937)

Gary Long was executive director of Sovereign Grace Ministries from 1979 to 2009. He argued for limited atonement in his *Definite Atonement*. Long's work is heavily dependent

630 B. Armstrong, *Calvinism and the Amyraut Heresy: Protestant Scholasticism and Humanism in Seventeenth-Century France* (Madison: University of Wisconsin Press, 1969). See above for the discussion of Amyraut and his theology.

631 Ibid., 166.

632 Ibid.

633 Ibid., 167.

634 Ibid., 167–69.

635 Ibid., 189–90.

upon secondary sources, which leads him historically astray at some points. For example, his very first sentence in chapter 1 is historically inaccurate in that he, following Nicole, affirms that Amyraut is the "father of Calvinistic hypothetical universalism."[636]

Long concludes in favor of limited atonement. The book has three appendices addressing three key universal atonement texts: 2 Pet 2:1; 1 John 2:2; and 2 Cor 5:19.[637]

John Frame (b. AD 1939)

Frame is currently the J. D. Trimble Professor of Systematic Theology and Philosophy at Reformed Seminary in Orlando, Florida. He previously taught at Westminster Theological Seminary and was one of the founding faculty members at Westminster Seminary California.

In his *Systematic Theology* Frame affirmed limited atonement.[638] He correctly noted there are only two views on the subject: either the atonement is limited to the elect alone or it is unlimited. After noting that many passages of Scripture make unlimited atonement seem "fairly obvious . . . there are some real problems with it."[639]

Frame advocated that if unlimited atonement is true, since the atonement is substitutionary in nature, then universalism would result: "If the atonement is universal, it guarantees salvation for everybody."[640] If one holds unlimited atonement, "you must hold a weaker view of what the atonement is."[641] For Frame, the atonement would then be something "less than a substitutionary sacrifice that brings full forgiveness."[642]

Frame lodged a second criticism against universal atonement: it does not actually save but "only makes salvation possible for those who freely decide to come to faith."[643] Frame has already rejected libertarian free will in chapter 35 of his *Systematic*. For Frame, "the atonement actually saves."

> Those who say that the atonement has an unlimited extent believe that it has a limited efficacy, a limited power to save. Those who believe the atonement is limited to the elect, however, believe that it has an unlimited efficacy. So everyone believes in some kind of limitation. Either the atonement is limited in its extent or it is limited in its efficacy.[644]

---

636 G. Long, *Definite Atonement*, 2nd ed. (Frederick, MD: New Covenant, 2006), 1.
637 Ibid., 67–110. Long was influential in persuading S. Lewis Johnson of limited atonement.
638 J. Frame, *Systematic Theology: An Introduction to Christian Belief* (Phillipsburg, NJ: P&R, 2013), 904–7.
639 Ibid., 905.
640 Ibid.
641 Ibid.
642 Ibid.
643 Ibid.
644 Ibid.

Frame considers the efficacy of the atonement to be the fundamental issue in the question of extent.

Frame's exegetical work on some of the passages concerning the extent of the atonement leaves something to be desired. With respect to John 10:11, 15, Frame deduced the atonement is only for the elect. This, of course, invokes the negative inference fallacy. He cited Rom 8:32–39 and concluded from it the eternal security of the believer. Rightly so, but this has nothing to do with the extent of the atonement. Paul is speaking of people who are already followers of Jesus and what is true of them in that state.

Concerning passages that employ "world" and "all," Frame attempted to dismiss them as referring to either a cosmic, ethical, or "all" as inclusive of Jews and Gentiles. He rightly noted that sometimes "all" is used hyperbolically and does not literally mean "all." This is not in dispute and it does not relieve the problem of the "all" passages with respect to the extent of the atonement. Frame interprets Paul as referring to "all Christians" or "all the elect" in 1 Cor 15:22.[645] Paul's point is only in Christ shall "all" be made alive. Again, this statement says nothing about the extent of the atonement. Speaking of 2 Cor 5:15, "and he died for all, that those who live might no longer live for themselves but for him who for their sake died and was raised," Frame missed Paul's point that Christ died for all, but only "those who live"—that is, those who are believers—should live not for their own sake but for the sake of Christ.[646] Most of the standard exegetical commentaries on this verse do not support Frame's reading of the Greek text here.[647]

Concerning 1 Tim 2:6 and 1 John 2:2, Frame interpreted the "all" in these verses as warranting the free offer of the gospel to all, not that Christ died for all.[648] But the context speaks clearly of actual atonement, not the offer of the gospel, though it is true that the gospel can be freely offered on the grounds of an atonement made for "all" people.

Frame interpreted Heb 10:29 and 2 Pet 2:1 as referencing members of the visible church who were not truly "united to Christ in a saving way."[649] From Heb 4:15 and 7:25 Frame argued that the intercessory ministry of Christ is only for those who believe. The priestly act of atonement and the priestly act of intercession are, for Frame,

645 Ibid., 906.

646 Ibid., 906–7.

647 See, for example, M. Thrall, "A Critical and Exegetical Commentary on the Second Epistle to the Corinthians," in *The International Critical Commentary*, vol. 1, *Introduction and Commentary on II Corinthians I–VII* (Edinburgh: T. & T. Clark, 1994), 411–12; M. Harris, "The Second Epistle to the Corinthians: A Commentary on the Greek Text," in *The New International Greek Text Commentaries* (Grand Rapids, MI: Eerdmans, 2005), 422–24; G. Guthrie, "2 Corinthians," in *Baker Exegetical Commentary on the New Testament* (Grand Rapids, MI: Baker, 2015), 303–6; R. Martin, "2 Corinthians," in *Word Biblical Commentary*, 52 vols. (Waco, TX: Word, 1986), 142–45.

648 Frame, *Systematic Theology*, 907.

649 Ibid.

coextensive. Christ only died for those for whom he intercedes, though nowhere in Scripture is this affirmed.

David Engelsma (b. AD 1939)

Engelsma pastored Protestant Reformed churches from 1963 to 1988 and was professor emeritus of the Protestant Reformed Seminary in Grand Rapids, Michigan, where he taught from 1988 to 2008. He is labeled a hyper-Calvinist by most other Calvinists, though he denies the label. In 1994 his important work on Calvinism and the free offer of the gospel appeared.[650] In it he argues against the well-meant offer of the gospel to all people.

Engelsma referred to Article 33 of the confessional articles of the Gospel Standard Churches. They argue that a call to an unconverted person to repent and believe would imply "creature power"—that is, the ability of that unconverted person to do what he was called to do. Thus, the call to the unconverted would imply free will and would be a denial of total depravity. Engelsma also asserted that such a call would deny limited atonement. If all are called to believe in Christ, then Christ must have died for all and must desire to be the Savior of all. But since Christ died only for the elect, only the elect are to be called in preaching.[651]

Engelsma denied that the call to the reprobate is in any way an expression of God's love for him or a desire of God to save him. God's purpose is single: to save the elect and the elect only. The general call of the gospel to the non-elect is not an expression of God's love for them, nor does it imply that Christ died for their sins.[652] God's well-meant offer of the gospel to the world cannot be wider in scope than the objective satisfaction of Christ on the cross. Christ only satisfied for the sins of the elect; hence the offer can only be genuinely made to the elect.

Engelsma asserted that the Protestant Reformed churches have been misrepresented as hyper-Calvinists by other Calvinists because of their denial of the well-meant offer of the gospel.[653]

Engelsma referenced the controversy in the 1960s surrounding Harold Dekker (AD 1918–2006), former academic dean and professor of missions at Calvin College.[654]

---

650 D. Engelsma, *Hyper-Calvinism and the Call of the Gospel: An Examination of the "Well-Meant" Offer* (Grand Rapids, MI: Reformed Free, 1994). Other Calvinists who have rejected the notion of a well-meant offer of the gospel include Herman Hoeksema and K. Schilder. See A. C. De Jong, *The Well-Meant Gospel Offer: The Views of H. Hoeksema and K. Schilder* (Franeker: T. Wever, 1954). High Calvinists who have accepted the notion of a well-meant gospel offer include K. W. Stebbins, *Christ Freely Offered* (Lithgow, NSW: Covenanter, 1978).

651 Engelsma, *Hyper-Calvinism and the Call*, 19.

652 Ibid., 24.

653 Ibid., 29.

654 The relevant articles on the Dekker controversy ran in the *Reformed Journal* from December 1962 to the May–June 1964 issue and included the following articles: "God So Loved—All Men!" (December 1962); "God So Loved—All Men! (II)" (February 1963); "God's Love for Sinners—One or Two?" (March 1963); "The Constraint of Christ's Love" (December 1963); "Redemptive Love and the Gospel Offer" (January 1964); "Telling the Good News to All Men" (March 1964); and "Limited Atonement and Evangelism" (May–June

Through Dekker's influence, the Christian Reformed Church seems to have allowed for the doctrine of universal atonement. Dekker grounded the doctrine of universal atonement in the doctrine of the well-meant offer. He was convinced that adherence to limited atonement impaired the principle of the universal love of God and tended to inhibit missionary zeal and activity. Dekker argued for God's universal love and a universal atonement:

> The universal love of God is also revealed in His invitation of the gospel, sincerely extended to all without reservation or limitation. Moreover, God's sincere invitation of the Gospel to all involves His desire that it be accepted by all . . . is the salvation which the atonement provides *available* to all men? Indeed it is. Otherwise the well-meant offer of the gospel is a farce, for it then offers sincerely to all men what cannot be sincerely said to be available to all.[655]

Engelsma admitted that Dekker proved conclusively that the doctrine of the universal offer implies universal atonement.[656] Dekker's reasoning is indeed difficult to refute:

> Consider the universal and sincere offer of the gospel . . . Can one really say that the divine love expressed in the gospel, in the good news of God's redemptive acts in Jesus Christ, is a *non-redemptive* love? How can a love which offers redemption be described as non-redemptive in character? Does that really make sense? The alternatives seem clear: *either the love of God expressed in the invitation of the gospel is redemptive or it is non-redemptive.* It seems to me that if it is non-redemptive, the gospel offer has no real meaning.[657]

Engelsma cannot be any clearer on the subject: "Paul . . . did not believe, nor did he ever preach, that God loved all men, was gracious to all men, and desired the salvation of all men, i.e., he did not believe or teach the well-meant offer of the gospel."[658]

Paul Helm (b. AD 1940)

Helm taught philosophy at the University of Liverpool and was appointed to the chair of the history and philosophy of religion, King's College, London, in 1993. He was

---

1964). The September 1964 issue contained a reply by Dekker to a letter concerning his doctrine of universal redemptive love and universal atonement.

655 Cited in Engelsma, *Hyper-Calvinism and the Call*, 61–62 (emphasis in original). See H. Dekker, "God So Loved—All Men!," 5–7; idem, "Limited Atonement and Evangelism," 24.

656 Engelsma, *Hyper-Calvinism and the Call*, 63.

657 Cited by Engelsma, *Hyper-Calvinism and the Call of the Gospel*, 96 (emphasis in original). See Dekker, "Redemptive Love and the Gospel Offer," 8–10.

658 Engelsma, *Hyper-Calvinism and the Call of the Gospel*, 53.

the J. I. Packer Chair of Theology at Regent College from 2001 to 2005, when he was appointed a teaching fellow. He publishes online at his website *Helm's Deep*.

Helm is known within and without Calvinist circles for his strong defense of limited atonement. He wrote a response to R. T. Kendall's *Calvin and English Calvinism* entitled *Calvin and the Calvinists*.[659] One of his early articles dealing specifically with the question of the atonement's extent is his "The Logic of Limited Atonement."[660]

Helm sought to respond to McLeod Campbell and J. B. Torrance's critique of limited atonement. Both objected to Owen's formulation of limited atonement on many grounds, not the least of which is it does not do justice to the biblical emphasis on the centrality of the love of God. For Helm, it is a misunderstanding of the atonement to suppose that God deals with all men in justice but with only some in mercy. The elect do not experience God's justice as it concerns them, but Christ satisfies justice for them. So it is not that some experience both love and justice while some experience justice only. "It is rather, according to the doctrine, that some experience love, some justice, neither both and each one or the other. The inequality is symmetrical."[661]

Acknowledging this, still a problem exists: the fact that some experience God's love in Christ and others do not. Helm admitted this. How can God consistently with his character accept Christ's satisfaction for some and not for others? Helm appealed to Paul in Rom 9:20. We simply have no right to question God, according to Helm.[662]

Helm attempted to rebut the claims of Campbell and Torrance by appealing to the nature of God's mercy. How can it be that there is mercy for some and not others? Helm deflected the morality aspect of the question by again appealing to Romans 9. He then attempted to respond to the logical part of the question. He thought the problem for Campbell is his misunderstanding of the logic of mercy as "undeserved love." If God has to exercise mercy as he has to exercise justice, then mercy ceases to be mercy. The logical character of mercy is vastly different from that of justice. "A justice that could be unilaterally waived would not *be* justice, and mercy which could not be unilaterally waived would not be mercy."[663]

In brief, if mercy is an act of the divine will, it is equally arbitrary whether that mercy is particular or universal. If on the other hand mercy is part of the divine nature, necessitated by who God is, whether that mercy is particular or universal its character as mercy is not compromised, according to Helm.

Helm defended Owen. He assigned God's love to God's will, as does Owen, and argued that it does not make love arbitrary or without reason. The origin is due not to

659 P. Helm, *Calvin and the Calvinists* (Edinburgh: Banner of Truth, 1998). See my critique of this work in the section on Calvin and my critique of Helm's chapter in *From Heaven He Came and Sought Her* below.

660 P. Helm, "The Logic of Limited Atonement," *Scottish Bulletin of Evangelical Theology* 3, no. 2 (Autumn 1985): 47–54.

661 Ibid., 49.

662 Ibid.

663 Ibid., 50 (emphasis in original).

God's reaction upon learning of human sin but to a determination of his will in accord with his character. By itself, it has no bearing at all on the scope of divine love.[664]

Helm admitted "such an exercise is, in a technical sense, 'arbitrary' but it is not arbitrary in the sense of being capricious, irresponsible, or irrational."[665]

For Helm, Campbell's logic is that any attribute necessary to God (love and justice) is necessarily exercised by God on all creatures on whom it is logically possible to exercise it. Helm said, "So far so good, but then notes the entailment of such an argument. The logical problem for Campbell is that this entails: any attribute necessary to God is necessarily exercised by God *equally* on all on whom it is logically possible to exercise it."[666]

Helm applied this to the creation. Why is it that a loving and wise God should ordain and create a universe with manifest angularities? Some are strong, weak, male, female, healthy, diseased, and so forth. Helm did not mention that many of these "angularities" are due to human sinfulness. If creation differentiations are commensurate with divine attributes, then it is presumably possible for there to be such with regard to God's redemptive purposes, which are entirely consistent with the divine attributes.[667]

Helm countered the argument that there is a difference between God being arbitrary about hair color, and so on, and eternal salvation by asking how such a claim can be argued. "Does not any distinction between Gods non-redemptive purposes, in which arbitrariness is permissible, and his redemptive purposes in which it is not permissible appear to be an arbitrary distinction?"[668]

To suppose that limited atonement makes the action of God arbitrary in an objectionable sense is to misunderstand both the nature of divine mercy and the nature of the divine will, according to Helm.[669]

Helm also stated in another work: "There is one immediately striking difference between Calvin and the approach to the atonement of Owen and others. Their starting point is not the atonement itself, as it was with Calvin, but the doctrine of God. The approach is much more obviously scholastic in its method."[670]

The dominant Reformed position on the atonement by Owen's time was its "highly juridical" nature.

> What dominates the discussion is the inexorable justice of God and how the atonement squares with that, or rather has to square with that. The focus on the atonement as the expression of the love and mercy of God is secondary.

664 Ibid., 52.
665 Ibid.
666 Ibid., 53 (emphasis in original).
667 Ibid.
668 Ibid.
669 Ibid., 54.
670 P. Helm, *Calvin at the Centre* (Oxford: Oxford University Press, 2010), 183.

> God may be love, but God is certainly justice, and the atonement is primarily an act of divine justice making mercy possible—whereas with Calvin the atonement is an act of divine mercy that is consistent with justice.[671]

Writing of the difference between Calvin and Owen, Helm stated:

> The reason that he [Calvin] provides for moving on from mere pardon to pardon by the atonement of Christ is not the requirement of divine justice that is characteristic of Owen's view: that justice demands satisfaction. The divine justice is not central to his argument, but the divine love. God sent his Son not because his justice required it, but because he loved us with unsurpassable depth and so wished to lavish on us an optimal expression of his mercy.[672]

The question in all of Helm's treatment here is whether love, grace, and mercy are natural to God's character. Let's begin with love. If one accepts the premise that God necessarily loves that which is good, then God loves man created in God's image. Man in that regard is considered by God to be "good." Thus, it follows that God must love man.

If Helm were to say that God loves that which is good, but not humanity as his image bearer, that would be an example of arbitrariness. If Helm were to circumscribe God's love for humanity within the boundaries of common grace, then such love would be a different kind of love. Helm might say that God does not love all, even with a love of common grace, to the same extent, since some die young and some live with pain and illness while others prosper. By this point, Helm's basic premise that God's love cannot be necessary is undercut. Helm is left with a revised objection to Torrance: God does not love all equally.

The core of Torrance's objection is that, under the terms of Owen, God initiates his dealing with man, even unfallen man, with law and not love or mercy. God's love is such that he does not need to be provoked to love or aroused by some action of humanity. But if love is not natural to God, then he needs to be prompted to love. But Scripture indicates that God's love flows freely from his very nature. If Owen is right, only law flows freely. Thus, Owen and Helm unwittingly attack the very character of God. God is law before he is love.

The Scripture does not indicate that God's love is a pure act of his will and is not naturally endemic to his nature while law is endemic to his nature. Just the opposite is the case with respect to love. The Scripture says God so loved the world. For Owen and Helm, "world" is equivalent to the elect, so they see God in a fundamentally different way. Like all Calvinists who assert a covenant of works, Owen and Helm

---

671 Ibid., 194.

672 Ibid., 195. Note that this parallels the critique by Torrance of Owen.

view God's relationship to humanity in the pre-fall state as essentially one of law. The same is true in the so-called covenant of redemption. Here again, it is law, not love, that functions as the fundamental mechanism of how God relates. What binds the Trinity together is a legal contract. What binds God to humanity is also a legal contract—the covenant of works.

This entire construct cuts to the heart of God's very character as revealed in Scripture from the very beginning: God is love. He actually loves his broken creation in such a way that God devised a remedy for brokenness—a way of salvation.

Calvin's approach is quite different from Owen and Helm. Commenting on Ezek 18:1–4, Calvin asserted that the passage should be understood in such a way

> that nothing is more unworthy than that God should be accused of tyrannizing over men, when he rather defends them, as being his own workmanship. When, therefore, God pronounces that all souls are his own, he does not merely claim sovereignty and power, but he rather shows that he is affected with fatherly love towards the whole human race since he created and formed it; for, if a workman loves his work because he recognizes in it the fruits of his industry, so, when God has manifested his power and goodness in the formation of men, he must certainly embrace them with affection. True, indeed, we are abominable in God's sight, through being corrupted by original sin, as it is elsewhere said, (Psalm 14:1, 2;) but inasmuch as we are men, we must be dear to God, and our salvation must be precious in his sight. We now see what kind of refutation this is: all souls are mine, says he: I have formed all, and am the creator of all, and so I am affected with fatherly love towards all, and they shall rather feel my clemency, from the least to the greatest, than experience too much rigor and severity.[673]

Calvin asserted the very thing Helm denies.

Alan C. Clifford (b. AD 1941)

Clifford is a leading British Amyraldian pastor who has written much on the subject of the extent of the atonement.[674] Clifford's summary view of limited atonement in the history of seventeenth-century England and beyond is reflected in the following letter to the editor of the *English Churchman*:

---

673 J. Calvin, "Commentaries on the Prophet Ezekiel," in *Calvin's Commentaries*, 22 vols., trans. T. Myers (Grand Rapids, MI: Baker, 1981), 12:216–17. See also Calvin's comments on Lam 3:33 in "Commentaries on the Book of the Prophet Jeremiah and the Lamentations," in *Calvin's Commentaries*, 22 vols., ed. J. Owen (Grand Rapids, MI: Baker, 1981), 11:422.

674 A. C. Clifford, ed., *Christ for the World: Affirming Amyraldianism* (Norwich, UK: Charenton Reformed, 2007); idem, *Calvinus: Authentic Calvinism: A Clarification* (Norwich, UK: Charenton Reformed, 1996); idem, *Atonement and Justification: English Evangelical Theology 1640–1790* (Oxford: Clarendon, 1990); idem, "Justification: The Calvin-Saumur Perspective," *Evangelical Quarterly* 79, no. 4 (October 2007): 331–48.

[T]he doctrine of limited atonement is as alien to Reformation Anglicanism as it is to the teaching of Amyraut and Calvin. In the seventeenth century, scholastic influences in Reformed theology affected this country as well as France. Thus the "over-orthodox" distorted Calvinism of Dr John Owen and many (but not all) of the Westminster divines was rejected by Richard Baxter and others. In the eighteenth and nineteenth centuries, the balanced biblicism of Calvin, the other Reformers, Amyraut and Baxter was maintained by the Nonconformists Matthew Henry, Isaac Watts and Philip Doddridge, and the Anglicans John Newton, Charles Simeon and Bishop Ryle. While I regret Ryle's espousal of episcopacy, his authentic Calvinism is unquestionably on target! According to this view of the New Testament, while ultimately only the elect effectually partake of salvation, the universally designed and sufficient atonement of Christ makes the gospel available to the whole world. This is true Christianity and true Calvinism![675]

Clifford does not mince words in this letter to the editor published one month later:

The Revd Edward Malcolm virtually concedes that Articles XV and XXXI are universalist when he admits that the compilers "are merely quoting Scripture." He then charges with having a "preconception" those who take them in their natural sense! If he thinks this is an Arminian view, the Anglican Clement Barksdale objected in 1653 that "You are mistaken when you think the doctrine of Universal Redemption Arminianism. It was the doctrine of the Church of England before Arminius was born. We learn it out of the old Church Catechism: 'I believe in Jesus Christ, who hath redeemed me and all mankind. And the Church hath learned it out of the plain scripture, where Christ is the Lamb of God that taketh away the sins of the world.'" Richard Baxter surely hit the nail on the head when he wrote, "When God saith so expressly that Christ died for all [2 Cor. 5:14–15], and tasted death for every man [Heb. 2:9], and is the ransom for all [1 Tim. 2:6], and the propitiation for the sins of the whole world [1 Jn. 2:2], it beseems every Christian rather to explain in what sense Christ died for all, than flatly to deny it." As for Mr Malcolm's citation of Calvin's seeming support for limited atonement, his partial quotation of this isolated statement ignores the fact that the reformer is discussing the implications of the Lutheran theory of consubstantiation rather than the extent of the atonement. Numerous other statements are consistently universalist (see my "Calvinus").[676]

675 A. C. Clifford, letter to the editor, *English Churchman*, June 6, 2000.
676 A. C. Clifford, letter to the editor, *English Churchman*, July 3, 2000.

Donald Macleod reviewed and critiqued Clifford's *Amyraldus Redivivus* in 2009.[677] His review is problematic in several places. For example, he chided Clifford for claiming Thomas Chalmers as moderate on the extent of the atonement, when we have seen that there is no doubt Chalmers held to universal atonement. Macleod spoke of Chalmers as "explicitly committed to Jonathan Edwards's theological determinism, and it is hard to imagine him arguing that the cross was set within an eternal divine counsel which simultaneously foreordained the hypothetical redemption of all and the actual redemption of some."[678]

Macleod seems unaware that Edwards was himself moderate on the atonement, as we have demonstrated.[679] Within Calvinism, one's commitment to theological determinism does not mandate a commitment to limited atonement.

Macleod correctly recognized that one may not infer the doctrine of limited atonement from the doctrine of election. But then he asserted "neither may we infer the doctrine of universal redemption from the doctrine of universal proclamation."[680] This is true in so far as it goes, but those who affirm universal atonement do not infer it from universal proclamation. They find it in Scripture and argue that the universal proclamation of the gospel cannot be genuine on the part of God or his messengers if there is no atonement for all people, since that would result in a situation where something was being offered that for some people clearly does not exist.

Macleod, following Owen, based the universal proclamation of the gospel on (1) the "organic link between Christ and the whole human race" and (2) the intrinsic sufficiency of the atonement adequate to expiate the sins of all the world.[681] But the link between Christ and humanity is, according to Owen, merely coincidental and necessary for Christ to die for the sins of the elect. Furthermore, a sufficiency of worth is insufficient for the salvation of anyone for whom there is no actual atonement. To suggest otherwise is mere word games.

Furthermore, Macleod seems unaware of Jonathan Moore's *English Hypothetical Universalism*, which demonstrated beyond any question that John Preston held to universal atonement. Macleod appealed to Preston's statement, "Go and tell every man without exception, that there is good news for him, Christ is dead for him."[682] Yet, as Moore demonstrated, the basis of this statement is Preston's Hypothetical Universalism. Macleod referenced *The Marrow of Modern Divinity*, along with Preston's version of the Great Commission, as being endorsed "by such magisterial Calvinists as Thomas

677 D. Macleod, "*Amyraldus Redivius*: A Review Article," *Evangelical Quarterly* 81.3 (July 2009), 210–29.

678 Ibid., 212.

679 It is improper for Clifford to label Edwards and all moderate Calvinists as "Amyraldian" since there is no evidence of a Saumur influence on Edwards's thought, unless perhaps indirectly through some of the Puritans like Charnock and others who held to a universal atonement.

680 Ibid., 218.

681 Ibid., 222–23.

682 J. Preston, *The Breast-Plate of Faith and Love*, 6th ed. (London: Printed by G. Burstow, 1651), 8.

Boston, Ebenezer Erskine and Adam Gib." Yet *The Marrow of Modern Divinity*, along with Erskine, Gib, and maybe Thomas Boston, all affirmed a universal atonement with limited particular intent.[683]

Macleod affirmed that God loves all people but warned that evangelists must choose their words carefully when expressing God's love to the sinner. Macleod spoke of "universal redemption," "universal pardon," and "universal salvation."[684] By "redemption" he meant atonement for everyone's sins, by "universal pardon" Macleod meant "potential pardon," and by "universal salvation" Macleod meant universalism, where all are saved in the end. He then informed his readers that Calvinists, and others who affirm universal atonement like Baxter and Wesley, affirm that after God has done all he does, he still requires human faith. One is at a loss to understand what this point has to do with his argument against universal atonement.

Macleod's historical fuzziness was revealed when he discussed Amyraldianism in the nineteenth-century United Presbyterian Church in Scotland. He cited the preamble to the 1879 Declaratory Act, which allowed exception to be taken to the teaching of the Westminster Confession on the extent of the atonement. According to Macleod, this carefully drafted act arose from the need to accommodate Amyraldianism.[685]

But as has been demonstrated in recent scholarship on Westminster, Amyraldianism was not placed outside the confessional boundary of the Westminster Confession. Macleod's assertion that Amyraldianism dissolved the bond between Scottish Presbyterian churches and their creed lacks historical demonstration.[686]

Curt Daniel (b. AD 1952)

Daniel is a Reformed pastor at Faith Bible Church in Springfield, Illinois, author, and lecturer on Reformed theology. His *History and Theology of Calvinism*, along with his doctoral dissertation "Hyper-Calvinism and John Gill," present the case for unlimited atonement from the earliest history of Reformed theology.[687] His fifty-page appendix at the end of his dissertation contains one of the most complete listings of quotations from Calvin proving beyond a shadow of doubt that Calvin did not affirm limited atonement.[688]

Daniel asserted the following historical narrative with respect to Calvinism and the extent of the atonement. Augustine believed in universal atonement. Gottschalk was probably the first to limit expressly the atonement only to the elect. Luther held to unlimited atonement. The English Reformers all believed in unlimited atonement

683 Ibid., 225.
684 Ibid., 226.
685 Ibid., 227.
686 Ibid., 228–29.
687 C. Daniel, *History and Theology of Calvinism* (Springfield, IL: Scholarly Reprints, 1993); idem, "Hyper-Calvinism and John Gill."
688 Daniel, "Hyper-Calvinism and John Gill," 777–828.

as expressed in Article 31 of the Thirty-Nine Articles. Within the Swiss Reformation, we find the same with Zwingli, Bullinger, and Musculus. Daniel asserted, "The evidence is overwhelming that John Calvin agreed with all the other Reformers that Christ died for all." "In this he was followed by Peter Martyr Vermigli, Zacharias Ursinus, and other Reformers." "Universal atonement was clearly the accepted viewpoint of Reformed theology up to about the year 1600." Beza is probably the first Reformer to explicitly teach limited atonement and probably the first Reformer to teach supralapsarianism.[689]

While Dort rejected Arminianism, many, like Davenant, affirmed dualism with respect to the atonement. John Owen formulated the classic defense of the strictly limited view. This was paralleled by Turretin on the Continent. Daniel argued that Bunyan held to unlimited atonement.

During the eighteenth century, men like Doddridge, Watts, and others taught a moderate Calvinism, while John Gill and the Hyper-Calvinists taught the opposite. A mediating approach came from the Marrow Men in the Scottish debate over the *Marrow of Modern Divinity*. Some of the Marrow Men taught dualism.

In the nineteenth century, William Rushton advocated a strict limited view of the extent of the atonement. New England theology and Albert Barnes held to universal atonement. While James Morison and Ralph Wardlaw in Scotland, along with Charles Hodge, Shedd, and Dabney in America, stressed particular aspects of the atonement in terms of intent, they asserted the universal aspects of the atonement, including Christ's bearing of sin for all people.

Daniel listed Griffith-Thomas, Lewis Sperry Chafer, R. T. Kendall, Robert Lightner, and Norman Douty among those who affirmed universal atonement in the twentieth century. He noted Louis Berkhof, John Murray, Rienke Barend Kuiper, and Gary Long made important contributions to the question on the limited side of the equation. Kuiper's *For Whom Did Christ Die?* improved on the limited atonement scheme, according to Daniel. Kuiper spoke of the universal benefits of the atonement to the non-elect, but the question is whether he means universal sin-bearing or only something along the lines of common grace, with the latter the more likely meaning.

Daniel asserted what scholars are now admitting: there is no one mainstream Reformed view regarding the extent of the atonement.[690] Daniel noted how most books on Calvinism paint the extent question as an either/or choice: either Christ died equally for all people or Christ died only for the elect. Scripturally and historically, it is more of a both/and balance.[691]

Daniel summarized the universal benefits of the atonement that Calvinists agree

689 Ibid., 360.
690 Ibid., 361.
691 Ibid.

on, regardless of their view of the extent question, with respect to the sins of humanity: (1) common grace, (2) delay of judgment, (3) Christ is now Lord of all according to Rom 14:9, and (4) universal free offer of the gospel.[692]

Daniel made a crucial point that has been verified in more recent scholarship—namely, that so-called four-point Calvinism historically preceded five-point Calvinism.[693]

Daniel corrects John Gill's faulty logic with respect to the love of God and the extent of the atonement. Gill had stated: "Those for whom Christ died, he loves with the greatest love; but he does not love every individual man with the greatest love; therefore he died not for every individual man."[694] Unlike Gill, Daniel asserted Christ died to provide salvation for all in a general sense (that is, to remove all legal impediments to them in case the Father chose to apply it to them), but he died with a special intent for the elect.[695]

Daniel critiqued the double payment argument and discussed the key objections to limited atonement: the "perishing" passages, 2 Pet 2:1, the "world" passages, the "all" passages, the "many" passages, the free offer of the gospel, and faith and assurance.[696]

We have already had reason to refer to Daniel's dissertation on many occasions, especially in the section above on John Calvin. Daniel's survey and critique of limited atonement from a historical perspective covers the following broad topics: (1) background, (2) the hyper-Calvinist defense of limited atonement, (3) limited atonement and the free offer, (4) Christ made sin, and (5) universal terminology suggesting general atonement.[697]

Martin Davie (b. circa AD 1957)

Davie served as the theological secretary to the Church of England Council for Christian Unity. In 1999 he delivered the Tyndale Doctrine lecture, which was published in 2001.[698] Davie interpreted "one died for all" in 2 Cor 5:14 as a reference to unlimited atonement. He referred to the back and forth on this issue among Calvinists themselves, but concluded:

> I can see the attraction of the Dort position. It is neat, tidy and leaves no loose ends. However, as Alister McGrath notes, "its critics tend to regard it as compromising the New Testament's affirmation of the universality of God's love and redemption" and I think that these critics are correct. The overall weight

692 Ibid., 364.
693 Ibid., 365.
694 J. Gill, *The Cause of God and Truth* (1855; repr. Grand Rapids, MI: Baker, 1980), 104.
695 Ibid., 368.
696 Ibid., 371–77.
697 Ibid., 496–607.
698 M. Davie, "Dead to Sin and Alive to God," *Scottish Bulletin of Evangelical Theology* 19.2 (2001): 158–94.

of New Testament teaching pushes us to the classic Anglican affirmation made in the Communion service in the *Book of Common Prayer* that on the Cross Christ made "a full, perfect, and sufficient sacrifice, oblation, and satisfaction, *for the sins of the whole world*."[699]

Arminian Theologians of the Twentieth Century

J. Rodman Williams (AD 1918–2008)

Williams was a pastor, theologian, and professor of renewal theology at Regent University in Virginia Beach, Virginia, from the mid-1980s. He earned a ThM and PhD from Union Theological Seminary. He was professor of systematic theology at Austin Presbyterian Theological Seminary and was president of the International Presbyterian Charismatic Communion and a participant in the Roman Catholic–Pentecostal Dialogue in the 1960s and following. Williams was the founding president of Melodyland School of Theology in Anaheim, California, and served as president of the Society for Pentecostal Studies in 1985. He is sometimes regarded as the father of modern charismatic so-called Renewal Theology. His most important work is the three-volume systematic theology, *Renewal Theology*.[700] Williams holds the distinction of writing the first complete systematic theology from a charismatic perspective.

Citing 2 Cor 5:18–21; 1 John 2:2; 1 Tim 1:15; and John 3:16, Williams asserted that the atonement was universal in extent but limited only to those who exercise faith in Christ. The objective and subjective aspects of the atonement must be kept in mind. Objectively, God has accomplished the atonement outside and apart from anything man does. Subjectively, the benefits of the atonement do not accrue to any individual until the point of faith.[701]

J. Kenneth Grider (AD 1921–2006)

Grider was an Arminian scholar of Nazarene extraction who wrote a theology from the Wesleyan Arminian perspective published in 1994.[702] In his survey of the various theories of the atonement, he spoke of the punishment theory in distinction from Anselm's satisfaction theory and the Grotian governmental theory. What Grider meant by the punishment theory is better known as the penal-substitutionary approach to the atonement: "The view of Calvin and Calvinism." Grider wrote as if this approach to the

699 Ibid., 193.

700 J. R. Williams, *Renewal Theology*, 3 vols. in 1 (Grand Rapids, MI: Zondervan, 1996).

701 J. R. Williams, "God, The World, and Redemption, vol. 1," in *Renewal Theology* (Grand Rapids, MI: Zondervan, 1988), 369–70.

702 J. K. Grider, *A Wesleyan-Holiness Theology* (Kansas City, MO: Beacon Hill, 1994). The relevant section on the extent of the atonement is found on pp. 326–35.

atonement was not around until Calvin. Calvin did affirm the penal-substitutionary understanding of the atonement, but he was not the first to do so. Grider correctly stated that Calvin himself held to an unlimited atonement.[703]

One of Grider's problems with penal substitution is "it is unfair to the nonelect."[704] This criticism is a misunderstanding of penal substitution. Many Arminians, including Arminius himself and John Wesley, have held this view of the atonement. Penal substitution does not entail limited atonement, as Grider thought. His beef is with the Reformed doctrine of election, not the nature of the atonement.

Grider distinguished between Christ being punished for us, which he considers unscriptural, and Christ suffering for us, which he considers biblical. Grider opted for the governmental view, which to his mind can incorporate all the biblical data and most of the other atonement theories.[705] He affirmed the "substitutionary" nature of the atonement, but he rejected the "penal" aspect.

Dave Hunt (AD 1926–2013)

Hunt was a Christian apologist, speaker, author, and founder of the website *The Berean Call* in 1992. Hunt's chief work dealing with Calvinism is *What Love Is This? Calvinism's Misrepresentation of God.*[706] Hunt and James White co-authored *Debating Calvinism.*[707]

Hunt's *What Love is This?* addressed the subject of limited atonement in chapter 13. Hunt appeared to take no notice of the fact that many Calvinists, past and present, did not affirm limited atonement. Further historical mistakes occur, such as Hunt's statement that Spurgeon rejected limited atonement.[708] Hunt makes some unnecessary and ill-advised judgments along the way, such as "[John] Owen was a brilliant man beyond the intellect of either Calvin or Luther."[709]

Hunt marshalled a number of good arguments against limited atonement. He correctly noted that a distinction must be made between atonement made and atonement applied. All are not saved because all do not believe. He cited the many biblical passages that are standard fare in the argument against limited atonement. He rejected the double payment argument as well as the argument that Christ's blood was "wasted" on the unlimited atonement view. He argued that "world" cannot be interpreted to mean "the elect," as many Calvinists are prone to do. The chapter concluded with an analysis of 1 John 2:2 in support of unlimited atonement. In chapter 14, Hunt addressed John 3:16; 1 Tim 2:4; 4:10; Heb 2:9; and 2 Pet 3:9.

---

703 Ibid., 328.
704 Ibid., 329.
705 Ibid., 330–31.
706 D. Hunt, *What Love Is This? Calvinism's Misrepresentation of God* (Sisters, OR: Loyal, 2002).
707 D. Hunt and J. White, *Debating Calvinism: Five Points, Two Views* (Colorado Springs, CO: Multnomah, 2004). This book is a point-counterpoint approach to the subject.
708 Hunt, *What Love Is This?*, 240.
709 Ibid., 244.

Hunt's presentation is more on a popular level, but he does quote numerous Calvinists and engage them. His final chapter returned to the title of the book and summarized his major thesis that Calvinism distorts the love of God for all people.

Thomas Oden (b. AD 1931)

Methodist theologian Thomas Oden's three-volume systematic theology is probably the most complete modern Arminian theology available. Oden's commitment to unlimited atonement is clear: "The atonement is addressed to all humanity, intended for all, sufficient for all, yet it is effectively received by those who respond to it in faith."[710]

I. H. Marshall (AD 1934–2015)

I. H. Marshall was a renowned New Testament scholar in the Methodist tradition. In his "Universal Grace and Atonement in the Pastoral Epistles," he argued the case for universal atonement. For example, concerning the key passage 1 Tim 2:6, he stated:

> Scholars agree that 1 Timothy 2:6 is a rewording of the saying of Jesus in Mark 10:45, with "all" replacing the "many" found in that text. Titus 2:14 is a paraphrase of the same text (with some influence from Ps. 130:8 and Exod. 19:5). A saying of Jesus that tells how the Son of Man came to give his life as a ransom for "many" has been reexpressed using more idiomatic Greek forms of expression.[711]

Marshall's most important article with respect to the extent of the atonement is "For All, for All My Saviour Died."[712] He treats exegetically and theologically the universal passages, particularly in the Pastorals, that seem to indicate an unlimited atonement. With respect to the universal language in the Pastorals, such as 1 Tim 2:4–6, Marshall stated:

> The purpose and effect of the phraseology in the Pastoral Epistles is not just to emphasize that Gentiles are included alongside Jews, but to magnify the grace of God who is concerned for all people and not just for some people. On the limited interpretation we have to do one or other of the following. We have to assume that readers would get the meaning "God wants to save all kinds of

710 T. Oden, *The Word of Life: Systematic Theology*, 3 vols. (New York: Harper Collins, 1989), 2:388.

711 I. H. Marshall, "Universal Grace and Atonement in the Pastoral Epistles," in *The Grace of God and the Will of Man*, ed. C. Pinnock (Minneapolis, MN: Bethany House, 1985), 59. Marshall's chapter is an excellent exegetical refutation of understanding 1 Tim 2:4–6 as "all kinds of people" rather than all people universally. See also Marshall on 1 Tim 2:4–6 in idem, *A Critical and Exegetical Commentary on the Pastoral Epistles*, ICC (Edinburgh: T. & T. Clark, 1999), 425–33.

712 I. H. Marshall, "For All, for All My Saviour Died," in *Semper Reformandum: Studies in Honour of Clark H. Pinnock*, ed. S. Porter and A. Cross (Carlisle, UK: Paternoster, 2003), 322–46.

> people, but of course it must be understood that he doesn't actually want to save everybody. It's not just that there may/will be people who reject salvation, but that he wants to save only some rather than all." Or we have to assume that this is the secret, unspoken thought of the writer. Such a limitation goes clean against the force of the actual statements and ends up by minimizing the grace of God rather than maximizing it.[713]

Marshall responded to the view that the New Testament's lack of the words "Christ died for you" in evangelistic settings is support for limited atonement. He rightly pointed out that this is "readily explained by the fact that most New Testament teaching is addressed to those who are already believers and examples of evangelistic preaching are few."[714] He noted that 1 Cor 15:3 "is surely a case of the preacher including his unsaved audience with him in an inclusive statement. It most certainly is *not* a statement that he died only for the sins of those who are already believers."[715]

Marshall addressed the point argued by some limitarians, such as Helm and Letham, that there is a difference in the logic of God's justice and mercy. The argument that God is under no obligation to show mercy to all and is therefore just in condemning some while showing mercy to others is flawed from Marshall's perspective.

First, the argument "that God may arbitrarily exercise mercy to some and not to others must be rejected as unjust. A Judge who treats one pregnant woman with mercy but shows none to another one in similar circumstances would not be tolerated." Second, "there are presumably no limits set to the capacity of God's merciful provision. . . . If God can show mercy to some, he has the ability to show mercy to all." Third,

> the biblical teaching about grace and mercy shows that it is motivated essentially by the need and plight and helplessness of the afflicted. . . . The mercy shown by God is not something arbitrary that arises purely from his own inscrutable purposes; on the contrary, it is aroused by his recognition of the need of helpless sinners.[716]

Aware that Calvinists will appeal to Rom 9:6–24 to argue that God's mercy is shown to some and not to others, Marshall pointed out that Paul's point in this passage is that God's promises do not fail simply because the Jews have failed to follow the Messiah. Paul's emphasis is on the fact that "mercy is God's prerogative and is not his rcsponsc to human works (Rom. 9.11–12, 16); consequently, it cannot be claimed as of

713 Ibid., 331.
714 Ibid., 336.
715 Ibid.
716 Ibid., 343.

right or as something deserved by anybody but remains the act of God in his freedom (Rom. 9.15)."[717]

By the time we get to the end of Romans 11, "Paul is declaring that God's purpose in the light of Christ is to 'have mercy on them all' (Rom. 11.32)."[718] "Paul's argument from past history that people cannot claim mercy on the basis of their works does not entail that his mercy is now selective and arbitrary. In fact the opposite is true."[719]

Marshall treated many more passages and issues than we can cover at this point. This chapter remains one of the best Arminian refutations of limited atonement available.

Representative Lutheran Theologians and the Extent of the Atonement[720]

Milton Valentine (AD 1825–1906)

Valentine was president of Pennsylvania College in Gettysburg, Pennsylvania, from 1868 to 1884 and was the third president and professor of systematic theology at the Lutheran Theological Seminary in Gettysburg from 1884 to 1903. His major theological work is the two-volume *Christian Theology*.

On the extent of the atonement, Valentine stated:

> *Lutheran*, and all non-Calvinistic theology says: *For all men*. And this in the sense, (1) *Negatively*, that there is no limitation either of its *sufficiency* or *efficiency* by any predestinating election of some to life and passing others by, as is involved in the conception of absolute decrees irrespective of foreknowledge and conditioning it. (b) *Positively*, that the atonement expresses God's eternal purpose, which He purposed in Christ Jesus, to provide forgiveness, eternal salvation, and all the means thereto, for real acceptance and use of all men—a provision in which, in both its nature and design, all men might be saved on condition of the assent of faith. The design of the atonement was to remove the oral and legal obstacles to the salvation of *all* men, so that it is applicable to one as well as another on terms that are open and impartial to all. This is a general or universal atonement.[721]

---

717 Ibid., 344.

718 Ibid.

719 Ibid.

720 See D. Scaer, "The Nature and Extent of the Atonement in Lutheran Theology," *Journal of the Evangelical Theological Society* 10 (1967): 179–87, for a helpful summary from a Lutheran perspective. All Lutherans since Luther have affirmed unlimited atonement.

721 M. Valentine, *Christian Theology*, 2 vols. (Philadelphia: Lutheran Publication Society, 1906), 2:158–59 (emphasis in original).

Valentine continued to argue that this universal scope must be viewed retrospectively as well as prospectively, by which he meant Christ died for the sins of all those who lived and died before his death on the cross. This is clear "from the universality affirmed of the atonement, as co-extensive with the fruits of Adam's sin (Rom. v. 18). (b) From passages distinctly referring to its retroactive bearing," such as Rom 3:25; Heb 9:15, 25, 26; 1 Pet 3:18–20; and Rev 13:8.[722]

Valentine found proof of a general atonement in:

1. Texts that directly affirm a universal provision for sin in Christ, such as John 1:29; 3:16; 6:51; 14:47; Rom 5:18–21; 2 Cor 5:14–15; Rom 5:9; Heb 2:9; 1 Tim 2:6; 4:10; and 1 John 2:2.
2. Texts that directly state salvation is offered to all, such as Isa 45:22; 55:1–3; Matt 11:28–30; Rev 3:20; 22:17; and 1 Tim 2:4.
3. Texts that affirm the guilt of the sinner who refuses the gospel call, such as Matt 23:37; Luke 14:17–24; John 3:19; Acts 7:51; Heb 2:3; Acts 13:46; and Heb 10:28–29.
4. Texts that affirm Christ died for some who will ultimately perish eternally, such as Rom 14:15; 1 Cor 8:11; Heb 10:29; and 2 Pet 2:1.
5. Texts that imply general atonement, such as God is no respecter of persons (Acts 10:34; Rom 2:11; 2 Chr 19:7); God declares he has no pleasure in the death of the wicked (Ezek 18:23–32; 2 Pet 3:9); and men themselves are responsible for their eternal damnation (Heb 3:7–19).
6. Texts that imply that limited atonement belittles the gospel and the grace of God.[723]

Valentine listed and answered common objections to general atonement:

1. God can be defeated in his purpose. Yet this is not the case if God's design was to provide a salvation conditioned on faith accepting the provision.
2. God's "general" will and his "special" will supposes different and conflicting purposes in the Godhead. The purpose of God's love for all is to open a way of salvation to all, but his further purpose is to save only those who are willing to accept God's loving provision.
3. All God's actions, with respect to their absoluteness, must be wholly from God himself. The conditioning of the results of the atonement represents his will as being determined by something outside himself. But the entire plan of salvation, including all parts, is entirely from God's self-determination and free love. "The true conception of God's sovereignty includes His ability to

722 Ibid., 2:159.

723 Ibid., 159–61.

adjust His work of redeeming love to the given nature of man, for the purpose of spiritual recovery."[724]

4. God makes provision for an end (the salvation of all people) that he knows will not be effected. But the end of God's purpose is twofold: the salvation of believers and the vindication of God's goodness with respect to unbelievers.
5. God's justice requires the actual salvation of all for whose sins Christ has made the satisfaction. This objection only works on a commercialistic, pecuniary, quantitative-equivalency approach to the atonement, which is not the biblical teaching. Furthermore, "Justice *owes* nothing to the sinner even under an atonement except *in the way* the atoning provision offers it."[725]
6. Some passages do teach that Christ died specifically for the elect, such as John 10:11–15; Acts 20:28; and Eph 5:25. But while these statements affirm a clear truth, they do not assert anything concerning the extent of the atonement being restricted only to these groups. This is merely begging the question. The affirmation of a wider extent is clearly made in the many positive statements concerning such in Scripture.[726]

Francis Pieper (AD 1852–1931)

Pieper was an influential Lutheran theologian whose four-volume *Christian Dogmatics* was published from 1950 to 1953. In answer to the question for whom Christ rendered satisfaction in atonement, Pieper said it was "for mankind, for all men."[727]

Conclusion

The twentieth century illustrates the numerous Calvinists who rejected limited atonement and who affirmed that Christ died for the sins of all people. As the twentieth century drew to a close, several ministries based in Reformed theology were influential in American evangelical Christianity and beyond. Three of the more significant include Ligonier Ministries, founded by R. C. Sproul in 1971; The Shepherd's Conference, founded by John MacArthur; and Desiring God Ministries, founded by John Piper in 1994. Each of these men is well known for his commitment to limited atonement.

During the last decade of the twentieth century, partly as a result of these ministries and partly due to other factors,[728] Reformed soteriology made great inroads

724 Ibid., 163.

725 Ibid., 164.

726 Ibid., 161–64.

727 F. Pieper, *Christian Dogmatics*, 4 vols. (St. Louis, MO: Concordia, 1951), 2:381. See also his chapter on "Universal Grace."

728 Such as Iain Murray and the Banner of Truth's selective reprinting of high Calvinist Puritan literature in the twentieth century.

among college and seminary students in evangelical institutions, especially among Southern Baptists.

The Twenty-First Century

Early in the twenty-first century, two new Reformed organizations arrived on the scene. The Gospel Coalition was founded in 2005 by D. A. Carson and Tim Keller. Together for the Gospel was founded in 2006 by Mark Dever, Al Mohler, C. J. Mahaney, and Ligon Duncan. Dever and Mohler are Baptists; Duncan is Presbyterian. The publication of Collin Hansen's *Young, Restless, and Reformed* in 2008 and the subsequent lead article about it in *Christianity Today* served to catapult the growing Reformed movement into the spotlight. Like the older Calvinists R. C. Sproul and John MacArthur, the leaders of the "new Calvinism" all affirm limited atonement.

The twenty-first century has witnessed a plethora of books published (and in some cases republished)[729] dealing with some aspect of Calvinism, usually from the TULIP perspective. Some of these books are written with the intent to further the resurgence of Calvinism while others are written to explain its doctrine. Most give little attention to the extent of the atonement in any serious discussion, expressing either overtly or by implication that Christ died only for the sins of the elect. The phrase "limited atonement" may or may not be utilized by these authors. One regularly observes phrases like "Christ died for the sins of his people" in these works, a common phrase indicating adherence to limited atonement where the speaker or writer intends that Christ died *only* for the sins of "his people."

The order of the following names generally appears according to dates of publication, not necessarily according to birth years.

O. Palmer Robertson (b. AD 1937)

Robertson taught at several major Reformed seminaries, including Reformed, Westminster, Covenant, and Knox, as well as served as principal of the African Bible College of Uganda.

He authored the chapter "Definite Atonement" in R. C. Sproul's *After Darkness, Light: Distinctives of Reformed Theology*.[730] He advanced the standard arguments in favor of limited atonement: (1) if the atonement is substitutionary, and if Christ

729 See, for example, D. Steele, C. Thomas, and S. L. Quinn, *The Five Points of Calvinism: Defined, Defended, Documented*, 2nd ed., updated and expanded (Phillipsburg, NJ: P&R, 2004). This work was originally published in 1963 by Steele and Thomas. See also R. C. Reed, *The Gospel as Taught by Calvin* (Edinburgh: Banner of Truth, 2009). This work was originally published in the early twentieth century.

730 O. P. Robertson, "Definite Atonement," in *After Darkness, Light: Distinctives of Reformed Theology*, ed. R. C. Sproul (Phillipsburg, NJ: P&R, 2004), 95–110.

propitiated the wrath of God for all, then all must be saved; (2) the double payment argument; (3) Christ purchased some sinners for himself; (4) the Father has given a select number of people (the elect) to the Son; and (5) Christ purchased the ends and the means of salvation, including faith, for the elect.

Palmer said concerning the purchase of faith: "If you have saving faith in Christ today, you can know that you personally were a part of the eternal plan of God for the salvation of sinners, and that Jesus Christ had you in mind when he suffered the punishment due to sin."[731]

He continued: "It follows, then, that those who have no faith are not those for whom he died." But such a statement is itself problematic for Reformed theology since even the unbelieving elect can resist the general call until such time as they receive the special, irresistible call. What Palmer would have to say is those who have no faith at the point of death are not those for whom Christ died.

For Palmer, "Christ died for all who will come, and all for whom he died will come."[732]

Robert Godfrey (b. circa AD 1946)

Robert Godfrey is president of Westminster Seminary (California) and professor of church history. He is a noted Reformed author. His PhD dissertation on the debate over the extent of the atonement at the Synod of Dort is an important historical contribution to the discussion.[733] Godfrey demonstrated the diversity with respect to the extent question that existed at Dort.

In 2009 Godfrey contributed a chapter entitled "The Reformation Consensus on the Atonement" to a multi-author book.[734] His discussion on the question of extent is surprisingly generalized, given his dissertation, as evidenced by this sentence: "Calvinists have asserted that if Christ was a substitute, a sacrifice, and a satisfaction for all people and every individual, then surely that must mean all people and every individual will be saved."[735] Godfrey is well aware that scores of Calvinists, including many at Dort and Westminster, rejected such an assertion and gave their arguments against it. Calvinists have never been monolithic when it comes to the question of the extent of the atonement, a fact that Godfrey well knows. He asserted that "the Calvinists have thought very carefully about this."[736] Such a statement is true of some, but the evidence in this volume suggests that others have not thought about it so carefully.

His statement, "It is interesting that Luther believed in election, but he never saw

731 Ibid., 97.

732 Ibid., 110.

733 R. Godfrey, "Tensions within International Calvinism: The Debate on the Atonement at the Synod of Dort, 1618–1619" (PhD diss. Stanford University, 1974).

734 R. Godfrey, "The Reformation Consensus on the Atonement," in *Precious Blood: The Atoning Work of Christ*, ed. R. D. Phillips (Wheaton, IL: Crossway, 2009), 145–62.

735 Ibid., 159.

736 Ibid.

the implication of it,"[737] assumes that election entails limited atonement, which is highly disputed within Reformed theology. When he quoted Heb 9:28 and interpreted it as meaning "not the sins of all, but of many—that is, the elect," he confused intent with extent and employed the negative inference fallacy.[738]

Godfrey defined the sufficiency of the atonement as its value and related it directly with efficiency.[739] He posits that the limitation in the atonement's extent is not about limiting the love of Christ.[740] But this is not entirely accurate either. Christ's love for the non-elect, however it is to be described, certainly falls short of a redemptive love in most of Reformed theology.

Richard Muller (b. AD 1948)

Muller has been professor of historical theology at Calvin Theological Seminary since 1992. He is considered one of the foremost authorities of Reformed thought in the sixteenth and seventeenth centuries. Muller's comments on the issue are important for the historical situation at Dort and beyond with respect to the extent question. Two fundamental questions needed to be answered, according to Muller.

First, posed by Arminius and answered at Dort, is the question "Given the sufficiency of Christ's death to pay the price for all sin, how ought one to understand the limitation of its efficacy to some?"[741] According to Arminius, the efficacy is limited by the individual person who chooses to believe or not to believe. According to Dort, efficacy was limited by God himself in pre-temporal election to God's elect. As we have seen, the final Canons of Dort do not define this limited efficacy in terms of a strictly limited extent for the atonement.

Second, is the value of Christ's death hypothetically universal in such a way that it could have been sufficient for all sin had God so intended, or, is the value of Christ's death such that if all would believe, all would be saved (an actual sufficiency)?[742]

Dort rejected the notion that Christ died *equally* for all such that he died for no person effectually. Dort did not reject the notion that Christ died for the sins of all men. Both the strict limitarian view of the extent and the Davenantian/Amyraldian/Hypothetical Universalism views remain consistent with the Canons of Dort, as Muller has noted.

Muller noted how both Calvin and Bullinger taught the sufficiency of the atonement

737 Ibid., 160.

738 Ibid.

739 Ibid.

740 Ibid., 161.

741 R. A. Muller, "Was Calvin a Calvinist?," in *Calvin and the Reformed Tradition: On the Work of Christ and the Order of Salvation* (Grand Rapids, MI: Baker, 2012), 61. See also his lecture at the H. Henry Meeter Center for Calvin Studies (Calvin College, Grand Rapids, MI) delivered on October 15, 2009, on the topic, "Was Calvin a Calvinist? Or, Did Calvin (or Anyone Else in the Early Modern Era) Plant the 'TULIP'?," 9–10. Available at https://www.calvin.edu/meeter/Was%20Calvin%20a%20Calvinist-12-26-09.pdf.

742 R. A. Muller, *Was Calvin a Calvinist? Or, Did Calvin (or Anyone Else in the Early Modern Era) Plant the "TULIP"?*, 9–10.

as a satisfaction for all sin.[743] One might ask, If Muller agreed that Calvin and Bullinger agreed on the point of sufficiency, why would Muller not list Calvin as a Hypothetical Universalist as he clearly does with Bullinger? There appears to be continuity between Calvin and Bullinger on this issue, according to Muller.

Muller made clear his view that the Salmurian theology falls within the boundaries of confessional Reformed orthodoxy.[744] He also pointed out how even Turretin admitted that the views of John Cameron and his Salmurian successors did not constitute heresy but lay within the boundaries of Reformed orthodoxy.[745]

Likewise, Muller noted how Amyraut's Hypothetical Universalism did not lead to the charge of heterodoxy against the likes of Davenant at Dort or those of a similar mind at Westminster. Muller stated, "The Westminster Confession was in fact written with this diversity in view, encompassing confessionally the variant Reformed views on the nature of the limitation of Christ's satisfaction to the elect."[746]

In *Calvin and the Reformed Tradition*, Muller contributed a chapter entitled "Calvin on Christ's Satisfaction and its Efficacy: The Issue of 'Limited Atonement.'"[747] Muller is certainly correct in his assertion: "In short, fixation on the anachronistic term 'limited atonement' and on the ancient but inherently vague language that 'Christ died for all people' or, by contrast, 'for the elect,' has led to fallacious argumentation on all sides of the issue."[748] Muller stated that the term "limited atonement" would have been "unintelligible to Calvin and, indeed, to the delegates to the Synod of Dort."[749]

Muller's critique of Kevin Kennedy's use of the term in *Union with Christ and the Extent of the Atonement* misses the point. Kennedy is clear on what he means by the use of "limited atonement"—that is, a limited imputation of sin to Christ. Muller himself fails to define what he means by "sufficiency" in his critique of Kennedy.[750] As we have

---

743 R. A. Muller, "John Calvin and Later Calvinism: The Identity of the Reformed Tradition," in *The Cambridge Companion to Reformation Theology*, ed. D. Bagchi and D. C. Steinmetz (New York: Cambridge University Press, 2005), 147.

744 R. A Muller, *Post-Reformation Reformed Dogmatics*, 4 vols., 2nd ed. (Grand Rapids, MI: Baker, 2002), 2:15; "Beyond Hypothetical Universalism: Moïse Amyraut (1596–1664) on Faith, Reason, and Ethics," in *The Theology of the French Reformed Churches: From Henri IV to the Revocations of the Edict of Nantes*, 198, 205, 208. Muller noted:

> Nearly all the older scholarship went astray from the actual evidence in its assumptions that hypothetical universalism per se ran counter to the Reformed confessions—notably, the Canons of Dort—and that Amyraut's form of hypothetical universalism, derived from the theology of his teacher, Cameron, was representative of hypothetical universalism in general (ibid., 205).

Warfield is an example of this sort of older scholarship that involves mischaracterization and historical lumping. See B. B. Warfield, *The Westminister Assembly and Its Work* (1959 repr.; Edmonton, AB, Canada: Still Waters Revival Books, 1991), 56, 144n94; *The Plan of Salvation* (1989; repr. Eugene, OR: Wipf and Stock, 2000), 118.

745 R. A. Muller, "Divine Covenanters, Absolute and Conditional: John Cameron and the Early Orthodox Development of Reformed Covenant Theology," *Mid-America Journal of Theology* 17 (2006): 36–37.

746 Muller, *Post-Reformation Reformed Dogmatics*, 1:76–77.

747 R. A. Muller, "Calvin on Christ's Satisfaction and Its Efficacy," in *Calvin and the Reformed Tradition*, 70–106.

748 Ibid., 73.

749 Ibid., 74.

750 Ibid., 75.

demonstrated, the term "sufficiency" is also ambiguous in Reformed theology. The question Muller has to answer with respect to Kennedy's work is simply, Did Calvin believe Christ suffered for all the sins of all people or for the sins of the elect alone?

This question is not anachronistic at all. Contrary to Helm and many high Calvinists on Calvin's view of the extent of the atonement, one should not assume that if Calvin did not debate a given subject, one cannot know whether Calvin held a position on that subject. Aquinas did not debate limited atonement, but nonetheless he held a position: unlimited atonement.

Muller errs when he avers:

> The problem for the doctrine of "limited atonement," therefore, lies in the fact that the sixteenth and early seventeenth-century debate concerned neither the objective sacrificial death of Christ considered as the atonement or *expiatio* offered to God for the price of sin, upon which all parties in the debate were agreed, or the unlimited value, worth, merit, power. Or "sufficiency" of the *satisfactio*, upon which all parties were also agreed, nor precisely, indeed, the limited *efficacia* or *applicatio*, inasmuch as all parties to the debate denied universal salvation.[751]

The issue was very much debated, as Davenant's writings make clear. The nature of the sufficiency had been redefined in the revision of the Lombardian formula, a point Muller overlooks.

My evaluation of Muller's treatment of Calvin's understanding of the extent question can be found in the section on Calvin above.

Robert Letham (b. AD 1947)

Letham is a Presbyterian, former pastor, and theologian who teaches systematic theology at the Wales Evangelical School of Theology. He has authored two significant works relating to the atonement and its extent[752] and advocates limited atonement. I have engaged at some length Letham's treatment of Calvin's view of the extent question in that section above, hence a limited treatment here.

Letham is rightly concerned about the dangers of the so-called covenant of redemption:

> To describe the relations of the three persons of the trinity as a covenant, or to affirm that there was a need for them to enter into covenantal—even

751 Ibid., 76.

752 R. Letham, *The Work of Christ: Contours of Christian Theology* (Downers Grove, IL: InterVarsity, 1993); idem, *The Westminster Assembly: Reading Its Theology in Historical Context* (Phillipsburg, NJ: P&R, 2009).

> contractual—arrangements is to open the door to heresy. . . . For all the good intentions of those who proposed it, the construal of the relations of the three persons of the Trinity in covenantal terms is a departure from classic Trinitarian orthodoxy.[753]

This is quite a strong statement on Letham's part concerning this aspect of federal Calvinism's theology. As we have seen, John Owen relied heavily on the covenant of redemption in support of limited atonement. Removal of this pillar of support severely weakens it.

Michael Horton (b. AD 1964)

Horton is the J. Gresham Machen Professor of Systematic Theology at Westminster West Seminary. He is also host of the weekly radio broadcast *White Horse Inn* and editor-in-chief of *Modern Reformation* magazine. Horton is an ardent defender of limited atonement.

Horton's *The Christian Faith* relies heavily on the concept of the covenant of redemption as an argument for limited atonement.[754] Three main answers to the extent question have been given in church history. The first is universalism, which Horton rejected. The second is that Christ died "to make salvation of every human possible." Horton identified this view with the Arminians and the Hypothetical Universalists. The third view "is that Christ died for all of the sins of the elect, thereby redeeming them at the cross." Horton prefers the term "particular redemption" rather than "limited atonement" for this view, which he affirms.[755]

Horton listed two major arguments for particular redemption: (1) it emphasizes the relationship between the Trinity and redemption, and (2) it emphasizes the efficacy and objectivity of Christ's saving work. With respect to the former, Horton relies on the covenant of redemption. He cited Eph 1:4–13; 2 Thess 2:13, 14; and Titus 3:5–8 as "explicit passages on this eternal pact."[756] Yet not a single one of these passages supports the notion of a covenant of redemption.

Furthermore, he attempted to use Rom 8:32–36; John 10:11, 15; Acts 20:28; Eph 5:25–27; and Matt 1:21 to support Christ's "intention to redeem his elect."[757] Here Horton has made two mistakes. First, he is extracting from these verses an abstract notion of the elect, lumping them all together as the believing elect and those who will believe at some point in the future. However, the New Testament always speaks of the elect as the body of believers as redeemed, never in the abstract of the elect as both

753 Letham, *The Westminster Assembly*, 236.
754 M. Horton, *The Christian Faith* (Grand Rapids, MI: Zondervan, 2011), 516–20.
755 Ibid., 516–17.
756 Ibid., 518.
757 Ibid.

believing and unbelieving. Second, Horton is committing the negative inference fallacy by assuming that since Christ is said to redeem a certain group of people, then Christ did not die for those not a part of these groups.

Horton's second argument for particular redemption concerning the efficacy and objectivity of Christ's saving work failed to distinguish properly between the intent, extent, and application of the atonement. Horton thinks that particular redemption does not limit the sufficiency of the atonement. "With the New Testament, advocates of particular redemption can cheerfully proclaim, 'Christ died for sinners,' 'Christ died for the world,' and 'Christ's death is sufficient for you,' acknowledging also with the Scriptures that the assurance 'Christ died for you' is to be given only to believers."[758] This is of course an understanding of sufficiency as hypothetical and intrinsic only; it is sufficient to pay for your sins *if God had so intended it to do so*, but God did not intend it do so for the non-elect, hence in reality, it is only truly sufficient for the elect.

In his *Putting Amazing Back into Grace*,[759] Horton attempted to connect some patristic writers to limited atonement, along with Luther. It appears Horton has confused the fact that these men are arguing against universalism, not a universal atonement.

Horton's historiographical method with respect to the patristics on the atonement's extent is so sloppy as to be embarrassing. There are no footnote references with which to check the quotations or their context. Most of his quotations don't support limited atonement in any way. Horton seems to be reading Reformed theology back into the writings of the church fathers.

Horton quoted Justin Martyr as saying:

> He endured the sufferings for those men whose souls are [actually] purified from all iniquity. . . . As Jacob served Laban for the cattle that were spotted, and of various forms, so Christ served even to the cross for men of every kind, of many and various shapes, procuring them by His blood and the mystery of the cross.[760]

The quotation comes from Justin's *Dialogue with Trypho*. For some reason, Horton has inserted the word "actually" into the text in brackets. The word does not appear in the original quotation. In addition, Horton has strung together two sets of texts from entirely different chapters, separated by the ellipsis.

The first part of the quote comes from chapter 41 where Justin talks about the offering of fine flour in the Old Testament being a figure of the Lord's Supper. The second

758 Ibid., 519.

759 M. Horton, *Putting Amazing Back into Grace*, 2nd ed. (Grand Rapids, MI: Baker, 2002), 290–95.

760 Ibid., 244.

part of the quotation comes from chapter 134. Here Justin stated the two marriages of Jacob were types of Christ and his death for Jews (Leah) and Gentiles (Rachel). For both of these, according to Justin, "Christ even now serves," which is a statement concerning the atonement. Rather than supporting limited atonement, the passage actually serves to support unlimited atonement.

Horton quoted Tertullian as saying: "Christ died for the salvation of His people . . . for the church." Nowhere in the writings of Tertullian does one find this exact quote. Horton appears to be drawing upon Gill's commentary on Tertullian at this point, where Tertullian is writing against Marcion. The context is a reference to Moses's willingness to sacrifice himself for the sin of the people when they had constructed the golden calf.[761] Nowhere in the actual quote does Tertullian say "His people" as in the Horton version. This is a reading of later Reformed theology into Tertullian. The passage in question does not even concern the extent of the atonement.

With respect to Cyprian, Horton cited this quotation:

> All the sheep which Christ hath sought up by His blood and sufferings are saved . . . Whosoever shall be found in the blood, and with the mark of Christ shall only escape . . . He redeemed the believers with the price of His own blood . . . Let him be afraid to die who is not reckoned to have any part in the cross and sufferings of Christ.[762]

I cannot locate this quotation anywhere in Cyprian's writings. It appears once again that Horton is dependent upon John Gill as a secondary source. The use of ellipses appears to indicate that Horton has taken individual statements from Cyprian, not just from the same work but from different works, and connected them apart from context. The words "are saved" in the first statement appear to be inserted into the quotation by Horton. For example, the first statement appears to be taken from Cyprian's letter to Father Stephanus: "For although we are many shepherds, yet we feed one flock, and ought to collect and cherish all the sheep which Christ by His blood and passion sought for."[763]

The second statement likely comes from Cyprian's letter to Demetrianus:

> What previously proceeded by a figure in the slain lamb is fulfilled in Christ, the truth which followed afterwards. As, then, when Egypt was smitten, the Jewish people could not escape except by the blood and the sign of the lamb;

761 Ibid., 245.

762 Ibid.

763 See Cyprian, "To Father Stephanus, Concerning Marcianus of Arles, Who Had Joined Himself to Novatian," in *ANF*, 5:369.

> so also, when the world shall begin to be desolated and smitten, whoever is found in the blood and the sign of Christ alone shall escape.[764]

By the "sign of Christ," Cyprian is referring to baptism.

The third statement in Horton's quotation of Cyprian comes from a different part of his letter to Demetrianus: "He redeemed believers with the price of His own blood." The final statement in Horton's quotation is taken from *On the Mortality*. The context concerns the fate of the unbaptized when they die and says nothing about the extent of the atonement.

Horton quoted Eusebius's *Demonstratio Evangelical Book 7*: "To what 'us' does he refer, unless to them that believe in Him? For to them that do not believe in Him, He is the author of their fire and burning. The cause of Christ's coming is the redemption of those that were to be saved by Him."[765]

This quotation is also a conflation of statements from different contexts and is not even an exact quotation of Eusebius's words. Eusebius's point is that Christ has brought salvation to the believing Gentiles and given them the Eucharist, but to those who remain unbelieving, Christ brings condemnation. There is nothing in the context that speaks to the extent of the atonement, much less affirms a limited atonement.

In fact, the third sentence in Horton's quotation comes from a different section that has the following statement in it: "And we say distinctly that the Word of God was He that was sent as the Saviour of all men." Contextually, Eusebius is actually affirming an unlimited atonement.

Horton turned to Jerome with this quotation:

> Christ is sacrificed for the salvation of believers . . . Not all are redeemed, for not all shall be saved, but the remnant . . . All those who are redeemed and delivered by Thy blood return to Zion, which Thou hast prepared for Thyself by Thine own blood . . . Christ came to redeem Zion [a metaphor for the church] with His blood. But lest we should think that all are Zion or every one in Zion is truly redeemed of the Lord, who are redeemed by the blood of Christ form the Church . . . He did not give His life for every man, but for many, that is, for those who would believe.[766]

Notice the ellipses. Once again, Horton has conflated a number of statements from different locations in Jerome. It also appears that Horton is dependent upon Gill at this point. Horton misses the context of the Lord's Supper in which Jerome

764 Cyprian, "Treatise V, An Address to Demetrianus," 5:464.
765 Horton, *Putting Amazing Back into Grace*, 245.
766 Ibid., 246–47.

makes the statement about Christ being sacrificed "for the salvation of believers." The final statement in the quotation is not a reference to the actual extent of the atonement but rather to the intent and application. Only those who believe will benefit from the atonement.

Robert Peterson (b. AD 1944) and Michael D. Williams (b. circa AD 1960)

Peterson and Williams co-authored *Why I Am Not an Arminian*, published in 2004. They correctly point out that modern-day Arminians who reject substitutionary atonement err. They then err themselves in arguing that limited atonement is an implication of substitutionary atonement. As noted above, this argument has been answered numerous times by leading Calvinists from the sixteenth century onward.

Peterson and Williams state something that few Calvinists who affirm limited atonement have been willing to state. They rightly point out that adducing such passages where Christ is said to have died for his "sheep" or his "church" are weak arguments for limited atonement since these passages cannot be interpreted to mean Christ did not die for others.[767] They also consider it weak to argue that election entails limited atonement. The case for limited atonement must be made from Scripture and not systematic theology.[768] This is an interesting point since more recent attempts to support limited atonement are based more in systematic theology and less in exegesis of the relevant passages.

Their case for limited atonement is threefold: Trinitarian harmony, exclusion passages, and efficacy passages. On the basis of Eph 1:3–14, the Trinitarian work of redemption "implies a definite or limited atonement." How and why this is the case from the passage itself, the authors do not say. They immediately link to John 17 and Jesus's high priestly prayer. Since Jesus prays only for the "elect" (a disputed point, as we have noted), it is logical to conclude that he died only for the elect.[769] Again, this argument has been answered by numerous Calvinists throughout history, as noted above.

Their second argument concerned exclusions in substitutionary atonement passages. The authors appeal to John 10, where Jesus lays down his life for the "sheep" and then stated, "You do not believe because you are not my sheep."[770] This fails to recognize that the text also states that the reason some were not Christ's sheep is their own unbelief. The passage says nothing about the extent of the atonement. The authors likewise appeal to John 17 where Jesus prays only for those who believe.[771]

The third argument is the efficacy of the work of the cross. Based on Rev 5:9, the

767 R. Peterson and M. Williams, *Why I Am Not an Arminian* (Downers Grove, IL: InterVarsity, 2004), 202.
768 Ibid., 202–3.
769 Ibid., 204–5.
770 Ibid., 205.
771 Ibid.

authors argued that Christ's atonement does not make salvation potential, but actual. From this passage, the authors set out a hermeneutical paradigm to interpret all the other passages on the extent of the atonement that make use of "world" and "all" in an effort to argue these words mean "all without distinction" rather than "all without exception."[772] This argument likewise has already been addressed above.

Peterson and Williams admitted their struggle with John 3:16 when it comes to limited atonement. They understand the passage to teach that "God assumes a saving posture toward his fallen world. When asked how we reconcile these passages with those that teach God's special love for the elect, we admit that our theology contains rough edges."[773]

R. Larry Shelton (b. circa AD 1941)

Shelton is professor emeritus at George Fox Evangelical Seminary in Portland, Oregon. His 2006 *Cross and Covenant: Interpreting the Atonement for 21st Century Mission* addresses the issue of the atonement from a non-Calvinist perspective.[774] We include Shelton in the discussion because of his discussion of the penal substitutionary and governmental aspects of the atonement.

Penal substitution interprets the acquittal of the sinner through the atonement either in terms of penalty transfer or as a payment of satisfaction to God. Limited atonement allows "justice to quantify the amount of merit needed to balance the celestial books with the merits contributed by the death of Christ."[775] Shelton seems to think that the only other option under a penal substitutionary scheme is universalism, since the merits of Christ are infinite in value. Shelton finds it difficult to hold together penal substitution and limited atonement.

Shelton mentioned H. Orton Wiley's view that penal substitution leads either to unconditional election or universalism.[776] Govermentalists view the atonement in some sense as penal, but "not in the more commercial sense seen in the doctrine of limited atonement."[777]

Shelton asserted that after Dort, the principle of love became subordinated to justice in Reformed theologians. How can forgiveness be applied when sin's penalty has already been paid? If one affirms a universal atonement, then universalism ensues. Limited atonement is the only logical solution. This shifts the basis of the atonement from love to justice.[778]

---

772 Ibid., 206–7.
773 Ibid., 212.
774 R. L. Shelton, *Cross and Covenant: Interpreting the Atonement for 21st Century Mission* (Tyrone, GA: Paternoster, 2006).
775 Ibid., 174.
776 Ibid., 189.
777 Ibid., 190; citing H. R. Dunning, *Grace, Faith and Holiness* (Kansas City, MO: Beacon Hill, 1988), 336–37.
778 Shelton, *Cross and Covenant,* 199.

Shelton has a point about scholastic high Calvinism that often became immersed in a commercial understanding of the atonement, but his point does not apply nearly so much to moderate Calvinists who reject a limited atonement. Shelton mentioned Calvin as one who taught the atonement was couched in legal categories yet motivated by love.[779] Shelton noted how Grotius, after attempting to modify the penal view because of its association with limited atonement, became an Arminian.[780]

G. Michael Thomas (b. circa AD 1966)

In recent years, several significant scholarly works have appeared that address the question of the extent of the atonement. Two of these are historical treatments of the question within Reformed theology, through roughly the end of the seventeenth century, and both acknowledge a significant strain of Reformed theologians who rejected limited atonement.

G. Michael Thomas's *The Extent of the Atonement: A Dilemma for Reformed Theology from Calvin to the Consensus 1536–1675*[781] is a book that should be read by all interested in this discussion. It demonstrates beyond doubt that many within the early Reformed tradition did not adhere to limited atonement and taught that Christ died for the sins of all people.

Since this work has been referenced many times in the sections dealing with the first generation of Reformers through the time of the Westminster Assembly, more will not be said here. Suffice it to say that Thomas's work is one of the most significant books historically dealing with the Reformed views on the extent of the atonement through 1675.

Jonathan David Moore (b. circa AD 1975)

Jonathan Moore's *English Hypothetical Universalism: John Preston and the Softening of Reformed Theology*[782] made the historical point that the famous Puritan John Preston held to unlimited atonement, along with many fellow Puritans.

Richard Muller's review of Moore's book contains important insights on the historical issue of the extent of the atonement. As Muller stated, "Moore resuscitates an issue recognized in the seventeenth century by Davenant, Baxter, and others, and noted with reference to the Westminster Assembly by Alexander Mitchell that there was an indigenous hypothetical universalism in British Reformed theology."[783]

779 Ibid., 199–200.

780 Ibid., 202.

781 G. M. Thomas, *The Extent of the Atonement: A Dilemma for Reformed Theology from Calvin to the Consensus 1536–1675* (Carlisle, UK: Paternoster, 2006).

782 J. Moore, *English Hypothetical Universalism* (Grand Rapids: Eerdmans, 2007).

783 R. Muller, "Review of *English Hypothetical Universalism: John Preston and the Softening of Reformed Theology*," *Calvin Theological Journal* 43 (2008): 149–50.

However, according to Muller, Moore's study contains two significant flaws, the second of which impinges on the discussion at hand. Moore

> underestimates the presence of non-Amyraldian or non-speculative forms of hypothetical universalism in the Reformed tradition as a whole and thereby, in the opinion of this reviewer, misconstrues Preston's position as a "softening" of Reformed theology rather than as a continuation of one trajectory of Reformed thought that had been present from the early sixteenth century onward. Clear statements of nonspeculative hypothetical universalism can be found (as Davenant recognized) in Heinrich Bullinger's *Decades* and commentary on the *Apocalypse*, in Wolfgang Musculus' *Loci communes*, in Ursinus' *catechetical lectures*, and in Zanchi's *Tractatus de praedestinatione sanctorum*, among other places. In addition, the Canons of Dort, in affirming the standard distinction of a sufficiency of Christ's death for all and its efficiency for the elect, actually refrain from canonizing either the early form of hypothetical universalism or the assumption that Christ's sufficiency serves only to leave the nonelect without excuse. Although Moore can cite statements from the York conference that Dort "either apertly or covertly denied the universality of man's redemption" (156), it remains that various of the signatories of the Canons were hypothetical universalists—not only the English delegation (Carleton, Davenant, Ward, Goad, and Hall) but also the [*sic*] some of the delegates from Bremen and Nassau (Martinius, Crocius, and Alsted)—that Carleton and the other delegates continued to affirm the doctrinal points of Dort while distancing themselves from the church discipline of the Belgic Confession, and that in the course of seventeenth-century debate even the Amyraldians were able to argue that their teaching did not run contrary to the Canons. In other words, the nonspeculative, non-Amyraldian form of hypothetical universalism was new in neither the decades after Dort nor a "softening" of the tradition: The views of Davenant, Ussher, and Preston followed out a resident trajectory long recognized as orthodox among the Reformed.[784]

This rather lengthy quote is crucial for the discussion at hand. Note especially Muller's statement that Preston's universalism is not a "softening" of the Reformed tradition with respect to the extent of the atonement but rather "a continuation of one trajectory of Reformed thought that had been present from the early sixteenth century onward." At the very least, this statement affirmed that at the very beginning of Reformed theology, there was a "trajectory" that held to universal atonement.

Muller asserted the same three years later:

784 Ibid.

> Given that there was a significant Hypothetical Universalist trajectory in the Reformed tradition from its beginnings, it is arguably less than useful to describe its continuance as a softening of the tradition. More importantly, the presence of various forms of hypothetical universalism as well as various approaches to a more particularistic definition renders it rather problematic to describe the tradition as "on the whole" particularistic and thereby to identify hypothetical universalism as a dissident, subordinate stream of the tradition, rather than as one significant stream (or, perhaps two!) among others, having equal claim to confessional orthodoxy.[785]

If, as asserted above, Calvin and Bucer did not hold to limited atonement (and if the same holds true for John Bradford), then among the first generation of Reformers on the continent and in England, unlimited atonement was actually the only game in town. Limited atonement does not begin to develop until the time of Beza in the late sixteenth century, after the death of Calvin.

Tom Barnes (b. circa AD 1961)

Barnes is a pastor and theology instructor whose *Atonement Matters* was published in 2008.[786] It is a popular treatment of the subject and argues for a strictly limited atonement. Barnes approached the topic from a biblical, theological, and practical angle. He is heavily dependent upon secondary sources, especially in his chapter covering the history of definite atonement. Consequently, he mistakenly identified many in church history as proponents of definite atonement who actually held to unlimited atonement.

Several problems with this book become evident in the introduction. For example, Barnes stated concerning general atonement: "This view argues that Christ died potentially for all persons without exception."[787] Clearly this is a misstatement. What he meant to say, as evident from the very next sentence, is that Christ died for all persons such that it is possible that all people can be saved. This is indeed what general atonement means. Barnes also misunderstood the Lombardian formula when he said it does not explicitly affirm unlimited atonement.[788]

Barnes made use of the standard arguments in favor of limited atonement, chiefly the intent-determines-extent argument and the double payment argument where substitutionary atonement is thought to entail limited atonement.

---

785 R. Muller, "Diversity in the Reformed Tradition: A Historiographical Introduction," in *Drawn into Controversie*, 24–25.

786 T. Barnes, *Atonement Matters* (Webster, NY: Evangelical, 2008).

787 Ibid., 22.

788 Ibid., 25.

Carl Trueman (b. AD 1967)

Trueman is professor of church history at Westminster Theological Seminary in Philadelphia. In his highly readable chapter, "Post-Reformation Developments in the Doctrine of the Atonement," Trueman laid out four main challenges to the classic Reformed position on the atonement expressed in the Heidelberg and Belgic Confessions: (1) Catholicism, (2) Arminianism, (3) Amyraldianism, and (4) Socinianism.

He raised the right question concerning the well-meant gospel offer if limited atonement is correct.[789] Trueman believes that the attempt to ground the well-meant offer in a universal atonement merely shifts the nature of the crucial questions from the atonement to God's intention in the atonement.[790] It seems as if Trueman here failed to distinguish between the intent and extent of the atonement and that he views the two as coextensive. This merely sidesteps the issue and does not answer the problem posed to those who adhere to limited atonement and the well-meant offer. That such is a problem for high Calvinism is admitted by Berkhof:

> It is said that, according to this doctrine, He offers the forgiveness of sins and eternal life to those for whom He has not intended these gifts. It need not be denied that there is a real difficulty at this point, but this is the difficulty with which we are always confronted, when we seek to harmonize the decretive and the perceptive will of God.[791]

Trueman proceeded to contrast the views of John Owen and Richard Baxter on the extent of the atonement. This chapter by Trueman is a very helpful analysis of the differences between Owen and Baxter on the extent question.

Trueman also authored a chapter in a recent, multi-author book on the extent of the atonement (*Perspectives on the Extent of the Atonement: 3 Views*), which will be discussed below.[792]

Kevin DeYoung (b. AD 1977)

DeYoung is a Calvinist pastor and popular author. He briefly addressed the issue of the extent of the atonement in *The Good News We Almost Forgot: Rediscovering the Gospel in a 16th Century Catechism*.[793]

789 C. Trueman, "Post-Reformation Developments in the Doctrine of the Atonement," in *Precious Blood: The Atoning Work of Christ*, ed. R. D. Phillips (Wheaton, IL: Crossway, 2009), 187.

790 Ibid., 189.

791 L. Berkhof, *Systematic Theology*, 462.

792 C. Trueman, "Definite Atonement View," in *Perspectives on the Extent of the Atonement: 3 Views*, ed. A. D. Naselli and M. A. Snoeberger (Nashville: B&H, 2015), 19–79.

793 K. DeYoung, *The Good News We Almost Forgot: Rediscovering the Gospel in a 16th Century Catechism* (Chicago: Moody, 2010), 82–84.

DeYoung quoted Ursinus in defense of limited atonement, not seeming to realize that Ursinus held to unlimited atonement, as has been demonstrated.[794] DeYoung succumbed to the false dilemma fallacy when he asserted: "If the atonement is not particularly and only for the sheep, then either we have universalism—Christ died in everyone's place and therefore everyone is saved—or we have something less than full substitution."[795]

Statements like: "I belabor this point not to belittle Arminian brothers and sisters but to give Jesus Christ His full glory"[796] are especially disconcerting as they express something of an elitist, triumphalist mentality. Do not all those Calvinists who affirm unlimited atonement, not to mention the non-Calvinists and Arminians who affirm it, seek to give Christ his full glory? In fact, many would argue that the unlimited atonement position gives Christ more glory than the limitarian view.

Timothy A. Williams (b. circa AD 1965)

Williams authored *The Heart of Piety: An Encouraging Study of Calvin's Doctrine of Assurance*, originally published in 2010.[797] Though the work is not focused on the extent question, it contains a helpful survey of twentieth-century literature on the extent of the atonement.

Dan Phillips (b. circa AD 1955)

Phillips authored *The World-Tilting Gospel: Embracing a Biblical Worldview and Hanging on Tight*,[798] a popular work that addresses the extent of the atonement in a few places. Phillips did not formally argue for limited atonement, but he appeared to assume it since he spoke consistently of Christ suffering for the sins of "his people," as, for example, in Isa 53:10–12.[799] He spoke of Jesus shattering man's pride "for mankind's own salvation."[800] Here "mankind" cannot refer to all people without exception but only to the elect within mankind, since it is only they for whose sins Christ died. Phillips stated, "Christ died as a substitute for his people,"[801] and "objectively, we saw that Jesus bore the sins of His people on the cross, and thus satisfied the justice of God."[802]

794 Ibid., 82.

795 Ibid., 83. We have already seen how many Calvinists in Reformed history have debunked this false dilemma.

796 Ibid., 84.

797 T. Williams, *The Heart of Piety: An Encouraging Study in Calvin's Doctrine of Assurance* (Raleigh, NC: Lulu, 2012).

798 D. Phillips, *The World-Tilting Gospel: Embracing a Biblical Worldview and Hanging on Tight* (Grand Rapids, MI: Kregel, 2011).

799 Ibid., 111.

800 Ibid., 121.

801 Ibid., 142.

802 Ibid., 145.

Kenneth Stewart (b. circa AD 1950)

Stewart is professor of theological studies at Covenant College in Lookout Mountain, Georgia. His *Ten Myths about Calvinism* was published in 2011.[803] This book deals with the "myths" that are perpetrated by Calvinists and non-Calvinists alike about Calvinism. Among the five reasons Stewart listed for why he wrote this book, one is the observable tendency to extremism in Calvinism.

Stewart demonstrated beyond doubt that the TULIP acrostic cannot be used as a yardstick in measuring what is truly Reformed.[804] He correctly observed the distortion concerning the extent of the atonement that occurs when a myopic focus on the modern TULIP construct rather than engagement with what actually occurred at Dort is the order of the day.[805] With respect to extent, Stewart noted that older Calvinist writers took pains to spell out the various senses and nuances of the extent of the atonement within Reformed theology, while more modern writers often fail to do so.

> Where Calvinist writers today show no such generous interest in defining and articulating their Calvinism, it may be an indication that they have accepted that they are now theologizing for an identifiable Calvinist narrow way, a Calvinism on the margins, rather than for the evangelical Protestant tradition as a whole. Such a tendency, if it in fact exists, represents a dramatic reversal, a self-imposed ghettoization compared even to the nineteenth century.[806]

This book is chock-full of historical analysis concerning Calvinism that is helpful to people on both sides of the theological aisle. His chapter "Recovering Our Bearings: Calvinism in the Twenty-First Century" is an important summary of where Reformed theology is today and the five Reformed "resurgences" from the French Revolution to 1990.[807]

Greg Forster (b. circa AD 1957)

Forster is a Reformed author whose *The Joy of Calvinism* was published in 2012.[808] Forster made it clear he is writing with the assumption that his readership consists of believers: "Throughout this book I speak of the promises of salvation with reference

803 K. Stewart, *Ten Myths About Calvinism* (Downers Grove, IL: InterVarsity, 2011).
804 Ibid., 75–96.
805 Ibid., 89–90.
806 Ibid., 89.
807 Ibid., 270–88.
808 G. Forster, *The Joy of Calvinism: Knowing God's Personal, Unconditional, Irresistible, Unbreakable Love* (Wheaton, IL: Crossway, 2012).

to 'you,' as in, 'when Jesus died and rose again, he saved you,'[809]—on the assumption that you, the reader, possess those promises."[810] But this way of expressing things is problematic. It implies salvation at the cross for the elect.

It is surprising to find Forster expressing pointblank that Calvinism itself implies no position one way or the other whether God loves the lost. He stated that Westminster took no position on it but that Dort explicitly endorsed God's love for the lost.[811] This is a misreading of historic Calvinism, as both Dort and Westminster imply God's universal love for all.[812]

Even more problematic is Forster's statement, "But I think there is another reason we tend to shrink from seeing God's love as personal. It's because God doesn't save every person."[813] Forster continued:

> But we could not say that Jesus's saving love—the love that does the work of salvation—was exercised on behalf of the lost. In fact, since Jesus knows the lost every bit as completely and as intimately as he knows his own people, the exclusion of the lost from Jesus's saving work would also have to be a personal exclusion. . . . We recoil in horror—I do as much as you—from this thought. . . . Because God is all-powerful, whatever he tries to do must succeed. Any "solution" to a theological problem that pictures God attempting to do something and failing must go right out the window. Whatever work God sets his hand to must be effective. . . . So the only way to solve this problem is to say that God's saving love is not directed at individuals personally. If we want to say God does not exclude specific individuals personally, then we must also say he does not save specific individuals personally. If the saving is personal, the excluding must also be personal. Therefore if we want God's saving work to be universal, it cannot be personal.

This statement indicates Forster's belief that if God intended for Christ to die for all people, then all people must be saved or God fails in his intention. This buys into a commercial theory of the atonement with its attendant problems, as we have seen previously. The universal atonement/personal salvation dichotomy is a false dilemma.

Forster misunderstood and misconstrued God's love and its dimensions even as expressed by those within his own Reformed tradition. To say that all other theological traditions other than Reformed theology operate on an approach to saving love that

809 Ibid, 47. This is one of the chapter subtitles in the book, following the title "God Loves You Personally."

810 Ibid., 27.

811 Ibid., 39.

812 See W. G. T. Shedd, *Calvinism: Pure & Mixed* (Edinburgh: Banner of Truth, 1986), 22–24.

813 Forster, *Joy of Calvinism*, 50.

does not and cannot embrace people as individuals rests on the assumptions that his notion of God's love is accurate, and it presumes that libertarian free will cannot enter into the equation—assumptions that would be rejected by all non-Calvinists. Forster's logic is as follows:

> If God's love is for all people, then either they're all saved (which we know is not true), or God's work fails in its purpose (which we also know is not true). God's saving love is either a personal love that embraces some people and not others, or it is not a personal love at all.[814]

Forster also trades on a confusion about Jesus's saving work on the cross as being "available versus effective."[815] Unless Forster wants to assert regeneration at the cross, he must affirm that salvation is made possible, even for the unbelieving elect, until they believe, at which point it becomes effective.

Forster's dependence on a commercial theory of the atonement is seen in his language, such as "Jesus purchased for you a place in God's kingdom,"[816] and his belief that in all traditions apart from Calvinism, "Jesus did his saving work impersonally," which "comes squarely into conflict with any meaningful concept of substitutionary atonement."[817] When he stated, "If Jesus died for all people and his death removed the sins of those for whom he died, everyone must be saved," he demonstrates his adherence to Owen's commercialism.

In fact, Forster can't escape his own logic here any more than Owen was able to escape his. Forster clearly stated, "Jesus died and rose again for you personally. And when he did, he actually saved you, personally. The actual saving happens at the cross and the empty tomb."[818] This is the hyper-Calvinism error of justification at the cross.

Further example of the sloppiness of Forster's thinking is evidenced when he stated: "Jesus made atonement only for the sins of those who are actually saved. If Jesus makes atonement for your sins, you are in fact, saved; therefore if you are not saved, he did not make atonement for your sins."[819] Has Forster completely forgotten about the unbelieving elect? Any number of unsaved readers might be reading his book who, in Forster's own system, are among the elect, meaning at some point in the future, they will indeed be saved. Thus, it is inaccurate and, in fact, false, to assert "if you are not saved, he did not make atonement for your sins."

Forster's last paragraph in the book is perhaps the most telling of all. In an effort to

---

814 Ibid., 52–53.
815 Ibid., 53.
816 Ibid., 55.
817 Ibid., 56.
818 Ibid., 58–59.
819 Ibid., 66.

magnify the glory of God, he goes to an unhealthy extreme in denigrating not only the bride of Christ but even God's character itself.

> With this picture we will never feel quite at home with the supreme love that saves us. We will always carry around the knowledge that in standing before a holy God, we are—and always will be, second rate. We are saved not because God loved us so much that he reordered everything in the universe for the sake of our salvation, but because he was able (fortunately!) to squeeze us into his agenda, to fit in our salvation with the other more important things he had going in the universe. We are not the crowning glory of God, but merely one of the gems in the cosmic crown of nature—and a gem that, in God's view, didn't need to be there.[820]

Terrance Tiessen (b. circa AD 1944)

Tiessen is a Reformed theologian and professor emeritus of systematic theology and ethics at Providence Seminary in Ontario. In a March 15, 2012, blog post[821] he explained how he had moved away from the limited atonement position as a result of his interaction with David Ponter.

In his book *Who Can Be Saved?: Reassessing Salvation in Christ and World Religions*,[822] Tiessen had argued the limited atonement position. His explanation of his personal journey away from limited atonement is interesting reading. Tiessen now affirms the classical moderate position on the extent of the atonement, citing Bruce Demarest's approach in his *The Cross and Salvation*.[823] Tiessen, like all moderate Calvinists, now agrees with Arminians on the specific issue of the extent of the atonement.

Tiessen now understands the problem with the high-Calvinist approach to the sufficiency question. He affirmed Calvin, Charles Hodge, and others within the Reformed tradition as adherents to unlimited atonement and rejected Owen's double payment argument.

Robert Peterson (b. circa AD 1949)

Peterson is professor of systematic theology at Covenant Theological Seminary in St. Louis, Missouri, where he has taught since 1990. He has authored many works related to the atonement, including *Calvin and the Atonement* and *Why I Am Not an*

---

820 Ibid., 153–54.

821 T. Tiessen, "For Whom Did Christ Die?," *Thoughts Theological: From the Pen of Terrance L. Tiessen* (blog), March 15, 2012, http://www.thoughtstheological.com/for-whom-did-Christ-die/.

822 T. Tiessen, *Who Can Be Saved?: Reassessing Salvation in Christ and World Religions* (Downers Grove, IL: InterVarsity, 2004).

823 B. Demarest, *The Cross and Salvation: The Doctrine of Salvation*, Foundations of Evangelical Theology, ed. J. S. Feinberg (Wheaton, IL: Crossway, 1997), 193.

Arminian, which he co-authored with colleague Michael Williams.[824] His *Salvation Accomplished by the Son: The Work of Christ* is his latest work on the atonement and is quite well done overall.[825]

Peterson's main line of thought with respect to the extent of the atonement is as follows: "Substitution implies efficacy, which implies particularity." "If this saving work is substitutionary, there are only two possibilities: either it is universal and everyone is saved, or it is particular and all whom God has chosen are saved. Universalism is unbiblical, therefore particularity is established."[826] In an appendix on the extent of the atonement, which originally appeared in *Why I Am Not an Arminian*, Peterson asserted his main point: limited atonement is an implication of substitutionary atonement.[827]

Peterson correctly noted that limited atonement, to be true, must not only be systematically consistent with Calvinism but must also be taught in Scripture, and the case must be made from Scripture and not only systematic theology. Peterson found support for limited atonement in Eph 5:25 and John 10:15.[828] But when talking about Christ's "sheep" or his "church," it is not at all unusual that Jesus and other biblical authors would say Christ died for them. This in no way implies or entails he did not die for others.

Peterson understands election to entail limited atonement. Actually, Calvinistic election only entails an intent to apply the atonement only to the elect, not an atonement exclusively *limited* to those who are elect.

For Peterson, limited atonement is implied in some passages that speak of Christ's substitutionary death. He found three evidences for limited atonement: Trinitarian harmony, exclusion passages, and efficacy passages.

An example of an exclusion passage is John 10:26: "Jesus follows his statements about dying for his sheep by a stark denial that some are his sheep. It would be difficult to maintain that he lays down his life to save them, for he has just excluded them from the number of his sheep."[829] Another exclusion passage is John 17, where, according to Peterson, Jesus did not pray for the world.

Concerning the efficacy of the atonement, Peterson asked whether the atonement makes salvation possible or effective. But this creates a false dichotomy. The atonement does both.

Peterson appealed to Rev 5:9 in support of limited atonement, but the verse says nothing about the extent of the atonement, only about the extent of the application.

---

824 R. Peterson, *Calvin and the Atonement* (Fearn, Scotland: Mentor, 1999); Peterson and Williams, *Why I Am Not an Arminian.*

825 R. Peterson, *Salvation Accomplished by the Son: The Work of Christ* (Wheaton, IL: Crossway, 2012).

826 Ibid., 410–11. The same argument is developed by A. T. B. McGowan, "The Atonement as Penal Substitution," in *Always Reforming: Explorations in Systematic Theology*, ed. A. T. B. McGowan (Downers Grove, IL: InterVarsity, 2006), 183–210.

827 Ibid., 566–75.

828 Ibid., 566–67.

829 Ibid., 570. Also in Peterson and Williams, *Why I Am Not an Arminian*, 205.

Since Peterson can find a few places where "world" is not used to denote "all without exception," he makes the unjustified move to interpret "world" in the atonement passages in a collective rather than a distributive sense.

Peterson's honest attempt to grapple with the tensions within his own theology is laudatory. He agreed with Arminians concerning John 3:16 and similar texts that speak of God's love for every person.

> We understand these passages to teach that God assumes a saving posture toward his fallen world. When asked how we reconcile these passages with those that teach God's special love for the elect, we admit that our theology contains rough edges. But we would rather have an imperfect theology and be faithful to the whole witness of Scripture than to mute the voice of some texts as Calvinists have sometimes done (John 3:16 and similar passages) and as Arminians do (the texts that teach God's special love for the elect).[830]

Peterson spoke of two types of biblical passages concerning the cross: those that speak of God's loving stance toward an evil world and others that speak of God's "effective love only for the elect." Peterson suggested the Scripture itself holds the two types of passages in creative tension, so he feels justified in doing so in his own theology.[831]

In reality, no tension exists. God loves the world, Jesus died for the sins of the world, and Jesus calls to himself all those who genuinely believe in him (the elect). The special love Jesus has for those who are his children is exhibited in how he relates to them and what he bestows upon them.

Myk Habets (b. circa AD 1966) and Bobby Grow (b. circa AD 1979)

Habets and Grow edited a multi-author volume published in 2012 entitled *Evangelical Calvinism: Essays Resourcing the Continuing Reformation of the Church*.[832] This work is one of the more important publications by moderate Calvinists in recent years. It charts the various Reformed theologies, identified by Habets and Grow as classical, federal, and evangelical. The work perfectly illustrates the diversity, both past and current, within Reformed theology with respect to the so-called five points of Calvinism.

The authors are concerned about the more mainstream forms of Calvinism today that tend to subordinate grace to nature, render the justice of God essential but the love of God arbitrary, and affirm a limited atonement, which is contrary to the plain sense of Scripture and is divorced from the doctrine of the incarnation.[833]

---

830 Ibid., 574.

831 Ibid., 575.

832 M. Habets and B. Grow, eds., *Evangelical Calvinism: Essays Resourcing the Continuing Reformation of the Church* (Eugene, OR: Pickwick, 2012).

833 Ibid., 10–12.

Habets and Grow map the Reformed topography in three broad areas: conservative Calvinists, represented by the likes of Charles Hodge; liberal Calvinists, represented by Schleiermacher; and Evangelical Calvinists, represented by Karl Barth. The doctrine of Scripture held by conservative Calvinists is mostly rejected by liberal and Evangelical Calvinists.[834] The largest of these three groups is the conservative branch.

Representative of the approach of these authors concerning the problem of limited atonement is Adam Nigh's comment:

> While Evangelical Calvinism discovers in Scripture that Christ died and accomplished atonement for all humanity, it does not affirm universal salvation . . . nor does it back away from the universal reach of Christ's atonement by reading the limited subjective appropriation of atonement on behalf of humanity into the eternal will of God through a doctrine of limited atonement precisely because such conclusions assume a causal necessity determining God's actions that is foreign to the testimony of Scripture and, indeed, to God's being.[835]

Following T. F. Torrance, Myk Habets's chapter expressed concern for "Nestorian tendencies" in the notion of limited atonement with "an overly forensic understanding in which atonement is thought of as a transaction external to God, rather than as the ultimate expression of the love of God for all."[836] Habets does not see how universal atonement leads to universalism without distorting the self-revelation of God as Holy Love, as Torrance had argued.[837] Anything short of a universal atonement circumscribes the incarnation in a way contrary to Scripture.

Jason Goroncy surveyed McLeod Campbell and P. T. Forsyth's atonement views. Calvinists in the seventeenth and eighteenth centuries overly focused on the objective nature of the atonement and its action on God, whereas in Forsyth's day the accent had shifted to an equally distortive subjectivism, according to Goroncy.[838]

In a concluding chapter, Myk Habets and Bobby Grow offer a number of theses to clarify their theology of the atonement's nature and extent.[839] Thesis 2 concerns the primacy of God's triune life as grounded in love, for Scripture teaches "God is

834 Ibid., 25. This basically renders inert claims by those like Al Mohler that Reformed theology preserves conservative Christianity and biblical inerrancy. See M. Worthen, "The Reformer: How Al Mohler Transformed a Seminary, Helped Change a Denomination, and Challenges a Secular Culture," *Christianity Today*, October 1, 2010, http://www.christianitytoday.com/ct/2010/October/3.18.html.

835 A. Nigh, "The Depth Dimension of Scripture," in *Evangelical Calvinism*, 91.

836 M. Habets, "There Is No God behind the Back of Jesus Christ: Christologically Conditioned Election," in *Evangelical Calvinism*, 184.

837 T. F. Torrance, *Scottish Theology: From John Knox to John McLeod Campbell* (Edinburgh: T. & T. Clark, 1996), 277.

838 J. Goroncy, "'*Tha mi a' toirt fainear dur gearan*': J. M. Campbell and P. T. Forsyth on the Extent of Christ's Vicarious Ministry," in *Evangelical Calvinism*, 263.

839 M. Habets and B. Grow, "Theses on a Theme," in *Evangelical Calvinism*, 425–55.

love." Habets and Grow stated it would be wrong to infer from this thesis that they are arbitrarily ranking the divine attributes and placing "love" at the top, as in open theism. "Theological reflection on 1 John 4:8 concerns God as relational and personal-Triune—not as a supreme form of *human* love."[840]

Thesis 3 asserted there is one covenant of grace. Following Calvin, the Scots Confession of 1560 clearly teaches the unity of Scripture based around the idea of a single covenant between God and humanity. Federal Calvinism moved this scriptural organizing principle to a theological systemic principle, with not one but three covenants: covenant of redemption, covenant of works, and covenant of grace.[841]

Thesis 6 asserted that grace precedes law. Federal Calvinism ends up distorting the gospel from good news to a new law.[842] Unlike Federal Calvinism, Evangelical Calvinism refuses to introduce a wedge between grace and law.[843]

Thesis 11 asserted Christ died for all humanity. Failure to accept this "theo-logic" leaves one "with the possibility that Christ could have assumed a particular (elect) humanity that was not truly representative of real sinful humanity which potentially injects Nestorianism into Reformed theology."[844]

Anthony Badger (b. circa AD 1966)

Badger is a graduate of Dallas Theological Seminary and a former pastor and professor at various institutions. His *Confronting Calvinism* was published in 2013.[845] In a chapter on limited atonement, he discussed and briefly responded to passages used to support limited atonement, stated the view of limited atonement, stated the view of unlimited atonement, engaged and negated eight major arguments used for limited atonement, and concluded that biblically one must distinguish between atonement procured and atonement applied. In the former case, Christ died for all; in the latter, the atonement is only applied to those who believe.[846]

David Gibson (b. AD 1975) and Jonathan Gibson (b. AD 1977)

One of the most recent scholarly treatments to advocate a strictly limited atonement is *From Heaven He Came and Sought Her,*[847] appearing in 2013 and edited by David Gibson and Jonathan Gibson. This book has been touted by many in the Reformed tradition as the definitive work on the subject, high praise indeed since such language has usually been reserved for John Owen's famous *Death of Death in the Death of Christ.*

840 Ibid., 429.
841 Ibid., 431.
842 Ibid., 434.
843 Ibid., 435.
844 Ibid., 445.
845 A. Badger, *Confronting Calvinism: A Free Grace Refutation and Biblical Resolution of Radical Reformed Soteriology* (Lancaster, PA: Printed by CreateSpace, An Amazon.com Company, 2013).
846 Ibid., 213–52.
847 Gibson and Gibson, *From Heaven He Came and Sought Her.*

The book includes twenty-three chapters written by a cadre of scholars and is a lengthy tome of seven-hundred three pages, including indices, published by Crossway. Twenty-one authors from a variety of backgrounds (including Presbyterian, Anglican, and Baptist) contribute chapters. The book's chief purpose is to defend the notion of definite atonement (limited atonement) by presenting supportive arguments and attempting to answer counter-arguments.

Because of the significance of this tome, I have provided an in-depth chapter-by-chapter review and critique of *From Heaven He Came and Sought Her* in a later chapter in this work. While the book will likely be too much for some laypeople to digest, I would encourage all theological students, pastors, and scholars to take the time to read and digest it. It is probably the most comprehensive defense of definite atonement available. On the surface it looks formidable, but it has a soft underbelly and is vulnerable to a number of criticisms.

Andrew Naselli (b. circa AD 1981) and Mark Snoeberger (b. circa AD 1972)

Naselli and Snoeberger edited the 2015 volume *Perspectives on the Extent of the Atonement: 3 Views.*[848] This work is the most recent book to address specifically the question of the extent of the atonement from all three major views. Three authors square off on the subject: Carl Trueman defends limited atonement, Grant Osborne defends unlimited atonement from an Arminian perspective, and John Hammett defends unlimited atonement from a multiple-intentions view of the atonement. This volume is a fair and effective presentation of the basic views on the subject.

In the introduction, Snoeberger wrote that the multiple-intention view is not precisely that of Amyraldianism or Hypothetical Universalism, but enough resemblance exists that they can be conflated under one heading.[849] Actually there is nothing new in the multiple-intention view that was not a part of Amyraldianism or Hypothetical Universalism. Among the patristic writers, some asserted multiple intentions in the atonement, and the notion is not foreign to Arminianism either.

Trueman approached the question of the atonement's extent "as an inference drawn from its nature and efficacy."[850] He built his case from the nature of Christ's mediatorial office and the unity between Christ's sacrifice and intercession. From this perspective, the atonement's limited extent is a "necessary inference" of the atonement's nature.

He rightly acknowledged that there is no single text in Scripture that teaches limited atonement. "It is the result of the cumulative force and implications of a series of strands of biblical teaching." Trueman listed two strands undergirding his position: (1) the particular intention of Christ's saving mission and (2) the objective efficacy of Christ's saving work. He then set these two against the biblical background on inten-

848 A. Naselli and M. Snoeberger, eds., *Perspectives on the Extent of the Atonement: 3 Views* (Nashville: B&H, 2015).
849 M. A. Snoeberger, "Introduction," in *Perspectives on the Extent of the Atonement,* 14.
850 C. Trueman, "Definite Atonement View of the Atonement," in *Perspectives on the Extent of the Atonement,* 21.

tion, efficacy, and atonement in Scripture. From this point, he is prepared to address "those texts that seem on the surface to militate against definite atonement."[851]

Though on the surface this approach may seem laudable, upon deeper inspection it appears to place theology before exegesis. Trueman's approach also reveals the fact that while there are no statements in Scripture affirming limited atonement, there are many that overtly affirm unlimited atonement. When push comes to shove, these verses wind up being forced into a limitarian framework in an effort to serve a particular theological scheme, as the other two authors in the book point out.

Trueman's treatment of Kevin Bauder's brief blog post "The Logic of Limited Atonement"[852] is quite revealing. Trueman spoke of Bauder offering a "recent objection" to limited atonement based on a distinction between provision and application. The question here is how Trueman is using the term "recent." If he means recent in that Bauder's post appeared just a few years ago (seven years from the time of the post to the time of Trueman's accessing it), then fine. But if he means that the argument against limited atonement based on a distinction between provision and application is "recent," then Trueman's statement is in error since this argument has been used by Calvinists who reject limited atonement for centuries.

Instead of addressing Bauder's logical points, Trueman merely informed the reader that he approached the matter from a different angle: particularity rather than limitation. However, there is ultimately no distinction between these two when it comes to the actual question, For whose sins did Christ die? Trueman failed to address Bauder's point.

When Bauder asked for a textual example of someone for whom Christ did not die, Trueman responded by appealing to John 17:12, where Christ supposedly excluded Judas from his prayer, and coupled this with 17:9, where Christ does not pray for those whom the Father has not given him. If Trueman's reading of John 17 is shown to be exegetically problematic, as I think has been shown, then Bauder's assertion still stands.

Trueman serves as a good example of how many contemporary limitarians argue the case for limited atonement, and his chapter is clear and concisely written.

Grant Osborne's chapter argued for unlimited atonement, surveying the standard passages that support the position.[853] Trueman found Osborne most lacking in his treatment of Christ's heavenly intercession, which is the very point on which Trueman hangs his hat in support of limited atonement. Most of Trueman's response hinges on this issue.

Hammett developed his view around three intentions for the atonement: universal,

851 Ibid., 23.

852 K. T. Bauder, "The Logic of Limited Atonement," ΤΩ ΧΡΟΝΟΥ ΚΑΙΡΩ: *"In the Nick of Time"* (blog), February 4, 2005, http://seminary.wcts1030.com/publications/Nick/Nick001.htm.

853 G. Osborne, "General Atonement View," in *Perspectives on the Extent of the Atonement*, 81–126.

particular, and cosmic, depending somewhat on Gary Shultz on the subject.[854] He correctly noted that a multiple-intentions approach to the atonement is not new. Hammett's arguments are generally well considered. In his section on "historical considerations," he erred in his assessment of Augustine as a proponent of limited atonement. He also wrongly placed Dabney and Shedd in the particularist camp, apparently overlooking the fact that both men held to universal expiation of sin with a particular intent to apply the atonement only to the elect, in the same vein as Hammett.[855]

Hammett rejected Trueman's notion that universal atonement disrupts the unity between the actual atonement and Christ's intercession. The argument is built on three assumptions: (1) that Christ did in fact die only for the elect, (2) that Christ interceded only for the elect, and (3) that Christ dies for and intercedes for the same number of people. Hammett correctly asserted that these assumptions are simply not supported in Scripture.[856]

Following Shultz, Hammett's appeal to 1 Cor 15:3 and Paul's preaching to the Corinthians before their conversion furnishes a strong argument against limited atonement.[857] Interestingly, this argument has been used in the past by Calvinists who affirm unlimited atonement against their limitarian brothers. The passage is overlooked or ignored in John Owen's *Death of Death in the Death of Christ* and was also overlooked or ignored in the recent book *From Heaven He Came and Sought Her*.

Another strength of Hammett's chapter is his focus on the role of the Holy Spirit in the subjective application of the atonement, a point often receiving little attention from limitarians.[858]

Trueman's response to Hammett is less concerned with dealing with Hammett's actual evidence and more concerned with fostering his notion that Old Testament typology of priesthood determines Christ's priestly work and leads to limited atonement. Trueman wrongly cited Hammett as downplaying the New Testament emphasis that atonement accomplishes the salvation that God intends for the elect.

> The hypothetical universalist must inevitably cut the immediate causal connection between the death of Christ and the actual accomplishment of salvation in the believer, as he must also cut the connection between the purpose of the death of Christ (to provide salvation for all) and the intercession of Christ (to provide salvation for only some).[859]

---

854 See G. Shultz, *A Multi-Intentioned View of the Extent of the Atonement* (Eugene, OR: Wipf & Stock, 2014).
855 J. Hammett, "Multiple Intentions View of the Atonement," in *Perspectives on the Extent of the Atonement*, 161.
856 Ibid., 165–66.
857 Ibid., 168–69.
858 Ibid., 174–76.
859 C. Trueman, "Response," in *Perspectives on the Extent of the Atonement*, 205–6.

I am at a loss to understand Trueman's point in this statement. All must acknowledge a distinction (chronological and otherwise) between the actual accomplishment of the atonement and its application. Would Trueman affirm the hyper-Calvinist error of justification at the cross? Furthermore, Hammett has made his case that there can be more than one purpose in God's intent of the atonement, even from within a Reformed soteriology.

The interaction among Trueman, Osborne, and Hammett is overall very helpful.

Before leaving our discussion of the twenty-first century, a word should be said about popular Calvinist authors who write in such a way as to imply that limited atonement is actually a part of the gospel. Recently a number of books have appeared from Calvinist authors dealing with the subject of "the gospel."

Greg Gilbert's *What Is the Gospel?* spoke eight times in four pages of Christ dying "for his people": "as a substitutionary sacrifice for his people," "for the sins of his people," "out of love for his people he willingly laid down his life, the lamb of God slain so his people could be forgiven." Christ died as the punishment "for his people's sins"; "Jesus bore all the horrible weight of the sin of God's people"; God "saw the sins of his Son's people resting on his shoulders"; "Jesus bore his people's sins and died in their place"; "the answer to all these questions is found at the cross of Calvary, in Jesus' substitutionary death for his people." "Just who are 'his people'?"[860] Gilbert continued in the next chapter to show that those who exercise repentance and faith constitute "his people."

Though Gilbert cited several Scripture passages that speak of Christ dying "for his people," such as Matt 1:21, or Christ dying for the "many," such as Mark 10:45, he mentioned none of the many Scriptures that speak of Christ dying for "all" and for the "world." Gilbert's brief section on the atonement is one-sided. He zeroed in on those passages that would seem to limit the atonement to a specific group of people and ignored those passages that seem to teach Christ died for all people.

When high Calvinists speak or write, as Gilbert, what they mean by "his people" is "elect people." Christ died on the cross for the sins of only "his people"—namely, the elect. Part of the problem here, in addition to a failure to consider the whole of Scripture on the subject, is a misinterpretation of Matt 1:21 by anachronistically retrojecting Reformed theology of the sixteenth and seventeenth centuries into a first-century text. Contextually, "his people" in Matt 1:21 is a reference to Israel, not the abstract body of the elect according to Reformed theology.

Of course, Gilbert is correct that Christ did indeed die for those who will ultimately be saved—that is, those who believe (the elect)—but he also died for the sins of those who will not ultimately be saved. Many other examples could be adduced from modern works by Calvinists.

---

860 G. Gilbert, *What Is the Gospel?* (Wheaton, IL: Crossway, 2010), 66–69.

Conclusion

Many works of a popular nature by Calvinists and non-Calvinists have been published or republished in the twenty-first century.[861] These works to varying degrees usually discuss the extent of the atonement from the TULIP framework, and the discussion is generally brief. It does not appear that interest in Calvinism, and especially the issue of the extent of the atonement, will wane any time soon.

---

861 The following are illustrative but not exhaustive: J. M. Boice and P. G. Ryken, eds., *The Doctrines of Grace* (Wheaton, IL: Crossway, 2002); M. Coate, *A Cultish Side of Calvinism* (Collierville, TN: Innovo, 2011); S. Ferguson, *By Grace Alone* (Lake Mary, FL: Reformation Trust, 2010); D. Johnson, *And the Petals Fall . . . A Rebuttal of TULIP Theology* (n.p., 2010); P. Lumpkins, *What Is Calvinism?* (Carrollton, GA: Free Church, 2013); J. Piper, *Fifty Reasons Why Jesus Came to Die* (Wheaton, IL: Crossway, 2006); R. C. Reed, *The Gospel as Taught by Calvin* (Edinburgh: Banner of Truth, 2009); D. E. Spencer, *TULIP: The Five Points of Calvinism in the Light of Scripture*, 2nd ed. (Grand Rapids, MI: Baker, 2009); J. Williamson, *L of the TULIP: A Case for Particular Redemption* (Baltimore: Publish America, 2009); and Hutson Smelley, *Deconstructing Calvinism: A Biblical Analysis and Refutation*, rev. ed. (Maitland, FL: Xulon, 2009), 149–70.

Part Two

The Extent of the Atonement in the Baptist Tradition

We have surveyed the history of the extent of the atonement from the church fathers through 2015. Part 2 surveys the extent question within Baptist life and thought from the seventeenth century to 2015. I will focus attention on English General and Particular Baptists through the end of the nineteenth century, then survey North American Baptists (excluding Southern Baptists) from ca. 1800 to 2015. At this point, I will turn to what Southern Baptists have said on the extent question from 1845 to 2015.

5

English General and Particular Baptists and the Extent of the Atonement

English Baptists came into existence in the early seventeenth century, birthed out of the English Puritan-Separatist movement. The earliest group, General Baptists, were more Arminian in theology and acquired this designation because they held to unlimited (general) atonement. Approximately thirty years later, the Particular Baptists arose, so designated because they were more Calvinistic in theology and by and largely held to limited atonement. Yet even Particular Baptists were not in lock-step on the issue of the extent of the atonement.[1]

1 W. Estep, following Glen Stassen, claimed that Particular Baptists modified their Calvinism under the influence of Menno Simons's *Foundation Book*, which they quoted in the First London Confession (1644; W. R. Estep, *The Anabaptist Story: An Introduction to Sixteenth-Century Anabaptism*, 3rd rev. ed. [Grand Rapids, MI: Eerdmans, 1996], 301–2; idem, *Why Baptists?: A Study of Baptist Faith and Heritage* [Dallas: Baptist General Convention of Texas, 1997], 49).

General Baptists[2]

What has Anabaptism to do with Arminianism? Perhaps more than most people think. The early English General Baptists certainly held to a theological position similar to what would come to be called Arminianism, with some historians suggesting that these distinctives originated in Arminius himself. William Estep, noted scholar of Anabaptism, suggested that English Anabaptism was clearly Arminian before Arminius.[3]

Jerry Sutton has proffered the suggestion of Anabaptist influence on the rise of the General Baptists via Arminius.[4] Clearly Anabaptism antedated Arminius by almost a century with its theological distinctives from Calvinism.

Sutton surveyed Arminius's interaction with Anabaptists and compared some of the notable Anabaptist leaders' views on soteriology with those of Arminius. Arminius knew of and interacted with Coonhert, who influenced the Dutch Mennonites, especially the Waterlander branch.[5]

In June 1599, the synods of North Holland and South Holland agreed to assign Arminius the task of "confuting" the Anabaptists "from Scriptures." Arminius reluctantly accepted and requested that any Dutch minister with Anabaptist tracts send them to Amsterdam where he could read, evaluate, and refute them. By 1601 Arminius had read all the Anabaptist books he could find, even asking for others to be sent to him that he might not have seen. In 1602 he reported to the North Holland Synod that he had begun the work. Yet Arminius never wrote the full refutation that he had been commissioned to write, and in 1606 he was granted a dismissal from the project.[6]

Sutton conjectured that one possibility as to why Arminius never completed the project was that he found himself in sympathy with the Anabaptists.[7] Anabaptist soteriology was more in line with that of Arminius than the high Calvinism of the Reformed at the beginning of the seventeenth century.

In a 1980 phone conversation Sutton had with noted Arminius scholar Carl Bangs,

2 For a survey of the General Baptists to 1660, consult B. R. White, "The English Baptists of the Seventeenth Century," in *A History of the English Baptists*, vol. 1 (Oxford: Baptist Historical Society, 1996), 15–58. For a survey of General Baptists through the mid-nineteenth century, consult W. Underwood, *The General Baptist Denomination: Its Past History, Distinctive Peculiarities and Present Condition* (Birmingham, AL: Henry James Tresidder, 1864). For a survey of General Baptists until the early nineteenth century, see A. Taylor, *History of the English General Baptists* (London: T. Bore, 1818). For a survey of English Baptists during the nineteenth century, consult J. H. Y. Briggs, "The English Baptists of the 19th Century," in *A History of the English Baptists*, vol. 3 (Oxford: Baptist Historical Society, 1994).

3 Estep, *The Anabaptist Story*, 267–303.

4 J. Sutton, "Anabaptism and James Arminius: A Study in Soteriological Kinship and Its Implications," *Midwestern Journal of Theology* 11 (2012): 54–87.

5 Ibid., 66.

6 Ibid., 66–67.

7 Ibid., 67.

Bangs confirmed that a document had been located in which Arminius did refute the Anabaptists. However, the refutation dealt with periphery matters and had no mention whatsoever of soteriology.[8]

Sutton concluded that a good case can be made that Arminius imbibed and espoused Mennonite and Anabaptist soteriology rather than the other way around. He further concluded: "If Arminius held to Anabaptist soteriology, and the General Baptists advocated Arminian soteriology, logic has it that the General Baptists advocated Anabaptist soteriology through an Arminian filter, so that English General Baptists after all have true Anabaptist roots."[9] This issue is of some significance not only for the discussion at hand but for Baptist history at large.

Thomas Grantham (AD 1634–1692)[10]

Grantham, the foremost English General Baptist of the latter half of the seventeenth century, affirmed unlimited atonement. Grantham had some similarities with Calvinism and some differences with Arminianism, as noted by J. Matthew Pinson.[11] He held to penal substitutionary atonement, as did Arminius. In his *Christianismus Primitivus*, he stated that Christ fulfilled the law by being a substitute "in the place and stead of Mankind."[12] To remedy the sin problem, God designed that Christ should be the physician to cure the malady of the sin of humanity. He did so by providing a plaster commensurate with the sore. As a result, said Grantham,

> none may cry out and say, I am undone, I am wounded with the unavoidable wound of Mankind: And there is no Balm for me, the Physician hath made the Plaister so narrow, that Thousands, and ten Thousands, cannot possibly have Healing by it; nay, he hath determined to see us perish without Remedy. Alas! there is none to save us, neither could we come whole and sound into the World; we are born to be destroyed, and destroyed we must be. To quell which hideous (and indeed most just) complaint . . . we are bid to behold the Lamb of God.[13]

Dan Taylor (AD 1738–1816)

Taylor was the leading General Baptist in his generation and founder of the New Connexion of General Baptists. He published forty-nine books, sermons, tracts, and

8 Ibid., 68.

9 Ibid., 86.

10 Some birth years are only approximations if unavailable.

11 J. M. Pinson, "The Diversity of Arminian Soteriology: Thomas Grantham, John Goodwin, and Jacob Arminius" (paper presented at the national meeting of the American Society of Church History, Florida State University, Tallahassee, FL, Spring 1998).

12 T. Grantham, *Christianismus Primitivus* (London: Printed for F. Smith, 1678), 62.

13 Ibid., 63.

pamphlets. He was famously involved in debate with Andrew Fuller over the nature and extent of the atonement. His support for unlimited atonement is well known.[14]

Since all General Baptists affirmed unlimited atonement, it is not necessary to survey their theological writings and sermons that demonstrate such. W. Underwood explained well the differences between the General Baptists and Particular Baptists in the mid-nineteenth century. Concerning the death of Christ, he stated,

> We believe that the death of Christ was voluntary and vicarious, and that in connection therewith His obedience and sufferings constituted a real atonement, satisfying the Divine law, reconciling the offended God to man and offending man to God; that the whole world, being guilty before God, is under condemnation to eternal death, yet that all penitents who trust in Christ have "redemption through His blood, the forgiveness of sins." But the distinguishing tenet from which we take our name, *general*, which was prefixed to our ancient church covenants, which we have inserted in many of our title-deeds, and which we would gladly "proclaim on the housetops," is *the love of God in Christ to all mankind.*[15]

Underwood contrasted this understanding with that of the Particular Baptists:

> When the high Particular Baptist says that Christ died only for a part of mankind, for his sheep or the Church; and when the lower one says that Christ died for the Church in one sense, and for the world in another, the General Baptist differs from both, . . . When the moderately Calvinistic Particular Baptist says that "redemption, while it *is particular*, has in addition a universal aspect," non-Calvinistic General Baptists are quite dazed with such a duplex presentment of it. When we are told that the Father's love to His offspring is all-embracing, and that the provision made for their salvation by the sacrificial mediation of the Son is unlimited, but that the required application of this salvation by the Holy Spirit is *purposely partial*, we seem to discern unequal sympathy and imperfect unity in the persons of the Godhead; and a trinity so disparate and divided we cannot accept.[16]

General Baptists did not consider themselves Arminians according to Underwood:

---

14 His biographer's description of the debates between Taylor and Fuller on the subject can be found in Adam Taylor, *Memoirs of the Rev. Dan Taylor* (London: Baynes and Son, 1820), 172–82.

15 W. Underwood, *The General Baptist Denomination, Its Past History, Distinctive Peculiarities, and Present Position* (London: Henry James Tresidder, 1864), 12 (emphasis in original).

16 Ibid., 15–16 (emphasis in original).

> On the other hand, I may state that, knowing little of Arminius beyond his name, and not liking all the little which we know, we never call ourselves his followers. . . . I am aware that there is a dictum with respect to dogmatic divinity similar to that which was uttered concerning philosophy, and as every man is pronounced to be either a Platonist or an Aristotelian, so it is supposed that every believer in Christ must be either a Calvinist or an Arminian. The supposition is erroneous, and the source of it is either prejudice or ignorance.[17]

It would seem that the key difference theologically between the General and Particular Baptists concerned the extent of the atonement. Underwood noted that Thomas Grantham

> admitted that there was not a more important point of difference among those churches than that which respects the extent of the ransom paid for mankind; but he contended that such difference would not justify a division because the points on which they agreed were more numerous and important than those on which they differed.[18]

Particular Baptists

Paul Hobson (d. AD 1666)

Hobson was a leading London Particular Baptist pastor and evangelist in his day. He was responsible for planting several churches in the Newcastle and Northumberland areas. He signed the 1644 and 1646 London Confessions.[19] In the 1644 and 1646 editions, the emphasis is on the application of the work of Christ to a certain number. Hobson lines up with this. The Westminster Confession divided its article on the extent of the sacrifice from the extent of the application in order to allow for the Amyraldian and Hypothetical Universalist positions on the extent of the atonement.

Hobson stated his belief "that Christ died for every man, but not for all alike." In support of the first proposition, he cited 1 Tim 4:10; Heb 2:9; and 2 Pet 2:1. Given that Genesis speaks of the sin of Adam as bringing death upon all humanity, God sent Christ "to step between the pronunciation of the curse and the act meriting, and the execution of the curse," so that man does not die immediately under God's curse. Christ bore the wrath of God and satisfied the justice of God, "and so Christ was the

17 Ibid., 18.

18 Ibid., 23–24.

19 For more on Hobson, consult W. T. Whitley, "The Reverend Colonel Paul Hobson," *Baptist Quarterly* 9 (1938–39): 307–10; and M. Bell, *Apocalypse How? Baptist Movements during the English Revolution* (Macon, GA: Mercer University Press, 2000), 82, 91–94, 104–5, 155–56, 238–40, 247–49.

Saviour of every man from the execution of that curse." Christ's death for all people has brought about a stay of execution, deferring God's wrath.[20]

We see clearly in Hobson the dual nature of the atonement: Christ died for the sins of all people, but he died especially or with particular intent to save only the elect. Hobson went on to state, "Christ tasted death for every man, and to deny it is heresie."[21]

Thomas Lamb (d. c. AD 1672 or 1686)

Lamb was a Particular Baptist and popular pastor and preacher in seventeenth-century England.[22] Benjamin Brook, in his *Lives of the Puritans*, said that "it is extremely obvious, that, upon the disputed points, he was a strict Calvinist."[23]

Lamb made it clear he affirmed a universal atonement. "So also affirmatively, say I, *Christ* gave himself a ransom and propitiation for the sins of all, and every man."[24] He affirmed Christ "suffered for all sins and transgressions of men against Gods most holy Law, so that now no man shall perish but through not believing remission of his sins through *Christ* alone."[25]

Lamb stated his agreement with the Arminian John Goodwin on the extent question: "Yet I deny not, but grant with him [John Goodwin], that the denial of Christ's Death for the sins of all, doth detract from God's *Philanthropy*, and deny him to be a lover of men, and doth in very deed destroy the very foundation and ground-work of Christian faith."[26]

Lamb argued that point that

> God commandeth no man to believe in Christ for salvation for whom there is no salvation in him; or that God on the contrary upon all occasions counseleth and chargeth men to take heed of uncertain, empty and vain dependencies, and from seeking help, peace and safety where they are not to be found.[27]

---

20 P. Hobson, *Fourteen Queries and Ten Absurdities about the Extent of Christ's Death, the Power of the Creatures, the Justice of God in Condemning Some, and Saving Others, Presented by a Free-Willer to the Church of Christ at Newcastle, and Answered by Paul Hobson a Member of Said Church* (London: Henry Hills, 1655), 6–14. See also the chapter on Hobson in R. Greaves, *Saints and Rebels: Seven Non-Conformists in Stuart England* (Macon, GA: Mercer University Press, 1985).

21 Hobson, *Fourteen Queries*, 101. A response to Hobson was written by William Pedelsden under the title *Sound Doctrine, or, The Doctrine of the Gospel about the Extent of the Death of Christ; Being a Reply to Mr. Paul Hobson's Pretended Answer to the Author's Fourteen Queries and Ten Absurdities: With a Brief and Methodicall Compendium of the Doctrine of the Holy Scriptures . . . : Also of Election and Reprobation . . . : Whereunto Is Added the Fourteen Queries and Ten Absurdities Pretended to be Answered by Mr. Paul Hobson, but Are Wholly Omitted in His Book* (London: Printed for Richard Moon, 1657).

22 B. Brook, *The Lives of the Puritans*, 3 vols. (1813; repr. Pittsburgh, PA: Soli Deo Gloria, 1994), 3:461–66.

23 Ibid., 3:466.

24 Thomas Lamb, *Absolute Freedom from Sin by Christ's Death for the World* (London: H. H., 1656), 254.

25 Ibid., 254.

26 Ibid., 248.

27 Ibid., 268.

He understood that if Christ only suffered for the sins of the elect, then God is commanding the non-elect to believe in Christ for a salvation that does not exist.

Lamb informed his readers that his view was challenged by other Calvinists who asserted that it denies election, supports free will, and that apostasy is possible. His response to this charge is telling.

> These as I have upon good reason knowingly denied them to be any natural consequences of the death of Christ for all men, yet nevertheless many who own the Death of Christ for all, do own these as true consequences, and these not only of more common and ignorant sort of people, but men of parts and good esteem for Learning.
>
> Hence it is that the opposers of Christs Death for all are animated to conclude these consequences undeniably to follow, and therefore reject it wholly as false Doctrine.
>
> Hereupon I have been pressed in my spirit to publish something in print, declaring and plainly proving that the Death of Christ for all hath not any affinity with these things, but is a Truth without them.[28]

John Bunyan (AD 1628–1688)

Bunyan is one of the most well-known seventeenth-century Particular Baptists and Puritans. He likewise held to unlimited atonement:[29]

> Christ died for all . . . for if those that perish in the days of the gospel, shall have, at least their damnation heightened, because they have neglected and refused to receive the gospel, it must need be that the gospel was with all faithfulness to be tendered unto them; the which it could not be, unless the death of Christ did extend itself unto them; John 3:16. Heb. 2:3. For the offer of the gospel cannot with God's allowance, be offered any further than the death of Jesus Christ doth go; because if that be taken away, there is indeed no gospel, nor grace to be extended.[30]

Speaking of Acts 3:23 and those who will be "cut off" from the people if they refuse to hear the preaching of the gospel, Bunyan stated, "But would God thus have

---

28 Ibid., x–xi.

29 D. Wenkel, "John Bunyan's Soteriology during His Pre-prison Period (1656–1659): Amyraldian or High Calvinist?," *Scottish Journal of Theology* 58 (2005): 333–52.

30 J. Bunyan, "Reprobation Asserted," in *The Whole Works of John Bunyan*, 3 vols. (Grand Rapids, MI: Baker, 1977), 2:348. See also "The Jerusalem Sinner Saved, or, Good News for the Vilest of Men," in *Works*, 1:90. Here Bunyan makes the "bold proclamation" to unbelievers, and says the Son "died for thee."

threatened, if Christ by his blood, and the merits of the same, had not paid full price to God for sinners, and obtained eternal redemption for them?"[31]

Bunyan said God's wrath will abide forever upon those who refuse Christ,

> for they want [lack] a sacrifice to pacify wrath for the sin they have committed, having resisted and refused the sacrifice of the body of Christ. Therefore it cannot be that they should get from under their present condition who have refused to accept of the undertaking of Christ for them.[32]

Bunyan expressed unlimited atonement in this short poetic verse:

> I gave my Son to do you good,
> I gave you space and time
> With him to close, which you withstood,
> And did with hell combine.[33]

He also stated:

> Yea, where is that, or he, that shall call into question the superabounding sufficiency that is in the merit of Christ, when God continueth to discharge, day by day, yea, hourly, and every moment, sinners from their sin, and death, and hell, for the sake of the redemption that is obtained for us by Christ?
>
> God be thanked here is plenty; but no want of anything! Enough and to spare! It will be with the merit of Christ, even at the end of the world, as it was with the five loaves and two fishes, after the five thousand men, besides women and children, had sufficiently eaten thereof. There was, to the view of all at last, more than showed itself at first. At first there was but five loaves and two fishes, which a lad carried. At last there were twelve baskets full, the weight of which, I suppose, not the strongest man could bear away. Nay, I am persuaded, that at the end of the world, when the damned shall see what a sufficiency there is left of merit in Christ, besides what was bestowed upon them that were saved by him, they will run mad for anguish of heart to think what fools they were not to come to him, and trust in him that they might be saved, as their fellow-sinners did. But this is revealed that Israel, that the godly may hope and expect. Let Israel therefore hope in the Lord, for with him is plenteous redemption.[34]

---

31 J. Bunyan, "Light for Them That Sit in Darkness," in *Works*, 1:429.

32 Ibid., 1:430.

33 J. Bunyan, "One Thing Needful," in *Works*, 3:734.

34 J. Bunyan, "Israel's Hope Encouraged," in *Works*, 1:607–8.

There are numerous other places in Bunyan's works where he affirms an unlimited atonement.[35]

Ben Rogers's article, "John Bunyan and the Extent of the Atonement,"[36] was written in response to my chapter on the extent of the atonement in *Whosoever Will*. Rogers critiqued my argument that Bunyan held to universal atonement and argued that he held to limited atonement. Two years later, Rogers also contributed a chapter on Bunyan in *Whomever He Wills*.[37] Interestingly, Rogers dropped his argument that Bunyan affirmed limited atonement in his chapter in this work. Rogers originally believed that Bunyan affirmed limited atonement, but in light of this fact, it may be that he now considers Bunyan's views as indeterminate because of the debated authorship of *Reprobation Asserted*, or has come to see Bunyan as moderate on the atonement.

Rogers is wrong on two counts and right on one issue. First, he erred in thinking Bunyan is indeterminate; second, he erred in thinking that Bunyan did not author *Reprobation Asserted*. It is reasonable to conclude Bunyan is the author and its contents are consistent with what Bunyan wrote elsewhere.[38] Nevertheless, Rogers got this right: whoever authored *Reprobation Asserted* did believe Christ died for the sins of all people.

Hyper-Calvinism among Particular Baptists in Eighteenth-Century England

The background and rise of hyper-Calvinism is too detailed and cannot be considered in any depth here. The story is perhaps best told by Peter Toon in *The Emergence of Hyper-Calvinism in English Nonconformity, 1689–1765*,[39] and Curt Daniel in "Hyper-Calvinism and John Gill."[40] Tobias Crisp, Joseph Hussey, John Skepp, John Gill, and John Brine are important names in the rise of hyper-Calvinism among Particular Baptists.

---

35 The following examples where Bunyan affirmed unlimited atonement can be culled from his works: Bunyan, "Justification by an Imputed Righteousness," in *Works*, 1:334; "Light for Them That Sit in Darkness," in *Works*, 1:408–9, 416, 429, 432; "Doctrine of Law and Grace," in *Works*, 1:526; 561–63; "The Saints Privilege," in *Works*, 1:667; "Some Gospel Truths Opened," in *Works*, 2:166–67; "A Vindication of Gospel Truths," in *Works*, 2:181, 194, 203, 208; "A Defense of the Doctrine of Justification," in *Works*, 2:297–98; 306–7; 309; 329–30; "Reprobation Asserted," in *Works*, 2:348–49; "A Few Sighs From Hell," in *Works*, 3:348; "Heavenly Footman," in *Works*, 3:384; "The Jerusalem Sinner Saved, or, Good News for the Vilest of Men," in *Works*, 1:90.

36 B. Rogers, "John Bunyan and the Extent of the Atonement," *Founders Journal* 82 (2010): 17–31.

37 B. Rogers, "Sovereign Grace and Evangelism in the Preaching of John Bunyan," in *Whomever He Wills: A Surprising Display of Sovereign Mercy*, ed. M. Barrett and T. J. Nettles (Cape Coral, FL: Founders, 2012), 316–36.

38 See Bunyan scholar, R. L. Greaves, who says no: "John Bunyan and 'Reprobation Asserted,'" *Baptist Quarterly* 21 (1965): 126–31; and P. Helm who says yes: "John Bunyan and 'Reprobation Asserted,'" *Baptist Quarterly* 28 (April 1975): 87–93.

39 P. Toon, *The Emergence of Hyper-Calvinism in English Nonconformity, 1689–1765* (London: Olive Tree, 1967).

40 C. Daniel, "Hyper-Calvinism and John Gill."

Tobias Crisp (AD 1600–1643)

Crisp was a Nonconformist pastor and popular preacher. After his death, his works were published under the title *Christ Alone Exalted*.[41] The first edition appeared in 1643. In 1690 his works were republished with additions by one of his sons and again in 1755 by John Gill. These included fifty-two sermons, fourteen of which were based on Isa 53:6. This publication created the "Crispian Controversy" and the "Antinomian Controversy," which would continue for at least ten years.[42]

In Crisp's defense of limited atonement, he "tended to speak rather too literally about the imputation of sins to Christ (and also of Christ's righteousness to the elect)."[43] Crisp was a doctrinal antinomian and held to eternal justification.[44] For him, justification may be viewed as occurring in three stages. First, the elect were, in the mind of God, justified in eternity on the basis of the covenant of redemption. Second, the elect were justified in Christ by virtue of his federal headship. Third, justification by faith occurs in time when the elect individual is assured of his eternal justification.[45] Unlike later hyper-Calvinists, Crisp did not hesitate to offer the gospel to all people and invite them to respond by faith in Christ.[46]

Joseph Hussey (AD 1659–1726)

Hussey was ordained a Presbyterian and was a pastor in Cambridge. He moved to a congregational form of church governance in 1694 and also became hyper-Calvinistic in his theology.[47] Hussey was careful to avoid the use of certain terms in his preaching to the lost. To speak of "offering" the gospel might imply innate ability on the part of people to respond. His book *God's Operations of Grace but no Offers of Grace* laid out his approach.[48]

Hussey believed in preaching the gospel to all but not offering the gospel to all indiscriminately, on the grounds that only the elect alone could respond in faith to the gospel.[49] Hussey denied that the non-elect had any duty to respond to the gospel,

41 T. Crisp, *Christ Alone Exalted in the Perfection and Encouragements of the Saints, Notwithstanding Sins and Trials. Being the Complete Works of Tobias Crisp D. D. Sometime Minister of the Gospel at Brinksworth in Whitshire Containing Fifty-Two Sermons on Several Select Texts of Scripture*, 4 vols. (London: R. Noble, 1791).

42 P. Toon, *Emergence of Hyper-Calvinism*, 49–54.

43 P. Toon, *Emergence of Hyper-Calvinism*, 56.

44 For a helpful discussion of "eternal justification" and its nuanced variations, consult O. Crisp, *Deviant Calvinism: Broadening Reformed Theology* (Minneapolis, MN: Fortress, 2014), 41–69.

45 P. Toon, *Emergence of Hyper-Calvinism*, 60.

46 Ibid., 63.

47 Ibid., 74–84.

48 J. Hussey, *God's Operations of Grace: But No Offers of his Grace* (London: D. Bridge, 1707). Hussey's *The Glory of Christ Unveil'd*, published in 1706, posited the human nature of Christ existed in heaven on the basis of the Trinitarian covenant of redemption.

49 Often hyper-Calvinists are caricatured today as if they do not believe in preaching to all. That is not accurate. Curt Daniel addressed this issue:

> In spite of their theological position on other points, the Hyper-Calvinists have stressed the primacy

since he has no ability to do so. For Hussey, inability equated to no moral obligation to believe the gospel on the part of the non-elect.

John Skepp (AD 1675–1721)

Skepp became a Baptist and pastored at Curriers' Hall, London. Skepp's role in the rise of hyper-Calvinism was his introduction of Hussey's theology to the English Particular Baptists. Toon stated that "Skepp stands, as it were, in the history of dogma, as the connecting link between Hussey's theology and the Hyper-Calvinism of many Particular Baptists through the eighteenth century."[50]

John Gill (AD 1697–1771)

Gill was a leading Particular Baptist pastor, theologian, and prolific author. He became pastor of the Baptist church at Horsleydown in 1719 and remained there until his death in 1771. Gill had great respect for Skepp, who participated at Gill's ordination. He was an extreme Calvinist in some of his views as well as a controversialist. "The High Calvinism of Richard Davis, hardened by controversy with Baxterianism and Arminianism, modified through the assimilation of Crispian doctrines, and severely conditioned by the influence of Hussey's 'no offers of grace' theology, was the theological environment in which Gill was nurtured."[51]

Gill was an ardent champion for limited atonement and is usually classed by scholars

---

> of preaching in a way that surprises many of their critics. Contrary to the opinion of some opponents, they nearly always believed that the Gospel is to be preached indiscriminately to all men. This is not a minority view either, nor a later development, for we find it from the very beginning. Hussey gave as the first answer to the question above ["How must we preach the Gospel, if we do not offer the Gospel?"], "We must preach the doctrine of salvation to all sinners, in general, within the hearing." The same opinion can be found in the special subject of our study, Dr. John Gill: "the Gospel is to be preached to all." Of course, this applies only to rational creatures; but as all men have the natural duty to hear and believe what God reveals to them, so the preacher has the duty to preach and proclaim to all. (Daniel, *Hyper-Calvinism and John Gill*, 448–49)

Daniel also stated: "With the exception of a few extreme Primitive Baptists, all Hyper-Calvinists have believed that we are to 'preach' the Gospel to all, but 'offer' it to none. Preach, explain, command—yes. Offer—no. Some have also quibbled over the word 'invite,' arguing that we can only invite 'sensible [convicted] sinners', not sinners in general. All this is related to anti-missionism" (C. Daniel, *The History and Theology of Calvinism* [Springfield, IL: Good Books, 2003], 89).

Along the same lines, Iain Murray said: "If God has chosen an elect people, then, Hyper-Calvinism argued, he can have no desire for the salvation of any others and to speak as though he had, is to deny the particularity of grace. Of course, Hyper-Calvinists accepted that the gospel be preached to all, but they denied that such preaching was intended to demonstrate any love on the part of God for all, or any invitation to all to receive mercy" (I. H. Murray, *Spurgeon v. Hyper-Calvinism: The Battle for Gospel Preaching* [Edinburgh: Banner of Truth, 2000], 89).

50 P. Toon, *Emergence of Hyper-Calvinism*, 88–89. Skepp's hyper-Calvinism can be seen in his *The Divine Energy: Or, The Efficacious Operations of the Spirit of God in the Soul of Man, in His Effectual Calling and Conversion: Stated, Proved, and Vindicated. Wherein the Real Weakness and Insufficiency of Moral Persuasion, without the Super-Addition of the Exceeding Greatness of God's Power for Faith and Conversion to God, Are Full Evinced. Being an Antidote against the Pelagian Plague* (London: Printed for Joseph Marshall, 1722).

51 P. Toon, *Emergence of Hyper-Calvinism*, 99.

as a hyper-Calvinist.[52] He was responsible for the republication of John Skepp's 1722 work *The Divine Energy*. Skepp had been a member of Hussey's church in Cambridge and was a close friend and mentor of Gill. Andrew Fuller was also troubled by Gill's over evaluation of the "effectual call" and his undervaluation of the "general call" in preaching. Referencing Gill's *Cause of God and Truth*, Clipsham stated the situation in stark terms: "Gill . . . went to great lengths to explain away the meaning of 'all' wherever it occurs in connection with the universal proclamation of the gospel, and studiously avoided the direct commands and exhortations in the Bible to repent and believe on Christ and be saved."[53]

Gill's argument against universal atonement was based on the presupposition that the objects of election and redemption are coextensive; hence only limited atonement can be the biblical position.[54]

One gets a taste of Gill's reasoning on limited atonement from his comments on 2 Cor 5:14–15:

> That the text does not say that Christ died for *all men*, but for *all*; and therefore, agreeable to other scriptures [Matt 1:21; John 10:15; Eph 5:25; Heb 2:9, 10], may be understood of all *the people* whom Jesus saves from their sins. . . . That it is said in the latter part of the text, that those for whom Christ died, for them also he rose again; who therefore ought to live. . . . Christ died for no more nor for others than those for whom he rose again; such for whom he rose again, he rose for their justification; if Christ rose for the justification of all men, all men would be justified, or the end of Christ's resurrection would not be answered; but all men are not, nor will be justified; some will be con-

52 Both T. Nettles and T. George have attempted to sanitize Gill of his hyper-Calvinism. See T. George, "John Gill," in *Theologians of the Baptist Tradition*, ed. T. George and D. Dockery (Nashville: B&H, 2001), 11–33. Though Nettles is correct to note Gill's distinction between preaching the gospel and actually offering salvation to all, J. L. Garrett is correct to point out, "Gill's rejection of 'offers' and 'tenders' with its implications for preaching means that he can hardly be removed from the ranks of the Hyper-Calvinists" (J. L. Garrett, *Baptist Theology: A Four-Century Study* [Macon, GA: Mercer University Press, 2009], 99). A. Sell stated, "No matter how much we may respect Gill for his prodigious labours . . . the fact remains that for all his assertion of the need to *declare* the gospel, he does seem to have underemphasized the gospel *call*" (A. Sell, *The Great Debate: Calvinism, Arminianism, and Salvation*, [Eugene, OR: Wipf & Stock, 1998], 82). R. Oliver reviewed Nettles's *By His Grace and for His Glory* and corrected Nettles's interpretation of Gill (*Banner of Truth* 284 [May 1987], 30–32). Iain Murray observed: "It is hard to see how Nettles' defense of Gill can be sustained" (*Spurgeon v. Hyper-Calvinism*, 131). It appears that in recent years Nettles has reluctantly backpedaled on his view of Gill: "Although I think the judgment should still be surrounded with cautions and caveats, there may be compelling evidence that Gill held to the distinctive Hyper-Calvinist tenet" (T. Nettles, "John Gill and the Evangelical Awakening," in *The Life and Thought of John Gill (1697–1771): A Tercentennial Appreciation*, ed. M. Haykin [Leiden: Brill, 1997], 153). Nettles has in view the denial of "duty faith" or the evangelical responsibility to believe the gospel. B. H. Howson has also observed Nettles's recent modifications (*Erroneous and Schismatical Opinions: The Question of Orthodoxy Regarding the Theology of Hanserd Knollys (c. 1599–1691)* [Leiden: Brill, 2001], 172).

53 E. F. Clipsham, "Andrew Fuller and Fullerism," *Baptist Quarterly* 20 (1963): 102.

54 J. Gill, *The Cause of God and Truth* (1735–1738; repr. Grand Rapids, MI: Baker, 1980), 98. See also his *A Complete Body of Doctrinal and Pratical Divinity: Or a System of Evangelical Truths Deduced from Scripture* (Parish, AK: Baptist Standard Bearer, 1987), Book 6, chapters 3 and 4.

demned: it follows, that Christ did not rise from the dead for all men, and consequently did not die for all men.[55]

Gill's most complete treatment of the extent question occurs in his *Body of Doctrinal and Practical Divinity*.[56] He strongly affirmed limited atonement. Gill adduced three groups of arguments against unlimited atonement: (1) unlimited atonement (Gill calls it "redemption") reflects negatively on God's nature and attributes, (2) unlimited atonement depreciates the grace of Christ in his work as redeemer, and (3) universal atonement is useless to those who are not saved.[57]

Concerning the first set of arguments, Gill believed that universal atonement does despite to the love of God. He queried: "What kind of love must that be, which does not secure the salvation of any by it?" Furthermore, God's love is invariable—but not according to the unlimited atonement scheme, since God loves sinners enough to die for them and wills that they should be save—and yet this love becomes wrath and God punishes them eternally. Finally, according to Gill, God's love is not sent to those who never hear the gospel. "Such love as this is unworthy of God."[58]

Gill suggested that universal atonement reflects negatively on God's wisdom. "Where is his wisdom in forming a scheme [unlimited atonement], in which he fails of his end?"[59] Just because Gill cannot conceive of any wisdom on God's part in an unlimited atonement does not establish his argument that there is no wisdom in it.

God's justice is also impugned by the unlimited atonement view according to Gill. Here Gill appealed to the double payment argument. Gill's error at this point is his commercialistic understanding of the atonement and failure to recognize that Scripture teaches the unbelieving elect remain under the wrath of God.

Gill asserted that God's omnipotence is defamed as he is unable "to carry his designs into execution."[60] But Gill forgot that God has attached a condition to the application of the atonement: it only is effective for those who believe the gospel. God's power is not diminished at all.

For Gill, God's immutability is called into question on the unlimited atonement view. God is "sometimes in one mind, and sometimes in another; sometimes his mind is to save them; and at another time his mind is to damn them."[61] This argument

55 J. Gill, *Cause of God and Truth*, 41–42 (emphasis in original).

56 J. Gill, *A Complete Body of Doctrinal and Practical Divinity*, 461–75.

57 Ibid., 463–67.

58 Ibid., 464. The problems with Gill's understanding of God's love should be evidenced. First, God's love does indeed secure the salvation of all who believe, even in an Arminian understanding of atonement. Second, Gill failed to recognize that God both loves and has wrath for the same individuals. Has he forgotten Eph 2:3, which speaks of the unbelieving elect as being under the wrath of God? Third, the problem of the unevangelized is as much a dilemma for Reformed soteriology as for Arminian soteriology.

59 Ibid.

60 Ibid.

61 Ibid., 465.

stands under the same critique as above concerning the love of God. In addition, Gill's argument here is undercut by those within the Reformed tradition who posit the notion of God's two wills: revealed and decretal.

Finally, Gill asserted universal atonement robs God of his glory. All moderate Calvinists and non-Calvinists would simply respond that the converse is true. Unlimited atonement redounds to God's maximal glory in that it magnifies all his divine attributes, including his love.

In Gill's second category of arguments against unlimited atonement (it depreciates the grace of Christ), he lists five arguments. First, Gill asked: what sort of love is it that dies for all but then withholds the means of grace from the majority of them such that they cannot be saved?[62] He is, of course, assuming his own Reformed soteriology to be true at this point. Gill might ask this question of his moderate Calvinist cohort as well, as it would seem to be more damaging to their soteriology.

Second, Gill suggested that universal atonement reflects negatively on the work of Christ, since "God is only made reconcilable, not reconciled, nor men reconciled to Him." Gill failed to understand the objective and subjective side of reconciliation as enumerated by Paul in 2 Cor 5:18–20.

Third, Gill presumed that if all for whom Christ died are not ultimately saved, then Christ's death was in vain. Appealing to Rom 8:32–33, Gill concluded the following: since those for whom Jesus died do not come under condemnation, and since many will come under condemnation, it must be true that Christ did not die for them. "Christ's death has no efficacy against condemnation."[63] This is a common argument in the limitarian arsenal. The answer is simple: Paul's audience and subject are believers. He is not speaking about all the elect considered in the abstract (the as yet unborn elect and the living unbelieving elect). Paul's point is that no condemnation accrues to *believers*, not that Christ did not die for all sinners. This argument has been adequately refuted by David Ponter.[64]

Fourth, Gill argued that the death of Christ and the post-resurrection intercessory ministry of Christ are of equal extent. In other words, according to Gill, Christ died for those for whom he did not pray. This argument is also exegetically fallacious, as we have seen. Fifth, if Christ died for all, then Christ will not "see the travail of his soul and be satisfied" a la Isa 53:11. This argument simply begs the question at hand.[65]

Gill's third category of arguments against unlimited atonement concerns its ineffectiveness for all those who are eternally lost. Gill asserted the argument that if Christ

62 Ibid.

63 Ibid., 466.

64 D. Ponter, "Romans 8:32 and the Argument for Limited Atonement," *Calvin and Calvinism*, May 26, 2011, http://calvinandcalvinism.com/?p=10318#more-10318.

65 Gill, *A Complete Body of Doctrinal and Practical Divinity*, 466.

died for those eternally lost, then his death was in vain.[66] The same, he argued, is true for all those who have never heard the gospel. Gill presumed that unlimited atonement entails uncertainty concerning the salvation of all people. This is a caricature of the non-Calvinist position. Non-Calvinists believe that the atonement makes possible salvation for all and guarantees the salvation of all who believe, though most Arminians would say that such salvation could be lost due to apostasy.

Finally, Gill asserted that salvation on the unlimited atonement view gives opportunity for those saved to think that they are saved by their own work and thus neglect to love, praise, and be thankful to Christ for their redemption. Here Gill has confused faith with a work.

Gill then launched into a treatment of the various texts that on the surface seem to support an unlimited atonement. These he considered under three classes: (1) the "all" or "many" texts, (2) the "world" texts, and (3) the texts that speak of Christ dying for those who are ultimately eternally lost.[67] Since all of these texts have either been addressed previously or will be addressed below, it is not necessary to engage Gill point by point.

John Brine (AD 1703–1765)

Brine became pastor of Curriers' Hall in London in 1729 and remained there until his death. He was actively involved in Particular Baptist life and continued the hyper-Calvinistic tendency among many Particular Baptists of the time. Brine wrote a response to Isaac Watts's views on universal atonement, presenting eight reasons Christ could only die for the elect.[68] His reasons were all based on his belief that election entails limited atonement.

Toon's summary analysis of the factors involved in the shift from high to hyper-Calvinism is helpful. He lists four factors.

1. After 1660 the majority of Puritans who were high Calvinists left the Church of England and became Nonconformists. The religious leadership was left in the hands of more moderate Calvinists and Arminians. "As the years passed by, High Calvinism became more and more the sole preserve of the Independents and the Particular Baptists."[69]
2. Hussey and later hyper-Calvinists fell prey to a rigid logic that election and irresistible grace entailed that Christ should not be offered to all people.
3. Most of the early hyper-Calvinists were self-educated, in a closed environment, and chose their theology before examining any alternatives.

66 Ibid.

67 Ibid., 467–75.

68 J. Brine, *The Certain Efficacy of the Death of Christ, Asserted* (London: Printed for, and Sold by Aaron Ward, at the King's Arms in Little-Britain, 1743), 4–80. See also Toon, *Emergence of Hyper-Calvinism*, 121–22, 138.

69 Toon, *Emergence of Hyper-Calvinism*, 146.

4. Obsession with the defense of the tenets of hyper-Calvinism led to a situation where "the evangelistic note of Scripture as basically an overture by God towards sinners was muted. This lack of interest in evangelism (and a reference to evangelism in their books is virtually impossible to find) came, as we have seen, with the deduction of the duty of ministers in preaching from the secret will of the Lord, the will of His decrees."[70]

C. H. Spurgeon spoke of John Gill's hyper-Calvinism and its influence on the churches: "The system of theology with which many identify his name has chilled many Churches to their very soul, for it has led them to omit the free invitations of the Gospel."[71]

It was this kind of extremism that would motivate Andrew Fuller in the late eighteenth century to move in the direction of a more evangelical Calvinism.

Daniel Turner (AD 1710–1798)

Baptist historian Robert Oliver documented a 1782 letter written by Particular Baptist Daniel Turner in which Turner stated he did not subscribe to particular redemption.

> Daniel Turner may have shared a love of liberty with John Ryland, but there were significant differences between the two men. In a letter written in 1782, Turner revealed that he did not subscribe to the doctrine of Particular Redemption. He wrote, "I am one who with the good Mr Polhill, Mr How[e], Dr. Watts and many others who hold the doctrine of Particular Election and general Redemption as it may be called." These were unusual sentiments for a Particular Baptist minister in the 1780's.[72]

Of further interest here is Turner's listing of Edward Polhill, John Howe, Isaac Watts, and many others as also affirming a general redemption.

Robert Hall (AD 1764–1831)

Robert Hall was a Particular Baptist leader and preacher known for his pulpit oratory. He was impressed with the divinity lectures of Alexander Gerard, a leader among moderate Calvinists. Hall was himself moderate on the question of the extent of the atonement.

---

70 Ibid., 148.

71 Whitley, *Calvinism and Evangelism in England* (London: Kingsgate, c. 1933), 28.

72 Daniel Turner, "Daniel Turner to Mr Mumm, Watford, 14 June 1782," Angus Library, Regent's Park College, Oxford, in R. W. Oliver, *History of the English Calvinistic Baptists 1771–1892* (Edinburgh: Banner of Truth, 2006), 62.

In a letter to a W. Bennett, dated January 10, 1810, Hall expressed his views on the extent of the atonement.

> I do think you have steered a happy medium between the rigidity of Calvinism and the laxness of Arminianism, and have succeeded in the solution of the grand difficulty—the consistency betwixt general offers and invitations, and the speciality of divine grace. This interesting question is handled with masterly ability. On this point, the representation of Calvinists has long appeared to me very defective, and that, fettered by their system, they have by no means gone so far in encouraging and urging sinners to the use of prayer, reading the Scriptures, self-examination, &c. as the scriptures justify. Here the Arminians, such of them as are evangelical, have had greatly the advantage of the Calvinists in pleading with sinners. I lent your book to B.—who is much pleased with it, and only wishes you had expressed yourself more fully in favor of the general extent of Christ's death. I think you have asserted it by implication, though I wish you had asserted it unequivocally; because I am fully persuaded that it is a doctrine of Scripture, and that it forms the only consistent basis of unlimited invitation. I think that the most enlightened Calvinists are too reserved on this head, and that their refusal to declare, with the concurrent testimony of scripture, that Christ died for all men, tends to confirm the prejudices of the Methodists and others against election and special grace.[73]

Robert Balmer[74] had three or four conversations with Robert Hall in 1819 and 1823. He recalled one conversation about the question of the extent of the atonement.

> On informing him that I had been perplexed with doubts as to the extent of the death of Christ, and expressing a wish to know his opinion, he replied, "There, sir, my sentiments give me the advantage of you; for on that point I entertain no doubts whatever: I believe firmly in 'general redemption;' I often preach it, and I consider the fact that 'Christ died for all men' as the only basis that can support the universal offer of the gospel."—"But you admit the doctrine of election, which necessarily implies limitation. Do you not think that election and particular redemption are inseparably connected?"—"I believe firmly," he rejoined, "in election, but I do not think it

73 S. Drew, ed., *The Imperial Magazine*, vol. 1, Second series (May 1831), 216–17.

74 R. Balmer (1787–1844), was a minister in the United Secession Church of Scotland, professor of pastoral theology, and later systematic theology. Balmer was pastor in Berwick-on-Tweed in Scotland for thirty years until his death. R. Balmer, *Academical Lectures and Pulpit Discourses, with a Memoir of His Life by Rev. Dr. Henderson, of Galashiels*, 2 vols. (Andersons: Scottish Nation, 1845), is his collected works.

involves particular redemption; I consider the sacrifice of Christ as a remedy, not only adapted, but intended for all, and as placing all in a saveable state and as removing all barriers except such as arise from their own perversity and depravity. But God foresaw or knew that none would accept the remedy, merely of themselves, and therefore, by what may be regarded as a separate arrangement, he resolved to glorify his mercy, by effectually applying salvation to a certain number of our race, through the agency of his Holy Spirit. I apprehend then, that the limiting clause implied in election refers not to the purchase but to the application of redemption." This representation seemed to me, at the time, to be encumbered with considerable difficulties; and I was not sure that I correctly apprehended it. Not choosing, however, to request Mr. H. to repeat or elucidate his statements, I asked him if he could refer me to any book where I should find what he regarded as the Scripture doctrine on the subject, stated and illustrated. He referred me to a book to which Dr. Smith, of Homerton, had, not many days before, referred me, in answer to a similar question,—Bellamy's "True Religion Delineated."

In the course of our conversation respecting the extent of Christ's death, Mr. Hall expatiated at considerable length on the number and variety of the Scripture expressions, in which it seems to be either explicitly asserted or necessarily implied, that it was intended, not for the elect exclusively, but for mankind generally, such as "the world," "all," "all men," "every man," &c. He made some striking remarks on the danger of twisting such expressions from their natural and obvious import, and on the absurdity of interpretations put on them by some of the advocates of particular redemption. He mentioned especially the absurdity of explaining "the world," John iii, 16, to signify the elect world, as the text would then teach that some of the elect may not believe. He noticed, further, that the doctrine of general redemption was not only asserted expressly in many texts, but presupposed in others, such as "Destroy not with thy meat," &c., and "Denying the Lord that bought them;" and that it was incorporated with other parts of the Christian system, particularly with the universal offers and invitations of the gospel.[75]

In a discourse on the atonement, Hall stated with respect to the atonement:

Who can conceive the extent of the vindication which the law of God received in the suffering of a person who was inseparably united with God; . . . In his

75 O. Gregory, ed., *The Works of the Rev. Robert Hall, A. M.*, 3 vols. (New York: J. & J. Harper, 1833), 3:76–77. This same account occurs in R. Balmer, *Academical Lectures and Pulpit Discourses*, 1:80–81.

> sacrifice all the moral purposes to be accomplished by the sufferings of the human race are fully answered and realized.[76]
>
> For this reason, and for others which might be mentioned, we have ground for believing that the divine Being never did, and never will, permit another such event to take place in the economy of providence; or allow that any other extended instance of the substitution of one person for a multitude of sinners should occur, or that the destinies of a whole race would be suspended on the voluntary interposition and matchless love of a great redeemer and benefactor.[77]

These examples are sufficient to show that there were even some Particular Baptists who did not affirm limited atonement.[78] Yet there was another Particular Baptist who, it seems, came to support universal atonement; one who wielded significant influence on nineteenth-century English and American Baptists, including the founders of the Southern Baptist Convention: Andrew Fuller.

Andrew Fuller (AD 1754–1815)[79]

Fuller was one of the giants among Baptists in England. Pastor, theologian, and author, Fuller, along with William Carey, was instrumental in the founding of the Baptist Missionary Society. His most famous work, *The Gospel Worthy of All Acceptation*, was published in 1785 and revised and republished in 1801.

Growing up amid the stifling influence of eighteenth-century hyper-Calvinism, Fuller saw firsthand its debilitating effects on preaching, evangelism, and missions. Through a careful study of the Scriptures and the influence of John Bunyan and Jonathan Edwards, Fuller moved away from hyper-Calvinism and developed two key theses that he argued brilliantly in his famous work *The Gospel Worthy of All Acceptation*.[80] First is

---

76 R. Hall, "The Substitution of the Innocent for the Guilty," in *The Atonement: Being Five Discourses* (New York: American Tract Society, 1840), 117.

77 Ibid., 121.

78 Thus, Peter Naylor's comment "that even those Particular Baptists who adopted the disjunction between 'sufficiency' and 'efficiency' never accepted that Christ laid down his life deliberately on behalf of all who happen to hear the gospel, or, indeed, for all men," is inaccurate historically (*Calvinism, Communion and the Baptists: A Study of English Calvinistic Baptists from the Late 1600s to the Early 1800s*, Studies in Baptist History and Thought 7 [Carlisle, UK: Paternoster, 2003], 169).

79 Some of the material in this section first appeared in my "Preaching for a Great Commission Resurgence," in *Great Commission Resurgence: Fulfilling God's Mandate in Our Time*, ed. Chuck Lawless and Adam Greenway (Nashville: B&H, 2010), 281–98.

80 A. Fuller, "The Gospel Worthy of All Acceptation, or the Duty of Sinners to Believe in Jesus Christ, with Corrections and Editions; to Which Is Added an Appendix, on the Necessity of a Holy Disposition in Order to Believing in Christ," in *Fuller's Works*, 3 vols., 2:328–416. Fuller's *Gospel Worthy* was first published in 1785, but a second edition with his revisions was published in 1801. The second edition appears in *Fuller's Works*.

the duty of all sinners to believe the gospel. All sinners should be encouraged through preaching to believe in Christ. Second, Fuller argued that it is the duty of preachers to offer the gospel to all people. Thus preachers should make every effort to exhort everyone to believe in Christ.[81] Key to understanding Fuller's two theses is the influence of Jonathan Edwards concerning the natural ability of sinners to respond to the gospel but their moral inability to do so.[82] This Edwardsian distinction provided Fuller with the theological groundwork for his *Gospel Worthy*.

Fuller exemplifies the fact that there is variety *within* the group of people who describe themselves with the "particular redemption" label. J. L. Dagg, a strict particularist himself, knew about this diversity in his own day. In addition to those Calvinists who maintain a strictly limited extent for the atonement, he spoke of some "people who maintain the doctrine of particular redemption," that "distinguish between redemption and atonement, and because of the adaptedness referred to, consider the death of Christ an atonement for the sins of all men."[83]

All Calvinists agree on the idea of Christ's *intent* or *effectual purpose* to save the elect alone, and they *all* also agree that this results in an eventual limited *effectual application* of the benefits to the elect. These categories necessarily relate to one another and are essential to their view of a pretemporal, Trinitarian, unconditional election to faith. They *all* adhere to these two categories of a limited effectual intent and a limited effectual application.

Where Calvinists differ is over the *extent* of the atonement, as Dagg himself observed. There are at least three particular redemption positions within Calvinism. One of these particular redemption positions affirms that Christ died for the sins of all people.

The chart that follows illustrates the three positions within the particular redemption camp. Where all Calvinists agree is on the atonement's *intent* and *application*. Where Calvinists disagree is over the *extent* of the atonement.

---

81 P. Morden, *Offering Christ to the World: Andrew Fuller (1754–1815) and the Revival of Eighteenth Century Particular Baptist Life*, Studies in Baptist History and Thought 8 (Carlisle, UK: Paternoster, 2003), 26–27. This work is an excellent biography of Fuller. As Morden noted, Fuller followed Jonathan Edwards's concept of natural and moral inability in sinners. All the unregenerate have natural ability to respond to the gospel, but none has the moral ability to respond to the gospel. Fuller believed no one can respond apart from electing grace and the regenerating work of the Spirit (44).

82 Ibid., 49. By "moral inability," Edwards and Fuller meant that no one would come to Christ apart from the work of the Holy Spirit. Morden correctly noted the "natural" and "moral" distinction has been criticized even by some in the Reformed tradition (ibid., 61). An excellent survey of Fuller's dependence on Edwards's distinction is G. Priest, "Andrew Fuller's Response to the 'Modern Question': A Reappraisal of *The Gospel Worthy of All Acceptation*," *Detroit Baptist Seminary Journal* 6 (2001): 45–73. Priest rejects a natural/moral distinction in Edwards and Fuller.

83 J. L. Dagg, *Manual of Theology* (Harrisonburg, VA: Gano, 1990), 326.

The Atonement	Particular Redemption Sense #1	Particular Redemption Sense #2	Particular Redemption Sense #3
INTENT	An Effectual Purpose in Christ to Save the Elect Alone	An Effectual Purpose in Christ to Save the Elect Alone	An Effectual Purpose in Christ to Save the Elect Alone
EXTENT	So much suffering for so much sin (Quantitative Equivalentism) (Intrinsic and extrinsic sufficiency for the elect alone)	Infinite value of suffering for so much sin (Nonquantitative Equivalentism) (Intrinsic sufficiency for elect and non-elect; extrinsic sufficiency for the elect alone)	Infinite value of suffering for infinite (all) sin (Nonquantitative Equivalentism) (Intrinsic and extrinsic sufficiency for elect and non-elect)
APPLICATION	A limited effectual application that corresponds to Christ's intent to save	A limited effectual application that corresponds to Christ's intent to save	A limited effectual application that corresponds to Christ's intent to save

In the first column is Dagg's own position. Christ's atonement is viewed as "so much suffering for so much sin." This is often labeled the "commercial" view or sometimes as the "equivalentist"[84] position (though I prefer to use the phrase "quantitative equivalentist" to identify this position). There is a quantifiable amount of suffering that Christ underwent that corresponds to the exact number of sins of the elect alone. The just suffering due for this quantifiable amount of elect sin corresponds to the degree of Christ's suffering and literal payment for sin on the cross.

The second column is the majority view among Calvinists in Reformed history from the late sixteenth century through today. John Owen, Francis Turretin, and a host of others held this view.

84 The "equivalentist" label is vague and unhelpful. One might think of an *identical* or *quantifiable* equivalency or a *moral* equivalency. The former is the commercial view, but all advocates of penal substitution acknowledge that Christ's death is *morally equivalent* to what God's justice requires of one and all sinners alike, though it is *not* an exact sort of punishment that each of them deserves. Remember the *idem-tantundem* debate between Owen and Baxter.

The third column is the view of the first generation of Reformed theologians, with the possible exceptions of Calvin and Bucer (though I think it is clear both held this view), and other moderate Calvinists, who are sometimes called dualists. This third view is yet another variety *within* the self-described particular redemption camp, as Dagg observed.

As Reformed scholars now affirm, the most hotly contested issue at the Synod of Dort was the extent of the atonement. The Genevan delegation strongly advocated for a strictly limited atonement while the English and Bremen delegations advocated for a universal atonement. Contrary to popular opinion, Dort did not *prescribe* the strict particularist view that Christ died only for the sins of the elect. The canons *allowed* for this view, along with the view that Christ died for the sins of all people. There was a deliberate ambiguity in the wording of the canons to allow both groups within the synod to sign. Dort did not take sides on the imputation of sin to Christ debate, but it only took sides on the issue of the effectual purpose of God to save his elect through the work of Christ and the effectual application of the Spirit, contrary to Remonstrant thinking on those points.

Where should one locate conceptually Fuller's position on the extent of the atonement? Fuller is an example of a particular Redemptionist who held to universal atonement.[85]

Fuller and Dan Taylor[86]

One of the most fascinating aspects of Fuller's *Gospel Worthy* concerns the influence of the General Baptist Dan Taylor on Fuller's view of the extent of the atonement.[87] In the first edition of Fuller's *Gospel Worthy*, written in 1781 but published in 1785, it is evident that he was committed to particular redemption (limited atonement) in the Owenic sense of that term.[88] However, following his debates with Dan Taylor, Fuller was persuaded that particular redemption in the sense of limited substitution (position 2 in the chart above) did not comport with Scripture. Taylor had argued the case for universal atonement and that universal invitations for sinners to believe the gospel

85 In the summer of 2014, Michael Haykin, Tom Nettles, and I engaged in a bit of a back and forth in blog posts over whether Andrew Fuller came to reject limited atonement by the time he published the second edition of *Gospel Worthy.* Haykin and Nettles argued that Fuller never abandoned his earlier commitment to limited atonement. These posts can be accessed at http://www.drdavidlallen.com/resources/. The titles are: "Gaining a Fuller Understanding: Response to Dr. Michael Haykin" (April 24, 2014); "Andrew Fuller on the Extent of the Atonement: A Response and Rebuttal" (May 5, 2014); "Response to Tom Nettles' 'Andrew Fuller and David Allen, Parts 1 & 2'" (June 1, 2014).

86 For narratives on Fuller's engagement with Taylor, consult J. W. Morris, *Memoirs of the Life and Writings of the Rev. Andrew Fuller* (Boston: Lincoln and Edmonds, 1830), 275–96; and Adam Taylor, *Memoirs of the Rev. Dan Taylor* (London: Baynes & Son, et. al., 1820), 172–82.

87 Some of the material in this section first appeared in my "Preaching for a Great Commission Resurgence," 281–98.

88 See A. Fuller, *The Gospel of Christ Worthy of All Acceptation* (Northhampton: T. Dicey & Co., 1785), 132–39.

could only be properly grounded in a universal provision in Christ's death. Taylor continued to point out that if limited atonement were true, then there is no provision at all for the non-elect in the death of Christ.

Fuller felt the brunt of this argument and could not answer it. He later confessed in 1803: "I tried to answer my opponent . . . but I could not. I found not merely his reasonings, but the Scriptures themselves, standing in my way."[89] As a Calvinist, Fuller's concept of redemption was still "particular" in the sense that the particularity was now located not in the *extent* of the atonement, but in the *design* and *application* of the atonement. Fuller believed the elect were determined to salvation in the elective purpose of God in eternity past. For Fuller, a universal atonement safeguarded the grounds for the universal offer of the gospel.

Proof for Fuller's shift can be found in a comparison of the first and second editions of *Gospel Worthy* where he discussed particular redemption.[90] The section on particular redemption in the first edition is almost completely rewritten in the second edition.[91] All references to particular redemption in the sense that Christ suffered only for the sins of the elect are excised by Fuller. Fuller abandoned his pecuniary (commercial) argument that Jesus's death was a literal debt payment. This commercial argument is one of the linchpin arguments for limited atonement. Fuller now argued against the concept of Christ's death as a literal debt payment, stating that if Christ's death were a literal debt payment, then it would be inconsistent with universal gospel invitations. It would also negate the principle of grace in that salvation could be claimed by the elect since Christ paid for it on the cross. Fuller believed that no inconsistency ensued from God's "special design" in the death of Christ in its application to the elect and the fact that all people everywhere were under obligation to believe the gospel. Only if limited atonement is maintained is there an inconsistency.[92]

The section on Particular Redemption in the second edition of *Gospel Worthy* is only about half the length of the first edition. Fuller has a lengthy quotation of Elisha Coles in the first edition where he quoted Coles twice as saying first that "Christ did not die for all," and then "The first act of faith is *not* that Christ died for *all*, or for *you* in particular: the one is not true; the other not certain to you."[93] He continued to quote Coles, stating there are many reasons to induce people to believe the gospel "without laying general redemption for the ground of their faith."[94] Fuller quoted

89 A. Fuller, "Six Letters to Dr. Ryland Respecting the Controversy with the Rev. A. Booth," in *Fuller's Works*, 2:709–10.

90 Morden, *Offering Christ to the World*, 73–74, illustrates some of the substantive changes. Morden's work is very important in showing Fuller's shift on the extent of the atonement.

91 See Fuller, *Gospel of Christ Worthy of All Acceptation*, 132–39; and "Gospel Worthy," in *Fuller's Works*, 2:373–75.

92 See Morden, *Offering Christ*, 68–76.

93 Fuller, *Gospel of Christ Worthy of All Acceptation*, 135.

94 Ibid., 135.

Witsius as saying "All, and every one in particular, therefore, to whom the gospel is preached, are not commanded immediately to believe *that Christ died for them*; for that is a falsehood."[95]

Every one of these quotations is excised in Fuller's second edition. There is no statement in quotation or by Fuller in this section of the second edition advocating limited atonement. In both editions Fuller quoted John Owen. In the first edition, following an Owen quote, Fuller spends another paragraph of eight sentences referencing statements in Owen's writings that demonstrate Owen saw no conflict between repentance and faith being incumbent "on all men in general, and this they [Owen, Coles, Witsius, and Ridgely] thought to be consistent with particular redemption."[96] This entire paragraph is excised in the second edition.

Furthermore, when Fuller quoted John Owen in the first edition, he referred to him as "the great Owen" and "the Doctor."[97] However, in the second edition, these titles evaporate and Fuller does not even name Owen in the text, choosing to introduce a single quotation from Owen with the words "says another."[98] In an interesting footnote, Alan Clifford in his *Atonement and Justification* stated: "Andrew Fuller opposed Gill's hypercalvinism and, in a letter to Jonathan Edwards' pupil Samuel Hopkins (1721–1803) dated 17 Mar. 1798, he lamented the continuing influence of Owen. (see Fuller's letter in the Angus Library, Regent's Park College, Oxford)."[99]

Fuller and the New Divinity Movement

The New Divinity exerted great influence on Fuller. The New Divinity interpreted "sufficient" with respect to the atonement to mean more than just "hypothetically" sufficient. They understood and used the term to mean an actual sufficiency in that Christ actually substituted himself for the sins of all people. This can be discerned in the writings of Joseph Bellamy and other New Divinity proponents.

Fuller's mature position on the extent of the atonement is all but identical to that of the New Divinity. Fuller had come to the place where he understood the atonement of Christ to be "sufficient" for the sins of all people because Christ actually substituted himself[100] for the sins of all people, even while continuing to maintain Christ's effectual purpose to apply the saving benefits of his death to the elect alone.

---

95 Ibid., 137 (emphasis in original).

96 Ibid., 138.

97 Ibid., 137.

98 Fuller, "Gospel Worthy," in *Works*, 2:375.

99 A. Clifford, *Atonement and Justification* (Oxford: Clarendon, 1990), 122.

100 G. Priest correctly noted that Fuller never abandoned penal substitutionary atonement but suggested that Fuller's use of governmental terms muddied the doctrinal waters of soteriology. See "Andrew Fuller's Response to the 'Modern Question,'" 50–51.

Fuller, Quantitative Equivalentism, and "Sufficiency"

Some assume that the only shift Fuller made was away from a "commercial" understanding of the atonement, (position 1 in the chart) and thus Fuller maintained his view of particular redemption in a sense that includes the notion that Christ only substituted himself for the sins of the elect (position 2 in the chart), just not in a quantitative equivalentist fashion.

However, in Fuller's section "On Particular Redemption" in *Gospel Worthy*, he said that Christ's death, in itself, is "equal to the salvation of the whole world, were the whole world to embrace it" and "the peculiarity [particularity] which attends it [to] consist not in its insufficiency to save more than are saved, but in the sovereignty of its application." Here it must be noted that Fuller is speaking about the actual extent of Christ's sin-bearing with respect to humanity, not the quantitative equivalentist issue of the tit-for-tat commercial view of the atonement with respect only to the sins of the elect.

Notice the difference in what Fuller said here compared with what he said above (approximately sixteen years earlier) regarding the death of Christ being of infinite value "if it had pleased God to have constituted them the price of their redemption." Here (in 1801) the death of Christ is not only of infinite value, sufficient for the whole world, but it is actually "equal to the salvation of the whole world." That is a horse of a different color altogether! Fuller has come full circle and abandoned limited atonement as understood and championed by Owen and Booth.

The question at hand is whether the later Fuller continued to believe in the variety of "particular redemption" that maintained a noncommercial yet limited imputation of sin to Christ with respect to his substitution—defined as Christ only suffered for the sins of the elect (position 2 in the chart). I am arguing the answer to that question is twofold: yes, the later Fuller maintained a noncommercial view of the atonement, but no, the later Fuller did not maintain a limited imputation of sin to Christ (limited atonement). He did not merely shift from 1 to 2 as others maintain, but he moved to position 3.

Fuller, Universal Atonement, and the Free Offer of the Gospel

Fuller's debates with Dan Taylor also concerned the grounds necessary for the free offer of the gospel. Taylor had argued that only an unlimited atonement could ground the free offer of the gospel.[101]

One might ask, how could the problem of the free offer of the gospel be helped merely by abandonment of a commercialistic approach to the atonement while still maintaining

101 See D. Taylor, *Observations on the Rev. Andrew Fuller's Late Pamphlet Entitled the Gospel Worthy of All Acceptation* (London: Paternoster-Row, n. d. [1786]); idem, *Observations on the Rev. Andrew Fuller's Reply to Philanthropos*, 2nd ed. (London: T. Bloom, 1788); idem, *The Friendly Conclusion Occasioned by the Letters of Agnostos to the Rev. Andrew Fuller Respecting the Extent of Our Saviour's Death* (London: W. Button, 1790).

limited atonement? It cannot. If Christ only substituted himself for the elect alone, then the salvation of the non-elect would be "naturally impossible," as Fuller said. However, Fuller went on to state:

> If there be an objective fullness in the atonement of Christ sufficient for any number of sinners, were they to believe in him, there is no other impossibility in the way of any man's salvation to whom the gospel comes than what arises from the state of his own mind.[102]

Throughout Reformed history, many within that tradition—long before Fuller—argued the case that the free offer of the gospel was not possible on a limited substitution scheme, and they were arguing the case against Reformed brothers, the vast majority of whom rejected a quantitative equivalentism.

For Fuller, the free offer of the gospel is grounded in the fact that Christ died for the sins of all people, not just the elect. This is further evidenced in Fuller's section "On Particular Redemption":

> There is no contradiction between this peculiarity [particularity] of design in the death of Christ, and a universal obligation on those who hear the gospel to believe in him, or a universal invitation being addressed to them. If God, through the death of his Son, have promised salvation to all who comply with the gospel; and if there be no natural impossibility as to a compliance [note the Edwardsian distinction between natural and moral ability in man here], nor any obstruction but that which arises from aversion of heart; exhortations to believe and be saved are consistent; and our duty, as preachers of the Gospel, is to administer them, without any more regard to particular redemption than to election.[103]

Fuller said there is no obstruction to salvation other than the aversion of the human heart. If particular redemption understood as limited substitution for the sins of the elect alone were Fuller's mature position, he could never have consistently made this statement. In such a case, there would have been a huge impossibility: no atonement exists for the sins of the non-elect any more than there is for fallen angels who have no atonement for their sins.[104]

This is Fuller's point of agreement with Dan Taylor, and he stated it clearly in Letter XII in his *Reality and Efficacy of Divine Grace*.[105] Fuller admitted he had been

102 Fuller, "Six Letters to Dr. Ryland, Letter III, 'Substitution,'" in *Works*, 2:709.
103 Fuller, "On Particular Redemption," in *Works*, 2:374.
104 Ibid.
105 Fuller, "Reality and Efficacy of Divine Grace, Letter XII," in *Works*, 2:550.

mistaken about the terms "ransom" and "propitiation" being applied only to those who were among the elect. Now these terms were "applicable to all mankind in general," an admission which clearly shows Fuller had abandoned limited substitution/atonement, not merely his earlier quantitative commercial views. No one affirming the kind of particular redemption that has a limited substitution component would ever say Christ's death serves as a "propitiation" and "ransom" for the sins of all people.[106]

It seems fairly clear that Fuller, at this point, was in agreement with Taylor concerning the extent of Christ's substitution; he died for every person.

Fuller and Abraham Booth

Abraham Booth's criticism of Fuller is well known. The two men had meetings together to discuss their differences during 1802. Fuller continued to argue that Christ's death, "merely referring to what it is in itself sufficient for, . . . was for sinners as sinners." This is Fuller's statement of unlimited atonement with respect to extent. But Fuller went on to note that with respect to the design or purpose of the atonement, it was for the elect alone. For Fuller, Christ's death, when considered in and of itself, was for sinners as sinners. Fuller thought it was for all sinners as such. I will develop this more in a moment from Fuller's Letter III on "Substitution" to John Ryland.

When we compare Booth's notion of the sufficiency of the atonement with Fuller, there is a difference. Booth said he was willing to admit the sufficiency "to have redeemed all mankind, had all the sins of the whole human species been equally imputed to him." Booth believed only in a hypothetical sufficiency, or a limited imputation of sin to Christ. Not so, the later Fuller.

Fuller and Richard Baxter

Booth charged that Fuller should be reckoned among the followers of Richard Baxter, who also believed in Christ's unlimited sin-bearing. Fuller responded to this in Letter VI to Ryland on "Baxterianism."[107] Note Fuller's actual words in paragraph three:

> Mr. Baxter pleads for "universal redemption;" I only contend for the sufficiency of the atonement, in itself considered, for the redemption and salvation of the whole world; and this affords a ground for a universal invitation to sinners to believe; which was maintained by Calvin, and all old Calvinists. I consider redemption as inseparably connected with eternal life, and therefore as applicable to none but the elect who are redeemed from among men.[108]

106 See "Reply to Philanthropos," in *Works*, 2:496, 2:550 respectively. See also *Works*, 2:555, where Fuller agreed with Taylor on John 3:16, Matt 22:1–11, and John 6:32 with respect to the extent of the atonement covering the sins of all people.

107 See A. Fuller, "Baxterianism," in *Works*, 2:714–15.

108 Ibid., 714.

One of Fuller's differences with Baxter was over the use of the term "redemption." Baxter connected the term "redemption" both with Christ's substitution for the sins of the world on the cross *and* the application to those who believe. Fuller reserved the term "redemption" only for the application of the atonement: those actually saved or possessing eternal life.[109] As demonstrated above, Fuller has already affirmed his support for an unlimited imputation of sin to Christ. Fuller never said he differed with Baxter over the issue of unlimited imputation.[110] Fuller wrote: "The particularity of redemption consists in the sovereign pleasure of God with regard to the application of the atonement; that is with regard to the persons to whom it shall be applied."

So we can say Fuller did maintain "particular redemption," even though he viewed Christ as satisfying for the sins of all people. If asked why we still call Fuller's view "particular redemption" when functionally his view amounts to a Calvinistic version of universal redemption, it is because that is the way Fuller *labeled* his own view. The point is there can be categorical agreement but differences in terminology. Like Baxter, but unlike Fuller, Jonathan Edwards was willing to call Christ's atonement a "universal redemption."

The bottom line is this: Baxter did indeed affirm an unlimited satisfaction for sins, just as Fuller did. However, Fuller disagreed with Baxter's use of the word "redemption" for the sufficient death of Christ on the cross for the sins of all people, not with Baxter's notion of Christ's unlimited satisfaction for sins.

Fuller's Letter III to John Ryland: "Substitution"

An analysis of Fuller's Letter III to John Ryland on "Substitution," written in 1803, two years after Fuller published his second edition of *Gospel Worthy*,[111] demonstrates Fuller's commitment to unlimited atonement.

This is one of six letters Fuller wrote in January, 1803, to his friend, John Ryland, concerning Fuller's ongoing dispute (1796–1806), chiefly over the atonement, with Abraham Booth, a former Arminian who had converted to Calvinism. Booth was especially critical of the influence he believed the New Divinity men in America were having on Fuller. Booth suggested that Fuller denied substitution. Fuller's third letter

109 As did some of the nineteenth-century American Calvinists, such as Robert Dabney. The distinction can be found in some American Calvinist writings at least as early as the first decade of the nineteenth century. See "Atonement and Redemption Not the Same" in *Sermons, Essays, and Extracts by Various Authors Selected with Special Respect to the Great Doctrine of Atonement* (New York: George Forman, 1811), 171–77.

110 It should be noted that Fuller was not influenced by Baxter, so it is unfair to charge him with "Baxterianism." He disagreed with Baxter over a great many things, not the least of which included "obscure terms," "artificial distinctions," the role of faith in justification, the gospel as a "new law" (Neonomianism), Baxter's sense of universal enabling grace, and the extent to which Baxter thought Calvinists and Arminians could be reconciled. Nevertheless, Fuller did state that he found several of his own sentiments in Baxter. With respect to the extent of Christ's death, Baxter, though he had his own peculiarities, did agree with Cranmer, Latimer, Hooper, Ussher, and Davenant, just as Fuller did.

111 A. Fuller, "Substitution," in *Works*, 2:706–9.

to Ryland denied this charge. This context is crucial in the interpretation of the letter. Fuller is not here remonstrating with Dan Taylor, the Arminian, but with a fellow Calvinist, who may have been the source of the false rumor floating around that Fuller had admitted in private he was no longer a Calvinist but an Arminian.

In paragraph two the important point is in the last sentence: "But, perhaps, Mr. B. [Booth] considers 'a *real*[112] and *proper* imputation of our sins to Christ,' by which he seems to mean their being *literally transferred* to him, as essential to this doctrine [substitution]; and if so, I acknowledge I do not at present believe it."[113] Here Fuller stated two things. First, he interpreted Booth's view on imputation to be that of transference ("sins being literally transferred" to Christ). Second, Fuller stated he does not affirm commercialism.

Paragraph four begins: "The only subject on which I ought to have been here interrogated is, 'The persons for whom Christ was a substitute; whether the *elect only*, or *mankind in general*.'" Fuller stated he intended to be "as explicit as I am able" in his answer. Here Fuller clearly and correctly identified the issue at hand. The issue is not whether Fuller believed in substitution; he clearly did.

In paragraph five, Fuller imagined a hypothetical question being asked of him: when the gospel is introduced into a country, "*For whom was it sent?*" His answer is twofold and takes into consideration his belief in God's revealed will and secret will. If answered in respect to the former, Fuller said the gospel "is sent for men, not as elect or as non-elect, but as sinners." "But if I had respect to the secret will or appointment of God as to its application, I should say . . . to take *out of it* a people for his name."[114] Here is Fuller's affirmation of particular redemption in the sense of God's ultimate *intent* in the atonement: to save the elect and them only. This statement alone indicates that in Fuller's mind there is a distinction between for whom atonement was made and for whom it was designed to save. But this does not implicate Fuller as a proponent of limited substitution. He said nothing about a limited extent, merely a limited intent and application.

Paragraph six continues this topic:

> In like manner concerning the death of Christ. If I speak of it *irrespective of the purpose of the Father and the Son, as to its objects who should be saved by it*, merely referring to what it is in itself sufficient for, and declared in the gospel to be adapted to, . . . It was for *sinners as sinners;* but if I have respect to the *purpose* of the Father in giving his Son to die, and to the *design* of Christ in laying down his life, I should answer, *It was for the elect only.*[115]

112 All italics in quotations of Fuller are his.
113 Fuller, *Works*, 2:706.
114 Ibid., 2:705.
115 Ibid., 2:707.

Fuller now moved from the question of "for whom was the gospel sent" and "in like manner" spoke of the death of Christ. Notice that semantically Fuller is contrasting what the atonement "is in itself sufficient for . . . and declared in the gospel to be adapted to," with its *purpose* and *design* that is for the elect only. What is it that is being contrasted? An atonement that is "for sinners as sinners" is being distinguished with an atonement that is, in intent and purpose to save, "for the elect only."

Fuller here noted a distinction between the *nature* and the *design* (application) of the satisfaction. What does Fuller mean by the term "sinners"? All sinners or some sinners? The context here and throughout the letter makes it clear Fuller intended the meaning "all sinners." Whenever Fuller intended to speak of elect sinners only, he carefully qualified the word "sinners" with "elect" or an equivalent term or phrase. For Fuller, "sinners as sinners" means "sinners qua sinners." If I say I love Americans as Americans, I don't mean only some Americans, but Americans qua Americans. There is no other distinction in mind. If one is an American, I love him by definition. Fuller's use of the term "sinners" must be universal as well as qualitative (as opposed to limited and quantitative). If a man is a sinner, Christ has substituted for his sin. This is the thrust of Fuller's explanation to Ryland of the argument against Booth.

Fuller then placed a footnote where he cited John Owen's distinction between what the atonement is in itself sufficient for, and what it is as applied. He further quoted Owen: "That it should be *applied* unto any, made a price for them, and become beneficial to them, according to the worth that is in it, is external to it, doth not arise from it, but merely depends upon the intention and will of God." Fuller rightly noted that it is on this ground that Owen "accounts for the propitiation of Christ being set forth in general and indefinite expressions."[116]

But does Fuller intend his quotation of Owen to indicate his agreement with Owen's notion of limited substitution? No, because contextually Fuller has already indicated the actual atonement was "for sinners as sinners," not that it was merely sufficient in terms of its intrinsic or internal value for all sinners. Nothing in Fuller's footnote on Owen's concept of sufficiency is used by Fuller to deduce a limited substitution. Fuller's view of sufficiency differed from Owen's.

Paragraph seven continues: "In the *former* of these views, I find the apostles . . . addressing themselves to sinners without distinction, and holding forth the death of Christ as a ground of faith to all men." Why does Fuller say "all men" here? This point is vital. If it is only the sins of some men, then those for whom Christ's death was not a substitution have no "ground of faith" for them. They are, as such, not savable. That, implied Fuller, is his challenge to Booth.

Fuller then appealed to two passages, Matt 22:4, where the servants are sent to call guests to the marriage supper, "Come, for *all things are ready*," and 2 Cor 5:21, "He

116 Ibid.

hath made Him to be sin for us who knew no sin, that we might be made the righteousness of God in Him."[117] Here Fuller did not appeal to the sufficiency of the atonement as the "ground of faith to all men" but the atonement itself as this ground of faith for all men. This is evidenced clearly by his quotation of 2 Cor 5:21. Fuller did not interpret the first clause of this verse in a limited fashion as do those Calvinists who affirm limited imputation of sin to Christ. Rather, he used the verse to support the contention that there is a ground of faith to all people in the death of Christ. What is that ground of faith? It is the substitutionary death of Christ for all.

In paragraph eight Fuller continued: "In the *latter* view" (Fuller's statements in paragraph six concerning God's secret will for the "purpose" and "design" of the atonement) God's "discriminating grace" is for the elect only. This is no affirmation of limited substitution because Fuller is speaking about "purpose" and "design" to effectually apply the satisfaction, not "extent." Notice here and elsewhere in this letter Fuller never answered the question he asked in paragraph four (whether Christ was a substitute for the "the elect only" or "mankind in general") with any statement affirming it was for the elect only. In fact, the context clearly indicates he is arguing for mankind in general.

Fuller continued to elaborate on his meaning in paragraph nine. He stated if his definition of substitution above is correct, then with respect to the "designed end" of the atonement, it "is strictly applicable [Fuller intends 'applied'] to none but the elect." Notice carefully the phrase "designed end" and the idea that it is only effectually applied to the elect. Fuller's next statement is very important in context:

> for whatever ground there is for sinners, as sinners, to believe and be saved, it never was the design of Christ to impart faith to any others than those who were given him of the Father. He therefore did not *die* with the intent that any others *should not die*.[118]

Notice Fuller clearly affirmed the limitation is not in the extent of the atonement but in its application. This is evidenced in that Fuller contrasted the "ground there is for sinners, as sinners, to believe and be saved" (unlimited substitution for sinners as sinners), with his point that "it never was the design of Christ to impart faith to any others" than the elect. Fuller did not say it never was the design of Christ to make expiation for, or substitute for, anyone other than the elect. Rather, he said it never was the design of Christ *to impart faith* to anyone other than the elect. Fuller distinguished the *intent*, the *extent*, and the *application* of the atonement.

Fuller asserted in paragraph ten that whether he can reconcile these two statements (Christ's death as ground for sinners as sinners to be saved and the fact that there never

117 Fuller, *Works*, 2:707.
118 Ibid.

was the design of Christ to impart faith to any other than the elect), he believed both are taught in Scripture and saw no inconsistency in them. If all Fuller meant by this was the reconciliation of an intrinsic sufficiency with the understanding that the intent of the atonement was for the elect alone, then there would be no reason to respond to Booth, for he affirmed the same. Much more is at stake.

It is Fuller's next statement in this paragraph that indicates he is speaking about something more than a mere sufficiency of value in the death of Christ. If the death of Christ was a substitution of such kind as to be

> equally required for the salvation of one sinner as for many—is not this the same thing as acknowledging that atonement required to be made for *sin as sin*; and, being made, was applicable to *sinners as sinners*? In other words, is it not acknowledged that God redeemed his elect by an atonement in its own nature adapted to all, just as he calls his elect by a gospel addressed to all?[119]

Notice first that Fuller spoke of substitution, not sufficiency. Second, Fuller spoke of this substitution as "equally required" for one or many sinners. Third, he asserted the atonement was made "for sin as sin" and "was applicable to sinners as sinners." He certainly did not say—indeed, he rejects the idea—that the atonement was made for the sins of the elect only, but for sinners as sinners. It is not possible in this context to interpret Fuller's use of "sinners" to be "elect sinners"; rather, it must mean "all sinners."

Fourth, Fuller spoke of the elect as being "redeemed" by an atonement "in its own nature adapted to all." Fuller does not say "sufficient" for all, though he believes that it is. Rather he said "adapted to all." How could such language be used by one who affirmed a limited substitution? How could the atonement be "adapted to all" and applicable to all, if it is only a substitution for the elect? Fifth, he draws a comparison ("just as") of atonement made with the call of the gospel addressed to the world. How could Fuller make these comments and draw this last comparison if he affirmed both a limited substitution and an unlimited gospel call? The grounds of his comparison would be undercut.

Paragraph eleven is vital to the question at hand. Here Fuller carefully distinguished between the intent, extent, and application of the atonement:

> If the speciality of redemption be placed in the atonement *itself*, and not in the sovereign *will of God*, or in the design of the Father and the Son, with respect to the persons to whom it shall be applied, it must, as far as I am able to per-

119 Ibid., 2:708. See C. Hodge, *Systematic Theology*, 2:544–45; and Dabney, *Systematic Theology*, 525, 527. Hodge used the almost identical wording of Fuller in making the same point. Both Hodge and Dabney did not affirm limited atonement and believed Christ substituted for the sins of all people.

> ceive, have proceeded on the principle of *pecuniary* satisfactions. In them the payment is proportioned to the amount of the debt; and, being so, it is not of sufficient value for more than those who are actually liberated by it; nor is it true, in these cases, that the same satisfaction is required for one as for many. But, if such was the satisfaction of Christ that nothing less was necessary for the salvation of one, nothing more could be necessary for the salvation of the whole world, and the whole world might have been saved by it *if it had accorded with sovereign wisdom so to apply it.* It will also follow that, if the satisfaction of Christ was in *itself* sufficient for the whole world, there is no further propriety in such questions as these—"Whose sins were imputed to Christ? for whom did he die as a substitute?"—than as they go to inquire who were the persons *designed* to be saved by him? That which is equally necessary for one as for many must, in its own nature, be equally sufficient for many as for one; and could not proceed upon the principle of the sins of some being laid upon Christ, rather than others, any otherwise than as it was the *design* of the Father and the Son, through one all-sufficient medium, ultimately to pardon the sins of the elect rather than those of the non-elect.[120]

Fuller queried if the "speciality [particularity] of redemption," "be placed in the atonement *itself*" (by which he means limited substitution) and not in either God's will or design, then with respect to the recipients (the elect), it must proceed on the "principle of pecuniary satisfactions," where the payment made is an exact equivalent of the debt owed.[121]

If this is the case, Fuller concluded that the satisfaction "is not of sufficient *value* for more than those who are actually liberated by it." Quite right. He also concluded that in these cases it is not true "that the same satisfaction is required for one as for many," as noted in paragraph ten. He continued: "If the satisfaction of Christ was in *itself* sufficient for the whole world," there is no need to ask such questions as whose sins were imputed to Christ or for whom did he die as a substitute, any more than asking the question "who were the persons *designed* to be saved by him?"[122] How can Fuller say this? He can do so because the satisfaction of Christ is for sinners qua sinners, or all sinners as such.

Fuller has already stated his affirmation that "the same satisfaction is required for one as for many." Fuller used the term "many" here as equivalent to the whole world. He concluded that if the atonement is limited in its extent, then with respect to the elect, it must proceed on commercial principles, thus negating Fuller's affirmation that

120 A. Fuller, "Six Letters to Dr. Ryland, Letter III," in *Fuller's Works*, 2:708.

121 Ibid.

122 Ibid.

the same satisfaction is required for one as for many. And if this is the case, Fuller further concluded it "is not of sufficient *value*" for anyone other than the elect. Fuller rejected commercialism, and in so doing affirmed universal substitution, not a non-commercial limited substitution. Otherwise Fuller's words become incoherent.

Fuller's next statement is crucial to note: "That which is equally necessary for one as for many, must, in its own nature, be equally sufficient for many as for one; and could not proceed upon the principle of the sins of some being laid upon Christ rather than others."[123] After making this point, Fuller again stated that the saving purpose and intent of the atonement was for the elect only. "To them, his substitution was the same, *in effect*, as if their sins had by number been literally transferred to him." Of course, Fuller has already made clear that he rejected this notion of commercialism and/or literal transference of sins, which is why he employed the conditional "if" and the phrase "*in effect*," which he placed in italics.

His point is that when it comes to actual substitution, it is not possible for Christ to substitute for some (the elect) and not for others. The only way a limited substitution can work is in a commercial or quantitative understanding of imputation of sins, and Fuller clearly has rejected such. However, it is possible for God to have a *design* in making an all-sufficient atonement for it to be applied only to the elect, and that is exactly what Fuller believed. Finally, he concluded the paragraph with the statement "All this I suppose to be included in the *design* of the Father and the Son, or in the 'sovereign application' of the atonement."[124]

Having established that it is not possible for Christ to have accomplished a limited substitutionary atonement, in paragraph twelve Fuller turned his attention to answer the question how it is that the sufficiency of Christ's death can provide the necessary grounds for the general (universal) gospel offer, "if the *design* was confined to the elect people?"[125] Notice Fuller did not say "if the *extent* was confined to the elect," but "if the *design* was confined to the elect." Fuller has demonstrated that he does not conflate these two concepts.

Fuller offered a threefold answer in paragraph thirteen:

> 1. It is a fact that Scriptures rest the general invitation of the gospel upon the atonement of Christ, 2 Cor. V. 19–21; Matt. xxii.4; John iii. 16. 2. If there were not a sufficiency in the atonement for the salvation of sinners, and yet they were invited to be reconciled to God, they must be invited to what is naturally impossible. The message of the gospel would in this case be as if the servants who went forth to bid the guests had said "Come," though, in

123 Ibid.
124 Ibid.
125 Ibid.

> fact, nothing was ready if many of them had come. 3. If there be an objective fullness in the atonement of Christ sufficient for any number of sinners, were they to believe in him, there is no other impossibility in the way of any man's salvation to whom the gospel comes than what arises from the state of his own mind.[126]

For Fuller, "objective fullness" equates to unlimited substitution. Interestingly this is the same language and use of Matt 22:4 that dozens of Calvinists who affirm unlimited substitution before, during, and after the time of Fuller, have used to make their case against a strictly limited atonement. God cannot offer to the non-elect what does not exist for them—namely, an atonement as the grounds for their salvation.

This was the crux of Taylor's argument and Fuller came to see it clearly and abandoned his view of limited substitution altogether, not merely a commercial notion of limited substitution. Here in this letter he now is attempting to answer Booth's charge that he had abandoned substitution completely. Fuller had not abandoned it; he had merely defined it differently than Booth because he now rejected a limited substitution, along with a commercial understanding of the atonement, both of which Booth affirmed.

As Fuller said concerning his debates with Dan Taylor in *The Reality and Efficacy of Divine Grace*, Letter X, published in 1790:

> He [Taylor] would not dispute, it seems, about Christ's dying with a view to the certain salvation of some, provided I would admit that, in another respect, he died for all mankind. Here, then, we seem to come nearer together than we sometimes are. The sense in which he pleads for the universal extent of Christ's death, is only to lay a foundation for this doctrine, that men, in general, may be saved, if they will; and this is what I admit: I allow, that the death of Christ has opened a way, whereby God can, consistently with his justice, forgive any sinner whatever, who returns to him by Jesus Christ; and, if this may be called dying for men, which I shall not dispute, then it is admitted, that Christ died for all mankind.[127]

It seems clear that Fuller was at this point in agreement with Taylor concerning the extent of Christ's substitution: "Christ died for all mankind."

---

126 Ibid., 709.

127 Fuller, "Reality and Efficacy of Divine Grace," in *Works*, 2:543–44. Later in this letter, Fuller spoke of the English Reformers who "fully avowed the doctrine of predestination, and at the same time spoke of Christ's dying for all mankind." Fuller not only affirmed this historically, but stated his own agreement with it as well. He then listed Cranmer, Latimer, Hooper, Ussher, and Davenant, all of whom were examples. Davenant was the leader of the English delegation to Dort and a signatory of the final canons.

We may summarize Fuller's view on the extent of the atonement by asking and answering four questions:

1. Did Fuller, especially in his later writings, distinguish between the intent, extent, and application of the atonement?

   Yes.
2. What did Fuller understand about the atonement with respect to Christ's substitution for sins?

   Fuller believed Christ substituted for all the sins of all sinners, insofar as he died for sinners qua sinners; but only the elect, according to the design and purpose of God in the atonement, will be saved.
3. What did Fuller see in the atonement that lays "a foundation for any sinner to come to God for salvation"?

   Christ's substitution for the sins of all mankind (i.e., sinners as sinners, which entails all sinners by definition).
4. What did Fuller mean when he spoke of the "sufficiency" of Christ's death?

   Context determines the answer to this. Sometimes Fuller refers to a sufficiency of worth and value. At other times he speaks of a sufficiency that is objective and the result of Christ's substitution for the sins of all.

In summary, the limited substitution interpretation of Fuller fails the congruency test and renders Fuller's statements incoherent. Fuller cannot be interpreted as excluding the non-elect in Christ's substitutionary work on the cross. He ruled out any sort of quantitative satisfaction or a limited substitution for the elect to the exclusion of the non-elect. He simply denïed both options.

Conclusion

A number of historians and theologians have concluded that Fuller did indeed come to hold a position of unlimited atonement. J. R. Willson, a high Calvinist, acknowledged Fuller's commitment to unlimited atonement in his 1817 *Historical Sketch of Opinions on the Atonement.*[128]

David Benedict, a nineteenth-century Baptist historian, speaking about the conflict between the "Gillites" and the "Fullerites," noted that the followers of Fuller were often considered Arminians by the Gillites. Yet, as Benedict rightly acknowledged, Fuller would not have differed much with Gill in other areas of Calvinistic soteriology, except with respect to the extent of the atonement.

128 J. R. Willson, *A Historical Sketch of Opinions on the Atonement, Interspersed with Biographical Notices of the Leading Doctors, and Outlines of the Sections of the Church, from the Incarnation of Christ to the Present Time; with Translations from Francis Turretin, on the Atonement* (Philadelphia: Edward Earle, 1817), 116.

> The Fuller system, which makes it consistent for all the heralds of the gospel to call upon men everywhere to repent, was well received by one class of our ministers, but not by the staunch defenders of the old theory of a limited atonement. According to their views, all for whom Christ suffered and died would certainly be effectually called and saved. These conflicting opinions caused altercations of considerable severity for a time, among the Baptists, who had hitherto been all united on the orthodox side. The Gillites maintained that the expositions of Fuller were unsound, and would subvert the genuine gospel faith. If, said they, the atonement of Christ is general in its nature it must be so in its effects, as none of his sufferings will be in vain; and the doctrine of universal salvation will inevitably follow this dangerous creed.[129]

James P. Boyce likewise thought Fuller held to a general atonement.[130] In the early twentieth century, Baptist historian H. C. Vedder stated:

> Fuller boldly accepted and advocated a doctrine of the atonement that, until his day, had always been stigmatized as rank Arminianism, viz., that the atonement of Christ, as to its worth and dignity, was sufficient for the sins of the whole world, and was not an offering for the elect alone, as Calvinists of all grades had hitherto maintained.[131]

Kerfoot served as the editor for the second edition of J. P. Boyce's *Abstract of Systematic Theology*. He made a comment concerning Andrew Fuller likely indicating Kerfoot's belief that Fuller held to unlimited atonement: "Andrew Fuller, we think, has done good service in emphasizing this general feature of the atonement, which high Calvinists, up to this time, had failed to do in their earnest insistence upon the limitations according to election."[132]

W. T. Whitley, the venerable Baptist historian of the first half of the twentieth century, stated that Fuller was teaching essentially what Baxter taught with respect to the extent of the atonement.[133]

W. Lumpkin has an interesting comment on Andrew Fuller that supports our contention that Fuller himself came to affirm universal atonement.

---

129 D. Benedict, *Fifty Years among the Baptists* (New York: Sheldon & Co., 1860), 141.

130 Tom Nettles, *By His Grace and for His Glory: A Historical, Theological and Practical Study of the Doctrines of Grace in Baptist Life*, 2nd ed., rev. and expanded (Cape Coral, FL: Founders, 2006), 153.

131 H. C. Vedder, *A Short History of the Baptists* (Philadelphia: American Baptist Publication Society, 1907), 249. Vedder erred in lumping all previous Calvinists together as affirming limited atonement, and he also erred in labeling Fuller's view "modified Calvinism."

132 J. P. Boyce, *Abstract of Systematic Theology*, 2nd ed., rev. and ed. F. H. Kerfoot (Philadelphia: American Baptist Publication Society, 1899), 274.

133 W. T. Whitley, *Calvinism and Evangelism in England Especially in Baptist Circles* (London: Kingsgate, c. 1933), 33.

> As the leading theologian of the era, Fuller sought to unite the doctrinal strength of Calvinism with the evangelical fervor of the old General Baptists. He did this through his theory of redemption, according to which he separated the doctrine of a general atonement from the doctrine of a particular redemption. Keeping the Calvinistic framework, he added to it the old General Baptist emphasis on a General Atonement.[134]

Robert Oliver acknowledged Fuller's shift on the atonement and spoke of the impact of Fullerism in the nineteenth century but seems vague on whether Fuller actually came to believe in an unlimited extent. "He [Fuller] went on to argue for a particular redemption, which depended upon its effects for its character. . . . Any limitation of the atonement was thus only to be seen in its application."[135] This statement may indicate Oliver thinks Fuller had come to affirm unlimited atonement with respect to the expiation of sin but continued to retain a limited application only to the elect.

Baptist historian W. Wiley Richards stated, "Limited atonement . . . was to be the most prominent position held until the middle of the nineteenth century. Through the influence of Andrew Fuller and others, limited atonement was supplanted by general atonement."[136] Likewise, P. E. Thompson, in his 2004 article "Baptists and 'Calvinism:' Discerning the Shape of the Question," affirmed the later Fuller's belief in a general atonement.[137]

Peter Morden pointed out how Fuller, in his reply to Dan Taylor, "Stated his revised position on the atonement clearly and openly."[138] Morden's conclusion is striking and important: Fuller's view of the extent of the atonement "could now properly be called 'general.'"[139]

> Fuller both clarified and modified his theology of salvation between the years 1785 and 1801, years in which this theology was a crucial motor for change in the life of the Particular Baptist denomination. The most important change was his shift from a limited to a general view of the atonement during his dispute with the Evangelical Arminian Dan Taylor.[140]

---

134 W. Lumpkin, *Baptist Confessions of Faith* (Philadelphia: Judson, 1969), 344.

135 R. Oliver, "The Emergence of a Strict and Particular Baptist Community among the English Calvinistic Baptists 1770–1850" (PhD diss., London Bible College, 1986), 160.

136 W. Wiley Richards, *Winds of Doctrine: The Origin and Development of Southern Baptist Theology* (New York: University Press of America, 1991), 193.

137 P. E. Thompson, "Baptists and 'Calvinism': Discerning the Shape of the Question," *Baptist History and Heritage* 39 (2004): 67–68.

138 Morden, *Offering Christ*, 70. For Fuller's reply, see "Reply to Philanthropos," in *Fuller's Works*, 2:488–89.

139 Morden, *Offering Christ*, 70.

140 Ibid., 75–76.

An 1811 volume entitled *Sermons, Essays, and Extracts by Various Authors: Selected with Special Respect to the Great Doctrine of the Atonement* is a multi-author work by American Calvinists devoted to demonstrating universal atonement.[141] This work contains sermons and essays by Calvinists in North America and England, including the likes of Jonathan Edwards Jr., John Smalley, Jonathan Maxcy, John Newton, and others. Also included is a chapter on "Three Conversations on Imputation, Substitution, and Particular Redemption," by Andrew Fuller. The work concludes with a one-page, two-paragraph chapter, "The Peculiarity of Redemption," taken from Fuller's section "Particular Redemption" in the second edition of *Gospel Worthy*. The inclusion of this material in a work specifically devoted to demonstrating that universal atonement is the biblical position illustrates, at the very least, that these authors believed the later Fuller held to the same doctrine. It is reasonable to conclude that either (1) Fuller had given permission for his works to be included in this volume, which would constitute clear evidence that Fuller held to unlimited atonement or (2) the editor(s) included these writings from Fuller because they themselves believed he held to unlimited atonement. In either case, there is no extant evidence that Fuller himself or any of his colleagues disputed his inclusion in this volume.

Finally, Fuller's first biographer, J. W. Morris, himself asserted—not once but three times—that Fuller had conceded the universality of the death of Christ for the sins of all people in his debates with Dan Taylor.[142]

The evidence seems quite strong that Fuller did indeed shift from a limitarian position to an unlimited view of the extent of the atonement. Fuller was a Particular Redemptionist who held to universal atonement. As the most important Particular Baptist in the late eighteenth and early nineteenth centuries, this point is seismic in its consequences for Baptist history and theology.

William Carey (AD 1761–1834)

William Carey, Baptist, Calvinist, and founder of the modern foreign mission movement, is a legendary figure. There is not enough material from Carey on the extent question to make a strict determination of his views. However, from what he did write, it seems likely that Carey had come to some understanding of the atonement as having actually paid for the sins of all people.

Carey and his fellow missionaries drew up "The Serampore Compact" in 1805 as a summary of their guiding principles. It stresses God's sovereignty in the missionary enterprise. But consider what this compact states in one place:

141 *Sermons, Essays, and Extracts.*

142 J. W. Morris, *Memoirs of Fuller*, 204, 206, 207.

> Fifthly. In preaching to the heathen, we must keep to the example of Paul, and make the greatest subject of our preaching, Christ Crucified. It would be very easy for a missionary to preach nothing but truths, and that for many years together, without any well-grounded hope of becoming useful to one soul. The doctrine of Christ's expiatory death and all-sufficient merits has been, and must ever remain, the grand mean of conversion. This doctrine, and others immediately connected with it, have constantly nourished and sanctified the church. Oh, that these glorious truths may ever be the joy and strength of our own souls, and then they will not fail to become the matter of our conversation to others. It was the proclaiming of these doctrines that made the Reformation from Popery in the time of Luther spread with such rapidity. It was these truths that filled the sermons of the modern Apostles, Whitefield, Wesley, etc., when the light of the Gospel which had been held up with such glorious effects by the Puritans was almost extinguished in England. It is a well-known fact that the most successful missionaries in the world at the present day make the atonement of Christ their continued theme. We mean the Moravians. They attribute all their success to the preaching of the death of our Saviour. So far as our experience goes in this work, we must freely acknowledge, that every Hindoo among us who has been gained to Christ, has been won by the astonishing and all-constraining love exhibited in our Redeemer's propitiatory death. O then may we resolve to know nothing among Hindoos and Mussulmans [Muslims] but Christ and Him crucified.[143]

Notice Carey's reference to "Christ's expiatory death and all-sufficient merits." Carey included Wesley with Whitefield, who preached "these doctrines." He spoke of the Moravians as being "the most successful missionaries in the world at the present day," and keep in mind that they were not Calvinistic and affirmed an unlimited atonement. Notice finally Carey's reference to the "all-constraining love exhibited in our Redeemer's propitiatory death."

Consider also this quotation from Carey in a letter dated April 10, 1796:

> I preach every day to the Natives, and twice on the Lord's Day constantly, besides other itinerant labours, and I try to speak of Jesus Christ and him

143 See G. Smith, *The Life of William Carey: Shoemaker and Missionary* (London: J. Murray, 1885), 444. This "Form of Agreement" was written by W. Carey, J. Marshman, and W. Ward and was printed at the Brethren's Press, Serampore, in 1805, and reprinted at the Baptist Mission Press, Calcutta, in 1874, with this title page: "Form of Agreement respecting the Great Principles upon which the Brethren of the Mission at Serampore think it their duty to act in the work of instructing the Heathen, agreed upon at a Meeting of the Brethren at Serampore, on Monday, October 7, 1805."

> crucified, and of him alone, but my soul is often much dejected to see no fruit. This morning I preached to a number from "to know the Love of God which passeth knowledge." I was much affected myself, filled with grief and anguish of Heart, because I knew they were going to Idolatrous and Mohammedan feasts immediately after, this being the first day of the Hindu Year; and the new Moon Ramadan of the Mohammedans. They are going I suppose to their Abominations at this moment, but I hope to preach to them again in the evening. I spoke of the Love of God in bearing with his Enemies, in supporting and providing for them, in sending his Son to die for them, and in sending the Gospel to them, and in saving many of them from eternal Wrath.[144]

The referent for "them" certainly seems like it includes all of the unbelieving nationals he eventually spoke to. Notice how Carey stated that God sent "his Son to die for them" in reference to all the unbelieving nationals.

Carey also wrote to Andrew Fuller in a letter dated November 1800 where he explained to Fuller how he shared the gospel with several of the people in one of the villages:

> You and I, and all of us are Sinners, and we are in a helpless state but I have good things to tell you. God in the riches of his Mercy became incarnate, in the form of Man. He lived more than thirty years on earth without Sin and was employed in doing good. He gave sight to the Blind, healed the Sick, the lame, the Deaf and the Dumb—and after all died in the stead of Sinners. We deserved the wrath of God, but he endured it. We could make no sufficient atonement for our guilt but he compleatly made an end of Sin and now he has sent us to tell you that the Work is done and to call you to faith in, and dependence on the Lord Jesus Christ.[145]

In these two quotes, it sounds like Carey is making "the bold proclamation," saying that God sent his Son to die for them (all in his lost audience) and other "enemies," some of which (not all) are saved from eternal wrath. If Carey accepted limited substitution (limited atonement), he would have to be equivocating on the term "sinners" and fudge on the inclusive term "we," as if he really didn't mean all those in his audience.

Carey spoke about how his preaching changed when he came to the mission field; "My Preaching is very different to what it was in England; but the Guilt and

144 T. G. Carter, ed., *Journal and Selected Letters of William Carey* (Macon, GA: Smyth & Helwys, 2000), 85.
145 Ibid., 149.

depravity of Mankind and the Redemption by Christ, with the presence of God's Mercy; are the themes I most insist upon."[146] Though this statement itself does not constitute proof of Carey's commitment to unlimited atonement, it is interesting in itself.

Carey reported a conversation with unbelieving nationals: "I then told them how God sent his son, to save Sinners, that he came to save them from Sin, and that he died in Sinner's stead, and that whosoever believe on him would obtain everlasting life, and would become Holy."[147] The word "them" definitely includes all those in his lost audience, so it sounds like he is using "sinners" to include them as well when he says "he [Christ] died in Sinner's stead," such that "whosoever [of them] believe on him would obtain everlasting life."

Carey may have had a governmental component to his view of penal substitutionary atonement:

> My great concern now is to be found in Christ. His atoning sacrifice is all my hope; and I know that Sacrifice to be of such value that God has accepted it as fully vindicating his government in the exercise of mercy to sinners, and as that on account of which he will accept the greatest offender who seeks to him for pardon. And the acceptance of that sacrifice of atonement was testified by the resurrection of our Lord from the dead and by the commission to preach the Gospel to all nations with a promise, or rather a declaration, that whosoever believeth on the Son shall be saved, shall not come into condemnation, but is passed from death unto life.[148]

Though one cannot say definitively that Carey held to unlimited atonement, it seems likely from these excerpts from his own writings that he did. Likewise, no one can say definitely that Carey held to limited atonement.

Richard Furman (AD 1755–1825)

Furman was elected first president of the Triennial Convention, the first national Baptist association of churches and he was the first president of the South Carolina State Baptist Convention. The early Furman held to a strictly limited atonement but apparently was influenced by Andrew Fuller and shifted to the general atonement position.[149]

146 Ibid., 84.
147 Ibid., 54.
148 Ibid., 251–52.
149 Richards, *Winds of Doctrine* (Lanham, MD: University Press of America, 1991), 58.

Andrew Broaddus (AD 1770–1848)

Broaddus was a nineteenth-century Calvinistic Baptist[150] who made it clear that he accepted universal atonement. Following his statements expressing his criticism of a commercial understanding of the atonement, Broaddus continued:

> These remarks on the *nature* of the atonement, lead to the question as to its *extent.* And here I take occasion to say, that a consistent and scriptural view of this subject appears to lead to the conclusion, that the atonement is *general* in its *nature* and *extent.* As opening a way for the salvation of sinners, considered *as sinners*, it is general in its nature; and as being of sufficient value for the salvation of the world, it is general in its *extent.* At the same time, it may be proper to remark, that *redemption*, considered as the result and application of the atonement, is limited, of course, to those who actually become the subjects of grace; in other words; to those who become believers in Jesus.[151]

Not only were there many Particular Baptists who affirmed universal atonement, not all of them interpreted election strictly according to the Dortian paradigm. One can find "striking depictions of election as being primarily a corporate reality" according to Philip Thompson. Thompson referenced *The Baptist Catechism* (1683/84), which was patterned closely after *The Westminster Shorter Catechism. The Baptist Catechism* rarely deviated from verbatim quotation of the *Westminster Shorter Catechism* articles. But the article on election demonstrates a noteworthy deviation. Westminster speaks of election as, "God having out of his mere good pleasure, from all eternity, elected some to everlasting life." *The Baptist Catechism* reads "God having out of his mere good pleasure, from all eternity, elected a people to everlasting life."[152] This is a significant departure from Westminster and just as easily can be interpreted to support corporate election as individual election.

Howard Hinton (AD 1791–1873) and James Haldane (AD 1768–1851)

John Howard Hinton (1791–1873) was a Particular Baptist pastor and denominational leader who served as President of the Baptist Union in 1837 and 1863 and was

---

150 For information on Broaddus's life, consult W. B. Sprague, *Annals of the American Baptist Pulpit*, 9 vols. (New York: Robert Carter & Brothers, 1860), 6:291–96.

151 A. Broaddus, "The Atonement," in *The Sermons and Other Writings of the Rev. Andrew Broaddus, with a Memoir of His Life*, ed. A. Broaddus (New York: Lewis Colby, 1852), 109. A contemporary biographer, Jeremiah Jeter, categorized Broaddus as "moderately Calvinistic," along the lines of Andrew Fuller (*Sermons and Other Writings of the Rev. Andrew Broaddus with a Memoir of His Life* [New York: Lewis Colby, 1852], 45 [emphasis in original]).

152 P. E. Thompson, "Baptists and Calvinism: Discerning the Shape of the Question," *Baptist History and Heritage* (Spring 2004), 73. See "The Westminster Shorter Catechism," in *The Book of Confessions* (Louisville, KY: The Office of the General Assembly, 1994), 182; and *The Baptist Catechism* (1683/1684; repr. Grand Rapids, MI: Baker, 1952), 20.

secretary of the Union from 1841 to 1866. He, along with the thirty-six churches of the Baptist Midland Association, published a circular letter in 1839 in which they advocated unlimited atonement, along with a discussion concerning the means of salvation: the Spirit and the Word.[153] This brought the ire of J. A. Haldane, who published a response.[154] Hinton followed with a rejoinder to Haldane.[155] This lively exchange illustrates the reality that at this point, both in England and America, Calvinists themselves were heavily engaged in debate over the extent of the atonement.

For our purposes, we are only interested in part two of Haldane's response to Hinton, since it addressed specifically the issue of the extent of the atonement. Here one finds all the standard arguments in favor of limited atonement. One has to wade through a fair amount of false dichotomies and logical fallacies to get to Haldane's point: the extent of the atonement is governed by the intent of the atonement. God intended to save only his elect, hence Christ died only for the elect. Haldane's edifice is built on two shaky foundations: John Owen's commercial understanding of the atonement and the supposition that the intent and extent of the atonement are coextensive.

Haldane, along with other critics of Hinton, essentially accused their Calvinist brothers of leaning toward Arminianism.[156] This accusation is obviously false since the circular letter is introduced with a listing of doctrines the churches affirm, and the list includes "Eternal and Personal Election,—Original sin,—Particular Redemption,—Free Justification by the Righteousness of Christ imputed,—Efficacious grace in Regeneration,—the Final Perseverance of the Saints."[157] This certainly does not sound very Arminian.

Notice especially the phrase "Particular Redemption." This phrase is often equated with "limited atonement." But as we have seen above, it is not uncommon, especially in the nineteenth century, to see Calvinist theologians affirming an unlimited atonement and at the same time a "particular redemption," namely, the salvation of the elect only. Hinton was a Particular Baptist, yet he, and others, like Andrew Fuller before him, held to unlimited atonement.

Hinton's rejoinder mostly addressed the issue of the role of the Holy Spirit in conversion. He referred Haldane to his writings on the extent of the atonement in his other works. There it is evident that Hinton affirmed an unlimited atonement.[158]

---

153 See also J. H. Hinton, "Whether Christ Died for All Men, Essay XII, " in *Theological Works of the Rev. John Howard Hinton, M. A.*, 6 vols. (London: Houlston & Wright, 1864), 2:361–77.

154 J. A. Haldane, *Man's Responsibility; the Nature and Extent of the Atonement; and the Work of the Holy Spirit in Reply to Mr. Howard Hinton and the Baptist Midland Association* (Edinburgh: William Whyte and Co., 1842).

155 J. H. Hinton, "A Rejoinder to Mr. Haldane," in *The Theological Works of the Rev. John Howard Hinton*, 1:125–82.

156 This is evidenced by comments made in critical reviews of Hinton coupled with positive reviews of Haldane in *The Primitive Church Magazine* 11 (November 1, 1841): 241–54; *The Primitive Church Magazine* 15 (March 1, 1842): 49–53, 67–68, 124–128.

157 Haldane, *Man's Responsibility*, 178–79.

158 See Hinton, "Whether Christ Died for All Men," 2:361–77.

Charles Spurgeon (AD 1836–1892)

Charles Haddon Spurgeon often has been cited, especially by Baptists, as a staunch Calvinist. While Spurgeon did indeed affirm limited atonement, at times it is clear he was inconsistent in his preaching on this issue. A. C. Underwood, in *A History of English Baptists*, wrote that Spurgeon's "rejection of a limited atonement would have horrified John Calvin."[159] Underwood is wrong on both counts: Spurgeon actually did affirm limited atonement, but John Calvin did not. According to Underwood, Spurgeon often prayed, "Hasten to bring in all Thine elect, and then elect some more." The mature Spurgeon confided in Archbishop Benson, "I'm a very bad Calvinist, quite a Calvinist—I look on to the time when the elect will be all the world."[160]

In a sermon on the atonement, Spurgeon appealed to the double payment argument as evidence for viewing the death of Christ as only for the elect, as well as securing assurance of salvation for all who have believed.

> There may be men with minds so distorted that they can conceive it possible that Christ should die for a man who afterwards is lost; I say, there may be such. I am sorry to say that there are still to be found some such persons, whose brains have been so addled in their childhood that they cannot see what they hold is both a preposterous falsehood and a blasphemous libel. Christ dies for a man, and then God punishes that man again; Christ suffers in a sinner's stead, and then God condemns that sinner after all! Why, my friends, I feel quite shocked in only mentioning such an awful error. Were it not so current as it is, I should certainly pass it over with the contempt that it deserves.
>
> The doctrine of holy Scripture is this, that God is just, that Christ died in the stead of His people, and that, as God is just, He will never punish one solitary soul of Adam's race for whom the Savior did thus shed His blood. The Savior did, indeed, in a certain sense, die for all; all men receive many a mercy through His blood. But that He was the substitute and surety for all men is so inconsistent, both with reason and Scripture, that we are obliged to reject the doctrine with abhorrence. No, my soul, how shalt thou be punished if thy Lord endured thy punishment for thee? Did He die for thee? O my soul, if Jesus was not thy substitute and did not die in thy very stead, then He is no Savior for thee! But if He was thy substitute, if He suffered as thy surety, in thy stead, then, my soul, "Who is he that condemneth?" Christ has died, yea, rather, has risen again, and sitteth at the right hand of God, and maketh intercession for us. There stands the master-argument:

159 A. C. Underwood, *A History of English Baptists* (London: Unwin Brothers Ltd., 1947).

160 A. C. Benson, *The Life of Edward White Benson*, 2 vols. (London: Macmillan & Co., 1900), 2:276.

> Christ "laid down his life for us," and "if, when we were enemies, we were reconciled to God saved by his life" (Romans 5:10). If the agonies of the Savior put our sins away, the everlasting life of the Savior, with the merits of His death added thereunto, must preserve His people, even unto the end.[161]

Spurgeon also spoke about the relationship of the death of Christ for us and our believing the gospel.

> I sometimes feel myself a little at variance with that verse—"Just as I am—without one plea But that Thy blood was shed for me." It is eminently suitable for a child of God, but I am not so sure to its being the precise way for putting the matter of a sinner. I do not believe in Jesus because I am persuaded that His blood was shed for me, but rather I discover that His blood was shed especially for me from the fact that I have been led to believe in Him. Jesus died with the special intent that we should be saved.[162]

Given this statement, it is surprising that Spurgeon would appeal to unbelievers in his congregation not only on the basis of the atonement of Christ but on the basis of Christ actually dying for their sins:

> Come, I beseech you, on Calvary's mount, and see the cross. Behold the Son of God, he who made the heavens and the earth, *dying for your sins*. Look to him, is there not power in him to save? Look at his face so full of pity. Is there not love in his heart to prove him willing to save? Sure sinner, the sight of Christ will help thee to believe.[163]

Notice the glaring inconsistency here. As one who believes in limited atonement, Spurgeon knows that there are always some of the non-elect in his audience when he preaches. For such people, there is no atonement. Yet Spurgeon addressed them and told them point blank that Christ died for their sins. This is nothing short of inconsistent for someone who holds to limited atonement.

In another sermon, "For Whom Did Christ Die?," Spurgeon said that Christ died for mankind, which normally would be understood as the whole world. He also said

161 C. H. Spurgeon, "The Death of Christ for His People," in *Metropolitan Tabernacle Pulpit*, 57 vols. (Pasadena, TX: Pilgrim, 1977), 46:6–7.

162 C. H. Spurgeon, "Faith and Regeneration," in *Metropolitan Tabernacle Pulpit*, 17:139.

163 C. H. Spurgeon, "Compel Them to Come In," in *New Park Street Pulpit*, 6 vols. (Pasadena, TX: Pilgrim, 1981), 5:23 (emphasis mine).

that Christ died for the "ungodly." Again, this is a broad word and could be construed as implying unlimited atonement. "We may fairly conclude that Christ died for men who needed such a death; and, as the good did not need it for an example—and in fact it is not an example to them—he must have died for the ungodly."[164] Given Spurgeon's belief in limited atonement, he must mean by this last statement that Christ died for the "ungodly elect."

Also in this sermon, Spurgeon asked and answered a question he posed to the crowd, which included unbelievers, concerning one who cannot believe Christ died for them. Spurgeon stated that if Christ did not die for the ungodly, then such a person makes God a liar.[165]

It is interesting that Spurgeon preached twice on Ps 147:3, once early in his ministry in 1855 and again late in 1890, just two years before his death. A comparison of these sermons reveals something quite interesting. In the 1855 sermon, Spurgeon is not shy about telling his audience, which includes nonbelievers, that Christ died for their sins:

> Now, in the silence of your agony, look unto him who by his stripes healeth thee. Jesus Christ has suffered the penalty of thy sins, and has endured the wrath of God on thy behalf. See you, yonder crucified Man on Calvary, and mark thee that those drops of blood are falling for thee, those nailed hands are pierced for thee, and that opened side contains a heart within it, full of love to thee.[166]

These statements would certainly give the impression that Spurgeon affirmed an unlimited atonement. He could not consistently speak in this fashion from a limited atonement perspective.

In the 1890 sermon, Spurgeon mitigated this bold language somewhat: "Healing for broken hearts comes by the atonement, atonement by substitution, Christ suffering in our stead. He suffered for every one who believeth in him, and he that believeth in him is not condemned, and never can be condemned, for the condemnation due to him was laid upon Christ."[167] Notice in this statement Spurgeon said Christ "suffered for every one who believeth in him." This is a statement commensurate with limited atonement. However, even here, Spurgeon did not say Christ died *only* for the sins of those who believe in him, though that is likely what he intends.

164 C. H. Spurgeon, "For Whom Did Christ Die?," in *Metropolitan Tabernacle Pulpit*, 20:497.
165 Ibid., 500.
166 C. H. Spurgeon, "Healing for the Wounded," in *New Park Street Pulpit*, 1:410.
167 C. H. Spurgeon, "Christ's Hospital," in *Metropolitan Tabernacle Sermons*, 38:281.

Clearly Spurgeon believed in limited atonement. But it is equally clear he was not always consistent with that belief in his own preaching.

Spurgeon once admitted his uncomfortableness in the debates over the atonement's extent within Calvinism:

> I always feel very fidgety when theologians begin making calculations about the Lord Jesus. There used to be a very strong contention about particular redemption and general redemption, and though I confess myself to be to the very backbone a believer in Calvinistic doctrine, I never felt at home in such discussions. It is one thing to believe in the doctrines of grace, but quite another thing to accept all the encrustations which have formed upon those doctrines, and also a very different matter to agree with the spirit which is apparent in some who profess to propagate the pure truth.
>
> I can have nothing to do with calculating the value of the atonement of Christ. I see clearly the specialty of the purpose and intent of Christ in presenting his expiatory sacrifice, but I cannot see a limit to its preciousness, and I dare not enter into computations as to its value or possible efficacy. Appraisers and valuers are out of place here.[168]

Given Spurgeon's avowal of his own Calvinism, it is certainly ironic that he should be vilified in his own day by many Calvinists who went so far as to accuse him of Arminianism. Iain Murray, in his fascinating volume *Spurgeon v. Hyper-Calvinism*, explained how many Calvinists viewed Spurgeon's ministry as a "second-hand ministry, deeply tainted with an Arminian spirit."[169]

Merger of General and Particular Baptists in England

1891 was a watershed year for General and Particular Baptists in England. After something of a courtship for some sixty years, the two groups finally united, primarily around the practical issue of missions. It was a slow train coming.[170]

In the last three decades of the eighteenth century, the stage was being set for the ultimate merger that would occur a hundred years later. The New Connexion General Baptists were reinvigorated with an evangelical orthodoxy, minus their for-

168 C. H. Spurgeon, "Rivers of Water in a Dry Place," in *Metropolitan Tabernacle Pulpit*, 21:388.

169 I. Murray, *Spurgeon v. Hyper-Calvinism*, 54.

170 The story is well-told by J. H. Y. Briggs in "Evangelical Ecumenism: The Amalgamation of General and Particular Baptists in 1891, Part 1," *Baptist Quarterly* 34, no. 3 (July 1991): 99–115; idem, "Evangelical Ecumenism: The Amalgamation of General and Particular Baptists in 1891, Part 2," *Baptist Quarterly* 34, no. 4 (October 1991): 160–79.

mer Socinian leanings, while the Particular Baptists, under the influence of Andrew Fuller and others, began to throw off the yoke of hyper-Calvinism. Both groups were increasingly concerned and committed to foreign missions and evangelism at home. The reorganization of the Baptist Union in 1832, followed by the back and forth on union possibility in the 1860s, '70s, and '80s, set the stage for an eventual reunion of the two denominations.

There was considerable cross-pollination between the two groups by the 1860s in terms of ministry and education. This continued over the next two decades. W. Underwood described the situation in an 1864 paper read before the Baptist Union of Great Britain and Ireland in the Cannon Street Chapel in Birmingham:

> "*General* Baptist churches are quite accustomed to choose *Particular* Baptist pastors; and a proportionate but not an equal number of General Baptists pastors are settled over Particular Baptist churches. The exchange of pulpits on both ordinary and special occasions is now of frequent occurrence, and the same sermons, if delivered verbatim, are as acceptable, so far as doctrine is concerned, in one place as in another."[171]

As time elapsed, the ranks of those occupying a *via media* between the extremes of an unmoderated high Calvinism and a tendency toward Unitarianism among some on the General Baptist side swelled in the Baptist Union.

John Clifford and Alexander Maclaren played strategic roles in laying the groundwork for reunion. Clifford had proposed a resolution in favor of amalgamation in October 1889 at the Baptist Union Assembly. According to Clifford, even where Calvinism was strong in certain churches and associations, some two-thirds of the members of these churches were not in full accord with the existing doctrinal statements that were Calvinistic. Even among many of these statements, the notion of limited atonement had long since been abandoned.

An interesting statement from London pastor Dawson Burns in *The Baptist Magazine* in March of 1889 tended to confirm that many Particular Baptists were not as entrenched in their commitment to five-point Calvinism as earlier generations may have been. He spoke of five-sixths of their churches and pastors as being "now in the main as 'General' in their doctrine as the General Baptists themselves."[172]

The final step of union occurred during the Association Meeting at Burnley in June 1891 where John Clifford served as president. Clearly some Calvinistic Baptists, like Spurgeon himself who was deeply disillusioned by the union for theological reasons, still held to limited atonement. Alexander Maclaren summed up the mood of the

171 Underwood, *The General Baptist Denomination*, 23.
172 Briggs, "Evangelical Ecumenism, Part 2," 174.

majority, however, when he remarked that it was no time to debate general or particular atonement when the whole world was asking if there was any atonement at all.[173]

Mennonite and Baptist Confessions—Sixteenth, Seventeenth, and Eighteenth Centuries

The Waterland Confession (1580) was a Mennonite confession. Article 7, "Of God's Predestination, Election and Reprobation," affirms a universal atonement:

> But inasmuch as this good God, as truly as he lives, does not delight in the destruction of any (f), nor wish that any should perish, but that all men should be saved (g) and attain to eternal salvation, so also he decreed and created all men for salvation (h); and when fallen, through his ineffable love (i) he restored them in Christ and in him ordained and prepared for all a medicine of life (k), if indeed Christ was given (l), offered (m) and died for a propitiation for all.[174]

Likewise, Article 8 affirms unlimited atonement: "We confess that the obedience of the Son of God (a), his bitter passion (b), death (c), effusion of blood (d), and unique sacrifice on the cross, is a reconciliation (e) and satisfaction for us all and for the sins of the whole world."[175]

Another influential Mennonite confession, The Dordrecht Confession (1632), affirms unlimited atonement in Article 9:

> Furthermore we believe and confess, that this is the same One, . . . who was sent into the world, and Himself delivered up the body prepared for Him, as "an offering and a sacrifice to God for a sweet smelling savour;" yea, for the comfort, redemption, and salvation of all—of the human race.[176]

By 1587/1588 a Separatist congregation began in London. Later, some of this congregation immigrated to Amsterdam, leaving the smaller body in London. This Separatist congregation produced *A True Confession* (1596) to guide both bodies. Though the confession stops short of affirming a strictly limited atonement, it does connect the atonement with the redemption of God's elect in Article 14:

---

173 A. Maclaren, *Missionary Observer* (August 1891): 320; cited in "Evangelical Ecumenism, Part 2," 177.
174 W. L. Lumpkin, *Baptist Confessions of Faith* (Valley Forge, PA: Judson, 1959), 47.
175 Ibid., 51.
176 Ibid., 69.

> That touching his Priesthood, being consecrated, he hath appeared once to put away sin, by offering and sacrificing of himself; and to this end hath fully performed and suffered all those things, by which God through the blood of that his cross, in an acceptable sacrifice, might be reconciled to his elect; & having broke down the partition wall, & therewith finished & removed all those legal rites, shadows, & ceremonies, is now entered within the vail into the holy of Holies. . . . [177]

In 1609 John Smyth produced the *Short Confession of Faith in 20 Articles.* Article 2 states: "That God has created and redeemed the human race to his own image, and has ordained all men (no one being reprobated) to life."[178]

The following year, The Helwys party produced *A Short Confession of Faith* (1610). Article 7 states: "Yea, much more . . . hath foreseen and ordained in him [Christ] a medicine of life for all their sins, and hath willed that all people or creatures, through the preaching of the gospel, should have these things published and declared unto them."[179] Likewise, Article 12 stated: "Moreover, as a High Priest . . . he hath finally given himself obediently (for the reconciliation of the sins of the world). . . . We acknowledge . . . that the obedience of the Son of God . . . is a perfect reconciliation and satisfaction for our sins and the sins of the world."[180]

In 1611, Thomas Helwys produced *A Declaration of Faith of English People Remaining in Amsterdam in Holland.* Lumpkin explained concerning this confession:

> Mennonite influence is readily seen in the confession for it shows a departure from the hitherto markedly consistent Calvinism of the Separatist movement. But it shows also decided signs of its authors' Calvinistic background. It is anti-Calvinistic on the doctrine of the atonement and anti-Arminian in its views of sin and the will.[181]

Article 3 states: "That by the promised seed of the woman, Jesus Christ, [and by] his obedience, all are made righteous. Rom. 5:19. All are made alive, 1 Cor. 15:22. His righteousness being imputed unto all."[182]

The followers of John Smyth produced a confession entitled *Propositions and Conclusions concerning True Christian Religion* (1612–14). Articles 22, 27, and 28 affirm

177 Ibid., 85 (some spelling modernized).
178 Ibid., 100. Lumpkin noted this confession was unique in two ways: it was anti-Calvinistic and anti-paedobaptist.
179 Ibid., 104.
180 Ibid., 105–6.
181 Ibid., 115.
182 Ibid., 117.

an unlimited atonement. Article 28 speaks of Christ "that He bought them that deny Him (2 Peter 2:1)."[183]

It is important to point out at this juncture that the earliest General Baptists did not embrace a full-orbed Arminianism, as Philip Thompson has noted. They were not as "vigorously anti-Calvinistic as they have often been portrayed."[184]

The Psalgrave Confession, "A Full Declaration of the Faith and Ceremonies professed in the dominions of the most illustrious and noble Prince Frederick V., Prince Elector Palatine," was translated by John Rolte and published in London in 1614. It strongly affirms an unlimited atonement: "Of the power of the death of Christ believe we, that the death of Christ, (while he being not a bare man, but the Son of God died) is a full and all-sufficient payment, not only for our sins, but also the sins of the whole world."[185]

The first well-known Baptist confession is The London Confession (1644). This confession is heavily dependent upon the 1596 Separatist work, A True Confession. Article 17 states, "Touching his Priesthood, Christ . . . hath appeared once to put away sin by the offering and sacrifice of himself, and to this end hath fully performed and suffered all those things by which God, through the blood of that his Crosse in an acceptable sacrifice, might reconcile his elect only."[186] Article 21 states, "That Christ Jesus by his death did bring forth salvation and reconciliation only for the elect."[187]

Lumpkin assumed these articles teach a strictly limited atonement. But a careful look at the wording reveals that such is not necessarily the case. What the two articles affirm clearly is that the death of Christ has provided "salvation" and "reconciliation" for the elect only. This wording does not mandate limited atonement; it only mandates, in good Calvinist fashion, that the actual benefits of the atonement redound only to the elect. Any Calvinist who affirmed an unlimited atonement could sign this statement of faith, and in fact, Paul Hobson, a Particular Baptist who clearly affirmed unlimited atonement, did just that.[188]

Lumpkin suggested that some London General Baptists

> seem to have responded to this confession in 1645 with a pamphlet called *The Fountaine of Free Grace Opened*, in which they defended their distinctive doctrine of a general atonement but distinguished themselves from "The

---

183 Ibid., 128.

184 Thompson, "Baptists and 'Calvinism,'" 65.

185 *A Declaration of the Pfaltzgraves: Concerning the Faith and Ceremonies Professed in His Churches*, trans. J. Rolte (London: Printed for Thomas Jones, and are to bee sold at his Shop in the Strand neere Yorke-House, 1637), fol. B3r (some language modernized).

186 Lumpkin, *Baptist Confessions of Faith*, 160.

187 Ibid., 162.

188 See M. Bell, *Apocalypse How? Baptist Movements during the English Revolution* (Macon, GA: Mercer, 2000), 82, 91–94.

Arminians" and denounced "scandalous aspersions" that they held to freedom of the will and denied a free election of grace.[189]

Another General Baptist confession appeared in 1651: *The Faith and Practice of Thirty Congregations*. Lumpkin said of this confession, "No consistently Arminian system is revealed; rather, some traditional emphases of Calvinism are set forth."[190] Article 17 states, "That Jesus Christ, through (or by) the grace of God, suffered death for all mankind, or every man; Heb. 2:9."[191]

In the late 1640s, Thomas Lover issued a confession that the General Baptists reissued in 1654: *The True Gospel Faith*.[192] Article 4 stated: "That God out of his love sent his son into the world to be born of woman, to die for the sins of all men under the first Covenant, John 3:16." Article 5 likewise stated, "That he did do the will of the Father, in laying down his life for all sinners, Phil 2:8 . . . . 1 Tim. 2:6, who gave himself a ransom for all."[193]

Particular Baptists produced the Midland Association Confession (1655), which was modeled on the London Confession. Article 7 states: "That Jesus Christ was, in the fullness of time, manifested in the flesh . . . gave Himself for the elect, to redeem them to God by his blood."[194]

The Somerset Confession (1656) is a Particular Baptist confession notable because it represents the earliest important effort at bringing together Particular and General Baptists. Lumpkin noted, "The Calvinism of the Western Association was not a rigid type. Collier, as a lay evangelist, was troubled by some of the same practical difficulties which the General Baptists said they saw in the doctrine of a restricted or particular atonement, ye he liked the Calvinistic framework."[195] Nevertheless, the confession affirms a limited atonement in Article 15: "THAT this man Christ Jesus suffered death . . . bearing the sins of his people on his own body on the cross . . . and by his death upon the cross, he hath obtained eternal redemption and deliverance for his church."[196]

The Standard Confession (1660) was, according to Lumpkin, "mildly Arminian"[197] and clearly affirmed a universal atonement. Article 3 states, "That there is one Lord Jesus Christ, . . . whom God freely sent into the World (because of his great love unto the World) who as freely gave himself a ransome for all, 1 Tim. 2:5,6. tasting death for every man, Heb. 2:9."[198]

189 Ibid., 147.
190 Ibid., 173.
191 Ibid., 178.
192 L. McBeth, *The Baptist Heritage: Four Centuries of Baptist Witness* (Nashville: Broadman, 1987), 70.
193 Lumpkin, *Baptist Confessions of Faith*, 192–93.
194 Ibid., 199.
195 Ibid., 201–2.
196 Ibid., 206.
197 Ibid., 221.
198 Ibid., 225.

The Second London Confession (1667 and 1688/89) is one of the most important Baptist confessions. This confession is strongly Calvinistic and seems on the surface to affirm a limited atonement but may actually be ambiguous, like the Westminster Confession, with respect to the extent question.[199] Chapter 8.5 states, "The Lord Jesus . . . hath fully satisfied the Justice of God, procured reconciliation, and purchased an Everlasting inheritance in the Kingdom of Heaven, for all those whom the Father hath given unto him." Likewise, chapter 8.8 reads, "To all those for whom Christ hath obtained eternal redemption, he doth certainly, and effectually apply, and communicate the same."[200]

The Second London Confession was instantly challenged by Collier and others. Collier had published his *Body of Divinity* in 1674. As a result of Nehemiah Coxe's challenge to Collier's theology, Collier wrote a supplement on *Election, Universal and Special Grace*, to which Coxe replied in 1677, followed by a rejoinder from Collier. The Baptist associations got involved and rival confessions were issued at London in 1677.[201]

General Baptists produced The Orthodox Creed (1678[9]). Lumpkin noted that this confession "approaches Calvinism more closely than any other General Baptist confession."[202] In this confession, a softened form of Calvinism presents predestination and election within a Christocentric framework.[203] It clearly affirms unlimited atonement in Article 18, "Of Christ dying for all mankind."

> God the father, out of his royal bounty, and fountain of love, when all mankind was fallen by sin, in breaking of the first covenant of works made with them in Adam, did chuse [choose] Jesus Christ, and sent him into the world to die for Adam, or fallen man. And God's love is manifest to all mankind, in that he is not willing, as himself hath sworn, and abundantly declared in his word, that mankind should perish eternally, but would have all to be saved, and come to the knowledge of the truth. And Christ died for all men, and there is a sufficiency in his death and merits for the sins of the whole world, and hath appointed the gospel to be preached unto all, and hath sent for his spirit to accompany the word in order to beget repentance and faith,: so that if any do perish, it's not for want of the means of grace manifested by Christ

199 The Second London Confession is an adaptation, in part, of the Westminster Confession. See W. J. McGlothlin, *Baptist Confessions of Faith* (Philadelphia: American Baptist Publication Society, 1911), 217: "The controlling influence in these changes was undoubtedly the Westminster Confession, the increasing stability and regularity of the Baptist churches, and the increasing desire for harmony with other Protestants."

200 Ibid., 262.

201 W. T. Whitley, *Calvinism and Evangelism in England Especially in Baptist Circles* (London: Kingsgate, [1933]), 21.

202 Lumpkin, *Baptist Confessions of Faith*, 296.

203 M. Medley, "A Good Walk Spoiled?: Revisiting Baptist Soteriology," in *Recycling the Past or Researching History?*, Studies in Baptist History and Thought 11, ed. P. E. Thompson and A. R. Cross (Carlisle, UK: Paternoster, 2005), 101.

> to them, but for the non-improvement of the grace of God, offered freely to them through Christ in the gospel.[204]

This confession speaks of both God's electing grace and "the grace of the Son in dying for all men."[205]

In 1691 A Short Confession or a Brief Narrative of Faith was published. The circumstances surrounding this confession are interesting. Lumpkin noted in the west country, during the last quarter of the seventeenth century, "there was a remarkable current away from Calvinism among some Particular Baptist Churches founded by Thomas Collier."[206]

Whitley explained how following the deaths of Collier (1691) and Coxe (1688), the 1677 confession was reprinted. Shortly thereafter, an assembly of representatives from Calvinistic Baptist churches throughout England and Wales met for consideration of how better to work together in ministry. The assembly encouraged churches to support the reprinted confession. However, Collier's influence was still felt in some of the churches he had planted and/or influenced, and not everyone was comfortable with the level of Calvinism in the confession. A second assembly was held in Bristol in 1690, and two years later the churches in the "west country" of England issued another confession explicitly repudiating the sections on election and reprobation of the 1677 confession and explicitly affirming a universal atonement in Article 6, "On the Extent of the death of Christ":[207]

> Concerning the extent of the death of our dear redeemer, we believe, that suitable to the great end of God the father in sending him into the world, to give himself a ransom for all mankind; for the world, the whole world; and that hereby the world hath its present being; and that thereby there is a way of reconciliation, acceptation, and salvation opened for all men: From whence we conclude, that if any man come short of obtaining reconciliation, acceptation, and salvation, it is not for want of grace in the father, nor a sacrifice in the son.[208]

In eighteenth-century England, one of the leading General Baptists, Dan Taylor, produced *Articles of Religion of the New Connexion* (1770). Article 3, "On the Person and Work of Christ," affirms unlimited atonement: "that he suffered to make a full atonement for all the sins of all men."[209]

---

204 Lumpkin, *Baptist Confessions of Faith*, 310–11.
205 Ibid., 303.
206 Ibid., 334–35.
207 Whitley, *Calvinism and Evangelism in England*, 23–24.
208 Lumpkin, *Baptist Confessions of Faith*, 336.
209 Ibid., 343.

Conclusion

History demonstrates the variety of Calvinism found even among Particular Baptists in England, especially concerning the extent of the atonement. English Baptist historian Thomas Crosby (AD 1685–1752) stated:

> And I know that there are several churches, ministers, and many particular persons, among *the English Baptists*, who desire not to go under the name either of *Generals* or *Particulars*, nor indeed can justly *be ranked under either of these heads*; *because they* receive what they think to be truth, without regarding with what human schemes it agrees or disagrees with.[210]

210 T. Crosby, *The History of the English Baptists*, 3 vols. (London: Printed and Sold by, the Editor, 1738), 1:174 (emphasis in original).

6

North American Baptists and the Extent of the Atonement

In this chapter, we shall consider key Baptists other than Southern Baptists on the subject. In the next chapter, we will consider the issue within Southern Baptist history from 1845 to the present.

North American Baptists from the Eighteenth to the Twenty-First Century

John Leland (AD 1754–1841)

Leland was a prominent early Virginia and Massachusetts Baptist leader who played a significant role in influencing Jefferson and Madison to include religious freedom in the Bill of Rights. After preaching an antislavery sermon, Leland left Virginia and came to Massachusetts in 1791, where he assisted in founding several Baptist churches in Connecticut.

Leland stated:

> I conclude that the *eternal purposes* of God and the *freedom of the human will* are both truths, and it is a matter of fact that the preaching that has

> been most blessed by God and most profitable to men is the doctrine of sovereign grace in the salvation of souls, mixed with a little of what is called Arminianism.[1]

Likely this "little" has reference at least to unlimited atonement. Leland himself was a Calvinist and may have been committed to limited atonement.[2]

David Benedict (AD 1779–1874)

Benedict served as a pastor for many years in Pawtucket, Rhode Island. Upon retirement, he pursued his love of Baptist history and published seven books. He chronicled the diversity of views among Baptists in Virginia and Kentucky. Benedict traced how the diverse theological perspectives in Virginia were transposed into Kentucky Baptist associations, organized as early as 1785.[3]

> The baptists in Virginia, at the time they began to send forth populous colonies of their brethren to the western country, were divided into Regulars and Separates, although the Separates were much more numerous. The *Regulars* were professedly, and some of them very highly Calvinistic; but the *Separates* were far from being unanimous in their doctrinal sentiments. A majority of them, however, were Calvinists, and of the rest, a part were much inclined to the Arminian side of the controversy; and some of the most distinguished among them, in opposing the high strains of Calvinism, which were incessantly, and in many instances dogmatically sounded by their orthodox brethren, had gone nearly the full length of the doctrine of Arminius. Others, with different modifications of the objectionable articles of both systems, were endeavoring to pursue a middle course. Such was the state of the Virginia Baptists, with regard to doctrine, at the period under consideration, and some of all those different classes were among the emigrants to the fertile regions of the west; but a majority of them were Separates in their native State. But the same people who had traveled together before their removal, so far as least as it respected their associational connection, pursued a different course when settled in Kentucky. The *Calvinistic Separates* united with the few *Regular baptists* among them, and established the Elkhorn Association, which, at its commencement, adopted the Philadelphia Confession of Faith; while those who inclined to the Arminian system, as well as those who

1 J. Leland, "A Letter of Valediction on Leaving Virginia, 1791," in *The Writings of the Late Elder John Leland*, ed. Louise F. Green (New York: G. W. Wood, 1845), 172 (emphasis in original).

2 See T. J. Nettles, *By His Grace and for His Glory*, rev. ed. (Cape Coral, FL: Founders, 2006), 87–88.

3 S. Lemke, "History or Revisionist History? How Calvinistic Were the Overwhelming Majority of Baptists and Their Confessions in the South until the Twentieth Century" *Southwestern Journal of Theology* 57 (2015): 233.

> adopted some of the Calvinistic creed in a qualified sense, united with the Association whose history we now have under consideration [the South district]. Thus the names of the *Regular* and *Separate* were transported beyond the mountains, and two separate interests were established in the neighborhood of each other.[4]

Benedict identified an association of Baptist churches formed in Western Pennsylvania called the "Covenanted Independent Baptists." "These churches are, as they say, called by some Semi-Calvinists, by others, Semi-Arminians."[5]

Luther Rice (AD 1783–1836) and Adoniram Judson (AD 1788–1850)

Judson and Rice are stellar names in the early Baptist missionary enterprise. Judson was not a writing theologian, and most of what he did write he destroyed or requested that it be destroyed. Since Judson was trained in the New Divinity tradition at Andover, and it appears his Congregationalist pastor father was cut from the same cloth, it is highly likely his influencers did not hold to limited atonement.[6] Article 5 of Judson's liturgy states that Christ "laid down his life for man . . . by which he made an atonement for all who are willing to believe."[7] This phrase is at least ambiguous as stated and does not clearly indicate Judson believed in limited atonement. In fact, it would appear that the statement that Christ "laid down his life for man" would indicate universal atonement since "man" here probably refers to "mankind." Notice Judson does not say anything about Christ dying only for the elect.

A key issue in this statement is the meaning Judson intended to attach to the word "atonement." If he meant to speak of the extent of the atonement, then the statement would be affirming limited atonement, but if he spoke only of the application of the atonement as being "for all who are willing to believe," then such would not necessitate limited atonement any more than it would necessitate unlimited atonement. The

---

4 D. Benedict, *A General History of the Baptist Denomination in America and Other Parts of the World* (New York: Lewis Colby and Company, 1848 [originally published in 1813 in two volumes]), 821. See also R. B. Semple, *A History of the Rise and Progress of the Baptists in Virginia*, rev. and ed. G. W. Beale (Richmond, VA: Pitt and Dickinson, 1810), available online at https://archive.org/details/historyofrisepro00semp.

5 D. Benedict, *A General History of the Baptist Denomination in America, and Other Parts of the World*, 2 vols. (Boston: Lincoln & Edmands, 1813), 1:602.

6 J. Willson, *A Historical Sketch of Opinions on the Atonement, Interspersed with Biographical Notices of the Leading Doctors, and Outlines of the Sections of the Church, from the Incarnation of Christ to the Present Time; with Translations from Francis Turretin, on the Atonement* (Philadelphia: Edward Earle, 1817), 163, noted: "Concerning the faculty and early student body of Andover Seminary, founded in 1808, the number of pupils is upwards of sixty; among all of whom, professor and pupils, there is probably not one who does not maintain the doctrine of general atonement." If this statement is accurate, it would likely confirm both Adoniram Judson and Luther Rice as Calvinists who affirmed universal atonement. In fact, Willson calls Andover "an American Saumur." Willson's book was published only nine years after the founding of Andover Seminary.

7 F. Wayland, *A Memoir of the Life and Labors of the Rev. Adoniram Judson*, 2 vols. (Boston: Phillips, Sampson, & Co., 1854), 2:469.

ambiguity of the word "atonement" in the context of the statement cannot be used to argue either way.[8]

Leonard Woods, the preacher who preached the missionary ordination sermon for Judson and Rice on February 6, 1812, clearly articulated a belief in unlimited atonement and, furthermore, developed this theological point as an important motive for missions and evangelism.[9] This is all the more interesting since Woods was a Calvinist, a Harvard graduate in 1796 at the top of his class, one of the founders of Andover Theological Seminary in 1808, and its first professor of theology. From its very foundation, Andover Seminary was moderate in its Calvinism. It was governed by trustees and a board of visitors, all of whom, though Calvinistic, affirmed an unlimited atonement.[10]

Woods's sermon text was Psalm 67. In the first paragraph, Woods pointed out that the psalmist expresses the heartbeat of God himself that all men may be saved.[11] Woods stated the purpose of his sermon: "I would persuade you to act, decidedly and zealously to act under the influence of Christian love."[12] The whole tenor of this sermon is wrapped around God's love for every human being on planet earth and how our love for the unsaved should motivate our missionary endeavors. The outline of his sermon consists of seven motives for missions and evangelism, the first of which is "the worth of souls." "The souls of all these are as precious as your own. The wisdom of God,—the blood of the dying Savior has so declared."[13] Woods's second motive that he urged on his hearers is "the plenteousness of the provision which Christ has made for their salvation."[14] "Were there anything scanty in this provision,—any deficiency in divine grace,—any thing circumscribed in the evangelic offer; our zeal for propagating the gospel would be suppressed."

---

8 T. Nettles rightly noted that Judson did not explicitly affirm limited atonement but then attempted, on the basis of Judson's comments about Christ's redemption and the elect, to say that this "certainly implies it" (*By His Grace and for His Glory: An Historical, Theological and Practical Study of the Doctrines of Grace in Baptist Life*, 2nd ed. [Cape Coral, FL: Founders, 2006], 100).

9 For confirmation of this, one can check *Sermon Preached at the Tabernacle in Salem February 6, 1812, on Occasion of the Ordination of the Rev. Messrs. Samuel Newell, Adoniram Judson, Samuel Nott, Gordon Hall, and Luther Rice, Missionaries to the Heathen in Asia, under the Direction of the Board of Commissioners for Foreign Missions* (Boston: Samuel T. Armstrong, 1812), which can be accessed at https://archive.org/details/sermondelivereda00wood. Woods's lengthy discussion on the question of the extent of the atonement (Lectures LXXXI and LXXXII) makes it clear he was a moderate Calvinist (Leonard Woods, "Lectures," in *The Works of Leonard Woods* [Boston: John P. Jewett & Company, 1851], 490–521). For example, Woods stated: "But this general design of the atonement, and the equal respect, above stated, which it had to the case of sinners universally, does not by any means imply, that all will be treated alike by the providence of God, or that all will share alike in the influence of the Holy Spirit. It does not imply, that the purpose of God respecting the actual bestowal of spiritual blessings, was the same as to all men. The general provision is one thing; the divine influence which disposes men to avail themselves of that provision, is another thing" (496). Here Woods distinguished between the extent of the atonement, which is universal, and the intent, which is restricted only to those who believe.

10 For a brief biography of Woods, consult D. B. Raymond, "Woods, Leonard," in *American National Biography*, eds. J. A. Garraty and M. C. Carnes, 24 vols. (New York: Oxford University Press, 1999), 23:813–45.

11 Woods, *Sermon Preached*, 10.

12 Ibid., 11.

13 Ibid., 12.

14 Ibid., 13.

The following statement by Woods clearly revealed his own affirmation of Christ's death for the sins of all people.

> But my brethren, the word of eternal truth has taught us that Jesus tasted death for every man; that he is the propitiation for ours sins, and not for ours only, but also for the sins of the *whole* world; that a rich feast is prepared, and all things ready; that whosoever will may come and take of the water of life freely. This great atonement is as sufficient for Asiatic and Africans, as for us. This abundant provision is made for them as well as for us. The door of Christ's kingdom is equally open to them and to us. Unnumbered millions of our race have entered in; and yet there is room. The mercy of God is an ocean absolutely exhaustless; and so far as his benevolence is a pattern for our imitation, and a rule to govern our exertions and prayers, *he wills that all men should be saved.*[15]

Notice here Woods affirmed God's universal saving will for all men and that God has provided the propitiation for the sins of all men. He quoted Heb 2:9, that Jesus "taste[d] death for every man" (KJV). All of this is grounded in God's saving love for humanity. Woods pleaded with his hearers to "exert yourselves to the utmost for the salvation of mankind; your exertions will fall far below the height of redeeming love."[16] This is not limited atonement.

Woods's third motive for missionary action was the biblical command to take the gospel to "every creature," which is "an exact expression of the heart of Jesus; a display of the *vastness* of his love." None of Woods's seven motives for evangelism include the usual things in contemporary Reformed writings and sermons, such as the glory of God, God's sovereignty, or the doctrine of election. There is no doubt he believed these things. Woods did not delve into the so-called secret will of God when it comes to motives for missions; he rather stayed within the revealed will of God and spoke of what the Bible clearly states about why we should do missions and evangelism: the fact that God loves all people, desires all to be saved, has made provision in the death of Christ for the sins of all people so they can be saved should they repent and believe, and we should give ourselves to missions and evangelism because of God's love for every lost soul on planet earth, our love for Christ, and our love for every single lost soul. As Woods said to Judson and Rice in his concluding charge in the sermon: "You go, we believe, because the love of God is shed abroad in your hearts by the Holy Ghost. . . . The cause in which you have enlisted, is the cause of divine love."[17]

15 Ibid., 13–14 (emphasis in original).
16 Ibid., 14–15.
17 Ibid., 26 (emphasis in original).

Woods's own sermon coupled with what we know of the writings of Judson and Rice make it clear that, as Calvinists, Judson and Rice held to the doctrine of election and they believed in the sovereignty of God in missions and evangelism. Whether they held to limited atonement is another question.

Evidence that Judson probably did not affirm limited atonement can be found in one of his addresses delivered while on furlough to the United States in March 1846. Speaking of the death of Christ, he stated: "But he did not yield; he suffered on for three more awful hours, until the Father saw that all was accomplished—that the price of our redemption was paid—that enough suffering had been endured to render it possible for every individual of our lost race to find salvation."[18] The sentence could not be uttered consistently by one who held to limited atonement.[19] The reason is obvious. According to limited atonement, Christ did not die for the sins of the non-elect. Thus it is not possible that "every individual of our lost race" could find salvation. No atonement was made for the non-elect, and salvation is not possible apart from the atonement of Christ.

David Jessee (AD 1783–1856)

Jessee became pastor of the Baptist Church at Castle Woods, Virginia, in 1803. James Taylor described Jessee's doctrinal beliefs concerning the extent of the atonement:

> In regard to the doctrines held and preached by him, it may be sufficient to say, that they coincided generally with those of the Regular Baptists. His views, however, in reference to the extent of the atonement, underwent a change. In the early part of his ministry he advocated the high-toned Calvinistic view of that subject; but in the latter years of his life he supported the view now generally adopted by the Baptists, viz., that the atonement is general in its nature.[20]

This statement is important for several reasons. First, it identifies Jessee with the Regular Baptists who were Calvinistic in theology. Second, it speaks of Jessee's shift away from limited atonement to general atonement. Third, note Taylor's statement that the view Baptists "now generally adopted" is not limited atonement but universal atonement. This was the situation according to Taylor in 1860, just fifteen years after the founding of the Southern Baptist Convention.

---

18 R. T. Middleditch, *Burmah's Great Missionary* (New York: E. H. Fletcher, 1859), 387.

19 It is possible Judson intends to speak of the intrinsic infinite sufficiency of the death of Christ, as many high Calvinists do, but even then as we have pointed out, such an account of sufficiency is woefully inadequate and by definition does not address the sins of the non-elect in any but a hypothetical way.

20 J. Taylor, *Virginia Baptist Ministers* (New York: Sheldon & Co., 1860), 289.

Francis Wayland (AD 1796–1865)

Wayland served as a professor at Andover Theological Seminary, was one of the founders of Newton Theological Institution, president of Brown University, and pastor of First Baptist Church in Boston and First Baptist Church of Providence, Rhode Island. He had a significant influence on early Southern Baptist leaders like Boyce and Manly.

In Wayland's *Notes on the Principles and Practices of Baptist Churches*, published just twelve years after the founding of the Southern Baptist Convention, he is quite clear on the shift away from limited atonement that had already taken place in Baptist life. Wayland wrote:

> The extent of the atonement has been and still is a matter of honest but not unkind difference. *Within the last fifty years a change has gradually taken place in the views of a large portion of our brethren.* At the commencement of that period Gill's Divinity was a sort of standard, and Baptists imbibing his opinions were what may be called almost hyper-Calvinistic. A change commenced upon the publication of the writings of Andrew Fuller, especially his "Gospel Worthy of all Acceptation." . . .
>
> It is difficult at the present day to conceive to what extent the doctrine of the limited atonement, and the views of election which accompanied it, were carried. I once knew a popular minister, who used to quote the passage, "God so loved the world," etc., by inserting the word *elect* before world: "God so loved the *elect* world," etc. I was, in the early part of my ministry, settled in a respectable town in Massachusetts. One of my members, a very worthy man, and the son of a Baptist minister, and reputed to be "very clear in the doctrines"—(this was the term applied to this form of belief)—had an interesting family wholly given up to worldliness. I wished to converse with them on the subject of personal religion, and mentioned to him my desire. He kindly but plainly told me that he did not wish any one to converse with his children on that subject. If they were elected, God would convert them in his own time; but if not, talking would do them no good, it would only make them hypocrites. He was, I believe, the last pillar of Gillism then remaining in the church. . . .
>
> In my last number I referred to the change which had taken place, in the opinions of Baptists, on the subject of the Atonement. The question mainly at issue was the *extent* of the gospel sacrifice; in other respects there has ever been, I believe, an entire harmony. It may be well to state briefly what I suppose to be the prevailing belief, in this doctrine, at present. In the northern and eastern States, it is generally held that the whole race became sinners in consequence of the sin of the first Adam; and that, on the other hand, the way of salvation was opened for the whole race by the obedience and death of the second Adam.

> Nevertheless, this alone renders the salvation of no one certain, for, so steeped are men in sin, that they all, with one consent, begin to make excuse, and universally refuse the offer of pardon. God, then, in infinite mercy, has elected some to everlasting life, and, by the influence of the Holy Spirit, renders the word effectual to their salvation and sanctification. In his offer of mercy he is perfectly honest and sincere, for the feast has been provided, and it is spread for *all.* This does not, however, interfere with his gracious purpose to save by his sovereign mercy such as he may choose. There is here sovereignty, but no partiality. There can be no partiality, for none have the semblance of a claim; and, if any one perishes, it is not from the want of a full and free provision, but from his own willful perverseness. Ye will not come to me, that ye may have life.[21]

Wayland apparently affirmed an unlimited atonement.

Edward T. Hiscox (AD 1814–1901)

Hiscox served as pastor of several Baptist churches in New England and New York. He is most known for his Baptist church manuals, some of which are still in publication today.

> American Baptists are decidedly Calvinistic as to substance of doctrine, but moderately so, being midway between the extremes of Arminianism and Antinomianism. Though diversities of opinion may incline to either extreme, the "general atonement" view is for the most part held, while the "particular atonement" theory is maintained by not a few. The freedom of the human will is declared, while the sovereignty of divine grace, and the absolute necessity of the Spirit's work in faith and salvation are maintained.[22]

Alvah Hovey (AD 1820–1903)

Hovey was a leader in the Triennial Convention, as well as professor and then president at Newton Theological Institution in Massachusetts from 1849 to 1899. Hovey is perhaps best known as the editor of the old American Commentary on the New Testament series that appeared in 1885. Hovey advocated that the intent of the atonement was to save the elect, but the extent of the atonement was for the sins of all people:

> These and similar portions of the Word of God indicate, not merely that the atonement is sufficient for all men, but also that it has been made so inten-

21 F. Wayland, *Notes on the Principles and Practices of Baptist Churches* (New York: Sheldon, Blakeman, and Co., 1857), 18, 19, 20 (emphasis in original).

22 E. T. Hiscox, *The Standard Manual for Baptist Churches* (Philadelphia: American Baptist Publication Society, 1890), 49.

> tionally; that God designed, by means of the atonement, to make provision for the pardon of all men,—to give them all a fresh probation and offer of life, by the economy of grace, as well as to lead some to repentance by the renewing power of his Spirit. Any other view of these passages seems to me unnatural, and therefore erroneous.
>
> If there were explicit statements in the Word of God, to the effect that Christ suffered for the elect only,—that he did not suffer for those who will be finally lost,—it would certainly be necessary for us to look for a different explanation of these passages; but we are not aware of any such statements, and therefore abide by their obvious import.[23]

A. H. Strong (AD 1836–1921)

Strong was an American Baptist pastor and professor of theology and president of Rochester Theological Seminary, where he taught for forty years. His influential *Systematic Theology* (1876) went through eight editions and was regularly used in Bible colleges and seminaries for many years. Strong was a moderate Calvinist on the extent of the atonement.

> The Scriptures represent the atonement as having been made for all men, and as sufficient for the salvation of all. Not the atonement therefore is limited, but the application of the atonement through the work of the Holy Spirit. . . . The atonement is unlimited,—the whole human race might be saved through it; the application of the atonement is limited,—only those who repent and believe are actually saved by it.[24]

Strong said of Calvin's view: "While in his early work, the *Institutes*, avoided definite statements of his position with regard to the extent of the atonement, yet in his latter works, the *Commentaries*, acceded to the theory of universal atonement. Supralapsarianism is therefore hyper-Calvinistic, rather than Calvinistic."[25] The first part of this statement is accurate. The latter part concerning supralapsarianism is not, for two reasons. First, supralapsarianism can *lead* to hyper-Calvinism but is not itself hyper-Calvinism. Second, though they are few and far between, there are supralapsarians like William Twisse, proculator of the Westminster Assembly, who affirmed an unlimited atonement.

---

23 A. Hovey, *A Manual of Christian Systematic and Christian Ethics* (Boston: Henry A. Young, 1877), 229–30. See also idem, *God with Us: Or, The Person and Work of Christ* (Boston: Gould and Lincoln, 1872), 166–77.

24 A. H. Strong, *Systematic Theology* (Valley Forge, PA: Judson, 1907), 771, 773. Strong referenced both John Calvin and Matthew Henry as taking this view.

25 Ibid., 777.

Arthur Pink (AD 1886–1952)

Pink was a Baptist pastor, evangelist, and Bible teacher with little formal training (six weeks at Moody Bible Institute). Pink edited the monthly magazine *Studies in Scripture* and generated more than two thousand articles. These formed the basis of his books, which were published posthumously. His biographer, Iain Murray, said, "The widespread circulation of his writings after his death made him one of the most influential evangelical authors in the second half of the twentieth century."[26]

Pink was an ardent Calvinist who vacillated between high and hyper-Calvinism as he sometimes denied God's universal saving desire, denied God's love for the non-elect, and held an extreme view of God's sovereignty. He was a strong advocate of limited atonement:

> To say that He [Christ] died for the human race is not only to fly in the face of this plain scripture, but is grossly dishonoring to the sacrifice of Christ. . . . No sophistry can evade the fact that these words give positive assurance that everyone for whom Christ died will, most certainly, be saved.[27]

Pink denied the sufficiency of the atonement as well, instead limiting it strictly to the elect: "The Atonement, therefore, is in no sense sufficient for a man, unless the Lord Jesus died for that man." Pink turned to William Rushton, a critic of Andrew Fuller, and quoted him as saying: "So then all their boasted 'sufficiency' of the Atonement is only an *empty offer* of salvation on certain terms and conditions; and such an Atonement is much too weak to meet the desperate case of a lost sinner." For Pink, "the Word of God never represents the *sufficiency* of the Atonement as wider than the *design* of the Atonement."[28]

Norman Douty (AD 1899–1993)

Douty was a Baptist pastor and itinerant preacher and teacher. His most important work is *Did Christ Die Only for the Elect? A Treatise on the Extent of the Atonement*,[29] published in 1972. Douty's book is an important twentieth-century contribution that argues for unlimited atonement from a moderate Calvinist perspective.

Douty accepted the dualistic aspect in the atonement's design according to the Lombardian formula: sufficient for all (full expiation of all sin) but efficient only for

26 I. H. Murray, *The Life of Arthur W. Pink*, rev. ed. (Edinburgh: Banner of Truth, 2004), xiii. See also Richard P. Belcher, *Arthur W. Pink: Born to Write* (Columbia, SC: Richbarry, 1982); Richard P. Belcher, *Arthur W. Pink: Predestination* (Columbia, SC: Richbarry, 1983).

27 A. W. Pink, *Studies in the Scriptures 1921–1925*, 17 vols. (Lafayette, IN: Sovereign Grace, 2004), 2:81.

28 A. W. Pink, *Exposition of the Gospel of John*, 2 vols. (Grand Rapids, MI: Zondervan, 1962), 2:220–21 (emphasis in original).

29 N. Douty, *Did Christ Die Only for the Elect? A Treatise on the Extent of the Atonement* (Eugene, OR: Wipf & Stock, 2007).

the elect. The book contains an interesting list of quotations from key figures from the patristic era to the modern church who affirmed unlimited atonement.

Douty evaluated the key passages, most in the New Testament, dealing with the extent of the atonement. The limitation of the atonement is not in respect to the imputation of sin to Christ but rather in the decree to apply the benefits of the atonement only to the elect. Douty's book is an attempted corrective to the decretal theology of high Calvinism as it plays out in the view of limited atonement.

Roger Nicole (AD 1915–2010)[30]

Roger Nicole was a leading twentieth-century proponent of limited atonement.[31] He was one of the founders of the Evangelical Theological Society and the International Council on Biblical Inerrancy. Nicole was a Swiss Reformed Baptist. He was professor of theology at Gordon Conwell Theological Seminary from 1949 until his retirement in 1986. He continued to teach theology at Reformed Theological Seminary (Orlando, Florida). Nicole authored more than one hundred articles and contributed to fifty books and reference works. His doctoral dissertation on Amyraut was published in 1981.[32]

Nicole's arguments for limited atonement are of the standard variety. Occasionally, his historiography was flawed, for example, when he wrongly asserted Charles Hodge and Robert Dabney held to limited atonement.[33]

Like so many on both sides of the aisle, Nicole's statement of the issue itself is flawed. For him, the question is the *design* of the atonement.[34] Design and extent are related, but in Nicole's mind they are one and the same. Hence if God *designed* the atonement only for the elect, then the *extent* of the atonement only covers the sins of the elect. As has been demonstrated, this is not an accurate assessment of the issue and the state of the question. The question as to the extent of the atonement is whether Christ substituted for the sins of all people or only for the elect. Nicole affirmed the latter but seems to have no category for a dual intent whereby God intends for Christ to die for all people (unlimited extent) but also designs that only the elect should be effectually redeemed (particular redemption).

---

30 Nicole is also addressed under the section on Calvin above as well.

31 His works addressing the extent of the atonement include R. Nicole, "John Calvin's View on the Extent of the Atonement," in *An Elaboration of the Theology of John Calvin*, 8 vols., ed. R. C. Gamble (New York: Garland, 1992), 8:119–47. This essay was also published earlier: R. Nicole, "John Calvin's View of the Extent of the Atonement," *Westminster Theological Journal* 47 (1985): 197–225. See also idem, "Covenant, Universal Call and Definite Atonement," *Journal of the Evangelical Theological Society* 38 (1995): 403–12; and idem, "Particular Redemption," in *Our Saviour God: Man, Christ and the Atonement*, ed. J. M. Boice (Grand Rapids, MI: Baker, 1980), 165–78.

32 R. Nicole, *Moyse Amyraut: A Bibliography with Special Reference to the Controversy on Universal Grace* (New York: Garland, 1981).

33 Nicole, "Covenant, Universal Call and Definite Atonement," 405.

34 Nicole, "Particular Redemption," 167.

Respecting the well-meant gospel offer, Nicole considered the essential prerequisite for a genuine offer to be: if the terms of the offer are observed, that which is offered is actually granted. Nicole thought limited atonement undergirds the sincere gospel offer: "It provides a real rather than a hypothetical salvation."[35] Actually just the opposite is the case. Nicole is here confusing an offer with a bare, conditional truth statement. The statement "If anyone repents and believes the gospel, he will be saved" is not an offer. It is not even a command or a call to anything. It is a simple conditional truth statement. Nicole failed to consider the issue in the light of God making the offer, not the preacher. If the offer is sincere on God's part to all people, including the non-elect, then on the limited atonement scheme, how can it be otherwise that God is offering the non-elect something that does not exist? There is no atonement made for their sins.

David Nettleton (AD 1918–1993)

Nettleton adhered to limited atonement but argued in his *Chosen to Salvation* that limited atonement is not a necessary corollary of election in a Calvinistic framework.[36]

John Reisinger (b. AD 1924)

A former Southern Baptist, Reisinger has been a Calvinistic Baptist evangelist and Bible teacher for more than fifty years. His brother, Ernest, was a Southern Baptist pastor and Calvinist with a passion to return the SBC to its Calvinistic roots.

In 2002, J. Reisinger published a sixty-two-page treatise entitled *Limited Atonement*.[37] Unfortunately, Reisinger's historiography is severely flawed. He argued that limited atonement was the historic doctrine of the church, though he said it was taught implicitly rather than explicitly. "Universal atonement is the new and novel doctrine when one looks at all of church history."[38] Reisinger deduced limited atonement from his brief study of four key words describing the atonement in the New Testament: ransom, substitute, reconciliation, and propitiation.[39]

Reisinger misrepresented the Arminian understanding of the nature and extent of the atonement, caricaturing it virtually beyond recognition.[40] The book concludes with an appendix entitled "*All* Equals *Many* but *Many* Does Not Equal *All*," where he attempted to show that Paul's use of "many" in Rom 5:12–19 does not mean "all without exception."

---

35 Nicole, "Covenant, Universal Call and Definite Atonement," 410.

36 D. Nettleton, *Chosen to Salvation* (Schaumburg, IL: Regular Baptist, 1983), 79.

37 J. Reisinger, *Limited Atonement* (Frederick, MD: New Covenant Media, 2002).

38 Ibid., 12.

39 Ibid., 14–26.

40 Ibid., 28–38; 45–47.

Leroy Forlines (b. AD 1926)

Forlines taught Bible and theology at Free Will Baptist Bible College, now Welch College. His best-known work, *Biblical Systematics* (1975), was revised and published as *The Quest for Truth* in 2001. His most recent work, *Classical Arminianism: A Theology of Salvation,* appeared in 2011, was edited by Matthew Pinson, and consists of earlier published material on Calvinism and Arminianism.[41]

In chapter 11 of his *The Quest for Truth*, Forlines argued for a penal-substitutionary understanding of the atonement. He critiqued the governmental view of the atonement, calling it "seriously inadequate."[42] He responded to objections raised by the governmental view against penal substitution.

Especially important is his critique of the notion that a penal substitutionary atonement entails limited atonement.

> The Calvinist may want to insist that the objection is valid and that Christ died only for the elect. The only way this argument could have any validity would be to deny the possibility of provisionary atonement. If there can be no provisionary atonement, it *does follow* that if Christ died for a person, his justification is *never provisionary* but always *real.* In explaining the view of limited atonement, Louis Berkhof comments: "The Calvinist teaches that the atonement meritoriously secured the application of the work of redemption to those for whom it was intended and their complete salvation is certain." A close look at what Berkhof said will show that it does not rule out the provisionary principle in atonement. He says that the atonement "makes certain" the salvation of those for whom it was intended. He did not say that the atonement automatically saved everybody for whom it was intended. Calvinists do not teach that the elect are justified before they experience faith. They teach that the person for whom Christ died will of a certainty be justified, but they do not consider a person justified until he experiences faith as the condition of justification. Thus, atonement is provisionary until the time it is applied. The *only way* to deny the provisionary nature of the atonement is to consider all people for whom Christ died to be justified *before* they experience faith.[43]

Forlines illustrates the fact that not all Arminians reject the penal substitutionary view of the atonement.

41 L. Forlines, *Classical Arminianism: A Theology of Salvation* (Nashville: Randall House, 2011).
42 L. Forlines, *The Quest for Truth* (Nashville: Randall House, 2001), 204.
43 Ibid., 206–7 (emphasis in original).

C. Gordon Olson (b. AD 1930)

Olson was professor of theology and missions at Northeastern Bible College (1967–90) and served in Baptist pastorates in New Jersey and New York City. He is currently an adjunct professor at Liberty University, Lynchburg, Virginia. In his 2002 *Beyond Calvinism and Arminianism*, Olson has a section dealing with the extent of the atonement, critiquing limited atonement and arguing the case for unlimited atonement.

Olson erred egregiously when he asserted: "Hyper-Calvinism *alone* holds to a 'limited atonement' in that Christ died only for the 'elect' and not in any real sense for all mankind."[44] It is certainly true that hyper-Calvinism affirms this, but Olson seems to be saying that all who hold this position are hyper-Calvinists, in which case, he is historically and theologically in error.

His statement that limited atonement never appeared in any creed before the Synod of Dort is true in one sense but needs qualification. Actually, Dort *allowed* for limited atonement but did not mandate it, as we have seen. Dort also allowed for an unlimited atonement as an unlimited expiation for sin with a limited intent to apply the atonement only to the elect. In point of fact, the earliest Reformed confession to affirm exclusively a strictly limited atonement is Turretin's *Formula Consensus* (1675).

Olson considered key passages of Scripture that are interpreted as supporting limited atonement, and then considered those passages that support an unlimited atonement.[45] He listed the following "serious implications" of the limited view:

1. Limiting God's love to the elect only.
2. Universal gospel offer is undercut.
3. Loss of personalization of the gospel presentation—limitarians offer it in general terms.
4. The requirement of faith is obviated. (Olson errs here. Calvinism does not deny that faith is the required condition for salvation.)

J. Ramsey Michaels (b. AD 1931)

Michaels is a Baptist theologian and New Testament scholar and author of major commentaries on 1 Peter, Revelation, Hebrews, and John. He taught New Testament at several theological seminaries (Gordon-Conwell, Andover-Newton, Fuller, and Bangor Seminary in Portland, Maine). He retired in 1994, though he still teaches on occasion.

Michaels affirms limited atonement. In "Atonement in John's Gospel and Epistles," he supported Roger Nicole's interpretation of passages within the Johannine corpus as suggesting limited atonement. With respect to 1 John 2:2, Michaels is critical of much of the Calvinistic exegesis of this verse. Nevertheless, he stated: "The point is not that

---

44 G. Olson, *Beyond Calvinism and Arminianism: An Inductive, Mediate Theology of Salvation*, 3rd ed. (Cedar Knolls, NJ: Global Gospel Ministries, 2012), 282.

45 Ibid., 283–91.

Jesus died for everyone indiscriminately so that everyone in the world is in principle forgiven but that all those forgiven are forgiven on the basis of Christ's sacrifice and in no other way."[46]

Earl Radmacher (AD 1931–2014)

Radmacher was an important leader in the Conservative Baptist Association of America. He served as president of Western Seminary in Portland, Oregon, from 1965 to 1990 and taught systematic theology. He authored numerous books, including *Salvation*, where he affirmed an unlimited atonement.[47]

Robert Picirilli (b. AD 1932)

One of the early twenty-first-century authors on the extent of the atonement is Robert Picirilli. He is a Free Will Baptist and Arminian theologian whose 2002 *Grace, Faith and Free Will: Contrasting Views of Salvation* argues for unlimited atonement.[48] Picirilli illustrates the fact that not all Arminian theologians affirm a governmental theory of the atonement. He clearly affirmed a penal substitutionary view of the atonement.[49]

Picirilli also understood the sufficiency of the atonement in the same way as moderate Calvinists: "The sufficiency of atonement can be affirmed only for those to whom it may be potentially applied."[50] No matter how intrinsically sufficient the atonement is in terms of worth and value, it simply cannot be said to be sufficient for the sins of people for whom Christ did not suffer since the atonement could never be applied to them.[51]

In response to Berkhof's argument that a universal extent of the atonement entails universalism, Picirilli made the important linguistic point that:

> It is typical of language usage to speak of an action as *actually* accomplishing what it was intended to accomplish, even if that action only made possible the accomplishment.
>
> In this way, the *potential* of an action is spoken of as contained in the action itself, even if some further condition or application is required. . . . Any action may linguistically be spoken of as containing its results.[52]

---

46 J. R. Michaels, "Atonement in John's Gospel and Epistles," in *The Glory of the Atonement*, ed. C. E. Hill and F. A. James III (Downers Grove, IL: InterVarsity, 2004), 117.

47 E. Radmacher, *Salvation*, in Swindoll Leadership Library, ed. C. Swindoll and R. Zuck (Nashville: Thomas Nelson, 2000).

48 R. Picirilli, *Grace, Faith and Free Will. Contrasting Views of Salvation: Calvinism and Arminianism* (Nashville: Random House, 2002), 83–137.

49 Ibid., 98. See also L. Forlines, *Biblical Systematics* (Nashville: Randall House, 1979), 149–73, who as an Arminian argues the case for a substitutionary view of the atonement over against a governmental view.

50 Ibid., 99.

51 As noted by Arminius, *The Works of James Arminius*, 3 vols., trans. J. Nichols and W. Nichols (Grand Rapids, MI: Baker, 1986), 3:77, 346.

52 Ibid., 3:93.

Picirilli appealed to moderate Calvinist W. G. T. Shedd for further support of his point,[53] along with Arminius's rejoinder to Perkins: "You confound the result with the action and passion, from which it exists . . . the obtainment of redemption with its application. . . . reconciliation made with God by the death and sacrifice of Christ, with the application of the same, which are plainly different things."[54]

Picirilli responded to the argument by Calvinists that saving faith is a gift from God given only to the elect, and hence the atonement is limited:

> This argument assumes a further doctrine that is not in evidence: namely, that saving faith is in fact a gift *as part of* the application of salvation rather than a condition for the application of salvation. To say it this way—which is precisely what Calvinists claim—is to expose it as unbiblical.[55]

Picirilli pointed out that Berkhof's statement concerning the state of the question of the atonement's extent is incorrect. Berkhof wrongly asserted that Arminians believe that God intended by the atonement to save all people. Rather, according to Picirilli, "What God intends to do, He does, His final purposes are never thwarted." The issue is about provision. This is what God intended to do in the atonement: make a provision for the salvation of all people such that those who meet God's condition of salvation, repentance and faith, will in fact be saved.[56]

Another argument in favor of unlimited atonement adduced by Picirilli is that condemnation of the unbeliever, biblically speaking, is the result of his refusal to believe God's witness concerning his Son, as, for example, in 1 John 5:10–11.[57]

For Picirilli, "The non-elect certainly *will* not accept the offer [of the gospel]. But in that certainty there is no necessity. The most coherent position is that the gospel offer is universal because the provision is universal and all who hear may, in fact, receive the salvation offered."[58]

God's provision of atonement is as broad as humanity's sin. Picirilli appeals to Rom 3:22–25 to make the point:

> (a) there is no difference,
> (b) because *all* have sinned,
> (c) being justified by His grace

53 W. G. T. Shedd, *Dogmatic Theology*, 2nd ed., 3 vols. (Nashville, TN: Thomas Nelson, 1980), 2:440, 477.
54 Picirilli, *Grace, Faith and Free Will*, 94; citing Arminius, *The Works of James Arminius*, 3:454.
55 Picirilli, *Grace, Faith and Free Will*, 97 (emphasis in original).
56 Ibid., 104.
57 Ibid., 118.
58 Ibid., 119 (emphasis in original).

—through the redemption that is in Christ,
—whom God set forth as a propitiation
—through faith, in His blood.

> Clearly, the propitiation and redemption purchased by the atoning death (blood) of Christ undergirds justification. This, in turn, modifies the "all" who have sinned, of whom Paul specifically says "There is no difference." The specific reason there is no difference is that all have sinned; that alone speaks strongly for atonement for all. And this, in verse 22, is cited as the reason justification is freely provided through Christ's atonement by faith. One may compare Romans 10:11, 12 where again the fact that salvation is by faith is connected to the fact that "There is no difference"; Acts 15:9 should also be noted.[59]
>
> God is no respecter of persons.
>
> An unconditional salvation of some versus others does mean that God treats some differently from others. And the passages that state this basic principle appear to be implying thereby that God deals with men on the basis of no predisposition on His part but solely on the basis of how they respond to Him who has dealt equitably with all.[60]

Picirilli also authored a chapter in *Grace for All: The Arminian Dynamics of Salvation.*[61] This is an excellent, clearly written article that articulates an Arminian understanding of the atonement's extent from a biblical/systematic approach. Picirilli carefully distinguishes between the atonement's intent and extent. He explains and summarizes the key Greek terms in the New Testament for the atonement, such as "ransom," "propitiation," and "reconciliation."[62]

With respect to Rom 5:18–19, Picirilli understands Paul's reference to "all men" in verse 18 and the "many" in verse 19 to refer to all humanity, with the meaning "that the *provision* or *basis* for justification and life is made for all, so that *all* encompasses all humanity . . . the New Testament can (as can any of us in normal discourse) speak of an event as *accomplishing* what is more technically said to be *made possible* or *grounded in it.*"[63] The same is true for 2 Cor 5:18–19.

59 Ibid., 120.
60 Ibid., 121.
61 R. Picirilli, "The Intent and Extent of Christ's Atonement," in *Grace for All: The Arminian Dynamics of Salvation*, ed. C. Pinnock and J. Wagner (Eugene, OR: Resource, 2015), 51–68.
62 Ibid., 52–61.
63 Ibid., 60 (emphasis in original).

Picirilli wrongly assumed W. G. T. Shedd held to limited atonement but rightly noted that Arminius was a "staunch defender" of penal satisfaction.[64] Speaking of God's intention in the atonement, Picirilli stated: "*Did God intend the atonement to save his people?* Yes, and this explains all the passages, frequently used to support the doctrine of limited atonement." "*Did God intend the atonement for the whole world?* Again, yes. . . . He intended to apply it only to those who appropriate its provision by faith."[65]

Finally, Picirilli spoke of the high Calvinist tendency to speak of the "sufficiency" of the atonement while denying its universality. If there is no atonement made for the non-elect, it is by no means sufficient for them by definition of the term "sufficiency." "Especially is it so, then, that an atonement that was intended by God to *accomplish* salvation for all for whom it was made, is not adequate to save those for whom it was not made."[66] An effective point indeed.

Tom Wells (b. AD 1933)

Wells is a pastor of The King's Chapel (Reformed Baptist Church) and writer in West Chester, near Cincinnati, Ohio. His work on the extent of the atonement, *A Price for a People*,[67] is a standard defense of limited atonement.

Wells reasoned from Rom 8:29–30 that there is a sense in which we were saved at the cross, since it was there our salvation was made certain. In another sense we were saved when we believed, when our salvation became real to us.[68] The problem here is Paul is referring to God's eternal plan and not to a specific historical event. Wells read more into the passage than is there. He failed to see the problem that, on his view, the passage would also teach that we are glorified at the moment of salvation.

Wells claimed "Christ's death does not 'create opportunities,' it establishes certainties."[69] This is a false dichotomy. As Henebury cogently remarked: "The truth is that God's Decree established certainties, while the Atonement is instrumental in the administering of the decree to both the elect and the non-elect. That is why the atonement had to have the whole of humanity (elect and non-elect) as its referents."[70]

Bruce Demarest (b. AD 1935) and Gordon Lewis (b. AD 1926)

Demarest is senior professor of Christian theology and spiritual formation at Denver Seminary, where he served from 1975 until his formal retirement in 2011. He is a

64 Ibid., 65.

65 Ibid. (emphasis in original).

66 Ibid., 66.

67 T. Wells, *A Price for a People: The Meaning of Christ's Death* (Edinburgh: Banner of Truth, 1992).

68 Ibid., 45–47.

69 Ibid., 50.

70 P. M. Henebury, "Christ's Atonement: Its Purpose and Extent, Part 1," *Conservative Theological Journal* 9 (2005): 108.

PhD graduate of the University of Manchester, under the tutelage of renowned biblical scholar F. F. Bruce.

Demarest is a moderate Calvinist. In his work, *The Cross and Salvation*,[71] he argued for an unlimited atonement within a Calvinist soteriology (though Demarest also rejected the notion that regeneration precedes faith). Demarest rightly considered a distinction between the provision of the atonement and the application of the atonement.

> We conclude that in terms of the atonement's *provision* Christ died not merely for the elect but for all sinners in all times and places. Christ drank the cup of suffering for the sins of the entire world. He died as a substitute, a propitiation, a ransom, etc. for the universe of sinners. The non-elect had their sins paid for on the cross, even though through unbelief they do not personally appropriate the benefits of his work. Christ, in other words, provided salvation for more people than those to whom he purposed to apply its saving benefits. The Atonement's universal provision removes every barrier between a holy God and sinners, unleashes in the world a power for good that restrains evil, guarantees the future resurrection of all people from the dead (John 5:28–29), provides an additional just basis for the condemnation of unbelievers, and offers motivation for the proclamation of the Good News to every creature. Arminians correctly emphasize the universality of the provision side of the Atonement.[72]

Demarest also co-authored a three-volume systematic theology, *Integrative Theology* (1990) with Gordon Lewis.[73] Lewis is the senior professor of Christian philosophy and systematic theology at Denver Seminary in Littleton, Colorado, where he has served since 1958. He served on the faculty of Baptist Bible Seminary from 1951 to 1958. He is also a past president of the Evangelical Philosophical Society and the Evangelical Theological Society.

The authors correctly distinguished between atonement as provision and the application of the atonement. "A twofold universal and particular purpose for the cross accounts coherently for three types of related passages": (1) The universal passages indicating that

---

71 B. Demarest, *The Cross and Salvation* (Wheaton, IL: Crossway, 1997), 189–95.

72 Ibid., 191–92 (emphasis in original). Notice the distinction that Demarest makes, as a moderate Calvinist, between God's *purpose* or *intent to save* and the *extent* of the atonement:

> In sum, regarding the question, For whom did Christ die? We find biblical warrant for dividing the question into God's purpose regarding the *provision* of the Atonement and his purpose concerning the *application* thereof . . . The *provision* side of the Atonement is part of the general will of God that must be preached to all . . . The *application* side of the Atonement is part of the special will of God shared with those who come to faith. (ibid., 193; emphasis in original).

73 For Gordon Lewis, see below in the chapter "North American Baptists and the Extent of the Atonement."

Christ died for the sins of all people, (2) the special intent passages where the "church" or "elect" are highlighted as receiving salvation through the atonement (such as Mark 10:45; John 17:9, 20, 24; Acts 20:28; Eph 1:4–7; 5:25; and 2 Tim 1:9–10), and (3) passages that combine a universal and particular focus, such as 1 Tim 4:10.[74]

Lewis and Demarest appear to be supporting a dual intent in the atonement such that Christ died for the sins of all people, which also provides for a general revelation and common grace to all, yet Christ died with the specific intent of bringing salvation only to the elect.

D. A. Carson (b. AD 1946)

Carson is a leading Baptist and evangelical scholar, theologian, and author who serves as research professor at Trinity Evangelical Divinity School, where he has taught since 1978. He is one of the founders of "The Gospel Coalition." Carson adheres to a Reformed soteriology, including limited atonement.

In a 1999 article and then in his book published one year later, *The Difficult Doctrine of the Love of God*,[75] Carson explained the relationship of the love of God, the extent of the atonement, and the offer of the gospel.

> In recent years I have tried to read both primary and secondary sources on the doctrine of the Atonement from Calvin on. One of my most forceful impressions is that the categories of the debate gradually shift with time so as to force disjunction where a slightly different bit of question-framing would allow synthesis. Correcting this, I suggest, is one of the useful things we may accomplish from an adequate study of the love of God presented in Scripture. For God is a person. Surely it is not surprising that the love that characterizes Him as a person is manifest in a variety of ways toward other persons. But it is always love. Both Arminians and Calvinists should rightly affirm that Christ died for all, in the sense that Christ's death was sufficient for all and that Scripture portrays God as inviting, commanding, and desiring the salvation of all, out of love (in the third sense developed in the first lecture). Further, all Christians ought also to confess that in a slightly different sense Christ Jesus, in the intent of God, died effectively for the elect alone, in line with the way the Bible speaks of God's special selecting love for the elect (in the fourth sense developed in the first lecture).
>
> Pastorally, there are many important implications. I mention only one. This approach, I contend, must surely come as a relief to young preachers in the Reformed tradition who hunger to preach the gospel effectively but who

74 G. Lewis and B. Demarest, *Integrative Theology* (Grand Rapids, MI: Zondervan, 1990), 409–10.

75 D. A. Carson, *The Difficult Doctrine of the Love of God* (Wheaton, IL: Crossway, 1999). This book is the published content of his lectures at Dallas Theological Seminary, which were also published as "God's Love and God's Wrath," *Bibliotheca Sacra* 156 (1999): 387–98. This is the fourth in a four-part article published in *Bib Sac*.

do not know how far they can go in saying to unbelievers things like "God loves you." When I have preached or lectured in Reformed circles, I have often been asked the question, "Do you feel free to tell unbelievers that God loves them?" Historically, Reformed theology at its best has never been slow in evangelism, as seen, for instance, in George Whitefield or virtually all the main lights in the Southern Baptist Convention until the end of the last century. Obviously I have no hesitation in answering this question from Reformed preachers affirmatively: of course, I tell the unconverted God loves them.

Not for a moment am I suggesting that when one preaches evangelistically one ought to retreat to passages of the third type (above), holding back on the fourth type until after a person is converted. There is something sleazy about that sort of approach. Certainly it is possible to preach evangelistically when dealing with a passage that explicitly teaches election. Charles Spurgeon did this sort of thing regularly. But I am saying that, provided there is an honest commitment to preaching the whole counsel of God, preachers in the Reformed tradition should not hesitate for an instant to declare the love of God for a lost world, for lost individuals. The Bible's ways of speaking about the love of God are comprehensive enough not only to permit this, but to mandate it.[76]

Similarly, Carson stated:

I argue, then, that both Arminians and Calvinists should rightly affirm that Christ died for all, *in* the sense that Christ's death was sufficient for all and that Scripture portrays God as inviting, commanding, and desiring the salvation of all, *out of love* . . . . Further, all Christians ought also to confess that, in a slightly different sense, Christ Jesus, in the intent of God, died effectively for the elect alone, *in line with the way the Bible speaks of God's special selecting love for the elect* . . . . This approach, I contend, must surely come as a relief to young preachers in the Reformed tradition who hunger to preach the Gospel effectively but who do not know how far they can go in saying things such as "God loves you" to unbelievers. When I have preached or lectured in Reformed circles, I have often been asked the question, "Do you feel free to tell unbelievers that God loves them?" . . . From what I have already said, it is obvious that I have no hesitation in answering this question from young Reformed preachers affirmatively: *Of course* I tell the unconverted God loves them.[77]

76 Carson, "God's Love and God's Wrath," 394–95.

77 D. A. Carson, *The Difficult Doctrine of the Love of God* (Wheaton, IL: Crossway, 2000), 77–78 (emphasis in original).

These statements are telling for many reasons. Notice Carson said that Christ's death "for all" is "in the sense that Christ's death was *sufficient* for all." Here Carson's meaning is dependent upon his usage of the word "sufficient." Upon first blush, one might assume that Carson believes Christ's death satisfied for the sins of every human being. In this case, he would be using the word "sufficient" to mean "extrinsic sufficiency," or in the classic sense. This possible reading is bolstered by the fact that Carson said "Arminians" should rightly affirm this fact as well. Arminians would indeed affirm it in the sense of an unlimited imputation of sin to Christ. But note Carson said "both Arminians *and* Calvinists should rightly affirm" it. No high Calvinist would ever affirm "extrinsic sufficiency" because they believe the death of Christ only satisfied for the sins of the elect. Thus, by his use of the term "sufficient," Carson may mean "intrinsic sufficiency."

All Calvinists and non-Calvinists can affirm the statement "Christ's death was sufficient for all," where "sufficient" is understood to mean Christ's infinite dignity and that the value of his death is capable of satisfying for the sins of all unbelievers. The problem is that moderate Calvinists and all non-Calvinists understand the term "sufficient" to mean not only that Christ's death *could have* satisfied for the sins of all unbelievers had that been God's intention but also that his death in fact *did* satisfy for the sins of all humanity. Carson probably rejects, along with all high Calvinists, this meaning of sufficiency. For them, Christ's death was *intended* only for the elect, and that intention also limits the imputation of sin to Christ (or the *extent* of his sufferings as well).

Carson's intended meaning here is ambiguous since his statement is capable of a number of different interpretations,[78] and his ambiguity may be deliberate.

Moreover, does Carson mean by the words "effectively" and "alone" that "Christ's death only results in the salvation of the elect?" If so, then no moderate Calvinist or non-Calvinist would disagree with the statement. Everyone agrees that the application of the atonement is only to the elect. This reading is potentially bolstered by the fact that Carson said "all Christians" (which includes non-Calvinists) should be able to affirm this. However, if this is his meaning, it is something of a tautology.

Carson could be read as meaning that Jesus died especially for the elect *alone*, where "alone" is explained in the immediately following clause: "*in line with the way the Bible speaks of God's special love for the elect.*" On this interpretation, the death of Jesus had a dualistic design: Christ died in one sense for the sins of all people, but in a special sense for the elect alone.

Here again, Carson is correct that all Christians can affirm this when the following implicit assumptions in his statements are made explicit. First, by his statement that

78 Carson has read G. Michael Thomas's work, *The Extent of the Atonement*, so he is no doubt familiar with these significant historical differences. See D. A. Carson, "God's Love and God's Wrath," 394.

Jesus "died for the elect alone" in line with "God's special selecting love for the elect," Carson means that the nature of the love God has for the elect is different from that which he has for the non-elect. This difference is exhibited in the fact that God has "selected" the elect to be the recipients of Christ's atoning death *in a way that is not true for the non-elect.* That is, God's love for his chosen children must in some way be different than his love for those who are not his chosen children.

Second, Christ's death for the non-elect brings them common grace. Assuming one leaves the meaning of "select" ambiguous, all non-Calvinists can affirm these statements *in so far as they go*. The problem is, for moderate Calvinists and non-Calvinists, his statements don't go far enough, since Carson does not specify for whose sins Christ suffered.

The following interpretation of Carson's words is also possible. If he meant to say that Christ actually died for the sins of the elect *only* and not for the sins of the non-elect, then logically Christ's death cannot be "sufficient" for the non-elect so that it is able to be applied to them. This limited sin-bearing is the position of all high Calvinists, and it is the crux of limited atonement (strict particularism).[79]

Notice Carson encouraged young Reformed preachers to tell "unbelievers" that God loves them, but he is silent on the subject of telling *unbelievers* that Christ *died for them* in the sense that his death satisfied the penalty for their sins. His theology may prohibit it. If this is Carson's intended meaning, then his statement that "all Christians" should be able to affirm this is erroneous. No moderate Calvinist or non-Calvinist believes that the death of Christ provided *only* common grace benefits for the non-elect.

It may be that the second interpretation is Carson's intended meaning. But if so, he is leaving too much to be read between the lines. Did Jesus's death on the cross satisfy for the sins of all humanity? Carson's paragraph ultimately does not answer the question in any explicit way.

But if Carson actually sides with high Calvinism, he must answer "no." With respect to the intent and extent of the atonement, high Calvinists believe the following: God loves all people (but not equally), God desires the salvation of all people, but Jesus only satisfied for the sins of the elect and no others. Moderate Calvinists and all non-Calvinists believe the following: God loves all people, God desires the salvation of all people, and Christ died for all people in the sense that his death satisfied for the sins of all people.[80]

---

79 In Mark Dever's audio interview with Carson, posted on Dever's *9Marks* website, it is clear that Dever (a high Calvinist) thinks Carson agrees with his limited imputation views. Dever attempts to pit Carson against Bruce Ware, professor at Southern Baptist Theological Seminary in Louisville, Kentucky, and a moderate Calvinist. The interview took place on February 25, 2009. "On Books with D. A. Carson," interview by Mark Dever, *9Marks*, February 25, 2009, http://9marks.org/interview/books-d-carson/.

80 The moderate Calvinists, however, argue that God's love for all is unequal, his saving desire is unequal; therefore Christ's *intention* in dying for the sins of all was also unequal.

Let's compare Carson with Calvin. Here is what Calvin had to say on John 3:16:

> And indeed our Lord Jesus was *offered to all the world.* For it is not speaking of three or four when it says: "God so loved the world, that he spared not His only Son." But yet we must notice what the Evangelist adds in this passage: "That whosoever believes in Him shall not perish but obtain eternal life." Our Lord Jesus *suffered for all*[81] and there is neither great nor small who is not inexcusable today, for we can obtain salvation in Him.[82] Unbelievers who turn away from Him and who deprive themselves of Him by their malice are today *doubly culpable*, for how will they excuse their ingratitude in not receiving the blessing in which they could share by faith.[83]

First, Calvin asserted that Jesus was "offered" to all the world. Non-Calvinists, moderate Calvinists, and most high Calvinists agree that God has a "universal saving will"[84] in that he desires the salvation of all people in his revealed will.

But this is not all that Calvin affirmed. Notice that he also said Jesus "suffered for all." The "all" here cannot mean the elect only since it is flanked with the quotation of John 3:16 with its "whosoever" and the statement that no one is inexcusable, "for we can obtain salvation in Him," followed by the statement that "unbelievers who turn away from Him . . . are doubly culpable" and fail to receive "the blessing in which they could share by faith."

Here Calvin clearly equated the "all" with "all unbelievers" and he said explicitly "Jesus suffered for all." Because of this, those who reject Christ are "doubly culpable." Why? Because they are rejecting the death of Christ on their behalf, which could provide them salvation if they were to believe.

Unlike Carson, Calvin had no qualms *explicitly* stating that "Jesus suffered for all." Not only did Calvin not employ the famous double payment argument, as do high Calvinists since Owen, he asserted that unbelievers are "doubly culpable" for their rejection of this "blessing" made available in Christ "in which they could share by faith." Calvin never used the double payment argument because he did not believe Scripture taught a limitation in the sin-bearing or the extent of Christ's death.

---

81 "Suffered for all" is an unlimited sin-bearing.

82 His death is actually *applicable* to all people since he "suffered for all" people.

83 J. Calvin, *Sermons on Isaiah's Prophecy of the Death and Passion of Christ* (1559; London: James Clark, 1956), 141 (emphasis added).

84 This expression is found three times in J. Piper's "Are There Two Wills in God?," in *Still Sovereign*, ed. T. R. Schreiner and B. Ware (Grand Rapids, MI: Baker, 2000), 107, 108, 122; and also in C. Daniel's *The History and Theology of Calvinism* (Dallas, TX: Scholarly Reprints, 1993), 208. B. Ware also used it affirmatively in "Divine Election to Salvation: Unconditional, Individual, and Infralapsarian," in *Perspectives on Election: Five Views*, ed. C. Brand (Nashville: B&H, 2006), 32.

John Piper (b. AD 1946)

Since we will evaluate Piper's view on limited atonement in more detail below, at this point we will simply note what Piper wrote in his "Going Beyond the Limits of Unlimited Atonement," in *Taste and See.*[85]

Piper asserted Christ's death was intended by God to obtain the willingness to believe.[86] He further stated:

1. There is no dispute that Christ died to obtain saving benefits for all who believe.
2. There is no dispute that Christ died so that we might say to all people everywhere without exception: God gave his Son to die for sin so that if you believe on him you may have eternal life (John 3:16).[87]

Piper thinks it is crucial to see what Arminians do *not* say. "They do not say that in the death of Christ, God intends to effectively save all for whom Christ died. They say only that God intends to make possible the salvation of all for whom Christ died."[88] From this Piper concluded "Arminians give man and not God the final determination of who is saved."[89]

David Wenkel critiqued Piper's theology of limited atonement.[90] He referenced Piper's official position on limited atonement according to "What We Believe About the Five Points of Calvinism," a 1998 online booklet available at desiringgod.org.[91]

1. Christ purchased for the elect the grace of regeneration and the gift of faith.
2. All men are the beneficiaries of the cross in some sense.
3. Christ died for all the sins of some men.

From these three propositions, Wenkel said Piper can tell all that Christ died for them, he just does not know how or to what extent. Wenkel pointed out how Piper's passion for God's glory sometimes short-circuits God's love when Piper said that God

---

85 J. Piper, "Going beyond the Limits of Unlimited Atonement," in *Taste and See* (Colorado Springs, CO: Multnomah, 1999), 325–27. Piper's *Five Points: Towards a Deeper Experience of God's Grace* (Fearn, Scotland: Christian Focus, 2013) also contains a discussion of limited atonement on pp. 37–52, but the argument here is essentially that in his chapter in *From Heaven He Came and Sought Her*, which we will take up below in a review of his chapter in that book. *Five Points* can also be found and is available for download at http://cdn.desiringgod.org/website_uploads/documents/books/five-points.pdf?1414777985.

86 Ibid., 325.

87 Ibid., 326.

88 Ibid.

89 Ibid. Actually, what Arminians, along with all other non-Calvinists, assert is that God sovereignly gives man the freedom to reject or accept the gospel offer.

90 D. Wenkel, "A Palatable Calvinism: Limited Atonement in the Theology of John Piper," *Journal of Dispensational Theology* 11 (2007): 69–83.

91 J. Piper, "What We Believe about the Five Points of Calvinism," *Desiring God* (blog), March 1, 1985 (rev. March 1998), http://www.desiringgod.org/articles/what-we-believe-about-the-five-points-of-calvinism.

is "committed to something even more valuable than saving all," that is, the "full range of God's glory."[92] For Piper, "Christ's dying for his own glory and his dying to show love are not only both *true*, they are both *the same*."[93] However, in another work Piper appears to make the love of God penultimate to God's glory.[94]

Wenkel pointed out that for Piper God's love is not demonstrated so much in Christ's sacrifice as in the infinite measure of God's glory. Yet Scripture places Christ's atonement in close proximity to the love of God as the motivating factor. Wenkel asserted: "It is a natural theological conclusion to stress the glory of the cross rather than the message of saving love, which according to Piper is only as broad as limited atonement."[95]

Wenkel highlighted a tension (contradiction?) in Piper's focus on God's infinite glory and joy displayed in sending his Son to die coupled with a universal love, "but it is unclear how a sinner can know God's love since it is not rooted in a substitutionary atonement."[96] Piper engaged in circular reasoning when he asserted faith is finding joy in the offer of the joy of the glorious cross. Yet how can one be sure that the sacrifice was for him?[97]

Piper's paradox is in attempting to hold two things together: our ability to say to all people without exception that "God gave Christ to die for sin such that if you believe, you may have eternal life," and yet on the other hand the denial that "God intended to make salvation possible for all persons."[98]

Wayne Grudem (b. AD 1948)

Grudem is a theologian, seminary professor, and author. He co-founded the Council on Biblical Manhood and Womanhood and served as the general editor of the ESV Study Bible. His *Systematic Theology* originally appeared in 1994 and has been widely used in Bible colleges and seminaries around the world.

Grudem's section on the extent of the atonement is concise, covering roughly ten pages. To his credit, he rightly pointed out that the state of the question is not so much the *purpose* of the atonement (critiquing Berkhof on that point) as it is the question of "what actually happened in the atonement." Did Christ pay for the sins of all people or not? That is the key question.[99]

One problem in this section is how he speaks of the "Reformed view" of limited atonement. Nowhere does Grudem acknowledge the debates *within the Reformed com-*

92 J. Piper, *The Pleasures of God*, rev. ed. (Sisters, OR: Multnomah, 2000), 313.
93 J. Piper, *The Passion of Jesus Christ* (Wheaton, IL: Crossway, 2004), 82 (emphasis in original).
94 Piper, *Taste and See*, 44.
95 Wenkel, "A Palatable Calvinism," 76.
96 Ibid., 77.
97 Ibid., 81.
98 Piper, *Taste and See*, 326.
99 W. Grudem, *Systematic Theology: An Introduction to Biblical Doctrine* (Grand Rapids, MI: Zondervan, 1994), 601.

munity since the end of the sixteenth century over this issue. He merely speaks as if all Calvinists affirm limited atonement and the rest who do not are non-Reformed. This is, of course, a major historical problem for Grudem.

Grudem first highlighted the standard texts used to support limited atonement, followed by texts that support what he calls "the Non-Reformed view (General Redemption or Unlimited Atonement)."[100] He asserted there are three points of agreement among all parties, one of which is "a free offer of the gospel can rightly be made to every person ever born."[101] It is true that all parties *agree* that the free offer can rightly be made to every person, but it is also true that all Arminians and other non-Calvinists do not agree that high Calvinism can hold this position with any consistency.

Grudem argued that those who affirm universal atonement cannot adequately answer the question, "When Christ died, did he *actually pay the penalty* only for the sins of those who would believe in him, or for the sins of every person who ever lived?"[102] Grudem asserted that those in hell suffer the penalty of their own sins, "therefore their penalty could not have been fully taken by Christ."[103] Here Grudem is trading on a commercialistic understanding of the atonement along with the double payment argument. He does not take into account that one must distinguish between the atonement's extent and its actual application.

Grudem attempted to blunt the force of the universal language in atonement passages by suggesting that these can usually be explained along the lines of the atonement is being *offered* to all the world. In addition to being exegetically problematic, Grudem entangles himself in contradictions when he asserted concerning 1 John 2:2 that John

> may simply be understood to mean that Christ is the atoning sacrifice that the gospel now *makes available for* the sins of everyone in the world. . . . It would be entirely consistent with the language of the verse to think that John is simply saying that Christ is the atoning sacrifice who is available to pay for the sins of everyone in the world. Likewise, when Paul says that Christ "gave himself as a ransom *for all*" (1 Tim. 2:6), we are to understand this to mean a ransom available for all people, without exception.[104]

How is Christ available to pay for the sins of "everyone in the world" when he has only made an atonement for specific people in the world, the elect? The same applies to Grudem's reference to 1 Tim 2:6. How can a ransom be available for all people "without exception" when there is no ransom for all people without exception?

100 Ibid., 595–97.
101 Ibid., 597.
102 Ibid. (emphasis in original).
103 Ibid.
104 Ibid., 598–99 (emphasis in original).

This is further seen in Grudem's appeal that Reformed people should not rush to criticize an evangelist who tells an unsaved audience,

> "Christ died for your sins," if it is made clear in the context that it is necessary to trust in Christ before one can receive the benefits of the gospel offer. In that sense the sentence is simply understood to mean "Christ died to offer you forgiveness for your sins." The important point here is that sinners realize that salvation is available for everyone and that payment of sins is available for everyone.[105]

But again, problems abound. All orthodox Christians affirm the necessity of belief in Christ before reception of the benefits of the gospel offer. That is not the point at issue. The sentence "Christ died for your sins" is actually understood to mean two things: (1) an objective satisfaction for the sins of the unbeliever has been made and (2) if the unbeliever will believe the gospel, then on the basis of that objective atonement made for his sins, he can receive the benefit, which is salvation. How can it be logically possible for an unbeliever, if he is among the non-elect according to Reformed theology, to receive a genuine offer of salvation when no atonement objectively exists for his sins? Salvation is not after all available to everyone, as Grudem has asserted. It is actually available only to the elect. Especially problematic is Grudem's final statement that "payment for sins is available for everyone." This is simply not the case on a limited atonement scheme, for obvious reasons. There is only a payment for the sins of the elect. All the non-elect have no payment for their sins. Even if they were to believe, they could not be saved.

Grudem's treatment of the other passages that teach universal atonement suffers from the same exegetical near-sightedness, as evidenced from his reliance on John Gill's tortuous interpretation of 2 Pet 2:1.

Stanley Grenz (AD 1950–2005)

Grenz was a Baptist theologian and ethicist. He was considered a leading evangelical theologian before his untimely death. For twelve years (1990–2002) Grenz held the position of Pioneer McDonald Professor of Baptist Heritage, Theology, and Ethics at Carey Theological College and at Regent College in Vancouver. He authored numerous works, including a systematic theology—*Theology for the Community of God*.[106]

Grenz affirmed a substitutionary atonement that is universal in scope: "As our expiation, Jesus' sacrifice covers all sin, so that God is able to forgive any and all."[107] He disavowed that universal atonement entails universalism:

105 Ibid., 602.

106 S. Grenz, *Theology for the Community of God* (Nashville: B&H, 1994).

107 Ibid., 456.

> Our wretched human situation consists not only of the sin that evokes God's displeasure, but also our own enmity against God. Through Christ, God is reconciled to us. But in our sin we remain at odds with him. From God's side, therefore, the atoning sacrifice of Jesus is universal; from the human side, however, its efficacy requires our response, namely, that we be reconciled to the God who has reconciled the world to himself (2 Cor. 5:19–20).[108]

Roger Olson (b. AD 1952)

Olson is professor of theology at George W. Truett Theological Seminary at Baylor University and is a self-proclaimed Arminian. Olson is one of the leading Arminian scholars today whose books on Arminian theology are must reading, especially for the Reformed who sometimes are prone to misunderstand Arminius and Arminianism. His book, *Against Calvinism*,[109] contains a section on the extent of the atonement (chapter 6).

Olson informed his readers that he is objecting to the following points made by Calvinists who affirm limited atonement:

1. Penal substitution should be understood to necessitate that Christ died only for the elect, otherwise universalism is entailed.
2. The sufficiency of the atonement rests solely in its value, while its efficiency is only for the elect since it was designed only for them.
3. The non-elect obtain some universal benefits from the atonement but not the expiation of sin since the atonement was never intended to make salvation possible for them.
4. If the atonement is universal in scope, the double payment argument entails that the penalty for sin is unjustly demanded twice (first paid by Christ on the cross then paid by all the non-elect in hell for eternity).[110]

Olson summed up his objections to limited atonement:

1. It is unsupported by Scripture.
2. It was never taught by the Christian Church until the late sixteenth century.
3. It contradicts the love of God for all people.
4. Limitarians wrongly conclude that universal redemption entails universalism.
5. Limited atonement entails that there can be no well-meant gospel offer to all indiscriminately.

108 Ibid.
109 R. Olson, *Against Calvinism* (Grand Rapids, MI: Zondervan, 2011).
110 Ibid., 136–50.

6. The "sufficiency" argument of high Calvinists (sufficient in value but not sufficient as a payment for all sins) is an illogical position from which to argue against the Arminian distinction between atonement accomplished for all but the application limited only to those who repent and believe the gospel.[111]
7. Many delegates at Dort and Westminster rejected limited atonement.
8. Scripture affirms unlimited atonement.[112]

Olson stated that:

> Arminians believe that any limitation of God's intention for everyone's salvation, including limited atonement, necessarily and inexorably impugns the character of God even where Calvinists insist otherwise. Arminians do not claim that Calvinists say God is not good or loving; they say Calvinism implies that necessarily, so that Calvinists should say it in order to be logically consistent with themselves.[113]

Kevin Bauder (b. AD 1955)

Bauder earned the PhD in systematic and historical theology from Dallas Theological Seminary and served as president of Central Baptist Theological Seminary in Minneapolis from 2003 to 2011. He is currently research professor of systematic theology at the seminary.

He published a blog post in 2005 entitled "The Logic of Limited Atonement."[114] Though a short piece, Bauder raised a strong point against the logical and theological confusion he thinks inherent to limited atonement.

The failure to distinguish properly between the atonement's provision and application is a crucial theological error of limited atonement. The logical error is discovered when one queries whether God intended to limit the atonement in its provision. Bauder correctly noted that one cannot answer this by appealing to evidence for limited application.

> Even if one recognizes (as Calvinists do) that part of God's intention through the death of Christ was to secure the application of salvation to the elect, such belief still does not reveal for whom God intended to provide salvation. This exposes the logical confusion in the argument for Limited Atonement.

111 Ibid., 137.

112 Ibid., 136–50.

113 Ibid., 67.

114 K. T. Bauder, "The Logic of Limited Atonement," ΤΩ ΧΡΟΝΟΥ ΚΑΙΡΩ: *"In the Nick of Time"* (blog), February 4, 2005, http://seminary.wcts1030.com/publications/Nick/Nick001.htm.

Bauder continued to show the logical fallacy involved in maintaining that unconditional election is incompatible with the rejection of limited atonement. Limited atonement includes an affirmation that God intended both to provide salvation for the elect only and to apply it to the elect only and a denial that God intended to provide salvation for the non-elect. This denial is what really defines limited atonement, according to Bauder.

Bauder considered the issue around three propositions:

1. Some persons are not persons for whom Christ intended to secure the provision of salvation.
2. All persons are persons for whom Christ intended to secure the provision of salvation.
3. Some persons are persons for whom Christ intended to secure the application of salvation.

Bauder stated:

> Those who reject Limited Atonement do not object to what it affirms, namely, that Christ died to provide salvation for the elect. The question is about the status of the non-elect: did Christ intend to provide salvation for them, or did He not? At this point, those who reject Limited Atonement answer with an affirmative. Christ did indeed intend to provide salvation for all people.[115]

The first sentence must be nuanced. Calvinists who reject limited atonement will be able to affirm this sentence. Non-Calvinists would agree only if it is understood that the elect are synonymous with those who genuinely believe the gospel. They would reject a Calvinistic understanding of unconditional election.

Bauder correctly asserted that proposition one and two directly contradict each other. Both statements cannot be true.

Concerning unconditional election, God only intended to apply salvation to the elect, hence proposition three. Bauder thinks there is not incompatibility of proposition three with either proposition one or two for the reason that the predicate of proposition three contains a different term. "In the first two propositions, the predicate is about those for whom Christ intended to provide salvation. In the third proposition, the predicate is about those to whom Christ intended to apply salvation. In other words, Unconditional Election is logically compatible with either Limited Atonement or General Atonement."[116] The argument that unconditional election entails limited atonement is not logically sound, according to Bauder:

---

115 Ibid.

116 Ibid.

> The statement that Christ would not die for someone whom He did not intend to save is really not a statement about Christ. It is a statement about what the speaker would do if he were in Christ's place. The same is true of the statement that Christ would not fail to elect someone for whom He shed His blood. Such arguments sound reasonable and they seem persuasive. Upon examination, however, their persuasiveness is found to be psychological rather than logical. They are speculations about how God would handle Himself if He were altogether such an One as us.[117]

Bauder concluded that if limited atonement is true, its truth cannot be established by an appeal to logical consistency.

> The strongest case for Limited Atonement would be made if its proponents could offer specific biblical texts that named particular individuals or groups for whom Christ did not die to provide salvation. Barring such evidence, the best that can be said for Limited Atonement is that it remains in doubt.[118]

Bauder's short article garnered the attention of Carl Trueman, who responded to it in his chapter defending limited atonement in the 2015 book *Perspectives on the Extent of the Atonement: 3 Views*.[119]

James R. White (b. AD 1962)

White is a Reformed Baptist author, debater in the area of Christian apologetics, and director of Alpha and Omega Ministries. He serves as an elder at Phoenix Reformed Baptist Church in Phoenix, Arizona. Two of his works address specifically the subject of Calvinism and each has a section on the extent of the atonement.[120]

White's *The Potter's Freedom* addressed the extent of the atonement in chapters 10 and 11. In chapter 10 White defined the issue of the atonement by correctly distinguishing between the *intention*, *scope*, and *effect* of the atonement.[121] Like many modern-day high Calvinists, White does not like the traditional sufficient/efficient formula and said it is "not fully Reformed." He thinks it carries some truth but complained that it "misses the most important issue": whether Christ intended to atone for every single human individual or whether it was intended to make atonement for the

117 Ibid.

118 Ibid.

119 C. Trueman, "Definite Atonement View of the Atonement," in *Perspectives on the Extent of the Atonement*, 31–32.

120 J. White, *The Potter's Freedom*, rev. ed. (Amityville, NY: Calvary, 2000); D. Hunt and J. White, *Debating Calvinism: Five Points, Two Views* (Colorado Springs, CO: Multnomah, 2004). *The Potter's Freedom* is White's rejoinder to Norm Geisler's *Chosen but Free* (Minneapolis, MN: Bethany House, 2001).

121 White, *The Potter's Freedom*, 232.

elect alone. This saying ("sufficient to save every single human being, but efficient to save only the elect") really says nothing to the point of the debate. No doubt White, like Beza and Owen, senses the need to revise the Lombardian formula away from its original sense of "sufficient for all" since it originally meant Christ actually atoned for the sins of all men.

White caricatured Arminianism by stating: "Historic Arminians saw that believing in the idea of substitutionary atonement would not fit with their system of theology."[122] This would come as quite a shock to Arminius himself, who held firmly to substitutionary atonement, not to mention John Wesley and a host of other Arminians past and present. White appears to be unaware that Hugo Grotius himself affirmed a substitutionary atonement in his explication of the governmental theory.[123]

White continued his caricature of Arminianism: "Modern Arminians are generally unaware of the history of Arminianism, and the fact that the phrases 'Jesus took the place of sinners' or 'Jesus died for us' or 'Jesus' death paid the penalty of sin' are 'borrowed from Calvinism.'"[124] These kinds of phrases can be found in all kinds of Arminian writers past and present. They are certainly not the sole property of Calvinism. White presupposes that substitution entails particular redemption and on this basis stated that Arminians reject substitutionary atonement and replace it with the governmental theory.[125]

White discussed Rom 8:31–34 and Hebrews 7–10 as affirming limited atonement. Yet nothing in either of these passages affirms limited atonement.[126] Perhaps the most egregious error White made is hermeneutical in nature. Referencing Gal 2:20, he stated, "But let us ask this question: can the justly condemned sinner who stands upon the parapets of hell in eternity to come, screaming in hatred toward the halls of heaven, say, 'I was crucified with Christ! He loved me and gave Himself up for me!' Surely not!"[127]

First and obviously, the context has to do with real or vital union with Christ. This is why Paul goes on to say, "it is no longer I who live, but Christ lives in me; and the life which I now live in the flesh I live by faith in the Son of God." No unbeliever can say,

---

122 Ibid., 233.

123 See, for example, G. Williams, who sought to correct this misunderstanding in some of the secondary sources concerning Grotius's view of divine justice and the governmental emphasis among Reformed writers. His doctoral dissertation is very helpful on this point: G. Williams, "A Critical Exposition of Hugo Grotius's Doctrine of the Atonement in *De satisfaction Christi*" (PhD diss., University of Oxford, 1999). See also his chapter "Punishment God Cannot Inflict: The Double Payment Argument *Redivivus*," in *From Heaven He Came and Sought Her*, 490–93.

124 White, *The Potter's Freedom*, 234.

125 Ibid., 235.

126 Among high Calvinists on Rom 8:32, there is a hasty term generalization. They convert the "us" into the general term "all," in the sense of "all" the elect irrespective of faith, thus arguing that "all for whom Christ died will be given all things." In the context, however, the "us" explicitly refers to the justified or believers. The idea is that since God gave his Son for those of us who believe, how much more will he give us (who believe) all things? Paul also uses the same form of the *a fortiori* argument in Rom 5:8–10.

127 White, *The Potter's Freedom*, 248.

"I have been crucified with Christ," even if it is an elect unbeliever, for none of them is "living by faith in the Son of God" (NKJV). If White considered the text and his own theological assumptions carefully, even he would have to say that Christ died for more people than can say "I have been crucified with Christ," since some of the elect are still in unbelief. The same goes with the passages that say Christ laid his life down for the church. That statement likewise only concerns believers. All parties (whether Calvinistic or not) grant that Christ died for more than are in a believing state. High Calvinists think Christ died only for those who will eventually come to believe, not only for those who presently believe. White, as is common in his argumentation,[128] is unwittingly placing union with Christ before faith and assuming that all the elect as such can therefore say "I have been crucified with Christ."

Second, it is a straw man concerning both Arminianism and moderate Calvinism. None of them use Gal 2:20 to advocate their position, because they all easily recognize that the verse obviously pertains to those in vital union with Christ. None of them think that the damned in hell can say "I have been crucified with Christ" but only that they can say "Christ has died for me." White's opponents assert the latter of all men, not the former. White argued as if these two propositions are the same and thus misrepresented his opponents, as well as the text.

White began engaging the theoretical topic of particular redemption with Calvin[129] rather than Scripture. White committed the negative inference fallacy by assuming that passages that seem to limit the extent of the atonement are to be interpreted as Christ dying *only* for those limited groups of people. White fails to note in most, if not all, of these cases the limitation is due to the use of personalized language where a specific group of people is being addressed or referenced. When a biblical author says "Christ died for us," one cannot logically infer that this statement means Christ died *only* for that group, as White does.

White appealed to the standard interpretation by many Calvinists of John 17:9 as proof of limited atonement. He presumed that Christ prayed only for the elect and not for the world in this chapter. Again, this presumes the negative inference fallacy. White's appeal to the use of "many" in Mark 10:45 as evidence of limitation in the atonement is based on a misunderstanding "many" as distinct from "all" rather than the correct meaning of "many" as distinct from "one" or "a few."

White identified what he considered to be three errors of Arminianism: rejection of "the biblical doctrine of the positive decree of God," rejection of the "biblical doctrine of the deadness of man in sin and his inability to do anything that is pleasing to God," and rejection of the "biblical doctrine of the atonement, including its *intention* and

128 White frequently speaks of all the elect as such being "saved at the cross."

129 White, *The Potter's Freedeom*, 253–62.

result."[130] Actually all three of White's assessments of Arminianism are in error, which can be demonstrated by a careful reading of Arminius himself as well as Arminian theologians past and present.

White's understanding of the atonement along commercialistic lines as well as his misunderstanding of what Arminians actually believe is evidenced in this statement:

> His blood may "buy" forgiveness, but our choice determines whether the entire work of Christ in our behalf will be a success or a failure. This empties the word "paid" of its meaning. If someone pays my bill, I no longer owe the money. The Arminian view leaves us with a contractual situation where Christ offers to pay the bill based upon the performance of the free act of faith.[131]

White correctly noted that the benefits of the atonement are not applied to the person until the point of regeneration. But he then turned right around and said that the certainty of application is grounded in God's decree of election, and Christ's substitution for the elect on the cross assures the benefits will be applied to each elect individual "who has received God's sovereign grace in eternity past."[132] These two statements would seem to be contradictory. White overlooks Eph 2:1–3, which declares that even the unbelieving elect remain under the wrath of God until regeneration. No one has "received" God's grace in eternity past. The only way this is not a contradiction is if White is referring to the mere fact of God's election of individuals in eternity past as constituting their appointment to receive his grace in the future.

In reference to 1 John 2:2, White stated: "The Reformed understanding is that Jesus Christ is the propitiation for the sins of all the Christians to which John was writing, and not only them, but for all Christians throughout the world, Jew and Gentile, at all times and in all places."[133] There are several problems with this statement. First, there is no monolithic "Reformed" understanding of "for the whole world" in 1 John 2:2, as we have seen. An entire segment of Reformed theologians and commentators who interpret this phrase as a reference to all people is ignored. Second, contextually this ignores the usage of the same phrase in 1 John 5:19, where "the whole world" clearly means all unbelievers on earth at the time of John's writing. Third, what is the justification for interpreting the phrase to refer to all believers "at all times and in all places"?

White's defense of limited atonement in both *The Potter's Freedom* and *Debating Calvinism* employs the standard arguments expressed at a popular level but intermixed with numerous logical fallacies and misinterpretations.

---

130 Ibid., 266 (emphasis in original).

131 Ibid., 267.

132 Ibid., 268.

133 Ibid., 274.

In all White's writings on Calvinism and the extent of the atonement, his tacit assumption is that God does not desire the salvation of the non-elect. One will recognize in his writings this dichotomy: either (1) God only wills the salvation of the elect or (2) God equally wills the salvation of all men. Consistently missing in his exchanges is the mainstream orthodox Calvinist position that (3) God desires the salvation of all men in his revealed will but only purposes to effect the salvation of the elect alone according to his secret will. White's arguments on the extent of the atonement always assume option 1, not option 3. This is certainly the case in his exchanges with Dave Hunt as well as in *The Potter's Freedom* when he deals with Matt 23:37; 1 Tim 2:4; and 2 Pet 3:9.

White's faulty interpretations of these passages and his assumptions about the will of God have not gone unnoticed by Calvinists themselves. Cornelis Venema (president of Mid-America Reformed Seminary), in his exposition on the free offer and Christ's disposition toward Jerusalem, takes the mainstream Calvinistic view of God's will when he said about Luke 13:34:

> It is difficult to see how this text could be taken in any other way than as an expression of Jesus' heartfelt desire that the inhabitants of Jerusalem find salvation. It seems clearly to express a desire that could only arise from a compassionate and earnest interest in their salvation.[134]

In contrast, Venema observed White's treatment of the parallel passage in Matt 23:37 and stated:

> White treats the parallel to this text [Luke 13:34] in Matthew 23:37, and tries to argue that in the context Jesus is not speaking about the salvation of all the inhabitants of Jerusalem but only of the leaders of the Jews. On his reading, the text does not express any desire for the salvation of the inhabitants of Jerusalem, some of whom may be non-elect. Though White's reading of Matthew 23:37 is rather unlikely, he neglects to note that the context in Luke 13:34 has to do with the issue of salvation or non-salvation, and that it speaks generally of many among the inhabitants of Jerusalem who forfeit their opportunity to enter into the kingdom while the door was open to them.[135]

---

134 Cornelis Venema, "Election and the 'Free Offer' of the Gospel (Part 2 of 5)," *The Outlook* 52.4 (April 2002): 19.

135 Ibid. For a refutation of the Gillite differentiation between "Jerusalem" and "thy children" (which White frequently uses when dealing with Matt 23:37), see David Silversides's treatment of the passage in *The Free Offer: Biblical & Reformed* (Glasgow: Marpet, 2005), 50–54. Silversides said,

> In this verse, Jerusalem evidently refers to the people of that city. It may have the leaders (denounced in the previous verses) especially in mind, but they were not solely responsible for the death of the prophets, or even of Christ himself; nor did the judgment fall only on them, as many ordinary people perished in the fall of Jerusalem (ibid., 50).

In White's treatment of the passages of Scripture touching on the will of God (e.g., Ezek 18:23; 33:11; Matt 23:37; John 5:34; 1 Tim 2:4; and 2 Pet 3:9), and those related to the death of Christ (e.g., John 1:29; 3:16; 1 Tim 2:6; 2 Pet 2:1), the tacit assumption seems always to be that God only wills the salvation of the elect.

Paul Martin Henebury (b. circa AD 1962)

Henebury is the founder and president of the Telos Biblical Institute. He authored two articles on the extent of the atonement, covering some of the key New Testament passages that seem to assert unlimited atonement and answering objections against them.[136]

Laurence M. Vance (b. circa AD 1963)

Vance is the director of the Francis Wayland Institute, adjunct instructor in accounting at Pensacola Junior College, and an adjunct scholar at the Ludwig von Mises Institute. He holds degrees in history, theology, accounting, and economics. He is also a prolific author.

Vance's *The Other Side of Calvinism* is a critique of Calvinism and contains a section on limited atonement.[137] Originally published in 1991, it was revised in 2007. Vance peppers his work with quotations from Calvinist sources demonstrating how at times some Calvinists have caricatured Arminianism. On occasion, Vance errs as well, such as when he wrongly claims the sufficient/efficient formula was coined by Augustine.[138]

Vance's treatment fares better when he addresses the standard arguments in favor of limited atonement.[139] One value of Vance's chapter on limited atonement is the collection of quotations from Calvinists, usually within the last one hundred years, respecting limited atonement and unlimited atonement that are patent examples of caricature, gross misrepresentation, and historical inaccuracy.

He continued,

> The older English pronouns of our Authorized Version (reflecting the singular and plural distinctions of the Greek) are helpful here. The word *thy* (singular) clearly relates to *Jerusalem* (singular). The *children* (plural), represented as chickens, are in view in the phrase *ye* (plural) *would not*, where the English reflects the plural of the Greek verb . . . It is the children that would not be gathered. Jerusalem is simply a collective description of the city and its people, as a body. The children of Jerusalem are nothing more complicated than those same people considered as a collection of individuals (ibid., 52).

Similarly, Carson noted that during the duration of Jesus's ministry, "he 'often' longed to gather and shelter Jerusalem (by metonymy including all Jews) as a hen her chicks (cf. Deut 32:11; Pss 17:8; 36:7; 91:4; Jer 48:40); for despite the woes, Jesus, like the 'Sovereign Lord' in Ezekiel 18:32, took 'no pleasure in the death of anyone'" (D. A. Carson, "Matthew," in *The Expositor's Bible Commentary*, 12 vols., ed. F. E. Gæbelein [Grand Rapids, MI: Zondervan, 1984], 8:486–87). As J. C. Ryle said, "We must be careful . . . not to confine 'ye would not,' to the Scribes, Pharisees, and rulers. The verse which follows [Luke 13:35] shows clearly that our Lord includes all the inhabitants of Jerusalem" (*Expository Thoughts on the Gospels: Luke*, 2:145).

136 P. M. Henebury, "Christ's Atonement: Its Purpose and Extent, Part 1," *Conservative Theological Journal* 9 (2005): 88–108; and idem, "The Extent of the Atonement, Part 2," *Conservative Theological Journal* 9 (2005): 242–57.

137 L. Vance, *The Other Side of Calvinism*, rev. ed. (Pensacola, FL: Vance, 2007), 405–73.

138 Ibid., 421.

139 Ibid., 422–32.

Conclusion

There can be no doubt that North American Baptists during this period were not in lockstep on the question of the extent of the atonement. The historical records indicate a wide variety on this issue within the Reformed camp.

The past thirty years has seen a rise in the influence of Calvinism in the overall evangelical world, especially in the United States. Generally speaking, the gatekeepers of this movement, people like D. A. Carson, John Piper, Al Mohler, Ligon Duncan, John MacArthur, R. C. Sproul, and others, are all strongly committed to limited atonement. Thus, probably a majority of the younger Calvinist students who self-identify as Reformed would be committed to limited atonement, at least in part due to the influence of these key leaders.

7

Southern Baptists and the Extent of the Atonement

The Southern Baptist Convention was birthed in Augusta, Georgia, in 1845.

The question of just how many Calvinistic Baptist churches in the South there were at the time depends upon the criteria used to make the determination: each church's doctrinal statement, the modern TULIP designation, and so on. Churches that rejected limited atonement but accepted the other basic doctrinal standards of Calvinism would rightly be considered Calvinistic. Our specific concern is with the question of the extent of the atonement, primarily from the time of the birth of the convention to the present.

Long before the founding of the Southern Baptist Convention, Baptists in the north and the south differed among themselves on the specific question of the extent of the atonement. According to Hackney, until the mid-eighteenth-century General Baptists, who affirmed universal atonement, were more numerous than Particular Baptists in New England and the Southern colonies.[1]

Baptist historian John Sparks noted how in 1775 the Kehukee Regular Baptist Association split. One group, composed of Separate Baptists and some Regular Baptists,

1 W. Brackney, ed., *Baptist Life and Thought: A Sourcebook*, rev. ed. (Valley Forge, PA: Judson, 1998), 97.

reorganized in 1777 under the name "United Baptists." The other group retained the name "Regular Baptists" and maintained its relationship with the Charleston Association.[2]

The Rapidan Association was also disrupted over Calvinism and Arminianism, especially over the issue of limited atonement. Sparks concluded that most Baptists

> were content to settle down on the formula of John Leland, himself a New England Separate Baptist who had settled in Virginia and in the Rapidan Association around the time of the Revolution. As Leland described it, the most successful preaching was "the Sovereign Grace of God, mixed with a little of what is called Arminianism."[3]

William Lumpkin related the following incident illustrative of the situation.

> In the May, 1775 General Association of the Separate Baptists in Virginia, the following question was discussed: "Is salvation by Christ made possible for every individual of the human race?" A warm debate followed, in which nearly every preacher tried to participate. . . . when a vote was taken toward the close of the day, it was found that the Calvinists had a small majority.
>
> That evening, the Arminians determined to see if their views would be a bar to fellowship, and the next day they learned to their dismay that this seemed to be the case. They then withdrew out of doors, taking the moderator with them. The Calvinists chose John Williams as their moderator. For some time the two groups were separate, communicating by messengers. Finally the Arminians offered what seemed to be a compromise: "We do not deny the former part of your proposal, respecting particular election of grace, still retaining our liberty, with regard to construction." To this the other party consented, and a happy reunion followed.[4]

Seventy years prior to the founding of the Southern Baptist Convention, a significant number of Virginia Separate Baptist ministers were not in accord with high Calvinism on the issue of particular election or particular redemption. They were "Arminian" on these points.

Most colonial Baptists who self-identified as Calvinists had adopted the "New Light Calvinism" of Jonathan Edwards and, subsequently, the modified Calvinism of Andrew Fuller. "Virtually all major eighteenth century colonial Baptists were modified Calvinists,"

2 J. Sparks, *The Roots of Appalachian Christianity: The Life and Legacy of Elder Shubal Stearns* (Lexington: University Press of Kentucky, 2001), 189.

3 Ibid. See J. Leland, "A Letter of Valediction on Leaving Virginia, 1791," in *The Writings of the Late Elder John Leland*, ed. L. F. Green (New York: G. W. Wood, 1845), 172.

4 W. Lumpkin, *Baptist Foundations in the South* (Nashville: Broadman, 1961), 103.

according to Michael Williams, who also stated, "Some of the colonial Baptists who emerged by 1790 could even be typified as 'Calminians' due to their unique blend of a softened form of Calvinism."[5] This obviously included a rejection of limited atonement.

John Asplund's *Annual Register of the Baptist Denomination* showed that in the late eighteenth century, of thirty-five associations in the US and frontier territories, seventeen formally subscribed to the Philadelphia Confession, and nine more held to the "Calvinistic system" or "Calvinistic sentiment." By the same token, even some within these associations, along with other associations which were more Arminian, embraced universal atonement. Some did not adopt any confession due in part to the diversity over the issue of Calvinism and Arminianism among the pastors and people of these churches. Asplund reported that the Sandy Creek Association held to no confession of faith at the time "as the generality of them hold to general provision [unlimited atonement]."[6]

Even though some Separate Baptists accepted many of the doctrines expressed in the Philadelphia Confession, Sparks noted they declined to endorse it not only because of scruples about man-made creeds but also because they "were still committed Arminians who preached a salvation available to all throughout the entire course of their ministries."[7]

Sparks recounted the role Shubal Stearns played in early American Baptist life.

> Doctrinally, from most available evidence it appears that Shubal Stearns was still a predictably mild Whitefield-style evangelistic Calvinist, but he was now exhibiting a strong General Baptist perspective as well. . . . Far more telling is the preamble of the short covenant that he almost certainly either wrote or dictated for another Baptist church he gathered and helped organize within five years of his own immersion. Copied at the church's reorganization in 1783, it reads verbatim as follows: . . . This brief statement was not copied by Stearns, and neither was the essence taken from the Westminster, First or Second London, or Philadelphia Confessions at all. It is a simple listing of the old General Baptists' Six Principles headed by a Separatist affirmation of the authority of Scripture and complemented by merely one Calvinistic article: that of the perseverance of the saints.[8]

As Thomas Kidd and Barry Hankins noted, most Baptist churches at the end of the eighteenth century espoused moderate Calvinist beliefs.

---

5 M. Williams, "The Influence of Calvinism on Colonial Baptists," *Baptist History and Heritage* 39 (Spring, 2004): 37–38.

6 J. Asplund, *The Annual Register of the Baptist Denomination in North America to the First of November, 1790* (Philadelphia: Thomas Dobson, 1792), 48–53; cited in Thompson, "Baptists and 'Calvinism,'" 62–63.

7 J. Sparks, *The Roots of Appalachian Christianity*, 107–8; citing R. Semple, *Rise and Progress of the Baptists in Virginia* (Lafayette, TN: Church History Research and Archives, 1976), 107–8.

8 Ibid., 45–46.

> They generally held to the doctrinal views of the English Baptist minister Andrew Fuller, who advocated a modified Calvinist view of the atonement. Fuller argued that Christ's death on the cross was "sufficient" to forgive the sins of all, but "efficient" only for the elect. In 1795, the Danbury Association entertained a query from a member church: "Are the non-elect in any sense bought by the blood of Christ?" It answered, "If by being bought, you mean to ask, whether the atonement is sufficient for the whole world; we answer in the affirmative: but if you mean to ask, whether the atonement of Christ has bought any of the fallen race, so as to release them from the curse of the divine law until they are regenerated, we answer in the negative." Some thought this position was quasi-Arminian, suggesting that Christ had somehow died for all mankind. Staunch Calvinists saw the atonement as sufficient for only those predestined to salvation. At the Powelton Baptist Church in Georgia, four members separated in 1791 because the church endorsed Fuller's theology of the atonement. Pastor Silas Mercer polled the congregation, asking whether it should "excommunicate a member for holding what is called a general provision." A majority voted in the negative, and they decided to expel the four hyper-Calvinist schismatics instead.[9]

G. W. Paschal described the situation in North Carolina with respect to Calvinism in the post-Revolutionary days:

> The rigid Calvinism which was preached in many of the Baptist Churches of the post-Revolutionary days absorbed the entire religious interest and was powerful in modifying the evangelic appeal which the churches made to the unconverted. The yearly meeting with its austere sermons emphasizing the doctrine of election and the helplessness of sinners failed to bring into the fellowship of the churches even the sons and daughters of their own members, and taught penitents to wait for some special divine interposition which should compel them to come in. The result was that some churches grew weaker and weaker year after year and finally passed out of existence, while the new denomination of Methodists entered the field and gathered rich harvests of eager souls.[10]

9 T. Kidd and B. Hankins, *Baptists in America: A History* (Oxford: Oxford University Press, 2015), 82.

10 G. W. Paschal, *History of North Carolina Baptists*, 2 vols. (Raleigh: The General Board North Carolina Baptist State Convention, 1955), 2:5. Paschal also noted that though many Baptist leaders tended to be strong Calvinists, the people in the pews were not. Some Associations, such as the Yadkin Baptist Association, rejected the notion of particular individual election along the lines of Dort. The Big Ivy Association only affirmed the Philadelphia Confession of Faith after the statement on election was removed (ibid., 2:432). Paschal also described a problem mainly in the Kehukee Regular Baptist Association that looked to the Philadelphia Association for guidance. The pastors of First Baptist Church in Philadelphia, Thomas Ustick and Morgan Edwards, had embraced a hyper-Calvinist "no offer" stance in 1796 but were unable to lead a majority of other pastors to be this extreme.

The debilitating effects of extreme Calvinism are well known in England and America in the eighteenth and early nineteenth centuries. Though Paschal's statement does not mention limited atonement specifically, it was certainly a plank in this system.

At the turn of the nineteenth century, many among the Regular and Separate Baptists were prepared to consider unification. In 1801 Regular and Separate Baptists in two Kentucky Baptist Associations joined together. The plan of the newly formed United Baptists included eleven principles (articles), including this statement: "The preaching (that) Christ tasted death for every man, shall be no bar to communion."[11] The Separates refused to accept the Philadelphia Confession in the proposed union with Regular (Particular) Baptists. In the eleven articles adopted in 1801, the doctrines of particular election and a limited understanding of the extent of the atonement were omitted.

The articles of faith of Baptist associations in south-central Kentucky and upper Cumberland in Tennessee in the early nineteenth century do not reflect any commitment to limited atonement. In the articles of faith of the Green River Association (1800), Russell's Creek Association (1804), Stockton Valley Association (1805), Gaspar River Association (1812), and Barren River Association (1830), there is no mention of limited atonement whatsoever. Likewise, there is no mention of irresistible grace and in only the Gaspar River Association is there any mention of election. What is affirmed in all these articles of faith, among other doctrinal tenets, is some form of total depravity and clear statements on the perseverance of the saints.[12]

In a discussion concerning the changing roles of Baptist Associations in Georgia in the first half of the nineteenth century, Jarrett Burch noted:

> By failing to differentiate Fullerite theology from Arminianism, the Primitive Baptists lumped all new methodologies into the category of heresy . . . any method that urged sinners toward active repentance confirmed the belief of a general atonement. According to their thought, a general atonement necessitated general redemption (i.e., if God intended to save everyone, all will be saved). Primitive Baptists could not visualize the preaching of a universal gospel, while believing in the particular and exclusive acts of God in calling his own to salvation. Any preacher who urged general appeal for salvation must not believe in a particular atonement.[13]

In addition to Primitive Baptists, other Georgia Baptist churches struggled with the extent of the atonement. For example, at the 1829 Ocmulgee Association meeting,

---

11 Sparks, *The Roots of Appalachian Christianity*, 200.

12 C. P. Cawthorn & N. L. Warnell, *Pioneer Baptist Church Records of South-Central Kentucky and the Upper Cumberland of Tennessee 1799–1899* (Gallatin, TN: Church History Research & Archives, 1985), 13–23.

13 J. Burch, *Adiel Sherwood: Baptist Antebellum Pioneer in Georgia* (Macon, GA: Mercer University Press, 2003), 89.

one of the issues concerned an inquiry from Walnut Creek Baptist Church in Jones County: "Did Jesus Christ suffer, bleed and die, on the Cross, for all mankind? Or only, for as many as the Divine Father gave Him in the Covenant of Grace?"[14]

In 1830 Cyrus White published a small work of nineteen pages on the atonement and its extent, arguing for unlimited atonement.[15] White was a Calvinist pastor who became convinced of universal atonement during the revival movement in the previous decade. His approach to the atonement was not that of moderate Calvinists who likewise affirmed an unlimited atonement but more in line with Arminianism. Burch stated that Georgia Baptist churches "that followed the regular and ordered tradition of Calvinism found this proposal unacceptable."[16]

Jesse Mercer reacted to White's proposal and published a series of letters refuting White's view,[17] and Georgia Baptists withdrew fellowship from White in 1830. In turn, White's association, the United Association, withdrew from the Georgia Baptist Convention.[18]

Among other issues of praxis noted by Burch, from 1828 to 1836 Georgia Baptist churches were torn by "factional fighting" and split over the doctrinal issue of the extent of the atonement.[19]

Burch's comment is illuminating:

> One should note that the confessions modeled after the Georgia Association [Georgia Baptist Convention] did not address the issue of limited atonement. Article four addressed only particular redemption. Therefore, those Baptists who accepted Andrew Fuller's view of the atonement could still be considered orthodox. The fourth article states, "We believe in the everlasting love of God to His people, and the eternal election of a definite number of the human race, to grace and glory: And that there was a covenant of grace or redemption made between the Father and the Son before the world began, in which their salvation is secure, and that they in particular are redeemed."[20]

14 *Minutes of the Ocmulgee Baptist Association* (Milledgeville, GA: Georgia Journal Office, 1829), 2, cited in Burch, *Adiel Sherwood*, 96.

15 C. White, *A Scriptural View of the Atonement* (Milledgeville, GA: Statesman and Patriot, 1830). White was an itinerant preacher and agent for the *Christian Index*, the Georgia Baptist paper. He was a Calvinist who moved from a limited atonement position to unlimited atonement.

16 J. Burch, *Adiel Sherwood*, 91. "During this time, Baptists in America continued to wrestle with Andrew Fuller's concept of a general provision, a view of the atonement similar to the creedal statement, 'sufficient for all, and efficient for the elect'" (ibid.).

17 J. Mercer published a series of letters in the *Columbian Star* (August 28–November 20, 1830) refuting White (*Ten Letters Addressed to the Reverend Cyrus White in Reference to His Scriptural View of the Atonement* [Washington, GA: News Office, 1830]).

18 Burch, *Adiel Sherwood*, 91.

19 Ibid., 108.

20 Ibid., 111. Burch also cited S. Boykin, *History of the Baptist Denomination in Georgia* (Atlanta: James P. Harrison and Co., 1881), 196.

This statement is significant in that Burch differentiates between the act of atonement and the specific application of the atonement to the elect according to eternal election. His point is that the confessional statement of Georgia Baptists does not affirm a strictly limited atonement to the exclusion of an unlimited atonement.

The 1831 heresy trial of Ephraim Moore (1793–1875) in the East Tennessee Baptist Association also illustrated the growing Baptist ambivalence toward strict Calvinism. W. Wiley Richards related the story. Moore preached free salvation to all who believed the gospel. The trial convened with Elder James Kennon as moderator. Kennon was known for his strict predestinarian views. After Moore admitted his belief in general atonement, the church voted to exclude him from the fellowship. Yet many members sided with Moore and eventually restored him to fellowship in 1843.[21]

In 1833, twelve years before the founding of the Southern Baptist Convention, Baptists in New Hampshire composed what would become the most used Baptist confession in Baptist life in America. Garrett said of this document: "One can conclude that the label 'moderately Arminian' would be as accurate as the term 'moderately Calvinistic.'"[22]

A comparison of the 1833 New Hampshire Confession with the 1742 Philadelphia Confession of Faith reveals just how much of the Calvinistic language in the Philadelphia Confession was left out of the New Hampshire Confession. Whole articles in the Philadelphia Confession articulating aspects of Calvinistic soteriology were excised in the New Hampshire Confession. Many Baptist churches in the south adopted the New Hampshire Confession.

In 1840 the first Baptist Association in Texas was founded: Union Baptist Association. The articles of faith reflect a moderate Calvinism, especially with respect to limited atonement. Article 6 stated:

> We believe that Christ died for sinners, and that the sacrifice which He made has so honored the divine law that the way of salvation is consistently opened up to every sinner to whom the gospel is sent, and that nothing but their own voluntary rejection of the gospel prevents their salvation.[23]

There is no statement mandating limited atonement here, though it is written with sufficient ambiguity to permit that viewpoint.

---

21 W. W. Richards, "Southern Baptist Identity: Moving Away from Calvinism," *Baptist History and Heritage* 31.4 (1996): 27. Richards noted: "A gradual erosion of the Calvinistic doctrines of depravity and atonement led Southern Baptists to construct a theological position of a weakened form of Calvinism. They reaffirmed their belief in the eternal security of the believer, but modified the remaining four doctrines."

22 J. L. Garrett, *Baptist Theology: A Four-Century Study* (Macon, GA: Mercer University Press, 2009), 132.

23 *Minutes of the First Session of the Union Baptist Association* (Houston: Telegraph Press, 1840), 8.

J. J. Burnett explained how representatives from the Holston, Tennessee, East Tennessee, and Nolachucky Baptist Associations assembled in August of 1843 to adopt a confession. Using the New Hampshire Confession as a guide, they affirmed an unlimited atonement and added emphatically that nothing in the articles was to be construed as affirming particular, unconditional election and/or reprobation.[24]

In 1845 the Sandy Creek Baptists adopted a confession that was very similar to the New Hampshire Confession, but with the articles "of Repentance and Faith" and "Of Sanctification" removed. This confession differed from their 1816 confession that spoke of effectual calling and eternal election. The article "Of God's Purpose of Grace" spoke of election as "consistent with the free agency of man,"[25] terminology that would later appear in the Baptist Faith and Message of 1925.

Writing in 1852 about Baptists in the Mississippi valley of the south in the late eighteenth century, John Peck noted that by 1785 there were three Baptist Associations in Kentucky: Elkhorn, Salem, and South Kentucky. Elkhorn and Salem were Regular Baptists; the South Kentucky Association were Separatists. Peck references a "portion" of the Regular Baptist pastors who came to Kentucky in this period "would be now regarded as hyper-Calvinistic in doctrine, especially in their limited views of the mediatorial office of Christ and the reservations they made concerning indiscriminate offers of mercy and salvation to all persons through faith in Christ."[26]

In some places there remained deep division between Regular and Separatist Baptists. Regular Baptists occasionally excluded pastors and churches from associations who refused to affirm limited atonement.[27]

Steve Lemke has demonstrated that high Calvinism was not the be-all and end-all for Baptists at the founding of the Southern Baptist Convention. Nor had it been for some time. It seems clear that some, though not all, of the founding fathers of the SBC were Calvinists who affirmed limited atonement. What also seems clear is that the majority of laypeople in Baptist churches in the south at the time were not strict five-point Calvinists. Most of them, it appears, did not affirm limited atonement. In fact, the historical record

24 J. J. Burnett, *Sketches of Tennessee's Pioneer Baptist Preachers, Being, Incidentally, A History of Baptist Beginnings in the Several Associations in the State Containing, Particularly, Character and Life Sketches of the Standard Bearers and Leaders of Our People,* First Series, 2 vols. (Nashville: Marshall and Bruce Company, 1919), 1:380–82.

25 G. W. Purefoy, *A History of the Sandy Creek Association from Its Organization in A.D. 1758 to A.D. 1858* (New York: Sheldon and Company, 1859), 199–214; here 205.

26 J. Peck, "Baptists of the Mississippi Valley," *The Christian Review* 70 (1852): 485. Peck stated that later, hyper-Calvinistic doctrines "became more prominent, and speculations were taught, until antinomianism [*sic*] in spirit, theory and practice prevailed to a ruinous extent among the churches in the Mississippi Valley" (486).

27 See A. W. Wardin, Jr., *Tennessee Baptists: A Comprehensive History, 1779–1999* (Brentwood: The Executive Board of the Tennessee Baptist Convention, 1999), 112–14. Elijah Hanks is a case in point: "When Elijah Hanks (1793–1871), pastor of the Knob Creek and Friendship churches, which were members of the Cumberland Association, began preaching that Christ tasted death for every man instead of dying only for the elect, three leading pastors of the association, including Garner McConnico and Peter S. Gayle, visited him around 1829. His refusal to change his views resulted in his churches being excluded from the association."

indicates that most Baptists in the south at the time of the founding of the SBC adhered to a theology somewhere between Calvinism and Arminianism.[28]

Baptist leaders and/or historians of the era prior to and up to fifty years after the founding of the SBC indicate that many Baptists in the north and south did not affirm limited atonement. We will look at several men, generally in chronological order according to their birth, to determine their views on the extent of the atonement.[29]

Southern Baptists from the Eighteenth to the Twenty-First Century

Jesse Mercer (AD 1769–1841)[30]

Mercer was a leading pre-Civil War Georgia Baptist, leader in the Georgia Baptist Association, and first president of the Georgia Baptist Convention, a position he held for nineteen years (1822–41). He was a four-time delegate to the Triennial Convention, founder of the Georgia *Christian Index*, which was originally the old *Columbian Star*, and one of the founders and first president of Mercer University. Few Baptists held any higher stature than this statesman.

With respect to limited atonement, his comments are crucial for the era in which he lived and wrote.

> It seems to be taken for granted that all those venerable fathers, who founded the Baptist Denomination in this state [Georgia], were as stern Calvinistic preachers as are the opposers of the *new plans*. But this is altogether a mistake. Abraham Marshall [son of Daniel] was never considered a predestinarian preacher. Some of them were so—seemed to be set for the defense of the gospel. Of these, Silas Mercer and Jeptha Vining were the chief. Abraham Marshall was never considered a *predestinarian* preacher. To use his own figure; he used to say, "he was *short legged* and could not wade in such deep water." He, with several others, was considered sound in the faith, though low Calvinists. Peter Smith and some others were thought rather *Arminian*; some *quite* so. . . . And here it may not be amiss to add, that the Baptists in the upper parts of South Carolina, in those

28 See S. Lemke, "History or Revisionist History? How Calvinistic Were the Overwhelming Majority of Baptists and Their Confessions in the South until the Twentieth Century?," *Southwestern Journal of Theology* 57 (2015): 227–54.

29 J. R. Nalls, "The Concept of the Atonement in Southern Baptist Thought" (ThD diss., New Orleans Baptist Theological Seminary, 1985), is a helpful summary of the views of key Southern Baptist theologians on the nature of the atonement, with a brief analysis of their views on extent.

30 Though Mercer died four years before the founding of the Southern Baptist Convention, his influence on the new convention was extraordinary and merits his inclusion here.

> days, comprehended mostly, it is believed, in the Bethel Association, were general provisionists. I think most of their ministers preached what is now called General Atonement.[31]

This work was published one year before the founding of the Southern Baptist Convention. Mercer himself shifted from his original commitment to limited atonement to the unlimited position.[32] Mercer's mature position on the extent of the atonement was the same as that of Andrew Fuller.[33]

William Bullein Johnson (AD 1782–1862)

Johnson was a leader among South Carolina Baptists, being a founder of the South Carolina State Baptist Convention in 1821 and succeeding Richard Furman as president. He served in that capacity until 1852. Johnson was instrumental in the founding of Furman University, the parent university of the Southern Baptist Theological Seminary.

He served as the first president of the newly formed Southern Baptist Convention in 1845, a position he held until 1851. He also served as chairman of the committee appointed to draft the constitution for the SBC. Johnson holds the distinction of being the only man to attend the initial meeting of the Baptist General Missionary Convention (1814), the Southern Baptist Convention (1845), and serve as president of both. In addition to pastoring churches, Johnson assisted in the founding of churches in Greenville and Columbia, South Carolina. While chancellor of Johnson Female University (1853–58), he was a pioneer in higher education for women.[34]

According to Roxburgh, Johnson could only be considered a moderate Calvinist at best.[35] He spoke of the atonement in governmental terms, which would be highly unlikely if he affirmed limited atonement. Tom Nettles confirmed the New Divinity's influence on Johnson.[36]

---

31 J. Mercer, "Reply to H.—No. 3," *The Christian Index*, February 25, 1836, 101 (emphasis in original). See also C. D. Mallary, *Memoirs of Elder Jesse Mercer* (New York: John Gray, 1844), 201–2. This quotation is also cited in J. D. Mosteller, *A History of the Kiokee Baptist Church in Georgia* (Ann Arbor, MI: Edwards Brothers, 1952), 37; and A. Chute, *A Piety above the Common Standard: Jesse Mercer and the Defense of Evangelistic Calvinism* (Mercer, GA: Mercer University Press, 2005), 68, though Chute misunderstands Mercer's language and indicates that Mercer believed in a strictly limited atonement.

32 Mallary, *Memoirs of Elder Jesse Mercer*, 290, 297–303. See also Richards, *Winds of Doctrines*, 58; and A. Chute, *A Piety above the Common Standard*, 71–72.

33 J. Mercer, "Excellency of the Knowledge of Christ Jesus the Lord," in *The Georgia Pulpit*, ed. R. Fleming (Richmond, VA: H. Kelly & Son, 1847), 46. In 1833 Mercer had stated he did not agree with Fuller but shifted sometime before his death in 1841.

34 See H. Woodson, *Giant in the Land: A Biography of William Bullein Johnson* (Nashville: Broadman, 1950); K. Roxburgh, "Creeds and Controversies: Insights from William Bullein Johnson," in *Baptist Identities: International Studies from the Seventeenth to the Twentieth Centuries*, in Studies in Baptist History and Thought 19 (Paternoster, 2006), 138–52; and R. J. Legendre, "William Bullein Johnson: Pastor, Educator, and Missions Promoter" (PhD diss., New Orleans Baptist Theological Seminary, 1995).

35 For the evidence for this based on Johnson's sermons and writings, see Roxburgh, "Creeds and Controversies," 150–51.

36 T. Nettles, "Boyce the Theologian," *Founders Journal* 69 (2007): 11–12.

Boyce published a series of eight articles in the *Southern Baptist* affirming the imputation of Christ's righteousness to the believer. Nettles thinks these articles were directed against the views espoused in the classroom at Furman University by J. S. Mims. Boyce also published seven articles on the subject by Johnson, who took the opposite view.[37] As president of the board of trustees, Johnson had previously responded to J. L. Reynolds's criticism of Mims in a letter where he defended Mims as orthodox. Johnson also wrote Mims a letter in which he stated: "In his opinion the doctrine of imputation had been gradually going out of use and that Baptists at least in this state [South Carolina] were becoming moderate Calvinists."[38] In a later letter to Mims, Johnson stated that the hyper-Calvinist brand of Calvinism that Reynolds affirmed would never be popular in South Carolina because "such views had never been embodied in the Convention Constitution, or the Constitution of the Institution, or prescribed to by the professors or W. B. Johnson."[39]

This excerpt from "The Sovereignty of God and the Free Agency of Man" may indicate that Johnson did not affirm irresistible grace:

> *Now, Now,* O fellow sinners, you have it in your power to place yourselves under influences, that are spiritual and saving; or under influences that are carnal and damning. You can read the Bible, or the book of Infidelity; the sermon of truth, or the novel of fiction; you can attend the party of sinful pleasure, or the meeting for holy prayer; you can go to the midnight revel, or to the house of God. You can lift up the prayer of the publican, or the howl of the bacchanal. You can utter the praise of the Most High, or belch out the blasphemy of the Arch fiend. How solemn the responsibilities that are upon you. Under what awful accountability does your free agency place you? The freedom to choose is the freedom to reject. O! Exercise this freedom aright. Pause, consider your latter end. "Choose you this day whom you will serve." Difficulties attend the decision. For their removal, search the scriptures, implore the teaching of that Holy Spirit, whom God will give to all that ask for in sincerity. And oh may He enlighten the eyes of your understanding, and give you to see Christ in the scriptures as your "wisdom, righteousness, sanctification and redemption."[40]

---

37 Nettles stated with respect to these articles written by Boyce: "They specifically criticized Socinianism, Arminianism, Pelagianism, the New Divinity, as well as a point by point refutation of William B. Johnson and his absorption in the New Divinity viewpoint" ("Boyce the Theologian," 12).

38 Letter to J. S. Mims, March 25, 1848, cited by R. J. Legendre, "William Bullein Johnson," 73 and by Roxburgh, "Creeds and Controversies," 150.

39 Letter to J. S. Mims, September 6, 1848, cited by R. J. Legendre, "William Bullein Johnson," 76 and by Roxburgh, "Creeds and Controversies," 150.

40 W. B. Johnson, "Free Agency of Man," *The Baptist Pulpit in the Unites States*, ed. J. Belcher (New York: Edward H. Fletcher, 1853), 126–27.

In an article written for the *Southern Baptist* in 1855, Johnson argued that some Baptists "believe in the Calvinistic scheme, and some in the Arminian. Some are hyper-Calvinists, and some are moderate Calvinists."[41]

This statement is important for several reasons. First, Johnson affirmed both Calvinists and Arminians make up the Southern Baptist Convention. Second, within the ranks of Calvinists, Johnson distinguished two groups: hyper-Calvinists (extreme Calvinists) and moderate Calvinists. Even within the Calvinist camp, not all agreed with limited atonement.[42] Third, Johnson wrote these words four years prior to the founding of The Southern Baptist Theological Seminary in Louisville, Kentucky, the first Southern Baptist seminary.

The first president of the Southern Baptist Convention in 1845 was certainly not a five-point Calvinist.

John L. Dagg (AD 1794–1884)

Dagg was a remarkable man who struggled physically with near-blindness and was also crippled. His formal education was limited, yet he holds the distinction of being the first Baptist to write a systematic theology in America, *Manual of Theology* (1857). He pastored in Philadelphia and later served as president of Mercer University in Georgia.

As mentioned before, Dagg was himself a high-Calvinist with respect to the atonement, but he clearly understood that within Reformed theology, and orthodox at that, was a group who affirmed "particular redemption" in the sense of final salvation but an unlimited atonement with respect to extent. He affirmed there is variety within the group of those who describe themselves by the label "particular redemption": "Other persons who maintain the doctrine of particular redemption, distinguish between redemption and atonement, and because of the adaptedness referred to, consider the death of Christ an atonement for the sins of all men; or as an atonement for sin in the abstract."[43]

R. B. C. Howell (AD 1801–1868)

Howell was pastor of First Baptist Church in Nashville, Tennessee, and then Main Street Second Baptist Church in Richmond, Virginia. He served five terms as president of the SBC and as editor of the Tennessee Baptist state paper, *The Reflector*, until 1848. Howell wrote two books on the subject of salvation: *The Way of Salvation*, first published in 1849, and *The Cross*, published in 1854.

In neither volume did Howell explicitly state that the atonement is limited in its extent. In the former, Howell spoke of the atonement as an "infinite satisfaction"

---

41 W. B. Johnson, *Southern Baptist* 7 (November, 1855); cited in Roxburgh, "Creeds and Controversies," 147–48.

42 This is not to say that all who believe in limited atonement should be classed as "hyper-Calvinists." It is true, however, that all hyper-Calvinists believe in limited atonement.

43 Dagg, *Manual of Theology*, 326. As noted above, the later Andrew Fuller appeared to be in this category, along with some other Particular Baptists in England and America.

and rejected a quantitative equivalency in the sufferings of Christ.[44] In discussing the substitutionary nature of the atonement, he cited numerous passages which reference Christ dying for "all." Concerning the death of Christ as a substitute, Howell stated: "He bare our sins; he died for all."[45]

In *The Cross*, Howell made one statement that also could be interpreted to reflect his belief in an unlimited atonement: "The sins of a rebellious world were pressing on his bursting heart."[46] When discussing the many nonsaving benefits which the cross brings to the world, Howell began the section by noting that Christ died for all. Nowhere does he distinguish between Christ's death for the sins of the elect and Christ's death for the rest of the world in terms of its nonsaving benefits. It appears Howell assumed that Christ died for the sins of all people.

J. M. Pendleton (AD 1811–1891)

Pendleton was a leading Baptist preacher, pastor, and theologian. He was one of the "great triumvirate" of the Landmark movement, along with A. C. Dayton and J. R. Graves. Pendleton was involved in the founding of Crozier Theological Seminary. His major theological work is *Christian Doctrines*, first published in 1878.

Pendleton considered it a "grand impertinence" to attempt to limit the atonement's sufficiency for all humanity. "So far as the claims of law and justice are concerned, the atonement has obviated every difficulty in the way of any sinner's salvation. . . . It places the world, to use the language of Robert Hall, 'in a salvable state.'"[47] Universal gospel invitations can rest only on the grounds of a universal provision in the atonement. Pendleton then quoted Andrew Fuller at length to support his contention.[48]

Pendleton stated:

> If, then, it is the duty of all men to believe, and if faith implies reliance on the atonement, and if the atonement was made for a part of the race only, it follows that it is the duty of those for whom no atonement was made to rely on that which has no existence. This is an absurdity. The more the point is considered, the more evident it will appear that the duty of all men to believe the gospel is inseparable from the "objective fullness" of the provisions of the atonement for the salvation of all men.[49]

---

44 R. C. B. Howell, *The Way of Salvation*, 5th ed. (Charleston, SC: Southern Baptist Publication Society), 87, 91.

45 Ibid., 90.

46 R. C. B. Howell, *The Cross* (Charleston, SC: Southern Baptist Publication Society, 1854), 19. For Howell's views on the atonement, consult C. M. Wren, "R. B. C. Howell and the Theological Foundations for Baptist Participation in the Benevolent Empire" (PhD diss., Southern Baptist Theological Seminary, 2007).

47 J. M. Pendleton, *Christian Doctrines: A Compendium of Theology* (Valley Forge, PA: Judson, 1878), 241–42.

48 A. Fuller, *The Complete Works of the Rev. Andrew Fuller*, 3 vols., ed. A. Belcher (Harrisonburg, VA: Sprinkle, 1988), 2:691–92.

49 J. M. Pendleton, *Christian Doctrines*, 244–45.

In a similar vein, Pendleton argued:

> In believing in Christ we not only believe primarily, that he died for sinners, but, secondarily, that he died for us as included among sinners. The latter belief is by no means to be made so prominent as the former, but it is essential to a joyous appropriation of the blessings of salvation. Now, if Christ did not die for all, and if it is the duty of all to believe in him, it is the duty of some—those for whom he did not die—to believe an untruth. This also reduces the matter to an absurdity for it cannot be the duty of any one to believe what is not true. We must either give up the position that it is the duty of all men to believe the gospel, or admit that the atonement of Christ has reference to all men.[50]

Pendleton was clearly committed to unlimited atonement.

J. R. Graves (AD 1820–1893)

Graves served as editor of *The Baptist* beginning in 1848 and was one of the leaders of the Landmark movement in Baptist life. In *The Work of Christ in the Covenant of Redemption* (1883), Graves appeared to affirm unlimited atonement. Christ's death made full provision for the sins of all people by removing "all legal and governmental obstructions, so that, in good faith, salvation by grace could be freely offered to all."[51] This is not the language used by limitarians.

James P. Boyce (AD 1827–1888)

Boyce was one of the founders of The Southern Baptist Theological Seminary in Louisville, Kentucky. He served as the seminary's first president and professor of theology.[52] His *Abstract of Systematic Theology*, published a year before his death, is one of the key systematic theology texts published in Southern Baptist life.

It is well known that Boyce studied under and was heavily influenced by Charles Hodge.[53] Boyce's discussion of the extent of the atonement is quite interesting.[54] He listed three theories: (1) universalism, which he rightly dismisses; (2) general atonement, by which Christ died for the sins of all men in an equal fashion. This is the traditional "Arminian" view; and (3) limited purpose: "That God designed only the actual salvation

50 Ibid., 245.

51 J. R. Graves, *The Work of Christ in the Covenant of Redemption; Developed in Seven Dispensations* (Memphis, TN: Baptist Book House, 1883), 103.

52 For the most recent biography on Boyce, consult T. Nettles, *James Petigru Boyce: A Southern Baptist Statesman* (Phillipsburg, NJ: P&R, 2009).

53 See, for example, W. W. Richards, "A Study of the Influence of Princeton Theology upon the Theology of James Petigru Boyce and His Followers with Special Reference to the Works of Charles Hodge" (ThD diss., New Orleans Baptist Theological Seminary, 1964).

54 J. P. Boyce, *Abstract of Systematic Theology* (Philadelphia: American Baptist Publication Society, 1887), 336–40.

of some; and that, whatever provision has been made for others, he made this positive arrangement by which the salvation of certain ones is secured." Boyce listed three points in favor of this theory and two difficulties with it, including that the offer of salvation is made to all men in Scripture, and that the death of Christ is spoken of in Scripture as for the "world" in such a way that contrasts the world with those who believe.[55]

Boyce then attempted to explain and reconcile universal general expressions on the extent of the atonement with God's definite purpose in saving the elect. He first mentioned Andrew Fuller's views on the atonement. He mischaracterized Fuller when he said that such a theory "accomplishes the desired end only by ascribing such a nature to the atonement, as makes it only a method of reconciliation for the people of God, and not actual reconciliation."[56]

Second, Boyce turned to a lengthy quotation from A. A. Hodge for a "better explanation."[57] He quoted Hodge as saying:

> Calvinists believe that the entire dispensation of forbearance under which the human family rests since the fall, including for the unjust as well as the just temporal mercies and means of grace, is a part of the purchase of Christ's blood. They admit also that Christ did in such a sense die for all men, that he thereby removed all legal obstacles from the salvation of any and every man, and that his satisfaction may be applied to one man as well as to another "if God so wills it."[58]

Boyce continued to quote Hodge:

> The design of Christ in dying was to effect what he actually does effect in the result. 1st. *Incidentally* to remove the legal impediments out of the way of all men, and render the salvation of every hearer of the gospel objectively possible, so that each one has a right to appropriate it at will. . . . 2d, *Specifically* his design was to impetrate the actual salvation of his own people,. . . . After the manner of the Augustinian Schoolmen, Calvin on 1 John 2:2, says "Christ died sufficiently for all, but efficiently only for the elect."[59]

A. A. Hodge was the son of Charles Hodge, the famous Princetonian professor of theology. Charles Hodge was also Boyce's professor at Princeton. A. A. Hodge is utilizing the same language his father used on the subject of the extent of the atonement.

55 Ibid., 336–37.
56 Ibid., 338. See discussion of Fuller above.
57 See A. A. Hodge, *Outlines of Theology*, 2nd ed. (New York: Robert Carter & Brothers, 1863), 416–17.
58 Boyce, *Abstract*, 338. See A. A. Hodge, *Outlines of Theology*, 416–17.
59 Ibid., 339.

When Charles Hodge spoke of "legal barriers/impediments" being removed, he made it clear he is affirming a universal substitution on the part of Christ for all people.

However, A. A. Hodge appears to be committed to a strictly limited atonement in his writings but continued to use the language of his father. This might indicate confusion of the issue on the part of A. A. Hodge. If all legal barriers have been removed by the death of Christ, then his death has to function as a substitute for the sins of all men.

Third, Boyce offered his own statement on the subject for clarification. He suggested it embraces no more than is actually implied in Hodge's statement, which Boyce quoted.

> It has only the advantage of recognizing more explicitly the relation of the atoning work of Christ both to the world and to the elect; a relation clearly indicated to be such that he can be called, in some general sense, the Savior of all men, though he bears this relation more especially to those who believe. 1 Timothy 4:10. The statement suggested is, that while, for the Elect, he made an actual atonement, by which they were actually reconciled to God, and, because of which, are made the subjects of the special divine grace by which they become believers in Christ and are justified through him; Christ, at the same time, and in the same work, wrought out a means of reconciliation for all men, which removed every legal obstacle to their salvation, upon their acceptance of the same conditions upon which the salvation is given to the Elect. According to this statement:
>
> 1. Christ did actually die for the salvation of all, so that he might be called the Saviour of all; because his work is abundantly sufficient to secure the salvation of all who will put their faith in him.
> 2. Christ died, however, in an especial sense for the Elect; because he procured for them not a possible, but an actual salvation.
> 3. The death of Christ opens the way for a sincere offer of salvation by God to all who will accept the conditions he has laid down.
> 4. That same death, however, secures salvation to the Elect, because by it Christ also obtained for them those gracious influences, by which they will be led to comply with those conditions.
> 5. The work of Christ, contemplated as securing the means of reconciliation, is a full equivalent to all that the advocates of a general atonement claim; for they do not suppose that more than this was done for mankind in general, while Calvinists readily recognize that this much has been done for all.

> 6. But, while the making of an actual atonement for the elect is not inconsistent with the securing of a method of atonement for all, the assertion that such was the special work done for them complies with the nature of the atonement as heretofore seen, and shows how Christ could be especially their Saviour, and also the Saviour of all.[60]

The following propositions are affirmed by Boyce in this quotation:

1. Christ can be called in a general sense "the Savior of all men."
2. Christ made a means of reconciliation for all men.
3. This means of reconciliation "removed every legal obstacle."
4. On the grounds of this removal of legal obstacles, the same condition of salvation applies to the non-elect as for the elect.
5. "Christ did actually die for the salvation of all."
6. The death of Christ provides the grounds for the sincere offer of salvation to all people.
7. The death of Christ is a "full equivalent" as all the advocates of General Atonement claim.

From this evidence, it would seem that Boyce cannot be claimed clearly to reside in the camp of limited atonement. Couple this with the fact that the Abstract of Principles, the doctrinal statement of Southern Baptist Theological Seminary, does not include a statement about limited atonement (or irresistible grace). Could this be because Boyce himself did not affirm limited atonement?

Tom Nettles, himself committed to limited atonement, is puzzled by Boyce's treatment of the extent of the atonement. He suggested that Boyce has introduced "an element of ambiguity" into the discussion. Boyce "virtually adopts the view [general atonement with particular application] he is seeking to displace." Nettles quoted Boyce's "legal obstacles" statement and asked: "If 'every legal obstacle' has been removed from all men, in what particular does Boyce's treatment of atonement differ from a general atonement?"[61]

The answer to Nettles's question is twofold: (1) In terms of extent only, there is no difference. (2) In terms of *intent*, there is a difference. Those who affirm "general atonement" do so with the meaning that Christ died *equally intending* the salvation of all people. Calvinists who affirm limited atonement assert that Christ's *intention* is to die only for the sins of the elect. Calvinists who reject limited atonement maintain this special intention for the elect but agree with non-Calvinists that in terms of extent

60 Ibid., 339–40.

61 T. Nettles, *By His Grace and for His Glory*, 2nd ed. (Cape Coral, FL: Founders, 2006), 153.

alone, Christ actually substituted for the sins of all people, hence all "legal obstacles" are removed.

Nettles took up this conundrum of Boyce's views on the extent of the atonement in his biography of Boyce. First, Nettles said that Boyce rejected the view of Andrew Fuller "that the atonement is general in its nature, but 'limited in its application.'"[62] Second, Nettles asserted Boyce's view "has every appearance of inconsistency with his earlier argument."[63] Third, Nettles tipped his hand and reveals why he thinks Boyce is inconsistent:

> The reader might well ask, how is it possible under Boyce's discussion of the nature of the atonement for him to write finally of a "means of reconciliation for all men, which removed every legal obstacle to their salvation" without it being effectual? They did not comply with the conditions, he answered. Ah, but compliance with the conditions is a blessing procured in a real reconciliation; forgiveness must come to all those for whom the legal obstacles have been removed. To conclude otherwise radically changes the nature of the atonement into something other than what Boyce described earlier.[64]

Here Nettles betrayed his commitment to a commercialistic understanding of the atonement. In fact, as he revealed in *By His Grace and For His Glory*, Nettles is a quantitative "equivalentist" with respect to the nature of the substitution of Christ on the cross for the sins of the elect. He believes there is a quantitative aspect to the atonement. This position is a minority position within Reformed theology, and even more a minority position among Baptists, past and present, who affirm limited atonement.

Boyce is not inconsistent as long as he intended by his language to indicate that there is a sense in which Christ did substitute for the sins of all people. It would seem this is a valid reading of Boyce, and if accurate, would remove him from the strict limitarian camp with respect to the extent of the atonement. Timothy George referenced Boyce's way of speaking about a universal aspect of the atonement "in a way not entirely dissimilar from Fuller."[65]

Most of Boyce's immediate successors on the faculty of Southern Seminary did not fully retain his Dortian Calvinism.[66]

---

62 T. Nettles, *James Petigru Boyce*, 461. Note here that Nettles seems to affirm Fuller did indeed view the atonement as general and yet in his rejoinder to my claim that Fuller held to unlimited atonement, he argued the opposite viewpoint.

63 Ibid., 464.

64 Ibid., 465.

65 T. George, "James Petigru Boyce," in *Baptist Theologians*, ed. Timothy George and David Dockery (Nashville: Broadman, 1990), 265.

66 J. L. Garrett, *Baptist Theology: A Four-Century Study* (Macon, GA: Mercer University Press, 2009), 150.

John A. Broadus (AD 1827–1895)

Broadus was professor of New Testament and homiletics at Southern Baptist Theological Seminary. In Broadus's memoirs of Boyce, he quoted approvingly E. E. Folk, the editor of the *Baptist Reflector*, following depiction of the theology of the new students at Southern Seminary whom Boyce taught in the post-Civil War 1800s: "The young men were generally rank Arminians when they came to the seminary" until they encountered the "strong Calvinistic views" of Boyce.[67]

This quote is important for the issue at hand. Notice Folk said the majority of new students at the seminary were "rank Arminians." How could this be if these men were coming from churches where five-point Calvinism was the norm?

B. H. Carroll (AD 1843–1914)

Converted to Christ from his atheism after being wounded in the Civil War, Carroll went on to a stellar career as a Texas Ranger, professor at Baylor University, and founder and first president of Southwestern Baptist Theological Seminary in Fort Worth, Texas.

Carroll appealed to John 1:29; 2 Cor 5:1–20; Heb 2:9; 1 Tim 4:9–10; and 1 John 2:2 as examples of universal atonement. He made the point "that no matter in what sense expiation was effective toward God for all men, it cannot result in universal salvation, since 'he that believeth not, shall be damned.'" Carroll continued:

> No matter in what sense expiation was for all men Godward, it can avail to usward by faith alone. The question of universal salvation is not therefore bound up with reconciliation Godward, whatever its extent, but with the ministry of reconciliation and our acceptance or rejection of the tendered mercy.[68]

Carroll analyzed James Boyce's section on the extent question in Boyce's *Abstract*:

> I hold James P. Boyce to be the greatest all-around Baptist ever produced by the South. While in his *Systematic Theology* he teaches that expiation of the sins of all men must mean universal salvation, yet before he closes his discussion he uses these remarkable words, which I cite:
>
> (1) While for the elect he made an actual atonement, by which they are actually reconciled to God, and because of which are made the subjects of the special divine grace by which they became believers in Christ, and are justified through him.

67 J. A. Broadus, *Memoir of James Petigru Boyce* (Louisville, KY: Baptist Book Concern, 1893), 265.

68 B. H. Carroll, "Colossians, Ephesians, and Hebrews," in *An Interpretation of the English Bible* (Grand Rapids, MI: Baker Book House, 1973 reprint), 86–92, for his complete discussion on the extent question.

(2) Christ at the same time and in the same work, wrought out a means of reconciliation for all men, which removed every legal obstacle to their salvation, upon their acceptance of the same conditions upon which the salvation is given to the elect.

(3) On page 297 he says,

The atoning work of Christ was not sufficient for the salvation of man. That work was only Godward, and only removed all the obstacles in the way of God's pardon of the sinner. But the sinner is also at enmity with God, and must be brought to accept salvation, and must learn to love and serve God. It is the special work of the Holy Spirit to bring this about. The first step here is to make known to man the gospel, which contains the glad tidings of salvation, under such influences as ought to lead to its acceptance.

For the purpose of comment I mark these paragraphs (1), (2), and (3). It seems difficult to reconcile (1) with (3) but (2) and (3) are in perfect harmony. In (1) he says that "for the elect he made actual atonement" . . . "they were actually reconciled to God." But in (3) he says that "the atoning work was not sufficient for the salvation of man, that work was only Godward, and only removed all the obstacles in the way of God's pardon for the sinner." This language applies of course to the elect. But in (2) he says, "Christ wrought out a means of reconciliation for all men which removed every legal obstacle to their salvation." Then for the elect the atonement "was not sufficient for the salvation of man and only removed all the obstacles in the way of God's pardon for the sinner," and if for "the nonelect the atonement wrought out a means of reconciliation," "removing every legal obstacle to their salvation," what is the difference Godward? What is the difference so far as Christ's work is concerned? Does not the difference come in the Spirit's work in connection with the application of the atonement and the ministry of reconciliation?[69]

Carroll then appealed to Baptist Calvinist William Buck's work *Theology: The Philosophy of Religion*, where Buck argued for an unlimited atonement.[70]

---

69 Ibid., 89–90.

70 Ibid. See W. Buck, *Theology: The Philosophy of Religion* (Nashville: Southwestern Publishing, Graves, Marks & Co., 1857), 46–56, 118. For more on Buck, consult J. H. Spencer, *A History of Kentucky Baptists*, 2 vols. (1886; repr. Gallatin, TN: Church History Research and Archives, 1984), 2:171–77. Buck pastored several churches, most notably the First Baptist Church in Louisville, Kentucky. Notice that the publisher of Buck's book, "Graves," is a reference to J. R. Graves and indicates he endorsed this book that promoted unlimited atonement.

A. H. Newman (AD 1852–1933)

Newman was a member of the founding faculty of Southwestern Baptist Theological Seminary, where he taught church history. He also served as a faculty member at Baylor University, Rochester Baptist Theological Seminary, McMaster University, Vanderbilt University, and University of Chicago. His description of the scene in Baptist life in 1894 follows:

> As regards the set of doctrines on which Augustine differed from his theological predecessors, and modern Calvinists from Arminians, Baptists have always been divided. The medieval evangelical sects were all, apparently, anti-Augustinian, and the Baptist parties of the sixteenth century followed in the footsteps of their medieval spiritual ancestors in this and other important particulars. Those Baptist parties of modern times whose historical relations with the medieval evangelical parties and the antipedobaptist parties of the sixteenth century are most intimate have rejected the Calvinistic system; while those that owe their origin to English Puritanism, with Wiclifism and Lollardism behind it and with the deeply rooted Calvinism of the English Elizabethan age as its leading characteristic, have been noted for their staunch adherence to Calvinistic principles, not, of course, because of any supposed authority of Calvin or of the English Puritan leaders, but because they have seemed to them to be Scriptural. Calvinistic and Arminian Baptists have both had periods of extreme development, the former sometimes scarcely escaping fatalism and antinomianism, the latter sometimes falling into Socinian denial of the deity of Christ and Pelagian denial of original sin. The great majority of the Baptists of today hold to what may be called moderate Calvinism, or Calvinism tempered with the evangelical anti-Augustinianism which came through the Moravian Brethren to Wesley and by him was brought to bear on all bodies of evangelical Christians.[71]

Newman indicated that a "great majority" of Baptists held to an unlimited atonement.

E. C. Dargan (AD 1852–1930)

Dargan was professor of homiletics at Southern Baptist Theological Seminary from 1892 to 1907 and pastor of First Baptist Church in Macon, Georgia, from 1907 to 1917. He served three years as president of the SBC (1911–13) and secretary of the Sunday School Board. He affirmed unlimited atonement.

71 A. H. Newman, *A History of the Baptist Churches in the United States* (New York: Christian Literature Co., 1894), 5–6.

Dargan considered as inadequate the notion that Christ paid the debt "for all who accept his services." He considered the scriptural view to be that Christ suffered the penalty of sin in humanity's place as a "sufficient and suitable substitute" for all the human race but only efficient for those who actually believe.[72]

Z. T. Cody (AD 1858–1935)

Cody was a Mercer University graduate who studied theology under James P. Boyce at Southern Seminary, earning the master of theology degree in 1887. He later completed the doctor of divinity degree from Bowden College. He served as pastor of several prominent churches in the South, including First Baptist Church in Greenville, South Carolina, and was editor of South Carolina's *Baptist Courier* from 1911 to 1935. He is described as "a theologian of the first rank" by the *Encyclopedia of Southern Baptists*.[73]

He wrote a fascinating and popular article in the *Baptist Courier* entitled "Are Baptists Calvinists?" The article was reprinted in *Baptist World* magazine and in *Christian Union Relative to Baptist Churches*, edited by James M. Frost.

> Are Baptists Calvinists? The answer to this question depends on what is meant by Calvinism. If by it is meant all that Calvin himself taught and practiced a negative answer is the only possible one; for Calvin believed in burning men for deadly heresy, in the union of church and state, in infant baptism and in a good many other things which have ever been rejected by all Baptists. But these things, while taught and practiced by the Genevan, are not now considered as essential to his system; and many feel that churches can reject them and still be called Calvinistic.
>
> The so-called "five points of Calvinism" are the essential doctrines of the system. Men have forgotten them now but they were once as familiar as the letters of the alphabet. They are, particular predestination, limited atonement, natural inability, irresistible grace and the perseverance of the saints. Now if this is the system that constitutes Calvinism it is again very certain that Baptists are not Calvinists. . . .
>
> But it can be very confidently affirmed that there is now no Baptist church that holds or defends the five points of Calvinism. Some of the doctrines are repugnant to our people. Could there be found a minister in our communion who believes in the theory of a limited atonement? . . .
>
> In answering our question, then, we would say that Baptists are not

72 E. C. Dargan, *The Doctrines of Our Faith* (Nashville: Sunday School Board of the Southern Baptist Convention, 1905), 139.

73 S. Lemke, "History or Revisionist History?," 238.

> Calvinists; and while Calvinism is an honored name, yet to wear it would detract somewhat from a greater honor that properly belongs to Baptists.[74]

This historical data makes it clear that any historiography suggesting that Baptists were Calvinists who affirmed all five points of the more modern TULIP schema until well into the twentieth century is flawed. As Steve Lemke pointed out:

> The threshold of evidence necessary to disprove the claim that the "overwhelming majority" of antebellum Baptists in the South were five-point Calvinists is rather low. The evidence need not show, for example, that (a) some Southern Baptists were not five-point Calvinists, or that (b) a few leading Southern Baptists were not five-point Calvinists, or that (c) some theologians or institutions affirmed five-point Calvinism. All the evidence need show is that there were a substantial number of Baptists in the South who were not five-point Calvinists. The evidence does clearly meet and exceed that threshold of evidence.[75]

E. Y. Mullins (AD 1860–1928)

Mullins served as president and professor of theology at Southern Baptist Theological Seminary in Louisville from 1899 to 1928. Through his administration, teaching, and writing, he became a leader in the Southern Baptist Convention, serving as president of the SBC from 1921 to 1924. It would be virtually impossible to overstate Mullins's influence on Southern Baptist life and theology in the twentieth century and beyond.

He was clearly a proponent of universal atonement.

> The atonement of Christ was for all men. His relation to mankind which has been set forth involves the consequence that he died for all. There are numerous passages of Scripture which leave no room for doubt. In John 3:16 it is declared that "God so loved the World" that he gave his Son; in Hebrews 2:9, "that by the grace of God he should taste death for every man;" in 2 Peter 2:1 it is declared in regard to false teachers, doomed to destruction, that they denied "even the Master that bought them." In I John 2:2 we read, "he is the propitiation for our sins; and not for ours only, but also for the whole world." In I Timothy 2:6 again we find the same statement in this form, "Who gave himself a ransom for all." In Titus 2:11 we read, "For the grace of God hath appeared bringing salvation to all men." In I Timothy 4:10 a distinction is

74 Z. T. Cody, "Are Baptists Calvinists?" *Baptist Courier*, February 16, 1911; reprinted in *Baptist World*, April 12, 1911, and in *Christian Union Relative to Baptist Churches*, ed. J. M. Frost (Nashville: Sunday School Board of the Southern Baptist Convention, 1915), 32–35.

75 S. Lemke, "History or Revisionist History?," 240.

> made between the race as a whole and those who believe. God is "the Saviour of all men, especially of them that believe."
>
> This last passage makes clear the fact that all men do not share equally in the benefits of the atonement of Christ. Those who remain in unbelief are not saved. Yet even they share many of the common blessings of life through the work of Christ. God's anger against human sin is restrained in order that men may repent. Every motive and appeal is provided in the gospel to induce them to do so.[76]

Mullins charged particularists with working from a false premise (God's "mere will") and arriving at the false conclusion of limited atonement by employing a "rigid logic."[77]

Edwin M. Poteat (AD 1861–1937)

Poteat had a colorful career as a pastor in churches in Maryland, Connecticut, and Pennsylvania; professor at Wake Forest College and Mercer University; and president of Furman University from 1903 to 1918. His *The Scandal of the Cross: Studies in the Death of Jesus* was published in 1928.

Though Poteat did not elaborate on the extent of the atonement, it is clear he affirmed universal atonement. He stated: "The redemption remains a fact, for what God in Christ did there He did for the whole race."[78]

A. T. Robertson (AD 1863–1934)

Robertson was Southern Baptists' premier Greek scholar who taught at Southern Seminary in Louisville. He authored the massive *Greek Grammar in the Light of Historical Research* as well as the six-volume *Word Pictures in the New Testament,* along with forty-three other books.

Robertson affirmed unlimited atonement, as can be seen, for example, in his comments on 1 John 2:2: "the propitiation by Christ provides for salvation for all (Heb. 2:9) if they will only be reconciled with God (II Cor. 5:19–21)."[79]

W. O. Carver (AD 1868–1954)[80]

Carver taught at Southern Seminary from 1896 until his retirement in 1943. He authored the article on the atonement in the *International Standard Bible Encyclopedia,* in which he rejected limited atonement:

---

76 E. Y. Mullins, *The Christian Religion in Its Doctrinal Expression* (Valley Forge: Judson, 1974 reprint), 336.

77 Ibid., 339.

78 E. M. Poteat, *The Scandal of the Cross: Studies in the Death of Jesus* (New York: Harper & Bros., 1928), 40.

79 A. T. Robertson, "The General Epistles and the Revelation of John," in *Word Pictures in the New Testament,* 6 vols. (Nashville: Broadman, 1933), 6:210.

80 Carver was more theologically liberal than his predecessors. See J. Duesing's assessment of Carver, "W. O. Carver, Southern Seminary, and the Significance of Adoniram Judson," *Footnotes* (blog), March 5, 2014, http://www.jgduesing.com/2014/03/05/w-o-carver-southern-seminary-and-the/.

> It is no longer possible to read the Bible and suppose that God relates himself sympathetically with only a part of the race. All segregated passages of Scripture formerly employed in support of such a view have now taken their place in the progressive self-interpretation of God to men through Christ who is the propitiation for the sins of the whole world. (1 Jn 2:2)[81]

W. T. Conner (AD 1877–1952)

W. T. Conner enjoyed a thirty-nine-year teaching career at Southwestern Baptist Theological Seminary as professor of systematic theology. Author of fifteen volumes and numerous articles,[82] his views on the extent of the atonement can best be seen in *Christian Doctrine* and *The Gospel of Redemption*, where it is clear he affirmed unlimited atonement.[83]

H. W. Tribble (1889–1967)

Tribble taught theology at Southern Seminary for twenty-two years, served as president of Andover Newton Seminary for three years, and then became president of Wake Forest College in 1950. In a 1936 work, *Our Doctrines*, he stated: "Christ died for the sins of all mankind."[84]

W. A. Criswell (AD 1909–2002)

Criswell pastored the prestigious First Baptist Church in Dallas, Texas, for more than fifty years, beginning in 1944. He was one of Southern Baptists' most well-known and well-loved preachers. He authored more than fifty books, most of them collections of his sermons through various books of the Bible. A two-time president of the Southern Baptist Convention, Criswell played a key role in the Conservative resurgence that swept the convention in the last quarter of the twentieth century.

Though Criswell was generally Calvinistic in his theology, he affirmed unlimited atonement.[85] In a sermon on 1 John 2:1–2 entitled "If Anyone Sin," Criswell stated:

> I've never been able to understand how the Calvinists, some of them, believe in a "limited atonement." That is, the sacrifice of Christ applied only to those who are the elect, but there is no sacrifice of Christ for the whole world—when John expressly says He is the sacrifice, the atoning, dedicated gift of God in

---

81 W. O. Carver, "Atonement," in *The International Standard Bible Encyclopaedia*, 5 vols., rev. ed., ed. J. Orr (Chicago: Howard Severance Co., 1915), 1:324.

82 According to W. Boyd Hunt, Conner's works were read more than those by Boyce, Dagg, and Mullins ("Southern Baptists and Systematic Theology," *Southwestern Journal of Theology* 1 [1959]: 47).

83 W. T. Conner, *Christian Doctrine* (Nashville: Broadman, 1937), 169–77. See also D. Dockery, "Southern Baptists and Calvinism: A Historical Look," in *Calvinism: A Southern Baptist Dialogue*, ed. E. R. Clendenen and B. Waggoner (Nashville: B&H Academic, 2008), 37–38.

84 H. W. Tribble, *Our Doctrines* (Nashville: Sunday School Board of the Southern Baptist Convention, 1936), 52.

85 Correctly noted by D. Dockery, "Southern Baptists and Calvinism," 39.

> our lives for the whole world [1 John 2:2]. And it is just according to whether we accept it or not as to whether the life of our Lord is efficacious for us in His atoning death.[86]

Theodore R. Clark (AD 1912–1999)

Clark became professor of theology at New Orleans Baptist Theological Seminary in 1949. In *Saved by His Life*, published in 1959, Clark affirmed unlimited atonement. Christ, in his death and resurrection, "furnishes the clue to the meaning of God's reconciling and saving work among all men."[87]

Clark's work is problematic, however, since he denied penal substitution, along with the inerrancy of Scripture. He was followed in this approach by Frank Stagg, professor of New Testament at New Orleans Seminary and later at Southern Seminary. Stagg likewise affirmed unlimited atonement. A third New Orleans Seminary professor of theology, Fisher Humphreys, also denied the penal substitutionary nature of the cross, although he did affirm some form of substitution in his 1978 *The Death of Christ*, as well as unlimited atonement.[88]

William W. Stevens (AD 1914–1978)

Stevens was Theophilus W. Green Professor of Bible and New Testament Greek at Mississippi College in Clinton, Mississippi. In *Doctrines of the Christian Religion*, he asserted that both universalism and limited atonement are "untenable views" on the extent of the atonement. The incarnation necessitated a universal atonement and Stevens appealed to texts such as John 3:16; 1 John 2:2; Heb 2:9; and 2 Pet 2:1 for support.[89]

Dale Moody (AD 1915–1992)

Moody taught systematic theology at Southern Seminary in Louisville from 1948 to 1984. In addition to his criticism of inerrancy, his views on apostasy were not in line with the Southern Baptist doctrinal statement or the Abstract of Principles that govern the faculty of Southern Seminary. These problems contributed to his early retirement.

Moody authored *The Word of Truth*, published in 1981.[90] Though he did not explicitly discuss the extent of the atonement, it was well known that Moody affirmed unlimited atonement. Moody also rejected the penal substitutionary model of the atonement.

---

86 W. A. Criswell, "If Anyone Sin" (sermon delivered at First Baptist Church, Dallas, TX, April 8, 1973).

87 T. R. Clark, *Saved by His Life: A Study of the New Testament Doctrine of Reconciliation and Resurrection* (New York: Macmillan, 1959), 32.

88 F. Humphreys, *The Death of Christ* (Nashville: Broadman, 1978), 94. See also idem, *Thinking about God* (New Orleans: Insight, 1974), 117.

89 W. W. Stevens, *Doctrines of the Christian Religion* (Grand Rapids, MI: Eerdmans, 1967), 191–92.

90 D. Moody, *The Word of Truth: A Summary of Christian Doctrine Based on Biblical Revelation* (Grand Rapids, MI: Eerdmans, 1981).

Robert H. Culpepper (AD 1924–2012)

Culpepper served as a missionary to Japan from 1950 to 1980 and then taught theology at Southeastern Baptist Theological Seminary in Wake Forest, North Carolina, for more than twenty years. In *Interpreting the Atonement*, published in 1966, he affirmed unlimited atonement: "The atonement is unlimited in its provision, but limited in its application."[91]

Charles Ryrie (AD 1925–2016)

Ryrie taught for many years at Dallas Theological Seminary and is well known as a theologian and author of the *Ryrie Study Bible*. Ryrie would be best described as a moderate Calvinist. The following excerpt on the extent of the atonement comes from his *Basic Theology*, originally published in 1986.[92]

> Because some reject does not invalidate the provision or mean that the provision was not made for them. If we say that a father provides sufficient food for his family, we do not exclude the possibility that some members of that family may refuse to eat what has been provided. But their refusal does not mean that the provision was made only for those who actually do eat the food. Likewise, the death of Christ provided the payment for the sins of all people—those who accept that payment and those who do not. Refusal to accept does not limit the provision made. Providing and possessing are not the same.[93]

James Leo Garrett (b. AD 1925)

Garrett is distinguished professor emeritus of systematic theology at Southwestern Baptist Theology Seminary. In his stellar academic career, he has taught at Southwestern Baptist Theological Seminary (1949–59, 1979–97), Southern Baptist Theological Seminary (1959–73), and Baylor University (1973–79). His theological magnum opus is the two-volume *Systematic Theology* published in 1995. He also authored the celebrated *Baptist Theology: A Four-Century Study*.[94]

Garrett approached the subject from a purely descriptive fashion in his *Systematic*. He first listed the New Testament texts used to support limited atonement, followed by those used to support unlimited atonement. Second, he briefly summarized the

91 R. Culpepper, *Interpreting the Atonement* (Grand Rapids, MI: Eerdmans, 1966), 123.

92 C. Ryrie, *Basic Theology* (Chicago: Moody, 1986). This material can be found online at http://www.bible-reading.com/atone.html#extent. Many would agree with Ryrie that one's view of the lapsarian question (order of the decrees) does not shed much light on the question of extent. This is true for a number of reasons, not the least of which is the fact that in the history of Calvinism both infralapsarians and supralapsarians have held to unlimited atonement.

93 Ibid., 318.

94 J. L. Garrett, *Systematic Theology: Biblical, Historical, and Evangelical*, 2 vols. (Grand Rapids, MI: Eerdmans, 1995); J. L. Garrett, *Baptist Theology: A Four-Century Study* (Macon, GA: Mercer University Press, 2009).

history of the question from Augustine, Prosper, Lombard, Calvin, Beza, Arminius, Dort, General Baptists, Particular Baptists, German Pietism, and Princetonian theologians. Finally, Garrett briefly listed twelve arguments for limited atonement and six arguments for general atonement. He concluded that the arguments for a general atonement "seem persuasive."[95]

Millard Erickson (b. AD 1932)

Erickson is distinguished professor of theology at Western Seminary in Portland, Oregon, and the author of the widely acclaimed systematic theology entitled *Christian Theology*, along with more than twenty other books. He was for many years professor of theology and academic dean at Bethel Seminary and previously taught at Southwestern Baptist Theological Seminary and Baylor University.

Erickson is a moderate Calvinist who affirmed universal atonement in a chapter on the subject in *Christian Theology*.[96] He stated, "The hypothesis of universal atonement is able to account for a larger segment of the biblical witness with less distortion than is the hypothesis of limited atonement."[97]

Erickson's chapter is generally very good but lacks proper nuance at certain points. He framed the discussion, not unsurprisingly since he is himself a Calvinist, from the perspective of the Dortian notion of election and the various lapsarian positions on the order of God's decrees.[98] Yet the actual question of extent is not really connected with either, as all Calvinists who reject limited atonement affirm unconditional election, and both supralapsarians and infralapsarians can be found throughout Reformed history who support unlimited atonement. Erickson correctly noted that the attempt to deduce limited atonement from the doctrine of election is unsuccessful.[99]

Erickson made some compelling arguments in favor of unlimited atonement. In reference to 1 Tim 2:6, he compares Paul's statement with the original statement in Matt 20:28 and notes:

> In 1 Timothy, Paul makes a significant advance upon the words of Jesus . . . but most significantly here, "for many" . . . becomes "for all." . . . When Paul wrote, the words of the tradition (i.e., as they appear in Matthew) may well have been familiar to him. It is almost as if he made a deliberate point of emphasizing that the ransom was universal in its purpose.[100]

95 Garrett, *Systematic Theology*, 2:65.
96 M. Erickson, *Christian Theology*, 3rd ed. (Grand Rapids, MI: Baker, 2013), 841–60.
97 Ibid., 761.
98 Ibid., 766.
99 Ibid., 760–61.
100 Ibid., 758.

Erickson acknowledged those texts that speak of Christ dying for "his sheep" and "his church." He went on to note:

> These texts, however, present no problem if we regard the universal passages as normative or determinative. Certainly if Christ died for the whole, there is no problem in asserting that he died for a specific part of the whole. To insist that those passages which focus on his dying for his people require the understanding that he died only for them and not for any others contradicts the universal passages. We conclude that the hypothesis of universal atonement is able to account for a larger segment of the biblical witness with less distortion than is the hypothesis of limited atonement.[101]

Clark Pinnock (AD 1937–2010)

Pinnock was a Baptist theologian who studied under F. F. Bruce. He taught at New Orleans Baptist Theological Seminary, Trinity Evangelical Divinity School, Regent College in Vancouver, and was professor emeritus of Christian interpretation at McMaster Divinity College from 1977 until 2002. Pinnock was a Calvinist whose theology gradually shifted to Arminianism and then later to an advocacy of open theism.

He edited two important volumes critiquing Calvinism, the first published in 1975 on the universality of God's grace entitled *Grace Unlimited*, and another in 1989, *The Grace of God and the Will of Man.*[102]

Grace Unlimited contains thirteen chapters written by various non-Calvinist authors and covering a number of biblical, historical, and theological issues related to Calvinism. The first two chapters, written by Vernon Grounds and Donald Lake, address, among other issues, the extent of the atonement. Grounds primarily surveys the notion of "grace" in salvation. He minces no words with respect to such passages like Rom 11:32; 1 Tim 2:6; Heb 2:9; 2 Pet 3:9; and 1 John 2:2 and their universality: "It takes an exegetical ingenuity which is something other than a learned virtuosity to evacuate these texts of their obvious meaning; it takes an exegetical ingenuity verging on sophistry to deny their explicit universality."[103]

---

101 Ibid., 761.

102 C. Pinnock, ed., *Grace Unlimited* (Minneapolis, MN: Bethany Fellowship, 1975); and C. Pinnock, ed., *The Grace of God and the Will of Man* (Minneapolis, MN: Bethany House, 1985). *Grace Unlimited* has recently been revised and updated by J. Wagner and published as *Grace for All: The Arminian Dynamics of Salvation* (Eugene, OR: Resource, 2015). Of the chapters that were retained, Wagner has updated and edited them. Six new chapters are included: R. Olson, "Arminianism Is God-Centered Theology," 1–17; G. Shellrude, "Calvinism and Problematic Readings of New Testament Texts or, Why I Am Not a Calvinist," 29–50; R. Picirilli, "The Intent and Extent of Christ's Atonement," 51–68; J. M. Pinson, "Jacobus Arminius: Reformed and Always Reforming," 146–76; V. Reasoner, "John Wesley's Doctrines on the Theology of Grace," 177–96; and S. Witzki, "Saving Faith: The Act of a Moment or the Attitude of a Life?," 242–74.

103 V. Grounds, "God's Universal Salvific Grace," in *Grace Unlimited*, 27.

Donald Lake's chapter, "He Died for All: The Universal Dimensions of the Atonement," is the only chapter dedicated completely to the subject of extent. He engaged Augustine, Calvin (whom he wrongly thinks held to limited atonement), and Barth in a bit of historical theology, then proceeded to look at some passages in John's Gospel and 1 John, as well as Paul's Epistles. Lake asserted: "A universal atonement truly honors God's grace and frees God from the charge that he is responsible, through election, for excluding some from his kingdom."[104]

In a final section on "limited atonement," Lake stated that Calvinists like Berkhof fail to recognize that the atonement is a universally valid offer of saving grace because Christ's atoning work for sin is complete. The issue of salvation turns not on a person's sin but his relationship to Christ. For Lake, all people are in a "saveable" state because there is an atonement for them should they believe.[105]

In *The Grace of God and the Will of Man*, multiple authors engage Calvinism. The chapters by I. Howard Marshall and Terry Miethe focus on the extent of the atonement. Marshall's chapter, "Universal Grace and Atonement in the Pastoral Epistles," is a stout analysis of four key passages in the Pastoral Epistles: 1 Tim 2:3–4; 2:5–6; 1 Tim 4:10; and Titus 2:11. With primary focus on 1 Tim 2:3–6, Marshall treated the passage under eight headings:

1. The word "save" and its cognates are used here in their normal spiritual sense.
2. The force of "*thelō*" should not be weakened.
3. The scope of "all" includes all men and women.
4. The scope of "all" is not confined to believers.
5. The alternation between "all" and "us" does not contradict universality.
6. The term "all" should not be narrowed to refer only to "the many."
7. "All" does not simply mean "all kinds of."
8. The grace of God is identified with his saving act in Christ.[106]

Marshall then considered the concept of "election" in the Pastoral Epistles. He makes the important point that whenever the term translated "elect" is used in the LXX and the New Testament for people, the reference is to people who are already God's people as members of Israel or the saved community—the church. The Reformed notion of a body of people called the "elect" considered in the abstract is not a biblical notion.[107]

Marshall's chapter is an excellent exegetical treatment of the passages in the Pastorals that support unlimited atonement.

---

104 D. Lake, "He Died for All: The Universal Dimensions of the Atonement," in *Grace Unlimited*, 43.

105 Ibid., 45–48.

106 I. H. Marshall, "Universal Grace and Atonement," in *Grace for All*, 54–64.

107 Ibid., 64–69.

Terry Miethe's chapter, "The Universal Power of the Atonement," surveyed eight arguments for limited atonement and eight arguments for unlimited atonement. He also considered Calvin's view on the extent of the atonement and concluded on the basis of Calvin's statements in his sermons and commentaries that he held to unlimited atonement.[108]

James E. Tull (AD 1938–1985)

Tull taught theology at Southeastern Baptist Theological Seminary from 1955 to 1985. He was basically liberal in his theological outlook.[109] His book, *The Atoning Gospel*, was published in 1982. Tull emphasized the representative nature of Christ's death over that of substitution. Though there is no direct statement of his view on the extent question, he spoke of Christ as the one who "represented all of humanity. He was the new man, the true man, the sinless representative of mankind,"[110] which likely indicates his belief in an unlimited atonement.

Paige Patterson (b. AD 1942)

Patterson is the president of Southwestern Baptist Theological Seminary in Fort Worth, Texas, and is a leading Southern Baptist preacher, theologian, churchman, statesman, and author. Patterson's stellar leadership in the SBC includes serving as president of two of its seminaries as well as president of Criswell College over a period of more than forty years. He served two terms as president of the SBC and appointed the committee that revised the Baptist Faith and Message doctrinal statement for Southern Baptists in 2000.

Patterson has been a strong defender of unlimited atonement in his preaching, teaching, and writing ministry. In addition to numerous statements in press reports over the years supporting unlimited atonement,[111] he articulated what he believed to be the biblical position in his chapter "The Work of Christ" in *A Theology for the Church*: "The idea of an atonement limited only to the elect is a concept that belongs to a logical system including other elements, such as irresistible grace, which many find appealing."[112] He also stated:

---

108 T. Miethe, "The Universal Power of the Atonement," in *Grace for All*, 71–96.

109 On Tull's liberalism, consult M. Williams and W. Shurden, eds., *Turning Points in Baptist History* (Macon, GA: Mercer University Press, 2008), 87.

110 J. Tull, *The Atoning Gospel* (Macon, GA: Mercer University Press, 1982), 115.

111 See, for example, "Patterson: Calvinism OK but Wrong," in a *Baptist Press* article published in the *Baptist Standard* (Nov. 24, 1999): "The Bible actually advocates 'the exact opposite' of a belief in limited atonement, he [Patterson] asserted. 'It says he died not only for our sins, but also the sins of the whole world. That is an unlimited atonement if I've ever read anything at all.'"

112 P. Patterson, "The Work of Christ," in *A Theology for the Church*, 2nd ed., ed. Daniel L. Akin (Nashville: B&H Academic, 2014), 585–86. See also idem, "Reflections on the Atonement," *Criswell Theological Review* 3 (1989): 307–20.

> The atonement of Christ is universal in scope but applicable only for those who receive him (John 1:10–12). It is universal or unlimited in its provision but limited in its application. It is sufficient for all, but efficient only for those who believe, who are the elect of God.[113]

Tom Nettles (b. AD 1946)

Nettles is a retired professor of church history at Southern Baptist Theological Seminary in Louisville. He plays a leading role in the Southern Baptist Founders Ministries. He authored an important book chronicling Calvinism in Southern Baptist life.[114] He has accurately noted the Calvinism of many of the founders and later leaders within the Southern Baptist Convention.

Yet it is important how many of these men he references did not affirm limited atonement. Nettles is quick to inform us of those who do, with evidence from their writings or sermons, but for the most part, with respect to those who do not state their views, Nettles does not acknowledge this directly, nor state that these men likely did not hold to limited atonement. The resultant impression one gets from reading *By His Grace and for His Glory* is that virtually all these men held to all five points of Calvinism as popularly understood—an impression not commensurate with the actual facts. Most of the Baptist leaders of the nineteenth century did hold to the doctrine of unconditional election, but when it comes to the notions of limited atonement and irresistible grace, the evidence indicates that many of these leaders rejected one or both.

Nettles's argument that most Baptist leaders held to the so-called doctrines of grace, by which is meant a five-point Calvinistic soteriology, does not have history on its side. For example, Nettles stated: "The first two generations of Southern Baptists held steadfastly to the theological system the *Religious Herald* called 'the Doctrines of Grace.'"[115] Nettles quoted F. H. Kerfoot's 1913 confession that included God's sovereignty, decrees, salvation as God's free gift, election in Christ from eternity, and perseverance.[116] But Kerfoot's wording of these doctrinal positions does not exhibit a strong "five-point" Calvinism. There is the absence of any mention of limited atonement. In point of fact, Kerfoot served as editor of Boyce's *Abstract of Theology*, and his notes indicate that his own brand of Calvinism was more moderate than that of Boyce.[117]

It is clear that many Southern Baptists who identified themselves as Calvinists in

113 P. Patterson, "The Work of Christ," 587.

114 T. Nettles, *By His Grace and for His Glory*.

115 T. Nettles, "Southern Baptist Identity: Influenced by Calvinism," *Baptist History and Heritage* 31 (1996): 17.

116 Ibid., 17–18.

117 F. H. Kerfoot, "The simple question is, what do the Scriptures teach? And it may be confidently claimed that they teach that Christ died for *all men*, as certainly as that they teach that he died especially for the elect. . . . Andrew Fuller, we think, has done good service in emphasizing this general feature of the atonement" (J. P. Boyce, *Abstract of Systematic Theology*, 2nd ed., rev. and ed. F. H. Kerfoot [Philadelphia: American Baptist Publication Society, 1899], 274; emphasis in original).

the nineteenth century did not include limited atonement in their "doctrines of grace."

Nettles devoted a chapter to limited atonement. After briefly considering some of the biblical texts that seem to teach against limited atonement, Nettles stated: "Historically, two streams of thought emerge from the writings of those who have defended limited atonement."[118]

One stream represented by Andrew Fuller and J. P. Boyce "affirms both the sufficiency of the atonement in it nature to save all men and the limitation of the atonement to the elect only in its intent." The second stream, represented by Abraham Booth and J. L. Dagg, "affirms that it is the nature of the atonement to save all for whom it is sufficient, and therefore its limitation in intent is necessarily a limitation of its sufficiency."[119] Nettles opted for the latter.

In this twofold analysis, Nettles failed to distinguish a kind of sufficiency that was part of the Reformed discussion on the extent of the atonement early on historically: an extrinsic, ordained sufficiency where Christ actually substituted for the sins of all people, even though only the elect would receive efficacious grace and be saved. Nettles appears to have no category in his thinking for this aspect of sufficiency.

Nettles argued the thesis that this kind of sufficiency language "is ultimately meaningless and misperceived the nature of the atonement."[120] He asked why the term "sufficient" is adopted. Because it is viewed as the ground for the free offer of the gospel. If Christ's death is sufficient only for the elect, on what grounds can salvation be offered to all? So argued Fuller.

Nettles contended that people are without excuse whether the atonement is sufficient or not. But this misses the point. That is not in question. The issue is what is being offered to the non-elect who are without excuse. On the limited atonement scheme, there is nothing to offer them since no atonement exists for them.[121]

Nettles claimed that it is a *non sequitur* to move from the deity of Christ as sacrifice to sufficiency for every individual person.[122] In the so-called sufficiency view of the atonement, Nettles posited a lack of precise distinction between atonement and either unconditional election or effectual calling—or both.[123]

> If he [Christ] died for all sufficiently . . . I cannot tell how one distinguishes this from the general atonement of the Arminians, who claim that Christ has died for all men, but its benefits accrue only to those who believe. The difference in the two does not lie in atonement, but in the Spirit's work of calling.[124]

118 Nettles, *By His Grace*, 340.
119 Ibid.
120 Ibid., 342.
121 Ibid., 344.
122 Ibid., 346.
123 Ibid., 348.
124 Ibid., 358.

Another error for Nettles is "an apparent necessity of separating objectivity from effectuality in order to maintain the concept of sufficiency for the whole world."[125] Nettles does not like the language of Christ "removing legal obstacles" that Shedd, A. A. Hodge, and Boyce used. He reverts to the double payment argument as evidence for a strictly limited atonement.[126] "Therefore, while confidently affirming the substitutionary and legal-penal aspects of atonement, one must also realize that applying this concept to all men without exception relegates the atonement to a nonefficacious state. This approaches the mistake of those who believe in general atonement and even contains elements of nonsubstitution."[127]

The sufficient for all but efficient only for the elect phrase

> does not distinguish this view from the view of general atonement. Much less should one affirm that the intent of Christ's death was the same for all men and that He has died indeed for all men without exception. When the necessary benefits of Christ's death does not actually terminate on all men, one should see the impossibility of such a view.[128]

In this quote, Nettles meant by "intent" the "efficacious purpose" of the atonement.

Nettles said it is proper to speak of a "quantitative, as well as a qualitative, element in the atonement."[129] Nettles, like John L. Dagg, is a quantitative equivalentist.[130]

Timothy George (b. AD 1950)

George is the founding dean of Beeson Divinity School in Birmingham, Alabama, and serves as an executive editor for *Christianity Today*. He is an adherent of limited atonement. His *Amazing Grace: God's Pursuit, Our Response*, appeared first in 2000, followed by a second edition in 2011.[131]

George suggested a replacement acronym for TULIP that he termed "ROSES":

- Radical Depravity
- Overcoming Grace
- Sovereign Election

125 Ibid., 349.

126 Ibid.

127 Ibid., 353.

128 Ibid., 357.

129 Ibid., 358.

130 In 2008 Nettles wrote an article entitled "Why Your Next Pastor Should Be a Calvinist," *Founders Journal* 71 (2008): 5–13. Though in this article he makes no reference to limited atonement specifically, it seems clear that Nettles's version of a Calvinist pastor is one who affirms a strictly limited atonement.

131 Timothy George, *Amazing Grace: God's Pursuit, Our Response*, 2nd ed. (Wheaton, IL: Crossway, 2011).

- Eternal Life
- Singular Redemption[132]

In his discussion of "singular redemption," George rightly pointed out that the attempt to shackle the many "all" verses in an atonement context with the meaning "all without distinction," as most Calvinists do, is "strained exegesis that is hard to justify in every case. Unless the context clearly requires a different interpretation, it is better to say that 'all means all,' even if we cannot square the universal reach of Christ's atoning death with its singular focus."[133]

George spoke of the "quagmire" of hyper-Calvinism. He listed five traits of the modern-day hyper-Calvinist:

1. They teach the doctrine of eternal justification.
2. They deny the free moral agency and responsibility of sinners to repent and believe.
3. They restrict the gospel invitation to the elect.
4. They teach that sinners have no warrant to believe in Christ until they feel the evidence of the Spirit's moving in their hearts.
5. They deny the universal love of God.

George calls hyper-Calvinism "a perversion of true evangelical Calvinism."[134]

Frank Page (b. AD 1952)

Page is a former pastor and the current president and chief executive officer of the executive committee of the Southern Baptist Convention. His *Trouble with the TULIP* was first published in 2000.[135]

This is a popular treatment of Calvinism that will provide any layperson with the basic distinctions between Calvinism and Arminianism, but it occasionally paints an inaccurate picture of what various Calvinists themselves actually believed about the extent of the atonement. For example, in describing limited atonement, Page quotes four Calvinists: Duane Spencer, Curt Daniel, R. B. Kuiper, and W. G. T. Shedd. Page appears to suggest that all these men affirmed limited atonement.[136] Actually Daniel and Shedd affirm an unlimited atonement and represent the group of Calvinists who are moderate on the extent question.

132 Ibid., 84.
133 Ibid., 94.
134 Ibid., 103–5.
135 F. Page, *Trouble with the Tulip*, 2nd ed. (Canton, GA: Riverstone Group, 2006).
136 Ibid., 24–25.

In 2011, Page appointed a task force consisting of several Southern Baptist theologians and pastors to address the issue of Calvinism in the SBC. The task force identified limited atonement as one discrepant issue. The group drafted and published a statement for the SBC outlining theological agreements and disagreements over Calvinism.[137]

David Dockery (b. AD 1952)

Dockery currently serves as president of Trinity Evangelical Theological Seminary and was former president of Union University, a Southern Baptist college in Jackson, Tennessee. Dockery is a leading Southern Baptist theologian and prolific author. In his *Southern Baptist Consensus and Renewal*, published in 2008, Dockery asserted his belief in universal atonement: "Atonement is realized when God takes upon Himself, in the person of Jesus, the sinfulness and guilt of humankind, so that His justice might be executed and the sins of men and women forgiven."[138] In another place he stated:

> The Bible teaches that God loves the world (John 3:16) and that the death of Christ was sufficient for the sins of the entire world (1 John 2:2). While the good news of the Gospel is to be preached to all and God's grace is available to all, it is only applicable for those who have trusted in Christ alone for forgiveness of sins (1 Tim 4:10).[139]

Ronnie Rogers (b. AD 1952)

Rogers is the senior pastor of Trinity Baptist Church in Norman, Oklahoma, and has written quite an interesting book entitled *Reflections of a Disenchanted Calvinist* in which he, as a former Calvinist, chronicled his dissatisfaction with the logic, exegesis, theology, and conclusions of Calvinism.[140]

Rogers believes the atonement is unlimited both in its value and its provision. It is not only sufficient to pay the penalty of all sin; it actually paid the penalty of all sin. God offers the gospel not just to all people groups and nations but to all people individually. Rogers asserted that God's secret will and his revealed will are "absolutely congruent and that God never gives the appearance of being or offering something that is absolutely contradicted by what he secretly knows—His secret will."[141]

---

137 Calvinism Advisory Committee, "Truth, Trust, and Testimony in a Time of Tension: A Statement from the Calvinism Advisory Committee," *SBC Life: Journal of the Southern Baptist Convention*, June 2013, http://www.sbclife.net/Articles/2013/06/sla5.

138 D. Dockery, *Southern Baptist Consensus and Renewal: A Biblical, Historical, and Theological Proposal* (Nashville: B&H Academic, 2008), 80.

139 Ibid., 83. Though it appears Dockery's intention in this statement is to affirm an unlimited atonement, the statement in and of itself is sufficiently ambiguous enough that a high Calvinist could affirm it by investing the term "sufficient" with the meaning of a hypothetical sufficiency only and not an actual sufficiency such that Christ died for the sins of all people.

140 R. Rogers, *Reflections of a Disenchanted Calvinist* (Bloomington, IN: Crossbooks, 2012).

141 Ibid., 26.

Rogers disaffirmed "that God's desire for everyone to experience eternal life, knowing that some will not trust Christ, in any way diminishes His sovereignty because He without constraint or coercion chose to create and grant man that opportunity."[142] Considering the love of God, predestination, and the extent of the atonement, Rogers pressed the point home that Calvinists face a difficult task in explaining to the non-elect on judgment day how it is that God can be said to love the non-elect in hell since he did not love them enough to provide them the remotest opportunity to escape eternal torment.[143]

Rogers did not draw a distinction between the moderate Calvinist position and the high Calvinist position on the extent of the atonement in conjunction with his point about the love of God for the non-elect. The Calvinist who affirms limited atonement would seem to fall victim to Rogers's critique since, in fact, God did not love the non-elect enough to provide an atonement for their sins. Hence it is impossible they could be rescued from hell.[144]

Rogers admitted that Scripture teaches God loves the elect "differently" than the non-elect. He also asserted that God's "love for the lost would be different had they become the elect through faith, which they in fact could have done."[145] Rogers considered it a "logical fallacy" and an "unbiblical deduction"

> to conclude that the Bible's affirmation of God's love for the elect means that he does not love all of the lost enough to provide for a *real* opportunity to be saved. This view of God's love is dramatically different than Calvinism's love for the lost, which does not allow them a chance to be saved, even though there seems to be an offer placed before them.[146]

Rogers disaffirmed that the distinctions in human love for spouse, children, and friends is analogous to distinctions in God's love for his elect and the lost, whom he does not offer a genuine chance to be saved (on the limited atonement scheme). He illustrated this point:

---

142 Ibid.

143 Ibid., 35.

144 The moderate Calvinist believes the same concerning predestination as the high Calvinist but also asserts that Christ died for the sins of all people out of love for all. The problem for this position, as Rogers sees it, is that God withholds his saving grace via his sovereign will in election and predestination, and hence the result is the same: the non-elect cannot be saved due to total depravity, which entails total inability on the part of anyone to believe the gospel unless God's saving grace is dispensed. In point of fact, this is indeed the case. The moderate Calvinist argues that his position includes a biblical perspective on the love of God for all, albeit such love is still discriminating in that God has a "special" love for the elect.

145 Rogers, *Reflections*, 36.

146 Ibid. (emphasis in original). Rogers needs to nuance this statement by noting that Calvinists assert that all people are "saveable," though, by entailment of limited atonement, such an assertion is logically impossible.

> . . . while it is true that I love my children differently from another man's children, I would not sit idly by and let his children be run over by a car, when I could have delivered them, and then try to convince the father of those children how much I loved them even in a different way than I love my children.[147]

Bruce Ware (b. AD 1953)

Ware is the T. Rupert and Lucille Coleman Professor of Christian Theology at Southern Seminary, where he has taught since 1998. Ware is a committed Calvinist and also committed to unlimited atonement.[148]

Gregg Allison (b. AD 1954)

Allison is professor of Christian theology at The Southern Baptist Theological Seminary. His *Historical Theology: An Introduction to Christian Doctrine* appeared in 2011 and is a very fine work.[149] He asked the right question—for whom did Christ die?—and fairly presented a brief summary of both sides of the extent debate.[150]

However, Allison's treatment is not without problems and needs to be nuanced. He rightly noted that Calvin's view is debatable and that later Reformed theologians embraced "a limited view of the atonement of Christ; that is, Christ did not die for the sins of every person, but only for the sins of the elect." He then stated: "The classic statement of this was set down in the *Five Articles of Calvinism* at the Synod of Dort in 1619." The antecedent of "this" is the previous statement that "Christ did not die for the sins of every person." The problem here is that Dort *allowed* for the limitarian position but did not *advocate* that position, as we have seen.

Allison has confused the *extent* question with the *intent* question at this point. Dort *advocated* the effectual *intent position*, against the Arminians, but left room for *diversity on the extent question*. Allison leaves the reader with the impression that Dort advocates "the limited atonement" position in the sense that "Christ did not die *for the sins of* every person." This is not quite accurate historically. Allison blurs the distinction between the *extent* and the *intent* at this point.

Furthermore, his quotation of Dort does not support the point he is attempting to make. The quotation *only* shows that those at Dort, contrary to the Remonstrants,

---

147 Ibid., 39.

148 See Bruce Ware, "Extent of the Atonement: Outline of the Issue, Positions, Key Texts, and Key Theological Arguments" (unpublished manuscript, n.d., available at http://www.epm.org/static/uploads/downloads/Extent_of_the_Atonement_by_Bruce_Ware.pdf). Ware delivered a paper on the extent of the atonement at the 2011 Evangelical Theological Society annual meeting in which he championed unlimited atonement. In that paper, Ware expressed his appreciation for and agreement with my chapter on the extent question in *Whosoever Will: A Biblical-Theological Critique of Five-Point Calvinism*. Ware supervised Gary Shultz's PhD dissertation advocating the "multiple intentions" view of the atonement (see below under "Gary Shultz").

149 G. Allison, *Historical Theology: An Introduction to Christian Doctrine* (Grand Rapids, MI: Zondervan, 2011).

150 Ibid., 404–8.

unanimously argued that the "*saving effectiveness* of the very precious death of his Son should extend to all the elect." The quotation goes on to say that it was "*the will of God* that Christ, by the blood of the cross . . . should *effectively* redeem . . . all those, and only those, who were chosen from eternity for salvation, and given to him by the Father." Dort advocated a *limited effectual intent to save* with a *limited application* but did not advocate the view that "Christ died only for the sins of the elect," as Allison seems to want to maintain. Of course, some delegates themselves advocated that very position, but the Canons of Dort do not.

Allison then noted that "the classical defense of the limited atonement view was voiced by John Owen," which leaves the reader with the impression that what Owen taught is what Dort advocated. It would be more accurate to state that Dort *allows for* Owen's view (to speak anachronistically), but *does not advocate it.*

Speaking of the Amyraldians, Allison stated they "dissented from this common limited atonement perspective." But as we have shown historically, the earliest position among the Reformed was unlimited atonement, along with the English variety of Hypothetical Universalism. He does not clearly state that Amyraut himself believed in a limited intent to save and an effectual application of the atonement, as Dort and all the Reformed believe.

While it is true that "a major difference arose in the Reformation and post-Reformation period: the limited atonement position versus the unlimited atonement position," this is too simplistic. One must consider the question from both the *intent* and the *extent.*

Regarding Shedd, Allison correctly noted Shedd's distinction between atonement and redemption. If Allison means to state that Shedd's understanding of the extent of the atonement was that it was unlimited *only* "in its value, sufficiency, and publication, but limited in its effectual application," and not unlimited in its actual satisfaction for the sins of all people, then he has erred with respect to Shedd's position, as we have seen above. All high Calvinists who advocate an internal sufficiency view of the atonement could agree with Allison's statement as it stands. That is not controversial among high Calvinists. But Shedd himself clearly asserted that the extent of the atonement in terms of actual satisfaction for sins was universal.

Allison summarized Shedd's view by saying: "Still, Shedd closely united the sufficiency of the atonement and the divine intention to apply it in redemption in the divine decree, so his position is rightly classified as limited atonement." This statement can only be correct if by it Allison is equating "limited atonement" with "limited intent to apply the atonement" and not the actual extent of the atonement. Otherwise, the statement is incorrect. Shedd may rightly be said to believe in a limited *redemption*, in the sense of an *effectual application* to the elect alone resulting from God's eternal purpose, but he may *not* be said to believe in "limited atonement." In fact, Shedd explicitly rejected "limited atonement" and specifically said *atonement is unlimited.*

Possible further evidence for Allison's misunderstanding may be the fact that he did not categorize Bruce Demarest as holding a limited atonement position in the same way as Shedd. If Shedd's adherence to a limited intent to apply the atonement qualifies him as a limited atonement advocate, then why does Allison not also identify Demarest as a limited atonement advocate? Demarest, like all Calvinists, agrees with a limited effectual purpose to apply Christ's death to the elect alone through the grant of faith, but Allison says Demarest basically held to a multiple intentions view, which amounts to (or is a variety of) the "unlimited limited atonement position." Allison correctly understands Demarest's distinctions between intent and extent. There is no difference here between Shedd and Demarest, or Dort, or with the early Reformers and some of the later Puritans who affirmed the same dualism with respect to the atonement.

These problems notwithstanding, Allison's treatment should be appreciated for his attempt to be evenhanded in addressing the two major views on the extent question from the perspective of historical theology.

Tom Ascol (b. AD 1957) and Founders Ministries

Tom Ascol is the pastor of Grace Baptist Church in Cape Coral, Florida. He is also the director of Founders Ministries. Here is the description of the organization from the "About" page on their website.

> Founders Ministries is a ministry of teaching and encouragement promoting both doctrine and devotion expressed in the Doctrines of Grace and their experiential application to the local church, particularly in the areas of worship and witness. Founders Ministries takes as its theological framework the first recognized confession of faith that Southern Baptists produced, *The Abstract of Principles*.[151] We desire to encourage the return to and promulgation of the biblical gospel that our Southern Baptist forefathers held dear.[152]

On that same page, here is their statement of purpose:

> The purpose of Founders Ministries is the recovery of the gospel of the Lord Jesus Christ in the reformation of local churches. We believe intrinsic to this recovery is the promotion of the Doctrines of Grace in their experiential application to the local church particularly in the areas of worship and witness. This is to be accomplished through a variety of means focusing on conferences and including publication, education, pastoral training and other opportunities

151 As we have seen, the *Abstract* only affirms three of the five points of Calvinism.

152 Founders, "About Us," accessed February 15, 2016, http://founders.org/about/.

consistent with the purpose. Each of the ministries will be developed with special attention to achieve a healthy integration of doctrine and devotion.[153]

Founders Ministries is committed to a strict five-point Calvinistic understanding of the gospel.

In direct response to the publication of *Whosoever Will: A Biblical-Theological Critique of Five-Point Calvinism* in 2010, Ascol published a book entitled *Whomever He Wills* in 2012, edited by Matthew Barrett and Tom Nettles.

Ascol penned a chapter in *Whomever He Wills* entitled "Calvinism Foundational for Evangelism and Missions."[154] In this chapter, he critiqued sections of my chapter on limited atonement in *Whosoever Will.* I have reviewed and critiqued this chapter as well in a post on September 12, 2012, which can be found on my blog site.[155]

At the center of my concerns with Founders Ministries is the distortion of the Baptist historical record with respect to Calvinism, especially on the question of how many early Southern Baptists actually affirmed limited atonement. A further concern is the failure of those in the Founders movement to strongly promote the biblical concepts of God's universal saving will and God's universal love.

With respect to the biblical concepts of God's universal saving will, universal saving love, and Christ's death for all people, Ascol's opposition to preachers indiscriminately telling everyone that "Christ died for you" seems the same as being against telling them that God is both willing and prepared to save them all. The use of the phrase "Christ died for sinners" (which for the high Calvinist means "Christ died only for elect sinners") as opposed to the use of the phrase "Christ died for you" leaves the impression with all sinners that Christ died for them. This is at the very least confusing and at worst disingenuous.

In fact, to oppose conveying to any and all sinners that God is both willing and prepared to save them is implicit hyper-Calvinism at the practical level. Note my use of the words *implicit* and *at the practical level.* Saying "Christ died for you" is equivalent to saying that God is willing, able, and prepared to save all and will do so if they come to Christ through repentance and faith because all the sins of all people have been imputed to Christ. Refusal to tell any sinner, "Christ died for your sins," implicitly questions God's saving will and saving love for that individual. I believe such a posture entails problems for evangelism, missions, and preaching.

Therefore, in light of the biblical and historical picture, it does not appear Ascol's conclusion that Calvinism has been a catalyst for missions and evangelism can be sustained without qualifications and/or modifications. One might just as easily say that

153 Ibid.

154 T. Ascol, "Calvinism Foundational for Evangelism and Missions," in *Whomever He Wills*, 269–89.

155 The multipart review of Ascol's chapter, published September 18, 2012, can be accessed in the "Resources" section of my website http://www.drdavidlallen.com.

the non-Calvinist doctrines the Moravians held in the eighteenth century had been a catalyst for missions and evangelism or the doctrines the Wesleyan Methodists held in the eighteenth and nineteenth centuries were a catalyst for missions and evangelism or the doctrines the Wycliffe Bible Translators held and hold (many of whom were and are non-Calvinists) in the twentieth century were a catalyst for missions and evangelism or that the essentially non-Calvinistic doctrines most Southern Baptists held in the twentieth century and continue to hold today and produced one of the greatest missionary forces on the planet were a catalyst for missions and evangelism.

One final point is worth noting concerning Ascol's historiography. Concerning the Synod of Dort, he wrote: "The Synod of Dort represents a watershed in the development of the orthodox Reformed view of the atonement. The second chapter, or canon, from that assembly's published confession clearly rejects *any understanding which* views Christ's death as indefinite, universal, or general in nature."[156] As noted above in the discussion of the Canons of Dort, this is simply historically inaccurate, as numerous Reformed historians have pointed out.

Daniel Akin (b. AD 1957)

Akin is the president of Southeastern Baptist Theological Seminary in Wake Forest, North Carolina. Akin leans Calvinistic in his theology but affirms unlimited atonement. In a 9Marks audio interview, in response to a question about the issue of the extent of the atonement by Mark Dever, Akin responded that he believes there is a double intention in the atonement: it provided for the sins of the world, but it actually secures the salvation of the elect.[157]

Ken Keathley (b. AD 1958)

Keathley is professor of theology at Southeastern Baptist Theological Seminary in Wake Forest, North Carolina. His 2010 *Salvation and Sovereignty: A Molinist Approach* contains a critique of limited atonement.[158]

Keathley summarized three views on the extent of the atonement: (1) general atonement, (2) limited atonement, and (3) unlimited atonement (singular redemption in Keathley's words).[159] It is difficult to distinguish the first and third view, as both affirm an unlimited atonement. Keathley linked the first view with the governmental theory of the atonement and the second and third views with the penal substitutionary

156 T. Ascol, "The Doctrine of Grace: A Critical Analysis of Federalism in the Theologies of John Gill and Andrew Fuller" (PhD diss., Southwestern Baptist Theological Seminary, 1989), 215 (emphasis mine).

157 Danny Akin, "Life and Ministry in the Southern Baptist Convention," *9Marks* (blog), October 29, 2010, http://9marks.org/interview/life-and-ministry-southern-baptist-convention/. The relevant segment begins at the forty-nine-minute mark.

158 K. Keathley, *Salvation and Sovereignty: A Molinist Approach* (Nashville: B&H Academic, 2010), 191–210.

159 Ibid., 194. Keathley noted a number of Arminians, such as Robert Picirilli and Matthew Pinson, have also adhered to the singular redemption view rather than the general atonement view.

theory of the atonement. But historically, early governmentalists like Grotius, and later John Wesley, clearly adhered to the penal substitutionary view as well, though many later governmentalists did not.

Keathley quoted Wesleyan theologian J. Kenneth Grider as stating that the view that Christ paid the penalty for sins "is foreign to Arminianism, which teaches instead that Christ suffered for us." Grider then succumbs to the double payment argument by assuming that if Christ paid for the sins of all people, then no one could be eternally damned. "Arminianism teaches that Christ suffered for everyone so that the Father could forgive those who repent and believe."[160]

Thus, according to Arminianism and the governmental view of the atonement, Christ died for *us*, not for our *sins*. Keathley rightly rejected this construct, but it is important to point out that not all Arminians, past or present, affirm the governmental view of the atonement at the expense of the penal substitutionary view. This has been demonstrated by Roger Olson in his *Arminian Theology*, who demonstrated that Arminius, Wesley, and many other Arminians affirmed penal substitution.[161]

Keathley defined the "singular redemption" view of the extent of the atonement in the words of Robert Lightner: "Christ died to make possible the salvation of all men, but to make certain the salvation of those who believe."[162]

After summarizing the standard arguments for limited atonement, Keathley offered five arguments in favor of "singular redemption," mostly drawing from Calvin and Robert Lightner. Keathley's second point should not be missed. It is much easier to reconcile the verses that seem to teach a limited atonement with those that teach an unlimited atonement than vice versa.[163]

Ray Clendenen (b. AD 1949) and Brad Waggoner (b. AD 1957)

Southeastern Baptist Theological Seminary, Founders Ministries, and LifeWay cohosted a conference on Calvinism in 2006. The conference brought together Calvinists and non-Calvinists to present papers on key issues of Calvinism and its role in the Southern Baptist Convention. The conference papers were published two years later as *Calvinism: A Southern Baptist Dialogue*, edited by Clendenen and Waggoner.[164]

The relevant two chapters dealing with the extent of the atonement were authored by David Nelson, who argued the case for unlimited atonement, and Sam Waldron,

---

160 Ibid., 194. See J. K. Grider, "Arminianism," in *Evangelical Dictionary of Theology*, 2nd ed. (Grand Rapids, MI: Baker, 2001), 97–98.

161 Olson, *Arminian Theology*, 221–41.

162 Keathley, *Salvation and Sovereignty*, 197.

163 Ibid., 205.

164 B. Waggoner and R. Clendenen, *Calvinism: A Southern Baptist Dialogue* (Nashville: B&H Academic, 2008). I wrote an extensive chapter-by-chapter review of this book: D. L. Allen, *Calvinism: A Review* (New Orleans: Center for Theological Research, 2008, http://www.baptisttheology.org/baptisttheology/assets/File/CalvinismaReview.pdf).

who argued the case for limited atonement. At the time, Nelson was a professor at Southeastern Seminary and Waldron was academic dean and professor of theology at Midwest Center for Theological Studies.

Nelson's chapter divides into three major sections, covering the design, nature, and extent of the atonement, with the bulk comprising the latter. With respect to design, 2 Cor 5:19 furnishes us with perhaps the best statement: "In Christ God was reconciling the world to himself." With respect to nature, Nelson rightly concludes the foundational metaphor, albeit not the only metaphor, for the atonement is penal substitution. With respect to extent, Nelson develops the subject under three headings: historical, exegetical, and theological.

One key significance of this chapter is Nelson's proof that limited atonement was not the position of the church before the Reformation. Following the work of Michael Thomas, he also shows that Dort was deliberately ambiguous in its language concerning the extent of the atonement. In fact, John Davenant, a signer of Dort, was one of many signers who rejected limited atonement and held to a form of universal atonement.

Furthermore, Nelson points out how many of the confessional statements of the seventeenth through the nineteenth centuries showed variety on the subject of the extent of the atonement, with some clearly affirming universal atonement. Nelson did make one common mistake with reference to the Westminster Confession when he said it "explicitly affirms" limited atonement.[165] In fact, although the majority of the Westminster Divines held to limited atonement, and the quotation Nelson makes can certainly be read in that way, the authors deliberately chose to use ambiguous language that would permit those who held to an unlimited atonement, such as Edmund Calamy, Henry Scudder and John Arrowsmith, among others, to sign.[166]

Exegetically, Nelson appeals to the standard verses that affirm unlimited atonement: John 3:16–18; 1 Tim 2:1–6; 2 Corinthians 5; Heb 2:9, 14–18; 2 Pet 2:1; 3:9; and 1 John 2:2. He correctly stated "In John 1 and 12 *kosmos* is used in the sense of both the earth and all the inhabitants of the earth, indicating that in the incarnation Jesus came to earth for the sake of saving all who would believe in Him."[167] Calvinistic attempts to make *kosmos* refer to something other than "all people" or "universe" "are strained and unnecessary."[168]

Theologically, Nelson makes several observations, affirmations, and denials. However one defines predestination and election, one's view of the atonement should not be controlled by a speculative order of the divine decrees. Nelson himself affirms unconditional

165 D. Nelson, "The Design, Nature, and Extent of the Atonement," in *Calvinism: A Southern Baptist Dialogue*, 126.

166 One may consult R. Muller's *Post-Reformation Reformed Dogmatics*, 4 vols. (Grand Rapids, MI: Baker, 2003), 1:76–80, to confirm this point.

167 Nelson, "Design, Nature, and Extent," 127–28.

168 Ibid., 128.

election but rejects double predestination, supralapsarianism, and eternal justification. He asks two pertinent questions of those who hold to limited atonement: (1) Do you hold to limited atonement primarily because of your view of the elective decrees? If so, one is prejudicing logic over exegesis. (2) Is the *will* of God or the *love* of God determinative for your view of limited atonement? If the former, what of the latter?

Nelson's view of the instrumentality of faith is that it has no meritorious value. He addresses two key limited atonement arguments: payment for unbelief and the double payment. "*If Christ died for sins, and unbelief is a sin, then must not all sin be atoned for?*" This objection makes a false assumption: the atonement works apart from faith. "*If Christ died for the sins of all people, as the general atonement doctrine holds, then are there not two payments offered for the sins of those in hell, the payment offered by Christ on their behalf and the payment of each condemned person himself in eternal death?*"[169] Although Nelson's answer to this double payment objection is correct (no one receives the saving benefits of the cross apart from faith, and according to John 3:18, unbelievers are condemned by their rejection of Jesus), it is insufficient because the argument above confuses pecuniary payments with penal justice, as before mentioned, and it fails to note also that the objection anachronistically imports categories of Western jurisprudence that are foreign to the New Testament. Furthermore, both payment for unbelief and double payment arguments are adequately rebutted by Calvinists themselves who accept an unlimited atonement (in the sense of unlimited expiation of the sins of mankind), as I have noted above.

One of the very few concerns I have with Nelson's chapter comes near the end when, after mentioning how limited atonement may "minimize or extinguish the free offer of the gospel," he then stated "the unlimited view of the atonement may promote a cheap offer of the gospel that may undermine the gospel altogether."[170] Obviously, the former statement is true. But it is not at all obvious that the latter statement is true. Nelson said this may result from

> homiletical silliness or it may be a deduction from general atonement to the belief that we may dispense with the doctrines of election and effectual calling, thus producing "inhumane" presentations of the gospel. By this I mean that our offers of the gospel sometimes seem to imply that God has nothing to do with salvation. By both our methods and our rhetoric, this seems apparent to me.[171]

Some of those who hold to unlimited atonement are guilty of their fair share of homiletical silliness, gimmicks, and rhetorical tricks. But are such cheap offers of the

169 Ibid., 134 (emphasis in original).
170 Ibid., 136–37.
171 Ibid.

gospel a corollary of unlimited atonement, or rather are they not the result of a *faulty deduction*? In other words, limited atonement *logically* leads to a minimization of the free offer of the gospel, for by definition, there is no satisfaction for sins in the atonement for the non-elect. This is a problem endemic to the doctrine itself, which can only be overcome by offering the gospel to everyone, *in spite of the fact that* there is actually no satisfaction available for all in Christ's death. There is no faulty deduction involved, only correct deduction given the doctrine.

On the other hand, there is satisfaction for sins in the atonement for *all people* in the unlimited view. Homiletical silliness, gimmicks or rhetorical tricks cannot *logically* be deduced from unlimited atonement. Such antics may be practiced sometimes by those who hold unlimited atonement but not as a logical corollary of the doctrine itself. Nelson made a telling statement when he said he admits he cannot say "either view of the atonement *causes* these aberrations." He should rather say something along these lines: "Limited atonement logically causes a problem for the free offer of the gospel. Unlimited atonement does not *cause* cheap offers of the gospel."[172]

In conclusion, Nelson's chapter is well written, cogently argued, and one of the best in the book.

Sam Waldron argues the case for limited atonement. This is the shortest chapter in the book, and I found it to be clear, concise, and to the point. However, problems surface immediately.

After clarifying what the question is not (it is not for whose benefit did Jesus die, is the atonement limited, or is the atonement sufficient to expiate the sins of the world), he concludes that the real question is, "In whose place did Christ substitute himself?" Waldron's comment that the question is not "is the atonement sufficient to expiate the sins of the world" is simply wrong. The question is very much about the sufficiency of the atonement. Strict particularists like Waldron limit that sufficiency to a mere intrinsic sufficiency that actually means the death of Christ *could have atoned for the sins of the world had God intended such, but he did not intend such; rather God intended the atonement only for the elect.*[173] To the non-elect this is no sufficiency at all. It is offering them forgiveness without an existing satisfaction for their sins.

We must distinguish between *intrinsic sufficiency*, which is the view of those who hold to strict limited atonement such as Waldron, and *extrinsic sufficiency*, which is the view of all four-point Calvinists, Arminians, and non-Calvinistic Baptists. He then seeks to answer the question "In whose place did Christ substitute himself?" under two headings: the proofs of particular redemption and the problems of particular redemption. Under these two, Waldron covers the main arguments in favor of limited

172 Ibid., 137.

173 S. Waldron, "The Biblical Confirmation of Particular Redemption," in *Calvinism: A Southern Baptist Dialogue*, 139–40.

atonement (particular redemption). A cursory look at his eleven footnotes indicates his dependence upon John Owen's *The Death of Death in the Death of Christ* and John Murray's *Redemption Accomplished and Applied.*

Waldron treats four issues under his first heading: (1) the substitutionary nature of the atonement, (2) the restricted recipients of the atonement, (3) the guaranteed effects of the atonement, and (4) the covenant context of the atonement. Waldron contends that "the nature of the atonement as substitutionary curse-bearing demands particular redemption."[174]

Following John Owen, Waldron presses the "double payment" argument against universal atonement. (This argument has already been presented and answered above.) He comments: "Vast support can be marshaled for the idea that the nature of the atonement requires that all those for whom Christ died are actually and ultimately saved."[175] The use of the phrase "vast support" is somewhat exaggerated given the over-all evidence. Those who hold to universal atonement can only do so "by muffling or receding" from the idea of penal substitution, according to Waldron. This is a common Calvinist gaffe that one often reads in the popular literature. It fails to recognize that many Arminians have been staunch defenders of penal substitution. Off the cuff one thinks of John Wesley.[176] Waldron's statement betrays a limited historical awareness and understanding of his own Calvinistic camp, since a host of Calvinists—including Calvin himself—have affirmed unlimited atonement and penal substitution.[177]

As further evidence for limited atonement, Waldron appeals to Rev 5:9–10, which says Christ has purchased with his own blood for God *men* from every tribe, tongue, people, and nation. Waldron confuses the extent of the atonement with the application of the atonement. Clearly the application is limited only to the elect who believe, which is the point of Rev 5:9–10. Even Bullinger, a leading sixteenth-century Calvinist, said in a sermon on Rev 5:9–10, this "signifies an universality, for the Lord has died for all: but that all are not made partakers of this redemption, it is through their own fault."[178]

Second Corinthians 5:14 asserts, according to Waldron, that substitutionary death means representative death; only those are saved for whom Christ suffered, thus he suffered only for the elect. But what does Paul mean by what he said in 2 Cor 5:14? Waldron, like John Murray,[179] appeals to 2 Cor 5:14–15 to sustain his case that Christ only died for all of the elect. He takes the pronoun "all" as "designating all those in

174 Ibid., 140.

175 Ibid., 141.

176 See Olson, *Arminian Theology.*

177 In addition to my discussion above under Calvin, See Daniel, "Hyper-Calvinism and John Gill"; and K. Kennedy, *Union with Christ and the Extent of the Atonement in Calvin*, Studies in Biblical Literature 48 (New York and Bern: Peter Lang, 2002).

178 H. Bullinger, *A Hundred Sermons upon the Apocalypse of Jesus Christ* (London: John Daye, 1573), 79–80.

179 Murray, *Redemption Accomplished and Applied*, 69–72.

Christ who are a part of a new creation (v. 18)."[180] When Paul speaks of "us," he is referring to those who have died and have been raised with Christ through faith. However, when Paul uses "all" three times in 2 Cor 5:14–15, there are three possible interpretations, only one of which supports limited atonement. Waldron takes the three instances of "all" to mean "believers" and the "them" to mean "believers." The second view takes the "all" to mean "all humanity" in all three occurrences.

Think of the verses paraphrased in this way: "Jesus, the one, died for all humanity, therefore all humanity died. He died for all humanity, so that they [the believing elect] that live shall no longer live unto themselves." "All" indicates universal atonement; "they that live" indicates the application of the atonement to the elect. A third approach takes Paul's words to form a parallel ABAB structure. In this case, the passage would be paraphrased thus: "Jesus, the one, died for all humanity, therefore all believers in Christ died spiritually with him. He died for all humanity, so that all believers who live in Christ spiritually should not live unto themselves."[181] Furthermore, the use of "world" in verse 19 does not and cannot mean "the elect" but the world of unbelieving humanity. While one can say Waldron's interpretation is a reasonable option, there are other options just as reasonable that would lead to a different conclusion. Furthermore, even granting his view of the passage, he cannot prove his own case, as limited atonement still cannot be logically deduced from the fact that Christ died for believers.

Waldron then argued that there is "an inseparable relation between the idea of substitution and the idea of representation" and associates this notion with 2 Cor 5:14b: "One died for all, then all died." He uses this association to prove the proposition that "if Christ died for someone, that person died on the cross." However, the reader should note the shift in the argument that occurs at this point. It is one thing to argue that 2 Cor 5:14–15 says that *believers* have died in Christ, and quite another thing to argue that *all* those for whom Christ died have also died in him. Contrary to Waldron, Paul is explicitly uttering the first proposition, and *not* the second. *On Waldron's own interpretation*, all he can establish from 2 Cor 5:14–15 (as well as from his citation of Rom 6:4–8) is that if Christ died for you *and you are believing*, then you have died and live in Christ. The "dying" and "living" ideas correspond to the "all things passing away" and the "all things becoming new." It is believers alone who have experienced this death, burial, and resurrection, and not *all those for whom Christ has died*. I don't think Waldron (or Murray) would want to say that *all* those for whom Christ died *are* new creatures. If so, then on their own presuppositions, *all the elect* would be new creatures *at the time of* Christ's death. This is the false doctrine of justification at the cross or, pushed further back according to decretal speculation, eternal justification. Waldron, as is frequent among five-point Calvinists and hyper-Calvinists, blurs the distinction

180 Waldron, "Biblical Confirmation of Particular Redemption," 143.

181 Ibid.

between *decretal* union and *real* (*vital*) union with Christ. Paul, in 2 Corinthians 5 and Romans 6, is saying that *believers* in *real* union with Christ have died in him and live unto him. These two things can be predicated of all in *real* or *vital* union with Christ. Participation in Christ's death and resurrected life cannot either be predicated of all humanity or of those in *decretal* union with Christ (all the elect *as such*).

The many passages that speak of Christ dying for his "sheep," "friends," "the church," and so on do not prove limited atonement as Waldron supposes. Even Robert Reymond, a supralapsarian hyper-Calvinist (all supralapsarians are not hyper-Calvinists), admitted:

> It is true, of course, that logically a statement of particularity in itself does not necessarily preclude universality. This may be shown by the principle of subalternation in Aristotelian logic, which states that if all S is P, then it may be inferred that some S is P, but conversely, it cannot be inferred from the fact that some S is P that the remainder of S is not P. A case in point is the "me" of Galatians 2:20: the fact that Christ died for Paul individually does not mean that Christ died only for Paul and for no one else.[182]

Consequently, that many verses speak of Christ dying for his "sheep," his "church" or "his friends" does not prove that he did not die for others not subsumed in these categories.

Dabney, a Calvinist respected by all, likewise noted that statements such as Christ died for "the church" or "his sheep" do not prove a strictly limited atonement, because to argue such invokes the negative inference fallacy: "The proof of a proposition does

---

182 R. L. Reymond, *A New Systematic Theology*, 2nd ed. (Nashville: Thomas Nelson, 1998), 673–74. "Hypers usually reject the idea of offers that are free, serious, sincere, or well-meant" (C. Daniel, *The History and Theology of Calvinism*, 89).

> 'Free offer' was the debated term in mainstream [or classic] Hyper-Calvinism, but 'well-meant offer' has been the debated phrase within the Hoeksema school. In essence, however, they are one and the same. The first simply brings out the aspect that God wishes to give something without cost, while the second points to God's willingness that it be accepted (C. Daniel, *Hyper-Calvinism and John Gill*, 410).

Since Reymond, like Gordon H. Clark (*Biblical Predestination* [Nutley, NJ: Presbyterian and Reformed Publishing, 1974], 130), explicitly rejected the well-meant offer or God's desire for the salvation of the non-elect in the free offer (*A New Systematic Theology*, 692–93), he is described here and in the chart below as a hyper-Calvinist, albeit a mild one. He was not as extreme as John Gill in other matters, or as extreme as Hoeksema and Engelsma. Unlike Hoeksema and Engelsma (but like Gill), Reymond affirmed God's general love and common grace. See R. L. Reymond, *'What is God?' An Investigation of the Perfections of God's Nature* (Fearn, Ross-shire, UK: Mentor, 2007), 100, 239. In this 2007 work, he is also critical of his earlier treatment of God's love in *A New Systematic Theology*, and thought the "Reformed tradition's pronouncements have been guilty of 'heresy by disproportion' when they subsume God's patient longsuffering and his redeeming love under his 'goodness' and fail to mention them in their definitions of God" (ibid., 244). He agreed with Donald MacLeod in thinking that "Reformed statements are guilty of shortchanging God's love in their definitions and descriptions of him" (ibid.). However, even with these concessions, the same question Iain Murray asked of David Silversides pertains to Reymond as well: ". . . but can the divine love, that the author wants to uphold, be without desire for the highest good of those [non-elect who are] loved?" ("Book Reviews," *Banner of Truth* 507 [December 2005]: 22).

not disprove its converse."[183] One cannot infer a negative (Christ did not die for group A) from a bare positive statement (Christ did die for group B), any more than one can infer that Christ *only* died for Paul because Gal 2:20 says that Christ died for Paul. This is the same kind of logical mistake that John Owen makes numerous times in his *The Death of Death in the Death of Christ*, and it is a logical fallacy constantly made by high Calvinists with regard to the extent of the atonement.

Waldron proceeded to argue that the guaranteed effects and the covenant context of the atonement demand particular redemption. The guaranteed effects of the atonement demand the application of the atonement to all the elect; they do not negate the fact that atonement was made for all men. The covenant context likewise does not do for Waldron what he wants it to do. God has placed a condition on his covenant: men must repent and believe the gospel in order to be saved.

Waldron's second section addresses three of the major problems with limited atonement: the biblical passages employing universal terminology with respect to the atonement, the free offer of the gospel, and the apostasy passages. I shall address only the free offer of the gospel. Waldron makes the typical high Calvinist comment: "The free offer of the gospel does not require us to tell men that Christ died for them."[184] He further stated: "This way of preaching is utterly without biblical precedent." Finally, he said: "If the free offer of the gospel meant telling unconverted sinners, 'Christ died for you,' then particular redemption would be inconsistent with the free offer. But nowhere in the Bible is the gospel proclaimed by telling unconverted sinners that Christ died for them."[185]

Such bold assertions are squarely contradicted in numerous places in the New Testament. They are contradicted by Paul's statement of the gospel in 1 Cor 15:3: "For I delivered to you first of all that which I also received: that Christ died for our sins" (NKJV). Paul is telling the Corinthians what he preached to them *before they were saved.* He preached to them, "Christ died for their sins." Waldron's statement is contradicted by Acts 3:26, which states: "To you first, God, having raised up His Servant Jesus, sent Him to bless you, in turning away every one of you from your iniquities" (NKJV). Peter is telling his unbelieving audience that God sent Jesus to bless *each* and *every* one of them and to turn *every one of them* from their iniquities. *This is equivalent to Peter saying: Christ died for you.* How could Jesus save every one of them (which is what blessing and turning away from iniquity involves) if he did not *actually* die for the sins of all of them? Certainly "each one" of the Jews Peter addressed must have included some who were non-elect.

As if this were not enough, what will Waldron do with Luke 22:20, 21? "Likewise He also took the cup after supper, saying, 'This cup is the new covenant in My blood, which is shed for you. But behold, the hand of My betrayer is with Me on the table'" (NKJV). Here Jesus clearly states his blood was shed for Judas, and yet Judas was not

183 Dabney, *Systematic Theology*, 521.

184 Waldron, "Biblical Confirmation of Particular Redemption," 149.

185 Ibid.

among the elect. It will not do to attempt to argue Judas was not at the table at this time as the text clearly states that he was. Calvin himself in numerous places explicitly says Judas was at the table.[186] If Jesus died for Judas, then his death was not restricted to the elect alone, for Judas was not elect.

Waldron's attempt to prove limited atonement falters historically, biblically, and theologically.

David Allen (b. AD 1957) and Steve Lemke (b. AD 1951)

I served as the dean of the School of Theology at Southwestern Baptist Theological Seminary (SWBTS) in Fort Worth, Texas, for twelve years, and currently serve as the dean of the School of Preaching at SWBTS. Lemke is the vice president and provost of New Orleans Baptist Theological Seminary. We coedited *Whosoever Will: A Biblical-Theological Critique of Five-point Calvinism*, which appeared in 2010.[187] This book grew out of the John 3:16 Conference held in 2008 at First Baptist Church, Woodstock, Georgia. The conference was jointly sponsored by Jerry Vines Ministries, Southwestern Baptist Theological Seminary, and New Orleans Baptist Theological Seminary. The purpose of the conference was to present papers on soteriology that offered a critique of traditional five-point Calvinism. The papers at the conference, along with others that were written at the request of the editors, were compiled and published in 2010.

I authored the chapter on limited atonement, addressing issues of definition, history, exegesis, theology, logic, and practical implications. This present work is an expansion of that chapter.

In a review of the book, Greg Wills of Southern Seminary stated the following concerning my argument in "The Atonement: Limited or Universal?" that Calvinists Charles Hodge and Robert Dabney both affirmed a universal atonement:

> Allen is right that most Calvinist preachers have held that Christ died for all persons in some sense. Calvin believed this. So did Edwards and Hodge and Boyce and Dabney. His death for all was such that any person, even Judas, if he should repent and believe the gospel, would not be rejected but would receive mercy. Most Calvinists have held that Jesus' sacrificial death was universal in that it made all men salvable, contingent on their repentance and faith in Christ. But Allen is incorrect to argue that such a position is not limited atonement, for these same theologians affirmed that the atonement was in important respects particular to the elect.[188]

186 See J. Calvin, *Tracts and Treatises*, 2:93, 234, 297, 370–71, 378; and also his commentary on Matt 26:21 and John 6:56. Augustine also believed Judas was at the table.

187 D. L. Allen and Steve Lemke, eds., *Whosoever Will: A Biblical-Theological Critique of Five-Point Calvinism* (Nashville: B&H Academic, 2010).

188 Greg Wills, "*Whosoever Will*: A Review Essay," *Journal for Baptist Theology and Ministry* 7.1 (Spring 2010), 16.

Wills continued:

> Charles Hodge and Robert Dabney argued that Owen's argument against double punishment was invalid to establish the truth of particular redemption, and they argued for universal aspects of the atonement. Both however taught that particular redemption was scriptural. Dabney appealed to the Bible's teaching on unconditional election as one of several "irrefragable grounds on which we prove that the redemption is particular." He held that certain aspects of the atonement were general, satisfaction and expiation, for example, but that others were particular, redemption and reconciliation. "Christ died for all sinners in some sense," Dabney summarized, but "Christ's redeeming work was limited in intention to the elect."[189]

Notice how Wills defined Christ's death: any person could be saved if he should repent and believe. But Wills does not mention how this can actually be the case on the limitarian scheme. No one disputes the fact that anyone who repents and believes the gospel can be saved. That is not the point at issue.

Wills does not seem to realize he has conceded the point for which I am arguing concerning Hodge and Dabney. Notice his definition of what it means to say that Calvinists have held that Christ died for all persons "in some sense." Wills stated that Christ's death "for all was such that any person, even Judas," is "saveable" should he repent and believe the gospel. That is exactly what I have argued. Christ's death is universal in that it actually satisfied for the sins of "all" (notice Wills's use of "all") should they repent and believe, including the likes of Judas, who was clearly among the non-elect. This is precisely the position of moderate Calvinists and all non-Calvinists with respect to the extent of the atonement.

Wills has contradicted his own position here. It is inconsistent to say that Judas is "saveable" if it is the case that Jesus only died for the sins of the elect. Those who hold to limited atonement do not believe that Christ's death paid for the sins of the non-elect. There is no remedy for the sins of Judas in the death of Jesus. Wills's statement is false, given a limited atonement: should Judas repent and believe he could in fact not be saved; he is not "saveable" because Christ did not die for his sins.

Whosoever Will also contains a chapter by Kevin Kennedy on Calvin's view of the extent of the atonement.[190] Kennedy cogently argued that the evidence from Calvin's own writings indicates he held to an unlimited atonement.[191]

---

189 Ibid., 17.

190 K. Kennedy, "Was Calvin a Calvinist? John Calvin on the Extent of the Atonement," in *Whosoever Will*, 191–212. This chapter is something of a summary of Kennedy's 1999 doctoral dissertation, which was later published as *Union with Christ and the Extent of the Atonement in Calvin.*

191 See above under the section on Calvin, where I reference and utilize Kennedy's work.

The *Journal of Baptist Theology and Ministry* is published by New Orleans Baptist Theological Seminary. The spring 2010 issue was devoted to the subject "Baptists and the Doctrine of Salvation." Section one contains three book review essays of *Whosoever Will*. Section two contains three review essays of Ken Keathley's *Salvation and Sovereignty*. In each section, a review from a Calvinistic perspective is included.[192]

Albert Mohler (b. AD 1959)

Mohler is president of Southern Baptist Theological Seminary, co-founder of Together for the Gospel, and one of the leading and influential spokesmen for Calvinism within the Southern Baptist Convention and the evangelical world at large. Mohler affirms limited atonement as can be gleaned from his published works where he speaks on the atonement's extent and his 2006 debate with Paige Patterson at the annual meeting of the Southern Baptist Convention. He also tacitly affirmed his commitment to limited atonement in a video shot in the setting of his own office and personal library. Holding up a volume from his library, he stated:

> One particular book here is of importance for me, and I think of it when I think of Together for the Gospel. This beautiful little volume is the first printing of John Owen's *Death of Death in the Death of Christ*. And this was sent to me from England by my dear friend Mark Dever as a gift upon my election as president of Southern Seminary, now almost 17 years ago.[193]

On Saturday, May 3, 2014, Mohler hosted his radio program "Ask Anything: Weekend Edition." A caller asked a question about the extent of the atonement, referencing John 3:16; 1 Cor 15:22; and 1 John 2:2. The caller stated if Jesus truly died for all the sins of mankind, and if even one ends up in hell, then that would make a mockery of the sufficiency of Christ's atoning blood.[194] There are several problems with the statement of the caller. He understands the atonement in commercial categories and thinks that if Christ died for an individual's sins, then the individual's sins must be forgiven. Implicit in the caller's statement is the notion that universal atonement entails universal salvation. Second, the caller does not understand the nature of the sufficiency of the atonement by failing to distinguish between intrinsic and extrinsic sufficiency. Third, the caller is conflating the extent of the atonement with its application, assuming the two are coextensive.

---

192 *Journal of Baptist Theology and Missions* 7 (Spring 2010).

193 A. Mohler, "Al Mohler: A Study Tour," *Together for the Gospel Online*, January 12, 2010, http://vimeo.com/groups/27420/videos/8693850.

194 A. Mohler, "Ask Anything: Weekend Edition," *AlbertMohler.com* (blog), May 3, 2014, http://www.albertmohler.com/2014/05/03/ask-anything-weekend-edition-05–03–14/. The caller's question begins at about the 9:53-minute mark, followed by Mohler's response.

In his response, Mohler did not disabuse his caller of these false notions. In fact, by his response, it would seem Mohler agreed with his caller's take on the issue. Mohler appealed to the different uses of "all" and "world" in atonement texts and asserted that no matter what view one takes, he must interpret these words differently in different contexts. He then made a statement along these lines: If Christ's saving work is applied to the world and all within it on the same basis, then all are saved, which is clearly not consistent with Scripture. But Mohler's analysis is flawed. His remark sidesteps the issue of the extent of the atonement completely. Notice Mohler is talking about the *application* of the atonement. The question on the table is the extent of the atonement. He has confused and conflated these two issues.

Finally, Mohler stated his own position: Christ died for those he has redeemed. He affirms limited atonement.[195]

Mark Dever (b. AD 1960)

Dever is the pastor of Capitol Hill Baptist in Washington, D.C. He is founder of *9Marks Ministries* and one of the co-founders of Together for the Gospel. In an article entitled "Which Confession?" Dever explained his views on the New Hampshire Confession of Faith, noting that it does not formally assert definite atonement.[196] He stated: "True, there was no necessity to affirm definite atonement in the document, but the New Hampshire drafters had cleverly muted that disagreement by using the first person plural approach, making statements about 'we' and 'us.'"[197] He continued:

> There was nothing in this I disagreed with. Christ did make a full atonement for our sins. Now I knew that some would be affirming this, thinking Christ also made a full atonement for the sins of the non-elect, but they also believed this. I have never thought that affirming definite atonement is necessary for salvation. Though I think it is biblical, I think I understand how many friends on this very point may believe in substitution as fully as I do, affirm that Christ's death is the only way to salvation, and yet think that in some way there is a secondary, non-salvific effectiveness latent in Christ's death, even worked by it, that is for all people. I am not persuaded that this opinion is correct. I will not have that opinion preached from our pulpit. We will not have an elder who wants to make a point of this. But I have come to think that our congregation is both richer and more useful by not requiring agreement on this point at the time of entering our congregation. And the New Hampshire Confession

195 Though it should be noted that Mohler's statement is true insofar as it goes: Christ did die for all he redeems. He also died for those who are not redeemed. Incidentally, Mohler is the only one of the six Southern Baptist seminary presidents who affirms limited atonement.

196 M. Dever, "Which Confession?," *The Founders Journal* 61 (Summer 2005), 6.

197 Ibid.

> gives us the freedom to have a wider evangelical membership, who then are led and taught by those who, like myself, have a more clearly and consistently biblical understanding of the atonement.[198]

Dever authored *The Gospel and Personal Evangelism*. He suggested three motives for evangelism: obedience to Scripture, love for the lost, and a love for God.[199] I agree completely. But Dever failed to mention two other critical motives affirmed in Scripture: (1) Christ's death for all men and (2) God's universal saving will. Of course, Dever cannot affirm Christ's death for the sins of all men because he holds to limited atonement. I assume he would agree with God's universal saving will, though he nowhere explicitly stated it in his book as far as I can tell (or in any of his other writings).

In a 2010 *9Marks* radio interview with Daniel Akin, president of Southeastern Baptist Theological Seminary in Wake Forest, North Carolina, Dever asked Akin about the extent of the atonement. In the process, Dever made this statement: "The hypothetical relation of the death of Christ to the non-elect is not part of the gospel. . . . The gospel is like [what] Paul could say 'He died for me.'"[200] This response is problematic. As a high Calvinist, Dever's response presumes limited atonement is true and thus Christ did in fact die only for specific people, the elect. Furthermore, it appears he is equating this belief with the gospel. What he means by "hypothetical" is unclear. If he is referring to Hypothetical Universalists, then they would respond that there is nothing "hypothetical" about the death of Christ for the non-elect. Christ did, in fact, die for the sins of all, including the non-elect. Finally, Paul states in 1 Cor 15:3 that his habit of preaching the gospel to the unsaved included the proposition "Christ died for our sins," which affirms unlimited atonement.

In a Twitter post on April 10, 2014, Kevin DeYoung (@RevKevDeYoung) reported Dever as saying, "We have no good news for unrepentant sinners. We only have good news for repentant sinners."[201] This statement reflects confusion between the gospel as objectively considered and our subjective response to it. The gospel remains objectively good news no matter our response to it, even as the gospel is an offer no matter our response when we hear it. The gospel will not benefit anyone eternally unless one appropriately responds to its offer of eternal life.

On a Q&A panel at T4G14, DeYoung referenced Dever's quote on the good news and said, "Of course we have the offer of good news." But again, this collapses the good news itself with the reception of the good news. The gospel is objectively good news to the entire world whether people subjectively receive what is offered in it or not.

---

198 Ibid., 6–7.

199 M. Dever, *The Gospel and Personal Evangelism* (Wheaton, IL: Crossway, 2007), 96.

200 Akin, "Life and Ministry." The relevant segment begins at about the fifty-minute mark.

201 Kevin DeYoung, Twitter post, April 10, 2014, https://twitter.com/revkevdeyoung/status/454071366250409984.

Malcolm Yarnell (b. AD 1962)

Yarnell is professor of theology at Southwestern Baptist Theological Seminary. He has provided critiques of Calvinist philosophy and theology in his seminal volume on free church theological method, *The Formation of Christian Doctrine*,[202] as well as in essays contributed to two major volumes in the SBC Calvinist controversy.[203] Yarnell works out his own affirmation of unlimited atonement in his appreciative reviews of the soteriology and evangelistic fervor of the first Anabaptist and first Baptist theologians in two European journals, *Baptist Quarterly* and *Theologie Evangelique*, as well as in his American review of the Synod of Dort in *SBC Life*. Yarnell also led in the fashioning of the popular statement, "Neither Calvinist nor Arminian but Baptist."[204]

Russell Moore (b. AD 1971)

Moore is the former dean and vice president of Southern Seminary in Louisville, Kentucky, and current president of the Southern Baptist Ethics and Religious Liberty Commission. He is an advocate of universal atonement.[205]

Eric Hankins (b. AD 1971)

In 2012, Eric Hankins, pastor of First Baptist Church, Oxford, Mississippi, and PhD graduate of Southwestern Baptist Theological Seminary, drafted a "Traditional Statement of Southern Baptist Soteriology." The statement articulated a non-Reformed soteriology and was published and signed by many Southern Baptists, including some entity heads, former SBC presidents, seminary presidents and faculty, pastors, and laymen.

I was asked to write an explanation for publication of Article 3, "The Atonement of Christ." The article consists of one proposition in affirmation and three in denial. It is the last denial that addresses specifically the question of the extent of the atonement.[206]

> We affirm that the penal substitution of Christ is the only available and effective sacrifice for the sins of every person. We deny that this atonement results in salvation without a person's free response of repentance and faith. We deny

202 M. Yarnell, *The Formation of Christian Doctrine* (Nashville: B&H Academic, 2007), 49–59, 73–106, 154–57.

203 M. Yarnell, "The Potential Impact of Calvinist Tendencies upon Local Baptist Churches," in *Whosoever Will*, 213–32; idem, "Calvinism: Cause for Rejoicing, Cause for Concern," in *Calvinism: A Southern Baptist Dialogue*, 73–95.

204 See M. Yarnell, "Les baptistes son-ils calvinistes ou non-calvinistes," *Theologie Evangelique* 12 (2013): 1–26; idem, "'We Believe with the Heart and with the Mouth Confess': The Engaged Piety of the Early General Baptists," *Baptist Quarterly* 44 (2011):1–23; idem, "The TULIP of Calvinism: In Light of History and the Baptist Faith and Message," *SBCLife*, April 2006, which can be accessed at http://www.sbclife.net/Articles/2006/04/sla8; idem, *Neither Calvinists nor Arminians but Baptists* (New Orleans: Center for Theological Research, 2010; co-authored with several non-Calvinist leaders in the Southern Baptist Convention).

205 R. Moore, "The Triumph of the Warrior King: A Theology of the Great Commission," *Russell Moore* (blog), March 5, 2008, http://www.russellmoore.com/2008/03/05/triumph-of-the-warrior-king-a-theology-of-the-great-commission-part-3. Moore has confirmed his views to me in personal conversation as well.

206 D. L. Allen, "Commentary on Article 3: The Atonement of Christ," *Journal of Baptist Theology and Ministry* 9 (2012): 41–48.

> that God imposes or withholds this atonement without respect to an act of the person's free will. We deny that Christ died only for the sins of those who will be saved.[207]

The "Traditional Statement" garnered the attention of the Southern Baptist leadership and resulted in a task force to consider the issue of Calvinism in the SBC appointed by Frank Page, president of the SBC Executive Committee. The task force drafted a statement on the issues that identified points of agreement and disagreement between Calvinists and non-Calvinists in the SBC entitled "Truth, Trust, and Testimony in a Time of Tension."[208] One of the key areas of disagreement concerned the extent of the atonement.

There are two direct statements on the atonement. The first appears in the "Truth" section of the document; the second in the "Tension" section. The first identifies where all agree on the atonement; the second points out the disagreement over the extent of the atonement.

> We affirm that the death of Jesus Christ on the cross was both penal and substitutionary and that the atonement He accomplished was sufficient for the sins of the entire world. We deny that there is anything lacking in the atonement of Christ to provide for the salvation of anyone.
>
> We agree that God loves everyone and desires to save everyone, but we differ as to why only some are ultimately saved.
>
> We agree that the penal and substitutionary death of Christ was sufficient for the sins of the entire world, but we differ as to whether Jesus actually substituted for the sins of all people or only the elect.

Notice in the second statement that all parties agree on God's universal love and his universal saving will. The key disagreement is over the extent of the atonement: "Whether Jesus actually substituted for the sins of all people or only the elect."

Matthew Harding (b. AD 1973)

Harding's Southwestern Baptist Theological Seminary PhD dissertation, "Atonement Theory Revisited: Calvin, Beza, and Amyraut on the Extent of the Atonement," was

---

207 Ibid. See also Eric Hankins, "A Statement of the Traditional Southern Baptist Understanding of God's Plan of Salvation," *SBC Today: Southern Baptist News and Analysis*, June 2012, http://sbctoday.com/wp-content/uploads/2012/06/A-Statement-of-Traditional-Southern-Baptist-Soteriology-SBC-Today.pdf.

208 "Truth, Trust, and Testimony in a Time of Tension: A Statement from the Calvinism Advisory Committee," *SBC Life: Journal of the Southern Baptist Convention*, June 2013, http://www.sbclife.net/Articles/2013/06/sla5.

completed in 2014.[209] Harding argued that Amyraut's understanding of a universal atonement paralleled Calvin, and that Beza went beyond Calvin in advocating a limited atonement.

Adam Harwood (b. AD 1974)

Harwood serves as associate professor of theology, director of the Baptist Center for Theology and Ministry, and editor of the *Journal for Baptist Theology & Ministry* at New Orleans Baptist Theological Seminary. He is a clear advocate of unlimited atonement, as evidenced by a well-written and insightful article, "Is the Gospel for All People or Only Some People."[210]

Jarvis J. Williams (b. AD 1978)

Williams is associate professor of New Testament interpretation at Southern Baptist Theological Seminary. His *For Whom Did Christ Die? The Extent of the Atonement in Paul's Theology*[211] is an attempt to support limited atonement by comparing material from Second Temple Judaism with Paul's letters.

This is a very uneven work. Material dealing with Second Temple Judaism is sometimes helpful. Material dealing with the extent of the atonement is historically and exegetically weak. The section dealing with the extent question is almost totally dependent on secondary sources. Williams failed to address or even acknowledge the exegetical and theological work of the many Calvinists such as Davenant, Baxter, Charles Hodge, Shedd, and Dabney who opposed limited atonement, many writing significant works against it. He shows no awareness of G. Michael Thomas's *The Extent of the Atonement*, a crucial work on the historical issues surrounding the question of extent within Reformed theology. Williams wrongly attributed the moniker of Arminianism to Ken Keathley's *Salvation and Sovereignty*.

Williams spent most of his time surveying Romans, with a section on divine and human agency in early Judaism, the Pseudepigrapha, and the Dead Sea Scrolls.[212] While this is interesting and helpful at times, there is little if any connection with the extent of the atonement. In fact, it appears as though he tried to force his preconceived thesis of limited atonement onto Second Temple texts—classic eisegesis. Most of the early Jewish works that he discussed have nothing to do with the extent question.[213]

209 M. Harding, "Atonement Theory Revisited: Calvin, Beza, and Amyraut on the Extent of the Atonement" (PhD diss., Southwestern Baptist Theological Seminary, 2014). See also M. Harding, "Atonement Theory Revisited: Calvin, Beza, and Amyraut on the Extent of the Atonement," *Perichoresis* 11 (2013): 49–73.

210 A. Harwood, "Is the Gospel for All People or Only Some People?," *Journal for Baptist Theology and Ministry* 11 (2014): 16–33.

211 J. Williams, *For Whom Did Christ Die? The Extent of the Atonement in Paul's Theology*, Paternoster Biblical Monographs (Milton Keynes, UK: Paternoster, 2012).

212 Ibid., 33–187.

213 Conversely, when it comes to those texts that actually speak, albeit indirectly, to his question, Williams seems unaware of their relevancy. For example, on the question of divine and human agency, he devoted only one para-

Williams covered "the purpose and benefits of Jesus' death" in chapter 4, of which the first several pages deal with animal sacrifice in the Hebrew Bible and human sacrifice in early Judaism, before even getting to Paul.[214] Pages 200–214 are a very limited study of seven key Pauline passages, most of which do not address the extent of the atonement directly. He failed to deal with those that do: Rom 5:18–19; 1 Cor 15:3; 1 Tim 2:3–6; and 1 Tim 4:10, to mention four. His treatment of 2 Cor 5:14–21 is limited to two pages and offers no exegesis. There is no treatment of 1 Cor 15:1–11, which indicates Paul understood the gospel to include his customary preaching "Christ died for our sins" to his unregenerate audiences, as he did in Corinth.[215]

This is all the more problematic in light of Williams's stated purpose "to offer a detailed, exegetical investigation of selected texts in Paul and in early Judaism that shed light on Paul's view of the extent of Jesus' death"[216] and his claim that his work is, to his knowledge, "the only monograph that concerns itself exclusively with arguing in favor of particular atonement from the Pauline letters by means of *exegetical rigor*."[217]

---

graph to *1 Enoch*, failed to mention the relevant passages, and neglects some of the secondary source scholarship on the issue. *1 Enoch* is a composite work, as Williams acknowledged. What he seems to be unaware of is the fact that scholars have written much about the issue of divine and human agency in the works that make up this corpus. See especially P. Sacchi, *Jewish Apocalyptic and Its History*, Journal for the Study of the Pseudepigrapha, Supplement series 20 (Sheffield, UK: Sheffield Academic, 1990), 83–83, 146, whose ideas are followed in expanded/modified fashion by G. Boccaccini, *Beyond the Essene Hypothesis: The Parting of the Ways between Qumran and Enochic Judaism* (Grand Rapids, MI: Eerdmans, 1998), 72–74, 133–35. In short, according to some scholars, the *Book of Watchers* (*1 Enoch* 1–36) teaches that sin is beyond human control and God must act to deliver humans from the evils they cannot help but commit, whereas the *Epistle of Enoch* (*1 Enoch* 92–105) emphasizes that humans are completely to blame for sin. While I think even this understanding of *1 Enoch* is somewhat simplistic, it is an important discussion relating at least indirectly to Williams's argument that he should engage if he is arguing that Jews believed "divine agency surrounds human agency," whatever he means by that.

The dearth of footnotes in the early Judaism portions of the book would seem to suggest that Williams consulted only a small number of the scholarly works on the literature. Given that he discussed the theology of one work (4 Ezra) twice in the same chapter, the conclusion seems unavoidable that he did not realize that this work appears in two collections (Apocrypha and Pseudepigrapha) under two different names. In one case, he discussed a book of the so-called Apocrypha, 2 Esdras, chapters 3–14 of which is a pseudepigraphon called 4 Ezra. In his treatment of the "Pseudepigrapha," however, he has a separate discussion of 4 Ezra. He does acknowledge in a footnote in the case of 2 Esdras that chapters 3–14 are known as 4 Ezra, but he seems completely unaware of the fact that this is the same 4 Ezra that he discussed in the following section of the chapter. He does not explain why he would deal with it twice or even refer the reader in a footnote to the other discussion. On the contrary, according to footnotes 7 and 19, he refers the reader to one translation of the work in one case and another translation in the other. Interestingly, his two discussions of the same work are quite different, which illustrates the highly subjective nature of his interpretation since not even he interprets the same text the same way twice.

Although he is correct in his contention that the martyrs in 2 Maccabees and 4 Maccabees are said to atone for Israel's sins, I fail to see how that supports limited atonement. There is simply no connection between 2 Maccabees and 4 Maccabees and the doctrine of limited atonement. The martyrs died on behalf of Israel only (not all the nations), but Israel is conceived corporately. These works do not seem to imply that the martyrs died only on behalf of certain individual members of Israel. While one may correctly contrast Paul's belief that Jesus died for the world with that of 2 Maccabees and 4 Maccabees that Jesus dies only for Israel, there is nothing that supports the idea of limited atonement in the Jewish texts or in Paul.

214 J. Williams, *For Whom Did Christ Die?*, 188–214.

215 James Morison discussed this text as evidence for unlimited atonement in his *The Extent of the Propitiation, or, The Question, For Whom Did Christ Die? Answered* (Kilmarnock: J. Davie, 1842), 14–16, 94. Morison cited several church fathers who took the same interpretation.

216 Williams, *For Whom Did Christ Die?*, 1.

217 Ibid., 2 (emphasis mine).

Williams's *Christ Died for Our Sins: Representation and Substitution in Romans and Their Jewish Martyrological Background* was published in 2015.[218] Williams continued his trajectory of limited atonement in more subdued tones. In the preface Williams acknowledged criticism of his previous work and has refined his thesis to a more modest proposal that martyr theology was one of several traditions influencing Paul's conception and presentation of the death of Christ.[219] Among his summary conclusions are the following three statements:

> In Romans, Paul suggests that Jesus, a Torah-observant Jew, innocently died for non-Torah-observant Jewish and Gentile sinners so that they would experience soteriological benefits, both as a result of his death for them and as a result of their identification with him by faith.[220]

> Paul's use of the Jewish martyrological traditions in Romans was an intentional missiological move on his part to contextualize the death of Jesus for Jewish and Gentile sinners to highlight the efficacious nature of Jesus' death for them.[221]

> While the Jewish martyrological narratives present Torah-observant Jews exclusively dying as substitutes for and as representatives of Jewish sinners, Paul uses the Jewish martyrological narratives to present Jesus, a Torah-observant Jew, as dying inclusively for Jewish *and Gentile* sinners who believe. According to Paul, Israel's God is the God of Jews and Gentiles (Rom 3:29–30), because "while we were yet sinners, Christ died for our sins" (Rom 5:8).[222]

In the first statement Williams seems to intend a limited atonement since Jesus died so that Jewish and Gentile sinners "would experience soteriological benefits." It appears the "would" is invested with the meaning of "will." If the latter compound clause—"both as a result of his death for them and as a result of their identification with him by faith"—is intended to convey limitation in both parts, then Williams is interpreting Paul as affirming a limited atonement.

In the second statement, I presume Williams intends to convey the notion of limitation in the death of Christ, though as worded it does not necessarily convey that meaning. Paul is addressing believers in Romans. When Paul talks about the efficacious nature of the atonement for and to those who are already believers, logically he is not

218 J. Williams, *Christ Died for Our Sins: Representation and Substitution in Romans and Their Jewish Martyrological Background* (Eugene, OR: Pickwick, 2015).

219 Ibid., x–xi, 184–88.

220 Ibid., 186.

221 Ibid., 187.

222 Ibid., 188.

committing himself to a strictly limited atonement in terms of the actual *provision* of the atonement but is speaking of the actual *application* of the atonement to them, which is, in fact, efficacious. Williams, however, appears to convey the meaning of strict limitation by his use of "efficacious."

In Williams's third statement, his position on limited atonement is clear: "Jesus died inclusively for Jewish *and Gentile* sinners who believe." "Inclusively" refers to Jewish and Gentile sinners; "who believe" delimits the category of sinners for whom Jesus died: *exclusively* for those who believe.

The problem is that nothing within Williams's treatment of the martyrological tradition, Isaiah 53, or Romans justifies, let alone mandates, this interpretation. Williams is likely operating from a commercialistic understanding of the atonement such that all those for whom Jesus substituted *must* have the atonement applied to them. This is simply not what Paul says in Romans or anywhere else in his letters.

Finally, Williams failed to reference Jintae Kim's PhD dissertation, "The Concept of Atonement in 1 John: A Redevelopment of the Second Temple Concept of Atonement."[223] Kim demonstrated that 1 John, building upon the Jewish traditions of forgiveness and cultic atonement in the OT and the Second Temple writings, combined these two traditions in its theology of atonement and forgiveness of sin. Despite the similarities between 1 John and these Second Temple and rabbinic traditions, including martyrological traditions, there are still decisive differences between them. The Second Temple writings and the later rabbinic traditions were particularistic in their focus (centered on Israel).

According to Kim, 1 John thoroughly universalizes and individualizes the national and corporate hopes of Israel by tying the two Jewish traditions (vicarious sacrifice and new covenant forgiveness) to Jesus's unique death and forgiveness of sin and extending the scope of efficacy of Christ's atonement to include the whole world. This is most clearly expressed in 1 John 2:2. The application of the term "Savior of the world" to Jesus in 1 John 4:14 emphasizes the universal efficacy of Christ's atoning death in connection with his role as "atoning sacrifice" in 1 John 4:10. Furthermore, John 1:29 points to the coming death of Christ as an atoning sacrifice for the sin of the world, which will be more fully explained in John 3:14–17.

The manner in which 1 John fuses these two Jewish traditional elements is unique compared to both the Second Temple writings and rabbinic writings. Like 1 John, Romans and Hebrews apply the universalizing of Jewish hopes to the atoning death of Jesus.[224] From the same Second Temple literature and martyrological traditions, Kim came to the opposite conclusion from Williams concerning the extent of the atonement in Romans and 1 John.

223 Jintae Kim, "The Concept of Atonement in 1 John: A Redevelopment of the Second Temple Concept of Atonement" (PhD diss., Westminster Theological Seminary, 2003).

224 Ibid., 200, 279, 292–93, 297.

David Platt (b. AD 1979)

Platt is the president of the International Mission Board of the Southern Baptist Convention. He was formally a pastor and on the faculty of New Orleans Baptist Theological Seminary, where he taught preaching.

Platt's Calvinism is well known and many assume he adopts the position of limited atonement. For example, Adam Harwood concluded such regarding Platt on the basis of comments made in Platt's "Divine Sovereignty: The Fuel of Death-Defying Missions" in *The Underestimated Gospel*.[225] At the very least, Platt's comments indicate he affirms a limited *design* or *intent* with respect to the atonement. Some of the trustees of the International Mission Board have indicated Platt responded specifically to questions about his view on the extent of the atonement and affirmed Christ died for the sins of all people.[226] This could indicate Platt holds to unlimited atonement like many in the history of Calvinism, assuming these trustees' understanding of Platt's response is in accord with Platt's intended meaning.

David Schrock (b. AD 1980)

Schrock is the pastor of Occoquan Bible Church in Woodbridge, Virginia. He completed his PhD dissertation, "A Biblical-Theological Investigation of Christ's Priesthood and Covenant Mediation with Respect to the Extent of the Atonement," at Southern Seminary under the direction of Stephen Wellum.[227] His dissertation, by his own admission, depends heavily on the progressive covenantalism explicated by Gentry and Wellum.[228] This is significant, as Gentry and Wellum's approach has received stringent critique from both Covenantalists and Progressive Dispensationalists.[229]

Schrock argued that an understanding of the typology of the priestly mediation of the new covenant is necessary for understanding the extent of the atonement and results in confirmation of limited atonement. For Schrock, a universal atonement does not match the priestly typology of the Old Testament. In fact, a universal atonement "destroys" the relationship of Old Testament type and New Testament antitype.[230] Accordingly, Jesus must offer an atonement that is particular only for the sins of the elect.

---

225 Harwood, "Is the Gospel for All People," 23; citing David Platt, "Divine Sovereignty: The Fuel of Death-Defying Missions," in *The Underestimated Gospel*, ed. Jonathan Leeman (Nashville: B&H, 2014), 69, 71.

226 Personal conversation of the author with some trustees.

227 D. Schrock, "A Biblical-Theological Investigation of Christ's Priesthood and Covenant Mediation with Respect to the Extent of the Atonement" (PhD diss., Southern Baptist Theological Seminary, 2013).

228 P. Gentry and S. Wellum, *Kingdom through Covenant: A Biblical-Theological Understanding of the Covenants* (Wheaton, IL: Crossway, 2012).

229 See the recent unpublished papers presented at the 2014 ETS on this topic by P. Gentry and S. Wellum, and C. Blaising and D. Bock's rather stringent critique: C. Blaising, "A Critique of Gentry and Wellum's *Kingdom Through Covenant*: A Hermeneutical-Theological Response," *The Master's Seminary Journal* 26.1 (Spring 2015): 111–27; D. L. Bock, "A Critique of Gentry and Wellum's, Kingdom through Covenant: A New Testament Perspective," *The Master's Seminary Journal* 26.1 (Spring 2015): 139–45. See also the three reviews by D. Bock, D. Moo, and M. Horton on September 11–13, 2014, at http://thegospelcoalition.org/article/kingdom-through-covenant.

230 Schrock, "A Biblical-Theological Investigation," 362.

Upon reading this dissertation, one is first struck by the biblical analysis of the Old Testament priestly ministry that is generally well done. However, Schrock's notion that the description of the priestly ministry in the Old Testament reveals a limited atonement and provides a typological/theological paradigm for deducing a limited atonement in the New Testament is shaky at best. The theological conclusions he drew at the end of each chapter simply aren't warranted by the textual ground he surveyed. There is no apparent connection.

Schrock also stated that one of the main reasons moderate Calvinists have not affirmed definite atonement is their failure to incorporate Christ's priesthood into their theological formulations.[231] This is wide of the mark given that many moderate Calvinists of the past (Davenant and Baxter to name two) did indeed incorporate Christ's priesthood into their theological formulations concerning the extent question.

Schrock concluded from the prophetic section of the Old Testament that "the prophetic expectation was a priest who would effect salvation for people from every nation, but not for every person. Thus, I concluded that the prophets support definite atonement and deny general atonement."[232] Based on Jesus as the perfect priest who is at once victor, mediator, and teacher derived from selected New Testament texts such as the Gospels, Hebrews, and Revelation, Schrock argued that Jesus "super-fulfilled the priestly type and died *for* his people and *against* his enemies."[233]

Schrock believes that every atonement text must be informed by the priestly ministry of Jesus. Since, as priest, Jesus only died for the sins of the elect, all the atonement passages that appear to speak of his death as for the "world," "all," and so on must be interpreted in this limitarian light. Schrock's exegetical and even theological treatment of key passages such as 1 John 2:2 and Heb 2:9 is severely limited. His attempt to co-opt Moses Stuart, who affirmed an unlimited atonement, misinterpreted Stuart's comments in their context. Here Schrock made the same mistake as Robert Candlish regarding Stuart.[234]

Schrock thinks that those who hold to a general atonement assert that Jesus died "for sin in the abstract."[235] This is inaccurate. I presume by this charge Schrock is himself dependent upon some form of a commercial understanding of the atonement. As demonstrated above from numerous Calvinists, a general atonement does not mean Christ died for some amorphous concept of "sin in the abstract."

Schrock does not explain how it is that "by nailing the law with all its legal demands to the cross (Col 2:13–15), Jesus effectively destroyed the judgment against his covenant people, and simultaneously won the right to judge all those whose sins were not expiated on Calvary." If thc law with all its legal demands is satisfied by Christ on the

231 Ibid., 352.
232 Ibid., 354.
233 Ibid. (emphasis in original).
234 See above under Robert Candlish.
235 Schrock, "A Biblical-Theological Investigation," 364.

cross, how can it be that such is the case only for the elect and not the non-elect? The Scriptures simply do not speak this way.

Schrock's major error is the failure to distinguish properly between atonement accomplished and atonement applied.[236] His discussion of the gospel as offered universally also leaves something to be desired. How is it that "the extent of the atonement must of necessity be coterminous with his priestly proclamation"?[237] Where is this stated in the New Testament? For Schrock, the multiethnic nature of Christ's covenant people (in other words, the elect viewed by Schrock in the abstract), impels the preaching of the gospel to all nations.[238] Schrock does not address the problem of how this preaching to all, including the non-elect, with its concomitant offer of salvation to all, can be sincere and genuine on the part of the preacher, and more importantly, on God's part, since there is no atonement made for the non-elect, hence there is nothing to offer them.

Schrock also authored a chapter in *Whomever He Wills* in response to my chapter critiquing limited atonement in *Whosoever Will*.[239] Since Schrock's chapter illustrates the perspective of many Southern Baptist Calvinists today, and since it is a direct response to my chapter, I will offer an extended critique.

Schrock's chapter is divided into five sections: "Christ's Death Is Particular," "Christ's Death Is Efficacious," "Priestly Arguments for Particular and Effective Atonement," "The Covenantal Nature of the Atonement," and "The Universal Impact of Definite Atonement."

Misunderstanding of Amyraldian and Moderate Calvinism

Schrock's chapter title, "Jesus Saves, No Asterisk Needed: Why Preaching the Gospel as Good News Requires Definite Atonement," is intriguing. What does he mean by "no asterisk needed" and preaching the gospel "requires" definite atonement? Schrock believes that "those who preach the gospel of Jesus Christ as the power unto salvation (Romans 1:16) must embrace and declare a cross which actually saves, and the only view that will support such preaching *in the long run* is definite atonement."[240] Schrock informs us that he will use the term "egalitarian" for all views of the atonement other than the definite atonement view (Arminian, Amyraldian, Molinist, and modified Calvinist [his categories]) because all these views assume that Christ's death makes equal provision both for those that would at some point believe, as well as those that never would be brought to belief. He stated that all these views "fail" because "they articulate a view of the atonement that is indefinite."[241]

236 Ibid., 366.

237 Ibid., 367.

238 Ibid., 368.

239 D. Schrock, "Jesus Saves, No Asterisk Needed: Why Preaching the Gospel as Good News Requires Definite Atonement," in *Whomever He Wills*, 77–119.

240 Ibid., 78 (emphasis in original).

241 Ibid.

This is the first of many serious errors in the chapter. The Amyraldian and moderate Calvinist views (and probably the Molinist view as well) do not promote a view of the atonement that is indefinite. As Calvinists, those who have held and hold today these views very clearly affirm a definite atonement in that the *intent* of Christ's death was to secure the salvation of the elect. Amyraldians and Hypothetical Universalists affirm that while the *sufficiency* of the provision is equally for all, the *intention* to apply it is not. To lump together Amyraldians, Molinists, and Hypothetical Universalists with Arminians is historically inaccurate and faulty.

Schrock makes another significant mistake when he asserts that all these views above borrow "the theological capital of definite atonement."[242] This is historically anachronistic since the limited atonement view developed in history within the Reformed camp *after* the Hypothetical Universalist position.

In section one, "Christ's Death Is Particular," Schrock asserted: "Textual proof for definite atonement begins with the straightforward statements that Christ died for a particular people."[243] He lists Matt 1:21; Titus 2:14; Acts 20:28; and Eph 5:25–27, and in a footnote he adds Rom 5:8–9; 1 Cor 15:3; 2 Cor 5:1–19; Gal 1:3–4; Titus 3:5–6; 1 Pet 2:24; 3:18. Of Titus 2:14, Schrock stated, "In this case, Paul goes further. He explicitly speaks of a people 'redeemed' and 'purified' by His death, for His own purposes."[244] Schrock failed to take into account that it would not be at all unusual to have these kinds of texts in the Bible when many of them occur in epistles addressed only to believers and not to the "world" as a whole. This is a point often overlooked in the discussion.

Here and throughout Schrock's chapter he continually employs vague terms like "His people," "the people of God," "a people," "all who are His," "His peculiar people," "them," "they," "His own," "the ones given Him," "His sheep," and "us." This kind of generalization blurs the distinction between believers and all the elect in the abstract. The "elect" are actually in two groups: (1) those who have believed and (2) those yet to believe. Schrock often conflates these two. But the texts he cited above pertain to *believers*. Schrock takes what is true of believers and then seeks to apply this to all the elect as an abstract class.

Concerning these texts, not a single one states Christ died *only* for the group mentioned in context. To infer such is to commit the negative inference fallacy. When Paul says in Gal 2:20 that "I live by faith in the Son of God, who loved me and gave Himself for me" (NKJV), are we to infer that Christ died *only* for Paul?

Schrock next tapped D. A. Carson's *The Difficult Doctrine of the Love of God*[245] and averred: "However, against egalitarians who indiscriminately universalize God's variegated love, Christ loves His bride in a way that He does not love the merchants

---

242 Ibid.

243 Ibid., 79.

244 Ibid.

245 D. A. Carson, *The Difficult Doctrine of the Love of God* (Wheaton, IL: Crossway, 1999), 16–21.

of Babylon who prostitute themselves with the Great Harlot (Revelation 17–19)."[246] The problem with this statement is that Amyraldians and moderate Calvinists don't indiscriminately "universalize" (I presume Schrock means to say "equalize" by his use of "universalize") God's variegated love. It is true that most Calvinists distinguish degrees in God's love in that they affirm an electing love and a general love. Many non-Calvinists would affirm the concept of degrees in God's love. One might say there is a sense in which no evangelical is properly an "egalitarian" in that all agree that God's love as understood to mean the giving of the benefits of salvation to people who meet God's condition of faith and indicates discrimination.

Dabney Misread

Schrock cited my appeal to the negative inference fallacy and my citation of Dabney. He said my point would be well taken if these "bare positive statements" (texts that speak of the extent of the atonement "for His people" or "for the church") were all there was.[247] "However, these texts are but visible geysers forced to the surface by the power of God's plan to save a particular people. As we will see below, the fountainhead of these verses is God's covenantal relationship with His particular people."[248] Nothing here mitigates or refutes what I have said at all.

Schrock then quoted Michaels: "Most references to Jesus death in John's gospel have to do with its benefits *for believers*, of Jesus' own disciples, and are thus fully consistent with 'particular redemption' as the early English Baptists understood it."[249] Again, this has nothing to do with the price of tea in China. We are not talking about the benefits of the atonement being limited only to those who believe. All agree with that. Nothing in Michaels's statement contradicts the notion of an unlimited atonement. Nothing in God's covenantal relationship with his people—that is, believers—mandates particular redemption as understood to mean a limited sin-bearing of Christ on the cross.

Schrock's critique of my "negative inference fallacy" and the Dabney citation is given in a lengthy footnote[250] where he appears to be dependent upon Greg Wills's critique of my chapter in his book review.[251] This critique deserves a detailed response, for both Wills and Schrock have made a significant error at this point. With respect to the negative inference fallacy and the extent of the atonement, the burden is on Schrock to prove that a simple positive can entail a universal negation. This is his claim. Schrock's problem is to prove from Scripture that Christ died *only for some people's sins* (a limited imputation of sin). But he offered no proof for that proposition.

246 Schrock, "Jesus Saves," 79.
247 Ibid., 81.
248 Ibid.
249 Ibid., 81–82 (emphasis in original).
250 Ibid., 80–81.
251 G. Wills, "Review of *Whosoever Will: A Biblical-Theological Critique of Five-Point Calvinism*," in *Journal for Baptist Theology and Ministry* 7 (2010): 15–18.

Schrock quoted Dabney as saying "Christ died for all sinners in some sense."[252] Schrock neglected to point out that Dabney means by this that Christ's death accomplished universal expiation for sins. Dabney makes this clear just a few pages later his *Lectures in Systematic Theology*, which I noted on page 83, footnote 78 of my chapter "The Atonement: Limited or Universal?" in *Whosoever Will.* Schrock referred to the "context" of the Dabney quote in an effort to refute my understanding of Dabney. Schrock quoted from pages 527, 528, 529, and 533 in Dabney's *Lectures* but apparently failed to see the direct statement by Dabney that Christ expiated the sins of all people. Here is Dabney's statement on John 3:16 in context:

> Verse 16: Christ's mission to make expiation for sin is a manifestation of unspeakable benevolence to the whole world, to man as man and a sinner, yet designed specifically to result in the actual salvation of believers. Does not this imply that this very mission, rejected by others, will become the occasion (not cause) of perishing even more surely to them? It does. Yet, (verse 17,) it is denied that this vindicatory result was the primary design of Christ's mission: and the initial assertion is again repeated, that this primary design was to manifest God, in Christ's sacrifice, as compassionate to all. How then is the seeming paradox to be reconciled? Not by retracting either statement. The solution, (verse 18,) is in the fact, that men, in the exercise of their free agency, give opposite receptions to this mission. To those who accept it as it is offered, it brings life. To those who choose to reject it, it is the occasion (not cause) of condemnation. For, (verse 19,) the true cause of this perverted result is the evil choice of the unbelievers, who reject the provision offered in the divine benevolence, from a wicked motive; unwillingness to confess and forsake their sins. The sum of the matter is then: That Christ's mission is, to the whole race, a manifestation of God's mercy. To believers it is means of salvation, by reason of that effectual calling which Christ had expounded in the previous verses. To unbelievers it becomes a subsequent and secondary occasion of aggravated doom. This melancholy perversion, while embraced in God's permissive decree, is caused by their own contumacy.[253]

Lest doubt remain, here are two more direct quotations from the very context of Dabney's *Lectures* from which Schrock himself quoted.

> In 1 John 2:2, it is at least doubtful whether the express phrase, "whole world," can be restrained to the world of elect as including other than Jews. For it is indisputable, that the Apostle extends the propitiation of Christ beyond those whom he speaks of as "we," in verse first. The interpretation described obviously

252 Schrock, "Jesus Saves," 80.

253 Dabney, *Systematic Theology*, 535.

> proceeds on the assumption that these are only Jewish believers. Can this be substantiated? Is this catholic epistle addressed only to Jews? This is more than doubtful. It would seem then, that the Apostle's scope is to console and encourage sinning believers with the thought that since Christ made expiation for every man, there is no danger that He will not be found a propitiation for them who, having already believed, now sincerely turn to him from recent sins.[254]

Schrock quoted from Dabney's page 528, as noted above. Here is Dabney's statement on that very page stating as clear as a bell his belief that Christ died for the sins of all people: "Redemption is limited, i.e., to true believers, and is particular. Expiation is not limited."

It is quite clear that Dabney believed "Christ made expiation for every man" and not for the elect only. Many other references could be given from his writings. Schrock's misreading of Dabney at this point and throughout is a major problem in his chapter.

Schrock said Dabney "also argues for the particular efficacy of the atonement." Exactly right. Dabney sees a distinction between "extent" and "application," which Schrock missed. Schrock continued to quote Dabney: "There is no passage in the Bible which asserts an intention to apply redemption to any other than the elect." Note carefully Dabney's use of the word "intention" and "apply" here. Dabney believed, as do all Calvinists, that God's *intention* in the atonement is that it be *applied* only to the elect. But Dabney clearly believed that Christ's death expiated the sins of all sinners. Schrock made the false assumption that my references to the universal aspects of Dabney's statements refer to common grace. He is missing Dabney's own stated position of universal expiation of sins. Part of what might be driving Schrock's misreading of Dabney here is the failure to understand that many nineteenth-century Calvinists distinguished between expiation and redemption, as we have demonstrated above. Expiation was unlimited whereas redemption was limited only to the elect. One sees this same distinction in the writings of Shedd as well as Dabney. Schrock has set up a false either/or distinction and attempted to shackle Dabney with it. More importantly, this either/or distinction is not supported by Scripture.

Schrock quoted Dabney again: "Christ's design in His vicarious work was to effectuate exactly what it does effectuate." Notice again Dabney's use of the word "design." "Design" and "intent" are synonymous. Christ's design in the atonement is that it would actually bring about the salvation only of the elect. Dabney believed that the atonement was limited in its *intent* and *application* but *not in its extent.* However, Schrock wrongly concluded from this last statement by Dabney "that Dabney argues for a limited atonement with 'temporal' (read: non-salvific) effects."[255] This is a major misread-

254 Ibid., 525.

255 Schrock, "Jesus Saves," 8.

ing of Dabney since he is clear here and elsewhere in his writings that he affirmed a universal sin-bearing in the death of Christ. Schrock has confused and thus conflated the issues of intent, extent, and application.

Schrock continued in his footnote,

> Allen's quotation implies that Dabney supports his egalitarian view, but such is not the case. Allen makes definite atonement appear to be a matter of logical gymnastics, but in fact, Dabney and his Reformed brethren pay very careful attention to the whole counsel of Scripture in order to affirm the particular saving and particular non-saving effects of the cross of Christ.

He then concluded this first paragraph of three in this footnote by citing a section of Greg Wills's review of *Whosoever Will*, specifically the section that deals with my chapter on limited atonement. My point in the Dabney quotation is to show that he held to unlimited atonement with respect to extent. Dabney did more than "imply" this; he stated it. It is not a matter of "logical gymnastics" but of straightforward statement on Dabney's part and on mine. Of course, Dabney, as I do, affirmed nonsaving effects of the cross. That is not the point.

Schrock continued paragraph two of his footnote: "Unfortunately, this is but one example where David Allen misrepresents those who defend definite atonement. Confusing matters, he puts defenders and opponents of particular redemption in the same list and concludes, 'All were Calvinists, and all did not teach limited atonement.'" He then noted the footnote where I explain that what they are not teaching is a limited imputation of sin to Christ, which is the hallmark of particular redemption when it is understood to mean a limited sin-bearing. Schrock attempted to substantiate this charge of misrepresentation in the next paragraph of his footnote by lengthy appeal to Wills's review of my chapter in *Whosoever Will*.

Before turning to Wills, I will address the charge of "confusion" in my list of Calvinists who reject limited atonement. My list contains no Calvinist who is a defender of the strict and narrow view of particular redemption. Schrock is mistaken and is assuming he has proven that Dabney does not believe what I am saying he believes. Furthermore, I presume Schrock is affirming that at least some of the names in my list are accurately represented as rejecting limited atonement. If that is the case, then he needs to deal with these. Suppose, for the sake of argument, that my list of dozens of Calvinists contains a few errors. Fine. Let's throw those out and deal with the remaining Calvinists on the list who are, in fact, affirming unlimited atonement with respect to extent and who are clearly acknowledged to be doing so by Reformed theologians/historians such as Richard Muller, Robert Letham, and Robert Godfrey. Knowledgeable Calvinists know that there are many such Calvinists in the history of

Reformed theology. What of them and their arguments? It is primarily their arguments I used in my chapter. I cannot find a single place in Schrock's chapter where he concedes the point that there is and has been debate on this issue *within the Reformed camp*. Schrock demonstrates a limited awareness of the complexity and diversity within the historic Reformed tradition.

Hence I am at a loss to understand what Schrock is referring to when he speaks of "confusion" in my list of names. Either he has failed to comprehend my statement that he just quoted making clear the distinction between affirming a limitation in the application of the atonement (which all Calvinists and non-Calvinists affirm) and a limitation in the sin-bearing of Christ for all people, or he is unaware of the history of Reformed theology on this subject. When I have carefully quoted and referenced in footnotes dozens of Calvinists who affirm unlimited atonement with respect to extent, the burden of proof is on him to show who on the list is actually a defender of limited extent. Showing in Dabney's writings where he affirms limitation in the intent or the application of the atonement while ignoring statements where he affirms universal sin-bearing is poor historical/theological method.

Since Schrock is dependent for his criticism in this section on Wills's review, let us now turn to him. Wills did not deal with the facts of my chapter. For example, he skirted the point of Christ dying for the sins of all people in my Calvinistic sources. He does not address my documentation about sufficiency. Like Schrock, he appears to miss altogether Dabney's points about universal expiation. My chapter does not engage in "universal aspects" of the atonement without carefully defining what is meant. I am speaking of the fact that Jesus died *for the sins of* all people, including the non-elect. I explicitly make clear in my chapter the number of major Calvinists of the past and present, almost fifty in fact, whom I mention, cite, discuss, or quote who affirm this specific universal extent of the atonement. Wills seems to ignore my purpose statement on page 65—that is, "The focus of this chapter is primarily on the question of the extent [as clearly defined by 'sin-bearing'] of the atonement." Wills attempts to yank the whole conversation back to the "intent" question while missing the significance of what these previous Calvinists said about the extent question.

In Schrock's third paragraph of footnote 13, he continues the "misrepresentation" charge and supports it by a lengthy quote from Wills's review of my chapter. Since I have already discussed this part of Wills's critique above in the section on *Whosoever Will*, the reader should refer to that section.

Intrinsic or Extrinsic Sufficiency?

The confusion continues when Wills asserted that I am incorrect to argue that such a position is not limited atonement. It most certainly is, and I was careful in my chapter to define the terms clearly so there would be no confusion. As I stated in my chapter and above, all Calvinists believe the atonement is limited at the point of application. They do not all believe it is limited at the point of extent.

Wills stated that the atonement was "sufficient for the sins of the world." At the very beginning of my chapter I was careful to distinguish between the two uses of "sufficient" by Calvinists in this debate through the centuries: intrinsic sufficiency (*sufficientia nuda*) and extrinsic sufficiency (*sufficientia ordinata*). The former means that Jesus's death was intrinsically sufficient enough to pay the sin debt of all people if God had so intended it to do so. When those who affirm particular redemption (as argued by John Owen) use the term, they by definition mean an "intrinsic, limited" sufficiency. Christ's death did not actually pay for the sins of the non-elect. It could have, but it did not. "Extrinsic sufficiency" means that Christ's death actually paid the sin debt of all people, not just the elect. All moderate Calvinists and all non-Calvinists agree that this is the biblical teaching with respect to the death of Christ.

I noted in *Whosoever Will* that moderate Calvinists like James Ussher, John Davenant, Nathaniel Hardy, and Edward Polhill distinguish between the senses of *sufficientia nuda* and *sufficientia ordinata* and argued for the latter. I also noted how Richard Baxter called John Owen's revision of the Lombardian formula (sufficient for all; efficient for the elect) a "new futile evasion." When Wills said that the death of Christ was "sufficient for the sins of the world," he means the former (*sufficientia nuda*) and not the latter (*sufficientia ordinata*). He then stated the death of Christ is "effective for the elect alone." Correctly stated. But then he said: "The key difference relates to the question of intent, not to the question of its universal sufficiency." *Au contraire!* True, the question of intent is indeed a key difference between Calvinists and Arminians. But the question of the universal sufficiency of the atonement is actually *the key issue in the debate over the extent of the atonement* between Calvinists, as well as between some Calvinists and non-Calvinists. It is precisely the universal sufficiency of the death of Christ that is at stake, as Henri Blocher correctly noted in reference to my chapter in *Whosoever Will* in his chapter in *From Heaven He Came and Sought Her* (see my evaluation of Blocher in the next chapter of this volume).

Everyone agrees that the death of Christ was intrinsically sufficient to save this world and a thousand worlds. But high Calvinists have not historically believed that the death of Christ is extrinsically sufficient to save the non-elect. They cannot believe such; the reason being there is no satisfaction in the death of Christ for the sins of the non-elect. On this view, the non-elect cannot consistently be viewed as "saveable," even if they should repent and believe. This is the key error of Schrock and Wills in footnote 13 of Schrock's chapter.

Jesus's High Priestly Prayer, the Negative Inference Fallacy, and False Dilemmas

Schrock next turned his attention to the technical expression "given me" used by Jesus in John's Gospel to speak of Jesus's mission. Elsewhere this phrase speaks of the particular group of people Jesus has received from the Father. Schrock asserted, "This particular language lends strong support for definite atonement."[256] Actually, there is little, if anything, in any of these kinds of statements in John's Gospel that lends support to any position on the question of the extent of the atonement. Schrock is merely making an assumption based on his inference that limited atonement is true. At best, these statements might be used to muster support for the doctrine of election, but even then they do not directly affirm the specific Dortian understanding of election. Schrock has committed a logical fallacy here.

Schrock discussed John 17 and Jesus's high priestly prayer as evidence for limited atonement. Robert Lightner called into question John Owen's notion (assumption) that since Jesus did not intercede for the "world" in John 17, he did not die for the sins of the world. This is a common argument in the limited atonement arsenal and has been addressed and answered even by a number of Calvinists, including the likes of Richard Baxter and John Bunyan. Robert Lightner called the assumption "unwarranted logically" and "unscriptural."[257]

Schrock found two problems with Lightner's approach. First, "canonically, it misunderstands Christ's priestly office, in which He fulfills all of His ministry."[258] Second, the "unscriptural" charge is "ironic because he [Lightner] takes no time to examine the office in type or fulfillment," which Schrock will do in the next section of his chapter. Schrock stated with respect to John 17:19, that "Jesus intends to die for the ones given Him by the Father." He continued, "Lightner overlooks the fact that in Christ's priestly prayer, He limits not only His intercession but also His crucifixion. . . . Jesus prays *and* dies for His own."[259]

The text itself does not state that Jesus dies *only* for those for whom he prays. No doubt, Schrock is correct to state that Jesus "intends" to die for the ones given him by the Father. Laying aside for the moment the possibility that in context this is most likely a reference to the disciples and even taking it as extending to the believing elect at the time, even then one is not warranted to draw the conclusion that the text means that Jesus *did not* die for the sins of all people, elect and non-elect. Here Schrock falls prey again to generalizing that election entails limited atonement. He assumes that if Jesus prays only for the elect, then he must have died only for the elect. The mistake here is a collapsing of the intercession of Christ into his expiation for sins. This merely begs the question of extent.

Schrock's approach here is refuted by Harold Dekker, former professor and academic dean at Calvin Theological Seminary, who wrote the following concerning Jesus's prayer in John 17:

256 Schrock, "Jesus Saves," 81–82.

257 R. Lightner, *The Death Christ Died: A Biblical Case for Unlimited Atonement*, ref. ed. (Grand Rapids, MI: Kregel, 1998), 103.

258 Schrock, "Jesus Saves," 83.

259 Ibid. (emphasis in original).

A word should be said about Jesus' prayer in John 17. Some correspondents have cited verse 9, where Jesus says, "I pray for them; I pray not for the world, but for them whom thou hast given me; for they are thine," to prove that Christ loved only the elect and not the world. But does it? Whom did Jesus designate by the words "those whom thou hast given me"? The elect? This is forced exegesis. The entire context, beginning with verse 4, makes it clear that those to whom Jesus referred in verse 9 are those who had come to believe in Him at that time, the actual persons whom the Father had given to Jesus in His earthly ministry up to that point, the ones of whom He said in verse 8 that they had received and believed His words. This interpretation is also supported by verse 20, where Jesus says, "Neither for these only do I pray, but for them also that believe on me through their word." Evidently right within the same prayer Jesus prayed not only for the limited number who were in view in verse 8, but also for the many who later would come through their word to share their faith.

What, then, did Jesus mean when He said, "I pray not for the world?" In the light of the foregoing, the explanation seems obvious. Surely Jesus did not mean that He did not love the world and under no circumstances would pray for it. We must observe that it was a certain prayer, with specific petitions, which He offered for those whom the Father had given Him, and which He declared He did not offer for the world. What were these specific petitions which He prayed? Chiefly that those who had come to believe in Him would be faithful, joyful, kept from the evil one, sanctified in the truth, and unified with those who would later come to believe through them. Would there have been any point in Jesus praying these things for the unconverted world? Certainly not. That He did not do so proves nothing about His disposition to the world, not even at that moment. He was simply praying in terms of the unique relationship which existed between Himself and His disciples, a relationship which the world did not share. Neither, therefore, could the world share in Jesus' prayer for the development and fruition of this particular relationship. However, in verses 21 and 23, part of the same prayer, Jesus did indeed pray for the world, He prayed the very thing which was alone appropriate to the world. He prayed that the world might believe—the same world about which John 3:16 teaches us that God loved it with a redemptive love, nothing less than the world of all men. To use the high-priestly prayer of Christ in John 17 as an argument for limitation in divine redemptive love is, it seems to me, clearly to misuse it.[260]

---

260 H. Dekker, "God's Love to Sinners: One or Two?," *Reformed Journal* 13 (1963): 14–15. See also Leon Morris, *The Gospel According to John* (Grand Rapids, MI: Eerdmans, 1971), 725, who argued the same point.

On pages 83–84, Schrock referred to John 10 and the Good Shepherd motif where Jesus refers to his sheep as "his own" and to the fact that he gave his life for his sheep. Schrock concluded from this that Christ died *only* for those given to him. Jesus's statements in John 10 in no way prove exclusivity. When we are told Jesus died for his "friends," does that prove he died only for them? Did he not die for his enemies as well? The point here is that simple positive statements cannot logically be used to infer category negations. Schrock continuously repeats the mistake of the negative inference fallacy in his chapter. I might also add that his ambiguous use of the phrases "limited atonement" and "particular redemption" in some places in his chapter leads him to commit the equivocation fallacy as well.

At the end of this section, Schrock cited Calvin's discussion in his commentary on John and concludes that Jesus's reference to the "sheep" as his "own" in light of John 6:37–39 and John 17 most likely refers "to the covenant people given to Him by the Father in eternity past."[261] Fine. But for the reasons stated above, this is no support for limited atonement. Schrock's last paragraph on page 84 is important. He combined John 13:1 and John 15:13. The loved ones of John 13:1 are set in contrast to Judas in 13:2. Schrock wrote,

> Thus, while there is in John a universal love for all the world (3:16), this does not mean that God's saving love extends to all people. Jesus "loved his own" and He died for his own. John 15 confirms this. Speaking of his particular love, Jesus says "Greater love has no one than this; that someone lay down his life for his friends."[262]

Clearly from this statement, according to Schrock the recipients of Christ's atoning love are not all people without exception but "His friends." This is a major misreading of John 3:16. John 3:16 appears to teach just the opposite: God's love for the world is demonstrated in that he "sent" his Son with the purpose that "whoever" believes in him will be saved. How can this be described as anything less than a "saving love"? God's saving love extends to all people. God desires the salvation of all as explicitly stated in John 3:16 and 2 Pet 3:9. What does not extend to all people is actual salvation since that is dependent upon fulfilling God's condition for salvation: repentance and faith. Since all people do not repent and believe, all are not saved. This fact, however, has nothing to do with a lack of God's love for them.

Before leaving Schrock's section on the particular nature of the atonement, I might point out that he has not attempted to incorporate or interpret any of the universal statements or metaphors found in John's Gospel. Words such as "light," "life," "bread," and "gift" as they appear in a general or universal context in John are important in a

261 Schrock, "Jesus Saves," 84.
262 Ibid.

consideration of the question at hand. It is interesting that Scripture routinely plays up the universal aspects of Christ's work, especially in John's Gospel.

The Efficacious Nature of the Atonement

Schrock wrote, "Historically, those who have defended penal substitution have usually embraced definite atonement."[263] In light of the large variety of Calvinists throughout Reformed history who have affirmed a form of unlimited atonement, coupled with the large number of non-Calvinists like John Wesley who affirmed unlimited atonement along with penal substitution, this statement needs qualification. In the footnote,[264] he mistakenly cited W. G. T. Shedd, who was actually moderate on the question of the extent of the atonement (assuming Schrock is citing Shedd as a proponent of limited atonement).

Schrock appealed to Owen's famous trilemma argument. He cited Clifford's critique of it along with my approving appeal to Clifford, then cited Carl Trueman's critique of Clifford. As I have noted in *Whosoever Will*, as well as this volume, Owen's trilemma argument has been criticized by Calvinists and non-Calvinists alike. Schrock's last sentence in the footnote is especially egregious: "It is the text of Scripture that must be 'defeated' in order to deny definite atonement."[265] Here Schrock is confusing his *interpretation* of Scripture with Scripture itself.

Owen's trilemma argument faces some problems, two of which appear to be insurmountable. The first is the problem of the issue of original sin. Notice it is not original "sins" but original "sin." If Christ died for original sin, then he died for at least one of the sins of the non-elect. If this is the case, then Owen's argument is defeated for Owen must admit that Christ died for some of the sins (original sin) of all men. Calvinist James Daane, in arguing that we can tell all in an unsaved audience that "Christ died for you," approached this type of argument. He wrote:

> Moreover, if we wholly reject every possible meaning of the statement, Christ died for you, what shall we do with original sin? Christ's death atoned for original sin, that one sin which is the fountain of all other sins, that one sin which entered the world, and as Paul teaches, brought death upon all men, that one sin which is every man's sin. One can, conceivably, say that Christ did not die for all the sins of every man, but one cannot say—and remain within Biblical teaching—that Christ did not die for that one sin which is every man's sin. Not every meaning of "for" can be rejected in the statement, "Christ died for your sins."[266]

263 Ibid., 88.
264 Ibid.
265 Ibid., 89.
266 J. Daane, "What Doctrine of Limited Atonement?," *Reformed Journal* 14 (1964): 16.

At the foundation of this problem is Owen's second problem: thinking of the imputation of sin to Christ as a transference of the guilt of specific transgressions. Would Owen consider the imputation of Christ's righteousness to believers as the transference of so many acts of law-keeping? It would seem not. Are believers credited with specific acts of righteousness on Christ's part? No, we are credited with a quality of righteousness. All of Christ's acts of obedience fall under the categorical class of "righteousness." Just as believers are not imputed with something like so many bits of righteousness but rather with righteousness categorically, so also Christ was not imputed with "sin-bits" but rather with sin in a comprehensive way. He was treated as though he were sinful. Owen, and it would seem Schrock as well, has a faulty notion of imputation. Christ died one death that all sinners deserve under the law. In paying the penalty of what one sinner deserves, he paid the penalty of what every sinner deserves. He suffered the curse of the law as defined by the law. Owen's trilemma argument undermines the true meaning of imputation and operates on the assumption of the transference of specific sins.

Charles Hodge, in contrast, has retained the proper understanding of imputation:

> What was suitable for one was suitable for all. The righteousness of Christ, the merit of his obedience and death, is needed for justification by each individual of our race, and therefore is needed by all. It is no more appropriate to one man than to another. Christ fulfilled the conditions of the covenant under which all men were placed. He rendered the obedience required of all, and suffered the penalty which all had incurred; and therefore his work is equally suited to all.[267]

At the end of this section Schrock wrote:

> If Christ *really* gave His life as a ransom for many (Matthew 20:28), if He *really* bore the curse in our place (Galatians 3:13), if He *really* became sin for us (2 Corinthians 5:21); then it must hold that there are some for whom He did not die. Otherwise, how could the ones He ransomed, freed from the curse, and imputed righteousness perish, unless the extent of His propitiation was less than universal [sic].[268]

Schrock's argument here entails that all the elect as a class (believing and unbelieving) were actually "freed from the curse" and "imputed with righteousness" at the cross. This is the error of justification at the cross of all the elect.

Schrock mentioned my critique of Owen's dependence on the double payment argument as relying heavily on a scholastic double payment for sins to defend definite

267 Hodge, *Systematic Theology*, 2:545.

268 Schrock, "Jesus Saves," 89.

atonement.[269] He then stated: "Greg Wills sets the record straight." Wills stated Owen "relies not so much on the double-payment argument as on the Bible's teaching." On page 15 of Wills's review, he stated that Owen placed "little weight" on the double payment argument. But the greater point Wills missed is that the concept of a "literal payment" for sins by Christ to God undergirds Owen's entire argument for double payment and for limited atonement. On page 16 of the review Wills stated that "Owen concluded repeatedly, all persons should be redeemed" if Christ atoned for the sins of all. Note the use of the word "repeatedly." On page 15 Wills said Owen "relies not so much on the double-payment argument" then on page 16 asserted, "Owen concluded repeatedly" based on the use of the double payment argument. These statements would appear to be incompatible.

A careful reading of Owen reveals he did indeed rely heavily on the double payment argument. It is one of the key linchpins of his whole attempt to argue for limited atonement. Virtually every contemporary Calvinist attempting to support limited atonement does so by appealing to Owen's double payment argument. Remove the errant commercial notion of a "literal payment" for sins and Owen's double payment argument collapses.

Priestly Argument for Definite Atonement

Schrock wrote: "Whatever the Bible teaches about Christ's priesthood will determine the nature and extent of Christ's atonement."[270] Not necessarily. Would it not be more proper to state that whatever Scripture teaches directly about the extent of the atonement will determine the question?

Schrock examined Old Testament priestly typology and from it found support for limited atonement. "The power of the argument is found in its comprehensive view of Scripture and the unity of the person and work of Christ."[271] This statement is footnoted, citing William Cunningham's *Historical Theology* and John Stott's *The Cross of Christ*. I found this interesting since Stott did not adhere to limited atonement. Noting that the Old Testament high priest always offered sacrifices for specific sinners, Schrock concluded with respect to Jesus as the antitype, "It is unmistakable that the high priest represents a particular people,"[272] and from this Schrock drew the further conclusion that the atonement is limited in its extent.

Schrock adduced four lines of evidence in an attempt to prove his point: (1) the priestly garments, (2) the location of the atonement, (3) the sacrifice itself, and (4) the relationship between intercession and atonement. With respect to the garments worn by the high priest, Schrock noted the names of the twelve tribes of Israel were engraved

269 Ibid.
270 Ibid., 90.
271 Ibid., 91.
272 Ibid.

on his ephod, "thus indicating his particular service for these peoples and not others." He concluded, "In this regard, the priestly attire 'visualizes' the particular nature of the atonement."[273]

Upon careful reflection, this analogy breaks down and actually works against Schrock's argument. Are we to assume that each and every member of each of the twelve tribes of Israel was genuinely a recipient of the benefits of the sacrifice made by the high priest such that upon their death they were redeemed and went to heaven? If just one did not, Schrock's analogy breaks down. I know of no Calvinist who would affirm such. In fact, it appears even Schrock himself does not affirm it since he mentions, "Under the Old Covenant, myriads of 'redeemed' Israelites died in the wilderness (Psalm 95), but now in the New Covenant, Christ has purchased redemption, justification (and faith), sanctification, and glorification for His particular people."[274] By placing "redeemed" in quotes, Schrock informs us he is assuming those who died in the wilderness were not genuinely redeemed. Were these not members of the twelve tribes whose names the high priest wore on his ephod? Did the high priest make sacrifices on the Day of Atonement for them? It would appear so. Schrock seems to contradict his own analogy.

The context of Numbers 14, which describes the debacle at Kadesh-Barnea, actually indicates God forgave the sins of those who rebelled (14:20) and that the deaths in the wilderness over the next thirty-eight years represented temporal discipline of God's covenant people and should not be interpreted salvifically.[275]

Schrock then turned to the subject of the location of the atonement in the Old Testament. He argued that typologically, the blood was applied to the altar in the old covenant, so that God is propitiated. Likewise Jesus applied his blood to the true altar in heaven (Heb 9:23–28). Thus all whom Jesus as high priest represented in his death are reconciled to God. Christ "is not making a mere provision for the salvation of all men by somehow qualifying all men for salvation, if only they will believe." "Christ is effecting propitiation before God as He applies his blood to the altar in heaven reconciling a God whose wrath goes out against each sin committed by those people whom Christ is representing. Consequently, temple typology rejects general atonement."[276]

The major problem here is the conflation of the extent of the atonement with its application. Schrock's appeal to the typology of Christ as our high priest simply cannot carry the freight he wishes to place on it. His description of dying for sin in general and dying for the specific sins of specific people borders on quantitative equivalentism, the notion that there is a quantum of sufferings in the death of Christ that corresponds

273 Ibid., 91–92.

274 Ibid., 105.

275 See my D. L. Allen, *Hebrews*, The New American Commentary (Nashville: B&H, 2010), 253–70, 365–69, for the argument in favor of this understanding of the text.

276 Schrock, "Jesus Saves," 93–94.

exactly to the number of sins of the elect whom he represents. Only a small minority of high Calvinists affirm quantitative equivalentism. Schrock's final statement "consequently, temple typology rejects general atonement" is a false conclusion in that he has not proven his premises upon which it rests. He merely extrapolates from typology to limited atonement.

Schrock's third category is the Old Testament sacrifices. He asserted that these different offerings "explain what Christ did on the cross, and when the question of extent/intent is applied to them, it becomes evident that they are harbingers of a particular redemption."[277] His major point here is that since the sacrifices of the Passover and Day of Atonement are only for those in the "covenantal community," then "there is nothing universal or general in these sacrifices which typify Christ (1 Corinthians 5:7)."[278] Schrock said those who affirm unlimited atonement may suppose that the high priest represented elect and non-elect in Israel in the old covenant, then Jesus the antitype will die for all people in the new covenant as well. He thinks this confuses the issue in two ways. First, the high priest does not represent spiritual Israel but Israel according to the flesh. "When egalitarians read categories of elect and non-elect back into the OT priesthood, they confuse the matter by conflating Christ's spiritual headship with Israel's ethnic constitution."[279] Second, "Christ will effectively save His covenant people in a way that the Old Covenant priests never could." Finally, Schrock compared Heb 10:14 with Heb 2:12–16 and concluded, "While taking on flesh and blood, Christ's obedience is not for all humanity, it is for His particular people."[280]

One must be careful with typology so as not to overreach. First, the type/antitype construct was never intended to account for all details of comparison/contrast between the two. Second, the fact that the Old Testament sacrifices were for all people in the covenant community actually argues for the opposite of limited atonement. If an Israelite under the old covenant was not ultimately redeemed, it was not for lack of atonement but for his own unbelieving heart. Third, I agree with Schrock that we should not read categories of elect and non-elect from the New Testament back into the Old. However, this seems to be precisely what he is doing in his argumentation. Neither should we read Old Testament categories of the sacrificial system into the New unless we have specific biblical justification to do so. Fourth, Schrock's two objections simply don't help his case in that they provide no evidence for limited atonement with respect to Jesus's sacrifice. Fifth, his statement that Jesus assumed human flesh not for the sake of humanity but only for the sake of the elect is misguided and also rests on a faulty conclusion. Note the difference in Schrock's view and the classical Christological view of the early church fathers, who said Christ suffers for the sins of all with whom he shares human nature.

277 Ibid., 95.
278 Ibid.
279 Ibid., 96.
280 Ibid.

By appealing to Heb 2:12–15, Schrock failed to mention the significance of the quotation of Ps 8:4–6 in Heb 2:6–8, followed by verse 9, which speaks of Jesus "tasting death for everyone," the grammar of which indicates that Christ's death was substitutionary in nature and universal in extent. Schrock's notion that Jesus's taking on human nature shared by all is merely coincidental because the elect are human is the argument John Owen and many Reformed theologians have made in an attempt to support limited atonement. Attempting to interpret the quotation, which speaks of all humanity immediately followed by Christ's death as being "for everyone," using the more limited terms found in Heb 2:12–16 is backward. The former governs the latter, not the other way around. Interestingly, unlike John Owen, who used Heb 2:14 to counter universalism by arguing limited atonement, John Calvin made no such use of Heb 2:14 to counter the same objection. For Calvin, what separates the elect from the non-elect is saving union with Christ, not limited atonement.

Schrock referred to Hebrews 9 several times in this section of his chapter in an effort to connect the priestly activity of Christ with limited atonement. It is also interesting to see what Calvin himself says about Heb 9:28: "Christ was sacrificed once to take away the sins of many people" (NIV). Commenting on this passage, Calvin stated, "He says many meaning all . . . as in Romans 5:15. It is of course certain that not all enjoy the fruits of Christ's death . . . , but this happens because their unbelief hinders them."[281] Calvin universalizes the term "many" rather than restricting it, like most do who defend limited atonement. Linguistically, "many" conveys the semantic concept of "more than a few," and in Rom 5:15 it is clear that "many" means "all without exception" as Calvin rightly noted.

Schrock's final category in this section concerns the issue of Christ's priestly intercession. His footnotes illustrate that he is dependent on William Symington's *On the Atonement and Intercession of Jesus Christ*. The key proposition Schrock is attempting to defend is this: Christ's atonement does not extend beyond those for whom he intercedes. Since I have basically addressed this above, I'll simply refer the reader to my comments at that point.

The Covenantal Nature of the Atonement

Schrock's fourth major section concerns the covenantal nature of the atonement. Jesus's death is rightly noted to inaugurate the new covenant, which the New Testament, especially Hebrews, affirms. Appealing to Heb 9:15–22, Schrock suggested there is a "textual restriction on the extent of the atonement" in verse 15 where those who are "redeemed" are also those who are "called." Schrock continued his error of conflating and thus confusing the atonement with its application. In the last sentence in this paragraph, Schrock

281 Calvin, *Hebrews*, 93–94. See Kennedy, *Union with Christ and the Extent of the Atonement*, 75–103; and my brief excursus on Calvin and Heb 2:14 and 9:28 in my *Hebrews*, 233–35.

noted that this passage in Hebrews "limits Christ's atoning benefits to those who are in covenant with Him—the non-elect remain outside Christ and under the judgment of God."[282] Notice the key word, "benefit," in this statement. Here Schrock gets it right. All Hebrews is saying is that the application of the atonement is for those who are in covenant with Christ; nothing is said in this passage about the *extent* of the atonement being limited. Schrock has drawn a false conclusion. "Christ's atonement did not simply make forgiveness possible; it decisively effected forgiveness and cleansing." Of course this is true. But the question is, *When* did forgiveness and cleansing occur? At the cross? In eternity past? No, forgiveness occurs at the point of faith, as Scripture teaches. Christ's atonement does indeed make forgiveness possible for the "elect," but it is not "effective" for them until they believe. Again, nothing here mandates limited atonement.

Under the heading "The Newness of the New Covenant," Schrock wrote, "Those who oppose particular redemption pay little attention to the covenantal structures of the Bible, and thus universalize the covenantal blessing of forgiveness, making it conditional upon faith."[283] This is an astounding statement given the New Testament is replete with verses that state salvation is conditioned upon faith. No one receives the covenant blessings unless he believes. Schrock stated that "making application of Christ's universal atonement dependent upon faith strips from Christ the honor of finishing and applying the covenant to each person individually."[284] How can this be when it is God himself who conditions the reception of salvation on faith? Schrock's statement that "egalitarians" "believe Christ purchased full forgiveness for everyone" is patently false.[285] All who believe in universal atonement, moderate Calvinist or otherwise, believe that full forgiveness is possible for everyone since Christ substituted for the sins of everyone, but actual forgiveness is only applied to those who believe. Whatever one's view of election and effectual calling, only those who are in the covenant by virtue of union with Christ experience the covenant blessings of forgiveness. Again, this in no way mandates particular redemption.

Schrock quoted approvingly Bruce Ware, who noted in the new covenant "there is no category for unbelieving covenant members."[286] He then followed with this statement: "Conjoined with a monergistic view of salvation, such a view of the New Covenant necessitates a particular and definite atonement."[287] I'm sure that this conclusion will come as some shock to Bruce Ware, who as a Calvinist himself rejects limited atonement. Only three sentences later, Schrock rightly stated, "all who are joined to Christ in His death will receive the blessings of this better covenant."[288] Exactly. The

282 Schrock, "Jesus Saves," 101.
283 Ibid., 103.
284 Ibid.
285 Ibid., 104.
286 Ibid.
287 Ibid.
288 Ibid.

blessings of the covenant require union with Christ. But Schrock in his next sentence fades back into the error of a commercial view of the atonement assuming "for those whom the Savior died, He truly saved!"

This is illustrated in the final paragraph of this section of Schrock's chapter where he spoke of Christ's death as having purchased faith. This is one of the linchpin arguments of John Owen for limited atonement. For Owen, not only is redemption purchased, but the means of redemption—faith—is also purchased only for the elect. Like Owen, Schrock treats faith like a commodity one can purchase. He seems unaware of the number of Calvinists who have critiqued this notion in Owen. One might also read Richard Baxter here as well, who responded to Owen by pointing out that Scripture never says that Christ died to purchase faith.[289] Like so many high Calvinists, it appears Schrock has mistakenly adopted a commercial theory of the atonement.

The Universal Impact of Definite Atonement

In his final section, Schrock addressed three vital subjects in the discussion: (1) the universal love of God, (2) the universal language of Scripture, and (3) the universal offer of the gospel.

Schrock stated that I equate God's love with his universal will to save all people. I do indeed. In fact, so does Reformed orthodoxy. Though I disagree with the notion of God's two wills (decretal and revealed), this concept is well known in Reformed orthodoxy. In God's so-called revealed will, God's love is indeed a universal saving love (John 3:16; 2 Pet 3:9, etc.). Schrock errs again by stating, "For egalitarians there is no place in the mind or heart of God for distinctive loves."[290] Since he has already lumped all who reject limited atonement into the egalitarian basket, Schrock's statement is untrue and misrepresents the beliefs of many of his fellow moderate Calvinists since they do indeed distinguish degrees in God's love. His statement is even untrue for many non-Calvinists who do the same.

What Schrock writes on pages 108–9 is especially troubling. Christians are not saved "because of some insipid universal love; it is because in His grace, God set His love on you before the foundation of the world."[291] It is the first part of this statement that is so troubling to me. "Insipid universal love"? My heart sinks just reading it. Place that comment alongside John 3:16: "For God so loved the world that He gave His only begotten Son, that whoever believes in Him should not perish but have everlasting life" (NKJV). Schrock then continued, Christ "does not throw the pearls of His sacrificial love at those from whom He does not expect, yes even engender, a return of love."[292] Pause and reflect on that statement. With echoes from Jesus's statement "Do not cast your pearls before

289 R. Baxter, *Universal Redemption of Mankind by the Lord Jesus Christ*, 42–43.
290 Schrock, "Jesus Saves," 106.
291 Ibid., 108–9.
292 Ibid., 109.

swine" Schrock applied the analogy to the non-elect. From these non-elect, Jesus neither "expects" a love response nor, in good Calvinist fashion, does he "engender" such a response within them. Schrock noted that Christ pursues his bride so that she "can experience the fullness of His love." He then stated: "This is far different from saying that God loves all, unconditionally, without exception."[293] Sadly, it certainly is. To top it all off, Schrock made a direct statement to anyone who is an unbeliever:

> Maybe today, you are reading this but don't know Christ: let all the kindnesses that God has given you—your gifts, joys, family, children, your very own life—and the promise of everlasting love lead you to repentance (Romans 2:4); trust in His Son and then you can experience the personal love of which Paul speaks.[294]

I must express my deepest concern about this statement in the sharpest of language. Such a message to the unsaved is bereft of the love of God and is virtually bankrupt. Is it *only* the "kindness" of God that is designed to lead us to repentance? Is it only the "promise" of some vague everlasting love offered to the unsaved? This is not only bad theology, it is bad Reformed theology. It borders on, if it is not outright, hyper-Calvinism.

It reduces the gospel message to bare statements about facts and conditional statements, in which God's own compassion and willingness that the unsaved be converted is entirely absent from the appeal. Can Schrock not even find it within himself to say to the unsaved "Jesus loves you!" or desires them all to be saved? The love of Christ for the unsaved has been shorn of its passion, and in its place comes an insipid, even embarrassing, appeal to the unsaved. God may love you; you will only know for sure if you believe. I doubt Schrock was converted under the preaching and teaching of such a limp and anemic expression of God's love for him.

This portion of Schrock's chapter is disappointing beyond words and illustrates why the discussion of this issue in the Southern Baptist Convention is so vital at this time. Limited atonement brings with it other errors into the church, both theological and practical. Schrock's brand of Calvinism is seriously problematic on the question of the love of God and the extent of the atonement.

Schrock next addressed the issue of universal language in Scripture. This is a difficult hill to climb for Schrock and all proponents of particular redemption due to the fact that there are so many New Testament passages that on a straightforward reading affirm unlimited atonement. He fosters two arguments to explain how the universal language of the New Testament supports definite atonement: the linguistic argument and the historical context of the apostles.

293 Ibid.
294 Ibid.

Schrock noted what all affirm: sometimes the Bible's use of "all" and "world" does not literally mean all people in the world. He rightly reminds us that context is the key. He praised John Owen for his "attention to the text" in determining the author's meaning. This is curious because Schrock seems oblivious to the many Calvinists, not to mention others, who have critiqued Owen for his failure in this very area. For example, as noted above in the section on John Owen, Neil Chambers demonstrated how, in circular fashion, Owen read his conclusion back into the reasons for his conclusion. His procedure constantly begs the question.

Furthermore, Schrock appears to miss the point that sometimes this universal language is stylized and hyperbolic. His appeal to Matt 3:5 is a case in point. The idea of limitation here is not "some of all kinds" of people, but rather that large groups are intended.

What Schrock and many others want to do is to use such stylized language to normalize all the nonstylized uses of "all" and "world" in atonement contexts. His appeal to the concept of "all without distinction" is meaningless. When "all" is used in this way, all "all" means is "all without any ethnic distinction." The use of this language is not meant to denote "some people of all kinds." Merely appealing to the notion of "all people without distinction" does not preclude the idea of all people without limitation. "All people" often means everyone without any ethnic distinction.

Consider Schrock's quote of Moses Stuart's commentary on Heb 2:9. He rightly pointed out that Stuart did not adhere to limited atonement but then wrongly concluded from Stuart's point that in some cases the phrase "for all" or "for all men" means all without distinction—Jews as well as Gentiles. It is not uncommon to find some Calvinists who affirm Christ died for all people to interpret the focus of some of these texts to indicate a focus on all without ethnic distinction. The error is concluding that therefore none of these texts means also "all without exception" or that there are no texts where "all" or "world" means "all without exception." Schrock has already conceded that Stuart affirmed unlimited atonement. Notice the conclusion Schrock drew from Stuart's point:

> Significantly, Stuart not only interprets the words of Hebrews 2:9 as a distributive (all without distinction), he principalizes his interpretation saying "the considerate interpreter, who understands the nature of the idiom, will never think of seeking, in expressions of this kind, proof of the final salvation *of every individual* of the human race."[295]

Schrock has made a significant error here in misreading what Stuart said. Stuart concluded that one cannot interpret this universal language as proof for universalism.

295 Ibid., 110 (emphasis in original).

He *did not* conclude that such language supports limited atonement. There is a world of difference between "universalism" and "universal atonement." Stuart rejected the former even as he accepted the latter.

Schrock's second argument concerning the use of universal language in Scripture is actually along the same lines as his previous argument. He attempted to show that "world" in the minds of the first-century apostles was more an ethnic designation for Jews and Gentiles. As we have already said, this does not vitiate the significance of the universal language. If the focus of "world" means "without distinction as to Jew and Gentile," then fine. In the culture of the apostles, all people in the world fell into one of those two classes. Again, this is no defeater for the interpretation of "all" and "world" in some contexts to mean "all unsaved people." Schrock mentioned John 3:16, stating that it is God's intention to save Jew and Gentile alike.[296] Does this mean God's "love" in that verse only extends to the elect among Jews and Gentiles? It would appear that is Schrock's interpretation.

There are many other universal passages in the New Testament that bear directly on the extent of the atonement. Schrock mentioned some of these but declined to consider them due to "space considerations." Fair enough. But Schrock's final statement in this section appears unwarranted, given the evidence: "based on the work of others, it is believed that similar conclusions would be found in these New Testament texts."[297]

The third part of Schrock's final section deals with the question of the universal offer of the gospel. He acknowledged that in the New Testament the offer of the gospel was made indiscriminately to all people without exception. He also acknowledged this is a problem for those who hold to limited atonement. He neglected to inform his readers that a significant group of Calvinists reject the concept of the universal or well-meant offer of the gospel. See, for example, David Engelsma's *Hyper-Calvinism and the Call of the Gospel: An Examination of the Well-Meant Gospel Offer*.[298] Schrock provided no definition of what the gospel offer is or entails. There is no affirmation that God desires the salvation of all men in his revealed will according to Reformed orthodoxy. This absence is telling.

In an attempt to reconcile definite atonement with a universal gospel offer, Schrock suggested five considerations. First, "Jesus makes universal invitations in the very same context where He affirms God's particular choice of some and rejection of others."[299] The verses he appealed to in no way support limited atonement and are more a part of the discussion concerning the nature of election. Second, Schrock raised the issue of those who have never heard the gospel. This is a thorny question no matter one's view of the extent of the atonement. The appeal to the Old Testament priests who made

296 Ibid., 112.

297 Ibid., 113.

298 D. Engelsma, *Hyper-Calvinism and the Call of the Gospel: An Examination of the "Well-Meant" Gospel Offer* (Grandville, MI: Reformed Free, 1994).

299 Schrock, "Jesus Saves," 114.

atonement and then went out to instruct the people followed by the question "Did Jesus really die to make provision for the sins of all men and then neglect to send His Spirit to give them the news?" fails to convince. Are we really expected to imagine that not one single person in Israel failed to be so instructed? What is the point of this contrived parallel? The reference to sending out the priests to instruct the people can only pertain generally. Thus by analogy this would be a picture of the church going out into the world to tell all people the good news. This is no argument for limited atonement. Third, Schrock stated the proclamation of the gospel was restricted before and during Jesus's lifetime, but after his crucifixion and resurrection, the gospel offer commanded by God to be offered to all the nations. What is the reason for this? There are sheep of other folds for whom Christ died (John 10:16).[300]

Fourth, the offer is "multi-intentional." It brings salvation and judgment. Agreed, but how does this support limited atonement, and what does it have to do with a genuine offer of salvation to all, including the non-elect? Furthermore, how could the offer of salvation bring judgment on the non-elect if they are rejecting what is not there for them to receive in the death of Christ? Judgment for rejecting the offer presupposes their ingratitude in rejecting a suitable provision for their salvation, does it not? Fifth, those who hold to a universal atonement transmute grace into something of a material commodity instead of something to be heard and believed. This point is the most bizarre of all to me and illustrates how Schrock does not seem to understand the contradiction his position entails. His quotation of moderate Calvinist James Richards illustrates the point.[301] Richards is making the powerful point that in the particularist gospel of limited atonement, God himself cannot offer salvation to the non-elect because there is no salvation to offer them—Christ did not die for their sins. They can't be redeemed even if they wanted to be. But the point is they cannot be offered that which does not exist for them. What is being offered the non-elect? Nothing. There is no salvation available for them because there is no atonement made for them. Schrock never mentioned that this critique has been pressed by moderate Calvinists since early in the seventeenth century. Nor does he seem to be aware that his question, "If God offers salvation to any who meet the condition of faith and repentance, is he not able to provide an eternal redemption?,"[302] borders on what hyper-Calvinists teach: the offer should not be made to any but those who give evidence of faith and repentance. Hyper-Calvinists teach that we should preach the gospel to all but only offer to those giving evidential signs of an interest in salvation. The Scriptures teach that the offer of the gospel is made unconditionally to all; it is the benefit of salvation that is conditioned upon faith and repentance.

300 Ibid., 116.
301 Ibid., 117.
302 Ibid.

Schrock concluded his final section with this statement: "Thus, the message we preach is not simply a sentimental invitation for whosoever may come."[303] I'll simply juxtapose to this statement these passages from John 3:16 and Rev 22:17–18: "For God so loved the world that He gave His only begotten Son, that whosoever believes in Him should not perish, but have everlasting life." "Both the Spirit and the Bride say 'Come!' Anyone who hears should say, 'Come!' And the one who is thirsty should come. Whoever desires should take the living water as a gift."

Schrock's conclusion is those who hold to universal atonement are guilty of "maligning" definite atonement. This is the last in a steady stream of words and phrases that tend to judge the actions, even motives, of some of those with whom Schrock disagrees. Notice the following phrases Schrock employed in this chapter: "Allen prides himself on defeating limited atonement"; "It is the text of scripture that must be 'defeated' in order to deny limited atonement"; "many who first mocked and rejected limited atonement"; "a movement away from biblical truth towards universal conceptions of the atonement"; and "many who malign definite atonement."[304] His use of "prides," "defeated," "mocked," and "malign" may suggest something of his attitude toward those who disagree with him on the extent of the atonement. Such language also appears to display the mistaken attitude of equating Scripture and one's interpretation of it.

Notice the contradiction and irony of his last paragraph compared to much that he has written in this chapter:

> May we seek to understand and appreciate the doctrine of definite atonement, not so that we can win a debate, but so that we can have greater confidence to go to the people for whom Christ died, people who today do not have street signs proclaiming the gospel to them, many who do not even know His name. Christ has died for these men, women, and children from every tribe, tongue, language and nation. We must go to them proclaiming without an asterisk: . . . Jesus Saves!

The irony here is that the message "Jesus Saves" does not apply to the non-elect. Not only that, but the message "Jesus Saves" is not an offer of the gospel nor a command to believe the gospel, nor is it an invitation to receive Jesus as Savior. The message "Jesus saves" never can apply to the non-elect. There is no remedy for their sins because Christ did not die for their sins. But even at that, isn't it true that the bare message "Jesus saves" conveys to an unsaved audience that Jesus is both able and willing to save them all? If so, how is that functionally different from saying "Jesus died for you"?

The problem I have with the preaching of some high Calvinists is that even they cannot escape from *implying* to all their listeners that Jesus died for them. But they don't

303 Ibid., 118.
304 Ibid., 81, 89, 107, and 119, respectively.

have a view of the atonement that can support such an implication. So they fudge and say to their audience "Jesus died for sinners." The audience interprets this to mean: "I'm a sinner, therefore Jesus died for me." But the high-Calvinist preacher means by this statement: "Jesus died for *elect* sinners." The word "sinners" here becomes a cypher for "the elect only." This is the inevitable position all who preach the gospel of limited atonement are in. Frankly, it is at best disingenuous and at worst deceptive to tell people "Jesus died for sinners" without explaining what one really means by this statement.

The irony of the title and subtitle of Schrock's chapter "Jesus Saves, No Asterisk Needed: Why Preaching the Gospel as Good News Requires Definite Atonement" is self-evident: definite atonement is not good news to the non-elect. Definite atonement is the gospel with an asterisk, whether overtly stated or not: *Jesus died for the sins of the elect only. If you believe, he died for you—and loves you too.

Gary Shultz (b. AD 1981)

Shultz wrote a doctoral dissertation in 2008 under the supervision of Bruce Ware at Southern Seminary on the subject of the extent of the atonement, which was published in 2014 under the title *A Multi-Intentioned View of the Extent of the Atonement.*[305] This is an important work on the subject as it is the first monograph to champion explicitly a multi-intentions view of the atonement in modern times.

Shultz's basic premise is that the atonement does not contain a single intention, the salvation of the elect, but multiple intentions are evident in Scripture, including the death of Christ for the sins of all people. It should be recognized at the outset that Shultz is writing from within the Reformed tradition and considers himself a Calvinist soteriologically. Shultz is a modern-day example of the theological position that has been evidenced in Reformed soteriology from the very beginning of the Reformed movement.

Shultz began with a helpful analysis of the issue. He correctly pointed out that there are only two positions: either Christ died for the sins of a limited number of people, or he died for the sins of all.

Shultz believes that the debate over extent centers on the question of God's intent, or purpose. This is indeed a significant part of the debate, but it is not the crux of the issue. The debate over extent centers on the answer to the question "For whose sins did Jesus die?" Calvinists differ with Arminians and other non-Calvinists over the question of God's intent in the atonement. But Calvinists who affirm universal atonement agree with Arminians and non-Calvinists on the actual extent of the atonement.[306]

Shultz correctly identified the false dilemma fallacy in those who wish to frame the question around the efficacy of the atonement versus the provisional nature of the atonement. For Shultz, limited atonement advocates err because they focus on a single

305 G. Shultz, *A Multi-Intentioned View of the Extent of the Atonement* (Eugene, OR: Wipf & Stock, 2014).

306 Ibid., 5.

purpose or intent in the atonement, while universal atonement advocates err because they don't subscribe to the notion that God's particular intention is to save only the elect. Schultz's work advocates both particular and general intentions in the atonement.

Shultz set the stage with a chapter on the historical background of the debate. While he correctly identifies the unlimited view as having been the majority view throughout church history, he errs in his claim that limited atonement has been a persistent minority view. As we have seen, that is simply not the case. The main reason for this claim is Shultz's view that Augustine tended toward limited atonement. Following a brief discussion of Gottschalk and the predestinarian debates in the ninth century, Shultz moved to the medieval period and concluded that Gregory of Remini and John Wycliffe held to particular redemption and Peter Lombard may have held it.[307] But, as we have seen, none of these men actually affirmed limited atonement. Wycliffe took an Augustinian reading of 1 John 2:2, but again, as we have demonstrated, this does not implicate one as an adherent of limited atonement, especially given other clear universal extent statements.

With respect to Calvin, Shultz thinks there is as much evidence to support a position of limited atonement as there is for universal atonement.[308] We have seen that such is not the case. Shultz thought that Beza's affirmation of limited atonement occurs as early as 1555, and since Calvin registered no disagreement with Beza, Shultz reasoned it is likely that Calvin held to limited atonement. This is problematic. There is no statement in Beza's 1555 *Tabula Praedestinationis* that affirmed limited atonement. One has to wait until 1586 for Beza's overt affirmation of limited atonement. Shultz relied on statements in Jinkins's "Theodore Beza" and Thomas's *The Extent of the Atonement* for his notion that Beza held to limited atonement in 1555. But Jinkins's and Thomas's statements make no such claim. Jinkins merely asserted that Calvin's view of predestination did not differ from Beza's, among other reasons, because Calvin never challenged Beza's view. This is certainly the case, but this is no assertion that Beza held to limited atonement. The same is true with Thomas's statement. Thomas simply stated, correctly I might add, that Beza's subordination of Christ and his work to God's decree of predestination "pointed the way to a doctrine of limited atonement."[309] Thomas does not state that Beza held to limited atonement at this point, though he would clearly do so later. Shultz has misinterpreted Jinkins and Thomas at this point.

Shultz provided an accessible summary of Arminius, Dort, and Amyraut on the extent question. He avoided the trap that many Calvinists fall into with respect to Amyraut's conditional and absolute notions of God's will. Unlike many caricatures of Amyraut's position, Shultz correctly pointed out that Amyraut distinguished between God's conditional and absolute will, but these are two aspects of God's one will, not

307 Ibid., 18.
308 Ibid., 25.
309 G. M. Thomas, *Extent of the Atonement*, 47.

two distinct wills in God.[310] Shultz also has a helpful summary of the positions of Richard Baxter and John Owen on the extent question. Finally, Shultz presents a very brief five-page summary of the debate from the nineteenth century to today.

Shultz concluded this section by rightly noting that a multiple-intention view of the atonement is not novel since it was held by many Calvinists from the very beginning of Reformed theological history. This perspective ties together and explains four important aspects of the atonement, according to Shultz:

1. Christ actually paid for the sins of all people.
2. Christ's death accomplishes universal aspects of creation that extend beyond his death for the elect and even for the non-elect.
3. Christ's atonement secures the salvation of the elect.
4. The general payment for all peoples' sin does not absolve those who do not believe but rather adds a further reason for the just condemnation.[311]

In chapter 3 Shultz demonstrated that the universal sufficiency of the atonement entails that Christ actually died for the sins of all people. This in turn guarantees the free offer of the gospel to all people and renders those who refuse to believe without excuse. Beginning with Isaiah 53, he treated all the major passages on the extent of the atonement, concluding that exegetically they can only be properly interpreted to teach that Christ actually died as a sacrifice for the sins of all people.[312] This is the strongest chapter in the book. One should especially take note of Shultz's treatment of Isaiah 53; John 3:16; 1 Cor 15:3; 2 Cor 5:14–21; 1 Tim 2:4–6; 1 Tim 4:10; Titus 2:11; Heb 2:9; and 2 Pet 2:1.

In chapter 4 Shultz chronicled the general intentions of the atonement. These include:

1. Grounding the universal offer of the gospel.
2. Making common grace possible.
3. Providing an additional basis of condemnation for those who reject the gospel.
4. Providing the supreme revelation of God's character as love.
5. Making Christ's cosmic triumph over all sin possible.[313]

This section contains an important discussion of the content of the gospel from 1 Cor 15:1–5. Here Paul indicates that "the content of the universal gospel call includes the fact that Christ died for all sins, and is therefore based upon an atonement that was for all sins. Part of the gospel is telling unbelievers that 'Jesus died for you.'"[314]

---

310 Shultz, *A Multi-Intentioned View*, 36.
311 Ibid., 53.
312 Ibid., 56–83.
313 Ibid., 89.
314 Ibid., 93.

Shultz also considered the role of the Holy Spirit in the call of the gospel. The Spirit convicts "the world" concerning the gospel message, and John explicitly connects the Spirit's work of conviction with Christ's death on the cross. "As John 16:7–11 explains, the Holy Spirit's work in the world is not only for the elect. . . . Limiting Christ's atonement to the elect results in separating part of the Spirit's work in the world from the Son's work on the cross."[315] Shultz noted that "Christ's payment for the sins of all people results in the Holy Spirit's work among both the elect and the nonelect, and this brings both grace and justice as it is received or rejected."[316]

Shultz asserted that common grace and natural gifting of human beings are wrought on the basis of the atonement.[317] Perhaps such is the case, especially with common grace, but no necessity for this being the case appears to be stated in Scripture.

Scripture emphasizes the atonement as the supreme expression of God's love toward humanity. Passages such as John 3:16; 1 John 4:9–10; and Rom 5:8, along with many others, illustrate this. Therefore, it would seem the atonement is accomplished for the sins of all people. For Shultz, the multi-intention view of the atonement properly recognizes the universal love God has for all and the particular love he has for the elect.

A universal atonement is necessary for Christ's cosmic triumph over sin to be realized. Passages such as Col 1:20 seem to indicate that even the non-elect are reconciled objectively in the atonement (though they remain subjectively unreconciled to God because they have refused to believe the gospel and hence remain in their sins). Limited atonement cannot ground Christ's reconciliation of all things since no atonement exists for the sins of all the non-elect.[318]

> That Christ's cosmic triumph over sin is only made possible by his payment for all sin is seen in four ways. First, we can see it in the nature of Christ's victory on the cross over all sin. . . . Second, it is evident in the nature of the reconciliation wrought by the cross, as the elect, the non-elect, and the creation are all reconciled to God, albeit in different ways. Third, the resurrection of all people, the elect and the nonelect, supports this truth. Finally, we see it in Christ's role as King, which is based upon his priestly work in the atonement as a sacrifice for all sin.[319]

Shultz distinguished between "salvific reconciliation" and "cosmic reconciliation" based on Col 1:21–23. John 5:26–28 and Rev 20:5–7 teach the resurrection of the

315 Ibid., 96.
316 Ibid., 100.
317 Ibid., 101–4.
318 Ibid., 111.
319 Ibid., 112.

elect and the non-elect. Since unbelievers will be raised in the eschaton, it would seem they are included in Christ's atonement just as those who have believed the gospel.[320]

Shultz also highlighted "particular intentions" in the atonement, which consist chiefly in securing the salvation of the elect. This chapter includes the standard Reformed arguments for understanding God's ultimate intent, or purpose, in the atonement as securing the salvation of those whom he has chosen before the creation of the world to redeem from their sins: the elect.

Shultz asserted that such a multi-intention view of the atonement is coherent, comprehensive, and consistent internally and externally with all aspects of scriptural teaching on the atonement.

Baptist Confessions in America

No survey of the question of the extent of the atonement among Baptists in general and Southern Baptists in particular would be complete without a review of the various Baptist confessions.

Lumpkin stated: "In Virginia and North Carolina, the earliest Baptists held Arminian views, and they seem generally to have acknowledged the Standard General Baptist Confession of 1660."[321] However, the influence of Regular and Separatist Baptists in the South after the mid-eighteenth century began to sway many General Baptists toward a more Calvinistic position. Most General Baptist churches were reconstituted along Calvinistic lines.[322]

However, it was often the case that these reconstituted churches did not accept limited atonement and retained their view of unlimited atonement. As we have already demonstrated, many Regular and Separatist Baptists churches and associations affirmed universal atonement.

One of the most important and influential eighteenth-century Baptist confessions in America is the Philadelphia Confession (1742). It was modeled on the Second London Confession (which was itself modeled on the Westminster Confession) and follows its wording closely at certain points.[323] While the Philadelphia Confession is often understood as affirming a limited atonement, a careful examination of the relevant section on the atonement reveals that the confession does not mandate or even

320 Ibid., 119.

321 Lumpkin, *Baptist Confessions of Faith*, 347.

322 Ibid.

323 For a comparison of the Baptist distinctives affirmed in the Philadelphia and Second London Confession that differentiated these Particular Baptists from some of the Presbyterian doctrines of the Westminster Confession, consult S. Lemke, "What Is a Baptist? Nine Marks That Separate Baptists and Presbyterians," *Journal for Baptist Theology and Ministry* 5 (2008): 10–39.

affirm a strictly limited atonement, but it does affirm a kind of particular redemption in the sense that the atonement secures the final salvation of "all those for whom Christ has obtained eternal redemption." The specific section addressing the atonement and its extent is chapter 8, sections 4 through 8:

> Chapter 8.4. This office the Lord Jesus did most willingly undertake, which that he might discharge he was made under the law, and did perfectly fulfil it, and underwent the punishment due to us, which we should have borne and suffered, being made sin and a curse for us; enduring most grievous sorrows in his soul, and most painful sufferings in his body; was crucified, and died, and remained in the state of the dead, yet saw no corruption: on the third day he arose from the dead with the same body in which he suffered, with which he also ascended into heaven, and there sitteth at the right hand of his Father making intercession, and shall return to judge men and angels at the end of the world.
>
> 5. The Lord Jesus, by his perfect obedience and sacrifice of himself, which he through the eternal Spirit once offered up unto God, hath fully satisfied the justice of God, procured reconciliation, and purchased an everlasting inheritance in the kingdom of heaven, for all those whom the Father hath given unto Him.
> 6. Although the price of redemption was not actually paid by Christ till after his incarnation, yet the virtue, efficacy, and benefit thereof were communicated to the elect in all ages, successively from the beginning of the world, in and by those promises, types, and sacrifices wherein he was revealed, and signified to be the seed which should bruise the serpent's head; and the Lamb slain from the foundation of the world, being the same yesterday, and to-day and for ever.
> 7. Christ, in the work of mediation, acteth according to both natures, by each nature doing that which is proper to itself; yet by reason of the unity of the person, that which is proper to one nature is sometimes in Scripture, attributed to the person denominated by the other nature.
> 8. To all those for whom Christ hath obtained eternal redemption, he doth certainly and effectually apply and communicate the same, making intercession for them; uniting them to himself by his Spirit, revealing unto them, in and by his Word, the mystery of salvation, persuading them to believe and obey, governing their hearts by his Word and Spirit, and overcoming all their enemies by his almighty power and wisdom, in such manner and ways as are most consonant to his wonderful and unsearchable dispensation; and all of free and absolute grace, without any condition foreseen in them to procure it.

Notice also the confession's statement in chapter 11.4: "God did from all eternity decree to justify all the elect, and Christ did in the fullness of time die for their sins, and rise again for their justification; nevertheless, they are not justified personally, until the Holy Spirit doth in time due actually apply Christ unto them." The statement does not state that Christ died *only* for the sins of all the elect. No doubt, many have inferred this, but it is important to point out that the confessional statement does not assert such. What the statement does assert is a kind of particular redemption that does not preclude a universal atonement. From this statement alone, it cannot be discerned whether the authors of the statement intended to assert *only* a strictly limited atonement, or whether they have worded the statement to allow for an unlimited atonement with respect to actual substitution for sins, as is the case with the Canons of Dort and the Westminster Confession.

In either case, Steve Lemke has correctly noted that the Philadelphia Confession was never widely adopted after 1845 by Baptist associations, state conventions, or educational institutions. It was "largely ignored by Southern Baptists after the mid-nineteenth century and remains something of an outlier in Southern Baptist experience for the last century and a half."[324]

The Articles of Faith of the Kehukee Association (1777) in North Carolina were designed to address the objections of the Separates to the Philadelphia Confession and to declare against Arminianism.[325] Glaringly absent from this confession is any statement about limited atonement. Election is stated to be individual and unconditional.

The Separatist Baptist Sandy Creek Association in North Carolina produced a confession called Principles of Faith of the Sandy Creek Association (1816).[326] Luther Rice was involved in the development of this confession. Rice was most likely a moderate Calvinist, as we argued earlier. Like the Kehukee Confession, there is no reference to limited atonement. As Thompson correctly pointed out, these principles were brief and appear to have been left undefined enough to allow latitude of interpretation of certain points.[327]

However, in 1845 the Sandy Creek Association revised their doctrinal confession to be essentially the same as the New Hampshire Confession. This change reflects "a clear and deliberate move away from the five-point high Calvinism that was pushed by Regular Baptists in the eighteenth century to a modified 'Calminian Baptist' view by the time of the founding of the Southern Baptist Convention."[328]

---

324 Lemke, "History or Revisionist History?," 244.

325 Lumpkin, *Baptist Confessions of Faith*, 354.

326 The confession can be found in the Minutes of the Sandy Creek Association for October 26, 1816, in G. W. Purefoy, *A History of the Sandy Creek Association*, 104–5.

327 P. Thompson, "Baptists and 'Calvinism,'" 74. See also Lumpkin, *Baptist Confessions of Faith*, 358, who confirms this.

328 As noted by Lemke, "History or Revisionist History?," 245. (See the Minutes of the Sandy Creek Association for September 26, 1845 in Purefoy, *A History of Sandy Creek Association*, 197–216.) The Sandy Creek Association did not use the Philadelphia Confession at all.

Another confession making no statement about limited atonement is the Terms of Union between the Elkhorn and South Kentucky, or Separate, Associations (1801). In fact, this confession makes no statement on the extent of the atonement at all.

The most important nineteenth-century Baptist confession is undoubtedly the New Hampshire Confession (1833). Less stringent than the Philadelphia Confession, it was designed to reflect a more moderate Calvinism. Like the previous three confessions, there is no reference to limited atonement. The document is constructed in such a way that one could affirm either limited or unlimited atonement and affirm the confession. Article 4 includes this statement that Christ "made atonement for our sins by his death."[329] Garrett stated the confession could just as well be described as "moderately Arminian" as "moderately Calvinistic."[330]

A comparison of the Philadelphia Confession with the New Hampshire Confession is revealing. The latter is clearly much more moderate in its Calvinism and likewise does not affirm limited atonement, a strict understanding of individual election along the lines of Dort, or irresistible grace, though the latter two are not overtly excluded by the confession.

In 1834, *A Treatise on the Faith of the Free Will Baptists* appeared. Chapter 6, "The Atonement and Mediation of Christ," states, "Christ gave himself a sacrifice for the sins of the world, and thus was made salvation possible for all men."[331] This statement clearly affirms unlimited atonement.

Henry Fish produced *The Baptist Scriptural Catechism* (1850). It is Calvinistic in tone, as illustrated by the distinction that Fish draws between the *design* of the atonement and the *sufficiency* of the atonement:

> Q. Did the atonement, in its saving design, embrace more than the elect?
>
> A. The elect only; . . . Matt. 1:21
>
> Q. And yet, was it not in its nature of sufficient value for the salvation of all mankind?
>
> A. It was, and hence God is said to have "sent his Son into the world," "that the world through him might be saved." John 3:17; Heb 2:9; John 1:29; 2 Cor 5:14–20; 1 Tim 2:6; 1 John 2:2.[332]

---

329 Lumpkin, *Baptist Confessions of Faith*, 362–63. For a more detailed analysis of how the New Hampshire Confession downplayed some of the more Calvinistic elements of the Second London Confession, see Yarnell, "Calvinism," 81.

330 Garrett, *Baptist Theology*, 151.

331 Lumpkin, *Baptist Confessions of Faith*, 372.

332 H. C. Fish, "Baptist Scriptural Catechism, 1850," *The Reformed Reader* (blog), accessed May 25, 2015, http://reformedreader.org/ccc/bsc.htm.

Notice there is no direct statement of limited atonement. Fish spoke of the "design" of the atonement as being for the elect only. Yet he spoke of its "nature" as "sufficient value for the salvation of all mankind." The key question here is what Fish means by "sufficient." If he means intrinsic sufficiency in terms of worth and value, then it is possible the catechism intends to suggest limited atonement. But if he intends to speak of an extrinsic sufficiency in the sense that Christ actually died for the sins of all, with salvation available to all who believe, then the catechism is not intended to teach a strictly limited atonement.

The doctrinal statements of the American Baptist Association (1905) and the North American Baptist Association (1950) both affirm unlimited atonement. The Confession of the Fundamental Fellowship (1921) and later the Goodchild Confession (1944) affirmed unlimited atonement: "We believe in Jesus Christ . . . making atonement for the sins of the world by his death."[333] The Articles of Faith of the Baptist Bible Union of America (1923) affirm unlimited atonement in Article 8.

The most important confession for Southern Baptists today is the Baptist Faith and Message, adopted in 1925 and slightly modified in 1963, 1998, and again in 2000. There is no statement affirming limited atonement in this confession. The framers of the original 1925 version all affirmed unlimited atonement: E. Y. Mullins, L. R. Scarborough, C. P. Stealey, W. J. McGlothin, S. M. Brown, E. C. Dargan, and R. H. Pitt served on the draft committee.

It is also true that there is no direct statement in the article on salvation that specifically affirms unlimited atonement. However, in Article 3, on the subject of humanity, the following statement is significant: "The sacredness of human personality is evident in that God created man in His own image, and in that Christ died for man; therefore every man possesses dignity and is worthy of respect and Christian love."[334]

The wording and context of this sentence strongly indicates an unlimited atonement. First, reference is made to "human personality," a phrase obviously referring to all humans. The ground for the sacredness of human personality is stated as "God created man in His own image." Here the word "man" clearly refers first to Adam and Eve as God's direct creation, and as progenitors of the human race, all humanity is subsumed in the word "man."

The second statement, "Christ died for man," draws its meaning contextually from the previous statement. Here "man" obviously means "all humanity." This is further confirmed by the third use of "man" in the sentence: "Therefore every man possesses dignity." Here "man" as modified by "every" refers to every individual human being on the earth. It cannot mean otherwise given the context.

In all three uses of the word "man" in this sentence, there is no limitation what-

333 Lumpkin, *Baptist Confessions of Faith*, 383.

334 Ibid., 395.

soever. In fact, context precludes any limitation. All humanity is indicated. Should one wish to interpret "died for" as including a provision of common grace, one would have to read a dual meaning into the statement: Christ died *for the sins of* the elect, and Christ died to bring common grace to the non-elect, all subsumed in the simple statement "Christ died for man." This does not seem to be the intent of the statement.

It would appear impossible to escape the conclusion that this article of the confession affirms universal atonement. By logical entailment, limited atonement is here denied.

This survey of creeds and confessions indicates several things. First, even among the Reformed, none of the major historical confessions mandated limited atonement only or excluded unlimited atonement. Second, some of the early Reformed confessions assert unlimited atonement, even though they also assert a limited *intent* on God's part in who will be redeemed—namely, the elect. Third, only a few Baptist confessions assert limited atonement exclusively in a way that rejects unlimited atonement. Even the majority of Particular Baptist confessions are written with a certain ambiguity on this specific issue.

Fourth, no Baptist confession from the eighteenth century and beyond asserts limited atonement, including the Abstract of Principles, the confession of Southern Seminary, founded only a few years after the birth of the Southern Baptist Convention in 1845. Fifth, this confessional evidence suggests that even many Calvinistic Baptists in the eighteenth and nineteenth centuries were moving away from limited atonement. Sixth, neither the 1689 London Confession nor the 1742 Philadelphia Confession, the only two major confessions that come near to affirming a limited atonement, even though neither affirms a strictly limited atonement, were very influential on Southern Baptists at the time of the founding of the new convention in 1845.[335]

Seventh, no Southern Baptist seminary has ever affirmed a confessional statement that includes limited atonement. The 1858 Abstract of Principles governing Southern Baptist Theological Seminary makes no mention of limited atonement. Though the 1742 Philadelphia Confession was available, the authors chose not to utilize it. Interestingly, one criterion that Basil Manly Jr. and the founding faculty of SBTS utilized in constructing the Abstract was that it would take no position about which there was division within the new Southern Baptist Convention.[336]

The authors devised the confession with sensitivity to both the moderate Calvinistic theology of Andrew Fuller, along with the New Divinity movement. Several leading Southern Baptists, such as William B. Johnson, first president of the

335 Though T. George has asserted that all 293 delegates in Augusta at the founding of the Southern Baptist Convention hailed from churches and associations that had adopted the Philadelphia/Charleston Confession of Faith (George, *Baptist Confessions, Covenants, and Catechisms* [Nashville: B&H, 1996], 11.)

336 J. P. Boyce, "Two Objections to the Seminary," *Western Recorder* 20 (1874): 2; and noted in R. A. Baker, ed., *A Baptist Source Book: With Particular Reference to Southern Baptists* (Nashville: Broadman, 1966), 140. See also G. Wills, *Southern Baptist Theological Seminary (1859–2009)* (New York: Oxford University Press, 2009), 31; and W. Mueller, *A History of Southern Baptist Theological Seminary* (Nashville: Broadman, 1959), 32.

Southern Baptist Convention, did not affirm limited atonement. The primary author of the first drafts of the Abstract, Basil Manly Jr., himself an advocate of limited atonement, was unable to persuade the other committee members to include limited atonement. The document underwent numerous revisions in the vetting process by the seminary faculty, a group of pastors, and a committee of Baptist educators. At most, the final document affirms four of the traditional five points,[337] though the doctrine of irresistible grace is not to be found specifically in the document either. Even Al Mohler, president of Southern Seminary and a high Calvinist himself, has described the Abstract as a three-point Calvinist document in that it does not affirm limited atonement or irresistible grace.[338]

Steve Lemke correctly noted that the SBC in general session never voted on or approved the Abstract to be a reflection of the convention's own doctrinal perspective. The New Hampshire Confession was always more popular with Southern Baptists than the Abstract.[339]

New Orleans Baptist Seminary (NOBTS) was founded in 1917. President Byron H. DeMent and faculty member W. E. Denham wrote the doctrinal confession for the seminary: The Articles of Religious Belief of NOBTS (1918). Both men were graduates of Southern Seminary, yet neither felt compelled to make use of the Abstract of Principles or its language. Steve Lemke, Provost of NOBTS, described the confession as affirming "2.5 to 3.0 points of classical Calvinism."[340]

It is not uncommon to hear some Calvinistic Baptists claim that the confessional documents of Baptists indicate a firm commitment to all the so-called five points of Dortian Calvinism (where Dort is understood to support exclusively limited atonement—a historical error, as we have seen).[341] History demonstrates otherwise. Lemke pointed out that "every major Baptist church manual or book on Baptist beliefs from 1853 through 1913 (though they were clearly aware of the *Philadelphia Confession*

337 See Wills, *Southern Baptist Theological Seminary (1859–2009)*, 32, 37–38.

338 J. A. Smith, Sr., "Mohler: Southern Baptists Need 'Table Manners' When Discussing Calvinism," *Southern News*, November 15, 2013, http://news.sbts.edu/2013/11/15/mohler-southern-baptists-need-table-manners-when-discussing-calvinism/.

339 Lemke, "History or Revisionist History?," 248–49, 251–52. The adoption of Southern Seminary and the Abstract of Principles was unusual "in that it was not done in the open convention session business, but in auxiliary meetings called the 'Education Convention' in 1857 and 1858. Thus neither the Abstract of Principles nor the adoption of Southern Seminary actually came to a full convention vote." Lemke cited Wills, *Southern Baptist Theological Seminary*, 31–52, and *SBC Annuals* for 1857 and 1858.

340 Lemke, "History or Revisionist History?," 250–51.

341 So, for example, Timothy George asserted, "Among Baptists in America the theology of Westminster was transmitted through the enormously influential Philadelphia Confession of Faith. Despite a persistent Arminian strain within Baptist life, until the twentieth century most Baptists adhered faithfully to the doctrines of grace as set forth in the Pauline-Augustinian-Reformed theology" ("Baptists and the Westminster Confession," in *The Westminster Confession into the 21st Century*, ed. Ligon Duncan, [Fearn, Scotland: Christian Focus, 2004], 1:155). Of course, it may be that George's use of "doctrines of grace" includes the moderate position on the extent of the atonement.

and the Abstract of Principles) promulgated and recommended the *New Hampshire Confession* as the confession that best expressed the perspective of Baptists."[342]

With respect to Baptists associated with the Baptist World Alliance, Paul Fiddes stated he could not find "a single example of limited atonement in any modern confession of faith."[343] Fiddes also noted that the earlier Baptist confessions "were rather undogmatic in their understanding of the *means* of atonement . . . It was not until the two major Baptist Confessions of 1677 and 1679, both under influence from the Westminster Confession, that there was an explicit statement of penal substitution."[344] Fiddes presumes that the doctrine of limited atonement is a logical consequence of the penal substitutionary view of the atonement.[345] This assessment is wide of the mark. However, if one takes a commercialistic view of the atonement such that the nature of Christ's substitution was for the sins of the elect in a quantitative equivalentist fashion, as one finds in Baptists such as J. L. Dagg and Tom Nettles, then the logical connection argument becomes stronger.

When it comes to Southern Baptists in particular, it is clear by the confessions they developed that they chose a theological approach that is somewhat of a mixture of Calvinism and Arminianism but leaning toward the Calvinist side with respect to total depravity, election, and perseverance.[346]

The shift against limited atonement in the early life of the Southern Baptist Convention began among those Baptists who first he ld it, not among the Arminians. Mercer and Furman both shifted from their original commitment to limited atonement to the unlimited position.[347] At the time of the formation of the Southern Baptist Convention, many aspects of high Calvinism were in dispute among Baptists, especially the doctrine of limited atonement. Though some of the original leaders of the early SBC were high Calvinists, they were by no means all high Calvinists, and the majority of the people who composed the early SBC were not high Calvinists or even moderate Calvinists in the sense that they affirmed the other four points of the TULIP.

Baptist historians have confirmed the diversity that existed among the earliest leaders of the Southern Baptist Convention with respect to Calvinism and especially limited atonement. Wayne Flynt, distinguished professor of history at Auburn University, likewise confirmed this theological moderation on the part of most Baptists in Alabama.

342 Lemke, "History or Revisionist History?," 252.

343 P. Fiddes, *Tracks and Traces: Baptist Identity in Church and Theology*, Studies in Baptist History and Thought 13 (Carlisle, UK: Paternoster, 2003), 239.

344 Ibid., 244.

345 Ibid., 243–44.

346 Lemke, "History or Revisionist History?," 243.

347 Richards, *Winds of Doctrine*, 58.

> No Biblical dispute shaped early Alabama Baptists so profoundly as Calvinism. . . . Although Baptists were Calvinists in the general sense of that term, they modified the doctrine. . . . If Charleston, South Carolina provides the clearest ancestry for Calvinism, Sandy Creek, North Carolina, lays firmest claim to the revival tradition. Ardent, charismatic, emotional, independent, Biblicist, the Sandy Creek tradition merged elements of both Calvinism and Arminianism.[348]

Albert W. Wardin Jr., in his history of Tennessee Baptists, stated, "In 1856 the *Baptist Watchman* maintained that Separate Baptist influence had triumphed and most Missionary or United Baptists held to a general atonement."[349] Note the year: 1856—just eleven years after the founding of the Southern Baptist Convention. The "United Baptists" resulted from the union of Regular Baptists and Separate Baptists in Kentucky, Virginia, and the Carolinas in the late eighteenth century and early nineteenth century. Generally speaking, from this group, though not only from them, emerged the formation of the Southern Baptist Convention in 1845.

Baptist historian Nathan Finn, dean of The School of Theology and Missions at Union University, confirmed these accounts of diversity among earlier Baptists on the Calvinism question and the extent of the atonement specifically.

> This does not mean Southern Baptists were uniformly Calvinist—if by Calvinist one means strict adherence to all "five points." For example, it is clear that the founding generation of Southern Baptists were debating the intent of the atonement, with some holding to more "limited/particular" understandings and others holding to more "general/unlimited" views. It is also clear, however, that there was minimal debate concerning the doctrines of election or perseverance.[350]

In light of the evidence, Finn's final statement concerning election needs to be nuanced. In some places, there was no small stir over the nature of election as well. In early Southern Baptist history, most churches and associations did not adhere to five-point Calvinism.

From the evidence we may infer the following generalizations. New light Calvinists in the colonial era in New England followed Jonathan Edwards, but in the Sandy Creek

348 W. Flynt, *Alabama Baptists: Southern Baptists in the Heart of Dixie* (Tuscaloosa: University of Alabama Press, 1998), 26–27.

349 A. W. Wardin, Jr., *Tennessee Baptists: A Comprehensive History, 1779–1999* (Nashville: Tennessee Baptist Convention, 1999), 148. Wardin also noted: "In its adoption of a new constitution in 1844, the Concord church [Brentwood, TN] eliminated references to election and effectual calling and instead declared, 'That the blessings of salvation are made free to all by the gospel'" (148).

350 N. Finn, "On the 'Traditional Statement': Some Friendly Reflections from a Calvinistic Southern Baptist," *Journal for Baptist Theology and Ministry* 10 (2013): 66–67.

area and churches associated with Sandy Creek, a one-point Calvinist framework (perseverance) prevailed. Richard Furman followed Andrew Fuller on the extent question: Christ's death substituted for all sinners, but the application of the atonement is limited only to the elect.[351] W. B. Johnson likewise reflected Fuller's views. R. B. C. Howell of First Baptist Church in Nashville, Tennessee, appears to be the most prolific and influential Baptist theologian in the pre-1845 group of southern Baptists. His view on extent is that of Andrew Fuller as well.[352]

Lemke summarized the evidence and concluded "that the Baptist confessions (particularly those affirmed in the South) from the early-nineteenth century through the early twentieth century were not overwhelmingly five-point Calvinist confessions, but in fact reflected various degrees of compromise between Arminianism and Calvinism."[353] Lemke's conclusion is difficult to resist in light of the evidence. The historical situation was such that Baptists were more Calvinistic than some non-Calvinist writers have been willing to admit, and they were less Calvinistic than some Calvinist writers have been willing to admit.

In spite of the insistence by Calvinists like Michael Horton and Arminians like Roger Olson that a hybrid of Calvinism and Arminianism is not possible,[354] Southern Baptists have demonstrated from the very outset of their existence that such is indeed the case.

---

351 J. A. Rogers, *Richard Furman: Life and Legacy* (Macon, GA: Mercer University Press, 1985).

352 W. B. Johnson, *The Gospel Developed through the Government and Order of the Churches of Jesus Christ* (Richmond, VA: H. K. Ellyson, 1846), reprinted in *Polity: A Collection of Historic Baptist Documents*, ed. M. Dever (Washington, DC: Center for Church Reform, 2001), 161–245.

353 Lemke, "History or Revisionist History?," 254.

354 M. Horton, "Preface," in R. Olson, *Against Calvinism* (Grand Rapids, MI: Zondervan, 2011), 10; R. Olson, *Arminian Theology: Myths and Realities* (Downers Grove, IL: InterVarsity Academic, 2006), 61–77.

Part Three

The Extent of the Atonement

A Critical Review

8

A Critical Review of *From Heaven He Came and Sought Her*

In the final two chapters of the book, I will examine and critique the latest scholarly work written in defense of limited atonement, *From Heaven He Came and Sought Her: Definite Atonement in Historical, Biblical, Theological, and Practical Perspective,* and summarize why unlimited atonement comports better with Scripture.[1] The book has been touted by some as the "definitive" scholarly word on definite (limited) atonement. David Wells said of it in his endorsement printed on the first page: "This is the definitive study." Free copies of the book were distributed to attendees at the 2014 Together for the Gospel conference.

David Gibson and Jonathan Gibson serve as editors of this substantive tome of 703 pages, including indices, published by Crossway. The work includes twenty-three chapters written by a notable cadre of twenty-one authors from a variety of backgrounds (including Presbyterian, Anglican, and Baptist) addressing the historical, biblical, theological, and pastoral perspective on the topic.

As with any multi-author volume, the chapters ebb and flow as to content, style, and relative substance. There is the occasional unavoidable overlapping of subject

1 D. Gibson and J. Gibson, eds., *From Heaven He Came and Sought Her: Definite Atonement in Historical, Biblical, Theological, and Practical Perspective* (Wheaton, IL: Crossway, 2013).

matter in various chapters as well. But this should not detract from what is overall a significant study on an often misunderstood subject.

The book's chief purpose is to defend the notion of definite atonement (more commonly referred to as "limited atonement" and also referred to as "particular redemption") by presenting supportive arguments and attempting to answer counterarguments.

Organizationally, the volume's fourfold structure (historical, biblical, theological, and pastoral) is probably the best way to approach the subject. The chapters in the first three sections are about equally divided (seven, six, and six), with each section totaling roughly 150 pages. The final pastoral section contains three chapters.

The table of contents is clear and provides a brief description of the major topic of each chapter. The "Select Bibliography" is only seven pages in length and is missing some significant works that probably should be listed, even for a select bibliography. Three indices (biblical references, names, and subject) provide the reader a helpful reference. These are reasonably helpful, though there are a few errors and omissions, which is practically unavoidable in a book of this size.

Even though the title of the book is a quotation from a well-known hymn, it engenders concern. "Her," in scriptural soteriology, is only used for Old Testament Israel as a whole and for the church in the New Testament as composed of believers. The pronoun is never used for the abstract class of all the elect who will inherit eternal life. The usage of "Her" in the title is indicative of the fact that these high Calvinists are continually equivocating between the abstract sense of the "elect" and the "elect" as believers. There is no usage in the New Testament of the elect considered in the abstract. It was reasoning along those lines—that is, what is true of elect believers is true of all the elect in the abstract—that was one of the conceptual doorways through which some Calvinists (the theoretical antinomians) entered into hyper-Calvinism in the late seventeenth and eighteenth centuries. One observes that many authors in this volume merely assume that what is true of the believing elect is *ipso facto* true of the class of the elect considered atemporally in the abstract. They assume the "Her" that Christ came for and sought is all of those elect who are appointed to eternal life, whether born or not yet born, whether believing or not yet believing, instead of the "Her" in the sense of the church that Samuel Stone's lyrics indicate. This is problematic.

J. I. Packer contributed the foreword, and it is vintage Packer; well written and full of high praise for the book. Many will remember Packer's introduction, mentioned earlier, to the Banner of Truth edition of John Owen's *Death of Death in the Death of Christ* more than fifty years ago. Packer referenced his earlier introduction to the 1959 Banner of Truth edition in the current foreword and informs us: "I am glad to be able to say nothing in it needs to be modified or withdrawn."[2] Thankfully,

2 J. I. Packer, "Foreword," in *From Heaven He Came and Sought Her*, 14.

Packer's more recent foreword is much less shrill than his earlier one, which was loaded with epithets for his non-Calvinist brothers and fell just short of denying them a seat at the table of salvation.[3] Of the present work, Packer gives it "top marks for its range of solid scholarship, cogency of argument, warmth of style, and zeal for the true glory of God."[4]

Editors Gibson and Gibson provide a well-crafted, two-page preface[5] outlining how they came to embrace definite atonement. They offer the book "with the prayer that it will paint a compelling picture of the beauty and power of definite atonement." They inform us, "The doctrine inhabits the poetic drama and the didactic propositions of Scripture."

The editors aim to provide a "depth and breadth of perspective" on the subject. Essays are written "irenically" and "dissenting voices are engaged firmly, but there is no shrillness of tone in our replies. There is no animosity of content in the critique of individuals and the movements associated with them." This is indeed as it should be.

However, the opening sentence of the last paragraph in the preface is surprising in this context and not a little troubling: "Precisely because it is articulating the gospel of God, this volume seeks to do away with all self-righteousness on the part of those who love definite atonement as they teach it for the good of the church."[6]

Given that some in the Reformed tradition, past and present, have unwisely made statements along the lines of "Calvinism is the gospel," it would seem the better part of wisdom not to say of the book that "it is articulating the gospel of God."[7] This should be especially so in light of the fact that definite atonement is the minority position in Christianity today, coupled with the fact that there have been many in the Reformed tradition itself, both past and present, who reject it. Since, however, the editors suggest

---

3 I have long been troubled by the shrill, critical tone of Packer's 1959 introduction to this edition of Owen's work. Here is a listing of the ubiquitous and sometimes uncharitable language that Packer employs about those who affirm unlimited atonement: unscriptural; destructive of the Gospel; unsound principles of exegesis; fallacious; dishonors the grace of God; dishonors God, cheapens the cross (3 times); makes Christ die in vain; destroys scriptural ground of assurance; anti-scriptural principle of self-salvation; grievous mistake; distorts the gospel; mental muddle; deprives God of his glory; trivializes faith and repentance; denies God's sovereignty; degenerate faith; cheap sentimentalism; degrading presentation; new gospel; superficial; makes Christ a weak and futile figure tapping forlornly at the door of the human heart, which he is powerless to open; shameful dishonor to Christ; and undermines foundation. Owen informs us that if we will listen to him, he will teach us how to believe the gospel and preach it.

Though not everything in this list is harsh (I would use some of Packer's terms in critique of his and Owen's view, such as "unscriptural," "unsound principles of exegesis," "fallacious," "destroys Scriptural ground of assurance," and "grievous mistake"), Packer's criticism here seems beyond the pale. Packer has never retracted any of this contumelious language that would apply to most fellow believers, including many within his own Reformed tradition.

4 J. I. Packer, "Foreword," 16.

5 D. Gibson & J. Gibson, "Preface," in *From Heaven He Came and Sought Her*, 17–18.

6 Ibid., 18.

7 Even Greg Welty, a high Calvinist, advised against calling Calvinism the gospel. See G. Welty, "Election and Calling: A Biblical Theological Study," in *Calvinism: A Southern Baptist Dialogue*, ed. E. R. Clendenen and B. Waggoner (Nashville: B&H Academic, 2008), 243.

to us it is "fair to ask for as much charity on the part of the reader as each writer has offered," I will give the benefit of the doubt at this point that they did not intend to convey the notion that definite atonement, or Calvinism, is the gospel.

The editors contribute an introductory chapter entitled "Sacred Theology and the Reading of the Divine Word." This is a helpful chapter that overviews the work and its intent to present a "biblico-systematic" approach. The metaphors of the production of a "web" and "map" to and through definite atonement succeed in aiding the reader to orient himself as to how the authors of the book are approaching the topic.[8]

The editors define definite atonement in a generic way that does not clearly articulate the heart of the concept as a limited substitution of Christ for the sins of the elect only.[9] This illustrates confusion on the actual state of the question. No doubt this limited substitution is indeed what the editors intend to convey by their definition. Yet, surprisingly, their definition could be affirmed by all Calvinists, including Amyraldians and English Hypothetical Universalists. What distinguishes the latter two groups of Calvinists from the authors of this book is their disagreement with the definition of the extent of the atonement as a limited satisfaction for sins. All Calvinists (high, Amyraldian, or English Hypothetical Universalists) agree on the intent of the atonement. Just as TULIP does not map Calvinism but is a point on the map, so the label "Hypothetical Universalism" does not map all Calvinists who adopt a position of unlimited satisfaction for sin.

Notice the definition speaks to the "intent" and "application" of the atonement, but it does not specifically reference the "extent."

The rest of the chapter makes clear why this is so: the authors, like all high Calvinists, cannot conceive of any category of penal substitution that does not *ipso facto* require definite atonement with respect to its actual extent as an unlimited satisfaction for sin (for example, pages 49–50, and the John Murray quote asserting there is no such thing as an unlimited atonement by insisting on the false either/or dichotomy between a limited efficacy and a limited extent).[10]

In an interview about the book, the Gibsons stated: "The ambitious claim of our book is that, penal substitutionary atonement, rightly understood, naturally entails definite atonement."[11] They further stated: "Our book contends that believing in penal substitution while rejecting definite atonement is a common misunderstanding of penal substitution."[12]

---

8 D. Gibson & J. Gibson, "Sacred Theology and the Reading of the Divine Word," in *From Heaven He Came and Sought Her*, 38–39.

9 Ibid., 33.

10 Ibid., 51.

11 D. Gibson and J. Gibson, interview by Fred Zaspel, *Books at a Glance* (blog), March 18, 2014, http://booksataglance.com/author-interviews/david-and-jonathan-gibson-editors-of-from-heaven-he-came-and-sought-her.

12 Ibid.

In short, the authors conflate, and thus confuse, the notions of intent and extent when it comes to the atonement. Hence the mere reference to "intent" in the definition[13] is considered sufficient to include extent as well, since for the editors and authors of this volume, intent and extent are coextensive.

It is refreshing to see that most of the authors repudiate a number of the usual historical mistakes when it comes to the extent of the atonement. Many of these are summarized in the introduction by the editors. First, they correctly note it "introduces distortion" and "lobotomizes history" to view the subject "through the lens of labels derived from prominent personal names in Reformation history."[14] Second, they distinguish between Amyraldianism and English Hypothetical Universalism, a distinction not always made in Reformed historical theology. Third, authors avoid the term "Calvinist" in preference for "Reformed" throughout the book, rightly noting that it is by no means certain Calvin himself affirmed definite atonement. Fourth, the authors wisely want to avoid couching the discussion in the anachronistic use of the acrostic TULIP, though appearing to succumb to Packer's notion that the five points stand or fall together, a notion all moderate Calvinists and many evangelical and Baptistic non-Calvinists like myself reject.[15]

The editors provide the reader with a useful survey of the chapters to come. The exegetical chapters attempt to locate the individual atonement texts within an overall theological framework,[16] which is a commendable method. The theological chapters aim to make four key points: the saving work of Christ (1) is indivisible, (2) is circumscribed by God's electing grace and purpose, (3) is centered on union with Christ, and (4) is Trinitarian.[17] The editors conclude with a survey of the pastoral chapters of the book.

Many within the Reformed tradition themselves will raise eyebrows at the following statement: "Proponents of a general, universal atonement cannot in fact, if being consistent, maintain a belief in the sincere offer of salvation for every person."[18] This is quite amazing in that the history of Reformed theology is replete with moderate Calvinists[19] pressing this very argument against their definite atonement brothers, with little in the way of rejoinder forthcoming. Whether this claim can be substantiated by the chapters that follow remains to be seen. We shall be especially interested in how those who write the theological and pastoral chapters address this issue.

---

13 D. Gibson & J. Gibson, "Sacred Theology and the Reading of the Divine Word," 33.

14 Ibid., 42.

15 Ibid., 43.

16 Ibid., 44.

17 Ibid., 45–49.

18 Ibid., 52.

19 My use of the term indicates all Calvinists who affirm Christ died for the sins of all men in an unlimited substitution, whether English, Amyraldian, or Baxterian Hypothetical Universalists.

Review of Michael Haykin, "'We Trust in the Saving Blood': Definite Atonement in the Ancient Church" (57–74)

Michael Haykin contributes a chapter on definite atonement in the ancient church. Though perhaps Haykin is known more as a scholar of Baptist history, he wrote a dissertation on the Pneumatomachian controversy in the fourth century. Historically, the normal point of departure to examine the question of the extent of the atonement would be the patristic era.

Before launching into a discussion of seven key church fathers, Haykin pointed out that the question of the extent of the atonement was not controversial in the early church. Hence "what can be gleaned about this doctrine in this era is mostly from implied comments rather than direct assertion."[20] This is an important point to make because in actual fact there is no overt assertion of definite atonement by any of the patristics, though there are several clear statements concerning universal atonement.

Haykin surveyed the following seven leading church fathers: Clement of Rome, Justin Martyr, Hilary of Poitiers, Ambrose, Jerome, and briefly Augustine and Prosper of Aquitaine.[21]

Clement of Rome

Haykin accepted Gill's "contextual equation" of "the elect of God" with "us" in 1 Clement 49:5 as "entirely justifiable."[22] But this is no proof Clement held to definite atonement in the sense that Christ died for the sins of the elect only. In fact, Haykin even pointed us to 1 Clement 7:4, where he says the blood of Christ "made available/won the grace of repentance for the whole world." This would appear to be a clear statement affirming a universal sin-bearing on the part of Christ for the world. Haykin concluded his brief analysis of Clement by noting the passages examined "provide glimpses of soteriological perspectives, one of which seems to be clearly in line with NT emphases on Christ's death being for the elect."[23] This is a far cry from asserting that Clement himself held to definite atonement.

Justin Martyr

Here Haykin referenced perhaps a dozen statements by Justin, none of which speaks specifically to the question of the extent of the atonement. Haykin concluded that "all of these references imply specificity in the extent of the atonement." Two things should be noted: (1) Haykin's use of "imply" is his admission that Justin Martyr

20 M. Haykin, "'We Trust in the Saving Blood': Definite Atonement in the Ancient Church," in *From Heaven He Came and Sought Her*, 60.

21 See chapter one of part one of this volume.

22 M. Haykin, "'We Trust in the Saving Blood': Definite Atonement in the Ancient Church," 61.

23 Ibid., 62.

does not overtly teach definite atonement, and (2) actually, contextually all these references do is imply specificity with respect to the application of the atonement to those who believe, not to a limitation of sin-bearing in the atonement for the elect only. Haykin then rightly pointed to a key text that indicates Christ died for the sins of all: Christ suffered "in the stead of the human race."[24] But Haykin concluded that these texts in Justin "do not provide an unambiguous statement regarding the extent of the atonement." The attempt to juxtapose Justin's clear statement about a universal atonement with his other statements and then conclude "they may well be interpreted as affirming a particularity in the extent of the atonement"[25] amounts to special pleading. There is particularity in the application of the atonement as all the church fathers affirm. But there is no statement limiting the atonement in its extent to the elect alone.

Hilary of Poitiers

Haykin quoted Hilary on Ps 129:9, including the statement that Christ "came to remove the sins of the world."[26] Noting that Hilary frequently used the first-person plural with regard to the atonement in his commentary on the Psalms, Haykin concluded "the concept of particular redemption is not outside the purview of Hilary's thought."[27] But this misses the point that when any author, biblical or otherwise, speaks of the atonement in the context of addressing believers or with reference to believers, the use of first-person plurals would be unavoidable and would in no way serve to indicate that the author was speaking only of those people. To assume such would be to invoke the negative inference fallacy. That Christ's death "has a special import for believers"[28] is not denied by anyone, but it certainly does not imply definite atonement.

Ambrose

Here Haykin noted that "close analysis of Ambrose's statements about the cross reveals the seeds of certain textual explanations . . . that would later be employed in defending definite atonement in the late sixteenth and seventeenth century."[29] But again, this is no argument that Ambrose held to definite atonement. Haykin, dependent upon Gill and Gill's translation of the original Latin, assumed Ambrose employed the double jeopardy argument John Owen used to support his case for definite atonement. But contextually, two things become evident.

---

24 Ibid., 64. Justin Martyr, "Dialogue with Trypho. a Jew," *The Apostolic Fathers, Justin Martyr, Irenaeus*, in *Ante-Nicene Fathers*, 10 vols., ed. A. Roberts and J. Donaldson, rev. by A. C. Coxe (1885; repr. Peabody, MA: Hendrickson, 2004), 1:247.

25 Ibid., 65.

26 Ibid., 67.

27 Ibid., 68.

28 Ibid.

29 Ibid., 70.

First, it is clear Ambrose affirmed universal atonement in the following quotation immediately preceding the citation by Haykin:

> Scripture said, too, in a marvelous fashion, "He has delivered him for us all," to show that God so loves all men that He delivered His most beloved Son for each one. For men, therefore, He has given the gift that is above all gifts; is it possible that He has not given all things in that gift?[30]

Here Haykin's dependence upon Gill for his point is problematic. Nothing in Ambrose would lead one to conclude he affirms definite atonement.

Second, Ambrose is not using the double jeopardy argument (a person being punished twice for the same crime) as Owen used it. As Shedd rightly noted, double jeopardy as Owen tried to use it is inadmissible because no one person is being punished twice.[31] In the section Haykin quoted from Ambrose, Ambrose made it clear that he is addressing believers (note the second-person "you"). He has already stated that Christ died for the sins of all men. Now he is addressing the benefits of that salvation to those who believe. Ambrose is rightly distinguishing between the extent of the atonement and the application of the atonement, which Owen and Haykin fail to do. Ambrose's meaning is believers can no longer be held liable to future punishment.

Jerome

Haykin cited Jerome's *Commentary on Matthew* (3.20) with reference to Matt 20:28. He admits there is ambiguity in Jerome's statement but said the words "hint that Jesus saw Christ's death to be for a particular group of people—believers."[32] Again, here the issue is whether Jerome has in mind the intent, extent, or application of the atonement. Nothing in this quotation affirms definite atonement nor precludes universal atonement.

Augustine

Haykin never said Augustine taught definite atonement but stated some of his comments "imply" it.[33] He appealed to Augustine's statements on John 10:26; 14:2; and 1 John 2:2. Many Calvinists themselves who affirm an unlimited atonement interpret 1 John 2:2 to refer only to the church.[34] Furthermore, Haykin failed to note the fact that it is clear Augustine thought that Jesus atoned for the sins of Judas![35]

---

30 Ambrose, "Jacob and the Happy Life," in *Seven Exegetical Works*. Fathers of the Church 65, trans. M. P. McHugh (Washington: Catholic University of America Press, 1970), 135–36.

31 W. G. T. Shedd, *Dogmatic Theology* (Nashville, TN: Thomas Nelson, 1980), 2:443.

32 M. Haykin, "'We Trust in the Saving Blood': Definite Atonement in the Ancient Church," 70.

33 Ibid., 71.

34 For examples, see my chapter "The Atonement: Limited or Universal?," in *Whosoever Will: A Biblical-Theological Critique of Five-Point Calvinism*, ed. D. L. Allen and S. Lemke (Nashville: B&H Academic, 2010), 61–107.

35 See Augustine's "Exposition of Psalm LXIX," Section 27, in *NPNF*, eds. P. Schaff and H. Wace (1892; repr. Peabody, MA: Hendrickson, 2004), 8:309.

I'll not take the space to recount the many times Augustine affirmed unlimited atonement through the use of such phrases as Christ died "for the sins of the whole world," how Christ's death is the "ransom for the whole world," and how Christ "paid the price for the whole world." See under "Augustine" above. In his *Exposition on the Book of the Psalms*, Augustine spoke of the "world" in relation to the atonement in such a way that precludes any possibility of meaning other than every person in the world.[36]

Haykin appealed to Raymond Blacketer for his take on Augustine. Interestingly, Blacketer correctly noted that "there is no single statement from the bishop of Hippo that explicitly declares that God's intention in the satisfaction of Christ was to procure redemption for the elect alone." But he then incorrectly concluded that this was "precisely the view that Augustine held."[37]

Blacketer, and perhaps Haykin, confused Augustine's statements about God's predestinarian will for the elect with his view on the actual satisfaction for all sin, which Christ accomplished in the atonement.

Prosper

Haykin also wrongly interpreted the early Prosper of giving "strong hints of a definite atonement in Augustine."[38] He quoted Prosper as saying that Christ died "for all" but also noted Prosper said "that He was crucified only for those who were to profit by His death."[39] Haykin failed to discern in what sense Prosper means these statements. In response to the objection that Christ "did not suffer for the salvation and redemption of all men," Prosper clearly affirmed Christ's death for the sins of all people but also affirmed that only those who believe will benefit from Christ's saving work: "Accordingly, since our Lord in very truth took upon Himself the one nature and condition which is common to all men, it is right to say that all have been redeemed and that nevertheless not all are actually liberated from the slavery of sin."[40]

Haykin further noted that Prosper, in his later career, "appears to have softened this commitment to definite atonement, or even rejected it in favor of an advocacy of the universal salvific will of God based on his reading of 1 Timothy 2:4."[41] But even in his earlier, so-called high Augustinian period, Prosper held to the same exegesis of 1 Tim 2:4 that he did in his alleged later departure phase. There is no evidence from his interpretation of 1 Tim 2:4 in *Call of the Gentiles* that Prosper departed from an alleged earlier position of definite atonement. All of this is a misreading of Prosper

36 Augustine, "Exposition of Psalm XCVI," in *NPNF*, 8:472. For evidence that Augustine clearly held to universal atonement, see the section on Augustine above.

37 R. Blacketer, "Definite Atonement in Historical Perspective," in *The Glory of the Atonement: Biblical, Historical and Practical Perspectives,* ed. C. Hill and F. James III (Downers Grove, IL: InterVarsity, 2004), 308.

38 M. Haykin, "'We Trust in the Saving Blood': Definite Atonement in the Ancient Church," 72.

39 Ibid., 72.

40 Prosper, "Prosper of Aquitaine: Defense of St. Augustine," trans. and annotated P. De Letter, S. J., in *Ancient Christian Writers,* 66 vols. (New York: Newman, 1963), 32:164.

41 M. Haykin, "'We Trust in the Saving Blood': Definite Atonement in the Ancient Church," 73.

and can be seen to be so when one carefully reads pertinent sections of his *Defense of St. Augustine*.[42] It is clear Prosper held to unlimited atonement and never held to definite atonement.

In conclusion, Haykin should be commended for the fact that he does not state any of these authors he surveyed clearly affirm definite atonement. But he must be faulted for several issues. First, the chapter is only a very brief survey of seven church fathers. Second, Haykin has missed significant counterfactual evidence that clearly shows some of these men held an unlimited satisfaction for sins and thus did not affirm definite atonement. Jerome is an example. He did not canvas the extant writings of his chosen church fathers with a view to engaging in an analytic/synthetic survey. Granted he cannot cover all the ground; no one could. But more ground surely needs to be covered than is reflected in this chapter. Third, he appears to be heavily dependent upon secondary sources (Gill and Blacketer) and fails to interact with other significant secondary sources. These are serious methodological problems.

Haykin's chapter has the feel of being rushed and too reliant on secondary sources. This certainly is not the norm for Haykin's writing. I appreciate his usual careful thoroughness. But in this case, his chapter is not a reliable guide on this subject.

Review of David S. Hogg, "'Sufficient for All, Efficient for Some': Definite Atonement in the Medieval Church" (75–95)

Hogg's chapter focuses on three figures (two prominent and one lesser known) in the medieval period. He began the chapter with the statement that it is "often assumed that expression and defense of definite atonement lacked clarity or support until the sixteenth and seventeenth centuries. With respect to the medieval church, such an assumption is inaccurate and misleading."[43] This statement itself is misleading. It is accurate in the sense that support for definite atonement can be found in Gottschalk, as Hogg noted. It is inaccurate in that outside of Gottschalk there is no support for definite atonement from either Peter Lombard or Thomas Aquinas, as Hogg attempted to show. Hogg has misinterpreted both on the issue.

Hogg noted that theologians during this era wrote about other Reformed doctrines in a manner "that is not only consistent with later Reformation expressions of definite atonement, but preparatory and foundational for this doctrine." Here Hogg is referring primarily to the Lombardian formula with respect to the atonement: sufficient for all but efficient only for the elect. This is a common refrain in his chapter. But, as we

42 Prosper, "Prosper of Aquitaine: Defense of St. Augustine," 32:149–51; 32:159–60; 32:164.

43 D. Hogg, "'Sufficient for All, Efficient for Some': Definite Atonement in the Medieval Church," in *From Heaven He Came and Sought Her*, 75.

shall see, medieval theologians do not write about the extent of the atonement in a way that is consistent with the stream of later Reformed theology that advocated definite atonement.

Hogg began his treatment with Gottschalk. Most of what he said about Gottschalk is fine. Gottschalk did indeed hold essentially the same position on definite atonement as many Calvinists hold today, but with no universal aspect. What Hogg is not as clear about is that Gottschalk and a few of his supporters were the only ones to hold this position during the medieval period.

One must remember that definite atonement asserts that Christ only shed his blood for the sins of the elect. This was not the position of the medieval church. Hogg is simply in error when he asserted that definite atonement "was presented to theological students as the dominant view."[44] Hogg appealed to Lombard's *Sentences*, which were used in all theological training as evidence. But this assumes Lombard taught definite atonement, and there is no clear evidence that he did.

When Hogg stated concerning Lombard, "For Peter, Christ died for the elect,"[45] I presume he intended to convey that Lombard believed Christ died only for the elect, and that Hogg is basing this on his interpretation of the Lombardian formula. But the formula does not state Christ died for the sins of the elect only. In fact, its original meaning was that Christ died for the sins of all but was only applied to those who believed (the elect). Lombard clearly affirmed in 3.20.5 of *Sentences* that Christ as priest offered himself for the sins of all with respect to the sufficiency of the satisfaction, but Christ offered himself for the elect as to its efficiency. This is the interpretation given the statement by medieval theologians and the earliest Reformers.

The Lombardian formula would later be revised from its original meaning and intent in the late sixteenth and early seventeenth century by Beza and others. Following Beza, some began to revise the formula to use hypothetical language such that Christ's death "could have been". instead of "was" a ransom for the sins of all people. John Owen was conscious of the fact that he was revising Lombard's formula by putting it in hypothetical terms to support his view of definite atonement. Richard Baxter took him to task for what he called Owen's "new, futile evasion." William Cunningham[46] acknowledged this revision in volume two of his *Historical Theology*.

Beza's criticism of the Lombardian formula launched a new stage in the development of the doctrine of limited atonement. Up until Beza, the Lombardian formula was accepted by Calvin and all Reformers as acknowledging that Christ died for the sins of all, but the atonement was only applied to the elect.

Hogg also erred when he stated that "To say, therefore, that God's elective purposes

44 Ibid., 80.

45 Ibid.

46 W. Cunningham, *Historical Theology*, 2 vols. (Edinburgh: Banner of Truth, 1994), 2:332.

in predestination are causative and thus bring about salvation in particular people is not only to say that God accomplishes what he decrees in foreknowledge; it is also to imply, if not to state plainly, that Christ died for the elect."[47] There is nothing in either that implies, much less "states plainly," that Christ died only for the elect. It is Hogg, not Lombard, who contends that the question of predestination necessitates definite atonement.[48] Notice how Hogg stated that Lombard believed the application of the atonement was "intended" for the elect.[49] This is an entirely different question than the extent of the atonement. Hogg, like most of the authors in this volume, failed to distinguish the intent of the atonement from its extent and its application.

Hogg concluded that, considered as a whole, Lombard's "theology is consistent with later articulations of definite atonement"[50] and that "the seeds of the doctrine of definite atonement were present in the schools and churches."[51] I thought Lombard affirmed definite atonement with his formula? It sounds like even Hogg is not convinced. Such would only be true if Lombard held to definite atonement, and there is no clear evidence that he did. In fact, there is clear evidence he did not.

Hogg completely misinterpreted the historical data when he said, "Definite atonement is not a minority view in the medieval church."[52] Of course it was! The only people who clearly advocated it was Gottschalk and those who supported him.

Speaking of Aquinas,[53] Hogg immediately informs us that Aquinas did not address the issue specifically.[54] In fact, Hogg even pointed out that Aquinas stated, on the basis of 1 John 2:2, that Christ died for the sins of the whole human race.[55] This is not definite atonement. Nevertheless, Hogg said Aquinas endorsed the idea that the blood of Christ was shed for the elect alone.[56] How could he, if he also affirmed Christ died for the sins of the "whole human race"? Hogg cannot have it both ways with Aquinas. Either Aquinas believed Christ died only for the sins of the elect or Christ died for the sins of the whole world.

Hogg's logic appears to operate along these lines:

> Aquinas believed in predestination.
> Belief in predestination entails belief in definite atonement.
> Therefore, Aquinas believed in definite atonement.

47 D. Hogg, "'Sufficient for All, Efficient for Some,'" 85.
48 Ibid., 88.
49 Ibid.
50 Ibid., 89.
51 Ibid.
52 Ibid.
53 Ibid., 89–95.
54 Ibid., 90.
55 Ibid.
56 Ibid., 90–91.

Hogg's appeal to Aquinas's use of "many" in *Summa*, Question 78, "The Form of the Sacrament," Article 3, provides no evidence for definite atonement. In context, Aquinas is addressing the preferred verbiage to be used at the Eucharist. His reference to "many" refers to elect Gentiles. Here is the context:

> Objection 8. Further, as was already observed (48, 2; 49, 3), Christ's Passion sufficed for all; while as to its efficacy it was profitable for many. Therefore it ought to be said: "Which shall be shed for all," or else "for many," without adding, "for you."
>
> Reply to Objection 8. The blood of Christ's Passion has its efficacy not merely in the elect among the Jews, to whom the blood of the Old Testament was exhibited, but also in the Gentiles; nor only in priests who consecrate this sacrament, and in those others who partake of it; but likewise in those for whom it is offered. And therefore He says expressly "for you," the Jews, "and for many," namely, the Gentiles; or "for you" who eat of it and "for many," for whom it is offered.

It is not possible to conclude from this, as Hogg does, that Christ's blood "was shed for the elect alone."[57] Aquinas's use of "many" is no proof of definite atonement. It rather speaks to the efficacy of the sacraments for believers as the context demonstrates. With respect to Aquinas's statements on 1 Tim 2:4, Hogg missed the fact that Aquinas takes the "will" to be God's antecedent will and "all men" means "all without exception." Aquinas is not saying that God wills "all kinds of men to be saved." This is a serious misreading of Aquinas.[58] Hogg asserted that Aquinas's theology is "in keeping with the doctrine of definite atonement."[59] It would seem such is not the case.

Hogg concluded with this statement: "It is true that these theologians did not define a comprehensive articulation of definite atonement, but it is also true that when the late sixteenth-and seventeenth century Reformers did, they were not breaking new ground but continuing to water seeds that had been planted long before them."[60]

This statement needs qualification. Not only did medieval theologians not define a "comprehensive articulation" of definite atonement, but with the exception of Gottschalk and a few others who agreed with him, the medieval theologians did not assert definite atonement.

Hogg's chapter would be more historically accurate had he concluded such. There are some serious methodological problems in this chapter. Hogg did not survey

57 Ibid.

58 Ibid., 94–95.

59 Ibid., 95.

60 Ibid.

the full range of Aquinas's statements on the question "For whose sins did Jesus die?" He missed the many points where Aquinas affirms an unlimited extent with respect to the atonement.

Review of Paul Helm, "Calvin, Indefinite Language, and Definite Atonement" (97–119)

Paul Helm's chapter attempts to defend the notion that Calvin's indefinite language is "thoroughly consistent with being committed to definite atonement, and which cannot be used as convincing evidence that he denied it."[61] His chapter brings nothing new to the table regarding Calvin's view and is essentially the same argument he made in 1982 in his *Calvin and the Calvinists*. However, much has transpired since then on the question at hand. Helm does reference Clifford and Kennedy on the unlimited side and Rainbow and Nicole on the limited side, all of whom appeared after 1982. However, he misses at least three important studies, all by Calvinists, which conclude Calvin held to unlimited atonement.

Curt Daniel's 1983 PhD dissertation, "Hyper-Calvinism and John Gill," contains an extensive fifty-page appendix entitled "Did John Calvin Teach Limited Atonement?" He provides dozens of in-context quotations with careful analysis. Daniel addresses and analyzes all the passages in Calvin that proponents of limited atonement cite as indicating Calvin held to definite atonement. His conclusion that Calvin held to an unlimited atonement seems to be beyond a reasonable doubt.

Helm also overlooks Peter Rouwendal's 2008 article.[62] Rouwendal's conclusion is striking. How could Calvin use the clear universal language with respect to the extent of the atonement if he indeed held to definite atonement? For Rouwendal, the universal propositions in Calvin's works do prove negatively that he did not subscribe to particular atonement. Rather enigmatically, Rouwendal believes that Calvin's universal propositions do indeed "falsify the conclusion that Calvin was a particularist, but are not sufficient to prove him a universalist."[63] This is quite problematic. Given that there are only two positions on the question of the atonement's extent, Rouwendal's demurral is unnecessary.

---

61 P. Helm, "Calvin, Indefinite Language, and Definite Atonement," in *From Heaven He Came and Sought Her*, 97.

62 David Ponter assessed Rouwendal's article in relationship to Nicole and Helm: "This is an exceptionally interesting article that argues for a basic three-fold classification schema of Particularism, Hypothetical Universalism and the Classical position (the Prosper-Lombard trajectory) within Reformed theology. It seems to me that his schema fits well with Richard Muller's divisions of Particularism, Speculative-Amyraldian Hypothetical Universalism, and Non-Speculative Hypothetical Universalism. Acknowledging this three-fold categorization takes our scholarship past the dated dichotomies of Nicole and Helm" ("Pieter Rouwendal on Calvin and Heshusius," *Calvin and Calvinism*, December 15, 2008, http://calvinandcalvinism.com/?p=1268).

63 P. L. Rouwendal, "Calvin's Forgotten Classical Position on the Extent of the Atonement: About Sufficiency, Efficiency, and Anachronism," *Westminster Theological Journal* 70 (2008): 328.

Additionally, Helm fails to interact with the research of David Ponter, one of the librarians at Reformed Theological Seminary in Jackson, Mississippi, whose website, *Calvin and Calvinism*, contains extensive quotations and analysis of Calvin's view of the extent of the atonement,[64] including an unpublished paper critiquing Nicole's arguments (and Helm's as well) for limited atonement.

Ponter's two-part historical essay on Calvin's view of the extent of the atonement that was published in the *Southwestern Journal of Theology*[65] has taken the debate on Calvin to a new level and must now be reckoned with by all who affirm Calvin held to limited atonement. Ponter concludes that Calvin held to unlimited atonement.

Helm's approach to the issue is confusing and fraught with problems. For example, he writes:

> while Calvin did not commit himself to any version of the doctrine of definite atonement, his thought is consistent with that doctrine; that is, he did not deny it in express terms, but by other things that he most definitely did hold to, he may be said to be committed to that doctrine.[66]

This borders on incoherence.

First, note carefully Helm's admission that Calvin did not commit himself to any version of the doctrine of definite atonement. I'm not sure how many versions there are of the view that Christ only substituted for the sins of the elect. I only know of one, with differences among later theologians between a quantitative and a qualitative equivalency. But either way, Helm correctly acknowledges that Calvin did not commit himself to definite atonement.

Second, Helm avers Calvin's thought is "consistent" with definite atonement, which Helm specifies as Calvin did not "deny it in express terms." But this is logically problematic. Can it be said my thought is consistent with the view that the moon is composed of green cheese if I do not "deny in express terms" the proposition that the moon is made of green cheese? The logical fallacy is self-evident.

Third, Helm stated that by means of other, related concepts that Calvin did affirm, he may be said to be "committed" to the doctrine of definite atonement. Helm is attempting to show that, by entailment, definite atonement results from some of the

---

64 See D. Ponter, "John Calvin (1509–1564) on Unlimited Expiation, Sin-Bearing, Redemption and Reconciliation," *Calvin and Calvinism*, March 1, 2008, http://calvinandcalvinism.com/?p=230.

65 D. Ponter, "Review Essay (Part One): John Calvin on the Death of Christ and the Reformation's Forgotten Doctrine of Universal Vicarious Satisfaction: A Review and Critique of Tom Nettles' Chapter in Whomever He Wills," *Southwestern Journal of Theology* 55, no. 1 (Fall 2012): 138–58; "Review Essay (Part Two): John Calvin on the Death of Christ and the Reformation's Forgotten Doctrine of Universal Vicarious Satisfaction: A Review and Critique of Tom Nettles' Chapter in Whomever He Wills," *Southwestern Journal of Theology* 55, no. 2 (Spring 2013): 252–70.

66 P. Helm, "Calvin, Indefinite Language, and Definite Atonement," 98.

other doctrines or concepts Calvin affirms. Unless all Calvin's universal statements can somehow be dispatched, Helm's entailment argument does not work. If such arguments work for Calvin, then they would entail Hypothetical Universalists also believed in definite atonement.

So, as Helm suggests, Calvin did not "commit himself" to definite atonement, but he may be said to be "committed to" definite atonement. He proceeds to justify this assertion on pages 99–101. I suspect most readers will find this incoherent at best and, at worst, logically flawed.

Helm argues that accumulating and assessing quotations of Calvin relative to the extent question is inappropriate since such proof-texting "abstracts from Calvin's deeper theological outlook."[67] Of course one needs to evaluate Calvin's statements in light of his full theology. That goes without saying. But this in no way negates the importance of looking carefully at what Calvin did say with respect to the extent question.[68] I wonder if Helm's approach here is in some way a result of the fact that there are so many universal statements in Calvin concerning the atonement's extent.

There are two ways to engage in historical inquiry. One method attempts to survey the data via induction. What did an author actually say about the specified subject? The other method, Helm's method, is deductive. This approach begins with certain presuppositions (i.e., Calvin held to limited atonement) and then attempts to discover such in the primary source material or at least show that the presupposition is not at odds with what one finds in the source material.

What Helm wants to do in his chapter is use Calvin's Reformed theology to reason to definite atonement. Helm seeks to answer the question whether definite atonement "fits better" than universal atonement in Calvin's teaching. In order to accomplish this goal, Helm develops three arguments.[69] First, Helm looks at "Providence and the Future." He admits that this argument may seem distant from debates about the question at hand. He is correct, for there is nothing in this section that can be found to remotely support definite atonement.

Second, Helm looks at "The Language of Aspiration," by which he means an expression on the part of Christ and Paul, which Calvin taps into, that stresses a desire for the eternal good of everyone, even when ignorant of God's decretal will. But again, there is nothing in this section that remotely supports the notion of definite atonement.

Helm makes a startling and deeply troubling statement: "In certain circumstances a person, even the person of the Mediator [Christ], may be distracted from the revealed will of God and instead express his immediate aspiration for the salvation of those who

67 Ibid., 100.

68 Moreover, as D. Ponter's two-part article on Calvin and the extent question in the *Southwestern Journal of Theology* argued, looking at Calvin's Reformed theological contemporaries is also relevant to the topic.

69 P. Helm, "Calvin, Indefinite Language, and Definite Atonement," 101–11.

may or may not be elected to salvation."[70] Christ may have been "distracted" from the revealed will of God? What sort of Christology is this? Frankly, I would be surprised if the book editors did not encourage Helm to delete this statement from his chapter, as it is so obviously problematic. But this statement seems problematic on another account. Some Calvinists wrongly assert that God does not desire the salvation of all people according to the revealed will of God. Drawing on the concept of God's two wills (or rather two aspects of his will), his revealed will and his decretal will, the vast majority of Calvinists argue that God desires the salvation of all in the revealed will but not in the decretal will. This is not the position of Helm and Blacketer in this volume, though it is of other contributors, such as Schreiner, Blocher, and Piper. Helm and Blacketer both deny the well-meant offer of the gospel.

Notice Helm stated that Christ himself, in certain circumstances, may be "distracted" from God's desire that all people be saved (normally considered his revealed will) and express his "aspiration" for the salvation of those who are the non-elect (those passed over in God's decretal will). One would have thought Helm would have expressed himself in the reverse: Christ may have been distracted from the decretal will and instead have expressed his desire for the salvation of those who may or may not be elected (all people would fall into one of these two categories).

Helm's third argument is "Universal Preaching." His argument attempts to show that Calvin's use of universal language with respect to preaching the gospel does not necessarily commit him to indefinite atonement. Quite right. Neither does it commit him to definite atonement, as Helm infers.

Helm is confusing the question of the intent of the atonement with its extent and application. Calvin clearly believed that God intended to effect the salvation of the elect only and therefore the elect only would actually have the atonement applied to them. Helm reasons from this, contrary to Calvin's other statements about universal extent, that Calvin also believed in definite atonement with respect to extent, though he has to admit that Calvin nowhere in his writings affirms a strictly limited atonement.

As Ponter correctly noted:

> The argument that the expiation carries within itself its own application or that it infallibly purchases faith and salvation is a post-Calvinian argument. For Calvin, faith and salvation are purchased by Christ for all the world, but the application is conditioned by faith which can be voided by the sinner's unbelief. In Calvin's wider theology, the gift of faith to some is determined, not by the extent or nature of the satisfaction, but by election, and then secondarily by the effectual call.[71]

---

70 Ibid., 107.

71 D. Ponter, "Review Essay (Part Two)," 261.

Helm proceeds to consider two biblical case studies in an attempt to show Calvin's thought is commensurate with definite atonement. The first is Ezek 18:23. Calvin's comments on this passage include discussion of the universal gospel offer in the light of the eternal decree. But again there is nothing in Calvin's statements here that Helm can point to that even hints at definite atonement. Helm assumes Calvin held to definite atonement and then reads Calvin's statements on the distinction between God's revealed and decretal will in light of that assumption.

Helm's second case study is 1 Tim 2:4 and Calvin's sermon on this passage. This is an attempt to extract definite atonement from Calvin's statements about the universality of gospel preaching. But again, he can find nothing in Calvin here to support the supposition that he held to limited atonement. Helm has assumed that Calvin's understanding of 1 Tim 2:4–6 took "all men" to mean "some men of all kinds" rather than "all men of every kind." There is no evidence for this from Calvin himself. Calvin is speaking not of the secret will of God (as Augustine had approached these verses) but of the revealed will.

From Calvin's own sermon on the Timothy passage it is evident that "all people" or "all nations" means something along the lines of "all men of all people and all nations" in a distributive sense.[72] This can be seen also in Calvin's commentary on this passage:

> For there is one God, the creator and Father of all, so, he declares, there is one Mediator, through whom access to God is opened to us, and this Mediator is not given only to one nation, or to a few men of a particular class, but to all, for the benefit of the sacrifice, by which he has expiated for our sins, applies to all. . . . The universal term "all" must always be referred to classes of men but never to individuals. It is as if he had said: "Not only Jews but also Greeks, not only people of humble rank but also princes have been redeemed by the death of Christ." Since therefore he intends the benefit of his death to be common to all, those who hold a view that would exclude any from the hope of salvation do Him an injury.
>
> The Holy Spirit bids us pray for all, because our one mediator bids all to come to Him, since by his death He has reconciled all to the Father.[73]

In fact, the Timothy passage actually asserts that the foundation for universal gospel preaching is a universal atonement. Calvin nowhere denies this.

Helm closes his discussion by noting three things. First, "given the opportunity to make the scope of Christ's work universal in intent, Calvin does not take it, as his exe-

72 J. Calvin, *Sermons on Timothy*, 160.

73 J. Calvin, "The Second Epistle of Paul the Apostle to the Corinthians and the Epistles to Timothy, Titus & Philemon," in *Calvin's New Testament Commentaries*, 12 vols., ed. D. W. Torrance & T. F. Torrance (Grand Rapids, MI: Eerdmans, 1994), 10:210–11.

gesis of 2 Cor 5:14 shows." Helm queries: "So if through his use of indefinite language Calvin presupposes a universal atonement . . . why, when he comes to the standard passages for 'universal atonement,' such as 1 John 2:2, does he not take the opportunity to state unequivocally that he is a proponent of universal atonement?"[74]

Second, Helm wants to distinguish between the world as composed of classes of individuals and the world as composed of individuals of a class. Helm stated:

> The question may be raised, would such indiscriminate language warrant a preacher asserting to all and sundry that "Christ died for you"? Only if the formulation were taken as an inference drawn from "Christ died for all" or "Christ died for the world," but not if from "Christ died for everyone in particular." The first premise, Calvin would hold, is true, while the second is false. That is, a distinction must be made between the world as comprised of classes of individuals, and the world as comprised of individuals of a class. Taken in the first way, the language would not be warranted, but in the second sense, the language is clearly warranted. Christ died for the world.[75]

This is an effort to explain away the universal language in 1 Tim 2:4–6 and to extract definite atonement from Paul's statement that Christ died for "all." But this is an abortive attempt. Attempting to force the meaning of "all without distinction" on the universal texts is to explode them with "grammatical gunpowder," as Spurgeon said in his sermon on this passage. The "all without distinction" concept often becomes code for "some of all without distinction." Thus "all" becomes "some of all sorts," an unwarranted move.

With respect to the NT texts that use universal language, the bifurcation of "all without distinction" and "all without exception" is ultimately a distinction without a difference. If I speak of all men without racial, gender, or other distinctions, am I not speaking of all men without exception? Whatever the distinction is and whatever the scope of the "all" is must be supplied by the context. The two phrases simply cannot be compartmentalized linguistically. The distinction is artificial.

Third, Helm mentions Calvin's explanation of the connection of universal preaching with election. But again, there is simply nothing here in Calvin that hints at definite atonement.

The long and short of Helm's chapter is to make the point that "definiteness in belief can bc allied with indefiniteness of expression."[76]

Helm stated:

---

74 P. Helm, "Calvin, Indefinite Language, and Definite Atonement," 116.

75 Ibid., 117.

76 Ibid., 119.

> May we not conclude, then, that the use of indefinite language is not only consistent with definite providence and definite election but that it is also consistent with being committed to the doctrine of definite atonement? Even though, as I have argued, Calvin does not commit himself to that belief. The use of indefinite language cannot therefore be used as an argument against such a commitment.[77]

Helm's conclusion is simply not warranted. The evidence he adduces neither supports the position that Calvin held to a limited satisfaction for the sins of the elect alone nor weakens the evidence suggesting he held to an indefinite atonement.

Helm retrojects a later version of substitutionary atonement into Calvin; one that is determined and defined by the dictates of a limited satisfaction for the sins of the elect alone along lines developed by John Owen and the revised version of the Lombardian formula. Helm actually fails to do what he desires to do: read Calvin historically as a theologian in his own context.[78]

Review of Raymond Blacketer, "Blaming Beza: The Development of Definite Atonement in the Reformed Tradition" (121–41)[79]

Raymond Blacketer attempts to ward off the challenge that Theodore Beza developed Calvin's theology into what became known as definite atonement. Blacketer believes there is "a clearly identifiable trajectory of thought in Christian tradition that can be described as particularist" and links this with God's "intention" to save only the elect.[80] Blacketer is thoroughly conversant with the literature on Beza, and his chapter is full of helpful and substantive footnotes.

The chapter contains several helpful points in the discussion. First, Blacketer cor-

77 Ibid.

78 Helm published a blog article on January 1, 2015, entitled "Hypothetical Universalism" (see P. Helm, "Hypothetical Universalism," *Helm's Deep: Philosophical Theology* [blog], January 1, 2015, http://paulhelmsdeep.blogspot.com/2015/01/hypothetical-universalism.html). Helm appears confused as to the state of the question concerning limited atonement. Helm understands Davenant to argue strongly for unlimited atonement but thinks the reason for doing so is unclear. He does not seem to grasp Davenant's focus on the nature of sufficiency. One gets the impression that, for Davenant, the universal benefits of the atonement are restricted to common grace and universal gospel preaching. Helm thinks Calvin held to limited atonement and sets him off against Davenant. In reality, Calvin and Davenant both affirmed universal atonement. Nevertheless, Helm's post illustrates the growing understanding of the role Hypothetical Universalism played early on in Reformed theology.

79 Blacketer makes the same arguments for limited atonement in "Definite Atonement in Historical Perspective," in *The Glory of the Atonement*, 304–23.

80 R. Blacketer, "Blaming Beza: The Development of Definite Atonement in the Reformed Tradition," in *From Heaven He Came and Sought Her*, 125.

rectly noted that the phrase "limited atonement" is misleading,[81] since it derives from the acronym TULIP, which was not used to describe the Canons of Dort until the early twentieth century. Second, he correctly noted that Amyraldianism, as a form of Hypothetical Universalism, was never considered to be outside the boundaries of confessional Calvinism.[82] Third, he rightly cautioned that one should be careful not to read the results of later debates back into Calvin's thought.[83] Fourth, Blacketer correctly identified the problem of some twentieth-century Calvin scholarship that attempted to read Calvin through the filter of Barth and neo-orthodoxy.[84] Fifth, he rightly noted the problems with attempting to pit Calvin against later Reformed scholasticism.[85]

However, his treatment is not without its problems. Blacketer erred logically and historically when he stated that Calvin's views on election and God's sovereignty extend the particularist trajectory "and exclude a universal, indefinite satisfaction and redemption obtained in some manner by Christ which would be potentially (not simply hypothetically) available to each human individual."[86] As we have seen historically, there is no "particularist trajectory" in the patristic era, the medieval period, or even in Calvin. Logically, such a statement forecloses on Calvin's view of the extent of the atonement by begging the question, something Blacketer has already indicated one cannot and should not do.

Blacketer confuses the question of "intent" with that of "extent" when he refers to this particularist trajectory "that identifies those to whom God intends to bestow the benefits of Christ's satisfaction as the elect alone."[87] Of course it is true that Calvin and the earliest leaders of the Reformed tradition believed this with respect to the intent of the atonement. Where Blacketer errs is in his assumption that they also believed this with respect to the extent of the atonement, something they in fact never state. This is Blacketer's assumption. He does not seem to distinguish between "intent" and "extent" here.

His statement concerning the death of Christ excluding what "would be potentially (not simply hypothetically) available to each human individual"[88] is also problematic. Hypothetical Universalism actually asserts the potentiality that each human individual could be saved if they were to believe because there is an atonement made for his sins. There is nothing "hypothetical" about the extent of the atonement for the sins of all people in Hypothetical Universalism. Thus I'm not sure what Blacketer means when he contrasts "potential" with "hypothetical."

81 Ibid., 121.
82 Ibid., 122.
83 Ibid.
84 Ibid., 123.
85 Ibid., 124.
86 Ibid., 125.
87 Ibid.
88 Ibid.

Blacketer considers Beza's analysis of 1 Tim 2:4, where he noted, like Calvin and Augustine before him, Beza interpreted this passage to refer to classes of people, "not every individual."[89] He stated that Augustine's "exegetical strategy" with texts using "all" in the context of atonement "means all classes" and "not every individual," and stated this was frequently Calvin's approach as well.[90]

But Blacketer did not note that Augustine never taught definite atonement and in numerous places clearly taught universal atonement. Not the least of the examples that can be culled from his writings, as I have previously noted, is Augustine's statement that Christ died for the sins of Judas. The same could be said with respect to Calvin's many statements about "all" or "world" where in several atonement contexts he clearly does not restrict their meaning.

Take Calvin's comments on Rom 5:18, for example: "Although Christ suffered for the sins of the world, and is offered by the goodness of God without distinction to all men, yet not all receive Him."[91] Likewise, consider Calvin's comments on Col 1:14: "He says that this redemption was procured through the blood of Christ, for by the sacrifice of his death all the sins of the world have been expiated."[92]

As I have pointed out in "The Atonement: Limited or Universal?" in *Whosoever Will*, some Calvinists interpret passages such as 1 Tim 2:4 to refer to classes of people while at the same time affirming a universal atonement. Blacketer erred in assuming that if one reads 1 Tim 2:4 in a restricted sense, then one must affirm limited atonement. He referred to Luther, who takes a similar reading of 1 Tim 2:4, but it is clear that Luther did not affirm definite atonement and did indeed affirm unlimited atonement. And again, contrary to Blacketer, Luther believed "God . . . genuinely wills (as scripture states) the salvation of all people."[93]

Blacketer is correct that Beza's *Tabula Praedestinationis* "does not contain an explicit doctrine of definite atonement."[94]

Blacketer attempts to deduce from Calvin's reading of 1 John 2:2 evidence that Calvin held to definite atonement: "This is strong evidence that Calvin did not teach a universal redemption that included every individual, but one that was particular to the elect."[95] Here Blacketer appears to be using the term "redemption" synonymously with "atonement." As above, he fails to recognize that a Calvinist may hold to a lim-

89 Ibid., 128.

90 Ibid., 128–29.

91 J. Calvin, *The Epistle of Paul the Apostle to the Romans and to the Thessalonians*, ed. D. W. Torrance and T. F. Torrance, trans. R. Mackenzie (Grand Rapids, MI: Eerdmans, 1960), 117–18.

92 J. Calvin, *The Epistles of Paul the Apostle to the Galatians, Ephesians, Philippians and Colossians*, ed. D. W. Torrance and T. F. Torrance, trans. T. H. L. Parker (Grand Rapids, MI: Eerdmans, 1996), 308.

93 R. Muller, "Predestination," in *The Oxford Encyclopedia of the Reformation*, 4 vols., ed. H. J. Hillerbrand (New York: Oxford University Press, 1996), 3:333. See also Martin Luther, *The Bondage of the Will*, trans. J. I. Packer & O. R. Johnson (Grand Rapids, MI: Revell, 2003), 170–71, 176.

94 Blacketer, "Blaming Beza: The Development of Definite Atonement in the Reformed Tradition," 132.

95 Ibid., 135.

ited reading of 1 John 2:2 and still affirm universal atonement. Such would seem to be the case with Calvin. If Blacketer had stated that with respect to the intent of the atonement, Calvin believed, based on passages like 1 John 2:2, that God intended the atonement should be applied only to the elect, he would have been correct.

Blacketer appears to suggest that Ursinus, Zanchi, and Musculus[96] all held to forms of definite atonement. This is incorrect, as all these men, regardless of what they believed about the intention of the atonement, are clear that they believed Christ satisfied for the sins of all people, or what can also be termed as "universal redemption" (Musculus's favorite phrase for it), and were thus Hypothetical Universalists,[97] as was Calvin.

Speaking of Calvin's sermon on 1 Tim 2:3–5, Blacketer stated that Calvin made the point repeatedly that God does not will the salvation of every individual, yet as far as the preaching of the gospel is concerned, Blacketer stated Calvin believed God does will the salvation of all (138). Actually, for Calvin, God does will the salvation of all people individually, and he makes his view clear in his comments on Lam 3:33:

> So also God, when he adopts severity towards men, he indeed does so willingly, because he is the judge of the world; but he does not do so from the heart, because he wishes all to be innocent—for far away from him is all fierceness and cruelty; and as he regards men with paternal love, so also he would have them to be saved, were they not as it were by force to drive him to rigor.[98]

Contra Blacketer, Calvin stated that God "wishes all" to be "innocent" in the sense that "he would have them to be saved." Calvin's use of "all" and "world" here makes it evident he referred to the world of the non-elect. Calvin affirms both the universal love of God and the universal saving will of God.[99]

Blacketer stated that by the time of Dort, "the majority of Reformed thinkers made increasingly explicit what was latent in the particularist strand of Christian thought, namely, that the divine intention [note carefully Blacketer's use of this word] in the sacrifice of Christ was to provide satisfaction specifically for the elect."[100] No doubt Blacketer intends by his use of the word "intention" to signify extent as well. Since God "intends" to save only the elect, Blacketer concludes the payment for sins on the cross was likewise only accomplished for the elect and later only applied to them; hence, definite atonement.

---

96 Ibid., 135, 139–40.

97 As R. Muller has documented in "Revising the Predestination Paradigm: An Alternative to Supralapsarianism, Infralapsarianism and Hypothetical Universalism" (Mid-America Fall Lecture Series, Dyer, IN, Fall 2008) and in other recent writings.

98 J. Calvin, "Commentaries on the Book of the Prophet Jeremiah and the Lamentations," *Calvin's Commentaries*, ed. J. Owen, 22 vols. (Grand Rapids, MI: Baker, 1981), 11:422–23.

99 J. Calvin, "The Lamentations of Jeremiah," in *Calvin's Commentaries*, 11:422–23. See below.

100 Blacketer, "Blaming Beza: The Development of Definite Atonement in the Reformed Tradition," 140.

But this is a leap in logic that is unfounded, one that appears to be made by most authors in this volume. Failure to distinguish properly between intent, extent, and application with respect to the atonement is a critical error when investigating the subject historically.

Finally, what Blacketer fails to point out historically is that Hypothetical Universalism chronologically preceded definite atonement on the Reformed scene. It is clear that for the first-generation Reformed, including Calvin, definite atonement (in the sense that Christ satisfied only for the sins of the elect) was not affirmed or articulated.[101]

Review of Lee Gatiss, "The Synod of Dort and Definite Atonement" (143–63)

Lee Gatiss takes us on a tour of the Synod of Dort, and an informative tour it is. Gatiss's chapter is one of the most important in the book. It is judicious, well-footnoted with primary and secondary sources, and clearly and engagingly written. The chapter lucidly demonstrates three truths, one or more of which have been and continue to be ignored or denied by many in the Reformed tradition. First, there were some Calvinists present at the synod who clearly affirmed that Christ died for the sins of all men. Second, the final Dortian Canons were worded in such a way so as not to exclude this position within orthodox Reformed doctrine. Third, early seventeenth-century Reformed theology on the question of the extent of the atonement was not monolithic by any stretch of the imagination.

The chapter is divided into three sections. Part one considers the historical context of Dort.[102] Gatiss stated his intention is to "put the Synod into historical context and note some of the diversity among the delegates."[103] He succeeds in doing so quite well in a three-page summary.

Part two addresses specifically the Canons of Dort on the death of Christ.[104] Gatiss rightly takes note of the fact that the Remonstrants were allowed to attend the early meetings of the synod but were dismissed in January over their "political posturing and obstructive maneuvering."[105] Nevertheless, Gatiss thinks the Remonstrants "were given a fair hearing" at the synod.

Gatiss does note Balcanquhall "did at times complain about their [Remonstrants] treatment at the hands of some delegates," but he attempts to brush this aside by stat-

101 With the possible exception of John Bradford and Martin Bucer, though J. C. Ryle stated Bucer was moderate on the extent of the atonement (Ryle, *Expository Thoughts on the Gospels: John 1–6*, 4 vols. [Grand Rapids, MI: Baker, 1979], 3:158). See chapter 3 above for more on Bucer.

102 L. Gatiss, "The Synod of Dort and Definite Atonement," in *From Heaven He Came and Sought Her*, 144–47.

103 Ibid., 144.

104 Ibid., 147–58.

105 Ibid., 148.

ing that the Arminian opinions were well known matters of public record. I think one will find that the record of what occurred at Dort indicates a fair amount of "political posturing and obstructive maneuvering" by the delegates as well. Here I think Gatiss's chapter needs some historical counterbalance from Arminian scholars.

Gatiss discusses the debates on the atonement's sufficiency and efficacy (the Lombardian formula) and the diversity of Reformed responses to the Arminian employment of the formula. He thinks the Arminian position on sufficiency takes the first part of the Lombardian formula and "pushes it further." I don't see how this can be the case since the original intention of the Lombardian formula was to express the fact of Christ's death for the sins of all people, an intention that was in the process of being reinterpreted by many in the Reformed tradition to support definite atonement.

Gatiss stated:

> Not only was the cross sufficient but it was actually effective in paying for each and every person, and indeed was designed by God to do so. . . . Thus the Arminian position on the atonement made an explicit claim not just about its extent but also about its purpose and intention in God's will.[106]

But the Arminian statement Gatiss quotes said nothing about God's intention in the atonement with respect to its efficacy. It is certainly true that the Arminian position was that Christ died with an equal intent to save all people, and this point all delegates at Dort disagreed with. All the Arminian statement, which Gatiss quotes, affirms is that God willed, or purposed, that the death of Christ, with respect to its extent, should be for the sins of all men, and it was this point that some of the delegates at Dort were in agreement with.

Furthermore, the final canon on this point (Article 2.3), which Gatiss quotes, stated: "This death of the Son of God is the only and most perfect sacrifice and satisfaction for sins, and is of infinite value and worth, abundantly sufficient to expiate the sins of the whole world."[107] (150). The operative word here is "sufficient." The majority of the delegates interpreted it to mean sufficient only in value to have paid the price for the sins of the whole world, but it in fact did not do so (definite atonement). Other delegates, like Davenant, interpreted sufficiency to mean that Christ's death actually did pay for the sins of all men. The language is deliberately ambiguous to permit both groups to sign.

Gatiss correctly points out that Article 5 places "the abundant sufficiency of Christ's sacrifice side by side with the necessity for indiscriminate evangelism, but without explicitly making a logical connection between them."[108] Gatiss then stated that

106 Ibid., 150.
107 Ibid.
108 Ibid., 151–52.

the delegates all concurred that those who are ultimately lost have no one to blame but themselves. This was certainly their statement, but as I have argued elsewhere, it is logically inconsistent and even incoherent to make this claim on the definite atonement scheme for the simple reason that nothing can be sufficient for someone (the non-elect) when it does not exist for him or function as the grounds for the indiscriminate offer of the gospel to him.

Gatiss turns to discuss the intentional efficacy of the atonement. He stated: "So the Synod said, more carefully, that the cross was somehow sufficient for all, but only intended to be efficacious for the elect."[109]

Under the subheading "Reformed Variations," Gatiss explains the British and Bremen delegations' minority reports to the synod on the question of extent. While agreeing with the special intention of the atonement for the elect, the British also argued that Christ "died for all, that all and every one by means of faith might obtain remission of sins, and eternal life by virtue of that ransom." In other words, Christ died conditionally for all but efficaciously only for the elect.

Gatiss spoke of Martinius, one of the Bremen delegates, as holding "Arminianizing opinions" and "inclined toward Remonstrant views" on the atonement.[110] Martinius would find this humorous, I suspect, since he clearly rejected Arminianism, as did all the delegates at Dort. If one speaks of Martinius's views as "Arminianizing," then one would have to do the same for Davenant and the British delegation, along with the Bremen delegation, since they all affirmed a form of Hypothetical Universalism. The only place Hypothetical Universalism agrees with Arminianism is on the specific question of the extent of the atonement: Christ actually substituted for the sins of all people. Gatiss's use of the label is at best uncharitable and at worst false.[111]

Gatiss thinks the final canons don't necessarily reflect British counterweight to Genevan dislike for the concept of a sufficiency whereby Christ died conditionally for all. I'm not so sure. Gatiss does state: "Without the British pressing the Synod on these points the Canons may perhaps not have been so carefully stated."[112] I think this accurately expresses the situation.

Following Jonathan Moore, Gatiss asserts: "Article II.8 affirmed that God 'willed that Christ . . . should *effectually (efficaciter)* redeem . . . all those, and those only, who were from eternity chosen,' but this left a back door open for Davenant and others by not technically denying an ultimately *ineffectual* universal redemption in addition to

109 Ibid., 154.

110 Ibid., 155.

111 R. Godfrey noted: "Martinius' statement [on the death of Christ] was almost a direct quotation of Ursinus . . . in no sense could Martinius rightly be associated with the Remonstrants or 'semi-Remonstrant' cause" (Godfrey, "Tensions within International Calvinism: The Debate on the Atonement at the Synod of Dort" [PhD diss., Stanford University, 1974], 196–98).

112 Gatiss, "The Synod of Dort and Definite Atonement," 157.

this."[113] Such a statement either fails to understand Davenant's position or unnecessarily questions his wholehearted approval of the canons witnessed by his own signature. No "technicality" was needed. This is precisely what Davenant believed and wrote about clearly. Davenant, along with all the other Hypothetical Universalists at Dort, needed no "back door" to sign the canons in good faith.

Gatiss's third section covers matters "After the Synod" and focuses on the Dutch Annotations and their treatment of four key texts: Isa 53:10–12; John 3:16; 1 John 2:2; and 1 Tim 2:1–6. He concluded "that there was careful exegetical work standing behind the doctrinal formulations of the Synod."[114]

Gatiss noted the Dutch Annotations echoed the Heidelberg Catechism, speaking of Christ's death in these terms: "When the heavy wrath of God for the sins of mankind lay upon him," and Christ "suffered so much for mankind."[115]

In his conclusion, Gatiss rightly noted (1) the canons carefully left certain questions undecided, (2) Davenant espoused a form of Hypothetical Universalism, and (3) the British delegation's Hypothetical Universalism exerted some influence on the synod.[116]

Gatiss affirmed the fact that Richard Baxter strongly committed to the Canons of Dort despite the fact that he held to an unlimited substitution for the sins of all people in Christ's death. This is further evidence of the elasticity of Dort's final statement on the issue.

In addition to the slightly biased statement on Martinius above, one might infer a smidgeon of bias in this statement in Gatiss's final paragraph. "Despite disagreements with other delegations, Davenant and Ward happily subscribed to the original pristine statement of 'five-point Calvinism.'"[117] I find the use of the word "pristine" interesting.

A final note on Gatiss's final sentence:

> The question, however, must be whether he [Richard Baxter] or Hypothetical Universalists today are as careful to avoid the slippery slope of Arminianism as the British at Dort were, and whether the Reformed are as willing now as they were at Dort to tolerate a certain amount of diversity within their robust internal debates.[118]

Perhaps Gatiss should have added to this slippery-slope comment the danger of "hyper-Calvinism" on the part of high Calvinists, since such is certainly historically warranted, and as he himself noted, according to Michael Thomas there were two

113 Ibid.
114 Ibid., 162.
115 Ibid., 160.
116 Ibid., 162–63.
117 Ibid., 163.
118 Ibid.

delegations at Dort "foreshadowing 'Hyper-Calvinism'" in their backing away from the notion of the obligation to evangelize everyone.[119]

Review of Amar Djaballah, "Controversy on Universal Grace: A Historical Survey of Moïse Amyraut's *Brief Triaitté de la Predestination*" (165–99)

Amar Djaballah's chapter on Amyraut is one of the strongest in the book. The author avoids the pitfalls of many who have read Amyraut through the filter of biased secondary sources. From well-documented primary sources, the author presents an accessible summary of Amyraut's position.

No one who reads this chapter should ever again speak of Amyraut or his position with such disdain and condescension as one sometimes finds among high Calvinists. Djaballah apparently is aware of the mistreatment Amyraut has sometimes received when he tells us Amyraut "should be studied as a member of the Reformed theological community, with whom one may differ, not as an adversary to reduce to silence."[120]

Djaballah rightly points out how English Hypothetical Universalism antedates Amyraldianism and that the two, though related, should be distinguished from each other.[121] He stated, "A form of Amyraldianism (Hypothetical or Conditional Universalism) is sometimes the default position on the atonement for most evangelicals with Reformed leanings."[122] Better perhaps to reverse this and say, "Amyraldianism, a form of Hypothetical Universalism, is sometimes the default position."

In the introduction, Djaballah informs his readers his intent "is not to provide a comprehensive critique of Amyraut's teaching on predestination and the atonement but rather to present a historical survey of Amyraut and his writings and the controversy that ensued as a result of their publication."[123] Djaballah attempts to avoid "hagiography on the one side and caricature and misrepresentation on the other."[124] He succeeds on both counts.

As to method, Djaballah proposes "to present the doctrine of 'Hypothetical Universalism' as expounded by Amyraut in the *Brief Traitté*" (1634; second edition, 1658) under five headings: (1) Amyraut's biography and background, (2) main tenets of the *Brief Traitté*, (3) synthesis of Amyraut's basic theses on predestination, (4) controversy over universal grace generated by his writings, and (5) Amyraldianism today.[125]

119 Ibid., 151.
120 A. Djaballah, "Controversy on Universal Grace: A Historical Survey of Moïse Amyraut's *Brief Triaitté de la Predestination*," in *From Heaven He Came and Sought Her*, 167–68.
121 Ibid., 166.
122 Ibid.
123 Ibid., 166–67.
124 Ibid., 167.
125 Ibid.

In the biography section, Djaballah charts the influence of Amyraut's teacher John Cameron, who taught theology at the Reformed Academy of Saumur. There is a brief but helpful paragraph covering the circumstances leading up to the writing of the *Brief Traitté* from Amyraut himself.[126] Of note is Djaballah's statement that Amyraut "gives the strong impression that he views the doctrines he expresses not only as consonant with Scripture but also as faithful to Calvin and the first generation of Reformers, and indeed as compatible with the Canons of Dort."[127]

The bulk of the chapter covers the main tenets of Amyraut's *Brief Traitté*.[128] Djaballah summarizes each chapter clearly and concisely. Of special interest for our purpose is the summary of chapter 7, "What is the Nature of the Decree by Which God has Ordained to Accomplish This Purpose, Either for its Extent or for the Condition on Which it Depends."[129]

Several things become clear from this chapter. First, Amyraut distinguishes between the effectual intent to apply and the extent of the atonement. Second, the sacrifice of Christ on the cross for sins has been made "equally for all" with respect to the extent of the satisfaction. Third, salvation for anyone is conditioned on faith. The basis of this is Amyraut's belief that (1) all are equal in creation and are equally sinners, (2) God's compassion to deliver mankind from sin is commensurate with the plight of mankind, and hence is universal, and (3) Christ took on human nature, hence the atonement was equally for all.[130] Amyraut affirms God's universal saving will. "This will to render the grace of salvation universal and common to all human beings is so conditional that without the fulfillment of the condition it is entirely inefficacious"[131] (183).

In Amyraut's chapter 9, Djaballah shows how Amyraut's view of predestination is in line with standard Reformed doctrine. As Djaballah noted, Amyraut is clear in his affirmation that "out of his mercy, God elects some to believe. In them he vanquishes all resistance . . . , conquers the corruption of their will, and brings them to faith willingly, abandoning others to the corruption and their ensuing perdition."[132] On what basis did God choose some to salvation and leave the rest to perish? Amyraut thinks Scripture does not answer this question. "God's decree and ensuing action are due solely to his will and good pleasure."[133] Amyraut also does not think God can be accused of partiality. As Djaballah summarizes, "God's granting faith to some does not put others in a position to complain about his decision."[134]

In section three Djaballah synthesized Amyraut's basic position on predestination.

126 Ibid., 172.
127 Ibid.
128 Ibid., 172 90.
129 Ibid., 179–83.
130 Ibid., 180.
131 Ibid., 183.
132 Ibid., 184.
133 Ibid.
134 Ibid., 185.

He noted that the distinction between God's will as secret and revealed is the key to understanding Amyraut on predestination and atonement.[135] "God's revealed will concerned a universal desire to save all men on the condition that they believe. God willed that his Son should make atonement for all on the condition that they believe."[136] For Amyraut there is no necessary cause and effect between salvation procured via the atonement and salvation applied. This is Amyraut's distinction between the extent and application of the atonement. Djaballah rightly noted that Amyraut's "Hypothetical Universalism" is hypothetical in the sense that salvation is effectual "only when and if the condition of faith is fulfilled."[137]

Section four addresses the controversy over Amyraut's theology in summary fashion. Three phases are traced, followed by the aftermath, covering the years 1634–75 and beyond. Amyraut's adversaries attacked him at several levels: he did not fall within the boundaries of the Synod of Dort, his position constituted a return to Arminianism, his treatment of Calvin was mistaken, and he was not faithful to Scripture on the topic at hand.[138] Amyraut was accused of heresy in 1637 and again in 1644–45 but was acquitted. The 1675 Helvetic Consensus, drawn up by theologians from Zurich and Geneva chiefly to thwart the spread of Amyraldianism, excluded universal atonement.

Djaballah concluded his chapter with a brief mention of some today who could be considered Amyraldian in their views, such as Alan Clifford in England and Bruce Demarest in America. As he said in the conclusion: "My aim has been to inform more than to pursue an argument, since Amyraut's views are so rarely understood from the primary sources."[139] In this goal, he is successful.

Review of Carl Trueman, "Atonement and the Covenant of Redemption: John Owen on the Nature of Christ's Satisfaction" (201–23)

The final chapter in the historical section concerns John Owen's dependence upon the concept of the covenant of redemption in his famous defense of definite atonement. Noted Owenic scholar Carl Trueman does the honors.

The chapter is well structured. Following an introduction, Trueman addressed the historical context of the debates between Baxter and Owen, followed by a discussion of the so-called covenant of redemption as a linchpin in Owen's argument for limited atonement. Even though these issues are somewhat theologically technical, Trueman

135 Ibid., 190.
136 Ibid., 190–91.
137 Ibid., 191.
138 Ibid., 192–93.
139 Ibid., 199.

keeps the discussion relatively accessible. For example, when he uses Latin phrases, he explains their meaning clearly.

Trueman reminds us that "competent proponents" of definite atonement don't generally argue from a few isolated texts but rather from the "implications of a series of strands of biblical teaching, from the foundations of redemption in the intra-Trinitarian relationship."[140] This is a noteworthy statement since it underscores the fact that there are no direct, overt statements in Scripture affirming Christ died only for the sins of the elect. Given this, proponents of definite atonement must operate on the "theological" level more so than on the "exegetical" level. Definite atonement is more of a theological deduction from Scripture and less an exegetically demonstrated construct.[141]

Trueman acknowledged criticism of Owen from a number of Reformed scholars, but stated he does not intend to revisit these; rather, he seeks "to tease out the way in which Owen's treatise indicates the interconnections that exist between various soteriological points."[142]

Trueman plunges us into the deep waters of the debates between Richard Baxter and Owen over the nature of justification and the atonement. Sympathetic to Owen, Trueman quoted one of the most important passages in Owen on the nature of the sufficiency of the atonement as reflected in the famous Lombardian formula. Trueman failed to take note of the late sixteenth- and early seventeenth-century revision of the Lombardian formula.

John Owen was conscious that he and others were revising Lombard's formula and preferred to put it in hypothetical terms: "The blood of Christ was sufficient *to have been made* a price for all."[143] This reinterpretation on his part and others was designed to support Owen's argument for definite atonement. Richard Baxter called Owen's revision of the Lombardian Formula a "new futile evasion," and he refuted Owen's position

---

140 C. Trueman, "Atonement and the Covenant of Redemption: John Owen on the Nature of Christ's Satisfaction," in *From Heaven He Came and Sought Her*, 202.

141 In another place, Trueman sought to respond to this critique:

> There are many who see limited atonement as a mere logical deduction from the doctrine of election and reprobation. That is far too simplistic a way of looking at it, because there is considerable exegesis underlying the notion of limited atonement and a great deal of sophisticated reflection upon the connections between Old Testament and New Testament in the development of the concept. Thus, to disagree with limited atonement you must disagree with the exegesis that underlies it and reject the understanding of the relationship between Old Testament types and New Testament antitypes. You should not dismiss limited atonement as a naïve, overly logical deduction from [the] doctrine of election, because that simply is not the case.

See C. Trueman, "Post-Reformation Developments in the Doctrine of the Atonement," in *Precious Blood: The Atoning Work of Christ*, ed. R. D. Phillips (Wheaton, IL: Crossway, 2009), 197–98. Granted, those who affirm limited atonement view it not "as a mere logical deduction," but it is certainly *primarily* a deduction on the basis of other theological considerations. The exegesis of biblical texts by high Calvinists like John Owen in support of limited atonement, on close inspection, is actually rather weak.

142 Trueman, "Atonement and the Covenant of Redemption: John Owen on the Nature of Christ's Satisfaction," 203.

143 J. Owen, "The Death of Death in the Death of Christ," in *The Works of John Owen*, 16 vols., ed. W. H. Goold (New York: Robert Carter and Brothers, 1852), 10:296 (emphasis mine).

thoroughly.[144] There are many examples of this revision in the writings of high Calvinists at the time. Note also that Cunningham acknowledged this revision in his well-known *Historical Theology*.[145]

Trueman next discussed Owen's concept of the "covenant of redemption."[146] The notion of a covenant of redemption is a seventeenth-century construct of federal theology. The covenant of redemption is an attempt to ground an *ordo salutis* (order of salvation) in the Trinity to undergird the certainty of fulfillment. It is the foundation of Owen's support for definite atonement.

The covenant of redemption can be outlined as follows:

1. God promises to Christ success in gaining the salvation of the elect.
2. This promise is the sole goal that the Son achieves and intends to achieve via the atonement. Thus—definite atonement.
3. The Son agrees to be the constituted representative of the elect.
4. A new relation between the Father and the Son is the basis of the Son's subordination to the Father in the work of redemption.
5. The incarnation is only undertaken with special saving reference to the elect.

Trueman explained for us Owen's trajectory of thinking from the covenant of redemption to his position that the death of Christ secures the "causal basis for all the conditions attached to salvation for the elect," including the purchase of faith for the elect.[147] For Owen, there can be no universality of extent and particularity in application.[148]

The eternal intention of the covenant of redemption causes Owen to interpret all potentially universalist statements concerning the extent of the atonement in the light of the covenant of redemption. Thus "world" becomes for Owen "world of the elect." Owen presupposes since all are not saved, all were never intended by God to be saved. Hence Christ died only for the elect. Game, set, match.

For whatever reason, Trueman offered no biblical justification for the Reformed notion of the covenant of redemption or for Owen's concept of faith as a purchase at the cross. In the eleven pages where he discusses the covenant of redemption, there is a paucity of biblical references. By my count there are only four biblical references in this entire section, three of which occur in a single quotation of Owen,[149] and even here Trueman stated Owen is making an "implicit" appeal to the terms of the covenant of redemption.

144 R. Baxter, *Universal Redemption of Mankind by the Lord Jesus Christ* (London: Printed for John Salusbury at the Rising Sun in Cornhill, 1694), 343–45.

145 W. Cunningham, *Historical Theology*, 2 vols. (Edinburgh: Banner of Truth, 1994), 2:332.

146 Trueman, "Atonement and the Covenant of Redemption: John Owen on the Nature of Christ's Satisfaction," 212–22.

147 Ibid., 220–21.

148 Ibid., 222.

149 Ibid., 218.

The covenant of redemption is a theological concept with no biblical evidence or justification. Furthermore, it would have been helpful had Trueman summarized the major arguments of those within the Reformed tradition, as well as those without, who find no biblical justification for either the covenant of redemption or the purchase of faith for the elect.[150]

For Owen, supposed biblical evidence comes from three primary places in the New Testament. First, Jesus's obedience to the will of the Father as expressed in the Gospel of John is taken to suggest a covenant of redemption in the Godhead in eternity past. Second, the statement in Luke 22:29 at the last supper is supposed to indicate the covenant of redemption. But here it is clear Christ is speaking of his fulfillment of the new covenant, not the covenant of redemption. Third, passages such as Heb 7:22; 10:5–7; and 12:24 are construed as support for the covenant of redemption. But here again, all these passages speak of the new covenant, as context makes clear.

Owen's *a priori* assumption behind the covenant of redemption is that all covenant relationships involving promise and obedience are covenant relationships from eternity. Nowhere is this stated in Scripture. There is a raft of theological problems here, most of which Trueman does not address. I shall mention ten.

1. There is no covenant within the Godhead revealed in Scripture. All covenants in Scripture are between God and men. What we have here is the positing of legal or contractual dealings within the Godhead—the Father demanding payment; the Son making the payment.
2. Covenants imply a prior state of non-agreement. How this could be posited within the Trinity is difficult to conceive. Oddly enough, Trueman speaks of the universal atonement position as creating dissonance in the Trinity. Actually it is just the opposite.
3. The covenant of redemption is a legal construct, but Scripture reveals Christ's atonement on the cross was based on love, not a legal agreement.
4. One might query, Where is the Holy Spirit in this eternal contract?
5. Scripture teaches that Christ's incarnation is in the stead of all humanity, not just the elect.
6. All temporal covenants mentioned in the Bible are subordinated to the covenant of redemption. The focus is on God's so-called secret or decretal will rather than his revealed will, which is where Scripture focuses.
7. Those like Owen who posit a covenant of redemption have a tendency to work from eternity into time. What is most speculative becomes the

150 As, for example, N. A. Chambers, "A Critical Analysis of John Owen's Argument for Limited Atonement in the Death of Death in the Death of Christ" (ThM thesis, Reformed Theological Seminary, 1998).

controlling element undergirding all else. This creates a tenuous connection with Scripture and is problematic.

8. When one reads Owen, it is obvious that the covenant-of-redemption structure is introduced prior to his examination of Scripture. His theological presupposition controls his exegesis.
9. There is a hermeneutical fallacy in this process. Promises made to the Messiah in the Old Testament are made to reflect promises made to the Son in eternity. Yet there is no scriptural basis for this.
10. Those like Owen who affirm the covenant of redemption state that the elect have a legal right to salvation both as to means and ends. How does this not destroy the principle of grace in salvation?

For Owen and the covenant of redemption, all the biblical terms for salvation, such as "ransom," "reconciliation," "redemption," and so on, must be understood as references only to the elect. In this approach, to die for is to save. It is simply not possible that Christ can be said to have died for the sins of anyone who is not ultimately saved.

These concerns notwithstanding, Trueman's chapter is a helpful summary of Owen's thought on the covenant of redemption and definite atonement. This chapter concludes the historical section of the book.

I offer the following as summary thoughts, impressions, and suggestions on the seven chapters in the historical section of *From Heaven He Came and Sought Her*.

1. There are some helpful chapters here, especially with respect to Dort, Amyraut, and Owen.
2. Haykin, Hogg, and Helm reflect inadequate historiography in their chapters.
3. The historical section ends in mid-seventeenth century. There is no reckoning with the major debates within the Reformed tradition from that time to the present.
4. There is no acknowledgment of the many within the Reformed tradition who did not hold to definite atonement, including many first-generation Reformers, Puritans, the Marrow Men, the Welsh controversy, Jonathan Edwards, the New Divinity, the nineteenth-century triumvirate of Hypothetical Universalist systematic theologians Charles Hodge, Robert Dabney, and W. G. T. Shedd, and a slew of Reformed theologians and exegetes in the twentieth century.
5. Also glaringly absent is any treatment of the rise and extent of hyper-Calvinism in the eighteenth and nineteenth centuries or acknowledgment that one cannot become a hyper-Calvinist without a commitment to definite atonement and its corollaries. Though a commitment to definite atonement

is not hyper-Calvinism, all hyper-Calvinists hold to definite atonement. Hyper-Calvinism cannot exist without definite atonement.

6. Finally, the historical section fails to indicate clearly the fact that the Hypothetical Universalist position within Reformed theology antedated both definite atonement and the Amyraldian disputes.

Review of Paul Williamson, "'Because He Loves Your Forefathers': Election, Atonement, and Intercession in the Pentateuch" (227–45)

The second major section of the book (chapters 9–14) addresses the biblical evidence for definite atonement. These chapters fail to note the salient fact that not once in the Old or New Testament is there a direct statement that says Christ died only for the elect. Such a statement in Scripture is necessary to prove definite atonement. In the absence of such a statement, the authors are forced on the defensive and must spend time explaining why the many universal passages on the atonement don't mean what they appear to mean. The authors inform us that the actual texts that speak of the universality of the extent of the atonement must be interpreted in light of the larger context of biblical theology, which, according to them, indicates a limitation in Christ's sin-bearing for the elect only.

This move, however, is problematic on four counts. First, it is in danger of *petitio principii*—that is, begging the question. Second, there is the constant refrain, assumed or stated, that the intent and the extent of the atonement are coextensive, though this is also a deduction made without a single biblical text that asserts this to be the case. Third, the authors of this section are reading the "universal" texts in light of the "limited" texts. No consideration is given to the possibility that many of these limited texts are expressed in this fashion because the biblical authors are writing specifically to believers. Fourth, the authors are superimposing a theology on these texts (eisegesis) rather than letting the texts speak for themselves (exegesis).

Paul Williamson addresses the issue of election, atonement, and intercession in the Pentateuch in chapter 9. He admits that "definite atonement is nowhere explicitly mentioned" in the Pentateuch but argues there are "certain hints" of this concept embedded within it.[151] This crucial admission is vital to note. Williamson states: "It would be inappropriate to infer some kind of general atonement from Israel's corporate experience of atonement. Any such atonement is accomplished and applied on the

151 P. Williamson, "'Because He Loves Your Forefathers': Election, Atonement, and Intercession in the Pentateuch," in *From Heaven He Came and Sought Her*, 228.

basis of Israel's divine election. . . . This does not imply, however, that each individual Israelite was thus equally atoned for and thus 'eternally forgiven.'"[152]

In response, no one says that each individual Israelite was equally atoned for and eternally forgiven any more than the unlimited atonement passages in the NT imply that each individual person for whom Christ died was equally atoned for and thus eternally forgiven. The last four words smuggle in the notion that the atonement's extent and application are coextensive and confuse the issue. This presumes that all for whom atonement is made must *ipso facto* be "eternally forgiven."

It is difficult to conclude that the Day of Atonement ritual (Leviticus 16) was in any sense limited. In fact, Williamson must admit that it was in some sense "all-inclusive."[153] Yet he makes the assumption that in Israel there were elect and non-elect. "Covenant and election circumscribed atonement. So a particular atonement may still be maintained for a 'mixed' covenant community."[154]

He also states, "To deduce a general, universal atonement in the NT from an atonement for a 'mixed' Israel in the OT is a non sequitur. . . . Atonement in the OT is therefore necessarily particular."[155] But these statements are problematic. First, they retroject a presumed Reformed understanding of individual election back into the text. But even granting this for the sake of argument, there is no necessity that election of some within Israel should preclude atonement being made for all. Second, by what logic is OT atonement "necessarily particular"? Where are the warrants for such an assertion? What Williamson should have said was, "Atonement in the OT is circumscribed by covenant and election, and is therefore necessarily particular in its application, not in extent."

Williamson discusses the Day of Atonement and typology within two Reformed covenantal frameworks: "New Covenant Theology approach" and the "Reformed Covenantal approach."[156] But one finds nothing in this section that supports definite atonement.

The bronze snake episode of Num 21:4–9 to which Williamson appeals[157] actually works against his case. He said, "It may be inferred that the bronze snake had a particular rather than a general focus; it was designed for the benefit of penitent Israelites, not impenitent rebels."[158] Note the key word "designed" here. Williamson fails to discern the simple fact that the limitation for Israel was not in the provision of the bronze snake (it was given for all Israel); rather, the limitation was in the application: only those who looked lived. There was a remedy for all Israel, and they would be healed if they would

152 Ibid., 229.
153 Ibid., 234.
154 Ibid., 235.
155 Ibid., 238.
156 Ibid., 235–38.
157 Ibid, 241.
158 Ibid.

only look. There is a remedy in Christ's death for all, and they will be saved if they will only believe. The extent (provision) is universal; the application is limited.

Contrary to Williamson's conclusion, there is no idea of definite atonement, even an undeveloped one, in the Pentateuch.[159] His assertion that election is the crucial theological prerequisite for atonement, even if true, does not entail definite atonement. It merely entails there is an atonement for those who are elect according to the Reformed understanding of election. It does not preclude an atonement made on behalf of those who never believe.

Review of J. Alec Motyer, "'Stricken for the Transgressions of My People': The Atoning Work of Isaiah's Suffering Servant" (247–66)

In chapter 10 Motyer treats us to a solid exegesis of Isaiah 53. I always try to read Motyer on any text of Scripture on which he writes. He is an excellent exegete. Here Motyer avoids the clutter of quotations from other commentators and stays with his exegesis of the text. It's smooth sailing until we come to page 252 where Motyer says a universal task is going to be accomplished successfully; it will be achieved by suffering, and the suffering and its result will exactly match each other. As the structure of Isaiah 52:14 displays: "The verse equates those who are appalled by the Servant's suffering with those who become the beneficiaries of his shed blood, and thus the verse introduces us to the concept of substitutionary atonement."[160] There is a world of difference between stating the text affirms substitutionary atonement, which it emphatically does, and stating the text affirms the suffering and its result will exactly match each other, which it does not. Motyer has smuggled in the notion of equivalency between intent, extent, and application—something that the text itself does not affirm.

Problems emerge again on page 261 when Motyer states, "Since universalism is ruled out by Isaiah's insistence on 'the many' . . . 53:4–6 commits the unprejudiced interpreter to an effective particularistic understanding of the atonement." Of course universalism in the sense of universal salvation is ruled out, here and throughout the Bible. Motyer here and in the next few pages failed to note that Isaiah's use of "many" does not linguistically necessitate the conclusion that (1) atonement was only made for some and/or (2) atonement was not made for all.

Mark 10:45 is clearly connected to Isaiah 53 according to Martin Hengel. "Here the imminent death of Jesus is interpreted in an inclusive, universal way as being 'for all

159 Ibid., 245.

160 J. A. Motyer, "'Stricken for the Transgressions of My People': The Atoning Work of Isaiah's Suffering Servant," in *From Heaven He Came and Sought Her*, 252.

men,' in connection with Isa. 53 and the covenant sacrifice of Ex. 24:8 (cf. also Zech. 9.11), as a representative atoning death 'for the many.'"[161] Hengel continued:

> It is also striking that the early kerygmatic formulae very soon qualify the universal "for all" and reduce it to "for us," meaning the community of believers. This is clear, for example, from a comparison of Mark 10.45 and I Tim. 2.6 with other surrender formulae or of Mark 14.24 with I Cor. 11.24 (cf. however, 10.17). This understandable tendency to reduce the scope of salvation to one's own community presumably already began with the events of Easter, which only affected a limited group.[162]

> Mark 10.45 probably also belongs in the context of that last night; it will have been used by him to elucidate his mysterious symbolic action. From both Mark and Luke we hear that Jesus spoke at the Last Supper about "serving." The saying over the cup and the saying about ransom are connected by the universal service "for the many," in the sense of "for all," which is presumably to be derived from Isaiah 53.[163]

Like Motyer, it is common for limitarians to appeal to "the many" in Isa 52:14–53:12 as evidence for limited atonement. But this is a misreading of the Hebrew text. As Joachim Jeremias pointed out concerning the pre-Christian interpretations of "the many" in Isaiah 53, "the many" is extended to include the Gentiles in *1 Enoch* and *The Wisdom of Solomon* and may refer to them primarily, if not exclusively, in Isa 52:14–15. But, Jeremias continued, in the Hebrew text there is no difference between "the many" of Isa 52:14–15 and Isa 53:11–12. All Jews and Gentiles are included.

> In fact, the Peshitta renders Isa. 52.15, "he will purify many peoples". *[sic]* If the Peshitta version of the Old Testament is pre-Christian (which is probable), then we have here an example of the inclusion of the Gentiles in the group of "many" for whom the atoning work of the servant is effective. . . . The "for many" of the Eucharistic words is therefore, as we have already seen, not exclusive ("many, but not all"), but, in the Semitic manner of speech, inclusive ("the totality, consisting of many"). The Johannine tradition interprets it in this way,

161 M. Hengel, *The Atonement: The Origins of the Doctrine in the New Testament* (Philadelphia: Fortress, 1981), 42.

162 Ibid., 71.

163 Ibid., 73. See also H. D. McDonald, *Forgiveness and Atonement* (Grand Rapids, MI: Baker, 1984), 127:

> Like the ransom Jesus paid (Matt. 20:28; cf. Mark 10:45; 1 Tim. 2:6), the shedding of the blood of the covenant is described as being 'for many.' This phrase does not set a limit to Christ's work. On the contrary, it suggests that the benefits of his self-sacrifice go beyond the lost sheep of the house of Israel.

for in its equivalent to the bread-word . . . it paraphrases "for many" as "for the life of the world" (John 6.51c).[164]

Another problem is Motyer's use of "unprejudiced." This is nothing more than an *ad hominem* attack on those who disagree with his interpretation and conclusion. In light of 53:6, others could just as easily say that any "unprejudiced" interpreter would be committed to a universal extent in the sin-bearing of the Suffering Servant.

But the problems continue. Motyer states: "The theological implications are profound: the atonement itself, and not something outside of the atonement, is the cause for any conversion."[165] This fails to consider further New Testament revelation on the role of the Holy Spirit in conversion, fails to recognize that the atonement saves no one until it is applied, fails to reckon with numerous Reformed theologians (Charles Hodge comes to mind) who disagree, and fails to distinguish properly between the extent and the application of the atonement.

Even Paul clearly indicates in Eph 2:1–3 that the believing elect he is addressing were under the wrath of God prior to faith. Notice the many times Paul makes the point that believers were once enemies, but now through faith we have peace, are justified, experience no condemnation, and so on. Such language necessitates an intervening condition. Justification at the cross is a false doctrine.

Motyer builds on the "many" statements in Isaiah 53 to argue definite atonement.[166] The many nations for whom the atonement is made "does not, however, commit us to universalism ('all without exception'), . . . so that even when 'many' seems to imply 'all,' it still effectively applies only on the individual level—to some in contrast to all."[167] Of course that is the case because the application is not coextensive with the extent. This does not, however, confirm definite atonement or negate universal atonement.

Motyer errs in this statement: "'Many,' then, has a certain specificity to it, while also retaining its inherent numerousness; it refers to those for whom the Servant made atonement and to whom he applies that same atonement (cf. Rev. 7:9)."[168] Here again Motyer assumes what he is trying to prove—namely, that the extent of the atonement is coextensive with its application. The text does not state this. Furthermore, this is a misinterpretation of the Revelation passage, which is so often quoted in favor of definite atonement but which actually has nothing to do with the extent of the atonement, only with the beneficiaries of the atonement.

As an aside, though Motyer does not quote others to support his exegetical conclusions, it is interesting that Calvin himself clearly affirms that the "many" of Isa 53:6

164 J. Jeremias, *The Eucharistic Words of Jesus* (Philadelphia: Fortress, 1966), 228–29.

165 Motyer, "'Stricken for the Transgressions of My People': The Atoning Work of Isaiah's Suffering Servant," 261.

166 Ibid., 264–65.

167 Ibid., 265.

168 Ibid.

means "all without exception."[169] More importantly, Paul uses "many" and "all" interchangeably in Romans 5, as the Greek text clearly shows.[170]

Motyer's chapter is an example of generally good exegesis coupled with reading one's theology into the text and drawing the wrong conclusions. Isaiah 53:6 is the heart of the passage, and it clearly asserts a parallelism between all those who have gone astray and the fact that "the Lord has laid on Him the iniquity of us all." There is indeed an equivalency in this passage but not as Motyer suggests. The equivalency is not between the sufferings of Christ and the elect only. The equivalency is clearly stated in 53:6 and is between those who have gone astray (all) and those (all) for whom the Servant suffers. This is even more clearly brought out by the inclusio Isaiah employs, beginning and ending the verse with the same Hebrew word *kullānū*, translated "all." The issue is not the meaning of "the many." The key is the meaning and use of "all" at the very linguistic heart of the five-stanza song—53:6. Definite atonement simply can't get past the "all" of Isa 53:6.

Review of Matthew Harmon, "For the Glory of the Father and the Salvation of His People: Definite Atonement in the Synoptics and Johannine Literature" (267–88)

Matthew Harmon authors the chapter on definite atonement in the Synoptic Gospels and Johannine literature. Harmon intends to argue three things: (1) Jesus died to display God's glory, (2) Jesus died to accomplish the salvation of his people, and (3) Jesus died for the sins of the world (where "world" does not mean "all without exception" but "all without distinction").[171]

In part 1 of his chapter Harmon attempts to find definite atonement in three key passages: John 6:22–58; John 17:1–26; and Rev 4:1–5:14.

John 6

From John 6:37–40, 44, Harmon pointed out that Jesus came to do the will of the Father. From verse 37, he noted the Father gives a specific group of people to the Son, and from verse 44 he noted no one can come to the Son unless the Father draws him. Harmon concluded: "Thus it is the Father's election of a specific group of people that defines who comes to the Son."[172]

169 Calvin, *Sermons on Isaiah*, 66, 70, 78–79.

170 Donald M. Lake discussed the shift between "all" and "many" in Rom 5:18–19, noting C. K. Barrett's observation, "By 'many' he can hardly mean anything different from the 'all men' of v. 12 (cf. also 1 Cor. 15:22). This inclusive use of 'many' is Hebraistic; in Old Testament usage 'many' often means not 'many contrasted with 'all' but 'many contrasted with one or some.'" See D. M. Lake, "He Died for All," in *Grace Unlimited*, ed. Clark H. Pinnock (Minneapolis, MN: Bethany Fellowship, 1975), 33.

171 M. Harmon, "For the Glory of the Father and the Salvation of His People: Definite Atonement in the Synoptics and Johannine Literature," in *From Heaven He Came and Sought Her*, 267.

172 Ibid., 270.

Several points call for explication.

First, Harmon is interpreting "all the Father gives me" as referencing election. This assumes two things: (1) the Reformed interpretation of election is correct and (2) this passage is referencing it. For the sake of argument, let's grant the first assumption for the moment. Even so, nothing in the passage speaks to "election." John 6 must be read in the light of the preceding context of chapters 1–5 as well as in its immediate context.

In John 1:6–9 John makes clear that God's intention in sending John the Baptist was that all might believe in Christ. Jesus, not John, is the "Light which gives light to every man coming into the world" (NKJV). Again in John 1:29, Christ comes that he might be the savior of the world. In John 3:16, God's love for the world is the motivation for his sending Jesus so that everyone who believes in him will have eternal life. John is establishing a universal desire on God's part for the salvation of the world and a universal remedy for such through Christ's death on the cross.

Second, when did this "giving" take place? Not in eternity past, for the use of the present-tense verb indicates contemporary action: the Father was in the very process of giving to the Son those who were believing on him.

Third, in what sense did God "give" people to his Son? Frequently in Scripture one finds the terms "gift" and "given" are idiomatically employed to denote God's favor expressing his redemptive work for mankind. See Ps 2:8 and Acts 4:25–26 as examples. Here the Gentile nations are said to be "given" to Christ as an inheritance. Yet this language clearly does not indicate that all the nations or all people in those nations are somehow "elected" to salvation in eternity.

John makes a connection between the "giving" and the "coming" in 6:37. Notice how verses 44–45 use different imagery but express the same meaning.

> "No one can come to Me, unless the Father who sent Me draws him: and I will raise him up in the last day. It is written in the prophets, 'And they shall all be taught by God.' Therefore everyone who has heard and learned from the Father comes to me." (NKJV)

Notice God's "drawing" is parallel to his "giving" in verse 37. How is the drawing accomplished according to vv. 44–45? By means of hearing, learning, and coming to the Lord. This is John's notion of what it means for some to be "given" to Christ. The refusal of unbelievers to come to Christ was due to their refusal to listen to the Father, as the context of John 5:37–38 and John 6 makes clear.

The reason many of the Jews did not come to Christ is not that they were not "given" to him by the Father but is found in their own stubborn hearts. John 5:40 said they were not willing to come to Christ, not that they could not come to Christ because they had not been "given" to him by the Father. Notice how John 5:43–47 speaks often of "belief."

Election is simply not in the picture in this passage. The "coming" of John 6:37 is synonymous with "believing," as verse 35 indicates. What does "all that the Father gives Me" refer to in verses 37 and 39? In verse 39 the phrase is equivalent to "everyone who looks to the Son and believes in Him" in verse 40. The phrase in verse 39 is equivalent to the phrase in verse 37. John is oscillating between believers viewed as a group and believers viewed as individuals, as the Greek text demonstrates. Thus the limited group of those given by the Father to the Son are those who have believed. It is incorrect to interpret the passage as teaching that certain persons are eternally elected to become believers.

What did Jesus mean when he said "will come to me" in verse 37a? Some Calvinist interpreters link the word "come" in verses 35, 37b, and 44 with "will come" in verse 37a. But this fails to recognize the two different Greek words used. *Hēkō* is the Greek word translated "will come" in verse 37a, while *erchomai* is the word used in verse 35 and 37b. Jesus appears to be thinking about all believers considered as a group in v. 37a.

What is intended by the phrase "will come to me"? Verse 39 answers the question. All believers are given by the Father to Christ, and they will reach final salvation in the eschaton via the resurrection in the last days. Thus it is final salvation that is in view, not pretemporal election.

There is a difference in saying John 6:44 indicates specific efficacious grace given only to the elect and in viewing it as meaning no one can come to believe in Christ unless the Father draws him via enabling grace. Jesus has declared numerous times, before he speaks of the "drawing" of the Father, that only believers possess eternal life (6:27–29, 40). What John affirms in chapter 6 is that God initiates and consummates the salvation process. Grace precedes human response.

There is nothing in this passage that affirms definite atonement.

John 17

Harmon's second key passage is Jesus's so-called high priestly prayer in John 17. Harmon's logic is this: intercession (for the elect only) = limited atonement (for the elect only). Since Jesus did not intercede for the world, he did not die for the sins of the world.[173]

This is a common argument in the limited atonement arsenal and has been addressed and answered, even by a number of Calvinists, including Richard Baxter (1615–91), Gryffith Williams (c. 1589–1672), Joseph Truman (1631–71), Nathaniel Holmes (1599–1678), Edward Polhill (1622–94), and W. G. T. Shedd (1820–94).[174]

---

173 Ibid., 272.

174 Baxter, *Catholick Theologie* (London: Printed by Robert White, for Nevill Simmons at the Princes Arms in St. Pauls Church-yard, 1675), 2:68–69; G. Williams, *The Delights of the Saints* (London: Printed for Nathaniel Butter, 1622), 37; J. Truman, *A Discourse of Natural and Moral Impotency* (London: Printed for Robert Clavel, 1675), 185–86; N. Holmes, "Christ Offering Himself to All Sinners, and Answering All Their Objection," in *The Works of Dr. Nathaniel Holmes* (London: Printed for the Author, 1651), 15; E. Polhill, "The Divine Will Considered in Its Eternal Decrees," in *The Works of Edward Polhill* (Morgan, PA: Soli Deo Gloria, 1988), 167–68, 170–71, 174; Shedd, *Dogmatic Theology*, 3:420–21.

Harmon writes:

> To claim that Christ atones for the sins of everyone but then applies that atonement only to the elect runs contrary to the totality of the work that Christ performs in order to glorify the Father. Such a claim also presents the persons of the Trinity working at cross purposes with each other.[175]

But Harmon offers no support for these claims. Why and how is it the case that atonement made for all humanity would not glorify the Father as an atonement made only for the elect? There is no disharmony in the Trinity. (I will address this claim more fully when we come to the theological chapters of the book.) Harmon is assuming what he is trying to prove: namely, that the atonement guarantees its application.

John 17 does not state that Jesus dies only for those for whom he prays. Laying aside for the moment the possibility that in context this is most likely a reference to the disciples, and even taking it as extending to the believing elect at the time, even then the conclusion is not warranted that the text means that Jesus did not die for the sins of all people, elect and non-elect (negative inference fallacy).

Harmon falls prey to generalizing that election entails limited atonement. He assumes that if Jesus prays only for the elect, then he must have died only for the elect. The mistake here is a collapsing of the intercession of Christ into his expiation for sins. This begs the question.

A better interpretation of John 17 was given by Harold Dekker, formerly professor and academic dean at Calvin Theological Seminary. I summarize his argument:

- Does John 17:9 indicate Jesus died for the elect only? The context beginning with v. 4 makes clear that those to whom Jesus referred in v. 9 are those who had come to believe in him up to that point in time. Verse 20 supports this, since there Jesus says he prays also for those who will (future) believe in him.
- When Jesus says he does not pray for the world (v. 9), what does he mean? Jesus prayed a specific prayer for those who had and would believe in him. There would have been no point in Jesus praying these specific things for the unconverted, because they could never be true for the unconverted until they were converted. The fact that he did not do so proves nothing about his disposition toward the world or the extent of his atonement for the world.
- This is made even clearer in John 17:21–23. Here Jesus does indeed pray for the world—namely, that the world might believe. Here the word

175 Harmon, "For the Glory of the Father and the Salvation of His People: Definite Atonement in the Synoptics and Johannine Literature," 272.

> "world" cannot be limited to the elect and means nothing less than the world of all people.[176]

David Ponter, in "Revisiting John 17 and Jesus' Prayer for the World,"[177] pointed out how, when it comes to John 17, the following are alleged, asserted, and assumed without any support from confirming evidence:

1. That this is a specific and effectual high priestly prayer on the part of Jesus.
2. That the "world" of 17:9 represents the world of the reprobate.
3. That those "given" in verse 9 represent the totality of the elect.
4. That the extent of the high priestly intercession delimits the scope of the satisfaction.
5. That the two parallel clauses in verses 21 and 23 are systemically overlooked or misread.

Ponter focused on number five. John 17:21 and 23:

> that they may all be one; even as You, Father, are in Me and I in You, that they also may be in Us, so that the world may believe [πιστευω] that You sent Me . . . I in them and You in Me, that they may be perfected in unity, so that the world may know [γινωσκω] that You sent Me, and loved them, even as You have loved Me. (NASB)

Ponter noted how Calvin took "world" in verses 21 and 23 as the world of the reprobate (non-elect) according to its usage throughout John 17. But when Calvin came to the verbs "to believe" and "to know," he interpreted them as referring to something other than true saving faith. Ponter pointed out that John Gill did the same thing in his interpretation of "world" in verse 21. Though it may mean the rest of the elect, Gill preferred to interpret it as meaning the remaining Jews and Deists (unbelievers) who will be forced to acknowledge Jesus as Messiah in the eschaton. Ponter viewed this as a strange and eccentric reading of the text. Where is the warrant for changing the normal meaning of "to believe" and "to know" in John's gospel such that they mean something other than saving belief and knowledge?

Ponter found a parallel usage in John 17:8: "For the words which You gave Me I have given to them; and they received them and truly understood [γινωσκω] that I came forth from You, and they believed [πιστευω] that You sent Me" (NASB). Jesus

176 H. Dekker, "God's Love to Sinners: One or Two?," *Reformed Journal* 13 (1963): 14–15. See also L. Morris, *The Gospel According to John* (Grand Rapids, MI: Eerdmans, 1971), 725, who argued the same point.

177 D. Ponter, "Revisiting John 17 and Jesus' Prayer for the World," *Calvin and Calvinism*, February 10, 2015, http://calvinandcalvinism.com/?p=15779.

uses the two verbs *believe* and *know* with the identical referent of the apostles who had come to know and believe that Jesus had truly been sent from the Father. This same point is repeated in verses 21 and 23 but now applied to the "world."

Ponter then considered 17:25: "O righteous Father, although the world has not known You, yet I have known You; and these have known [γινωσκω] that You sent Me" (NASB). This same approach can be found in other places in John's Gospel. Consider 6:69: "And we have *believed* and have come to *know* that You are the Holy One of God" (NASB, emphasis added). Likewise John 16:27: "For the Father Himself loves you, because you have loved Me, and have *believed* that I came forth from the Father" and John 16:30: "Now we know that You know all things, and have no need for anyone to question You; by this we *believe* that You came from God" (NASB both; emphasis added).

It would appear these expressions have something of a thematic or formulaic meaning for John according to Ponter. Calvin and Gill have assumed and asserted that "world" in verse 9 denotes the non-elect rather than the world of humanity in opposition to God and the church. Context and usage mitigate against their interpretation. Ponter concluded:

> However, once the meaning of *kosmos* throughout the chapter is allowed to assume its normal meaning, and once the meanings of the verbs *believe* and *know* are allowed to be read consistently (as defined by context and usage rather than atextual interpolations), then according the standard rules of hermeneutics, the strict particularist reading of this passage really has no footing in this chapter.[178]

Ponter's final point to support his exegesis of the passage is that the prayer is for the world's salvation, as evidenced by the use of the subjunctives in Greek: "That the world may believe," and "that the world may know." Jesus prays that future believers be unified for a major purpose: that the world may believe and know that Jesus has been sent from the Father. Ponter concluded that the exegesis of John 17 better supports an unlimited atonement.

High Calvinists insist that if Christ dies for a particular person, then he prays for that particular person. But this argument can be inverted. All would have to agree if Christ prays for a particular person, he must have died for that person. John 17:21 and 23 clearly assert Christ prays for the world, therefore he must have died for the world.

Revelation 5:9–10

Harmon's third passage is Rev 4:1–5:14. Key here is Rev 5:9–10, which Harmon assumes teaches limited atonement. It simply does not. All the passage does is indicate who the

178 Ibid. (emphasis in original).

redeemed are and where they are from (every tribe, tongue, nation). One must assume the atonement and its application are coextensive to find evidence for definite atonement in Revelation 4–5, which is, of course, what Harmon does.

Election Circumscribes Atonement

Harmon concludes that election circumscribes atonement, not the other way around.[179] He takes "his people" in Matt 1:21, coupled with Matt 20:28 and Matt 26:28, and deduces definite atonement. He does not seem to consider the possibility that the referent of "His people" is likely the Jews viewed ethnically and not some abstract Reformed notion of election. He avoids passages like Luke 22:20–21, where Christ includes Judas in the group of those for whom his blood is shed. As I have mentioned before, both Augustine and Calvin affirm Judas was at the table and Augustine clearly states that Jesus suffered for Judas's sins.

Harmon correctly states: "Particularism and universalism are complementary realities, not contradictory ones."[180] Precisely. But his comment is in reference to the extent of atonement combined with universal proclamation. He means to argue for the intrinsic sufficiency (value) of the atonement as the grounds for a universal preaching of the atonement. Since this is the burden of Piper's final chapter in the book, I will address this issue at that point.

Johannine Literature

At this point Harmon shifts to the Johannine literature, where he spends the most time. He points out how John includes statements about God's election of a particular people to receive the benefits of Jesus's death in John 10. Yet he cannot produce any statement in John 10 that asserts definite atonement.

"World" in Johannine Literature

Harmon concludes by noting the key for the universal language in John is not that the atonement is for all people but that it extends beyond Jews to include people from every tribe and tongue.[181] He attempts to support this point by a discussion of the word "world."[182]

Something of his faulty methodology is evidenced by his comment on John 1:29: there is nothing in the context to restrict the usage of "world," but the "numerous other restricted uses must be brought to bear."[183] But why "must" this be so? How is it that

179 Harmon, "For the Glory of the Father and the Salvation of His People: Definite Atonement in the Synoptics and Johannine Literature," 271.

180 Ibid., 281.

181 Ibid.

182 Ibid., 282–87.

183 Ibid., 283.

in every single atonement passage that uses the word "world," most Calvinists inform us that the word must be restricted because in some other contexts it is restricted?

With respect to the use of *kosmos* in the Gospel of John, the word characteristically means human beings in rebellion against God. See John 1:29 where it is the sins of the "world" that must be atoned for. In John 3:16 the world is spoken of as being loved and condemned, and then some are saved out of it. The latter two outcomes occur because of either belief or unbelief according to 3:18. John 3:19 is consistent with this.

A comparison of 1 John 2:2 with 1 John 5:19 illustrates how Harmon's treatment of *kosmos* in 1 John 2:2 is in error. In 2:2 Christ is the propitiation for the sins "of the whole world." In 5:19 "the whole world" lies under the sway of the wicked one. The phrase translated "the whole world" in both passages is identical in Greek. "World" in 1 John 5:19 must mean "the unbelieving world," as in all people with the exception of believers. The word does not and cannot mean "some of all kinds" of people but of necessity must refer to all unbelieving people without exception.

The same meaning attaches to 1 John 2:2. Christ is the propitiation of "our sins" (believers) and of the sins of "the whole world" (all unbelievers). The atonement is unlimited. Harmon does not appear to have followed his own advice: "Only the context can determine what *kosmos* means, not *a priori* assumptions."[184]

Like all the chapters in this section, Harmon bases virtually his entire case on the supposition that universal terms with respect to the extent of the atonement signify "all without distinction" and not "all without exception." (See my comments on the problems with this in previous reviews and below in the review of Jonathan Gibson.)

John 10: Christ and His Sheep

Harmon stated in a footnote regarding John 10:15: "It simply will not do to assert that a text like this does not explicitly 'say that Christ died *only* for the church, or that he did not die for the non-elect,' as does David L. Allen."[185] Yet he affirms my basic assertion: "True, the claim that Jesus laid down his life for his sheep does not logically demand that he died only for the elect." He then attempts to blunt the force of this fact. What Harmon cannot demonstrate is where the text logically demands that Christ died only for the sheep. According to standard logical protocol, all things must be established by good and necessary consequence.

By what logic does one exclude Jesus's critics from the scope of his death by the revelation that they are not his sheep? There is nothing in Jesus's statement that limits the scope of his death. As long as the Pharisees and other unbelievers refuse what Jesus is saying, they are incapable of receiving the saving benefits of his death. Even if Jesus's statement indicates that his critics are not now nor ever will be among his sheep, such

184 Ibid., 287.
185 Ibid., 277.

does not affirm or entail limited atonement. To assert that the statement does teach or entail limited atonement is to succumb to the negative inference fallacy.

Even from Harmon's perspective, he must believe that Jesus died for more than just those who are Christ's sheep since he believes Christ died for the unbelieving elect who are not yet his sheep. Harmon's error here is taking what applies to believers and extrapolating the predication to all of the elect in the abstract. What are the exegetical grounds for reading "sheep" in John's context as the abstract class of all the elect? There are none.

John 10 and Logic

Here is the argument Harmon desires to set out from John 10:

> Christ died for his sheep.
> Pharisees are not his sheep.
> Therefore Christ did not die for them.

The burden of this section, and indeed most of the chapter, is an attempt to employ this kind of logical argument without explicitly stating it. But his logical argument is invalid.

Consider this parallel example from D. A. Carson:

> All orthodox Jews believe in Moses.
> Smith is not an orthodox Jew.
> Therefore Smith does not believe in Moses.[186]

The conclusion does not follow, and the syllogism is logically fallacious. Analogies could be added *ad infinitum*.

> John loves Mary.
> Bill is not Mary.
> Therefore John does not love Bill.

No matter how you parse it, it is invalid logic, and no sound argument can be grounded in an invalid logical argument. It does not matter what interpretation of the sheep one takes in John 10, the argument is invalid.

Harmon wrongly concluded from John 10 that Christ died only for those given to him. Jesus's statements in John 10 in no way prove exclusivity. When we are told Jesus

186 D. A. Carson, *Exegetical Fallacies*, 2nd ed. (Grand Rapids, MI: Baker, 1996), 102.

died for his "friends," does that prove he died only for them? Did he not die for his enemies as well? The point here is that simple positive statements cannot logically be used to infer category negations.

Conclusion

1. Harmon does not engage the many Reformed authors who critique the standard interpretation of these passages as limited to the elect only. Where is reference to Charles Hodge, Robert Dabney, or W. G. T. Shedd on many of these universal texts?
2. It appears Harmon is dealing in supposed implications from his own presuppositions, which he brings to the text from the Reformed system.
3. The burden of proof is on Harmon to show why and how in every atonement passage where universal terms are employed the meaning of these terms should be restricted and thus transmuted into limited terms on the basis of a few examples where contextually the terms are restricted. This is simply not possible exegetically.
4. John employs words such as "light," "life," "bread," and "gift" as they appear in a general or universal context. These are important in a consideration of the question at hand. Scripture routinely plays up the universal aspects of Christ's work, especially in John's Gospel. There are far more universal terms and statements with respect to the extent of the atonement than there are restricted terms and statements.
5. Harmon continuously repeats the negative inference fallacy in his chapter.

Review of Jonathan Gibson, "For Whom Did Christ Die? Particularism and Universalism in the Pauline Epistles" (289–330)

Jonathan Gibson's chapter 12 is one of the heftiest in the book, weighing in at forty-plus pages. This is to be expected since there is so much material in the Pauline Letters that impinge on the question at hand.

Following a two-page introduction, he divides his chapter into five sections: (1) particularistic texts (four pages); (2) universal texts (twenty-five-plus pages); (3) texts that deal with those perishing, false teachers, and offended brothers for whom Christ died (two pages); (4) Christ died for "all" and for the "world" (five pages); and (5) definite atonement and evangelism (one page). This is followed by a summary conclusion.

Gibson's chapter is helpful in many ways, chiefly in his effort to cover the key texts in Paul in a reasonably substantive way. Romans 5:12–21 and 2 Cor 5:14–19 receive more lengthy treatment. The writing style is clear, and the chapter contains a number of helpful footnotes. Gibson attempts a fair and balanced treatment of the texts.

As a minor quibble, the section dealing with McCormick seems to me to be a bit of a rabbit trail that unnecessarily interrupts the flow and has little to do with the question at hand.

Tension in Paul?

Gibson sees a tension in Paul between particular and universal atonement texts.[187] His thesis is "I will demonstrate that the universalistic elements in Paul's atonement theology complement rather than compromise the possibility of interpreting Christ's death as definite atonement."[188] I would argue it is the other way around. The few limited texts in Paul's atonement theology compliment rather than compromise the many universal texts that clearly affirm an unlimited atonement.

In section one, Gibson lists six "particularistic texts" that he believes indicate Christ died only for the elect.[189] He is attempting to interpret the many universalistic texts in light of the fewer restricted texts. There is no tension between these texts, nor do the particularistic texts affirm definite atonement. It would be normal and natural for Paul, when writing to believers, to speak of "Christ's death for us." Given this kind of context, to infer from this that Christ died only for "us" is to invoke the negative inference fallacy.

Gibson acknowledges the negative inference fallacy argument is "prima facie, entirely fair"[190] but attempts to blunt it in three ways. First, he states that the argument is too simplistic because to attempt to deduce universal atonement from this argument is a *non sequitur*. The problem here is that the argument is not used to deduce unlimited atonement. That comes from an exegesis of the relevant texts. The negative inference fallacy is the logical *non sequitur* that Gibson himself is using in an attempt to deduce limited atonement from these so-called limited texts. His attempt to turn the tables is unsuccessful.

Second, Gibson attempts to show that Paul absolutizes the universality of sin with "all" language that is "indisputably unambiguous." He follows this up by saying there is no statement in Paul such as "there is not one for whom Christ did not die."[191] He then said: "Yet when it comes to Paul's 'universalizing' the target audience of Christ's atonement, he employs deliberately ambiguous language: 'many,' 'all,' and 'world,' may mean 'all without exception,' but the terms may equally mean 'all without distinction.' Context must determine the meaning in each particular case."[192]

187 J. Gibson, "For Whom Did Christ Die? Particularism and Universalism in the Pauline Epistles," in *From Heaven He Came and Sought Her*, 290.

188 Ibid., 291.

189 Ibid., 291–95.

190 Ibid., 292.

191 Ibid., 293.

192 Ibid.

Gibson trades on the "all without distinction" versus "all without exception" notion throughout this chapter. It is the key argument he makes in the attempt to interpret the universal passages in a restricted manner. But is this a valid distinction?

Several points need to be made in response. First, there is nothing ambiguous about Paul's use of the word "all" and "world." Keep in mind that these universal verses were routinely interpreted by the Church to teach universal atonement from the time of the early church fathers to the end of the sixteenth century. Second, with respect to the statement that Paul never says "there is not one for whom Christ did not die," this is an argument from silence. Why would Paul make such a statement in the light of his many statements about the universal scope of the atonement? Gibson fails to note there is also not one statement where Paul says Christ died only for the sins of some people. Finally, Gibson's third argument against the validity of the negative inference fallacy is to state that the onus lies on proponents of universal atonement to explain why Paul sometimes employs limited language.

The answer to this final point is quite easy to make, and I have already stated it above. It would be normal for Paul to use restricted language when addressing the church to speak of Christ's death "for us." Gibson has already acknowledged the validity of the negative inference fallacy as a logical argument. He has not demonstrated how it is that the argument does not apply in the way he treats the so-called limited texts.

Actually, the onus lies on Gibson and all particularists to explain why Paul would employ so much universal extent language in atonement texts as he does. Note again the length of the section dealing with the particularist texts (four pages) compared with the length of the section dealing with the universal texts (more than twenty-five pages).

In section two, Gibson addresses many of the universalistic texts that speak of Christ dying for "many," "all," and the "world."[193] The key argument in this section is the fact that "all" and "world" are not always used in an inclusive sense of every person on the planet. This is, of course, denied by no one (at least, no one I know).

The problem is that Gibson wants to take this point and then use it to restrict every single use of these terms in atonement contexts to mean something along the lines of "all nations" or "some of all kinds of people," and so on.

"All Without Distinction" vs. "All Without Exception"?

Let's parse the phrase "all sinners without distinction." All sinners means every human being. "Without distinction" means every human being regardless of ethnicity, gender, and so on. It is not possible to change the meaning of this phrase into "some of all kinds of people." Yet this is exactly what Gibson is doing. The "all without distinction"

193 Ibid., 295–321.

concept becomes code for "some of all without distinction." Thus "all" becomes "some of all sorts," an unwarranted move by Owen[194] and here followed by Gibson.

Ask yourself what the statement "all without distinction" means in the context of the atonement passages. The answer is it means "all kinds of people"—that is, all people of every kind, not some people of every kind. The problem with applying this distinction to passages like 1 Tim 2:4 is the use of "all" in the text gets transmuted into meaning "some of all kinds of people." Since the adjective "all" modifies "men" in the Greek text of 1 Tim 2:4, it is not possible to change "all" into "some men of all kinds," thus making the "all" modify "kinds" not "men" properly considered.

Yet this is the semantic shift Gibson makes: "all" becomes "some." Apparently for some Calvinists, since "all" sometimes means "all of some sorts" or "some of all sorts," it can never mean in any atonement context all humanity including each and every person. The logical fallacy is evident. In context, Paul is asking Christians to pray for actual people, not for classes of people. The point is this: don't exclude anyone from your prayers, no matter their social status.

Augustine disagreed with Gibson on this with respect to 2 Cor 5:18–21:

> Of this death the Apostle Paul says, "Therefore all are dead, and He died for all, that they which live should not henceforth live unto themselves, but unto Him which died for them and rose again." Thus all, without one exception, were dead in sins, whether original or voluntary sins, sins of ignorance, or sins committed against knowledge; and for all the dead there died the one only person who lived, that is, who had no sin whatever, in order that they who live by the remission of their sins should live, not to themselves, but to Him who died for all.[195]

Here it is evident that Augustine makes no use of the "all without distinction" concept and in fact states clearly that the extent of Christ's death extended to "all" who were dead in sins.

Calvin and Spurgeon likewise disagree with respect to 1 Tim 2:4–6. From Calvin's own sermon on the Timothy passage it is evident that "all people" or "all nations" means something along the lines of "all men of all people and all nations" in a distributive sense.[196]

This can be seen also in Calvin's commentary on this passage, which Gibson quotes:

> For there is one God, the creator and Father of all, so, he declares, there is one Mediator, through whom access to God is opened to us, and this Mediator is

194 Owen, "The Death of Death in the Death of Christ," 10:197.

195 Augustine, "The City of God," in *NPNF*, 2:425.

196 J. Calvin, *Sermons on Timothy* (Edinburgh: Banner of Truth, 1983), 160.

> not given only to one nation, or to a few men of a particular class, but to all, for the benefit of the sacrifice, by which he has expiated for our sins, applies to all. . . . The universal term "all" must always be referred to classes of men but never to individuals. It is as if he had said: "Not only Jews but also Greeks, not only people of humble rank but also princes have been redeemed by the death of Christ." Since therefore he intends the benefit of his death to be common to all, those who hold a view that would exclude any from the hope of salvation do Him an injury.
>
> The Holy Spirit bids us pray for all, because our one mediator bids all to come to Him, since by his death He has reconciled all to the Father.[197]

Calvin's statement that the term "all" here "refers to classes of men but never to individuals" must be read carefully in the context. What Calvin means is "all men of all nations" in a distributive sense. Nowhere in Calvin's writings does he use this distinction to deduce limited atonement as Gibson does.

The attempt to distinguish between the phrases "all without distinction" and "all without exception" is ultimately a distinction without a difference. To speak of all people without racial, gender, or other distinctions is to speak of them as all without exception. The distinction itself and the scope of the "all" must be supplied by the context. To compartmentalize the two phrases linguistically is to create an artificial distinction.

What about 1 Cor 15:3–11? Gibson fails to discuss one of the most important Pauline texts that speaks to the question of the extent of the atonement: 1 Cor 15:3–11. In 1 Cor 15:3 Paul writes: "For I passed on to you as most important what I also received: that Christ died for our sins according to the Scriptures." Here Paul is reminding the Corinthians of the message he preached to them when he first came to Corinth (Acts 18:1–18). He clearly affirms the content of the gospel he preached in Corinth included the fact that "Christ died for our sins."

Notice carefully Paul is saying this is what he preached pre-conversion, not post-conversion. Thus the "our" in his statement cannot be taken to refer to all the elect or merely the believing elect, which is what Calvinists who affirm definite atonement are forced to argue. The entire pericope of 1 Cor 15:3–11 should be kept in mind. Paul returns to what he had said in verse 3 when he gets to verse 11: "Whether then it was I or they, so we preach and so you believed" (NASB). The customary present tense in Greek used by Paul when he says "so we preach" along with the aorist tense in Greek for "believed" makes it clear Paul refers to a past point in time when they believed what it was his custom to preach.

197 J. Calvin, "The Second Epistle of Paul the Apostle to the Corinthians and the Epistles to Timothy, Titus & Philemon," in *Calvin's New Testament Commentaries*, 10:210–11. See also C. Spurgeon, "Salvation by Knowing the Truth," in *The Metropolitan Tabernacle Pulpit*, 26:49–50.

What did Paul preach to them in his evangelistic efforts to win all the unsaved to Christ? He preached the gospel, which included "Christ died for our sins." And so they believed. First Corinthians 15:3 is one of the strongest passages supporting unlimited atonement.

Review of Jonathan Gibson, "The Glorious, Indivisible, Trinitarian Work of God in Christ: Definite Atonement in Paul's Theology of Salvation" (331–73)

In this chapter Jonathan Gibson attempts to demonstrate definite atonement in Paul's soteriology. His basic thesis is that definite atonement emerges from the Pauline Letters when one approaches the issue in a biblico-systematic fashion. "Definite atonement is a theological conclusion reached on the other side of comprehensive synthesis."[198]

Strikingly, Gibson announces: "When exegesis serves the domain of constructive theology . . . one may argue not only that Paul's theology allows for a definite atonement but that it can point in no other direction."[199] Bold words. Can Gibson deliver?

With Eph 1:3–14 as an anchor text, Gibson sketches five main components of Pauline soteriology: God's saving work is (1) indivisible, (2) circumscribed by God's grace, (3) encompassed by union with Christ, (4) Trinitarian, and (5) doxological.[200] No evangelical Christian would disagree with Gibson's broad categories. The disagreement will come from what he deduces from them.

Gibson illustrates the first component from Titus 3:3–7, concluding from verses 5–6 that redemption applied flows from redemption accomplished in a cause-effect manner. From Rom 5:9–10 and 8:29–30 he builds on election and the indivisible saving work of God. He rightly critiques Barth for collapsing redemption applied into redemption accomplished but seems unaware of the fact that this is what he and all Calvinists who affirm definite atonement actually do,[201] despite his protestations otherwise.

Gibson critiques what he considers to be the opposite error from Barth—namely, forcing a disjunction between the moments of redemption (as is the case in semipelagianism and Arminianism, Amyraldianism, and English Hypothetical Universalism).[202] With respect to the latter two groups, Gibson wrongly states that their adherents fail to maintain the connection between redemption accomplished and redemption applied.

Gibson rightly denies any justification at the cross. But unless there is an interven-

198 J. Gibson, "The Glorious, Indivisible, Trinitarian Work of God in Christ: Definite Atonement in Paul's Theology of Salvation," in *From Heaven He Came and Sought Her*, 332.

199 Ibid.

200 Ibid., 335–36.

201 Ibid., 344.

202 Ibid., 345.

ing condition (not mere temporality) before one is justified, there seems no escape from this position. Many Calvinists, such as Charles Hodge for example, clearly distinguish redemption accomplished and redemption applied.

Gibson's second Pauline soteriological component, election, is treated on pages 346–49. Gibson appears to deduce that election = definite atonement. Here he avers that Arminianism, Amyraldianism, and Hypothetical Universalism result in a situation where "God's general universal love trumps his special love for the elect to the extent that the latter becomes a mere 'afterthought.'"[203] This statement is false with respect to the latter two groups, and in my judgment is also incorrect with respect to Arminianism.

Gibson's third soteriological component from Paul is union with Christ.[204] Working from Rom 5:12–21; 6:1–11; and 2 Cor 5:14–21, Gibson concludes that union with Christ is key to Paul's soteriology.

From these passages, Gibson draws five theological conclusions.

1. Affirming the distinct but inseparable dimensions of union with Christ counters Barth's collapsing of one aspect into another.[205]
2. Union with Christ counters attempts to force a disjunction between redemption accomplished and applied, which in turn necessarily renders the efficacy of Christ's death contingent upon faith.[206]
3. Affirming union with Christ at the moment of redemption accomplished counters any disjunction between the effect of Christ's substitutionary death and the effect of his resurrection.[207]
4. Union with Christ means that Christ's substitutionary atonement is a representative atonement and not merely a bare "instead of" atonement.[208]
5. Union with Christ means that the particularity of the atonement must take place prior to the moment of redemption applied.[209]

There are several problems with these conclusions.

First, what does it mean to affirm "distinct but inseparable dimensions" of union with Christ? If there is some distinction between redemption accomplished and applied, as Gibson admits, then what's the problem? If the distinction is merely chronological, as Gibson seems to assert, then how is the logic of the definite atonement scheme any different from Barth?

203 Ibid., 349.
204 Ibid., 349–60.
205 Ibid., 357.
206 Ibid., 357–58.
207 Ibid., 358–59.
208 Ibid., 359.
209 Ibid., 359–60.

Second, there is no forced "disjunction" between redemption accomplished and applied. This is a distinction that Scripture itself makes. Third, Gibson states this "disjunction" necessarily renders "the efficacy of Christ's death dependent upon faith." "Efficacy" is another word for "application." Biblically, Christ's death is not applied until faith is present. No one receives the application of the atonement until he exercises faith. Even the unbelieving elect remain under the wrath of God until they believe according to Eph 2:1–3.

Fourth, there is no union with Christ at the moment of redemption accomplished other than in the mind of God. Actual union with Christ takes place at the moment of justification. Fifth, we must ask why it is that union with Christ means that the particularity of the atonement must take place prior to redemption applied? Where is this stated in Scripture? Gibson offers no warrant for this claim.

The major problem with this section, and indeed the chapter, is that Gibson has fallen into the trap of the false dilemma fallacy. Gibson's logic is as follows: either Christ died for all men such that all are rendered saveable were they to believe or Christ died to effect the salvation of the elect. If Christ died to effect the salvation of the elect, then he did not die for the sins of all men.

In other words, the logic is either A or B. Not A, therefore B. Gibson's reductionist approach doesn't work. The extent of the atonement is not either/or. It is both/and. Christ died for the sins of all men, and he died to effect the salvation of all who believe.

A further problem with Gibson's discussion of union with Christ is he fails to interact with Kevin Kennedy's *Union with Christ and the Extent of the Atonement in Calvin*, where Kennedy concluded Calvin held to an unlimited atonement.

Gibson's fourth component of Pauline soteriology has to do with the Trinity. "A Trinitarian approach moves us towards a doctrine of definite atonement."[210] Gibson argues that any form of unlimited atonement creates "dissonance" in the Trinity. This charge is problematic on several accounts. First, it assumes there can be only one purpose of God in the atonement: the salvation of the elect. Second, note this sentence with respect to Hypothetical Universalists: "They force the conclusion that Christ died for everyone as their 'general Savior' to offer an atonement that would never actually atone."[211] Here Gibson is again conflating the extent of the atonement with its application. I suspect he is working off a commercial understanding of the atonement, like John Owen, which necessitates that the atonement must be applied to those for whom it is made.

Third, Gibson argues that since the Holy Spirit does not bring the gospel to all the unevangelized, then somehow there is dissonance between the Spirit, the Father, and the Son. But this overlooks the fact that it is first Christians who bring the gospel to the unevangelized, and then the Holy Spirit works through the means of the Word.

210 Ibid., 368.

211 Ibid., 370.

The "problem" of the unevangelized is as much a problem for the Calvinist as it is for the non-Calvinist.

Finally, Gibson's charge concerning disunity among the Trinity, especially with respect to the Holy Spirit, presupposes a Reformed understanding of anthropology (total depravity = inability) and the irresistible nature of the efficacious call. All non-Calvinists would disagree at these levels as well.

Ultimately, Gibson is trading on a false dilemma. He wrongly assumes that the Father did not intend for the Son to provide a satisfaction for all sin and thus imports dissonance in the Trinity that does not exist.

Gibson's threefold response to what he considers problems with the position of Hypothetical Universalists like Davenant of old, and more recently Daniel, whom he quotes,[212] is weak. First, he brings up the unevangelized argument again and states, "In this regard, the Spirit underperforms and in so doing brings disharmony into the Trinity."[213] Second, he suggests it is difficult to avoid the fact that the Son ends up with a "confused" or "split" personality.[214] This fails to reckon with what most Calvinists affirm concerning the distinction between God's revealed will and his decretal will. Third, he suggests that the notion of a dual intent with respect to the extent of the atonement "gives the impression that there exist two 'economies' of salvation."[215] This is an impression or inference on his part, one that all Hypothetical Universalists deny and justify their denial in their writings.

Where is the Hypothetical Universalist who has argued that the Son desired the salvation of anyone contrary to the wishes of the Father? Hypothetical Universalists would, I suspect, consider Gibson's analysis a caricature of their position. After Jonathan Edwards spoke of "the great provision that is made for the good of their [lost sinner's] souls" and how "he [Christ] invites them to accept of this provision," he then added:

> All the persons of the Trinity are now seeking your salvation. God the Father hath sent his Son, who hath made way for your salvation, and removed all difficulties, except those which are with your own heart. And he is waiting to be gracious to you; the door of his mercy stands open to you; he hath set a fountain open for you to wash in from sin and uncleanness. Christ is calling, inviting, and wooing you; and the Holy Ghost is striving with you by his internal motions and influences.[216]

212 Ibid., 369.
213 Ibid.
214 Ibid., 369–70.
215 Ibid., 371.
216 J. Edwards, "The End of the Wicked Contemplated by the Righteous," in *The Works of Jonathan Edwards*, 2 vols. (Edinburgh: Banner of Truth, 1992), 2:212. Edwards, unlike Gibson, sees no disharmony in Christ making provision in his death for all lost sinners, even those who will finally be damned, since Edwards also believed all the members of the Trinity are seeking their salvation.

Interestingly, Calvinists who oppose the notions of common grace and God's universal love use the same argument Gibson makes and posit the identical Trinitarian disharmony in an effort to discredit these notions. Curt Daniel makes that point in the extended context of what Gibson quotes on page 369. Most Calvinists affirm both common grace and universal love and yet see no disharmony in the Trinity, even as they affirm special love and grace for the elect alone in God's "secret will." Universal atonement, God's universal love and desire for the salvation of all people, and the universal offer of the gospel in no way entails any intra-Trinitarian disunity.

Gibson's fifth Pauline component concerns God's glory. He bluntly states: "A salvation intended but never realized can bring God no praise."[217] But how can this be sustained? If, as many Calvinists argue, God is glorified via the damnation of the non-elect, how is it that he cannot be glorified if in his love he made atonement for the sins of all men such that at the judgment they are doubly culpable for rejecting the gospel? Indeed, this is Calvin's point with respect to his comments on John 3:16. If a limited atonement can redound to God's greater glory, as some Calvinists claim, then an unlimited atonement can redound to God's maximal glory.

Gibson informs us early on that he is not "imposing" a systematic grid over the universal text while privileging the particularistic texts.[218] Yet one completes this chapter with the sense that, unfortunately, that is just what has happened. Gibson spoke of exegesis, yet from his previous chapter he was unable to furnish a single Pauline text that directly affirms definite atonement. He is, in one sense, forced to deduce definite atonement theologically from Paul in this chapter, since the exegetical data are not on his side.

Gibson's false dilemma fallacy excludes any possibility that Christ could die for the sins of all people.

Review of Tom Schreiner, "'Problematic Texts' for Definite Atonement in the Pastoral and General Epistles" (375–97)

The final chapter in the biblical section is authored by Tom Schreiner, professor of New Testament interpretation at Southern Seminary. I have known Dr. Schreiner for many years. He is one of Southern Baptists' top scholars. He was kind enough to write an endorsement a few years earlier for my book *Lukan Authorship of Hebrews*,[219] and we have recently co-chaired the Holman Christian Standard Bible Translation Oversight Committee for LifeWay Christian Resources.

217 Gibson, "The Glorious, Indivisible, Trinitarian Work of God in Christ: Definite Atonement in Paul's Theology of Salvation," 371.

218 Ibid., 333.

219 D. L. Allen, *Lukan Authorship of Hebrews*, NAC Studies in Bible and Theology (Nashville: B&H Academic, 2010).

Schreiner addresses key problematic texts for definite atonement: 1 Tim 2:4–6; 1 Tim 4:10; Titus 2:11–14; 2 Pet 2:1; 2 Pet 3:9; and Heb 2:9. Like the authors in previous chapters, he bases virtually his entire argument on interpreting the universal language in these texts utilizing the "all without distinction" vs. the "all without exception" model. I have already addressed most of these texts and the "all without distinction" proposal in some detail in previous chapter reviews.

Schreiner believes God's desire for people to be saved and his intention to save only the elect are compatible elements in biblical soteriology.[220]

1 Timothy 2:4–6

Schreiner stated, "God desires to save all kinds of people."[221] It is difficult to discern here whether Schreiner affirms God's universal saving desire, but I believe that to be the case. Schreiner claims, in response to I. H. Marshall, that "the Reformed view does not exclude individuals from God's saving purposes, for people groups are made up of individuals."[222] The operative word here is "purposes." All orthodox Reformed theologians assert God's universal saving "desire" or "will," and it appears Schreiner confirms his agreement here. Yet Schreiner does not appear to see that on his definite atonement scheme, by entailment every non-elect individual, regardless of what people group he is in, is excluded from any opportunity of salvation. This would seem to cut across the grain of God's universal saving desire.

1 Timothy 4:10

Here Schreiner rightly rejects Skeat's interpretation of the Greek word *malista* ("especially") as "namely";[223] the supposed universalist meaning of the text;[224] and Baugh's proposition that "Savior" refers not to spiritual salvation but to how God relates graciously to all humanity.[225]

Schreiner interprets the text to refer to God's salvific desire toward all kinds of people—that is, "all kinds of individuals from diverse people groups."[226]

> It seems, then, that Paul is saying here that God is potentially the Savior of all kinds of people—in that, as the living God there is no other Savior available to people—but that he is actually the Savior of only believers. . . . The possibility of God being a Savior for all kinds of people exists because there

220 T. Schreiner, "'Problematic Texts' for Definite Atonement in the Pastoral and General Epistles," in *From Heaven He Came and Sought Her*, 375.
221 Ibid., 377.
222 Ibid., 378.
223 Ibid., 380–81.
224 Ibid., 382.
225 Ibid., 383.
226 Ibid., 385.

> is only one living God (4:10b) and one Mediator available to the people (2:5–6).[227]

Schreiner continues:

> Definite atonement may be affirmed alongside other biblical truths, such as God's salvific stance to the world and the possibility for people to be saved if they believe in Christ. Those who hold to a definite intention in the atonement to save only the elect also believe that God desires people to be saved . . . that he is available as Savior to all people (1 Tim. 4:10), that Christ's death is sufficient for the salvation of every person, and that all are invited to be saved on the basis of Christ's death for sinners (1 Tim. 1:15).

There are several problems here as I see it. First, it seems strange and strained to say that the text means "all kinds of people" instead of "all people." Second, as I have argued in earlier reviews, the "all without distinction" and "all without exception" hermeneutical framework for all the atonement texts simply does not work. Third, Schreiner admits that the text indicates Jesus is potentially the savior of all kinds of people. But Reformed theologians who affirm definite atonement argue that Christ is not potentially the savior of anyone or any group; he is actually the savior of the elect.

Fourth, with respect to the "possibility for people to be saved if they believe in Christ," there is no possibility of the non-elect being saved if they were to believe in Christ because there is no atonement made for their sins. This is simply a logical impossibility. Fifth, how can Christ be available as Savior to all people when he has only made an atonement for some of the people: the elect? Again, this is a logical impossibility. Sixth, what does it matter to say that Christ's death is intrinsically sufficient in terms of its worth or value to save "every person" if it is not extrinsically sufficient to save every person because it did not satisfy for the sins of every person?

Seventh, while it is true that all are invited to be saved "on the basis of Christ's death for sinners," what Schreiner means by "sinners" seems to entail elect sinners only since Christ did not die for the sins of the non-elect. Hence he does not explain how it is possible for salvation to be offered to "all" when there is no satisfaction for the non-elect. This is especially problematic since eternal life is being offered to all people that hear the gospel call within all people groups.

Titus 2:11–14

Here again Schreiner argues for the "all without distinction" interpretation.

---

227 Ibid., 385–86.

2 Peter 2:1

Schreiner rejects the traditional interpretation that the word "bought" refers to Christ's death on the cross for the sins of false teachers. He opts for a "phenomenological" reading: "It appeared as if the Lord had purchased the false teachers with his blood (v. 1), though they actually did not truly belong to the Lord."[228]

Feeling the pinch of the strained nature of this exegesis, Schreiner asks, "Is this an artificial interpretation introduced to support a theological bias?"[229] He then mentions "the Arminian reading" of this text, which is somewhat inaccurate since Calvinists who affirm unlimited atonement also interpret this text as do Arminians. The Lutheran theologian Francis Pieper likewise rejected Schreiner's interpretation.[230]

By conflating the intent, extent, and application of the atonement, Schreiner wrongly concludes that universal atonement here compromises the doctrine of the perseverance of the saints.[231]

2 Peter 3:9

Schreiner rightly rejects John Owen's interpretation that the meaning of "any" and "all" must be constrained by the "you" earlier in the verse, and hence "any" and "all" refer to those wavering within the church and not to all people (though he thinks the restrictive meaning is "possible").[232] Schreiner's explanation revolves around the distinction of God's two wills: decretive and permissive.[233] This is of course problematic for those who don't accept this distinction. I must also demur at the statement, "It is clear from many texts that he [God] decrees the salvation of only some."[234]

Hebrews 2:9

The latter part of Heb 2:9 states that "by God's grace, he might taste death for everyone." Here again Schreiner appeals to the context as support for his "all without distinction" rather than "all without exception" model. He acknowledges that the immediate context of the Psalm 8 quotation is speaking of all humanity but states

---

228 T. Schreiner, "'Problematic Texts' for Definite Atonement in the Pastoral and General Epistles," in *From Heaven He Came and Sought Her*, 390. See T. Schreiner, *1, 2 Peter, Jude*, New American Commentary (Nashville: B&H, 2003), 331, on phenomenological language in 2 Pet 2:1. He makes a similar argument for Rom 14:15 in his *Romans*, Baker Exegetical Commentary 6 (Grand Rapids, MI: Baker, 1998), 735: "Paul refers to believers phenomenologically, that is, at the level of appearances, rather than at the level of true spiritual reality." R. B. Kuiper takes the same approach in *For Whom Did Christ Die?: A Study of the Divine Design of the Atonement* (Eugene, OR: Wipf & Stock, 2003), 38. For Schreiner's comments on God's universal saving desire as taught in 2 Pet 3:9, see *1, 2 Peter, Jude*, 380–83.

229 Schreiner, "'Problematic Texts' for Definite Atonement in the Pastoral and General Epistles," 391.

230 F. Pieper, *Christian Dogmatics*, 4 vols. (St. Louis, MO: Concordia, 1951), 2:21: "The objection that these passages refer to cases that cannot actually occur would destroy the whole argument of the apostle."

231 Schreiner, "'Problematic Texts' for Definite Atonement in the Pastoral and General Epistles," 392.

232 Ibid., 393.

233 Ibid.

234 Ibid., 394.

"though the author refers to human beings in general, he does not put any stress on all human beings without exception."[235] The point here is not what is stressed. The point is what is actually stated. Psalm 8 is speaking of "all without exception."

Hebrews 2:10–18 begins a new subparagraph. Schreiner wants to utilize the specific references to the benefits of the atonement to believers in these verses to constrain the meaning of "all" and "everyone" in the previous verses. This is hermeneutically problematic in my view.[236]

Summary Evaluation of Chapters 9–14, "Definite Atonement in the Bible"

Thankfully, the authors in this section do not resort to the exegetical error of John Owen in arguing that "world" means the elect in places like John 3:16. Yet once it is understood that "all without distinction" and "all without exception" is an invalid and ultimately unworkable distinction, the load-bearing wall for the argument of definite atonement is removed and the superstructure erected on it collapses.

The muscle of any theological position is only as strong as the exegetical basis upon which it is built. Unfortunately, the authors of this section have not succeeded in shoring up definite atonement's faulty exegetical foundation. Hermeneutics, exegesis, and logic undercut definite atonement biblically.

Review of Donald Macleod, "Definite Atonement and the Divine Decree" (401–35)

Donald Macleod begins a six-chapter section on "Definite Atonement in Theological Perspective." There is much helpful material in these chapters. Probably the most significant is the interaction with the Amyraldian and English Hypothetical Universalism views within the orbit of Reformed theology. This is commendable and opens the door for further dialogue to occur.

However, this interaction is not without its problems, as there appears to be a fair amount of misunderstanding and mischaracterization of these positions. Macleod begins his chapter by noting: "The focus of this chapter is the link between the divine intention of the atonement and its extent."[237] Here he rightly acknowledges a distinction between the intent and extent of the atonement, but as we shall see, he appears to

235 Ibid., 395.

236 For more on this passage, see my excursus: "Hebrews 2:14 and the Extent of the Atonement in John Calvin and John Owen" in *Hebrews*, The New American Commentary (Nashville: B&H, 2010), 233–35.

237 D. Macleod, "Definite Atonement and the Divine Decree," in *From Heaven He Came and Sought Her*, 401.

misunderstand the connection between the two. He uses the oft-quoted statement by Berkhof: "Did the Father in sending Christ, and did Christ in coming into the world to make atonement for sin, do this with the design or for the purpose of saving only the elect or all men? That is the question and that only is the question."[238]

But this sends the discussion off the rails at the very beginning. Note the words "design" and "purpose." All Calvinists, whether they believe in definite atonement or universal atonement, would affirm Berkhof's statement because they believe that the ultimate purpose of God in the atonement is the salvation of the elect. Macleod, like Berkhof, assumes that if the issue can be stated in this fashion, then the game is over. Definite atonement is established because intent and extent are assumed to be coextensive. Macleod is reading the issue through the filtered lens of Berkhof, and he appears to be reading Amyraldianism through the lens of Warfield's mischaracterization of Amyraldianism.

The chapter is divided into five major sections: "Arminianism,"[239] "Eternal Predestination,"[240] "Supra- and Infralapsarianism,"[241] and "Karl Barth's Supralapsarianism; and Hypothetical Universalism."[242] This final section is the longest sustained discussion of Hypothetical Universalism in the book.

Of these five sections, the middle three, while interesting in and of themselves, offer little help to the argument for definite atonement.

All orthodox Christians affirm eternal predestination; the debate occurs over how this is accomplished. Eternal predestination simply does not entail limited atonement nor does it contradict unlimited atonement. Even if Reformed theology's notion of election is correct, which we can grant at the moment for the sake of argument, all that entails is that there is an atonement for the elect, not that there cannot be an atonement for the sins of the so-called non-elect. To argue otherwise is a logical fallacy.

The intra-family debate within Reformed theology over supra- and infralapsarianism is interesting but again offers no help in proving definite atonement. Calvinists from both groups have affirmed definite atonement while others of both camps have affirmed unlimited atonement. One thinks immediately of William Twisse, proculator of the Westminster Assembly, who was both supralapsarian and an advocate for unlimited atonement.

The section on Karl Barth is especially unnecessary since I suspect the majority of the Reformed, along with the non-Reformed, would agree with Macleod's critique of Barth. There is simply no help for the argument of definite atonement by exposing Barth's problems on the issue of election.

238 Ibid., 402.
239 Ibid., 402–6.
240 Ibid., 406–9.
241 Ibid., 409–13.
242 Ibid., 422–34.

Arminianism

Macleod asks, "How can blood-bought souls perish?"[243] He turns to "Scottish Arminian James Morison" for an answer. This is interesting for three reasons. First, Morison was a Calvinist before he shifted to more Arminian views on the atonement. Morison himself denied becoming an Arminian. "I am not an Arminian; call me a low-Calvinist, or a no-Calvinist, if you like, but I am not an Arminian."[244]

Second, Macleod could have turned for an answer to the many Calvinists within the Scottish church who rejected definite atonement, such as the famous Thomas Chalmers. Third, Macleod references Morison with respect to the assertion that in the death of Christ, "while all objective legal obstacles to their salvation have been removed, other internal obstacles remain."[245]

One gets the impression that this point is an exclusive Arminian point. Actually this language of "legal obstacles" being removed can be found in many Calvinists who affirm unlimited atonement (John Davenant, Charles Hodge, Robert Dabney, W. G. T. Shedd, and Andrew Fuller come to mind), as Macleod acknowledges later on,[246] and even in some who maintain a strictly definite atonement, like A. A. Hodge. One wonders why Macleod does not engage the arguments of these Calvinists with respect to Christ's death removing legal obstacles.

Macleod states that Arminianism posits "no commitment on God's part to overcome human unbelief."[247] This is a caricature of Arminianism since their notion of prevenient grace functions in just this way. Of course, Macleod is operating from the Reformed concept that total depravity = total inability.

A major error in Macleod's chapter is his charge that James Morison's description of prevenient grace is "pure Pelagianism."[248] A careful reading of Morison reveals he clearly believed in the necessity of God's enabling grace prior to human response to the gospel. This is not Pelagianism. Macleod has caricatured Morison here.

Also problematic is Macleod's point that the "peculiarity" of Arminianism "makes no provision for redemption from its [sin's] power."[249] He then quotes Charles Wesley's hymn, "And Can It Be," and says the hymn "challenges every element of Arminian theology."[250] Of course, this suggests that Wesley the Arminian did not understand his own theology. It appears Macleod may lack nuance in his own understanding of Arminianism.

---

243 Ibid., 403.

244 O. Smeaton, *Principal James Morison: The Man and His Work* (Edinburgh: Oliver & Boyd, 1902), 114. See also A. Robertson, *History of the Atonement Controversy in Connexion with the Secession Church* (Edinburgh: Oliphant, 1846), 161–74, 323–25, for the specifics on Morison.

245 Macleod, "Definite Atonement and the Divine Decree," 403.

246 Ibid., 431.

247 Ibid., 403.

248 Ibid., 404.

249 Ibid., 406.

250 Ibid.

Macleod makes the following statements:

> Limiting the saving benefits of the atonement to definite, special objects of God's love is not a violation of the mind of Christ but an expression of it. . . . At the last judgment, those who are "passed by" and hear Christ declare "Depart from me," nevertheless this "carries the assurance that judgment will not be without mercy."[251]

Mercy for whom? How the person standing before Christ at the last judgment, with no atonement made for his sins, unelected, unloved by God in a saving manner, can hear the words "depart from me" and yet this judgment "not be without mercy" is beyond me.

Problems with Macleod's chapter continue when he considered God's universal love.[252] Macleod noted that in Arminianism God's universal love is extended "equally" to every member of the human family.

> God has provided a Savior suited to the needs of every human being and that he has commissioned his ambassadors to plead with every human being to accept the services of this Savior. This is all that Arminians believe; and the Reformed believe it all—every jot and tittle of it.[253]

I must ask how it is that Macleod can affirm these things with any consistency.

First, no Calvinist, high or moderate, believes God's universal saving love is extended "equally" to every member of the human family.[254] The old Reformed distinction of God's love of benevolence and his love of complacency evidences my point. Second, advocates of definite atonement cannot coherently assert that Christ is a Savior "suited to the needs of every human being." Christ is only salvifically suited to the needs of the elect since he only atones for their sins. Third, Macleod appears to be unaware of the problem he and all high Calvinists have when pleading with "every human being" to accept Christ—namely, he has no gospel to offer the non-elect for Christ did not die for their sins. He is offering the non-elect salvation that does not exist in Christ for them.

Hypothetical Universalism (422–34)

Macleod, citing Muller, rightly noted there is variety within Hypothetical Universalism.[255] Macleod seems to assume that Hypothetical Universalism, like Arminianism, is historically

---

251 Ibid., 407.
252 Ibid., 408.
253 Ibid.
254 See D. A. Carson, *The Difficult Doctrine of the Love of God* (Wheaton, IL: Crossway, 1999).
255 Macleod, "Definite Atonement and the Divine Decree," 422.

a latecomer to Reformed theology. Actually, as Muller has demonstrated, Hypothetical Universalism predates definite atonement in the Reformed camp and did not arise with English Hypothetical Universalism.

Macleod asserts that it is the "secret will" of God under discussion in debate on the extent of the atonement.[256] How can this be when the secret will of God is secret? Actually, it is Scripture that is operative in the discussion. One cannot interpret Scripture in light of the "secret" will but the "revealed" will, which strongly suggests unlimited atonement.

Macleod acknowledges the critique of definite atonement by Arminians and English Hypothetical Universalists with respect to the universal offer of the gospel.[257] He said the great evangelists of Reformed orthodoxy "were not embarrassed by the alleged inconsistency" and "wasted no time prying into the secret counsels of the Almighty or arguing with him that there was no point in pleading with every sinner since only the elect were to be saved." But Macleod fails to mention the scourge of hyper-Calvinism historically in this very vein.

One troubling feature in this chapter is what appears to be Macleod's misunderstanding of Hypothetical Universalism. In a discussion on the importance of not trying to pry into the imponderables of God's secret will but rather engaging in indiscriminate preaching, he noted that Hypothetical Universalists fare no better than their high-Calvinist counterparts: "Hypothetical Universalism provided no solution. How could they put their trust in a hypothetical redemption? How could they believe at all unless they were elected to faith?"[258]

Macleod's first question appears to misunderstand just what it is that is "hypothetical" in Hypothetical Universalism. For all Hypothetical Universalists, the atonement is not hypothetical for the non-elect, it is actual. What is hypothetical is the conditionality of faith: if anyone believes, he shall be saved based on the fact that there is an atonement for sin. Conditionality is operative in all orthodox Christian approaches to salvation: faith is a necessity.

With respect to the second question above, as Calvinists, all Hypothetical Universalists believe in election and the necessity of effectual calling. Macleod's wording in the above quotation ("elected to faith") may suggest his belief that faith is a gift purchased by Christ on the cross for the elect only. This is, of course, the view John Owen advocated, and he is followed by many Calvinists to the present day.

But Owen's argument is flawed at several levels.

1. Where in Scripture are we informed that faith is a gift purchased for the elect? Salvation is purchased, but never faith.

256 Ibid., 428.
257 Ibid., 429–31.
258 Ibid., 431.

2. This approach treats faith as a commodity. Such a notion is an example of category confusion and is foreign to Scripture. Faith becomes something of an object instead of a relational response.
3. If faith is purchased for the elect, then the elect have a right to the means of salvation. Grace is vitiated.
4. This faith-as-purchase notion is grounded in the notion of a covenant of redemption between God and Christ in eternity. (See my critique of this in the review of Carl Trueman's chapter.)
5. Faith as a gift is not equivalent to faith as a purchase.
6. There is simply no causal link between the atonement and faith. In fact, Owen said if faith is not purchased by the cross, then universal atonement is "established."

Macleod asks: "Is it not fatally incoherent that God should simultaneously decree that the cross of Christ should redeem all the non-elect and provide him with grounds for their greater condemnation?"[259]

It did not seem so to Calvin, who stated this very point in his comments on John 3:16.

These problems notwithstanding, Macleod's chapter should be read by all to gain understanding in how Calvinists attempt theologically to describe and define definite atonement.

Review of Robert Letham, "The Triune God, Incarnation, and Definite Atonement" (437–60)

The chief burden of Letham's chapter is to demonstrate that all forms of universal atonement create Trinitarian disharmony.[260]

Letham lumps Amyraldians with Arminians when he states that

> the atoning death of Christ does not of itself secure the salvation of anyone in particular, since it is contingent on the human response in the case of Arminianism or on the particular work of the Spirit in terms of Amyraldianism. Moreover, since the atonement is not intrinsically efficacious, it cannot yield a doctrine of penal substitution.[261]

259 Ibid., 434.

260 R. Letham, "The Triune God, Incarnation, and Definite Atonement," in *From Heaven He Came and Sought Her*, 439.

261 Ibid., 440.

This statement is problematic on several counts. First, Letham accuses Arminianism of making election a "rubber stamp" to a human decision.[262] This is a caricature of Arminianism. Second, note the operative phrase "of itself." Interestingly, I recall Charles Hodge and W. G. T. Shedd stating that the atonement "of itself" secures the salvation of no one. No one is saved until, through the work of the Holy Spirit, they are brought to faith in Christ. This is the way the NT expresses the matter. Letham's approach confuses extent with application. Third, it is incorrect to argue that lack of intrinsic efficacy negates penal substitution. On what logic is this conclusion based? Letham may be slipping into the web of a commercialistic view of the atonement here.

It appears Letham assumes that, for Amyraut, Christ died equally for all in terms of intent as well as extent.[263] This is true for Arminians but not true for Amyraut and his followers. When Amyraut spoke of Christ dying "equally" for all, it is clear he meant that his death was equally sufficient for all, not in the sense of intention or purpose.[264] Amyraut believed Christ died with the special intent of saving only the elect.

Letham said the "key problem" with Hypothetical Universalism is that "it posits disruption in the Trinity."[265] Hypothetical Universalists don't "posit" disruption in the Trinity. What Letham means is that in his opinion the position of Hypothetical Universalism "entails" disruption in the Trinity. Proof of this critique is the burden of pages 440–44. He is arguing that Davenant's construct entails conflict and incoherence, but Davenant is arguing that the Trinity acts in unity to accomplish a dual intent in atonement and redemption.

Letham's critique of Amyraldianism and English Hypothetical Universalism illustrates his point that the question about the intent of the atonement is inescapably one about its nature. For Amyraldianism and Hypothetical Universalism, the atonement cannot be intrinsically efficacious since the results of Christ's death do not accrue to all.[266]

Yet nowhere does Scripture say the atonement is intrinsically efficacious. Intrinsically sufficient, yes; intrinsically efficacious, no. "Consequently, the church down through

---

262 Ibid.

263 Ibid., 438–40.

264 As Proctor said,

> In the statement that Christ died *pro omnibus equiliter* (explained Daillé, *Apologiae* ii 632), the theologians of Saumur meant the adverb to signify that there is none for whom Christ did not die; it does not mean that all are equal in affection or will of God in giving Christ to die. Cf. Drost, *Specimen* 25: Amyraut and Testard explained the death of Christ for all equally in terms of sufficiency . . . Amyraut explained the two uses of the adverb in *De Grat* (Gen) 223.

See L. Proctor, *The Theology of Moïse Amyraut Considered as a Reaction Against Seventeenth-Century Calvinism* (PhD diss., University of Leeds, 1952), 376n78; J. Daillé, *Apologia pro duabus Ecclesiarum in Gallia Protestantium Synodis Nationalibus*, 2:632; and M. Amyraldo [Amyraut], *Specimen Animadversionum in exercitationes de gratia universali* (Saumur: Jean Lesnier, 1648), 223.

265 R. Letham, "The Triune God, Incarnation, and Definite Atonement," in *From Heaven He Came and Sought Her*, 440.

266 Ibid., 439.

the ages has confessed both the inseparability of the works of God and the appropriations."[267] True. The church has also confessed unlimited atonement.

Letham concludes that for all forms of Hypothetical Universalism, the Trinity is of two minds: (1) Christ should die for all, (2) but in contrast determining that some, not all, will be saved.[268] Here he appears to be dependent on Warfield's skewed understanding and critique of Hypothetical Universalism.

Letham said the problem of Hypothetical Universalism is highlighted in Davenant. From the premise that universal gospel preaching needs to be grounded on a coterminous provision, he taught that the death of Christ was the basis for the salvation of all people. "Each person is salvable. Therefore the scope and intent of the atonement is universal. Christ paid the penalty not for the sins of particular individual persons but for the whole human race."[269]

Letham noted the Lombardian formula, "sufficient for all, efficient for the elect," meant for many particularists only a sufficiency that was equivalent to infinite value. Letham rightly noted that Davenant held that God actually provides salvation for all. The sufficiency is ordained by God in the evangelical covenant.[270]

Letham continues,

> This universal provision in the atonement, for Davenant, overshadowed and preceded a decree whereby God determined salvation for the elect. No actual reconciliation or salvation comes before a person believes. In this, God makes available or withholds the means of application of salvation to nations or individuals, according to his will. Only the elect receive saving faith. This decree, differentiating between elect and reprobate, conflicts with God's decision that Christ atone for each and every person by his death. God decides first one thing, then another.[271]

Letham's assessment of Davenant's position[272] appears to be incorrect. Davenant taught, on the basis of 2 Cor 5:18–20, that God was reconciled to the world objectively but not all people in the world are subjectively reconciled to God. Davenant's understanding of this universal provision did not "overshadow" God's decree to save the elect.

Citing Jonathan Moore, Letham posits conflict in Davenant between God's decree to save only the elect and his decree to provide universal atonement. In short,

---

267 Ibid., 442.
268 Ibid.
269 Ibid., 443.
270 Ibid., 443–44.
271 Ibid., 444.
272 Ibid.

Hypothetical Universalism is inherently inconsistent. The problem here can be traced to Warfield's misreading of Amyraut's concept of the divine decrees. Warfield, and apparently Letham, thinks that Amyraut posits four absolute (secret will) decrees sequentially, with the first two conditional. This conditionality is viewed as something man does in the process.

Letham thinks that Amyraut taught Christ died for all equally and for no one in particular. When Letham states, "According to Amyraut, Christ died with the intention of saving all people,"[273] he (Letham) is mistaken. Amyraut makes it clear Christ died with the special intention of saving only the elect. Letham has Amyraut teaching that God ordained that the death of Christ would be applied to the elect in such a way that the decree of election appears late in the sequence of the four decrees. Yet for Amyraut, the first two decrees appear in the revealed will of God and are conditional while the second two decrees are absolute. Furthermore, the final two decrees are not logically dependent upon the first two decrees. Letham has misconstrued what Amyraut teaches about the divine decrees.

Here is the bottom line: the attempt to overlay an ordering of the decrees in an infralapsarian or supralapsarian scheme on Amyraut and Davenant in an attempt to understand Amyraut and Davenant's approach is misguided and engages in a category fallacy. Letham wants to frame Amyraut's language to suggest that the decrees were a part of God's decretal will and yet conditioned by the actions of men. For Amyraut, the first two decrees were a part of God's revealed will. Since there are different kinds of decrees, there is no conflict, unless Letham wants to assert that God's revealed will contradicts his secret will.

Letham thinks the positions of Amyraut and Davenant entail conflict in the divine decrees. But for Amyraut and Davenant, the Trinity works together in perfect harmony (general and special love, common and special grace, external and internal call, the free offer of the gospel and the provision to obtain a universal basis for the salvation of all men, along with a basis for the certain salvation of the elect).

Finally, Letham's critique of the Torrance brothers scores some points, but two things should be noted. First, Letham may disagree that the incarnation, for T. F. Torrance, entails atonement for all humans,[274] but let's not forget that this was the position of the church fathers and the medieval church. Second, Letham is correct to note Torrance's error in claiming Calvin rejected the Lombardian formula, but then errs himself when he concludes from this that Calvin held to definite atonement.[275] This fails to take into account the revision of the formula after Calvin's death by supporters of definite atonement (see the previous review of Hogg's chapter), as well

273 Ibid., 438.
274 Ibid., 447.
275 Ibid., 453.

as the overwhelming evidence from Calvin's writings that he did not hold to definite atonement.

Review of Garry Williams, "The Definite Intent of Penal Substitution" (461–82)

Garry Williams writes the next two chapters on penal substitution and the double payment argument. The upshot of these two chapters is an attempt to argue that penal substitution entails definite atonement and that the double payment argument (that God cannot demand payment for sin twice) is a valid construct and supports definite atonement.[276] Williams boldly stated, "Insistence on an atonement made for all without exception undermines belief in penal substitutionary atonement."[277]

First rattle out of the box, Williams comes across as a bit condescending when he states his chapter is "simply intended to show brothers that at this point they are wrong." It would have been better to word this along the lines of showing brothers "reasons why perhaps they may be wrong in their assessment."

Williams devotes the major portion of his chapter (462–72) to an evaluation and critique of Archbishop Ussher's (seventeenth century) and Broughton Knox's (twentieth century) views of the extent of the atonement in relationship to penal substitution. Both were Calvinists who affirmed that Christ died for the sins of all people.

Archbishop Ussher

Williams states that Ussher is rightly categorized as a Hypothetical Universalist "given his insistence that Christ's death was intended to make satisfaction for every person, should he or she believe."[278] This wording can be tricky. What Ussher believed and what Williams is intending to convey about Ussher is that Christ died for the sins of all people, such that if any person believes he will be saved because there is an atonement made for his sins. As I have noted in previous reviews, what is "hypothetical" about Hypothetical Universalism is not the extent of the atonement but the conditionality of the application of the atonement—faith of the individual.

Williams identifies three underlying concerns for Ussher. First is the preaching of the gospel. Ussher believed that an atonement that was not universal in extent could not be the basis for the offer of the gospel to all people.[279] Second, Ussher differentiates

---

276 G. Williams, "The Definite Intent of Penal Substitution," 461. See also G. Williams, "Penal Substitution: A Response to Recent Criticisms," *Journal of the Evangelical Theological Society* 50 (2007): 71–86.

277 G. Williams, "The Definite Intent of Penal Substitution," in *From Heaven He Came and Sought Her*, 461.

278 Ibid., 462.

279 Ibid., 463.

between the extent of the atonement and the application of the atonement.[280] Third, Williams claims Ussher taught that Christ did not make satisfaction for any individual specifically, but for human nature qua nature.[281] It is this third point about Ussher where I think Williams gets it wrong. Williams appears to be reading Ussher's use of the word "nature" to indicate something differentiated from "person." This is not what Ussher means.

His critique of Ussher on this point is lengthy,[282] and it appears Williams misunderstands Ussher's use of the term "nature" in context. Ussher is not distinguishing "nature" from "personhood," as Williams contends. Rather, in context Ussher contrasts the nature of man with the nature of the fallen angels and rightly points out that Christ did not assume angelic nature but only human nature. It is obvious what Ussher means here—Christ suffered the punishment due to humanity as composed of individual people.

Williams wants to take this in a direction foreign to Ussher's meaning and intent. He asserts: "On Ussher's view, Christ is a person and made satisfaction as a person, but he did not make satisfaction for persons as such."[283] Consequently, Williams thinks that Ussher's position "logically denies penal substitution."[284] Williams spends the next three-and-one-half pages tearing down the straw man that Ussher believes human nature is the object of atonement and not sinful human persons.

Broughton Knox

Williams stated that Knox, like Ussher, is concerned about the well-meant gospel offer and how such is necessitated by an unlimited atonement. Also noted is Knox's point that a commercialistic/pecuniary approach to the atonement undermines definite atonement.[285]

Williams noted correctly that Knox distinguishes (not "separates," which is the term Williams uses) the extent of the atonement from its application.[286] Williams writes as if Knox's distinction between the intent, extent, and application of the atonement is something new and invalid. As we have seen, the distinction antedates the Reformation.

Williams rejected any notion of a distinction between the intent and extent of the atonement yet offered no biblical justification to prove his point. His argument rests solely on the notion that God's will "makes them [Christ's sufferings] what they are

280 Ibid.

281 Ibid., 464. Note Williams's dependence upon C. Gribben, "Rhetoric, and Theology: James Ussher and the Death of Christ," *The Seventeenth Century* 20 (2005): 53–76.

282 Williams, "The Definite Intent of Penal Substitution," 465–68.

283 Ibid., 465.

284 Ibid., 466.

285 Ibid., 468–69.

286 Ibid., 471.

and thus makes them definite."[287] This is simply a *non sequitur*, as well as an assertion without support.

Specificity of the Atonement in Scripture

Williams addressed a few NT and OT texts that he adduces support definite atonement. But not a single one of the verses he cites directly or even indirectly hints at such.

He makes much of the point that "sin" (generic) and "sins" (specific) are not mutually exclusive in use. This is correct. His conclusion, however, does not follow and is in need of nuance: "Although none of these NT writers were self-consciously addressing our question, they evidently held that Jesus died bearing specific sins committed by particular people."[288]

Actually, the NT authors were self-consciously addressing the question of the extent of the atonement in several places. If by "specific" Williams means all specific sins but not in some quantifiable manner, and if by "particular" he means all people individually and not some people individually, then the statement is correct. If, as I suspect, Williams means by "particular people" only the elect, then the statement is an example of begging the question—Williams is assuming what he is trying to prove.

Williams attempted to glean from the instructions given concerning various Levitical offerings that "Levitical atonement was definite atonement."[289] His examples all come from the cases of individuals who bring offerings, which, by definition, are definite to that individual.

This says nothing about the extent of the atonement for the nation of Israel or beyond. It is the logical fallacy of assuming that individual offerings in the OT prove definite atonement. It also ignores the Day of Atonement ritual, which addressed the sins of all the people and works against definite atonement.

Conclusion

Williams concluded the chapter with a false dilemma (either/or) statement: "An indefinite atonement must either embrace universalism or it must contradict the biblical doctrine of penal substitution."[290]

This conclusion is unwarranted. Williams trades on a commercialist view of the atonement, which fails to consider the proper biblical notion of imputation of sin, combined with a failure to distinguish properly between the atonement's extent and application. Williams's notion that the death of Christ demands forgiveness be provided to those for whom Christ died is simply not justified biblically or theologically.

287 Ibid.
288 Ibid., 474.
289 Ibid., 479.
290 Ibid., 481.

Review of Garry Williams, "Punishment God Cannot Inflict Twice: The Double Payment Argument *Redevivus*" (483–515)

In chapter 18 Garry Williams addresses the double payment argument.

Owen's Double Payment Argument

Classically formulated by John Owen, the double payment argument asserts that God's justice does not allow the same sin to be punished twice, first in Christ and then in the sinner. Owen's defense of this argument employs a commercialistic understanding of the atonement, for which he has been righty criticized by Calvinists and non-Calvinists alike.

Williams begins with John Owen's statement of the double payment argument, followed by a brief recitation of some Calvinists and non-Calvinists who reject it. Williams outlines the aim of his chapter: to reexamine and restate the double payment argument.[291] He will attempt to extricate the argument from its entanglements with commercialism by reworking it "without the commercial concepts" in the hopes of salvaging it for the defense of definite atonement. He intends to argue that "punishment should be defined as *suffering inflicted as a fitting answer to sin.* This definition will establish against its critics a double punishment argument that could proceed without any commercial language."[292]

The bulk of this chapter (487–506) is given over to an analysis of the nature of metaphor, and specifically the metaphor of punishment as debt repayment. While there is interesting material here, most of this section is extraneous to the argument at hand. The crucial material to support the contention that the double payment argument is a valid construct is found on pages 506–15.

Williams makes an important concession when he states "It is true that the double punishment argument is viable only if the idea of definiteness is retained; if unquantifiability means indefiniteness, then the argument fails."[293] Williams thinks this is a false choice and proceeds to show why.

The gist of John Owen's double payment argument is that "debt" language in Scripture moves beyond the metaphor and actually describes the mechanism for the payment of sin. Owen, and Williams, assumes that since the satisfaction is for "sins" plural, and not for "sin" in abstraction, it therefore must be definite (limited to only the elect). The transaction is commercial: so much is owed, and so much is paid. If Christ paid for all sins, then God cannot demand a second payment from any sinner. Seems like an open and shut case.

---

291 G. Williams, "Punishment God Cannot Inflict Twice: The Double Payment Argument *Redevivus*," in *From Heaven He Came and Sought Her*, 486.

292 Ibid., 486 (emphasis in original).

293 Ibid., 499.

Problems with the Double Payment Argument[294]

The metaphor is pushed beyond its legitimate point of analogy and becomes, for Owen and Williams, the actual mechanism whereby sin is paid for. Williams's dependence upon Owen's treatment of the parable of the unforgiving servant in Matthew 18 leads him to misinterpret the point of the parable. The context of the parable is not atonement but forgiveness between brothers by way of a commercial debt metaphor. The point of the parable is the mechanism for forgiveness, not the mechanism for satisfaction of sins.

Williams concludes that Christ's satisfaction is a "repayment." The mistake is viewing God as a creditor from the fact that sin is metaphorically described as a debt.[295] Sin as debt is about obligation, not about the death of Christ being a payment to a creditor (God). Nowhere in Scripture is God ever viewed as "creditor" who is paid a debt via the death of Christ.

At this point in the discussion Williams should be credited for his accurate portrayal of Hugo Grotius's view of the nature of the atonement.[296] Often Grotius is misunderstood and mischaracterized as teaching something less than penal substitution. Williams noted and rebutted this error.[297]

As part of his argument, Williams posits that it is "both possible and necessary to hold together the idea of an unquantifiable punishment and an inherently definite atonement."[298] Recall Williams's conclusion in his previous chapter that only "sins" were laid on Christ at the cross, not "sin" generically.

This is fundamentally an unnecessary and even flawed bifurcation. No one claims that Christ dies for "sin" without dying for "sins." Of course Jesus did not die for some abstract notion of sin. He died for real people—all of them. He accomplished this by becoming "sin" for us (2 Cor 5:21). Christ died for "the one and the many," for "sins" and for "sin." In suffering the one death that one and all sinners categorically deserve, he made satisfaction for *all the sins* of *all the sinners*. The same can be said of *any* other given sin and *any* given sinner.

Even Charles Hodge said,

294 For a recent critique of the double payment argument from a Calvinist, consult O. D. Crisp, *Deviant Calvinism: Broadening Reformed Theology* (Minneapolis, MN: Fortress, 2014), 213–33. Crisp makes use of R. L. Dabney's criticisms of the double payment argument. See also M. Lynch, "Not Satisfied: An Analysis and Response to Garry Williams on Penal Substitutionary Atonement and Definite Atonement" (unpublished paper, Calvin Theological Seminary, Spring 2015), 12–25. As Lynch rightly pointed out against Williams, "Reformed theologians have insisted on an infallibility of the application of Christ's satisfaction to the elect, but this infallibility is not to be found in or grounded on the *nature* of satisfaction. To rest infallibility of application on the nature of Christ's atoning work assumes not only a crass pecuniary logic regarding the satisfaction, but also collapses the distinction between election and the work of Christ" (18).

295 Williams, "Punishment God Cannot Inflict Twice: The Double Payment Argument *Redevivus*," 490–93.

296 Ibid., 490–92.

297 I highly recommend Williams's excellent PhD dissertation on Hugo Grotius: "A Critical Exposition of Hugo Grotius's Doctrine of the Atonement in *De satisfaction Christi*" (PhD diss., University of Oxford, 1999).

298 Williams, "Punishment God Cannot Inflict Twice: The Double Payment Argument *Redevivus*," 499.

> Christ fulfilled the conditions of the covenant under which all men [not just the elect] were placed. He rendered the obedience required of all [not just the elect], and suffered the penalty which all had incurred [not just the elect]; and therefore his work is equally suited to all [not just the elect].[299]

This view described by Hodge is not the position that Christ's death is "an internally unspecified penal satisfaction narrowed only by its application," or a view that it "is not an actual, defined answer to any sin committed by any individual," as if Christ's death is "detached from any crime," as Williams suggests.[300] These descriptions by Williams are straw men.

Like Owen, Williams appears to be operating from a sort of quantitative transference view of imputation: specific guilt for specific sins of the elect alone is laid on Christ. But this is problematic. While our sins are imputed to Christ, before our conversion we remain under the wrath of God, as Paul states in Eph 2:1–3. As Dabney said, God holds the unbelieving elect subject to wrath until they believe. Williams mentioned this problem[301] but failed to address this objection by Dabney and others that the living unbelieving elect are under the wrath of God.

Williams also failed to address how God can *justly* postpone the grant of faith to the people for whom Christ died, if Christ literally "purchased" faith for them. Hodge said, "The moment the debt is paid the debtor is free, and that completely. No delay can be admitted, and no conditions can be attached to his deliverance."[302]

Owen's and Williams's Faulty View of Imputation

Would Owen consider the imputation of Christ's righteousness to believers as the transference of so many acts of law-keeping? It would seem not. Are believers credited with specific acts of righteousness on Christ's part? No, we are credited with a quality of righteousness, or treated as though we had obeyed God's law categorically by virtue of our union with Christ. All Christ's acts of obedience fall under the class or moral category of "righteousness."

Just as believers are not imputed with something like so many particular acts of righteousness but rather with righteousness categorically, so also Christ was not imputed with all the particular sinful acts of some people, like so many "sin-bits," but rather with sin in a comprehensive way. He was treated as though he were sinful, or categorically guilty of the sin of the whole human race.

Owen, and it would seem Williams as well, has a faulty notion of imputation. The

299 Hodge, *Systematic Theology*, 2:544–45.

300 Williams, "Punishment God Cannot Inflict Twice: The Double Payment Argument *Redevivus*," 507–8.

301 Ibid., 486.

302 Hodge, *Systematic Theology*, 2:470–71.

truth is, Christ died one death that all sinners deserve under the law. In paying the penalty of what one sinner deserves, he paid the penalty of what every sinner deserves. He suffered the curse of the law as defined by the law. Owen's double payment and trilemma arguments undermine the true meaning of imputation and operate on the assumption of the transference of specific sins.

Owen's trilemma *necessarily* operates on the assumption that there was a *quantitative* imputation of sins to Christ. The biblical idea of imputation does not work that way, and most Reformed people do not even think of the imputation of Christ's righteousness to believers in that *quantitative* way.

Charles Hodge, in contrast, has retained the proper understanding of imputation:

> What was suitable for one was suitable for all. The righteousness of Christ, the merit of his obedience and death, is needed for justification by each individual of our race, and therefore is needed by all. It is no more appropriate to one man than to another. Christ fulfilled the conditions of the covenant under which all men were placed. He rendered the obedience required of all, and suffered the penalty which all had incurred; and therefore his work is equally suited to all.[303]

Williams is at odds with Hodge.[304]

Misreading of Fuller and Dabney

Williams is also at odds with Andrew Fuller, whom he quoted.[305] Williams said, "Fuller distances the nature of the atonement from its design and application."[306] Why? Because Fuller had come to believe in unlimited expiation at the time he wrote the letters to Dr. Ryland that Williams quotes from.

Williams thinks he has Fuller and Dabney over a barrel with his false either/or dilemma.[307] He failed to recognize that both men did not think in terms of a quantitative imputation of sin to Christ, unlike Owen! Williams stated that both "locate the specificity exclusively in the application of Christ's work."[308] How can this be? If the specificity is "exclusively" in the application, it cannot be in the extent. Fuller and Dabney are actually advocates for an unlimited imputation of sin to Christ view and not for a quantitative or limited imputation of sin to Christ position.

---

303 C. Hodge, *Systematic Theology*, 2:544–45.

304 Williams fails to note his dissimilarity with Hodge in his brief footnote about Hodge: "Punishment God Cannot Inflict Twice: The Double Payment Argument *Redevivus*," 511.

305 Williams, "Punishment God Cannot Inflict Twice: The Double Payment Argument *Redevivus*," 506–7.

306 Ibid., 507.

307 Ibid., 509.

308 Ibid., 510.

Williams, Commercialism, and Sufficiency

Williams is committed to two contradictory ideas. He rightly argued against the notion that Christ died for sins in some sort of a quantitative-equivalentist fashion. Yet simultaneously Williams affirmed a limitation in the sins imputed to Christ such that only the sins of the elect are so imputed. But this carries Williams back to where he does not want to go: a commercialistic/pecuniary view of the atonement resulting in a limited sufficiency in the death of Christ, despite what he said on page 499. A gospel that speaks only of a bare infinite value in Christ's death is "cold comfort" to those for whom Christ did not die, as Ussher said:

> A bare sufficiency in Christ does not serve the turn; this would be a cold comfort. Suppose a man who was in debt, afraid of every sergeant and every sheriff, should be told, "Sir, there is money enough in the king's account to discharge all your debts." This may be very true, but what good is that to him? What comfort does he have by it unless the king offers to come and freely assume his debt?[309]

On the definite atonement scheme of Williams, the nature of the atonement can never be sufficient for the non-elect. Williams cannot have it both ways.

Williams is dependent on Owen's articulation of the compatibility of identical satisfaction and delayed application on the basis of the covenant of redemption.[310] However, as pointed out in my review of Trueman's chapter, the so-called covenant of redemption lacks biblical support and is problematic on numerous counts. Appeal to the covenant of redemption does not answer the problem for definite atonement that the Scripture teaches in Eph 2:1–3 the unbelieving elect remain under the wrath of God.

Williams's commercialism is further evidenced as he trades on the false dilemma fallacy when he asserts, "If God punishes all sin, then Christ must have died for the sin of unbelief, and if he did that for all without exception, then all without exception must be saved."[311]

What of Original Sin?

Williams's tacit dependence upon Owen's trilemma argument faces some insurmountable problems, not the least of which is the issue of original sin. Notice it is not original "sins" but original "sin." If Christ died for original sin, then he died for at least one of the sins of the non-elect. If this is the case, then Owen's argument is defeated for Owen must admit that Christ died for some of the sins (original sin) of all men. It seems that

309 J. Ussher, "The Satisfaction of Christ," in *The Puritan Pulpit: The Irish Puritans*, ed. Don Kistler (Orlando, FL: Soli Deo Gloria, 2006), 117.

310 Williams, "Punishment God Cannot Inflict Twice: The Double Payment Argument *Redevivus*," 511.

311 Ibid., 515.

either Owen must say that Christ died for *some of the sins (original sin) of all men*, or he must take the view that Christ only underwent punishment for *some of the sins of some men* (a position not listed in his trilemma).[312]

Throughout Williams's chapter he insists on Christ dying for "actual sins," especially on page 508. What he never deals with is the subject of Christ dying for original sin.

Williams, Ussher, and Dabney

Williams also tries to drive a wedge between Ussher and Dabney. He says, "Unlike Ussher, Robert L. Dabney defended the belief that 'Christ's redeeming work was limited in intention to the elect.'"[313]

All Dabney means is a limitation *in the intent to apply*. Does Williams think Ussher was an Arminian? Of course Ussher agreed with the idea that Christ had an effectual intent to apply his death to the elect alone that corresponded to God's purpose in election. All Calvinists, including the broad spectrum of Hypothetical Universalists, agree with that. It's just the case that Ussher grounded the efficacy *in Christ's intercession on behalf of the elect*, not in the death or satisfaction in itself.

Ussher said, "For the universality of the satisfaction derogates nothing from the necessity of the special grace in the application: neither doth the speciality of the one any ways abridge the generality of the other."[314]

At the end of the same work, he wrote,

> And therefore we may safely conclude out of all these premises, that "the Lamb of God, offering himself a sacrifice for the sins of the whole world," intended by giving sufficient satisfaction to God's justice, to make the nature of man, which he assumed, a fit subject for mercy and to prepare a medicine for the sins of the whole world, which should be denied to none that intended to take the benefit of it: howsoever he intended not by applying his all-sufficient remedy unto every person in particular to make it effectual unto the salvation of all, or to procure thereby actual pardon for the sins of the whole world.[315]

Conclusion

The double payment argument remains a flawed concept, even with the attempted restatement. Williams wants to proceed without the problematic gaps involved in

312 As argued, for example, by Calvinist J. Daane, "What Doctrine of Limited Atonement?," *Reformed Journal* 14 (1964): 16.

313 Williams, "Punishment God Cannot Inflict Twice: The Double Payment Argument *Redevivus*," 485.

314 J. Ussher, "The True Intent and Extent of Christ's Death and Satisfaction on the Cross," in *The Whole Works of the Most Rev. James Ussher*, 17 vols., ed. C. R. Elrington (Dublin: Hodges, Smith, and Co., 1864), 12:553.

315 Ibid., 12:558–59.

commercial language, but he ultimately cannot get away from commercial categories and concepts driving his arguments. Owen conceived of Christ's death as a "literal payment," and therefore his double payment and trilemma arguments function on a quantitative conception of the imputation of sin to Christ.

Postscript

Williams makes a subtle Christological error on page 498 and wrongly thinks it is compatible with Turretin's statement that he quotes on page 499. Williams said, "We must ascribe the properties of one nature [of Christ] to the other because they are both united in one person."[316] You'll notice that is precisely what Turretin does not say in the quote on page 499. Turretin rightly said that the properties of Christ's natures were really communicated to the person, not necessarily to the other nature.

I think Williams erred on the communication of properties. For example, if, as Williams said, we must ascribe the properties of one nature to the other (nature), then Christ's human nature must be said to be omnipresent, or ubiquitous (among other confusions). This is the confusion that caused some Lutherans to adopt ubiquitarianism.

Turretin has the Antiochian stress and concern for Christ's real humanity, while the Alexandrians had the stress and concern about the unity of Christ's person. We should indeed be zealous about both. Turretin, to protect Christ's real humanity and therefore the identification of his nature with our nature, does not ascribe the properties of Christ's divine nature to his human nature, but Turretin does ascribe the properties of either nature to Christ's person.

In other words, all that can be predicated of either of Christ's natures can be predicated of his person, but what is true of either nature may not necessarily be predicated of the other nature (Jesus, in his human nature, was not omnipresent). Think of Christ as (1) a person, (2) divine nature, and (3) human nature. Here is what we can correctly say about Christology: Everything that is true of 2 and 3 is true of 1. But what is true of 2 is not necessarily true of 3.

Williams goes too far and basically says one must ascribe the properties of 2 to 3. That is incorrect. Granted, in some cases, what is true of 2 may be true of 3 (given the image of God in man), with some significant qualifications due to the creator/creature distinctions, but in most cases we must not ascribe the properties of one of Jesus's natures to the other nature.

This issue is not directly related to Williams's argument, but it indicates where Williams's errs in his doctrine of Christology as well as in his interpretation of Turretin.

316 Williams, "Punishment God Cannot Inflict Twice: The Double Payment Argument *Redevivus*," 498.

Review of Stephen Wellum, "The New Covenant Work of Christ: Priesthood, Atonement, and Intercession" (517–39)

Stephen Wellum addresses the subject of priesthood, atonement, and intercession in an effort to demonstrate that only definite atonement takes account of Christ's unified priestly work: Christ only dies for the sins of those for whom he intercedes.

In the introduction, Wellum states: "all general atonement views must divide Christ's unified priestly work, redefine Christ's relation as Priest to his people, and ultimately make ineffective his work as the Head of the new covenant—all points which Scripture will not allow."[317] Wellum proceeds to address three issues: (1) crucial methodological/hermeneutical issues central to the argument, (2) OT priests accomplish a particular and unified work, and (3) Christ, like the OT priesthood, achieves a particular and effective work for his covenant people.[318]

Section One

In section one Wellum discusses "Priesthood and Typology," and "Priesthood and Covenants." Wellum is quite correct to point out that an understanding of the nature of Christ's priestly work must be viewed in the light of covenantal structures, especially the new covenant.[319] He quotes Waldron and Barcellos: "What is the scope, extent, and design of the new covenant? Is it a general covenant made with everyone, making salvation possible for everyone, if they will take it? Or, is it a limited covenant made only with certain persons and assuring their eternal salvation?"[320]

As Wellum clarifies, one could ask the question, "Whom does Jesus, as High Priest, represent in his death and apply the fruits of that covenant to?" Wellum believes that all general atonement views remove the work of Christ from its new covenant context. Notice this statement carefully: "Christ's atoning work cannot be extended to all people without also extending the new covenant benefits and privileges to all. . . . All general atonement views must either redefine the nature of the new covenant or argue that Christ dies as the covenantal Head of another covenant, whatever that is."[321] Here is Wellum's key assumption: the atonement's extent and application must be coextensive. Those for whom Christ died must receive the covenant benefits.

But where in Scripture is that stated? There is no place in Scripture that asserts Wellum's point. As we shall see, even his attempt to derive it typologically fails.

317 S. Wellum, "The New Covenant Work of Christ: Priesthood, Atonement, and Intercession," in *From Heaven He Came and Sought Her*, 518.

318 Ibid., 519.

319 Ibid., 522.

320 Ibid.

321 Ibid.

Section Two

In section two Wellum discusses the unified work of the old covenant priests.[322] Here he offers a helpful summary of the work of the Levitical priests. One finds only one place in the section where Wellum seeks to critique advocates of a general atonement,[323] and it becomes evident he is following John Owen's argument that all for whom Christ dies he intercedes, and all for whom he intercedes he dies. Owen and Wellum think this group is coextensive and applies only to the elect. The logical fallacy of this argument will become evident below.

Section Three

Wellum's third section addresses the unified work of Christ as new covenant priest. Here he moves into a full-blown critique of unlimited atonement.[324] His basic thesis is, "A crucial problem with all general atonement views is that they fragment Christ's priestly work of offering and intercession."[325]

Wellum asserts that Robert Lightner's argument that Christ's intercession is limited to his heavenly intercession only for the believing elect is in error, as is Gary Shultz's argument that Christ's intercession may be viewed as salvific for the non-elect. Wellum's reasons all revolve around his own preconceived notion that the extent of the atonement as well as Christ's intercession is limited only to the elect, an unproved assertion on his part.

Wellum has to depend on typology to get where he wants to go, and in the process he has to ignore many passages in the NT that assert the unlimited scope and nature of Christ's atonement. Direct biblical statements trump typologizing.

Wellum acknowledges the counterarguments general atonement advocates make to his argument[326] and attempts to respond to them. But here again, he is dependent upon OT typology that since OT priesthood represented only covenant people, so Christ's atonement extended only to the elect.

Wellum misinterprets Heb 2:5–18 by failing to note the text builds on the author's quotation of Psalm 8 and the solidarity of humanity with Christ in his incarnation, leading to the statement that Christ "tasted death for every one" in Heb 2:9. In the following section in Hebrews, the benefits of this death are described as accruing to those who have believed in Christ. Hebrews 2:5–18 does not assert that the atonement and the benefits of the atonement are coextensive. This is Wellum's assumption.[327] Hebrews limits Christ's atoning benefits to those who are in covenant with Christ. Nothing is said in Hebrews about the extent of the atonement being limited.

322 Ibid., 523–28.
323 Ibid., 527.
324 Ibid., 530–38.
325 Ibid., 530.
326 Ibid., 532–35.
327 Ibid., 532–33.

The New Testament is replete with verses that state salvation is conditioned upon faith. No one receives the covenant blessings unless he believes. God himself conditions the reception of salvation on faith, according to Scripture. Actual forgiveness of sins is only applied to those who believe.

Whatever one's view of election is, only those who are in the covenant by virtue of union with Christ experience the covenant blessings of forgiveness. How does one enter into union with Christ? The scriptural answer is, by faith. This, however, in no way mandates definite atonement.

Wellum's appeal to the typology of Christ as our high priest simply cannot carry the freight he wishes to place on it. Caution should be exercised so as not to read categories of elect and non-elect from the NT back into the OT. Neither should we read OT categories of the sacrificial system into the NT unless we have specific biblical justification to do so.

While Wellum considers objections from contemporary scholars, I do not see where he addresses the critique of his position made by the likes of Baxter, Bunyan, Shedd, Polhill, Decker, and many others within the Reformed ranks.

Definite Atonement and Jesus's Prayer in John 17

Wellum supposes that if Jesus's intercession (John 17) is limited to the elect, then he dies only for the sins of the elect. But nowhere does the text itself state that Jesus dies only for those for whom he prays. Further, John 17 makes no mention of the death of Christ. Laying aside for the moment the possibility that in context this is most likely a reference to the disciples, and even taking it as extending to the believing elect at the time, even then one is not warranted to draw the conclusion that the text means that Jesus did not die for the sins of all people, elect and non-elect.

To assert that the phrase "those whom you have given me" refers to the elect is forced exegesis. The context makes clear that those to whom Jesus referred in verse 9 are the disciples, and possibly all those who had already come to believe in him during his earthly ministry. Verse 20 likewise supports this understanding, for there Jesus says he prays not only for those who have believed in him but also for those who would believe in the future.

When Jesus says he does not pray for the world at this point, the meaning is obvious. This specific prayer is focused on specific people. He was praying for believers to exhibit certain spiritual characteristics that only believers could display. What point would there have been for Jesus to pray these things for the unconverted?

Here is the critical point. That Jesus did not pray for the "world" at this point does not prove he did not pray for the world of the unbelieving at other points. To assert such is to invoke the negative inference fallacy, which Wellum appears to do. But the kicker is that in verses 21 and 23, Jesus did pray for the world. He prayed that the world might believe. To extract the "elect" somehow from this word "world" in this context is obviously eisegesis.[328]

Wellum falls prey to generalizing that election entails limited atonement. The mistake here is a collapsing of the intercession of Christ into his expiation for sins, an unwarranted move biblically that begs the question.

In addition to the logical fallacies of begging the question and negative inference, Wellum also commits the fallacy of affirming the consequent in his treatment of Jesus's intercessory prayer. His logic is as follows:

> All prayed for = all died for
> Therefore,
> All died for = all prayed for.

The logic is obviously fallacious. Consider this example:

> If a man is dead, he is not breathing.
> Therefore,
> If a man is not breathing, he is dead.

The latter is a false inference and is not necessarily true. The man could be holding his breath.[329]

Also lurking behind Wellum's arguments is his commitment to a commercialistic view of the atonement, which we have already discussed in previous reviews.

Conclusion

As Doug Moo said in his review of Gentry and Wellum's *Kingdom Through Covenant*, "I am less certain of the argument for particular atonement, whose relevance to the key argument is not immediately obvious."[330] The same may be said for Wellum's chapter here.

Review of Henri Blocher, "Jesus Christ *the* Man: Toward a Systematic Theology of Definite Atonement" (541–82)

Blocher's chapter is the final chapter in the section on theology, and appropriately so since he attempts to develop something of a systematic theology of definite atonement.

---

328 See my critique of this line of exegesis above on Matthew Harmon's chapter.

329 D. Ponter, "Some Invalid and Unsound Arguments for the Assertion That All Died-For Are All Prayed-For," *Calvin and Calvinism*, February 28, 2013, http://calvinandcalvinism.com/?p=12337.

330 See D. Moo, "Kingdom through Covenant: A Review by Doug Moo," *The Gospel Coalition*, September 12, 2012, http://www.thegospelcoalition.org/article/kingdom-through-covenant-a-review-by-douglas-moo.

The chapter is divided into five major sections, the first and last of which don't deal specifically with the question at hand.

Section one, "Prolegomena" (542–47), is a brief introduction to systematic theology, covering three areas: tradition, reason, and Scripture. This is a helpful section but somewhat tertiary to the question at hand. Section two (547–61) addresses the extent question from a historical theology perspective. Here Blocher briefly discusses Augustine, Calvin, Andrew Fuller, Charles Hodge, Karl Barth, and Bruce McCormack. Section three (561–76) compares definite atonement with Hypothetical Universalism in five areas: (1) use of Scripture; (2) the love of God and gospel invitation; (3) Trinitarian harmony, the universal gospel offer, and personal assurance; (4) the double payment argument; and (5) the sufficiency question. Section four (576–80) addresses the subject of Christ's organic unity with humanity and its impact on the extent of the atonement. Section five (580–81) briefly considers the extent question and time (historical sequencing), and like the first section, is really tertiary to the main question.

My evaluation and critique will focus on sections two through four and will be a bit lengthier than previous chapter reviews. I am especially grateful that Blocher engages some of my critique of definite atonement in *Whosoever Will*[331] at numerous points in his chapter.

Difference between Definite Atonement and Hypothetical Universalism

Blocher asks where the decisive difference lies between Hypothetical Universalism and definite atonement:

> Where then does the decisive difference lie? In the relationship with election. Is the purpose of the atonement identical for all, elect and reprobate? Hypothetical Universalism answers yes; definite atonement answers no. Or, in the transaction that took place on the cross, which is described by such phrases as "bearing sins," "satisfying divine justice," "paying the ransom-price," are the reprobate included as well as the elect? Hypothetical Universalism: Yes; definite atonement: no. Or, did atonement secure eternal life in such a way that those for whom it was accomplished according to its main purpose and operation shall infallibly receive it at the end? Definite atonement, yes; Hypothetical Universalism: no.[332]

With respect to the first question, it is not accurate to say that Hypothetical Universalism asserts the purpose of the atonement is identical for all. The extent of the atonement is

331 Allen, "The Atonement: Limited or Universal?," 61–107.

332 H. Blocher, "Jesus Christ *the* Man: Toward a Systematic Theology of Definite Atonement," in *From Heaven He Came and Sought Her*, 548–49.

identical for all, but the intent (purpose) according to Hypothetical Universalism is the same as with definite atonement: to secure the salvation of the elect. With respect to the third question it is also inaccurate to state that Hypothetical Universalism does not affirm that the atonement secures eternal life "according to its main purpose" since supporters of Hypothetical Universalism affirm that this is accomplished in the application on the grounds of both God's special intent and the atonement's extent.

Blocher's wording in this paragraph is somewhat confusing. If we speak of the nature of the satisfaction, it is for all men. If we speak of the intention, from the Hypothetical Universalism perspective, it is unequal. Atonement secured the legal basis of salvation. The only difference between definite atonement and Hypothetical Universalism is the extent of sin-bearing that causes Hypothetical Universalists to talk differently about "intent" of the atonement. Hypothetical Universalists believe God intended Christ to die for the sins of all people (unlimited atonement), but that God also intended only to give effectual grace to the elect (effectual purpose).

Misreading of Augustine, Calvin, and Andrew Fuller and Charles Hodge

Augustine. Blocher said that Augustine's case is "complex" and that there is no unified doctrine of atonement that stands out in Augustine's writings.[333] Actually, this is not the case. Augustine is clear in his affirmation that Christ died for the sins of all people, including Judas.[334] Blocher tries to use Augustine's textual interpretation of some passages to indicate his adherence to definite atonement. However, this fails to recognize that many Hypothetical Universalists interpret these passages as Augustine did, yet they clearly held to universal atonement. Does Blocher think Augustine had a different definition of predestination and grace than the Hypothetical Universalists? The later Augustine affirmed the same definition of predestination as Hypothetical Universalists, and all Calvinists I might add.

Calvin. With respect to Calvin, I have already addressed this issue in the review of Blacketer's chapter. Blocher is heavily dependent on Nicole's outdated work on Calvin's view of extent. Much research on Calvin's view has transpired since Nicole's 1985 article. Blocher speaks of defenders (plural) around Calvin, like Beza. Here I must inquire: "Who else?" Blocher does not name anyone. The recent work of Richard Muller and others have shown that virtually all the first-generation Reformers held to universal atonement. Beza's affirmation of definite atonement does not appear until some twenty-five years after Calvin's death.[335]

333 Ibid., 549.

334 Augustine, "Exposition on the Book of the Psalms," in *NPNF*, 8:309.

335 Consult D. Ponter's two-part article on Calvin's view of the extent of the atonement, where he shows beyond a reasonable doubt that Calvin affirmed universal atonement ("Review Essay [Part One]" and "Review Essay [Part Two]").

Andrew Fuller and Charles Hodge. Blocher also appears to misread both Andrew Fuller and Charles Hodge, whom he assigns to the definite atonement camp, in disagreement with my placing them in the Hypothetical Universalism camp.[336] Blocher thinks many of my quotations "fail to convince because the flexibility of the language used by definite atonement supporters is not recognized."[337] Concerning my approach to Fuller, Blocher said "some complements are needed to achieve a proper balance."[338]

Actually it is the other way around. Blocher fails to recognize the flexibility of the dualism of intent and extent in Fuller and Hodge. He confuses Hodge's clear statement about Christ's sin-bearing for the world with the issue of the universal offer.[339] For Hodge, it is the universal nature of the atonement that grounds the universal offer, which is Hodge's point in the very quotation Blocher cites.[340]

Hodge clearly states that though Christ did not die "equally" for all men (as in Arminianism), yet he died for his "sheep" and "church," (as in Calvinism) and "He did all that was necessary, so far as a satisfaction to justice is concerned, all that is required for the salvation of all men" (Hypothetical Universalism). If Christ's death accomplished "all that is required for the salvation of all men," then it cannot be a limited substitution as in the definite atonement scheme. Hodge affirmed Christ's universal sin-bearing.[341]

Hodge carefully distinguishes between the purpose, design, and intent of the atonement from its extent.[342] W. G. T. Shedd likewise shares the same theology.[343] Rather than demonstrating Fuller and Hodge to be in the definite atonement camp, Blocher's analysis actually demonstrates the opposite.

Recall Blocher's point about theological method at the beginning of his chapter. Showing in Hodge's writings where he affirms limitation in the intent or the appli-

---

336 For the evidence that the later Fuller came to reject limited atonement, see above under "Andrew Fuller (AD 1754–1815)," and P. Morden, *Offering Christ to the World: Andrew Fuller and the Revival of Eighteenth Century Particular Baptist Life*, Studies in Baptist History and Thought 8 (Waynesboro, GA: Paternoster, 2003), 26–27. See also my "Preaching for a Great Commission Resurgence," 292–94.

337 Blocher, "Jesus Christ *the* Man: Toward a Systematic Theology of Definite Atonement," 551.

338 Ibid., 552.

339 Ibid., 554.

340 Ibid., 555.

341 Hodge, *Systematic Theology*, 2:555. Notice also how Robert Dabney, Hodge's contemporary, cites Hodge as affirming universal expiation (R. L. Dabney, *Systematic Theology* (1878; repr. Edinburgh: Banner of Truth, 2002), 527). Dabney also wrote, "Certainly the expiation made by Christ is so related to all, irrespective of election, that God can sincerely invite all to enjoy its benefits, that every soul in the world who desires salvation is warranted to appropriate it, and that even a Judas, had he come in earnest, would not have been cast out." See also Dabney's comment, "Redemption is limited, i.e., to true believers, and is particular. Expiation is not limited" (ibid., 528). Dabney stated, "Christ made expiation for every man" (ibid., 525).

342 Hodge, *Systematic Theology*, 2:545–46.

343 Shedd, *Dogmatic Theology*, 3:418, affirms the same unlimited sin-bearing in the atonement: "The expiation of sin is distinguishable from the pardon of it. The former, conceivably, might take place and the latter not. When Christ died on Calvary, the whole mass, so to speak, human sin was expiated merely by that death; but the whole mass was not pardoned merely by that death. The claims of law and justice for the sins of the whole world were satisfied by the 'offering of the body of Jesus Christ once for all' (Heb. 10:10)."

cation of the atonement while overlooking statements where he affirms universal sin-bearing is, in fact, a theological method not up to par with that expressed in his prolegomenon.

Definite Atonement and Hypothetical Universalism Compared

In section three Blocher addresses five matters:

1. Scripture, including Heb 2:9, and the negative inference fallacy.
2. The love of God and the gospel invitation.
3. Trinitarian harmony, the universal gospel offer, and personal assurance.
4. The double payment argument.
5. The sufficiency question.

We can only touch on each of these briefly.

The Use of Scripture

Blocher suggests that Hypothetical Universalists overlook "natural understandings" of texts that on the surface support unlimited atonement.[344] He takes up Heb 2:9 as an example. He asserts "man" is not part of the original. That is merely a translational issue. The text says that Christ died for "every one." Whether "man" does or does not occur in the text is immaterial.

Blocher then moves to the following context of the passage that speaks of those who benefit from the atonement in an attempt to limit the meaning of Heb 2:9 to the elect. This fails to consider the preceding context of the quotation of Psalm 8, which connects the incarnation to the work of Christ for all people. It also fails to recognize the biblical distinction between the extent of the atonement, which is unlimited, and its application, which is limited.

Blocher noted my point about the negative inference fallacy being employed by those who hold to definite atonement. "Fair enough," he states. He then sidesteps the issue and attempts to turn the tables: "Nevertheless, the tendential logic that springs from such rather favors definite atonement."[345] This assertion is not backed up with any evidence.

Blocher concludes, "Piecemeal exegesis does not yield a clear-cut answer to the choice between definite atonement and Hypothetical Universalism. The evidence must

344 Blocher, "Jesus Christ *the* Man: Toward a Systematic Theology of Definite Atonement," 562.

345 Ibid., 563.

be digested by theological reflection."[346] Of course, all would affirm this. But such a statement assumes that those who affirm Hypothetical Universalism engage in "piecemeal exegesis" while those who affirm definite atonement "digest" the exegesis by "theological reflection."

It is my observation that piecemeal exegesis is often the fault of some who argue for definite atonement. Definite atonement is a theological deduction from Scripture, not so much a doctrine derived from clear exegesis of Scripture.

The Love of God and the Gospel Invitation

Blocher rightly affirms God's universal love and universal saving will[347] and sees how affirming the former necessarily entails the latter, unlike Helm and Blacketer. He said, "The love of God for all also refers to their ultimate salvation. Such statements as Ezekiel 18:32 and 2 Peter 3:9 (an implicit restriction to the elect is little likely) declare such a will."[348]

Trinitarian Harmony, the Universal Gospel Offer, and Personal Assurance

I have already addressed the issue of Trinitarian harmony and the universal gospel offer in previous reviews of chapters in *From Heaven He Came and Sought Her*. The discussion of personal assurance is brief, and I will skip it here.

In this section Blocher offers an inadequate response to Gary Shultz's point about the gospel content of Paul's kerygma to the unconverted Corinthians, "Christ died for our sins," in 1 Cor 15:1–3. He attempts two defeaters: (1) Paul does not reproduce the wording verbatim and (2) "for us" may have meant Paul's team and any who would join them.[349] Yet Paul's statement clearly implies he preached Christ died for the sins of all. Here Paul reminds the Corinthians of the message he preached to them when he first came to Corinth (Acts 18:1–18). He clearly affirms the content of the gospel he preached in Corinth included the fact that "Christ died for our sins."

Notice carefully Paul is saying this is what he preached pre-conversion, not post-conversion. Thus the "our" in his statement cannot be taken to refer to all the elect or merely the believing elect, which is what the high Calvinist is forced to argue. How else, from a Reformed perspective of limited atonement, could Paul preach to all people that Christ had died for their sins? He could not do so with any consistency.

The entire pericope of 1 Cor 15:3–11 should be kept in mind. Notice how in verse 11 Paul returns to what he had said in verse 3: "Whether then it was I or they, so we preach and so you believed" (NASB).The customary present tense in Greek used by

---

346 Ibid.

347 Ibid., 563–65.

348 Ibid., 564–65.

349 Ibid., 568.

Paul when he says "so we preach," along with the aorist tense in Greek for "believed," makes it clear Paul refers to a past point in time when they believed what it was his custom to preach.

What did Paul preach to them in his evangelistic efforts to win all the unsaved to Christ? He preached the gospel, which included "Christ died for our sins." And so they believed.

Double Payment Argument

Blocher attempts to blunt the problems with double payment.[350] Since I have addressed this issue in a previous review, I will not deal with it here. I will, however, raise one smaller issue. Blocher responds to Gary Shultz's point about universal reconciliation in Colossians 1.[351] Blocher quotes Shultz: "In order for Christ to reconcile all things to the Father, He had to pay for all sin, including the sin of the non-elect. Otherwise, some sin would be outside his atoning work and thus outside His cosmic triumph." Blocher then states that Shultz presumably would not assert that Christ died for the sins of fallen angels, "and therefore his cosmic triumph does not require his payment for the sins of all his enemies." Shultz spoke of "all sins," which in context means "all human sins," including the sins of the non-elect. Blocher takes this and extends it beyond what Shultz said to include the fallen angels.

Atonement and Sufficiency

Since I have addressed this issue in other chapter reviews, I shall be brief. Blocher argues the atonement is sufficient for the salvation of reprobates (the non-elect) "since it made certain the gift of faith."[352] This is problematic. Blocher is trading on an intrinsic sufficiency of value, not an actual sufficiency or ransom price paid for all such that were one of the non-elect to believe, he would be saved. It is impossible that such could be the case for, by definition, there is no atonement for the non-elect. The atonement is in no way sufficient for the sins of the non-elect because no atonement exists for their sins.

Christ the Redeemer as Man

Blocher attempts to argue that the headship of Christ over "his" people necessitates definite atonement. Blocher finds "a tension" with Andrew Fuller's insistence that Christ's death, considered irrespective of "the appointment of God, with regard to its application," was "for man, not as elect or non-elect, but as sinners."[353] "What is this 'sin' in Fuller's sentence, against which the wrath of God was discharged? . . . The

350 Ibid., 570–74.
351 Ibid., 574.
352 Ibid.
353 Ibid., 577–78.

'price paid' metaphor refers to the transaction itself, not to latter application."[354] But no tension exists as Blocher fails to recognize Fuller affirmed unlimited expiation and distinguished the atonement's extent from its application.

For Blocher, Christ died as the "Head" of a new humanity. "Considering the largest community in which the structure of headship is established, and most radical import—the human *genus*—we may affirm both definite atonement and a universal reference."[355]

Blocher believes Christ's headship as the New Adam grounded such propositions as man, in a generic sense, was redeemed on the cross; the "world" was reconciled (2 Cor 5:19); and "every human being qua human being is concerned."

"How is humanity involved?" Blocher queries. Christ appropriates "man" in a generic sense of humankind: "He creates in himself Jews and Gentiles 'into one new *Anthropos* . . . .' Considering the dimension of unity of humankind, he deserves to be called 'the Savior of the world (John 14:42).'"[356] What of those who do not believe? For Blocher, the bond of human solidarity entails that Christ's work, as Head of the genus, concerns all people. All are called to believe in Christ. If they refuse, they "cut themselves off from humanity as a genus: they confirm for themselves the Adamic condemnation."[357]

Blocher concludes this section: "Highlighting the organic dimension, the corporate character, of humanity illuminates the foundation in atonement of universal invitation, and why faith is required for enjoyment."[358] But exactly how such is possible on Blocher's terms is difficult to see. No foundation exists for a universal invitation because no foundation exists for the salvation of all who are considered to be the non-elect. What one hand gives, the other takes away in Blocher's system of definite atonement. Blocher's affirmation of definite atonement, a "universal reference," and a universal gospel call is problematic.[359]

Conclusion

While I appreciate Blocher's chapter in many ways, I can't help but sense that he engages in a systemic misreading of some of the primary sources. His failure to note clear universal satisfaction language in Augustine, Fuller, and Hodge, not just universal offer language, is problematic.

In summary, there are six common presuppositions undergirding the arguments of these chapters in the systematic theology section of *From Heaven He Came and Sought Her*:

354 Ibid., 578.
355 Ibid.
356 Ibid., 579.
357 Ibid.
358 Ibid., 580.
359 Ibid., 578.

1. Limited intent entails limited extent. This is the notion that God's intention in the atonement (to save the elect) entails a limitation in Christ's sin-bearing such that there is an imputation of the sins of the elect only to Christ at the cross.
2. Election entails limited extent. God's salvific intention is expressed in the divine decree of election, and election entails the notion that atonement is only made for the sins of the elect.
3. Penal substitution entails limited extent.
4. Hypothetical Universalism in all forms entails Trinitarian discord.
5. Old Testament priestly typology entails New Testament definite atonement.
6. There are only two options: either definite atonement or universalism.

We have seen in the reviews of the chapters in the theological section that (1) these are theological deductions and (2) none has clear scriptural support.

Review of Daniel Strange, "Slain for the World?: The 'Uncomfortability' of the 'Unevangelized' for a Universal Atonement" (585–605)

The final three chapters in *From Heaven He Came and Sought Her* address practical matters. In this chapter, Daniel Strange deals with the issue of the unevangelized.

Introduction

In his introduction, Strange thinks universal atonement presents "insurmountable theological difficulties."[360] He suggests that unlimited atonement cannot be the basis of a well-meant gospel offer for those who never hear the gospel since "it makes no offer at all, thus making it 'limited.'"[361] But this is certainly no fault of universal atonement. It is not universal atonement that makes the offer; it is Christians who make the offer on behalf of God.

According to those who hold to universal atonement, there is an objective remedy for the sins of all people, regardless of whether it is offered or not, whether they hear the gospel or not, or whether they believe it once they hear it or not.

Strange continues:

> As a result, further questions might be raised as to this atonement's "objective" qualitative nature (especially if a "penal" rather than a "governmental"

360 D. Strange, "Slain for the World?: The 'Uncomfortability' of the 'Unevangelized' for a Universal Atonement," in *From Heaven He Came and Sought Her*, 587.

361 Ibid., 587.

> theory of the atonement is espoused), and ultimately of God's character and sovereignty. Christ has provided a *de jure* salvation for all, but *de facto* it is not accessible to all and is limited in its scope.[362]

The "objective nature" of the atonement is what it is whether people ever hear the gospel or not. God's character is not impugned if the gospel does not come to the unevangelized. Romans 1 seems to make that clear. Rather, it is the church's character that is impugned for lack of obedience to get the gospel to all the nations. Interestingly, the same kind of argument with respect to God's character—namely, his universal saving love—could be made against definite atonement.

This chapter is divided into two sections: (1) the question of the unevangelized in relation to universal atonement and (2) the question of the unevangelized in relation to definite atonement.

The Unevangelized and Unlimited Atonement

Strange immediately appeals to John Owen's *Death of Death* with a lengthy quotation. Owen concluded either people can be saved apart from hearing the gospel, or the atonement must be constructed in such a way that both the character of God and the unity of the economy of the Godhead is questioned.[363]

This is a false dichotomy. It is not an either/or situation. I have addressed both issues of the character of God and Trinitarian disharmony in previous chapter reviews, so I will not cover that ground here. Strange proceeds to attempt to show that the atonement's objective accomplishment and subjective application is an untenable distinction.[364] He queries: Can a universal atonement properly be called such when there are conditions on its application and when not all for whom it is made hear about it?

Of course it can. The nature of conditional acceptance in and of itself indicates not all will meet the condition. Furthermore, the condition of repentance and faith for the atonement's application is placed by God himself.

Strange attempts to argue that those who affirm universal atonement are in the same position as those who affirm definite atonement with respect to the offer of the gospel. The unevangelized have no offer at all.[365] But there is a world of difference. Universal atonement provides the grounds for the universal offer of the gospel to all. Definite atonement does not. As I have pointed out numerous times in these chapter reviews, what is definite atonement offering the non-elect? Nothing. There is no gospel to offer them because there is no atonement made for their sins. On their view, the unevangelized are not offerable (able to be offered consistently).

---

362 Ibid.

363 Ibid., 589.

364 Ibid., 591.

365 Ibid., 592.

Referencing Robert Reymond, Strange states that universal atonement eviscerates Christ's atoning work from its infinite intrinsic worth.[366] Not at all. Proponents of universal atonement affirm the atonement's infinite intrinsic worth and its extrinsic sufficiency to save all who believe, including every person on planet Earth were they to believe because there is an atonement made for every person.

Strange asks, in what way is this category of people (those who never hear the gospel) saveable if they don't have the opportunity to respond? The answer is really quite simple: they are not saveable unless they believe the gospel, and they can't believe it unless they hear it. They are, nonetheless, culpable before God since they have the witness of both creation and conscience à la Rom 1:18–32. The nature of God's objective atonement is not called into question on the universal atonement position, as Strange suggests.

Strange then launches into a discussion of Pinnock and Hackett on the issue. He states they are "internally consistent" in making connection between universal atonement and universal accessibility.[367] Pinnock's inclusivism is in error, as Strange rightly noted.[368]

Strange appealed to Miller's study of John 1:9 suggesting that the "light that shines in the world" is directed to those who respond to it. Here the "world" does not mean "world" but effectively means the elect.[369] In previous reviews, I have already pointed out the problematic nature of this kind of exegesis.

Strange spoke of another difficulty for the universal atonement position—the motivation for missions and evangelism "if everyone has access to respond to Christ outside of the human messenger."[370] But the vast majority of people who hold to universal atonement also reject inclusivism.

The Unevangelized and Definite Atonement

Strange devoted four pages to this final section. He attempted to demonstrate that definite atonement is commensurate with urgency in evangelism and possesses intrasystematic consistency and intra-Trinitarian harmony. His basic position is simple: God has ordained that those chosen for salvation will hear the gospel. He attempts to link the universality of sin with the particularity of grace as seen in the history of revelation and the revelation of history.[371] Strange rightly noted that defenders of universal atonement will question the biblical and theological presuppositions of his case. Strange's

366 Ibid., 593.
367 Ibid., 594.
368 Ibid., 597.
369 Ibid., 599.
370 Ibid.
371 Ibid., 602.

appeal to Acts 16:6–8 to support definite atonement is strained at best.[372] In fact, the passage has nothing to do with the extent of the atonement.

That some proponents of definite atonement throughout history have shown an urgency in evangelism cannot be denied. What needs to be added is that many advocates of definite atonement throughout church history have certainly lacked urgency in evangelism because of their Calvinism, albeit a distorted version of it.

Strange assumes William Carey held to definite atonement but offers no basis for this claim.[373] Clearly Carey was a Calvinist, but as far as I am aware, there is no firm evidence in his writings that he held to definite atonement. (See my treatment of Carey above.)

Conclusion

Strange's chapter does not succeed in supporting definite atonement or in showing universal atonement to be untenable. That some people groups are without the gospel is no less an acute problem for universal atonement as for definite atonement.

Review of Sinclair Ferguson, "'Blessed Assurance, Jesus Is Mine'? Definite Atonement and the Cure of Souls" (607–31)

Sinclair Ferguson's chapter addresses the issue of assurance in pastoral ministry from the perspective of limited atonement. The bulk of the chapter is an analysis and critique of the nineteenth-century Scottish Presbyterian pastor McLeod Campbell's view of definite atonement and assurance. Campbell's *The Nature of the Atonement* is his critique of penal substitutionary atonement and advocacy for a general atonement.

McLeod Campbell on the Nature and Extent of the Atonement

Campbell's key error, which Ferguson likewise assumes, is that penal substitution necessitates definite atonement. For Campbell, the only way to justify the biblical position of general atonement was to deny penal substitution.

Ferguson's choice of Campbell to address the connection of the extent of the atonement with assurance of salvation is rooted in Campbell's pastoral ministry. Campbell was deeply concerned about the lack of assurance of salvation he saw in many of his church members. He concluded that this was due to federal theology's emphasis on limited atonement "and that assurance was the fruit of recognizing evidences of grace as marks that one was among the elect."[374]

372 Ibid.

373 Ibid., 604.

374 S. Ferguson, "'Blessed Assurance, Jesus Is Mine'? Definite Atonement and the Cure of Souls," in *From Heaven He Came and Sought Her*, 612.

Response to Campbell's Criticism of Penal Substitution and Definite Atonement

Ferguson lists and responds to five of Campbell's criticisms of penal substitution and definite atonement:

1. It makes justice a necessary attribute of God but love an arbitrary one.[375]

Campbell argued that the atonement must be universal or God's character is impugned for loving some and not others. Ferguson thinks Campbell has confused character and relationship. Ferguson responds that it is "just for the loving God to hate sin and even to reveal that he hates sinners. No intelligible interpretation of Mal 1:2–3 . . . can make these words mean that God loves Jacob and Esau in the same sense and in the same way."[376] Ferguson accuses Campbell of confusing justice with punitive justice. The former is an essential attribute of God while the latter is a relational response due to sin.

2. Federal Calvinism makes the divine-human relationship essentially legal rather than filial.[377]

Ferguson responds in two ways. First, filial relationship is a legal standing in Scripture as revealed in Pauline "adoption" language. Second, it is questionable whether federal Calvinism views "the Edenic relation as fundamentally legal, but not gracious."[378]

3. Forgiveness is logically prior to repentance and prior to the atonement itself.[379]

Ferguson's critique is chiefly that Campbell has confused a divine disposition of grace with a divine act of forgiveness.[380]

4. The atonement is not a penal substitution.[381]

According to Ferguson, Campbell viewed the atonement as an act of expiation for sins, but not penal substitution. There is no imputation of our guilt and punishment to Christ. Rather, via the incarnation and crucifixion, Christ perfectly repents for us.

J. B. Torrance, in his introduction to Campbell's *Nature of the Atonement*, disputes this claim by Ferguson and argues that Campbell did affirm penal substitution.

375 Ibid., 614–16.
376 Ibid., 615.
377 Ibid., 616–18.
378 Ibid., 617.
379 Ibid., 618–20.
380 Ibid., 619.
381 Ibid., 620–23.

Ferguson rightly points out that this concept of Christ's "repentance" is something of which the Bible itself never speaks as the "central key" to the atonement.[382]

5. Definite atonement prohibits assurance of salvation.[383]

From Campbell's viewpoint, how can one have assurance of salvation if one does not know that Christ died for him? Ferguson is certainly correct to point out in response that the assurance of faith is not obtained prior to our salvation.[384] However, Ferguson errs in footnote 70 when he states that the reprobate have the same warrant to believe in Christ as do the elect. Likewise, his claim that on no occasion in the NT did the apostles preach the gospel in terms of "Christ died for you, therefore believe" is inaccurate.[385]

First, from a limited atonement perspective, how could the reprobate have the same warrant to believe in Christ? There is no atonement made for their sins, hence no grounds exist on which they would ever be accepted by God if they were to repent and believe the gospel. The Reformed notion of total depravity and its entailment that no one will believe unless given efficacious grace does not lessen this problem at all.

Second, 1 Cor 15:1–11 makes it clear that Paul's normal method of bringing the gospel to any group for the first time was to preach that "Christ died for our sins." See my remarks on this in the review of Blocher's chapter above. Ferguson's attempt to extricate federal theology from Campbell's criticism with respect to assurance only partially succeeds. Whereas Campbell overplays the criticism, Ferguson underplays it.

Definite Atonement and Christian Assurance

A final, short section rounds out the chapter entitled "Definite Atonement and Christian Assurance."[386] Here Ferguson asserts that definite atonement is not only well able to sustain Christian assurance but in fact grounds it. Actually, it is not the question of the extent of the atonement that grounds Christian assurance but the nature of the atonement and the Savior who made it that grounds it for all who repent and believe the gospel.

Neither Ferguson's appeal to the double payment argument nor his appeal to disruption in the Trinity offer support for definite atonement. Since I have already dealt with both of these issues in previous chapter reviews, I will not do so here in detail.

Ferguson's footnote 94 erects a straw man argument against Hypothetical Universalists. His assertion that Trinitarian disharmony is entailed in all forms of universal atonement overlooks the biblical distinction yet interrelationship among the

382 Ibid., 621.
383 Ibid., 623–28.
384 Ibid., 624.
385 Ibid.
386 Ibid., 628–30.

intent, extent, and application of the atonement. Ferguson states that according to Hypothetical Universalists, "the Father sets forth the Son as a real propitiation for the sins of some for whom that propitiation never actually propitiates. This remains a non-propitiating propitiation, which creates a double jeopardy."[387] No, the propitiation concerns all sins and sinners, as 1 John 2:2 indicates. Ferguson fails to see the point that the atonement in and of itself does not secure its own application. The atonement is only applied to those who meet God's condition for salvation (not propitiation), which is repentance and faith. Romans 3:25 makes this clear: the propitiation is "through faith in His blood." Propitiation is not applied until faith.

In the Hypothetical Universalism approach, God intended that Christ substitute for the sins of all people, hence the extent of the atonement is unlimited, but God also intended that the atonement only be applied to the elect via the special call. For all other non-Calvinist proponents of universal atonement, God intended that Christ substitute for the sins of all people, hence the extent of the atonement is unlimited. God desired that the benefits of the atonement accrue to all people, though God also intended that the atonement be applied only to those who believe.

Review of John Piper, "'My Glory I Will Not Give to Another!' Preaching the Fullness of Definite Atonement to the Glory of God" (633–67)

The final chapter in *From Heaven He Came and Sought Her* covers the subject of preaching and definite atonement. John Piper does the honors. This chapter is a fitting conclusion to the book as Piper attempts to show that preaching definite atonement redounds to the glory of God.

Introduction (633–37)

Piper asserts three things as foundational for his chapter:

1. The glory of God is the heart of the gospel and the end for which God created the world.
2. The central task of ministry and preaching is the magnifying of the glory of God. Every sermon should be expository according to Piper, to which I utter a hearty "Amen!"
3. The cross is the climax of the glory of God's grace.

I have no qualms here.

387 Ibid., 629.

Definite Atonement Is a Significant Part of the Glory of God's Grace (637–39)

Piper thinks that the wording of Eph 1:4–6 and Rev 5:9 points to definite atonement. "God does not raise everyone from spiritual death. He raises those whom he 'predestined for adoption as sons' (1:5). . . . This means that in the atonement God designed and secured spiritual life and its resulting faith, for those whom he predestinated to sonship."[388]

There are five problems here.

1. These texts say nothing about the extent of the atonement.
2. Piper is assuming that predestination entails definite atonement. Nowhere in Scripture is this connection made.
3. He buys into the Council of Dort's notion, later developed by John Owen, that faith is something purchased by the atonement for the elect. Nowhere in Scripture is faith said to be purchased for the elect at the cross.
4. Piper appears to think and speak about the elect in an abstract sense. Piper's generalization blurs the distinction between the believing elect and all the elect in the abstract. Actually, the elect must be considered in two groups—those who have believed and those who have yet to believe. Piper is conflating these two. But he does not seem to realize that the texts he cites pertain to believers, not the elect in the abstract. Piper is reading Reformed theology into the text. He takes what is true of believers in Eph 1:4–6 and then seeks to apply this to all the elect as an abstract class; an illegitimate hermeneutical move.
5. With respect to Rev 5:9, even Heinrich Bullinger, a leading sixteenth-century Calvinist, in a sermon on Rev 5:9–10 said this "signifies an universality, for the Lord has died for all: but that all are not made partakers of this redemption, it is through their own fault."[389]

The Love of God and Definite Atonement (639–42)

Piper argues for a "unique love of God for his elect that accounts for the unique effect of definite atonement in saving them."[390] He continues: "Others are not made alive. Therefore, this love is a distinguishing love. It is not given to all. It is given to sinners who are predestined for sonship."[391]

Notice the logical fallacy in this argument. Granting for the sake of argument that we can distinguish different kinds of love (God's saving love for the elect and general love for the non-elect), how does this support or entail definite atonement? It does not.

388 J. Piper, "'My Glory I Will Not Give to Another!' Preaching the Fullness of Definite Atonement to the Glory of God," in *From Heaven He Came and Sought Her*, 639.

389 H. Bullinger, *A Hundred Sermons upon the Apocalypse of Jesus Christ* (London: John Daye, Dwelling over Aldersgate, 1573), 79–80.

390 Piper, "'My Glory I Will Not Give to Another!' Preaching the Fullness of Definite Atonement to the Glory of God," 640.

391 Ibid.

Piper succumbs to the negative inference fallacy in his argument. He presumes that a special love for the elect entails no atonement for the non-elect.

Piper demonstrates an inability to distinguish properly between the Arminian and Amyraldian views on God's love. He states concerning both Arminians and Amyraldians: "The preciousness of this personal love is muted where it is seen as an instance of the same love that Christ has for those who finally perish. It is not the same."[392] Amyraldians (and all other Hypothetical Universalists, I might add) distinguish degrees or senses in God's love for the elect and non-elect just as those who support definite atonement do. Piper has mischaracterized Amyraldians on this.

From a Reformed perspective, God's love for the elect is greater in degree but also in purpose since it involves a purpose to save only a select number of people. Non-Calvinists would of course disagree with this limited purpose. Additionally, most non-Calvinists believe it is not necessarily wise to talk about degrees in God's love, especially when the analogies given come from human life and love. Perhaps God's love should not be measured by degrees of love as found among humans since God's love is perfect and ours is not.

In this same vein, in his sermon on "For Whom Did Christ Die?" Piper attacks Arminianism as a theology of self-salvation. He said, "In order to say that Christ died for all men in the same way, the Arminian must limit the atonement to a powerless opportunity for men to save themselves from the terrible plight of depravity."[393] This is a caricature of the Arminian position.

The New Covenant and Definite Atonement (642–48)

Piper states that Christ secured not only the possibility that all who believe will be saved, but also that all who are called will believe. This is what makes the atonement definite according to Piper. He continues, "The faith of God's chosen and called was purchased by the 'blood of the covenant' (Matt. 26:28)."[394]

> The term definite atonement refers to this truth—when God sent his Son to die, he had in view the definite acquisition of a group of underserving sinners, whose faith and repentance he obtained by the blood of his Son. This is a divine purpose in the cross—to purchase and create the saving faith of a definite, freely chosen, unworthy, rebellious group of sinners.[395]

392 Ibid., 641.

393 J. Piper, "For Whom Did Christ Die? And What Did Christ Actually Achieve on the Cross for Those for Whom He Died?," *Monergism,* May 25, 2015, http://www.monergism.com/thethreshold/articles/piper/piper_atonement.html. Piper adjusted this wording in *Five Points: Towards a Deeper Experience of God's Grace* (Ross-Shire, UK: Christian Focus, 2013), 40.

394 Piper, "'My Glory I Will Not Give to Another!' Preaching the Fullness of Definite Atonement to the Glory of God," 642–43.

395 Ibid., 643.

Actually, all Calvinists who affirm an unlimited atonement could easily agree with Piper's statement, with one exception: his claim concerning faith as purchased by the cross.

It is erroneous to state that what makes the atonement definite is only God's intent to save all the called who will believe. All Amyraldians and Hypothetical Universalists believe this as well. What makes the atonement "definite" as the term is used by all the authors in *From Heaven He Came and Sought Her* is the affirmation that Christ only substituted for the sins of the elect.

One must properly distinguish between the atonement's intent and extent. Piper is confusing intent and extent in his statement above.

Faith Purchased by Christ on the Cross

Several times in this section, and the entire chapter, Piper spoke of "faith" being "purchased" by the atonement. This is the argument developed by John Owen in his *Death of Death*. Faith is purchased by Christ on the cross and bestowed on the elect unconditionally. The importance of this argument for Owen can be seen in his admission that if this is not true, then universal atonement and free will is "established."

For Owen (and Piper), God designs that not only the goal (salvation of the elect) but the means to that goal (faith) are purchased by Christ in the atonement. Faith is bestowed by God "absolutely upon no condition at all" according to Owen.[396] Thus the elect have a right to the means of salvation purchased for them by Christ. All of this is rooted in Owen's concept of the covenant of redemption, which Piper never mentions but which underlies his argument. The covenant of redemption is a contract in eternity past between the Father and the Son to save the elect through the means of the Son's death on the cross. The Son agrees to die for the elect only.

---

396 J. Owen, "The Death of Death in the Death of Christ," 10:203. For Baxter's refutation of Owen's idea of Christ purchasing faith infallibly for all for whom he died, see *Universal Redemption*, 412–28; and *Catholick Theologie*, 2:69. Andrew Fuller also rejected the idea of Christ "purchasing repentance and faith, as well as other spiritual blessings," since it entails that God is "under such a kind of obligation to show mercy to sinners as a creditor is under to discharge a debtor, on having received full satisfaction at the hands of a surety" (A. Fuller, "The Gospel Its Own Witness," in *The Complete Works of the Rev. Andrew Fuller*, 2:82). Fuller "acknowledges he never could perceive that any clear or determinate idea was conveyed by the term *purchase*, in this connexion; nor does it appear to him to be applicable to the subject, unless it be in an improper or figurative sense" (ibid.; emphasis in original). For Chambers's refutation of Owen's argument on the purchase of faith, see "A Critical Examination of John Owen's Argument for Limited Atonement in 'The Death of Death in the Death of Christ'" (ThM thesis, Reformed Theological Seminary, 1998), 195–217, 221–33. Chambers noted:

> Owen's talk of "purchase" could well be seen as having a distorting effect on the biblical idea of faith, by reifying it, making it a thing or object or commodity, instead of a relational response. The phrase "purchase of faith" is a category confusion, for trust, like love, can only be given by the subject, not bought, and arises in the subject (ibid., 228).

Phil 1:29 is the key text used to argue that faith has been directly purchased for the elect by Christ. The relationship between the grant to believe and Christ is never exactly stated. And, given what the passage says, if it can be affirmed that our suffering for Christ is not a direct purchase of the atonement, then neither is the grant to believe. Thanks to David Ponter for this insight.

There is no biblical statement affirming such a covenant. Piper cannot demonstrate anywhere from Scripture the notion that faith is something "purchased" for the elect at the cross. Such language finds no support in the NT. Where Owen and Piper err is in thinking that faith as a gift is equivalent to faith as a purchase. There is no causal link between the death of Christ and subjective faith. In Piper's scheme, faith becomes something of a commodity, an object instead of a relational response. This is a category confusion on his part.

"Gift" is the language of grace. "Purchase" is the language of rights. Owen's notion of the "purchase of faith" is a theoretical construct dependent on the so-called covenant of redemption and a commercialistic understanding of the atonement. In fact, Owen even states that the elect are owed salvation and have a "right" to it.[397]

Four-Point Calvinism? (648–56)

Piper critiques the views of Bruce Ware, professor of theology at Southern Seminary, Gary Shultz, Senior Pastor of First Baptist Church Fulton, Missouri, and theology professor at Baptist Bible Theological Seminary and Liberty University, and Gerry Breshears, professor of systematic theology at Western Seminary, who co-authored a book on the atonement with Mark Driscoll. Piper recognizes that so-called four-point Calvinism is not new (the section heading here reads "A Modern Appearance of an Old Error"—assuming the section headings are his and not the editor's).

Piper chooses not to address any of the historical material on this subject as do many in *From Heaven He Came*. Ware has not published on the subject, and Piper is basing his discussion on Ware's unpublished class notes and some personal correspondence. Furthermore, Piper admits he has not read Shultz's dissertation but is basing his critique on a twelve-page article by Shultz published in 2010. Finally, the relevant material on the atonement in the Breshears/Driscoll volume is less than twenty pages,[398] and the relevant material on extent is only four pages.

The uninformed reader might get the impression from Piper that moderate Calvinism (four-point Calvinism) is somehow a latecomer or even an aberration in Reformed theology. Notice how Piper refers to the "traditional Reformed view of definite atonement."[399] On the same page one finds this section heading: "Is a Revision of the Historic Reformed View of Definite Atonement Necessary?" Limited atonement is *a* traditional view within Reformed theology, but it is not *the* traditional view, nor is it the oldest view within the Reformed camp. Moderate Calvinism was the original position of early Reformed theology. Virtually every one, if not all, of the first gen-

397 J. Owen, "The Death of Death in the Death of Christ," 10:223–24.

398 Mark Driscoll and Gerry Breshears, *Doctrine: What Christians Should Believe* (Wheaton, IL: Crossway, 2010), 267–70.

399 Piper, "'My Glory I Will Not Give to Another!' Preaching the Fullness of Definite Atonement to the Glory of God," 656.

eration among the Reformed held it. Furthermore, Richard Muller, among others, including some in this book, have demonstrated that Amyraldianism and Hypothetical Universalism are within the boundaries of confessional Reformed theology.

Piper's approach is to indict Ware on the charge of the double payment argument. He thinks Ware "has failed to distinguish between a penal sentence and the actual execution of that sentence."[400] I have already critiqued the double payment argument in a previous chapter review. Suffice it to say that the double payment argument has been critiqued by many within the Reformed tradition, including J. Davenant, R. Baxter, E. Polhill, C. Hodge, R. Dabney, and W. G. T. Shedd.

Piper misses Ware's point about the elect remaining under the wrath of God until they repent and have faith (Eph 2:1–3). Of course the sentence has not been carried out on them. The point is, as Piper himself admits, "Until the point of faith, they were heading to hell."[401] Piper explains the time delay between the atonement and the application of the atonement with the analogy of a prisoner whose debt has been paid, but the paperwork takes time to process and be applied to the prisoner. This is a very poor analogy and does not explain the fact that even the unbelieving elect remain under the wrath of God and would be eternally lost should they die before they believe, as Piper has admitted. No other meaning can be assigned to Eph 2:1–3.

Are People in Hell Now Reconciled to God through Christ?

Piper's further attempts to explain the difference between the wrath of God for the unbelieving elect and the non-elect in hell are also problematic. He returns to his critique of Ware at this point. At issue for Piper is Ware's use of the term "reconciliation."[402] Piper fails to discern that the biblical concept of reconciliation à la 2 Cor 5:18–21 involves both objective and subjective reconciliation.[403] By the death of Christ on the cross, there is a sense in which God is reconciled to the world in that the payment for sin has been made. But 2 Cor 5:18–21 goes on to explain that in addition to this objective reconciliation, there must occur a subjective reconciliation whereby people turn to God through Christ by repentance and faith.

All unbelievers in hell were the beneficiaries of God's objective reconciliation through Christ's death on the cross. Had they repented and believed the gospel, they would have been saved. But the Scripture is clear that no one is saved by this objective reconciliation alone. There must be subjective reconciliation as well. This is Ware's point, which Piper criticizes.

Although I might word some of Ware's points differently (I would agree with Piper's

400 Ibid., 650.

401 Ibid.

402 Ibid., 652–55.

403 See L. Morris's defense of this point in his excellent treatment of reconciliation in *The Apostolic Preaching of the Cross*, 3rd rev. ed. (Grand Rapids, MI: Eerdmans, 1965), 214–50.

demurral at using the term "peace with God" to describe those in hell), in essence Ware is correct in what he affirms about reconciliation.

Definite Atonement and the Free Offer of the Gospel

Piper asserts his belief that the free offer of the gospel to all people is one of the "benefits" or "intentions" of God in the atonement.[404] Scripture teaches the "free offer" of the gospel to all. But this is not something that the atonement itself "accomplished," especially on Piper's view of things. In fact, this is one of the key problems with definite atonement and is one of two main reasons why so many in the Reformed tradition, like Bruce Ware, reject it (the other being the exegetical evidence is clearly against limited atonement).

Piper correctly states that Shultz argues one cannot preach the gospel sincerely to all people on the platform of definite atonement: "If Christ did not pay for the sins of the non-elect, then it is impossible to genuinely offer salvation to the non-elect, since there is no salvation available to offer them."[405] Piper takes strong umbrage at this claim. This claim articulated by Shultz has been made by many in the Reformed tradition since the days of the ascendency of limited atonement in the late sixteenth century.

Piper, quoting Roger Nicole, totally misses the point of Shultz's argument: "If the terms of the offer be observed, that which is offered be actually granted."[406] Certainly no one disputes this. All Calvinists and all non-Calvinists agree with this statement. Piper attempts to justify the validity of an "offer" if the one offering "always and without fail gives what is offered to everyone who meets the terms of the offer."[407] But is this all that is necessary? What would constitute a valid offer? At least four elements would seem to be necessary.

1. The one offering sincerely desires to give something.
2. The one offering possesses that which he offers.
3. The one offering desires that the thing offered be accepted.
4. The recipients of the offer are able to fulfill the condition of the offer.

The key point Shultz is making is that one has to be able to give what is offered to any and everyone who comes. The simple fact is, according to definite atonement, if one of the non-elect were to respond to the offer, it would be impossible for God to give salvation for no atonement exists for the non-elect to be given to any one of them.

Piper, following John Murray, attempts to blunt the force of this by arguing that

404 Piper, "'My Glory I Will Not Give to Another!' Preaching the Fullness of Definite Atonement to the Glory of God," 657–64.
405 Ibid., 658.
406 Ibid., 658–59.
407 Ibid., 659.

what is offered in the gospel is Christ. This is a clever sidestepping of the issue. Of course it is Christ who is offered! But on what grounds is Christ offered to all? He can be offered only on the grounds that he has paid the price for every person's sin. Furthermore, though Piper himself does not make the claim, it will not do to argue that the non-elect will not come since they are not given the effectual call. This, too, sidesteps the issue.

Here is an example of Piper's logic:

> What is offered to the world, to everyone who hears the gospel, is not a love or a saving achievement designed for all and therefore especially for no one; but rather, what is offered is the absolute fullness of all that Christ achieved for his elect. This fullest of all possible achievements is offered to all—because Christ is offered to all. And thus definite atonement turns out to be the only ground of a fully biblical offer of the gospel.[408]

1. What is offered is offered to the "world, to everyone who hears the gospel."
2. What is offered is not something "designed" for all.
3. What is offered to the whole world is the "absolute fullness of all that Christ achieved for his elect."

How, by any stretch of logic, can that which Christ designed and achieved only for the elect be offered to everyone in the world? Piper's conclusion, "And thus definite atonement turns out to be the only ground of a fully biblical offer of the gospel," is totally unwarranted. This claim is astounding to me. Piper thinks that all Calvinists and non-Calvinists who affirm unlimited atonement do not have grounds for offering the gospel in a "fully biblical" manner.

Piper turns from a consideration of the validity of the universal offer to the genuineness of that offer.[409] First, he mentions those who appeal to God's foreknowledge as problematic for the sincerity of the gospel offer. I do not know of a single Calvinist or non-Calvinist who makes the argument that the offer of salvation to all cannot be sincere since Christ knows who will accept and who will not. The reason the offer cannot be sincere on a definite atonement scheme is because the non-elect are being offered something that does not, in fact, exist for them.

Second, Piper states that the "bottom line objection" is not what God knows but what God desires. Piper takes the position of most Calvinists by arguing that God is able to desire something sincerely, yet nevertheless decide that what he desires will not come to pass. But again, Piper engages in a subtle shift away from the issue at hand. The issue

408 Ibid., 659–60.
409 Ibid., 661–64.

is not the question of God's two wills, as many affirm in Reformed theology. The issue is God offering something to the non-elect that does not exist for them to receive.

Piper never answers this question. He rather engages in futile evasions. His argument here is off point and is simply a red herring. I might also add that it is ultimately incoherent to argue that we do not offer people the possibility of salvation. Even on the Reformed understanding of salvation, salvation for the elect is both possible and inevitable because of election and efficacious calling. Unless one wants to argue for justification in eternity or justification at the cross (hyper-Calvinist errors), then one has to affirm Christ's death makes salvation possible until the point of faith when that salvation is applied to the elect.

Piper's Conclusion: Preach the Fullness of Definite Atonement

Piper concludes that the aim of preaching is to display the fullness of God's glory. "The glory of the cross is the fullness of its definite achievement. Therefore, we diminish the glory of the cross and the glory of grace and the glory of God when we diminish definite atonement."[410] Just the opposite is true. There is no statement in Scripture that says Christ died only for the sins of the elect. There are many statements that affirm Christ died for the sins of all.

When we fail to preach the gospel of 1 Cor 15:3, which includes preaching the fact of Christ's death for the sins of all people, we diminish the glory of the cross and the glory of grace and the glory of God—and the glory of God's love.

God's glory is indeed what it is all about. Unlimited atonement brings God not just "greater glory" but maximal glory.

Among the reviews of *From Heaven He Came and Sought Her* is one by Michael Lynch, PhD student under Richard Muller at Calvin Theological Seminary.[411] Lynch is a moderate Calvinist. Lynch found many of the same problems with this book as I have enumerated above. "Even so, the book contains confusing claims that call into question whether this book can be recommended as a consistent and accurate defense of definite atonement. *From Heaven He Came and Sought Her* lacks sufficient precision over how definite atonement relates to redemption accomplished in distinction from redemption applied."[412] Lynch found the most glaring deficiency in the book to be the ambiguity over the definition of definite atonement in the introductory essay:

> Generally speaking, the book's *de facto* definition often amounts to little more than this: God intended or designed to savingly *apply* the benefits of the death of Christ to the elect alone. That God designed the death of Christ to be sav-

---

410 Ibid., 667.

411 M. Lynch, "Book Review of *From Heaven He Came and Sought Her*," *Calvin Theological Journal* 49 (2014): 352–54.

412 Ibid., 352.

> ingly applied only to the elect is hardly controversial among any confessional Reformed theologian, whether he or she affirms hypothetical universalism or not. Instead, the book only obfuscates the real issue that advocates of definite atonement should be arguing, namely, that Christ made a satisfaction only for the sins of the elect.[413]

He correctly pointed out that "this confusion over what is and is not definite atonement unfortunately persists not merely in the introductory essay but throughout the whole."[414]

Lynch had further concerns about some of the historical misreadings in the chapters by David Hogg and Michael Haykin. Lynch does not find the book to surpass Owen's classic *The Death of Death in the Death of Christ* "in terms of precision or cogency of argument."[415]

---

413 Ibid., 353.
414 Ibid.
415 Ibid., 354.

9

Why Belief in Unlimited Atonement Matters

A significant portion of this work has been an exercise in historical theology. The following chart lists representative names, most of whom are discussed above, in the four categories Arminianism, Classic/Moderate Calvinism, High Calvinism, and Hyper-Calvinism.[1] Compare this chart with the one in the introduction listing and defining each of these four categories.

1 Not every group is captured within these categories. Baptists who are non-Calvinists for the most part do not consider themselves Arminians since they differ on matters such as eternal security but agree with them on the extent question. Also, there is much diversity within each of the groups listed. Some high Calvinists are higher than others, but they all affirm general love, general grace, and the free offer of the gospel. Some in the hyper-Calvinist category are more extreme than others. A name is listed in the hyper-Calvinist group if they (1) deny that God loves the non-elect in any sense, *or* (2) deny common grace, *or* (3) deny the well-meant offer, *or* (4) deny human responsibility to evangelically repent and believe the gospel (i.e., "duty-faith").

Notable Representatives on the Extent of the Atonement

Arminianism	Classic/Moderate Calvinism	High Calvinism	Hyper-Calvinism
J. Arminius, S. Episcopius, J. Goodwin, H. Grotius, J. Horn, D. Whitby, J. Wesley, R. Watson, T. Grantham, A. Clarke, J. Taylor, T. Summers, W. B. Pope, J. Miley, H. O. Wiley, D. Moody, I. H. Marshall, H. Hammond, J. Griffith, S. Loveday, G. Cockerill, S. Ashby, M. Pinson, J. M. Hicks, P. Marston, R. Forster, J. Dongell, S. Harper, S. Hauerwas, W. Willimon, S. Grenz, J. Cottrell, L. F. Forlines, R. Picirilli, J. Walls, R. Shank, R. Dunning, S. Witzki, J. K. Grider, R. Olson, G. Osborne	J. Calvin, P. Vermigli, W. Musculus, J. Oecolampadius, G. Zanchi, A. Marlorate, H. Bullinger, U. Zwingli, M. Luther, Z. Ursinus, J. Kimedoncius, D. Paraeus, R. Rollock, T. Cranmer, H. Latimer, M. Coverdale, J. Ussher, J. Davenant, E. Culverwell, S. Ward, J. Hall, L. Crocius, J. H. Alsted, M. Martinius, J. Cameron, M. Amyraut, J. Daillé, J. Preston, G. Bucanus, R. Baxter, E. Polhill, R. Harris, J. Saurin, E. Calamy, S. Marshall, R. Vines, L. Seaman, H. Scudder, J. Arrowsmith, T. Adams, J. Bunyan, S. Charnock, J. Howe, W. Bates, J. Humfrey, J. Truman, G. Swinnock, J. Edwards, D. Brainerd, A. Fuller (later writings), J. C. Ryle, T. Chalmers, R. Wardlaw, A. Strong, N. Douty, A. C. Clifford, M. Erickson, B. Demarest, C. Daniel, B. Ware	T. Beza, W. Perkins, W. Ames, S. Rutherford, E. Reynolds, J. Owen, F. Turretin, H. Witsius, T. Goodwin, O. Sedgwick, D. Dickson, J. Durham, H. Knollys, B. Keach, H. Collins, T. Ridgley, E. Coles, A. Booth, C. Spurgeon, J. L. Dagg, A. Kuyper, B. B. Warfield, W. Cunningham, J. Girardeau, H. Bavink, A. A. Hodge, L. Berkhof, L. Boettner, J. Murray, K. Stebbins, G. Bahnsen, I. Murray, E. Hulse, J. I. Packer, R. Nicole, R. C. Sproul, D. Wilson, M. Horton, D. Steele, C. Thomas, R. K. M. Wright, W. Grudem, S. L. Johnson, S. Storms, G. Long, J. MacArthur, J. Piper, A. Mohler	R. Davis, J. Hussey, J. Skepp, J. Gill, J. Brine, W. Gadsby, W. Huntington, J. C. Philpot, J. Wells, W. J. Styles, W. Rushton, A. Pink (early writings), Herman and Homer Hoeksema, H. Hanko, G. Clark, J. Gerstner (later writings), D. Engelsma, J. Robbins, V. Cheung, G. Ella, R. L. Reymond

The historical evidence on the extent of the atonement from the Reformation until 1650 can be summarized in four statements. First, nearly all, if not all, of the earliest Reformers, including Calvin, held to a form of universal atonement.[2] Second, limited atonement as a doctrinal position was developed in the second and third generation of Reformers, beginning primarily with Beza. Third, the Synod of Dort debated the issue extensively and the final language of Dort was deliberately left ambiguous on the subject so as to allow those among the delegates who rejected strict particularism and who held to a form of universal atonement to sign the final document. Fourth, the Westminster Assembly consisted of a significant minority of delegates who rejected limited atonement and affirmed a form of universal atonement.

The controversy that took place within the second and third generations of Reformed theologians was not the rejection of limited atonement but the introduction of limited atonement. In fact, chronologically, after the introduction of limited atonement, Calvinism slowly began to open the door to the rejection of the free gospel offer.[3] When the free offer was finally and explicitly rejected, hyper-Calvinism was born.[4] One should note hyper-Calvinism is not a necessary corollary of limited atonement, though many Calvinists past and present have been led down its path, which began with limited atonement.

This diversity on the extent of the atonement continued to develop in the seventeenth through nineteenth centuries in both England and America. Many Calvinists across denominational lines were moderate on the extent question. By the time of the founding of the Southern Baptist Convention in 1845, many Baptists were moderately Calvinistic in their theology, but there was simply no uniform agreement among them on the extent of the atonement, election, or irresistible grace. The historical evidence makes it no longer tenable to argue that virtually all of the early Southern Baptist leaders and laypeople alike were strict five-point Calvinists.

This work has sought to demonstrate that it was not unlimited atonement expressed in any variety, whether Hypothetical Universalism, Arminianism, Amyraldianism, Baxterianism, or otherwise, that was the theological innovation intruding on an already accepted limited atonement. The situation is just the reverse. Limited atonement is the innovator in church history. This point is vital to understand.

---

2 There is still some question in the minds of some scholars about the views of Martin Bucer and John Bradford.

3 In fact, there were already some extreme delegates to the Synod of Dort from Gelderland and Friesland who rejected indiscriminate gospel offers. See R. Godfrey, "Tensions within International Calvinism: The Debate on the Atonement at the Synod of Dort, 1618–1619" (PhD diss., Stanford University, 1974), 210; and G. M. Thomas, *The Extent of the Atonement: A Dilemma for Reformed Theology from Calvin to the Consensus (1536–1675)* (Carlisle, UK: Paternoster, 1997), 149.

4 See C. Daniel, "Hyper-Calvinism and John Gill" (PhD diss., University of Edinburgh, 1983), 514. It is not as though hyper-Calvinists were against preaching to all (contrary to popular opinion). Rather, they were against the idea that God is "offering" Christ to all and that preachers should indiscriminately do the same (ibid., 448–49; and I. H. Murray, *Spurgeon v. Hyper-Calvinism: The Battle for Gospel Preaching* [Edinburgh: Banner of Truth, 2000], 89).

The famous TULIP acronym as it appears in popular literature by Calvinists and non-Calvinists alike is unhelpful and counterproductive in setting out a Reformed soteriology. It actually did not enter into use until early in the twentieth century, most likely in a 1905 lecture by Dr. Cleland Boyd McAfee, a Presbyterian minister in Brooklyn.[5] The first influential popularization of the acronym was by Loraine Boettner in his *Reformed Doctrine of Predestination*.[6] This is especially true for the "L" in TULIP. "Limited Atonement," in its theological definition, means a limited substitution for sin. This is rejected by moderate Calvinists. However, all moderate Calvinists affirm, with all other Calvinists, whether high or hyper, that the atonement is "limited" in its application only to the elect because of God's elective purpose. If you ask a moderate Calvinist if he believes in "limited atonement" in the sense of the atonement accomplished, he would say "no." If you ask a moderate Calvinist if he believes in "limited atonement" in the sense of God's ultimate intent to save only the elect, he would say "yes." If you ask a moderate Calvinist if he believes in a "limited atonement" in the sense of its application, he would say "yes," as would all Arminians and non-Calvinists. The historical survey of moderate Calvinists who spoke on this subject confirms this reality.

One might ask why it was necessary to spend so much time on the historical aspect of this question. Although truth cannot be determined by counting noses, it is necessary to demonstrate the many in every generation of Reformed history who have rejected limited atonement. I have significant disagreements with many of these men in other areas of their Calvinism, not to mention their views on ecclesiology and baptism, but these disagreements do not negate the truth and significance of what they, as influential historic Calvinists, are admitting and affirming on the subject of the extent of the atonement.[7] Much has been written on the extent question in recent years, and much of it relies on modern secondary sources. There is often ignorance or confusion about the views of the early church, the early Reformers, the diverse opinions on the subject within the Puritan movement,[8] and eighteenth- and nineteenth-century Great Britain and New England.

Generally speaking, most modern Calvinists see only two basic theologies: Calvinism and Arminianism. For them, there is no middle ground. Within Calvinism itself they have two categories: high Calvinism and Amyraldianism (which is often filtered through unreliable secondary sources, which often incorrectly lump Hypothetical Universalism and Baxterianism in with it). All that is left falls under the banner of Arminianism. These kinds of distinctions are far too simplistic.[9] Calvinist Curt Daniel was right when he

---

5 W. Vail, "The Five Points of Calvinism Historically Considered," *The Outlook* 104 (1913): 394.

6 See L. Boettner, *The Reformed Doctrine of Predestination*, 3rd ed. (Grand Rapids, MI: Eerdmans, 1932), 59–60, 150–61.

7 As distinguished from what they say about Christ's intent and the nature of the application.

8 Few know about the views of John Howe and Stephen Charnock, for example. They both held to a Calvinistic form of universal redemption (see above).

9 Regarding the two categories within Calvinism, Muller has observed that the Ursinus, Bullinger, Musculus,

asserted: "Those who posit that there is no middle ground between Arminianism and Calvinism ignore the plain facts of church history."[10] For too many Calvinists today, middle ground views are simply rejected as being Arminian.

In light of the historical evidence, extreme claims of some high Calvinists and Arminians that no middle ground exists between Calvinism and Arminianism are unfounded. Michael Horton, for example, asserted, "There is no such thing as 'Calminianism.'"[11] Arminian Roger Olson takes the same tack as Horton.[12] R. C. Sproul's famous statement falls in this category: "I think that a four-point Calvinist is an Arminian."[13] The absurdity of this statement is now self-evident.

The fatal flaw in this logic is the failure to recognize that Anabaptism, Lutheranism, and moderate Calvinism antedated high and hyper-Calvinism. Chronologically, with respect to limited atonement, high Calvinism was late to the game and hyper-Calvinism was even later.[14]

Likewise, the historical record exposes the extremism of some high Calvinists and all hyper-Calvinists, especially when Calvinism is equated with the gospel itself. For example, Kuiper stated, "Next to the Bible itself the clearest and purest expression of this doctrine is found in the five points of Calvinism."[15] Compare this kind of statement with that of Calvinist Baptist Andrew Fuller in reference to his Calvinist opponents: "The writings of Calvin himself would now be deemed Arminian by a great number of our opponents."[16] John Gadsby recorded that his father, William Gadsby, "always considered, and often stated publically, that Andrew Fuller was the greatest enemy the church of God ever had, and his sentiments were so much cloaked with the sheep's clothing."[17]

The whole lapsarian project, with its concomitant extremist speculation concerning

---

Davenant, Ussher, and Preston trajectory is distinct from the Saumur model, even though all of them held to a form of "hypothetical universalism" (R. Muller, "Review of *English Hypothetical Universalism*," *Calvin Theological Journal* 43 [2008]: 149–50). Further, in his *Post-Reformation Reformed Dogmatics: The Rise and Development of Reformed Orthodoxy, ca. 1520 to ca. 1725*, 4 vols. (Grand Rapids, MI: Baker, 2003), 1:76–80, Muller stated that the Amyraldian view is compatible with Dort and the Westminster Confession. This means that there are, according to Muller, *at least three* branches *within* the Calvinistic position, a notion that has only begun to take hold in Reformed historiography over the past twenty years, yet many popular Calvinist books take virtually no notice of this understanding and continue to operate from an outdated historiography.

10 C. Daniel, "Hyper-Calvinism and John Gill," 732.

11 M. Horton, "Preface," in Roger Olson, *Against Calvinism* (Grand Rapids, MI: Zondervan, 2011), 10.

12 R. Olson, *Arminian Theology: Myths and Reality* (Downers Grove, IL: InterVarsity Academic, 2006), 61–77. Steve Lemke is correct in his assertion that both Horton and Olson are committing the logical error known as the "fallacy of false alternatives" ("Using Logic in Theology: The Fallacy of False Alternatives," *SBC Today: Southern Baptist News and Analysis*, June 3, 2011, http://sbctoday.com/using-logic-in-theology-the-fallacy-of-false-alternatives/).

13 R. C. Sproul, *The Truth of the Cross* (Stanford, FL: Reformation Trust, 2007), 140–41.

14 C. Daniel stated that "hyper-Calvinism was the intruder into Reformed theology" ("Hyper-Calvinism and John Gill," 768–69).

15 R. B. Kuiper, *For Whom Did Christ Die? A Study of the Divine Design of the Atonement* (Eugene, OR: Wipf & Stock, 2003), 70.

16 A. Fuller, "The Gospel Worthy of All Acceptation," in *The Complete Works of the Rev. Andrew Fuller*, 2:168.

17 J. Gadsby, *A Memoir of the Late Mr. William Gadsby* (Manchester: J. Gadsby, 1844), 34.

an *ordo salutis*, began in modern times with Theodore Beza[18] and William Perkins. Limited atonement is a part of this cocktail too.

Consider the difference between John Owen and John Calvin on the issue. For Calvin, Christ's death sufficiently paid the price for the sins of all people, and so all may receive God's offer of salvation. Muller correctly noted: "Yet, as we have seen, Calvin also consistently points to Christ's death as full payment for the sins of the world, undergirding, as it were, the indiscriminate proclamation of the gospel."[19] This was also the view of all first-generation Reformers, and has been the view of all moderate Calvinists since. Behind this was a particular understanding of the Lombardian formula "sufficient for all, but efficient for the elect only," namely, that Christ's death paid for the sins of all people, yet "efficient for the elect alone" in the sense that the benefits of the atonement are applied only to those who believe—namely, the elect. Calvin and all the early Reformers understood the Scriptures to teach that people perish not for a lack of an atonement for their sins but because of their own unbelief. Of course, regarding the efficiency side of the formula, all Calvinists affirm that the special grace necessary to bring the unbelieving elect to a state of belief is, at the time of the Spirit's effectual calling, "irresistible."

For Owen, on the other hand, Christ's death had no direct relationship or reference to the sins of the non-elect. There is a limited sin-bearing in the death of Christ: he died only for the sins of the elect. Owen and Calvin differ with respect to the sufficiency aspect of the Lombardian formula.

The same difference is found in Andrew Fuller when contrasted with Abraham Booth on the issue of sufficiency. Fuller came to see the problem of the free offer of the gospel from the platform of limited atonement in his debates with the General Baptist Dan Taylor. As a result, he rejected limited atonement and rewrote the section on the extent of the atonement in his second edition of *The Gospel Worthy* accordingly.[20]

Fuller and Booth clashed over this issue. Booth, like Owen, operated from a revised Lombardian Formula to make the sufficiency of Christ's death a hypothetical suffi-

18 Beza bought into some shaky exegesis and translations (mistranslations) of certain verses that were later used by federal Calvinists to support the system. For example, Muller stated: "Beza, by way of contrast, moves the text into new doctrinal associations by way of philological issues and re-translation. He renders the text 'Ego vero paciscor vobis, prout pactus est mihi Pater meus regnum,' rendering *diatithemi* as *paciscor*, 'to make a covenant' and, given the tenses of the verbs, we have, 'I make a covenant with you [present] . . . as my father has made a covenant with me [past]'" ("Toward the Pactum Salutis: Locating the Origins of a Concept," *Mid-America Journal of Theology* 18 [2008]: 40). See also M. Elliott's critique of Beza at this point, referencing Muller's statement above: "Beza has to leave '*regnum*' hanging in the verse. Can one really 'covenant a kingdom?' Is it not a fallacy typical of the theological exegete to see *diatithemi* and make its meaning follow that of the cognate substantive (*diatheke*)?" (M. W. Elliott, *The Heart of Biblical Theology: Providence Experienced* [Farnham, UK: Ashgate, 2013], 133).

19 R. Muller, *Calvin and the Reformed Tradition* (Grand Rapids, MI: Baker Academic, 2012), 82. See also ibid., 105: "Since Christ paid the price for all sin and accomplished a redemption capable of saving the whole world, his benefits are clearly placed before, proffered, or offered to all who hear."

20 See D. L. Allen, "Preaching for a Great Commission Resurgence," in *Great Commission Resurgence: Fulfilling God's Mandate in Our Time*, ed. Chuck Lawless and Adam Greenway (Nashville: B&H, 2010), 281–98.

ciency. For Booth, the death of Christ is only sufficient for those whom Christ substituted for on the cross: the elect. He wrote:

> While cheerfully admitting the sufficiency of Immanuel's death to have redeemed all mankind, had all the sins of the whole human species been equally imputed to him; and had he, as the Universal Representative, sustained that curse of the law which was due to all mankind; yet we cannot perceive any solid reason to conclude, that his propitiatory sufferings are sufficient for the expiation of sins which he did not bear, or for the redemption of sinners whom he did not represent, as a sponsor, when he expired on the cross. For the substitution of Christ, and the imputation of sin to him, are essential to the scriptural doctrine of redemption by our adorable Jesus.—We may, therefore, safely conclude, that our Lord's voluntary substitution, and redemption by his vicarious death, are both of them limited to those, for whom he was made sin—for whom he was made a curse—and for whose deliverance from final ruin, he actually paid the price of his own blood.[21]

Notice Booth's two kinds of sufficiency: hypothetical and actual. Booth, like Owen before him, has knowingly revised the Lombardian Formula.

All Calvinists would have to say that Jesus died for a particular people (his elect), but they need not say that he died for them *alone* or *only*, in the sense of having their sins alone imputed to him. "Particular redemption" is vague terminology historically speaking, since the term "redemption" can either reference the ransom price paid or the liberated/forgiven state that believers alone enjoy. This is why theologians talk of "redemption *accomplished*" and "redemption *applied*." One can believe in "particular redemption" in the sense that Christ purposes to effect the forgiven state (redemption *applied*) of all those appointed to eternal life (the elect) through an *unlimited* ransom price (redemption *accomplished*). Particular Redemptionists in this latter sense need not embrace Owen's limitation in redemption accomplished. All Calvinists who affirm an unlimited atonement also believe in a kind of particular redemption.

There is no particularity in the *imputation* of sin to Christ. Rather, the particularity, according to moderate Calvinists, is in God's special will in the case of the elect, such that he wills (according to his decree) *to apply* that all-sufficient death to the elect alone by granting them the *moral* ability to believe.[22] The particularity according to Arminians and other non-Calvinists lies in the application of the atonement only to those who believe the gospel.

---

21 A. Booth, "Divine Justice Essential to the Divine Character," in *The Works of Abraham Booth*, 3 vols. (London: Printed by J. Haddon, 1813), 3:61.

22 See R. Wardlaw's explanation in *Discourses on the Nature and Extent of the Atonement of Christ* (1843; repr. London: Forgotten Books, 2013), 207–8.

Thus, in summary, there are three views concerning the extent of the atonement among Calvinists.

1. The atonement is limited quantitatively (equivalentism) to the elect only. (John L. Dagg and Tom Nettles are examples.)
2. The atonement is limited in its design and extent to the elect only. (John Owen and Al Mohler are examples.)
3. The atonement is limited in its ultimate design or intent to be applied to the elect but is unlimited with respect to the satisfaction of the sins of all men. (John Davenant, Charles Hodge, Millard Erickson, Bruce Demarest, and Bruce Ware are examples.)

If, according to orthodox confessional Calvinism, God can will not to save all even though he is willing to save all, why cannot he will that Christ's death be a provision for all and yet give faith to some only? This is asked by Neil Chambers, a moderate Calvinist, who affirms unlimited atonement within the Reformed framework of moral inability and a compatibilist understanding of free will. His point is well-taken. Even within a Reformed framework, the analogy is valid (though from a non-Reformed framework, everyone has the ability to believe the gospel once it is heard due to God's provision of enabling grace through the Word and the work of the Spirit).

The Problem Stated, or Ambiguity and Equivocation in High Calvinism

Some Calvinists who affirm limited atonement maintain that Christ's atonement is sufficient for all people, even though it only satisfied for the sins of the elect.[23] In recent years in books, blogs, and other media, high Calvinists have attempted to address this issue.

The sufficiency argument of those who hold to limited atonement proceeds in this fashion: Christ died only for the sins of the elect. Nevertheless, the death of Christ is sufficient for all people in the sense of its infinite worth and value. Therefore we should preach the gospel to all people since it is sufficient and since we don't know who the elect are. Anyone who believes the gospel will be saved.

Here is the problem: How can Christ's substitutionary death be said to be sufficient

23 "Sufficient": adequate; enough; as much as needed; equal to what is needed or required; fully capable; ample; plenty; suitable; abundant; made or suited to the purpose of.

> If "atonement" is taken to mean the value or sufficiency of Christ's death, only a very few theologians involved in the early modern debates taught limited atonement—and if atonement is taken to mean the actual salvation accomplished in particular persons, then no one taught unlimited atonement (except perhaps the much-reviled Samuel Huber) (Muller, *Calvin and the Reformed Tradition*, 60–61).

for the sins of the entire world, when, according to limited atonement, no atonement for sins exists for the non-elect? What strict Calvinists are actually saying is that the atonement *would* or *could be* sufficient for all had God intended it to be sufficient for them. But God, according to them, did not intend the atonement to be made a ransom price on behalf of the non-elect, thus there is no satisfaction made for their sins. The sufficiency can only be understood to be a statement about the atonement's infinite intrinsic value, such that it could hypothetically be satisfactory for all, but it is not "extrinsically" or "actually" satisfactory for all.

The Problem Unrecognized by Many Calvinists

Many Calvinists don't seem to recognize the gravamen of this issue or are reluctant to address it. One can understand why: it renders the notion of limited atonement theologically problematic beyond repair. The only response to the dilemma is to use sufficiency language in broad, undefined ways in an attempt to cover over the problem. Many Calvinists who affirm universal atonement have for centuries pressed this issue with their high Calvinist counterparts, and the silence in response is deafening.[24]

Consequences of the Problem

Several consequences flow from the question of the sufficiency of the atonement and its extent:

1. If limited atonement is correct, Jesus did not substitute himself on the cross for the sins of the non-elect.
2. Therefore, it is impossible that the non-elect could ever be saved since there

24 For example, this very issue was addressed by John Davenant, leader of the English Delegation at Dort, and signatory of the Canons of Dort. Davenant spoke of an "ordained sufficiency," by which he meant that God designed and intended the atonement to satisfy for the sins of all men and not just the elect. Davenant was one of several at Dort who affirmed a universal atonement in terms of its extent. Matthias Martinius, delegate from Bremen, also argued the same position as Davenant. He said, "Nor here will it be enough to assert such a sufficiency of redemption as could be enough; but it is altogether such as is enough, and such as God and Christ have considered enough. For otherwise the gospel command and promise are destroyed" (See Edward D. Griffin, "An Humble Attempt to Reconcile the Differences of Christians Respecting the Extent of the Atonement," in *The Atonement: Discourses and Treatises* [Boston: Congregational Board of Publication, 1859], 371). In fact, as we have seen above, historians of Dort acknowledge that the final canon on the extent of the atonement was deliberately worded with ambiguity so that both those who held to a limited satisfaction for sins and those who held to a universal satisfaction for sins could sign it in good conscience. It should be noted that though these moderate Calvinists agree with their Arminian and non-Calvinist brothers on the extent of the atonement, they disagree over the special intent of Christ in making an atonement, since all Calvinists argue that God, from eternity, intended only to save the elect.

is no atonement made for their sins. They are in the same unsaveable state they would be if Jesus had never come at all. Or, as others have argued, they are no more saveable than fallen angels.

3. It is impossible that the atonement can ever be described as sufficiently able to save the non-elect in any way other than hypothetically: something can't be sufficient for anyone for whom it is nonexistent. To suggest otherwise is simply to engage in semantic word games, obfuscation, or equivocation.
4. Further complications emerge concerning the preaching of the gospel. How can preachers universally and indiscriminately offer the gospel in good faith to all people, which clearly includes many who are non-elect, when there is no gospel to offer them—that is, when there is no satisfaction for all their sins? The usual response from strict Calvinists is that we don't know who the elect are, so we offer the gospel to all. But this misses the point and the problem. The issue is not that we don't know who the elect are. That is a given. The issue is we are offering something to all people, including those who turn out to be non-elect, that indeed does not exist for all to whom the offer is made. An offer made to all sinners entails contradiction as the preacher knows that the satisfaction for sins by Christ on the cross was not made for all to whom the gospel comes, but he pretends and speaks as if there is a legitimate offer to all to whom the gospel is preached.
5. The problem is even more acute with respect to the gospel offer when it is understood that it is God himself making the offer through us.[25] Second Corinthians 5:18–20 makes it clear that it is God offering salvation to all people through the church *on the grounds of the atonement of Christ*. If he himself has limited that substitution to only the elect, how can he make such an offer genuinely to all people? It would appear such is not possible.
6. If Christ did not die for the sins of all people, what exactly is it unbelievers are guilty of rejecting? There is no atonement for their sins for them to reject. Unbelief of the gospel, by its very definition, involves rejection of God's provision of grace through Christ's death.
7. Scripture makes use of universal exhortations to believe the gospel. Limited atonement deprives these commands of their significance.

25 "This distinction between noetically-limited heralds and the noetically-perspicuous God serves to obscure the real question involved. In addition such a distinction neglects the truth that God speaks in and through the instrumentality of the preacher" (A. C. De Jong, *The Well-Meant Gospel Offer: The Views of H. Hoeksema and K. Schilder* [Franeker: T. Wever, 1954], 123).

For all who affirm limited atonement, the atonement can only be sufficient for those for whom it is efficient. Forget the fact, according to all Calvinists, that the non-elect will not be saved given God's discriminating purpose of election; this particular problem involves the fact that there is no atonement made for them in the first place. Double jeopardy indeed.

The Problem Illustrated in the Southern Baptist Calvinism Advisory Committee Statement

I was privileged in 2012 to be a part of the SBC's Calvinism Advisory Committee and the resulting statement, "Truth, Trust, and Testimony in a Time of Tension." I believe it is a helpful statement and serves as a good launching pad for further discussion. Documents of this nature sometimes contain some understandable ambiguity for the sake of unity. Let me state at the outset that I believe every signatory of the statement acted with a clear conscience and in good faith.

Consider the following two statements on this issue of "sufficiency" in "Truth, Trust, and Testimony in a Time of Tension" on the subject of the atonement of Christ:

> We affirm that the death of Jesus Christ on the cross was both penal and substitutionary and that the atonement He accomplished was sufficient for the sins of the entire world. We deny that there is anything lacking in the atonement of Christ to provide for the salvation of anyone.[26]

In the section on "Tensions," the following statement occurs: "We agree that the penal and substitutionary death of Christ was sufficient for the sins of the entire world, but we differ as to whether Jesus actually substituted for the sins of all people or only the elect."[27]

In the spirit of the document's call for continued dialogue, here is a question for those who affirm limited atonement: How can one affirm both of the above statements consistently? Notice in both statements the language "sufficient for the sins of the entire world" is used. As argued above, how can the atonement in any meaningful sense be said to be sufficient for the sins of the non-elect since there is no atonement for the sins of the non-elect? It would seem Calvinists who affirm limited atonement are forced to use the word "sufficient" only in a hypothetical way, which does not solve the problem.

---

26 Calvinism Advisory Committee, "Truth, Trust, and Testimony in a Time of Tension: A Statement from the Calvinism Advisory Committee," *SBC Life: Journal of the Southern Baptist Convention*, June 2013, http://www.sbclife.net/Articles/2013/06/sla5.

27 Ibid.

In fact, it creates a logical problem, a theological problem, and a practical problem with respect to preaching and evangelism.

All who affirm limited atonement face the problem of the free offer of the gospel. In their system, the atonement is actually only sufficient for those who believe.

Strict Calvinists wind up clouding the issue of sufficiency when they tell us that Christ's death is sufficient in the sense that if anyone believes the gospel, he will find a sufficient atonement for his sins. Therefore, all people are saveable, insofar as if anyone believes, he will be saved. Well of course. No one doubts that. That proposition is true as far as it goes because it only speaks to the causal relationship between faith and salvation: anyone who truly believes will certainly be saved. But strict Calvinists exhibit their confusion on this issue when asked why this is so. Their response: because there is an atonement of infinite value able to be applied to the one who believes. Of course there is. But ask the question this way: suppose one of the non-elect should believe. Could he be saved? Not according to the limited atonement position because no satisfaction for sins exists for the non-elect.[28]

Imagine that Christ had not died at all on the cross. Now, in such a scenario, imagine this statement: "If anyone believes in Christ, he shall be saved." Such a statement is meaningless and is, in fact, false. In this scenario, there is no means provided for anyone to be saved regardless of whether they believe or not. This is precisely where the non-elect stand in this world in relation to the cross of Christ and their sin in the limited atonement scheme.

My argument is simple: if there is no atonement for some people, then those people are not saveable. If no atonement exists for some, how is it possible that the gospel can be *offered* to those people for whom no atonement exists? If anyone is not saveable, he is not offerable. One cannot offer salvation in any consistent way to someone for whom no atonement exists. Strict Calvinists cannot have it both ways. Either Christ has substituted for the sins of all men or he has not.[29]

This is the huge blind spot most strict Calvinists exhibit. Most Southern Baptists have long staked their claim that all people can be saved because Christ died for all.[30] Universal atonement grounds the free offer of the gospel to all people.

---

28 Some may try to parry the issue by arguing that the non-elect will not believe because they cannot believe apart from effectual calling. There are two problems with this response. First, it begs the question whether the Reformed understanding of total depravity as total inability and the Reformed notion of effectual calling are correct. Second, even if these are correct, the problem is not lessened: one cannot offer something to another in good faith when that "something" does not exist.

29 See my critique of D. A. Carson on his ambiguous use of "sufficiency" with respect to the extent of the atonement above and in D. L. Allen, "The Atonement: Limited or Universal?," in *Whosoever Will: A Biblical-Theological Critique of Five-Point Calvinism*, ed. D. L. Allen and S. Lemke (Nashville: B&H Academic, 2010), 89–91.

30 This is certainly the implication of the following statement in the Article on Man in the *Baptist Faith and Message*: "The sacredness of human personality is evident in that God created man in His own image, and in that Christ died for man; therefore, every person of every race possesses full dignity and is worthy of respect and Christian love."

Scripture and the Extent of the Atonement

In my attempt to read broadly in this area over the past several years, I have observed a particular strategy of high Calvinists when it comes to the actual key biblical texts dealing with the extent of the atonement. They often inform the reader that there are two kinds of texts in the New Testament that play a key role in the question of extent. There are those texts that use words like "all" and "world" with reference to the death of Christ. Then there are those texts that speak of Christ dying for his "sheep" or for the "church." Then something like the following claim is either assumed or asserted: the Bible equally affirms a limited aspect to the atonement and an unlimited aspect. The limited texts can only be contextually understood to refer to Christ dying only for the sins of those mentioned in the restricted group. The universal texts are either speaking of the gospel offer, which is for all the world, or using terms like "world" and "all" to refer to (1) all the elect (where the elect believing and unbelieving throughout history are meant), (2) Jews and Gentiles, or (3) all kinds or groups of people in the world.

This claim, whether assumed or asserted, is unsubstantiated. First, as virtually all high Calvinists agree, there is not one single text in Scripture that affirms a strictly limited atonement. Second, there are far more texts that speak of the universal aspect of the atonement rather than the limited aspect. This notion that there is an "equal" number of texts that address the subject is simply false. Third, as I have attempted to demonstrate in this work, it is not hermeneutically or contextually possible to interpret "world" and "all" in the disputed texts in a limitarian fashion where there is no contextual reason to assign such a restricted meaning.

This is a linguistic/exegetical issue. Sometimes the Bible uses the words "all" and "world" in a sense that does not mean, "all without exception." This point is not in dispute. The problem lies in the invalid hermeneutical/exegetical legerdemain that transmutes the words "all" or "world" into something less than all humanity in the New Testament passages where it is used in direct and indirect reference to the extent of the atonement.

Passages like John 1:29,[31] John 3:16, and 1 Tim 2:4–6 simply cannot be shackled with the limiting lexical chains that restrict the meaning of "world" and "all" to something less than all humanity. This is a huge linguistic mistake. As many Calvinists have rightly pointed out, "world" in Scripture never means "the elect." Context usually makes it clear whether "all" or "world" means "all without exception" or whether the focus is on all classes of people, which would still include all without exception. It is simply not exegetically possible to interpret "all" and "world" in the three texts listed above, and several others, in a limited fashion.

31 Leon Morris correctly noted that in passages like John 1:29, the reference is to the totality of the world's sin, rather than to a number of individual acts of sin (*The Gospel According to John*, 148).

Of course it is true that in writing to the church, New Testament authors speak of the atonement in reference to their audience. Thus it is not surprising to find them saying things like Christ died for the church, and so on. Why would we require the biblical authors to note in every instance when they speak of the death of Christ in relationship to believers that they also mean to affirm Christ died for the sins of all people? Why would we assume that such is the case unless we bring a preconceived theology to the text?

Calvinists often appeal to Paul's preaching in Acts to support the contention that the Apostles never used such language as "Christ died for your sins." They conclude from this lacuna that Paul never employed such a phrase in evangelistic preaching or witnessing, and this is evidence for limited atonement. But is such a conclusion valid?

First, this is an argument from silence. It does not conclusively prove Paul, Peter, or anyone else did not say it, nor is it a valid argument that they did not believe it. Second, all the sermons in Acts are condensed versions of the actual sermons given. Third, with respect to Peter's sermon in Acts 3, how else could he tell his hearers to "repent and be baptized in the name of Jesus Christ for the forgiveness of your sins" (Acts 3:19) if he did not somehow connect the death of Christ on the cross as accomplishing the means for their forgiveness and salvation? Are we to think that Peter's hearers did not understand that what Peter was saying in essence was that since Christ died for their sins, the door is opened for them to repent and believe? Furthermore, if Peter believed in limited atonement, how could he say "it was for you first that God raised up his Servant, and sent him to bless you by turning every one of you [*hekastos* in Greek meaning 'each one, every one'][32] from your wicked ways" (Acts 3:26)? For any of the non-elect present in his audience, there was no atonement for them, so it would be impossible for them to be saved, even if they wanted to. It would also be disingenuous on Peter's part to give anyone such false hope.

Paul did indeed tell unsaved people that Christ died for their sins, and furthermore it was his consistent practice to do so according to 1 Cor 15:3: "For I passed on to you as most important what I also received: that Christ died for our sins according to the Scriptures." Here Paul is reminding the Corinthians of the message he preached to them when he first came to Corinth (Acts 18:1–18). He clearly affirms the content of the gospel he preached in Corinth included the fact that "Christ died for our sins." Notice carefully that Paul is saying this is what he preached pre-conversion, not post-conversion. Thus the "our" in his statement cannot be taken to refer to all the elect or merely the believing elect, which is what the high Calvinist is forced to argue. Notice how Paul connects what he says in verse 3 with verse 11: "Whether then it was I or they, so we preached and so you believed." Paul's use of the customary present tense in Greek

32 W. Bauer, *Greek-English Lexicon of the New Testament and Other Early Christian Literature*, trans. and rev. F. W. Danker, W. F. Arndt, and F. W. Gingrich, 3rd ed. (Chicago: University of Chicago Press, 2000), 298.

("so we preach") coupled with his use of the aorist tense in Greek ("believed") makes clear he refers to a past point in time when the Corinthians believed what it was Paul's custom to preach. According to verse 3, Paul's custom was to preach to the unsaved "Christ died for our sins."

The assertion that Paul did not preach a universal atonement is false based on 1 Cor 15:3–11. What do we mean when we preach to the unsaved, "Christ died for your sins"? Do we not intend to convey that God desires to save all and that God is prepared to save any and all since Christ's death is actually sufficient to save them? One wonders if a reluctance to say "Christ died for you" implicitly expresses a reluctance to tell unsaved people that God is willing to save them all and is prepared to do so as well if they will repent and believe.

Finally, this argument that the apostles never used such language as "Christ died for your sins" is a double-edged sword. Neither is it *explicitly* said in the NT scriptures by any evangelist to a lost person that "God loves you," even though all orthodox Calvinists affirm that the idea is *implied*. Shall we conclude that the apostles and inspired authors did *not* believe in God's universal benevolent love since they nowhere *explicitly* said to the lost, "God loves you"? Hyper-Calvinists use that sort of argument on the love of God, and high Calvinists use a parallel argument when they appeal to the absence of explicit "Christ died for you" language in the NT. Both are fallacious.

The Love of God and the Extent of the Atonement

Limited atonement cuts across the biblical revelation of the love of God. If God determined that Christ died only for the sins of the elect, then it is clear that he loves the elect more and in a drastically different way as compared to the non-elect. John Frame spoke of God's temporal love for the non-elect, which is to be distinguished from his saving love, which only terminates on the elect.[33] Passages such as John 3:16 that teach God's love for all the world must be taken at face value. How can God be said to love someone in the gospel offer when he has not provided a means for their salvation via an atonement?

One should distinguish where and how it is that high and moderate Calvinists differ on the issue of God's love for the elect and non-elect, and where they agree. Both agree to distinguish God's love for the elect from the non-elect in the sense that God only provides the necessary saving grace through the effectual call to redeem the elect. All Calvinists, because of their doctrine of unconditional election, must talk about God's love in ways that distinguish between different kinds of God's love for the elect

33 J. Frame, *The Doctrine of God* (Philadelphia: P&R, 2002), 417–20.

and non-elect.[34] Some prefer to say that God has a "special" or "saving" love for the elect that he does not have for the non-elect.

Both agree, at least most in both camps agree, that humanity has the natural capacity to believe but does not have the moral capacity to believe apart from the effectual calling, which comes only to the elect. But moderates assert that God's love for his world, as the Scripture teaches, extends to the point of Christ dying for the sins of all humanity, such that if anyone does believe, they shall be saved, based on an extrinsically sufficient atonement made for all. On this construct, no one perishes for lack of an atonement for his sins. On the high Calvinist construct, the non-elect could not be saved even if they wanted to because limited atonement by definition asserts there is no atonement for their sins. This would seem to run counter to the biblical revelation of the omnibenevolence of God and Christ for the entire world.

All non-Calvinists find this notion of God's "saving love" or "special love" as defined by Calvinists to be problematic. God's love is expressed in actual relationship with all believers in a way that is not the case with unbelievers. But it is a different matter to suggest, as all Calvinists do, that God places a saving love on some individuals and not on others. From a non-Calvinist perspective, Scripture does not make such a distinction.[35]

Henry Sheldon's point about this notion of God's "special love" is worthy of consideration:

> Predestinarians are wont to descant on the special love of God, as though a love which is entirely independent of relative worthiness of its objects, and passes by some to fasten exclusively upon others, constitutes a pleasing mystery. However, a love of this kind belongs to a pathological condition. It is quite possible to limited beings in whom feeling and reason are not necessarily in true coordination. But to impute it to God, whose feeling never outruns His all-perfect intelligence, is without any rational warrant. The differing measures of His love must be supposed to correspond to the differing realities of its objects. He is not liable to untruth in His feelings any more than He is liable to error in His intellectual perceptions.[36]

John Peckham's monograph, *The Love of God: A Canonical Model*, is an excellent treatment of the subject with significant bearing on the extent of the atonement. Peckham inductively analyzed all the texts in Scripture that speak directly or indirectly to the love of God. He examined the transcendent-voluntarist and immanent-

34 See Carson, *The Difficult Doctrine of the Love of God* (Wheaton, IL: Crossway, 1999).

35 In this vein, corporate election of Israel in the OT should not be used as a paradigm for NT salvific election.

36 H. C. Sheldon, *System of Christian Doctrine* (Cincinnati: Jennings and Graham, 1903), 433.

experientialist models of divine love within theology today and found elements of truth as well as weaknesses in both.

Scripture teaches God universally seeks a relationship of reciprocal love, but he also enters into a particular relationship only with those who respond appropriately to his love.[37]

"God's love for the world is volitional, but neither necessary nor exclusively volitional."[38] Peckham argued that such passages as Exod 33:19 and Rom 9:15–18 do not support the notion that God's love is *exclusively* volitional in an arbitrary election of some people to receive salvation while mercy is withheld from others.[39]

Malachi 1:2–3 speaks of God's "love" for Jacob and "hatred" for Esau. Reformed theologians interpret this passage as election and rejection. But Peckham countered that in this context the Hebrew word translated "love" does not mean "choose." Exegetically, in every other biblical instance that speaks of God's "hatred" toward people, such a disposition is prompted by their evil actions.[40] God's response is not arbitrary but evaluative. God's treatment of Israel in compassion and grace "is a model of what he will bestow on all sinners who accept his love (Jn 3:16; Rom 10:13; 1 Jn 1:9)."[41] This carries over into Paul's comments on this passage in Romans 9.

Peckham stated: "Many passages in the canon explicitly present God's call and election as conditional on response, yet no passage clearly depicts either God's call or election as unilaterally effective."[42] According to Matt 22:1–4, the called are not always the chosen. Jesus describes the chosen as those who accept the invitation. "The divine-human love relationship enjoyed by the elect, then, requires appropriate response (compare Rom 10:9, 12–13; 11:22–23)."[43]

There is no example in Scripture of causally determined love. Scripture regularly depicts God's love and human love as voluntary.[44] Peckam further argued that God's love is evaluative. "Throughout Scripture, God enjoys, delights in, appreciates and finds value in humans. God's love for humans is explicitly linked to evaluative pleasure and/or displeasure semantically and thematically."[45] Likewise, God's displeasure in Scripture is never stated to be arbitrary but is always motivated and prompted by evil.[46]

Peckham spoke of God's love as "foreconditional," by which he means "God's love

37 J. Peckham, *The Love of God: A Canonical Model* (Downers Grove, IL: InterVarsity, 2015), 67.
38 Ibid., 90.
39 Ibid., 98–100.
40 Ibid., 105.
41 Ibid., 106.
42 Ibid., 109.
43 Ibid., 110.
44 Ibid., 113.
45 Ibid., 118–19.
46 Ibid., 126.

is freely bestowed prior to any conditions but not exclusive of conditions."[47] He is careful to note the absolute priority of divine love in the divine-human relationship. God's love initiates all love. Human love is neither primary nor meritorious in God's eyes. Peckham rightly noted that unmerited love is not the same as unconditional love. "Something may be conditional, yet unmerited, contingent on response but not thereby earned or deserved when it is received."[48]

For Peckham, unconditional love is not greater than conditional love. "When God finally cuts off those who have rejected him, it is only in response to their *final* decision to shut him out. When (insofar as he is committed to respecting their free will to love or not love) there is nothing more he could do (Is 5:1–7)."[49]

Peckham contends that Scripture indicates

> a reciprocal love relationship between God and each individual cannot be unilaterally determined by God. This is not due to any divine defect or lack of power but due to the nature of love itself, which, according to this [canonical] model, requires significant freedom. . . . If significant freedom is a necessary condition of love, it is impossible for God to determine that all beings *freely* love him.[50]

Peckham also contends that there is both a conditionality and an unconditionality to God's love as revealed in Scripture. This is due to the objective and subjective aspects of the love of God. God's subjective love is that which inheres in his character regardless of human response. God's objective love is his love that is affected by the response of people. God's objective love "describes his (interactive) love relationships with creaturely objects and thus refers to that love which initiates relationship with creatures and evaluatively corresponds to, and is affected by, the dispositions and actions of its object. It is thus (fore)conditional and requires reciprocal love for its permanent continuance."[51]

God's subjective love is unconditional and grounds God's objective foreconditional love. In the subjective sense, God's love is described in Scripture as eternal. The objective aspects of God's love are relational and predicated on human response to God's prevenient, unmerited love. "God's love is thus unconditional in that his character of love is unchanging and he always wills to love all (subjective love), but conditional with respect to divine evaluation and relationship (objective love)."[52]

47 Ibid., 191.
48 Ibid., 202.
49 Ibid., 203.
50 Ibid., 207–8 (emphasis in original).
51 Ibid., 212.
52 Ibid., 213.

God's subjective love is everlasting, unconditionally constant, and grounded in his eternal character of love.[53]

Scripture indicates God's love is both universal and particular.[54] God's love for the world is foreconditional and universally relational. God loves all people and desires all to come to a saving relationship with him through Christ.[55] God loves every individual foreconditionally for the purpose of loving them particularly in a reciprocal love relationship.

Why is God's love particular? Reformed theology argues that this is the case because of God's selective choice of some, the elect, for salvation, upon whom he sets his saving love. Peckham agrees that Scripture differentiates between God's universal and particular love but believes that God has given humanity "significant freedom" to choose to love God in return or to reject him. Some are loved by God more intimately than others, receiving the blessings of his saving love, not because of an arbitrary sovereign election but because of human rejection of God's love.

If Peckham's interpretation of the canonical data on the love of God is correct, then the notion of a limited atonement is precluded and for obvious reasons. How could God be said to love, in any meaningful sense of the term, those for whom he did not provide atonement for their sins? How could God be said to desire the salvation of all people if he did not provide atonement for all people? Since no one can possibly be saved apart from the atonement of Christ, it is simply contradictory to speak of God's universal love and his universal saving will on the limited atonement platform.[56]

John 3:16 clearly indicates God's saving intentions are as broad as the world. John clearly connects God's act of atonement for sins with God's love in 1 John 4:9–10. Canonically, the logic of Romans 1–11 demonstrates this as well. In Rom 1–3, Paul demonstrates the scope of human sinfulness is universal. In Rom 11:32, the scope of God's mercy is universal. That Paul may be referring to the people groups of Jews and Gentiles does not change the fact that God's purpose is to show mercy to all within both people groups.

Many in the history of the Reformed tradition have subordinated God's love to his sovereignty. At the heart of this approach lies a fundamental misreading of the intra-Trinitarian nature and relationship of perfect love and how that is expressed to the world through Jesus Christ. God's nature is such that he loves all individuals and desires their eternal salvation. Consequently, God has provided atonement for the sins of all.

---

53 Ibid., 214.

54 Ibid., 235–47.

55 See Carson, *The Difficult Doctrine of the Love of God*, 17, 76. The illogic of Carson's attempt to try to embrace God's universal love with particular election and limited atonement in the specific context of preaching and evangelism is brought out by J. Walls and J. Dongell, *Why I Am Not a Calvinist* (Downers Grove, IL: InterVarsity, 2004), 188–91.

56 As Walls and Dongell noted in *Why I Am Not a Calvinist*, 55, "In our judgment, it becomes meaningless to claim that God wishes to save all while also insisting that God refrains from making the salvation of all possible."

Furthermore, given that love is intrinsic to God's nature, to posit an arbitrary distinction between his saving love for the elect and his general, albeit nonsaving, love for the non-elect is actually to impugn the character of God as revealed in Scripture.

The love of God is indeed a difficult doctrine for the high Calvinist's doctrine of limited atonement.

Logic and the Extent of the Atonement

Some read verses that say Christ died for his "sheep," "church," or "friends" and draw the conclusion that since these groups are limited, so the atonement must be limited. This line of argument is logically flawed because it invokes the negative inference fallacy, which says the proof of a proposition does not disprove its converse. When Paul says "Christ died for me" in Gal 2:20, we cannot infer that he died only for Paul. This is the logical mistake made by all high Calvinists on this point. There is no statement in Scripture that says Jesus died only for the sins of the elect.

Some argue that if Jesus died for the sins of all people, then all people will be saved. This is a false conclusion for several reasons. First, the Scripture is clear that all will not be saved. Second, it confuses the extent of the atonement with the application of the atonement. No one is saved by the death of Christ on the cross until they believe in Christ. This point was made by Shedd, a Calvinist with impeccable credentials.[57] As stated above, Eph 2:1–3 makes clear that even the elect are under the wrath of God and "have no hope" until they believe.

Third, as 2 Cor 5:18–21 makes clear, reconciliation has an objective and subjective aspect to it. The death of Christ objectively reconciles God to the world in the sense that his justice is satisfied and he stands ready to pardon, but the subjective side of reconciliation does not occur until the atonement is applied when the individual repents of sin and puts faith in Christ. Along these lines, don't miss Col 1:19–20, which speaks of Christ's universal reconciliation of all things. This of course does not mean "universalism," but it does mean that Christ's death on the cross is a crucial aspect of his Lordship over all people and things (Phil 2:9–11). Every knee shall bow.

Fourth, one key argument used by Calvinists for limited atonement is the double payment argument (see John Owen). As noted above, in essence, it argues that justice does not allow the same sin to be punished twice. There are at least four strong arguments against this: (1) it is never found in Scripture, (2) it confuses a commercial understanding of sin as debt with a penal satisfaction for sin (the latter is the biblical view), (3) even the elect are still under the wrath of God until they believe (Eph 2:1–

57 W. G. T. Shedd, *Dogmatic Theology* (Nashville, TN: Thomas Nelson, 1980), 2:477.

3), and (4) it negates the principle of grace in the application of the atonement since nobody is owed the application.

Fifth, another logical/theological argument used to support limited atonement is the triple choice argument. It is built on the double payment argument. Either Christ died for all the sins of all people, or all the sins of some people, or some of the sins of all people. If Christ died for the sins of all, then why are not all saved? The argument sounds good logically, but it is flawed. Scripture never says a person goes to hell because no atonement was provided for him. People are said in Scripture to perish because they do not believe. Even though Christ died for all, he does not apply salvation to all. Faith in Christ is the condition for salvation. Finally, the argument quantifies the imputation of sin to Christ, as if there is a ratio between all the sins of those Christ represents and the sufferings of Christ, an unnecessary move given the extrinsic sufficiency of Christ's death for the sins of the world.

Sixth, we have seen that many high Calvinists succumb to disjunctive thinking on the question at hand. "Either Christ came to save or he came to make salvation possible" is one example.[58] Biblically, both are true. Even from an Arminian and non-Calvinist standpoint, Christ came both to make salvation possible for all men and to save all who believe.

Preaching, Evangelism, Missions, and the Extent of the Atonement

There are some negative practical implications for ministry entailed by limited atonement with respect to preaching and evangelism. These may be listed under three headings.

Diminishing of God's Universal Saving Will

Calvinists have trouble defending God's universal saving will from the platform of limited atonement. The basic issue is this: if Christ did not die for the non-elect, how can this be reconciled with passages of Scripture such as John 17:21, 23; 1 Tim 2:4–6; and 2 Pet 3:9 that affirm God desires the salvation of all people? Moderate Calvinists and non-Calvinists have no trouble here since they affirm Christ did indeed die for the sins of all people, hence God can make the well-meant offer to all. Without belief in the universal saving will of God and a universal extent in Christ's sin-bearing, there can be no well-meant offer of the salvation from God to the non-elect who hear the gospel call.

58 See L. Gatiss, *For Us and for Our Salvation* (London: Latimer Trust, 2012), 112.

The Well-Meant Gospel Offer

We are to express and display God's love for humanity in the way we command all men to repent, in our preaching of the gospel, in our compassionate invitations, and in our indiscriminate offerings of Christ to all. Christ's own heart and ministry, in this respect, is our pattern. We are to point the lost to the sufficiency of Christ to save them. In addition to Christ's express evangelistic commands and God's will that all be saved, Christ's actual sufficiency in his atonement for all should also form a basis for our evangelism.

Limited atonement undermines the well-meant gospel offer. We are to evangelize because God wills all men to be saved and has made atonement for all men, thus removing the legal barriers that necessitate their condemnation. Christ died not only for "sinners" but for the sins of all sinners. When high Calvinists use the terminology "Christ died for sinners," the term "sinners" becomes something of a code word for "the elect only." In order to be consistent with their theology, Calvinists must resort to the deliberately vague statement "Christ died for sinners."

Second Corinthians 5:19–20 states, "That is, in Christ, God was reconciling the world to Himself, not counting their trespasses against them, and He has committed the message of reconciliation to us. Therefore, we are ambassadors for Christ, certain that God is appealing through us. We plead on Christ's behalf, 'Be reconciled to God.'" Here we have God himself offering salvation to all. But how can he do this according to limited atonement since there is no provision for the salvation of the non-elect in the death of Christ?

Furthermore, how can God make this offer with integrity? It seems difficult to suppose he can. Without belief in the universal saving will of God and a universal extent in Christ's sin-bearing, there can be no well-meant offer of salvation from God to the non-elect who hear the gospel call. It would be like being invited to the Master's banquet table where no chair, table setting, and food has actually been provided. This implicates and impugns the character of God in the making of the offer of salvation to the non-elect because in fact there is no salvation to offer: Christ did not die for their sins.

John Murray and Ned B. Stonehouse attempted to blunt the force of this argument by offering a response in *The Free Offer of the Gospel.*[59] They state that the real point in dispute is whether it can properly be said that God desires the salvation of all people. Murray and Stonehouse adopt the "two wills" posture: God's decretive will and his revealed will. They argue that one can only say that God desires the salvation of the reprobate (non-elect) in God's revealed will, otherwise contradiction ensues.[60]

---

59 J. Murray and N. Stonehouse, *The Free Offer of the Gospel* (Phillipsburg, NJ: Lewis Grotenhuis, n.d.). This short work appears also in The Fifteenth General Assembly of the Orthodox Presbyterian Church *Minutes*, 1948, Appendix, 51–72.

60 Ibid., 3.

Thus, in the offer of the gospel to the world, there is more than a "bare preceptive will of God" involved, but rather "the disposition of loving kindness on the part of God pointing to the salvation to be gained through compliance with the overtures of gospel grace." The authors argue that when "God desires" the salvation of all people, this expresses a genuine attitude of loving kindness inherent in the free offer to all.[61]

Murray and Stonehouse mention a number of passages in support of their approach, including Ezek 18:23, 32; 33:11.[62] But they are candid enough to state that when they speak of God's decretive will, "it must be said that God absolutely decrees the eternal death of some wicked and, in that sense, is absolutely pleased so to decree."[63] In fact, in reference to the Hebrew word *chaphez*, the authors state: "And neither is there evidence to show that in the word *chaphez* there is here any comparative notion to the effect that God takes greater pleasure in saving men than he does in damning them."[64] The authors continue:

> Obviously, however, it is not his decretive will that all repent and be saved. While, on the one hand, he has not decretively willed that all be saved, yet he declares unequivocally that it is his will and, impliedly, his pleasure that all turn and be saved. We are again faced with the mystery and adorable richness of the divine will. It might seem to us that the one rules out the other. But it is not so.[65]

Unlike some limitarians, Murray and Stonehouse do not believe that 2 Pet 3:9 should be interpreted as restricted to the elect.[66] God wills the salvation of all sinners. But, of course, that is God's revealed will, not his secret will, according to Reformed theologians like Murray and Stonehouse. Calvin too asserts the same in his exegesis of 2 Pet 3:9:

> It could be asked here, if God does not want any to perish, why do so many in fact perish? My reply is that no mention is made here of the secret decree of God, by which the wicked are doomed to their own ruin, but only of his loving-kindness as it is made known to us in the Gospel. There God stretches out His hand to all alike, but he only grasps those (in such a way as to lead to Himself) whom He has chosen before the foundation of the world.[67]

---

61 Ibid., 4.

62 Ibid., 5–15.

63 Ibid., 19.

64 Ibid.

65 Ibid.

66 Ibid., 23–25.

67 J. Calvin, "The Epistle of Paul the Apostle to the Hebrews and the First and Second Epistles of St. Peter," in *Calvin's New Testament Commentaries*, 12 vols., ed. D. W. Torrance & T. F. Torrance (Grand Rapids, MI: Eerdmans, 1994), 12:364.

To all those outside of Reformed theology, the notion that God "desires" and "wills" things on the one hand that he nils on the other via his decretive will borders on being illogical and nonsensical. We are informed "we should not entertain any prejudice against the notion that God desires or has pleasure in the accomplishment of what he does not decretively will," but rather respect the mystery. The universal (revealed) will of God that all be saved demonstrates "that there is in God a benevolent loving kindness towards the repentance and salvation of even those whom he has not decreed to save. This pleasure, will, desire is expressed in the universal call to repentance."[68]

The authors' appeal to "mystery" to explain this conundrum wears thin quickly with most people. Even more troubling is their example of Jesus himself, who "willed the bestowal of his saving and protecting grace upon those whom neither the Father nor he decreed thus to save and protect."[69] Where is the scriptural support for this claim?

Murray and Stonehouse conclude that the full and free offer of the gospel is a grace bestowed upon all and is a manifestation of love in the heart of God.

> The grace offered is nothing less than salvation in its richness and fullness. The love or lovingkindness that lies back of that offer is not anything less; it is the will to that salvation. In other words, it is Christ in all the glory of his person and in all the perfection of his finished work whom God offers in the gospel. The loving and benevolent will that is the source of that offer and that grounds its veracity and reality is the will to the possession of Christ and the enjoyment of the salvation that resides in him.[70]

But one must ask how can this possibly be the case if there is no atonement to ground the offer to the non-elect? Even on a revealed will/decretal will construct, it is simply impossible that God can be offering something in good faith to those who are non-elect when what is being offered does not exist. Without an objective atonement for the sins of all people, Murray and Stonehouse are left with a logical impossibility, no matter how they slice it.

Saving faith accepts that Christ died for me. Without a universal atonement it is not possible for anyone to know from the gospel itself that Christ died for him. In limiting the atonement, particularists necessarily limit the offer of the gospel. The crucial question for all high Calvinists is how is it possible to maintain the free offer of the

---

68 Murray and Stonehouse, *The Free Offer of the Gospel*, 26. See also D. J. MacLean, *James Durham (1622–1658) and the Gospel Offer in Its Seventeenth-Century Context*, Reformed Historical Theology 31 (Göttingen: Vandenhoeck and Ruprect, 2015).

69 Ibid.

70 Ibid., 27.

gospel without grounding it in universal atonement? Hyper-Calvinists saw this inconsistency and simply rejected the free offer of the gospel entirely.[71]

Preaching and the "Bold Proclamation"

The bold proclamation of the gospel is an old term used to refer to telling people individually or corporately that "Christ died for your sins." Notice how some Calvinists use coded language here. Those who believe in limited atonement will say "Christ died for sinners," which is code for "elect sinners." This is confusing at best and disingenuous at worst.

Anything that makes the preacher hesitant to make the bold proclamation that "Christ died for your sins" is wrong. If one thinks it is true that Christ only suffered for some, preaching will be deeply affected. The preacher does not know who the elect are, so he must preach to all as if Christ's death is applicable to them, even though, as his position entails, he knows and believes all are not capable of salvation. This makes the preacher operate on the basis of something that is actually untrue. This is a problem for the pulpit. From the standpoint of preaching, the free and well-meant offer of the gospel for all people necessarily presupposes that Christ died for the sins of all people.

Calvinists point out that they preach to all because they don't know who the elect are. Certainly true, but this misses the point. Belief in limited atonement puts the preacher in the difficult position of preaching to all people as if Christ's death is applicable to them even though all are not capable of salvation since the non-elect have no atonement made for them. This creates a situation where preachers operate on the basis of something that is not true in every situation. In addition, how will such a preacher respond to the following question from an unbeliever: "When you say Christ died for sinners, does that mean Christ died for me?" There is no way to answer that question with a firm "yes" from the platform of limited atonement. On the other hand, preachers who affirm universal atonement can boldly proclaim Christ died for their sins.

Everyone agrees that doctrine matters. Doctrine informs praxis. This is not an issue of whether someone is committed to preaching and evangelism. This is not a question of whether one is passionate about preaching and evangelism. I take it for granted that Calvinists as well as non-Calvinists desire to obey the Great Commission. That being said, and for the reasons stated above, I am arguing that a belief in limited atonement

---

71 For works written by high Calvinists on the free offer of the gospel, consult E. Hulse, *The Free Offer: An Exposition of Common Grace and the Free Invitation of the Gospel* (Haywards Heath, UK: Carey, 1973), 14–15; De Jong, *The Well-Meant Gospel Offer*; K. W. Stebbins, *Christ Freely Offered: A Discussion of the General Offer of Salvation in the Light of Particular Atonement* (Strathpine North, Australia: Covenanter, 1978); D. Silversides, *The Free Offer: Biblical and Reformed* (Glasgow: Marpet, 2005); and D. H. Gay, *Particular Redemption and the Free Offer* (Biggleswade, UK: Brachus, 2008); D. H. Gay, *The Gospel Offer Is Free: A Reply to George Ella's Rejection of the Gospel Offer*, 2nd ed. (Biggleswade, UK: Brachus, 2012).

necessarily entails a hindrance to preaching and evangelism.[72] Paul said the content of the gospel he preached included the fact that "Christ died for our sins" (1 Cor 15:3). Limited atonement denies and distorts a crucial aspect of the gospel: that Christ died for the sins of the world.

Erskine Mason, a nineteenth-century Calvinist pastor, summed up well the importance of a universal atonement for preaching:

> I confess, my brethren, I do not understand the gospel, if this is not one of its cardinal doctrines; if the indiscriminate offer of Jesus Christ, and of pardon and eternal life through him, is not made to the race, and as truly and honestly and sincerely made to one individual as another of the race. . . . If the entire population of the globe were before me, and there should be one in the mighty assembly for whom there was no provision, I could not preach the gospel; for how could I say in sincerity and honesty to all and to each, come and take of the waters of life freely?[73]

Conclusion

It would only take one clear statement in Scripture that Christ died for the sins of all people to confirm unlimited atonement no matter how many statements indicate Christ died for a specific group of people. Likewise, it would only take one clear statement in Scripture that Christ died *only* for the sins of the elect to confirm limited atonement. Yet, as all Calvinists who defend limited atonement admit, there is not one single statement in Scripture that overtly states Christ died only for the sins of the elect. There are easily a dozen New Testament texts overtly stating Christ died for the sins of all people.

The burden of proof is on the advocates of limited atonement to prove that a simple positive statement, "Christ died for some people's sins," can entail a universal negation: "Christ did not die for all people's sins." The hill that must be climbed is to prove, exegetically from Scripture, that Christ died *only for some people's sins* (a limited imputation

72 High Calvinists may bring up Spurgeon to refute this claim. As we have seen, there was a certain inconsistency with Spurgeon between his theology of limited atonement and his practice of preaching as if Christ had in fact died for all people. I have observed through the years that high Calvinists don't preach limited atonement; they preach as if they believed in an unlimited atonement. In what can only be interpreted as a sad remark concerning the ministry of the far famed Puritan John Owen, William Goold, in the preface to volume 8 of *The Works of John Owen*, 16 vols., ed. W. H. Goold (New York: Robert Carter and Brothers, 1852), stated:

> John Rogers, in his singular work, "The Heavenly Nymph," records the cases of two individuals, Dorothy Emett and Major Mainwaring, who ascribed their conversion to the preaching of Owen when he was in Dublin. Mr Orme remarks, that the circumstance confutes a saying attributed to Owen, that he never knew an instance of a sinner converted through his instrumentality; though the saying might so far be true, that he himself might be ignorant of the extent of his own usefulness. (viii)

73 E. Mason, "Extent of the Atonement," in *A Pastor's Legacy: Being Sermons on Practical Subjects* (New York: Charles Scribner, 1853), 281.

of sin), in light of all the passages that employ terms like "world" and "all" in the various extent passages. This is a steep hill indeed. If limited atonement fails exegetically, then no amount of theological flying buttresses will support it.

There is no credible biblical support for limited atonement. There is no sustainable theological support for limited atonement. There is no bulletproof logical support for limited atonement. It is difficult to understand why some Calvinists cling so tightly to limited atonement when faced with the exegetical data. I'm reminded of Irving Kristol's statement: "When we lack the will to see things as they really are, there is nothing so mystifying as the obvious."[74]

The problems associated with a limitarian understanding of the atonement are legion. For biblical, theological, logical, and practical reasons, we deny that Christ died only for the sins of those who will be saved. Limited atonement truncates the gospel because it saws off the arms of the cross too close to the stake.

Christ died for the sins of all, because of his and the Father's love for all, to provide a genuine offer of salvation to all, and his death not only makes salvation possible for all but actually secures the salvation of all who believe through the regenerating work of the Holy Spirit. There is a provision of forgiveness for all to whom the gospel comes. There is a provision of forgiveness for all who come to the gospel.

---

74 I. Kristol, "'When Virtue Loses All Her Loveliness'—Some Reflections on Capitalism and 'The Free Society,'" *The Public Interest* 21 (Fall 1970), 3.

Subject Index

T

Y

Name Index

N

O

Scripture Index